M000159450

Film Choreographers and Dance Directors

Film Choreographers and Dance Directors

*An Illustrated Biographical Encyclopedia,
with a History and Filmographies,
1893 through 1995*

by LARRY BILLMAN

McFarland & Company, Inc., Publishers
Jefferson, North Carolina, and London

Front cover photos: Top left: Tony and Sally DeMarco sail across the floor in **Crazy House** (Universal, 1943). Bottom left: Mikhail Baryshnikov and Gregory Hines created the choreography for **White Nights** (Columbia, 1985). Right: Antonio Gades, the star choreographer of **Blood Wedding**, **Carmen** and **El Amor Brujo**.

Back cover photo: Bob Fosse and Gwen Verdon perform in **Damn Yankees** (Warner Bros., 1958).

Frontispiece: Jack Cole (looking slightly cross-eyed) coaches Marilyn Monroe (looking slightly baffled) for "My Heart Belongs to Daddy" in *Let's Make Love* (Twentieth Century–Fox, 1960).

British Library Cataloguing-in-Publication data are available

Library of Congress Cataloguing-in-Publication Data

Billman, Larry.
    Film choreographers and dance directors : an illustrated
biographical encyclopedia, with a history and filmographies, 1893
through 1995 / by Larry Billman.
      p.   cm.
    Includes index.
    ISBN 0-89950-868-5 (case binding : 50# alkaline paper) ∞
    1. Dance in motion pictures, television, etc.— History.
2. Choreography — Filmography.   3. Choreographers — Biography.
I. Title.
GV1779.B55   1997
793.82'092'2 — dc20   96-31756
[B]   CIP

Manufactured in the United States of America

McFarland & Company, Inc., Publishers
  Box 611, Jefferson, North Carolina 28640

For Tomo, who has choreographed the beat
of my heart and directed the dances in my
head for thirty years — with love

TABLE OF CONTENTS

ACKNOWLEDGMENTS

This book is the collective effort of hundreds of people and dozens of institutions. Without their input, it would be a very small, sparse volume of misinformation.

I have to thank SSDC (the Society of Stage Directors and Choreographers), Grover Dale and the L.A. Dance Foundation, and PDS (the Professional Dancer's Society), who were all extremely helpful and cooperative, proving their worth to dancers and choreographers. Because of this book, Grover Dale and Alan Johnson became partners-in-crime, supplying endless information and support. They also became valued friends.

There are two books which actually inspired me to begin this one: the landmark *Tap!* by Rusty E. Frank and *Hoofing on Broadway* by Richard Kaslan. I encourage you to read them both. Through a great stroke of luck, the Beverly Hills Library houses the unpublished manuscript of *Dancing in Commercial Motion Pictures*, an unbelievable treasure trove of facts, names and dates, written by Mary Jane Hungerford, "submitted in partial fulfillment of the requirements for the degree of Doctor of Philosophy in the Faculty of Education of Columbia University" in 1946. It is evident that she interviewed many of the leaders in film choreography, and I am deeply indebted to her. Doctor Hungerford — wherever you are — I salute you!

Within the entertainment and dance communities, my gratitude to Ed Balin, Margie Chachkin, Roy Clark, Mart Crowley, Johan Filinger, John Frayer, Teri Garr, Joe Giamalva, Naomi Graham, Anders Hatlo, Maria Gahva Henley, Pam Killinger, Dorothy Kloss, Adrian and Ruby Le Peltier, Julie MacDonald, Keith Merryman, Lee Mims, Tim O'Brien, Dabina O'Donnell, Robert Osborne, Katie Peck, Jan Phillips, Alyson Reed, Zack Reed, Diane Salzberg, Tad Schnugg, Kathi Sharpe-Ross, Benjamin "Buddy" Spencer, and Teresa Taylor-Campbell. And from the families of those honored in these pages, I thank Ava Astaire McKenzie, Milly Castle, Sandy Hanna, Joy Griffiths, Valentina Oumansky, and Tina Taylor.

Special thanks go to Miriam Nelson and Sylvia Lewis, two beautiful ladies who have "done it all" and started my career and life on the right foot. And to James Robert Parish, a master of film writing, who encouraged, guided, and helped me with his expertise and friendship. This book simply would have not happened without him.

My deepest thanks to the choreographers who answered my letters and phone calls, often filling out time-consuming questionnaires, so that the information on their lives and careers would be correct. Choreographers who extensively shared their histories and memories in interviews and personal anecdotes in writing were Elizabeth Aldrich, Johnny Almaraz, Peter Anastos, the late Donn Arden, Julie Arenal, Rick Atwell, Bob Banas, Maggie Banks, Earl Barton, Toni Basil, Jim Bates, Hal Belfer, Patricia Birch, Lionel Blair, Kim Blank, Marc Breaux, Kevin Carlisle, Alan Carter, Gene Castle, the late Chris Chadman, Marge Champion, Felix Chavez, Russell Clark, Hope Clarke, Gene Columbus, Robin Cousins, Don Crichton, Grover Dale,

Jacques d'Amboise, Rita D'Amico Hyde, Graciela Daniele, Danny Daniels, Danny Dare, Michael Darrin, Gemze DeLappe, Miguel Delgado, Paul DeRolfe, Angie Blue DeShon, Matthew Diamond, Joanne Divito, Kathryn Doby, Carla Earle, Sarah Elgart, Daniel Esteras, George Faison, the late Ernest Flatt, Bill Foster, Damita Jo Freeman, Larry Fuller, Miranda Garrison, Troy Garza, Myrna Gawryn, D.J. Giagni, Jeanette Godoy, Gillian Gregory, Dorain Grusman, Bruce Heath, Lynne Hockney, Peggy Holmes, Carl Jablonski, Jerry Jackson, Brad Jeffries, Alan Johnson, Dan Kamin, Shirley Kirkes, Mark Knowles, Edmond Kresley, Bill and Jacqui Landrum, Barry Lather, Ted Lin, Anita Mann, Burch Mann, Claude Marchant, George and Ethel Martin, Stan Mazin, Donald McKayle, Roger Minami, Arthur Mitchell, Jerry Mitchell, Gene Nelson, Phineas Newborn III, Fayard Nicholas, Charlene Painter, Vincent Paterson, Steven Peck, Paul Pellicoro, the late Michael Peters, Arlene Phillips, Helene Phillips, Alex Plasschaert, Dennon and Sayhber Rawles, Jack Regas, George Reich, Christopher Riordan, Alex Romero, Herb Ross, Janet Roston, Alton Ruff, Alex Ruiz, Dom Salinaro, Otis Sallid, Dorian Sanchez, Shanda Sawyer, the late Buddy Schwab, the late Lee Scott, Shabba Doo, Adam Shankman, Dan Siretta, James Starbuck, Tony Stevens, Patsy Swayze, Tad Tadlock, Andre Tayir, Wilda Taylor, Lynne Taylor-Corbett, Myles Thoroughgood, David Toguri, Joe Tremaine, Jerry Trent, the late James Truitte, Gwen Verdon, Tam G. Warner, Onna White, the late Billy Wilson, the late Lester Wilson, Dee Dee Wood and Michelle Zeitlin. It was an honor to be working in conjunction with you on this project. There are too many who have died since they corresponded with me and as I received new obituaries, the feeling that I had lost another friend often overwhelmed me. Here it is dear friends, a too-brief documentation of your life and work. I hope you are proud. We will see you in the movies!

To those I did not manage to get in touch with, I apologize. I hope that this book will encourage them or friends and family members to contact me so that they too can be represented in detail and truth for future volumes.

I thank the Academy of Motion Picture Arts and Sciences for their wonderful Margaret Herrick Research Library where I was able to dig and prod for days. Alison Pinsler, Scott Miller, and the entire staff there tirelessly combed through over six hundred individual files to help me track down the elusive information I sought. Also in the United States, the Billy Rose Theatre Collection at the New York Public Library at Lincoln Center, and the Anaheim, Beverly Hills, Los Angeles, and Santa Ana, California, public libraries rewarded me with cooperative staffs and helpful material. In London, the Kensington Central Library was also helpful and rewarding. Special thanks go to Katherine Oxenham at the Westminister Research Library — a remarkable lady in a remarkable place.

The American Dancer, The Dance and *Dance Magazine* provided a wealth of information — as they have for dancers throughout the years — as well as *LA Dance* magazine, published by the L.A. Dance Foundation. And I am terribly grateful to the handful of writers who have documented dance in film throughout the years, especially the late Ted Hook, Roy Clark, Ann Barzel, the late Viola Hegyi Swisher, Don Bradburn, and Kevin Grubb. Their monthly columns in *Dance Magazine* beginning in the late 1940s finally began to document who did what. For the first time choreographers, assistants and dancers were listed for their contribution to film. In the '90s, Tony Selznick began to do the same for *LA Dance*. A deep bow — sometimes, you were the only references I had.

My gratitude to all of the book stores I visited, searching for stills and out-of-print books on dance and film musicals which might provide some clues. In California: Larry Edmunds Books (thank you, Pete Bateman), Aladdin Books, Cinema Collections, Collectors Book Store and Eddie Brandt's Saturday Matinee; in New York: Jerry Ohlinger's Movie Material Store and Movie Star

News; and in London: Foyles, Dance Books, Dress Circle, Dillons, and Zwemmer (where the salesclerk laughed when I asked if they had any books on the British Film Musical; "What is the British film musical?" she asked, guffawing.) In Barcelona, Cinelandia unearthed photographic treasures, interest and friendship of all sorts.

I am compelled to take a moment to congratulate and thank Ted Turner and all of his staff at Turner Pictures who are committed to the preservation and distribution of our movie musical heritage. As the holders of the MGM and Warner Bros. film libraries, they lead the industry in quality product with the videos and laser discs which they continue to release for MGM/UA. In particular their **Busby Berkeley Disc**, **Cavalcade of MGM Shorts**, the **Dawn of Sound** series and the "Collector's Edition" of **That's Entertainment! III** have made available unseen (for decades) dance treasures for our education and enjoyment.

And finally, my deepest gratitude to my "support group," the friends and family who helped with patience, phone numbers, credits, newsclippings (mostly obituaries, unfortunately), love, and energy: Forrest Bahruth, Harry and La Vone Billman, Dick DeNeut, Clare Graham, Tsuyoshi Hashimoto, Debra Lowell, Hiroshi Misago, John and Mary Jo Ludin, Roy Luthringer, Richard and Ava McKenzie, Margie Schultz, and Cid Stoll. And to my daughters, Sekiya and Saadia, whose interest and keen eyes kept adding film credits to my lists and who shared this learning experience with me. If you notice anyone remaining in the movie theater to the bitter end of the credits, it's probably them.

ABOUT THIS BOOK

While doing research for a book on Betty Grable, I had difficulty finding the names of the choreographers and dance directors who were responsible for the musical numbers in some of her films — and this in the career of a lady who was basically a dancer! Now Betty Grable was certainly remarkable, and energetic, but she did not have that special talent to create her own dance routines. She relied on other men and women to invent the movement sequences which presented and expanded on her modest dance talents and contributed to her success.

In the seemingly unending research on the history of American film, little or no attention has been paid to the people who made the movies dance. Composers and lyricists have received credit for the tunes they wrote, but sparse acclaim has been accorded to the men and women who brought those songs to the screen, made them move, made them dance — most often creating original scenarios in which to frame them. We can read about the famous stars who twirled and tapped, shimmied and swayed; yet we know very little about the people who directed (and often taught) them to do so.

In film credits, we can easily find the editor, costume designer, art director, and Technicolor consultant, but it is difficult (if not impossible) to find the name of the person who created the dances. The average audience member realizes that someone had to write the words the actors speak, design and create the costumes they wear, and supervise the performances and filming. I would hope to heighten general awareness that someone also made the actors dance.

As Richard Kislan wrote in *Hoofing on Broadway*, an excellent book about the history of stage dance, "Nothing in the American Musical Theater has been more inaccessible to its public than the record of its dance tradition." The history of dance in film has likewise been ignored. Kislan defends the lack of documentation of live dance with the observation that "The inequity stems from the very nature of dance as an ephemeral art tradition passed on from one generation to another by demonstration, practice, and personal supervision." Movie historians, however, cannot use the same excuse. It all exists there for us to see — and re-see.

Dance direction and choreography in film comprise an important part of our international film heritage. The exceptionally talented people in this field have been called many things ("dance directors," "choreographers," "musical sequence stagers"), but their work has been basically the same.

In film musicals, they created the concept for the musical sequences (which usually comprised the bulk of the film's running length), often directing the sequences themselves. They broke the primitive format of merely photographing stage dance and developed ways to use the camera as their inventive "eye" — giving us the rich filmed heritage of Busby Berkeley, Larry Ceballos, and Dave Gould.

They decided how the sequence would be enacted on film — would it merely be "business" or did it call for actual dance steps? How did it look and feel? How would it be photographed? The transition from pointless dance number to integrated plot exposition was made by pioneers like Fred Astaire and Hermes Pan.

They defined the musical arrangements of the songs with the arrangers, leaving us with the distinctive syncopation of Hermes Pan's numbers and Jack Cole's oriental and Afro-Cuban–influenced musical dances.

They experimented with technical effects and worked closely with art directors to bathe their dance sequences in unique color and decor, with Gene Kelly and Eugene Loring leading the way in both groundbreaking areas.

They drastically influenced the design of the costumes, so that the clothes would move correctly and not inhibit the performers as they danced. They helped to create the stars' personae, as their musical performances were often a major part of each film. And they made the movie musical what is was — something that sang and danced and *moved*. Sometimes, they made it soar!

They also added movement and dance to non-musical films. Whenever you see a movie in which the actors are dancing, a choreographer created that scene, a task that required attention to the featured players' ability (or lack thereof), the background movement of the extras, the style of the period, and the delicate business of timing the dialogue to the movement. We have to remind ourselves that every harem dance, royal ball, party scene, high school prom, and disco or nightclub sequence had a choreographer to create its patterns, rhythm, and adaptation to the camera. They also invented "specialized movement" for the actors in order to enrich character, heighten dramatic effect, and allow the inventive combat sequences of today's films.

During the Golden Era of the major film studios, dance directors were on the studio staff. In addition to creating or supervising all of the dance sequences for the musicals, they were responsible for teaching movement to the actors. Dance directors coached stars to add grace to their performances. As Academy Award–winning costume designer Edith Head once told Miriam Nelson at Paramount: "We should have a class where you dance directors teach our young actors to *walk!*" They often did. When a non-dancing star was assigned to a dancing role or one which required specialized movement, a dance director became teacher, coach, movement creator, camera designer, and confidante. The film choreographers often became the stars' best friends because of the close work they did with the delicate ego. Marilyn Monroe hardly took a breath without Jack Cole.

Staff dance specialists often served as assistant or second unit directors, herding extras through battle sequences, exoduses from Egypt, and entrances into Rome. In contemporary films, "action sequences staged by" or "martial arts choreography by" are now common credits, but in the early years of filmmaking these chores were routinely assigned to dance directors because of their "eye" and their ability to move large groups of people.

Choreography was one of the first equal opportunity employers in films. While women often designed the costumes or edited the films, they also worked in near-equal numbers with men creating dance. African Americans and Hispanics were eagerly accepted into film because of their talents and knowledge which contributed to the authenticity and rich detail of a film. Sadly, Asians have been allowed minimal contributions to American films, as their music and dance are not widely accepted by the Western world. Gays heavily populated the film dance world — as they do in classical and theater dance — bringing their sensibilities and talents to the screen in rich abundance. The very nature of the specifics of dance helped to give its purveyors of varying nationality, gender, and sexual lifestyles entrée into the world of film.

As of the writing of this book, film producers are reluctant to make musicals. Target audiences for the cinema (fourteen-year-old males) just don't go to see them: no one dies, no one curses, no one has explicit sex on table tops or in elevators. The body count is nil, and car crashes and the destruction of buildings or property are difficult to work into the musical score. But choreographers continue to add delicious coloring and details to contemporary filmmaking, whether by creating a pastiche of an earlier period or by adding rhythmic excitement to a sequence. Fight scenes, "alien" movement, pantomimes, social dance sequences, erotic couplings, and satirical statements are all being created by movement makers in contemporary film. Perhaps more choreographers are working in film now than ever before.

I wanted to finally document who these people are and what they have done. I happen to feel that they have made major contributions to our film heritage. From the 1920s to the present day, the men and women who have created dance movement on film are an impressive group.

The book is arranged as follows (after an Introduction):

BIBLIOGRAPHY

The Bibliography lists books, articles, and interviews that were of use in compiling this work and are presented here for the reader's further interest and study.

PART I. A HISTORY OF DANCE ON FILM (essentially decade by decade)

Beginning at the turn of the century, the films, choreographers, and innovations are described for each period: dance styles, contributions to overall filmmaking, innovations in camera and editing techniques, special effects, musical number and design creation — with selected critical comments. A filmography follows the coverage of each decade, listing important or interesting films and detailing choreographers, specific musical numbers of interest, outstanding performances, and appropriate videotape information, if available.

PART II. BIOGRAPHIES OF CHOREOGRAPHERS AND DANCE DIRECTORS

Dance directors and choreographers are listed alphabetically and photographs are provided. Details of birthdate and birthplace, dance training, early professional experiences as a performer, significant contributions to dance on film, awards and honors, date and place of death (where applicable), and published biography or autobiography information are given. Choreographic credits follow: stage, television, music video, nightclub/concert, ballet/dance pieces, and miscellaneous (ice shows, circus, theme parks, etc.), to allow the reader to realize the full scope of each subject's talent and contributions to dance in general. Film credits are then listed, noting year of release, studio, any special credit, and co-creators. An attempt has been made to include international contributions — primarily European. Asia and Latin America are not well represented.

The Appendix to Part II is an alphabetical list of the films with their choreographers.

PART III. INDEX

All film and show titles, people, places, and selected subjects mentioned in the book are entered alphabetically, with page numbers cited.

For purposes of classification, movie titles in this text are printed in **bold** type, operas and ballets are printed in ***bold italics***, stage plays and written works are in *italics*, and television shows, song titles, and other forms of entertainment are in "quotation marks." I hope that this clarifies the many titles listed for the reader.

INTRODUCTION

I began my career in the entertainment business as a performer in films, theater, night-clubs, and television shows during the 1960s and 1970s. As a dancer, I had the opportunity to study with or work for some of the best choreographers and dance directors of the time: Donn Arden, Barbette, Toni Basil, Jack Cole, Rita D'Amico, Ron Fletcher, Bob Fosse, Lester Horton, Gene Kelly, Michael Kidd, Hugh Lambert, Sylvia Lewis, Eugene Loring, Jonathon Lucas, Anita Mann, Hermes Pan, Jack Regas, Jaime Rogers, James Truitte, and David Winters.

But my first real insight into film choreography and musical staging came in 1969, when I assisted Miriam Nelson on the Warner Bros. comedy **The Great Bank Robbery**, set in the Old West. Although the film was not technically a musical, it did have several songs in it, plus one major scene which took place at a "Town Hall Dance" party. Watching Miriam plot and plan the big musical number involving Zero Mostel, Kim Novak, and the Mitchell Boys Choir, I was amazed at her knowledge of the camera (shots, angles, etc.), as well as her attention to plot, character, period, and overall mood of the film. She worked closely with director Hal Averback every step of the way, discussing her concepts and showing him all of the action and dance we created as we rehearsed. After Miriam and I blocked out each musical sequence on the sound-stage, it was my job to teach the actors their movement patterns and dance steps.

Miriam's work involved not only the major musical sequences: she worked with the actors on all specialized movement throughout the film. One job I eagerly volunteered for was to teach Kim Novak how to twirl tassels from her bare breasts — a seduction sequence which was filmed only for the European release as it was still the puritanical sixties. The ever-ladylike Miriam graciously turned my offer down and spent hours in Ms. Novak's trailer teaching her to twirl like a pro. Ah, a cutting room floor treasure!

When it came time to shoot the big "Town Hall Dance" party, Miriam was suddenly whisked away to Columbia to direct Ingrid Bergman, Goldie Hawn, and Walter Matthau in a rock 'n' roll dance sequence in **Cactus Flower**. I was left alone to finish the picture.

The "Town Hall Dance" scene involved Kim Novak, Clint Walker, Akin Tamiroff, Ruth Warrick, and about 70 extras and dancers. As the scene was to depict the passage of time over the course of an evening, they had to perform several social dances of the 1890s: the Varsovienne (a French folk dance which is commonly used for dialogue sequences because both partners face front), square dances, waltzes, and polkas. I worked privately with Ms. Novak and Mr. Walker — two hardworking human beings whose experience with dance was limited, but whose professionalism was not — staging their dance movements so that they could deliver dialogue and allow their reactions to register for the camera while performing some complicated social dance patterns. Ruth Warrick and Akim Tamiroff were also easy to work with and learned quickly. I was very happy not to have the ever-energetic Mostel in the sequence!

On the day of the actual shooting, I was given about one hour with the actors, dancers, and extras to block out large patterns of movement for each dance sequence. We had divided the dialogue into three separate sequences, deciding beforehand which dialogue would be appropriate for each dance pattern. The entire cast and crew waited patiently while I taught the dancers and the pressure begin to mount. When the director asked if we were ready to shoot, I answered, "Yes," and immediately heard the cry of "Places!"

Since dialogue was being spoken and recorded, there could be no music played. I alone heard the music through a headset. I would have to direct the dancing actors by waving my arms so that they would be in sync with the music, which would be added to the soundtrack later. This was a surprise to me, since we had not discussed it beforehand, but I pretended that I did this all of the time.

And so before me stood more than 70 human beings, their eyes focused on me. "We're rolling!" was spoken, the cameras turned, and the sea of humanity started dancing. I counted silently with my mouth and waved my hands like a conductor, while Clint and Kim danced and said their dialogue, Akim and Ruth registered reactions, and the dancers whirled about the set. I was sweating bullets. On screen, the sequence goes by in a flash, but I remember the planning, the organization, the cooperation — and the responsibility.

My second up-close experience with film choreography came when Howard Jeffrey was assigned the job of staging the musical numbers in **Willy Wonka and the Chocolate Factory** (Paramount, 1971). He hired me as a member of his "skeleton crew"—a group of six dancers with whom he could experiment and create the musical numbers and staging before he went to Europe where the movie would be filmed. He would teach the actors in Germany what we had done in California. On a bare stage at Twentieth Century–Fox in Century City, six of us stood in for the actors—singing and creating the movement as Howard staged each sequence, working with a pianist to create the concept, form, and musical arrangement.

Because the film did not have a large budget to compete with the lavish **Oliver!** (1968) its creative concept for the musical sequences was to have the songs flow simply in and out of the action, performed by few cast members. It had been decided that the film would not contain major dance sequences. The director, Mel Stuart, and Howard had decided that none of the characters in Roald Dahl's wonderfully delicate book should burst into a song and tap dance, but rather, perform the songs as "Musical Reality."

With the incredible Betty Walberg creating the dance arrangements at the piano on the soundstage, for one month the skeleton crew worked under Howard's direction, performing pieces of business, creating patterns of movement, and defining the shape of each musical sequence. Whenever we would improvise and start to perform complicated dance steps, Howard would gently remind us of the concept and make us walk or gesture to bring the songs to life. The only actual dance steps in the film were performed by Jack Albertson, who was a real hoofer and could make the dance steps seem to spring from his joy.

It was fascinating to be there at the beginning: watching entire scenes take shape, singing "The Candy Man" for the first time, and being privy to the basic concept of the creative team which would eventually be filmed and captured on celluloid forever.

Although the film industry, critics, and audiences alike do not seem to want to understand the art of choreography, it is very simple. It literally means to "write with dance." The term has since been used to include people who create sequences in mime, martial arts, and other specialized forms of movement.

Choreography and dance direction are very special arts. You either have the desire and ability to do it, or you don't. These creators combine their knowledge of dance, their own personal background and style of movement, awareness of the camera and what it can do, period, mood, and just sheer art. Many people sit down and place words in order on the blank sheet before them to create a screenplay, but not many can make that blank sheet dance, causing audiences to react with emotion and admiration.

The film choreographer is responsible for so much of each film's style, pace, movement, and character. The classic movie musicals are loved for their dancing as much as anything else. Today's films contain unobtrusive movement or dance sequences which often become the most memorable part of the movie.

During my research for this book, I wrote to author Alvin H. Marill, whose excellent book *Movies Made for Television* was one of my sources, asking him for updated choreographic credits for movies made for television. In his prompt return letter, he wrote, "For space purposes I cut down on the technical credits for each movie, and unfortunately the choreographer had to go." In the current film reviews in *Variety* and *Hollywood Reporter*, choreography credits are not listed. *Sight and Sound* is, at present, the only English-language publication which continues to list choreographic credit. In such respected annual publications as *Screen World*, *Film Review*, and *Film Yearbook*, you can only sporadically find the name of the person who created the dance sequences, as from time to time choreographic credits are eliminated.

The present work is intended to correct this lapse in reference coverage.

The history of dance on film has been neglected for too long. Most often, it is the dancing stars who have been discussed and examined, for the general public has been able to respond to those celebrities they admire and pay their hard-earned money to see. Very few moviegoers have realized who the people behind the concepts, the choreography, and the filming of dance in the movies are. Most seem to believe the dancers make up the steps as they go along. In this, choreographers and dance directors share the endless frustration of the screenwriter. As the authors of the movement sequences, they have been relegated to the back row of recognition. Perhaps that is because of the power of film — the power that makes us *want* to believe that the actors and actresses are making it up as they go along.

Some of the dancing stars did make it up — not as they went along, but with weeks (sometimes months) of planning and creation. Many of the stars simply repeated variations of routines they had refined over many years in vaudeville or stage shows. However, though they may have been responsible for the creation of their personal dance steps, they usually worked in conjunction with another dance director or choreographer, one who could help them conceive and shape the musical numbers. And when it came time to receive credit for their dance creations, even the great dancing stars often found themselves standing in the shadows with the rest of the choreographers.

This is one of the reasons that many great choreographers and dance directors worked only briefly in film. The frustration of not having complete control over the musical sequences, or of seeing their work incorrectly photographed and edited by others, sent many back to the stage, television, or ballet world, where they could have more control over their work.

But there were many who continued working in the movie industry, leaving behind an incredible volume of work which is available to all of us through the longevity of film — and now, the growing libraries of videotapes and laser discs.

Choreographers are a specific classification of artist. When asked, "Why did you become a choreographer?" most of those I interviewed answered simply, "I was always a choreographer...a director." They spoke of shows they had conceived, directed, and choreographed in their backyards as children, the ideas for the music and dance simply pouring out of their heads. They remembered endless dance routines they created in their bedrooms. Brad Jeffries' mother,

Sandy Hanna, reminisced over the phone: "Oh, he's been dancing since he was about four years old. I had to get him a portable record player so he could carry it around. And he was always putting on shows. I remember many late nights having to run out and find some dry ice for his Halloween displays on the front lawn." They all had to study and perfect their craft, but the inclination was simply there. Their unique collection of talents allowed them to move easily into the ranks of director, as so many have, for it is basically the same art form: creating, organizing, visualizing, and collaborating. They are authors of movement.

Their methods of working vary greatly. Some begin with the plot and the characters, allowing themselves to get inside of the dramatic motivation and exploring how those people would move. Others use dancers to create the movement — a living palate on which to paint the dancing pictures. Many arrive at rehearsals with a concrete plan: large hunks of dance steps, patterns and staging. Some allow the music to guide them emotionally as their bodies move in their personal physical reactions to the rhythms. There are those who work to counts (the famous "a 5–6–7–8" from *A Chorus Line* is the musician's loving tribute to choreographers); others work to percussive vocal sounds like Jack Cole's "oom-cha" here and "ba-donk" there. Although the methods vary, the end result is the same: a scenario or emotion told in movement.

The Academy Awards

The Academy Award for Best Dance Direction was awarded in only three years, 1935–1937. Following are the nominees, with the winner listed first. Four "Special Awards" were given from 1949 through 1968.

In 1935 two musical numbers were cited per nomination and a certificate, rather than an "Oscar" statuette, was given. Dave Gould won for the "I've Got a Feeling You're Fooling" number from **Broadway Melody of 1936** and the "Straw Hat" number from **Folies Bergère**. Busby Berkeley was nominated for the "Lullaby of Broadway" and "The Words Are in My Heart" numbers from **Golddiggers of 1935**. Bobby Connolly was nominated for "Latin from Manhattan" from **Go into Your Dance**, and "Playboy from Paree" from **Broadway Hostess**. Sammy Lee was nominated for "Lovely Lady" and "Too Good to Be True" from **King of Burlesque**; and Hermes Pan for "The Piccolino" and "Top Hat" from **Top Hat**. Leroy Prinz was nominated for "Elephant Number — It's the Animal in Me" from **The Big Broadcast of 1936**, and "Viennese Waltz" from **All the King's Horses**. And Benjamin Zemach was nominated for the "Hall of Kings" number from **She**. (It is unknown why the other nominees had to submit two numbers for nomination while Zemach is only listed with one.)

In 1936 only one number was cited per nomination, and Oscar statuettes were given. Seymour Felix won the Award for "A Pretty Girl Is Like a Melody" number from **The Great Ziegfeld**. Busby Berkeley was nominated for "Love and War" from **Golddiggers of 1937**; Bobby Connolly was nominated for "1000 Love Songs" from **Cain and Mabel**; Dave Gould was nominated for "Swingin' the Jinx" from **Born to Dance**; Jack Haskell was nominated for "Skating Ensemble" from **One in a Million**; Russell Lewis was nominated for "The Finale" from **Dancing Pirate**, and Hermes Pan was nominated for the "Bojangles of Harlem" number from **Swing Time**.

In 1937 Hermes Pan won the Award for the "Fun House" number from **A Damsel in Distress**. Busby Berkeley was nominated for "Finale" from **Varsity Show**; Bobby Connolly was nominated for "Too Marvelous for Words" from **Ready, Willing and Able**; Dave Gould was nominated for "All God's Chillun Got Rhythm" from **A Day at the Races**; Sammy Lee was nominated for "Swing Is Here to Stay" from **Ali Baba Goes to Town**; Harry Losee was nominated for "Prince

Igor" from **Thin Ice**, and Leroy Prinz was nominated for the "Luau" number from **Waikiki Wedding**.

Four special awards have been given. In 1949 Fred Astaire was saluted with "A Special Award for his unique artistry and his contributions to the technique of motion pictures." In 1951 a Special Award went to Gene Kelly "In appreciation of his versatility as an actor, director and dancer, and specifically for his brilliant achievements in the art of choreography on film." In 1961 Jerome Robbins was honored for **West Side Story**: "For his brilliant achievements in the art of choreography on film." And in 1968 a Special Award went to Onna White for **Oliver!**, citing her "Outstanding achievement in choreography."

*　　　*　　　*

The reader may wish to gain further information about dancers and choreographers directly from the professional societies in the field. The four most important are

Career Transition for Dancers (CTFD)
5757 Wilshire Blvd., 6th Floor
Los Angeles, Calif.

L.A. Dance Foundation
(formerly Choreographers Resourcenter — CRC)
627 North Palm Drive
Beverly Hills, Calif. 90210

Professional Dancers Society (PDS)
270 N. Canon Drive, Suite 103
Beverly Hills, Calif. 90210

Society of Stage Directors and Choreographers (SSDC)
1501 Broadway, 31st Floor
New York, New York 10036-5633

BIBLIOGRAPHY

The following books and newspaper and periodical articles were sources for much of the information in the book. I applaud and thank the following authors for gathering bits and pieces of this fascinating history and including it in their work for posterity.

BOOKS

Altman, Rick. *The American Film Musical.* Bloomington: Indiana University Press, 1989.

Ames, Jerry, and Siegelman, Jim. *The Book of Tap.* New York: McKay, 1977.

Anderson, John Murray, and Abercrombie, Hugo. *Out Without My Rubbers.* New York: Library, 1954.

The Annual Obituary. Chicago and London: St. James, 1988–1992.

Astaire, Fred. *Steps in Time.* New York, Harper, 1959.

Babington, Bruce and Evans, Peter William. *Blue Skies and Silver Linings—Aspects of the Hollywood Musical.* Manchester, England: Manchester University Press, 1985.

Barnett, Lincoln. *Writing on Life: Sixteen Close-ups.* New York: Sloan, 1951.

Barrios, Richard. *A Song in the Dark.* New York: Oxford University Press, 1995.

Bloom, Ken. *American Song—The Complete Musical Theater Companion,* New York, Facts on File, 1985.
_____. *Hollywood Song—The Complete Film and Musical Companion.* New York: Facts on File, 1995.

Brooks, Tim, and March, Earle. *The Complete Directory to Prime Time Network TV Shows—1946–Present.* New York: Ballantine, 1988.

Cagney, James. *Cagney by Cagney.* New York: Doubleday, 1976.

Casper, Joseph Andrew. *Stanley Donen.* Metuchen, N.J.: Scarecrow, 1983.

Castle, Charles. *The Folies Bergere.* New York: Franklin Watts, 1985.

Chaplin, Saul. *The Golden Age of Movie Musicals and Me.* Norman: University of Oklahoma Press, 1994.

Chujoy, Anatole, and Manchester, P.W., comps. and eds. *The Dance Encyclopedia.* New York: Simon and Schuster, 1967.

Cocchi, John. *Second Feature.* New York: Citadel, 1991.

Connor, Jim. *Ann Miller, Tops in Taps.* New York: Franklin Watts, 1981.

Croce, Arlene. *After Images.* New York: Knopf, 1977.
_____. *The Fred Astaire and Ginger Rogers Book.* New York: Galahad, 1972.

Danilova, Alexandra, and Brubach, Holly. *Choura, the Memoirs of Alexandra Danilova.* New York: Knopf, 1986.

Davis, Ronald L. *The Glamour Factory.* Dallas: Southern Methodist University Press, 1993.

Delamater, Jerome. *Dance in the Hollywood Musical.* Ann Arbor: UMI Research, 1981.

DeMille, Agnes. *America Dances.* New York: Macmillan, 1980.
_____. *And Promenade Home.* New York: Da Capo (reprint), 1980.
_____. *The Book of the Dance,* New York: Golden, 1963.
_____. *Dance to the Piper.* New York: Da Capo (reprint), 1980.
_____. *Portrait Gallery.* Boston: Houghton Mifflin, 1990.

Ebsen, Buddy. *The Other Side of Oz.* Newport Beach, Calif.: Donovan, 1993.

Edwards, Anne. *The DeMilles, an American Family.* New York: Abrams, 1988.

Feuer, Jane. *The Hollywood Musical.* London: Macmillan, 1993.

Fitzgerald, Michael G. *Universal Pictures.* New Rochelle, N.Y.: Arlington House, 1977.

Fordin, Hugh. *The World of Entertainment.* Garden City, N.Y.: Doubleday, 1975.

Frank, Rusty E. *Tap!* New York: Morrow, 1990.

Franks, A. H. *Ballet, a Decade of Endeavor.* New York: Pitman, 1956.

Gadan, Francis, and Maillard, Robert. *A Dictionary of Modern Ballet.* London: Methuen, 1959.

Ganzl, Kurt. *The British Musical Theatre, 1865–1984.* New York: Oxford University Press, 1984.

Gottfried, Martin. *All His Jazz: The Life and Death of Bob Fosse.* New York: Bantam, 1990.

Green, Stanley. *Encyclopedia of the Musical Film.* New York: Oxford University Press, 1981.

_____. *Encyclopedia of the Musical Theatre.* New York: Da Capo, 1976.

_____. *Hollywood Musicals—Year by Year.* Milwaukee: Leonard, 1990.

Grubb, Kevin Boyd. *Razzle Dazzle: The Life and Work of Bob Fosse.* New York: St. Martin's, 1989.

Harvey, Stephen. *Directed by Vincente Minnelli.* New York: Harper & Row, 1989.

Haskins, James. *Black Dance in America—A History Through Its People,* New York, HarperCollins, 1990.

Haskins, Jim, and Mitgang, N.R. *Mr. Bojangles.* New York: Morrow, 1988.

Higham, Charles. *Cecil B. DeMille.* New York: Scribner, 1973.

Hirschhorn, Clive. *Gene Kelly.* New York: St. Martin's, 1984.

_____. *The Hollywood Musical.* New York: Crown, 1981.

Hungerford, Mary Jane. "Dancing in Commercial Motion Pictures." Ph.D. diss., Columbia University, 1946.

Jamison, Judith, with Kaplan, Howard. *Dancing Spirit.* New York: Doubleday, 1993.

Kamin, Dan. *Charlie Chaplin's One Man Show.* Metuchen, N.J.: Scarecrow, 1984.

Kislan, Richard. *Hoofing on Broadway.* New York: Prentice Hall, 1987.

Knox, Donald. *The Movie Factory: How MGM Made "An American in Paris."* New York: Praeger, 1973.

Kobal, John. *Gotta Sing Gotta Dance.* Rev. ed. London: Spring, 1983.

_____. *People Will Talk.* New York: Knopf, 1985.

_____. *Rita Hayworth: The Time, the Place and the Woman.* New York: Norton, 1977.

Koegler, Horst. *The Concise Oxford Dictionary of Ballet.* Updated ed. New York: Oxford University Press, 1987.

Kreuger, Miles. *The Movie Musical from Vitaphone to 42nd Street.* New York: Dover, 1975.

Leonard, William Torbett. *Broadway Bound: A Guide to Shows That Died Aborning.* Metuchen, N.J.: Scarecrow, 1983.

Lemmon, David. *The Benson and Hedges British Theatre Yearbook.* London: Andre Deutsch, 1992.

Loney, Glenn. *Unsung Genius: The Passion of Dancer-Choreographer Jack Cole.* New York: Franklin Watts, 1984.

Long, Richard A. *The Black Tradition in American Dance.* New York: Rizzoli, 1989.

Maltin, Leonard. *Leonard Maltin's Movie Encyclopedia.* New York: Dutton, 1994.

Marill, Alvin H. *Movies Made for Television.* Westport, Conn.: Arlington House, 1980.

Martin, John. *The Dance.* New York: Tudor, 1946.

Martin, Tony, and Charisse, Cyd. *The Two of Us.* New York: Mason/Charter, 1976.

Medved, Harry, with Randy Dreyfuss. *The Fifty Worst Films of All Time.* New York: Popular Library, 1978.

Minnelli, Vincent, with Hector Arce. *I Remember It Well.* New York: Doubleday, 1974.

Mordden, Ethan. *The Hollywood Musical.* New York: St. Martin's, 1981.

_____. *The Hollywood Studios.* New York: Knopf, 1988.

Morrow, Lee Alan. *The Tony Award Book: Four Decades of Greatness.* New York: Abbeville, 1987.

Mueller, John. *Astaire Dancing.* New York: Knopf, 1985.

Parish, James Robert. *The Fox Girls.* New Rochelle, N.Y.: Arlington House, 1971.

_____. *The Paramount Pretties.* New Rochelle, N.Y.: Arlington House, 1972.

_____. *The RKO Gals.* New Rochelle, N.Y.: Arlington House, 1974.

_____. *The Slapstick Queens.* New York: Castle, 1973.

Parish, James Robert, and Stanke, Don. *The Glamour Girls.* New Rochelle, N.Y.: Arlington House, 1975.

_____ and _____. *Hollywood Baby Boomers.* New York: Garland, 1992.

_____ and _____. *The Leading Ladies.* New Rochelle, N.Y.: Arlington House, 1977.

Parish, James Robert; Stanke, Don; and Mank, Gregory W. *The Hollywood Beauties.* New Rochelle, N.Y.: Arlington House, 1978.

Parker, David L., and Siegel, Esther. *Guide to Dance in Film.* Performing Arts Information Guide Series, vol. 3. Detroit: Gale Research. 1978.

Pike, Bob, and Martin, Dave. *The Genius of Busby Berkeley.* Reseda, Calif.: Creative Film Society, 1973.

Previn, André. *No Minor Chords.* New York: Doubleday, 1991.

Prevots, Naima. *Dancing in the Sun: Hollywood Choreographers 1915–1937.* Ann Arbor: UMI Research, 1987.

Ragan, David. *Who's Who in Hollywood.* New York: Facts on File, 1992.

Robertson, Allen, and Hutera, Donald. *The Dance Handbook.* Boston: Hall, 1988.

Rozsa, Miklos. *Double Life.* New York: Wynwood, 1982.

Rubin, Martin. *Show Stoppers: Busby Berkeley and the Tradition of Spectacle.* New York: Columbia University Press, 1993.

Schatz, Thomas. *The Genius of the System.* New York: Pantheon, 1988.

Schultz, Margie. *Eleanor Powell: A Bio-Bibliography.* Westport, Conn.: Greenwood, 1995.

Shawn, Ted, with Poole, Gray. *One Thousand and One Night Stands.* New York: Da Capo, 1979.

Silverman, Stephen M. *Dancing on the Ceiling: Stanley Donen and His Movies.* New York: Knopf, 1996.

Stacy, Jan, and Syvertsen, Ryder. *Rockin' Reels.* Chicago: Contemporary, 1984.

Stearns, Marshall, and Stearns, Jean. *Jazz Dance.* New York: Macmillan, 1968.

Straight, Raymond, and Henie, Lief. *Queen of Ice, Queen of Shadows.* New York: Stein and Day, 1985.

Taylor, John Russell, and Jackson, Arthur. *The Hollywood Musical.* New York: McGraw-Hill, 1971.

Terry, Walter. *The Dance in America.* New York: Harper, 1956.

Tharp, Twyla. *Push Comes to Shove.* New York: Bantam, 1992

Thiel-Cramer, Barbara. *Flamenco*. Linigno, Sweden: Remark, 1991.

Thomajan, Dale. *From Cyd Charisse to "Psycho": A Book of Movie Bests*. New York: Walker, 1992.

Thomas, Tony. *The Films of Gene Kelly*. Secaucus, N.J.: Citadel, 1974.

_____. *That's Dancing!* New York: Abrams, 1984.

Thomas, Tony, and Terry, Jim, with Berkeley, Busby. *The Busby Berkeley Book*. New York: New York Graphic Society, 1973.

Towers, Deirdre. *Dance Film and Video Guide*. Princeton, N.J.: Dance Horizons/Princeton, 1991.

Variety's Who's Who in Show Business. New York: Garland, 1985.

Video Hound's Golden Movie Retriever. Detroit, Washington, and London, Visible Ink, 1994, 1995.

Walker, Kathrine Sorley. *Dance and Its Creators: Choreographers at Work*. New York: John Day, 1972.

Wayburn, Ned. *The Art of Stage Dancing*. New York: Belvedere (reprinted), 1980.

White, Joan, ed. *20th Century Dance in Britain*. London: Dance, 1991.

Willis, John. *Screen World Annuals*. New York: Crown, 1949–1994.

_____. *Theatre World Annuals*. New York: Crown, 1943–1993.

Zorina, Vera. *Zorina*. New York: Farrar Strauss Giroux, 1986.

ARTICLES

Alpert, Hollis. "West Side Story." *Dance Magazine*, October 1960.

Anderson, Jack. "Danny Daniels Says Grumble." *Dance Magazine*, December 1965.

_____. "The Fabulous Career of Bronislava Nijinska." *Dance Magazine*, August 1963.

_____. "His Only Dogma Is 'No Dogma.'" *Dance Magazine*, November 1969.

_____. "Valerie Bettis, Choreographer and Modern Dancer, Is Dead." *New York Times*, September 28, 1982.

Armstrong, James. "Marge Champion: San Francisco Hoofer." *Dance Magazine*, July 1976.

Arvey, Verna. "Dancing for the Camera." *The American Dancer*, January 1936.

Bailey, Peter. "Michael Peters: The Dance Whiz Behind 'Thriller.'" *Ebony*, June 1984.

Barnes, Clive. "Kenneth Macmillan's Legacy." *Dance Magazine*, January 1993.

Barzel, Ann. "Anthony Z. Nelle, the Chronicle of a Dance Director and Producer." *Dance Magazine*, August 1945.

_____. "Let's Talk About 'Teacher.'" *Dance Magazine*, June 1962.

_____. "Looking at Television." *Dance Magazine*, multiple issues, 1954–1968.

Bayes, Atholie. "Dancers Become Actresses." *The American Dancer*, June 1937.

_____. "If You Can Dance You Must — Says Harry Losee." *The American Dancer*, November 1937.

Bell, Joseph N. "Donn Arden's Art: Beauty, Disasters Wrapped in Extravagance." *Los Angeles Times*, July 15, 1988.

Boroff, David. "Joe Layton — Man in Motion." *Dance Magazine*, September 1959.

_____. "West Side Story." *Dance Magazine*, April 1957.

Bradburn, Don. "Los Angeles Seen." *Dance Magazine*, multiple issues, 1982–1983.

Brennan, Judy. "Choreography Glides Back into Focus on Silver Screen." *Los Angeles Times*, August 1994.

Bruce, Leon. "Classic Hindu Dancer." *Dance Magazine*, March 1959.

Calvin, Kenneth W. "The Big Idea of Fanchon and Marco." *The Dance*, March and April 1929.

Clandon, Laura. "Meet Herbert Ross." *Dance Magazine*, January 1958.

Clark, Roy. "Alex Romero Compares Hollywood and Broadway." *Dance Magazine*, January 1962.

_____. "Better Known as Maggie." *Dance Magazine*, September 1962.

_____. "Hollywood and Las Vegas." *Dance Magazine*, multiple issues, 1957–1965.

_____. "30 Years of Nick Castle." *Dance Magazine*, February 1964.

Cole, Jack. "Three Definitions ... Dance Director, Choreographer, Stager of Movement." *Dance Magazine*, April 1949.

Como, William. "For the Worlds of After Dark." *Dance Magazine*, December 1962.

Constantine. "Dance Theater in Hollywood." *Dance Magazine*, April 1948.

_____. "'Dancing Is a Business' — LeRoy Prinz." *Dance Magazine*, September 1944.

Cooper, H.E. "The Black Crook." *The Dance*, September 1926.

Copland, Roger. "Broadway Dance." *Dance Magazine*, November 1974.

Cox, Dan. "Jeffrey Hornaday Breaks Tradition." *Dance Magazine*, December 1985.

_____. "Video Fever!" *Dance Magazine*, October 1984.

Crain, Llewellyn. "Dancer Opens His Own Doors to 'Fame.'" *Los Angeles Daily News*, May 25, 1985.

Dalzell, Allan Cameron. "Hale, Hale, the Troupes All Here." *The Dance*, 1930.

David, Martin A. "Sallid Saves Passion for 'Healing' Works." *Los Angeles Times*, April 13, 1986.

DeMille, Agnes. "Laurey Makes Up Her Mind." *Dance Magazine*, March 1963.

deVries, Hilary. "It's Been So Entertaining." *Los Angeles Times*, May 1, 1994.

Dewey, Lucia. "Spashing into Film Industry with a 'Duck,' Choreographer Sarah Elgart." *DramaLogue*, August 7–13, 1986.

Dougherty, John. "The Romance of Sujata and Asoka." *Dance Magazine*, October 1962.

Dunning, Jennifer. "Ballet's Former 'Bad Lad' Is Back with His Own Troupe." *New York Times*, December 15, 1982.

Dwan, Robert. "A Legend in His Own Feet." *Los Angeles Times*, July 26, 1981.

Egan, Carol. "Larry Fuller: His Dues Are Paid." *Dance Magazine*, February 1980.

Estrada, Ric. "Reflections on a Broadway Flop." *Dance Magazine*, January 1968.

Everette, Walter. "Putting the Dance on Ice." *Dance Magazine*, February 1946.

_____. "Want a Dance Job?" *Dance Magazine*, February 1943.

Farber, Stephen. "'The Turning Point': A Revolution for Hollywood." *New West*, November 21, 1977.

Fatt, Amelia. "Flamboyant Maestro." *Dance Magazine*, October 1969.

Felix, Seymour. "Dance Director's Grief." *The Dance*, January 1929.

_____. "Speeding Up the Show." *The Dance*, November 1928.

_____. "What About Chorus Boys?" *The Dance*, February 1929.

Francis, Roland. "The New Extra Girl." *Photoplay*, December 1929.

Fuller, Graham. "Gene Kelly." *Interview*, May 1994.

Galligan, David. "Eleanor Powell Remembers Astaire, Toscanini, MGM." *Drama-Logue*, January 15–21, 1981.

Garafola, Lynn. "The Unexpected Choreographic Career of Elizabeth Aldrich." *Dance Magazine*, March 1995.

Gold, Ronald. "It's 'Non-Choreography' but 'All Dance'!" *Dance Magazine*, July 1968.

Goldstein, Patrick. "Shrimp and Crew: Street-wise Bugaloo." *Los Angeles Times*, March 25, 1984.

Goodman, Saul. "Dancing Along with Mitch." *Dance Magazine*, September 1963.

_____. "Meet Linda and Stuart Hodes." *Dance Magazine*, July 1962.

Greenhill, Janet. "Joe Tremaine and L.A. Jazz." *Dance Teacher Now*, March 1994.

Grubb, Kevin. "Basil Blasts Off." *Dance Magazine*, March 1988.

_____. "Dancefilms '85." *Dance Magazine*, December 1984.

_____. "Dancetera/Broadway and Beyond." *Dance Magazine*, multiple issues, 1983–1988.

_____. "Dancing with the Nouveau Reich." *Dance Magazine*, March 1984.

Gruen, John. "American Dance Machine: The Era of Reconstruction." *Dance Magazine*, February 1978.

_____. "Smuin Sets Sail on Broadway." *Dance Magazine*, January 1988.

Guerrero, Dan. "Ortega Spices 'Salsa.'" *Drama-Logue*, May 5–11, 1988.

Haithman, Diane. "With a Song in Its Heart." *Los Angeles Times*, April 26, 1992.

"Hanya Holm, The Life and Legacy." *The Journal for Stage Directors and Choreographers*, 1993.

Harper, Ray. "The Magic of the Rasch Cane." *The Dance*, January 1928.

Hawkins, William. "Something About Gwen Verdon." *Dance Magazine*, August 1956.

"Hollywood Dance Directors." *Dance Magazine*, February 1947.

Hooks, Ted. "Hollywood Commentary/Hollywood and Las Vegas." *Dance Magazine*, multiple issues, 1947–1957.

Horosko, Marian. "Tap, Tapping and Tappers." *Dance Magazine*, October 1971.

Horton, Lester. "A Choreographic Design for 'Atlantis.'" *Dance Magazine*, July 1947.

Hungerford, Mary Jane. "How to Get the Most from Screen Dancing." *Dance Magazine*, June 1948.

_____. "Must Screen Dances Be 'Incidental'?" *Dance Magazine*, June 1947.

Hunt, Dennis. "'Hot City' Cashes In on Disco Craze." *Los Angeles Times*, August 5, 1978.

"It Takes Two to Tango." *People*, March 22, 1993.

Joel, Lydia. "Conversation with Peter Gennaro." *Dance Magazine*, August 1964.

_____. "Dancer-Choreographer-Show Director Now Film Director Herb Ross Talks Shop." *Dance Magazine*, December 1967.

Kaplan, Larry. "The Man Who Made the Ballerina Prima." *Arts and Entertainment*, June 1993.

Kelly, Gene. "Making a Cineballet for 'American in Paris.'" *Dance Magazine*, August 1951.

Knight, Arthur. "Dance in the Movies." *Dance Magazine*, multiple issues, 1955–1960.

_____. "Dance in the Movies — Paging Oscar!" *Dance Magazine*, March 1958.

_____. "Gene Nelson, Agnes DeMille and 'Oklahoma!'" *Dance Magazine*, July 1955.

_____. "Hermes Pan, Who Is He?" *Dance Magazine*, January 1960.

Knowles, Jocelyn W. "Lessons with Carmelita Maracci." *Dance Magazine*, May 1964.

Koegler, Horst. "Portrait of Aurel Von Milloss." *Dance Magazine*, May 1960.

Kutner, Nanette. "How the Charleston Came to Broadway." *The Dance*, December 1925.

Lang, Harry. "He Didn't Know How!" *Photoplay*, June 1930.

Levenson, Lew. "Dances Staged By —?" *The Dance*, December 1928.

Lewis, Emory. "Helen Tamiris: Plain and Fancy." *Dance Magazine*, June 1955.

Livingston, D.D. "Taps for Bill Robinson." *Dance Magazine*, January 1950.

Loney, Glenn. "Geva Talks About Yesterday, Today and Tamara, Too." *Dance Magazine*, January 1973.

Lowell, Sondra. "The Days When Talent Was Tapped." *Los Angeles Times*, September 12, 1979.

Luft, Herbert G. "Ernst Matray, a Career of More Than 65 Years." *Films in Review*, January 1976.

McDonagh, Don. "Léonide Massine, Choreographer, Dies." *New York Times*, March 17, 1979.

McKairnes, Jim. "He's Dancing as Fast as He Can." *Moviegoer*, August 1984.

MacMahon, Audrey. "Footwork + Headwork = Carl Randall." *The Dance*, April 1928.

Marshall, Sidney. "The New Hollywood Dancing Girl." *The Dance*, December 1929.

Maynard, Olga. "Nureyev, The Man and the Myth." *Dance Magazine*, May 1973.

Mazo, Joseph H. "Matt Mattox; the Master's Voice." *Dance Magazine*, March 1993.

"Michael Peters Makes Music Move." *Dance Magazine*, September 1984.

Miller, M.L. "See It with Music." *The Dance*, June 1929.

Mitchell, Curtis. "Old Forms to New Music." *The Dance*, April 1926.

Mueller, John. "The Astaire Illusion." *Dance Magazine*, November 1987.

Nagrin, Daniel. "In Quest of a Dance." *Dance Magazine*, September 1951.

Narodny, Ivan. "The Dancie Arrives." *The Dance*, December 1929.

_____. "Dancies Preferred." *The Dance*, April 1930.

Nelson, Gene. "Gene Nelson: Working in Hollywood." *Dance Magazine*, May 1956.

Nevins, Catherine. "What Can Sound Pictures Do for Dancing?" *The Dance*, November 1928.

Norman, Shirley. "The Stage of Fashion — Roger Minami." *Vegas Visitor*, January 21, 1972.

O'Steen, Kathleen. "Choreographers Kick Up Storm over Vid Credits." *Variety*, October 7, 1992.

Ostlere, Hilary. "'Guys and Dolls,' Part One; Choreographer Christopher Chadman." *Dance Magazine*, September 1992.

Palatsky, Eugene. "Ernie Flatt in Action." *Dance Magazine*, December 1964.

Perlmutter, Donna. "Carmelita Maracci: An Appreciation." *Dance Magazine*, November 1987.

Philp, Richard. "Miss D's Day." *Dance Magazine*, December 1987.

Pierre, Dorathi Bock. "Hermes Pan — Dancing to Fame." *The American Dancer*, September 1936.

_____. "Hollywood Recognizes the Dance." *The American Dancer*, April 1936.

_____. "Johnny Boyle." *The American Dancer*, September 1937.

_____. "Katherine Dunham — Cool Scientist or Sultry Performer?" *Dance Magazine*, May 1947.

_____. "Larry Ceballos Returns from England." *The American Dancer*, June 1938.

Pikula, Joan. "Daniel Ezralow, Determined to Dance." *Dance Magazine*, April 1982.

_____. "Tommy Tune: Stretching Out in Space." *After Dark*, August 1975.

Porter, Keyes. "Seymour Felix — His Ideas on Dance Direction." *The Dance*, October 1927.

Provenzano, Tom. "Hooking Up with 'Five Guys Named Moe' (Plus Three)." *Drama-Logue*, July 22–28, 1993.

_____. "Learning Dance History with Michael Peters." *Drama-Logue*, September 28, 1993.

Rasch, Albertina. "The New World Ballet." *The Dance*, February 1929.

Rawlings, Paul. "Close-up of Bambi Linn and Rod Alexander." *Dance Magazine*, June 1958.

_____. "Grover Dale's Road to Broadway." *Dance Magazine*, July 1960.

Redelings, Lowell E. "The Hollywood Scene — Men Behind the Scenes." *Hollywood Citizen News*, November 11, 1951.

_____. "The Hollywood Scene — Women Behind the Scenes." *Hollywood Citizen News*, April 4, 1949.

Reiner, Jay. "Who's That Tap-Tap-Tapping on the Floor?" *Los Angeles Herald Examiner*, August 5, 1980.

Reiter, Susan. "John Carrafa: Read My Feet." *Los Angeles Times*, January 29, 1989.

Roberts, W. Adolphe. "Natacha Natova the Versatile." *The Dance*, September 1928.

Roman, Robert C. "Busby Berkeley." *Dance Magazine*, February 1968.

_____. "Hide Your Daughters, Here Comes Russell Markert." *Dance Magazine*, September 1969.

_____. "Jessie Matthews — England's Dancing Divinity of the Thirties." *Dance Magazine*, September 1966.

_____. "Ruby Keeler: Back to Broadway After 40 Years." *Dance Magazine*, December 1970.

Rosenwald, Peter J. "Breaking Away '80's Style." *Dance Magazine*, April 1984.

Russell, Nina. "Michael Bennett's 'Coco.'" *Dance Magazine*, February 1970.

Saber, Gai. "Funny Feet." *The Dance*, April 1927.

Sammy Kicks as Joan Wants Leroy but Uses Eddie to Master Steps." *Variety*, July 1933.

Sandler, Ken. "Break Dancers Twist, Turn Way Uptown." *Los Angeles Times*, March 25, 1984.

Scheur, Philip K. "Dancing Isn't Decoration." *Dance Magazine*, May 1946.

_____. "Hollywood Hoofer." *Dance Magazine*, January 1947.

Schoen, Elin. "The Broadway Baby — Live from New York." *New York Magazine*, July 23, 1979.

Scott, Tony. "Leroy Prinz, Man in Motion." *Variety*, Thirty-Sixth Annual Anniversary edition, 1969.

Service, Faith. "Ernest Belcher, the Teacher of 'It.'" *The Dance*, August 1928.

Shaner, Daniel. "'One and Only' Jeff Calhoun." *Drama-Logue*, December 4–10, 1986.

Silver, Gordon R. "Stepping Stars — Who Teaches the Stars to Dance?" *The Dance*, December 1929.

Small, Lina. "Matthew Diamond's Cutting Edge." *Dance Magazine*, October 1980.

Smith, Judy MacGregor. "Spotlight on William Milie." *Dance Magazine*, July 1974.

Smith, Rod. "Michael Smuin, Dancing in the Light." *San Francisco*, February 1984.

Sobel, Bernard. "Hollywood Dance Directors." *Dance Magazine*, February 1947.

_____. "1, 2, 3, — Kick!" *The Dance*, January 1929.

_____. "Ziegfeldiana." *Dance Magazine*, September 1947.

Sommer, Sally. "Steve Condos, 1918–90." *Village Voice*, October 2, 1990.

Stevenson, Salli. "Jaime Rogers; 'Fame's New Kid on the Block.'" *Los Angeles Times*, 1985.

Stock, Alice Demetrius. "He Speaks Fluent Body Language." *The Gazette*, February 20, 1994.

Stoop, Norma McLain. "Footloose: On Location with Herbert Ross." *Dance Magazine*, March 1984.

_____. "Spotlight On: Tony Stevens." *Dance Magazine*, May 1974.

Swisher, Viola Hegyi. "Bob Fosse Translates Sweet Charity from Stage to Screen." *Dance Magazine*, February 1969.

———. "Franz, Otherwise Known as Michel Panaieff, Tells About His Swanhildas." *Dance Magazine*, December 1967.

———. "Hollywood and Las Vegas." *Dance Magazine*, multiple issues, 1965–1982.

———. "The One and Only, Genuine, Original Hugh Lambert." *Dance Magazine*, March 1968.

———. "Rod Alexander: Back Where He Is Happy to Belong." *Dance Magazine*, June 1967.

———. "Tapper into Tape: Dancer-Choreographer-Teacher Danny Daniels." *Dance Magazine*, April 1980.

———. "To Thine Own Self Be True." *Dance Magazine*, April 1966.

———. "Triana!" *Dance Magazine*, July 1970.

———. "Xanadu." *Dance Magazine*, August 1980.

"Ten Dance Directors Have Corner on Staging in Motion Pictures." *Variety* October 19, 1933.

Terry, Walter. "The Alchemy of Dance Creation." *Dance Magazine*, January 1952.

Udavich, Mim. "I, Latina." *Vibe*, December 1993.

Valis-Hill, Constance. "Matt Mattox Comes of Age." *Dance Magazine*, November 1983.

Vargo, Mike. "A Crash Course in Chaplinism." *In Pittsburgh*, January 14–20, 1993.

Vaughan, David. "Dan Siretta: Rediscovering the American Musical." *Dance Magazine*, February 1978.

———. "Frederick Ashton." *Dance Magazine*, May 1974.

Vernon, Jacques M. "Will Precision Troupes Always Be Popular?" *The Dance*, February 1929.

Watts, Richard, Jr. "Musical Comedy and Revue Dancing—How Did It Develop?" *The Dance*, January 1929.

Wheelock, Julie. "Tapping the Source of Inspiration." *Los Angeles Times*, June 26, 1988.

Williamson, Liz, and Moore, Mike. "That Eclectic, Elusive Dance Called Jazz." *Dance Magazine*, February 1978.

Zadan, Craig. "Haworth, Hayworth—A Mistake Is a Mistake." *After Dark*, November 1971.

Zimmer, Elizabeth. "Out There with Karole Armitage." *Dance Magazine*, May 1986.

Ziony, Ruth Kramer. "George Reich, Master of Revels at the Latin Quarter and Points East." *After Dark*, November 1968.

TELEVISION SHOWS

"Bob Fosse: Steam Heat." *Dance in America*, PBS, 1990.

"Everybody Dance Now." *Dance in America*, PBS, 1991.

"MGM—When the Lion Roars." Turner Pictures, 1991.

"Story of a People—Expressions in Black." SI Communications, 1991.

INTERVIEWS

JOHNNY ALMARAZ—May 20, 1994 (by telephone)

DONN ARDEN—July 20, 1992, Mission Viejo, Calif.

EARL BARTON—May 21, 1994 (by telephone)

TONI BASIL—August 25, 1992, Los Angeles, Calif.

JIM BATES—April 25, 1996 (by telephone)

HAL BELFER—April 8, 1993—Las Vegas, Nev.

LIONEL BLAIR—May 7, 1993, Kensington Close Hotel, London

KIM BLANK—1994 (by telephone)

DANNY DARE—May 31, 1993 (by telephone)

RON FLETCHER—May 19, 1993 (by telephone)

ALAN JOHNSON—August 22, 1994, and October 13, 1994, Los Angeles, Calif.

DAN KAMIN—March 11, 1996, Hollywood, Calif.

SYLVIA LEWIS—January 29, 1992, Brea, Calif.

ARTHUR MITCHELL—June 23–25, 1995, Orlando, Fla.

JERRY MITCHELL—May 24, 1994 (by telephone)

MIRIAM NELSON—July 24, 1992, Santa Monica, Calif; October 9, 1994, Los Angeles, Calif.

FAYARD NICHOLAS—October 2, 1992 (by telephone)

STEVEN PECK—March 25, 1993, Fullerton, Calif.

ALEX ROMERO—November 3, 1996, Hollywood, Calif.

ALEX RUIZ—October 17, 1994 (by telephone)

SHABBA DOO—June 3, 1994 (by telephone)

JAMES STARBUCK—June 30, 1993, Beverly Hills, Calif.

TONY STEVENS—August 23, 1993, New York, N.Y.

TAM G. WARNER—January 12, 1994 (by telephone)

Part I. A History of Dance on Film

THE BEGINNINGS: 1893-1930

The history of film choreography begins at the turn of the century, along with the birth of the moving pictures themselves.

As early filmmakers sought to find subjects that moved, dance was one of the first to be captured on the new medium. Moving trains, running horses, and animated humans brought gasps from those first audiences as they appeared on the flickering screen. What "moved" better than dancing? It flowed, it twirled, it leapt, it pulsed and throbbed with the rhythm of life. As with the earliest dramatic and comedy films which simply photographed stage performances, these early dances were existing routines from shows that the dancers were appearing in. The idea of creating something special for the camera lay in the future. But those early dancers had to create — or have created for them — their dance routines. Thus the art of choreography was first documented for the ages.

The very nature of dance on film has long been a topic for discussion. Arlene Croce, noted dance critic, wrote in her book *After Images*:

> Dance in film is a subject that has taken on a semblance of controversy owing to the insistence of some writers that a conflict between dance and film exists.... people dancing in the movies are demonstrating one kind of human activity the camera can capture as well as any other. Movies can also invent dances that cannot be done anywhere except on film.... Most successful screen dances lie somewhere between total cinematic illusion and passive recording.... A cleanly photographed dance can be pretentious and boring; a complex cinematic extravaganza can be utterly devoid of kinetic charm.

These early filmmakers simply realized the power of the dance and aimed their cameras at it. Many popular Broadway music hall dancers of the day made the trek to Orange, New Jersey, to be filmed in the historic Black Maria (the first documented soundstage). Carmencita and the Nicholas Sisters of music hall fame and even South Sea island dancers from the Barnum and Bailey Circus and American Indian dancers from *Buffalo Bill's Wild West Show* were filmed performing their existing routines.

The very first press demonstration of projected film in the Edison Vitascope system was

Before there was a ***Will Rogers Follies*** (or a Tommy Tune), there was this knee-slapping, show-stopping number, performed by the Russell Markert Girls in **King of Jazz** (Universal, 1930).

presented as the eighth and last act of the variety bill at Koster and Bial's Music Hall, Broadway and 34th Street, New York, on April 23, 1896. Dance routines were an important part of that historic event.

Annabelle Moore is the most famous of the early film dancers. Her **Sun Dance** (1894) was shown as part of that first press demonstration. Many of the popular routines she created and performed on the music hall stage of the day were filmed (**Butterfly Dance, Flag Dance, Serpentine, Tambourine Dance**, etc.), and credit should be given to her as perhaps the screen's first choreographer. As her stage dances had been created with intricate lighting, some of her films were even hand-tinted to try and duplicate the excitement. A review from an early film critic praised her work:

> The arc began to sputter and out from the wall stepped a girl clad in garments more picturesque than protective and began to execute the intricacies of the **Butterfly Dance** … as the sputtering grew louder and the grinding more fervent she began … lifting her skirts by means of a stick in each hand and waving them in fanciful lepidopteral imitation.

In the short films popular in the nickelodeons, countless young girls *en pointe* (**Little Miss Lillian — Toe Danseuse**, Edison, 1903), barefoot Greek freestyle dancers (the Leander Sisters in **Cupid and Psyche**, Edison, 1897, or Ella Lola's **La Trilby**, Edison, 1898), and the ethnic wigglings of Little Egypt and others (**Imperial Japanese Dance**, 1894; Ella Lola's **Turkish Dance**, 1898; **Princess Rajah Dance**, 1904) were viewed with awe. In that first decade, theatrical dances were the most filmed: James Grundy in **Cake Walk, Buck and Wing Dance** and **Breakdown**, three dancers from the London company of *Gaiety Girls* in **The Carnival Dance** (all Kinetoscope, 1894), and many others—performing variety and vaudeville dancing (called "skirt dancing") and jostling tap-dance routines. These dancers earned from five to fifty dollars, depending on the length of the dance and the dancer's reputation. They usually performed their dance in one take.

When the photoplay was first created, dances continued to add movement and interest, even serving as the subject of the primitive stories, as in **The Messenger Boy and the Ballet Girl** (1905) and **Dancing Lessons** (1913). French film pioneer Georges Méliès often used dance for his experimentation, being the first to add technical effects (color, optical illusions, etc.) The kinetic nature of dance made it seem perfect for the new medium, and filmmakers actively sought out dancers for their cameras.

The inherent eroticism of dance also made it perfect for the "peep show" aspect of early cinema—which continues into the filmmaking of today. Scantily clad young women (and often, men) could writhe and gyrate under the guise of cultural authenticity, expressing their advertised "pagan desires" in "forbidden ceremonies." Young boys peering into these exotic delights could expand and explore their budding sensuality, much as they would with their dedicated perusal of *National Geographic Magazine* in the next decades. The beauty and sensuality of the moving body made it a natural for the moving pictures.

Most of the famous classic dancers of the time refused to be in films, thinking that the medium was temporary and tawdry. Only Loie Fuller (**Fire Dance**, 1906) and Anna Pavlova (**The Dumb Girl of Portici**, 1916) left their fabled images on commercial film for us to see from those early years—although it is argued that Isadora Duncan appeared in a show dance titled **Animated Picture Show**.

As films became feature length, many popular song-and-dance stage stars happily appeared in those early silents: Gaby Delys and Harry Pilcer (**Her Triumph**, 1915), Vernon and Irene Castle (**The Whirl of Life**, also 1915) and Ann Pennington (**Antics of Ann**, 1917), bringing their existing stage routines to film. Many of the early female acting stars also had dance experience and background, so a wide range of dance could be used—from ballet to interpretive—as screenwriters devised exotic or vulnerable heroines and used dance to enrich their characters.

In most dramatic and adventure films there was often a scene containing some sort of dance: a party, a period ballroom scene, a biblical orgy, or a nightclub or theater sequence. D.W. Griffith's **Intolerance** (which used members of the Denishawn school in 1916) and all of Theda Bara's and Nazimova's biblical epics contained dance sequences. Hula girls, ballerinas, chorus girls, and dancing slave or wild gypsy girls were often the heroines of the early films. Many silents even used the word "Dance" in their titles: **On with the Dance**, **The Idol Dancer**, **Dancin' Fool**, and **The Spanish Dancer**. In this enticing new form of entertainment, the sensual lure of the dancing female was used and exploited: "To most people a dancer was a romantic figure and script writers found no difficulty in filling their lives with excitement and adventure for purposes of movie drama" (*Dancing in Commercial Motion Pictures*).

Dance was also effective to heighten comedy sequences. Charles Chaplin, with his extensive English music hall, vaudeville and dance background, knew the dramatic and comic possibilities which could be expressed through dance and is perhaps the first film star who choreographed routines for himself and his co-stars. He explored the comic opportunities of dance in such films as **Tango Tangles** (1914), in which Chaplin fights for the attention of a hat check girl while chasing and sliding among the dancing couples—a scene photographed in an actual ballroom. In **Tillie's Punctured Romance** (1914), Chaplin and Marie Dressler's hilarious burlesque tango allows slapstick details no dialogue could. While trying to escape the clutches of a department store official in **The Floorwalker** (1916), Chaplin performs some classic ballet

technique. **Sunnyside** (1919) finds him floundering in the midst of a troupe of interpretive dancing girls in a comic dream. In **The Pilgrim** (1922) he offers a comic dance-pantomime of the
story of David and Goliath, and in **The Gold Rush** (1925), Chaplin's "Table Roll Dance" is a
brilliant parody of a dance. With Chaplin's self-taught background, he never thought to take a
"dances by" credit on his films. The status of onscreen credits was still in its infancy in those
early days of moviemaking, with everyone simply contributing his talents to the final product
without consideration of billing. It was not until **Limelight** (1952) that Chaplin took screen
credit for his dance inventions for the first — and only — time.

The dancing stars left their images behind for us to enjoy and to note as part of the his-
Along with Chaplin, another early film giant, Douglas Fairbanks, must be credited with
some of the earliest choreography and staging for his memorable fight scenes. A heroic athlete
who began his career on the stage, Fairbanks filled his most memorable action films (**The Mark
of Zorro**, 1920; **The Three Musketeers**, 1921; **Robin Hood**, 1922; and **The Thief of Baghdad**, 1924) with sweeping and stylized movements, daring gymnastics, and intricate combat
sequences, all created by an expert.

One of the most important aspects of dance on film has been the historical documentation
of social dance over the last one hundred years. However, that aspect hardly went through the
minds of the dance creators of the time; they simply expressed a part of the life around them.
In the earliest one and two-reelers, social dances were readily photographed: **The Bowery Waltz**
(1897), **The Maypole Dance** (1903), **Cakewalk on the Beach at Coney Island** (1904), etc.
With the arrival of feature-length films, social dance became an important part of the story within
scenes set at ballrooms, masquerades, parties, and dancehalls. Often, these scenes introduced
major plot complications.

The history of social dance itself parallels the evolution of the rules of courtship. From the
waltz with its keep-your-distance rules to the mutually joined groins of contemporary writhing,
social dance vividly illustrates the social and sexual morés of the times. And so another need for
dance in film surfaced as filmmakers strove to depict dramatic and romantic situations through
dance.

Rudolph Valentino's tango in **The Four Horsemen of the Apocalypse** (1921) used dance
to define the sensual man-woman relationship a decade before Fred Astaire and Ginger Rogers
would explore and redefine it. Valentino himself became film's first dancing male sex symbol,
and we can only assume that he created his own choreography pieced together from the dance
steps and combinations he had learned in his youth.

Dance also illustrated the changing roles of men and women. For example, after dozens of
female stars were cast as virginal ballerinas in early films, Joan Crawford's "Charleston Series"
(beginning with the silents **Paris**, 1926, and **Pretty Ladies**, 1927, and culminating in the talkies
Our Dancing Daughters, 1928, and **Our Modern Maidens**, 1929) personified the liberated
and hedonistic flapper of the era, dancing frantically at a wild party or speakeasy — document-
ing American women's acceptance of their own sensuality.

As on the stage, the creative forces in film recognized the power and opportunities of dance.
But they soon realized that someone would have to choreograph or stage these sequences, for
the dance backgrounds or creative powers of the actors themselves were limited. Dance directors were needed to arrange those dances for the camera or to create original movement routines.

The dancing stars left their images behind for us to enjoy and to note as part of the history of the cinema, but few details remain from those early days about the choreographers and
dance directors, except for the creative input supplied by two dance pioneers in California:
Ernest Belcher and Theodore Kosloff. Both had emigrated from Europe (Belcher from England,

Theodore Kosloff coaches Dorothy Adams and Jeanne Dodd for a Hollywood Bowl production of **Carmen**, 1937.

Kosloff from Russia), had appeared as performers on the American vaudeville circuits, and had fortuitously settled in California, where they opened landmark dance schools which would change the very direction of serious dance training in America. Their students included dozens of future dancers and choreographers who would change dance in America and throughout the world through their participation in ballet, musical comedy, television, and film.

Cecil B. DeMille was one of the first directors to consistently utilize dance for period and atmosphere. Realizing the value of their expertise and what they could contribute to his work, DeMille gave both Belcher and Kosloff their start in film collaboration. The other moviemakers in southern California quickly availed themselves of these men's prodigious talents, and they became the first studio-contracted dance directors. They are the roots of the dance-on-film tree.

Kosloff, because of his dark, brooding good looks, made dozens of films for DeMille as an actor and supervised the dancing in as many. His first film appearance was in Paramount's 1916 **To Have and to Hold**, "in which his walk down a huge staircase as a court jester brought an avalanche of letters" (*Dancing in Commercial Film*). In *DeMille*, biographer Charles Higham describes DeMille's fascination with Kosloff: "Kosloff had all of the qualities DeMille admired in a man. He was fearless and superbly built — limbs like that of a Michelangelo carving. His noble profile and aristocratic bearing was almost overpowering." For DeMille, Kosloff created a dance solo for himself as the Aztec prince in **The Woman God Forgot** (1917); Geraldine Farrar's dance in **Carmen** (1919); and a sensational four-minute "Worship of the Golden Calf" number in **The Ten Commandments** (1923). He was later featured prominently in DeMille's only musical, **Madame Satan** (1930), creating and starring in an electrifying "Ballet Mechanique." Kosloff also served as Marilyn Miller's ballet master in her two film appearances (**Sally**, 1929, and **Sunny**, 1930), as he had coached the Broadway dancing star in New York.

In the May 1922 issue of *Motion Picture*, Kosloff's contributions were described: "For the studio he occupies a unique position. For C.B. DeMille, he acts as a choreographic advisor. All the actors playing in one of the DeMille productions are required to pass his test as to their body movements and grace. He teaches them how to walk; if it is necessary, he instructs them in dancing. He watches all groupings of characters *en scene*, advises the art director as to detail. In short, he is C.B.'s ballet master." Despite his classic Russian ballet training, Kosloff's film specialties were usually pagan orgies and exotic movement pieces for DeMille.

When DeMille's niece, Agnes, convinced her uncle that she wanted to dance, he arranged an audition for her for Kosloff's school. Agnes had watched Kosloff film his dance sequence in **The Woman God Forgot** (1917). In her book *Dance to the Piper*, she tells how she, too, had been stunned by his physical presence: "naked in feathers, leaning on a feathered spear.... His gestures were real classic pantomime, involving clenched fists and the whites of the eyeballs, a positive style which gave the camera something to focus on.... Every expression was performed with a force that could have carried him across the room and over the wall. I was awe struck. I went home and doubled the number of knee-bends I performed every night before bed." She was accepted into his school, and her illustrious career began.

For the famous DeMille orgies, Kosloff often worked with more than 200 dancers. He used his own students and members of the Denishawn school, even casting Ted Shawn in a featured dance role in **Don't Change Your Husband** (1919).

If Kosloff was the stunning sexual animal of early filmed dance, Ernest Belcher was its first cultured dance master. A gentle, soft-spoken man, Belcher worked for most of the major studios during his career (Fox, Goldwyn, Paramount, Warner Bros.) and several of the minors (Associated Producers and Producers Distributing Corporation). Above and beyond his multiple dance creations, he coached and trained actors and actresses for the dance sequences in their films, staged period sequences — even going as far as teaching the actors how to bow in **Beau Brummell** (1924) — and also was responsible for what are considered to be the first serious ballet sequences captured on film in **Salome vs. Shenandoah** (1919) and the Lon Chaney silent version of **Phantom of the Opera** (1925). In these early years of filmmaking, choreographers collaborated on all types of movement with the director and actors, not only dance. Belcher's work on **Phantom** also included staging the movement and pantomime for large groups of people and coaching the actors in their physical reactions to the Phantom and his deeds.

The 1924 catalogue from Belcher's Celeste School of Dancing, then located at West 15th Street in downtown Los Angeles, claimed that "ninety percent of the most beautiful artistic dancing scenes in films are arranged and staged by this director." As Belcher was a ballet master and trained in various ethnic dances, his choreographic contributions to film included a wide spectrum of dance and movement forms, including multiple ethnic and period social dances: a Hungarian dance in **Silken Shackles**, a balloon and scarf number in **The Far Cry**, a German polka in **The Sea Beast**, and a charleston in **Padlocked** (all 1926); an 1880 quadrille in **Heart of Maryland**; and an "Egyptian fantasy" in **What Happened to Father** (both 1927). He created dance routines for many stars, including Spanish dances for Pola Negri in **The Spanish Dancer** and for stepdaughter Lina Basquette in **The Christian** (both 1923), the "Celeste Tango" for Ina Anson and Rod LaRoque in **Gigolo** (1926), and a waltz for Leatrice Joy and Nils Asther in **Blue Danube** (1927).

Respected by cost-conscious producers—it was said that he could take a request for a sequence at 8:00 a.m. and have it filmed by noon, even with retakes—Belcher was already exploring the possibilities of movement and dance on film in its earliest days. In December 1929, Belcher was quoted in "Stepping Stars, Who Teaches the Dancers of the Screen?" in *The Dance*:

> There is a great difference between directing stage dances and screen dances. On the screen, you have to plan on important dramatic action going on simultaneously with your dance.... Another thing—and this is vastly important—before the all-seeing camera, certain leg and arm movements done at precisely the same time are quite apt to result in a very noticeable flickering on the screen. For years I have been trying to eliminate this by observing closely just what those combinations are.

Belcher used many of the technical effects available at the time. "For dance scenes in **Mother o' Mine** (Associated Producers, 1921) figures on a center elevation are extremely hazy, others closer to the camera appear practically nude in the dim light. The whole effect is one of delicate artistry rather than sensuous vulgarity and it is produced by use of special lighting, wind and steam" (*Dancing in Commercial Motion Pictures*, 1946).

In addition to the film contributions of Belcher and Kosloff, their highly successful schools became an important part of the film community and the foundation of West Coast dance education. Actors and actresses and the children of important moviemakers attended the schools for the training and the prestige. The most promising students were given jobs in the casts of the vaudeville units, prologues and films that Belcher and Kosloff were working on, and their ballets at the Hollywood Bowl. These works produced many of the dance leaders of the future: Merriel Abbott, Rod Alexander, Marge and Gower Champion, Cyd Charisse, Agnes DeMille, Paul Godkin, Carmelita Maracci, Matt Mattox, Edna McRae, James Starbuck, Maria Tallchief, and Gwen Verdon. While his students worked their way to the top, Kosloff enjoyed great financial success; by the 1940s he was a wealthy California landowner.

In a very diplomatic statement made in 1944, Belcher explained that his exit from film work was due to the changes in the creative freedom of the dance director. In the silent years, he had been allowed great freedom in his work, with little interference from directors and producers. That changed as the silents gave way to the talkies, and Belcher found he could not work within the restrictions of the new era.

According to his step daughter, film star Lina Basquette, Belcher left films in the mid–'30s "because Ernest was not the type to 'push and shove'—would not play the 'Tinseltown game' of chicanery.... he would never receive the renown that he deserved as a choreographer and producer of magnificent dance sequences.... I firmly believe that if Ernest had taken on an exotic Russian label and played the 'social scene' ... he would have become more famous and monetarily successful" (letter from Basquette to Naima Prevots, quoted in Prevots' book *Dancing in the Sun*).

This talented, polite gentleman also was a victim of Hollywood's early politics. Basquette was married to Sam Warner (of the Warner brothers) and partially had been responsible for Belcher's work at the studio in the first place. When Sam died, Basquette's battle with the Warner family over the estate found her blackballed by the studio. She feels that Belcher suffered by association.

Kosloff's reign with DeMille was slowly usurped by LeRoy Prinz, a budding dance director who was beginning his prolific career during the period. Ambitious, resourceful, and able to handle multiple tasks, Prinz was hired by DeMille not only to supply dance and period movement but often to act as the second unit director, herding extras, staging battles, and coaching the stars in their movement. Kosloff began to devote his energies to his school and to classical dance for stage and concert.

Film choreographers and historians owe a great debt to both of these men, who paved the way for all that would come later. Unfortunately, by the next decade, both men would limit their film work to concentrate on their schools.

Denishawn, another important West Coast school and dance troupe, contributed dancers and choreographers to the early films. Founded by interpretive dance pioneers Ruth St. Denis and Ted Shawn in 1915, the "School of Dancing and Related Arts" soon became another popular adjunct to the film community. Members of the Denishawn troupe created multiple dance sequences for films, though much of their work is undocumented.

Ted Shawn had made his film debut with partner Norma Gould in a one-reel film **Dances of the Ages** in 1913, also creating the scenario around the dances they performed. As a famous dance figure he was paid the unheard-of fee of $500 for four hours of work in **Don't Change Your Husband** (1919). His wife, Ruth St. Denis, had been captured on film even earlier (before she was "Sainted") in **Dance — Miss Ruth Dennis** in 1894. Denishawn dancer Margaret Loomis, who would become a silent screen star, danced in **The Sheik** (1921) and received $50 for her onscreen talents, but was paid $35–$50 as a consultant or as a trainer who helped groups to execute a director's ideas. In later years, Shawn, St. Denis, Loomis, Norma Gould, and others of the Denishawn troupe would say that the work in films was demeaning to their art — but they happily accepted the salary. It has been documented that St. Denis choreographed **The Lily and the Rose** for D.W. Griffith in 1915 and collaborated with Shawn on Griffiths' 1916 work **Intolerance** (although Shawn continually denied it) and Theda Bara's **Cleopatra** (Fox, 1917). Regarding the latter, St. Denis denied that she doubled for the vamp star. Even Denishawn member Martha Graham left her image on film in a dance sequence from **Male and Female** (1919).

Another important early film dancemaker, Eduardo Cansino, arrived in America from Spain as a member of the famed Dancing Cansinos. After the troupe's great success on the vaudeville circuit as the first Spanish dancers to make an impact in the United States, Eduardo moved to Hollywood in 1927 to open a school. He soon became involved in films as a freelance choreographer and dance coach. In John Kobal's *Rita Hayworth*, Eduardo Cansino's son Vernon recalled, "Dad had a very successful business choreographing over at Warner Bros. He directed the dance numbers for films where they needed Spanish flavors like **Song of the Flame**, **Noah's Ark**, **Golden Dawn** and **Under a Texas Moon**. Over at MGM he did the dances for Ramon Novarro and Renee Adoree in her last picture, **Call of the Flesh**. And he had Irene Dunne there to teach her a dance for a movie she never made over at RKO." He eventually was signed as Dance Director by Fox but, along with Belcher and Kosloff, perhaps made a greater contribution to dance on film with his many generations of teaching in Hollywood. Among his former students who would achieve film success were Margo, Betty Grable, Grace Poggi, and his daughter, Rita Hayworth.

Other early California dance directors included Marion Morgan, a former Los Angeles schoolteacher. Creating interpretive dances, Morgan formed a dance troupe which appeared in **Don Juan** (1926), **The Night of Love**, and **The Private Life of Helen of Troy** (both 1927). An article written by Earle Wallace in 1927 mentions her prominence in films:

> Almost every picture, it seems, has a dance shot here or there, and this, of course, keeps many dancers busy. Marion Morgan is devoting her entire time to the exclusive production of dance sequences for the screen. She keeps a large unit of girls constantly busy.

An entirely new avenue of dance opportunities opened with the introduction of sound.

Believe it or not, there had been some silent musicals: the operettas **Mademoiselle Modiste** (1926) and **The Student Prince**, (1927), for example. The movie musical officially began in 1927 with **The Jazz Singer**, a historic film which used sound for its musical sequences, choreographed by Ernest Belcher. A November 1928 article in *The Dance* ("What Can Sound Pictures Do for Dancing?") promised,

> The new sound-recording devices will provide another field of expression for the dance. Trained dancers will be in demand by the studios.... For the talkies will record the music to which dances are done and the public will see the dance at the same time as they hear the music. Therefore the correct dance must be performed.

The article also contained the prophetic words, "Warner Brothers have engaged Larry Ceballos, who has staged various musicals in New York, to do the dancing numbers of their future pictures. The fact that they consider this phase of production via Vitaphone of sufficient importance to engage a well-known dance director speaks for itself."

Ethan Mordden in *The Hollywood Musical* writes about the instant need for dance directors for films:

> Dance was sudden, strange and necessary in 1929. In the scramble to shoot and release musicals, Broadway choreographers were brought in for the kicklines and hoofing that added nothing to character or action.... Anyway, who would film dance in Hollywood? The choreographer? The cameraman? The director? Too often, directors who knew nothing of dance took charge, filming a number from several angles simultaneously and letting an editor paste it together with absurd reaction shots from bystanders. Obviously, dance would work best when an inventive director pulled the motion into his overall conception or when a smart choreographer took over the camera for the numbers.

Hollywood now looked to the New York stage to find its stars and dancemakers. California had a new "Gold Rush" as the Easterners arrived to create the movie musical. They had no master plan. They simply dreamed of recreating the success they had achieved with their stage musicals. So the Broadway musical of the time became the basis for dance in the first musical films.

As for the integration of dance in the Broadway musical itself, the beginning of that phenomenon is most often credited to a show called *The Black Crook* in 1866. The legend goes that a ballet troupe was stranded when their theatre burned down, and their dances, costumes, and imaginative scenic effects were incorporated into a dramatic presentation. Their dance routines were simply inserted into the show, combining a "book" show with musical sequences for the first time. *The Black Crook* was also touted to be "New York's first absolute leg show — beautiful, novel, and well presented."

As the American musical grew and changed shape over the years, the influences of ballet, minstrel show, tap, and social (or ballroom) dancing all came together in precision or "line" dancing, the style most prevalent in the early Broadway musicals of the 1920s.

The line dance had been made popular around 1910 by an Englishman, John Tiller, with his troupe, The Tiller Girls. In *The Dance*, February 1929, Tiller was described as "a wealthy English manufacturer whose hobby was dancing and the production of amateur shows. He organized marches and folk dances, and on one occasion is said to have produced a maypole dance in which two hundred children danced in rhythmic unison." He first opened a school, imported an Italian ballerina, and began experimenting with units of dancers, which eventually became "the pony ballet ... a part of every English musical show." The troupe was brought to America in 1918 by producer Charles Dillingham and subsequently by Oscar Hammerstein, Florenz Ziegfeld, and George White to appear in their shows to great success. American Gertrude Hoffman added acrobatics and athletics to the marching and kicking of the Tillers and gained acclaim with the Gertrude Hoffman Girls, while Billy Watson added spice with "the organization of husky, capable-looking ladies of forbidding bulk" in Billy Watson's Beef Trust.

American dance directors of the period simply duplicated that successful formula — a line of girls or boys all performing the same steps with precision which delighted audiences of the period: The Chester Hale Girls, Fanchon and Marco's Fanchonettes and Sunkist Beauties, Russell Markert's Sixteen American Rockets, Allan K. Foster troupes, Albertina Rasch Girls, and a dozen others.

In addition to the precision line dances, the dance menu on the musical comedy stage of the period included social dances, tap, toe-tap, legomania, eccentric, acrobatic, and shimmy. Dance directors used existing routines of the stars of the show; precision routines they and their collaborators devised; or lines of dancers who arrived with their own routines.

The art of choreography, the actual creation of the dance steps, was in its infancy. These early dance supervisors were not encouraged to innovate. Their job was simply to repackage the old, successful routines to different music, with the dancers wearing different costumes. The only variations asked of dance directors were the geometric patterns within which the precision routines comprised of simple steps could be performed. Ned Wayburn, one of the most successful Broadway dance directors and producers who also had an important dance studio and school in New York (where Fred and Adele Astaire were students), actually had a formula of ten steps from the entrance to the exit for successful routines.

In "Dances Staged By?," a fascinating article in *The Dance*, December 1928, the distinguishing points of the some of the leading dance directors of the day (who would all contribute to early film musicals) were noted:

> [Seymour Felix's] numbers are coherent. They frequently add to the story, when they are not merely atmospheric.... Felix is a stickler for beauty and a veritable maniac for perfect morals. He wants manly men and goes out and gets them.... Chorus girls tell me that Felix gives them more opportunity for individuality than any other man.... Busby Berkeley loves mass effects. He likes to break his numbers up into parts. In this respect he is unlike Bobby Connolly or Sammy Lee, both of whom strive for long

In 1928, Fanchon coaches two of her Sunkist Beauties in a "bow knot."

routines which sweep from an opening consecutively to a climax…. Jack Haskell … knows his dance technique and can impart it to his ensembles…. he is best at creating pictures…. Mass movement is his forte…. Unlike Berkeley, who struggled up from the ranks with Sammy Lee and Bobby Connolly, Haskell has the attitude of the dilettante toward his work…. He believes in pictures, groupings, much adagio and acrobatic work, in contrast to the less subtle "hot" dancing of many others. Much of

> Haskell's work is colored by his frequent visits to Europe whence he returns with much folk dancing ideas.... Edward Royce is the great protagonist of the graceful, pictorial school. His chorus work has less vigor than some of the younger men, but it has a charm which sometimes is lacking in their creations.

As the musical form itself began to change through the work of Jerome Kern, George Gershwin, and others, these dance directors also contributed to that evolution. Among the Broadway dance directors who began innovating and slightly deviating from the norm of the line dance with their dance direction and choreography were Busby Berkeley (who experimented with various rhythms for the chorus to "challenge" each other with); Albertina Rasch (whose girls were the first to incorporate ballet technique into their precision routines); David Bennett (originating the "domino" routine still performed by the Rockettes); Bobby Connolly (who used lots of tap dancing in his routines and created the sensational "Varsity Drag" in the show *Good News*, 1927); Seymour Felix (one of the first who strove to integrate dances that furthered the plot into the show); and Sammy Lee (who insisted on girls with extensive dance training, adding complicated acrobatic routines to the dancing line).

In the September 1944 issue of *Dance Magazine*, LeRoy Prinz described his contribution to the evolution of stage (and eventually screen) dance: "In the early musical shows on Broadway, every show had a Tiller routine with all 100% precision and all individuals good. No one got a ripple of applause or held their own. Those routines seemed flat to me. One day I got the idea of having the last girl in the line start one beat behind and never catch up. I used this idea in one of the *Vanities*. The audience literally rolled in the aisles. It was the first time I had a hit number by making a bad routine out of a good one." Prinz also had a technique called the "conglomeration effect" which broke up the effect of the precision line "by using different steps for different dancers in the line, an accomplishment as much a reflection of sophisticated spatial manipulation as a clever division of labor among dancers of unequal ability ... 'a matter of every dancer going to town and doing something different usually for the last sixteen or thirty-two bars of music.'" (*Hoofing on Broadway*).

When the first films began to sing and dance, dance directors were brought from Broadway along with the successful properties to continue the dance heritage on film. At first, they were given the credit "dances staged by," "dance direction" or "dances and ensembles by" because they did just that. They adapted, directed, and staged the choreography which already existed.

Bennett, Berkeley, Ceballos, Connolly, Fanchon, Felix, Hale, Lee, Prinz, and Rasch were all invited to Hollywood to join Ernest Belcher, Eduardo Cansino, and Theodore Kosloff to help create the first popular form of the movie musical, the revue. Films such as **The Fox Movietone Follies** (staged by Fanchon and Edward Royce), **Hollywood Revue of 1929** (Sammy Lee, Natacha Natova, Albertina Rasch) and **The Show of Shows** (Larry Ceballos and Jack Haskell) in 1929, **Paramount on Parade** (David Bennett, Marion Morgan) and **King of Jazz** (John Murray Anderson, Russell Market) in 1930, featured all of the stars under contract to each particular film studio and dance interludes provided by precision line dancers and dance specialty acts.

Fanchon, one of the most successful producers of lines across the country with her brother, Marco, began in films coaching stars and supplying their lines of dancers to shorts and features. Starting as a vaudeville team, they built a powerful show business empire which included supplying all of the live shows to the Fox West Coast chain of theatres, a school (where Ethel Meglin would teach and create the famous Meglin Kiddies) and production factory in Hollywood. One of Fanchon's earliest documented film chores was creating a ballroom scene for Rudolph Valentino and the cast of **The Eagle** (1925) in the period style of Catherine the Great.

Mae Clark leads the line of girls in a rehearsal under the watchful eye of Busby Berkeley (at rear) for **Night World** (Universal, 1932).

In discussing her coaching of stars for film roles in *The Dance*, October 1929, Fanchon said, "In film work you usually teach just a few steps at the beginning of the dance and then perhaps a few at the end — in short, only those necessary for close-ups. For the body of the dance — the long shots, you know — a double is usually rehearsed." A multitalented choreographer, director, producer, lyricist, and librettist, Fanchon would progress to "supervise" musical sequences in films and become one of Hollywood's first female producers.

Russell Markert, Allan K. Foster, and David Bennett would desert films after only a few efforts and return to their highly successful stage careers. Ned Wayburn remained behind in New York, presumably not willing to jeopardize his great success with something as "iffy" as the motion pictures. But the others stayed.

In 1929, one man arrived from Broadway and stayed to change the face of film forever.

Although Seymour Felix had created the dance routines for the stage version, for the filming of the Broadway stage success **Whoopee** (1930), Busby Berkeley was brought from New York to Hollywood. Berkeley had also broken the "precision line look" on the musical theater stage with character effects, although not with varying movement or spatial relationships. In *Hoofing on Broadway*, Berkeley's innovation is described: "Contemporary observers credit him with 'tampering' with the unity and precision of the chorus line by introducing 'the little girl at the end of the line', who, as the perennial underdog who had to work harder and kick higher to fit in, was a surefire avenue to laughter, sympathy and applause." Those character details would surface in his film work.

He also understood what the camera could do. A concise description of the difference between live performances and film was written by Viola Hegyi Swisher in *Dance Magazine*, February 1969 ("Bob Fosse Translates **Sweet Charity** from Stage to Screen"):

> Looking at live theater, the collective audience eye establishes and exercises its own liberty of action and scope. Being a selective and highly independent viewing agent, it freely indulges its tendency to dart at will from here to there, although a stage director has ways of influencing and guiding this viewing instrument. By lighting, for instance. But the film director and his camera have, between them, powers more dictatorial. By offering the audience eye no alternative choice of what to look at, the film director *cum* camera can tell movie viewers exactly where to look, how little or how much to see…. the camera almost literally forces the director to decide on a focal point for its single eye.

Berkeley somehow realized all of this some 40 years earlier and guided his audiences through wonderlands of movements, patterns, feminine beauty, and incredible scope.

The recognized transition of photographed dance begins with Berkeley's numbers in **Whoopee** (filmed in 1929, but released in 1930). The dancers were photographed from overhead and created patterns heretofore unseen by any audience (except possibly Broadway stage hands who might have been working in the "flies"). Berkeley realized that the camera could add variation and movement, and he envisioned dance numbers specifically for the new film idiom. In the *NY Times* review of **Whoopee** (October 1, 1930), critic Mordaunt Hall observed: "There are fascinating groups of dancers, photographed from directly above, that are remarkably effective."

Despite the full credit usually given to Berkeley, there were other experimentations going on with photographed dance. In an article about those early musicals ("See It with Music," *The Dance*, June 1929) writer M.L. Miller comments on **Fox Movietone Follies**: "As an instance of what the screen can do with production effects there is the 'Under the Sea' number…. here the dancers are seen as flapper fish and seaweed nymphs, apparently under water, in slow and distorted movement. Trick photography has, of course, helped, just as it will in hundreds of dancing sequences to be shot in the future."

John Murray Anderson, who was not really a choreographer or dance director, but whose use of lighting and theatrics made him one of the American theater's acknowledged masters of staging, contributed only one epic to the film musical genre before he returned to the stage. His experimentation with the camera, pre-recorded sound, effects, and early Technicolor in **King of Jazz** had the industry talking. Florenz Ziegfeld was originally offered the job, but when he turned it down, star Paul Whiteman suggested Anderson. In "He Didn't Know How," a June 1930 article in *Photoplay*, wherein writer Harry Lang explains that **King of Jazz** was Anderson's first film and that he learned as he worked, one of his experiments is described: "A dancer, his body painted brilliant black, like patent leather, dances atop a huge drum. From one side, a red light is focused on him; from the other, a green glare, and from the front, a white ray. And, as a result, on the background behind the dancer will appear three dancing shadows — one black, one red and one green. It is the old 'multiple shadow' effect — a thing that has bothered directors before…. But Anderson, instead of trying to get away from the multiple shadows, used them!"

Larry Ceballos reviews the troops in a 1920s Warner Bros. publicity shot (photograph courtesy of Joy Griffiths).

In his autobiography, Anderson himself described this first film effort:

> I was really at a loss to know where to begin when I hit upon the idea (not very orig-
> inal perhaps) of interviewing all the best technical experts on the lot.... I asked each
> if he had any pet ideas and effects that he had dreamed up, but had never been given
> the opportunity of carrying out.... Having completed my directorial job, I was now

faced with the problem of putting the picture together, for nobody but myself knew precisely what it was all about. Here again I started something new. I taught the cutters to work with a Metronome, and only changed "angles" at the beginning of a musical phrase. In this way, although an audience was not perhaps conscious of it, the film actually kept cadence with the music.

Despite the critical acclaim the film received and a contract for more films, Anderson left Hollywood and did not return until a new challenge, in the form of creating spectacles for swimming star Esther Williams, brought him back some 24 years later. Had he stayed, he undoubtedly would have contributed greatly to dance and film innovation.

Larry Ceballos was another innovative creator whose contributions would be eclipsed by Berkeley's powerful legacy. Ceballos started in film as a dancer, who "earned $300 from Vitagraph Studios in 1913 for a half an hour's work. He improvised an acrobatic waltz in evening clothes for a cabaret scene" (*Dancing in Commercial Motion Pictures*). Born into a circus family, Larry began his career performing with the Ringling Brothers and Barnum and Bailey Circus, also studying ballet from a teacher with the troupe. He then toured in vaudeville and appeared on the Broadway stage as a musical comedy performer. He was slated to perform in a show in England when the dance director for that show suddenly became ill. Ceballos took over the dance direction and continued in that job for five years. After success with staging dances on Broadway, he arrived in Hollywood in 1927 to put his work from *The Music Box Revue* on film, at the momentous time that sound was also arriving. For his work on **Lights of New York** (1928), the first all-talking feature, he was given the first opening title credit as dance director on the screen.

As a dancemaker who envisioned his work directly for one camera, Ceballos created, directed, and edited his musical numbers on the soundstage, receiving notice for **The Show of Shows** (1929) with a February 1930 *Photoplay* review praising, "If the picture has one especially grand thing, it is the succession of novel and beautiful stage pictures and routines devised by Larry Ceballos and Jack Haskell." His concepts were much simpler than Berkeley's, Dave Gould's, and Haskell's: "First I try to be logical in the telling of my story. Then I get a simple set so the dancers are seen instead of the set. I try always to have simple but effective movement which is far more successful than a lot of conglomerate counter-movements which distracts the eye." (*American Dancer*, 1938).

Skillful and expedient in his work (he reportedly taught extras to perform an African dance in a half hour for **Notorious Lady**, 1927), his asking fee was $200 a day, whereas other dance directors earned only $100. He is justifiably remembered for his imaginative "Tiptoe through the Tulips" and "Painting the Clouds with Sunshine" numbers in **The Gold Diggers of Broadway** (1929), "The Land of Let's Pretend" and "Welcome Home" from **On with the Show** (also 1929), and the "Floradora Sextette" for Alice Day, Lila Lee, Myrna Loy, Patsy Ruth Miller, Marion Nixon, and Sally O'Neill in **The Show of Shows** (1929).

The rest of the musical numbers in the film musicals from 1927 to 1930 were basically filmed stage performances.

Although D.W. Griffith, Thomas Ince, and others had experimented extensively with camera techniques, most of the early song and dance sequences were statically and unimaginatively photographed. Up until Berkeley's arrival, dance directors were given three choices for their musical sequences: the long, full shot, the medium shot, and the close-up. Little experimentation had been done with angles or a moving camera. Often, the dancers moved out of the frame or, worse yet, lost their heads or feet. The camera was usually positioned at a distance and the dances were filmed from the viewpoint of an audience in the theater. Effects such as negative printing, "underwater" ripples, and medium shots were sparingly used, but basically the dances were filmed as stage sequences. Exceptions, such as **The Cocoanuts** (Allan K. Foster, 1929) which possibly contains the first overhead shot of dancers (The Gamby-Hale Ballet Girls), and "The Hoosier Hop" from **It's a Great Life** (Sammy Lee, 1930), which includes double-exposure, low and high angle shots, and other effects, illustrate the first attempts at dance-and-camera experimentation.

Most of the dance directors had little or no input with the film's director; they simply supplied the dance sequences to be filmed at the director's discretion. When these early sequences are viewed now, we can see exactly how the dancing in the stage musicals of the period looked. In the next decade, Hollywood would tamper with stage show transfers in an effort to make them "movies," but the best remaining records we have of the Broadway musical stage of the day are these early musical films. They are excellent archival material for theatrical and film dance history. Dancing stars such as Ann Pennington and Marilyn Miller recreated their successful dance routines from Broadway on film.

The choreography itself was primitive. The legions of boys and girls did basic tap steps, marched, created formations, and sloppily performed precision drills. The various choruses were never mixed — troupes such as the Albertina Rasch Ballet performed ballet (with the ads from **Sally** promising "39 Albertina Rasch Girls who toe-dance more perfectly than other choruses can clog") — and specialty acts performed acrobatics, eccentric dancing, and toe-tapping, while the Ensemble tapped, hopped, and kicked.

As the stage musical continued to evolve, people with dance talents began to create the dance routines and actually choreograph the musical numbers. But many of the pioneers of the early years in film musicals (1927-1930) were basically people who could design a number and tell the dancers *where* to do their steps, for *how long* and in *which* direction. They didn't "do" steps.

That would all change as the movie musical transformed its shape and began to grow into what we recognize as the beginning of the Golden Age. As this transformation took place, the dance directors and choreographers would be among the most influential in those innovations.

Selected Filmography

Note: These are the author's personal choices and do not necessarily reflect critical, artistic or economic success. Listings include film title, choreographer/dance director, studio, year of release, available video or laser disc, followed by author's reason for recommending its viewing. As dance and film are both visual arts, the best way to understand the changes is to see the films. Many classic dance sequences are now available on video and/or laser disc. Others are not. Please join me in writing to the video release companies in an effort to get many "lost treasures" available to all of us.

The Hollywood Revue of 1929 (Sammy Lee, Natacha Natova, Edward Royce) MGM, 1929, Laser Disc:"The Dawn of Sound," MGM/UA — A great chance to see the Musical Stage Dance Form of the period, with its planned-to-be-precision line dancing and specialty dance acts.

It's a Great Life (Sammy Lee) MGM, 1930, Laser Disc: "The Dawn of Sound, Volume II," MGM/UA — A peek at "The Hoosier Hop" diffuses the belief that Busby Berkeley was the only person

experimenting with camera angles, techniques and special effects. The choreography is primitive and laughable, but the technical collaboration is not.

King of Jazz (John Murray Anderson, Russell Markert) Univ, 1930, Video:MCA — Dazzling musical number concepts from Anderson and one of the most sensational adagio dances ever captured on film in a "Rag Doll" dance by Marion Statler and Don Rose.

Madame Satan (Theodore Kosloff, LeRoy Prinz) MGM, 1930, Video:MGM/UA — Cecil B. DeMille's one and only musical, highlighted by a spectacular — and bizarre — "Ballet Mechanique," starring and choreographed by Kosloff, with Prinz staging.

Paramount on Parade (David Bennett, Marion Morgan) Par, 1930 — A barrage of musical numbers from all of Paramount's stars of the day.

Phantom of the Opera (Ernest Belcher) Univ, 1925, Video:Critic's Choice — Belcher's historic input to films not only includes the excellent Ballet sequences, but his staging and choreographing of the chase scene.

The Show of Shows (Larry Ceballos, Jack Haskell) WB, 1929, Laser Disc: "The Dawn of Sound," MGM/UA — In a startling onslaught, specialty dancers rush toward the camera during the "Lady Luck" finale, frantically performing their routines as if they were told, "Okay kids, you got 32 bars ... and your life depends on it!"

Sunnyside Up (Seymour Felix) Fox, 1929 — "Turn on the Heat" dance madness as the girls remove Eskimo costumes and begin writhing. Their dancing frenzy causes the igloos to melt, and the frozen wasteland becomes a tropical paradise! But this dance is too hot — a brush fire begins, and the girls' only escape is to jump into the pool in front of them as a water curtain shoots upward. And we thought Michael Jackson's music videos were "out there"?

Whoopee (Busby Berkeley) Goldwyn, 1930, Video:HBO — Watch and be amazed as Berkeley plays camera tricks which will revolutionize the film musical and cinema itself. Also, a sassy turn by Ethel Shutta in "Stetson."

THE 1930s

After the overabundance of extravagant revues in the 1930 releases, musical films fell into disfavor with audiences. They wanted more than a mere series of unrelated songs, dances, and sketches. Broadway book show successes such as *The Desert Song* (1926), *Good News* (1927), *Rosalie,* and *Whoopee* (both 1928) would be transplanted in front of the camera to try and win audience favor ... and the original backstage musical achieved success with MGM's **Broadway Melody** (1929), the first film musical to win the Academy Award as best picture.

The dance numbers in **Broadway Melody** were unimaginatively photographed stage routines created by George Cunningham, but the story appealed to audiences. It was Busby Berkeley who would take the genre to new heights with his dance direction for Warner Bros.' **42nd Street** in 1933. In the October 1979 issue of *Esquire*, the film was capsulized as "the movie where Busby Berkeley's genius for kitsch was allowed to blossom forth in all its surreal splendor — the high point of which is the moment when the skyline of Manhattan bursts into dance."

42nd Street was an original film musical which Warner Bros. was not initially enthusiastic about. The studio knew that box office receipts for musicals had fallen off drastically because of the audience's apathy to the revue format. But when this film was released, as much as the audiences enjoyed the story, the snappy comedy dialogue, and the bright performances by the actors, it was the musical numbers that were the big surprises. **42nd Street** made a star of Busby Berkeley. His musical sequences for the film contained very little dance (except for Ruby Keeler's solos) but rather created moods, told stories, and paraded dozens of beautiful girls before the camera. These were not comely chorines statically staged in a distant row across the front of a stage, they came at you, allowing the audience to revel in the close-ups of their freshness and beauty.

Girls, violins, neon and unseen miles of electrical wiring: "The Shadow Waltz" from Warner Bros.' **Golddiggers of 1933** (Busby Berkeley).

In an interview, Berkeley said:

> If you go through all of my pictures you will see very little actual dancing. It wasn't because I didn't know how to create it and do it, but I wanted to do something *new and different.* Something that has never been seen before. Had they ever seen seventy or a hundred pianos waltzing? Had they ever seen lighted violins before? The same goes for all my various formations ... it isn't particularly the steps but what you do with them.... Musical numbers are musical numbers. If they employ a certain amount of dance, fine, and if they employ other rudiments or props or something else that's effective, that's fine if it entertains an audience [Bob Pike and Dave Martin, *The Genius of Busby Berkeley*].

Later film critics and theorists would call Berkeley's work vulgar, sexist, camp, tasteless, voyeuristic; Berkeley himself would be called everything from "a naive surrealist" to "the exemplar of purely cinematic images," while one critic crowned the praise with: "He belongs with Eisenstein, Griffith, Norman McLaren and a few others as a master of cinema as dynamic, kinetic experience, generating wonder at the audacity of his spacial imagination as it dissolves the proscenium stage solidity into a vertiginous world of shifting plains, ambiguous dimensions and extraordinary patterns of metamorphosis" (*Blue Skies and Silver Linings — Aspects of the Hollywood Musical*).

"Berkeley seems to have appreciated instinctively that film space is completely fictional and may be rearranged at will from shot to shot without any necessity for literal continuity... Berkeley's concepts are inconceivable in any medium other than film. He remains one of the cinema's originals," British author John Russell Taylor wrote in *The Movies* in 1976. Berkeley could picture his visions so completely that he used only one camera (rather than the usual three or four assigned to cover the action from various viewpoints) and directed the musical numbers himself.

On top of his expertise with the camera, Berkeley also would innovate filmed musical numbers with intricate scenarios. Not content with the mere song-and-dance routines which were the norm at the time, with **42nd Street** he began creating stories told in movement and song, and the original film musical continued to grow and change shape. If **Broadway Melody** had popularized the backstage musical genre, **42nd Street** forever changed the filming of musical sequences. Berkeley's dance scenarios were often lurid, adding a memorable darkness to musicals of the '30s. Because of his creativity and knowledge of the camera, he went on to direct films, becoming one the first dance directors to take the reins of an entire film.

42nd Street also made a film star of Broadway dancer Ruby Keeler. Her rather clumsy tap style was compensated for by her natural and sweet persona. As the first tap-dancing star of the screen, she successfully continued in films for ten years. However, audiences never fully realized that she also created her own dance routines in collaboration with Berkeley. In the landmark book *Tap!*, she described the process: "In **42nd Street**, I did my own choreography. In pictures, there was always a dance director; but he took care of the big numbers. I always did my own routines — it was always my dancing. Of course when I was with a partner, like Lee Dixon or Paul Draper, we would work it out together."

The "backstage story" began its reign as the film musical's most successful format and continued with such classics as **Footlight Parade** (1933), **Dames** (1934) and the **Goldiggers** series (Berkeley), the **Broadway Melody** series (Dave Gould), **Dancing Lady** (Sammy Lee and Eddie Prinz, 1933), and **The Great Ziegfeld** (Seymour Felix, 1936). The musical numbers created for these films took place on a stage, with those stages getting bigger and bigger and containing incredible effects that no real stage could accommodate. As the technique of film grew, dance directors were offered moving cameras, multiple angles and sizes of shots, dissolves, wipes, and ever-increasing mechanical scenic miracles. Like the competing techno-fects of today's successful moviemaking, audiences of the '30s were impressed with "the-bigger-the-better" depiction of musical numbers. Although the dancing itself was not elaborate, the elevators, turntables, moving sidewalks, pools, fountains, staircases, and gigantic cascading draperies challenged the dance directors and caused the studios to build enormous soundstages. In some cases, they tore down walls so that two soundstages could be combined to hold the fantastic mechanics and seemingly endless space required. Dance on film reached baroque proportions. It wasn't about what one human body could do — it was about the effect hundreds of bodies could make in patterns and mass.

In spite of his busy schedule at Warner Bros., Berkeley continued work with the Eddie Cantor series of musicals at Samuel Goldwyn that he had started with **Whoopee**, supplying lush, fanciful, and erotic routines for the newly formed Goldwyn Girls. By 1934 Warner Bros. and Goldwyn were fighting over Berkeley's services.

Berkeley's innovations with the camera were already being mirrored by most of the important dance directors of the time such as Larry Ceballos, Bobby Connolly, Dave Gould, Sammy Lee, and LeRoy Prinz. Their work was soon being compared to Berkeley's, as evidenced by the *Hollywood Reporter's* review of **Moonlight and Pretzels** (July 25, 1933)—"Bobby Connolly staged some lovely sprightly dance numbers, particularly the clock episode and Bus (sic) Berkeley can be proud of his picture disciples" — and by *Variety's* December 12, 1933, review of **Sitting Pretty**: "The Pickens Sisters and the Larry Ceballos Girls are in for singing and production numbers. Girls most important item is a black and white fan dance in abbreviated costumes, with overhead shots of the waving fans giving an effect similar to the water ballet overheads of **Footlight Parade**, and very striking on the production work." Although a backlash eventually began from critics (the 1934 review of Harold Hecht's work on **Bottoms Up** praises the musical number for *not* being spectacular, filmed from the ceiling, etc.), Berkeley reigned supreme.

His unique position at Warner Bros. is described in *The Genius of the System*: "He signed a new seven-year contract in February 1934 that identified him as a director, but Berkeley's work was so specialized and distinctive — and commercially successful — that he was given a remarkable degree of authority. He conceived, designed, choreographed, directed and even edited the musical numbers himself." Despite his penchant for going over budget, producer Hal Wallis was to draft a memo acknowledging Berkeley's status: "The Title **Dames** is to be followed by the name of the Director and Busby Berkeley in equal-size type."

Even the coming attractions for his films began to feature his name. For **Footlight Parade**, the previews proclaim: "Busby Berkeley's most glamorous ensembles!" and the 1960s reissue of a double bill titles the films as **Busby Berkeley's Footlight Parade** and **Goldiggers of 1935**. For **Footlight Parade**, Berkeley got Jack Warner to spend $38,000 to build a pool for the spectacular "By a Waterfall" number. The finale of the "Shanghai Lil" number (in which the cast members form images of the Stars and Stripes and President Franklin D. Roosevelt) was so popular that a version with the Union Jack and King George was filmed for release in Britain and one with the French Flag and Marshall Foch for France.

Screenwriter Robert Buckner, who worked at Warner Bros. at the time, was quoted in *The Glamour Factory*: "If you hired Berkeley, you got his girls with him. They had done the routines so many times that they didn't have to rehearse. He'd just say to them, 'All right girls, 13-A,' and they'd go right into it. Buzz knew exactly how to put a musical together.... There was no nonsense about him, no waste of time. He was a businessman, and that's why he was so successful."

Berkeley's "girls" were ranked in a complicated order. There were the prestigious "Close-up Girls," the "Full Figure Shot Girls," the "Medium Shot Girls," and "Background Girls." They were ranked by their physical beauty, not their dance expertise, with lots of envy, bickering, and jostling for position understandably going on among them. Of course, he also used dozens of men, but only as background or filler. Berkeley is remembered by his dancers as intensely loyal to his favorites, giving them constant work. He is also remembered for his ribald jokes. (Said Melba Marshall in John Kobal's *People Will Talk*: "And he had one of the best senses of humor I've ever known. He would break the tension immediately ... he would say ... dirty little things like: 'O.K. girls, now come on, spread your pretty little legs' and it would get a giggle out of everyone.") Though he used hundreds of girls during the decade, only a few (Lucille Ball, Virginia Bruce, Paulette Goddard, and Betty Grable) would go on to subsequent film success.

As the major studios all rushed to sign up dance directors under the jurisdiction of their music departments, the battle of the dance directors began. Oddly enough, two of the superstar dance directors of the early musicals, Berkeley and Dave Gould, could barely perform a dance step. "Berkeley was a cameraman — he was not a dance director. This is a terrible thing to say, but I think he did a time step and a break!" said dancer Sheila Ray. Gene Kelly simplified it in **That's Dancing!** (1985): "Rather than choreographing his dancers, Berkeley maneuvered them." Berkeley and Gould merely took the steps from the stars, chorus, or dance assistants,

"I didn't raise my daughter to be a human harp!" protested one mother over this Busby Berkeley fantasy in "Spin a Little Web of Dreams" from **Fashions of 1934** (Warner Bros.).

adjusted and adapted them, and staged the numbers for the camera. In "Dancing for the Camera" by Verna Arvey for *The American Dancer* in January, 1936, the process was explained:

> In some studios, the dances are not actually created by the men who are supposed to create them. They simply plan the formations. Then they engage clever chorus girls. When the time comes for them to build their dances, they select the cleverest dancer from the chorus and say, "Show me a step." The girl does one, spontaneously. If they like it, they include it. If not, they call on another dancer. In this way, most of the screen's dance ensembles are formed. Their attractiveness lies in the interesting formations and in the photographer's ingenuity.

For the next fifty years, dancers, teachers, coaches, and assistants would create the dance numbers with little or (usually) no credit. There was no sinister plot involved on behalf of the studios or dance directors. Every department in a major studio during the mid-1930s to mid-1950s had a "supervisor" who always received credit, while subordinates often did the actual work. This is not to demean the talent of the supervisors or directors. They truly knew what to do for the camera with the various elements of the musical numbers, therefore attaining fame for their efforts. The actual creation of the dance steps, however, was often the uncredited work of others. The new administrative title created one of the mysteries of who actually did what in creating the dance routines in film — a mystery that continues today.

"Ten Dance Directors Have Corner on Staging in Musical Pictures," began an article in *Variety* on October 10, 1933. It continued: "Through the cycle of musical pictures, started by Warners **42nd Street** ... dance directing until recently was a closed shop with four men, Busby Berkeley, Larry Ceballos, LeRoy Prinz and Sammy Lee having a corner on the business.... Battle of the dance directors has been hot and heavy at times, with few of them ready to admit that the other fellow has anything. Most of the animosity has been caused by the studios' lack of knowledge of number production, the major lots feeling that only one or two men knew how to transfer a musical number to the screen. Then, too, studios were caught unprepared when musicals did a revival." The article stated that finally the job slot was opening up, with David Bennett, Seymour Felix, Jack Haskell, and Albertina Rasch being given opportunities to create lush musical sequences.

Berkeley, Prinz, Felix, Gould, and others also were obviously excellent self-promoters and began creating a niche at their respective studios. The power struggles at the major studios were intense, and the dance directors hoped to build their own dynasties. Some of them were excellent in dealing with the studio moguls, while others were not as politically motivated or adept. Already homophobia was rampant amidst the politics of the studio, with such gay dance directors as Jack Haskell feeling the bigotry ("Jack Haskell was treated like a fool by Darryl F. Zanuck," LeRoy Prinz remarked in his *Oral History*). The Good Ole Boys Club was already alive and well in Hollywood.

Albertina Rasch, the only female in the superstar ranks, was a Vienna-born classical ballerina who parlayed her talent into supplying most of the prestigious Broadway shows and vaudeville houses of the 1920s and 1930s with her ballet choreography and lines of dancers. By the time she was transferred to Hollywood, Rasch already had such a famous reputation on Broadway that her name was included in Lorenz Hart's lyrics in two Rodgers and Hart shows — "When I Go on Stage" from *She's My Baby* (1928) and "Rich Man, Poor Man" from *Spring Is Here* (1929) — and used as a punchline in cartoons of the period: "Breaking out in a Rasch." Humorist S.J. Perelman would later describe old, tired chorines performing outdated routines as "the D.A.R. — the Daughters of Albertina Rasch."

The Albertina Rasch Girls became a staple of most of MGM's 1930s musicals and historical dramas, adding beauty and the "class" of their ballet work, plus greater demands on the dancers themselves. Dancer Sheila Ray remembered, "When I used to work for Albertina Rasch over at MGM I'd roll over out of bed on to the floor and then get up, because she'd have you using different muscles that you'd never used before! She'd forget to let you rest.... I didn't enjoy working for her. On the other hand we all loved working with Busby and Bobby Connolly, because he was so sweet; and then later on for Jack Donohue, because he was always kidding around." (John Kobal, *Gotta Sing Gotta Dance.*)

In a December 1929, *Photoplay* article by Roland Francis about the rigors of being a dancing extra in musicals, "Madame" Rasch and her work methods were described:

> The Albertina Rasch Girls at MGM are a bit different. Madame Rasch was trained in the exacting schools of the ballet in Europe, and she was a famous premiere ballerina at the Metropolitan Opera House. Her girls are larger and apparently stronger than the others. They must be. When they train for dance numbers there is no music. Only the rhythmical hand-clapping of Madame Rasch...They have little time for flippancy. Madame Rasch would undoubtedly "fire" one of her girls if a smart-crack answer were given to a question. Like most Europeans she is a believer in discipline.

Rasch was a forceful, secure task-master and held her own with the brash male dance directors of the day. Bernard Sobel wrote in the September 1947 issue of *Dance Magazine*, "Albertina

Rasch made stage history when she introduced her ballet groups. She was a terrific worker and contributed greatly to the success of several Ziegfeld productions. Her displays of temper, however, were frightening. She used words as flagellants; spoke so cruelly to the dancers that Ziegfeld, who was always kind to the girls, would walk out of rehearsals embarrassed." She was famous for drilling her girls with a cane (in a 1928 article for *American Dancer*, Ray Harper quoted her: "Perhaps you have noticed that I am not using music while the girls are working on their routines? It's a little theory of mine. You see, I want them to get the sense of rhythm and timing without any—what you might say—artificial aid"). Her remarkable temperament and techniques made her the prototype for many "ballet master/mistress" characters who would be portrayed in films of the future. When interviewed by a reporter she snapped, "Will you please say that I am not the second Pavlova, or the third Genée, or the fourth Karsavina, or the fifty-seventh variety of anybody else? I am simply Albertina Rasch, first and last."

And when she spoke, the entire industry listened. In multiple articles from 1925 through 1930 in *The Dance*, a popular magazine of the time, Rasch expounded on her many ideas. On creating a truly "American" ballet: "The European ballet is a twin-sister of the opera; ours can only be a twin-sister of the popular stage, our musical comedy, motion picture or vaudeville type—a light entertainment.... There is something typically American in our atmosphere that makes us different from the children of the old world, and that is our racial rhythm, our climatic temperament, and, above all, our impressionistic mode of thinking." on the new techniques required for filmed dance: "Dancing on the natural stage is three-dimensional, while the film dance is only two-dimensional.... A girl dancing for films has to behave like a bride who is being photographed for a newspaper Sunday supplement: constantly conscious of her look and pose, so that it will make a good picture. It is a consciousness of the frontal effect."

Rasch's personal views about dance on film were primitive, as evidenced by further comments in a lengthy article ("Dancies Preferred") in *The Dance*, April 1930:

> The film ballet is an accomplished success, out of its experimental phase, of a year ago.... A ballerina performing a dance for the camera and microphone must be more conscious of her facade, florid design and conventionalized poses ... for the simple reason that she is posing for a machine and not for living eyes.... You see, the film dance in its essential form can be fifty percent more a floating and flying affair than the natural dance. Dancing for a camera can be performed with far more effective aerial illusions.... My levitation choreography follows a principle of yogi magic by exploiting the rhythmic means in a fused plastic form, kinetic color and synchronized sound designs, which brings about the optical illusion of levitation—the floating dance.

In her autobiography, Russian ballerina Alexandra Danilova would later recount working with Mme. Rasch on a 1931 London production of *Waltzes from Vienna*:

> At the first rehearsal, she asked me, "Do you know any tricks?" "What do you mean?," I said; I didn't understand. "Well," she said, "everybody has their tricks. Do you do some special kind of kicks, or maybe thirty-two fouettés?" "Good God, no," I said. I couldn't grasp her method of choreography. She explained, "All my girls have tricks of their own—we sort of stop in the middle of a number and each girl comes to the center and takes her turn, does her trick. So, what is it you will do?" And I said, "Anything you will choreograph." Finally, she asked me, "Can't you remember some movements from your ballets?" And I said, "Yes," and showed her a few of my variations. What a strange choreographer she is, I thought. Somehow, we hodgepodged a waltz—I don't think it was anything very good.

The Albertina Rasch Dancers in MGM's Broadway melody of 1936. Rasch was one of the first to feature ballet in her precision line dance work (Tillers-on-Tot).

Despite Danilova's opinion, critics of the day admired Rasch's "lavish standards" (*Variety*, December 21, 1938). Critics and audiences alike expected that a "Rasch Ballet" would expose them to culture and the arts.

Another, less successful classical troupe, the Gamby-Hale Ballet Girls, was formed by ballerina Maria Gambarelli and Chester Hale. This troupe danced in **The Cocoanuts** (1929) and **Hooray for Love** (1935) before bouréeing off into obscurity.

The struggle for self-promotion among the early dance directors was fierce. In the April 1930 issue of *The Dance* devoted completely to the new opportunity in dance — "The Movies" — Rasch and Chester Hale took out full-page ads advertising their schools, and commercial endorsements noted that the Albertina Rasch dancers used Max Factor's make-up exclusively in their appearance in **The Rogue Song** and the Chester Hale Girls always wore "Man o' War" dance rompers. Albertina even endorsed "Lucky Strike" cigarettes in an eye-catching ad which featured an imposing photograph of Mme. Rasch in a glamorous turban stating: "In training so many dancers, I must emphasize the importance of physical fitness. I urge athletic slenderness. 'No sweets'— I insist, 'Just light a Lucky instead'…. Then too, as dancing is strenuous, the wind must be protected — and Luckies never tax one's wind or irritate the throat."

Busby Berkeley took out elaborate ads in the trade papers of the day, listing his glowing reviews and his major contributions to the films ("The last 32 minutes! A word about the last 32 minutes of **Footlight Parade**…. The man who is responsible for taking these last 32 minutes of musical score, visualizing a presentation and translating it to the screen — the man who creates these numbers as you see them on the screen, stages them, directs them and shoots them, is — Busby Berkeley!") Johnny Boyle placed ads in the *Hollywood Reporter*, July 11, 1933: "Johnny Boyle of the Jack Donahue-Johnny Boyle dance studio in New York — teacher of Wheeler and Woolsey, Ruby Keeler, Joe E. Brown, Will Rogers, Marilyn Miller and Jack Haley...original dance routines in soft shoe — eccentric — broken rhythm — buck, etc. especially arranged for the screen's new musical comedy technique." The film studios began using the fierce competition by replacing one dance director with the other, faithfully described as part of the gossip of the day in the trade papers.

The dance directors' screen assignments were written about with the same excitement as the casting of the stars. For example, *Motion Picture Herald*, June 9, 1934: "Goldwyn Engages Felix: Seymour Felix has been engaged by Samuel Goldwyn to direct and stage the production numbers for **The Treasure Hunt** starring Eddie Cantor [retitled **Kid Millions**— auth.]... The new plan of Mr. Felix is to pantomime songs and dramatize them without resorting to precision numbers." On July 24, 1933, *Variety* announced that "Sammy Kicks as Joan Wants LeRoy but Uses Eddie to Master Steps." The headline referred to the brouhaha at MGM when Sammy Lee protested that LeRoy Prinz, originally signed to create the musical numbers for **Dancing Lady** with Joan Crawford, left for a Paramount assignment. When Crawford insisted that Prinz stage her numbers, LeRoy sent his brother, Eddie, to do the task, eliminating one of Lee's routines. In 1934, "difficulties" between Jack Haskell and Paramount resulted in LeRoy Prinz taking over his chores for **Search for Beauty.**

Promotional films were made about these new celebrities, usually showing them selecting the girls for their choruses. (And they had plenty to choose from: The bus depots and train stations of Hollywood were flooded with young girls from all over America arriving daily for that big chance to dance in a Hollywood musical.) Like Flo Ziegfeld before them, the best-known dance directors were perceived as authorities on beauty, and dozens of magazine articles detailed the qualities they looked for in the girls they hired. For an audition at Paramount, David Bennett listed his requirements — which sound vaguely like rating horseflesh:

> To get into my chorus...a girl must be close to five feet four inches in height and weigh from between 105 to 115 pounds. In selecting from those who meet these height and weight requirements, I look first at their teeth. Good teeth are the initial beauty essential of the chorus girl.... Posture has much to do with my selection. If a girl doesn't sit well, I know she has let herself get slouchy. She probably has been too lazy to brace herself properly at the waist, where vital organs are (Richard Kislan, *Hoofing on Broadway*).

A writer then described Berkeley's qualifications: "When Berkeley looks at a girl, he looks at her face and her figure. He looks at her arms and hands, watches the way she handles them. If they're beautiful but handled clumsily, she's 'out.' If they're all right, he looks at her legs. And they have to be good!" Bobby Connolly and Sammy Lee both had height and weight parameters, but also mentioned training and dance ability, which began to play a more important part for a girl to get a slot in the once untrained chorus.

Sammy Lee's work focused primarily on displaying beautiful girls, although he admitted, "I consider her dancing ability. The first essential here is a definite sense of rhythm. Without this, she can do nothing, even if she knows the steps." ("1,2,3 — Kick!" *The Dance*, January 1929). For his work on **Meet the Baron** (1933), the *Hollywood Reporter* (October 2, 1933) noted, "The shower bath number, 'Wearing a Great Big Smile' is well handled, and will give the hinterland yokels who haven't seen some of the more elaborate undressing numbers in other musicals, a round of gasps."

The tap-challenge sequence from perhaps Busby Berkeley's finest dance scenario, "The Lullaby of Broadway," from **Gold-diggers of 1935** (Warner Bros.).

These early dance director giants were a colorful lot. They dressed for success in suit, tie, and often a hat, looking more like the film's director than someone who was going to perform difficult physical work like modern choreographers. Trying to fit into the *au courant* notion of successful film producers and directors of the day, they often adapted a tough, despotic style of leadership, behaving in the Eric Von Stroheim school of dictatorship. On film, they were portrayed as hard-boiled dance-making machines ... or else as temperamental, hysterical, effeminate "artistes"—always good for a laugh in those days of stereotypical characterization.

Seymour Felix was one of the toughest. During his heyday as a leading Broadway dance director, Felix contributed multiple articles to *The Dance* detailing his work methods ("Speeding Up the Show," "Dance Director's Grief," "His Ideas on Dance Direction," etc). Felix's major contribution to the evolution of show dance had been more integration of the dances into the plot, and his writing contains many references to "Showmanship" and "Salemanship." In "What About Chorus Boys?" (February 1929) Felix described his standard of hiring male dancers for his chorus "I like regular fellows, real men. I detest handsome men. To a great part of the audience they give a sickening impression. They look like collar advertisements, as if they were paid for their good looks—and no real man wants to be paid for his prettiness." Accompanying photographs reveal Felix to be a very ordinary looking man, with a rather prominent nose.

In John Kobal's book *Gotta Sing Gotta Dance*, dancer and showgirl Gwen Seeger talked about working with Felix on **Kid Millions** (1934):

Seymour Felix, I think, was the hardest person that I ever worked for ... he would have us do that number over and over again until we almost dropped. He kept himself going with coffee and aspirins. And he was just so keyed up constantly.... You'd go for six or seven hours without stopping.... Well Felix went mad. He screamed and hollered at this kid who started to pee in her pants. So Lucille Ball got very angry at Seymour Felix. He was a little man. He was about 5' 1" I think ... and Lucille Ball, who was about 5' 9" or 5' 10", got up and walked down and put her finger in his face and scolded him, and he said something to her, and she just picked him up and put him under her arm, walked off the stage and took him outside.... She carried him out like a suitcase!"

Felix once asked the men at an audition to "plié across the floor." When the male dancers began squatting and moving slowly across the room, the angry Felix shouted, "What are you doing?" One of the braver dancers answered, "You asked us to 'plié' across the floor," to which Felix answered "I don't know. It's one of those French words." He had meant to say "chainé" (a moving series of turns).

Speaking to John Kobal in *People Will Talk*, Hermes Pan recalled:

Seymour was of the Sammy Lee school, New York stage. You'd never think he was a dance director to look at him. He looked like a shoe salesman.... As a matter of fact, most of the dance directors of that period were sort of the hard-boiled, slangy types with the cigar, who would shout at the girls, "Get your fannies on...Get the lead out!" They were always sort of the nasty type.... LeRoy Prinz would make some girls hysterical. He would just love to have them in tears. And that seemed to be the thing, to swear at the girls and be nasty.

Whatever his personal tics or work methods, Seymour's work on **The Great Ziegfeld** (1936) would cause the *New York Times* to trumpet, "The picture achieves its best moments in the larger sequences devoted to the Girls — ballet, chorus and show. At least one of these spectacular numbers, filmed to music of Irving Berlin's 'A Pretty Girl Is Like a Melody' with overtones of 'Rhapsody in Blue,' never has been equalled on the musical comedy stage or screen. And some of the others, notably the circus ballet led by Harriet Hoctor, are scarcely less effective."

Dave Gould, who would win the first Oscar for dance direction in 1936 for the "Straw Hat Number" (**Folies Bergère**) and "I've Got a Feeling You're Fooling" (**Broadway Melody of 1936**), would co-create some of the 1930s' most memorable dance sequences. Dorathi Bock Pierre, in her May 1936 *American Dancer* article, described him as "a very pleasant young man of short stocky build who is deeply and seriously interested in the significance of dancing in the motion pictures." Some of his views were recorded:

He points out that motion pictures have not developed a single dancer or dance director; that all those who have risen to any fame or popularity have come to pictures after a long apprenticeship on the stage.... Today, dance as a pure art form can only be used in fantasy, the dream or imaginative ideas in a picture such as the dances in **Midsummer Night's Dream**. He also feels that the technique of having the camera create the dance can only be utilized for this same purpose.... Mr. Gould thinks that dancing in pictures is only at the beginning of its importance and popularity.... I asked Mr. Gould what he thought of the possibility of the modern dance in pictures. He said that it was still too unknown to the huge rural public to whom pictures played.... As the numbers form in his mind and he works them out, he rehearses them about eight weeks, and then they make a test picture of them, without makeup or costume. When they are run off they can see necessary changes.

Later under contract to RKO-Radio Pictures, Gould would go on to direct the dances for the first two Fred Astaire-Ginger Rogers films (**Flying Down to Rio**, **The Gay Divorcee**), introducing assistant Hermes Pan to his association with Astaire. Hal Borne, rehearsal pianist for Astaire, later remembered,

> Well, with all due respect to Dave Gould—he must have had something to get where he was. He just didn't have what Hermes did. First of all, Dave Gould was not a dancer, which is right off the bat two strikes on you. I think he could do a time-step and that was about it. He was strictly an idea man and it caught up with him. I think Gould was more interested in camerawork. It was very easy for Hermes to take over because Hermes was such a talented dancer and his ideas for choreography were exactly what Fred wanted, and then too, Hermes was a younger man than Dave Gould." (Arlene Croce, *Ballet Review*, 1972)

In later years, Gould was slowly going blind. At one rehearsal he mistook a garment-loaded clothesrack at the back of the soundstage for a group of dancers and shouted, "Why isn't that group of people joining the others?" LeRoy Prinz, in his *Director's Guild of America Oral History* (1978) called Gould: "the only choreographer or dancer who had two left feet."

Prinz was hardly one to talk, as his dance expertise included merely a time step. In the June 1939 issue of *Dance Magazine*, the colorful raconteur and businesslike professional wrote an article titled "3 Routines a Week," in which he described his work methods:

> First, I must get the script and read it and conceive "great" ideas to fit spots in the story. It is rare that there is any dance routine or idea contained in the story.... I stage around one hundred and fifty routines each year. Each must be "terrific" and different from anything that has ever been done.... My next job is to sell the producer on the idea. I have to present to a producer at least a dozen dance ideas for his picture and out of them he'll probably use three.... I go back to my office and sketch out the dance in complete detail for the benefit of the production department. This department figures the cost.... Incidentally, it might be well to point out here that a dance director is not concerned alone with big ensembles of girls ... in **Give Me a Sailor**, Betty Grable and Jack Whiting did a supposedly impromptu routine. But the dance director has to work out that routine.... Insofar as "Great ideas" go, Hollywood dance ensembles are in a period of decided change. The huge dance ensembles as the audiences sees in pictures like **The Great Waltz**, **Alexander's Ragtime Band** and **My Lucky Star** are going out of favor with producers because they are very expensive. Personally, I think they're worth the cost.

Prinz surrounded himself with experts in all fields of dance and rated such glowing reviews as, "LeRoy Prinz's dance ensembles bear the mark of genius ... the dance routines are original, elaborate, and the sky's the limit" in the *Hollywood Reporter* (September 2, 1933, for his contributions to **Too Much Harmony**).

Credits on these early films read: "dance direction," "dances staged," or "arranged/directed by." Although recognition is most often given to Agnes DeMille for using the title "choreography by" on her original stage production of *Oklahoma!* in 1943, the term was previously used in 1936 by George Balanchine for his title on the stage production of *On Your Toes*. As magazine quotes from the 1920s prove, the word was known and used to describe the creation of stories in dance. In April 1949, Jack Cole wrote a satirical article, "3 Definitions ... Dance Director, Choreographer, Stager of Movement," for *Dance Magazine* in which he chided Balanchine for using the term: "Choreographer—the title as a program credit came into being the time that folk ways hit the St. James Theatre, six to eight years ago…. Riding in on the tail … were the Russian gentlemen who figured they could pick up a few dollars from the musical stage between their annual rearrangements for the ballet — aided and abetted by the more knowing producers who confuse snob appeal with progressive theater." Prior to those first usages, there had been many dance directors who did have the ability to create dance steps, but they were still billed as "dance director" or "dances by."

After Berkeley, the other major innovations of the thirties arrived when the film musical introduced two of the greatest dancing stars in movie history: Fred Astaire and Ginger Rogers.

Fred Astaire was not only one of film's greatest dancing males, he also was one of the industry's most important choreographers and dance directors — creative roles the general public never fully understood.

Before Astaire made his film debut in **Dancing Lady** (MGM, 1933), he had had an important musical comedy stage career with his sister, Adele. He had begun choreographing their stage routines early in their vaudeville appearances. When Adele retired to marry into British royalty, Fred decided to try the movies. For his second film, he was luckily paired with RKO contractee Ginger Rogers in **Flying Down to Rio** (also 1933) as minor leads. Their onscreen charisma, coupled with Astaire's innovations in choreography and musical number concepts for film, would make them the number one box office musical stars for ten years.

Another lucky pairing happened when fledgling choreographer Hermes Pan was assigned to work with Dave Gould and Astaire on **Flying Down to Rio**. Pan's association, friendship, and collaboration with Astaire lasted until Astaire's death in 1987.

Hermes Pan, a self-taught dancer who primarily learned his unique rhythmic style from black friends while growing up in Memphis, Tennessee, appeared in the choruses of two Broadway shows (*Animal Crackers*, 1928, and *Top Speed*, 1929, in which he also assisted LeRoy Prinz) before creating an act with his sister, Vasso. One of his favorite stories concerning the "tough" years was about the time he left his mother as collateral for an unpaid hotel room while he and Vasso moved onto the next town to perform and earn the rent. Finally settling in Los Angeles, he staged the numbers for a second-rate touring company and eventually assisted LeRoy Prinz and David Bennett on two Hollywood stage shows, where his work was noticed by an RKO talent scout and he was brought to films.

The innovations that Astaire and Pan brought to films would have a lasting effect. Before them, most dance sequences had been isolated performance pieces, stopping the flow of the screenplay. Astaire and Pan tried to create not gratuitous dance, but dance that extended the plot and explored the characters and their relationships (Pan told Tony Thomas in *That's Dancing*: "We spent a great deal of time trying to figure out how to get into a musical number gracefully.") Not only did their dance numbers come out of story and character situations, but the greatest composers of the time (George Gershwin, Irving Berlin, and Jerome Kern) were commissioned to write music for the team. Their staging and choreography for Fred and Ginger defined the new male-female relationship in dance (dance as seduction), also refining the "dance as narrative" technique which would blossom in the '40s and '50s with Gene Kelly's, Jack Cole's, and Eugene Loring's ballets and Astaire's own work in such films as **Yolanda and the Thief** (1945) and **Ziegfeld Follies** (1946).

The press of the day was intelligent enough to notice the difference in the Astaire-Rogers films in the way that dance was presented. For **Top Hat** (1935) the *Time Magazine* review said: "When Hollywood revived musical films three years ago, dancing was monopolized by director Busby Berkeley and his imitators. Thanks more to Fred Astaire than any other single influence, the character of musical comedy in the cinema has completely changed." And *Variety* wrote, "It might also be noted that Hermes Pan, who staged the production numbers, has kept away from the animated pinwheels and revolving swastikas which often make audiences crosseyed. In addition, he has made a marked effort to subjugate the chorus to the principals. Smart."

Astaire and Pan were among the first to insist on prerecorded music (prior to that, dancers performed to live orchestras, seated far away in the soundstage), tap sounds placed on the soundtrack after the film was completed (with Pan supplying the sounds for Rogers), sufficient rehearsal time for the dances during preproduction, and complete control of the concept, design, dance steps, photographing, and editing of each dance sequence. They also insisted that the dances be filmed in full figure, showing Astaire's and Rogers' entire bodies in as few takes as necessary, so that the audience would understand the immediacy and reality of what they were doing—no camera tricks. The movement of the camera was choreographed along with each dance sequence, with Pan standing beside the camera directing its movement during filming.

In *Tap!*, Hermes Pan is quoted:

> Now, before **Flying Down to Rio**, no one had ever seen a dance number on the screen from beginning to end. You might see dancing, but then the camera would cut down to the feet, then to the face smiling, and then to a table at somebody applauding. But you never saw the whole dance routine. When we were working on the first number, "The Carioca," I said right away: "This number should be shot without a cut. I mean no cutting away from it or cutting to the feet." We discussed it with the director and the cameraman, and we said: "Now we want head to foot, a tight full figure all the way through. And if you have to cut in the figure, just change angles so it's still full figure."

Astaire and Pan would also imaginatively experiment with Fred's solos. Within the format of the Astaire-Rogers films, Astaire would be expected to perform at least one number without Rogers, so to avoid repetition, they begin to explore concepts for the numbers, with the ideas coming to them in the rehearsal hall, on the studio lot, on the golf course, or in the middle of the night. As Astaire was a superb musician, he and Pan combined his expertise on the drums, piano, and accordion with dance steps in several solos. Astaire's love of golf ("The Golf Solo" in **Carefree**, 1938), the syncopation of machines ("Slap That Bass" in **Shall We Dance**, 1937), and dueling shadows ("Bojangles of Harlem" in **Swing Time**, 1936) became the conceptual basis for three of their most sensational creations. These numbers also found their core in simple behavioral movement, which swelled and expanded to become full-blown dance sequences.

While Astaire concentrated on the choreography for himself, his partner, Pan, created the rest. Astaire insisted that the background be unobtrusive, and Pan willingly complied, agreeing that busy crowds of extras or cluttered sets would detract from the dance. Dave Gould did the chorus staging in **Flying Down to Rio**, but Hermes Pan was responsible for the choreography of other dancers involved in the subsequent Astaire-Rogers films, such as Betty Grable and Edward Everett Horton in **The Gay Divorcee** (1934) and all of the ensemble work. It was the auspicious beginning of a choreographic career that would span four decades.

As Pan explained in an interview with John Kobal in *People Will Talk*: "**Flying Down to Rio** was the first time that dancing as such had ever been seen on the screen; a routine set to music, an intimate dance number especially. Before that, it had been mostly scenes, but I think that Astaire and Rogers were the first ones who did a dance routine. Before that, everyone was still in the Berkeley School ... Sammy Lee and Bobby Connolly and Dave Gould."

By the time Astaire and Pan made **Carefree** in 1938, they had been experimenting with special effects, as noted by *Variety* in its August 31, 1938, review: "In the dream sequence, as result of a sedative administered by Dr. Astaire, the team does one of its best double numbers ('I Used to Be Color Blind' is the tune), wherein a slow-motion camera points up the poetry of their terpsichorean motion. The idea was done once before by the elder Fairbanks in a dream chase sequence, but the slow motion, for terp effect, has been surprisingly neglected until now. It's a socko production variety." The number was originally planned to be filmed in color, but RKO's economics kept Astaire from making his color debut until the next decade.

During the '30s, Astaire and Rogers made **Flying Down to Rio**, **The Gay Divorcee**, **Roberta**, **Top Hat**, **Follow the Fleet**, **Swing Time**, **Shall We Dance**, **Carefree** and **The Story of Vernon and Irene Castle** before dissolving the successful teaming to pursue individual career goals, being reunited for the last time in **The Barkleys of Broadway** in 1949.

Astaire's contributions to film choreography were summarized in his 1987 *Dance Magazine* obituary by John Mueller:

> ...his dances contain some of the most excruciatingly complicated choreography ever put on film — an amazing and endlessly revisitable world of rhythmic nuance and subtle inflection. When two dancers from the New York City Ballet, under the direction of Jerome Robbins, tried to duplicate one of Astaire's duets, they found they still hadn't gotten all of the details after twelve hours of work...Because the movie system usually listed someone else as the dance director or choreographer for his films, it is the impression that many of Astaire's dances were choreographed by others. This was an illusion Astaire never sought to propagate and, when asked, would deny vigorously. In fact, although he often used choreographic assistants and occasionally danced in numbers, particularly production numbers, arranged by others, the vast majority of his dances were his own creation: enduring choreographic masterpieces, dazzling in their musicality, wit, rhythmic intricacy, inventiveness, and originality, that were nowhere else approached in Hollywood and only rarely equalled in the history of dance.

As Fred Astaire was the leading male dancer of the era, Eleanor Powell became his female counterpart, her dance routines greatly overshadowing anything else in her films: script, music or co-stars. Introduced on film in **George White's Scandals of 1935**, Eleanor Powell recreated her sensational Broadway solo routines on film, while Busby Berkeley, Bobby Connolly, Dave Gould, Sammy Lee and Albertina Rasch would stage the dancers around her and position the camera. Powell's routines were similar and she did not experiment with special effects, camera movement or motivation of the dance, as they were usually performed within an "Onstage" context. She insisted on being photographed full-figure, with as few cuts as possible. The variations on the unique tap dancing she created were made within the routine itself.

In *People Will Talk*, Powell discussed many thoughts in an interview: "Every dancer in motion pictures owes a debt of gratitude to Fred Astaire because he brought dancing to the screen in the right way. Prior to his and Ginger's films, a dancer would come on in a nightclub scene and would go into a dance and two steps later there'd be Joan Crawford's hand over the screen and a voice saying: 'Come and sit Down.' And then the leading man sits down and looks at her and they talk some more and then suddenly everybody applauds and the dancer is bowing and that was it for him, nothing! This is what the dancer had in films, so I never had an aspiration of coming to motion pictures." She luckily did agree to appear in films to document her personal style of rapid-fire tapping, ice-skating-speed turns and supple back bends. Powell's solos made use of such inventive "partners" as a dog, horse, Matador's cape, lariats, drum sticks and other unusual items as she creatively searched for new ways to present her basic tap style: "My dancing was solid, very masculine. I had a very low tap; I worked from the ankle down. It was really hard work."

As England tried to enter the musical film sweepstakes, expatriate American tap expert and

Fred Astaire and Hermes Pan lightheartedly create a publicity pose of how dance directors work (1937).

choreographer Buddy Bradley arrived in Britain with his talents and American sense of dance to create a series of films for Jessie Matthews, England's female dancing star. Bradley had been uncredited for his contributions to a series of Broadway shows and found the climate of Europe more conducive to acknowledging African-American talents. He is the first black choreographer to receive film credit, and he imparted his talent and knowledge to generations of British dancers.

Rachel Low, writing about Bradley's major contributions to dance on film in British musicals, wrote in *Film Making in 1930s Britain*: "It was in **Evergreen** [1934] that Buddy Bradley, a black American dancer and dance director who had directed [Matthew's] dance numbers in several Cochrane stage shows and was to do so in a number of her films, introduced the infinitely extendable stage into British films, in which performers are seen on a realistic stage which then proceeds to lose its proscenium arch and expand at will."

As the concepts and photographing of musical sequences evolved, the innovative choreographers and dance directors were being joined by directors whose sense of rhythm and movement were compatible. Former stage director Rouben Mamoulian had made a landmark musical in 1929 (**Applause**) and continued to influence the staging and filming of musical numbers with **Love Me Tonight** (1932), starring Maurice Chevalier and Jeanette MacDonald. Although not a choreographer, Mamoulian brought new sophistication to the genre by weaving the songs into the plot and filming them fluidly and innovatively. When Vincente Minnelli was later complimented for bringing sophistication to musical films, he instead credited Mamoulian's influence — "The way Mamoulian took one number, 'The Son of a Gun Is Nothing But a Tailor' and neatly created the most effective plot denouement I'd ever seen in a musical film."

The major innovations to musical and dance sequences might have ended here, but the utilization of dance during the 1930s was great.

During this decade the major studios formulated their house styles for musical films. The musical numbers at Warner Bros., although supposedly happening as part of a stage production, broke the proscenium and fluidly and elaborately depicted lengthy scenarios. Goldwyn's Eddie Cantor series often used dreams as the settings for out-of-this-world, Busby Berkeley–staged numbers. MGM's and Fox's dance numbers were nearly always stagebound, but on a stage the size of a battleship. RKO's dance sequences were often set in an art-deco nightclub, again the size of a football field. Paramount's musical numbers were more modest, with smaller casts and settings. Universal found more success with their monster genre, so their musical formula was undefined.

But no longer did choreographers, directors, and photographers simply film staged song and dance. They opened it up, moved the camera with the dancers, experimented with trick photography, and created and refined the film musical in all aspects, led by the innovations and successes of Berkeley, Astaire, and Pan.

Comprising a popular musical film genre of the period which generously utilized dancing and musical staging were the MGM stage-transferred operettas like **The Merry Widow** (1934), **Rose Marie** (1936), **Sweethearts** (1938), and **New Moon** (1940), usually starring another popular team: Nelson Eddy and Jeanette MacDonald. Although Eddy and MacDonald did not dance themselves, they were often backed or surrounded by choruses of dancers. Dance direction for these films was handled by Albertina Rasch, Dave Gould, Ernst Matray, Chester Hale, and Val Raset, utilizing ballet and period movement.

This group of dance directors also supplied the period movement and social dance scenes for the lavish non-musical film versions of such classic novels as **David Copperfield** (1935), **A Tale of Two Cities** and **Anna Karenina** (1935) and **Camille** (1937), which were a popular element of Metro Goldwyn Mayer's film output of the times.

The importance of period social dance to the plots of these dramas was highlighted in a special study guide prepared for **Anna Karenina** (Ernest Belcher, Chester Hale and Marguerite Wallman) by William Lewin:

One of the highlights of the direction is the ballroom scene, where, Anna and Vronsky fascinate each other as they dance the mazurka. From the rhythmic motion of arriving couples at the grand staircase we make a delightfully smooth transition to the Waltz. The major domo announces the mazurka…. Interwoven with his calling of the mazurka is the ironic episode of Kitty's pursuit of Vronsky, Levin's pursuit of Kitty, and Vronsky's pursuit of Anna. Through the strings of the harp we see dancers moving in rhythmic patterns. As Vronsky changes partners, dancing first joyfully with Anna, then boldly with Kitty, the actions and reactions make a fluid cinematic design.

At Paramount, musical stars Bing Crosby, Dorothy Lamour, George Raft, Martha Raye, Buddy Rogers, and Shirley Ross made a series of progressively sophisticated musical films which integrated the songs within the story and allowed resident dance director LeRoy Prinz the opportunity to experiment with musical staging. Dance masters such as the Nicholas Brothers and Louis DaPron began to give Prinz's films their most exciting dance sequences, choreographing their own numbers, which were then directed or staged by Prinz. In June 1939, *Dance Magazine* columnist Paul Francis noted, "Paramount uses quite a bit of dancing in its pictures, though most of it ends up on the cutting room floor. The can-can in **Zaza** was excellent, as were the folk dances in the last Bing Crosby picture, but they never survived preview — the can-can because of censorship and the other because of footage."

Samuel Goldwyn found great success with lavish musical comedies starring Eddie Cantor. Starting with the innovative stage transfer **Whoopee** in 1930, Busby Berkeley created lavish, lurid production numbers for **Palmy Days** (1931), **The Kid from Spain** (1932), and **Roman Scandals** (1933), original screenplays which always found the effete, harmless Cantor surrounded by dozens of scantily-clad Goldwyn Girls in Berkeley's macho cinematic fantasies. The series continued with Seymour Felix on **Kid Millions** (1934) and Robert Alton (brought to Hollywood for the first time from great Broadway success) on **Strike Me Pink** (1936). Alton would receive his due acclaim in the next decade.

The campus musical, which began with the stage-transferred **Good News** in 1930, continued to be a popular film musical form with **College Humor** and **Sweetheart of Sigma Chi** (1933); **College Rhythm** (1934); **Collegiate**, **Pigskin Parade**, and **College Holiday** (1936); **Life Begins in College** and **Varsity Show** (1937); **Freshman Year** (1938); and at least a dozen others. They utilized the dance direction talents of Busby Berkeley, Nick Castle, Jack Haskell, LeRoy Prinz, and Geneva Sawyer and featured dancers Johnny Downs, Dixie Dunbar, Betty Grable, and Eleanore Whitney. The basis for most of the choreography was the social dances of the period (the Shag, the Shim Sham, the Big Apple). As contemporary reviews noted, the cinema students spent most of their time shagging through the action of the film — and not much time on higher learning. The screenplays themselves hinged on the winning of the Big Game, followed by the stupendous musical finale.

For the Alice Faye musicals at Twentieth Century–Fox, dance directors George Hale (**George White's Scandals**, 1934), Sammy Lee (**365 Nights in Hollywood**, 1934, and **King of Burlesque**, 1936), Jack Donohue (**Music Is Magic**, 1935), Jack Haskell (**Sing, Baby, Sing**, 1936, and **Wake Up and Live**, 1937), Seymour Felix (**On the Avenue**, 1937, **Alexander's Ragtime Band**, 1938, and **Rose of Washington Square**, 1939), Carl Randall (**You're a Sweetheart**, 1937), and Nick Castle and Geneva Sawyer (**Sally, Irene and Mary**, 1938) supplied the numbers. The Fox musicals usually had a backstage setting with the musical numbers performed on stage and not integrated into the action. Very few "story" numbers were created at Twentieth Century–Fox, as was being done at Warner Bros., RKO, and Paramount, so the dance directors were not given

The Albertina Rasch Dancers perform "The Mariachi" in MGM's **Girl of the Golden West** (1938).

opportunities to further plot or explore characterization in dance, but rather challenged to come up with constant variations for the onstage routines.

Shirley Temple arrived at Fox in 1934, giving rise to a need for choreographers and dance directors to create routines for "America's Sweetheart"—who luckily could tap! She had studied ballet and tap with Ernest Belcher, so her training was extensive. Bill "Bojangles" Robinson, one of America's finest tap-dancing male stars, appeared many times with the little Miss Temple and created memorable routines for the unlikely duo, working in conjunction with Nick Castle, Geneva Sawyer, Jack Donohue, and Sammy Lee. Despite the tragic racial discrimination of the time, Mr. Robinson's unique talent was fortunately allowed to be captured on film for the ages because of his screen association with the beloved moppet.

Usually called the greatest tap-dancer of all time, Bill Robinson always wore wooden-soled shoes with which he could produce the cleanest tap sounds. With his up-on-the-toes, lighter-than-air technique he "brought an end to the era of flat-footed hoofing." (Sammy Davis, Jr., in **That's Dancing!**).

In the book *Tap!*, Fred Kelly, Gene's brother, related a charming anecdote about Robinson's work with the extraordinary child star: "I asked Bill Robinson in later years if Shirley was as good a dancer as she seemed to be in the movies. He said: 'Aw, Fred, that girl was so perfect it was embarrassing. I'd show her a step and the next day I come down and start to do the step and she'd say: "Uncle Bill, yesterday you started on the other foot."'"

Choreographer Jack Donohue and dancer Buddy Ebsen set out to create a dance routine to "At the Codfish Ball" for little Miss Temple and Ebsen in **Captain January** (1936). After they worked for three days with a dance-in, Shirley arrived in a limousine to see the number. They performed it for her, asked if she liked it, and then suggested that she learn the routine. "Is it set?" the seven-year old asked without batting an eye. When Ebsen admitted there might be some changes, she said, "Let me know when it's set and I'll learn it." Her waiting limousine whisked her away. Once the routine was set, the talented star learned it in two half-hour sessions.

As the film industry struggled to create varied musical options, Fox experimented with Sonja Henie, the Norwegian Olympic skating champion, in 1936 with **One in a Million** (Nick Castle, Jack Haskell). Dance on ice was a new challenge. Classically trained Harry Losee was responsible for creating most of Miss Henie's ice routines and continued to create ice numbers for the film industry and touring ice shows. For each subsequent Henie film, the challenges grew; such innovations as watered ice to reflect the skaters and continually increasing complexities in the creation and photographing of routines tested Losee's skill and imagination. In an article of the period, Losee's work was described:

> Some of Losee's figures are stunning, if merciless upon the skaters. Losee himself is not a skater and has never before designed routines for skaters, but for this reason, perhaps his approach is fresher than it might otherwise be. It is extremely interesting to watch him give specific, technical instructions in moments of difficulty in a craft that is not his own, and to see them, furthermore, prove to be right. His inventions are ingenious and sprightly, and if they look half as swell on film as they looked in rehearsal they will make the finished picture of genuine dance interest.

Other experimentations with dance and movement on ice were often praised, as in this March 8, 1939, *Variety* review of the collaboration between classically trained Val Raset and ice skating specialist Frances Claudet on **Ice Follies of 1939**: "The ice numbers are new and novel material for screen presentation.... The reflections in the ice as the performers glide through their numbers will quickly catch audience attention. Camera movement and angles add much to impress ... the rink sequences have been tinted and toned in laboratory printing to remove any glare from the ice surface ... as the title suggests, it's the ice show and spectacle that count."

A surprising benefit of the prolific output of dance during the thirties was the creation of musical two-reel short subjects from numbers left on the cutting room floor. *The Hollywood Reporter* blared (November 9, 1933): "Leftover Dance Footage Gives Majors Headaches — It is estimated close to a quarter of a million feet of unused song and dance have been shot by the majors in making of their pictures to appease the present yen for musicals." Brief scenarios or introductions were written and filmed, and an entirely new batch of film product reached the local theaters.

In terms of dance styles and techniques used during the 1930s, the bulk of dance on film was the "pick-'em-up-and-slap-'em-down" variety of hoofing. The dancers themselves had come from vaudeville and the Broadway stage, often self-taught, and their technique was primitive. Although film dance had been elevated to an art form by such artists as Astaire, Powell, Robinson, Hal Leroy, the Nicholas Brothers, and Louis DaPron, the chorus continued to stomp and flap. Social dances such as the Charleston, tango, bolero, shag, and Waltz gave what little variation there was to 1930s film dance.

Although dance in commercial film surprisingly utilized three of the major forces in dance during the 1930s (Ted Shawn, Ninette DeValois, and Bronislava Nijinska — but for only one film each), most of the ballet work was created by Albertina Rasch and Aida Broadbent. Other

European classical ballet innovators to begin their film contributions in the '30s were Anton Dolin, Robert Helpmann, David Lichine, Marguerite Wallman and George Balanchine.

The Goldwyn Follies (1938) introduced Balanchine's genius to films for the first time when he choreographed ballets for his soon-to-be-wife, Vera Zorina. Zorina described his work methods in her autobiography:

> His impulse was always music.... He played a piece over and over again on the piano until it was entirely in his head. He had no scraps of paper, no diagrams with choreographic notes, but would begin choreographing by lightly touching a dancer's hand and telling him or her how or where to move.... George effortlessly became a master at filmmaking, a field in which he had never worked before.... Rather than choreograph a full ballet from beginning to end, as he would have for the stage, he choreographed with the camera in mind.

This work method caused producer Samuel Goldwyn to eliminate a planned and rehearsed *An American in Paris* ballet from the film when Balanchine kept moving Goldwyn from set to set and camera set up to camera set up trying to show him the work. Without seeing the ballet in one piece, Goldwyn simply didn't understand it.

Claiming that there was "too much ballet," Goldwyn insisted that Balanchine combine ballet with "modern" dancing. (Wrote Zorina: "What he meant by 'modern' in 1937 was something like the terrific tap dancing of Eleanor Powell or the sublime dancing of Astaire and Rogers; he did not mean the Martha Graham kind of modern.... I am certain that in the late 1930s the average person in America thought of ballet as something bizarre and foreign.") Balanchine created a ballet based on the Romeo and Juliet theme, represented by tap versus ballet dancers, which pleased Goldwyn. For *Undine*, his other dance contribution to the film, Balanchine and cameraman Gregg Toland closely collaborated and had a trench dug, placing the camera below floor level so that the film audience would see the dancers in an elongated view, just as a theater audience would. Balanchine's vision of Zorina rising from the waters in *Undine* would be the inspiration for the hippo rising out of the pool in "Dance of the Hours" in Walt Disney's **Fantasia** (1940).

His next film was **On Your Toes** (1939), a film version of his great stage success. Although Zorina claimed that Balanchine demanded — and got — "carte blanche on his contract, making us virtually autonomous, so that some of the ballets are like separate artistic units in otherwise undistinguished pictures," in June 1939, Anatole Chujoy wrote in *Dance Magazine* about Balanchine's battles on the film:

> It is being said on excellent authority that Balanchine insists on Ray Bolger being signed for the part he played on Broadway.... Knowing Balanchine, I'd wager that he'd rather not do the picture at all than do it with second-rate material. If this happens, if Balanchine cannot come to an agreement with Warners, **On Your Toes** will be produced according to the accepted formula for the production of musical comedies, and the motion picture audience will have the doubtful privilege of seeing a splendid musical comedy reduced to the tinsel glamour of a super-B extravaganza reminiscent of every worse effort of every film producer in Hollywood. The situation of the ballet choreographer...in the movies is radically wrong. Those in charge do not realize the potentialities of ballet in film.

He was eventually saddled with Eddie Albert, a non-dancing male lead, for the *Slaughter on Tenth Avenue* ballet. Zorina wrote that Balanchine used "a superb black tap dancer and cut back and forth from Eddie Albert's face and torso to the tap dancer's legs and feet. It worked perfectly. I'm afraid the dancer was kept secret." [Note — the author believes the dancer's name was Herbie Harper, a protégé of Buddy Bradley, who had assisted Balanchine on the original stage production.]

Balanchine and others from the ballet world would continue into the 1940s with minimal film work as they devoted most of their energy and talent to the classical dance world. Ballet was simply not commercial at the time.

On top of the prolific film work they did, most of the top dance directors created all of the live stage dance in Hollywood, further integrating themselves into the film community. While prologues (live shows themed to and performed in conjunction with a film at the major theaters across the country) were the vogue, Sid Grauman hired Busby Berkeley, Larry Ceballos, and Albertina Rasch to create them for his Chinese and Egyptian theaters in Hollywood. Fanchon and Marco supplied hundreds of "ideas" (their term for prologues) for the entire Fox West Coast chain of theaters.

Despite the tremendous input of the decade, the movie industry never understood dance directors: *what* they did, *how* they did it, or the importance of their contribution to films. They were a group without a union, receiving no health and welfare benefits, pensions, guaranteed screen credit, or other recognition shared in most film crafts. The competitive nature of the dance directors themselves did not help their position as they fought for the crown, and the growing jealousy on the part of producers and directors over their visibility and popularity begin to fester.

With the success of musical films and their dance sequences, the Academy of Motion Picture Arts and Sciences (AMPAS) finally voted on December 12, 1935, to acknowledge achievement in dance direction. They bestowed an Academy Award for best dance direction for three years (1935–1937), the first year basing the nominations on two musical numbers created by the individual and subsequently awarding nominations for only one number. The winners were Dave Gould in 1935 (**Folies Bergère** and **Broadway Melody of 1936**), Seymour Felix in 1936 (**The Great Ziegfeld**), and Hermes Pan in 1937 (**A Damsel in Distress**).

In "Hollywood Recognizes the Dance," an article in *The American Dancer*, April 1936, Dorathi Bock Pierre congratulated the academy on finally recognizing dance directors and choreographers with a category of their own, admitting, "The argument has often been propounded by people connected with the picture industry that an audience interested in dancing is a very small one, according to them confined almost entirely to dancers, and that all they can hope to do with dancing in pictures, or all they want to do, is to give a suggestion here and there, and to show a pretty face or shapely figure; otherwise the interest of the spectator will wander." While describing all of the nominated dance numbers, when she reached the title song from **Top Hat**, choreographed by Hermes Pan, she revealed, "Audiences composed of the ordinary untrained spectator are all enthusiastic about this number, and still the studios say, 'People are not interested in seeing a dance, they would be bored....'"

In *The Genius of Busby Berkeley*, Berkeley has a story to tell about the upset over his "Lullaby of Broadway" dance sequence from **Golddiggers of 1935** not winning:

> Everyone expected I would receive an Oscar for it, but they gave it to someone else [Dave Gould]. The Dance Directors section of the Academy ... were so infuriated...that they gave me a big dinner at the Trocodero. About two hundred and fifty people attended with studio brass and many of my old pals who were dance directors. It was quite an affair, and they presented me with a beautiful plaque as a tribute. The inscription on this reads: "Presented to Busby Berkeley, Guest of Honor, at the first Annual Dinner of the Dance Directors Section of the Academy of Motion Pictures

Edward A. Prinz (center) visits his sons Eddie (l) and LeRoy (r) while the boys are engaged on their duties as dance directors at Paramount (1935). Prinz, Sr., is described as a "nationally known dance teacher" and has operated his school in St. Joseph, Missouri, for more than 43 years (photo courtesy of the Academy of Motion Picture Arts and Sciences).

Arts and Sciences on December 7, 1936, in recognition for his outstanding contribution to the pioneering and development of musical productions in motion pictures." This testimonial is signed by all of the leading choreographers.... I appreciate it as a very nice tribute, because they all thought I was the best of the bestest.

In 1936 Dave Gould and Seymour Felix went before the academy board and tried to get a special award presented to Berkeley for his contributions to motion pictures in general. It is reputed that the Screen Director's Guild of America objected to the term "dance director." They refused to accept that audiences had come to see a film because of its dances, rather than its other aspects (despite Berkeley ads to the contrary). The award was quietly disbanded in 1939, and the academy's recognition for dance contributions officially ended.

Many years later, on September 10, 1979, AMPAS presented a retrospective evening of film clips saluting those long-ago awards, with panel discussions by Hermes Pan, Eleanor Powell, LeRoy Prinz, and moderator Gene Nelson. The printed program contained interesting observations:

> The Best Dance Direction award may have been one of the most short-lived of Academy Awards ... but it was surely one of the most entertaining, not only in terms of what it was for but the manner in which it was handled. Each dance director was invited to nominate two dance numbers for whose direction he was responsible, and these numbers were then screened for the entire Academy membership which was asked to cast ballots on a point system rating the merit of the nominated achievements as to originality of idea, execution and entertainment value [750 individual musical numbers were offered for consideration — auth.]. For the first year...which was given in the form of a Certificate of Merit rather than an Oscar, all the nominated dance numbers were screened at Grauman's Chinese Theater.... The public was invited to attend, and copies of the ballots were distributed to them.... On June 8, 1939, along with many changes created by the formulation of the various film guilds, the Academy's Board of Governors voted to drop the Best Dance Direction category from the Awards.

In future years, honorary Academy Awards would be given to Fred Astaire in 1949, Gene Kelly in 1951, Jerome Robbins (**West Side Story**, 1961), and Onna White (**Oliver!**, 1968) for their contributions to dance on film — a questionable reward to the people who made the American musical film what it was.

Without a union and diffused by battling egos, the dance directors politically stumbled. The dancers themselves never really knew quite what to do. In 1935, a dancer's union was formed ("The newly formed Screen Dancers' Guild of Los Angeles held their first annual Christmas Show at the Carthy Circle Theatre on December 15, to raise funds for jobless screen dancers. The Guild, which originated as a strictly male organization, has voted to accept into membership girl dancers in films"—*American Dancer*, February 1939). They struggled to survive for one year, with most opposition coming from the Screen Actors' Guild (SAG), who would not recognize the specialized work that dancers performed. When a vote was taken in the 1940s for dancers to either be represented by SAG or SEG (Screen Extras Guild), the leaderless and bickering dancers selected the less prestigious (and lower-paid) SEG. The "powers that be" never seemed to understand — or champion — the art of dance on the screen. The irony, of course, is that contemporary critics and audiences alike watch the musical films of the '30s specifically to see the musical numbers.

New restrictions on the creativity of the dance directors arrived with the adoption of the Production Code and censorship watchdogs Joseph Breen and Will Hays in 1934. Gone were the transparent costumes and nudity of the Busby Berkeley fantasies, and restrictions on dances were detailed: "Dancing in general is recognized as an art and as a beautiful form of expressing human emotions. But dances which represent sexual actions, whether performed solo or with two or more; dances intended to excite the emotional reaction of an audience; dances with movement of the breasts, excessive body movements while the feet are stationary, violate decency and are wrong." (*Motion Picture Production Code*, 1930.)

Despite the new political barriers, the 1930s left us a film legacy of dazzling dance numbers and virtuosity by Fred and Ginger, Shirley and "Bojangles," and Ruby Keeler; the early tap creations of Nick Castle and Geneva Sawyer; the spectacular "A Pretty Girl Is Like a Melody" from **The Great Ziegfeld** (1936); and the dizzying kaleidoscopic work of Busby Berkeley. Dancers were starting to need training to perform a variety of styles, and the calibre of dancing talent rose as the major dance schools in Hollywood boomed. Film audiences were exposed to the creativity of George Balanchine, Larry Ceballos, Bobby Connolly, Seymour Felix, Sammy Lee, Hermes Pan, LeRoy Prinz, and Albertina Rasch. Dancer-choreographers started their film careers: a very young Ann Miller, the dazzling Condos and Nicholas Brothers, the charming Ray Bolger, Louis DaPron, Buddy Ebsen, George Murphy, and the tap-dancing star who would further ratt-a-tatt her way into film history in the 1940s, Eleanor Powell.

Ernest Belcher and Theodore Kosloff had left the now highly competitive field to devote all of their energies to their schools and preparing the next generation of dancing greats. Many others shared their genius in one or two films and then hurried back to the security and autonomy of the musical stage, the classical dance world, or their successful schools. Benjamin Zemach, after being nominated for an Oscar for his inventive work in **She** (1935), the first of the three films he choreographed, returned to modern dance and theatre to explore Israeli dance.

Despite the defections, in ten years dance on film had leapt light years ahead.

Selected Filmography

The Big Broadcast of 1936 (Fayard Nicholas, LeRoy Prinz, Bill Robinson) Par, 1935 — In specialty appearances, the budding Nicholas Brothers and the legendary Bill Robinson are given opportunities by Prinz to show us their stuff. And oh, what stuff!

The Big Broadcast of 1937 (Louis DaPron, LeRoy Prinz) Par, 1936 — An early look at the superb dance talents of DaPron (in a duet with Eleanore Whitney), which he would later channel into creating dance sequences for others.

The Big Broadcast of 1938 (LeRoy Prinz) Par, 1937 — Martha Raye's comic talent and Prinz's staging and direction make "Mama, that Moon is Here Again" a laugh-out-loud number for Raye and a chorus of sailors who lift, pull, throw, and threaten to tear her limb-from-limb.

Born to Dance (Dave Gould, Eleanor Powell) MGM, 1936, Video:MGM/UA — Eleanor taps her way into our collective memories in several smash-

ing numbers, but the finale, "Swingin' the Jinx Away," would serve as the prototype for all military-big-guns-firing-marching-bands-parading numbers till the end of time.

Broadway Melody of 1936 (Dave Gould, Buddy Ebsen, Eleanor Powell, Carl Randall, Albertina Rasch) MGM, 1935, Video:MGM/UA — Eleanor Powell's second film appearance confirms her film stardom with some dazzling solo work — surrounded by choruses staged by Gould, Randall and Rasch — but the joyful "Sing Before Breakfast" performed by the tap wizardress and Buddy and Vilma Ebsen on a tenement roof is this film's "feel good" moment.

Captain January (Jack Donohue) Fox, 1936, Video:CBS/Fox — Shirley Temple and Buddy Ebsen in a charming tap dance duo, showing both of them off to advantage.

A Damsel in Distress (Fred Astaire, Hermes Pan) RKO, 1937, Video:Turner Home Ent — Contains

Dave Gould (squatting at far left) gives directions to the dancers for the "Finale" of **Broadway Melody of 1938** (MGM).

Pan's Oscar-winning amusement park romp for Astaire, with George Burns and Gracie Allen.

Dancing Pirate (Eduardo Cansino, Russell Lewis) RKO, 1936, Video:Matinee Classics — Excellent dancers Charles Collins and Steffi Duna head several colorful, Spanish-flavored dance ensembles in this early Technicolor film. The "Cape Dance" is a stunning use of whirling red capes amidst black, grey, and white costumes.

Flying Down to Rio (Fred Astaire, Dave Gould, Hermes Pan) RKO, 1933, Video:Turner Home Ent — Astaire, Rogers, Gould, and Pan all come together to make history — and girls on airplane wings are the icing on this dance cake.

42nd Street (Busby Berkeley, Ruby Keeler) WB, 1933, Video:MGM/UA — Berkeley's second giant step (after **Whoopee**) with an inventive scenario and surrealistic staging for the title tune.

The Gay Divorcee (Fred Astaire, Dave Gould, Hermes Pan) RKO, 1934, Video:The Nostalgia Merchant — contains the incomparable "Night and Day" adagio by Astaire and Rogers and one of the longest musical numbers in films, "The Continental," which tested Gould's versatility in how many ways he could present the same material — and almost succeed. "Let's K-nock K-neez" by Betty Grable and Edward Everett Horton is also a hilarious example of '30s dance eccentricity.

Going Hollywood (George Cunningham, Albertina Rasch) MGM 1933, Video:MGM/UA — All right, if you buy real-life-worldly Marion Davies as a naive girl's schoolteacher, then you will buy her as a simple farm girl with Bing Crosby clunking amongst swaying daisies, dancing scarecrows, and hoedowning couples in "We'll Make Hay While the Sun Shines." I regret that Bing enters the soundstage while Davies is filming the finale, "Our Big Love Song," for I would love to see where Cunningham and Rasch were going with Marion dressed as Catherine the Great (in a dress the size of a mobile home) walking amidst back-bending and lute-strumming Chinese chorines.

Goldiggers of 1933 (Busby Berkeley) WB, 1933, Video:MGM/UA — The foolishness and glitter of

"We're in the Money" juxtaposed with the poignant power of "My Forgotten Man" are only two examples of Berkeley's versatility.

Golddiggers of 1935 (Busby Berkeley) WB, 1935, Video:MGM/UA — The chilling scenario and patterns of movement in "Lullaby of Broadway" — as Gene Kelly says in **That's Dancing!**, "The most incredible tap dance sequence ever filmed. A monument to the genius of Busby Berkeley" — make this film memorable.

The Goldwyn Follies (George Balanchine, Sammy Lee) UA, 1937, Video:HBO — Balanchine's less-than-successful film debut is an endless bore of a film, but it marks the first serious introduction of classical ballet into popular American film.

The Great Ziegfeld (Seymour Felix) MGM, 1936, Video:MGM/UA — The "Big One" — girls and turntables and stairs and Austrian drapes, with everything going on forever. Deserving of the Oscar it won for dance direction.

Hollywood Party (Seymour Felix, Dave Gould, George Hale, Albertina Rasch) MGM, 1934, Video:MGM/UA — In a film which cannot decide whether it is a feature film or a series of shorts, evolving filmed dance direction and staging of a Berkeley-esque title tune — with Buck Rogers–like telephone operators (who seem to be impaled by microphones) on turntables and shot from overhead — collides with a stagebound operetta scenario and staging of "Hello" (performed by petal-tossing Grecian girls, cellophane-draped chorines, and Zulus — ending in a funny tango between Jack Pearl and Jimmy Durante). But a movie with the Three Stooges, Laurel and Hardy *and* Mickey Mouse simply has to be seen.

Just Around the Corner (Nick Castle, Bill Robinson, Geneva Sawyer) Fox, 1938, Video:CBS/Fox — "I Love to Walk in the Rain" is the highlight of this film which marked the beginning of Shirley Temple's "fade-out" as she grew too big for her tap shoes.

The Little Colonel — (Jack Donohue, Bill Robinson) Fox, 1935, Video:CBS/Fox — Bill Robinson and Shirley Temple match talent and charm in some of the screen's most enduring images, performing Robinson's famous "Stair Dance."

Murder at the Vanities (Larry Ceballos, LeRoy Prinz) — Par, 1934, Video:MCA — Bizarre backstage murder mystery, containing the infamous "Marijuana" production number.

My Lucky Star (Harry Losee) Fox, 1938, Video:CBS/Fox — Dance on ice continues to expand in an imaginative *Alice in Wonderland* ice ballet for Sonja Henie and skating chorus.

On Your Toes (George Balanchine) WB, 1939 — *Slaughter on Tenth Avenue* is one of the few preservations on film of Balanchine's innovative stage and ballet work. A tough one to find, however. Hopefully, Warner Bros. will soon release it on video for all to see.

Rosalie (Dave Gould, Eleanor Powell, Albertina Rasch) MGM, 1937, Video:MGM/UA — Powell's tap wizardry fronts the imagination of Gould and Rasch — plus a look at nearly every dancer and extra in Hollywood in 1937!

Shall We Dance (Fred Astaire, Harry Losee, and Hermes Pan) RKO, 1937, Video:Turner Pict. — Although Astaire made an unconvincing ballet dancer partnering bizarre ballerina Harriet Hoctor, his solo to "Slap That Bass" and his rise to the challenge of dancing on roller skates with Ginger Rogers to "Let's Call the Whole Thing Off" make this film a dance-variety delight.

Strike Me Pink (Robert Alton) UA, 1936 — Alton's first film offering, mimicking the camera tricks of Busby Berkeley but adding elegance and class to the onscreen African-American dancers, plus a very bizarre depiction of "Shake It Off with Rhythm."

Sweethearts (Ernst Matray, Albertina Rasch) MGM, 1938, Video:MGM/UA — The lavish title number and "Jeanette and Her Little Wooden Shoes" impress in MGM's first three-color Technicolor operetta. Don't expect Nelson Eddy to dance, he can barely walk!

Top Hat (Fred Astaire, Hermes Pan) RKO, 1935, Video:RKO — A classic number for Astaire and a male chorus to the title song, plus a dazzling "Cheek to Cheek" for Astaire and Rogers are the film's highlights.

THE 1940s

Building upon the innovations of the 1930s, the 1940s were the beginning of the Golden Age of the movie musical, with more musicals produced during this decade than at any other time. The tragedy of World War II created the need for escapism at the movie theater, and the movie musical supplied it by the reel, along with dance by the mile.

The movie musical was the antithesis of the reality that Americans had first tried to escape during the Depression in the '30s. Now, with a war ravaging the world, most of the able-bodied young men were taken away from their homes, and the rest of the adult population worked diligently in less-than-glamorous jobs. Escape into the fantasy of the movie musical became emotionally necessary. The children of that era were exposed to hours of musical films, as the children of later generations would be exposed to onscreen violence.

On stage and in the films of the times, bursting into song was the absent-minded revelation of a character's inner feelings, a revelation which was then blown out of all proportion into a verse, a 32-bar chorus, and then the dance. The children of the era grew up believing that the greatest goal in life was to simply feel so good that you could twirl on a shiny floor like Fred Astaire or breeze down a sidewalk like Gene Kelly, not giving a damn what the neighbors might think. Your joy (and talent) would be so great, so overwhelming, that the neighborhood would join in, instinctively knowing the lyrics and choreography.

It was the collaborative challenge of the screenwriter, director, and choreographer to make that transition work: from simple words to a full-blown production number.

The 1940s were filled with music, from Broadway stages, radios, record players, and movie screens. Singing was something that nearly everyone could do: in the shower, driving in the car, and singing along at home with the radio or the record player. But dancing? Ah, only the gods could dance. Mere mortals could not keep up with Kelly or Astaire or Hayworth, Powell, Miller or Grable. The masses had to be satisfied watching the great ones dance. And satisfied they were.

During the 1940s, dancing propelled the movie musical—tap, ballet, jazz, ballroom, jitterbugging, and more sophisticated ethnic variations. Non-musical films usually contained a nightclub, ballroom, school dance, or party scene which also required dance expertise. With the need for technically skilled and versatile dancers so great, the studios now had chorus dancers under permanent contracts. These dancers went from film to film — often not remembering the title of the picture, simply completing a day's work. The dance department of each studio gave classes to all the budding actors and actresses in the studio's talent school. Dance creators had their hands full as nearly every major film star also danced onscreen during the '40s (Greta Garbo, Bette Davis, Clark Gable, John Wayne, Paulette Goddard, Maureen O'Hara, etc.). The dream factory became a dancing machine!

Each and every department at the film factories now had a titular head, and the dance directors reigned supreme in the music departments of the major studios. Along with overseeing the dance requirements of each film the studio produced, the dance director also served as the administrative head for the department, hiring people to teach classes or coach dancing stars on their routines, and assigning specialists to create original dance. Many were capable of choreographing and staging the musical sequences themselves; others were not. There were now people who created tap, ballet, jitterbug, ethnic, water, and ice-dancing sequences. They rarely received credit, however, for the credit went to the dance director, who was now under a

The history of American social dance has been captured on film. Here, Ginger Rogers and Rand Brooks try a 1930s Fox-Trot in **Lady in the Dark** (Paramount, 1944).

long-term contract to the studio. The dance director hired and fired, supervised the work — and got the credit.

The details of dance credits continued to be multi-layered and elusive. The making of **The Jolson Story** at Columbia in 1946 illustrates the complicated layers of the system.

As Jack Cole was dance director for Columbia at the time, contractually he was responsible for the overall dance direction and would receive on-screen credit for the film. Cole's expertise was jazz dance, so Val Raset was brought in to create the old-fashioned Broadway and vaudeville sequences. Audrene Brier and Matty King were next hired to teach Larry Parks, the film's star, to move like Jolson. Miriam Nelson, a dancer and former assistant to Danny Dare at Paramount, was then asked to create a number for the film because of her tap expertise. Evelyn Keyes, portraying "Julie Benson" (a fictitious name invented for Jolson's real-life wife Ruby Keeler, who refused to allow the producers the use of her name), was to perform a dance to "Liza." During the dance she becomes frightened of the high staircase she is dancing on, she freezes, and Jolson saves the day by rising from his seat in the audience and singing. After Miriam created the tap sequence, Cole, Jolson, Keyes, and the film's producers came to see it one day on the set in the soundstage. When Miriam finished performing the rather difficult number, she waited patiently while all of the principals discussed it. Finally, it was agreed that the number would be used, but that Miriam herself would have to perform it in all the medium and long shots, for it was too difficult for Keyes. Everyone filed out, with only Jolson taking the time to congratulate Miriam on her work. In the released film, Miriam performed her own choreography. Her name is nowhere to be found in the credits.

But, with this huge burst of activity, the new exploration of dance styles and the emergence of more versatile dancers and creators, the innovations in film dance soared. As most of the technical experimentation had happened in the 1930s (camera angles and techniques, multiple exposures, slow motion, color, etc.), the historic dance changes of this decade were primarily within the techniques and styles themselves. Meanwhile, the innovators of the previous decade continued to add richness to the musical film legacy.

The Judy Garland-Mickey Rooney series of MGM musicals stole Busby Berkeley from Warner Bros. to direct and create the musical numbers (**Babes in Arms**, 1939, **Strike Up the Band**, 1940, and **Babes on Broadway**, 1941). Personal problems and Garland's reluctance to work with him eventually found him only in charge of the "I Got Rhythm" finale in **Girl Crazy** (1943), but his daring approach to the visualization of musical sequences continued.

Musical arranger Roger Edens described some typical Berkeley excitement on "Do the La Conga," a major song-and-dance sequence in **Strike Up the Band** (1940):

> Then Berkeley got crazy and decided on blowing the whole number up ... using every possible camera angle he could think up ... then decided to complicate matters even further by announcing that he would shoot the whole number in one take! With Six Hits and a Miss as vocal backup for Judy, Paul Whiteman and his orchestra, with Mickey on drums and 115 dancers (one of which was Marjorie Keeler, Ruby's sister), Berkeley rehearsed the cast and crew for thirteen days, and it was ready ... and it worked ... and without a hitch! [Hugh Fordin, *The World of Entertainment*].

For MGM, Berkeley also supplied his staging brilliance to **Ziegfeld Girl** and **Lady, Be Good** (1941), and **Born to Sing** (1942); he directed **For Me and My Gal** (1942) and **Take Me Out to the Ballgame** (1949). He returned briefly to Warner Bros. to direct **Cinderella Jones** (1946).

Decades later, Berkeley's '40s contributions would be best remembered for the riot of color, girls, strawberries, bananas, and Carmen Miranda he created for "The Lady in the Tutti Frutti Hat" in **The Gang's All Here** (1943), his only work at Twentieth Century–Fox during the decade. Although several countries banned the number, it wasn't until years later that psychologists told us that the bananas were huge phallic symbols being waved at poor Miss Miranda and several of the floor patterns Berkeley photographed from overhead represented vulvas. Contemporary audiences simply had a swell time watching it.

Several of the once superstar (and Oscar-nominated) dance directors of the thirties (Larry Ceballos, Seymour Felix, Dave Gould, and Sammy Lee) continued to contribute, although they were now relegated to less prestigious projects, often at minor studios such as Republic and Monogram. Aida Broadbent continued at RKO, while Albertina Rasch retired in 1939, keeping her position in the film industry as the wife of composer Dimitri Tiomkin.

The classic 1930s combination of Fred Astaire and Ginger Rogers had ended in 1939 with **The Story of Vernon and Irene Castle**, a biography of an earlier pair of America's dancing sweethearts. Now, "Gingerless" (as Astaire titled the chapter in his autobiography *Steps in Time*), Astaire moved from studio to studio and from partner to partner, adapting his choreography to the strengths — or weaknesses — of each one: Eleanor Powell, Rita Hayworth, Virginia Dale, Joan Leslie, Lucille Bremer, Olga San Juan, and Judy Garland. At last, he reunited with Ginger in **The Barkleys of Broadway** (1949). He was finally given a special award by the Academy of Motion Pictures Arts and Sciences in 1948: "For his unique artistry and his contributions to the technique of musical pictures." Astaire's forties creations incorporated the jitterbug, the Big Apple, jive, and other social dances of the period, as well as adapting his tap expertise into a more jazz-like style.

Separated from Hermes Pan for most of the decade, Astaire successfully worked with new collaborators (Robert Alton, Bobby Connolly, Danny Dare, Eugene Loring, Val Raset, and David Robel), and three of his solos during the decade were among his best: the "Firecracker" dance in **Holiday Inn** (1942), the drunken glass-smashing, bar-leveling "One for My Baby" in **The Sky's the Limit** (1943), and the technically complicated triumph fronting a chorus of Astaires to "Puttin' on the Ritz" in **Blue Skies** — a number which was to be "Astaire's Last Dance" as he announced his retirement from the screen in 1946. But when Gene Kelly, the original male star of **Easter Parade** (1948), was injured and forced to withdraw, Astaire was lured out of retirement. As the musical numbers for the film had been conceived and plotted for Kelly by Robert Alton, Astaire's comedic talents were expanded with a Kelly-inspired "A Couple of Swells" song-and-dance routine with Judy Garland. Had Alton been devising musical sequences for the usually top-hat-white-tie-and-tails bedecked Astaire, this brilliant stretch — which Astaire would continue to explore in the next decade — probably never would have happened. (More about Alton, Kelly, Loring, Powell, and other Astaire collaborators later).

Hermes Pan was contracted by Twentieth Century–Fox and began his dazzling color-splashed series of work with Alice Faye, Betty Grable, June Haver, Rita Hayworth, Carmen Miranda, and Caesar Romero, often appearing on-screen partnering the leading lady. He periodically was reunited with Astaire during the decade, as in **Second Chorus** (1940), **Blue Skies** (1946) and **The Barkleys of Broadway** (1949), but new challenges allowed him to adapt his genius to new dance techniques.

In 1941 he created the numbers for Sonja Henie's **Sun Valley Serenade** and was challenged with ice dancing for the first time:

> Zanuck told me that they had decided not to spend much money on her pictures because she was giving everybody such a hard time. This was particularly the case in the "Black Ice Ballet".... This was a number that I created.... I got together with the set man and he said, "Well, we'll flood it with nicozine dye." Anyway, Henie was very difficult to work with ... she would get into a sit spin and ... she would stay in it for about 5000 years. And I'd say, "When I count to eight, Henie, *leave* the spin. Because there are about sixteen boys coming down on you and they'll run into you."...and she got into a beautiful sit spin, and those sixteen boys came down on her ... and you can't stop them when they're on skates ... and they hit Henie and she flew over there,

down into the nicozine dye. And when she got up, she was *black*. Her face and her costume were covered in it [John Kobal, *People Will Talk*].

Eleanor Powell's name was top-billed in a series of musicals, and in **Broadway Melody of 1940** she co-starred with Astaire in a one-time-only miracle of dance on film which still rates cheers when viewed today.

In *People Will Talk*, she described the initially strained creative process with Astaire for their dance numbers:

> We had no choreographer at all. What made it so difficult was that nobody could do what I was doing but me. Up to the time Fred worked with me, he always had a young lady that he could teach.... In fact, Hermes Pan used to take the girl's part ... but me being my own choreographer and Fred being his own on **Broadway Melody**, who was going to tell who what to do? I said: "Mr. Astaire, I have a number and there's something wrong in the middle of it. If I did it for you, would you please help me with the center part of it? It just doesn't feel right." I thought that might be one way we could get on our feet! So I did it, got to the middle and stopped. And he jumped out of his chair real quick and said: "Oh, I see what you mean," and he did a little something and then he stopped and ran right back to the chair.

The ice had been broken, and the two superstars improvised to create movie dance magic together.

Cinema writer Dale Thomajan salutes Powell in *From Cyd Charisse to **Psycho**—A Book of Movie Bests*, singling out her work in **Ship Ahoy** (1942) under the heading "The Best Number in an Otherwise Mediocre Musical":

> Midway through this modest black-and-white programmer ... Smartly dressed in turban and whippy skirt, Eleanor Powell swings into action, skipping, kicking, and cartwheeling ... tables, chairs, flying rings, even a diving board get into the act as Eleanor serves up two-and-a-half minutes of the most expert and endearing dancing you will ever see.... Finally, with miraculous precision, she and Dorseyman Buddy Rich exchange one small drum (thrown), one drumstick (bounced), one handshake (firm), and a pair of smiles (absolutely dazzling)—all this occurring bing-bang-bing in a matter of seconds—then suddenly "I'll Take Tallulah" is over and you find yourself wondering, as you're putting your socks back on, if it all really happened.

Eleanor Powell was not the only dance virtuoso to leave her legacy of specialized and unique dance styling on film during the 1940s. Another mile-a-minute tap wizardress, Ann Miller, starred in a series of "B" musicals for Columbia, with the unique tap numbers she created being the highpoint of the low-budget films. Whereas Powell's technique and style impressed, Miller's sizzled with raw sensuality and knock-yourself-out energy. When Cyd Charisse injured herself during rehearsals in **Easter Parade** (a film project distinguished by *two* lucky breaks), Miller got her chance to dance with Astaire. She was contracted by MGM for further prestigious film roles in the next decade.

Male hoofer-choreographers Ray Bolger, Buddy Ebsen, Hal LeRoy, and George Murphy continued to collaborate with dance directors and perform their individualized styles in multiple film roles.

By this time vaudeville was dead, and the highly popular nightclubs of the period offered exposure to specialty dance acts and teams who were now given opportunities in films. The tapping Condos Brothers and the ballroom-team sensations Veloz and Yolanda, Tony and Sally

DeMarco and Don Loper and Maxine Barratt arrived on the set to appear in nightclub sequences with their own choreography, which had often taken years to refine and perfect. It was inexpensive talent for the studios and added marquee-value names to many low-budget films without extensive rehearsal costs, and their dancing expertise usually stopped the show.

These specialty appearances also afforded greater visibility to African-American dancers and choreographers. For decades, black artists had enjoyed success on stages and in venues such as the Cotton Club, the Apollo Theater in Harlem, and the black vaudeville circuit. Finally, their appearances on film made a huge impact on audiences around the world. Although a black film industry had begun in the 1920s, it wasn't until the late 1930s and throughout the 1940s that these sensational dance artists were widely introduced to general audiences in shorts and features. Their musical numbers in major studio releases were usually isolated from the script and could be removed for Southern showings, but all-black musicals such as **Cabin in the Sky** and **Stormy Weather** (both 1943) finally gave extensive exposure to some of America's most talented performers. The Nicholas Brothers, Buck and Bubbles, the Four Step Brothers, the Harlem Congaroo Dancers, and Tip, Tap and Toe followed Bill "Bojangles" Robinson into movie history with their artistry.

Dozens of new Caucasian dancing stars of various backgrounds and styles were also forging careers during the war years. This group basically concentrated on performing and relied on others to supply the choreography and staging of their work. Some (Lucille Bremer, Johnny Coy, Johnny Downs, Joan McCracken, and Marc Platt) would have brief success for one reason or another, but others (Cyd Charisse, Dan Dailey, Rita Hayworth, Danny Kaye, Donald O'Connor, Peggy Ryan, and Vera-Ellen) would find favor with film audiences for extensive careers.

Another popular performer-choreographer arrived on screen in 1942 and became the next major influence in dance on film: Gene Kelly.

Discovered on Broadway in *Pal Joey* in 1940 and immediately brought to Hollywood, Kelly's unusual combination of classic dance training, athleticism, and unsophisticated masculinity made a great impact on the film musical. If Fred Astaire was dancing's elegant gentleman, Kelly was its boy next door. Bringing Stanley Donen with him from Broadway as a partner and co-creator, Kelly drastically changed the face of the musical film during the 1940s. "In his working-man clothes and trademark white socks, Kelly remade dance on film from a European art form into an American one with his snappy paper-tearing, roller-skating, puddle-stomping footwork." (Hilary de Vries, *Los Angeles Times*, May 1, 1994).

With his star status allowing him major input into the dance contents of his films, Kelly was single minded about his goal. In September 1962 he told *Dance Magazine,* "When I came to Hollywood, it was as an actor-dancer, certainly not as a choreographer. But soon after my first picture I realized that no director in Hollywood was seriously interested in developing the cinematic possibilities of the dance. No one cared about finding new techniques or improving the old ones. I decided that that would be my work."

From his very arrival in films with **For Me and My Gal** (1942), Kelly studied the effect of filmed dance and realized that speed, distance, and the dancer's environment were all altered by the camera. While a close-up gave strength to actors, it weakened the power of the dancer. Remembering what he had learned on Broadway from director John Murray Anderson, he began to develop mood and coloring for his dance numbers. He also concentrated on developing the character of his role *through* dance, rather than abandoning it and becoming merely a graceful dancer. In 1994 he told Graham Fuller for *Interview,* "I did **Cover Girl** (1944) ... and that's when I began to see that you could make dances for cinema that weren't just photographed stage dancing. That was my big insight into Hollywood, and Hollywood's big insight into me."

The two angels of American film dance, Fred Astaire and Gene Kelly, finally appear together in the "Babbit and the Bromide" number from **Ziegfeld Follies** (MGM, 1945).

Creating in conjunction with the camera and the other technical elements of the film medium, Kelly and Donen took chances, experimented, and stretched the concept of dance on film with such innovations as double image (**Cover Girl**, 1944), a live dancer with animation (**Anchors Aweigh**, 1945), gymnastics and athleticism (**Living in a Big Way**, 1947, and **The Pirate** and **The Three Musketeers**, 1948), the introduction of the female lead through a dialogueless dance montage of the various sides to her character (**On the Town**, 1949), and filming outdoors in actual locales (**On the Town**).

The individual contributions of Kelly and Donen are impossible to separate:

> After Minnelli the greatest discoveries in Arthur Freed's great gallery are surely Gene
> Kelly and Stanley Donen, considered first as a two-headed monster and then individ-
> ually. Kelly's gifts as a musical director are difficult to assess because we do not know,
> it is impossible to know, and no doubt they themselves did not and do not know, exactly
> how much Kelly and Donen each contributed to their joint works.... Since they were
> both dancers and are both choreographers, one might expect their films to be dance-
> dominated, but not at all. (Taylor and Jackson, *The Hollywood Musical*).

Two other important elements of their creative collaborations were assistants Carol Haney and
Jeanne Coyne (who was married to both Donen and Kelly). Due to Kelly's movie-star power,
most credit comes his way.

Donen stayed at Columbia after **Cover Girl** (1944) and choreographed five films before
joining Kelly at MGM for **Anchors Aweigh** (1945). After seven years as choreographer and co-
director with Kelly on multiple films, Arthur Freed gave him a chance to become a full-fledged
director with **Royal Wedding** (1951). Due to harrowing experiences on **Easter Parade** and **Summer Stock** with Judy Garland, the female lead originally cast, director Charles Walters dropped
out. "I'm terrible sorry, but I can't go through it again," he told Freed. "I've just spent a year
and a half with her, and I'm ready for a mental institution." Donen collaborated two more times
with Kelly on **Singin' in the Rain** (1952) and **It's Always Fair Weather** (1955) and went on to
a successful direction career using his dance background to make fluid and rhythmic films.

Kelly would continue to experiment with the musical form into the next decade, creating
some of Hollywood's most remarkable dance musicals, not only as star and choreographer, but
also director.

One of Kelly's most heroic innovations was his use of extended dance pieces (called "ballets" or "dance as narrative") in most of his later '40s films: ***Slaughter on 10th Ave.*** from **Words
and Music** (1948), ***The Pirate Ballet*** from **The Pirate**, and ***A Day in New York*** from **On the
Town**. At first edited because of the studio's fear that audiences would not sit still that long,
Kelly's dance pieces got longer and longer as his imaginative work disproved the studio's fear,
finally reaching its culmination in his magnificent **An American in Paris** ballet in 1951. Bosley
Crowther in his *New York Times* review of the film praised it as "...a truly cinematic ballet —
with dancers describing vivid patterns against changing colors, designs, costumes and scenes ...
conceived and performed with taste and talent. It is the uncontested high point of this film."

While Fred Astaire choreographed for himself and his partners and Hermes Pan created
the ensemble dances, Kelly was the first dancing star to conceive the musical numbers and create the choreography for all of the dancers in his films, not only for himself.

The comparisons between Kelly and Astaire were inevitable. Cyd Charisse, who was fortunate enough to dance with both of them, had her opinion quoted in the book *That's Dancing*: "Kelly is the more inventive choreographer of the two. Astaire, with Hermes Pan's help,
creates fabulous numbers — for himself and his partner. But Kelly can create an entire number
for somebody else.... I think however that Astaire's coordination is better than Kelly's. He can
do anything — he is a fantastic drummer. His sense of rhythm is uncanny. Kelly, on the other
hand, is the stronger of the two. When he lifts you, he lifts you!"

Ann Miller, another lucky co-worker with the pair, was quoted in *Dance Magazine*, January 1947:

> Fred Astaire has done the most to bring all three kinds (tap, ballet and ballroom)
> together. He started it. But when he tries — as he did once — to do ballet, he's just

about the world's worst. Gene Kelly *has* lifted tap dancing one step higher. In actual execution he may not be as good as Astaire, but he has taken the principles of choreography and adapted them, making a story out of each routine…. Gene is really a four-in-one combination of producer, director, actor and dancer — and that's hard to beat.

Kelly's intense and diverse dance education also differentiated his work from Astaire's. Although Astaire had taken some classes as a child, he was basically self-taught, observing the many dancers around him on the vaudeville circuit and devising a style of his own. Kelly's background in ballet and his greater physical strength allowed his work to be more expansive and athletic, with airborne variations that Astaire could only suggest.

In *The American Film Musical*, a primarily psychological evaluation of the genre, author Rick Altman writes: "One fact seems immediately striking: unlike other male dancers, Gene Kelly never had a stable female partner with whom he could establish a duet style, as Astaire did with Ginger Rogers…. The Gene Kelly who stands out, performing numbers which only he could bring off, is not a Gene Kelly making love, but a Gene Kelly showing off. Always confident of his own abilities, Kelly seems at his best when he is clowning." Agreeing with the basic truth in this observation, it becomes obvious that the differences between Astaire and Kelly were not only in their dance styles but in their conception of dance numbers. Astaire *did* partner better than any other dancer on film. If it wasn't a female, it was a top hat and cane, a hat tree, a framed photograph, or a broom. Kelly is at his most magnificent performing dazzling solos while children or female co-stars and the audience watch in awe.

Whatever the comparisons, Astaire and Kelly (genuine admirers of each other's talent) finally appeared together during the decade in a brief sequence in **Ziegfeld Follies** (1946). Astaire, when asked by the press to name his favorite partner, would often tactfully answer, "Gene Kelly."

One of the best musical film directors of the decade, Vincente Minnelli, made his first excursion to Hollywood, to stage the "Public Enemy Number One" number in Paramount's **Artists and Models** in 1937. He was brought back to films by MGM as a dance director. When he explained that he did not choreograph, his contract was rewritten to specify that he would direct the musical numbers. Perhaps he could not devise a dance combination, but Minnelli, with his fanciful talents in art and costume design and sophisticated sense of style and photographing dance, co-created some of the most superb musical sequences in films of the decade in collaboration with choreographers: **Ziegfeld Follies** ("This Heart of Mine" and "Limehouse Blues" with Robert Alton and Astaire), **Meet Me in St. Louis** ("Under the Bamboo Tree" with Charles Walters, 1944) and a dramatic sequence which literally dances, the waltz scene in **Madame Bovary** (with Jack Donohue, 1949):

> Although Flaubert devoted a scant few pages in the novel to the ball at the chateau, Minnelli's instincts told him that in cinematic terms this would be the dramatic highlight of the picture — the occasion for Emma's (Jennifer Jones) illusions and Charles' (Van Heflin) forebodings to converge in a turbulent sea of music and movement…. These contradictions collide with breathtaking force…. Emma's introduction to the dance, shown in long, flowing takes, is rudely punctuated by shots of an increasingly drunken Charles…. Once Rudolphe (Louis Jourdan) pulls Emma into the dance, exhilaration heightens imperceptibly into chaos…. Minnelli draws the viewer into her delicious vertigo, describing circles within circles as the dancers whirl inside the orbit of his spinning camera…. "The lady's going to faint," cries Rudolphe as Emma pants in his arms, which prompts the improbable command, "Break the windows!" … the panes

smash in perfect cadence to the accelerating waltz while Emma careens past.... Floundering is a sea of dancing couples, Charles staggers toward his spinning wife while Minnelli whips the camera into a final froth.... Emma flees the room as the orchestra soars to its last crescendo. Timed and choreographed to the last millimeter, this episode paradoxically celebrates the perilous lure of letting go [*Directed by Vincente Minnelli*].

Remembered later by actors as a director who had little or no contact with them and their performances but rather concentrated on the "look" of each sequence, Minnelli deeply understood the translation of musical sequences onto film. They offered him endless opportunities to design and stage for the screen. His musical sequences were never stagebound, but rather, steeped in brilliantly colored detail and defined only by the camera's limitless vistas.

The new choreographers and dance directors who gained prominence in the 1940s had all started their work on stage the previous decade. They brought their more extensive dance training and staging expertise with them to films, enriching the styles which were now expanding.

Robert Alton, after his successes on Broadway with *Too Many Girls* (1939) and *Pal Joey* and *Panama Hattie* in 1940, and one film (**Strike Me Pink**, 1936), was contracted by Columbia for collaboration with Astaire on **You'll Never Get Rich** in 1941. Alton's work on the Broadway show *Hold Your Horses* had received a prophetic review from the *Hollywood Reporter* on September 27, 1933: "...and there must be loud applause for the dance direction.... Bob Alton has staged a number of cleverly designed dances with not a tap in a chorusful that are beautiful and amusing. He could teach the movies plenty." And teach them he did.

While creating the numbers for the **You'll Never Get Rich** chorus, Alton's expectations that Hollywood dancers meet the level of the Broadway dancers he had worked with raised a ruckus:

> "I insisted that they do tap and ballet dancing both, and do it well," he told one reporter, "and they came back with the claim that I was working them too hard. It seems that heretofore the average dancing girl in pictures merely had to walk through a routine, looking beautiful. She never really had to dance." The dancers threatened to strike unless their pay was raised from $55 a week to $66 a week with a $5.50 bonus for any day [in] which they had to do lifts. They won [John Mueller, *Astaire Dancing*].

Alton was next contracted as dance director by MGM to create the lush musical sequences in **Ziegfeld Follies**, **The Harvey Girls** and **Till the Clouds Roll By** (1946), and **Good News** (1947), **Easter Parade** and **Words and Music** (1948), and his distinctive work became a valuable part of MGM producer Arthur Freed's musical unit signatures, along with Conrad Sallinger's orchestrations, Roger Eden's musical layouts, and Kay Thompson's vocal charts.

Alton, who was once identified by Cecil Smith as "'the truest and best representative in our time of the historic qualities of American popular theatre dancing' ... offered audiences bright, sexy, and happy dancing unencumbered by serious purpose or symbolic meaning. He sensed what the audience wanted and gave it what it liked." His flowing, graceful style included the entire body in his choreography, something which had made his Broadway work so successful, extending the dance movements to include the arms and hands and filling the stage with movement. Alton's film numbers were always elegantly staged without relying on tricky camera angles or effects, and he moved large numbers of dancers easily and with precision. "I have exactly six minutes in which to raise the customer out of his seat. If I cannot do it, I am no good." (*Hoofing on Broadway*).

Alton's working style was simply described by the man himself in a 1952 interview: "I study

Bride Rita Hayworth is surrounded by bridesmaids in "The Wedding Cake Walk," staged by Robert Alton in **You'll Never Get Rich** (Columbia, 1940).

the script, listen to the music, and then go away and dream about it for a while. When I have the ideas I need, I get together with the designers, begin rehearsals, and work out from there the final arrangements of both dances and music. It's just as simple as that. The ideas come, and I put them to work."

Donald O'Connor talked about Alton in *Tap!*: "But it wasn't until I worked with Gene Kelly and Bob Alton that I started to dance as, what I called, a total dancer. Alton was a painter with choreography. The man was incredible. He didn't know how to hoof. I'd have to put in my own taps and stuff. So it wasn't until I started working with Bob Alton and Gene Kelly that I started dancing from the waist up, using my arms, my hands, and synchronization in that way." Alton's camera work was fluid, his musical numbers filmed with a grand sweep and flow.

Alton's staging expertise is lauded in *The World of Entertainment!* by author Hugh Fordin. Referring to Alton's creation of the "On the Atchison, Topeka and the Santa Fe" number in **The Harvey Girls** (1946):

> It takes place on acres of open ground, a train arrives, travelers get off; there are milling crowds — a choreographer would have his hands full if he were to mount this for the theatre. But in motion pictures, stage space is limitless. Alton's conception of a number such as 'Atchison' far exceeded his talents as a choreographer. His eye was more on movement than on dance steps. He had the rare gift of moving people to a musical cadence without ever making them look theatrical and unreal.

Another side of Alton is beautifully documented by Agnes DeMille in *Dance to the Piper*. DeMille was fired from one of her early Broadway shows, *Hooray for What!* (1937), and "the only pleasant episode connected with this experience was a conversation I had with Robert Alton, my successor." She goes on:

> One day, toward the end, he sat me down in the theater and told me what mistakes I had made. He was neither pompous nor boasting; he spoke out of friendly good will and a vast experience. I have profited from his remarks ever since and I remember him with gratitude.... His rules for rehearsals are as follows; I repeat them for the benefit of all young choreographers:
>
> 1. Begin with something technical and definite.
> 2. Begin on time. Be prompt.
> 3. Do not let the chorus sit down.
> 4. Never let them make a mistake. Do not pass over a fault. Stop them in the middle of a bar if necessary and correct.
> 5. Polish as you go along.
> 6. Never seem in doubt.
> 7. Never let the bosses see anything unfinished. If you have only eight bars to show them, show them this much and no more. If you have not this much, get up yourself and demonstrate.
>
> Alton worked ... at a speed suggestive of a radio sports commentator, with a whistle between his teeth. The dancers adored him. No time was wasted in his rehearsals. Slick, finished and speedy, the work went together. There were no great moments of dramatic revelation, but each routine was solidly built and effective.

Alton was responsible for bringing Charles Walters to films by suggesting him to Gene Kelly for **Dubarry Was a Lady** (1943). Walters, after dancing in nightclubs and on Broadway for Alton, choreographed some of the most memorable musical films of the 1940s: **Meet Me in St. Louis** (1944), **The Harvey Girls** (with Alton, 1945), and **Ziegfeld Follies** (the "Madame Crematon" number, 1946). Walters' numbers were not filled with intricate dance, but rather "staging" which included the camera in the dance. Musing on his days at MGM, he later told author John Kobal (*Gotta Sing Gotta Dance*), "I suppose one of the things that made Metro musicals so alive and inventive was that we didn't study other people's work or what was happening in the theatre then, even though most of us came from the stage. I don't remember seeing anyone else's films, so I don't know whether or not I was influence by the people working around me."

He made the transition from choreographer to director with **Good News** (1947) and continued to stage the musical numbers (and even dance in some of them) throughout his directorial career. "Walter's choreographic use of the camera, the way in which it takes us into his confidence and includes us in his own excitement with the dance, has been characteristic of his work, no matter who actually choreographed the numbers of his later films. Whether as a director or as a choreographer he had taken the dance to the audiences." (John Kobal, *Gotta Sing, Gotta Dance*).

Dale Thomajan names **Good News** (1947) "The Best MGM Musical Not to Involve Fred Astaire, Judy Garland, Gene Kelly or Vincente Minnelli" and writes, "Who could have predicted that **Good News** would be so terrific—that every number would turn out to be a genuine classic of songwriting, musical arrangement, staging and performance?" Without naming Alton, he happens to praise the man's abilities to create movement sequences which show the best of his performer's (sometimes limited) abilities: "'The Varsity Drag' ... a treat from beginning to end. The dancing here seems to be executed as much with arms as with legs (lots of syn-chronized semaphoring) and there's a nice bit that combines the formality of a reception line with square-dance elements and chorus-girl kicks." And a tip of the hat to former choreogra-pher Charles Walters in his first direction effort: "The cast forming a human wedding cake as the camera tracks in over the bottom layer ... then up to a second tier ... and higher still to pre-bride-and-groom June (Allyson) and Peter (Lawford) who kiss, steal a peek at the camera to see if they're being observed, discover they are, and then decide, what the hell, to kiss again as the movie ends. In 1947 one wept in dumb joy. One still does."

Tap dancing continued to be a major movement staple of most of the 1940s musicals. Like the classic positions and combinations of ballet, tap dances were created from the basic steps, rhythms, and combinations that had been devised over the years. Most of the tap dancing greats had been self-taught, but now they were teaching and passing on their unique expertise. Refined on stage and screen in the 1930s, tap reached new heights by adapting well to the swing sounds of the decade.

One of the film's top tap specialists was Nick Castle. Eventually working for most of the studios during his career, he initially assisted Jack Haskell and was placed under contract to Twentieth Century–Fox during the 1930s and 1940s. With a generous scope of dance expertise, Castle was also an excellent idea man for musical number concepts, and his library of song-and-dances shows a stunning variety. Because of his flair for comedy, he successfully worked with the Ritz Brothers and would go on to stage all of the Dean Martin and Jerry Lewis Paramount films of the following decade.

Because so many of Twentieth Century–Fox's musicals were set at the turn of the century, Castle (like the costume designers, musical arrangers, and others of the time) did not aim for authenticity:

> In **Nob Hill** (1945), one of Twentieth Century's numerous contributions to the war
> boom in period musicals, Castle includes a bit of everything — can-can, tap (well in
> advance of authentic steps), exhibition ballroom, Bunny Hug, acrobatics and sponta-
> neous street dancing. Castle's influence, like that of Pan, is not conducive to faith in
> the authenticity of historical material in Fox musicals. His aim has always been to cre-
> ate entertaining sequences even when he had to stretch history [*Dancing in Commer-
> cial Motion Pictures*].

Not only could Castle create original dance routines for stars like Alice Faye, Betty Grable, Jack Haley, and Shirley Temple, he also had a genius for staging the already created routines of the dancing star-choreographers. In *Tap!*, Ann Miller spoke about his talent: "I worked with most of the great tap choreographers: Nick Castle, Louis DaPron, Willie Covan, Hermes Pan.... Nick Castle was a fantastic tap dancer. He used to work a lot with The Condos Brothers and The Nicholas Brothers. Nick Castle was a great dance director, he really was. And he danced!"

In an interview with the author, Fayard Nicholas also had nothing but praise for his col-laborations with Castle. Prior to the Nicholas Brothers being signed to a Twentieth Century–Fox contract, Fayard alone created all of the choreography for himself and his brother, Harold. Working with a dance director was new for him, but Fayard found that on top of Castle's incred-ible tap expertise and showmanship, "he always had wonderful ideas." While collaborating on the "I've Got a Gal in Kalamazoo" number in **Orchestra Wives** (1942), Castle suggested the fantastic stunt of Fayard scaling a wall. "I said: 'Walk up the wall? Are you crazy?'" He asked Castle to do it first, but Castle said: "I can't do it ... but I know you can." "So, we tried it. On the first take, something was wrong with the camera — a hair on the lens or something. We got

Even America's top singing stars needed choreography. Appropriate Latin dance shenanigans by dance director Nick Castle are performed by the Andrews sisters as they sing "Rhumboogie" in **Argentine Nights** (Universal, 1940).

it on the second take and I said: 'Oh, happy day!'" Castle also asked the brothers not to rehearse the sensational finish of their featured number in **Stormy Weather** (1943) — in which they bounded over one another. "No rehearsals — just do it! We did it — in one take! And I said: 'Oh, happy day!'"

Another tap master, Louis DaPron, was a resident dance director at Universal, creating the sensational tap routines for Donald O'Connor and Peggy Ryan (who were Universal's B musical movie answer to MGM's Mickey Rooney and Judy Garland), and the Jivin' Jacks and Jills, an energetic troupe of dancers who performed ensemble work in most of the films. "They used to make those Universal musicals in thirty minutes," Dan Dailey is quoted in *The Glamour Factory*, with Maxene Andrews (of the Andrews Sisters) adding, "Our pictures were made in ten days.... We had to do most of our choreography, which we made up as we went along." Without the luxury of the large MGM, Fox, and other major studio budgets for preparation and filming time, DaPron had to oversee and create the musical sequences for dozens of films each year.

Starting his career in films as an on-screen partner for Eleanore Whitney at Paramount in the 1930s, DaPron continued dancing on screen in featured roles and specialty numbers while simultaneously choreographing. On top of his expertise in tap, he incorporated contemporary dances of the time (jitterbug, lindy, truckin', Suzi-Q, peckin', big apple, etc.) into the youth-oriented film dance sequences. Peggy Ryan remembered working with DaPron in *Tap!*: "During many of those Universal movies, our choreographer was the great Louis DaPron. Oh, what a dear Louis was. I always thought he was very shy, he didn't come on real strong, you know — his feet talked for him…. Louis was wonderful. He did the most innovative things with his feet. Things I've never seen before or after. On the beat and off the beat. His gift was boundless. He was a dancer's dancer."

Castle and DaPron were joined by John Boyle, Willie Covan, Harland Dixon, and Hermes Pan as Hollywood's top tap instructors to create and teach the dance combinations if the stars were not responsible for creating their own dances. John Boyle, a walking encyclopedia of tap who was James Cagney's coach and teacher on **Yankee Doodle Dandy** (1942), was given the task of teaching Donald O'Connor complicated routines whenever O'Connor had difficulty learning Louis DaPron's choreography. Willie Covan was named the head dance instructor at MGM after Eleanor Powell's insistence to studio mogul Louis B. Mayer. Ann Miller remembered her work with Covan: "Buz Berkeley was one of the greatest of all dance directors, but he couldn't tap. He couldn't dance. He had to hire somebody to come in and do the work for him. That's how he happened to hire Willie Covan. Buz had the ideas, but he would have somebody else work on the tap and the actual dancing. I worked with Willie Covan once and it was probably the best thing I've ever done: 'I've Gotta Hear that Beat' [in **Small Town Girl**, 1953]…. I think he was wonderful, he made a lot of contributions." (*Tap!*).

Tap teachers and dance assistants would continue to create the dancing for other non-capable dance directors like LeRoy Prinz into the 1950s. In his autobiography, James Cagney described the filming of **The West Point Story** (1950): "This very effective number, "Brooklyn," was staged by a little red-haired girl named Ruth Godfrey, who had been with Jack Cole. She put the entire involved sequence together in about ten days." As Warner Bros. dance director, Prinz is credited with the dances in **The West Point Story**, and there is no mention of Ruth Godfrey, who assisted Prinz in dozens of films.

Prinz maintained a staff of experts on various forms and styles of dance for his work: Paul Haakon (ballet), brother Eddie Prinz and Lou Wills, Jr. (tap), Hal Belfer (acrobatics and adagio), José Fernandez (Latin), and Ruth Godfrey (modern and jazz). Miriam Nelson recalled that Prinz asked her to assist and co-create routines for her husband, Gene Nelson, in **The Daughter of Rosie O'Grady** (1950). When Prinz realized that his budget would not accommodate her as a staff member, he told her she could get on the payroll if she appeared in the movie. She did, in the "A Farm Off Broadway" number.

Prinz also would bring in specialists for numbers with international themes. In an interview for this book, Hal Belfer remembered assisting Prinz on **My Wild Irish Rose** (1947), saying that an Irish champion jig dancer had been brought from Ireland for the film. "I learned the steps from her and then taught them to the dancers. LeRoy was a great camera technician. It was so easy to read his charts…. 'For eight bars, take this group of dancers this direction … then we cut to this angle, so for eight bars, move this group in this direction, etc.' He was so organized and professional."

Ernst Matray, a man with an impressive European stage and film background as actor, director, and screenwriter, arrived in America with a dance troupe. Although first signed by MGM as an actor, his thick European accent limited his acting roles, and he was pigeon-holed as a dance director for the bulk of his work in American film. Assisted by his wife, Maria — who probably had the more extensive dance background and ability to create steps and combinations — Matray directed multiple sequences in a wide range of musical forms during the decade.

> The Matrays were seldom given screen credit, since their work consisted most often
> of folk and period dance which MGM consistently failed to credit…. Not only has

(L to R) Jeanne Cagney, James Cagney, Joan Leslie, Walter Houston, Rosemary DeCamp and flag waving chorus make America's patriotic blood boil in "You're a Grand Old Flag" from **Yankee Doodle Dandy** [Johnny Boyle, Seymour Felix, LeRoy Prinz, Warner Bros., 1942].

their work been largely unrecognized because it was not given screen credit but sometimes it was eliminated entirely from the film as was the case with lovely Armenian dances in the park done for **The Human Comedy** (1943). The ballet choreography in **Florian** (1936), both featured and credited, is the best known work of this couple, though not the most representative [*Dancing in Commercial Motion Pictures*].

For one of their RKO credits, **Dance, Girl, Dance** (1940), *Variety* singled Ernest Matray out for praise (August 28, 1940) with,

> In the true sense of the word, this is a drama with music, rather than a musical comedy. Hence there's little on the song-and-dance production side notable. Only one of these scenes is striking, this being the rehearsal of what is called the American Ballet. Vivian Fay, from Broadway extravaganza, is the ballerina in this and does a bangup job in front of an expertly trained classical troupe. Ernst Matray, dance director, rates a bow for this sequence.

Jack Donohue, after working with Shirley Temple at Fox and spending several years creating dances for films in England, joined the MGM dance department in the 1940s and began to specialize in creating and staging musical numbers for Frank Sinatra, Jimmy Durante, Red

Skelton, and other comedians and performers on the studio lot. He also created many of the imaginative water numbers for Esther Williams, a never-ending challenge for the MGM creative staff. Although he was not an innovator in terms of dance styles or techniques, Donohue's staging of musical numbers and success with non-dancers showed the promise of the excellent comedy direction career he would eventually enjoy.

Film dance of the time also grew with the introduction of the ethnic, jazz, and modern dance styles and techniques which were revolutionizing the dance world itself. In ethnic dance, many choreographers had begun traveling the world to study the dance forms of the Caribbean, Africa, Asia, and Latin America. What they learned, they brought to the screen.

World War II gave birth to Nelson Rockefeller's "good neighbor" policy, and with the politics came the opportunity for films, musical scores, and dance directors to expand into the rhythms and dance idioms of Latin America. Such films as **Down Argentine Way** (Nick Castle, Geneva Sawyer, 1940), **That Night in Rio** and **Weekend in Havana** (Hermes Pan, 1941), **Pan-Americana** (Charles O'Curran, 1945), **Thrill of Brazil** (Nick Castle, Jack Cole, Eugene Loring, 1946), **Carnival in Costa Rica** (Léonide Massine), and **Fiesta** (Eugene Loring, 1947) expanded the film dance repertoire with variations of sambas, tangos, congas, merengues, and other popular Latin social dances. Despite the still occasional fictitious representations of the dances of Mexico, Cuba, and South America, choreographers began to utilize authentic varieties of dance in their work, either by researching on their own, or by calling in authorities on every type of dance to create authentic choreography. Authentic classical Spanish dance celebrities Carmen Amaya, Carmelita Maracci, Antonio and Rosario, and Antonio Triana joined Eduardo Cansino and briefly shared their talents on and off screen with film audiences.

Among the above-mentioned choreographers was a man who would innovate dance on film in many directions: Eugene Loring. A man with diverse talents in theater, dance, and art, Loring first created a sensation dancing in his own ballet *Billy the Kid* in 1938 and in Agnes DeMille's *Rodeo* in 1942. Originally, MGM producer Arthur Freed wanted DeMille after her sensational success with *Oklahoma!* but when she was unavailable because of stage commitments, Robert Alton suggested Loring. Loring had extensive background and study in Spanish dance, so he brought his ballet and ethnic expertise to films and was to be a major force in the filmed version of the "dream ballet" of the 1940s.

DeMille had successfully explored the Freudian psyche through movement in her landmark ballets for the stage versions of *Oklahoma!* (1943) and *Carousel* (1945). No longer were dream dances fantasy excursions into sugar-plum-fairy land; rather, they became nightmarish journeys into the character's deepest fears and repressions. The movie musical and non-musical films began including dream sequences galore. With the growing popularity of psychology and psychoanalysis, Alfred Hitchcock's **Spellbound** (1945) had created a sensation with its dream sequences, designed by the latest sensation of the art world, Salvador Dali.

The surrealism of Dali inspired Loring when he found a perfect place for a ballet in **Yolanda and the Thief** (1945). At first a bit intimidated by working with Fred Astaire, Loring devised a unique ballet including such elements as bed sheets that encompass Astaire as the nightmare begins and running the film backwards so that Lucille Bremer could emerge from and then disappear into a pond. *New York Times* critic Bosley Crowther had nothing but praise for the dance sequences: "A dream-ballet number, expanded against Daliesque decor, with Mr. Astaire as the dreamer, is a thing of pictorial delight. And a rhythm dance, done to the melody of ... 'Coffee Time,' puts movement and color to such uses as you seldom behold on the screen." Loring would later expand his "Dream Ballet" exploration to its height with **The 5,000 Fingers of Doctor T** in 1953.

After the success of Agnes DeMille's "Dream Ballet" on the Broadway stage in *Oklahoma!*, the films followed with dream sequences galore. Here, June Allyson bows to Robert Walker in a musical dream sequence from **Her Highness and the Bell-boy** (Charles Walters, MGM, 1945).

Loring would also contribute to dance on film — and American dance in general — with his historic American School of Dance in Hollywood, which he opened in 1947. Los Angeles now had a variety of schools and teachers which could more than aptly prepare Hollywood dancers for the new demands. The Falcon Studio and the schools of film-related dance figures Louis DaPron, David Lichine, Michel Panaieff, and Carmelita Maracci upgraded the opportunities of dance education by leaps and bounds. Like Belcher, Kosloff, Denishawn, and Fanchon, Loring and the many superb teachers who taught at the school over the years prepared generations of future dancers and choreographers for careers in all forms of dance. Offering more than a dozen types of dance techniques, Loring's motto was "no form of dance which is a sincere expression of feeling and which has a communicable technique is excluded." With classes in drawing, art structure, and choreography, and guest courses from a wide range of personalities who were in Los Angeles for one reason or the other, the American School of Dance was one of the most influential schools on the West Coast.

Along with Loring, inclusion of ethnic dance helped to introduce another giant to films: Jack Cole. A fascinating "upstart" from the modern dance world, Broadway, and nightclubs, Cole studied ethnic dance (and dance in general) voraciously and mixed jazz, primitive, latin, and Hindu dance styles to create the legendary style of his own. For the first time, Cole, who utilized exciting isolation of various parts of the body in his work, asked film dancers to use their hips, their groins, and their libidos.

Eugene Loring provided some of his most memorable ballet sequences in **The 5,000 Fingers of Doctor T** (Columbia, 1952).

"When I first came to California and the movies, I was exploding with enthusiasm. I saw no reason why dancing and musical numbers need be so pedestrian and unimaginative, so pretentious and dull, so enormous and hilariously stupid. After a little experience, I was astounded that they came off as well as they did." Under contract first to Columbia, Cole was responsible for shaping Rita Hayworth's "Love Goddess" persona with his sensual choreography for **Tonight and Every Night** (1945), **Gilda** (1946), and **Down to Earth** (1947). "I remember the first thing I did with her, I did something on **Cover Girl**. Val Raset was really first doing the picture. He's a very dear, old-fashioned ballet man who was not adjusted to doing that kind of film at all. Seymour Felix was a very old-fashioned 'girl' dance director from the old days; and Gene Kelly was doing his own thing. And finally they had to do something with Rita, and Harry Cohn asked Gene who they could get and they got me." (*People Will Talk*)

Ann Miller worked with Cole on **Eadie Was a Lady** (1945) and **Thrill of Brazil** (1946) and rhapsodized over him in *Tap!*: "I also worked with Jack Cole…. Oh honey, he was fantastic. He wasn't a tap dancer, he was a dance director. He did a lot of East Indian work. The lady from the ballet, Agnes DeMille — everybody got tired of that after a while, and Jack came along and made everybody bend over and do a lot of real primitive things. He absolutely rejuvenated dancing. Totally revitalized it and redid it." He also caused constant havoc with the censorship boards of the day with his honesty in movement.

Alan Johnson, who assisted Cole on the stage vehicle *Zenda!* (1963), called him "*the* innovator" in an October 1971 *Dance Magazine* interview, "…even more so than Agnes DeMille or Jerry Robbins. Before Cole, it was all step-turn-tap. Cole changed that. Through him, we learned how the dance should feel, that dance was a dancer dancing with his whole being, and that choreography has to be reconceived and tailored for the medium it's using. Dance — it isn't just steps."

While most of the major studios had a chorus of dancers under contract for their musicals during the 1940s, Cole convinced colorful mogul Harry Cohn that Columbia Studios should have a dance "Ensemble." In February 1944, he created that unique group, comprised of Francine Ames, Nita Bieber, Patricia Cummings, Ruth Godfrey, Gloria Maginetti, Ethel Martin, Rod Alexander, Bob Hamilton, Charles Lanard, George Martin, Alex Romero, and Paul Steffan. Later that initial group would be augmented by such future dance greats as Anita Alvarez, Hal Belfer, Paul Godkin, Harriet Ann Gray, Carol Haney, Matt Mattox, Buzz Miller, and Gwen Verdon. They had strenuous daily classes in Cole's technique, and when they weren't filming, the studio allowed Cole to present them in nightclubs around the country. In Cole's *New York Times* obituary, the group was mentioned: "In the Forties at the Columbia lot, Jack Cole taught and trained an entire generation of dancers through a jazz influenced style that came to represent American Show Dancing throughout the world and that was wildly copied everywhere."

Constantly striving to move dance on film into new areas, Cole was always vocal with his criticisms:

> "Everybody considers dancing as merely decorative — and that's how it's staged in a theatre or shot in a studio.... We move just enough so as not to disturb the composition of a set." This convention, he continued, may be traced in films all the way back to Busby Berkeley and his passion for "making wallpaper with real people.... The trouble is that, outside of ballet, nothing intelligent is ever expected of dancers or dance." He described his working methods on **Down to Earth** (1947): "The whole musical set-up comes first — the point of each number, what it contributes to the story, who must dance it, and why. Also into what classification each naturally falls: intimate, comic, decorative, spectacular. Then you take each number separately and attack it from all angles ... coordinating your musical findings with your conception of camera set-ups and dancer's movements" [*Dance Magazine*, May 1946].

In the same article, Cole seriously examined the partnership that movement and the camera could enjoy. "The camera offers enormous latitude to the choreographer if he learns its power, its whims and its evils.... The difficulty of obtaining presence on the screen is enormous.... Dynamics are lost and movement outlined in space is emphasized. It has the power to make mediocre dancers seem brilliant and strong and brilliant stylists seem weird and distorted." Agnes DeMille, a great fan of Cole and his work, wrote about him in *America Dances*, "Jack Cole was the first commercial choreographer to put a lasting stamp on the national style ... astonishing and vital handling of rhythm. In Hollywood, Jack Cole made some excellent dances that were filmed with great intelligence, chiefly because he himself designed the camera work and supervised it step by step." Watching Cole's numbers now, we can see his influence of how they were staged, directed, filmed, and edited — the camera angles are severe and dramatic, the pacing razor-sharp, and the stylized dancing still on the cutting edge.

Besides demanding a strong technique, Cole's influence on dancers and what was expected of them also moved the art on stage and film into new directions: "I just try to touch the dancer at the center of his emotions. I try to remind him of what he is — a dancer, and actor, a real person. If you're ashamed of this or that emotion, you can't dance ... when you dance you must bring real emotion to whatever you're doing. Isn't that what dancing is about — emotion, life — and not just patterns in the air?" (Ric Estrada, "Reflections on a Broadway Flop," *Dance Magazine*, January 1968.)

Rita Hayworth dances onscreen with choreographer Jack Cole in **Tonight and Every Night** (Columbia, 1945) to the song "What Does an English Girl Think of a Yank?"

Like Michael Bennett decades later, Cole — with his fascinating combination of tough guy and sinuous enchanter — appealed to both men and women, weaving a hypnotic hold on his dancers. Matt Mattox related (*Dance Magazine*, November 1983), "You always did everything full out. You never marked the movement. By doing this, you gained stamina and strength. You also learned to do everything to a precision count. It is because of this that his ensemble work is so neat and clean." Mattox remembered how, during the filming of a number performed on a staircase without hand railings in **The "I Don't Care" Girl** (1952), he and Marc Wilder became so intent during a camera run-through with Gwen Verdon dancing in for star Mitzi Gaynor that an accident occurred:

> Gwen turned and kicked at us, and Marc and I fell backwards, forgetting that there were no boys waiting to catch us. Marc ended up rolling backwards down fourteen stairs, and I fell onto my back after passing through seven feet of space.... Whatever Jack wanted, Jack would get because we loved to do what he created, and we respected him for the master he was.... Jack opened my eyes to a new kind of dance. It reached down and grabbed your insides and made you aware of an emotional experience within yourself and with the people you worked with.

While Cole was leading the way for Caucasian dancers, African-Americans were being led by primitive dance pioneer Katherine Dunham. In the 1940s, she was taken from success in the nightclub and concert worlds to add her talents to feature films: **Pardon My Sarong** and **Star Spangled Rhythm** (1942), **Stormy Weather** (1943), and **Casbah** (1948), usually appearing

Dance director Jack Cole (seated) rehearses Marc Platt and Rita Hayworth for **Down to Earth** (Columbia, 1947).

onscreen with her dance troupe. After years of intense study of African and Caribbean dance, Dunham, with her talent and perseverance, made historic contributions to American dance. When she began to create her dance troupe, black dancers primarily did tap dancing or were merely asked to shimmy and writhe, without any formal training. Dunham started from scratch with an entire generation of African-American dancers, changing the face of black commercial dance forever.

"I don't see any color in what we do," she said in a February 1956 interview in *Dance Magazine*. "It's only a fortunate accident that I've hit upon and used material chiefly of people with Negro background. But I would feel I'd failed miserably if I were doing dance confined in technique or audience-satisfaction to race, color or creed." Defending the sensuality of her dances, "Miss Dunham points out that it is an important part of the lives that she, as an anthropologist has studied.... And by adding to dance a social awareness, she says, 'I think I am making it a part of the expressive lives of the people who come to see it.'" And her film work introduced that sensuality to generations of moviegoers.

During the 1940s, ballet began to receive major exposure in commercial film, with the work of many European dance leaders finding its way onto the screen.

Léonide Massine, a giant of the ballet world, first put his genius on film with the 1941 Warner Bros. shorts **The Gay Parisian** and **Spanish Fiesta** (which were filmed versions of his already existing ballets), returning to Hollywood in 1946 to stage the numbers for Vera-Ellen in **Carnival**

in Costa Rica. He spoke to *Dance Magazine* (August 1946) about his wish to create and dance in a full-length feature film ballet with Vera-Ellen (**The Blue Danube**). Although he predicted success for ballet on film, it was not the film he spoke about that accomplished this breakthrough.

It was **The Red Shoes** in 1948, choreographed by Massine and Robert Helpmann, which captured the world of the ballet and became the most popular ballet film until **The Turning Point** in 1977, some thirty years later. The film catapulted glowing British ballerina Moira Shearer to film stardom, and although she was announced to be the star of a succession of dance roles in the next decade (**Hans Christian Andersen**, **Royal Wedding**, **Les Girls**, **Brigadoon**), her personal life kept her out of a lasting film career, and her subsequent films (**The Tales of Hoffman**, **The Story of Three Loves**, and **The Man Who Loved Redheads**) did little to fulfill her promise. The film itself, however, changed the commercial future of serious dance.

Not statically filmed stage ballet, **The Red Shoes** was completely cinematic. The collaboration between choreographers Helpmann and Massine and writer-producer-directors Michael Powell and Emeric Pressburger included imaginative camera work, multiple special effects, and atmospheric lighting. Bosley Crowther reviewed **The Red Shoes** in the *New York Times* and wrote of the climactic twenty-minute ballet: "The cinema staging of this ballet, conceived in cinematic terms, is a thrilling blend of movement, color, music and imagery ... fresh choreography, arranged by Robert Helpmann, spark[s] impressions that are vivid and intense." *Dance Magazine* awarded Powell and Pressburger their 1948-49 Season award "for use of ballet in films," calling it "obviously a milestone on the road to the yet unaccomplished ballet film, will be the launching point for those millions who are to be the ballet audiences of tomorrow."

The popular acceptance of **The Red Shoes** encouraged Americans Gene Kelly and Eugene Loring to use ballet in extended dance sequences. It took ballet away from the "cultural elite" of the 1940s and allowed the masses to enjoy it without shame. It also created a generation of ballet dancers, as little girls enrolled in ballet classes by the thousands. Although small boys still felt the urge to snicker at the sight of men in tights, the romantic awe of their little girlfriends helped them to accept the exposure to classic dance. **The Red Shoes** finally made ballet a successful option in commercial films.

From the European ballet world, Balanchine, Andrée Howard, David Lichine, Cleo Nordi, David Paltenghi, Michel Paneiff, Massine, and Helpmann joined Americans Kelly, Loring, and Bernard Pearce to create ballet sequences for films during the decade as the dance vocabulary expanded and ballet-trained personalities became film stars. There had been a brave but neglected film with a ballet background filmed in 1946 by little Republic Pictures — **Specter of the Rose**, choreographed by Tamara Geva — but it would take **The Red Shoes** to place classical ballet into the moviegoing vernacular of the masses.

The rest of the dance output in musicals of the decade was prolific, if not innovative. If the dance directors and choreographers were not allowed to explore new musical sequence concepts, technical advances, and camera collaborations, they were expected to create dazzling variations on several themes.

Military-themed musicals rolled out of the studios by the caisson. **Buck Privates** (Nick Castle), **Rookies on Parade** (Nick Castle, Louis Dapron), and **Navy Blues** (Seymour Felix) in 1941; **When Johnny Comes Marching Home** in 1942 (Louis DaPron, the Four Step Brothers); **This Is the Army** (Nick Castle, LeRoy Prinz, Robert Sidney) in 1943; **Hey Rookie** (Louis DaPron, Stanley Donen, Ann Miller, Val Raset), **Four Jills in a Jeep** (Don Loper), and **Here Come the Waves** (Danny Dare) in 1944 were but a few. Choreographers had to meld marching with hepcat variations, with Hermes Pan creating the ultimate military close-order drill with Alice Sullivan for an unlikely Betty Grable and chorus of WACS in **Pin Up Girl** (1944).

Robert Helpmann, Léonide Massine and Moira Shearer in the film that "legitimized" ballet on film, **The Red Shoes** (Rank, 1948).

Skating stars Vera Hruba-Ralston and Belita joined the already established Sonja Henie, and dance on ice was explored in **Iceland** (James Gonzalez, Carlos Romero) and **Ice-Capades Revue** (Harry Losee) in 1942; **Lady, Let's Dance** (Dave Gould and Michel Paneiff) and **Lake Placid Serenade** (Jack Crosby and Felix Sadowski) in 1944; and **The Countess of Monte Cristo** (Louis DaPron) in 1948.

Paramount's "Sarong Songs" and other tropically based films needed dances: **Song of the Islands** (Hermes Pan, 1942), **Rhythm of the Islands** (Lester Horton, 1943), **Rainbow Island** (Danny Dare, 1944), **Song of the Sarong** (Carlos Romero, 1945), etc. Although the choreography was loosely based on authentic Polynesian steps and rhythms, its main objective was to give love-starved GIs an opportunity to ogle scantily clad girls wiggling seductively. Hope's, Crosby's and Lamour's "Road" trips to exotic locales also needed numbers: **Road to Singapore** (LeRoy Prinz, 1940), **Road to Zanzibar** (Prinz, 1941), **Road to Morocco** (Paul Oscard, 1942), **Road to Utopia** (Danny Dare, 1945), and **Road to Rio** (Billy Daniel, Bernard Pearce, 1947), with vaudeville routines for Bob and Bing and pagan ceremonies for Dot and the girls receiving dance creators' input.

At Twentieth Century–Fox, the blonde domination continued with Vivian Blaine, Alice Faye, Betty Grable, June Haver, and Carole Landis as they alternated the aforementioned Latin American good-neighbor-policy Technicolor explosions with their ongoing series of good-old-

Vera Hruba-Ralston, Republic's answer to Sonja Henie, is the centerpiece of this iced musical sequence, as dance on ice is explored by Harry Lossee in **Lake Placid Serenade**, 1944.

days musicals. World War II audiences enjoyed returning to the simple times of the turn of the century. Experts on vaudeville and period dancing such as Nick Castle, Danny Dare, Fanchon, Seymour Felix, Sammy Lee, and Hermes Pan supplied the dances for **Tin Pan Alley** (1940), **My Gal Sal** (1942), **Sweet Rosie O'Grady**, **Coney Island** and **Hello, Frisco, Hello** (1943), **Irish Eyes are Smiling** (1944), **The Dolly Sisters** (1945), and the rest of the garishly colored, escapist fare. The choreography and dance direction were basically recreations of nostalgic tap, waltz, and line dances, always set in an "on stage" situation. It was the same old thing, really, only this time in eye-popping color.

It was MGM who allowed its dance directors and choreographers to experiment with the camera and the ever-increasing technical innovations. MGM utilized more and more ballet, often in surreal settings (**Yolanda and the Thief**). They also allowed Astaire to compete with dozens of pairs of dancing shoes (**The Barkleys of Broadway**) and Gene Kelly to film a musical on location for the very first time (**On the Town**). With the support of supervising producer Arthur Freed, the dancing at MGM sailed and soared.

Not as many short musical films were being made by the major studios in the 1940s, but a new abbreviated musical film form began: soundies. Popular singers and musicians of the day were filmed performing one musical number, often using dancers, which needed the expertise of a choreographer. These films would eventually be shown on early television and pave the way to the music video of the 1980s.

With the popularity of the nightclub as a major part of American social life, dozens of musicals required choreographers to create club routines for films — some based on the most famous nighteries of the era: **Trocodero** (Larry Ceballos, 1944), **Billy Rose's Diamond Horse-shoe** (Hermes Pan) and **The Stork Club** (Billy Daniel) in 1945, and **Copacabana** (Larry Ceballos, 1947). If they were not allowed to break out of the confining nightclub stage–sized space, the choreographers had to continually use their imaginations to create conceptual variations on a theme which had been used in films for over twenty years. Many non-musical films also used club settings, with dance directors staging songs and musical sequences for the likes of non-dancers Lauren Bacall, Lizabeth Scott, Ida Lupino, and other club sirens. Because of the war, those clubs often had exotic locales from Europe to Africa — and appropriate musical staging.

Dance continued to be used prolifically in non-musicals and even received notice by critics (*McCalls* review of **Romance of Rosy Ridge**, 1947, choreographed by Jack Donohue: "The folk songs and 'Play Party' dances are sheer enchantment!") In June 1959, *Dance Magazine* film critic Arthur Knight neatly wrote about the use of dance in non-musical film forms:

> One of the chief functions of dance, at least so far as the film makers are concerned, would seem to be the quick establishment of a locale or an atmosphere.... Rarely are they functional, or built integrally into the plot. More often ... the dance opens the picture. Everything is light and gay as the villagers skip and clap their way through a few dozen measures.... Then suddenly someone rushes in with the news that the woods are on fire. *Exeunt omnes.* The dance is abandoned, never to be resumed. The plot has taken over. Even when these atmospheric dances are inserted somewhere along the way ... one is often genuinely surprised to note that the credits include a choreographer (frequently well-known). What happens, all too often, is that in the preparation of a picture the producer decides that a nice, lively dance number could be used at this point in the story for color, visual variety, and production values. The choreographer is hired, handed an outline of the plot, and told to come up with something extraordinary, something that will be a memorable high point in the picture. Enchanted with the prospect, he creates an eight-minute sequence, complete in itself.... The producer is delighted. They assemble a hundred or so of the best dancers in Hollywood and rehearse the sequence for six weeks. Another two weeks is spent on the shooting. And what ultimately comes out on the screen is perhaps ninety seconds of assorted leaps and turns, broken by lines of dialogue between the hero and his sweetheart. "The picture ran too long," is the usual explanation and the first thing that gets cut is the dance sequence.

Nevertheless, these frustrating experiences continued to give employment to choreographers and dancers — and contributed to that mythic cutting room floor treasure trove.

In the rash of forties dramas set in India, authentic East Indian dancers Ram Gopal, Chandra Kaly, Mayura, and Sujata and Asoka (along with researcher Jack Cole) moved from concert and nightclub success to the Rajah's palace on the backlot. No longer was the hootch dance a figment of someone's imagination. Suddenly, the movies were giving their patrons "culture."

Among the non-musical films of the period which benefited from the addition of dance were the financially successful "Harem Scarum" epics of Universal: **Ali Baba and the Forty Thieves** (1943); **Sudan** and **Cobra Woman** (1944); **Salome, Where She Danced** (1945); and **Tangier** (1946). Luring the audience to "SEE Pagan Ceremonies" and "WITNESS Forbidden Dances of Desire" performed by Maria Montez, Yvonne DeCarlo, and other sensual creatures, these escapist adventures used the incredible talents of Lester Horton, West Coast modern dance innovator.

Horton was under contract to Universal as a dance director to supply ethnic, classic, and operatic staging and dance movement to their films. The films he worked on hardly stretched his abilities, but the salary did pay the bills for his more esoteric efforts, such as his brilliant company of dancers and his Dance Theatre in Hollywood, where many future leaders of black American dance (Alvin Ailey, Carmen DeLavallade, James Truitte) and modern dance (Bella Lewitsky, Joyce Trisler) were studying and performing.

Assigned to create the dances for a Montez pot-boiler called **Siren of Atlantis**, Horton approached the assignment with his usual dedication and attention to detail. The final result was diplomatically described in an article he wrote for *Dance Magazine* in July 1947: "Bella Lewitsky was assistant dance director. Together we draughted the dances in authentic flavor in various ways. Each proved inappropriate to the total direction of the film or lacking in the needed photogenic qualities. A synthesis of North African and Arab materials ultimately provided the motifs of movement which could meet the demands." Horton was possibly saying that the producer wanted more hootch than the authentic Berber music, costume, movement, and ethnic dance drama Horton had so painstakingly researched and planned to use.

The popular westerns of the forties nearly always contained a saloon sequence — complete with a singing madame and can-can girls — or a campfire-lit hoedown. The Roy Rogers/Dale Evans Western series at Republic kept Larry Ceballos continually occupied during the decade, using his ingenuity to devise variations to the genre.

The choreographers of the next generation were now dancing in films, often assisting, learning their craft from the camera, rather than from the stage as the previous dancemakers had done. This would be a very unique group of people who, unfortunately, would begin their solo choreographic careers just as the movie musical was falling out of favor. Many of them would instead make their mark on stage or in television. This new group included Ernest Flatt, Paul Godkin, Miriam Nelson, Jack Regas, and Donald Saddler — as well as many members of Jack Cole's group (Rod Alexander, Hal Belfer, Carol Haney, George and Ethel Martin, Matt Mattox, Alex Romero, and Gwen Verdon).

Instead of the flashy, self-promotional publicity of the 1930s, dance directors were receiving recognition through press exposure of a different nature. Although most film critics still had difficulty differentiating the dancer from the dance and the bulk of reviews praised (or damned) the star, rather than the choreographer, film dance began to be noticed by the dance world. Quality interviews, profiles and background information on Hollywood's dance directors in the 1940s began appearing in *Dance Magazine*.

In their February 1947 issue, "nine noted choreographers discuss potentialities and failures of screen dancing." Jack Cole: "The camera is more than kind to mediocrity and savagely unsuccessful in transmitting a highly personal and stylistic artist." Nick Castle: "On the screen, a number reaches its highest value when the camera is used to emphasize important movements and moods." Charles O'Curran: "Films present peculiar problems, but they are replete with opportunities for the dance director." LeRoy Prinz: "I try to have each dance presented as authentically as possible, but I find it necessary to inject little touches that will give it commercial value." Eugene Loring: "In order to be successful on the screen, a dancer must be able to do something else besides dance if he expects to establish himself as a prominent personality." Robert Alton: "The present fault of the camera is that it still loses the dancer's face, which, strangely enough, is one of the most interesting parts of a dance routine. The process of cutting to the feet and various parts of the body is, however, a thing of the past." Billy Daniel: "'Stage dancing' transferred to the screen will become most important for Hollywood dance sequences because the public has indicated that it prefers this type to ballet or ballroom. Ballet can only become important when the general public is ready to accept it, and so far, there has been no indication that the average movie fan will pay money to watch ballet." Hermes Pan: "There will be more and more dances with a message on the screen, and, certainly, they will work smoothly into the plot.... With the coming of modern ballet and a new lens, the dancer will have greater opportunities on the screen than he now has on the stage." Gene Kelly: "Never forget that we are dealing with a three-dimensional art in a two-dimensional medium. Until we have three-dimensional cameras, dancing will never have the kinetic force in movies that it has on the stage."

In June 1947, Mary Jane Hungerford wrote "Must Screen Dances Be 'Incidental'?" for *Dance Magazine*, coining the phrase "Cinedance" and writing that the "Nutcracker Suite" in Walt Disney's **Fantasia** was actually "an extended Cinedance.... Here is an art to tantalize the creative capacity of the most imaginative choreographer. It should make him forever impatient of having his fancy chained to the comparatively narrow range of action which humans can normally perform." In an article written one year later, Hungerford wrote a treatise on appreciation of motion picture dance with a check list for the reader. She also pondered the question of *who* actually did *what* while trying to evaluate the meaning of the credit "dance director:" "Sometimes the dance director given screen credit has simply located and hired a folk dance group or an exhibition ballroom team and acted as intermediary between them and the cameraman and the picture director during the shooting.... In other instances, the same credit ... may be used for the person who created the entire choreography."

Attention was finally being paid by the press and appreciative audiences, but politically, the art of dance direction continued to be unprotected. In the early '40s, a small group of dance directors attempted to organize and create a guild, for they were still unprotected from erratic salaries; they still received no health, welfare or pension benefits; and their work could be tampered with by directors, producers and stars.

Danny Dare, a former Broadway and vaudeville performer who was dance director at Paramount from 1941 to 1945, explained the attempt in a letter to the author in May 1993:

> In 1944 I organized the Dance Director's Guild. I negotiated with the MPPA (the studios) and signed a contract giving us recognition.... We held meetings for about six months before this and I had been elected President. There weren't too many Dance Directors interested. They didn't understand the value of residuals, pensions, etc. The ones I remember were Stanley Donen, LeRoy Prinz and brother, Josephine Earl, Miriam Franklin [aka Nelson] and a short Russian Mickey something [Raset]. Buzz [Berkeley] was no longer a Dance Director, he directed. Bob Alton traveled in different circles. Seymour Felix and Sammy Lee moved in different circles. At any rate, the contract with the studios was signed, meetings were held, negotiations were started about minimum salaries, royalties, guarantees, credits, etc. Records of the meetings were kept (I think Josephine Earl was the Secretary). About six months later my contract with Paramount called for them to make me a full director. I was called to the front office ... and told they had too many directors under contract and couldn't give me a picture to direct. However, would I like to be a producer? I was disappointed but didn't have much choice. So I became a producer. END OF STORY. Being a Producer, I couldn't function as Pres. of the Dance Director's Guild. LeRoy Prinz was elected Pres., and the organization disintegrated.

Despite Dare's passion and valiant attempts, once again the various interests and factions of the dance directors would not allow them to come together and join strengths.

Choreographers were also deeply involved in the sexual politics of the times. Along with dancers, male choreographers continued to fight the perception of the effete "tutu and tights"

Paramount publicity photo of Danny Dare watching Billy Daniel and Dorothy Dalton "jump for joy" (1938).

artistes on stage and in film. Homosexuality was still not accepted in the primarily heterosexual world of filmmaking, and most male choreographers and dance directors were suspect, which also undermined their positions of power. Rumors ran rampant about *this* director and his protégé choreographer or *that* dancing star and *that other* choreographer. Coupled with the general misconception of what the art of choreography actually was, misunderstandings or disagreements could be dismissed with the labels of "fairy" or "faggot." Many of the choreographers of the period flamboyantly displayed their masculinity, like the successful dance directors of the previous era, with multiple (and well-publicized) romances and marriages to beautiful showgirls, prolific casting couch tactics and womanizing, highly visible drunkenness, truck driver's vocabulary, and other questionable, supposedly heterosexual behavior. Tough-skinned individuals like Jack Cole simply lived their lives as they chose, being able to face detractors (as Cole would later portray a choreographer proving his masculinity on film in **Designing Woman** in 1957). Others would align themselves with successful gay directors and producers whose closeted personal lives may have been gossiped about but whose box-office success assured their positions. As for the female choreographers, they often had to play the rampant casting couch game with actresses or find a powerful protector by becoming wife or mistress to an important man within the industry.

Amidst these various politics, in 1950, *Film Daily Yearbook* discontinued listing dance directors and their credits.

Selected Filmography

Anchors Aweigh (Stanley Donen, Gene Kelly) MGM, 1945, Video:MGM/UA — Kelly dances effortlessly with an animated mouse and charmingly with a little Mexican girl, and even makes "The Voice," Frank Sinatra, look good hoofing — plus he gives the greatest display of athletics since Douglas Fairbanks.

Black Narcissus (Mayura) Rank, 1947, Video: VidAmerica — Jean Simmons' brief dance unleashes her character's sensuality in this classic tale of bridled passions, bringing her "nubile" reviews — as well as making her a star.

Broadway Melody of 1940 (Fred Astaire, Bobby Connolly, Eleanor Powell) MGM, 1940, Video: MGM/UA — The tap number by Astaire and Powell to "Begin the Beguine" is the final statement on tap in film — and the fluid camerawork and mirrored walls and floors ain't bad either!

Cover Girl (Jack Cole, Stanley Donen, Seymour Felix, Gene Kelly, Val Raset) Col, 1944, Video: Col — A chance to observe collective input from a master group. Kelly and Donen show their promise with the "Alter-Ego" dance and the exuberance of "Make Way for Tomorrow."

The Dolly Sisters (Seymour Felix) Fox, 1945 — Felix scores a new "high" in "lows" with the vulgar

racism of "Darktown Strutter's Ball" and the absurd hilarity of showgirls dressed as cosmetics in "Powder, Lipstick and Rouge."

Down Argentine Way — (Nick Castle, Fayard Nicholas, Geneva Sawyer) Fox, 1940, Video:Key Video — Castle supplies just the right dancing to finally make Betty Grable a star, and the Nicholas Brothers nail the title tune with a tap dance that defies gravity.

Down to Earth (Jack Cole) Col, 1947, Video: Col — Cole creates some dances from his wildest nightmares. Often claimed to contain the first modern ballet on the screen.

Girl Crazy (Busby Berkeley, Jack Donohue, Charles Walters) MGM, 1943, Video:MGM/UA — Wonderful musical staging by Donohue and Walters, giving a "Preview of Coming Attractions" of their directorial talents, as well as a slam-bang finale from Berkeley.

Good News (Robert Alton, Charles Walters) MGM, 1947, Video:MGM/UA — Seamless musical staging and energetic dance numbers from even non-dancers.

The Harvey Girls (Robert Alton, Charles Walters) MGM, 1946, Video:MGM/UA — Alton creates the

Showgirls outlandishly dressed as (clockwise from top right): "Mascara," "Lady Lipstick," "Patsy Powderpuff," "Patricia Powder" and "Rosy Rouge" in the bizarre "Powder, Lipstick and Rouge" production number from **The Dolly Sisters** (Seymour Felix, Twentieth Century–Fox, 1945).

perfect musical number: "On the Atchison, Topeka and the Santa Fe," which "dances" with barely a dance step.

Hellzapoppin' (Richard Barstow, Nick Castle, Eddie Prinz) Univ, 1941 — The best lindy hop routine ever captured on film, performed with screen-bursting exuberance by the Harlem Congaroo Dancers. Probably created by the members of the dance team and staged by Castle and Prinz, this dance sequence has got to be seen to be believed. A piece of American dance history!

The Kid from Brooklyn (Bernard Pearce) RKO, 1946, Video:Goldwyn — Vera-Ellen nearly dances herself into a frazzle in some hyper-kinetic dance offerings.

Kismet (Jack Cole) MGM, 1944 — This non-musical version of the story gives a glimpse of what Cole would do with the musical version 11 years later. The East Indian dance techniques and color and sensuality of the solo he did for Marlene Dietrich are sensational ... disguising the fact that it is *not* Dietrich dancing.

The Kissing Bandit (Robert Alton, Stanley Donen) MGM, 1948 — A fiery "Pas de Trois" by Cyd Charisse, Ricardo Montalban, and Ann Miller inserted at the last moment saves this turkey with its fire and fun.

Mister Big (Louis DaPron) Univ, 1943 — DaPron's energy and talent serves stars Donald O'Connor and Peggy Ryan well. C'mon Universal, where are the videos?

Moon Over Miami (Hermes Pan, The Condos Brothers) Fox, 1941, Video:Key Video — The Condos Brothers join Grable in a joyful tap celebration, and Pan's staging of "Kindergarten Conga" makes you want to jump up and join the absurd shenanigans.

On an Island with You (Jack Donohue) MGM, 1949, Video:MGM/UA — Pagan ceremonies, smooth adagios with Cyd Charisse and Ricardo Montalban and some cool swimming sequences for Miss Williams.

On the Town (Stanley Donen, Gene Kelly) MGM, 1949, Video:MGM/UA — The first real all-dance musical: sprawling, soaring, skipping, and shaking all over.

The Pirate (Robert Alton, Gene Kelly, Fayard Nicholas) MGM, 1948, Video:MGM/UA — Kelly at his most athletic and graceful in "Niña," most

physical and erotic in **The Pirate Ballet** and joining Judy Garland in an honestly funny "Be a Clown."

The Red Shoes (Robert Helpmann, Léonide Massine) Rank, 1948, Video:Par — The fairy tale that made an entire generation of little girls squeeze into toe shoes. The extended ballet is fanciful and beautifully choreographed and photographed. A milestone in dance on film.

Siren of Atlantis (Lester Horton, Bella Lewitzky) UA, 1948 — The atmospheric dances by Horton give this dramatic hogwash most of its mystery and power.

Stormy Weather (Nick Castle, Katherine Dunham, Fanchon, Fayard Nicholas, Bill Robinson, Clarence Robinson) Fox, 1943, Video:CBS/Fox — A gloriously preserved tap capsule of black dance of the 1930s and 1940s, created by some of its most artistic leaders.

Strike Up the Band (Busby Berkeley) MGM, 1940, Video:MGM/UA — "Do the La Conga" is an invigorating look at contemporary dance, and Mickey Rooney conducting an all-fruit orchestra is a terrific example of Berkeley's vivid imagination.

Sun Valley Serenade (Hermes Pan, Fayard Nicholas) Fox, 1941, Video:CBS/Fox — A smashing reflective black ice ballet for Sonja Henie, and the Nicholas Brothers' and Dorothy Dandridge's ultimate version of "Chattanooga Choo Choo."

Tonight and Every Night (Jack Cole, Val Raset) Col, 1945, Video:Col — Raset supplies the old-fashioned numbers while Cole supplies the sizzle, building Rita Hayworth's Love Goddess persona with "You Excite Me" and creating one of the most unique dances on film with the "Radio Dance" for sensational Marc Platt.

Words and Music (Robert Alton, Gene Kelly) MGM, 1948, Video:MGM/UA — Elegant stage pieces by Alton and the landmark **Slaughter on 10th Ave.** Ballet performed by Kelly and Vera-Ellen.

Yankee Doodle Dandy (John Boyle, Seymour Felix, LeRoy Prinz) WB, 1942, Video:WB — Painstakingly detailed recreation of period stage sequences and a glimpse at what George M. Cohan's dancing style might have been — complete with dead arms.

Yolanda and the Thief (Fred Astaire, Eugene Loring) MGM, 1945, Video:MGM/UA — Loring's dream ballets are visual treats for the eyes and puzzles for the mind, stylishly performed by Astaire and Lucille Bremer.

Ziegfeld Follies (Robert Alton, Fred Astaire, Eugene Loring, Charles Walters) MGM, 1946, Video:MGM/UA — Astaire and Alton supply two of cinema's most wonderfully visual dance-as-narrative landmarks: "This Heart of Mine" and "Limehouse Blues." Enjoy watching the dance ensemble

try to get gracefully onboard the turntable in "This Heart of Mine"!

Ziegfeld Girl (Busby Berkeley) MGM, 1941, Video:MGM/UA — Berkeley takes tiny Judy Garland and Lana Turner and sleep-walking Hedy Lamarr and almost makes them believable showgirls, surrounded by authentic beauties who seem to descend from heaven in stunning costumes by Adrian.

THE 1950S

After the prolific musical output of the 1940s, the 1950s saw a huge change in the movie musical genre and in films themselves when they were challenged by two of the most influential innovations of the twentieth century: television and rock 'n' roll.

At the beginning of the decade, the studios still had their dance directors: Alex Romero (MGM), Hal Belfer (Universal), Josephine Earl and Charles O'Curran (Paramount), Jack Cole and Stephen Papich (Twentieth Century–Fox), and LeRoy Prinz (Warner Bros.). The collapse of the movie industry itself would soon cause choreographers to look for work elsewhere as studio dance departments were eliminated. Creative dance makers became freelancers once again.

Although the quantity of film musicals produced during this decade would pale in comparison to the previous one, the quality reached a level of perfection. After more than twenty years of experimentation the dance inventors now knew exactly what they were doing: combining inventive choreography, camera technique, story telling, music, design, and technically proficient dancers to create the best library of dance on film for history to marvel at.

While the choreographers and dance directors innovated and continued to change dance on film, they were still unappreciated. In 1952, Lowell E. Redlings wrote in his "The Hollywood Scene" column in the *Hollywood Citizen News*: "From the moment images began to move about on a movie screen — long before the public even dreamed of talkies or full-length stories on celluloid — the dance has been an important part of motion picture entertainment. Yet, even today there is little understanding among the general public and even in some Hollywood quarters [regarding] the role the dance director plays in the making of a movie."

Dance Magazine assigned well-respected critic Arthur Knight to begin a monthly "Dance in the Movies" review column, and although he would sometimes defend dance directors ("Choreographers like Jack Cole and Eugene Loring, who have contributed enormously to film dance and dancers, must still struggle for the obviously necessary cooperation between director and choreographer"), he also would often ignore them. In his November 1956 review of French director Rene Clair's **The Grand Maneuver**, he gushed, "As always, Clair has put considerable emphasis upon the dance elements in his story. The film seems to swing from lantern-lit *bal musette* to provincial ballroom to secluded bistro, offering tantalizing glimpses of the varied social dances of the period." Knight failed to credit a choreographer. *Dance Magazine* also finally acknowledged the large amount of dance work being done on the West Coast with monthly columns about film and television, written by Ted Hook and Roy Clark (and eventually Viola Helgi Swisher, Don Bradburn, and Kevin Grubb in subsequent decades) which notated

choreographers, assistants and dancers in film, an invaluable source for research on this decade.

Along with being misunderstood and largely unrecognized, the choreographer's work was still being edited by others. Despite the success of **The Red Shoes** and other films with extended dance sequences, producers still got nervous about lengthy dances. Often, intricate dance sequences were not performed by the stars of the film but instead featured brilliant but little-known (to the moviegoing public) dancers. When a film's running length was deemed too long, it was easier to remove entire dance sequences, rather than painstakingly snipping bits of dialogue and action to shorten a film.

The censors of the time also caused havoc with the new honesty-in-dance movement, costume design, and sensual performances. Jack Cole's lusty work regularly went under the knife, and a number that Billy Daniel staged for Jane Russell in **The French Line** (1954) caused the censors to threaten its removal, with the Catholic Legion of Decency condemning the film. This controversy may have helped the film's box office receipts, but it frustrated the choreographers who were trying to contemporize photographed dance. Somewhere there must be a Deleted Musical Number Heaven full of unseen glories.

But the movie musical had other troubles.

At the end of World War II, the country had a very different attitude about filmgoing. The escapism of the '30s and '40s was replaced by a grittier, more realistic style of film, introduced by European directors such as Vittorio DeSica. The frothy, nonsensical musicals began to lose their popularity, and the film studios scrambled to find new formulas. They also felt the oncoming competition of television, so they began searching for ways to compete with the new enemy.

New film processes such as 3-D, Cinerama, VistaVision, and CinemaScope were trumpeted to try and lure audiences away from their television screens, adding new challenges for photographers, directors, and choreographers. Although wide-screen processes had been briefly tried in the 1920s, they now became the norm as studios rushed to buy the latest cameras and movie houses installed new screens. These wide-screen processes meant learning new techniques. A solo dancer was lost on the wide ribbon on the screen; chorus people to the left and right of the soloist suddenly loomed 30 feet high; images had a tendency to "shatter" if a body moved too quickly across the screen. Stanley Donen (now a director) compared the new techniques to designing for fresco rather than canvas. It was time for new homework for the dance masters.

Hermes Pan's work on the new wide screen in **Meet Me in Las Vegas** (1956) was praised by critic Arthur Knight:

> His staging of the Frankie Laine number, a torrid ballad titled "Hell Hath No Fury," might well give pause to other dance directors.... He spots Laine well up front, close to the camera, against a perfectly plain black background. Black panels and a dramatic cross-lighting permit sudden appearances or disappearances of the five red-clad dancers working together in beautiful unison behind him. It is one of the simplest and cleverest dances yet devised for the CinemaScope screen, and particularly notable for the effective use of its small ensemble.

Working with Todd-AO for the first time on **Can Can** (1960), Pan easily adapted and found it beneficial:

Opposite: A gaggle of future choreographers in this dance number from **Tea for Two** (Warner Bros., 1950): Front row (L to R): Carol Haney and behind her, Ward Ellis, Cass Jaeger, Patrice Wymore, Gene Nelson, Doris Day, Jack Boyle, Virginia Gibson, Jack Regas and Dee Turnell. In the back row (above Doris Day's head) is Ernest Flatt (photo courtesy of Jack Regas).

> I never liked to do tricks with the camera nor do I like an excessive amount of cut-
> ting during a dance routine. With Todd-AO, there is really no need for either of these.
> You have a screen that is roughly the size of the stage proscenium, and a camera that
> permits you to get very close to your dancers and yet show them in full figure. What
> I like best about the new system is that you can stage a number more or less as you
> would see it from "out front" [*Dance Magazine*, January 1960].

The television musical variety shows also took the edge off of musical films. Families could
watch popular singing and dancing (and many of the films' biggest) stars for free in their homes.
On television, choreographers were challenged and given opportunities each week to experiment with concepts for dance sequences and camera collaboration. The movie musical fell into
hard times.

Some of the dancemakers from previous eras bravely tried to save the genre with inventive
work. The seemingly indestructible Fred Astaire, for example, met the challenges of the era in
a series of successful films with new partners: Leslie Caron, Cyd Charisse, Audrey Hepburn,
Betty Hutton, Jane Powell, and Vera-Ellen. Again, their various talent levels and dance techniques caused him to invent and create. But it was his collaboration with choreographers Robert
Alton, Nick Castle, Michael Kidd, Eugene Loring, Hermes Pan, and Roland Petit that would
stretch his capabilities. Although constantly threatening retirement, he continued singing and
dancing and creating throughout the 1950s, incorporating the modern techniques of knee-slides,
isolation, and even rock 'n' roll into his classic work. Television itself also gave him a challenge
and an opportunity to innovate. In 1958, his first television special, "An Evening with Fred
Astaire," allowed him to conquer the newest visual medium.

Gene Kelly likewise stretched his imagination and inventive partnership with the camera,
creating the masterpieces for which he is best remembered: **An American in Paris** (for which
he won his "special" Oscar, 1951), **Singin' in the Rain** (with the trailer promising "the unbelievable, the sensational ***Broadway Ballet***. It's the most thrilling dance number ever staged!"
1952), **Brigadoon** (1954), **It's Always Fair Weather** (1955), and his landmark all-dance film,
Invitation to the Dance (1956). Kelly's ballets became feasts for the eyes, and his solos incorporated the best of his unique talents, with the simplicity of jumping in puddles in **Singin' in
the Rain** crowning his exploration of the range of human expressions through dance.

Kelly's dance-as-narrative concepts reached their peak in this decade, producing a body of
work which will be enjoyed by endless audiences and examined by generations of film and dance
critics and students. With assistants Carol Haney and Jeanne Coyne (who would become his
wife), he mixed the dance vocabularies of ballet, jazz, and musical theater readily and inventively, embracing and brilliantly utilizing the new wide-screen techniques of the era.

It was not without a constant battle, however. In 1994, Kelly told Hilary deVries in the
Los Angeles Times:

> The executives didn't know how to read a musical script — they still don't! There would
> be a line like "I love you" which was followed by "Three minutes of song and dance"
> and they never quite understood that. One time, somebody upstairs insisted that we
> write out the dances, so I got together with other choreographers and wrote out, 'Four
> bars then into a glissade, arabesque, boy takes girl in his arms, lifts her down into a
> fish…" It's a classic dance language, but of course it was Latin to them, and we soon
> went back to the old way.

Jack Cole, now dance director at Twentieth Century–Fox, was given the challenge of boost-
ing Betty Grable's faltering box office dominance in **Meet Me After the Show** (1951), **The**

Ann Miller performs barefooted for the first time in "The Lady from the Bayou" (under the direction of Hermes Pan) from **Hit the Deck** (MGM, 1955), surrounded by (L to R) Roy Palmer, Bert May, Frank Radcliff, Buddy Bryan and Art Mendez (photo courtesy of Buddy Bryan).

Farmer Takes a Wife (1953), and **Three for the Show** (1955). With his assistant, Gwen Verdon, his work stretched Grable's capabilities and showed new depths of her humor and sensuality. For his efforts on **On the Riviera** (1951), a Danny Kaye film, the *Hollywood Reporter* oozed, "Jack Cole's stylized dances ... are a welcome change from stereotypical terpsichorean forms." At Twentieth Century–Fox, he also created sensational routines for up-and-coming dancing star Mitzi Gaynor (**The "I Don't Care" Girl**, 1953) and continued Fox's blonde domination by devising sensual choreography for their newest bombshell, Marilyn Monroe, in **Gentlemen Prefer Blondes** (also 1953). Though basically a non-dancer, Monroe could understand and interpret Cole's erotic body language. As he had done for Rita Hayworth, Cole created a screen persona for Miss Monroe that fairly sizzled in her musical numbers. Cole's sense of humor and erotic tension was perfect for the fifties, poking fun at America's breast obsession, while continuing his unique jazz-based work for the dancing corps. In Arthur Knight's *Dance Magazine* review of **Gentlemen Marry Brunettes** (1955), Cole's contributions were praised:

> There is also an Afro-Hollywood ballet to the tune of "Ain't Misbehavin'" that permits Cole the smart, swift-paced pattern shifting, the spread legged toe balancing and frantic wrist wavings that have become virtually his trademark ... as the plot unwinds interminably, you find yourself wishing they could just skip the story and give us more of Mr. Cole's agile and amusing contributions.

Cyd Charisse and Fred Astaire in *The Girl Hunt* ballet from **The Band Wagon** (MGM, 1953), as Astaire continues to expand his style in Michael Kidd's choreography.

Betty Grable and John Carroll struggle over a bottle of demon rum in a dream ballet deleted from **The Farmer Takes a Wife** (Twentieth Century–Fox, 1953), choreographed by Jack Cole.

As part of his job description as dance director, Cole also gave input to films he did not actually choreograph. With an impressive archive of dance history and material, and a probing mind, Cole offered detailed suggestions for the John Phillip Sousa biography **Stars and Stripes Forever** (1952) for musical sequences which were historical and innovative. Producer-writer Lamar Trotti accepted the suggestions and then went ahead to produce a very generic musical of the period, choreographed by Nick Castle and Stephen Papich. In 1955, Cole's stage success **Kismet** was translated to film by MGM, and he flamboyantly choreographed **Designing Woman** (and portrayed "The Choreographer" onscreen — creating an exciting dance-as-combat sequence) and collaborated with Gene Kelly on **Les Girls** in 1957. As the movie musical ground to a halt, however, he eventually abandoned the restrictions and frustrations of Hollywood for greater challenges in New York.

Hermes Pan continued to produce a large volume of varied dance offerings during the decade. When asked by author John Kobal, in an interview for *People Will Talk*, "What did you think of some of those people like Bob Alton, Michael Kidd ... were you worried at all?" The ever-gracious Pan replied, "I loved it. Anything I see that is good gives me a lift.... I loved Michael Kidd. He was so talented. And I loved Jack Cole's work because he had a new look. And he would inspire *me*. So, I would love to see anything by Jack, or Jerome Robbins. To me they were inspirations, and I would think that dancing really can be good." And Pan's contributions to the fifties were good: **Three Little Words** and **Let's Dance** (1950), **Texas Carnival** (1951),

Lovely to Look At (1952), **Kiss Me Kate** (1953), **The Student Prince** (1954), **Hit the Deck** (1955), **Meet Me in Las Vegas** (1956), **Silk Stockings** and **Pal Joey** (1957), and **Porgy and Bess** (1959).

Jack Cole's hope for the future, as he had expressed it in *Dance and Dancers*—"for musical pictures, the dance director, a properly equipped one — very rare — should be the director" — was coming true. In the August 1954 issue of *Dance Magazine*, Arthur Knight commented,

> It is therefore with particular pleasure that we note a new type coming forward in the studio — the dance director turned film director. True, only a few have as yet become established names in the field — Gene Kelly, Charles Walters and Stanley Donen — but they seem to presage a whole new trend. As the dance assumes a more prominent and integral position in the development of a story, it is increasingly important that the director have some knowledge of what his dances can accomplish. No small part of the charm of **Lili** was Charles Walters' ability to bring the film to a climax in an imaginative and whimsical ballet sequence.

The above-mentioned Kelly, Walters, and Donen followed Busby Berkeley into handling the reins of an entire film with varying degrees of success. Other choreographers such as Robert Alton, Larry Ceballos, Bobby Connolly, Ralph Cooper, Jack Donohue, Arthur Dreifuss, Dave Gould, LeRoy Prinz, and Wendy Toye would be joined in the following decades by Debbie Allen, Earl Barton, Patricia Birch, Gower Champion, Bob Fosse, Gregory Hines, Jeffrey Hornaday, Alan Johnson, Gene Nelson, Kenny Ortega, Jerome Robbins, Herbert Ross, Shabba Doo, and David Winters. Unfortunately, Jack Cole was never given the opportunity.

Busby Berkeley continued into the 1950s, creating fanciful sequences for **Two Weeks with Love** (1950, also director), **Call Me Mister** (1951, also director), **Two Tickets to Broadway** (1951, with uncredited Gower Champion, also director), **Million Dollar Mermaid** (1952, staging of the water ballets), **Easy to Love** (1953) and **Rose Marie** (1954, staging of the "Totem Tom Tom" number). He was still up to his flamboyant shenanigans.

On **Small Town Girl** (1953, with Willie Covan, Ann Miller, and Alex Romero), musical arranger André Previn reminisced in his autobiography, *No Minor Chords*, about working with the legendary Berkeley ("He was a man who venerated the camera and adored setting problems for it, then coming up with solutions.") Previn goes on to fantasize a Berkeley monologue in prose:

> ...behind the careening camera, his eyes blazing, shouting directions and exhortations while the playback music added to the atmosphere of panic. "Great, great," he would scream, "the green smoke is perfect, let's have more, yes, that's lovely, now, whip the mirrors around, wonderful, just right, get those prisms ready for the waterfall, oh boy, that's perfect," and suddenly the head swerved and the voice screamed in anguish, "Goddammit, you silly bitch, can't you dance any faster?"

Previn recalls that for a fantasy musical sequence, Berkeley envisioned Jane Powell making an entrance in a buggy pulled by forty eagles — which, due to budget restraints, became a huge ox. When the ox was first brought onto the set, Buzz walked around him and announced, "Nice and big, but I want him painted gold." Not satisfied that the ox had been completely gilded, Berkeley knelt down to "give close scrutiny to the ox's nether regions.... The ox had had it, in spades — enough was enough. He took careful aim and peed right on Mr. Berkeley.... The fact that Buzz was wearing a white suit was a nice touch, but the force, trajectory, and amount of stream overshadowed everything else; it was awe-inspiring."

For "I've Gotta Hear That Beat," another number in the film, "he devised a dance in which Ann Miller, tapping madly, cruised around a huge floor which had dozens of holes in it." The holes had been drilled so that dancers or extras lying on their backs under the floor holding musical instruments could "whip their arms out at precisely the moment the lyrics dictated.... It must have been over 100 degrees under the floor, and completely dark, and the hapless extras had to be hauled out periodically for air and light." Interviewed during filming, Berkeley reasoned, "Why did I have Ann Miller dance through the musicans with their arms sticking up through holes cut in the floor? Because it was interesting to watch, interesting to photograph. I could have had her come out on the stage and do a buck-and-wing routine, call it a dance, and that would have been that. But I always try for the new and different. They don't think about those things today."

Previn's final description captures Berkeley and the madness and genius he personified: "There was Ann Miller, spangled and glittering, whirling around dangerously, avoiding the holes in the floor; there were the subterranean instrument holders, gasping for air; and above it all, Buzz, on the seat of a huge camera crane, shouting imprecations, screaming instructions, hurling the camera at an alarming speed, Ben Hur during the chariot race, Errol Flynn leading the Charge of the Light Brigade, General Custer heading right into Indians at full gallop."

Other prolific dance directors of the 1940s continued their work into the 1950s (Robert Alton, Nick Castle, Billy Daniel, Charles O'Curran, LeRoy Prinz) but, for the first time, film was creating choreographers and dance directors of its own. Jack Baker, Earl Barton, Hal Belfer, Bill Foster, Alex Romero, Lee Scott, and Kenny Williams began their careers in this uncertain time. In January 1952, *Dance Magazine* observed: "Incidentally, one of the real services being performed by films is the training of outstanding choreograpter assistants, among the most promising at the moment being Ernest Flatt and Alex Romero."

Although film would breed other innovators, it was the dance world and the Broadway stage that continued to supply the creators who were given the greatest opportunities. It was a constant source of frustration for the Hollywood-based choreographers.

To compete by presenting something that could not yet be seen on television, major Broadway hits were finally transferred lovingly to the screen—**Oklahoma!** (1955), **The King and I** and **Carousel** (1956), **The Pajama Game** (1957), etc., allowing glimpses of some time-honored choreography from Broadway greats Agnes DeMille, Jerome Robbins, Michael Kidd, and Bob Fosse. During the 1930s and 1940s Hollywood had consistently shifted and rearranged Broadway transfers, deleting songs and dances, changing the story, casting Hollywood personalities in roles they could not sing or dance and generally mucking up the successful shows. But in the 1950s, audiences were finally promised: "Uncut! Just as seen on Broadway for its sold-out 400 performances!" And this meant importing the innovative choreography intact, rearranged only for the camera.

Agnes DeMille's first film experience working for her uncle Cecil on **Cleopatra** (1934) had been a hideous, humbling experience. In *The DeMilles: An American Family*, author Anne Edwards relates how Agnes, determined to "bring a touch of class to the dance sequences," was reduced to performing a seductive dance on the back of a bull. With plucked eyebrows, a brief costume and brown body makeup, she entered precariously writhing on the bull until DeMille stopped the filming, shouting, "Oh, no! Oh, no! ... I am so disappointed ... it has no excitement ... no thrill, no suspense, no sex.... What I would like is something like the Lesbian Dance in **The Sign of the Cross**." The on-duty censor sighed, "Boy! If we hadn't had the Christians singing hymns like crazy we would never have got away with it." Agnes was fired by her uncle.

Bambi Linn (wearing the bridal veil) approaches her wedding with trepidation in Agnes DeMille's landmark ***Dream Ballet*** from **Oklahoma!** (Magna), which finally reached the screen in 1955, 12 years after it revolutionized dance in the American musical.

Her next film assignment was to create the court dances for MGM's **Romeo and Juliet** (1936). Hired by director George Cukor, she worked for sixteen weeks, creating an intricate ballet which was reduced to fuzzy background movement while the camera lovingly focused on the star, Norma Shearer. "When I saw a cut version of what actually had been filmed I went outside the projection room and lay down in the grass and was very, very sick" (*The DeMilles: An American Family*). In *The Hollywood Musical*, authors John Russell Taylor and Arthur Jackson defend Cukor's cuts: "Her distress is understandable, but obviously Cukor was right: the function of the dances in this sequence are not to exist and be recorded as a self-sufficient, coherent entity, but to form part of a more complex filmic whole, to be, though a finished creation to their choreographer, merely so much raw material for the director." Asked to remain at MGM and do **Marie Antoinette**, she instead took off in her own direction and revolutionized not only modern ballet but also musical comedy.

Recognized for demanding that her dancers project characters rather than their own personalities, DeMille with her concepts and choreography for *Oklahoma!, Carousel, Allegro* and other revolutionary musicals in the theater, had seriously influenced dance on film in the previous decade. Though it was often publicized that DeMille was coming to Hollywood to recreate her Broadway successes (or original works) onscreen, her major work did not arrive on film until 1955 when **Oklahoma!** was finally produced. DeMille's concepts extended the dance into dramatic situations, completely integrating the musical form. The basis of her movement came out of the characters, their emotional attitude, and the story situation. No one danced for dance's sake in DeMille's work. Although her Freudian approach to the dream ballet had been widely copied on screen before her ballet from **Oklahoma!** was filmed, her work still contained original surprises, such as the introduction of the dance-in, in which the leading lady, Shirley Jones, walks to her dance persona, Bambi Linn, and as they touch, Linn takes over the role. Previously, film makers had tried to disguise dance-ins, covering them with hair or veils or using moving, long distance shots of them, interspersed with close-ups of the star waving her arms. DeMille's psychological introduction of the dance-in brought new emotional depth to the entire work. The 1955 audience understood and accepted.

Jerome Robbins, a prolific ballet choreographer who would also find success in the musical theatre and eventually pioneer with DeMille a new breed of genius (the director-choreographer), finally had his work preserved on film in **The King and I** (1956). Because of the lack of control that film choreographers had, Robbins obviously preferred the total authority he enjoyed in the worlds of ballet and theatre. The films were still controlled by directors and studio heads. Robbins could work in the ballet and the musical as an auteur; in film, he was a member of a team. Although he was to create one of the milestones in dance films (**West Side Story**) in the next decade, in reviewing his career, we find that the bulk of his work was dedicated to the live performance arts, as was DeMille's. Again, Robbins' creative core was the human condition, his characters taking the audience along on the emotional journey their dance depicted. Whereas DeMille gave us dancing cowboys and fishermen from the past, Robbins devised dancing sailors and gang members, denizens of the contemporary world.

Another Broadway innovator, Michael Kidd, began with stage successes transferred to the screen: **Where's Charley?** (1952), **Guys and Dolls** (1955), and **L'il Abner** (1959, restaged for film by Dee Dee Wood). One of Kidd's major original film musicals (**The Band Wagon**, 1953), choreographed in collaboration with Fred Astaire, was reviewed — with reservations — at the time of its release by *Dance Magazine*: "The **Girl Hunt Ballet**, a witty and episodic satire of the Mickey Spillane mystery story, is the film's high spot and one of the most brilliant works of Michael Kidd's career ... [it] is ingenious in its use of camera trickery, fascinating in its counterpoint of spoken word and dance — but quite impossible to accept as the finale of a *stage* musical."

Fred Astaire's relationship with Michael Kidd was at first uncertain. In *After Dark* (December 1975), screenwriter Betty Comden remarked that Astaire seemed uneasy working with Kidd, unsure about Kidd's more classical approach to dance: "It reminded me of the lack of common ground between the movie hoofer and the ballerina, which we had in our script." Costume designer Mary Ann Nyberg also recalled,

> Astaire was admittedly petrified about working with Michael Kidd, who had come to the unit with the reputation of not only being the hottest choreographer on Broadway, but also being one of the brightest lights in American Ballet. Astaire began arriving early at the studio to warm up for his numbers, Kidd was always there before him. No matter how early Astaire arrived, Kidd was always there before him. When it reached the point when both of them were getting to the studio before five in the morning, Astaire turned to the choreographer and said, "Look, this is ridiculous" and discovered that Kidd was just as nervous about working with Astaire as Astaire was about working with Kidd. They reached a truce [*After Dark*, December 1975].

Though **The Band Wagon** would later be acknowledged for its innovation, it was the athletic exuberance of another original screen musical, **Seven Brides for Seven Brothers** (1954), that once more changed the face of film dancing. Filling the new, wide CinemaScope screen with lusty, expansive movement and ingratiating characterization, Kidd would continue moving back and forth from Hollywood to Broadway, joining the stage director–choreographer ranks

Gemze DeLappe as "King Simon of Legree" in Jerome Robbins' ***Small House of Uncle Thomas***, captured on film in **The King and I** (Twentieth Century–Fox, 1950).

and invigorating both entertainment mediums. When Kidd suggested casting the seven brothers of the title with some of the best male dancers of the day (Jacques d'Amboise, Matt Mattox, Marc Platt, and Tommy Rall), the studio heads were unsure. "They kept saying to me in words of one syllable, 'You can't have a bunch of guys jumping around; the audience will think you've got some pansy backswoodsmen!'" (Ronald L. Davis, *The Glamour Factory*). Instead,

Kidd's work tumbled and leapt, bounded and jostled with athletic energy rather than classical grace. The movie's prevue proclaimed, "The new look in musical comedy ... four rollicking dance numbers to give the show a Sock!"

From the modern dance world, Valerie Bettis arrived with a unique choreographic *and* acting contract at Columbia Studios. Primarily creating the dances for Columbia goddess Rita Hayworth during her brief film career, she also played supporting roles with her glamorous blonde looks and whiskey voice. Jack Cole said in *People Will Talk*,

> Valerie was a dancer, and a good one, who wanted to be an actress, and that always makes problems. Already they were competing ladies: Valerie was a little younger, very expert in her own right, but Valerie always did numbers for her like Valerie Bettis would do. Valerie was a *very* fine modern dancer of the Hanya Holm crew in New York, but Rita Hayworth wasn't a dancer in that way, nor did she pretend to be. She was a beautiful lady and you always had to treat her like the most beautiful showgirl who could move. You couldn't treat her like a dancer, because you couldn't put that burden on her.

Bettis's unorthodox movement simply did not work as well on Hayworth as Cole's had, and when her acting career did not take off, she returned to the concert stage.

Helen Tamiris and Hanya Holm, two more leaders of American modern dance of the period who had successfully transferred their talents to musical theatre stage innovation and success, were brought to films in the '50s. They were hardly given the respect they deserved. Holm was assigned a remake of **The Vagabond King** (1956), in which Holm's legendary talent, which was to score great success on stage in such landmarks as *My Fair Lady* (1956) can barely be assessed. *Dance Magazine* reviewed Holm's single film in November 1956: "A good deal of the dancing also fell to the editor's shears—what comes out on the screen might have been arranged by almost anyone.... Miss Holm deserves another chance under happier auspices."

Tamiris, after innovative contributions to the stage smashes *Up in Central Park* (1945) and *Annie Get Your Gun* (1946), restaged the dances for the film version of her **Up in Central Park** in 1948. In 1952, she worked on an original musical, **Just for You**, with non-dancers Bing Crosby and Jane Wyman as her stars. Like Holm, Tamiris found her first film job frustrating ("Most of Tamiris' work has been cut out of **Up in Central Park** and Universal is cutting back its budget on dance directors. A trend?"—"Via the Grapevine" column, *Dance Magazine*, June 1948). Both Holm and Tamiris high-tailed it back to Broadway and the concert stage after these unrewarding film assignments.

With the dwindling volume of musicals being produced, the decade included some of the last dancing stars placed under contract to the major studios. They joined the already established Fred Astaire, Ray Bolger, Cyd Charisse, Dan Dailey, Betty Grable, June Haver, Rita Hayworth, Danny Kaye, Gene Kelly, Ann Miller, Donald O'Connor, and Vera-Ellen to vie for the shrinking dance roles. From the European ballet world Leslie Caron, Taina Elg, Zizi Jeanmaire, Lilliane Montevecchi, and Juliet Prowse were placed under contract and had varying degrees of success and exposure. American dancers Richard Allan, John Brascia, Kelly Brown, Jacques d'Amboise, Sally Forrest, Virginia Gibson, Susan Luckey, Allyn McLerie, James Mitchell, Tommy Rall, Bobby Van, Helen Wood, and Patrice Wymore and former choreographers Michael Kidd, Gwen Verdon, and Carol Haney were featured in one or more high profile musical films. Mitzi Gaynor, Shirley MacLaine and Sheree North left their dance shoes far behind and went on to sustained careers because of their comedic or dramatic abilities and appeal.

Four of the new featured dancers also brought highly imaginative choreographic abilities along with them to change the film musical.

In **My Sister Eileen** (L to R) Bob Fosse, Janet Leigh, Betty Garrett and Tommy Rall perform Fosse's early film choreography to "Give Me a Band and My Baby" (Columbia, 1955).

Bob Fosse arrived to the movies in the 1950s as a successful club and stage performer, hoping to follow his idol, Fred Astaire, into a film career. In one of his 1953 films, **Kiss Me Kate**, supervising choreographer Hermes Pan allowed Fosse to choreograph his own section of the number "From This Moment On" with partner Carol Haney, giving film audiences a dazzling glimpse of Fosse the choreographer. That same year, dance director Gower Champion allowed Fosse to shape his own dances in **Give a Girl a Break**, as did Alex Romero in **The Affairs of Dobie Gillis**. Without the standard leading-man looks of the period and the declining musical opportunities, after several roles it became obvious that Fosse had no future as a film performer, so he abandoned Hollywood for New York. There, with Gwen Verdon — another film expatriate who finally found her due recognition on the stage — he began creating the dances for a series of hit musicals, two of which would be filmed during the '50s (**The Pajama Game**, 1957, and **Damn Yankees**, 1958). He also created all of the dances and musical staging for himself, his costars and ensemble in the original musical **My Sister Eileen** (1955).

From early performances in burlesque and nightclubs, Fosse had developed a very personal style that had bits of Astaire, Kelly, and Cole in it, but was fueled by a never-ending fascination for the female which ignited his freedom of sensual dance expression. His distinctive style and dance vocabulary would grow with each show, until he too joined the ranks of director-choreographer on the Broadway stage. His stylized from-the-hip, hat-over-one-eye work was distinguished by its economy (the power of a single gesture), humor, non-musical rhythm breaks (often performed by clusters of moving humanity writhing, talking and taunting the audience or camera), and all of his dances built from tight, controlled intensity to explosions of expansive expressions of freedom through dance. With Fosse, everything was contrast: fast to slow, little to big, contained to explosive. His genius would come into full blossom several decades later.

In *Dance Magazine*, August 1957, Carol Haney, one of the stars of **The Pajama Game** who had assisted Gene Kelly on many films, spoke about the collaboration between original stage director George Abbott, Fosse, and film director Stanley Donen when the property was transferred to the screen:

> My "Steam Heat" number, for example … was done exactly as we did it in the theatre. It was supposed to be presented on a stage … and I thought Stanley was very wise not to try to trick it up for the movie. On the other hand, for a scene like the big "Once a Year Day" number — the picnic dance which we did on location in a park — Bob Fosse rechoreographed his original dance completely to involve more people and all the space you can cover with a camera. And Stanley, who knows about dance, photographed it in wonderful travelling shots that captured all of the dynamism of the movements and at the same time provided enough air around the performers to make their movements significant. You see, you just can't set up your camera and photograph a dance…. You have to know just where to place it, which angle will make it exciting and alive. I know because I've tried.

Fosse was fortunate to work in his early films under the tutelage of such masters of dance on film as Pan, Donen, Romero, Haney, Verdon, and Champion, who could inspire him for his future film dance explorations.

Marge and Gower Champion appeared in 1950s movies as the first-ever husband and wife dancing film stars. Although they had both previously danced in films, it was their phenomenal success in nightclubs and on stage which would bring them back to Hollywood as stars, allowing them to offer creative input on both sides of the camera. Their extensive dance training (from Ernest Belcher, Marge's father) and Gower's inventions of fluid floor patterns and lifts presented a never-ending whirl of movement and grace, breaking the stiffness of previous ballroom teams and evolving into classic adagio teamwork. With input from Marge and in collaboration with other choreographers, Gower created their dances in **Mr. Music** (1950), **Show Boat** (with Robert Alton, 1951), **Everything I Have Is Yours** (with Nick Castle) and **Lovely to Look At** (with Hermes Pan, 1952), **Give a Girl a Break** (with Bob Fosse, 1953) as well as **Three for the Show** (with Jack Cole) and **Jupiter's Darling** (with Hermes Pan, 1955). In a television interview on Dave Garroway's "Wide Wide World" show in 1956, Champion spoke about preferring to work in film. ("Most enlightening was the comment that in the movies dancer and choreographer have a wider scope. More difficult steps can be done. Things one would not dare before the one-shot television camera can be tried a number of times in a movie. Mistakes can be eliminated and only the successful accomplishments are welded together for the whole" — Ann Barzel, *Dance Magazine*).

Champion ended the fifties choreographing the one film in which he and Marge did not appear (**The Girl Most Likely**, 1957), with Arthur Knight evaluating his work on the film:

> But every once in a while the story is shoved aside and Gower Champion comes in to stage another dance sequence. And each time that happens, the screen fairly springs alive with his brisk, clean, humorful and original routines…. In style and general approach, Champion seems a good deal closer to Jack Cole than to any other dance director currently working in films. Like Cole … he seems happiest with a minimum

Kelly Brown flies high as Bob Banas approaches on the right in Gower Champion's energetic choreography for "Balboa," in **The Girl Most Likely** (RKO, 1957), the only film Champion choreographed for other performers.

> of props and fussy background details.... Again like Cole, Champion stages numbers that are full of clean, vigorous movement and piquant humor.... Where Champion differs from Cole — and it is a significant difference — is in the muscular exuberance of his work. Cole is always superbly controlled, every action carefully plotted and smoothly executed; Champion's dancers seem to move with a youthful enthusiasm that is no less carefully choreographed, but choreographed to retain the spark of spontaneity.

The film gave a glimpse of the energy and highly commercial inventiveness of his musical number concepts which would make him one of Broadway's most successful director-choreographers in the 1960s and 1970s. Marge retired from performing in 1960 to raise their sons, but worked as his valued assistant until their divorce in 1971, going on to a solo choreographic career of her own. When receiving a *Dance Magazine* award in 1964, Gower expressed his gratitude with anecdotes about his work:

> Marge and I have a phrase we use quite often when something particularly marvelous happens to us and it is, "Well, here we are, a lousy dance team, and we've made it." We said it when we bought our first home in California, when we signed an important movie contract, and I really feel like saying it now.... As the kids will tell you, I'm the only successful pigeon-toed dancer in America.... My dances are ... quite simple and they require a high degree of performance.... I've told this to the kids many times — if they don't sell them, the dances don't work.... They said that *Bye Bye Birdie* [1960] had "hackneyed" choreography ... but my favorite of all time was that "Gower Champion, although his technique is solid and his sense of line precise, is always just faintly gauche." O.K.? I adore that line.

Gene Nelson, the final male dancer-choreographer film star of the fifties, arrived during the decade to create all of his own dance routines for the last series of Warner Bros. musicals. Under contract first to Twentieth Century–Fox, he danced in **I Wonder Who's Kissing Her Now** (1947), but he had to leave Hollywood and be "discovered" on Broadway in *Lend an Ear* (Gower Champion's first stage choreographic success in 1948) to be brought back to films by Warner Bros. Nelson's style combined tap, jazz, ballet, gymnastics, and his skills as a former ice skater with an easy-going onscreen charm. As Warner Bros. had never experimented with the musical genre in terms of technical innovations or integration of story, character, and musical sequences, Nelson was challenged by the basically stagebound presentations of song and dance:

> Warner Bros. didn't really believe that it was possible to make a musical without having an out-and-out theatrical or show business background, which seemed to justify the dance scenes by presenting them as rehearsals, dress rehearsals and the "show" ... the author needed only to insert one line in the screenplay — such as "opening night of the show" and that was a reason to do an irrelevant number with any liberties one desired — an advantage, obviously, but not necessarily good. It is all too easy to over-extend oneself on a motion picture "theatre" stage.... In the choreographer's earnest desire to entertainment and reach for excitement, he has overlooked the fact that by taking "believability" away from the scene he has also taken away a great portion of the entertainment value [*Dance Magazine*, May 1956].

With then wife Miriam, Nelson strove to create dozens of innovative, athletic tap dances and numbers, under the jurisdiction of resident dance director LeRoy Prinz. After being let go by Warner Bros. in 1955, he finally received onscreen credit for the choreography (that he had been creating all along for himself) for Universal's **So This Is Paris** (1954, with Lee Scott). Arthur Knight observed in *Dance Magazine*, "Not only does the film mark the dancing debut of Tony Curtis, the teen-ager's delight, but it is also, I believe, the first film choreography for his co-star, Gene Nelson.... His high-spirited grace, his muscularity — and his over-insistent flashiness as well — are present in every routine, no matter who happens to be performing ... he seems to be a mighty handy man to have around."

That same year, Nelson got the opportunity to make his most enduring film and to work with Agnes DeMille on **Oklahoma!** Arthur Knight described the combination of the acrobatic tap-dancing star and the modern ballet innovator: "What might have produced a disastrous head-on clash of personalities ... quickly resolved itself into a particularly neat demonstration of the kind of artistic collaboration necessary to the production of a motion picture" (*Dance Magazine*, July 1955). Three weeks before filming began, they met for the first time — both confessing that they had never seen the other's work. Together, they created the scenario of Nelson's big number ("Kansas City"), the actual dance steps, and even the casting and characterizations of the other dancers involved. In the book *That's Dancing!* Nelson reminisced: "Agnes invented a lot of the choreography on the spot. She didn't know much about tap dancing and we would discuss bits of business and she'd say, 'Show me some steps.' I would and then she'd say, 'That's good, let's do that.'"

Although Nelson was never given a female partner to match his abilities (he costarred with the lovely — but technically lacking — June Haver, Doris Day, and Virginia Mayo) and was late in the time frame of the movie musical, he managed to leave behind some sensational solos (the "gym number" in **She's Working Her Way Through College**, 1952, for instance). He also never lost his awe for the medium, as he noted in Tony Thomas's *That's Dancing!*: "It's a marvelous medium for dancers.... You can do wonderfully imaginative things with film — it's like

Gene Nelson pretends to teach Phyllis Thaxter a dance step in this publicity photo taken at Warner Bros. circa 1955.

being a magician…. In my heyday I could only do about four pirouettes without starting to fall, but with film I could do a dozen by cutting and editing. The magic of film is that you can create anything you want."

Never receiving full credit for his creative contributions, Gene Nelson took his extensive knowledge of film and its technique to become a successful television and film director in the '60s.

Gene's wife, Miriam (née Franklin) Nelson, began in films as one of those stroke-of-luck stories. Accompanying Gene to Hollywood where he would film the show he was touring in, **This Is the Army** (1943), on her second day in California, she happened to meet Billy Daniel with whom she had worked on Broadway and who was now dancing in films. "C'mon over to Paramount and see how they make movies," he invited. When she arrived on the studio lot, she heard her name yelled from the commissary by Buddy DeSylva. DeSylva had produced her last stage show — and was now the president of Paramount. He told her to "go on upstairs" and fifteen minutes later, she had a seven-year contract at Paramount, where she would eventually act, dance, and begin assisting Dance Director Danny Dare. When Gene started making films at Warner Bros. she joined him there and worked as one of LeRoy Prinz's legion of assistants, coaching Doris Day, co-creating Gene's routines, and making several appearances on film.

She was eventually to create one of the most enduring dance images on American film in the drama **Picnic** (1955). The emotional moment when Kim Novak was to succumb to the potent charms of drifter William Holden was told in dance to the tune of "Moonglow." Through discussions with director Joshua Logan, it was decided that the moment would take place in the moonlight at the Labor Day picnic, with Holden sensuously swaying to the far-off strains of a band. Novak was to see him, become transfixed, and join him in a sensual dance. In an interview with the author, Nelson recollected that it was not easy to take two non-dancers and make them feel comfortable with the simple movement. "Kim complained. She had to walk down a series of steps and then move across the ground to join him. She complained that her high-heeled shoes kept sinking into the sand and said she couldn't do it. I said I would show her ... and luckily, I did it. We finally had to place wooden boards and cover them with sand to create a path that led to him." Viewed today the dance still crackles with emotion, with *Premiere* magazine noting in September 1993 that the film "contains the sexiest dance scene in movie history ... it smoldered ... it draws the viewer in with suggestion, the heat, the holding back."

Rod Alexander, another product of film choruses and a member of the prestigious Jack Cole ensemble at Columbia, created two rousing screen dance efforts before he deserted film to become one of television's first major dancer-choreographer stars with his wife, Bambi Linn. In **Carousel** (creating everything else but Agnes DeMille's restaged *Louise's Ballet*) and **The Best Things in Life Are Free** (with Bill Foster) in 1956, Alexander's work was bold and lyrical, and it filled the wide screen.

In other musical films of the decade, there were last attempts at the previously successful "nostalgia" films for Betty Grable: in **Wabash Avenue** (Billy Daniel, 1950) and for Doris Day in **On Moonlight Bay** (1951) and **By the Light of the Silvery Moon** (LeRoy Prinz and Donald Saddler, 1953). However, ballet had now arrived onscreen in a big way because of the success of **The Red Shoes**.

The same British team which had scored such groundbreaking success with **The Red Shoes** collaborated on **The Tales of Hoffman** (1951), incorporating singing, fantastic settings and costumes, and a cast of balletic greats. Eugene Loring continued his ballet creativity in **The 5,000 Fingers of Dr. T** (1953) and **Meet Me in Las Vegas** (1956), and Michael Kidd's previously mentioned work in **The Band Wagon** (with Fred Astaire, 1953) combined the techniques of ballet with popular culture in *The Girl Hunt Ballet*. David Lichine and Michel Panaieff had by now settled in Hollywood, opening successful schools and occasionally creating classic ballet sequences for films, often appearing in them.

Gene Kelly, against all advice, created the earlier mentioned 22-minute ballet in **An American in Paris**. In the August of 1951 issue of *Dance Magazine*, Kelly wrote about their goal with the elaborate sequence: "We wanted to do a ballet without an actual story line or plot, a ballet that *suggested*, rather than narrated, a ballet which said more with things unsaid, than with things said." Selecting French painters for each section of the ballet ("Because the boy who is the central figure in the film is a painter, we decided to create decors, designs and costumes in the varied styles of those French painters who are supposed to have influenced him in his work"), Kelly, with the impeccable taste of director Vincente Minnelli, created an unmatched visual masterpiece ... and was rewarded with a special Academy Award.

With his great success with **An American in Paris**, in 1952 Kelly announced an all-dance film, **Invitation to the Dance**, to star Leslie Caron, Nora Kaye, and himself. After many stops, starts, and continuing frustration, MGM allowed him to make it in 1953 with featured dancers Igor Yousekevitch, Claire Sombert, Tamara Toumanova, and Kelly. The studio's lack of confidence in the film's commercial potential, the deletion of one entire ballet ("Dance Me a Song"), and MGM's financial woes kept it from being released until 1956. *Dance Magazine*'s film critic, Arthur Knight, reviewed the film in June 1956:

> As the years went by, one began to hear rumors — of sequences dropped and sequences added, of a cartoon dance that was taking an interminable time to produce, of soaring budgets.... Then one heard that the studio was re-editing, changing, shortening, popularizing the film, and that Kelly himself despaired of what they were doing to his picture.... And yet, seeing this (film), one can only wonder why MGM hesitated so long over its release, for Gene Kelly has filled his film with moments of great verve and imagination and an abundance of the kind of genial, rhythmic routines that he does best.... More than any other dance director in Hollywood, he is conscious of the camera's ability to augment or heighten the effect of a dancer's movement.... The distressing thing is that MGM, after having commissioned the work, had so little confidence in the public as to delay the release of this pleasant and often ingenious picture until now. Perhaps what threw them was Kelly's obvious artistic sincerity in making the film in the first place.

Roland Petit came to America from France to create a sensation with his Ballets de Champs Elysées. Petit, an upstart who revolutionized classical dance with his sensual, earthy, and quirky choreography, forever changed the pas de deux by adding passion and humor to technique. No longer were ballerinas merely supported, lifted, and spun by adoring — and passive — partners. They were caressed, kissed, balanced precariously, and sometimes manhandled by partners (usually Petit) who reveled in the man-woman relationship. He also combined musical comedy, the music hall, pantomime, cutting-edge fashion, and sardonic humor with his work. Petit took classic ballet, eroticized and electrified it, and created the battle of the sexes *en pointe* for his leading ballerina and wife, Jeanmaire.

After premiering his company in the United States to unprecedented notice by the press and public, Petit was signed by Howard Hughes in 1951 to film his ***Carmen***. Petit and the entire company were kept on a retainer for nearly a year, then released when Hughes decided not to film the ballet. Originally, George Balanchine had been announced to create the ballets for **Hans Christian Andersen** (1952) with stars Danny Kaye and Moira Shearer, but when Shearer became pregnant, Balanchine dropped out — and Petit and Jeanmaire were given their opportunity for film immortality. Petit's ballets for **Hans Christian Andersen, The Glass Slipper** and **Daddy Long Legs** (1955), and **Anything Goes** (1956) for Jeanmaire and another French dancing gamine, Leslie Caron, added large doses of sensuality to the form, taking filmed ballet in a new direction.

Other figures from the European ballet community to try their hand at the film medium with varying degrees of success were Alan Carter (**The Man Who Loved Redheads**, 1955), William Chappell (**The Prince and the Showgirl**, 1957), Pauline Grant (**Happy Go Lovely**

A robust men's section from the "June Is Bustin' Out All Over" number from **Carousel** (L to R): Buddy Bryan, Bill Foster, Ward Ellis and Fred Curt, choreographed by Rod Alexander (Twentieth Century–Fox, 1956).

with Jack Billings, 1951; **Melba**, 1953, and **Let's Be Happy** with Alfred Rodrigues, 1957), Tatjana Gsvosky (**Magic Fire**, 1956), Alfred Rodrigues (**Oh, Rosalinda**, 1956), and Mary Skeaping (**The Little Ballerina**, 1951).

Because producers still misunderstood assigning the proper style and dance background to their dance needs, classical choreographers were handed unlikely projects. Jaroslav Berger, the renowned artistic director of Switzerland's Bern State Theater, was hired to create a dance sequence for the biblical epic **Solomon and Sheba** (with Jean Pierre Genet, 1959). Saddled with Gina Lollobrigida as his prima ballerina and a sordid excuse for an orgy, his one piece of commercial film work would earn such future evaluations as:

> Miss Lollobrigida rehearsed for a month to prepare for the dance, with among other things, a hula hoop. On screen, as the festivities begin, Miss Lollobrigida wiggles her hips and performs a mild striptease.... 150 oil-skinned dancers stand on top of rocks, twisting about and flexing their muscles.... Other Sheban beauties are tossed skyward like high school sophomores at their first party.... Ten minutes of "Soul Train" on any given week is easily more erotic.... The net result is perhaps the most amazing five minutes in the American cinema. No description could possibly do it justice. You'll have to see it to believe this one [*The Fifty Worst Films of All Time*].

Two Europeans who fared better were William Chappell (**Moulin Rouge**, 1952) and Claude Grandjean (**French Can Can**—aka **Only the French Can**, 1956), who were responsible for truly original depictions of the can-can on screen. Working in close collaboration with American John Huston and Jean Renoir of France, two of film's greatest directors, they created

Gene Kelly, Claire Sombert, and Igor Yousekevitch in **Invitation to the Dance** (MGM, 1956), Kelly's landmark all-dance film.

original choreography especially for the mood, using colors and inventive camerawork, truly making dance an integral part of the films' success.

Andrew Sarris called **French Can Can** "the most joyous hymn to the glory of an art in the history of cinema," and Dale Thomajan wrote that it contains "The Best Extended Sequence" in his book of movie "Bests":

> What follows is a sequence that once seen is never forgotten ... to have seen **French Can Can** in a good 35mm print is to have been to Movie Heaven.... Last and best of all is the cancan itself, heralded by the emergence of dancing girls from seemingly everywhere: One drops over the edge of a balcony; others fly across tabletops and into and out of the laps of patrons; some materialize from backstage — one dancer literally bursts through a wall. A splendid commotion ensues as the girls fight their way through hordes of exuberant customers to converge on the dance floor and begin the show.... Renoir's cinematographer, Michel Kelber, shoots the cancan ... from virtually every camera position, angle and distance imaginable and the dancer's costumes ... create an intoxicating kaleidoscope of whirling colors.

The other films of the decade were a varied lot for dancemakers.

Three-D, a technique which seemed to promise at last the full use of the three-dimensional possibilities of dance, flickered briefly on the screen from 1952 to 1954 as one of the gimmicks

The Prince (dancer-choreographer Roland Petit) offers his love (and a candelabra) to mermaid Jeanmaire in *The Little Mermaid* ballet from **Hans Christian Andersen** (Samuel Goldwyn, 1952).

the studios used to fight television. If choreographers had complained that dance on film was two-dimensional, here was their chance to add that third dimension. Choreographers who got the opportunity (and challenge) to work with the medium were David Paltenghi (**The Black Swan**) in 1952; Betty Arlen (**Cat Women of the Moon**), Jack Baker (**Those Redheads from Seattle**), Josephine Earl (**Sangaree**), Lester Horton (**The 3-D Follies**), Olga Lunick (**Son of Sinbad**), LeRoy Prinz (**House of Wax**), and Lee Scott (**Miss Sadie Thompson**) in 1953; Billy Daniel (**The French Line**), Ron Fletcher (**Top Banana**), and Sylvia Lewis (**Drums of Tahiti**) in 1954; and Hermes Pan (**Kiss Me Kate**) in 1955. Rather than using the new technique to change the shape of film itself, the studios asked choreographers to create dance numbers that merely kicked at or tossed props and flung arms into the faces of the special glasses–adorned crowd. Studios planned to use 3-D for other films (among them the highly innovative musical **Red Garters**, choreographed by Nick Castle), but audiences soon complained about wearing the special glasses, and the experiment was over within four years, with only occasional films (**The Mask**, choreographed by Don Gilles in 1961, and **Captain E-O**, choreographed by Jeffrey Hornaday and Michael Jackson in 1987) later using the technique.

In the category of non-musical films, the "Harem Scarums" of the forties became low-budget "Tits-and-Sand" epics in the fifties. Actress-dancer-choreographers Carmen DeLavallade, Sylvia Lewis, and Wilda Taylor were often hired to portray Houris or Nautch dancers — with the stipulation they would also choreograph their own dance sequences. Along with their performance and choreography work they also worked as dance-ins for the female stars, and their gorgeous torsos were often used in print ads, joined to the heads of the less-than-perfectly-formed female stars.

Like the films of Cecil B. DeMille from decades earlier, the hugely successful biblical epics of the time—**David and Bathsheba** and **Quo Vadis** (1951), **The Robe** and **Salome** (1953), **Demetrius and the Gladiators**, **The Silver Chalice**, **Sign of the Pagan** and **The Egyptian** (1954), **The Prodigal** (1955), and **The Ten Commandments** (1956)—offered dancing respites from the pious tales with orgies, writhing slaves, princesses dancing for their lives, and barbarian tribes filling a throne room with color, rhythm and legitimately bared flesh. Valerie Bettis, Jack Cole, Ruth Godfrey, Stephen Papich, LeRoy Prinz, Alex Romero, Lee Scott, and Kenny Williams created the dances, many of them across the new wide screens.

The choreography was now more intricate and authentic, based on well-researched Asian and African dance. The choreographer's work, however, continued to be controlled by the whim of the director or producer. Ballet legend Serge Lifar was originally approached in 1950 by composer Miklos Rozsa to choreograph the dances for **Quo Vadis**. Sadly, Lifar's only contribution to commercial film to that point had been **Ballerina** (1938). When Lifar's schedule would not permit him to create the dancers for the film in Rome, Rozsa hired another classical choreographer from the Rome and La Scala opera houses, fellow Hungarian Aurel Milloss. About one of the dance sequences Rozsa wrote in his autobiography, *Double Life*:

> ...the dances were under way and everything seemed to be going well. Of course in pictures nothing ever goes well for long, as I should have known. A telegram arrived from MGM, summoning me back to Hollywood immediately.... I did not know then that my departure would mean disaster for the wonderful scene that the "Bacchanale"could have been.... I begin to get alarming letters ... they couldn't get [producer Mervyn] LeRoy to come and see it. It was important that he did see it, because it wasn't just a set piece but an integral part of a larger scene. At last word came. The day before shooting of the scene LeRoy had seen the dance. It was much too elaborate; all he wanted was a few girls prancing about behind the Emperor and his wife. Everything else could go. That was that.... The "Bacchanale," which could have been a tremendous Roman spectacle, was reduced to shots of a few limp showgirls.

As for other forms of ethnic dance being used in dramatic films, the Voodoo rites in **Lydia Bailey** (Jack Cole, 1952) and **The Mississippi Gambler** (Gwen Verdon, 1953) used Afro-Cuban dance movements to add excitement and authenticity to the films. Cole went to Haiti to study authentic voodoo rituals and sizzled onscreen with Carmen DeLavallade, but "unfortunately for Cole's intentions, the impact of the ritual dance was continually vitiated by [director Jean] Negulesco's — or the film's editor's — decision to intercut the dance sequence with shots of watcher's faces, filled with foreboding and terror.... Obviously, Negulesco and others were afraid audiences would rush to the toilets or the popcorn concession if they had to look at a serious, threatening dance for longer than two minutes at a time" (Glenn Loney, *Unsung Genius*). Cole's valiant efforts, however, were noticed by the *New York Times*: "A voodoo dance on the plantation grounds makes a compelling spectacle."

Film audiences were also given a chance to see what all the shouting was about for Spanish dance sensation José Greco in four films of the decade: **Manolete** (1950), **Sombrero** (1953), **Around the World in 80 Days** (1956), and **Holiday for Lovers** (1959). Although not specifically created for the films, Greco's exciting choreography was on view in his "specialty" performances.

Hot Blood (1956), a film which *The Motion Picture Guide* dubs a "strange dramatic musical"

An odd mixture of East Indian, Moroccan, and sheer Hollywood styles mix in 1959's **Sign of the Gladiator** (American International, choreographed by Claude Marchant).

(and goes on to praise: "The musical numbers are staged surprisingly well by a director mainly known for his gritty dramas"), was directed by Nicholas Ray and produced by Columbia. Matt Mattox and Sylvia Lewis were contracted to create the dance sequences, as the leading male character was a gypsy dancer. Lewis described the background of the film in a letter:

> Poor Nick Ray! … I recall he had spent months with a Gypsy tribe in N.Y. and thoroughly researched the culture and was in love with the project. Matt and I spent weeks of pre-production working out the dances for the two unknown (until a few days before shooting) stars. Nick was thrilled with the stuff we did which we would perform for him for approval. All the while, Matt tried like crazy to convince Nick that he and I should do the roles. By the time he was saddled with those two pathetic stars [non-dancers Cornel Wilde and Jane Russell were cast], I think Nick agreed … with some capable actors (and dancers) in the leads, Nick could have had an interesting picture.

Mattox and Lewis ended up doing all of the dancing themselves in longshots, for Wilde and Russell were not capable of the complex dance challenge. "The 'whip dance' you saw where it was obvious when they cut to me was a complete re-shoot … they had to bring back all those extras to re-do the number because Nick had shot me so close, without an attempt to disguise the 'double.' What a gig!"

Jack Baker, Hal Belfer, Josephine Earl, Kenny Williams and other studio-contracted dance directors supplied movement supervision to many of the films at their respective studios, most often not receiving credit. A waltz here, a hoedown there, and continuing staging for nightclub "thrushes" kept them earning their weekly salaries, without much creative challenge or rewards.

As if the competition of television and the destruction of the film industry itself were not enough, rock 'n' roll then reared its world-shattering head.

Whereas the 1940s had created a group of singing stars who at least attempted to dance (the Andrews Sisters, Doris Day, Jane Powell, Frank Sinatra) the rock 'n' roll decade produced mere singing stars. Elvis Presley moved his hips, but the rest of the stars simply stood and sang. Arthur Knight protested in his *Dance Magazine* review of **Let's Rock** (1958), "Big-screen audiences are introduced to the talents of ... a paralyzing assortment of rock 'n' roll combos — trios, quartets and sextets of shoulder-shrugging, finger-snapping, glassy-eyed youngsters who mouth their inane lyrics with utter incomprehension. Also on hand ... is young Peter Gennaro, charged with the organization of some suitably frantic dances to accompany the vocal gyrations of these teen-age werewolves." Opportunities for dance in the first few rock musicals being produced were limited.

Slow to pick up on this new musical revolution, Hollywood finally began making musicals which capitalized on the current musical trends. Earl Barton, who had danced in the film **Seven Brides for Seven Brothers**, was one of the first to be responsible for creating the dance numbers for such "trendies" as **Rock Around the Clock, Cha-Cha-Cha Boom!**, and **Don't Knock the Rock** (1956), doing his very best to incorporate good dancing into films which dealt with contemporary music forms. *Dance Magazine* (December 1956) recognized his efforts:

> The movies rarely seem to devote much attention to ballroom, or social, dancing. In most pictures, whenever such a dance interlude is inserted it is either a big production number or an opportunity for the hero to tell the heroine that he loves her.... **Cha-Cha-Cha Boom!** (Columbia), like its predecessor **Rock Around the Clock**, is an exception to this neat rule ... it has both topicality and a-typicality to recommend it.... Actually, the dance itself— performed here by Dante DePaulo ... and Sylvia Lewis, who attacks each number as if she had just discovered her hips — the dance is a curious, prancing combination of sexy come-on and staid stand-offishness.... One doesn't dance *with* a partner but *around* him ... at the end of the film, when Perez Prado's frantic calisthenics finally crowd the floor with *cha-cha-ers*, it is as if St. Vitus had suddenly visited the sex-starved inmates of a mental institution.

Usually, the featured rock 'n' roll performers were plopped into the film, statically performing their latest hits, with disgruntled dancers moving uncomfortably behind them.

Alex Romero created Elvis's first — and finest — dance movement in the title tune from **Jailhouse Rock** (1957). After making his film debut in the western drama **Love Me Tender**, this would be Elvis's second musical. Romero simply approached the number from a classic standpoint. He knew that Elvis was capable of dancing, so he conceived the number as a raucous song-and-dance with the male lead (Elvis) fronting a group of excellent male dancers. Although the number is consistently shown to depict Elvis at his best, Romero received no onscreen credit. A letter of apology for the "oversight" from producer Pandro S. Berman printed in *Variety*, December 10, 1957, was supposed to erase Romero's disappointment in not being credited for the film's finest moment.

After that, Elvis's image (and perhaps Colonel Tom Parker's request that Elvis "not move around so much") seemed to inhibit him and the collaboration of future choreographers. Only David Winters could seem to get Elvis rocking in his collaborations with "the king" in the next decade.

An athletic hoedown from **The Second Greatest Sex**, Universal's 1955 attempt to get into MGM's **Seven Brides for Seven Brothers** market (choreographed by Lee Scott).

The film musical was at the crossroads. The once-popular musical form itself had changed, budgets were tightened, the dancing choruses were smaller and the imagination harnessed.

Popular music continued to offer dance possibilities. Scopitone, a type of rear-projection screen meant to replace the non-visual juke box in restaurants and bars, allowed choreographers some work, creating musical numbers for popular singing stars of the day. The fad did not enjoy immense popularity, but it would re-emerge as the music videos of the '80s.

LeRoy Prinz continued to stage his old-fashioned "proscenium-locked parades" at Warner Bros.; Twentieth Century–Fox refused to experiment with book musicals; and the minor studios (Monogram, PRC, Republic, and Eagle-Lion) had fallen into financial troubles, so the high output of the '40s slowed to a dribble in the '50s.

But that dribble was filled with classics.

Despite the "special" awards to Astaire and Kelly, the Academy of Motion Picture Arts and Sciences continued to ignore annual nominations for dance creations. "The Academy has not *yet* found reason to give a yearly award for the best dancing or dance direction — a reflection of the general attitude prevalent in the film industry toward the importance of dance and dancers" (Arthur Knight, *Dance Magazine*, August, 1954).

In 1956, James Selva — the head of Selva and Sons, a manufacturer of dance shoes and supplies — through his publication *Dancer's Notebook*, and a group called Dance Alliance, once again tried to talk the academy into adding two new categories to their annual awards: "best dancer" and "best choreography." Petitions with over 15,000 signatures arrived at the academy before their December 10, 1957, Board of Governor's meeting. Nevertheless, the board voted unanimously against the proposal.

Arthur Knight once again expressed his frustrations in his March 1958 *Dance Magazine* "Dance in the Movies" column:

> Perhaps it might be pertinent to ask who made the greater contribution to the artistic success of a musical film (the basis for the Academy's Awards), its choreographer or, say its music arranger? Last year **The King and I** walked off with five major awards, among them an Oscar to Alfred Newman and Ken Darby for "best scoring, musical." But nothing at all went to Jerome Robbins, whose ballet sequence, *The Small House of Uncle Thomas*, was not only the high-point of the picture but a high-point of the entire cinematic year.... Does it really make any difference if a dancer or a choreographer receives an Oscar? The answer is that it does. Quite apart from the personal prestige which makes Oscar the most coveted prize in the industry, there is also an implicit recognition of dance itself as an integral part of film production—as integral as set design or sound recording.

At the end of the lengthy column, Knight printed the address of the academy and urged readers to write in protest, "Enough letters from you, the audience, the ticket-buyers, may force its Board of Governors to reconsider their unfortunate position, their failure to provide any suitable recognition for dance achievement in what is at once one of the most popular and characteristic of American film forms."

As of the writing of this book, choreographers still have not been recognized for excellence on a regular basis by the AMPAS.

Selected Filmography

An American in Paris (Gene Kelly) MGM, 1951, Video:MGM/UA—Kelly makes all of his experimentation and daring pay off in one of the most glorious ballets ever conceived for the camera—plus "I Got Rhythm" and "By Strauss," two "charm" pieces for Kelly which bridge the ages.

The Best Things in Life Are Free (Rod Alexander, Bill Foster) Fox, 1956—Alexander scores with a wonderful jazz ballet for Sheree North and Jacques d'Amboise to "Birth of the Blues."

Carousel (Rod Alexander, Agnes DeMille) Fox, 1956, Video:CBS/Fox—Another peek at greatness with DeMille's restaged *Louise's Ballet* plus Alexander's original shenanigans for "June Is Bustin' Out All Over," which nearly busts the screen with its Michael Kidd–like energy.

Damn Yankees (Bob Fosse) WB, 1958, Video: Warners—One of Fosse's stage masterworks rethought for the camera, and the only complete film record we have of Gwen Verdon's magnificence ... plus a chance to watch Fosse dance with her in "Who's Got the Pain?"

Easy to Love (Busby Berkeley) MGM, 1953, Video:MGM/UA—Berkeley proves the width of his creativity with a water-ski number for Esther Williams which is soaring and moving, plus charm-

ing staging for Tony Martin and some little old ladies in "That's What a Rainy Day Is For."

The 5,000 Fingers of Dr. T (Eugene Loring) Col, 1953, Video:Col—Once again, Loring is in Freudland with some of the most imaginative dream/dance sequences on film.

French Can Can—aka **Only the French Can** (Claude Grandjean) United Motion Picture Org, 1956, Video:Interama—In acclaimed French director Jean Renoir's only musical, Grandjean fully integrates inventive and raucous can-can variations that build until they literally burst through posters. His other French music hall sequences are steeped in period and character.

Gentlemen Prefer Blondes (Jack Cole) Fox, 1953, Video:CBS/Fox—Cole's characteristic "girly" movements fit like a glove on Marilyn Monroe, and his concept for "Diamonds Are a Girl's Best Friend" creates a classic number—imitated by Madonna in her music video "Material Girl"—and helps to define Monroe's on-screen charisma.

The Girl Most Likely (Gower Champion) RKO, 1957, Video:United Home Video—Gower's "Balboa" number is one of the most having-fun, splashing, jumping, soaring romps in filmed dance history.

Give a Girl a Break (Gower Champion, Stanley Donen, Bob Fosse, Bill Foster) MGM, 1953, Video:MGM/UA — A real dance treat, filled with Champion's inventiveness from beginning to end … and a delight to see Champion and Bob Fosse together.

Hit the Deck (Ann Miller, Hermes Pan) MGM, 1955, Video:MGM/UA — Simply good clean fun. Sassy Ann whips through a couple of jazzy pieces, and Pan's overall musical staging is charming — including a "Fun House" duo for Debbie Reynolds and Russ Tamblyn that echoes his Academy Award–winning number for Fred Astaire, George Burns, and Gracie Allen in **Damsel in Distress**.

The "I Don't Care" Girl (Jack Cole, Seymour Felix) Fox, 1953 — Finally some serious dancing for Mitzi Gaynor supplied by Cole in some bizarre musical number concepts which seem to be from another (much better) film.

It's Always Fair Weather (Stanley Donen, Gene Kelly) MGM, 1955, Video:MGM/UA — Kelly, Dan Dailey, and Michael Kidd combine to create remarkable "male bonding" sequences before the term existed. Dancing on trash can lids, roller skates, and taxi rooftops, the dances constantly soar and surprise. Kelly's superb use of the widescreen format is a must-see.

Jailhouse Rock (Alex Romero) MGM, 1957, Video:MGM/UA — The title song is the best number Elvis ever did on film, unfortunately never improved upon — nor matched — during the rest of his film career.

Just for You (Helen Tamaris) Par, 1952, Video: Par — Modern dance and Broadway great Tamaris is handed two of the strangest concepts for musical numbers on record — a ballet about a bullfighter and his temptations, performed to Jane Wyman singing "Maiden of Guadalupe," and a by-the-lake romp by dozens of schoolgirls and that nifty song-and-dance gal, Ethel Barrymore. Ouch! This one you gotta see.

The King and I (Jerome Robbins) Fox, 1956, Video:CBS/Fox — All right, **The Small House of Uncle Thomas** is one of the greatest dance pieces in the history of the world, but check out the staging of the "March of the Siamese Children" if you want to see movement, music, rhythm, charm, and character that will bring tears to your eyes.

Kiss Me Kate (Bob Fosse, Ann Miller, Hermes Pan) MGM, 1953, Video:MGM/UA — Pan creates some smashing dance sequences for Ann Miller and

Tommy Rall, and Fosse's style is introduced in "From This Moment On," a fat piece of dance.

Les Girls (Jack Cole, Gene Kelly) MGM, 1957, Video:MGM/UA — Cabaret sensations that never existed in real life — except for Cole's cabaret shows. The only regret is that Kelly didn't stop being the boy next door for a minute and try more of Cole's isolations and funk.

Million Dollar Mermaid (Busby Berkeley, Audrene Brier) MGM, 1952, Video:MGM/UA — The Berkeley magic takes to the water and the air, creating Esther Williams' most memorable image — Venus rising from the water, surrounded by sparklers. Buzz, you beautifully crazy guy!

Miss Sadie Thompson (Lee Scott) Col, 1953, Video:Col — Scott adds the sensuality missing from the rest of this filmed version of *Rain* with his steamy "The Heat Is On" for Rita Hayworth, surrounded by sweating, hollering Marines.

My Sister Eileen (Bob Fosse) Col, 1955, Video:Col — Fosse on his own on film for the first time, making Janet Leigh and Betty Garrett twirl and appeal — plus a challenge dance between Fosse and the underappreciated Tommy Rall which defies description.

Oklahoma! (Agnes DeMille, Gene Nelson) UA, 1955, Video:CBS/Fox — The world finally got to see what all the shouting had been about over DeMille's landmark work. It was worth the wait. A masterpiece is captured on film for all time.

On the Riviera (Jack Cole) Fox, 1951 — Inventive, bizarre musical concepts by Cole, well performed by Rod Alexander, Danny Kaye, Ethel Martin, Matt Mattox, and Gwen Verdon.

The Pajama Game (Bob Fosse) WB, 1957, Video: Warners — Hooray! Fosse's remarkable work for the Broadway stage lovingly captured on film for the ages — and the bonus is watching Carol Haney add fun to sex.

Picnic (Miriam Nelson) Col, 1955, Video:Col — What do you remember from this film? The steamy dance that Kim Novak and William Holden do at the lake, right? That's film choreography.

Red Garters (Nick Castle) Par, 1954, Video:Par — In the only stylized Western musical on film, Nick Castle brings an infectious sense of joy and energy to the numbers.

Royal Wedding (Fred Astaire, Nick Castle) MGM, 1951, Video:MGM/UA — Astaire figures out how

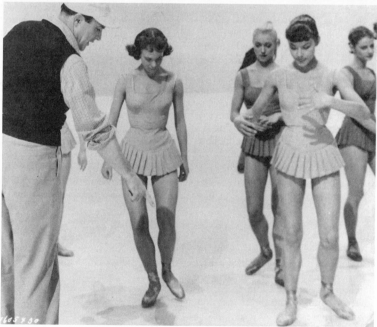

Top: Dan Dailey, Gene Kelly and Michael Kidd present themselves to David Burns at the end of "March! March!" in **It's Always Fair Weather** (choreographed by Kelly and Stanley Donen, MGM, 1955). ***Bottom:*** Gene Kelly instructs young ballerinas for "Dance Me a Song," a deleted sequence from Kelly's 1956 MGM all-dance film **Invitation to the Dance**.

Even "The King" dances! Clark Gable whirls Jean Willes around, as Eleanor Parker looks on in **The King and Four Queens** (UA, 1956 — unfortunately choreographer unknown).

to dance on the ceiling in this technical milestone while Castle helps the hard-working Jane Powell look like a real dancer in some breezy, bright numbers.

Salome (Asoka, Valerie Bettis, Lee Scott) Col, 1953, Video:Col — Bettis and Scott supply modern techniques and eroticism for Hayworth's "Dance of the Seven Veils" in this otherwise tepid biblical epic.

The Second Greatest Sex (Lee Scott) Univ, 1956 — Scott's tribute to **Seven Brides** proves his remark-

able talent in this low-budget pleaser. Where is the video, MCA/Universal?

Seven Brides for Seven Brothers (Michael Kidd) MGM, 1954, Video:MGM/UA — Who said men don't dance? Kidd proved they do — and still rate cheers in movie houses throughout the world. His scenario for "The Barn Raising Dance" has more exposition, character, wit, and energy than the entire script. A landmark dance epic in all respects.

She's Working Her Way Through College (Gene Nelson, LeRoy Prinz) WB, 1952 — Gene Nelson's gymnastic number in the college gym clears the way for Michael Kidd, **Footloose**, and a whole new soaring acrobatic style of dance.

Silk Stockings (Fred Astaire, Eugene Loring, Hermes Pan) MGM, 1957, Video:MGM/UA — The Astaire man just never stopped, and Pan and Loring surround, support, and supplement him and Cyd Charisse with primo treasures.

Singin' in the Rain (Stanley Donen, Gene Kelly) MGM, 1952, Video:MGM/UA — Despite raves for the ***Broadway Ballet***, its the staging, filming, and performance by Kelly of the title tune that make this film a classic, plus some sensational tap and comedy offerings from the underrated Donald O'Connor.

Small Town Girl (Busby Berkeley, Willie Covan, Ann Miller, Alex Romero) MGM, 1953, Video:MGM/UA — Very unusual numbers: Bobby Van hopping for three minutes, and Ann Miller tapping amidst disembodied arms. (André Previn remembered the filming of this number in his autobiography: "As usual, Buzz was endlessly patient and solicitous of all the technical people, the light movers, the camera pullers, the track layers, and almost completely incognizant of the human travail required. It was a scene worthy of Fritz Lang's **Metropolis**.")

There's No Business Like Show Business (Robert Alton, Jack Cole) Fox, 1954, Video:CBS/Fox — It was called "garish, overblown and lumbering" by critics, but as a kid I saw this flick 17 times, and I still pull out the video to get a "good old days" fix. In this grandaddy of Irving Berlin songfests, Alton creates graceful and gorgeous production numbers while Cole almost sends Monroe over the edge of her limitations — and good taste — in "Heat Wave," aiding me and several million other young lads toward puberty.

Three for the Show (Gower Champion, Jack Cole) Col, 1955, Video:Col — Cole's love of commedia dell'arte and men running with chandeliers peaks in this one, but Grable outdoes Monroe's "Heat Wave" in "How Come You Do Me Like You Do?" thanks to the master.

Three Little Words (Fred Astaire, Hermes Pan) MGM, 1950, Video:MGM/UA — Two numbers with Vera-Ellen and Astaire ("Mr. and Mrs. Hoofer at Home" and "Thinking of You") are worth the price of admission to this tepid bio-pic.

Wabash Avenue (Billy Daniel) Fox, 1950 — Daniel pumps up the volume on Grable and makes her sizzle as she never has before.

THE 1960s

Hollywood's new sixties look at reality and the ever-growing youth rebellion finally made the movie musical obsolete, and dance on film was in chaos. Arthur Knight titled the December 1962 installment of his monthly "Dance in the Movies" article in *Dance Magazine* "The Year They Almost Stopped Dancing."

In this new world people simply did not burst into song and dance. On film, they now defied authority, grovelled in lower-class lifestyles, searched for truth, and stabbed young women in the shower. Ethan Mordden, in *Medium Cool*, his excellent analysis of the films of the 1960s, astutely wrote: "The blockbuster musical was out of reach. The form itself had grown too big for its public, and too tame. Moviegoers didn't want Lee Marvin creditably getting through 'Wandrin' Star.' That's a party turn, not a musical. A musical is Astaire and Garland doing 'A Couple of Swells.' But that was over."

Terry McMillan wrote how her generation felt about musical films while growing up in the '60s: "Sometimes we would mimic people like Doris Day and Fred Astaire and laugh like crazy because they were always so damn happy while they sang and danced.... What I hated more than anything was when in the middle of a movie the white people always had to start singing and dancing to get their point across." To be able to sing and dance was not a goal for young people any longer. To the new rock 'n' roll generation, white men could still jump — but they suddenly couldn't sing.

Nevertheless, choreographers continued to contribute what they could to the richness of films. Rarely were they now put under contract to the studios to stage musical numbers or movement for dialogue scenes, or to handle dance departments or classes. As the system itself buckled and crashed, studios were eliminating their contract players, so the need for a talent school did not exist. Twentieth Century–Fox continued with Hal Belfer as resident dance director for its talent pool, while Tommy Mahoney created musical sequences for Walt Disney's films, television show, and new theme park, Disneyland.

With the box office success of the Broadway transfers of the '50s (**Oklahoma**, **Carousel**, **The King and I**, etc.) the big dance movies of the '60s were again adapted from Broadway hits. Proven stage successes seemed to be the only musical formula that the crumbling studios would risk producing. And with the Broadway transfer, stage choreographers, rather than Hollywood-based dancemakers, were given the opportunity to translate the dance to film.

Alex Romero, who had collaborated with the best (Robert Alton, Gene Kelly, Jack Cole) during his apprenticeship as a film assistant, was now under contract to MGM as dance director and was assigned most of their original musicals. He was not, however, given the opportunity to translate a major stage success to film. In an interview with writer Roy Clark for *Dance Magazine* (September 1962), he discussed the many differences beween choreographing for films and for Broadway:

> The movie is cast according to box office appeal.... The choreographer is never consulted before casting... (but) told what to do, how long a number can run, and then, when all is through, he may well be in for a lot of surprises.... Very few Hollywood choreographers have a clause in their contracts permitting them to call the shots [Romero, however, did have that power].... It is considered that too much dance will weaken the plot.... Hollywood choreographers have to contend with reaction shots in practically every dance number. These are views that cut away from the dance to a person or persons watching it ... in the majority of cases, the editor picks the high spot of the choreography for the break.... Eighty percent of Hollywood's dance jobs are not ... dance numbers at all.... In Hollywood the choreographer is responsible for a specific amount of footage of film. His job begins and ends there. The New York choreographer has a responsibility to the entire production. Obviously the two cannot be compared. Each appreciates the other's values, and can study the other's techniques.

The stage choreographers who were given the "plum" of translating a stage success to film had to contend with all that Romero talked about — and more — with varying degrees of success. Transfers such as **West Side Story** (Jerome Robbins, assisted by Tommy Abbott, Maggie Banks, Howard Jeffrey, and Tony Mordente, 1961), **Gypsy** (Robbins' original stage work adapted to the screen by Robert Tucker, 1962), **The Music Man** (Onna White with Tommy Panko, 1962), **Bye Bye Birdie** (White, 1963), **Oliver!** (White with Panko, 1968), **The Unsinkable Molly Brown** (Peter Gennaro, 1964), **A Funny Thing Happened on the Way to the Forum** (Jack Cole's original work adapted to the screen by George and Ethel Martin, 1966), **Half a Sixpence** (Gillian Lynne, 1967), **How to Succeed in Business Without Really Trying** (Bob Fosse's original work adapted to the screen by Dale Moreda, 1968), **Sweet Charity** (Bob Fosse, 1967), **Funny Girl** (Herbert Ross, 1968), and **Hello, Dolly!** (Michael Kidd, 1969) represented the major musical theater dance output of the decade. The only film choreographers given a

Bye Bye Birdie (Columbia, 1963): Bobby Rydell and Ann-Margret lead the kids in Onna White's "Cool" choreo.

chance to reinterpret other people's original stage work for the screen were Charles O'Curran (**Bells Are Ringing**, 1960), Jack Baker (**Paint Your Wagon**, 1969), and the ever-creative Hermes Pan: **Can Can** (1960), **Flower Drum Song** (1961), **My Fair Lady** (1964), and **Finian's Rainbow** (1968).

West Side Story allowed Jerome Robbins to take his landmark stage concept and adapt it to the screen with great critical and box-office success, as well as an Oscar for his genius. Robbins adapted and revised his original stage work for the film, as well as creating new choreography for the screen. His previous film work had been restaging **The King and I** for the screen, and when he started his second film, he had great reservations:

> I'll admit that I have resisted Hollywood for years. I don't find most Hollywood musicals to be of a serious nature, and that's putting it mildly. Dance hasn't been very successful on the screen. My feeling is that dance calls for a reference — that is, a limitation of space, a frame, and three dimensions.... What the audience does get, most of the time, is sex, charm, and daring, but not the genuine energy that dance should have. I'd make an exception in behalf of Michael Kidd's ballets in **Seven Brides for Seven Brothers**. Astaire? He's all to himself, of course, and what really comes through, I'd say, is his personality [*Dance Magazine*, October 1960].

With **West Side Story** Robbins learned how to collaborate with the camera. Also serving as codirector, he filled the screen with dancing and dramatics never seen before — or since. After the film won 10 Academy Awards, the revised trailer featured Robbins' contributions with, "thrill to the sensational dancing by internationally famed choreographer Jerome Robbins."

West Side Story, perhaps the most honored and successful dance film of all time, took the "on location" experiments that Gene Kelly and Stanley Donen had done in the forties and fifties and expanded on them, making the cracked sidewalks of New York sizzle with sensational movement. Again using Kelly's groundwork of masculine performance and character, the dancing men were portrayed as brave, tough, and macho and the male cast contained eight future film choreographers (Tommy Abbott, Bob Banas, José DeVega, Tony Mordente, Jaime Rogers, Andre Tayir, Bobby Thompson, and David Winters). The young people of the day could relate to the revamped *Romeo and Juliet* tale of misunderstood youth, struggling against the conventions and old rules of the unfeeling adults around them. It was as if the James Dean icons of the fifties were now singing and dancing against the wind, instead of howling at it. And the dancing was simply spectacular. ("Perhaps the most striking aspect of it is the sweep and vitality of the dazzling Jerome Robbins dances.... This pulsating persistence of rhythm all the way through the film — in the obviously organized dances — gives an overbeat of eloquence to the graphic realism of this film and sweeps it along"— Bosley Crowther, *New York Times*.)

Stanley Kauffmann titled his October 1961 review "West Side Glory" and continued, "Here at last is a film in which dance is not stuck in like raisins in a cake, and neither is it a photographed record, like most ballet films. The whole work was *composed* from beginning to end in terms of its music and its movements. Robbins is one of the few ballet choreographers who are interested in commenting on contemporary American life."

While the theatre and dance worlds praised Robbins' brilliance, members of the film community have not been so gracious. Associate producer Saul Chaplin recently wrote in his autobiography *The Golden Age of Movie Musicals and Me*:

> I attended rehearsals, as usual, and was both amazed and appalled by what I witnessed. Jerry was by far the most exciting choreographer I had ever watched. He seemed to have an endless stream of exciting ideas. He would try one, then replace it with another.... He would then come up with something that was even more thrilling. He had the most facile, quicksilver mind I had ever seen at work. At the same time, he was such an insane perfectionist that it was impossible for any of the dancers to achieve the standards he demanded immediately. To make matters worse, he had a very low tolerance point ... he heaped such verbal abuse on the dancers that the place took on the atmosphere of a concentration camp. They didn't dance out of joy, they danced out of fear.

Regarding the never-ending question of *who* (Robert Wise or Jerome Robbins) directed *what* on the film, Chaplin contends that Robbins shot "The Prologue," "America," "Cool" and "Something's Coming." At one point Robbins was fired for having to re-record much of the score because he had changed the tempi, slipping badly behind in the schedule and filming too much unusable footage. "His only defender seemed to be Robert Wise," Chaplin wrote. "He proved utterly impractical as a film-maker and that's unfortunate. With his incredibly creative mind and keen eye, he unquestionably would have been a major force in the art of the cinema.... Yet he is the only person I have ever met in my entire career that I vowed never to work with again."

Peter Gennaro, recreating his stage hit *Unsinkable Molly Brown*, was interviewed during filming by *Dance Magazine* (August 1964) and spoke about his second Hollywood chore: "Having Chuck Walters, an ex-dancer and choreographer, as my director was a joy. He was appreciative, understanding and yet gave me full freedom.... I never planned being a choreographer. I started to teach while I was dancing and one thing led to another.... I've gotten several offers

Choreographing a rock fight was only one of Jerome Robbins' challenges in the musical landmark **West Side Story** (UA, 1961). Front row (L to R): Bobby Thompson, Andre Tayir, Jay Norman, Rudy Del Campo. Back row: Jose DeVega, Nick Covacevich (aka Navarro), Jaime Rogers, Eddie Verso (photo courtesy of Bobby Thompson).

to do more. But I don't want to do just anything. In fact, I'm not sure that I want to do anything other than TV now." Despite the success of Debbie Reynolds' bravura performance and Gennaro's work, he returned to the stage and television work he preferred and never made another film.

Another successful stage innovator, Onna White, received a rave review for her first film work in **The Music Man** by *Dance Magazine*, July 1962:

> Onna White, also from the original production, was brought out to re-create her choreography for the camera. And she has risen admirably to the challenge. Her dancers seem to be everywhere at once — marching, gliding, cartwheeling about the huge sets with the utmost abandon. The camera rolls back as they advance, rushes in for a detail, or perches high in the air to reveal a special pattern. The bubbling vitality, elan, and humor that Onna White brings to her dances is something that Hollywood needs today far more than Broadway. We hope she will stay awhile.

She did stay, and went on to garner one of the few Oscars for choreography, a special award for **Oliver!** in 1968.

Another major stage-to-screen transfer during the decade was **Finian's Rainbow** (1968); however, it cannot be included in the above-mentioned successes. Although the 1947 hit show had great difficulty in finally reaching the screen, the entire industry had high hopes for the project, Fred Astaire's last screen musical. The choreography by Hermes Pan was edited, and often completely eliminated, by the director, up-and-coming "wunderkind" Francis Ford Coppola, who was doing his first screen musical and trying to adapt it to some of the changing camera and editing techniques of the time. Because Coppola felt that the dances were "too dancey," Pan was fired from the project and replaced by Claude Thompson and, in some cases, improvising cast members. In a May 1984 article from *Dance Magazine* about Astaire and his many contributions to dance on film, **Finian's Rainbow** is pegged as

> The Apocalypse ... the dances generally are presented with the same impatient insensitivity as in ... **Flying Down to Rio** of thirty-five years earlier. They are a phantasmagoria of arty angles, disorienting and purposely mismatched cuts, and abrupt uninformative close-ups. Dance is photographed and edited as if it were a car chase in a Roger Corman movie. It is the new (old) Coppola approach, not Astaire's, that dominates Hollywood films now.

Another former stage success filmed during the decade was **Billy Rose's Jumbo**. The musical numbers were staged by Busby Berkeley, with aerial sequences created by circus legend Barbette. Originally produced onstage in 1935 as the last production at New York's famed Hippodrome Theater (with Barbette in the cast), it finally arrived on film in 1963. With very little actual dancing, **Jumbo** contains some of the most successful musical sequences in the widescreen format, due to its director, former choreographer Charles Walters, and the imagination of Barbette and Berkeley. Arthur Knight wrote in his regular "Dance in the Movies" column in *Dance Magazine*, December 1962:

> ...under Charles Walters' bubbling direction, the entire film seems to dance. It is so exhilarating to see again a picture that moves, that soars, that swings high with the aerialists, and circles with the equestriennes, that mingles with the clowns, and goes behind the bars for the lion act ... no dancers, all of them move well — they seem to have created no problem for Busby Berkeley, an old hand at this sort of thing, when it came to integrating them into the lively and elaborate circus routines. He makes them *look* as if they are dancing ... the result is irresistible.

With **Sweet Charity** (1969), the ever-experimenting Bob Fosse brought Gwen Verdon with him to the project to coach Shirley MacLaine in the title role Verdon had done so successfully on the stage. Fosse did all he could to make the project a screen translation. In an extensive article by Viola Hegyi Swisher in *Dance Magazine*, he discussed the various adaptations and changes he felt he needed to make for the screen:

> Most often the camera called for changes in forms and patterns ... other changes came about because I thought I could do a little better than before. In this work you keep developing and something once very difficult becomes easy after you've grown a bit.... More and more during filming, as I got used to the mobility of the camera I took advantage of it. And now I'm least satisfied with the things I shot just as they were in the stage show.

Two other stage-to-screen transfers (**Camelot**, 1967, and **Paint Your Wagon**, 1969) nearly eliminated all of the dancing. The director of both films, Joshua Logan, seemed to have an aversion to dance; his earlier **South Pacific** (1958) starred one of the best dancers in film musicals, Mitzi Gaynor, but mostly harnessed her talents in uninventive musical staging. Broadway-based

Choreographer-cum-cigarette: Bob Fosse coaches Shirley MacLaine for "If They Could See Me Now" from **Sweet Charity** (1968).

choreographer Buddy Schwab bravely worked on **Camelot**, trying to add a dance vocabulary to the endless, mind-numbing, widescreen closeups of its principals, Vanessa Redgrave's naive wish to "improvise" most of her movement, and Logan's heavy-handed direction. Schwab satirically wrote "Choreographed?" next to the film title on a questionnaire he filled out for this book before his untimely death.

In the case of **Paint Your Wagon**, which had found its success primarily due to Agnes DeMille's rousing "Americana" choreography in the first place, the lack of dance was particularly unfortunate. Although DeMille was announced to create the film version for MGM in Cinerama in 1953, Jack Baker was eventually assigned the task, over a decade later, of organizing what little movement or staging Logan retained when the property finally reached the screen. He did not comment on his unchallenging chore of trying to add movement to the walking, swaying, meandering gold miners.

There were a few original big budget screen musicals during the '60s which contained varying degrees of dance opportunities: **Pepe** (Eugene Loring and Alex Romero, 1960), **The Wonderful World of the Brothers Grimm** (Alex Romero, 1962), **Thoroughly Modern Millie** (Joe Layton, 1967), **The Happiest Millionaire** (Marc Breaux and Dee Dee Wood, 1967), **Inside Daisy Clover** (1966), **Doctor Dolittle** and **Goodbye Mister Chips** (Herbert Ross, 1967 and 1969), **The Night They Raided Minsky's** (Danny Daniels, 1968), **The One and Only Original Family Band** (Hugh Lambert, 1968), and **Star!** (Michael Kidd, 1968).

While working on **Doctor Dolittle**, Herb Ross was given ample print to express many of his views on dance, actors and film in *Dance Magazine* (December 1967): "For the theatre and movies, much of my work has been in the area of movement for non-dancers.... Part of the way I approach the problem is by trying to make the actor comfortable in the kind of movement that comes most easily to him. Then I can slowly go further and further" (the same approach that animal trainers use to create their acts). **Dolittle** would eventually have sixteen musical sequences "as well as the 'lead-ins' and 'lead-outs' to these.... In fact, about ninety minutes, or approximately half of what appears on the screen, will have been directed by him. 'But,' says Ross, 'there is no specific dance action in the entire film. We've not yet found a title that really explains a job like that. Yet film and theatre choreographers do it all the time.'"

Funny Girl (1968), with its multiple onstage musical sequences, offered more dance opportunity to Ross. Receiving the billing "director of musical numbers" in an attempt to describe to the audience the scope of his work, he was perhaps at his most innovative during *offstage* musical sequences, as he explained to *Dance Magazine* writer Lydia Joel (December 1967):

> There are many possible approaches to staging musicals for the theatre and for the movies. Some directors like to stress the differences between the spoken and the sung or danced sections. I belong to those who believe that the musical is moving in the direction of increased integral elements and should continue to do so more and more.... There are a number of us knocking ourselves out trying to integrate mime, dance movement, acting, and singing so that one is never conscious of numbers going on and off. I was sure, for instance, that the success of **West Side Story** would make a difference in the films that followed it. I hoped it would pave the way for more imaginative musicals. I even expected that dancers would help change theatre and film. But the truth is that there are still only a handful of writers, producers, directors, and especially, those men who have the final okay, who are sufficiently aware and flexible to see how dance can be of help to them.

As Michael Kidd had filled the screen with new energy, vitality and dazzling widescreen usage in the 1950s, his former assistants, Marc Breaux and Dee Dee Wood, carried the torch

Sally Ann Howes and Dick Van Dyke front an energetic group of British dancers (Antonia Ellis is to the left of Howes) in the "Toot Sweet" number from **Chitty Chitty Bang Bang** (Marc Breaux and Dee Dee Wood, UA, 1968).

into the '60s, creating sensational dance sequences for **Mary Poppins** (1964) and **Chitty Chitty Bang Bang** (1968), two original screen musicals. Arthur Knight's October 1964 *Dance Magazine* review of **Mary Poppins** praised the team: "For all these glittering excellences, it is still the musical sequences — and particularly the dance sequences — that lift **Mary Poppins** into a very special class ... the muscular acrobatics demanded by Marc Breaux and Dee Dee Wood in their choreography of the film's two spectacular ballets." Their dances strutted, swirled and soared — always with a whimsical sense of humor. Two of their best numbers ("Step in Time" from **Poppins** and "Me Old Bamboo" from **Chitty**) were fronted by agile comic and dancer Dick Van Dyke in a perfect collaboration of creators and executor.

When **The Sound of Music** (again Breaux and Wood) became the box-office champ of 1965, the film studios, in their panic for revenue, believed that bigger was better and began creating huge films with huge budgets. These monsters, usually offered in road-show engagements complete with intermission and inflated prices, tried to turn movie-going into an "event" rather than the casual part of the weekly schedule it had been for Americans during the forties and early fifties.

Hello, Dolly! (1969) was one of the hoped-for blockbuster stage-to-screen transfers of the decade. Plagued by troubles and a soaring budget, its progress was widely chronicled by a negative press in the beginnings of the how-much-it-costs-and-how-much-trouble-it-is-in advance media coverage of today's films. With Barbra Streisand, the only genuine musical superstar of the decade, in a role which many critics felt was miscast, rumblings of unhappy costar Walter Matthau, Gene Kelly directing his biggest budget musical, and a mind-boggling (at the time) budget being used for the biggest exterior set ever built on the financially panicked Twentieth Century–Fox backlot, choreographer Michael Kidd also experienced his share of the bad rap.

In a *Life* magazine cover article of February 14, 1969, illustrated by gorgeous color photos but written in flagrantly negative prose focusing on the production's problems, some of the classic confrontations of choreographer and various collaborators were detailed in the general press for the first time. During rehearsal of the title number in the elaborate "Harmonia Gardens" set with Streisand and the male dancing chorus, the train on Streisand's dress was deemed too long and too heavy. Costume designer Irene Sharaff was called to the set to watch a run-through:

> Again both Streisand and the dancers tripped on the train of the dress, "See what I mean?" said Kidd. Sharaff: "No Michael, I don't see what the problem is." "It's simple, Irene, Barbara trips on it, the dancers trip on it." "Perhaps if you changed the movements, Michael, the dancers wouldn't step on it." "The dress is so heavy Barbra won't be able to kick at the end of the number." "But Michael," Irene Sharaff said as if to a child, "is the kick necessary?" "I think it is, yeah," Kidd said. He seemed unfazed by Irene Sharaff's recalcitrance. When she suggested they wait until the dress is finished, he answered, "Sure, Irene … and if the dress doesn't work, there'll be some changes made."

Production designer John DeCuir was then summoned to battle about the restrictions to the pattern of movement that the layout of his restaurant setting created for Kidd. Defending his design with, "But, Michael, the set is supposed to be a restaurant," DeCuir was challenged by Kidd with, "And I'm saying, John, that people aren't going to pay $3.50 a ticket to see someone gumming down a lamb chop."

As the studios tightened their financial belts, choreographers were forced to find work on a per-film basis. It became a struggle to the new up-and-coming choreographers who wanted to work on film. Most of the promising, talented artists of the time (Rod Alexander, Tony Charmoli, Ernie Flatt, Peter Gennaro, Tom Hansen, Jonathon Lucas, Jack Regas, Bob Sidney, and James Starbuck) found that television offered them an outlet for their creativity — and a constant paycheck. With such weekly programs as "Your Hit Parade," "Your Show of Shows," "Omnibus" and the musical-variety shows of Dinah Shore, Perry Como, and others, the demands for new concepts and choreography for musical numbers kept them busy and made their work available to millions. Television also offered employment to the legions of dancers who had come to Hollywood for the shrinking film jobs. The choreographers of the period managed to do a few films, but the quality and the challenge of the films they worked on were limited.

While financially panicked Hollywood refused to experiment with all-dance films, Europe continued to produce them. In 1962 **The Lovers of Teruel**, choreographed by Milko Sparemblek, delighted — and shocked — filmgoers with its sensuality and surreal settings. From Spain, **Los Tarantos** (1964) exploded on the screen, giving audiences a final chance to see the legendary Carmen Amaya in her most extensive appearance on film and introducing the power and creativity of the next king of Spanish dance, Antonio Gades.

Romeo and Juliet (1966), showcasing the choreography of Kenneth MacMillan for the first time on film and introducing the newest ballet sensation Rudolph Nureyev, partnering the legendary Dame Margot Fonteyn, came from Britain, with Jacqueline Maskey writing in *Dance Magazine*,

> A number of people who were less than rapturous in their reception of Kenneth MacMillan's full length ballet for the Royal Ballet (and there were *quite* a few) will be pleasantly surprised by the film version. And not because the ballet has been re-worked for the camera eye or freed from its stage connections … it is the nature of the camera, functioning as a selective eye, which enhances…. Moments of emotional climax are given greater points by the close-up; sprawling pageantry is made more orderly by confinement within a frame. The camera delivers specifically to the spectator moments of which he can be only generally aware in the theatre.

From France, **Black Tights** (1962) featured four of Roland Petit's innovative stage pieces from the repertoire of his Ballet de Paris: ***The Diamond Cruncher***, ***The Devil in 24 Hours***, ***Cyrano De Bergerac*** and ***Carmen***. *The Motion Picture Guide* praises the film: "You must be a balletomane to be able to sit through this much dance without wanting to get up and do a pirouette yourself, if only to work out the kinks in your legs. Technically brilliant and beautifully danced, **Black Tights** will remain as one of the best of its genre."

France also experimented with the musical form with **The Umbrellas of Cherbourg** (which had no dance, 1964) and **The Young Girls of Rochefort** (which seemed to be all dance, choreographed by Norman Maen, 1967). In the latter, Maen created soaring variations of jazz-based routines for male leads Gene Kelly, George Chakiris, and Grover Dale and what seemed to be the entire population of the little pastel-painted town. Filmed entirely on location, the streets, parks, and public square were alive with British and French dancers in sequences that paid tribute to **On the Town** and **West Side Story**. The casting of two non-dancing, non-singing female leads (sisters Catherine Deneuve and Francoise Dorleac) caused critics to complain, and although **Umbrellas** was a major hit, **Young Girls**, "a tribute to the American musical," was unwelcomed internationally.

Other important dance figures placing their imprint on film for the first time during the decade were American modern innovator Ann Halprin (**Revolution**, 1968) and the groundbreaking African-American ballet pioneer Arthur Mitchell (**The Day the Fish Came Out**, 1967). Along with the aforementioned Kenneth MacMillan and Roland Petit, European ballet figures Dirk Sanders and Maurice Béjart (**Belles et Ballets**, 1960), Jack Carter (**The Masque of the Red Death**, 1964), and Willy Dirtl (**Die Fledermaus**, 1964) participated in film. But it would continue to be the dance world that allowed them to exercise their genius.

Back in the United States, what was left of the film musical was in a state of flux as they tried to grapple with the growing popularity of rock 'n' roll. As Broadway and musical theatre also struggled, it seemed that television (the other "villain") was the only medium able to incorporate the new music, personalities, and philosophy.

Now that American music and social dance had drastically changed with the acceptance of rock 'n' roll into mainstream popularity through the nationwide exposure of radio, recordings, and television, the studios searched for a new formula for their more economically budgeted musical films. The tailored-for-drive-in youth epics from American International Pictures needed choreography, as did Elvis's pelvis. The new musical stars did not dance (and it wasn't considered "cool" to do so) so producers, writers, directors, and choreographers worked at defining the new rock musical form ("Two features have been released spotlighting the Twist and writers have rewritten party scenes in various scripts to include the fad dance" — Roy Clark, *Dance Magazine*, January 1962). Some of the films were a definite throwback to the more traditional style with songs coming out of the situation, music specifically composed for the film, and production numbers. Others presented the star's latest recordings in a performance setting with no relationship to the script or characterization. Sometimes within one film (usually Presley's), both styles were used, mixing ungracefully.

Ludmilla Tcherina and Stevan Grebel in the 1962 French all-dance film **The Lovers of Teruel** (Minarch, choreographed by Milko Sparemblek).

From the very beginning of film, social dance had been included in screen choreography, but the new rock steps and styles were changing commercial choreography itself. The highly popular rock television shows ("American Bandstand," "Soul Train," "Hullabaloo," "Shindig," "Shivaree," "Where the Action Is," etc.) weekly exposed a wide audience to the latest dances created in streets and clubs across the country. Traditional choreography simply did not work to the new music.

On these films, the older choreographers most often acted as dance direcors, arranging and staging the movements that the dancers improvised. Some, such as Hal Belfer, seemed to thrive with the new dance technique demands: "Hal Belfer, chief Watusi consultant on the MGM lot is interviewing dancers who can Frug, Watusi, Swim, Crawl, Twist and do character type dancing" (*Dance Magazine*, March 1965). Budding film choreographers David Winters, Andre Tayir, and Toni Basil entered the scene. They specialized in rock movement and dancing, were contributing prolifically to television's weekly rock 'n' roll shows, and began to contribute to film. They were the first group of dancemakers to actually choreograph rock movement.

The Elvis Presley series at MGM and Paramount used varying amounts of dance, movement, and staging. As part of the formula, Elvis was most often surrounded by a bevy of minimally clad go-go girls, rather than the traditional mixed dancing chorus. When the films had a period or show business setting, male dancers were more amply used. The Presley series was among the last of the traditional musicals produced in America and used a variety of dance directors: Jack Baker, **It Happened at the World's Fair** (1963) and **Spinout** (1966); Earl Barton, **Roustabout** (1964), **Harum Scarum** (1965), and **Frankie and Johnny** (1966); Hal Belfer, **Kissin' Cousins** (1964); Jonathon Lucas, **The Trouble with Girls** (1969); Charles O'Curran, **King Creole** (1958), **G.I. Blues** (1960), **Blue Hawaii** (1961), **Girls! Girls! Girls!** (1962), and **Fun in Acapulco** (1963); Jack Regas, **Paradise, Hawaiian Style** (1966) and **Live a Little, Love a Little** (with Jack Baker, 1968); Alex Romero, **Double Trouble** (1967), and David Winters, **Viva Las Vegas!** (1964), **Tickle Me** (1965), and **Easy Come Easy Go** (with Miriam Nelson, 1967). These films were cranked out like the 1940s musical "B" movies of Monogram, Republic, and PRC.

Ann-Margret, the new female screen sensation of the sixties, had musical talents, so all of her films used dance sequences, usually choreographed by her former dance teacher, David Winters, and coached and refined by her "associate" and friend, Maggie Banks. The male dancers of the time now got a better chance for employment, for if Elvis was framed by nubile beauties, Ann-Margret was usually the center of attention from a group of frenetic males. Winters helped to create her sex-kitten onscreen persona, and later, he would stage and direct her to great live performance success. From a Broadway stage career as a child to a major role in the film **West Side Story**, Winters started teaching dance classes in Hollywood. Attending his classes became the "in" thing for the young actors and actresses of the time (Ann-Margret, Richard Chamberlain, Teri Garr, Joey Heatherton, Julie Newmar) to do, as well as all of the working dancers. Winters' assistants and featured dancers Toni Basil and Anita Mann would go on to successful solo choreographic and directing careers.

Viva Las Vegas! (1964) finally brought the king and the sex kitten together, with Winters channeling the natural combustion into some quintessential rock musical numbers. With veteran musical film director George Sidney at the helm, an ample budget, and a script which melded onstage performance sequences with original songs that actually furthered the plot, **Viva Las Vegas!** came very close to dragging the movie musical into the present.

The AIP **Beach Party** movies (staged by Winters, Jack Baker, Tommy Mahoney) and films starring such new rock sensations as Fabian in **High Time** (Miriam Nelson, 1960), Sonny and Cher in **Good Times** (Andre Tayir, 1967), and Connie Francis in **When the Boys Meet the Girls** (Earl Barton, 1965) challenged the choreographers to test the rock musical genre with their dances and musical staging. Some of the films still called for traditional musical dance sequences while others (with little or no thought or budget for rehearsals) simply used atmosphere wiggling. **When the Boys Meet the Girls**, a remake of **Girl Crazy** starring new pop singer Connie Francis, received a vitriolic review in *Time* magazine (January 21, 1966):

Choreographer Nick Castle gives Ann-Margret a sizzling film musical introduction in "Isn't It Kinda Fun?" from the 1962 remake of **State Fair** (Twentieth Century–Fox), backed by (L to R) Jimmy Huntley, Howard Kreiger, Jack Dodds, Herman Boden, Marc Wilder, Roy Clark, Jack Tygett, and Jerry Staebler.

> In this remake, MGM cooks the goose that laid the golden egg. Rarely have so many charmless performers been assembled. Zing, freshness, warmth, humor and yay-team vitality have been banished — presumably to please a new generation that will never know what it missed.... The brains behind **The Boys** undoubtedly believe that the movie reflects changing tastes, but they seem to confuse updating with down grading.

Choreographer Earl Barton tried his very best to mix contemporary musical staging with one classical song-and-dance production number ("I Got Rhythm") that got the clunky Francis and costar Harve Presnell out of the way so that the chorus could dance. In 1988, writer Kevin Grubb singled out **Head** (Toni Basil, 1968), starring the Monkees: "Even by today's futuristic music video standards, the film boasts fascinating, if technically rough, concepts rooted in movement and psychedelia."

As during the 1940s when jitterbugging specialists were hired for films, go-go dancers were now hired to improvise their dance specialties for the cameras. These dancers came primarily from the discothèques springing up in L.A. and New York and had little or no formal dance training. However, they had a large repertoire of the popular dances of the times (twist, pony, mashed potato, jerk, etc.). Suddenly classically trained dancers were forced to learn all of the latest dance crazes in order to keep themselves employed in film and television.

The new rock 'n' roll choreography was finding a smoother transition with live performers. In Detroit, at the Motown "Talent Factory," Cholly Atkins, former dancer and nightclub star (as half of the famed tap duo Coles and Atkins), was hired to mold, teach, and choreograph for all of the artists under contract. He created a new form of vocal choreography for the groups which changed the face of contemporary choreography. Atkins called it "an organized presentation" and it was smooth, sensual and simple — created to focus attention on the lead singer and the lyrics — while the back-up singers smoothly melded into a continual backdrop of movement. The rising black artists had not yet become film celebrities, but their work can be seen in a variety of "youth" films, in which they appeared as guest artists. Pioneer Atkins would not receive onscreen credit until 1989 (**Tapeheads**), yet his work was often seen on film and television and seriously affected the staging and choreography of the entire genre worldwide from his work with the Supremes, Temptations, Jackson Family, and all of Motown's stars.

In England, Cliff Richard, Britain's most successful pop star, made a series of musicals which aided America's Herbert Ross and Britain's Gillian Lynne in their film careers. These films were a definite throwback to the Hollywood musicals of the 1950s, as England experimented with how to handle its rock stars on film. The musical numbers created by Ross (**The Young Ones**, aka **Wonderful to Be Young**, 1962, and **Summer Holiday**, 1963) and Lynne (**It's a Wonderful Life**, aka **Swinger's Paradise**, 1965) were inventive, polished, and joyful — heralding the career that former ballet dancer Ross would eventually have as a leading film director. It was British director Richard Lester who defined what the rock musical — as well as the music video in the '80s — would become, with his fluid camera work, inventive and irreverent staging, and direction in 1964's groundbreaking Beatles musical **A Hard Day's Night**. The "staging" was done by the camera and in the editing room. Actual dance was not included.

British choreographers began contributing more significantly to dance on film. After merely being asked to mimic Hollywood or Broadway for decades, choreographers Lynne, Gillian Gregory, Norman Maen, and Paddy Stone rose from the dancing ranks to create musical numbers which equaled the best of Hollywood. The standard of excellence among British dancers itself began to rise — leading to their musical theater boom in the 1970s and 1980s.

In the non-musical films of the 1960s, the Love Generation had also appeared on the American scene, so drug-induced hippie orgies needed staging (*Dance Magazine*, May 1967: "Disjointing time through movement in multiple rhythms, Hal Belfer staged a choreographic freakout for Mimsy Farmer in **Riot on Sunset Strip**") and there was still the occasional party scene for choreographers to stage.

Among the dramatic films to need dance sequences, **The King of Kings** (1961), one of the last major biblical epics, incorporated Salome's "Dance of the Seven Veils" as an important part of its scenario. Composer Miklos Rozsa once again wrote in detail about the painful experience in his autobiography *Double Life*:

> The studio had told me not to discuss the dance with [producer Samuel] Bronston, as he wouldn't know anything about it. When we got to Madrid, I tried the writer, but he was very evasive and quickly left town. The director [Nicholas Ray] was even more vague. When pressed, he told me that the choreographer [Betty Utey] was his wife. She had once been a dancer with Hermes Pan ... and, although she had never done any choreography before, felt she could do this. Bronston had found his Salome [Brigid Bazlen] in Chicago. She was a schoolgirl of about sixteen, a bit plump, who, somewhat surprisingly, had never acted or danced before. I was almost in tears. Here was a choreographer who had never choreographed and a dancer who had never danced ... the picture, ... to be fair, had its moments, although Salome's dance wasn't one of them. The poor Chicago schoolgirl simply ran about aimlessly from pillar to post making seductive movements. The first preview was so disastrous that the editor boiled the scene down to a couple of minutes, which of course wrecked the music.

A Hermes Pan Roman orgy sequence in **Cleopatra** (Twentieth Century–Fox, 1963).

One major dramatic film of the decade, **They Shoot Horses, Don't They?** (1969), was based on dance itself: the relentless dance marathons of the 1930s. Choreographed by Tom Panko with technical expertise offered by Noble "Kid" Chissell (an actual marathon dance champion), the entire cast, including stars Jane Fonda, Susannah York, Red Buttons, Gig Young, and Michael Sarrazin, were forced by director (and "sadistic dance master") Sydney Pollack to run around the set each morning before shooting, "to re-create the physical and mental grind of the marathon and heel-and-toe derby ... until their faces and bodies had the look he wanted; a painful mixture of fatigue and frenzy" (*Life*). The realism helped earn Academy Award nominations for director Pollack, actresses Fonda and York, and an Oscar for best supporting actor for Young, as well as painful memories for the scores of dancers who worked on the film. In conversation with the author, dancer John Frayer bitterly remembered, "We all *tried* to get off the picture. Every morning, we would beg to be let go. Oh God, it was a nightmare."

Two films in the late '60s brilliantly displayed the future opportunities for dance in nonmusical films. British director Ken Russell hired Terry Gilbert to add period feeling and sensuality with dance sequences in **Women in Love** (1968), the successful film which made Russell a bankable name in the industry. Russell would continue to collaborate closely with choreographers in his future work. The auspicious teaming of comedy writer–director–star Mel Brooks and choreographer Alan Johnson on **The Producers** (1967) resulted in its hilarious "Springtime for Hitler" production number. While Brooks eventually lampooned everything from racial stereotypes to the classic western and horror film genres, Johnson satirized the non-sensical musical staging of Broadway and films. Their work previewed the successful comedy film-and-dance integration of the following decades: dance as satire.

Busby Berkeley began enjoying a renaissance during the decade. After a retrospective in San Francisco in 1965, his thirties films began to be shown at revival/art houses all over the country as the new generation discovered his "hallucinatory" work, often viewing the films in a hemp-smoke haze and exclaiming, "Far out!" We began to dip into the past for film dance treasures.

Berkeley even appeared as one of the cameo stars (along with Ruby Keeler, Dorothy Lamour, and others) in a bizarre 1970 film, **The Phynx**. Former Berkeley girl Lois Lindsay was also recruited for the chorus and recalled about the filming: "They turned to Buzz and they said, 'Mr. Berkeley, would you give the girls a step, a dance step for an entrance?' Well, Buzz has never danced in his life. Not except for one step he had given us way long ago. And so he turned to us and said, very seriously, 'Okay girls, now we'll make our entrance like this' (a basic tap step). That's all he'd ever done and that's all we ever did" (*People Will Talk*).

At the time of Berkeley's death in 1976, producers Irwin Winkler and Robert Chartoff were preparing a film titled **Busby**, based upon his life and work. It was never produced.

Politically, Bob Fosse fought new battles. Ever championing the rights of dancers and choreographers, his battles began with his stage work. In 1961, Fosse went to the American Arbitration Association and filed against producer Robert Whitehead regarding his work on *Hail the Conquering Hero*. Whitehead drastically changed two of Fosse's numbers, and when Fosse objected, he was replaced by Todd Bolender. As the contract had read, "complete artistic control," Fosse claimed that Whitehead forfeited the rights to use his choreography by making changes. The following year, while preparing *Little Me*, he refused to go into production, holding out until the producers recognized his right to be represented by a union (SSDC, the Society of Stage Directors and Choreographers).

Now, he took on the movies. While filming **Sweet Charity**, he asked approval from the Directors Guild of America for the onscreen credit "Choreographed and directed by." *Dance Magazine* explains:

> Up to that point, the DGA had a long-standing rule that the last card — and it must be a separate card — before the first scene in a motion picture shall read: "Directed by...." The only exceptions are, "written and directed by..." or "Produced, written and directed by..." Directors have been trying for a long time to protect the uniqueness of their credit by fending off such cards as "Dances directed by...," or, for that matter, "Choreography directed by..." [February 1969].

Fosse eventually was given "Directed and choreographed by" credit.

As the workload continued to shrink, promising talents went back to New York or concert stages, or stretched their skills in television. The movie industry and the very form of film itself were still in transition, and film choreography faced its next challenge.

Selected Filmography

Billy Rose's Jumbo (Barbette, Busby Berkeley, Charles Walters) MGM, 1963, Video:MGM/UA — The staging, filming, and editing of "Over and Over," "The Circus Is on Parade" and "This Can't Be Love" proves once and for all the supreme sense of style and rhythm Berkeley and Walters pos-sessed. Please don't ask "Billy Rose's Jumbo WHAT?"

Bye Bye Birdie (Onna White) Col, 1963, Video: Col — An ample look at White's energetic, fun-filled work as she cheerfully mocks rock 'n' roll.

Thanks also to Gower Champion's original concepts.

Can-Can (Hermes Pan) Fox, 1960, Video:CBS/Fox — Good stuff from a master, plus a superb group of dancers.

Chitty Chitty Bang Bang (Marc Breaux and Dee Dee Wood) UA, 1968, Video:UA — An overblown original sixties "biggie" that is saved by its musical sequences. Thanks, Marc and Dee Dee. It's a shame you didn't write the script.

The Cool Ones (Toni Basil) WB, 1967 — Hip and hot dancing which helps you forget this terrible script.

Flower Drum Song (Hermes Pan) Univ, 1961, Video:Univ — As good as the "Love Look Away" dream ballet and the rest of the dances are, it's Pan's staging of "Sunday" which makes you smile.

Funny Girl (Herbert Ross) Col, 1968, Video: Col — The seamless musical numbers which literally are halfway finished before you realize Streisand is singing; the humor of the roller skating sequence; and the pregnant bride, all help to make this musical the gem it is.

Half a Sixpence (Gillian Lynne) Par, 1967, Video: Par — A swell dance show from Tommy Steele, Grover Dale, and choreographer Lynne, introducing the new breed of super British dancers to the world in style.

Hello, Dolly! (Michael Kidd) Fox, 1969, Video: CBS/Fox — The last of the '60s musical epics has nearly *everything* wrong with it — but the dancing.

Hootenanny Hoot (MGM, 1963) and **Kissin' Cousins** (MGM, 1964) (Hal Belfer), Video:Both MGM/UA — A duo from Belfer which were among the last of the dance treats in the rock 'n' roll vein, before somebody decided dancing wasn't cool.

Mary Poppins (Marc Breaux and Dee Dee Wood) Disney, 1964, Video:Disney — The film is episodic, slow, and a musical without a love story. It's the relentless energy and inventiveness of "Step in Time" and the wonderful dance with the penguins to "Jolly Holiday" which earned this film its Academy Award. Don't let anyone tell you differently.

The Music Man (Tom Panko, Onna White) Col, 1962, Video:Col — All of the charm and joy of White's original stage work for the property was lovingly retranslated on film for the ages to enjoy. "Shipoopi" especially soars.

The Night They Raided Minsky's (Danny Daniels) UA, 1968, Video:UA — Some hilarious "Burleycue" chorus shenanigans and wonderfully corny comedy sketches devised by Daniels.

The Producers (Alan Johnson) Embassy, 1967, Video:Embassy — The first major dot on the roadmap to dance as satire. Busby Berkeley's influence on Adolf Hitler comes back with a vengeance, as brilliantly conceived and written by Mel Brooks and visualized by Johnson.

Star! (Michael Kidd) Fox, 1968, Video:CBS/Fox — Overblown, overlong, and over its head. They should simply eliminate all of the dialogue and show the wonderful period numbers created by Kidd and performed by a sterling cast.

State Fair (Nick Castle) Fox, 1962, Video:CBS/Fox — Look out! Here comes Ann-Margret! And we have Castle to thank for realizing her boiling-point capacity in the wiggle-fest he created for her in "Isn't It Kind of Fun?"

Summer Holiday (Herbert Ross) WB, 1963 — While American musicals were festering and dying, Britain got a future master to create the dances and numbers for a wonderful little musical starring Britain's Elvis, Cliff Richard, and his musical contingent. Its a shame Elvis never got such a good musical in his filmography.

Sweet Charity (Bob Fosse) Univ, 1969, Video: Univ — Like a kid with a new toy, Fosse nearly scuttles this dance masterpiece as a first-time director with his MTV quick-cut dizziness, but Shirley MacLaine, Chita Rivera, Paula Kelly, Ben Vereen, Buddy Vest, LeeRoy Reams, and Sammy Davis, Jr. — plus one of the most splendid dance ensembles ever captured on film — impeccably perform Fosse's memorable musical sequences.

Thoroughly Modern Millie (Joe Layton) Univ, 1967, Video:Univ — Layton's humor and talent spills out all over this film. The actors talk much too long and they don't dance enough, but when they do, it's a joy. Carol Channing being thrown in the air by acrobats?

The Unsinkable Molly Brown (Peter Gennaro) MGM, 1964, Video:MGM/UA — Debbie Reynolds' tomboy energy and Irish Jigs with Grover Dale and Gus Trikonis are great, but watch for the humor, heart, and character revelations in "Belly Up to the Bar, Boys." A classic.

West Side Story (Tommy Abbott, Maggie Banks, Howard Jeffrey, Tony Mordente, Jerome Robbins)

Tommy Rall partners Barbra Streisand in the ***Swan Lake*** spoof in **Funny Girl** (Herbert Ross, Columbia, 1968).

UA, 1961, Video:MGM/UA — Robbins transposed his masterpiece on film and got an Academy Award for his efforts. It is still being argued exactly what contributions Robert Wise and Robbins made to the film as codirectors. Watch it and decide for yourself.

When the Boys Meet the Girls (Earl Barton) MGM, 1965 — Barton strikes gold with one of the last of the good dance numbers to "I Got Rhythm" as rock eats up the genre.

The energetic "Waiter's Gallop," choreographed by Michael Kidd in one of the last of the big dance films, **Hello, Dolly!** (Twentieth Century–Fox, 1969). Front row (L to R): Bobby Thompson, Gary Menteer, Ian Gary and Jimmy Hibbard. Second row: Alex Plasschaert, Howard Jeffrey, Jim Hutchinson and Jerry Trent.

The Young Girls of Rochefort (Gene Kelly, Norman Maen) WB/Seven Arts, 1967 — George Chakiris, Grover Dale, and Gene Kelly dance boldly on some of the most impossible surfaces ever used by dancers — and speak and lip-sync in French! This film was almost ignored upon its release; take a look at it now and marvel at the brave effort (available in Japan on laser disc, it is almost certain to arrive upon our shores).

THE 1970s

In this decade, the integration and use of dance in the highly successful **American Graffiti** (Toni Basil, 1973) was to lead the way to the film-dance integration of the future. Although not a musical, the film used a nostalgic rock score and period social dances by Basil to tell its story. "It began an entire new trend back to the oldies but goodies of an earlier era. Directors began to use oldies to add mood and texture to their films, whether or not they were set in the present. Rock music took on a deeper meaning for those who lived through its birth." (From *Rockin' Reels*.)

Dance on film was going back to its beginnings: these were not dance numbers building to a "socko" finish, but rather, behavioral movement for actors revealing character, period, locale, and plot advancement. Film actors and actresses no longer were the gods and goddesses of dance, performing physical movements that were out of the reach of the audience. In the realistic scenarios of contemporary film, they were mere mortals — the more "mere," the better. Dance went back to the common man, rock 'n' roll was here to stay, and choreographers came back into demand. And suddenly, the 1950s were big box-office!

From Broadway, **Grease** (the longest running musical of the time) was transferred to the screen in 1978, with its choreography and musical staging by Patricia Birch supplying most of the magic. As they had on Broadway, Birch's musical numbers made the audience laugh, boogie in their seats, and completely accept the absurdity of the characters bursting into song and dance. In a June 1978, *Dance Magazine* interview during filming, Birch said,

> One of the first things they asked me was "How many dancers do you want?" and I said, "Waddaya mean, how many dancers do I want? There should be nothing that resembled quotes dancers unquotes in this film or it'll blow the whole thing. *But*, if you'll let me find twenty dancers from both coasts that I think are interesting as *characters* as well as top dancers, you got to carry them through the film and make them part of that high school, and have me just as interested in them when they're banging their lockers around as when they're dancing, if you allow this, then I want twenty dancers."

Under Birch's direction, those twenty dancers and the principal cast helped to make **Grease** the highest grossing musical film of all time.

During the 1970s, dancing also moved back into the lives of young people with the disco era. Not since the 1940s had social dance played such a major role in American society, and the films reflected that. America was dancing once again — in clubs, at school dances, on television, and on film.

Soundtrack record album sales spurred the last throes of the movie musical, dinosaurs in their size lumbering toward extinction. *L.A. Magazine* wrote, "Streisand got in first with **A Star Is Born** (1976). The movie may have been a dog to some, but, boy did Columbia Records clean up with the album!"

Saturday Night Fever (Jeff Kutash, Jo Jo Smith, Deney Terrio, Lester Wilson, 1977) suddenly reinvented the movie musical. It seemed to come out of nowhere, unheralded and unprepared for the great success it would have. Generated by a hit soundtrack written and performed by the Bee Gees, it had one of the most successful original musical scores created for film. The characters did not burst into song, but rather into dance as the lyrics were sung off-camera by the pop stars. Although the dance steps and technique were contemporary and the set was filled with smoke, haze, and flashing disco lights, the dance sequences were filmed in the classic style: full-figure, with the camera choreographed to move with the dancers. The script (a tale of desperate, bitter, alienated young people who struggled for recognition in the smoky, mirror-ball-lit dance club) was in direct opposition to the sheer elation of the dance sequences. But the image of the dancing, white-suited Tony Manero (John Travolta), his right arm pointed toward heaven and his left hip aiming toward hell, became a sign of the times. The film popularized the new dance-as-competition genre and made a star of John Travolta. Fred Astaire publicly proclaimed that he was a fan of the white-suited young man who was the world's newest dancing star, and an (unproduced) film was planned to pair the two.

With the use of contemporary dance, collaboration between multiple experts now became necessary. The credits on **Saturday Night Fever** created a controversy when several people

Annette Cardona, John Travolta, and Eve Arden rock out in **Grease** (Patricia Birch, Paramount, 1978).

publicly announced that they had created the dances in the film. Disco dance expert Jo Jo Smith received onscreen credit as "dance coordinator," while unbilled street and club dancers Deney Terrio and Jeff Kutash both claimed responsibility for teaching Travolta his dances. Terrio and Kutash gained recognition from their association with the hit film, going on to choreography careers of their own. Lester Wilson, who received onscreen credit for the film and was one of the most beloved of contemporary choreographers, was too much of a gentleman to ever publicly deny the claims. While Terrio and Kutash probably created Travolta's work, it is obvious that Wilson must have staged Travolta's dances and created the miles of dance for the rest of the performers.

The potential of record sales also generated two other big pop musicals in 1978: **Sgt. Pepper's Lonely Hearts Club Band** (Patricia Birch) and **Thank God It's Friday** (Joanne Divito). Featuring recording stars the Bee Gees, Peter Frampton, and Donna Summer, the films were based on their pop soundtracks.

Choreographers now scrambled to find street dancers for their ensembles and input, while professionally trained dancers scurried to disco class. Social dancing dictated the dance in these trendy films, so choreographers and dancers had to keep abreast of the latest steps, the latest attitudes and "moves." Toni Basil, who pioneered the search in 1970, described to Kevin Grubb of *Dance Magazine* (March 1988) what she saw when she infiltrated the clubs where the primarily black men competed:

> I learned that there was no one club where they danced. You just had to be at the right
> place at the right time, and you *might* see one of them…. I saw this guy who ran up

George Burns tries out Patricia Birch's choreography in **Sgt. Pepper's Lonely Hearts Club Band** (Universal, 1978), flanked by Peter Frampton and the Bee Gees.

> the wall ... like the Nicholas Brothers and did a back flip! I hooked up with this gay kid ... named Lamont DeFontaine, who was doing a high-attitude pose dance called the Vogue. He was a little apprehensive about it, but he started taking me to more places.

Her search eventually unearthed such innovators as Don Campbell, Fluky Luke, Poppin' Pete, Puppet Boozer, and Shabba Doo. ("Dancing was all a lot of these guys knew. They were as much a part of the street as a ballerina is part of the barre.") (Kevin Grubb wrote in *Dance Magazine*, March 1988), "She learned that, while they were brilliant soloists, as a group their guarded, street-hustler instincts kept them from working together." Basil's perseverance finally won out when she worked with (and also appeared in) a seven-member group called The Lockers in 1970. Their appearance on television's "Saturday Night Live" "put street dance on the map and brought it forever out of the closet."

It was only the name that had been closeted, for the tradition was a long and glorious one. Many ground-breaking dancers had been street dancers from the very beginnings of American dance — creating tap, jitterbug, jive, and the constantly evolving variation of what is now dubbed "street dance." The heritage and tradition of self-taught and improvised dance was simply being carried on from Bill Robinson, the Nicholas Brothers, Tip, Tap and Toe, the Four Step Bros., and countless others over the past century. Popular singer-dancers James Brown, Michael Jackson, and M.C. Hammer would continue the tradition into the next decades.

At first, dance critics and technically trained dancers would reject street dance as an art form. But some recognized the truth: "A double toure is a trick, a foueté is a trick ... we all know that is a trick. So if someone gets up and does 'The Running Man' into a back aerial and spins on their back, its a trick. And they're all valid and they all have their place in dance," commented choreographer Jamale Graves in the 1991 PBS documentary "Everybody Dance Now."

From The Lockers, Shabba Doo would go on to collaborate and innovate in all forms of entertainment. While discussing the very concept of street dance and its deep American roots, Shabba Doo said that the techniques of street dance were just as rigid as classic ballet, developed with dedication and intensity over the years and passed on from dancer to dancer. There were no formal schools for the technique as yet. The clubs and streets around the country served as showcase, workshop, and class for the thousands of young dancers who dedicated their lives to it. This was dance as competition in real life—a chance for kids from the ghetto to excel in something, borne from the philosophies and rhythms of rock 'n' roll.

Although roller skating on film had been a challenge for dancemakers before—Fred Astaire and Ginger Rogers in **Shall We Dance** (1937), Gae Foster's Skating Vanities troupe in **Pin Up Girl** (1944), Donald O'Connor in **I Love Melvin** (1953), and Gene Kelly in **It's Always Fair Weather** (1955)—America was now roller skating to the disco beat. **Roller Boogie** (David Winters, 1979) and **Skatetown U.S.A.** (Bobby Banas, 1979) captured the temporary madness on film for posterity. Rather than creating the onstage patterns of the ice skating film "boom" in the forties, the choreographers now moved the cameras out onto the rink floor, in the middle of the action, zooming and moving along with the skaters. The exhibition roller skaters of the era hired for the films combined adagio partnering, adaptation of ice techniques and tricks, and disco arms and hands—plus the ever-pulsating hips.

Other rock musicals of the decade which were enriched by choreographer's input included **Sparkle** (Lester Wilson, 1976), an original story of a rock 'n' roll sister act's struggle for fame. **Tommy** (1975), a record album by The Who that become a concert and then a film, was staged by Gillian Gregory, with *Time Magazine* (March 31, 1974) noticing "some lavish production numbers whose very excess is their own meaning." It was not until its sensational 1993 stage revival that the property would "dance." In the biographical rock 'n' roll genre, David Winters staged concert sequences for the updated **A Star Is Born** (1976) and Toni Basil did the same for **The Rose** (1979), creative assignments Winters and Basil were handling offscreen as well.

The filming of **The Rocky Picture Horror Show** (choreography by David Toguri, 1975), a mildly successful camp stage satire on monster films, went by almost unnoticed in the 1970s. Slowly the film began to reach cult status in midnight showings all over the world. As of the writing of this book, the film is still shown internationally, with audience members faithfully performing the choreography along with the film cast—a first. If we couldn't dance along with Astaire and Kelly, we could perform Toguri's satirical movements.

In the continuing stage-to-screen transfers of the decade, already established choreographers and some new artists brought their creativity to the screen. In the category of traditional musical works, Jerome Robbins was represented with the recreation of his atmospheric stage dances in **Fiddler on the Roof** by Tommy Abbott and Sammy Bayes (1971). Robbins protégé Howard Jeffrey had little opportunity to show his stuff in **On a Clear Day You Can See Forever** (1970), while Lee Theodore supplied sweeping dance sequences to **Song of Norway** that same year. **Man of La Mancha** (Gillian Lynne, 1972), **Lost in the Stars** (Paula Kelly, 1974), and **A Little Night Music** (Patricia Birch and Larry Fuller, 1977) offered little challenge to the talented choreographers. Onna White added her talents to **1776** and **The Great Waltz** (1972) and created especially imaginative dance numbers for **Mame** (1974), with Lucille Ball, the film's star, praising White during filming: "She makes the camera dance! Her camera moves are fantastic — her vitality is in every shot!" (*After Dark*, October 1973). In the rock musical transfers of the seventies, Sammy Bayes did the staging for **Godspell** (1973), Rob Iscove added excitement to **Jesus Christ Superstar** (1973), and African-American modern dance innovator Louis Johnson supplied his talents to **The Wiz** (1978), with Carlton Johnson and Mabel Robinson.

Twyla Tharp, who had injected the most excitement into the dance world since Jerome Robbins, was introduced on film with another rock musical transfer, **Hair** (1979), with some very non-traditional movement. As Julie Arenal had done with the original stage production, Tharp created movement and dance for the cast that was quirky and came from the core of characterization rather than dance-for-dance's-sake. Also dancing in the film, Tharp began her multiple film collaborations with director Milos Forman. *Time Magazine* recognized their efforts: "(Forman's) camera and editing are in perfect harmony with Tharp's shaggily informal dance patterns; rarely has a musical's choreography flowed so naturally out of the movement of the nonmusical scenes."

With the success of the Broadway revival of *No, No Nanette*, tap dancing was suddenly back in vogue on stage in the also struggling Broadway musical. The stage production brought film dance greats Busby Berkeley (who "supervised" the production) and Ruby Keeler (who starred) back into the spotlight and sent countless kiddies to tap class. Two British film musicals, **The Boy Friend** and **Bugsy Malone**, capitalized on that nostalgic success.

The Boy Friend (Christopher Gable, Terry Gilbert, Gillian Gregory, and Tommy Tune, 1971), a British and American stage success of the 1950s which paid tribute to the 1920s, was finally filmed as British director Ken Russell's homage to Berkeley and the 1930s film musicals. Russell and the multiple choreographers filled the screen with dance, but without the luxury of their predecessors' budgets. The numbers were rehearsed immediately prior to filming, with Russell explaining in an interview, "We did our choreography the day before. Why should dancers have 6 months to learn a number they can pick up in an afternoon?"

Bugsy Malone (Gillian Gregory, 1976), a very original film musical, reinvented the genre of the '30s gangster films with an all-child cast. *Time Magazine's* September 6, 1976, review commented:

> First of all, **Bugsy Malone** is a gangster movie, done in the vintage style. So far, so good. It is also a musical. Curious, but not without precedent. Most everything is played straight. Fair enough. But it is played by kids. Entirely by kids. The average age of the cast is twelve. At first the whole thing seems like an eccentric stunt. But as the film, done with care and affection, gets going, it works surprisingly well.

With only a six-week rehearsal period, choreographer Gregory and director Alan Parker managed to take the young — and mostly non-dancing — cast of 200 American and British children and create a glorious batch of musical numbers.

The biggest nostalgia film musical successes of the decade were the **That's Entertainment** films produced by MGM. Editing together numbers from the great MGM Library of musical films, **That's Entertainment!** (1974) surprisingly scored big at the box-office. It introduced new generations to the magic of film choreography (Alton, Astaire, Berkeley, Castle, Donen, Kelly, Pan, Powell, Rasch and Walters) and rated cheers and sighs from the older crowd as the Great American movie musical passed before their eyes once again. The film's ad campaign slogan ("Boy, do we need it now") was painfully true. **That's Entertainment! Part 2** (1976) was filled with more of the same, but had the added lure of Astaire and Kelly creating their last original film choreography. In his *Los Angeles Times* review (May 16, 1976), Charles Champlin noted, "The sheer energy and artistry of the MGM dance numbers is nowhere better remarked than in the 'From This Moment On' sequence from **Kiss Me Kate**, performed by Ann Miller, Tommy Rall, Bobby Van, Jeanne Coyne, and a young pair named Bob Fosse and Carol Haney. Watching it with awe for the joyous effort, you realize all over again what the movies did to broaden the base for enthusiasms once thought to be elitist."

Hopeful film producers tried several original non-rock musicals in an attempt to keep the genre alive. **Tom Sawyer** (Danny Daniels, 1973), **Huckleberry Finn** (Marc Breaux, 1974), **Funny Lady** (Herbert Ross, 1975), **Movie, Movie** (Michael Kidd, 1978), and **New York, New York** (Ron Field, 1977) benefited from some excellent musical sequences from masters, although Broadway dance creator Fields' major contribution to **New York, New York** (the elaborate "Happy Endings" production number) was originally edited out of the already-too-long film. It was reinstated when the "uncut" version was released on video. Broadway and modern dance innovator Donald McKayle arrived on film with the last of the live-action-and-animation Disney original musicals, **Bedknobs and Broomsticks** (1971).

Hermes Pan, represented in the decade by such greatness in the **That's Entertainment** films, created musical sequences for **Lost Horizon** (1973), voted one of the worst films ever made and receiving painfully brutal reviews. (Arthur Cooper, *Newsweek*: "One lavish production number, 'Living Together, Growing Together' may indeed be the silliest choreography ever put on film." *The Motion Picture Guide* went even further: "The choreography by Pan received widespread criticism. Originally there had been a 'fertility dance' featuring muscular bikini-clad men dancing in a 'ring-around-the-rosy' fashion. Supposedly the preview audience laughed so hysterically it was cut from the print.")

Despite the critical pounding, future choreographer D.J. Giagni shared his personal memories of the experience in a letter to the author:

> It was the first film I was ever in, and I *loved* working with Hermes. He was truly from the old school. We would arrive on the set (the reconstructed **Camelot** set on the Warner Bros. back lot) at 10:00 a.m. and have coffee and donuts for about an hour then work for about 1½ hours and stop for more coffee, then work another ½ hour and go to lunch. The afternoon was even shorter!... But I loved working with Hermes so much that I promised myself that when I choreographed I would grow a beard like Hermes had at the time so I could look important thinking and scratching my beard. And I have the beard to this day.

Pan's personal frustrations over the project were the lack of qualified Asian dancers for the cast. As he had reluctantly done in **Flower Drum Song** (1961), he was forced to use Caucasians in "yellow face," a distasteful practice which would not draw serious industry attention until the Asian-American theatrical community protested in 1991 when *Miss Saigon* arrived on Broadway, with a non-Asian leading man.

Europe continued to supply the all-dance films of the decade. **Peter Rabbit and the Tales of Beatrix Potter** (choreographed by Sir Frederic Ashton, 1971) and **Don Quixote** (1973) with choreography, performances, and co-direction by Rudolph Nureyev and Sir Robert Helpmann unfortunately made little impact at the box office. *Time Magazine*'s July 5, 1971, review of **Peter Rabbit** praised, "Fortunately a British gentleman of Potterian sympathy has found an ideal adaptation — the dance. Using members of the Royal Ballet, choreographer Frederic Ashton has literally given **Peter Rabbit and the Tales of Beatrix Potter** a new dimension ... (the characters) spring and caper like Steiff toys given the spark of life." *Playboy*'s review of **Don Quixote** said, "Make no mistake: Rudolph's smashing solos are the whole show."

Baby gangsters perform Gillian Gregory's "Charleston" in the innovative **Bugsy Malone** (Paramount, 1976).

The highly publicized first-time Russian-American film collaboration on the 1976 remake of **The Blue Bird** (Igor Belsky, Leonid Jacobson) promised more than it delivered in terms of dance on film. With George Cukor directing and actresses Ava Gardner, Elizabeth Taylor, Jane Fonda, and Cicely Tyson portraying leading roles, Bolshoi Ballet star Maya Plisetskaya was first announced with great fanfare to dance the title role. After Natalia Kasatskina, the original choreographer, left the project, Plisetskaya, because of a difficult performance schedule, also dropped out. Budding ballerina Nadia Pavlova instead took the role, and other Russian dance stars, Valentina Ganibalova and Alexander Godunov, were cast, supported by members of the Leningrad Kirov Ballet. Despite all of the hype to the dance world before its release, the final print drew the following notice: "For all its strong dance cast, **The Blue Bird** is not a balletic picture. Although there is one entertainment sequence, dancing is integrated with acting in the Maeterlinck classic." (*After Dark*, May 1976).

Ballet made a commercial comeback on the screen in 1977 with **The Turning Point**. With classic choreography by Ashton and Balanchine among others, this film allowed director Herbert Ross and his wife and assistant, Nora Kaye, the opportunity to finally utilize their lifelong love of classical dance and his knowledge of capturing dance with the camera. Not since **The Red Shoes** had ballet been "box office." The commercially successful film combined a strong story, the best of classical dance, and excellent performances with the box office power of Shirley MacLaine and Anne Bancroft. It made ballet accessible to new generations of audiences. It also made a star of Mikhail Baryshnikov, ballet's first movie hunk.

When presenting Herbert Ross and Nora Kaye an "Award of Distinction" for the film's "profoundly influential extension into cinema," *Dance Magazine* editor William Como said, "Of **The Turning Point**, I have no hesitation in stating (backed as I am by statistics) that it was a veritable turning point in American ballet.... It immediately increased the dance audience by more than three million. Ballet schools around the country reported a startling rise in student enrollment. Public awareness of dance had been stimulated beyond all expectations."

Other filmed ballet contributors during the decade were Robert North and Ann Ditchburn with **Slow Dancing in the Big City**, 1978, a story whose leading female character (also Ditchburn) was a ballerina suffering from tendinitis and struggling to her goal of dancing the leading role in a modern ballet. Russian ballet giants Yuri Grigorovich and Maya Plisetskaya had their original stage work reinterpreted in commercially released 1979 film versions of **Spartacus** and **Ivan the Terrible** (Grigorovich) and **Anna Karenina** (Plisetskaya). Other important figures from the dance world also participated in non-musical offerings: David Blair (**The Private Life of Sherlock Holmes** 1970), Gemze DeLappe (**Justine**, 1970) and Stuart Hodes (**Voices**, 1979).

In non-musical films, filmmakers returned to the original use of dance in silent films: for period flavor, humor, character exposition, fantasy sequences, and pageantry, with the dramatic epics **King Kong** (Claude Thompson, 1976) and **The Godfather, Part 2** (Jerry Jackson, Steven Peck, 1974) benefiting from dance sequences.

The comic possibilities of dance first probed by Charles Chaplin were further explored, particularly in Steven Spielberg's **1941** (1979), in a clever parody of 1940s dances created by Paul DeRolf and Judy Van Wormer. Pauline Kael wrote in *The New Yorker,* November 1980: "The U.S.O. Jitterbug is one of the greatest pieces of film choreography I've ever seen."

The example of dance as satire set by Alan Johnson in **The Producers** (1967) continued with Johnson creating hilarious musical sequences for Mel Brooks's **Blazing Saddles** (1974), **Young Frankenstein** (1974)—about which *Time Magazine* rhapsodized in its December 30, 1974, review: "Brooks is always at his best making fun of the stupidities of popular entertainment (recall 'Springtime for Hitler' in **The Producers**) and this scene, with scientist and subject in top hat and tails performing 'Puttin' on the Ritz,' is some sort of deranged high point in contemporary film comedy"—and **High Anxiety** (1977). Rob Iscove supplied the dancing "spoofs" for Brooks's **Silent Movie** (1976). Johnson also collaborated with Gene Wilder on **The Adventures of Sherlock Holmes' Smarter Brother** (1975) and **The World's Greatest Lover** (1977). The film audiences who had laughed *at* the dance sequences in musical films now laughed *with* them in these comedies, as they brilliantly spoofed themselves.

In England, flamboyant director Ken Russell continued to use dance sequences in his controversial dramatic and biographical films, with Terry Gilbert adding atmosphere and sexuality to **The Devils** (1971) and **The Music Lovers** (1971), and Gillian Gregory contributing her creativity in **Mahler** (1974) and **Valentino** (1977)—which was Rudolph Nureyev's bid for film stardom. About the latter, *Time Magazine's* review (October 17, 1977) stated, "...in the Charleston and ballroom dancing sequences, Nureyev shows the audience what might have been: an erotic figure far more alive than the glittery props and people who surrounded him."

It was Bob Fosse's work which perhaps left the most imaginative dance images on film from the seventies. Although a writer in *Dance Magazine*, May 1984, accused Fosse of giving in to current trends ("Dance in recent films tends to be a series of two-second gestural effects frenetically photographed"), all of the promise he had shown as a stage and film choreographer came to fruition in the 1970s. After his less-than-totally-successful debut as a film director with **Sweet Charity** in 1969, **Cabaret** (1972) completely rethought the stage success and recreated the decadence of 1930s Germany in drama, song, and dance. Fosse discussed his objectives for the film in *New York Magazine*:

> I had to break away from movie musicals that just copy the Broadway show. Or movie musicals that copy conventions of the stage. **Singin' in the Rain**, **An American in Paris**, all the Gene Kelly, Fred Astaire musicals — they're classics. But they represent another era. Today I get very antsy watching musicals in which people are singing as they walk down the street or hang out the laundry.... In fact, I think it looks a little silly. You can do it on the stage. The theater has its own personality — it conveys a removed reality. The movies bring that closer.

With an Academy Award for his first complete film masterpiece, Fosse became the prestigious name in film circles he deserved to be, also winning Tony and Emmy awards that same year in a first-time "Triple Crown" sweep. After success with a straight dramatic film (**Lenny**, 1974), he also became one of America's first autobiographical directors (joining Italy's Federico Fellini and France's Francois Truffaut) with **All That Jazz** (1979). The gritty, completely contemporary musical drama used dance as it had not been used before to paint the brilliantly dark autobiographical portrait of an obsessive choreographer and his work. One of the most exhilarating collaborations of camera and dance was the opening audition sequence in which dancers seemed to melt into one another as they performed pirouettes.

With the shrinking of the movie musical and the demise of the musical variety show on television, choreographers were hard-pressed to find ongoing employment. Roy Clark in his monthly *Dance Magazine* column about Hollywood reported, "Whether the tight economic situation is to blame or whether, as one choreo put it, the TV biggies 'want all the money to themselves,' steady employment ... has been hard to come by this season" (1970); and "Dancers and choreos are suffering from our depressed economy and industry slowdown. At this writing, only five Fall variety shows are scheduled for all three national networks combined" (1971). Choreographers vied for the also-shrinking stage jobs, continued performing, or went into new fields of employment within the industry: editing, foley, casting. Some even developed other talents. D.J. Giagni wrote to the author and honestly expressed the dilemma which continues today:

> I haven't worked that much on film — there is not much film choreography anymore. As a family man with two children I had to give up choreography because either I wasn't good enough or lucky enough but I couldn't make a living from the stage (my real love). The time commitment far exceeds the financial rewards unless the show is a hit. Sadly I never had that. I make fine handcrafted furniture for a living now and choreograph if the project is interesting.

The theatrical community mourned when Jack Cole died in 1974. For all of his creativity and the lasting influences he had made on dance, film, and the stage, he never received an Emmy, Oscar, or Tony Award for his immense contributions. In November 1979, an auction of the over 2,500 pieces of Cole's incredible dance collection was held at Sotheby's in London. Long-time companion and executor of Cole's estate, David Gray, remarked, "I would have preferred not to break up the collection, but of the institutions in this country, one wanted the books, another only the artifacts. In other words, only bits and pieces. I'm keeping a few mementos, photographs ... certain correspondence. But literally everything else is gone."

In the eighties Ron Field was working on *Once a Star*, "The story of famous movie stars of the 1940s — told from the point of view of Jack Cole." By 1987, the title was changed to *Rehearsal on Stage Ten,* but the project never reached production. It was only the American Dance Machine which kept Cole's legacy alive.

Bob Fosse faces his dancers (flanked by assistants Gene Foote and Kathryn Doby) and gives instructions for the highly erotic airline commercial number in **All That Jazz** (Fox/Universal, 1979), his brilliant semi-autobiographical final film.

The weak political status of dancemakers was once again confirmed with the releases of **That's Entertainment!** and **That's Entertainment! Part 2.** As the credits rolled after the two dance explosions, there were no choreographers listed.

Selected Filmography

All That Jazz (Bob Fosse) Fox, 1979, Video:CBS/Fox — Decadent, daring, and dazzling. Oh God, Bob, we really miss you.

The Boy Friend (Christopher Gable, Terry Gilbert, Gillian Gregory, Tommy Tune) MGM-EMI, 1971, Video:MGM/UA — Ken Russell's rainbow of dreaded excess, salvaged by some wonderful dancing.

Cabaret (Bob Fosse) AA, 1972, Video:CBS/Fox — Fosse gets it all right this time, gets an Oscar, and shows his stylized best in all of the musical sequences, which slip out of the drama and catch you unprepared.

Grease (Patricia Birch) Par, 1978, Video:Par — A blast to the past, energized and witticized by Birch's work.

Hair (Twyla Tharp) UA, 1979, Video:MGM/UA — What do you remember about this film? The cops on the dancing horses, right? Proves the potential power of movement on celluloid … and the sense of Tharp.

Jesus Christ Superstar (Rob Iscove) Univ, 1973, Video:Univ — Energy and daring, jumping, rocking and rolling. It's good stuff.

Mame (Martin Allen, Onna White) WB, 1974, Video:WB — For the first time, the world didn't love Lucy — and it's a shame, because White's work is wonderful. This film also freezes in time one of the last big job opportunities for Hollywood's dancers.

1941 (Paul DeRolf, Judy Van Wormer) Univ, 1979, Video:Univ — In this granddaddy of budgets gone awry, look for the wonderful jitterbug sequence that says everything the rest of the movie should have said.

The Rocky Horror Picture Show (David Toguri) Fox, 1975, Video:CBS/Fox — Probably the most well-known choreography and staging in history. Thousands perform it on Saturday night all over the world. A phenomenon which is helped greatly by Toguri's witty work.

Roller Boogie (David Winters) UA, 1979, Video: MGM/UA — Winters takes the endless circles of the roller skating rink and tries everything he can: conga lines, Busby Berkeley camera angles, multiple images, slow motion, and a corps of the best skaters of the time in this basically old-fashioned Mickey-and-Judy scenario. It's a real hoot to watch, with Linda Blair winning my award as "Best Sport of the '70s" to try and keep up with skating pro Jim Bray — and wearing some of the funniest outfits and hairdos of the time.

Saturday Night Fever (Jeff Kutash, Jo Jo Smith, Deney Terrio, Lester Wilson) Par, 1977, Video: Par — The contemporary dance movie of the decade, making a star out of John Travolta and giving us all hope.

Thank God It's Friday (Joanne Divito) Col, 1978, Video:Col — Primarily remembered as disco diva Donna Summer's film debut — and farewell. In this disco daze of a movie, choreographer Divito and performer Chick Vennera create a dance in a parking lot which says it all — plus has you rooting for the character for the rest of the film. Too bad the producers didn't let her do a dance for all of the characters. Another monument to the opportunities of dance on film.

That's Entertainment!(Robert Alton, Fred Astaire, Busby Berkeley, Nick Castle, Bobby Connolly, Willie Covan, Stanley Donen, Jack Donohue, Seymour Felix, Dave Gould, Gene Kelly, Michael Kidd, Ann Miller, Hermes Pan, Eleanor Powell, Albertina Rasch, Charles Walters) MGM, 1974, Video:MGM/UA — Practically the history of film choreography at MGM. How tragic that we had to go backwards to see great dancing, rather than allowing the creative artists of the future to have their time on film. But we did — and it's dazzling. Watch the chorine's shoulder strap break during Clark Gable's "Puttin' on the Ritz"…she stops dancing, chatters to the girl next to her, but nothing stops Gable!

That's Entertainment, Part II (Robert Alton, Fred Astaire, Busby Berkeley, Nick Castle, Jack Cole, Bobby Connolly, Stanley Donen, Jack Donohue, Bob Fosse, Dave Gould, Gene Kelly, Ann Miller, Hermes Pan, Eleanor Powell, Alex Romero, Charles Walters) MGM, 1976, Video:MGM/UA — Another scrumptious helping of the "Good Old Days" — plus new work by Astaire and Kelly. They don't do much, but then again, they don't have to.

The Turning Point (Alvin Ailey, Frederick Ashton, George Balanchine, Jean Coralli, John Cranko, Michel Fokine, Lev Ivanov, Harald Lander, Kenneth MacMillan, Alexander Minz, Dennis Nahat, Jules Perrot, Marius Petipa) Fox, 1977, Video: CBS/Fox — It may have taken the 13 dance geniuses listed above to create the original stage choreography, but it took one man to capture it so brilliantly on film: Herbert Ross.

The Wiz (Carlton Johnson, Louis Johnson, Mabel Robinson) Univ, 1978, Video:Univ — Again, too big, too long, and Diana Ross is simply too old, but Johnson's work provides any excitement there is. A good look at some of the best African-American dancers of the era.

THE 1980s

The eighties continued to be filled with dance on film for three reasons: nostalgia, the wide acceptance of social dance, and the greatest opportunity for dancemakers to create on film since the invention of the camera: the music video.

Contemporary life in America became increasingly stressful and complicated. Americans had lost the last shreds of their innocence in the 1970s and were now floundering through the

"Me" decade, searching for truth, love, and a good paycheck. To escape, moviegoers continued to flock to films which took place in another time — usually the 1950s and 1960s. Choreographers were in demand once again, as the films used social dances of those periods to create their nostalgic atmosphere as well as supplying humor and social commentary.

Social dancing continued to be important in the everyday life of the young. The acceptance of dance skills by young males as a social strength contributed to the new popularity of dance. With break dancers performing on city streets, popular dance shows on television ("Dance Fever," "Solid Gold," "Soul Train," etc.) and an ever-growing club life for the young, street and club dance reached new heights in technique and exposure.

This huge demand for filmed dance created work opportunities for the new generation of choreographers and dance directors which included Paula Abdul, Jamale Graves, Jeffrey Hornaday, Kenny Ortega, Vincent Paterson, Michael Peters, Otis Sallid, Susan Scanlan, Lynn Taylor-Corbett, and Anthony Thomas whose work was introduced to movie audiences in the eighties. The greatest opportunities however, were offered in music videos rather than feature films.

MTV, a new television network, which premiered August 1, 1981, popularized the music video. With a limited budget, the struggling network asked record companies for free promotional music videos for their "all-music television" — and the rest is history. At first produced in limited quantity to spur record sales, music videos now became an industry. Not only did they give exposure to artists and help sell records, but the videos themselves became commercial successes. They were sold in video stores, shown widely on other television networks worldwide, and given awards for excellence. The careers of many budding directors and choreographers started in music videos and moved to feature films. In previous decades, the evolution of stage dance had influenced dance on film; now it was the music video, producing the greatest impact on filmed dance since the 1930s innovations of Busby Berkeley and Fred Astaire.

Brief musical shorts featuring popular recording artists of the day performing a single song had began with soundies in the 1940s. In the fifties, Scopitone was invented; for 25 cents, patrons could see their favorites perform. With the new technology of video, the form took a giant step. In the mid '70s, Earl Barton had produced a series of single-song pieces and tried to sell them to television, but the networks were reluctant to air all-music programs. The popular musical variety television shows of the time still included inane dialogue and comedy sketches. All-music programs were suspect in the '80s. Without the once popular musical variety television shows of the previous decades, exposure for the recording artists had diminished, and the need for the music video was born.

Dance, at first, was used sparingly behind and around basically non-dancing stars. Many in the industry attribute the acceptance of enriched dance in the new form to the historic collaboration between choreographer Michael Peters, director Martin Scorcese, and the unique song-and-dance talents of Michael Jackson on the video "Beat It." "Beat It" also changed the face of the basically white artist exposure on MTV as Michael Jackson began to dominate the music industry. Jackson, Peters, and director John Landis would then expand the form to a 13½-minute long mini-film of song, dance, effects, and creativity in 1983 with "Thriller." "The dance helps in telling the story," said choreographer Peters. "It's energetic. It makes them (the viewer) feel that they want to dance. Someone will look and say, 'God, I wish I could do that.' I want people to do that" (*Dance Magazine*, October 1984).

From the originally direct approach of using dance and the camera to reflect the song, choreographers and directors now began to explore more abstract ways in which to illustrate the music. Toni Basil pioneered in the form with **Head** (1968) and videos for her own recording career. The careers of pop singer-dancers Paula Abdul, Madonna, Janet Jackson, M.C. Hammer,

Choreography as body language: Arlene Phillips directed the Village People to front a gym filled with hunky young men to spell out "Y.M.C.A." in **Can't Stop the Music** (EMI, 1980).

and Prince were enhanced by MTV exposure in such ground-breaking musical numbers as "Knocked Out," "What Have You Done for Me Lately?," "Nasty," and "When Doves Fly." Many non-dancing stars soon realized the power of dance and enlisted choreographers to co-create some of their best work: Lionel Ritchie's "All Night Long" (choreographed by Susan Scanlan), Billy Joel's "Uptown Girl" (Michael Peters), and Stevie Nicks' "Stand Back" (Jeffrey Hornaday).

Dance was now used lavishly, giving exposure and challenges to choreographers and employment to a new generation of dancers. It also offered carte blanche for experimentation from the dancemakers. Basil remarked to *Dance Magazine* in March 1988 (Kevin Grubb, "Basil Blasts Off"): "When I got involved with commercial films it was impossible to choreograph for the medium. Directors would constantly make us choreograph for a proscenium and then try to put it on film or video. All the film technique I'd been learning on my own was virtually useless until video became popular ten years later."

Music videos were complete scenarios within themselves. They didn't come out of anything, nor did they have to segué into anything else. The soundies and Scopitone films had been quite primitive, with the numbers focusing on the singers or instrumentalists in a one-set performance location. Usually filmed in the old proscenium style with few cameras, angles or technical effects, dance was used as a "back-up," simplistically illustrating the lyrics or theme of the song. But, with the new technical advances in film, on a music video the sky was the limit—or rather, the imagination level of the creative team and the budget were. Choreographers collaborated conceptually with the directors and the stars to create individual musical numbers with imaginative visuals. The staging, direction and editing of music videos forced directors and choreographers to reexamine how dance itself was to be used in film and be one of the major innovations of the decade. "It's an incredible tool that anybody can use," said Michael Peters. "You can expand and really collaborate with an artist. It's so new and so experimental that there are no parameters on it. Nobody's saying, 'This is the form.' It's really open-ended." (Dan Cox, "Video Fever," *Dance Magazine,* October 1984.)

These were not cheaply filmed musical numbers. They were full-blown expensive production numbers approaching the scale of the MGM golden years in terms of creativity and budget. As film director Martin Scorcese—who eagerly accepted the challenge of the music video—stated, "The American musical is an art form." Music videos became compact versions of the movie musical. In the future, retrospectives will most probably be created to illustrate the prolific and inventive work of choreographers in the '80s and '90s in these videos, with commercially released compilations not unlike the **That's Entertainment!** trilogy of films which saluted the movie musical.

As the effects in film had grown to boggle the audience's minds with explosions, speeding space ships, dissolving people, and the total destruction of galaxies, choreographers now felt the need (or were pressured by the studios) to be larger than life—bigger, louder, faster—in their creativity. Kevin Grubb commented in *Dance Magazine,* July 1987, about the dangers involved in this new F/X usage on stage and in film: "The demands of F/X musical choreography on dancers is controversial and merits discussion. At the heart of the matter are injuries that ... occur at alarming rates."

Whereas dance-ins had been previously used in films to perform for non-dancing stars, now dance-ins with specific dance skills (turns, acrobatics, gymnastics, leaps, etc.) were used as an integral part of the choreography. With the new quick-cut style of filming dance (called "montage editing"), dancers were hired to perform fantastic stunts which when melded into the editing process made it appear as if superhuman people were performing the dancing, pushing the human body beyond its limits. Paula Abdul's music videos featured extraordinary single stunts by young male dancers who could complete nearly uncountable pirouettes or staggering gymnastic feats. Often, one solo dance routine would be performed by dozens of people in bits and pieces of expertly edited cuts. Filmmakers in the '20s dazzled audiences by offering various dance acts of mind boggling tricks and skills, one following the other. Contemporary filmmakers now presented them shot-by-shot.

Choreographers were collaborating with film technique as never before. On "Dance in America: Everybody Dance Now," a 1991 segment of PBS' "Great Performances," the choreography and filming and editing techniques for music videos were discussed and illustrated in depth, featuring the leading choreographers of the medium at the time.

In the program, Martin Scorcese discussed directing Michael Jackson's historic "Beat It," choreographed by Michael Peters:

> The dance steps themselves were worked out to combine with the camera movement
> so that the camera itself is dancing and the dolly grips were as important as some of

the dancers. I wanted to make something classical the way the great choreographers moved in the late '40s, early '50s and the films that I saw growing up.... Some of the dance music videos disturb me because it's really lots of quick cuts and flashes and I don't really see the dance.... But we are clashing two forms. Maybe the video itself is the dance. You know, the piece of film itself and the impression that it gives to the mind when you're flashing by on those channels ... maybe it speaks another language to a younger generation. Who knows?

Rosie Perez (who was choreographing television's "In Living Color" at the time) stated her personal opinions: "Videos to me are like a fantasy, like a dream. And when you dream, you dream so rapidly, so fast, so therefore the movement has to be the same thing. It like has to hit you and go, hit you and go, hit you and go."

Vincent Paterson remarked: "There is a power in using dance in a very quick-cut, chopped up, edited version. Dance is not always used in that ... format, but it can be used merely for energy or excitement, as much as a visual or costume change or lighting design." Michael Peters capsulized it with: "Music videos are indicative of what we are, the way our culture has gone — instant gratification ... my attention span is *this* short so you better do it really fast because otherwise I'm gonna hit that remote button and change the channel!"

In a similar discussion in *Dance Magazine*, October 1984, Susan Scanlan had said, "It's just butchering the dance. To butcher the choreography to four counts, four counts, four counts — that's posing. I'll go to see a dance video now and you don't know whether the guy knew three steps or what." Lynn Taylor-Corbett agreed: "Anything conceptual is just lost."

In 1981, Toni Basil created "Word of Mouth," one of the first long-form videos, and British director Jack Bond attempted to make a feature-length music video with **It Couldn't Happen Here** (1988) starring the Pet Shop Boys and choreographed by Arlene Phillips. Although critics likened the film to the work of Jean-Luc Goddard and Ken Russell, audience reaction indicated that contemporary audiences liked their music videos in short bursts, rather than ninety minutes of "MTV from hell." Not released theatrically outside the United Kingdom, the film did not receive the international exposure it deserved.

As the music video became more and more inventive — even paying loving homage to the movie musical and dance forms of the past, as Michael Jackson, Janet Jackson, and Paula Abdul have done so successfully — the film musical itself strayed off into uneven directions. The financially uncertain film companies tried desperately to find out just exactly what the filmgoers wanted.

Nevertheless, the '80s saw a new shot in the arm for dance-themed films with the box-office smashes **Flashdance** (Jeffrey Hornaday, 1983), **Footloose** (Lynn Taylor-Corbett, Dorain Grusman, and Charlene Painter, 1984) and **Dirty Dancing** (Kenny Ortega, 1987), all landmarks in their use of imaginative dance direction. In all three films, dance was used as liberation and a form of expression by the leading characters, allowing them to excel and triumph, with audiences cheering along the way. Not only did these films imprint some of the most vivid images on our collective memories, they also produced hit songs. The bean counters smiled.

Jeffrey Hornaday, the choreographer of **Flashdance**, had previously gathered extensive camera and editing knowledge making music videos in Mexico. To prepare for the film, Hornaday "rented a video system, put on the music, and just danced spontaneously while the film was going. I would think of the character, what she'd be feeling as she danced. I did this for a week. When a certain point of view would emerge, I'd set that dance on the dancer." (*Dance Magazine*, October, 1983).

He talked further about making the film in *Dance Magazine* (December, 1985):

Street dancer Jennifer Beals suspiciously eyes a ballerina on her way to an important dance competition in **Flashdance** (Jeffrey Hornaday, Paramount, 1983).

> There's no such thing as flashdancing. It was a title the writer came up with for the movie. You know, in the script, all it said for the dance number was, "And now she does a dance onstage." Adrian [Lyne, the director] and the scene designer and I would come up with a general premise, and I'd go into the studio and devise it. So flashdancing was really more an element of filmmaking. It's not rooted in a form out there in the world…. In **Flashdance** I choreographed cut for cut. We did the choreography for a specific camera angle to last a certain length of time, to correspond with the previous and outgoing cut.

Variety said (4/15/83): "Watching **Flashdance** is pretty much like looking at MTV for 96 minutes. Virtually plotless, exceedingly thin on characterization and sociologically laughable, pic at least lives up to its title by offering an anthology of extraordinarily flashy dance numbers…. This may be the first main line commercial film to incorporate trendy break dancing into its proceedings, and aspects of disco, Aerobicize and even Kabuki new wave are provocatively on view — the closest feature film equivalent to music promo videos."

Whereas **Flashdance** was about a character who was a dancer, **Footloose** was about an ordinary young man who challenged a town's laws against dancing. Director Herb Ross chose Lynne Taylor-Corbett to choreograph **Footloose** after seeing her work *Great Galloping Gottschalk* at American Ballet Theatre: "I thought she'd be good for this because of the wit and sense of humor she displayed in that comedy duet for two men. I didn't want a choreographer who was only interested in dance numbers. I wanted one who was interested in humanity." Taylor-Corbett, who approached the film with the challenge that "the choreography must serve the script and be very realistic, which excluded many choreographic possibilities," experimented with her non-dancing leads, Kevin Bacon and Lori Singer, by watching them dance in clubs and building on their natural physical responses to music. Denying that **Footloose** was a dance film, but rather "dance as a metaphor for freedom," Ross and Taylor-Corbett worked with the leads and young Brigham Young University and Utah State College students "more from an actor's viewpoint than a dancer's" (*Dance Magazine*, March 1984).

For her efforts, Taylor-Corbett received Kevin Grubb's praise in *Dance Magazine*, May 1984: "The opening of dozens of dancing feet cutting the rug to Kenny Loggin's title song is Taylor-Corbett at her most inventive. A scene in which ... Christopher Penn learns to dance with the help of a Walkman is genuinely funny and touches on the innocence of Middle America without caricaturing it."

The popular social dances of the day differed greatly from the social dances of the past. They were performed solo, as Kevin Grubb noted in "Dance Films '85" (*Dance Magazine*, December 1984): "Neither style emphasizes partnering and — as illustrated by Marine Jahan in **Flashdance** and Sony Walkman in **Footloose**— today's recreational dancing is an insular sport cut off, except for occasional slams and thrusts, from human contact."

But **Dirty Dancing** was about partner dancing of the early 1960s, contemporized and eroticized by choreographer Kenny Ortega and its cast.

> Ortega shines in that his staging is barely noticeable to the untrained eye. He took social dance forms and sculpted them in a kinetic way for the camera. Rather than rely on postproduction tricks or slip in doubles as in the film **Flashdance**, the producers use dance as a language, trusting its basic value. Director (Emile) Ardolino says that "dance is used to advance plot and to reveal character. Dance is a metaphor for what was about to happen across the country, both politically and sexually." ...The simplicity of showing an "old fashioned" social dance blossom into a wilder, freer, physical expression makes the film highly accessible" [Deirdre Towers, *Dance Magazine*, October 1987].

Flashdance and **Footloose** had both used highly publicized dance-ins for their stars (Marine Jahan for Jennifer Beals and Peter Tramm for Kevin Bacon), frustrating dancing actors and actresses looking for leading roles in films. **Dirty Dancing**, with its talented leads Patrick Swayze, Jennifer Grey, and Cynthia Rhodes, enhanced the careers of its technically proficient performers. It also gave a diverse career opportunity to choreographer Kenny Ortega's assistant, Miranda Garrison. Kelly Bishop (from the stage success *A Chorus Line*) had been hired for the role of Vivian, the "bungalow bunny," but when the actress playing the role of Jennifer Grey's mother became ill, Bishop was moved into the role. Producer Linda Gottlieb recalled what happened next in *Premiere* Magazine: "Our assistant choreographer, Miranda Garrison, wanders over. I notice that she looks different. She's put on makeup, changed out of her leotards. She looks sort of sexy. Sort of like — Vivian. 'Let me read for that part,' she begs. We read her. She is wonderful. She will alternate between being Patrick Swayze's onscreen temptation and, when she is not shooting, his offscreen dance coach. On low-budget films everybody does everything."

As **Saturday Night Fever** had done for John Travolta in the '70s, **Dirty Dancing** made a star of Patrick Swayze, who previously had appeared in non-musical film and television roles. The classic ballet training and background Swayze had been encouraged to hide so that his macho movie actor image would not be damaged served him well this time...and women all over the world swooned, voting him "The Sexiest Man Alive." His mother, Patsy Swayze, created the dance sequences for several successful non-musical films during the decade (**Urban**

Cowboy, 1980, **Big Top Pee Wee**, 1988) as well as creating and producing a "How-To-Dance" video featuring her famous and talented son and his wife (also a dancer and choreographer), Lisa Niemi.

Not only were choreographers experimenting with hip new camera techniques, they were also dealing with the "needle-drop" trend of best-selling soundtracks for the musical basis of their work. Original musical scores were not being created for musical films; instead, individual numbers from various rock stars were collected and combined for a film's score. This new procedure assured the studios of best-selling soundtrack albums. It was difficult for the choreographers to build a number physically and emotionally, since the rock songs stayed at one level and then merely faded out, never being intentionally arranged to support, build or aid a musical sequence on film. The endless beat of the new rock hits only allowed endless numbers which locked, bopped, hip-hopped and popped — then simply faded out, rather than building to an emotional climax.

Trying to compare or compete with the new music video filming and editing techniques greatly influenced the filming of **A Chorus Line** (Jeffrey Hornaday, 1985), which everyone hoped would be *the* dance film of the decade, emulating its stage success. Getting the longest running musical onto the screen had a long and troubled history. Original creator Michael Bennett spent years developing the film for Universal, but his concepts to put his "baby" on film were simply not what the studio wanted: a documentary approach or a sequel. Bennett instinctively knew that the property could not simply be transposed from stage to film. When discussions bogged down, Bennett walked away from his contract — and a film career.

Because of the success of his participation in **Flashdance**, Jeffrey Hornaday was hired to collaborate with director Richard Attenborough, who was filming his first musical. During the making of the film, Tony Fields, playing the role of Al in the film, praised Hornaday in *Dance Magazine* ("Jeffrey Hornady Breaks Tradition," by Dan Cox, December 1985): "Jeff has a style of taking what was, what is, and what will be, and making it all come together." But Alyson Reed, a very capable dancer with a wide range of dance technique and skills, balked when Hornaday wanted to use other girls in quick-cuts of pirouettes and acrobatics during her performance as Cassie in her "Let Me Dance for You" solo. Writer Dan Cox, in the same *Dance Magazine* article, described Hornaday's approach to dance on film: "Hornaday likes to use the camera. He ignores the full-figure, single-angle shots made popular by the deans of dance films, Fred Astaire and Gene Kelly, in favor of a variety of camera angles mixed rapid-fire into a collage. One pirouette might be seen from seven different perspectives, but never for more than a split second at a time. Thus, the dance movement itself is blurred; the urgency of the moment is prominent."

Critics and fans who had eagerly awaited the film were disappointed (*People Magazine*: "Jeffrey (**Flashdance**) Hornaday's half-hearted attempt to update the dancing for the '80s also misfires"). Nevertheless, it contains some excellent choreography and performances, and in future years it may be appreciated for its blessings.

The press of the day was filled with plans to transfer other stage successes to the screen. CBS Theatrical purchased *Stepping Out* for Cher, Shirley Maclaine, and Mary Tyler Moore (it would be made in 1992 with a very different cast); Tri Star bought *I'm Getting My Act Together and Taking It on the Road* to star Dolly Parton and be directed by Herbert Ross, and *Dreamgirls*, starring Whitney Houston, would be directed by Bob Fosse. In 1982, **Annie** (Joe Layton and Arlene Phillips) and **The Best Little Whorehouse in Texas** (Tony Stevens) were two stage musicals which actually made it to the screen. They were the last of the spectacular musical shows to be filmed.

Top: Dance as liberation: Patrick Swayze lifts Jennifer Grey in a "swan lift" in the highly successful **Dirty Dancing** (Kenny Ortega, Vestron, 1987). *Bottom:* Robust "Aggies" (L to R): Stephen Moore, Jerry Mitchell, David Warren Gibson, Douglas Robb, Jeff Calhoun and Ed Forsyth, stomp their way through Tony Stevens' choreography in **The Best Little Whorehouse in Texas** (Universal, 1982).

Joe Layton, whose innovative theater and television work had won him multiple awards and a major place in the industry as a director and choreographer, was billed with "Production numbers supervised by" on **Annie**. His approach to the integration of dance was quite focused: "Choreography is like writing a piece of material with words. If you translate words into moods, attitudes, style, and motion, you have choreography. Dance as decoration simply doesn't cut it anymore. I used to hope my dance numbers would stop the show. Now I think of the whole piece. Even if you are a choreographer and not a director, too, that's a 'must' attitude. You are not a department. You are part of the continuation of the story" (*Dance Magazine,* November 1978).

In discussing his work on **Whorehouse**, Tony Stevens remembered that much of what he had created in the rehearsal hall for the rousing "Aggies" dance number had to be drastically changed once he arrived on the actual movie set. When it came time to edit the film, the studio (Universal) suddenly got cold feet about the dance numbers and begin eliminating everything that did not contain the film's stars, Dolly Parton and Burt Reynolds. So much of what Stevens felt was his best work found its way to the cutting room floor. The male chorus of the film contains many budding choreographers, among them Jeff Calhoun, Jeffrey Hornaday, Mark Knowles, Jerry Mitchell, Vince Paterson, and Dennon Rawles.

Other stage-to-screen transfers of the eighties were the revival of the old-fashioned **The Pirates of Penzance** (staged by Graciela Daniele with contemporary humor in 1983) and the pop success **Little Shop of Horrors** (Pat Garrett, 1986). Most of the major stage musical hits were now imports from Britain, and even though Gillian Lynne was announced as being signed to do *Les Miserables* on film in 1989, it did not happen.

Original screen musicals came in many shapes, sizes and degrees of success. For example, The disco era moaned its last in 1980 with **Can't Stop the Music** (Arlene Phillips) and **Xanadu** (Kenny Ortega and Jerry Trent), two films which attempted to copy the success of the classic movie musical and update the form. **Can't Stop the Music** combined the lavish production values of earlier musicals with the music and attitudes of the '80's, but was crucified by critics. (*Newsweek*, July 7, 1980: "…ushers in a new concept in entertainment — it's the first all-singing, all-dancing horror film, the **Dawn of the Dead** of the disco generation. If this movie doesn't scare you, you're already dead.") **Xanadu** went even further. It was a big-budget attempt to pair a popular songster of the day (Olivia Newton-John) with a musical film icon (Gene Kelly). It combined contemporary and conventional dance, the pop appeal of roller skating, lasers and other disco effects — and hoped to get a hit soundtrack out of the results. Hopefully, both films are sealed in a time capsule somewhere and will be seen by future generations.

Xanadu introduced up-and-coming choreographer and director Kenny Ortega to the master, Gene Kelly. Although not a classically trained dancer, Ortega had a varied theater background, coming to films after being noticed for his work with the avant-garde rock theater group The Tubes, who appeared in **Xanadu**. Kelly welcomed the ambition and talent of the younger man, forming a mentor student relationship which would serve Ortega well in his future. Ortega fondly remembered Kelly showing him hours of his past work, discussing options, camera work, and the many details of his choreography.

While working on **Xanadu**, Ortega tried to explain how his street-dance background influenced his choreography: "My dance traces back to the non-professionals in discotheques and clubs; to non-pro rock and roll dancers who are now 'moving off' to a new kind of music. It fiddles along with the lead guitar. It does riffs…. It's like a tap dancer does *his* riffs. My dancers and I — instead of just moving to that musical riff tempo and snapping our fingers in a regular metronomic beat — create our own phrases. Our own riffs. Body riffs" (*Dance Magazine*, August 1980).

Gene Kelly graciously shares the spotlight in a soft-shoe routine with dance novices Michael Beck and Olivia Newton-John in **Xanadu** (Kenny Ortega and Jerry Trent, Universal, 1980).

The other choreographer on the film, Jerry Trent, was responsible for the more lyric, classical dance form sequences in the film. He told Viola Hegyi Swisher for *Dance Magazine* (August 1980) that he had learned something from this first major film assignment: "I've learned that for all the camera's ability to see some things your human eyes doesn't [sic] see, you as choreographer have to remember that the camera doesn't have a mind at all — except yours."

Choreographic artists with a sense of the past and a base in the present were able to imaginatively recall other eras through eighties sensibilities. **Pennies from Heaven** (Danny Daniels, 1981) harked back to the thirties with evocative dances and staging, viewed with the new sardonic attitude. Despite this viewpoint, the film was a sincere tribute to Robert Alton, Fred Astaire, Busby Berkeley, Nick Castle, Louis DaPron, Hermes Pan, and others. With former choreographer Herbert Ross directing (he calls the film "the most complete, in terms of realizing the dream") and Daniels' exquisite tap expertise and creativity (assisted by his son, Daniel Joseph Giagni, and Randy Doney), the film was one of the few dance dramas ever to be produced in Hollywood. The opulence and mindless frivolity of the performers within the musical numbers were the antithesis of the Depression-era setting and bleak hopelessness of the story and characters. Another period musical, **Victor/Victoria** (Paddy Stone, 1982) looked back at the past with a loving giggle and played sexual games in its humorous period nightclub musical numbers.

Original musical pastiches of later rock 'n' roll times included **Grease 2** (Patricia Birch,

Steve Martin leads a bevy of blonde-wigged beauties in **Pennies from Heaven** (Danny Daniels, MGM, 1981).

1982), which tried to match the extraordinary success of the first film; **La Bamba** (Miguel Delgado, 1987); **Hairspray** (Edward Love, 1988); **Shag** (Kenny Ortega); and **Great Balls of Fire** (Bill & Jacqui Landrum, 1989). All used a well-researched social dance vocabulary of the time but theatricalized it to glorious proportions.

Fame (Louis Falco, 1980) was completely contemporary, taking advantage of Falco's concert dance daring and experimentation. **The Blues Brothers** (Carlton Johnson, 1980) was also contemporary, but the musical numbers were inserted in the dated performance setting manner. In a *Dance Magazine* review of **Popeye** (1980), controversial director Robert Altman's only musical film, the depth of expertise and intricate collaboration between movement experts now called upon was evident — and the recognition perceptive: "Hovey Burgess' Circus Technique, Roberto Messina's stunt work and Sharon Kinney's modern dance adds up to the most uniquely choreographed film musicals to ever come to the screen."

The original musical sequel **Staying Alive** (Dennon and Sayhber Rawles, 1983) tried to pull **Saturday Night Fever** into the '80s and big box-office, taking Tony Manero," John Travolta's character, from the discos to the Broadway stage. Critics complained that its MTV style of quick-cut photography defeated the strength of its dancing. It was difficult, they said, to assess the skills of the choreographers and the dancers, with all of the flash, smoke, and hysterical editing. Directed by Sylvester Stallone, the film was called "A terpsichorean **Rocky**.... choreographers Dennon and Sahyber Rawles limit Travolta's dancing to unimaginative jazz steps, a few firmly planted lifts, and one or two leaps (filmed in slow motion, of course) that attempt to capture the same kind of macho dynamism as the **Rocky** films. Ultimately, the dance numbers look more like fight scenes than dance choreography" (Kevin Grubb, *Dance Magazine*, October 1983).

More than ever before, the new film choreographers had to be able to create a wide range of dance styles with other original American film musicals ranging from the traditional (**The Great Muppet Caper**, Anita Mann, 1981, and **The Muppets Take Manhattan**, Chris Chadman, 1984) to pop (**Streets of Fire**, Jeffrey Hornaday, 1984, **School Daze**, Otis Sallid, 1988, and **Sing**, John Carrafa, Otis Sallid, 1989).

As American society redefined its male images to include male dancers as sex symbols, the star power of two male dancing film star–choreographers of the decade, Mikhail Baryshnikov (a Russian ballet star) and Gregory Hines (an African-American tap dancer), allowed dance to be used as a major part of their films.

Whereas Bill "Bojangles" Robinson had only been given the opportunity to star in musical films, Gregory Hines's multi-dimensional appeal allowed him to move from musical to drama to comedy in a variety of film roles. One of the last to rise from the ranks of a dance act (with brother, Maurice, and their father), Hines found success on Broadway and was quickly cast in films. Along with his performance talents, he brought his choreographic expertise to intricate tap-dancing sequences, dubbing it "improvography."

Hines exposed his tap-dancing expertise to new generations of film audiences with **The Cotton Club** (Claudia Asbury, George Faison, Hines, Henry Le Tang, Michael Meacham, Arthur Mitchell, and Michael Smuin, 1984 — more about this film later) and **Tap** (Hines and Le Tang, 1989). **Tap** captured the greatness of tap masters Harold Nicholas, Sandman Sims, Steve Condos, Savion Glover, Sammy Davis, Jr., and Hines, and was directed by Nick Castle, Jr., dedicated to his brilliant father who had spent his life defining tap on film.

Baryshnikov, introduced on film in **The Turning Point**, melded Hines' tap expertise with his balletic prowess when they costarred in **White Nights** (Twyla Tharp, Baryshnikov, Roland Petit, and Hines, 1985), using their diverse dance styles to advance the plot and reveal their characters and nationalities through dance. In the film, Baryshnikov effectively used dance to express the frustrations of his Russian-dancer character:

> Baryshnikov performs a stirring, earthy solo.... Photographed in the dimness of a half-lit stage ... Baryshnikov's angry turns and clenched fists evoke more than ... frustration with Soviet repression; there's a good deal of Baryshnikov himself here. Choreographed by him with some help from (Twyla) Tharp, the dance is not long or expansive, but so charged with emotional honesty that viewers can't help reflecting on Baryshnikov's actual defection from the Soviet Union eleven years ago" [*Dance Magazine*, November 1985].

Baryshnikov's next film, **Dancers** (1987), focused on ballet and the relationships within a ballet company and was not nearly as successful. Other classical dance–based films of the decade were **Nijinsky** (Sir Kenneth MacMillan, Léonide Massine, 1980) and **Six Weeks** (Ann Ditchburn, 1982).

While the original musical drama **The Cotton Club** was being filmed, the dance world anticipated it greatly. It promised to recreate the historic dance wealth of the famed nightclub and legendary African-American artists who had performed there.

Michael Smuin, Tony award–winning Broadway choreographer, prolific ballet creator, and one of the choreographers on **The Cotton Club**, began his collaboration with director Francis Ford Coppola with **Rumble Fish** (1983). Rather than creating traditional dance pieces, Smuin was challenged in that film to create unique movement sequences. Coppola contacted him to stage the fight scenes in the film, saying, "I've seen your ballets. You do great violence, really poetic violence. I want to get some of that into what I'm doing." When he told Smuin to go

John Travolta and Cynthia Rhodes, flanked by the newest generation of screen dancers, in **Staying Alive** (Dennon and Sayhber Rawles, Paramount, 1983).

ahead and write the fight scene, Smuin protested, "I'm not a writer!" to which Coppola responded, "You write ballets. Go ahead and write the fight scene." "So I spent three days underneath that goddamn bridge," Smuin remembered (*San Francisco*, February 1984). "It was 110 degrees. I was just miserable out there. And I wrote out the whole fight. I'd just walk through things.... I let my imagination go. I did it like it was a dance, just the way I saw it. I put it all down on about three pieces of paper and handed it to him." A critic would later dub the fight scenes "beautifully balletic."

Coppola's first collaboration with a choreographer — Hermes Pan on **Finian's Rainbow** — was less than successful, but Smuin was filled with praise for the flamboyant director during the **Cotton Club** filming. "My relationship with Francis has been nothing short of wonderful. He's completely supportive of my work. For a non-dancer, his dance instincts are astute," he told Kevin Grubb in "Dancefilms '85" (*Dance Magazine*, December 1984). That article detailed the use of multiple choreographers on the film:

> George Faison, who left **The Cotton Club** shortly after it began shooting (but is given credit in the film nonetheless) was replaced not only by Smuin, but also by noted Broadway choreographer Henry LeTang ... Dance Theatre of Harlem artistic director Arthur Mitchell, Claudia Asbury and Michael Meacham. Gregory Hines is given a special credit as "Tap Improvographer" for A Capella tap numbers he performs. "I'm estimating we shot about twenty-two numbers," says Le Tang, who choreographed all of the picture's tap routines, "and those are only the ones *I* did. I have no idea what numbers Michael and Arthur worked on.... There was an enormous amount of everything — dancing, singing, specialty acts — we shot enough for three movies." Smuin remains doubtful, however, that all the choreographers will be satisfied with what dances are used in the film. "We've shot so much that's absolutely gorgeous, but you've

got to keep in mind that there's more to this film than just the dancing. How much
of the choreography will be in the final cut will be determined by Francis and God.

When the film was released, however, the endless reaction shots, quick cuts, and snippets
of dance, determined by God — or Francis? — dashed everyone's hopes. Somewhere, there are
hours of sensational choreography and dancing gathering dust.

In 1980, Coppola had even attempted to create a new musical production unit at his
Zoetrope Studios in Hollywood, signing Gene Kelly to be in charge of assembling the creative
team. Coppola was quoted in *Variety*: "We hope the new venture will recall earlier years when
the Freed unit had such talents as Kelly himself, Judy Garland, Frank Sinatra, Esther Williams,
Ann Miller, and directors [sic] such as Joe Pasternak, Vincente Minnelli, Stanley Donen, George
Sidney, and Freed." After spending nearly $2 million, the unit produced **One from the Heart**
(choreographed by Kenny Ortega and musical number supervision by Kelly, 1982) and planned
Sex and Violence as their second film before the glorious plan went bankrupt.

Break dancers now regularly appeared on street corners in America's major cities and on
television, bringing the greatest influx of new dance styles since the 1940s. Popping, locking,
boogie, hip-hop, floating, Egyptian, freestyle and other terms were invented by the kids to
describe their styles, born of the South Bronx neighborhood ghettos in the early seventies. The
young dancers created their own steps to compete in genuine "gang warfare" (perhaps an after-
effect of the influence of **West Side Story**?). They spent hours perfecting their skills for the next
rivalry on the streets or in the clubs, jealously guarding their combinations from piracy by competing dancers or groups. As the new dance style came up from the underground and began a
crossover into commercial entertainment, a new breed of dancers and choreographers arrived
on film and television screens. The new style was described in "Break Dancers Twist, Turn Way
Uptown" (*Los Angeles Times*, March 25, 1984): "Break dancing changes the entire gravity of dance
from top to bottom not just with their bodies, but *on* their bodies."

As street dancing and disco contests became an outlet for non-violent competition among
gangs and ethnic groups, a rash of dance-as-competition original film musicals flooded the mar-
ket: **Breakin' 1** (Jaime Rogers), **Breakin' 2: Electric Bugaloo** (Bill Goodson), and **Body Rock**
(Russell Clark, Dona Davis-Clark, Joanne Divito, Susan Scanlan) in 1984; **Girls Just Want to
Have Fun** (Bill Goodson, Steve LaChance, and Otis Sallid) and **The Last Dragon** (Torrance
Mathis, Ernie Reyes, Ron Van Clief, Lester Wilson) in 1985; **The In Crowd** (Jerry Evans, Peggy
Holmes, Lynne Taylor-Corbett, and Linda Weisburg) in 1988, and the aptly titled **Dance to
Win** (Paula Abdul, Jerry Evans) in 1989. The leading characters were either fighting to get on
a popular television dance show, fighting for their group to win the street dance contest or fight-
ing for their lives. Suddenly, it was cool to have dance as a social skill.

While working on **Beat Street**, another of the dance-as-competition films, Lester Wilson
spoke to *Dance Magazine*, April 1984, and argued against the notion that break dancing was
purely improvisational: "What these kids do today is carefully thought through. To choreograph
this film, I had to study their movements closely, see how they could be captured by the camera — adding a turn, an arm, a stop — showing them how they could develop their own movements further. The discipline involved was to have them go over specific movements again and
again until I captured it on film most effectively." He combined professional dancers with the
novices in a break-dance ballet and predicted: "Break dancing will continue to develop as an
idiom, just as modern dance and ballet have continued to explore and assimilate new kinds of
movement."

Like so many of the musicals of the 1940s which used dance teams and soloists performing

In one of the dance-to-win films, Donovan Leitch (son of Rock icon Donovan) shows off for his class in **The In Crowd** (Jerry Evans and Lynn Taylor-Corbett, Orion, 1987).

their own routines, for the first time films began to list multiple choreographers. The complexities of the street and social dance of the period required that various specialists be hired to do portions of dance sequences, usually bringing their own dancers with them. **Fast Forward** (1985), another dance as competition film, with its record-breaking tally of seven choreographers (Rick Atwell, Aimee Covo, Felix, Pamela Poitier, Gary Porter, Robin Summerfield, and Charlie Washington), illustrates this trend. As with the social fabric of American society, there were now so many factions and interest groups within social dance styles that these specialists were required. There were few (if any) dancers who could do it all. The promising aspect was that young dancers were being rewarded for their hours of practice and creativity by being offered screen exposure for their art.

    Fast Forward was originally to be choreographed by Michael Peters. When Peters was unavailable, director Sidney Poitier selected Rick Atwell, a former Harkness Ballet dancer who submitted an audition tape of his work. "Sidney talked to me in terms of dramatic intention, what the numbers had to say," Atwell recalled for Kevin Grubb of *Dance Magazine* ("Dancefilms '85," December 1984). He used a cast of eight dancers to play the dance team "who came from completely different backgrounds. It wasn't easy to find the common denomination in each of them that made them look as if they'd been dancing together for years."

    Unfortunately the hyperactive camera work and edits, weak scenarios, needle-drop soundtracks, limited budgets, and the fear of classic musical film formats and traditional musical numbers somehow diluted the excellent work of the choreographers and the dancers in these films. A review of **Fast Forward** in the *Motion Picture Guide* sums up the genre: "The choreo by Rick

Atwell was first rate, but (the film) was a rewind most of the time as it was passé before it began and had very little to do with reality among teenagers...."

After the phenomenal success of his work in **Dirty Dancing,** Kenny Ortega (with Miranda Garrison) went on to explore the contemporary Latin dance scene in **Salsa** (1988). His valiant attempt was appraised in a *Los Angeles Times* review: "(Ortega) could easily claim self-defense in killing director Boaz Davidson. Certainly Davidson's penchant for cutting away from dancers to close-ups of elbows murders whatever artistry Ortega has evolved.... **Salsa** just might be the hottest dirtiest dancing of the season, but we'll never know." Ortega moved on to direction himself (**Newsies, Hocus Pocus**) to further control the integrity of his work.

John Carrafa, interviewed by Susan Retter for the *Los Angeles Times* (January 29, 1989) while working on his first film, **Sing** (1989, with Otis Sallid), spoke about reconstructing the tap dances from the film **Singin' in the Rain** for Twyla Tharp's 1985 stage production. "I realized how much I could learn from watching old films. It's all right there for anybody who really wants to find out how to do this." But too often it seemed that all that Robert Alton, Fred Astaire, Busby Berkeley, Gene Kelly, and Hermes Pan had introduced to musical cinema techniques was now ignored as filmmakers experimented with what they *hoped* "the kids will pay money to see." As with the music industry, the inmates were running the asylum.

The most satisfying dance film of the '80s for buffs of earlier musicals was MGM's **That's Dancing!**, assembled lovingly in 1985 by the team who had produced **That's Entertainment!** and **That's Entertainment! Part II**. With Gene Kelly acting as "creative advisor," the film featured most of Hollywood's dance greats, briefly mentioned choreography, and tried to be contemporary with clips from music videos and break-dance films. *Variety* stated in its January 23, 1985 review: "MGM and Jack Haley, Jr. amply demonstrate once more what audiences once liked about movies, but face the problem of what audiences like now ... the wonderful work of Fred Astaire and Ginger Rogers and on through an absolutely complete list of the greats ... the moderns shown are embarrassingly clumsy by comparison, especially the group from 'Fame,' jumping up and down on cars. Whatever that was, it wasn't dancing."

A book was published in conjunction with the film, containing interesting observations about dance on film from some of the greats of the dance world for future film dancemakers to consider. Gene Kelly was quoted:

> There seems to be a common misapprehension that dancing and the motion picture are well suited to each other — they are not. The dance is a three-dimensional art form, while the motion picture is two-dimensional. I would compare dancing basically to sculpture and the motion picture to painting. So the difficulties we have in transferring a dance onto film are simply the ones of putting a 3-D art form into a 2-D panel.... You have to construct a dance so that it can be cut and edited, and do it in a way that won't disturb the viewer. You learn to use the camera as part of the choreography. It's possible that a lot of fine dancing has been ineffectual in the movies because it was photographed unimaginatively. Filming dance will always be a problem because the eye of the camera is coldly realistic, demanding that everything look natural — and dancing is unrealistic. That's the challenge, and all art is a compromise between your ideas and whatever means you have at your disposal.

George Balanchine added his thoughts: "Films should be a product of greater imagination and fantasy than the theatre because of the larger scope which elements of time and space have in motion pictures. I also think the responsibility of anyone working in film is greater than in the theatre because he is addressing people all over the world. This is why I think a serious, creative, inventive approach to films is an absolute necessity."

The most serious dance films of the decade occurred when Spain was heard from once again internationally with a series of all-dance films from star-choreographer Antonio Gades and director Carlos Saura: **Blood Wedding** (1981—"considered to be the dance film of the decade"—*Motion Picture Guide*), **Carmen** (1983), and **El Amor Brujo** (1986 —"Gades and Saura have opted for a more direct approach in this film than in their two previous collaborations ... neither a cinematic rendering of a set choreography ... nor an exterior plot intertwined with that of a ballet ...the film uses dance as an integral part of the protagonist's lives"). With co-creator Saura and partner Christina Hoyos, Gades took the promise he showed in the 1970s with **Los Tarantos** and blossomed with these three dance blockbusters. Combining classic Flamenco and ballet, innovative camerawork, and dramatic scenarios, settings, and decor, he created films that dazzled audiences and critics alike around the world. Dale Thomajohn, in his colorful style, asked, "The best movie version of **Carmen**? Hell, this was the best movie of the 1980s," singling out "an especially exciting a cappella dance interlude provided by the ensemble being drilled ... their feet captured in close-up, they stomp back and forth across the studio floor.... When my mother and I attended a screening ... in the 2,400-seat auditorium of a Boca Raton college, at the conclusion of this dance one-sixth of the audience, an old man, shouted 'Bravo!'" The innovative cinematic explorations of Spain also produced **The Court of the Pharoahs** (José Granero, 1985), a daring film which told the story of a theatrical troupe who dared to perform a politically forbidden dance under the Franco regime. One scarcely viewed Chinese film (**Illusory Thoughts**, 1988) allowed Hong Kong–born American dancer and choreographer Patrick Chu — also the film's producer, writer, director and star — to fill the screen with all-dance in this personal exploration of his "thoughts on life, love, religion, and art."

Cuba produced its first musical comedy film, **Patakin** (Victor Cuellar, 1985), and Nicaragua was also heard from with **The Spectre of War** (Alberto Mendez, 1989), a film about a professional dancer who is injured in revolutionary fighting, ending his dance career. "Dance as politics" became a new genre.

Another unique (and brave) film came from Argentina in 1988. **Tango Bar,** choreographed by a raft of leading tango specialists (Nelson Avila, Santiago Ayala, Lilliana Belfiore, Doris Petroni, Carlos Rivarola, Nelida Rodriquez, and Norma Viola), used a brief plot to weave fascinating versions of the tango's evolution from its beginning as a turn-of-the-century social dance to a balletic interpretation. Film clips from Chaplin to Astaire and Rogers were interlaced for a fascinating, history on film of the Buenos Aires dance craze.

From England, original musicals ranged from contemporary (**Absolute Beginners**, David Toguri, 1986) to traditional (**Bert Rigby, You're a Fool**, Larry Hyman, 1989) with highly imaginative dance and staging input in both. Successful Great Britain–based choreographers from the London Contemporary Dance Theatre company, Robert North, Micha Bergese, Anthony Van Laast, and Tom Jobe, began creating dance sequences for films (**Slow Dancing in the Big City**, **High Spirits**, **Excalibur**, **Nutcracker**).

In 1982, Australian tap expert and stage star David Atkins choreographed **Pirate Movie** and **Star Struck** and choreographed and starred in **Squizzy Taylor**, leading Australia into the film musical genre.

In the non-musical films of the decade, dance became a powerful vehicle for filmmakers to portray fantasy or make sardonic or humorous statements. The visions of people singing and dancing on the street which were accepted — and welcomed — up until the mid–1950s were now greeted with guffaws. And the film and dance makers used that to their advantage.

The dance-as-satire genre generated major laughs with such fare as the whimsical dance

Antonio Gades embraces Laura Del Sol in a still from the Flamenco film **Carmen** (Orion, 1983).

input of Danny Daniels in **Indiana Jones and the Temple of Doom** (about which *Time* magazine said, "Another production number commences with Indy and Willie scrambling on the floor to find the antidote and the diamond among flying ice cubes, bullets, balloons, and feet as the chorus girls giddily scatter through the chaos. Wow!"—May 21, 1984). Other films featuring work in this genre were **To Be or Not to Be** (Alan Johnson and Charlene Painter) and **Monty Python's The Meaning of Life** (Arlene Phillips) in 1983; **Top Secret** (Gillian Gregory) and **Privates on Parade** (Gillian Gregory) in 1984; **Cocoon** (Gwen Verdon), **National Lampoon's European Vacation** (Gillian Lynne), and **Lust in the Dust** (Stan Mazin) in 1985; **Three Amigos** (Shirley Kirkes) and **Haunted Honeymoon** (Graciela Daniele) in 1986; **Earth Girls Are Easy** (Russell Clark, Sarah Elgart, ISO, and Wayne "Crescendo" Ward) and **The Naked Gun** (Jerry Evans) in 1989.

Writer-director John Hughes, who began his prolific career during the '80s, used dance and musical numbers in all of his early films, collaborating with a wide range of choreographers, selecting them carefully for their particular expertise to supply the right mood and movement for each: **The Breakfast Club** (Dorain Grusman, 1985), **Pretty in Pink** (Kenny Ortega, 1986), **Ferris Bueller's Day Off** (Wilbert Bradley, Kenny Ortega, 1986), and **Uncle Buck** (Miranda Garrison, 1989).

To show the hilarious suburbia of which the young newlyweds tried to become a part in **She's Having a Baby** (1988), Tony Stevens got his chance to collaborate with Hughes. Stevens was asked to create multiple patterns and variations in movement which became (through cooperative efforts between Hughes and Stevens in editing and finding an appropriate song) a whimsical lawn mower ballet.

In the wide range of period dramas and comedies produced during the 1980s, international choreographers supplied rich movement details to comment on the lifestyles of the various decades. For the 1920s filmmakers offered **Maxie** (Matthew Diamond, 1985) and **Good Morning, Babylon** (Gino Landi, 1987); for the 1930s, **Johnny Dangerously** (Tony Stevens, 1984) and **The Color Purple** (Claude Thompson, 1985); and for the 1940s, **Hope and Glory** (Anthony Van Laast, 1987) and **Who Framed Roger Rabbit?** (David Toguri and Quinny Sacks, 1988). To evoke the style of the 1950s and 1960s, **Peggy Sue Got Married** (Toni Basil and Chrissy Bocchino, 1986) enhanced a prom setting to put audiences in the mood.

Adventure and fantasy films generously used choreography: **Romancing the Stone** (Jeffrey Hornaday) in 1984; **Santa Claus: The Movie** (Pat Garrett), **Mata Hari** (Lucy Igaz, Senanda Kumar), and **The Emerald Forest** (José Possi) in 1985; **Labyrinth** (Charles Augins), **Legend** and **Highlander** (Arlene Phillips), and **The Golden Child** (Michael Smuin) in 1986; **The Running Man** (Paula Abdul), **Red Riding Hood** (Barbara Allen), and **Sleeping Beauty** and **Snow White** (Jacob Kalusky) in 1987; **High Spirits** (Micha Bergese), **Jane and the Lost City** (Gillian Gregory), **The Lair of the White Worm** (Imogen Claire), **Serpent and the Rainbow** (Carmen DeLavallade and Juan Rodriquez), **Red Heat** (Ginger Farley), **Willow** (Eleanor Fazan), and **Salome's Last Dance** (Arlene Phillips) in 1988; and **The Karate Kid Part III** (Paula Abdul and Pat E. Johnson) and **Farewell to the King** (Anne Semler) in 1989.

The horror-thriller genre began using dance and acknowledging its contributors: **Fright Night** (Dorain Grusman) in 1985; **Killer Party** (Malcolm Gale) in 1986; **Evil Dead 2** (Andrea Brown, Susan Labatt, Tam G. Warner) and **Hell Squad** (Andrea Hartford) in 1987; **Bloody Pom Poms** (Lucinda Dickey) in 1988; and **Fright Night, Part 2** (Russell Clark) and **Phantom of the Opera** (Tony Fields, Gyorgy Gaal) in 1989.

Pioneered in California by former choreographer Ron Fletcher, film star Jane Fonda, and diet guru Richard Simmons, the physical fitness craze was now a part of American life, and suddenly, aerobic dancing made its way into films. Choreographers were needed to create fitness videos, as well as the 1984 made-for-TV film **Getting Physical** (Jerry Evans) and the 1985 features **Perfect** (Natalie Brown, Kim Connell, and Jerry Jackson), **Gimme an "F"** (Steve Merritt), and **Heavenly Bodies** (Brian Foley). These films found a way to justify a rock soundtrack — and give young males a legitimate excuse to ogle fit, tight young ladies bouncing and stretching in form-fitting leotards.

Matthew Broderick rocks out to "Danke Schoen," courtesy of choreographers Wilbert Bradley and Kenny Ortega in **Ferris Bueller's Day Off** (Paramount, 1988).

In the '80s, strippers became "erotic dancers," and multiple clubs sprang up across America. **Stripper** (1986), an excellent documentary on the women who chose this newly accepted profession, featured choreography by the dancers. With the new freedom in film (and that teenaged male audience), scriptors took their cue from those early screenwriters who realized dancers were sympathetic characters, then combined that realization with the new opportunity to show flesh. Films (often made direct-to-video) such as **Takin' It Off** (1984), **Strip for Action** (1986), and **Midnight Dancer** and **Takin' It All Off** (1987) featured erotic dancers, but choreographic credits were not found. In **Dressed to Kill** (1980) director Brian DePalma allowed Angie Dickinson to freely express her sexuality and then get savagely butchered in the elevator. Thus a brand-new "Women in jeopardy" film genre arrived. Horror and dance combined for a rash of dramas about strippers who must die. Although many of the films simply allowed the actresses to improvise their writhing, Ted Lin was nearly a one man industry during the late eighties with **Stripped to Kill** (1987) and two 1989 films, **Dance of the Damned** and **Stripped to Kill II: Live Girls**.

America's phobia of openly appreciating the male body was also relaxing, and with the opening of Chippendales and other ladies-only nightclubs in the early eighties, male strippers moved into the limelight. For the first time in American history, women were allowed to ogle and howl, paw, and stuff money into the flimsy g-strings of pumping male dancers. Choreographers were needed to refine the pumping — taking it from sleaze to a slickly produced-and-choreographed stage fantasy presentation. Dancemaker Nick Denois pioneered at Chippendales, followed by Nancy Gregory and then Steve Merritt, with Ted Lin also creating a *U.S. Male Revue*. In film, **Perfect** and **Gimme an "F"** contained male stripper sequences, along with **A Night in Heaven** (Deney Terrio, 1983), the made-for-TV films **For Ladies Only** (Paul DeRolf, 1981) and **Lady**

Killers (Jerry Evans, 1985) and a direct-to-video feature **The Life and Loves of a Male Stripper** (choreographer unknown).

Despite the above-mentioned unknown dancemakers, a promising trend of the '80s was that choreographers more often received onscreen credit. With new rules and goals from all of the film craft unions, film credits now listed most everyone. The irony, of course, is that people started receiving credit for thirty two bars of the twist in a prom scene, when during the '30s and '40s the credits for dance directors and choreographers who created nearly half of the film's content were often buried, ignored, or missing.

Choreographers were approaching their work from a different angle. Not often asked to create traditional song-and-dance numbers, they were recruited to add behavioral and specialized movement for the cast and mood of the films. As dance itself had changed, so had the input of dance specialists.

One of the new choreographers to surface in the 1980s was Sarah Elgart, who had taken her avant-garde dance concert concepts and work into film. In 1986 she collaborated on three films, **Howard the Duck**, **Fire with Fire**, and **Modern Girls**. A literate, talkative woman, she spoke about her work in the August 7, 1986, issue of *Drama-Logue* with perception and clarity:

> It's staging.... It isn't the kind of dance that looks as if it took years of sweating in the studio. There was a fight scene (in **Howard the Duck**) I had to choreograph with two of my dancers and two actors. That was really interesting for me because it was kind of a choreographed gesture/fight scene but with spoken language — and again dealing with where that line crosses over between what is dance and what is real life.... When I started out I was frequently more concerned with movement than space because I didn't understand that a camera could completely alter a field of depth just by changing a lens. I like to be allowed behind a camera...

In another article in the *Hollywood Reporter* she talked about the variety of chores a choreographer must be prepared to tackle: "In '**Fire with Fire**,' I was brought in to help actors develop their characters. The film revolves around a dance with Catholic school girls and reform school boys. I coordinated the dance, which concentrates on four couples. It was important in this sequence that we execute individual gestures and movements that enable the actors to learn to be their characters."

The title "choreographer" itself was changing. Originally meaning "one who writes with dance," the title was now bestowed on creators who "wrote" scenarios with movement of all sorts. No longer was it acceptable for actors to merely suggest character, combat, or specialized movement. As film collaboration matured, other types of movement specialists were brought in to join the creative team and began to find their way into on-screen credits.

Fight scenes were now especially elaborate, detailed, and dangerous, with the intricate forms of the various Asian martial arts. After decades of creating sensational swordplay, acrobatics, gymnastics, and athletics without being credited, specialists were finally given onscreen credits, in the realm of "choreography." Previously lumped under "stunts," these creators often staged and directed a large amount of a film's running time in the new action films. And attention was being paid to their contributions. Pioneered by the uncredited Bruce Lee and Chuck Norris, '80s action stars Steven Seagal, Jean Claude Van-Damme, and Sho Kosugi asked for — and got — credit for their martial arts choreography, along with Jun Chong, Pat E. Johnson, Harrison Mang, Torrance Mathis, Ernie Reyes, Michael Stone, and Ron Van Clief. Other specialized creators — for creature movement (Peter Elliot), boxing (Ron Stein), swimming (Mike

Alan Johnson directs Mel Brooks in musical staging for "The Inquisition" in **History of the World, Part I** (1981) (photograph courtesy of Alan Johnson).

Nomad), roller skating (Phil Gerard), and fight scene staging (Rick Prieto, George Chung, Jimmy Nickerson)—also received "choreography" credits during the '80s.

In 1984 a group of more than one hundred choreographers approached the Directors Guild of America and asked to be represented. After agreeing to include them into its membership, the Directors Guild was unable to reach an agreement with the Alliance of Motion Picture and Television Producers. They remained unionless.

On August 19, 1988, the Academy Foundation presented yet another event at the AMPAS recalling the Academy Awards for best dance direction from 1935–1937. Nearly ten years after the previous retrospective, the nostalgic evening contained memories from Hermes Pan and Ruby Keeler, introductions of Marge Champion, Cyd Charisse, Ann Miller, Gene Nelson, Miriam Nelson, the Nicholas Brothers, Sheree North, and Onna White, and dazzling film clips to remind all of the contributions made to film by choreographers and dance directors — and a bitter reminder of how the industry refused to acknowledge them. It was all right to wallow in "remember when?," but not good enough for "and the award goes to."

While television, films made for television and cable, and direct-to-video created new job opportunities for dancemakers, the major innovative dance work of the '80s was in the realm of music videos. Awards for choreography are given annually in the MTV Music Video Awards. Music videos perpetuated the old habits, however, most often not crediting the choreography — the very art which helped to make the form unique.

AIDS, the scourge of the creative arts world, began to take its toll of film choreographers as promising careers were stifled and silenced.

Mel Brooks (with Stan Mazin on his direct left and Jerry Trent and Ted Sprague on his right) leads the madness in Alan Johnson's hilarious "Inquisition" number in **History of the World, Part I** (Twentieth Century–Fox, 1981).

Selected Filmography

Absolute Beginners (David Toguri) Orion, 1986, Video:HBO — Musical numbers make this film the unique contemporary musical that it is. Over most everyone's head, it is what **Tommy** might have been.

Amadeus (Twyla Tharp) Orion, 1984, Video: HBO — Tharp's staging of the opera sequences is brilliant — and disturbing — just like the rest of this groundbreaking musical biography.

Annie (Joe Layton, Arlene Phillips) Col, 1982, Video:Col — Good stuff from two major talents in an overblown version of the Broadway hit.

Bert Rigby, You're a Fool (Larry Hyman) WB, 1989, Video:WB — Charming musical numbers devised by Hyman in this feel-good little film.

The Best Little Whorehouse in Texas (Tony Stevens) Univ, 1982, Video:Univ — The best little parts in the worst little mistake since Burt Reynolds embarrassed himself in **At Long Last Love** are the exuberant dancing from the youthful hookers and patrons, plus an Academy Award nomination–winning soft shoe for Charles Durning. Stevens told me that Durning never missed his daily "dancer's warm-up."

Big (Patricia Birch) Fox, 1988, Video:CBS/Fox — When Tom Hanks and Robert Loggia dance on the giant piano keyboard in the toy store, the sheer joy of childlike freedom created by Birch pastes a smile on the audience's faces which lasts throughout the entire feel-good film.

The Blues Brothers (Carlton Johnson) Univ, 1980, Video:Univ — And you thought **1941** was long? The final nail in the movie musical's coffin as those renowned musical comedy masters John Belushi, Dan Aykroyd, and John Landis show us the results of no control. Only choreographer Johnson had a clue.

The Cotton Club (Claudia Asbury, George Faison, Gregory Hines, Henry LeTang, Michael

Julie Andrews, a girl-playing-a-boy-playing-a-girl, fronts the male chorus in some "Razzle Dazzle" period nightclub numbers, created by Paddy Stone in the gender-bending **Victor/Victoria** (MGM, 1982).

Meacham, Arthur Mitchell, Michael Smuin)— Orion, 1984, Video:Embassy — Snippets of what must have been incredible stuff in its original form. I'd like to also acknowledge Maurice Hines's creativity and input. The final train sequence makes you realize Coppola thought he was making a musical. The one film in recent memory from which an entire **That's Dancing** type of film could be created with the sensational dancing which ended up on the cutting room floor.

Dirty Dancing (Kenny Ortega) Vestron, 1987, Video:Vestron — The film that the world — and the movie industry — had been waiting for but didn't know it. Wonderfully erotic period social dance performed by a magnificent cast. Gave dancing a good name once again. Thanks, Kenny!

El Amor Brujo (Antonio Gades) Orion, 1986, Video:Pacific Arts — The best of Spanish dance captured on film. The performances, atmosphere, and choreography in this shattering ballet are superb.

Fame (Louis Falco) MGM, 1980, Video:MGM/UA — Falco's "Hot Lunch Jam" takes over the New York streets and gives this film its most memorable sequence.

Ferris Bueller's Day Off (Kenny Ortega, Wilbert Bradley) Orion, 1986, Video:Par — Kenny scores again (with Bradley's help) with "Danke Schoen," one of the most uplifting musical sequences in recent film history.

Flashdance (Jeffrey Hornaday) Par, 1983, Video: Par — Sensational, fractured photographed dancing which was to telegraph the frantic camera techniques of the future. Made the first ghost dancer-star out of Marine Jahan.

Gimme an "F" (Steve Merritt) Fox, 1985, Video: Fox — Some of the best dancing in contemporary film, combining cheerleading, aerobics, and one of the only erotic film dance numbers performed by a male to date.

History of the World, Part 1 (Alan Johnson) Fox, 1981, Video:CBS/Fox — Inquisition nuns and priests in an Esther Williams number? Mel Brooks's madness brought to life by Johnson's talent.

The In Crowd (Jerry Evans, Lynne Taylor-Corbett, Linda Weisburg)— Orion, 1988, Video: Orion — A charming retelling of the popularity of "American Bandstand"–type teen dancers featuring several wonderful and whimsical recreations of social dances of the 1960s, plus a genuine challenge dance between the two male leads that isn't afraid — it simply dances.

She's Having a Baby (Tony Stevens) Par, 1988, Video:Par — Screenwriter and director John Hughes does it again: realizing the power, humor, and versatility of a musical number, he lets choreographer Stevens create a delightful suburban "lawn mower" ballet to pay tribute to many of the absurd musical sequences of the past, while making a telling statement about the times.

That's Dancing! (Robert Alton, Fred Astaire, Busby Berkeley, Ray Bolger, Johnny Boyle, Bobby Connolly, Stanley Donen, Bob Fosse, Dave Gould, Michael Jackson, Ruby Keeler, Gene Kelly, Ann Miller, Fayard Nicholas, Hermes Pan, Michael Peters, LeRoy Prinz, Bill Robinson, Charles Wal-

ters, Lester Wilson) MGM, 1985, Video:MGM/UA — Once again into the fray to find some gems…and the inclusion of music videos and street dancing is appropriate. We're goin' *on*, folks!

Those Lips, Those Eyes (Dan Siretta) UA, 1980, Video:MGM — In this hardly seen little gem of a film, Siretta recreates some marvelously tacky summer stock staging and choreography.

Top Secret (Gillian Gregory) Par, 1984, Video:Par — Hilarious concepts and execution, featuring Val Kilmer, who gives a sensational light musical performance with Gregory's dances getting major laughs.

White Nights (Mikhail Baryshnikov, Gregory Hines, Roland Petit, Twyla Tharp) Col, 1985, Video:Col — Two dance greats fortunately captured strutting their stuff in a fascinating battle of styles.

THE 1990s— AND BEYOND

As the '90s began, Hollywood tried once again to be hopeful about the movie musical, despite constant critical apathy for the form.

In an editorial, "Cartoons Yes, Humans No," writer Kurt Anderson speculated in the November 22, 1993, issue of *Time Magazine* why the movie musical was simply unacceptable:

> Trained by TV to be literal-minded and by the zeitgeist to be a bit cynical, today's younger generation began driving the traditional musical toward extinction more than two decades ago. The genre's zenith came, not coincidentally, at the last moment of the baby boomers' cultural powerlessness, during the 1950s, when a big Hollywood musical appeared every few months…. As a creator of **The Little Mermaid**, **Beauty and the Beast** and **Aladdin** for Disney, [Alan] Menken has almost single-handedly revived the movie musical, albeit in cartoon form…. It seems that people at the end of the 20th century can accept a movie character bursting into song only if that character is nonhuman. And the main audience for today's new musicals is children, who tend to come with very little disbelief in need of suspending.

With the new success of the Disney animated musical films (**Beauty and the Beast**, **Aladdin**, and **The Lion King**), Steven Spielberg announced that *Cats* would be filmed as an animated feature, completely disregarding the fact that much of the show's success was based on the wonder of the human body in movement. But animated films were once again box-office and the movie musical was accepted by audiences if teapots, genies, and lovable animals sang and danced. The suspended reality was acceptable from nonhumans in the fantasy framework. For the first time, Disney gave choreographic credit for one of their all-animated features — to Brad Flanagan for their 1992 blockbuster **Aladdin**— although, ever since **Snow White and the Seven Dwarfs**, choreographers had always created the dance sequences and filmed them with

Jean-Claude Van Damme battles James Lew with the agility of Baryshnikov in **Timecop** (Universal, 1994) as martial arts choreography becomes important.

live dancers (among them Marge Champion, Roland Dupree, Roy Fitzgerald, and Margaret Kerry), which were then animated.

If contemporary audiences would accept animated characters singing and dancing, then live-action versions of successful cartoons could employ song-and-dance routines — and they did. For **Dick Tracy** (1990), Disney commissioned Stephen Sondheim to write an original musical score, hired pop star Madonna to perform it and Jeffrey Hornaday to choreograph and stage the sequences, and then edited them into bits, pieces, and flashes — intercut with speeding cars, blasting guns, and shots of nearly everything but the dancing. Eleanor Powell's gratitude to Fred Astaire sixty years before for photographing dance properly almost mocked the backwards use of dance on film. More complete (and hilarious) musical sequences added comic highlights to **The Addams Family** (Peter Anastos, 1991) and **Addams Family Values** (Anastos and Adam Shankman, 1993), **The Flintstones** (1994), and **Casper** (1995, both Shankman). They combined the dance creativity of the choreographers and new technical effects to create musical sequences like something from a vintage Warner Bros. Looney Tunes cartoon. **The Mask** (Jerry Evans, 1994) was even brave enough to include a full-blown production number in which the hero, played by new comic superstar Jim Carrey, tries to woo his ladylove, "romancing her and dancing up a storm in one of the film's inventive bits of pyrotechnic choreography" (*Variety*, July 28, 1994). *Drama-Logue* praised the "inspired setpieces — the Mask singing 'Cuban Pete' to turn a mob of would-be captors into a rhythmically swaying conga line is a memorable slice of comic lunacy." The trend to translate successful cartoon-like television shows of the '60s and '70s onto the big screen for the Generation X audience also brought humorous choreographic collaboration: **The Beverly Hillbillies** (Brad Jeffries, 1993), **The Coneheads** (Saul Ybarra, 1994), and **The Brady Bunch Movie** (Joe Cassini, Margaret Hickey Perez, 1995).

On the other hand, real people singing and dancing received constant critical drubbing. In the June 17, 1994, review of the new laserdisc release of **Paint Your Wagon**, the *Entertainment Weekly* critic wrote: "Did you ever watch **West Side Story** and suddenly find the idea of gang members ballet dancing just ridiculous? If so, you're going to have a similar problem seeing the scum of the Old West two-stepping in this musical tale of the California Gold Rush."

The original musicals **Stepping Out** (Danny Daniels), **For the Boys** (Joe Layton), and **Shout** (Michelle Johnston) in 1991 and **Newsies** (Peggy Holmes, Kenny Ortega) in 1992 attempted to reintroduce the form to the new generation of filmgoers. The critics weren't sure what they liked. About **Newsies**, *Variety* praised the choreography — "it's only in the vigorous **West Side Story** style dancing choreographed by Ortega and Peggy Holmes that the film sporadically comes alive"— while *People* complained, "The choreography by director Kenny Ortega, who choreographed **Dirty Dancing**, has a dated, clodhopping style." The 1994 issue of *Film Review* summed it up with, "If for nothing else, this must go down in the annals of history as the bravest film of '92 … Director/choreographer Kenny Ortega's rousingly clichéd songfest has it all: music, romance, slapstick, courage, a few decent villains, a good story and above all some splendid dance sequences. The songs stink … but **Newsies** still makes it as one of the more irresistible stinkers of the year." These Generation X critics were not helpful, dubbing musicals "old-fashioned" and "sentimental," and the uncertain studios, after that first important weekend in '90s box-office calculations, abruptly pulled these films from release. They moved quickly to cable television and video.

Gene Kelly, interviewed extensively by Hilary deVries for the *Los Angeles Times* upon the release of **That's Entertainment! III** (1994), voiced his theories about why the musical had declined: "Kids today are sorry they can't do musicals like we did, and the reason is there is no romantic music. It's hard to do a musical without singing 'I love you,' and it's hard to do a romantic pas de deux to hip-hop music using quick-cut shots from the feet to the eyes to the legs or whatever."

Many felt that the 1992 romantic comedy **Sleepless in Seattle** (Miranda Garrison) was actually a musical. Although the actors did not dance or lip-synch, the nostalgic songs on the soundtrack enriched and motivated the scenario. The film was a surprise hit, and the soundtrack was a smash.

In his July 18, 1994, *Variety* review of the fantasy **North** (choreographed by Patricia Birch), Leonard Klady dared suggest, "[Director Rob] Reiner even pulls off a fantasy song-and-dance sequence that suggests **North** might have made a dandy musical."

Despite the success of stage musicals, music videos, video sales and rentals of classic musicals, and lovingly remastered and restored versions on laser disc, large-scale stage musicals floundered in their attempt to be filmed as studio heads balked at the finances involved. One hundred million dollar budgets were all right for action/buddy/techno-fects films like **The Terminator**, **Die Hard**, and **Aliens**, but few filmmakers had the courage of their convictions to mount a full-scale musical. The movie business was now concentrating on the "business": putting all of their energy into high-concept screenplays, sequels of proven successes, prime release date bookings, and demographics.

Plans for future musicals, however, were constantly announced in the show business trade papers. In December of 1993, composer/producer Andrew Lloyd Webber announced that he would begin producing film versions of his phenomenal stage successes *Aspects of Love*, *Cats*, *Evita*, *Joseph and the Amazing Technicolor Dreamcoat*, *Phantom of the Opera*, and *Starlight Express*. *Phantom* had been ready for filming with Michael Crawford — and then abandoned. *Evita* was announced several times, and Paula Abdul did pre-production work on a version to star Meryl

Streep. When Streep suddenly defected, the project floundered. Oliver Stone planned to begin filming in 1995 with Michelle Pfeiffer, but also abandoned the project in June 1994. As of this writing, **Evita** is finally being filmed, starring Madonna and Antonio Banderas and choreographed by Vincent Paterson.

In 1993, writer-director James L. Brooks created a 40 million dollar original musical, **I'll Do Anything**, with choreography by Twyla Tharp. After the film was completed, it was tested in multiple showings, and the film was finally released in 1994 without any of its musical numbers.

Writer-director John Hughes, whose work in the '80s had been enriched by dance sequences, abandoned dance input when he struck it rich with **Home Alone** (1990). He continued throughout the early '90s in that vein with **Home Alone 2**, **Dennis the Menace**, and **Baby's Day Out**, reusing the basic premise of a youngster sadistically bashing older people. Music and dance left his work, and yet, in 1994, he announced that was he planning remakes of **Damn Yankees** and **The Pajama Game**, stating that he "loved musicals."

Michael Ritchie finalized plans to film the longest running stage musical, **The Fantasticks** (Michael Smuin, still not released), and Nick Castle, Jr. was developing an original screenplay, **Harold Square**. **Dancing Still**, the inspiring story of choreographer Barry Martin, was purchased by Touchstone Pictures. After a tragic 1981 auto accident in South Africa, Martin became a quadraplegic, but returned to triumphantly dance with his own Deja Vu company in New York in 1991.) **Dirty Dancing** screenwriter Eleanor Bergstein sold an original screenplay, **It Only Happens with You**, about couples meeting at a New York ballroom dance studio, which was eventually filmed as **Let It Be Me** (Miranda Garrison, not yet released).

A tale which illustrates contemporary moviemakers' attempts at musicals began on June 3, 1994, when *Variety* printed the announcement that director Paul Verhoeven and screenwriter Joe Eszterhas (known for their highly successful collaboration on **Basic Instinct** in 1992) would began production on **Showgirls**. While the title may have triggered memories in the minds of older musical fans of **Ziegfeld Girl**, **Give a Girl a Break**, and other rags-to-riches backstage stories, the new script was described as "the controversial rock 'n' roll musical about a lap dancer who enters the ruthless world of show dancing in Las Vegas." The article continued, "Actresses will have to be nude for much of the film … since '**Showgirls**' is the story of a young woman who 'lapdances' in a nude bar but aspires to become a glitzy showgirl, nudity will be as plentiful as neon in this Vegas romp."

Expecting a battle with the MPAA over the film's eventual rating, Verhoeven told *Variety*, "It's not something special for me to do something that should be NC-17 or should be an R. I always worked in a very free way in Europe, and it's only in the United States that made me get into a lane where these fights are necessary. I make the movie as I feel it and mostly as the material dictates it." He noted, and *Variety* reported, that "some observers feel the part could offer the same short-cut to stardom that **Basic Instinct** brought to Sharon Stone" (whose notoriety was primarily based on the actress exposing her naked crotch during an interrogation scene, which one Hollywood wag called "the most famous parting since Moses and the Red Sea"). Elizabeth Berkley, a young television actress with a dance background, was eventually cast to star "once she signs a contract that she'll do the required nude scenes in the film." (*Variety*, September 8, 1994). Marguerite Derricks was signed to choreograph.

MGM-UA took the challenge of releasing a major NC-17 film. With a huge publicity campaign, the film opened in October 1995, and after a promising first week attended by curiosity seekers, critics and audiences alike rejected it. The cliché-ridden script, badly filmed and edited dancing, absurd musical number concepts, and obvious exploitation of all of the actresses involved threaten to make **Showgirls** the this-you-gotta-see film of the '90s. Musicals (and Elizabeth Berkley's career) took several giant steps backwards.

Erotic dance (with lapdancing thrown in to reflect contemporary adult entertainment trends) continued to be plentifully used in films of the mid '90s: **Exotica** (Claudia Moore), **Female Perversions, Headless Body in a Topless Bar, Lap Dancing, Striptease** (Marguerite Derricks), etc. Aside from the box-office lure of nudity, it offered complex female characters as sexual morés shifted and searched for expression in the age of safe sex.

Use of dance in the movie musical was being rethought by choreographers. In August 1994, Vincent Paterson told Judy Brennan for the *Los Angeles Times* that he felt the dance collaboration should be "something with more of an edge.... The idea is to do a musical, to incorporate one art into another, so that the movement doesn't look like some big dance number.... That's the message we're playing with in film. To bring choreography in but to make it ... something you don't even notice."

A new, flourishing gay cinema produced several musicals during the decade. Canada was brave enough in 1993 to make the first "AIDS musical," **Zero Patience** (Susan McKenzie), with *Variety* praising, "The best song ... a deliciously catchy pop tune neatly visualized with underwater ballet and a bit of poolside acrobatics." And from "down under," **The Adventures of Priscilla, Queen of the Desert** (Mark White, 1994), an outlandish story of three men heading across Australia to appear in a drag act, found commercial success. **To Wong Foo, Thanks for Everything, Julie Newmar** (Kenny Ortega, 1995) was America's drag queen odyssey, with Wesley Snipes, John Leguizamo, and Patrick Swayze (**Dirty Dancing**'s "Sexiest Man Alive" in another brave career move) shaking their spangles.

As with all forms of filmmaking, the musical was changing and evolving, with dance input reflecting those changes.

In 1993, a television version of **Gypsy** (Jerome Robbins' original choreography and staging recreated by Bonnie Walker, with Peggy Holmes) got reviews which seemed more like love letters. They all mentioned that the once-named "Boob Tube" might become the vehicle for the return of the musical genre. **Bye Bye Birdie** (Ann Reinking) followed in 1995.

Perhaps some brave commercial film producer will be able to translate the excitement of the music video or sensational rock concerts (Madonna's "Blonde Ambition" tour, done by Vincent Paterson, or Michael Jackson's "Dangerous" tour, created by Kenny Ortega) to a feature-length film as the movie industry continues to struggle with its art-versus-commercialism debates and goals. Only time will tell.

The first all-dance film of the decade was **George Balanchine's The Nutcracker**, a long awaited filming of the New York City Ballet's most economically successful ballet. Adding Macauley Culkin (a highly successful child actor of the day) for name value, the film began to disappoint even before its December, 1993 release. In a highly publicized battle, Culkin's father protested the added narration by Kevin Costner (more name value insurance for the tentative Warner Bros. producers) and removed Macauley from the film's promotion. Greater disappointment came when reviewers saw the film. Unanimously they proclaimed it beautifully conceived and danced — and badly underlit and filmed. *Time* magazine's December 6, 1993, review summarized the feelings of many critics and audiences:

> Dance is the last place to try anything but stable, even conventional, camera work ...the action is blurry.... The choreographic patterns are unreadable and even...brilliant dancing loses some of its definition. In the end the visual failure breaks the spell and blunts the ballet's appeal. The best solutions to filming dance were worked out in 1930s musicals.... Fred Astaire — who insisted on clarity above all else — would groan.

In 1995, once again it was Spain and Carlos Saura who gave filmgoers a lavish all-dance treat with **Flamenco**. A dazzling montage of dozens of Flamenco artists, the choreography was created by the dancers themselves, with no single choreographer receiving credit.

Another anticipated film dance "meal" of the decade was **That's Entertainment! III** (1994), the fourth compilation (including **That's Dancing!**) of more of MGM's song-and-dance treasures. Whereas the first three had been feasts, this version turned out to be more of a snack, for most of the treasures had been previously used and the cupboard was nearly bare. In this one, however, outtakes were included to allow musical film fans peeks at lost wonders from the creativity of some of the best film choreographers (Robert Alton, Gene Kelly, Michael Kidd, Charles Walters, etc.). The studio originally wanted to release it on television or video but gave it a brief theatrical release. Jason McCloskey said in his *Drama-Logue* review, "For the MTV club generation, it offers startling proof that dancing did not in fact originate with Michael Jackson.... What [it] underscores is how brilliant — and hard-working — these dancers/singers were, and how immensely skilled they were in riveting our attention without benefit of today's typical three-second cuts." Other reviewers criticized it for its old-fashioned "hokum," and young audiences stayed away. It will probably be most remembered within the industry for the legal battles MGM/Turner Pictures had with widow Robyn Astaire for usage of footage of Fred Astaire. Once again, no choreographers were given credit in what was basically an all-dance film. Members of the SSDC picketed the film in New York. When a deluxe "director's cut" edition of the film was released on video and laser disc with complete, unedited numbers and more outtakes, MGM/Turner Pictures rectified their oversight by printing the choreographers' names on an enclosed brochure.

It took a little Australian film in 1992, **Strictly Ballroom**, to generate excitement and hope in the future of the dance film. Robert Horton, in *Film Comment*, praised the film: "...one of the best indicators for a future to the musical film (if there is a future to the musical film) that I've seen lately.... **Strictly Ballroom** in its own modest way, reaffirms that movies are dances.... This is necessary in an age in which movies no longer know how to dance — and we're not talking about musicals either. This film *moves*, zipping along where so many new American movies get mired in committee thinking and star turns and laborious 'backstory.'" Choreographer John "Cha Cha" O'Connell — aided greatly by the performances and choreographic input of stars Paul Mercurio and Antonio Vargas — created a satiric, swirling, passionate picture of the highly competitive (and most often, grotesque) professional ballroom dancing world. As with **Dirty Dancing**, the young lovers' rehearsals served as the opportunity to reveal their characters and the development of their relationship (dance as liberation for the plain-Jane heroine and release from the strict confines of ballroom dance's rules for the hero), and the final dance was their triumph (dance as competition).

In the dramatic and comedy films of the nineties, the work of the film choreographer was allowed to blossom. Although the line dance was gone, dance on film was back to its original use, and choreographers were hired to create moods, reflect periods, and add grace and character to the actors.

In a July 1994 article by Judy Brennan in the *Los Angeles Times* titled "Choreography Glides Back into Focus on Silver Screen," it was noted that in 1993, 43 movies had choreographed sequences — "But the presence of choreography is often subtle, playing on the audience's subconscious conditioning from all of those TV music videos ... of having music and dance incorporated into their lives." Vincent Paterson was quoted: "'People always think of choreography as ballet or Broadway or a dance movie like **Flashdance**. But choreography is becoming more and more an integral part of filmmaking.... Because of MTV we've become so accustomed to

Paul Mercurio and Tana Morice "Paso Doble" into film dance history in **Strictly Ballroom** (John "Cha Cha" O'Connell, Miramax, 1992).

music and dance, most people don't realize its role or remember it when they do see it on the screen.'"

Film comedy masters Jim Abrahams and Jerry and David Zucker had nearly always included a choreographer on their creative team to add whimsical musical sequences to their films: **Airplane!** (Tommy Mahoney), **The Naked Gun** (Jerry Evans) and **Top Secret** (Gillian Gregory) in the '80s and continuing the successful formula into the '90s with **Naked Gun 2½** (Miranda Garrison and Johnny Almaraz, 1991) and **Naked Gun 33⅓: The Final Insult** (Garrison, 1994). Mel Brooks spoofed the entire **Robin Hood** film genre with **Robin Hood: Men in Tights** (1993) with Cindy Montoya-Picker creating the comic dance sequences for a rap group of African-American "Merry Men" and Brooks reunited with Alan Johnson on **Dracula: Dead and Loving It** in 1995. Other dance as satire successes early in the decade were **The Tall Guy** (Charles Augins, 1990) and **Death Becomes Her** (Brad Jeffries, 1992), which benefited greatly from satiric take-offs on stage musical production numbers.

In comedy or dramatic films with musical backgrounds, onstage performance pieces continued to win audience favor. Choreographers created a variety of musical sequences for **The Lemon Sisters** (Anita Mann, 1990), **The Five Heart Beats** (Michael Peters, 1991), **The Bodyguard** (Sean Cheesman, 1992), and **Leap of Faith** (Mary Ann Kellogg, Sharon Kinney, 1992). The song-and-dance sequences in **Sister Act** (1993) and **Sister Act II: Back in the Habit** (1994) were responsible for much of the comedy films' success. Lester Wilson, Lisa Mordente, Eartha Robinson and Michael Peters invented hilarious pastiches of bad nightclub acts and rollicking rock 'n' roll church showstoppers for Whoopi Goldberg and her singing nuns.

After the disco and break dance eras of solo dance, older social dance forms performed by partners came back into vogue, in life and onscreen. The inherent romanticism and eroticism of social dance became the basis of several films of the decade, and dance as seduction became a major force.

The endless sensual sambas of **Wild Orchid** (Morleigh Steinberg, 1990) and many of the graphic sex scenes of the decade had to be choreographed—something Jack Cole would have approved of. **The Mambo Kings** (Kim Blank, Michael Peters, 1992) used its musical sequences to great dramatic effect, even pulling a musical number from **Neptune's Daughter** (Jack Donohue, 1949), re-editing it and interspersing it with dramatic contemporary footage to start the film off with an emotional bang. *Rolling Stone*'s March 1992 review commented on the film's unique collaboration: "Michael Ballhaus' camera work, Stuart Wurtzel's production design, Ann Roth's costumes, Claire Simpson's editing and Michael Peters' choreography combine miraculously to create a palace of idealized memory where people tired of jobs, prejudice and frustration can find a sultry night of paradise."

Tangos were used prolifically in major dramatic films of the decade to add romance and eroticism and explore the characters' relationships. The 1992 Academy Award–winning "best foreign film" **Indochine** (Chris Gandois) used a mother-daughter pas de deux between Catherine Deneuve and Linh Dan Pham. In **The Cemetery Club** (Ron Tassone, 1993), Danny Aiello wooed Ellen Burstyn with dance. In the 1994 box-office blockbuster **True Lies** (Lynne Hockney), an opening tango represented the suave, sophisticated side of the "ordinary-guy-who-is-actually-James-Bond" character played by Arnold Schwarzenegger—as well as a charming new dimension of the hulking action hero.

Scent of a Woman (1992), the film which finally won a "best actor" Oscar for Al Pacino, concentrated its entire ad campaign on a pose from the sultry tango performed by Gabrielle Anwar and the blind character portrayed by Pacino, but credit for the choreography was nowhere to be found in the printed credits. One had to wait until the end credits to find out that Jerry Mitchell and ballroom expert Paul Pellicoro had co-created it.

The story of the creation of the sequence illustrates the intense collaboration between the various specialists involved. Pellicoro spent many months coaching Pacino and Anwar in the classic Argentine tango, and Mitchell was called in (after Tommy Tune turned the job down) to shape the sequence. "I approached Al Pacino from an actor's point of view," he said in an interview with the author. He staged the dance number "without a proscenium" on the dance floor, and when it was completed, he showed director Martin Brest, saying, "You choose your 'front,' I have my favorites, but from every angle you can see the emotion." After the number was filmed, the editors asked Mitchell to videotape himself and a partner doing the dance so that the number could be edited on the correct beat and angle of each sequence. In an article devoted to the popularity of the tango in film ("It Takes Four to Tango"—*People Magazine*, March 22, 1993) Mitchell described his work: "It's the first time you see the human side of Al Pacino's character," while the sequence itself was touted as "…one of the most delicious dance scenes in recent memory."

The lambada, a brief international dance phenomenon of the decade, caused filmmakers to release two dance-as-competition films in 1990: **Lambada: The Forbidden Dance** (Feliz Chavez, Miranda Garrison) and **Lambada** (Shabba Doo), to try and capitalize on the rage. Vogueing, another social dance rage, was explored in **Paris Is Burning** (1991), a successful documentary on the members of the black, gay clubs in Harlem who used dance to compete and express themselves. Popular artists such as Madonna (with the collaboration of choreographer Vincent Paterson) exposed middle America to this dance style in a successful song-and-music video and helped to place it in the lexicon of American social dance.

Al Pacino and Gabrielle Anwar in the memorable Tango sequence from **Scent of a Woman**, created by Jerry Mitchell and Paul Pellicoro (Universal, 1992).

As Valentino had done on the silent screen, John Travolta added his personal dance expertise to several films of the '90s, but without credit. For **Pulp Fiction** (1994), he devised an audience-pleasing dance contest number for him and Uma Thurman — with *Los Angeles* Magazine naming it "best disco choreography for a hit man" (March, 1995). While working on **White Man's Burden**, a crew member related, "Every day, John would show up with a new dance. The cast and crew would line up to learn his 'dance of the day' including the Hitchhiker and the Mashed Potato," (*US*, March 1995).

Otis Sallid went to Europe and trained German, Yugoslavian, and British dancers for **Swing Kids**, a film which used dance as politics: German kids doing American social dances in protest against Hitler. During the two-month rehearsal period, Sallid made dancers out of the non-dancing leads and jitterbuggers out of the European dancing cast. In the *Entertainment Weekly* review (March 12, 1993), the critic gave Sallid praise for his hard work: "The dancing, for all of its gymnastic splendor, comes off as wilder, sexier, less meticulously choreographed than it usually does in Hollywood swing-dance sequences." But they failed to mention Sallid's name.

Martial arts, mime, and even "alien" sequences continued to require the artistry of movement specialists who could combine technique and training and tailor it to the film's needs. Collaboration between actors, directors, and movement specialists reached new heights during the decade, with such contributions as Dan Kamin's expertise in comic silent screen mime and movement for the acclaimed performances of Robert Downey, Jr., in the title role of **Chaplin** (1992) and Johnny Depp in **Benny and Joon** (1993). Kamin's experiences followed the classic frustrations of the movement creators before him: "My credit of 'comedy choreographer' took some working out," Kamin wrote in a letter to the author, "...as the DGA would not allow several other titles we proposed for my work creating the comedy scenes.... 'Choreographer' might

Johnny Depp serves Dan Kamin during work sessions of **Benny and Joon** (MGM, 1993) (photo courtesy of Dan Kamin).

be a bit misleading — I usually have to get into a lengthy explanation of what I actually did. The fact is, the work I did on the two films crossed many movie-role boundaries — the director, the actors, the writer." After Kamin coached Downey for almost one year ("We did exercises to alter his posture. To mobilize his body; to loosen his arms and legs. To make his body do things it had never done before ... changed his whole posture in order to become the Little Tramp"), Downey dubbed Kamin "relentless. He's probably the truest example of a perfectionist I've ever met. He'd do the stuff all day long himself ... almost like if *he* did it enough, I'd get it.... It was like skydiving in labor." Building each sequence through movement to recreate Chaplin's gestures and grace, and eventually even revising the script with his "design" of the comedy scenes, Kamin shares onscreen credit for "Chaplin choreography" with Johnny Hutch and dance choreography by Kate Flatt and Susanne McKenrick.

For **Bram Stoker's Dracula** (1992), Francis Ford Coppola once again invited Michael Smuin (with Morleigh Steinberg) to join his creative team in order to design stylized movement for three vampire brides who tempt the character played by Keanu Reeves. "It wasn't necessarily dancing that Francis wanted," Smuin was quoted in *Dance Magazine* in 1991:

It was more like ceremonial walking on air and on the walls and ceiling and flying. It certainly needed a choreographer's touch to bring it to life the way he wanted to see it. At one point he said take the three girls and make them into a spider. So with belts and loops and ropes and things we managed to put some interesting things together. Certainly weird, but yet beautiful and grotesquely lyrical.

Period dances added authenticity and embellishment to dozens of dramatic films. Elizabeth Aldrich, an American authority on nineteenth century social dance who began enriching film in the late seventies, continued to contribute, to the Merchant Ivory Films **Mr. and Mrs. Bridge** (with Charlotte Gossett, 1990) and **Remains of the Day** and Martin Scorsese's **The Age of Innocence** in 1993. Aldrich's assignment was "to create dances that compliment the action while remaining in the background ... in the tearoom scene in **Remains of the Day**, where the waltzing couple seems to merge into the period decor, her contribution is so unobtrusive as to go practically unnoticed. When this happens, Aldrich counts the job as a success." (*Dance Magazine*, March 1995). *Variety* noticed the contributions of a dancemaker in their review of 1994's **Princess Caraboo**: "A ball planned to introduce the princess to England's Prince Regent is a gem of art design and choreography ... credit is due to Anthony Van Laast for staging the period dances" (August 29, 1994).

Ice choreographer Robin Cousins (**Fire and Ice**, 1985) contributed to **The Cutting Edge** (1992). *Film Annual* observed about its leading lady, Moira Kelly, "Amazingly, Ms. Kelly couldn't skate at *all* before signing up for the film: her ease on the ice is attributable to the expert tutelage of Robin Cousins." Aside from Cousins' skill as tutor, his input regarding skate-ins for the two non-skating leads, camera collaboration, and sheer artistry provided the film's multiple ice sequences.

The choreographers of the '80s were now becoming the directors of the '90s. Such multi-talented artists as Debbie Allen, Patricia Birch, Grover Dale, Graciella Daniele, Matthew Diamond, Rob Iscove, Vincent Paterson, and Otis Sallid moved into stage, music video, and television direction, using their skills to receive Tony and Emmy nominations and awards for their work.

Within the first five years of the decade, the deaths of Donn Arden, Christopher Chadman, Louis Falco, Tony Fields, Spencer Henderson III, Joe Layton, Edward Love, Tommy Mahoney, Steve Merritt, Michael Peters, Scott Salmon, Buddy Schwab, James Truitte, Billy Wilson and Lester Wilson sent the industry into saddened shock. And on February 2, 1996, Gene Kelly joined Fred Astaire, Busby Berkeley, and other giants in dance-in-film heaven.

Screen credit was still not assured for choreographers' work. In 1991, Lou Conte was asked to choreograph a jitterbug sequence in **A League of Their Own** for Columbia. When Conte went to see the film and found that his name was not included on the credits, his agent phoned the producers to be told that the "deal memo" (which was in addition to his contract) Conte had signed did not include onscreen credit. Because of the principle of the issue Conte eventually sued Columbia. Conte was assured that his name would be added to the video release and any television screenings of the film.

The battle for recognition for the art of choreography continued, and the '90s will perhaps prove as significant for their politics as for their creative output. For the first time, dancers and choreographers united to help one another toward professional goals and fair treatment in the industry which had ignored them from the very beginning.

An organization called Dance Alliance was founded in 1990 to aid and unify dancers working in film and television. In 1991, Grover Dale founded the Choreographers Resourcenter (CRC)—which became the L.A. Dance Foundation in 1996 in Los Angeles. Joined and supported

by Debbie Allen, Alan Johnson, Kenny Ortega, Vincent Paterson, and other influential choreographers, the group offered seminars and workshops to young dancers and budding choreographers which allowed them to expose their work to influential peers and participate in a wide
range of topics — from "The Next Generation of Musical Movies" to "Making the Move into
Feature Film Production." Budding choreographers were encouraged to get their skills in camera and editing techniques, along with dance expertise. It was a new era for dance on film, and
the dancemakers needed additional skills and experience to compete with their highly technically trained co-workers. Whereas the choreographers of the past had learned about the camera while working in front of it, this new generation was offered the opportunity to receive their
training behind it, beforehand.

Dale was quoted in *Variety*, December 6, 1991, about his reasons for creating a support
group for choreographers:

> Currently, if you walk onto a union set where a production number is being choreo-
> graphed, everyone on the set has pension and welfare and a wage standard except us....
> People still think choreographers just make up steps. Actually, we mold, shape and
> craft six minutes of a sequence, figure out the emotional structure behind it and how
> to illuminate the idea, and direct the lighting and costuming. We're becoming direc-
> tors and initiators of new projects.

The ball was rolling, and the energy was coming together in unity.

In October 1992, a group of choreographers held a press conference protesting the "lack
of respect" for their work from the AMPAS. In a compilation video called **Oscar's Greatest
Moments**, released by the academy, sections of musical numbers from the first twenty-one Oscar
ceremony productions were used without any choreographic credits. Debbie Allen stated: "This
one instance is only a symptom of the greater problems we're facing. We're targeting this tape
because we believe it's time that the industry gave us equal time and respect along with all other
creators. After all, the industry goes to great lengths to make sure it credits the caterer on the
set, but not the choreographer." The academy tried to soften their obvious snub by printing a
full-page ad in the trade papers in December, finally listing the contributing choreographers
along with hundreds of other participating classifications.

On the evening of March 9, 1993, a meeting was held at Screenland Studios in North Hollywood to explain a union contract for choreographers, staging directors, and assistants. After
two years of weekly meetings by choreographers, assistants, agents, and attorneys, the rules and
regulations of the Media Choreographers Council/Society of Stage Directors and Choreographers (MCC/SSDC) were printed and a contract for producers devised. The founding members of the new union were Kim Blank, Russell Clark, Miranda Garrison, Peggy Holmes, Manette
LaChance, Vincent Paterson, and Tony Selznick.

At the meeting, congratulatory letters and telegrams arrived from those who could not
attend, but added their full support: Paula Adbul, Debbie Allen, Marge Champion, Joe Layton, and Gwen Verdon. Impassioned speeches were given by agents Julie MacDonald, Tim
O'Brien, Teresa Taylor-Campbell, and Zack Reed and choreographers Russell Clark, Grover
Dale, Peggy Holmes, Alan Johnson, Manette LaChance, and Kenny Ortega. The passion and
energy in the room ran high. After a nearly seventy-year history of indecision, fierce competition, and fear, this new breed of creative artists had created a solidarity.

After the announcement was made that Debbie Allen was working under the new union
contract's stipulations on the 65th Academy Awards television show (with the full cooperation

In **Stepping Out** (Paramount, 1991), Liza Minnelli demonstrates Danny Daniels' choreography to (L to R) Jane Krakowski, Bill Irwin, Julie Walters, Carol Woods, Sheila McCarthy and Ellen Greene.

of producer Gilbert Cates), pledges for union membership came from Anita Mann, Onna White, Stan Mazin, Shabba Doo, and a host of others.

Film choreographers, staging directors, and assistants are now protected by a union. The new generation has finally united to gain the respect and recognition they deserve.

The snub by the industry when the "best dance direction" category was deleted from the Academy Award nominations in 1939 lives on, so recognition has had to come from other organizations and peer groups.

Founded in 1980, the Professional Dancer's Society (PDS), a non-profit group whose goals are to build "The Gypsy Manor" (a retirement home for needy dancers) and create scholarships for young dancers, had begun to honor choreographers. Academic Dance memorial scholarships were established in the names of Robert Alton, Nick Castle, Jack Cole, Seymour Felix, Carol Haney, and Lester Horton. Starting with a citation to LeRoy Prinz at their annual picnic, a Gypsy Lifetime Achievement Award was created and given to choreographers Louis DaPron (1987) and Hermes Pan (1988) at small luncheons attended by members. As factions within the group stressed the need for funds for their goals, the award was changed to be given to "names" which would increase attendance at ever-growing events. The award was subsequently given to Donald O'Connor and Sammy Davis, Jr., Debbie Reynolds and Onna White, Bob Hope and Cyd Charisse, Ann Miller and Mickey Rooney, Ginger Rogers and the Nicholas Brothers, Shirley MacLaine and Milton Berle, and Juliet Prowse and Mitzi Gaynor. As the ceremonies have grown to become excellent fund-raisers, choreographers have been nearly forgotten. They simply don't sell seats.

In 1990, a National Academy of Dance was created to bestow awards for excellence in dance and choreography for films, television and stage — and the dance world rejoiced. It started as an idea from dancer Wade Collings, and Los Angeles television producer Gregory Willenborg ("long dreaming of an awards show, similar to the Grammys, specifically for dance") joined the battle. With the cannily dangled carrot of a television "special" sale (ABC, July 1990), the event on January 19, 1990, at the newly opened San Diego Convention Center received support from the financial community and nearly ecstatic participation from the film-dance world. Shirley MacLaine gushed at the ceremony, "I have been waiting a lifetime for this night ... possibly several!" with presenter-performers Ann-Margret, George Chakiris, Cyd Charisse, former first lady Betty Ford, Ann Miller, Liza Minnelli, Mickey Mouse, the Nicholas Brothers, Juliet Prowse, Chita Rivera, Tony Stevens, Onna White, and Lester Wilson creating a spectacular presentation and show of support. Choreography awards were given to Paula Abdul for best music video ("Cold Hearted") and best television ensemble ("The Tracey Ullman Show"); to Kenny Ortega for film (**Dirty Dancing**); to Tommy Tune for stage (*Grand Hotel*); and to Walter Painter for television ("Disney/MGM Studios Theme Park Opening"). Other awards went to the Dance Theater of Harlem (outstanding modern dance company) and Patrick Swayze (**Dirty Dancing**), and "Hall of Fame" inductions to Martha Graham and Sammy Davis, Jr.

It never happened again.

In 1994, the Film Society of Lincoln Center presented a series of tributes to dance directors and offered separate evenings on Herbert Ross, Jack Cole, and Michael Kidd, with film clips and guest commentators. Writing about the Jack Cole tribute (February 4, 1994) in *LA Dance Magazine*, Alan Johnson reported:

> The prevailing sentiment of the evening was that this kind of acknowledgement was long overdue. Jack Cole was responsible for bringing a style, a vocabulary, and a technique to dance that never existed before.... His influence is reflected in the work of Bob Fosse and Michael Bennett. His visual sense dictated the style of the sets, costumes, lighting, and the use of the camera. His movement, use of music, and interjections of the double entendre evoked as many laughs as any Neil Simon comedy. During a question-and-answer period, someone asked; 'Is there anywhere to learn this technique?" [Longtime Cole associate and collaborator] Ethel Martin paused and answered; 'No. We're all too old and too tired."

In 1993, Michael Peters and Alan Johnson began a campaign to get the AMPAS to once again create a category for dance direction. Having won an Emmy for his television work for **The Jacksons: An American Dream** and creating the proper movement framework for Angela Bassett's sensational performance as Tina Turner in **What's Love Got to Do with It?** (1993), Peters was well aware of film's dependency on dance expertise. Choreographers were recognized with awards in all other forms of entertainment: stage, television, music video, and cabaret.

MTV started a new "Movie Awards" in 1995 and even included a "best dance sequence" category. Nominated that first year were Jim Carrey and Cameron Diaz for **The Mask**, Arnold Schwarzenegger and Tia Carrere for **True Lies**, John Travolta and Uma Thurman for **Pulp Fiction**, and the Brady Kids for **The Brady Bunch Movie. Pulp Fiction** was the winner and dance was recognized by the MTV generation, but without a mention of the choreographers.

A dance awards ceremony was created by the L.A. Dance Foundation and the first one was held on September 18, 1994. Along with an annual Heritage Award (titled "The Fosse" award after the man who posthumously received the first one — accepted by Bebe Neuwirth) and a Dance Educator's award to Joe Tremaine, five film choreographers were nominated: Elizabeth Aldrich for **The Age of Innocence**, Michael Peters for **Sarafina!** and **What's Love Got to Do with It?**, Lester Wilson for **Made in America**, Kenny Ortega and Peggy Holmes for **Hocus Pocus**, and Otis Sallid for **Swing Kids**. In an evening filled with solidarity (with hundreds of dancers, choreographers, and interested entertainment industry members present), history (the presence of Michael Kidd, Fayard Nicholas, Archie Savage, and Onna White), and pride, Otis Sallid (**Swing Kids**) and Michael Peters (**What's Love Got to Do with It?**) received the award in a tie. After emotional speeches from Debbie Allen, Gregory Hines, and others, Rebecka Peters' acceptance speech for her son, Michael, who had died only 23 days prior to the event, elevated the event with her inspirational message about the pride he felt by being honored by his peers.

The second ceremony, on October 15, 1995, featured the "Fosse" lifetime achievement award posthumously bestowed on Jack Cole, the Dance Educator's award given to Patsy Swayze, new "alternative dance" award going to Toni Basil, and a television commercial category. The motion picture nominations were Graciela Daniele for **Bullets Over Broadway**, Jerry Evans for **The Mask**, Greg Rosati for **Blue Sky**, Adam Shankman for **The Flintstones**, and Mark White for **The Adventures of Priscilla, Queen of the Desert**, with Evans winning for **The Mask**.

In 1977, authors John Russell Taylor and Arthur Jackson had written, "Screen choreography can be as simple as you like, or as complicated as you like. When Fred Astaire begins to walk along the station platform in **The Band Wagon** singing 'By Myself' that is choreography, though he only walks and sings, because the walk and the camera movement are exactly timed to provide a sort of delicate visual counterpoint to the song." That magical bond between dance and the camera has provided the motion picture with some of its most memorable moments: John Travolta's glorious cock-of-the-walk prowl in **Saturday Night Fever**; the breaking open of the set for the rush of the corps toward the fountain in **An American in Paris**; the dissolves from dancer to dancer in the pirouettes during the audition sequence in **All That Jazz**. That's dance on film.

Dance on film awaits the next "Golden Age" so that it can flower once again. Until then, talented choreographers and dance directors will work and innovate in live stage shows and rock concerts, television, music videos, and the occasional film. They will financially support themselves continuing to perform, teach, or take their talents to other aspects of entertainment. In the meantime, we can treasure and take pleasure in reviewing the past through videos, laser discs, and special screenings of the big-time dance films. Their beauty only grows with age. The achievements of those dance directors and choreographers continue to amaze new generations.

Selected Filmography

The Addams Family (Peter Anastos) Par, 1991, Video:Par — Anastos captures a sense of the bizarre cartoon beginnings of the family in his waltz scene and campy "The Mabushka" number.

Death Becomes Her (Brad Jeffries) Univ, 1992, Video:Univ — To set the black comedy tone of this film (unfortunately behind its opening credits), Jeffries creates an overly precious stage number for delicious Meryl Streep and a flock of dutiful chorus boys which begs, borrows, steals — and invents.

The Fisher King (Robin Horness) TriStar, 1991, Video:Col — The swirling waltz fantasy in Grand Central Station personifies the madness — and romance — of this unique film.

The Mambo Kings (Kim Blank, Jack Donohue,

Michael Peters) WB, 1992, Video:WB — Choreographers Blank and Peters and director Arne Glimcher collaborate to raise the hair on the back of your neck with a sound/dance and editing sensation as Armand Assante joins Tito Puente's band while a murder takes place in a crowded, smoky club.

The Mask (Jerry Evans) New Line Cinema, 1994, Video:New Line — Two inventively hilarious dance numbers in one colorful Looney Tunes of a film. While the leading character's face had to be animated by multiple special effects, Evans helps up-and-coming comedy star Jim Carrey broadly physicalize through dance.

Naked Gun 2½: The Smell of Fear (Johnny Almaraz, Miranda Garrison) Par, 1991, Video:

During an historic **Tap** challenge, Gregory Hines shows his stuff to (L to R) Arthur Duncan, Pat Rico, Harold Nicholas, Steve Condos, Sandman Sims, Henry LeTang and Sammy Davis, Jr. (Tristar, 1988).

Par—Almaraz and Garrison create a dance sequence which extends the madness in this spoof, rating some of the biggest laughs in the film.

Newsies (Peggy Holmes, Kenny Ortega) Disney, 1992, Video:Buena Vista—Trying to update the movie musical using the wrong script, the wrong cast, and the wrong situation (as Gene Kelly said: "Musicals are about romance"), Ortega fills the screen with exuberant dance and gives a work opportunity to dozens of Hollywood's finest young male dancers.

Scent of a Woman (Jerry Mitchell, Paul Pellicoro) Univ, 1992, Video:Univ—In one scene, the choreographers' expertise and the work of Al Pacino and Gabriel Anwar give the film its emotional core. Memorable Astaire-Rogers stuff and a grand example of how dance can enrich characters, emotions, and story.

Showgirls (Marguerite Derricks) MGM/UA, 1995—The first "NC-17" rated musical. Director Paul Verhoeven proudly boasted: "I love nudity, especially female nudity. I love to look at naked girls. I love tits and ass. Mostly tits." (*Movieline*, October 1995). Choreographer Derricks reportedly had to remove her clothes at the first rehearsal to

make the dancers feel comfortable. Recommended only as "High Trash," a **Beyond the Valley of the Dolls** for dance.

Stepping Out (Danny Daniels) Par, 1991, Video: Par—Tap-master Daniels gives Liza Minnelli and a cast of superb actors tap routines that are real and charming. At the moment when Bill Irwin and Sheila McCarthy tap through the snow as they rehearse their routine for the upcoming Benefit, fond memories of Gene Kelly, Fred Astaire, Judy Garland, and others dancing down the streets warm us and make us wish for yesterday's purity.

Strictly Ballroom (Paul Mercurio, John "Cha Cha" O'Connell, Antonio Vargas) Miramax, 1992, Video:Touchstone—Although the initial dance sequences are erratically photographed and edited, the climactic "Paso Doble" is a gem, combining technique and emotion to create a dance Home Run.

Swing Kids (Otis Sallid) Touchstone, 1993, Video:Buena Vista—Sallid gets a group of real kids to display the energy and sexual tension of social dance from another era, translated brilliantly into contemporary terms.

The Tall Guy (Charles Augins) Miramax, 1990, Video:RCA/Col — Augin's sense of humor augments the whimsy of this film, particularly in the delightfully absurd "Elephant Man" number.

Tap (Gregory Hines, Henry LeTang) TriStar, 1989, Video:Col — Sensational tap pieces performed by legends. It's a shame it's all photographed so darkly.

That's Entertainment! III (Robert Alton, John Murray Anderson, Fred Astaire, Busby Berkeley, Nick Castle, Jack Cole, Bobby Connolly, George Cunningham, Stanley Donen, Jack Donohue, Seymour Felix, Dave Gould, Gene Kelly, Michael Kidd, Sammy Lee, Eugene Loring, Ann Miller, Hermes Pan, Eleanor Powell, Alex Romero, Charles Walters) MGM, 1994, Video:MGM/UA — Back to the past once again for delicacies for the future. The split-screen juxtaposition of Cyd Charisse's and Joan Crawford's two versions of "Two Faced Woman" illustrates the importance of concepts for musical sequences. Joan loses — and would her "blackface" be red!

True Lies (Lynne Hockney) Fox, 1994, Video: CBS/Fox — Hockney supplies a charming tango for Arnold Schwarzenegger and Tia Cararre at the start of the film to establish the proper tongue-in-cheek tone. At the finish, Arnold ("I'll be back!") sweeps wife Jamie Lee Curtis into his arms for a smile-generating reprise.

Part II. Biographies of Choreographers and Dance Directors

The library of commercial film has amazingly captured a wide variety of work. There are aerial choreographers, ice choreographers, mime, water, ballet, jazz, tap, modern and ethnic artists listed. In the 1980s, specialized movement (martial arts, alien, animal, combat, etc.) advisors began finally to receive on-screen credit. Commercial film has managed to capture the work of most of the dance world greats — perhaps briefly — but, nevertheless, their work exists on film.

The choreographers and dance directors are listed alphabetically. An attempt has been made to give ample attention to each listing. Each piece of dance on film is as important as the next — for our enjoyment, our education and the advancement of dance into the future. Some artists have more information available than others, hence the more complete listing. If such information as birthdate and place, dance education, performance experience, etc. is not listed, it is simply because it could not be found. Any information or corrections that readers might have would be greatly appreciated so that future editions may be more complete.

To give as full a portrait as possible of each artist, the author has attempted to list birthdate, place of birth, dance education (as every dancer and choreographer is a product of dance educators), performance credits, associations and influences. Awards, literary works, school or university affiliations and positions held on major dance or theatre associations are also noted whenever applicable or available. Performance or non–dance related credits will also be found. Choreographic credits for stage, television, ballet, music video, concert/nightclubs, and miscellaneous (arena shows, theme parks, etc.) follow, and then film credits, upon which the greatest emphasis has been placed. This is important because the individual's contributions to dance in general may have been prolific, whereas the opportunity to work in film may have been limited.

The history of film choreography is filled with people with a single credit. Upon the demise of the movie musical in the 1950s, steady work for choreographers at the major studios ceased. Choreographers were no longer under contract to the studios but brought in for a single assignment. Without a studio contract or affiliation, they were usually not hired again.

The researcher comes to realize that the entire procedure of hiring choreographers for film has been hit-and-miss — and continues to be. Most producers do not fully understand what a choreographer contributes to their project. They rarely plan in their budget for the services of one. Without a union, there had been no minimum guarantee set, nor rules or regulations of any sort. In the case of nonmusical films that require choreography for a social dance scene, many producers and directors have not planned for it (or are not even aware that such expertise will be needed) until they begin to film the sequence. A choreographer is then hastily secured from a variety of sources: a relative, spouse or lover of someone involved, one of the featured actor's dance teachers or friends or, very often, one of the actors or actresses themselves who have dance ability. The producers have also traditionally tried to pay the least amount for the work (again, without having any union guidelines to help them), hence the history is filled with people who have one or two credits and then seem to vanish.

Until the 1970s, choreography credits for nonmusical films were rarely given. As the various unions requested credit for individuals performing specific skills on films, movie credits became more detailed and choreographers benefited. If the caterers and drivers could be listed, why not the people who created the dance sequences? The choreographers of today usually receive on-screen credit, as well as their assistants. Researching the 1900s–1940s was very difficult, since there is little record of each individual's work. Credits have been gathered from books, magazine articles, interviews and résumés supplied by the choreographers themselves.

• All major films commercially released in the United States appear in the following biographical listings; 16mm dance films made for schools and libraries do not, however. Such information may be found in *Dance Film and Video Guide*, compiled by Deirdre Towers (1991).

• Assistant or associate credits are given whenever possible.

• Movies made-for-television are included in the film credits, as they are released commercially around the world and shown regularly in re-runs on television as movies. Films released directly to video are also included, although not notated as such.

• For brevity, Short Subject films will be notated as (S), Made-for-Television as (TV), Broadway as (Bdwy), Off Broadway as (OB), Out of Town or Touring Production as (OOT), Revival as (Rev), Director as (Dir), Producer as (Prod), Nomination as (Nom), Assistant as (Asst), Associate Choreographer as (Assoc).

• Film dates are the United States release date.

KEY TO OTHER ABBREVIATIONS

Film Studios and Production Companies

AA — Allied Artists
ABF — Associated British Films
ABPC — Associated British Pictures Corporation
AIP — American International Pictures
BIFD — B.I.F.D. Films
BIP — British International Pictures
BN — British National
Brit Ntl — British National
Col — Columbia
Crown Intl — Crown International
Disney — Walt Disney Productions
First Ntl — First National
Fox — Twentieth Century–Fox and Fox Pro-
ductions
Gau/Brit — Gaumont/British
GFD — General Films Distribution
Grand Ntl — Grand National
LFP — London Films
MGM — Metro Goldwyn Mayer
Mon — Monogram
Par — Paramount
PRC — Producers Releasing Corporation
Rank — J. Arthur Rank
UA — United Artists
Univ — Universal and Universal International
WB — Warner Bros.
? — I simply do not know

Countries

Fr — France   Ital — Italy   Swed — Sweden
Ger — Germany   Pol — Poland
GB — Great Britain   Span — Spanish

Organizations

ABT — American Ballet Theatre   MET — Metropolitan Opera
AMPAS — Academy of Motion Pictures Arts   PDS — Professional Dancers Society
   and Sciences   SHARE — Share Happily and Reap Endlessly
CLO — Civic Light Opera   SSDC — Stage Society of Directors and
CRC - Choreographer's Resourcenter   Choreographer
DGA — Director's Guild of America   St. Louis Muny — St. Louis Municipal Light
LACLO — Los Angeles Civic Light Opera   Opera

Locations

LA — Los Angeles   NJ — New Jersey   NYC — New York City
LV — Las Vegas   NY — New York   SF — San Francisco

EXPLANATION OF SCREEN CREDITS

In the ever-changing world of authority and expertise, credits for choreography and dance direction have been given various titles. People who worked from the early days of film into the 1970s as assistants were never given credit, when in fact, they often created the material. In today's film credit vernacular, they would be listed as "Associate Choreographers."

The following is an attempt, in layman's terms, to define the responsibility of the following artists:

MUSICAL NUMBERS STAGED BY: Songs and minor dance sequences created: scenario, action, patterns, positioning and movement of people, stage business.

DANCE DIRECTOR, DANCE DIRECTION BY, DANCES STAGED BY, DANCES ARRANGED BY: The patterns, positioning and movement of people, the scenario of the dance number, adaptation for the camera of sequences which involve actual dance steps. Sometimes control of the camera.

CHOREOGRAPHY, DANCES BY: The creation of the actual dance steps, the style and technique of performance, the sequence of the steps and the positioning and direction of the dancers throughout the sequence.

ASSISTANT CHOREOGRAPHER: Working with the dancemaker responsible for the actual steps and staging, the assistant helps to figure out the logistics of the dancing; teaches and trains the dancers; acts as the representative when the choreographer is not available and sometimes creates actual dance steps, under the direction and supervision of the choreographer.

ASSOCIATE CHOREOGRAPHER: Actually creates dance and movement sequences, in "association" with other choreographers. They are often given this credit because of specific dance expertise (ethnic, country-western, tap, etc.) needed for a particular sequence not within the overall choreographer's expertise.

The following film credits were gathered from multiple sources: printed material, individuals' résumés, and mentions in discussions, interviews and biographies. Not every film was watched to see if the person was given on-screen credit. The author has made no assumptions and has not "invented" a credit without reading it first or hearing it from another source. Assistant and Associate credits are given whenever possible; usually the information came from the dancemaker themselves.

MERRIEL ABBOTT

b. Chicago, Illinois, 1893
d. Chicago, Illinois, November 6, 1977

Affectionately known as "Teacher" by all of her students and dancers, this renowned choreographer and producer actually began as a kindergarten teacher. When new educational theories advocated dance as part of a physical education program, she began studying with Andreas Pavley and Serge Oukrainsky in Chicago. After trying for a dance career in New York (and further study with Theodore Kosloff), she returned to Chicago to teach at the Pavley-Oukrainsky school and then opened her own school in 1922, with students eventually including Marilyn Miller, Ginger Rogers and June Taylor. She began her line of dancers in the late '20s ("pretty girls, magnificently drilled in clever routines that utilized ballet, tap and acrobatic dances") in her first live shows at the Chicago Theater. The line appeared throughout America and toured internationally, becoming so famous that "Abbott Dancers" became a generic term, used as the punchline to a joke in a 1930s *New Yorker* cartoon. Along with extensive film and stage work during the 1930s and '40s, she installed a line of dancers as the permanent attraction at the Empire Room of the Palmer House in Chicago when it opened in 1933. Discontinuing the dancers in 1956, she was contracted as the entertainment director for the Hilton Hotel chain, booking acts and producing all of the shows at the Palmer House in Chicago until her death in 1977. Giving early employment, exposure and career direction to such dance teams as Marge & Gower Champion, Francois & Giselle Szony and Veloz & Yolanda, her approach to choreography and showmanship was capsulized in *Dance Magazine*, June, 1962: "Numbers must have a meaning — dramatic, romantic or comic. Or the dance must astound with brilliant pirouettes or castanets or aerial somersaults. Miss Abbott has been a longtime admirer of acrobatics, and has recognized the fascination that physical prowess holds for an audience. There were many beautifully set acrobatic dances in the days when she was setting routines." Married to orthopedic surgeon Dr. Phillip Lewin and mother of one son, Frank, her assistant choreographers throughout the years included Richard & Edith Barstow and George Tapps.

Stage: George White's Scandals (Bdwy '29), *Fine and Dandy* (OOT '30), *Clowns in Clover* (Bdwy '33), *Smiling Faces* (OOT '32)

Nightclub/Concert: Palmer House (Chicago), Les Ambassadeurs (Paris), Copacabana Casino (Rio de Janeiro, '35)

Film (All credits are for routines for The Merriel Abbott Dancers):

1931 **The Milky Way**—Vitaphone (S)
      Night Club Revels—Vitaphone (S)
1932 **Smiling Faces**—Vitaphone (S)
1933 **Sky Symphony**—Vitaphone (S)
1939 **Love on Tap**—MGM (S)
      Man About Town—Par (with LeRoy Prinz)
1940 **Buck Benny Rides Again**—Par (with LeRoy Prinz, assisted by Richard Barstow)
      Love Thy Neighbor—Par
1942 **Priority Blues**—Soundies Corp (S)
      Sports a la Mode—Soundies Corp (S)
1944 **Swing Fever**—MGM (with Ernst and Maria Matray)

TOMMY ABBOTT

b. Waco, Texas, 1934
d. New York, New York, April 8, 1987

Primarily known for his meticulous restaging of Jerome Robbins' work, Abbott began his dance training in Waco with Elmer Wheatley, a local teacher. After graduating from high school in Texas he went to New York, enrolling in the School of American Ballet. His first Broadway show, *West Side Story* (1957), took him to Hollywood for the film version, playing the role of "Gee Tar," which he originated on the stage, as well as assisting Robbins. In 1961–62, he toured with Robbins' Ballets: USA, again assisting. After another Broadway show, *A Family Affair* in 1962, he assisted Robbins on *Fiddler on the Roof* ('64) and then began staging Robbins' shows and ballets around the world. In 1973 he was named Regisseur for the New York City Ballet and continued recreating Robbins' original works until his premature death in 1987.

Stage: West Side Story (Bdwy '64, '80 & '85 revs), *Fiddler on the Roof* (London, Tel Aviv, Amsterdam)

Ballet/Dance Pieces: Restaging Robbins' originals—"The Concert," "Afternoon of a Faun," "Move," "New York Export: Opus Jazz"

Film:

1961 **West Side Story**—UA (with Maggie Banks, Howard Jeffrey, Tony Mordente, Jerome Robbins—also appeared)

1971 **Fiddler on the Roof**—UA (adapting Jerome Robbins' original choreography, with Sammy Bayes)

PAULA ABDUL

b. Los Angeles, California, June 19, 1963

This performer-creator is the first choreographer to achieve superstar pop performer status. She started dance lessons at the age of 8 in California with Dean Barlow, continuing with Bella Lewitsky and Joe Tremaine. In 1982, while studying sportscasting at Cal State Northridge, she became a Laker Girl (the dance squad for the LA Lakers basketball team) and began choreographing their routines. The Jackson Family saw her work and hired her to do a music video and concert for them. The next step was a series of successful music videos for Janet Jackson. About Jackson's video "Nasty" she said: "I more or less choreographed that video in an hour in my bathroom with a mirror that I only saw from the waist up." She continued teaching dance and movement to rock stars, coaching them and staging their concerts. "When I was choreographing for other artists I knew in my heart that I wanted to be doing the entertainment, but I knew that choreography was going to be my base, something that I would always come back to." Her growing fame led her to choreograph for films and television shows. In 1988 she recorded her first album, "Forever Your Girl," which went triple platinum and gave her the opportunity to choreograph her own music videos and concert tours. She created the first music video to utilize tap dancing ("Straight Up"), combined contemporary dance steps with classic dance technique and training and her music videos often pay tribute to the choreographic greats of the Golden Era who inspired her: "Cold Hearted" (Bob Fosse), "Opposites Attract" (Gene Kelly) and through the wonder of contemporary technical effects, she even danced with Kelly in a Diet Coke commercial. She made her film debut in **Junior High School** (1977) and among her many honors are two Emmys and the 1987 American Music Video Award for "Best Choreography." In 1992, she married actor Emilio Estevez, but they divorced in 1994. On the PBS television show "Dance in America: Everybody Dance Now" (1991) Abdul stated: "Choreography is my thing that I will always come back to."

TV: The Dolly Parton Christmas Special, "The Tracey Ullman Show" ('87–89, Emmy Award), Emmy Awards Show ('89), American Music Awards ('89 & '90), 62nd Academy Awards Show ('90); commercials for Michelob Lite and Diet Coke

Music Video (Partial listing): "Torture"—The Jacksons; "When I Think of You," "Control," "Nasty" (MTV Award '87), "What Have You Done for Me Lately?"—Janet Jackson; "Dragnet"—Dan Aykroyd and Tom Hanks; "Notorious"—Duran Duran; "Goldmine"—The Pointer Sisters; "Velcro Fly"—Z.Z. Top (American Music Video Award '87); "Land of 1,000 Dances"—Dan Ackroyd, "Roll with It"—Steve Winwood; "Knocked Out," "The Way You Love Me," "Straight Up," "Forever Your Girl," "Cold-Hearted," "Opposites Attract," "Alright," "My Love Is for Real," etc.—Paula Abdul

Nightclub/Concert: "Victory" Tour—The Jacksons ('84), Aretha Franklin Tour, "Faith" Tour—George Michael, "Under My Spell" tour—Paula Abdul ('91–92)

Film:

1983 **Private School**—Univ

1986 **A Smoky Mountain Christmas**—Sandollar Prods/ABC (TV)

1987 **Can't Buy Me Love**—Touchstone (assisted by Carlton Jones)

    The Running Man—TriStar

1988 **Action Jackson**—Lorimar

    Bull Durham—Orion

    Coming to America—Par (assisted by Cindy Montoya-Picker)

1989 **Dance to Win**—MGM (with Jerry Evans)

    The Karate Kid Part III—Col (assisted by Cindy Montoya-Picker, with Pat E. Johnson)

    She's Out of Control—Weintraub Ent. Group (assisted by Cindy Montoya-Picker)

1991 **The Doors**—TriStar (with Bill & Jacqui Landrum)

RITA ABRAMS

1975 **At Long Last Love**—Fox (with Albert Lantieri—also appears, "dance coordinator" credit)

1976 **Nickelodeon**—Col (also appeared)

JEFF J. ADKINS

Dancer and choreographer who began dance studies with his mother. Stage appearances include productions of *Cats*, *West Side Story*, *Paint Your Wagon* and *Showboat*. He danced on numerous television specials and in the films **A Chorus Line**, **Body Double** and **Footloose.**

Film:

1990 **Ski Patrol**—Paul Maslansky/Triumph

SANDY HENDRICKS ADLER

1979 **Van Nuys Blvd.**—Crown

PATRICK ALAN
1988 **Colors**— Orion

ALFREDO ALARIA
Spanish-born dancer and choreographer who achieved international success in nightclub extravaganzas around the world during the 1950s–60s with his Ballet Alaria. His sensuous, gender-bending concepts and choreography in cabarets were repeated in his **Diferente** film credit, in which he played a homosexual dancer. Although the film was shown at the Cannes Film Festival, the repressive atmosphere of Franco's Spanish rule of the day did not allow it to receive wide exposure or promotion.
Stage: *Marcela and I* (Madrid '62)
Nightclub/Concert: Casino de Paris, *Ca C'Est L'Amour—Lido de Paris* (Stardust Hotel, LV '59), Grove Theater (LV)
Film:
1961 **Diferente**— Compton Cameo (also appeared)

ELIZABETH ALDRICH
b. Appleton, Wisconsin, February 26, 1947
Acclaimed dance and etiquette historian, lecturer, choreographer and author who specializes in 19th century and ragtime dance. A graduate of the New England Conservatory of Music and a student of Renaissance dance, Aldrich began choreographing for film when a friend introduced her to producer Ismail Merchant to create period movement for Merchant Ivory Productions. Discussing her work on the ballroom scenes using non-union amateurs for the economic Merchant Ivory films (*Dance Magazine*, March, 1995) she admitted, "I try to stay away from dancers. Their body stance isn't natural; they don't look like real people. Even if it takes longer to teach nondancers the steps, I prefer taking the time, because in the end the effect is more appropriate." As an author, she has written *From the Ballroom to Hell: Grace and Folly in 19th-Century Dance* and is currently managing editor for Oxford University Press' forthcoming 6-volume *International Encyclopedia of Dance*. She served as a dance core consultant on PBS' 8-part series "Dancing," and conducts lecture workshops and demonstrations internationally.
Ballet/Dance Pieces: Works for the Court Dance Company of New York, New York Baroque Dance Company, American Ballroom Theater and Taller de Danzas Antiguas (Santiago, Chile)
Film:
1979 **The Europeans**— Levitt-Pickman
1981 **Quartet**— WB
1990 **Mr. and Mrs. Bridge**— Miramax (with Charlotte Gossett)

1993 **The Age of Innocence**— Col (*LA Dance Awards* nom)
     The Remains of the Day— Col
1995 **Jefferson in Paris**—Touchstone (with Beatrice Massin, "Sally's Dance" credit)
1996 **Surviving Picasso**— WB

GEORGE ALEXANDER
1992 **Best of the Best 2**— Entertainment

ROD ALEXANDER
b. Powers County, Colorado, January 23, 1922
"When I begin a new piece, I consciously try to avoid using movements and ideas that have become trite. I try to have an emotional point of view on my subject, and the movement comes from that point of view," said Alexander, one of television's first dancing stars, when analyzing his approach to choreography in *Dance Magazine*, June 1958. Growing up in Colorado, he created and performed in kiddie shows. He moved to to California as a young man, he studied various forms of dance with Ernest Belcher, Nick Castle, Jack Cole, Hanya Holm, Lester Horton, Carmelita Maracci and Edna McRae in Chicago, often paying for his lessons by working as a welder. He started his performance career in film choruses in 1938 (**The Heat's On, Ziegfeld Follies, Tars and Spars** and **Down to Earth**, etc.) and was a member of Jack Cole's dance group at Columbia Studios (1945–48). Moving to New York, he appeared on Broadway in *Inside U.S.A.* and *That's the Ticket* (OOT '48), and *Great to Be Alive* ('50, also assisting Helen Tamaris) and first worked with Bambi Linn. Wed to Linn on April 2, 1950, they created a nightclub act and after gaining notice at New York's Plaza Hotel, were signed for TV appearances. As lead dancers on Max Liebman's "Your Show of Shows" (1952–54) and "Max Liebman Presents," he found television success both choreographing and performing with Miss Linn. In 1958 he formed Rod Alexander's Dance Jubilee, and toured the United States and internationally until he and Linn separated and the group disbanded in 1959. Spending two years in Hawaii and Japan (1964–66) creating stage shows, he returned to the United States and his prolific television work. In *Dance Magazine* (Jan. '67) he was quoted: "The serious dancing started when I was 20 years old and the choreography began as soon as I could get some bodies to work on."
Stage: *Arabian Nights* (Jones Beach '54), *Shinbone Alley* (Bdwy '57), *13 Daughters* (Bdwy '61), *Asphalt Girl* (Tokyo '64, also supervised the script and lyrics for the first Western-style musical in Japan)
TV (partial listing): "Your Show of Shows," "Max Liebman Presents": "Best Foot Forward," "Lend an Ear," "Naughty Marietta," "The Follies of Suzy,"

"Good Times," etc. ('55, Emmy nom); "Arthur Godfrey's Talent Scouts," "Arthur Murray Dance Party," "The Victor Borge Show" ('51), "The Steve Allen Show," "Jack and the Beanstalk," Connie Francis Special ('61), "The Hollywood Palace" ('66–67)

Nightclub/Concert: Act for Ann Sothern ('55); production numbers at the New Frontier Hotel (LV '56), Cafe de Paris (NY '58)

Film:
1956 **The Best Things in Life Are Free**— Fox (with Bill Foster)

Carousel— Fox (with Agnes DeMille, assisted by Bill Foster)

Dance Americana— USIA (S) (with Rod Alexander's Dance Jubilee Troup— also danced)

AURORAH ALLAIN
1990 **The Adventures of Ford Fairlane**— Fox (assisted by Cindy Montoya-Picker)

RANDY ALLAIRE
1987 **Teen Wolf Too**— Atlantic Releasing

DAVID ALLAN
1989 **The January Man**— MGM/UA

BARBARA ALLEN
1987 **Red Riding Hood**— Cannon
1990 **Me and Him**— Col (also appeared)

DEBBIE (DEBORAH) ALLEN
b. Houston, Texas, January 16, 1950
A multi-talented lady who is among the major creative forces of the '80s and '90s. Her love of dance began as a child and, after private lessons with Patsy Swayze, she began studies at the Houston Ballet Foundation at the age of 14. After graduating from Howard University, she went to New York and made her professional debut off–Broadway in *Ti-Jean and His Brothers* and danced with George Faison's company. She appeared on Broadway in *Purlie* ('70), *Raisin* ('73), *Ain't Misbehavin'* and became a star as "Anita" in the 1979 revival of *West Side Story* and continued to find acclaim in *Sweet Charity* ('86 rev). As a featured actress, she appeared in the films **The Fish That Saved Pittsburgh** ('79— which she also choreographed), **Fame** ('80), **Ragtime** ('81), **Jo Jo Dancer, Your Life Is Calling** and frequently on television: "Fame" series (which she also choreographed and directed), "3 Girls 3" ('77), "Roots: The Next Generation" and

"Ebony, Ivory and Jade" ('79). Moving into new areas of responsibility, she produced and directed the TV series "A Different World" and also produced "The Boys" (ABC '92). Miss Allen was one of the choreographers given a tribute on the 1984 Emmy Awards show and has the distinction of working under the first film choreographer's union (MCC/SSDC) contract for the 65th Annual Academy Awards ('93). In 1995, she starred on TV in "In the House" and was the winner of the Soul Train "Lady of Soul" award.

Stage: Bayou Legend (OB '74), *Fame* stage show (European tour '83, also dir, prod and appeared), *Carrie* (Bdwy '88)

TV: "Fame" Series (Emmy winner for "Come One— Come All" Episode '81–'82 and "Class Act" episode in '82–83), Debbie Allen TV Special ('89), "Motown 30: What's Going On" ('90, Emmy nom), "African American Odyssey" ('90), "Stompin' at the Savoy" ('92, also dir), 63rd–67th Academy Awards ('91–95, '93 NAACP Image Award winner for 65th production)

Film:
1979 **The Fish That Saved Pittsburgh**— UA (also appeared)

1990 **Polly**— Disney (TV) (also dir)

1995 **Forget Paris**— Castle Rock (with Lisa Estrada)

SHAUN ALLEN
1985 **Pink Nights**—? (also appeared)

JOHNNY ALMARAZ
b. Bakersfield, California, May 3, 1945
After studying dance at the McFarland School of Dance in Bakersfield, Johnny made his debut at the age of 8 in a dance recital at the Pomona Fair ("Between the cows and the pigs") and his subsequent career took him all over the world as a performer, choreographer and now, casting director ("It's all been so much fun," he wrote, "I wouldn't change a thing in my life … I've been able to do everything I've wanted to do— and still am"). Relocating to Hollywood as a teenager, he studied with Bob Banas, Roland Dupree, Carlton Johnson, Claude Thompson and David Winters and began appearing on stage (Ann-Margret's nightclub act, *Catch My Soul* in Los Angeles), in films: **Billie, Mrs. Brown, You've Got a Lovely Daughter, The Cool Ones, Bedknobs and Broomsticks** and on TV (the Andy Williams, Jonathon Winters and Tom Jones shows, Elvis Presley special). He created his first choreography with a number for Ann Miller on "The Jonathon Winters Show" and assisted Toni Basil, Michael Bennett, Ron Field, Anita Mann, Walter Painter, Jaime Rogers, Claude Thompson and Lester Wilson. In 1970, he went to Paris to tour

Europe in Sylvie Varten's act and stayed there for twelve years, appearing in Peter Goss's modern dance company, fashion shows for Cartier and multiple stage and television shows. Returning to America in 1982, he switched careers to casting feature and commercial films, eventually opening his own office. When Miranda Garrison invited him to assist her on **The Rocketeer** in 1990, he returned to the business of creating dance. When asked to cite major influences in his life, his list is as eclectic as his talents: "My mom, my fourth grade teacher, Mrs. Washburn, Audie Murphy, *West Side Story*, Bob Banas — and **Pinocchio** for the magic of dreams and wishing on a star."

TV: ABC Fall Television Promo; commercials for Ross and Marshalls

Miscellaneous: Fashion shows for Cartier (France)

Film:

1989 **Eddie and the Cruisers II: Eddie Lives!**—Alliance — Aurora/Scotti (assistant to Claude Thompson)

1990 **The Rocketeer**— Touchstone (asst to Miranda Garrison)

1991 **Naked Gun 2½: The Smell of Fear**— Par (with Miranda Garrison)

1992 **A River Runs Through It**— Col (with Miranda Garrison)

1995 **Amberwaves**— Amberwaves Partners Prod (also casting)

JOHN ALTON

1943 **The Sultan's Daughter**— Mon (with Nico Charisse)

ROBERT ALTON (ROBERT ALTON HART)

b. Bennington, Vermont, January 28, 1897
d. Los Angeles, California, June 12, 1957

Master dance director, choreographer, director and producer who revolutionized American show dance. Famous for never preparing ahead ("First, he has the music played several times to get the rhythm and tempo; then he memorizes the words, and with those fixed in his mind he tries to interpret in dance form just what the lyrics mean..." With all this firmly in my mind I call a rehearsal. I say 'Do this.'" And it's a step. I don't know why. It's always been that way.... My poor memory for dancing comes in handy because in that way, I rarely repeat myself," *Hoofing on Broadway*). As a young boy, he left home to "run away with the circus" as a contortionist but his father caught him and brought him back. Channeling his show business dreams into dance, he studied with Ralph MacKernan in Springfield, Mass., and spent his summers in New

York studying with Bert French and Mikhail Mordkin. He debuted as a dancer with Mordkin's company and appeared on Broadway in *Take It from Me* ('19), followed by *Greenwich Village Follies* ('24) and *Some Day* in 1925, which closed out of town. He and his wife, Marjorie Fielding, then created a dance act and later had a line of girls in vaudeville. When his wife took a year off to have a baby, Alton began dance direction at St. Louis movie theaters, also teaching at Clark's Dance School in St. Louis where his students included Donn Arden and Betty Grable. Successful staging at New York's Paramount Theatre led to a choreographic career which would encompass most of the major Broadway hits of the 1930s and '40s, collaborating with Cole Porter, Rodgers & Hart & Rodgers & Hammerstein. Learning stage direction from John Murray Anderson, Alton's Broadway work aided the careers of Ray Bolger, John Brascia, Don Crichton, Betty Grable, Gene Kelly (he remembered seeing Kelly for the first time when his mother brought him to Alton "wearing knickers"), Sheree North, Vera-Ellen, Charles Walters and many future film dancing stars when he took them to Hollywood with him. He changed the face of Broadway choreography by breaking up the chorus (which had up to that point been a precision line) into small groups and featuring solos and his musical staging was always elegant and detailed. He choreographed his first film in 1936 and continued to be one of Hollywood's leading choreographers during the golden age of the movie musical with his lush musical numbers, serving as dance director at MGM from 1944-'51. He also directed the non-musical film **Merton of the Movies** (MGM '47). In 1957, he was working on the film version of **Pal Joey** for Columbia when he died and was replaced by Hermes Pan.

Stage: Hold Your Horses (Bdwy '33), *Anything Goes, Keep Moving, Life Begins at 8:40* and *Thumbs Up* (Bdwy '34), *Ziegfeld Follies* (Bdwy '34,'36,'43), *At Home Abroad* (with Harry Losee and Gene Synder) and *Parade* (Bdwy '35), *The Show Is On* (with Harry Losee) and *White Horse Inn* (Bdwy '36), *Between the Devil* and *Hooray for What?* (Bdwy '37), *Leave It to Me* and *You Never Know* (Bdwy '38), *Aquacade Revue, Dubarry Was a Lady, One for the Money, The Streets of Paris* and *Too Many Girls* (Bdwy '39), *Higher and Higher, Panama Hattie* and *Two for the Show* (Bdwy '40), *Sons o' Fun* (Bdwy '41), *By Jupiter, Count Me In* and *Pal Joey* (Bdwy '42), *Dancing in the Streets* (OOT '42), *Early to Bed* (Bdwy '43, also dir), *Laffing Room Only* (Bdwy '44), *Pal Joey* (Bdwy rev '52, also dir, Tony Award), *Hazel Flagg* and *Me and Juliet* (Bdwy '53), *The Vamp* (Bdwy '55, also dir, Tony nom)

TV: "Ford Star Jubilee" (also prod), "You're the Top — A Tribute to Cole Porter" ('56), Donald O'Connor Special ('60)

Robert Alton appears on screen, partnering Greta Garbo in her last film, **Two Faced Woman** (MGM, 1941).

Nightclub/Concert: *Let's Play Fair* (Casa Mañana '38), *The Big Show* (Casa Mañana '39), three Casino De Paris shows, *Salute to Cole Porter* ('56) and production numbers for the New Frontier Hotel (LV '55–56, assisted by George Chakiris); acts for Rhonda Fleming, Judy Garland and Kay Thompson

Miscellaneous: New York Paramount ('33), *Billy Rose's Aquacade* (Cleveland & NY World's Fair '39), Benefits for the U.S Armed Forces during World War II

Film:
1936 **Strike Me Pink**— UA
1941 **Two Faced Woman**— MGM (also appeared as Greta Garbo's dance partner)
   You'll Never Get Rich— Col (with Fred Astaire)
1944 **Bathing Beauty**— MGM (with Jack Donohue & John Murray Anderson)
   Broadway Rhythm— MGM (with Jack Donohue, Don Loper, George Murphy, Charles Walters)
1946 **The Harvey Girls**— MGM (with Ray Bolger, Charles Walters)
   Till the Clouds Roll By— MGM (assisted by Alex Romero)
   Ziegfeld Follies— MGM (with Eugene Loring, Fred Astaire, Charles Walters, assisted by Harry Rogue)
1947 **Good News**— MGM (with Charles Walters)
1948 **Easter Parade**— MGM (with Fred Astaire, Nick Castle)
   The Kissing Bandit— MGM (with Stanley Donen)
   The Pirate— MGM (with Gene Kelly, Fayard Nicholas)
   Words and Music— MGM (with Gene Kelly, assisted by Alex Romero)
1949 **The Barkleys of Broadway**— MGM (with Fred Astaire, Hermes Pan, assisted by Alex Romero)
   In the Good Old Summertime— MGM
1950 **Annie Get Your Gun**— MGM (assisted by Alex Romero)
   Pagan Love Song— MGM (also dir, assisted by Alex Romero)
1951 **The Belle of New York**— MGM (with Fred Astaire, assisted by Marilyn Christine, Alex Romero)
   Show Boat— MGM (with Gower Champion)
1953 **Call Me Madam**— Fox (assisted by Ward Ellis)
   I Love Melvin— MGM
1954 **The Country Girl**— Par (assisted by Ernest Flatt)
   There's No Business Like Show Business— Fox (with Jack Cole, assisted by Ernest Flatt)

White Christmas— Par (assisted by Bea Allen, Joan Bayley, Les Clark and Ernest Flatt)
1955 **The Girl Rush**—RKO (also co-prod, assisted by Bea Allen, Joan Bayley, Ernest Flatt)
1974 **That's Entertainment!**— MGM (with others)
1976 **That's Entertainment Part 2**— MGM (with others)
1985 **That's Dancing**— MGM (with others)
1994 **That's Entertainment! III**— MGM (with others)

ROBERT ALVAREZ

Dancer-choreographer who worked with Paula Abdul in music video and live performances and toured with Dance Caravan in 1990, demonstrating The Lambada.
Film:
1991 **Rich Girl**— Studio Three Film Corp.

CARMEN AMAYA

b. Barcelona, Spain, circa 1913
d. Bagur, Spain, November 19, 1963
Along with La Argentina, Rosario & Antonio and José Greco, Carmen Amaya was responsible for creating international awareness of Flamenco and Spanish classical dance. Born into a family of dancers, she began dancing professionally in Spain at the age of 7 and appeared in Paris at the Folies Bergere the next year. She created a sensation at the Barcelona World's Fair of 1929 and at the outbreak of the Spanish Civil War in 1936 she moved to Mexico and then, to Buenos Aires, Argentina, where her great success caused a theater to be named after her. Dubbed "The Queen of the Gypsies," she made her New York debut in 1941, touring Europe and the United States with her own company and appearing on Broadway and in concert halls, nightclubs, and films. Her final film appearance was with Antonio Gades in **Los Tarantos** ('64). One week before her death from a kidney ailment, she was awarded the Medal of Isabela la Catolica by the Spanish government.
Film (Credits are for her dance troupe's appearances):
1944 **Follow the Boys**— Univ (with Louis DaPron, George Hale, Joe Schoenfeld, Frank Veloz)
1945 **See My Lawyer**— Univ (with Louis DaPron)
1964 **Los Tarantos**— Sigma III (with Antonio Gades)

JEAN PIERRE AMIEL

1982 **The Dark Crystal**— Univ

PETER ANASTOS

b. Schenectady, New York, February 23, 1948

Founder, choreographer and co-director of Les Ballets Trockadero de Monte Carlo, the successful all-male comedic ballet troupe started in 1974, Anastos appeared with the company under the stage name of "Olga Tchikaboumskaya" and created a series of hilarious ballet satires. He began his dance training in Schenectady with Marilyn Ramsey and danced with Ballet North. Moving to Manhattan, he continued his studies with Elizabeth Ivantzova-Anderson, Wilson Morelli and Vera Nemtchinova. Regarding his work with Ballets Trockadero, Arlene Croce wrote in the *New Yorker* in 1977: "Anastos is … very close to Robbins; he has the skill to use Robbins against himself. *Another Piano Ballet* is the funniest ballet since *The Concert*, which happens to have been the first Robbins piece to Chopin's music. Anastos doesn't parody *The Concert*, of course, but by providing it with a sequel, twenty one years later, he brings the cycle to an end." Resident choreographer and artistic director for New Jersey's Garden State Ballet from 1979–'89, he collaborated with Mikhail Baryshnikov on ABTs *Cinderella* and the Emmy Award nominated CBS television special "Baryshnikov in Hollywood." Choreographer-in-residence for the Santa Fe Opera in 1983, he was named artistic director of the Cincinnati Ballet in July, 1994. As a writer, Anastos' articles and dance reviews have appeared in *Dance Magazine, Dance Ink, Ballet Review, Christopher Street, New York Times* and *Los Angeles Times*. Anastos is the recipient of two Guggenheim Fellowships (1981 and 1991) and four NEA fellowships.

Stage: *Chess* (Ntl tour '89), *When She Danced* (NY '90), *I Hate Hamlet* (Bdwy '91)

TV: "Baryshnikov in Hollywood" ('82, with Mikhail Baryshnikov, Emmy nom)

Ballet/Dance Pieces (Partial listing): For Les Ballets Trockadero De Monte Carlo (1974–'78): "Yes, Virginia, Another Piano Ballet," "Ecole de Ballet," "Go for Barocco," "Isadora Dances," "Don Quixote," "Les Biches," "Walpurgis Nacht," "Pharaoh's Daughter," "Forgotten Memories," "Siberiana" and "Pieriniana;" "Cinderella" ('83, with Baryshnikov for ABT), "The Gilded Bat" (Ballet West, '90), "The Silver Screen" (American Ballroom Theatre), "Sweet Dreams" (Milwaukee Ballet, '93), "Peter Pan" (Cincinnati Ballet, '94)

Film:

1991 **The Addams Family**—Par (assisted by Victoria Hall)

1993 **Addams Family Values**—Par (with Adam Shankman, "Tango" credit)

JOHN MURRAY ANDERSON

b. St. John's, Newfoundland, September 10, 1886

d. New York, January 30, 1954

Famed director, musical stager, producer, librettist and lyricist who was educated in Edinburgh, Scotland and Lausanne, Switzerland. He studied to be an accountant and arriving in New York, changed his career to an antique dealer. But his love for the theater got the better of him. With a partner, Cynthia Perot, he performed as a ballroom dance team at the Palais Royal and in vaudeville and began staging "Galas" for high society. Called "The Founding Father of the American Revue" by Vincente Minnelli, he became one of the legendary Broadway Revue Directors with his first show, *The Greenwich Village Follies of 1919*, and he continued to specialize in innovative stagecraft (elevators, revolves, treadmills, color and design coordination, etc.) and lighting effects. During a 36-year period he created (and in some cases wrote and produced) 34 musical comedies and revues (29 on Broadway and 7 in London) plus staged 7 circuses for Ringling Brothers and Barnum and Bailey, 4 aquacades for Billy Rose, 11 pageants, 61 movie house presentations and countless nightclub revues (primarily at Billy Rose's Casa Mañana and Diamond Horseshoe in New York). Anderson often worked in collaboration with choreographer Robert Alton and aided the careers of scenic and costume designers Minnelli, Howard Greer, Charles LeMaire and Adrian as well as introducing modern dance choreographers to the Broadway stage (Martha Graham, Doris Humphrey and Jack Cole). He also wrote over 60 songs for his productions.

Autobiography: *Out Without My Rubbers* (1954)

Stage (All Broadway credits as director): *Greenwich Village Follies* ('19–24), *What's in a Name?* ('20), *League of Notions* ('21), *Jack and Jill* ('23), *Dearest Enemy* ('25), *Hello Daddy* ('28), *Bow Bells* and *Fanfare* ('32), *Life Begins at 8:40* and *Thumbs Up!* ('34), *Ziegfeld Follies* ('34, '36, '43), *Billy Rose's Jumbo* ('35), *Home and Beauty* ('37), *Aquacade Revue* and *One for the Money* ('39), *Two for the Show* ('40), *Sunny River* ('41), *Laffing Room Only* ('44), *The Firebrand of Florence* and *Spring in Brazil* ('45), *Three to Make Ready* ('46), *Heaven on Earth* ('48), *John Murray Anderson's Almanac* ('29, '53), *New Faces of 1952* and *Two's Company* ('52)

Nightclub/Concert: (Partial listing): *Let's Play Fair* (Casa Mañana, NY '38), *The Big Show* (Casa Mañana '39), *Nights of Gladness, Nights of Madness* (Diamond Horseshoe, NY '40), *Billy Rose's Aquacade, Violins Over Broadway, On Ze Boulevard, Toast of the Town* (Diamond Horseshoe, NY '45)

Miscellaneous: Ringling Brothers and Barnum and Bailey Circus ('42–51)

Film:

1930 **King of Jazz**— Univ (with Russell Markert, also dir)

1944 **Bathing Beauty**— MGM (with Robert Alton, Jack Donohue, staged swimming sequences)

1952 **The Greatest Show on Earth**— Par. (with Barbette, Richard Barstow—"Circus Musical and Dance Numbers Staged By" credit)

1994 **That's Entertainment! III**— MGM (with others)

ADOLFO ANDRADE

1986 **Tangos: The Exile of Gardel**—(Fr/Argentine) (with Margarita Balli, Susana Tambuti, Robert Thomas)

JERRY ANTES

b. Seattle, Washington

Handsome and versatile dancer, singer and actor who had a successful career as a performer in films: **Rear Window** ('54), **The Opposite Sex** and **Bundle of Joy** ('56), **State Fair** ('62), **Under the Yum Yum Tree** ('63), **Mary Poppins** ('64) and television: as a "regular" on the Danny Kaye, Edie Adams, Rosemary Clooney and Judy Garland shows. A member of the prestigious Desilu Workshop from 1960-61, he was featured in Anna Maria Alberghetti's, Mitzi Gaynor's, Betty Hutton's and Debbie Reynolds' nightclub acts, *Vive les Girls* at the Dunes Hotel, Las Vegas, and the 1971 national tour of *No, No, Nanette*. In addition to assisting Gene Kelly on "Dancing Is a Man's Game," a 1959 TV special, he choreographed one film for Columbia and commercials during the 1960s for Cascade Studios. For the past several years, he has been featured in the *Palm Spring Follies*.

Film:

1955 **A Lawless Street** (aka **The Marshall of Medicine Bend** and **My Gun Commands**)— Col

ANTONIO (ANTONIO RUIZ SOLER)

b. Seville, Spain, November 4, 1921

d. Madrid, Spain, February 5, 1996

As the outstanding male Spanish dancer of his day and paving the way for José Greco and Antonio Gades, Antonio began his studies with Manuel Real ("Realito"). Making his stage debut with his cousin, Rosario Perez, in Liége, Belgium, in 1928, they were first billed as The Kids from Seville, and subsequently, as Rosario and Antonio. They arrived in America in 1940 and created a sensation on stage and films, becoming an internationally famous Flamenco team with their explosive dance routines. Separating from Rosario in 1953 he formed his own company to explore combining Spanish dance with ballet, collaborating often with Léonide Massine. The company performed its "Farewell Tour" in 1978 and he focused on teaching until his death. Antonio's film credits during the 1940s are for the creation of his on-screen routines with Rosario.

Biography: *Antonio and Spanish Dancing* by Elsa Brunelleschi (1958)

Nightclub/Concert: The Kids From Seville (multiple appearances '28–39), Rosario and Antonio ('40–'53), act for Anita Ekberg and Anthony Steele ('58)

Film:

1941 **Antonio and Rosario**— Col (S)

Sing Another Chorus— Univ (with Larry Ceballos, appeared with Rosario)

Ziegfeld Girl— MGM (with Busby Berkeley, appeared with Rosario)

1944 **Hollywood Canteen**— WB (with LeRoy Prinz, Frank Veloz, appeared with Rosario)

1945 **All Star Musical Revue**— WB (S) (with Busby Berkeley, LeRoy Prinz, Frank Veloz, appeared with Rosario)

Pan-Americana— RKO (with Charles O'Curran, appeared with Rosario)

1949 **Make Mine Laughs**— RKO (with Ray Bolger, appeared with Rosario)

1952 **Duende y Misterio del Flamenco**—(Span)

1954 **Flamenco**— Suevia Films (Span) (also appeared)

1959 **Honeymoon** (aka **Luna Da Miel**)— Gau/Brit (with Léonide Massine, also appeared)

1973 **The Three-Cornered Hat**—(Span)

ARTHUR APPEL

1939 **The Wizard of Oz**— MGM (asst to Bobby Connolly)

1941 **The Big Store**— MGM

1946 **Dragonwyck**— Fox

RON ARCIAGA

1991 **Fires Within**— MGM

DONN (DONALD) ARDEN

b. St. Louis, Missouri, July 17, 1915

d. Palm Springs, California, November 2, 1994

Colorful personality whose lavish extravaganzas dominated New York, Los Angeles and Las Vegas nightclub stages from 1950–80 and whose productions ("Conceived, staged and directed by") were seen at the Lido in Paris for 42 years. Arden began dance studies in St. Louis at Clark's Dance School (with fellow student Betty Grable), studying with Robert Alton, who Arden credits as being his mentor. At the age of 15 he won a Charleston contest with Ginger Rogers and joined a Fanchon and Marco "Blue Room Revue." Performing as a "Sin-

Jerry Antes and Jack Regas frame Betty Hutton in her nightclub act (1953) (photo courtesy of Jack Regas).

gle" in speakeasies and vaudeville, he added two sets of twins for even greater success (Donn Arden and the Artist's Models), learning how to create all of the dance and staging material for the act. After boldly telling a club owner that ("...the badly trained chorus ruined his act. When asked if he thought he'd be any better at directing the dancers, Donn said, 'Yes,' and proved it!") at the age of 18, he created his first "Line" at the Lookout House in Cincinnati. He stopped dancing in 1940 and produced house "Lines" and production numbers for theaters and nightclubs across the country. With

Antonio and Rosario, "The Kids from Seville," in **Make Mine Laughs** (RKO, 1949).

his first ice show at the Hotel New Yorker, producer Earl Carroll invited him to come to the West Coast to stage Carroll's Hollywood revues in 1947. In 1949, he founded Arden-Fletcher Productions with Ron Fletcher and finally decided to move west. Starting at the Desert Inn, Las Vegas, in 1950 and then creating all of the spectacular shows at the Moulin Rouge in Hollywood from '53 he became America's most successful nightclub stager and director, famed for his opulent spectacles. He preferred being called a dance director, rather than a choreographer ("Anyone can make up dance steps!") and is listed in the *Guinness Book of World Records* for having his name on a marquee the longest of any producer-director. His film credits are all uncredited filmed versions of existing nightclub sequences.

Nightclub/Concert (Partial listing): Hotel New Yorker Ice Revue ('43–46), Rio Cabana, Chicago ('45), Lido de Paris (France '48–90, Stardust Hotel, LV '58–91), Desert Inn, LV (multiple numbers '50–63 and productions *Hello America!*, *Pzazz*, etc.), Moulin Rouge, Hollywood ('53–60), Marine-

land Starlight Spectacular ('60), *All About Dames* (Latin Quarter, NY), *Hallelujah Hollywood!* ('73–'81) and *Jubilee* (Ballys, LV '81–current), *Hello Hollywood Hello* (MGM, Reno '78); also multiple acts for stars including Betty Grable and Eleanor Powell

Miscellaneous: Holiday on Ice ('68–70)

Film (Credits include the locale of original stage work filmed):

1955 **Cinerama Holiday**—Cinerama Corp (Lido de Paris and Desert Inn, Las Vegas)

Paris Follies of 1956—AA (aka **Fresh From Paris**, Moulin Rouge, Hollywood)

1959 **Imitation of Life**—Univ (Moulin Rouge, Hollywood restaged by Bill Chatham)

JULIE ARENAL
b. New York, July 22, 1942

Modern dancer, choreographer, director and teacher who studied dance with Maggie Black, Leon Danielian, Martha Graham, Igor Yousekevitch and at Bennington College. Making her professional debut with the Anna Sokolow Dance Company at the American Dance Festival in New London, Conn., she subsequently danced with the John Butler, Jack Cole, José Limon and Sophie Maslow companies. After assisting Sokolow at Lincoln Center, she made her solo choreographic debut with the Theatre Company of Boston's production of *Marat/Sade*. Her choreography for the first major rock musical *Hair* in 1968 ("It's 'non-choreography' but 'all dance'") broke new ground for the musical stage ("I'd say to the kids, 'If you had one chance to be remembered in this world, what pose would you take?' And they'd give me some crazy thing, and we'd use that.... It's very hard for dancers to hide their training ... like placement and turnout and precision. And they forget about creating that image. They don't allow the movement to speak to you." *Dance Magazine*, July, 1968). She subsequently staged and directed productions of the musical in London, Belgrade and Los Angeles. Director of the NY Express Break and Boogie Dance Co. she also taught movement for actors at the Herbert Berghof Studios in New York and appeared in the film **Beat Street**. Married to actor Barry Primus since 1961, her ecclectic career has since moved into direction.

Stage: *Marat/Sade* (Boston), *Hair* (Bdwy '68), *Indians* (Bdwy '69), *Isabel's a Jewel* (London, '70, also dir), *Gun Play* (OB '71), *2008½* (OB '74), *I Took Panama* (OOT '77), *The Sun Always Shines for the Cool* (OB '79), *Funny Girl* (Tokyo '79–80, also dir), *Jesus Christ Superstar* (Stockholm '80, also dir), *Abyssinia* (OB '87), *Half a World Away* (OB '87, also dir), *Pancho Diablo* (NY Shakespeare Festival '87)

TV: "Gypsy Fever" (ABC '78), "Mid-Summer Night of Music" (Italy '86); commercials for Sears, McDonald's (winner of the "El Cervantes" award)

Music Video: "Self-Control"—Laura Branigan; "Breakout"—Starpoint; "Stepping Out"; video for Crystal Gayle.

Ballet/Dance Pieces: "Fiesta" (Ballet Hispanico '72), "Boccaccio," "A Private Circus" (Ballet Hispanico), "Fun to Be You and Me," "The Referee" (SF Ballet), "El Arbito" (Ballet Nacional De Cuba); Multiple works for her NY Express Break and Boogie Dance Co. including "On the Move" and "The City" (Spoleto Festival '84)

Film:
1978 **King of the Gypsies**—Par
1981 **Four Friends**—Filmways
1982 **Soup for One**—WB
1984 **Once Upon a Time in America**—Ladd/WB
1992 **Mistress**—Rainbow/Tribeca
1995 **Steal Big, Steal Little**—Chicago Pacific Ent

GIORGIO ARESU

Italian dancer and choreographer currently working in Europe in multiple television and stage projects.

TV: "1,2,3," "The Saturday Night Show" (Spanish TV)
Film:
1989 **Berlin Blues**—Cannon

ALEX ARIZPE
1991 **Rush**—MGM/Pathé

BETTY ARLEN

Arlen began her career as a Wampas Baby star of 1921 and appeared in **She's Working Her Way Through College** ('52).
Film:
1953 **Cat Women of the Moon**—Astore (also appeared)

KAROLE ARMITAGE
b. Madison, Wisconsin, March 3, 1954

Titled "The complete contemporary dance artist" in *Dance Magazine*, May, 1986, this innovative dancer and "cross-current" choreographer was praised as, "She may be the only dancer in the world whose background spans Balanchine training ... and a long association with Merce Cunningham. Add to this odd mixture her passion for Motown music and black social dance, developed as a student listening to the radio while she commuted a daily 120 miles ... for ballet lessons with Tatiana Dokoudovska." As a teenager, Armitage moved with her family from Kansas to Europe and made her debut dancing with the Geneva Ballet (1972–'74). She returned to America and joined Cunningham's company and in 1978, she began creating choreography for performances in Manhattan. In 1981, she left Cunningham and formed her own company. Her unique movement exploration and performance style drew attention in France, where Rudolph Nureyev asked her to create works for the Paris Opera Ballet. After devising ballets for ABT, the Tasmanian Dance Company and others, she formed Armitage Ballet in 1986 and continues to challenge the viewer with choreography that was once described as: "Explodes like a Molotov cocktail hurled defiantly at the audience." Also exploring filmed dance, she credits George Balanchine and Merce Cunningham as her dance mentors, with a variety of artists, filmmakers and musicians affecting her creativity, "I have often choreographed right to the beat, in the sense of making the quarter notes swing; it gives the dance a lot of pizzazz and drama. I think it is accepted now that dance is a completely independent art. It can accompany music fully or have no direct relationship to it.... When you make art, you don't do it only as entertainment. It's also addressing contemporary culture. For this reason, I was once interested in punk."

TV: "The South Bank Show" ('86)

Ballet/Dance Pieces: (Partial listing) "Drastic Classicism," "The Watteau Duet," "The Mollino Room," "Do We Could," "Parafango," "The Elizabethan Phrasing of the Late Albert Ayler," "Romance;" for the Paris Opera Ballet: "GV 10" and "Les Anges Ternis"

Film:
1990 **Without You I'm Nothing**— Electric Pic
1992 **Kuffs**— Univ
1993 **Chain of Desire**— Mad Dog Pictures (also appeared)

DIANE ARNOLD

1979 **The Man in the Santa Claus Suit**— Dick Clark Prod/NBC (TV)

CLAUDIA ASBURY

b. Houston, Texas

Born into a family of professional dancers, Claudia moved to New York to enrich her training and appear in a series of Broadway shows, beginning in 1974 with *Mack and Mabel* and subsequently in *So Long 174th Street* ('76), *The Act* ('77) and *Evita* ('79). While appearing in *Sophisticated Ladies* ('81), she began her choreographic work, serving as assistant to Michael Smuin. On the West Coast, she appeared on TV in "The Carol Burnett Show" and was assistant choreographer on the national tour of *A Musical Jubilee*.

Miscellaneous: City Lights (Great Adventures Theme Park, NJ '78, also dir)

Film:
1984 **The Cotton Club**— Orion (with George Faison, Gregory Hines, Henry LeTang, Michael Meacham, Arthur Mitchell, Michael Smuin)

SIR FREDERICK ASHTON

b. Guayaquil, Equador, September 17, 1906
d. Eye, Suffolk, England, August 18, 1988

Acclaimed dancer-choreographer whose interest in dance began when, at the age of 11, he saw Pavlova perform in Lima, Peru. When his family moved to England he was further dazzled by the Diaghilev Ballets Russes. After graduation from school in 1924, he worked as a foreign correspondent for an export merchant in London and studied classic ballet with Léonide Massine and Marie Rambert. Rambert encouraged his first choreographic effort, "A Tragedy of Fashion" as part of *Riverside Nights*, a London revue in 1926. For Marie Rambert's Ballet Club he continued his choreographic career and briefly joined Ida Rubinstein's company in Paris in 1927 before returning to Rambert. Producer-impressario Charles Cochran asked him to choreograph for nightclubs and theatrical revues in London, working in collaboration with tap choreographer Buddy Bradley. This work in the commercial theater would add depth to his contributions to the world of Ballet. In 1933 he was asked to create works for the Vic-Wells Company and in 1935 joined the company as a premier danseur and choreographer. The company moved to Covent Gardens to become Sadler's Wells. In 1946, he choreographed **Cinderella** for the company, having the distinction of being the first British Choreographer to create a full length ballet. He was named associate director of the Royal Ballet and when Ninette DeValois retired in 1963, he became full director. Ashton's prolific choreographic output is distinguished by his mastery of pas de deux and the lightness, precision and lyricism of the Royal Ballet style he created. His film career included several substantial original works for the screen or the filming of existing stage pieces. On **The Loves of Isadora** (1978), he tried to reconstruct from memory the dances he had seen Isadora Duncan perform for its star, Vanessa Redgrave, and choreographer, Litz Pisk. As the first in British dance to receive the honor of being Knighted in 1962, he also received the *Dance Magazine* Award in 1970. With a choreographic career which spanned nearly four decades, he retired from the Royal Ballet in 1970.

Biography: Frederick Ashton— A Choreographer and His Ballets by Zoe Dominic and John Selwyn Gilbert (1971), *Frederick Ashton and His Ballets* by David Vaughan (1977)

Stage: Riverside Nights (London '26), *Ballyhoo* (London, '32, with Buddy Bradley), *The Gay Hussar* (London '33), *Four Saints in Three Acts* (NY '34), *The Flying Trapeze* (London, '35, with Buddy Bradley), *The Fleet's Lit Up* (London '38), *A Midsummer Night's Dream* (Old Vic, London '54), **Manon** ('47) and **Orfeo ed Euridice** (Royal Opera, London '53)

Ballet/Dance Pieces (Partial listing): Over 100 ballets for Ballet Rambert, the Royal Ballet, Ballets Russe de Monte Carlo, New York City Ballet and the Royal Danish Ballet including "Four Saints in Three Acts" ('33), "Mephisto Valse," "Facade," "Les Patineurs," "A Wedding Bouquet," "Homage to the Queen," "Ondine," "La Fille Mal Gardee," "Devil's Holiday," "Illuminations," "Daphnis and Chloe," "Tiresias," "Sylvia," "Rinaldo and Armida," "Birthday Offering," "Romeo and Juliet," "La Valse," "Madame Chysantheme," "Marguerite and Armand," "The Dream," "La Chatte Metamorphoseé Infemme" ('86)

Nightclub/Concert: Trocadero (London)

Film:
1932 **Dance Pretty Lady**— BI/Wardour ("Technical advisor on ballet scenes" credit)

1935 **Escape Me Never**— UA
1951 **The Tales of Hoffman**— The Archers-LFP/Lopert (assisted by Alan Carter, Joan Harris, also appeared)
1953 **The Story of Three Loves**— MGM
1960 **The Royal Ballet**— Rank/UA (also assoc dir)
1968 **The Loves of Isadora** (aka **Isadora**)— Univ (with Litz Pisk)
1971 **Peter Rabbit and the Tales of Beatrix Potter**— EMI/MGM (also appeared)
1977 **The Turning Point**— Fox (with Alvin Ailey, George Balanchine, Jean Coralli, John Cranko, Michel Fokine, Lev Ivanov, Harald Lander, Kenneth MacMillan, Alexander Minz, Dennis Nahat, Jules Perrot, Marius Petipa)

ASOKA

b. Germany

Dancer and choreographer who appeared in concert, TV, films and on stage with wife Sujata and helped to introduce the classic dances of India to international audiences. Although born in Germany, his interest in the dances of India led him to move and study there in the 1930s. His intense research included religious rituals, folk dances, classic dances, court dances and he was eventually given approval to stay in monasteries with Buddhist monks in Tibet to learn their as yet-unseen rituals and dances. Upon his release from a detention camp in the Himalayas (where he had been held as an "enemy alien" from 1939 to 1944 by the British) he met Sujata, a leading Hindu dancer. They began their performing partnership in 1946 and were married in March 1947. After debuting in India, they began their successful international career at the Lido de Paris in 1948 and then in Canada and the United States the following year. They toured internationally for more than a decade in concert and nightclubs, as well as teaching Indian dance and yoga. With acting and dancing contracts in Hollywood from 1952 to 1954, Asoka choreographed the team's multiple film appearances. When Hollywood's brief fascination with Indian locales and screenplays ended, they returned to their international live appearances and teaching, becoming naturalized U.S citizens in 1955.

TV: Multiple appearances on the Liberace, Ed Sullivan and Dinah Shore shows (1950–60s)

Ballet/Dance Pieces (Partial listing): "Agui Puja" (Fire Purification), "Rama and Sita," "Ajanta Frescoes," "Royal Mogul Wedding"

Film (All credits except two are for the team's on-screen routines):
1947 **Calcutta**— Par (with Roberta Jonay, danced with Sujata)
1952 **Aladdin and His Lamp**— Mon

Caribbean Gold— Par (danced with Sujata)
1953 **Desert Legion**— Univ (danced with Sujata)
The Diamond Queen— WB (danced with Sujata)
The Flame of Calcutta— Col (danced with Sujata)
King of the Khyber Rifles— Fox (with Steven Papich, danced with Sujata)
Salome— Col (with Valerie Bettis, Lee Scott, danced with Sujata)
Fair Wind to Java— Rep
1954 **Bengal Brigade**— Univ (danced with Sujata)

MICHELE ASSAF

"I've taught for 10 years, and I originally got jobs choreographing — whether it was stage or film or whatever — through teaching. People heard about me and asked for me. Now there's a lot more dance in everything, and people are aware of dance from all the music video. But before, I think the producers didn't know enough, so they would call in teachers ... and I happened to be a choreographer and it worked out," stated this dancer, actress, choreographer, teacher and director in a 1993 SSDC roundtable discussion. Beginning as a performer, her film appearances include **A Chorus Line** ('85). Describing her work as "athletic, sensual, a combination of contemporary styles with a foundation of jazz, modern and ballet" her multi-talents and commercial adaptability have taken her all over the world. When asked if she considered working on TV commercials as "selling out," Assaf quickly answered, "It's not about the dance. It's about the product. That's something that's very important for choreographers — It's not the choreographer as star, it's not about making your choreography look great, it's about making the product look great. When I do a ballet, I'm going to create the most incredible movement that I'm capable of."

Describing her work as "athletic, sensual, a combination of contemporary styles with a foundation of jazz, modern and ballet" the talents of this dancer, actress, choreographer, teacher and director talents have taken her all over the world to choreograph, direct and teach in Australia, Italy, Japan. Film appearances include **A Chorus Line** ('85).

Stage: Starmites (Bdwy '89, Tony nom), *Saint Seiya* (Tokyo '91), *Sweet Charity* (Tokyo '92, also dir), *It's a Bird, It's a Plane, It's Superman* ('92 Goodspeed Opera House rev), *Strider* (OB), *Street Heat* (LA), *Scenes from an Execution* (LA '93), *Jesus Christ Superstar* (Royal Ballet of Flanders), *Can Can* ('95 Goodspeed Opera House rev), *Bring in the Morning* (NY '95)

TV: "The Guiding Light," Italian TV Awards (Milan), Mick Jagger's Australian and Japanese TV

Sujata and Asoka perform an East Indian dance interlude in **Bengal Brigade** (Par, 1954).

specials, "Well, Well, Well," "One Life to Live," "Odiens" (Italy), "Telegato" (Italy '88), "Festival Barre" (Italy), 1993 Tony Awards (asst to Walter Painter), "Through Thick and Thin" (After-School Special)

Music Video (Partial listing): "Primitive Cool"— Mick Jagger; "Babylon"—Justine John; "Too Turned On" and "All Night Passion"—Alisha; "Betty's Bein' Bad," "Shakin'" and "Out Goin' Cattin'"—Sawyer Brown

Nightclub/Concert: Mick Jagger ('88 Japan and Australia tours, '89 World tour), Soul Sisters ('93–'94 European tours)

Film:

1981 **Twirl**—NBC (TV) (also appeared)
1988 **Last Rites**—MGM (with Lee Ann Martin)
       Spike of Bensonhurst—FilmDallas

FRED ASTAIRE (FREDERICK AUSTERLITZ)

b. Omaha, Nebraska, May 10, 1899
d. Beverly Hills, California, June 22, 1987

Dancer, singer, actor, choreographer, composer and author who is responsible for reshaping the movie musical and dance on film with his innovations and dedicated professionalism. As a child, he began brief formal dance training at 5 with Claude Alvienne at New York's Grand Opera House and started in vaudeville with his sister, Adele, two years later. After headlining for ten years, they became international musical comedy stars in ten shows from *Over the Top* (Bdwy '17) to *The Band Wagon* (Bdwy '31). When Adele retired from the theater to marry in 1931, he starred in *The Gay Divorce* (Bdwy '32 & London '33). He made his film debut at the age of 33 in **Dancing Lady** and his subsequent 40-plus year career firmly established him as the screen's most famous dancer. He began choreographing for his act with Adele and their stage shows and occasionally choreographed for other shows, often being brought in as a "Dance Doctor" to cure ailing musical numbers for such stage stars as Marilyn Miller, Noel Coward and Ginger Rogers. In his series of nine film musicals with Ginger Rogers at RKO in the 1930s, he insisted that his dances be photographed in full figure shots and with very few cuts. The choreography was devised especially for the camera, rather than photographed stage routines and the camera was choreographed to move with the dancers. To bridge the transition between dialogue and the musical numbers, he and collaborator Hermes Pan created patterns of movement which went from character action to actual dance. He also helped integrate song and dance to evolve naturally out of the action, rather than being an isolated piece of entertainment—leading the way to the fully integrated musical of the 1940s. Often uncredited for choreography, he always worked out his own dance routines with Pan, conceiving the numbers and creating the actual steps. Attempting

Fred Astaire surrounded by dancing men (future choreographer Jack Regas is to Astaire's left) in "If Swing Goes, I Go Too," a number written by Astaire and unfortunately deleted from **Ziegfeld Follies** (MGM, 1945) (photo courtesy of Jack Regas).

to never repeat himself in his solo dances, he spent weeks working with various props to come up with a "Gimmick" for each solo (drums, brooms, mops, coat racks, revolving rooms, etc.) Since 1947, his name has been associated with a chain of dance schools. Among the most honored of film innovators, he received a special Oscar in 1949, the *Dance Magazine* Award in 1959, The Film Society of Lincoln Center Honors in 1973, The Kennedy Center Honors in 1978 and the American Film Institute's Life Achievement Award in 1981.

Autobiography: *Steps in Time* (1959)

Biography: *Starring Fred Astaire* by Stanley Green and Burt Goldblatt (1973), *Astaire — The Man, the Dancer* by Bob Thomas (1984)

Related Works: *The Fred Astaire & Ginger Rogers Book* by Arlene Croce (1972), *Astaire Dancing* by John Mueller (1985)

Stage: *Over the Top* (Bdwy '17, with Allan K. Foster), *The Passing Show of 1918* (Bdwy, with Jack Mason), *Apple Blossoms* (Bdwy '19, with Edward Royce), *The Love Letter* (Bdwy '20, with Edward Royce), *For Goodness Sake* (Bdwy '22, with Allan K. Foster), *The Bunch and Judy* (Bdwy '23, *Stop Flirting* and *London Calling* (London '23), *Sunny* (Bdwy '25, with David Bennett, Theodore Kosloff, John Tiller), *Lady Be Good* (Bdwy & London '25, with Max Scheck), *Funny Face* (Bdwy & London '27, with Bobby Connolly), *Smiles* (Bdwy '28, with Ned

Wayburn), *Girl Crazy* (Bdwy '30, with George Hale), *The Band Wagon* (Bdwy '31, with Albertina Rasch), *The Gay Divorcee* (Bdwy '32, London '33, with Carl Randall, Barbara Newberry)

TV: "An Evening with Fred Astaire" ('58, with Hermes Pan, Emmy award), "Another Evening with Fred Astaire" ('59, with Hermes Pan), "Astaire Time" ('60, with Hermes Pan, Emmy Award), "Think Pretty" ('64), "The Hollywood Palace" (1965–70), "The Fred Astaire Show" ('68, with Herbert Ross)

Nightclub/Concert: Act for Adele and himself at the Trocodero Nightclub, (NY '25)

Miscellaneous: Staged dance numbers for Irene Castle after the death of her husband, Vernon (1921) and created touring U.S.O. shows for himself during World War II

Film (For all films except four (*), Astaire did not receive screen credit for his choreography):

1933 **Flying Down to Rio** — RKO (with Dave Gould, Hermes Pan)

1934 **The Gay Divorcee** — RKO (with Dave Gould, Hermes Pan)

1935 ***Roberta** — RKO (with Hermes Pan — "Dances arranged by" credit)

      Top Hat — RKO (with Hermes Pan)

1936 —**Follow the Fleet** — RKO (with Hermes Pan)

      Swing Time — RKO (with Hermes Pan)

1937 **A Damsel in Distress**— RKO (with Hermes Pan)

Shall We Dance— RKO (with Harry Losee, Hermes Pan)

1938 **Carefree**— RKO (with Hermes Pan)

1939 **The Story of Vernon and Irene Castle**— RKO (with Hermes Pan)

1940 **Broadway Melody of 1940**— MGM (with Bobby Connolly, George Murphy, Eleanor Powell, Albertina Rasch)

Second Chorus— Par (with Hermes Pan)

1941 **You'll Never Get Rich**— Col (with Robert Alton)

1942 **Holiday Inn**— Par. (with Danny Dare)

You Were Never Lovelier— Col (with Peggy Carroll, Val Raset)

1943 *****The Sky's the Limit**— RKO (with Bernard Pearce, "Dances arranged by" credit)

1945 **Yolanda and the Thief**— MGM (with Eugene Loring)

1946 **Blue Skies**— Par (with Hermes Pan, David Robel)

Ziegfeld Follies— MGM (with Robert Alton, Gene Kelly, Eugene Loring, Charles Walters)

1948 **Easter Parade**— MGM (with Robert Alton, Ann Miller)

1949 **The Barkleys of Broadway**— MGM (with Robert Alton, Hermes Pan)

"Special Award": Academy Award statuette to Fred Astaire "for his unique artistry and his contributions to the technique of musical pictures."

1950 **Let's Dance**— Par (with Hermes Pan)

Three Little Words— MGM (with Hermes Pan)

1951 —**The Belle of New York**— MGM (with Robert Alton)

Royal Wedding— MGM (with Nick Castle)

1953 **The Band Wagon**— MGM (with Michael Kidd)

1955 *****Daddy Long Legs**— Fox (with Roland Petit, David Robel —"Dances staged by Fred Astaire and David Robel" credit)

1957 *****Funny Face**— Par (with Eugene Loring)

Silk Stockings— MGM (with Eugene Loring, Hermes Pan)

1961 **The Pleasure of His Company**— Par (with Hermes Pan)

1968 **Finian's Rainbow**— WB (with Hermes Pan, Claude Thompson)

1974 **That's Entertainment!**— MGM (with others)

1976 **That's Entertainment II**— MGM (with others)

1985 **That's Dancing**— MGM (with others)

1994 **That's Entertainment! III**— MGM (with others)

CHOLLY ATKINS (CHARLES ATKINSON)

b. Pratt City, Alabama, September 30, 1913

Tap dancer, choreographer and Rock-vocal movement pioneer who won a Charleston contest in Buffalo, New York at the age of 10, starting him on his extraordinary career. He appeared on Broadway in *The Hot Mikado* and in the films **San Francisco** ('36), **Strike Me Pink** ('37) and **The Big Broadcast of 1938**. With Charles "Honi" Coles, he formed Coles and Atkins, an unchallenged "Class" tap-soft shoe dance act which appeared in night clubs, theaters, TV and concerts for over 20 years. On Broadway they appeared in *Gentlemen Prefer Blondes* ('49). Unfortunately their artistry was only captured on film once in **Rock 'n' Roll Revue** ('52). When they broke up the landmark dance team, Atkins began working with black vocal groups, starting with the Cadillacs in 1953 and becoming responsible for shaping an entire vocal choreography vocabulary whose impact is still felt around the world. The style had been started by Paul Robinson of the Temptations, but when Atkins joined Motown's Artistic Development Department staff for all of their rising artists in 1965, he refined and organized it, combining the earthy Soul movements of James Brown, contemporary street dance and adding his urban sophistication and dance vocabulary to create patterns of movement. He taught stage etiquette and choreographed for most of the major African-American recording artists of the 1960s and '70s, creating their unique movement styles by combining bits of ballroom, jazz and even tap steps to create routines which were practiced by adoring teenaged fans and moved into social dancing of the period. Atkins finally received the accolades he has so deserved for decades when he won a Tony Award for his choreography for the Broadway success *Black and Blue*. He currently lives and teaches in Las Vegas.

Stage: *Black and Blue* (Bdwy '89, Tony Award)

TV: Staging for all the Motown groups for their appearances on such shows as "American Bandstand," "The Ed Sullivan Show," The Grammy Awards Shows, "Hullabaloo," "Soul Train," "Shindig," "Shivaree," "T.C.B.," "Where the Action Is," etc.

Nightclub/Concert: Acts for the Cadillacs, the Four Tops, Aretha Franklin, Marvin Gaye, Gladys Knight and the Pips, Martha and the Vandellas, Smokey Robinson and the Miracles, the Supremes, the Temptations; revues at the Maxim Hotel (LV)

Film:

1952 **Rock 'n' Roll Revue**— Studio Films (S) (also appeared)

1965 **Beach Ball**— Par (with Rita D'Amico, uncredited for The Supremes' appearance)

1988 —**Tapeheads**— Ave Pictures (with Eddie Batos)

DAVID ATKINS

b. Australia

Described in a review of the 1994 recording of his latest Australian stage success *Hot Shoe Shuffle* as "a talented hoofer/choreographer/actor ... the nearest thing Australian dance theatre has to Tommy Tune. However, physically they are worlds apart, Tune well over six feet tall and Atkins just over five," Atkins is one of Australia's leading stage and screen dance creators. Appearing onstage in *A Chorus Line*, *Cats* and his own original dance shows: *Dancin' Man*, *Dynamite*, *Dancin' Dynamite* and *Hot Shoe Shuffle*, he also starred in the Australian films **Squizzy Taylor** and **Personal Services**. His film choreography credits reflect his major participation in Australian film musicals.

Stage (Also dir and star): *Dancin' Man*, *Dynamite*, *Dancin' Dynamite* (Australia), *Hot Shoe Shuffle* (Australia, Bdwy and London, '94, Olivier Award nom '95)

Film:
1982 **Pirate Movie**— Fox
      Squizzy Taylor— Filmways (also appeared)
      Star Struck— Cinecom Intl
1987 **High Tide**— TriStar

TEDDY ATLAS

1989 **Triumph of the Spirit**— Triumph

RICK (RICHARD) ATWELL

b. St. Louis, Missouri, July 29, 1949

Dancer, choreographer and director who began his dance studies with Tatiana Dokoudovska at the Kansas City Conservatory of Music. He made his professional debut at the age of 10 in the 1959 Kansas City Starlight Opera production of *Flower Drum Song*, later relating that he knew he wanted to be a choreographer even then, creating numbers backstage with the older children in the production. A member of the St. Louis Muny Opera in 1967, he moved to New York and broadened his dance repertoire studying with David Howard, Luigi, Matt Mattox and Patricia Wilde. That same year he joined the Harkness Ballet and remained a member until 1972 while simultaneously appearing on Broadway in *The Rothchilds* and *Georgy* ('70) and *The Selling of the President* ('72, in which he also assisted Ethel Martin). He studied acting with Gene Frankel and Mary Tarcai and appeared off Broadway in *Cowboys #2*, *Lady Audley's Secret*, *Turkey Delight* and *An Evening with Pat Carroll*. Stock appearances include *Hit the Deck*, *Half a Sixpence*, *Death of a Salesman*, *Butterflies Are Free*, *Bye Bye Birdie* and the national tour of *Pippin*. He danced in the film version of **Annie**. His first choreographic work was *Tenderloin* for Equity Library Theater in

New York. He was nominated for an award by *Backstage Magazine* for his work on *Sarava* on Broadway in 1979.

Stage: *Tenderloin* (OB), *Two by Two* (OOT '72), *Sarava* (Bdwy '79, also dir), *Streetheart* (Studio 54 Cabaret, NY '84), *I, Jan Cremer* (Amsterdam), *Council of Love* (Berlin)

TV: "Dancin' to the Hits," Suzanne Sommers Special, "Physical Fitness" CBS Special

Nightclub/Concert: Acts for Tovah Feldshuh, Bonnie Franklin, Gotham, Suzanne Sommers and S.R.O.

Ballet/Dance Pieces: "Playgrounds" (Carlotta Portello and Co.)

Film:
1985 **Fast Forward**— Col (with assistants Aimee Covo, Felix, Pamela Poitier, Robin Summerfield, and "Dance Consultants" Gary Porter, Charlie Washington)

CHARLES AUGINS

b. Arlington, Virginia

London-based dancer, choreographer, director and actor who began his dance studies at the age of 9 with tap classes at the Arlington Recreation Department and progressed to ballet at 17 with the Jones-Haywood School of Ballet in Washington. He danced with the Baltimore City Ballet, Talley Beatty and D.C. Repertory Dance companies and taught jazz at Boston University and ballet and jazz at the Boston Conservatory. From 1974–76 he was director of dance for the Ellington School of the Arts and made a cultural study trip to the Bolshoi and Kirov Ballet Schools in Russia. He danced on Broadway in *Never Jam Today* ('68) and the all-black revival of *Guys and Dolls* and in the off-Broadway revue *Let My People Come*. In 1978 he moved to London to direct, choreograph and star in *Bubbling Brown Sugar* and has remained home-based in Britain for the past eighteen years. His choreography and direction on the London-originated (and Olivier Award-winning) hit *Five Guys Named Moe* brought him international recognition. Along with his multiple directing and choreography credits, he continues to appear as an actor on British television, film and stage.

Stage: *Bubbling Brown Sugar* (London, also dir and star), *Porgy and Bess* (Glyndebourne Festival Opera), *Kiss Me Kate* (Bristol Old Vic), *Snap Shots* (Edinburgh Festival), *Chorus Girl* (London), *Dangerous Corner*, *Dash*, *The Blue Angel*, *This Is My Dream* (Theatre Royal), *Eastward Ho!* (London '81), *Five Guys Named Moe* (Lyric Theatre, London '91; Bdwy '92)

TV (All British TV credits): "All God's Children Got Rhythm," "We've Been Waiting," "6:55," "The Hot Shoe Show" ('82), The Selena Duncan Series; Pointer Sisters Pepsi Commercial

Film:
1986 **Labyrinth**— TriStar (with Cherly McFadden, also appeared)
1990 **The Tall Guy**— Miramax (also appeared)

AUGIE AULD
b. 1905
d. 1983
Hawaiian hula dancer and choreographer who introduced the popular standard "Lovely Hula Hands" in 1940 and appeared in the films she choreographed, as well as **Rainbow Island** ('44).
Film:
1938 **Hawaii Calls**— RKO (also appeared)
1945 **The Moon of Manakoora**— Soundies Corp (S) (also appeared)

EMILIO "STRETCH" AUSTIN
1991 **Strictly Business**— WB

CHRISTINE AVERY
1994 **Funny Bones**— Hollywood Pictures

PHYLLIS AVERY
b. New York, November 14, 1924
Dancer, actress and choreographer who appeared in the films **Queen for a Day** ('51), **Ruby Gentry** ('52), **The Best Things in Life Are Free** ('56) and **Made in America** (1993). Also costarred in the TV series "The Ray Milland Show" and "Mr. Novak." Married to actor Don Taylor, they have two daughters.
Film:
1945 **Sensation Hunters**— Mon

NELSON AVILA
Appeared partnering Nelida Rodriguez in *Tango Argentino* on Broadway (1984) and in London (1991).
Film:
1988 **Tango Bar**— Castle Hill (with Santiago Ayala, Lilliana Belfiore, Doris Petroni, Carlos Rivarola, Nelida Rodriguez, Norma Viola, also appeared)

SANTIAGO AYALA
1988 **Tango Bar**— Castle Hill (with Nelson Avila, Lilliana Belfiore, Doris Petroni, Nelida Rodriguez, Carlos Rivarola, Norma Viola)

SHLOMO BACHAR
Director and choreographer of the Hadarim Dance Company, an Israeli folk troupe.
Film:
1980 **The Jazz Singer**— Associate Film Distribution (with Donald McKayle, members of the Hadarim Dance Company appeared)

JACK BAKER
b. New York, June 21, 1916
Prolific choreographer of film, television and nightclub acts during the 1950s and '60s. The son of Walter Baker, owner of a dance studio in New York, Jack also studied with Lisa Gardener, Phil Hayden and Vera Stolska. He made his professional debut on Broadway in *Panama Hattie* in 1940 and continued in ten Broadway shows, among them *Oklahoma!, Let's Face It, Something for the Boys, Ziegfeld Follies* and *By Jupiter*. After moving to the West Coast in 1945, he danced in films and assisted Jack Donohue and other choreographers. One of his major film dance roles was as "The Heavy" in the **Slaughter on Tenth Ave.** Ballet in **Words and Music** (1948) with Gene Kelly and Vera-Ellen. He began his solo choreographic career in 1951 contracted by Paramount as dance director and continued to work for nearly every studio in Hollywood as the film musical changed with the intro of rock 'n' roll, often assisted by his wife, former dancer Sheila Meyers. After multiple television choreographic credits, he made the transition to director of "Here's Lucy" (1968).
Stage: *The Best of Burlesque* (LA '60, with Wilda Taylor), *Victory Canteen* (LA '71, also dir)
TV (Partial listing): "Mission: Impossible," "Mannix," "The Untouchables," Kraft Music Hall, "Mayberry R.F.D." ('69), "The Hollywood Palace," "Desilu Playhouse," "Here's Lucy"; the Ames Brothers, Jack Benny, George Burns, Rosemary Clooney, Perry Como, Bob Hope, Dean Martin, Dinah Shore and Andy Williams shows; specials for George Burns ('59), Bob Hope and Ginger Rogers ('60); commercials for Zenith
Nightclub/Concert: Acts for the Andrews Sisters, the Ames Brothers, George Burns, Betty Garrett & Larry Parks, Mitzi Gaynor, Liberace, Debra Paget, Irene Ryan, the Sportsmen and Mamie Van Doren; Bob Hope U.S.O. tours
Film:
1953 **The Caddy**— Par
       The Stars Are Singing— Par
       Those Redheads from Seattle— Par
       Tropic Zone— Par
1954 **Jubilee Trail**— Rep
1955 **Sincerely Yours**— WB
       Timberjack— Rep
1957 **Beau James**— Par (assisted by Pat Denise)
       Ten Thousand Bedrooms— MGM
       This Could Be the Night— MGM
1958 **Guns, Girls and Gangsters**— UA
       Marjorie Morningstar— WB (assisted by Pat Denise)

1959 **Born Reckless**— WB
1960 **Sex Kittens Go to College**— AA
1962 **The Road to Hong Kong**— UA (with Sheila Meyers)
    The Scarface Mob— Desilu/Cari Releasing (with Sheila Meyers)
1963 **Come Blow Your Horn**— Par (with Maggie Banks, Nick Castle)
    It Happened at the World's Fair— MGM
1964 **Robin and the 7 Hoods**— WB (assisted by Pat Horn)
1965 **Beach Blanket Bingo**— AIP
    Dr. Goldfoot and the Bikini Machine— AIP (assisted by Christopher Riordan)
    Harlow— Par (also appeared as "The Choreographer")
    How to Stuff a Wild Bikini— AIP
    Sergeant Deadhead— AIP
1966 **Ghost in the Invisible Bikini**— AIP (assisted by Christopher Riordan)
1968 **Live a Little, Love a Little**— MGM (with Jack Regas)
    Spinout— MGM
1969 **How to Commit Marriage**— Cinerama
    Paint Your Wagon— Par
1975 **Train Ride to Hollywood**— Billy Jack/Taylor-Laughlin

TROY BAKER

1996 **Split Second**— Indie

GEORGE BALANCHINE (GYORGI MELITONO-VITCH BALANCHI-VADZE)

b. St. Petersburg, Russia, January 9, 1904
d. New York, April 30, 1983

Because of his strong faith in the talents of American dancers this innovator changed the face of classical dance in the United States. The son of a Georgian composer, he entered the Imperial School of Ballet in St. Petersburg, Russia, at the age of 10 and made his debut in 1915 in *Sleeping Beauty*. He enrolled in the Marinsky Conservatory of Ballet and Music in 1921, studying piano and music theory with the intentions of becoming a concert pianist. Already choreographing at the age of 16 while still in school, he formed Soviet State Ballet in 1923 and left Russia in 1924 to tour Germany and France with the company (including Alexandra Danilova and Tamara Geva). In Paris, he was engaged as ballet master by Serge Diaghiliev, choreographing ten major works for the company. In her book *America Dances*, Agnes DeMille wrote: "He sought employment in the popular music halls of Western Eu-

rope and was there exposed to types of work his elders had been protected from and which, under continuing Imperial conditions, he might never have seen." He observed "Adagio" dances, "…for it was in the music halls that Balanchine learned the acrobatic stunts he later incorporated into the classical techniques, and through his genius, the tossing, carrying, wrapping and writhing found their way into meaningful designs." Balanchine later would say, "Thank God when I first began to choreograph in Paris, I didn't speak French. Fifty years later, somebody read my reviews. If I'd read them in the twenties, I would have gone back to Russia!" In 1929, he was invited to Copenhagen as ballet master for the Royal Dutch Ballet and made his film choreographic debut (as well as dancing in) **Dark Red Roses** in Britain in 1930. After helping Col. de Basil to create the Ballets Russes de Monte Carlo, he formed his own Les Ballets in 1933. In 1934, he was invited to open a school in New York (The School of American Ballet) and created **Serenade** as his first American ballet. He helped introduce ballet to musical comedy when he staged the dances in *Wake Up and Dream* in London and came to America to change the dance vocabulary of the American musical stage. Started American Ballet with Lincoln Kirstein in 1935, which became the ballet "wing" of the Metropolitan Opera, where he choreographed from 1935–38. Temporarily abandoning the ballet world to work on the Broadway stage and in Hollywood, he created original choreography in films until 1942 for Vera Zorina (who became his third wife), although in later years, some of his ballet work was filmed for commercial release. Returning to New York in 1946, he and Kirstein founded Ballet Society which became the New York City Ballet in 1948. In the book, *That's Dancing*, he spoke about his work on film: "The responsibility of anyone working in films is greater than in the theater because he is addressing people all over the world…. Creating dance for movies imposes completely new problems on the choreographer. It renders his task far more intricate and difficult, gives him new riddles to solve, and opens a wide range of possibilities for the exercise of his invention." Often named as the most brilliant choreographer of the twentieth century, he is praised for his pure ballet creations, using his dancers as tools and never allowing the dance to be overshadowed by costumes, scenics or music. Won the *Dance Magazine* Award in 1950 for his ballet **The Firebird** and again in 1959 and the 1978 Kennedy Center Honors. He appears on film as the choreographer in **I Was an Adventuress** (1940).

    Autobiography: *How I Became a Dancer and a Choreographer* (1954)

    Biography: *George Balanchine, Balletmaster* by Richard Buckle and John Taras, (1988)

Related Works: *Balletmaster — A Dancer's View of George Balanchine* by Moira Shearer, (1987)

Stage: *Wake Up and Dream* (London '29), *Cochran's 1930 Revue* (London, with Serge Lifar), *Ziegfeld Follies of 1936* (with Robert Alton) and *On Your Toes* (Bdwy '36), *Babes in Arms* (Bdwy '37, with Fayard Nicholas), *The Boys from Syracuse, Great Lady* and *I Married an Angel* (Bdwy '38), *Cabin in the Sky* (also dir), *Keep Off the Grass* and *Louisiana Purchase* (Bdwy '40 with Carl Randall), *The Lady Comes Across* and *Rosalinda* (Bdwy '42), *The Merry Widow* and *What's Up?* (Bdwy '43, also dir), *Dream with Music* and *The Song of Norway* (Bdwy '44), *Mr. Strauss Goes to Boston* (OOT '45), *The Chocolate Soldier* (Bdwy '47), *Where's Charley?* (Bdwy '48), *Courtin' Time* (Bdwy '51), ***The Rake's Progress*** (NY Met, '53), *On Your Toes* (Bdwy '54 rev) and *House of Flowers* (Bdwy '54, replaced by Herbert Ross), *A Midsummer Night's Dream* and *The Winter's Tale* (Shakespeare Fest, Stratford, Conn. '58), *Romeo and Juliet* and *The Merry Wives of Windsor* (Shakespeare Fest, Stratford, Conn. '59), *On Your Toes* (Bdwy '82 rev, with Donald Saddler)

TV: "One, Yuletide Square" ('52), "Noah and the Flood" ('62), "NYC Ballet: Coppelia: Live from Lincoln Center" ('77, Emmy nom)

Ballet/Dance Pieces (Nearly 200 works — Partial listing): "La Nuit" ('20), "Apollo," "Prodigal Son," "Balustrade," "Serenade," "La Baiser de la Fee," "Elegy," "La Sonnambula," "Orpheus," "Firebird," "Jones Beach" (with Jerome Robbins), "Scotch Symphony," "Agon," "Allegro Brillante," "Stars and Stripes," "Liebeslieder Waltzes," "La Valse," "Bugaku," "A Midsummer Night's Dream," "Ballet Imperial," "Western Symphony," "Don Quixote," "Harlequinade," "Jewels," "Ragtime," "Dances at a Gathering," "Who Cares?," "Donizetti Variations," "Variations for Orchestra" ('82)

Miscellaneous: Ringling Brothers and Barnum and Bailey Circus ("Circus Polka" '42)

Film:

1930 **Dark Red Roses** — New Era Films (also appeared)

1938 **The Goldwyn Follies** — Samuel Goldwyn (with Sammy Lee)

1939 **On Your Toes** — WB

1940 **Fantasia** — Disney (with Marge Champion)
I Was an Adventuress — Fox (also appeared)

1941 **Louisiana Purchase** — Par (with Jack Donohue)

1942 **Star Spangled Rhythm** — Par (with Danny Dare, Katherine Dunham, choreographed Zorina's dance to "That Old Black Magic")

1967 **A Midsummer Night's Dream** — Showcorporation (also conceived the production)

1977 **The Turning Point** — Fox (with Alvin Ailey, Frederick Ashton, Jean Coralli, John Cranko, Michel Fokine, Lev Ivanov, Harald Lander, Kenneth MacMillan, Alexander Minz, Dennis Nahat, Jules Perrot, Marius Petipa)

1993 **George Balanchine's The Nutcracker** — WB

MARGARITA BALLI

1986 **Tangos: The Exile of Bardel** — (Fr/Argentine) (with Adolfo Andrade, Susana Tambutti, Robert Thomas)

BOB (ROBERT) BANAS

b. New York, September 22, 1933

A highly in-demand performer whose talent and bright-eyed, youthful looks kept him featured in television, stage and film work before he made the transition to choreography. He began his career at 13, dancing with Ballet Intime and Tamara Lepko's Ballet Company and made his professional debut in the 1952 LACLO production of *Carousel* as "Enoch Snow, Jr." He appeared on Broadway in *Peter Pan* ('54) and continued musical theater work in such shows as the LACLO productions of *Brigadoon* ('54), *Kiss Me Kate* ('55) and *Annie Get Your Gun* ('57) and a 1956 production of *Can Can* at the Civic Playhouse in Los Angeles, directed by Busby Berkeley. Studying a wide variety of dance styles from Jack Cole, Lester Horton, Matt Mattox, Bronislava Nijinska and Michel Panaieff, he also took acting classes at the Player's Ring in Hollywood. He was featured in over twenty films, including **Babes in Toyland, The Best Things in Life Are Free, Bye Bye Birdie, Daddy O, Don't Knock the Twist, Girl Happy, Hound Dog Man, The King and I, Kissin' Cousins, Let's Make Love, L'il Abner, Made in Paris, The Pajama Game, The Unsinkable Molly Brown** and **West Side Story**. During the 1960s he started his choreographic work on "The Judy Garland Show" and alternated between performing ("Polka Parade," "Shindig," the Frank Sinatra, Carol Burnett, Milton Berle, Danny Kaye and Red Skelton shows) and choreographing on television, returning briefly to Broadway in *The Happy Time* in 1968. He taught at many Hollywood schools, including Steven Peck's. Citing Gene Kelly and Fred Astaire as influences in his life, he also names dancemasters Michel Panaieff and Jack Cole as mentors. His direction credits include the TV show "Something Else" in 1970 and live benefit shows in Los Angeles.

Stage: *On a Clear Day, You Can See Forever* (Greek Theatre, LA '68), *We're in the Money* (LA '87), *Crazy Words, Crazy Tune* (LA '92)

TV (Partial listing): "Dr. Kildare" ('61), "Shivaree" ('65), "Kraft Summer Music Hall" ('66), "Swinging Country" ('66, also assoc prod.), "The

Jonathan Winters Show" (The Bob Banas Dancers '67–68), "Malibu U" (The Bob Banas Dancers '67), "The Action Faction" ('69), "Something Else" ('70, also dir), "Quincy," "The Bad News Bears," "Barnaby Jones," "Mork and Mindy," "Mission: Impossible," "I'll Get By"; specials for Tennessee Ernie Ford, Tony Martin, Frank Sinatra, Lindsay Wagner and Jonathan Winters

Ballet/Dance Pieces: "LA Dance Currents" ('74), "Bolero" (LA Ballet Society ('75)

Nightclub/Concert: *Ziegfeld Follies* ('64, Thunderbird Hotel, LV, with Dick Humphreys), the Cork Club (Houston); acts for Gladys Knight and the Pips, Gordon McRae and Tommy Sands

Miscellaneous: Industrials for Chrysler Motors, etc.

Film:

1963 **The Skydivers**— Crown Intl
1976 **Eleanor and Franklin**— ABC (TV)
1979 **Skatetown U.S.A.**— Col
1980 **The Day the Bubble Burst**— Fox (TV)
1983 **Heart Like a Wheel**— Fox
1985 **Tuff Turf**— New World
1986 **Down and Out in Beverly Hills**— Touchstone
1989 **Always**— Univ (with Gillian Gregory)
Teen Witch— Trans World Ent (with Russell Clark)
Summer Job— SVS Films
Under the Boardwalk— New World

MARGARET "MAGGIE" BANKS

b. Vancouver, B.C., Canada, 1924

This dancer-choreographer with Scottish parents started her dance career studying ballet as a child with June Roper in Vancouver. At the age of 12, she went to London and received a full scholarship to study with Ninette DeValois and the Sadler's Wells School of Ballet. At 14, she joined the corps of American Ballet Theatre and rose to soloist and then, principal, dancing with the company for six years. She guested with Ballets Russes and the Markova-Dolin company and then toured in *Annie Get Your Gun* and appeared on television in "Your Show of Shows" ('51) which exposed her to jazz and commercial dance. After marrying dancer Tommy Wonder, they toured with a dance act (Tommy and Maggi) on the Merriel Abbott circuit of supper clubs for five years (1951–56). When the act — and the marriage — dissolved, she moved to Hollywood, where she taught. Her extensive film and television career began as assistant to Jack Cole, Gene Kelly, Charles O'Curran, Hermes Pan, David Winters and extensively with Nick Castle (who said: "Maggie is the only ballerina I've ever seen who can lay out the

beats…she's got a great sense of rhythm.") She finally received on-screen credit for assisting ABT co-worker and friend Jerome Robbins on **West Side Story** (1961). A longtime association and friendship with Ann-Margret began when they worked together on **State Fair** (1962). Maggie choreographed the show-stealing "Bachelor in Paradise" number on the 1962 Academy Awards TV show and continued as Ann-Margret's personal dance coach-choreographer for most of her film, television and live work for the next decade. Another film sensation who depended on Maggie's expertise and friendship was Marilyn Monroe, with Maggie being signed to stage a "Dream Sequence" for the never-completed **Something's Got to Give** in '62. Relocating to Reno in 1973, she opened a ballet school and in 1984, founded the Nevada Festival Ballet, of which Ms. Banks is also artistic director. In 1986, she was awarded the Governor's Award for Dance by the Nevada State Council on the Arts and is listed in the Nevada Women's Hall of Fame.

Stage: *Silk Stockings* (Circle Arts Theatre, San Diego '61, asst to Roland Dupree)

TV: "Dancing Is a Man's Game" ('59, assistant to Gene Kelly), as assistant to Nick Castle: "The Andy Williams Show" ('63–66), "The Judy Garland Show" ('63), Tennessee Ernie Ford Specials, "The Hollywood Palace," Golden Globes Award Show; solo choreographed the 35th Academy Awards Show ('62), the Dinah Shore Show

Nightclub/Concert: Ann-Margret's act (assistant to David Winters, '67)

Ballet/Dance Pieces: For Nevada Festival Ballet: "Swan Lake," "Gaite Parisienne," "Giselle," "Coppelia," "Swan Lake," "Les Sylphides," "Carmen," "Firebird," "Aurora's Wedding," "Classically Swingin'" ('94)

Miscellaneous: SHARE "Boomtown" shows, multiple industrials

Film:

1956 **Anything Goes**— Par (assistant to Nick Castle)
1960 **Can-Can**— Fox (assistant to Hermes Pan, with Gino Malerba)
Let's Make Love— Fox (assistant to Jack Cole)
1961 **The Children's Hour**— UA
West Side Story— UA (with Tommy Abbott, Howard Jeffrey, Tony Mordente, Jerome Robbins)
1962 **Girls! Girls! Girls!**— Par (asst to Charles O'Curran)
Mr. Hobbs Takes a Vacation— Fox
State Fair— Fox (assistant to Nick Castle)
Two for the Seesaw— UA
1963 **Come Blow Your Horn**— Par (with Jack Baker, Nick Castle)
Dime with a Halo— MGM

1964 **Kitten with a Whip**— Univ (assistant to David Winters)

The Pleasure Seekers— Fox (assistant to Robert Sidney)

Sunday in New York— MGM

Viva Las Vegas— MGM (assistant to David Winters)

1965 **Bus Riley's Back in Town**— Univ (assistant to David Winters, with Toni Basil)

1966 —**Made in Paris**— MGM (assistant to David Winters)

Stagecoach— Fox

The Swinger— MGM (assistant to David Winters)

BORIS BARANOVSKY

1994 **Police Academy: Mission to Moscow**— WB

BARBETTE (VANDER CLYDE)

b. Round Rock, Texas, December 19, 1904
d. Austin, Texas, August 5, 1973
Legendary cross-dressing aerialist who later became an Aerial Ballet creator and director of circus sequences in film. As a kid in Texas he learned to wire walk on his mother's clotheslines. When a local circus advertised their need for a replacement for a high-wire act, 14-year-old Vander auditioned. Since it was an all-female act (The Alfaretta Sisters — World Famous Aerial Queens), he was required to perform in drag. After appearing with Erford's Whirling Sensation, he took the stage name "Barbette" and debuted his single act in New York's Harlem Opera House in 1919. In 1923 he went to Paris to appear at the Casino de Paris, where silent film star Sessue Hayakawa was headlining. Barbette became a star in European Revues (Paris Alhambra, Casino de Paris, Folies Bergere and the London Palladium) during the 1920s and '30s — with his talent and beauty celebrated in the writing of Jean Cocteau ("Ten unforgettable minutes. A theatrical masterpiece. An angel, a flower, a bird"), Anton Dolin and other leaders of the European art community of the time. Broadway appearances include headlining at the Palace in 1927 and in *Billy Rose's Jumbo* ('35) at the Hippodrome Theatre. He also appeared in Cocteau's experimental film **The Blood of a Poet** ('30). After a tragic fall in the late thirties, in which he broke his back and legs, Barbette then coached aerial acts, creating routines for films and live performances and also produced a troupe of girls (The Barbettes) who performed "Web" and "Iron Jaw" routines in circuses internationally. In 1942, John Murray Anderson hired Barbette to collaborate with him when he staged Ringling Bros.

and Barnum and Bailey Circus and, in 1959, film director Billy Wilder contacted Barbette to coach Jack Lemmon and Tony Curtis with their female impersonations for the classic comedy **Some Like It Hot**. Purportedly despondent over being relegated to retirement in Austin, Texas (and living with his sister), Barbette ended his colorful life with sleeping pills at the age of 69. In 1993, performance artist John Kelly created a stage work based on Barbette (*Light Shall Lift Them*) at the Brooklyn Academy of Music's Next Wave Festival.

Miscellaneous: Ringling Bros. and Barnum and Bailey Circus ('42–51), *Disney on Parade* ('69–70)

Film:

1952 **The Greatest Show on Earth**— Par (with John Murray Anderson, Richard Barstow — aerial ballets, uncredited)

1959 **The Big Circus**— AA (with Patricia Denise)

1963 **Billy Rose's Jumbo**— MGM (with Busby Berkeley, The Barbettes appear)

LYNETTE BARKLEY

Stage: *The Gifts of the Magi* (OB '85)
Film:
1986 **Playin' for Keeps**— Univ (with Ronn Forella)
1987 **Orphans**— Lorimar

ROSEMARY BARNES

1989 **The Perfect Model**—Chicago Cinema

CHARLES BARON

1947 —**The Fabulous Dorseys**— UA

GEORGE BARON

1958 **Hello London**— Regal Intl (with Ted Shuffie)

B.H. BARRY

1989 **Lost Angels**— Orion

R.G. BARSI

Teacher at Paris' Ecole De Danse.
Film:
1973 **Last Tango in Paris**— UA

RICHARD BARSTOW

b. Ashtabula, Ohio, April 1, 1905
d. New York, May 2, 1981
Richard Barstow has the distinction of being one of the few (or, perhaps, only) choreographers to be written about in *Ripley's Believe It or Not*. Born with a congenitally deformed foot, he began physical

therapy at the age of 5 and eventually took dance lessons at a dancing school across the street from the family home in Astabula. At the age of 7 his talent encouraged his mother and four of his siblings to create a vaudeville act: The Five Barstows. As "Dickie Barstow — The Iron-Toed Boy," he was mentioned in Ripley's collection of odd feats as being able to stand supported by one toe wedged into the neck of a Coca-Cola bottle and jump from a height of eight feet, landing on his toes! When the family act disbanded, he performed as a toe-tap dancer at nightclubs and theaters with his sister, Edith, and they also appeared in the Vitaphone short **The Gem of the Ocean** (1934). In 1938 he secured a new partner, Bonnie Bradley. He began his choreographic career assisting Merriel Abbott. Initially choreographing for the Merriel Abbott Dancers, he went on to choreograph several stage shows, TV and films, but made his greatest creative contributions to the Ringling Bros. and Barnum and Bailey Circus, which he staged and directed from 1949 to '78 (with Edith choreographing until her death on January 6, 1960). It all began when John Ringling North saw one of Barstow's shows at Billy Rose's Diamond Horseshoe and phoned him, asking if we would like to choreograph for the Circus. "But I've never seen a circus," Barstow replied."You've got a dog, haven't you?" asked Mr. North — and the 29 year association began. A memorial tribute was held for this colorful creator at the Palace Theatre in New York on May 26, 1981.

Stage: Barefoot Boy with Cheek (Bdwy '47), *Sally* (Bdwy '48 rev), *New Faces of 1952* (Bdwy, which he recreated on film in '54), *This Was Burlesque* (OB '69), *Annie Get Your Gun* (Jones Beach '78, also dir)

TV: "The Ed Wynn Show" ('49), "The Ford Star Revue" ('50–51), "Garroway at Large," "Eddie Cantor Comedy Theatre" ('54–55), "The Jimmy Durante Show" ('54–57), "The Milton Berle Show"

Nightclub/Concert: Production shows for the Diamond Horseshoe and Latin Quarter nightclubs (NY), *Stop and Go-Go* (Hilton, Chicago, '65); acts for Milton Berle, Janet Blair & the Blackburn Twins, Eddie Cantor, Judy Garland, Brenda Lee, Jane Morgan and Ed Wynn

Miscellaneous: Champagne on Ice (Belita's Ice Revue, London '53), Ringling Bros. and Barnum and Bailey Circus ('49–77, dir and staged with Edith); industrials for General Motors (*Motorama—* New York Auto Show '53), *Symphony of Fashion* (St. Louis), etc.

Film:
1934 **The Gem of the Ocean** — Vitaphone (S) (appeared with Edith)
1940 **Buck Benny Rides Again** — Par (with Merriel Abbott, uncredited)

1941 **Hellzapoppin'** — Univ (with Nick Castle and Eddie Prinz, uncredited)
1952 **The Greatest Show on Earth** — Par (with John Murray Anderson and Barbette, uncredited)
1953 **The Girl Next Door** — Fox (with Michael Kidd, uncredited)
1954 **A Star Is Born** — WB (with Jack Donohue, assisted by Jack Harmon)
New Faces — Fox

EARL BARTON (ERWIN JAY BARER)

b. Pittsburgh, Pennsylvania, July 6, 1929

"Since I started out as a dancer, I always did the choreography for my own dances," explained this performer and choreographer who helped the film musical make its transition to rock 'n' roll during the 1950s and '60s. He began dance classes at Gene Kelly's school in Squirrel Hill, Pennsylvania, and when Earl was 14, his family moved to California. There he studied ballet with Eugene Loring, Madame Nijinska and Michel Panaieff; modern with Lester Horton and tap with Johnny Mattison. At 16, he made his professional debut in a series of five musicals at Los Angeles' Greek Theatre ('45). Upon graduation from high school, he immediately went to New York and danced in all of the major TV shows there, building a successful career (featured in the "Saturday Night Revue," *Dance Magazine,* Oct. 1953, wrote:"Barton is a top dancer worth watching"). He created a solo club act and was booked into such well-known nighteries as the Palmer House in Chicago, the Thunderbird Hotel, Las Vegas, and the Prince George Hotel in Toronto, also touring Europe. On film, he was featured as one of the "Suitors" in **Seven Brides for Seven Brothers**. His choreographic skills began to receive notice when Dinah Shore was so impressed with a number he had done for himself at NBC that she hired him to create the dances on one of her shows — he remained for three seasons. His staging and choreography continued in all entertainment mediums, with his strong jazz style successfully integrating the new Rock movement. Accepted into the DGA in 1966, he wrote, produced and directed documentaries about Maharishi Mahesh Yogi and **Those Hollywood Stuntmen** and a feature for Crown Intl. (**Trip with the Teacher**). In the mid '70s, he created thirty-minute musical films ("The Music Store") featuring Jefferson Airplane, Vic Damone and José Feliciano which were pioneering forms of music videos. With his 1990 bride, Jeannie, he became a proud father of a daughter in 1991 and was expecting a second child due in December 1994.

Stage: Can Can (LA '56, also the Hacienda Hotel, LV)

TV: "Broadway Open House" ('50–51, also appeared), "Your Hit Parade," "The Dinah Shore Chevy Show," "Manhattan Tower" and "Inside Beverly Hills" ('56), "The Frank Sinatra Show" ('57), "The Frances Langford Show" (The Earl Barton Dancers, '57–59), "The Milton Berle Show" ('59), "The Dean Martin Show," "The Kate Smith Show" ('60), "The Steve Allen Show" ('61), "The Lively Ones" ('62–63), "The Edie Adams Show" (also prod); specials for Lorne Green and Danny Thomas

Music Video: Multiple Scopitones (The Christy Minstrels, "When the Boys Meet the Girls," etc. '65)

Nightclub/Concert: Las Vegas: Tropicana Hotel (a series of original musical comedies opening the hotel on April 3, 1957 and continuing until '60), *Summertime Frolics* (Dunes Hotel, '61), the Earl Barton Dancers at the Riviera Hotel ('62), Bonanza Hotel ("Opening" show starring Lorne Green); acts for Edie Adams, Eve Arden, Augie & Margo, Jack Costanzo, the Crosby Brothers, Elaine Dunn, the Earl Twins, Frankie Laine, Debra Paget, the Wilda Taylor Trio, Shani Wallis, Nancy Wilson and Patrice Wymore

Film:
1956 **Cha-Cha-Cha-Boom!**— Col
      Don't Knock the Rock— Col
      Rock Around the Clock— Col (also appeared)
1959 **The Five Pennies**— Par (assisted by Lizanne Truex)
1961 **Twist Around the Clock**— Col
1964 **Roustabout**— Par
1965 **Harum Scarum**— MGM
      When the Boys Meet the Girls— MGM (assisted by Wilda Taylor)
1966 **Frankie and Johnny**— MGM (assisted by Wilda Taylor)
1967 **Doctor, You've Got to Be Kidding**— MGM
1981 **Jacqueline Susann's Valley of the Dolls**— CBS/Fox (TV)

GILLIAN BARTON
1995 **Rob Roy**— UA

TONY BARTUCCIO
1988 **Ground Zero**— Ave Entertainment

MIKHAIL (NIKOLAIEVICH) BARYSHNIKOV
b. Riga, Latvia, January 27, 1948

"That is why I *came* here to the States — to expand my vision," said this classical dancer, actor and choreographer who created international headlines when he defected from Russia in 1974. His work in America earned him the highest praise from critics and ballet fans alike, while his masculine appeal allowed him to become Ballet's biggest male movie star. He began his training at the Latvian Opera Ballet School at 12 and at 15 he was admitted to the Vaganova School in Leningrad. At 19 he became a soloist with the Kirov Ballet — skipping the rank of corps completely. While appearing as a guest artist with the Bolshoi Ballet in Toronto in June, 1974, he defected and joined ABT, where he also began choreographing. Other guest appearances included the Australian Ballet, Hamburg Opera, Paris Opera and Eliot Feld companies. With a passionate objective to diversify his career, he became a media celebrity, starring on TV in "Baryshnikov at the White House" (Emmy Award, '75), a featured role in the film **The Turning Point** (in which he was nominated for an Oscar for "Best Supporting Actor," '77), more TV exposure in "Baryshnikov on Broadway," "Baryshnikov in Hollywood" ('82) and "Dance in America: Baryshnikov Dances Balanchine" (Emmy Award, '89) and two additional films — in which he starred and choreographed. He joined the NYC Ballet in 1978 and became artistic director of ABT in 1980, producing and staging classic works for the company. In 1990 he co-created the White Oak Project with Mark Morris, serving as artistic director and performing with the group, and toured extensively in 1993 with Twyla Tharp. He received the *Dance Magazine* Award in 1978 and the New York City Liberty Award in 1986 and is the first choreographer to have a perfume named after him.

Biography: Bravo Baryshnikov by Alan LeMond (1978)

TV: "Baryshnikov in Hollywood" ('82, with Peter Anastos, Emmy nom)

Ballet/Dance Pieces (Partial listing): "Don Quixote," "The Nutcracker," "Giselle," etc.

Film:
1985 **White Nights**— Col (with Gregory Hines, Roland Petit, Twyla Tharp, also appeared)
1987 **Dancers**— Cannon (also appeared, "After Coralli, Perrot and Petipa" credit)

TONI BASIL (ANTONIA CHRISTINA BASILOTTA)
b. Philadelphia, Pennsylvania

When Bette Midler was asked about this lady who pioneered the research and refinement of street dance — incorporating it into her routines and changing the face of contemporary theatrical dance — she replied, "What do you say about a woman who is practically *the* most influential choreographer of

Two dance greats of the century, Mikhail Baryshnikov and Gregory Hines created the choreography — and excitement — for **White Nights** (Columbia, 1985), in which their "Challenge" (Ballet vs. Tap) added great dimension to plot and character, as well as giving the film sheer entertainment value.

popular music?" Toni's father Louis Basil's career as a successful orchestra conductor moved the family all over the United States. At 5 she began ballet class in New York with Madame Swoboda and by 11 she started tap lessons in Chicago with Edna MacRae. When her father's career settled the family in Las Vegas, she started jazz lessons with Christina Carson Devore and Joyce Roberts, making her professional debut at the Sahara Hotel (where her father was conducting) with the Joyce Roberts Dancers and also being a cheerleader at Las Vegas High School. After moving to Los Angeles to attend Dental Technician's school, she danced in films (**Bye Bye Birdie**, **Viva Las Vegas**— also "dance-in" for Ann-Margret), and began her professional choreography career at 17 assisting David Winters on the TV shows "Shindig" and "The T.A.M.I. Show."

When Winters went to New York to do the series "Hullabaloo," Basil was offered a TV job to solo choreograph. Recalling that her interest in film began with an introduction from Rolling Stones' member Brian Jones, she credits the Living Theater and Les Ballets Africain as being the two greatest influences in her work. She directed rock stars in concert, discovered and danced with The Lockers ('70) and became a recording artist herself with a Gold Record for her album "Word of Mouth" and Double Platinum Award for the single "Mickey" ('82). Leading the way for Paula Abdul and others, she was the first recording artist to direct and choreograph her own music videos, two of which ("Mickey" and "Word of Mouth") reside in the permanent collection of New York City's Museum of Modern Art (MOMA). Also a dramatic film actress: **Five Easy Pieces**, **The Last**

Picture Show, **Easy Rider**, **Slaughterhouse Rock**, **Rockula**, **Mother, Jugs and Speed**, **Greaser's Palace**, etc. Nominated for MTV and Grammy Awards, her ongoing fascination with — and study of— street dance continues, with her 1993 stage piece *Shockin' the House: Two Decades of L.A. Street Dance* receiving praise from the *Los Angeles Times* (Sept. 10, 1993): "Basil allowed glimpses of unexplored riches: dancers who momentarily devastated you with their beauty,talent or style." In 1995 *LA Dance* presented her with a special "Alternative Dance" award.

Stage: *Toni Basil at the Roxy* ('76), *Follies Bizarre* with Devo ('78), *Toni Basil at the Fox Venice*, *Shockin' the House* ('93)

TV: "Romeo and Juliet '70," "Cotton Club '75" special, "Sesame Street," "The New Smothers Brothers Comedy Hour," "Saturday Night Live," "Dick Clark's The Rock and Roll Years," "F-TV" ('85), VH1 Awards ('95); commercials for Diet Coke (featuring Manhattan Transfer), Right Guard, Schlitz Malt Liquor, 7-Up, Suntory Beer, etc.

Music Video: (Partial listing): "Word of Mouth," "Mickey," "Shopping from A to Z," "Over My Head"— Toni Basil; "When Problems Arise"— Fishbone; "You Took Advantage of Me," "Get Closer"— Linda Ronstadt; "Once in a Lifetime," "Cross-Eyed and Painless"— Talking Heads; "Time Will Tell"— David Bowie; "Day and Night," "In My Life"— Bette Midler; "Energy"— Melissa Manchester; "When Women Are Lonely"— Peter Wolf; "Sorry"— Arsenio Hall; "North on South Street"— Herb Alpert; "Girls on My Mind"— David Byrne; "Nut Bush," "Wild Thing"— Tina Turner; "We Want the Funk"— Gerardo; "Ed Wood" video

Nightclub/Concert: *Doo Dah Daze* (Flamingo Hotel, LV, '75, with Bob Thompson), *At the Kitchen* (Sahara Hotel, LV, '77), Bette Midler ("Detour," "Tour for the First Depression," "Divine Madness" and "Experience the Divine" tours), David Bowie ("Diamond Dogs" and "Glass Spider" tours), Jesse Johnson, Pee Wee Herman, Melissa Manchester ("Energy" tour), The Pointer Sisters ("Fire" tour), Van Halen, Tina Turner ("Private Dancer" Tour), Gerardo ('91 tour), Julia Migenes ('95 tour)

Film:
1964 **The T.A.M.I. Show**— AIP (assistant to David Winters
1965 **Village of the Giants**— Embassy (also appeared)
1967 **The Cool Ones**— WB
1968 **Head**— Col (also appeared)
1973 **American Graffiti**— Univ
1979 **The Rose**— Fox (assisted by Kenny Ortega)
1980 **Divine Madness** WB
1986 **Peggy Sue Got Married**— TriStar (with Chrissy Boccino)
1990 **Rockula**— Cannon (with Russell Clark, also appeared)

1991 **Delirious**— MGM/Pathe (assisted by Miranda Garrison)
Mobsters— Univ (assisted by Miranda Garrison)
1995 **Something to Talk About**— WB
1996 **The Kings of Caroline**—?
That Thing You Do!— Fox

JEANETTE BATES
1944 **Between Two Women**— MGM
The Thin Man Goes Home— MGM
1948 **Another Part of the Forest**— Univ
1953 **Remains to Be Seen**— MGM
1954 **Rose Marie**— MGM (with Busby Berkeley)

JIMMY (JAMES) BATES
b. Los Angeles, California, February 22, 1938
Dancer, actor and choreographer who literally grew up in the entertainment media," making his movie debut at the age of three in a **Henry Aldrich** film. He made early film appearances dancing with Gene Kelly in **Living in a Big Way** ('47) and as the child who watches Fred Astaire in the "Drum Crazy" number in **Easter Parade** ('48). Over the years he studied dance at the Meglin Studio, with Nick Castle and at Eugene Loring's American School of Dance. A member of the Loring Dance Players in 1956 and appearing onstage in *RSVP* in Hollywood in 1960, his acting film credits include **The Wistful Widow of Wagon Gap, Andy Hardy Comes Home** and **Run Silent, Run Deep**. He found himself in demand dancing in films (**Bye Bye Birdie, Kissin' Cousins, Unsinkable Molly Brown, What a Way to Go!**, etc.) and on many major TV shows of the '60s ("The Lucy Show," Tennessee Ernie Ford specials, "Polka Parade," etc.) before beginning his choreographic career. When asked about the transition, he replied, "I always wanted to direct and before I knew it, I was staging." During the 1970s, he staged and directed The Young Americans and other popular, youthful song and dance groups. He eventually moved into producing-directing and in 1995, created *Chem TV*, a touring rock and roll concert show for young people. Married to dancer-choreographer Judy Newhouse since 1959 when they met on a USO tour, they are the proud parents of Robert and Erin.

Stage: Ntl companies of *West Side Story, Grease, Oklahoma!, Guys and Dolls, The Music Man* (also dir for all entries)

TV: The Young Americans ('70), "The Mac Davis Show" ('76), "The Lucy Show," "The New Mickey Mouse Club," "The Flip Wilson Show," "The American Teacher Awards," "AFI Salute to Steven Spielberg," "The American Presidential Inaugural Gala," etc.

Nightclub/Concert: Shindig (Tour '65); acts for Thelma Houston, Ronnie Milsap, Anne Murray, Dolly Parton, Joan Rivers, etc.

Miscellaneous: Industrials for Mattel, IBM, Hallmark, the Marriot Corporation, Allstate Insurance, Pepsi Cola, etc.

Film:

1975 **Smile**— UA (assisted by Judy Bates)

EDDIE BATOS

1987 **Dutch Treat**— Cannon

1988 **Tapeheads**— Ave Pictures (with Cholly Atkins)

SAMMY (DALLAS) BAYES

b. 1940

Dancer-choreographer and director who studied at Stephens College in Columbia, Mo. and eventually became Choreographer-in-Residence there. Among his performance credits are the Broadway and film versions of **Fiddler on the Roof**.

Stage: Canterbury Tales (London '68 & Bdwy '69, Tony nom), *Heathen!* (Bdwy '72), *Shelter* (Bdwy '73), *Rainbow Jones* (Bdwy '74), *Fiddler on the Roof* (Bdwy '90 rev and Imperial Theater, Tokyo, recreating Jerome Robbins' original work), *West Side Story* (Takarazuka, Japan)

Film:

1971 **Fiddler on the Roof**— UA (with Tommy Abbott, adapting Jerome Robbin's original work, also appeared)

1973 **Godspell**— Col

JOAN BAYLEY

1959 **Journey to the Center of the Earth**— Fox

RALPH BEAUMONT

Choreographer and teacher who attended college in San Francisco and received his theater training at New York's American Theatre Wing. After appearing on Broadway in scores of shows (among them *Guys and Dolls*, '50 and *Can Can*, '53), in films and on TV, he joined the creative team, eventually becoming a director-choreographer of multiple stage projects.

Stage: Saratoga (Bdwy '65), *The Yearling* (Bdwy '65), *The Royal Flush* (OOT '67, restaging Jack Cole's work), *The Most Happy Fella* and *Gentlemen Prefer Blondes* (London '70, also dir), *Enrico* (Italy '70), *A Funny Thing Happened on the Way to the Forum* ('71 Bdwy rev), etc.

Film:

1970 **Myra Breckenridge**— Fox (assisted by Larri Thomas)

MAURICE BÉJART (BERGER)

b. Marseilles, France, January 1, 1927

With *Dance Magazine* (July, 1961) calling his work "a mixture of ballet, pantomime, motion pictures, revue, musichall, circus, Kabuki and Peking Opera," Béjart's bold, daring and sensual works make him one of the 20th Century's most influential dance/theater figures. He began his study of dance at the Marseilles Opera Ballet School while receiving a Bachelor of Letters degree from the University of Marseilles. Moving to Paris in 1945, he studied with Leo Staats and danced with the Paris Opera Ballet. He then joined Roland Petit (1947–'49), Britain's International Ballet (1949–50) and the Royal Swedish Ballet (1951–52). In 1953, he organized Ballets Romantique, which became Les Ballet de L'Etoile in '54 (and eventually Ballet Theatre de Maurice Béjart in '57) and made his debut as a choreographer. His works were called "shocking" and "erotic" and they were captured on film in **Belles et Ballets**— in which he also danced with the group. In 1959 he was appointed director of Theatre Royal de la Monnaire in Brussels and changed the name of the company to Ballet of the 20th Century in 1960. His work in Belgium included creating multiple "teleballets" which successfully explored the collaboration of dance and the camera. He then founded Ballet Lausanne, which continues to stimulate the dance world into the 1990s. Béjart has choreographed over eighty ballets and written three novels. Winner of multiple international awards, including the *Dance Magazine* Award in 1974, the Japan's Art Association Praemium Imperiale Award in 1993 and the Deutscher Tanzpries in 1994.

Autobiography: Un Instant dans la Vie D'Autrui (1979)

Stage: (For the Paris Opera): **The Seven Deadly Sins, The Tales of Hoffman, Tannhauser, The Damnation of Faust**

TV: "Orpheus" for French TV ('59, also appeared), multiple "teleballets" for Radiodiffusion Television Belge (Belgium, early '60s)

Ballet/Dance Pieces (Partial listing): "Petit Page" ('46), "Baudelaire," "Bolero," "Don Giovanni," "Kabuki," "Le Sacre Du Printemps," "Loves of a Poet," "The Magic Flute," "Nijinsky, Clown of God," "Orpheus," "Pyramide," "Ring un Den Ring," "Isadora," "Mephisto Waltz," "Leda," "L'Impromptu," "Malraux," "5 Noh Plays of Yukio Mishima," "The Miraculous Mandarin," "Cinema, Cinema," "M" ('93)

Nightclub/Concert: Voila l'Homme, (Fontaine des Quartres Saisons, Paris '56)

Film:

1952 **The Firebird** (aka **Eldfageln**)—(Swed)

1960 **Belles et Ballet**— Hermes (Fr) (with Dirk Sanders, also appeared)

Ernest Belcher, one of film's first dance pioneers, in a studio portrait, circa 1925.

1983 **Les Uns et les Autres** (aka **Bolero**)— Double 13 (with Nicole Daresco, Rick Odums, Micha Van Joecke, Larry Vickers)

ERNEST BELCHER

b. London, England, June 8, 1882
d. Los Angeles, California, February 24, 1973

One of the true pioneers of dance on film and dance education in America. At 16, he started dance classes in London: ballet with Francesca Zanfretta and Alexandre Genée, also period and folk dancing, Spanish, Indian and Eastern Oriental dance. Other interests and studies included architecture, music, piano and water color drawing. He made his professional stage debut in *On the Heath* at the Alhambra Theatre in 1909 and toured the British Isles in *The Blue Bird* ('10). While performing an act with his first wife, Celia Celeste, in English Music Halls, he began his film work, creating dances for the Selsoir Motion Picture Company of London from 1911–12. After arriving in America with the Golden Dancers in 1914, he worked in New York and appeared on the Keith-Orpheum Circuit with his act and a new partner, Lisa Graham. When diagnosed with tuberculosis, he moved to California to cure himself in 1915. There, he met and married Gladys Basquette, mother of budding film star

Lina Basquette. Cecil B. DeMille, D.W. Griffith and Mack Sennett gave him his first opportunities to work in American films in 1917, performing multiple tasks: creating dance routines, staging period sequences and training and coaching stars John Barrymore, Marion Davies, May McAvoy, Colleen Moore, Pola Negri, Ramon Novarro, Mary Pickford and others. Opening his first dance school in Los Angeles in 1916 ("boasting two pupils who paid and three who did not"), he established many "firsts" in American — and eventually international — dance training: a systematic grading ("The Ernest Belcher Eight Grade System"), the intense goal of building up male dancers and, with his varied work in films, concert and prologues productions, he offered professional experience for his students. The schools (which often had 2,000 students) had a faculty teaching ballet, tap, acrobatics, physical culture, "moderne" dance, hula, ballroom and Spanish dance, and were continual sources for film casting and training of movie celebrities. Students over the years included Rod Alexander, Hal Belfer, daughter Marge Champion, future son-in-law Gower Champion, Cyd Charisse, Yvonne DeCarlo, Nanette Fabray, Paul Godkin, Betty Grable, Rita Hayworth, Carmelita Maracci, Matt Mattox, Rita Moreno, Maria Tallchief, Shirley Temple, Gwen Verdon and Loretta Young. By his own count, he worked on over 200 films in those very early days of Hollywood. Unfortunately, it is impossible to verify those credits, although in 1923, he was named "Ballet Master of Movieland" by WAMPAS (the Western Association of Motion Picture Advertisers). He aspired toward investigating the possibilities for ballet in films and the establishment of the first American ballet company and from 1922, his annual concerts at the Hollywood Bowl were groundbreaking events. Writing a series of monthly articles, ("The Technique of Dance") for *The American Dancer* from 1931 to 1933, by the mid–30s, Belcher's gentle, refined nature was at odds with the intense competition between the other dance directors, so he withdrew from film work and devoted all of his energies toward his schools and students. In 1944 Ann Barzel wrote: "Ernest Belcher has been the most prominent 20th century English teacher in America." Dance on Film owes him a great debt for his talent, experimentation and the ranks of future film dance creators he trained and inspired.

Biography: A section of *Dancing in the Sun* by Naima Prevots (U.M.I. Research Press, 1987)

Stage: Carmen, Aïda (Hollywood Bowl), 1936 Los Angeles Civic Light Opera productions of *Maytime, The Merry Widow, Naughty Marietta* and *The Desert Song*

Ballet/Dance Pieces (Partial listing): 17 ballets for the Hollywood Bowl including: "A Grande Valse De Conert," ('30), "Rosamunde," "Gavotte Royale,"

"Valse Viennese-Wiener Blut," "Le Cid" (all '31); "Eylsia (A Greek Divertisement — Tribute to the Los Angeles Olympics)" and "Samson and Delilah" ('32) and "Carnival of Venice" ('34)

Nightclub/Concert: The Embassy and Montmarte (Hollywood '31)

Miscellaneous: Prologues for Grauman's Million Dollar Theater

Film (Partial listing):

1918 **We Can't Have Everything**— Famous Players/Lasky

1919 **Broken Blossoms**— Griffith/UA
     Salome vs. Shenandoah— Mack Sennett

1920 **The Furnace**— Real Art
     The Idol Dancer— Griffith
     Jenny Be Good— Real Art

1921 **Doubling for Romeo**— Goldwyn-Cosmopolitan
     Mother o' Mine—Associated Producers
     Small Town Idol— Mack Sennett

1922 **The Blind Bargain**— Goldwyn
     Heroes of the Street— WB

1923 **Bella Donna**— Par
     The Christian— Goldwyn-Cosmopolitan
     Enemies of Women —Par
     Souls for Sale— Goldwyn
     The Spanish Dancer— Par
     Temple of Venus— Fox

1924 **Beau Brummel**— WB
     The Hunchback of Notre Dame— Univ.

1925 **Phantom of the Opera**— Univ

1926 **La Bohéme**— MGM
     The Dancer of Paris— First Ntl
     The Far Cry— WB
     Gigolo— Producers Distribution Corp
     Irene— First Ntl
     Padlocked— WB
     The Sea Beast— WB
     Silken Shackles— WB

1927 **The Blue Danube**— Par
     The Devil Dancer— Pathé
     Heart of Maryland— WB
     The Jazz Singer— WB
     Serenade— First Ntl
     Twinkletoes— First Ntl
     What Happened to Father— WB

1928 **Show Folks**— Pathé

1929 **General Crack**— WB
     The Godless Girl— MGM
     Hollywood Revue of 1929— MGM (with Sammy Lee, Natacha Natova, Albertina Rasch, Ernest Belcher's Dancing Tots appeared)
     Making the Grade— Fox

1930 **The Dancers**— Fox

1931 **Gems of MGM** (S)— MGM

1935 **Anna Karenina**— MGM (with Chester Hale, Marguerite Wallman)

1939 **The Little Princess**— Fox (with Nick Castle)

HAL (HAROLD BRUCE) BELFER

b. Los Angeles, California, February 16, circa 1920

Dancer, choreographer, writer, producer, director and teacher whose diverse career has kept him in demand for over five decades. Teased about being "Born in fifth position," he was urged by his mother to begin dance studies to overcome his shyness. He studied ballet with Ernest Belcher and Carmelita Maracci and tap with Willie Covan, Louis DaPron and Harriett and Al Durea. At the age of 7 he won an RKO "Fred Astaire Dance Contest" and made his professional debut as a child on a Bebe Daniels' radio show. He also appeared for Fanchon and Marco in their Christmas and Easter revues at the Los Angeles Paramount Theatre. As a teen he began adagio dancing with various partners at the Shooter and Ross Ballroom and won their "Fred Astaire Award." After performing a solo act in West Coast clubs, he served with the Medical Corps in Burma, China and India during World War II, creating shows to entertain the servicemen. When word of his expertise reached the attention of Major Melvyn Douglas, he was assigned to the Entertainment Production Unit for the Tea and Rice Circuit. After his tour of duty, he studied cinematography and editing at USC and was selected to be in Jack Cole's group of contract dancers at Columbia. His film choreographic career had begun when he assisted LeRoy Prinz at Warner Bros. before and after the War and when he created and choreographed *The Smart Set*, a hit revue at Ciro's in Hollywood ('48), its success started his solo choreographic career. In 1949 he was signed as head of the dance department at Universal, creating a talent development program and training such young contract players at the time as Tony Curtis, Rock Hudson, Piper Laurie and Lori Nelson ("I taught movement and lip synching class"). He then became head of 20th Century–Fox's dance dept. of the new talent division in 1961 and later, the MGM TV dance dept. After staging Lena Horne's nightclub act at the Sands Hotel in Las Vegas in 1955 he was so much in demand that he eventually relocated to Nevada for his producing, directing and editing work. In the mid–60s, he created dozens of Scopitone musical shorts, among them "Tijuana Taxi"— thought to be Scopitone's first all-choreographic work. In 1968 he became a production coordinator/choreographer for Krofft Enterprises and in 1970, he was named executive producer for Premore Productions and won a Film Advisory Board Award for Excellence for his production of the TV show "Imagine That." When interviewed for this book he admitted — with a smile — "Lou Wills, Jr. and I are the only two who could do a full twisting 'Butterfly.'"

Hal Belfer, far right, attends a production meetting about a 1949 U.S.O. tour he is staging with (L to R) Jackie Coogan, Donald O'Connor, Jack O'Connor and Patricia Medina to promote Universal's new film, **Francis**.

Stage: *The Great Waltz* (Bdwy '34, with Albertina Rasch and LACLO productions of the same show in '49 and '53), *Showgirls of 1962* (West Coast)

TV: Abbott & Costello, Ben Blue, Donald O'-Connor and Ritz Brothers editions of "The Colgate Comedy Hour" (early '50s), "Saturday Night Revue" ('54), "The Frankie Laine-Connie Haines Show" ('55, also appeared), the Bob Hope and Jack Benny Shows, "The Untouchables," "Mr. Novak," "The Perils of Pauline" (pilot '68), "H.R. Pufnstuf" ('69); commercials for Kellogg, Schlitz, Solo Cup

Music Video: Over 26 Scopitone musical numbers for Vikki Carr, Vic Damone, James Darren, Damita Joe, Barbara McNair, Lou Rawls, Debbie Reynolds, Bobby Rydell, Neil Sedaka, Frank Sinatra, Jr.

Nightclub/Concert: *The Smart Set* (Ciros, LA '48), *Belles of 1962,* (Mexico City and Lake Tahoe); created "Lines" for the Riviera ('55-56), Sands ('55), Thunderbird and Flamingo (The Flamingoettes, also served as Entertainment Director '56-60) Hotels (LV), *George Arnold Ice Revue* (LV '58); acts for Harry Belafonte, Yvonne DeCarlo, Judy Garland, June Havoc, Lena Horne, Brenda Lee, Peggy Lee, Dean Martin & Jerry Lewis, Tony Mar-

tin, the Mills Brothers, Dinah Shore, Adam "Batman" West, Patrice Wymore, etc.

Miscellaneous: *Contempo* (Dupont Industrial '64)

Film:

1942 **Yankee Doodle Dandy**— WB (assistant to LeRoy Prinz)

1947 **That's My Gal**— Rep (with the Four Step Brothers)

My Wild Irish Rose— WB (assistant to LeRoy Prinz)

1948 **One Sunday Afternoon**— WB (assistant to LeRoy Prinz)

1949 **The Gal Who Took the West**— Univ

1950 **Buccaneer's Girl**— Univ

Double Crossbones— Univ

The Milkman— Univ

Wyoming Mail— Univ

1951 **Comin' Round the Mountain**— Univ

Flame of Araby— Univ

The Golden Horde— Univ

Little Egypt— Univ

1952 **The Black Castle** —Univ

Has Anybody Seen My Gal?— Univ

Lost in Alaska— Univ

Meet Danny Wilson— Univ

The San Francisco Story— WB
Scarlet Angel— Univ
Son of Ali Baba— Univ
The World in His Arms— Univ
1953 City Beneath the Sea— Univ
Fort Algiers— UA
Girls in the Night— Univ
Take Me to Town— Univ
1959 Juke Box Rhythm— Col
1961 All Hands on Deck— Fox
The Commancheros— Fox
Pirates of Tortuga— Fox
Tender Is the Night— Fox
1962 Don't Knock the Twist— Col (assisted by Elaine Joyce)
Five Weeks in a Balloon— Fox
1963 Hootenanny Hoot— MGM
Take Her She's Mine— Fox
1964 The Brass Bottle— Univ
Get Yourself a College Girl— Col (assisted by Pete Menefee)
A Global Affair— MGM
I'd Rather Be Rich— Univ (with Miriam Nelson)
Kissin' Cousins— MGM (assisted by Pete Menefee)
Your Cheatin' Heart— MGM (assisted by Pete Menefee)
1965 The Art of Love— Univ
Fluffy— Univ
1967 The Love Ins— Col
The Ride to Hangman's Tree— Univ
Riot on Sunset Strip— AIP
Rosie!— Univ
1968 The Pink Jungle— Univ

LILLIANA BELFIORE

b. Buenos Aires, Argentina, October 12, 1952

Studied at the Institute of Superior Arts and danced with Ballet Festio Argentino (1967-68), the Contemporary Ballet ('70), Ballet Teatro Colon (1971-75) and the London Festival Ballet before she founded her own dance company.

Ballet/Dance Pieces (Partial listing): "Griselda, a Butterfly's Dream"

Film:

1988 **Tango Bar**— Castle Hill (with Nelson Avila, Santiago Ayala, Doris Petroni, Carlos Rivarola, Nelida Rodriguez, Norma Viola)

IGOR BELSKY

b. Leningrad, Russia, March 28, 1925

While still training at the Leningrad Choreographic School, Belsky was accepted into the Kirov Ballet in 1942 and became one of the fabled company's leading character dancers. Married to Lyud-mila Alexeyeva, another Kirov soloist, he began choreographing in 1959 (**Coast of Hope**) as one of the most promising Soviet choreographers "seeking for a new idiom to interpret contemporary themes" (*The Dance Encyclopedia*). From 1963–72, he was chief choreographer for the Leningrad Maly Theatre and then served as artistic director for the Kirov.

Ballet/Dance Pieces (Partial listing): "Coast of Hope" ('59), "Seventh Symphony," "The Humpbacked Horse," "Swan Lake," "Eleventh Symphony," "Gadfly" ('67), more

Film:

1976 **The Blue Bird**— Fox (with Leonid Jacobson)

DAVID BENNETT

b. Albany, New York

Staging and choreographing during the early years of the development of the American Musical Theater, Bennett worked extensively with composers Jerome Kern and Rudolph Friml. He began his career operating a dance school in Albany and when the school burned to the ground, he went to Manhattan to try his luck. After only six weeks of dancing in the chorus of a Broadway show, he did his first dance direction work on *The Wild Rose* (1902). In 1922 he observed some black children performing a Charleston in Alabama, returned to New York and collaborated with lyricist Irving Caesar on a song, introducing it in a nightclub revue and popularizing the dance. With the staging of the "Totem Tom Tom" number in *Rose Marie* (1924), his career soared ("Once having seen it who can forget it? He is a creator— many imitate him. No sooner did he devise the original idea of having the girls crumple up against each other ... than many other managers in town had something similar to offer in the hope of similar success"— *The Dance*, December, 1925). After being replaced by Hermes Pan on a 1932 Hollywood production of *9 O'Clock Revue* (which started Pan on his prolific career), Bennett's documented career suddenly ends.

Stage: *The Wild Rose* (Bdwy '02, with Adolph Newberger), *A Skylark* (Bdwy '10), *Nobody Home* and *Very Good Eddie* (Bdwy '15), *Flo Flo* and *Leave It to Jane* (Bdwy '17), *Oh Look!* (Bdwy '18), *Nothing But Love* (Bdwy '19), *Lady Kitty Inc.*, *Pitter Patter* and *Poor Little Rich Girl* (Bdwy '20), *It's Up to You*, *June Love* and *The Right Girl* (Bdwy '21), *Queen o' Hearts* (Bdwy '22), *Adrienne*, *The Battling Butler*, *Hello Everybody*, *Hi Little Widows*, *The Magic Ring* and *Wild Flowers* (Bdwy '23), *London Calling* (London '23), *Betty Lu*, *Dear Sir*, *The Dream Girl*, *Marjorie*, *Rose Marie*, *Top Hole* and *Vogues of 1924* (Bdwy '24), *Sunny* (with Fred Astaire, Theodore Kosloff, John Tiller), *The City Chap*, *Dancing*

Honeymoon, Florida Girl and *The Daughter of Rosie O'Grady* (Bdwy '25), *Earl Carroll's Vanities of 1925, 1926, 1927* (Bdwy), *Oh Please!* and *Criss Cross* (Bdwy '26), *Go to It, Golden Dawn, Lovely Lady, Lucky* (with Albertina Rasch), *The Manhatters* and *My Princess* (Bdwy '27), *Three Cheers* (Bdwy '28), *9 'O Clock Revue* (Hollywood '32, replaced by Hermes Pan), *Provincetown Follies* ('36, with Lee Morrison)
Nightclub/Concert: Club Alabam' (NY '23)
Film:
1930 **Follow Thru**— Par
      Honey— Par
      Let's Go Native— Par
      Paramount on Parade— Par (with Marion Morgan)
      Safety in Numbers— Par
1933 **Sons of the Desert**— MGM

MICHAEL BENNETT (MICKEY DIFIGLIA)
b. Buffalo, New York, April 8, 1943
d. Tuscon, Arizona, July 2, 1987
Michael Bennett's landmark concepts for the Broadway stage changed the shape of musical theater. Unfortunately his brilliance was not to be captured on film; plans for filming his own masterpiece **A Chorus Line** for Universal fell through when he simply walked out of his "three picture deal" and his unique creation was filmed by another director (Richard Attenborough) and choreographer (Jeffrey Hornaday). He began dance lessons at the age of 3 and by the age of 12, he had already decided to become a choreographer and director. Leaving high school during his senior year, he toured Europe in *West Side Story* and then danced in the Broadway choruses of *Subways Are for Sleeping* ('61), *Here's Love* ('63) and *Bajour* ('64). He danced in industrials and on TV in "Hullabaloo" ('65–66) and began choreographing on Broadway with *A Joyful Noise* ('66), receiving his first Tony nomination. After his only film credit, he said in a 1970 *Dance Magazine* interview, "I've been offered a lot of pictures as a choreographer, but I'd rather wait and go to Hollywood as a director-choreographer. You get more freedom that way. When you are only a choreographer, there are too many people telling you what they want. You can't create what you feel." He became a stage director-choreographer in 1971 and proceeded to create many of Broadway's most memorable shows of the 1970s and 80s, among them *A Chorus Line*— the longest running musical on Broadway. He also directed the Broadway drama *Twigs* ('71). Received the 1976 *Dance Magazine* Award and won seven Tony awards for his stage work— before AIDS robbed the American musical theater of one of its greatest innovators.

Biography: *One Singular Sensation* by Kevin Kelly (1990)
Related Works: *A Chorus Line and the Musicals of Michael Bennett* by Ken Mandelbaum (1989)
Stage: *A Joyful Noise* (Bdwy '66, Tony nom), *Henry, Sweet Henry* (Bdwy '67, Tony nom), *Promises, Promises* (Bdwy '68, Tony nom), *Coco* (Bdwy '69, Tony nom), *Company* (Bdwy '70, Tony nom), *Follies* (Bdwy '71, also co-dir, Tony Awards for choreo and dir), *Seesaw* (Bdwy '73, with Bob Avian, Grover Dale, Tommy Tune, also dir, Tony Award for choreo), *Bette Midler on Broadway* (Bdwy '73), *A Chorus Line* (Bdwy '75, with Bob Avian, also creator and dir, Tony Awards for choreo and dir, Pulitzer Prize for script), *Ballroom* (Bdwy '78, with Bob Avian, also dir, prod, Tony Award for choreo), *Dreamgirls* (Bdwy '81, with Michael Peters, also dir and prod, Tony Award for choreo), *Scandals* (workshop '85, with Jerry Mitchell)
TV: "The Dean Martin Show" (number for Joey Heatherton, '65), "Kraft Music Hall" ('67), "The Ed Sullivan Show" ("Sunny" number for Fran Jeffries, '68), "Pinocchio" (Hallmark Hall of Fame)
Film:
1968 **What's So Bad About Feelin' Good?**— Univ

JACQUES BENSE
1984 **Le Bal**— Almi Classics (with D'Dee)

LEONETTA BENTIVOGLIO
Italian dancer, choreographer and author of *Contemporary Dance* and *The Theater of Pina Bausch*, both published in 1985.
Film:
1981 **City of Women**— Gaumont/New Yorker

LILI BERDEN
1962 **The Small World of Sammy Lee**— Brit Lion

JAROSLAV BERGER
Artistic director of Switzerland's Bern State Theater.
Film:
1959 **Solomon and Sheba**— UA (with Jean Pierre Genet)

MICHA BERGESE
b. Garmisch, Germany, February 19, 1945
German-born dancer and choreographer who has achieved success and recognition in Great Britain. He began studying music at the Andrew Hardie

School and then dance at the London School of Contemporary Dance. He joined the London Contemporary Dance Theatre in 1970, creating his first choreography in 1972 and becoming one of the company's leading dancers in 1973. In 1980, he left the company to return to school at London University, studying arts administration and forming his own all-male company, Mantis, in 1981. In 1985, he appeared in the film **The Company of Wolves**.

Ballet/Dance Pieces: "Outside-In" ('72, with Anthony Van Laast), "Nema," "Solo Ride" ('78)

Film:
1988 **High Spirits**— TriStar
1994 **Interview with the Vampire**— Geffen

BUSBY BERKELEY (WILLIAM BERKELEY-ENOS)

b. Los Angeles, California, November 29, 1895
d. Palm Desert, California, March 14, 1976

"In the theatre your eyes can go any place you want. But in a picture the only way I could entertain an audience was through the single eye of the camera. But with that single eye I could go anywhere I wanted," said this dance and film director who innovated the filming of musical numbers with his fluid camerawork and intriguing patterns and scenarios in a 1969 *NY Times Magazine* interview. Born to theatrical parents, he grew up amidst touring players and made his stage debut at the age of 5. He attended the Mohegan Lake Military Academy in New York for five years, which gave him the basic material for the endless drill formations he would later create on film. He made his Broadway debut performing a comic role in *Irene* ('19) and after experience as a director of stock dramas and comedies in New England and Canada, he was talked into directing a musical in Boston by its producer. He became a Broadway dance director with *Holka Polka* in 1925 and as a great self-promoter with ideas and energy, he continued staging the dances in fifteen Broadway shows. He later confessed that although he had never taken a dance class, he learned the five basic positions of ballet while creating a dance number in *A Connecticut Yankee* (1927) in which the Queen was to teach ballet positions to the ladies of the court. As he paced the stage, pretending to be deep in thought, he said to one of the dancing girls: "I think I'll have the Queen start off by showing the first position" and she said, "Oh, you mean like this," and pointed her feet in a certain way. He moved to other girls, calling out the next four positions. "In this way, and without knowing it, I learned the first five positions of dance." In *Present Arms* ('28), for which he was also dance director, he appeared and introduced the song "You Took Advantage of Me." His stage suc-

cess brought him to Hollywood in 1930 for **Whoopee**. Realizing the camera's potential ("A great part of my work has not been the work of a choreographer strictly speaking, for me, if I dare to say it, it is the camera that must dance"), he created a new visual vocabulary for the movies, insisting to producer Samuel Goldwyn that he direct the musical numbers himself. Famous for overhead camera work, kaleidoscopic patterns and inventive musical scenarios, Berkeley was one of the few film dance directors whose name was used in the film ads to attract audiences and usually received the credit: "Numbers created and directed by." As a natural step from his innovative camera work in his musical numbers (using only one camera and editing as he filmed), he became a full-fledged film director. After a series of tragic consequences almost as bizarre as some of his lurid musical scenarios (eight marriages to six women, multiple suicide attempts, drunk driving and manslaughter charges in the deaths of three people — plus stays in psychiatric wards) he retired from films. Tributes by the San Francisco Film Festival and the Museum of Modern Art in New York brought him out of retirement in 1965 and he made a triumphant comeback as production supervisor on the 1971 Broadway revival of *No, No Nanette*. He was also honored by the Thalians in 1971. In the book *That's Dancing*, Gene Kelly paid him this tribute: "Berkeley showed what could be done with a movie camera ... he was the guy who tore away the proscenium arch. He tore it down for movie musicals. Many get credit for it but it was Berkeley who did it. And if anyone wants to learn what can be done with a movie camera, they should study every shot Busby Berkeley ever made. He did it all." The *American Thesaurus of Slang* defines "A Busby Berkeley" as "a very elaborate number."

Biography: *The Busby Berkeley Book* by Tony Thomas and Jim Terry (1973)

Stage: *Holka-Polka* (Bdwy '25), *Sweet Lady* and *The Wild Rose* (Bdwy '26), *A Connecticut Yankee*, *Earl Carroll's Vanities of 1927* and *Lady Do* (Bdwy '27), *Good Boy*, *Present Arms* and *Rainbow* (Bdwy '28), *Pleasure Bound* and *A Night in Venice* (Bdwy '29), *The Street Singer* (Bdwy '29, also dir), *International Revue*, *Nine-Fifteen Revue* and *Sweet and Low* (Bdwy '30), *Glad to See You* (OOT '44, dir only), *Can Can* (LA '56, dir only), *No, No Nanette* (Bdwy '71 rev, Production Supervisor)

Film:
1930 **Whoopee**—UA
1931 **Flying High**— MGM
       Kiki— UA
       Palmy Days— UA
1932 **Bird of Paradise**— RKO
       The Kid from Spain— UA
       Night World— Univ

Busby Berkeley surrounded by scantily-clad lovelies on the set of **Footlight Parade** (Warner Bros., 1933).

1933 **Footlight Parade**—WB (with Ruby Keeler, work completed by Larry Ceballos when Berkeley had a scheduling conflict)

      42nd Street—WB (with Ruby Keeler)

      Gold Diggers of 1933—WB

      Roman Scandals—Samuel Goldwyn

1934 **Dames**—WB (with Ruby Keeler)

Fashions of 1934—WB

Twenty Million Sweethearts—WB

Wonder Bar—WB (with Hal LeRoy)

1935 **Bright Lights**—WB (with Larry Ceballos, also dir)

      Go Into Your Dance—WB (with Bobby Connolly, Ruby Keeler)

Gold Diggers of 1935— WB (also dir, Academy Award nominations: "Lullaby of Broadway" & "The Words Are in My Heart" numbers)
I Live for Love— WB (also dir)
In Caliente— WB (with Tony DeMarco)
Stars Over Broadway— WB (with Bobby Connolly)
1936 **Gold Diggers of 1937**— WB (Academy Award nom: "Love and War" number)
Stage Struck— WB (also dir)
1937 **Hollywood Hotel**— WB (also dir)
The Singing Marine— WB
Varsity Show— WB (with John "Bubbles" Sublett, Academy Award nom: "The Finale" number)
1938 **Garden of the Moon**— WB (also dir)
Gold Diggers in Paris— WB
1939 **Babes in Arms**— MGM (also dir)
Broadway Serenade— MGM (with Seymour Felix)
The Wizard of Oz— MGM (with Ray Bolger, Bobby Connolly, uncredited)
1940 **Strike Up the Band**— MGM (also dir)
1941 **Babes on Broadway**— MGM (also dir)
Lady, Be Good— MGM (with the Berry Bros, Eleanor Powell)
Ziegfeld Girl— MGM
1942 **Born to Sing**— MGM (with Sammy Lee)
Calling All Girls— WB (S) (numbers from **Footlight Parade**, **Gold Diggers of 1935** and **Wonder Bar**)
For Me and My Gal— MGM (with Bobby Connolly, Gene Kelly, George Murphy, also dir)
1943 **Cabin in the Sky**—MGM (with John "Bubbles" Sublett, staging of one number, uncredited)
The Gang's All Here— Fox (also dir)
Girl Crazy— MGM (with Jack Donohue, Charles Walters, "I Got Rhythm" number)
Three Cheers for the Girls— Vitaphone (S) (with Bobby Connolly)
1946 **Cinderella Jones**— WB (also dir)
1948 **Romance on the High Seas**— WB (uncredited)
1949 **Take Me Out to the Ballgame**— MGM (with Stanley Donen, Gene Kelly, also dir)
1950 **Two Weeks with Love**— MGM (also dir)
1951 **Call Me Mister**—Fox (with Steve Condos and John Wray, also dir)
Two Tickets to Broadway— RKO (with Gower Champion, Ann Miller, also dir)
1952 **Million Dollar Mermaid**— MGM (with Audrene Brier, "Fountain" and "Smoke" Numbers credit)
1953 **Easy to Love**—MGM
Small Town Girl— MGM (with Willie Covan, Ann Miller, Alex Romero)
1954 **Rose Marie**— MGM (with Jeanette Bates, staged "Totem Tom Tom" number)

1963 **Billy Rose's Jumbo**— MGM (with Barbette, Charles Walters, second unit director)
1974 **That's Entertainment!**— MGM (with others)
1976 **That's Entertainment Part II**— MGM (with others)
1985 **That's Dancing**— MGM (with others)
1994 **That's Entertainment! III**— MGM (with others)

LINDA BERNABEI-RETTER
Dance, choreographer and teacher who toured on the 1990 Dance Caravan demonstrating the Lambada and is currently a member of the Tremaine Dance Center faculty.
Film:
1991 **Body Moves**— Prism Ent

THE BERRY BROTHERS
Ananias: b. New Orleans, Louisiana, 1912 d. 1951
James: b. New Orleans, Louisiana, 1914 d. 1969
Warren: b. Denver, Colorado, 1922 d. 1996
Sensational "flash act" trio who found fame in nightclubs, stage and films. Encouraged by their mother, they perfected their unique dance style with their only formal lessons coming from eccentric dancer Henri Wessels. Their father, a very religious man, did not at first approve of their show business aspirations but eventually relented and taught them the Cakewalk and the Prancing Strut. When the family moved to Hollywood, Ananias and James entered an amateur contest in 1925 and James appeared in some **Our Gang** shorts. In 1929 Ananias and James opened as a duo at the Cotton Club and played to great success for four-and-a-half years. The duo appeared on Broadway and on tour in *Blackbirds of 1930* (where Ananias was praised in the *Brooklyn Eagle*: "Ananias Berry stops the show. No one, black or white, can dance as he does. As a kid, he has gone further already than most dancers ever get.") Their growing fame prompted them to be a hired as part of the "Opening" show at Radio City Music Hall in 1932. When Ananias briefly left the act in 1934, younger brother Warren was taught the sensational routines and when Ananias returned one year later, the three brothers finally danced together. In 1938, they shared the Cotton Club bill with the Nicholas Brothers. They returned to Broadway in *Shuffle Along* in 1951 and shortly, Ananias died tragically at the age of 39 and the act dissolved. They never wore taps and their routine consisted of two sections: a strut (with roots in cakewalk) and a cane section, with great emphasis on dynamics — moving quickly between posed immobility and flashing action (called "freeze and melt").

Stage: *Blackbirds of 1928, 1930* (Bdwy), *Shuffle Along* (Bdwy '51)

Nightclub/Concert: The Cotton Club ('29, '36 and '38), Roxy Theatre (NY '36), Moulin Rouge, (Paris '37)

Film (Choreographic credits are for film appearances):

1936 **The Music Goes 'Round**— Col (Ananias only, with Larry Ceballos)

1941 **Lady, Be Good**— MGM (with Busby Berkeley, Eleanor Powell)

1942 **Panama Hattie**— MGM (with Danny Dare, Sammy Lee)

1948 **Boardinghouse Blues**— All-American Pictures

1949 **You're My Everything**— Fox (Ananias and Warren only, with Nick Castle)

ZINA BETHUNE

b. New York, February 17, 1945

Making her professional debut as an actress at the age of 6 Off Broadway, she began her dance training at 7 at Balanchine's School of American Ballet, also eventually studying with Robert Joffrey and Milton Feher. Alternately dancing and acting, the multi-talented teen danced in NY City Center's ***Nutcracker*** ('56), on Broadway in *The Most Happy Fella* and received glowing press notices for her performances in TV's "This Property Is Condemned" and "Little Women" ('58) and in the 1960 film **Sunrise at Campobello**. She enjoyed her greatest exposure as "Gail Lucas" on the TV series "The Nurses" (1962–65) which led to another film role, **Who's That Knocking at My Door?** ('68). A lifetime of fighting physical disabilities (scoliosis, lymphedema) climaxed when she had replacement operations in Denmark for dysplastic hips. After being on crutches for six months, she bravely returned to the dance world in 1982, forming Bethune Ballet. She subsequently founded Bethune Theatredanse and Dance Outreach, to bring dance to the handicapped. She also danced with the Robert Haddad Dance Company and triumphantly returned to the Broadway stage in *Grand Hotel* in 1991.

Stage: *Cradle of Fire* (LA '93)

Film:

1988 **The Boost**— Hemdale (also appeared)

VALERIE BETTIS

b. Houston, Texas, December 20, 1919

d. New York, September 26, 1982

Dancer, actress and choreographer who is credited with being the first modern dancer to choreograph for a classical ballet company when she created ***Virginia Sampler*** for the Ballets Russes De

Monte Carlo in 1947. She started her dance studies at the age of 10 in Houston and continued at the University of Texas. At 18 she moved to New York to study with Nenette Charisse and Hanya Holm, making her stage debut with Holm's company in 1937, also choreographing for the troupe. After her solo debut in a 1941 recital in New York she started her own dance company. With her smoldering blonde looks, "flamboyant theatricality" and smoky baritone voice, she switched genres and found success as a musical comedy performer on Broadway in *Inside U.S.A.* ('48) and *Bless You All* and *Great to Be Alive* ('50). As one of the performer-choreographer dance pioneers on television, she was finally brought to Hollywood under an unique contract as actress, dancer and choreographer for Columbia Pictures. After her film work, she continued teaching in New York until her death. In the *Dance Magazine* July 1974 review of a revival of her ballet ***Streetcar Named Desire*** (originally created in 1952) by the National Ballet of Washington at Kennedy Center, John Green wrote: "...has the uncanny ability to pinpoint and crystalize an emotion via movement ... Miss Bettis is not a mimic. She is an inventor, and what she invents is, finally, always truer to dance than to mere plot." Winner of the *Dance Magazine* Award in the "Modern Dance" classification in 1949, she had once been described by Edwin Denby of the *New York Herald Tribune* as a dramatic dancer "not unlike Bette Davis in her effect." ***Streetcar*** has been revived in 1982 and 1994 by the Dance Theatre of Harlem.

Stage: *Glad to See You* (OOT '44), *Beggar's Holiday* (Bdwy '46), *Peer Gynt* (ANTA '51), *Ulysses in Nighttown* (OB and London '58), *If Five Years Pass* (OOT '62, also dir), *Pousse Cafe* (Bdwy '66), *Final Solutions* ('68)

TV: "Paul Whiteman's Goodyear Revue" ('49, also appeared), "Our Town," "The Women," "The Sound and the Fury," "George Gershwin's 135th Street," "As I Lay Dying" ('65)

Ballet/Dance Pieces: "Prairie Barn" ('41), "And the Earth Shall Bear Again," "The Desperate Heart," "Dramatic Incident," "Virginia Sampler," "As I Lay Dying," "Yerma," "Streetcar Named Desire," "The Golden Round," "Winesburg, Ohio," "Early Voyages," "On Ship," "Echoes of Spoon River," "Next Day," "Domino Furioso," "Green Mansions" ('81)

Film:

1951 **The Dance of Life**— Univ (S) (with José Limon, also appeared)

1952 **Affair in Trinidad**— Col (also appeared)

1953 **Let's Do It Again**— Col (with Lee Scott, also appeared)

Salome— Col (with Asoka, Lee Scott)

1954 **Athena**— MGM

Valerie Bettis with Ray Milland, emoting in **Let's Do It Again** (Columbia, 1953).

JACK BILLINGS

Light comedy supporting actor in British films of the 1940s and '50s (**The Body Said No**, **The Wedding of Lili Marlene**, etc.).

Film:

1946 **Springtime** (aka **Spring Song**)—Brit Ntl (also appeared)

1950 **Mystery at the Burlesque** (aka **Murder at the Windmill**)—Mon

1951 **Happy Go Lovely**—RKO (with Pauline Grant)

NIGEL BINNS
1996   **Captain Cosmos**—DB Films

PATRICIA BIRCH
b. Scarsdale, New York, 1934

Describing her approach to dancework in 1979 as: "I don't just stage dances, I end up in the middle of the whole mess ... I'm not one for intricate steppy steps ... I want to preserve the energy of authentic dances." Patricia Birch is a dancer, choreographer, teacher and director whose contributions to the Broadway musical during the 1970s were highly influential, before she moved into directing. Although "shuffled off to ballet school" at the age of 3, it wasn't until she was 9 that she seriously began studying dance. At 12 she attended the Perry-Mansfield Summer School of Theater and Dance in Colorado where she studied with Merce Cunningham, who sent her to study at the School of American Ballet and Martha Graham School. She danced as a soloist with the Martha Graham Company in 1950, continuing on-and-off through 1970, eventually directing the company. Her musical theater performance career began at NY City Center Light Opera Company in revivals of *Brigadoon, Oklahoma!* and *Carousel* and she appeared on Broadway in *Goldilocks* ('58) and *West Side Story* ('59). She also appeared off Broadway in *Fortuna* and *The Carefree Tree* ('56 — which she also choreographed) and in concert in Valerie Bettis' ***Domino Furioso***. Her diverse performance experiences exposed her to greatness: "Martha [Graham] was the bigger influence, but I learned a lot of comedy from Agnes [De-Mille]." Starting her choreographic career on stage and TV, she recalled her 1972 intro to film choreography, "['Electric Company' composer] Joe Raposo called ... to say he was doing this movie called **Savages** and they need a dance for Kathleen Widdoes. It turned out to be called "Stomping on the Spaniel" or something, and we put the record on a record player and we made a dance." In a 1993 SSDC roundtable discussion, she described the challenges in film, "You work with the director. The first thing you've got to forget about is proscenium. In film you can work 180 degrees — or, God knows, when we were working in one of those football fields, we were working practically 360 degrees. So, you're working in circles, and it's a whole different thing. You try to choreograph in such a way that they're going to have all these choices to make in the editing. And then, you hope your intention was clear. A lot of times we get shut out as choreographers; sometimes we're welcomed in. Sometimes it's handed over to us; sometimes it's 'Thank you very much, that was a lovely dance. Bye Bye.' I found the most helpful thing to do with those guys is to say, 'What are we doing here?,' so that you can give them what they want." Later admitting "I've never been a person who just comes in to choreograph. I've always been part of the overall scheme of things," she naturally progressed to direction (**Grease 2**, '82). Her talents as a TV director have been recognized with "Best Direction" Emmy Awards for "Great Performances: Celebrating Gershwin" ('88) and "Natalie Cole—Unforgettable with Love" in 1992. Member of the dance faculties of the Juilliard School and the Martha Graham School, she is married to William Becker and the mother of three.

Stage: *The Carefree Tree* (OB '56, also appeared), *You're a Good Man, Charlie Brown* (OB '67 & Bdwy '71), *Up Eden* (OB '68), *F. Jasmine Adams* and *The Me Nobody Knows* (Bdwy '71), *Grease* (Bdwy '72, Tony nom, Drama Desk Award), *A Little Night Music* (Bdwy '73), ***The Losers*** (American Opera Center at Juilliard), *Over Here!* (Bdwy '74, Tony nom), *Candide* (Bdwy '74 rev), *Diamond Studs* (OB '75), *Truckload* (Bdwy '75, also dir), *Pacific Overtures* (Bdwy '76, Tony nom), *Happy End* and *Music Is* (Tony nom) (Bdwy '77), *Hot Grog* (OB '77), *Gilda Radner, Live from New York* (Bdwy '78), *They're Playing Our Song* (Bdwy '79), *Really Rosie* (OB '80, also dir), *El Bravo* (OB '81, also dir), *Zoot Suit* and *American Passion* (Bdwy '81), *The Cradle Will Rock* ('83 rev), *Rag Dolly* (Russia '85, also dir), *Roza* (OOT '86), *Street Scene* (Bdwy '90), *What About Luv?* (NY '92, also dir), *Anna Karenina* (Bdwy '92, "Musical sequences staged by"), *Smilin' Through* (OB '94, also dir), *Houdini* (work in progress '94, also dir), *Bard in Berlin* ('94, also co-dir), *I Sent a Letter to My Love* (Primary Stages '95, also dir)

TV: "Saturday Night Live," The Academy Awards Show, "The Electric Company," "Celebrating Gershwin" ('88, Emmy for dir), "Natalie Cole—Unforgettable with Love" ('92, Emmy for dir), "Christmas with Flicka," "Dance in America: 20th Anniversary of Great Performances"

Film:
1972 **Savages**—Angelika
1975 **The Wild Party**—AIP
1977 **A Little Night Music**—New World (with Larry Fuller)
       Roseland—Boxoffice International
1978 **Grease**—Par
       Sgt. Pepper's Lonely Hearts Club Band—Univ (assisted by Greg Rosatti)
1979 **Gilda Live**—WB
1981 **Zoot Suit**—Univ (assisted by Greg Rosatti)
1982 **Grease 2**—Par (assisted by Greg Rosatti, also dir)

1988 **Big**— Fox
      Working Girl— Fox
1990 **Stella**— Touchstone
1991 **Awakenings**— Col
      Billy Bathgate— Buena Vista
      Sleeping with the Enemy— Fox
      This Is My Life— Fox
1992 **Used People**— Fox
1994 **The Cowboy Way**— Univ
      North— Castle Rock

ERNESTO BITTNER

1959 **Caverns of Vice** (aka **Das Nachtlokal Zum Silbermond**)— Gala (Ger)

DAVID BLAIR (BUTTERFIELD)

b. Halifax, Yorkshire, England, July 27, 1932
d. London, England, April 1, 1976

Classical ballet dancer-choreographer who briefly appeared on the London musical comedy stage in *Bob's Your Uncle*, but found his greatest success as "first rank male dancer" with the Sadler's Wells Ballet (which became the Royal Ballet). He started his dance studies at the age of 8 at Mme. Ibbetson's school in Halifax. His sister lost interest in dance and young David, who has accompanied her to class, asked if he could have his parents' hard-earned money for the classes himself. In 1941, he began performing in the Sunshine Dance Competitions and by the time he was 14, he had won six silver cups and forty-five gold medals. In 1946 he received a Royal Academy of Dancing scholarship to the Sadler's Wells School, joining the company three years later as an "infant prodigy." He rose to principal dancer in 1956 and eventually partnered Margot Fonteyn to great acclaim. His dance expertise can be seen in the films **An Evening with the Royal Ballet** ('63) and **Romeo and Juliet** ('66 — in which he dances the role of "Mercutio"). Given the title "Commander of the Order of the British Empire" by Queen Elizabeth in 1965, he was announced as the artistic director for the Norwegian National Ballet but died before taking the position.

TV: "Swan Lake: Live from Lincoln Center" ('76, Emmy nom)

Ballet/Dance Pieces: (for Atlanta's Municipal Theater): "Swan Lake" ('65) and "Sleeping Beauty" ('66); for American Ballet Theatre): "Swan Lake" ('67), "Giselle" ('68), "Sleeping Beauty" ('74)

Film:
1970 **The Private Life of Sherlock Holmes**— Mirisch/UA

LIONEL BLAIR (OGUS)

b. Montreal, Canada, December 12, 1931

"I never wanted to be a choreographer ... it just happened!" said this successful actor, dancer and (reluctant) choreographer during an interview for this book. When he was 5, his father wanted to move from Montreal to the United States and his mother wanted to move to London — his mother won. In England, young Lionel made his performance debut as a child in *The Wizard of Oz* as a "Munchkin" and appeared on the London stage as an actor (*Watch on the Rhine*, Shakespeare at Stratford On Avon, etc.) until the age of 15. He began performing in musicals (*Kiss Me Kate, Annie Get Your Gun*) and as a self-taught dancer he did an act with his sister, Joyce, staged by Buddy Bradley. In 1952 he made his film dancing debut in **Where's Charley** and subsequently danced in **The Limping Man** ('53 — "dancing on a Xylophone!"), **King's Rhapsody** and **Gentlemen Marry Brunettes** ('55 — working with Jack Cole) and **The Cool Mikado** ('63). Featured acting roles continued in **The World of Suzie Wong** ('60), **A Hard Day's Night** ('64), **Maroc 7** ('67) and **Absolute Beginners** ('86) as well as in most of the films he choreographed. While dancing for choreographer George Carden on the "Jimmy Jewel and Ben Warriss" TV show in the early '50s, Carden wanted to leave the series and suggested Lionel as choreographer. "I made pretty pictures with beautiful girls and was known as the glitziest choreographer on TV. You know, tits and teeth!," he laughingly recalled, his dancers becoming a staple of British television. After this successful phase of his career he returned to what he loved best: performing. He appeared with good friend Sammy Davis, Jr. on television and in Royal Variety Performance (1961— a show in which he appeared eight times, as well as acting as associate producer for several times), also partnering Chita Rivera in "Night of 1000 Stars" in a tribute to Astaire and Rogers. Often dubbed "England's Fred Astaire" because of his graceful tap style, he gained added acclaim with his highly successful cabaret act and appearances on television as the Host of "Name That Tune," as captain of the men's team on "Give Us a Clue" and the BBC radio show "Don't Call Us." He continues to act and direct English stage productions (*Lady Be Good, Mr. Cinders, Season's Greetings, Rosencrantz and Guildenstern Are Dead, There's a Girl in My Soup*, etc.) and in 1993, toured in *Don't Dress for Dinner*. Lionel and his wife, Susan, have three children.

Autobiography: Stage Struck

Stage: 4 sets of Tiller Girls in various productions

TV: The Lionel Blair Dancers on "Blackpool Night Out," The Jo Stafford Show ('64), "Thank Your Lucky Stars," ('65, also appeared), "Spotlight"

and "Picadilly Palace" ('67), "Sunday Night at the London Palladium," Robert Goulet Special ('69), "Saturday Spectaculars"
Nightclub/Concert: Winstons (London '56)
Film:
1960 **In the Nick** — Warwick/Col
     Jazz Boat — Warwick/Col
1962 **The Main Attraction** — 7 Arts/MGM (with Donald Saddler, also appeared)
1963 **Play It Cool** — AA (also appeared with The Lionel Blair Dancers)
1966 **Promise Her Anything** — Par (also appeared)
1968 **Salt and Pepper** — UA (also appeared)
1969 **The Magic Christian** — Grand Films — Commonwealth Unit (also appeared)

SANDRA BLAIR
1989 **Chorus of Disapproval** — South Gate/J & M

MARLA BLAKELY
Music Video: Videos for Randy Newman and ZZ Top (MTV Award)
Nightclub/Concert: Bette Midler's "Divine Madness" Tour (with Toni Basil), Manhattan Transfer
Film:
1988 **Mac and Me** — Orion

KIM BLANK
b. Long Beach, California, January 16, 1956
After early dance lessons at the Terry Dagg School of the Dance and the Mona Frances School of Ballet, at 13 Kim saw a concert of Carlton Johnson's company ("It was a jazz ballet on pointe, it sort of opened my eyes") and she applied for — and got — a scholarship to Roland Dupree's Dance Academy in Hollywood. Learning various styles from Joe Bennett, Jerry Grimes, Gene Marinacchio and Claude Thompson, she also studied with Michael Peters, eventually joining his workshop in the late '70s. While an English literature major at UCLA she continued to find inspiration from Judith Jamison ("I left the theater at intermission and could hardly breathe"), Lester Wilson (his production of *$600 and a Mule*) and other live performances ("Dragging along a surfer friend up from Orange County"). In 1981, she joined the LA Knockers — a street/dance theater group headed by Jennifer Stace and Joan Wulfson — performing around L.A. and in Japan, for which she also began choreographing. Film appearances include **Americathon**, **Barton Fink**, **What's Love Got to Do with It?** and **Forrest Gump**, music videos: "Thriller," "Smooth Criminal" and "Dancing on the Ceiling" and on television in two Academy Award shows, the Emmy Awards and "The Jackson Family Honors." Along

with her performing and choreography, she began exploring physical wellness, teaching at Jane Fonda's Fitness Studios and is currently involved with Seldenkrais. She especially enjoyed the intense collaboration between Michael Peters, the dancers, actors and herself while filming **The Mambo Kings** and continues her involvement in Latin dance. When asked what she did with her English literature degree, she replied, "I am still listening to people and approaching the world as I learned to do studying literature."
Stage: *Kiss of the Spider Woman* (Bdwy '93, assistant to Vincent Paterson)
TV: "General Hospital," "Hanna," "Nightingale's"; commercials for Jourdan, Long John Silver's and Revlon
Music Video: "Lean on Me" — Thelma Houston and The Wimans; "Have You Had Your Love Today?" — The O'Jays and The Jazz
Film:
1991 **Hook** — Univ (with Vincent Paterson, Smith Wordes, "Additional choreography by" credit — worked with Julia Roberts as "Tinker Bell")
1992 **The Mambo Kings** — WB (with Jack Donohue, Michael Peters, "Ballroom Sequences Staged By" credit)
1994 **There Goes My Baby** — Orion

LOLA BLANK
1991 **The Super** — Fox

ANGIE (ANGELA) BLUE (DESHON)
b. Duluth, Minnesota, May 14, 1914
Crediting her mother, her early Catholic upbringing, Hermes Pan ("My boss and wonderful friend") and Betty Grable (dance-in for and friend from 1941–60) as the influences in her life, Angie Blue's career ran the gamut of film dance. After studying with Mr. and Mrs. Piper and Mildred Eaton, she made her professional debut at the Doric Theatre in 1922, won a talent contest in 1924 and formed an act with sister, Theodora: the Blue Sisters. They toured Florida, Georgia (The Sweet Papa Bozo Show) and the Keith circuit in California from 1924–29. That same year, she made her choreographic debut at Denfield High School in Duluth with "Lady of Spain" ("replete with castanets"). Moving to Hollywood, she made her film debut in **Footlight Parade** (1933). After many appearances as a dancer, Hermes Pan hired her to assist him and be a dance-in for Joan Fontaine in **A Damsel in Distress**. Taking a brief respite from dance, she married Charles DeShon, had a son, Dennis, and Hermes Pan talked her into coming back to assist him at 20th Century–Fox on **That Night in Rio**.

On her next film, **Moon Over Miami**, she was reunited with Betty Grable—whom she had first met on the set of **The Gay Divorcee**—acting as coach and dance-in for the star. Placed under contract to Fox as dance director, she remained there from 1941–54, working with Pan, Seymour Felix, Billy Daniel and other choreographers; running the dance department of the contract talent school and solo choreographing ("only small things at 20th when they didn't want to bring in a choreographer") until 1962, when she fulfilled a life-long dream and became a nun at the Carmelite Monastery in Carmel, California. In 1968, she returned to public life.

Film:
1937 **Something to Sing About**—Grand Natl (with John Boyle, Harland Dixon)
A Damsel in Distress—RKO (assistant to Fred Astaire, Hermes Pan)
1941 **Moon Over Miami**—Fox (assistant to Hermes Pan)
That Night in Rio—Fox (assistant to Pan)
A Yank in the R.A.F.—Fox (assistant to Geneva Sawyer)
1942 **Footlight Serenade**—Fox (assistant to Pan)
Song of the Islands—Fox (assistant to Pan)
Springtime in the Rockies—Fox (assistant to Pan)
1943 **Coney Island**—Fox (assistant to Pan)
Sweet Rosie O'Grady—Fox (assistant to Pan)
1944 **Pin Up Girl**—Fox (assistant to Pan)
1945 **Diamond Horseshoe**—Fox (assistant to Pan)
The Dolly Sisters—Fox (assistant to Seymour Felix)
1946 **The Shocking Miss Pilgrim**—Fox (assistant to Pan)
1947 **Mother Wore Tights**—Fox (assistant to Seymour Felix)
1948 **Green Grass of Wyoming**—Fox
That Lady in Ermine—Fox (assistant to Pan)
When My Baby Smiles at Me—Fox (assistant to Seymour Felix with Les Clark)
1949 **Dancing in the Dark**—Fox (assistant to Seymour Felix and "ghosted" for Betsy Drake)
1950 **My Blue Heaven**—Fox (assistant to Seymour Felix, Billy Daniel)
Wabash Avenue—Fox (assistant to Billy Daniel)
1951 **Call Me Mister**—Fox (assistant to Busby Berkeley)
1952 **Belles on Their Toes**—Fox
1955 **Hit the Deck**—MGM (assistant to Hermes Pan)
1956 **The Swan**—MGM
1957 **Silk Stockings**—MGM (assistant to Her-mes Pan and Eugene Loring with Dave Robel and Pat Denise)

LARRY S. BLUM

Stage appearances include *A Chorus Line*.
Film:
1988 **18 Again!**—New World

IVICA BOBAN

1991 **Rosencrantz and Guildenstern are Dead**—Cinecom ("Mime Choreography" credit)

CHRISSY (CHRISTINE A.) BOCCINO

Dancer and choreographer who danced on Broadway in *A Joyful Noise, Henry, Sweet Henry* ('67) and *A Chorus Line*. Las Vegas cabaret appearances include David Winters' *Youthquake* (Riviera Hotel '68) and Toni Basil's *Doo Dah Daze* (Flamingo Hotel '75). Her most recent film appearance was as "Mother Teresa" in **Naked Gun 33⅓** ('93).
Film:
1986 **Peggy Sue Got Married**—Univ (with Toni Basil, "staging" credit)
1988 **Beetlejuice**—WB
1990 **Madhouse**—Orion

RICHARD (RYSZARD) BOLESLAWSKY (AKA BOLESLAWSKI AND BOLESLAVSKY)

b. Warsaw, Poland, 1889
d. New York, New York, 1937
Director-choreographer who is best remembered as co-founder with Maria Ouspenskaya of the American Laboratory Theatre in 1925. He began his career performing with the Moscow Art Theatre. Emigrating to America in the early 20s, he directed a series of productions on Broadway: *Sancho Panza* (1923), *The White Eagle* and *Ballyhoo* (1927), *Falstaff* (also choreo) and *Mr. Moneypenny* (1928). The American Laboratory Theatre worked in the same fashion that the Moscow Art Theatre had, with each production (among them *Twelfth Night, The Trumpet Shall Sound* and *Big Lake*) viewed as a "collective education." He relocated to Hollywood in 1930 and after one dance director assignment, directed numerous films (**Storm at Daybreak, Fugitive Lovers, Hollywood Party, Metropolitan, Operator 13, O'Shaughnessy's Boy, The Garden of Allah**, etc.). He died while directing ***The Last of Mrs. Chaney***.

Stage: *Falstaff* (with Ted Shawn) and *The Three Musketeers* (with Albertina Rasch, Bdwy '28)
Film:
1930 **The Grand Parade**— Pathé

RAY (RAYMOND WAL-LACE) BOLGER

b. Dorchester, Massachusetts, January 10, 1904
d. Los Angeles, California, January 15, 1987
Bolger has the distinction of being the only American eccentric/comic dancer to gain full star status on stage, television and in films. Unable to afford formal dance classes, he first learned tap dancing from Dinny Haley, a friendly watchman who was a retired tap dancer. Bolger finally took ballet lessons from Senia and Regina Roussakoff in Boston, performing bookkeeping services for their dance school. He made his stage debut at 18 in a Roussakoff recital and toured for two years with the Bob Ott Musical Comedy Repertory Company throughout New England. With Ralph Sanford he formed A Pair of Nifties and the team managed to get a booking at the Rialto Theater in New York. He danced at a nightclub and then debuted on Broadway in *The Merry Whirl* (1926), continuing onstage in *A Night in Paris, Ritz Carlton Nights* (a Gus Edwards Revue for two years), *George White's Scandals of 1931 and 1932* and was finally featured in *Life Begins at 8:40* ('34), which prompted a New York critic to write: "He is an engaging comedian whose dancing never fails to steam up the audience." He gained full stardom in *On Your Toes* ('36), being dubbed "The Jazz Nijinsky" because of his work in the ballet **Slaughter on Tenth Avenue**, choreographed by George Balanchine. When Fred Astaire created a sensation on the screen, the film studios rushed to sign male dancers for films and Bolger began making films at MGM. Originally signed to play the "Tin Woodman" but, after showing the producer that the "Scarecrow" offered greater dance possibilities, he switched roles and gained film immortality in **The Wizard of Oz** (1939). He alternated between films at RKO, Warner Bros. and MGM and the Broadway stage in *Keep Off the Grass, By Jupiter, Three to Make Ready* and created musical theater history with *Where's Charley* in 1948 (in which his rendition of the number "Once in Love With Amy" often required dozens of encores), recreating the success on film in 1953. Other Broadway roles include *All American* and he starred on television in "Where's Raymond?" from 1953–55. His unique blend of ballet, tap, eccentric dance and comedy required that he create most of his solo routines himself.

TV: "Where's Raymond?" (aka "The Ray Bolger Show," with Sylvia Lewis)

Film (Credits are for his solo routines in each film):
1936 **The Great Ziegfeld**— MGM (with Seymour Felix)
1937 **Rosalie**— MGM (with Dave Gould, Eleanor Powell, Albertina Rasch)
1939 **Sweethearts**— MGM (with Ernst Matray, Albertina Rasch)
        The Wizard of Oz— MGM (with Busby Berkeley, Bobby Connolly)
1940 **No, No Nanette**— RKO (with Aida Broadbent)
1941 **Four Jacks and a Jill**— RKO (with Aida Broadbent)
        Sunny— RKO (with Leon Leonidoff)
1943 **Stage Door Canteen**— UA
1946 **The Harvey Girls**— MGM (with Robert Alton, Charles Walters)
1949 **Look for the Silver Lining**— WB (with LeRoy Prinz)
        Make Mine Laughs— RKO (with Antonio)
1952 **April in Paris**— WB (with LeRoy Prinz, Donald Saddler)
        Where's Charley?— WB (with Michael Kidd)
1961 **Babes in Toyland**— Disney (with Jack Donohue, Tommy Mahoney)
1985 **That's Dancing!**— MGM (deleted dance number from **The Wizard of Oz**)

ADOLPH BOLM

b. St. Petersburg, Russia, September 25, 1884
d. Hollywood, California, April 16, 1951
Acclaimed Russian dancer and choreographer who "is considered to be one of the great pioneer figures of the American ballet scene" (*Concise Oxford Dictionary of Ballet*). Graduating from the Russian Imperial Ballet School in 1904, he joined the Maryinsky Theatre Ballet and after organizing and dancing in Pavlova's first tours, he was promoted to soloist in 1910. He danced with Diaghilev's Ballets Russes and in 1911 he left the Maryinsky and danced exclusively for Diaghilev, also beginning his ballet staging and choreography work. After his second Ballets Russes tour to America, he remained there, creating his own company (Ballet Intime Adolph Bolm) and staging operas and ballets for the Metropolitan and Chicago Civic Operas (for which he was also ballet master and premier danseur). Relocating to Hollywood in 1930, he worked briefly in films and created ballets for the Hollywood Bowl. In 1933 he joined the San Francisco Opera Company and opened a school. After serving as ballet master and regisseur general for Ballet Theatre in New York (1942–43), he returned to Hollywood to teach and write his memoirs until his death.

Biography: A section of *Dancing in the Sun* by Naima Prevots (1987)

Stage: *Miss 1917* (Bdwy '17), *Le Coq d'Or* (Met '18), *Petrouchka* (Met '19), *The Birthday of the Infanta* (Chicago Opera '19)

Ballet/Dance Pieces (Partial listing): "Sadko" ('16), "Elopement," "Little Circus," "Les Nuages," "Krazy Kat," "Apollon Musagéte," "Ballet Méchanique" (aka "The Spirit of the Factory," Hollywood Bowl, '30), "Scheherazade" and "Bach Pieces" (Hollywood Bowl '36), "The Christmas Carol" (SF Opera '36)

Miscellaneous: *Spanish Choreographic Episode* (a Prologue for the Rivoli Theater, NY '19), etc.

Film:

1931 **The Mad Genius**— WB
1934 **The Affairs of Cellini**— Fox
1941 **The Men in Her Life**— Col
       The Corsican Brothers— UA

SUSAN BONAWITZ-COLLARD

1994 **Nell**—Fox

NATALIA BORISOVA

1968 **The Party**— UA (featuring Serge Jarott and General Platoff's Don Cossack Ca)

BARBARA BOURGET

1993 **Tomcat: Dangerous Desire**— Ent Securities LTD/Rep

SISSY BOYD

1995 **Four Rooms**— Buena Vista

JACK BOYLE

b. New York, December 11, 1916
d. Los Angeles, California, November 30, 1969
Dancer, actor and choreographer who appeared on Broadway before coming to Hollywood as an assistant dance director in 1941. He continued to work in films as an actor: **Youth on Parade, My Best Gal** ('43), **Cover Girl** ('44), **Shine on Harvest Moon** ('45), **The French Line** ('54), **The Best Things in Life Are Free** (playing a choreographer —'56), and **Billy Rose's Jumbo** ('63) while using his dance direction talents with television work into the Sixties. Married to actress Joanne Dale.

TV: "The Red Skelton Show" ('55–62)

Film:

1943 **Melody Parade**— Mon
       Nearly Eighteen— Mon

       Spotlight Scandals— Mon (also appeared)
1944 **Alaska**— Mon (with Felix Sadowski)
       Ever Since Venus— Col
       Hot Rhythm— Mon
       She's a Sweetheart— Col
       Sweethearts of the U.S.A.— Mon
1945 **Sunbonnet Sue**— Fox
1946 **Freddie Steps Out**— Mon
       High School Hero— Mon
       Swing Parade of 1946— Mon (also appeared)
1947 **Sarge Goes to College**— Mon
1948 **Campus Sleuth**— Mon
       Ladies of the Chorus— Col
       Mary Lou— Col
1949 **Slightly French**—Col

JOHN "JOHNNY" BOYLE

b. Wilkes-Barre, Pennsylvania, 1916
d. Los Angeles, California, October 16, 1965
"We needed steps — and Johnny had them," recalled Buddy Ebsen in his autobiography about this artist. "He was a walking and dancing catalogue of all the steps, traditional or newly invented, that any hoofer had ever danced since the year one, and he executed them to perfection." Boyle, a self-taught dancer made his first public appearances in dance contests in Pennsylvania, following in the dancing footsteps of his mother and sister who won all of the Irish jig and reel contests in Wilkes-Barre. He worked in minstrel shows, vaudeville (as part of Boyle and Brazil and also an act with his wife) and was featured on Broadway in *The Cohan Revue of 1916* and in Vitaphone shorts. Working briefly in England as a choreographer during the mid '30s, he returned to America for film work. Once described by Harland Dixon as "A great teacher but lacked style and personality," Boyle started a dance school with Jack Donahue in New York in 1927 and one in Hollywood in 1933, coaching future greats Buddy and Vilma Ebsen, Ruby Keeler, Marilyn Miller, George Murphy, Eleanor Powell, Ginger Rogers and Fred and Dorothy Stone, among others. James Cagney insisted that Warner Bros. hire Boyle to recreate George M. Cohan's dance style and routines for him in the Academy Award winning film **Yankee Doodle Dandy** ('42). Rating a rather bizarre description in *Who's Who in Dance, 1940*: "Specialty: imitates all stars of tap with dolls fastened to hands and tiny shoes on fingers. Gives lecture-demonstrations on the history of tap," he was often called "Jack" Boyle and his career has been confused in several published works with the man in the previous listing and a cameraman named "John Boyle" who also worked during the same time. With partner Hiram Brazil, he is credited

with inventing echo dancing—with one dancing on the downbeat and the other on the upbeat. Father of a son and daughter who also appeared with him as a trio.

Stage: *Castles in the Air* and *No Foolin'* (Bdwy '26), *Excess Baggage, Padlocks of 1927, Piggy* and *Strike Up the Band* (Bdwy '27), *Well, Well, Well* (Bdwy '28), *Boom Boom, Pleasure Bound, Great Day* ("doctoring" LeRoy Prinz' choreography) and *Top Speed* (with LeRoy Prinz) (Bdwy '29), *Stand Up and Sing* (London '30), *Shoot the Works* (Bdwy '31, also appeared), *Americana* (Bdwy '32), *Burlesque* (UCLA '62)

TV: "Shower of Stars" ('58)

Ballet/Dance Pieces: Gershwin's "Rhapsody in Blue" (the first ballet in tap, NY, date unknown)

Film:

1932 **Hello Good Times**— Vitaphone (S) (with Albertina Rasch, also appeared)

1935 **Sweet Music**— WB (with Bobby Connolly)

1936 **Double or Nothing**— Vitaphone (S) (also appeared)

Forbidden Music— Gau/Brit

Jack of All Trades— Gau/Brit (with Philip Buchel, Jack Hulbert)

Keep Your Seats Please— ABF (GB)

1937 **Broadway Melody of 1938**— MGM (coach to Eleanor Powell)

Something to Sing About— WB (with Angie Blue, Harland Dixon, also danced—uncredited)

1938 **Dark Sands**— GFD (GB)

1941 **Where Did You Get That Girl?**— Univ

1942 **Dancing Dolls**— Soundies Corp (S)

Yankee Doodle Dandy— WB (with Seymour Felix, LeRoy Prinz)

1944 **Bowery to Broadway**— Univ (with Louis DaPron, Carlos Romero)

The Bridge of San Luis Rey— UA (with Antonio Triana)

Minstrel Man— PRC

1945 **The Naughty Nineties**— Univ

1950 **West Point Story**— WB (with Ruth Godfrey, Gene Nelson, Eddie Prinz, LeRoy Prinz, Al White, Jr., "Mr. Cagney's dances created by" credit)

BUDDY BRADLEY (CLARENCE BUDDY BRADLEY)

b. Harrisburg, Pennsylvania, July 25, 1913
d. New York, July 17, 1972

Brilliant black tap dancer, choreographer, producer and director who achieved his due success as an expatriate in Europe in the 1920s and '30s. Self-taught from dance routines he had seen in vaude-ville and nightclubs, he made his professional debut in the chorus of Connie's Inn, a New York nightclub: "During the day, I ran an elevator, but at night, I hung around 'The Hoofers Club.' By 17, I was pretty good. We stole steps from each other." He made his New York stage debut in 1926 in a revue with Florence Mills and began teaching in 1928, coaching tap specialists Fred & Adele Astaire, Jack Donohue, Paul Draper, Eddie Foy, Ruby Keeler, Ann Pennington, Eleanor Powell and Pat Rooney. Due to his natural talent for choreography and ability to construct an exciting dance sequence, he created many routines for the stars in Broadway musicals of the time but never received credit. After appearing on Broadway in *Blackbirds of 1928* and re-choreographing *Greenwich Follies of 1928* (originally done by Busby Berkeley) he was brought to England for a London production of *Evergreen* in 1930 by famed London producer and impressario C. B. Cochran. His full credit for that show is believed to be the first received by a black artist for a show with an entirely white cast. He also made his English stage debut at the London Pavilion on March 1, 1931 in *Cochran's 1931 Revue*. He was signed as dance director for Cochran and Gaumont-British Pictures, beginning his successful association with British musical star Jessie Matthews who later wrote: "All of my numbers were 50–50 collaborations. Buddy and I worked together on all of my musicals from *Evergreen* on. He was a superb rhythm dancer and I worked on my tap with him. Even though in most of my numbers, I danced alone, Buddy shared the choreography credit with me." Because of his acclaimed work on Matthews' films, he was signed by 20th Century–Fox to choreograph **Alexander's Ragtime Band**— but when he arrived in the United States to begin work, the script was not completed and filming was postponed. He returned to England for film commitments there and never got to contribute to the American movie musical. Bradley did many stage shows in Italy, France, Spain and England, collaborating with Frederick Ashton, Anton Dolin and Léonide Massine. His career eventually moved into television in Britain, where he produced and directed. The *Manchester Guardian* once called him "The Gauguin of the dance."

Stage: *Greenwich Follies of 1928* (Bdwy with Chester Hale, Ralph Reader, uncredited), *The Little Show* (Bdwy '29, with Danny Dare created the sensational "Moanin' Low" number for Clifton Webb, uncredited), *Evergreen* (London '30), *Hold My Hand* (London '31), *Cat the and Fiddle* and *Ballyhoo* (with Frederick Ashton) (London '32), *Nice Goings On* (London '33), *Mr. Whittington* (Bdwy '33, with Jack Donohue, Jack Buchanan), *Lucky Break* (London '34), *This'll Make You Whistle, The Flying Trapeze* (with Frederick Ashton) and

Anything Goes (London '35), *Happy Returns* (London '38), *Full Swing* (with Jack Hulbert) and *Big Top* (London '42), *La-Di-Da-Di-Da* (with John Regan and Fred A. Leslie) and *Something in the Air* (London '43, with Jack Hulbert), *It's Time to Dance* (London '45, also appeared), *Sauce Tartare* (London '49), *Sauce Piquante* (London '50), *Divorce Me Darling* (London '65, with Harry Naughton), *That's What's Happening, Baby* (OB '67)

Ballet/Dance Pieces: "High Yaller" (Sadler's Wells)

Nightclub/Concert: Cabaret act for Vera Zorina and Anton Dolin

Film:

1931 **Out of the Blue**— Gau/Brit (with Jessie Matthews)

1933 **Good Companions**— Gau/Brit (with Jessie Matthews)

1934 **Evergreen**— Gau/Brit (with Matthews, also appeared, "Dances and ensembles arranged by" credit)

Waltzes from Vienna (aka **Strauss' Great Waltzes**)— Gau/Brit

1935 **Brewster's Millions**— UA

First a Girl— Gau/Brit (with Matthews, Ralph Reader)

Radio Parade of 1935 (aka **Radio Follies**)— Gau/Brit (with The Buddy Bradley Girls)

1936 **It's Love Again**— Gau/Brit (with Matthews)

1937 **Gangway**— Gau/Brit (with Matthews)

Head Over Heels in Love— Gau/Brit (with Matthews)

1938 **Sailing Along**— Gau/Brit (also appeared)

This'll Make You Whistle— GFD (GB)

1940 **The Spider**— Gau/Brit

1944 **Fiddlers Three**— Ealing

1945 **Flight from Folly**—WB

1946 **Walking on Air**— Gau/Brit

WILBERT BRADLEY

b. Jackson, Mississippi, April 28, 1926

While studying medicine at Wilson Jr. College in Chicago, this African-American artist had the opportunity to see many unique dancers appear at the Regal Theatre, kindling his interest in dance and theater. After seeing Katherine Dunham's group in 1944 in Hollywood, he returned to Chicago and auditioned for her, receiving a scholarship to begin dance studies at the Dunham school with Lavinia Williams and Talley Beatty. He joined the group and toured with them, also appearing with the troupe in the Italian film **Mambo** in 1954. Sensing new opportunities, he left the Dunham company and remained in Europe, working as an actor in films and television and forging a career as a choreographer, first assisting Hermes Pan on **Cleopatra** ('63) and going on to a solo career creating exotic

dance sequences for the popular Italian "Sword and Sandal" epics of the '60s. Returning to the U.S. in 1968, he joined the Free State Theater Company as an actor and choreographer and is currently resident choreographer for Chicago's Kennedy-King College and the ETA Black Theater group.

Film:

1963 **Cleopatra**— Fox (assistant to Hermes Pan)

Samson and the Seven Miracles of the World— AIP

1964 **Hercules, Samson and Ulysses**— MGM

Queen of the Nile— Max/Colorama

Sandokan the Great— MGM (also appeared)

1965 **The Snow Devils**— MGM (also appeared)

1986 **Ferris Bueller's Day Off**— Orion (with Kenny Ortega)

KIM BRANDSTRUP

1995 **Angels and Insects**— Samuel Goldwyn (GB)

SHIMON BRAUN

1974 **Kazablan**— UA

MARC (CHARLES) BREAUX

b. Carenco, Louisiana, November 3, 1934

Multi-talented dancemaker who, with his wife, Dee Dee Wood, created some of the most memorable dance sequences on film in the 1960s. As a youth he moved to New York with thoughts to become a chemist, but instead followed his interests in dance and theater. He studied modern dance with Doris Humphrey and Charles Weidman, ballet with Helene Platova and Elizabeth Anderson-Ivantzova and received dramatic training at the Neighborhood Playhouse. Making his professional stage debut in *That's the Ticket* (OOT '48) he then appeared on Broadway in *Kiss Me Kate* and *Ballet Ballads* ('48), *The Barrier* ('50), *Catch a Star* ('55), *L'il Abner* ('56, in which he assisted Michael Kidd and met and married Miss Wood) and as one of the sensational whip-cracking desperados in *Destry Rides Again* ('59—again for Kidd). He continued his work with Kidd, co-choreographing *Subways Are for Sleeping* ('61). With his rough-hewn masculine looks, he moved from dance roles to dramatic appearances in *Fire Exit* (OB) and enacted the role of "Tybalt" in a TV version of *Romeo and Juliet*. Relocating to the West Coast in 1962 for choreographic assignments with Wood, their screen dance contributions dazzled audiences as the film musical took its last giant gasps. After separating from Wood, he returned briefly to the stage in the 1971 touring revival of *A Funny Thing Happened on the Way to the Forum* and became a director of many television shows: "The Sound of Children" ('69), "The Hollywood Palace" ('69–70), The King Family Special, "The New Dick Van Dyke Show" ('71–74), "Fred Astaire Salutes the Fox Musicals," etc.

Stage: *Do Re Mi* (Bdwy '60, with Dee Dee Wood), *Subways Are for Sleeping* (Bdwy '61, cochoreographer with Michael Kidd), *Lovely Ladies, Kind Gentlemen* (Bdwy '70), *Minnie's Boys* (Bdwy '70), *A Funny Thing Happened on the Way to the Forum* ('71 rev, also appeared), *Snoopy!!!* (OB '82)

TV (Partial listing): "The Fred Waring Show" (three seasons, also danced), "The Bell Telephone Hour," "Music from Shubert Alley" ('59, with Wood, also appeared), "The Andy Williams Show," Pat Boone Special ('61), "The Hollywood Palace," "Danny Thomas' Wonderful World Of Burlesque" ('65), Carol Burnett Special ('66), "Bing Crosby's Goldilocks" ('69, also dir), "Of Thee I Sing" (with Wood, '72)

Miscellaneous: *Disney on Parade* (Touring arena show, with Wood)

Film:
1962 **40 Pounds of Trouble**— Univ (with Wood)
1964 **Mary Poppins**— Disney (with Wood)
1965 **The Sound of Music**— Fox (with Wood, assisted by Phil Laughlin and Larri Thomas)
1967 **The Happiest Millionaire**— Disney (with Wood)
1968 **Chitty Chitty Bang Bang**— UA (with Wood)
1974 **Huckleberry Finn**— UA (assisted by Garrett Lewis)
1976 **The Slipper and the Rose—The Story of Cinderella**— Univ
1978 **Sextette**— Crown Intl (assisted by Jerry Trent)

CEDRIC BRENNER
1996 **What a Drag (Pedale Douce)**— AMLF (Fr)

AUDRENE BRIER
b. Los Angeles, California, 1917
A child actress at the age of 3 and a protégé of Gus Edwards, she worked on stage and film as an actress while studying ballet with Ernest Belcher and tap with Nick Castle. After making films as an actress in England at 21, she returned to America and decided to devote her energies to dance and began film chorus work. Making the transition into choreography, she assisted Castle and Geneva Sawyer on **Little Miss Broadway** ('38). She signed a contract with Columbia in 1941, assisting Jack

Cole on **Down to Earth** ('47) and staging the musical sequences for Larry Parks in **The Jolson Story** and **Jolson Sings Again**. In a *Hollywood Citizen News* profile on April 4, 1949, her creative process was described:"She works up her actions, dances, or whatever they can be called, for Larry Parks from the Jolson songs themselves, not from the pictures in which Joly has worked. Sometimes she works alone until she has the number down; sometimes she and Larry work it out together. They don't get much in the way of credit for their creations though." Married to 20th Century–Fox production assistant Norman Rockett, she remained with Columbia until 1950, when she began free-lance work, often assisting Nick Castle.

Film:
1938 **Little Miss Broadway**— Fox (assistant to Nick Castle and Geneva Sawyer)
1946 **The Jolson Story**— Col (with Jack Cole, Miriam Nelson)
1947 **Down to Earth**— Col (assistant to Jack Cole)
     Sweet Genevieve— Col
     Two Blondes and a Redhead— Col
1949 **Jolson Sings Again**— Col
1951 **On the Sunny Side of the Street**— Col
1952 **Million Dollar Mermaid**— MGM (with Busby Berkeley, "Underwater Choreography" credit)
1956 **Bundle of Joy**— RKO (assistant to Nick Castle, with Dick Humphreys)
1958 **Rock-A-Bye Baby**— Par (assistant to Nick Castle)

AIDA BROADBENT
b. Manchester, England
Classical ballet dancer, choreographer and teacher who moved from England to Vancouver, Canada, at the age of 2 and began dance training there. After making her professional debut in a Leon Leonidoff production in Vancouver, she moved to the United States at 15 and appeared in concert in the U.S. and the Orient with her own company. As a member of Ernest Belcher's ballet group, she appeared at the Hollywood Bowl and in films (**La Bohéme**, 1926, etc.) as prima ballerina. She also danced as a soloist in the Fanchon and Marco Revues at the Los Angeles Paramount Theater (1933–35), with the Albertina Rasch ballet, and at Grauman's Chinese Theater, often under the stage name "Aida Barona." Her first choreographic works were with Fanchon and Marco's touring Hollywood Symphonic Ballet (1934–36) and their productions of *Prometheus* and *Hollywood* at the Hollywood Bowl in 1935 (in which she was also prima ballerina). She began her film work as a dance director at RKO two years later, doing uncredited coaching chores for their stars. As the resident choreographer

In 1929, Audrene Brier was a 12 year old student at the Meglin Studios, appearing at the Hillstreet Theater, in Los Angeles.

for the Los Angeles Civic Light Opera (1939–61), she choreographed dozens of shows and trained her own ballet company, among her dancers being the young Mitzi Gaynor. She also directed the dances at the Toronto Exposition in 1951. As one of the film's first female choreographers, she coached and created dances for stars Ray Bolger, Betty Grable, Ann Miller and Anna Neagle. The dancing corps of her LACLO work contained dozens of future dancing greats who all remember her with fondness. Up until the late 1980s she taught ballet at the Hollywood YMCA.

Stage: *Watch Out Angel* (OOT '45), *The Red Mill* (Bdwy rev '45), *Gypsy Lady* (Bdwy '46); for the Los Angeles Civic Light Opera — Partial listing: *Gypsy Baron* ('39), *Show Boat*, *The Merry Widow* and *The Red Mill* ('40), *The Chocolate Soldier* ('41 and '50), *Bitter Sweet* ('42), *Gypsy Baron* ('43), *New Moon* ('44), *The Desert Song* and *Rose Marie* ('45), *The Fortune Teller* and *Roberta* ('46), *Three Musketeers* and *Rosalinda* ('47), *Naughty Marietta* ('48), *The Great Waltz* and *Song of Norway* ('49), *Rose Marie* ('50), *The Merry Widow* ('51 and '61), *Song of Norway* ('52 rev, with George Balanchine), *The King*

Aida Broadbent (far right) demonstrates "proper instruction on pointing of the toe" for the publicity cameras (1942).

and I ('58); *West Side Story* (Vancouver CLO '64)

TV: "The Jimmy Durante Show" ('54–57), "The Eddie Cantor Comedy Theatre" ('54–55)

Nightclub/Concert: Act for Jimmy Durante

Ballet/Dance Pieces: "Prometheus," "Hollywood" (Hollywood Bowl '35, with Fanchon, Marcel Silver), "Grand Canyon Suite" (Hollywood Bowl '37), "Blue Danube," "Rhapsody in Blue," "Merry Wives of Windsor"

Film:

1938 **You Can't Take It with You**— RKO (uncredited)

1940 **Irene**— RKO

Melody and Moonlight— Rep

No, No, Nanette— RKO (with Ray Bolger)

1941 **Four Jacks and a Jill**— RKO (with Ray Bolger)

     Sis Hopkins— Rep

1943 **Cowboy in Manhattan**— Univ

1944 **Storm Over Lisbon**— Rep (with Lisan Kay, The Aida Broadbent Girls appeared)

1945 **Tell It to a Star**— Rep

ANDREA BROWN

1987 **Evil Dead 2: Dead By Dawn**— Rosebud Releasing (with Susan Labatt, Tam G. Warner)

NATALIE BROWN

1985 **Perfect**— Col. (with Kim Connell, Jerry Jackson, also appeared)

PHILIP BUCHEL

English dancer and choreographer who contributed greatly during the birth of British film musicals in the 1930s with his performances and dance creations. From the late 1940s onward, he collaborated with his wife, Betty.

Film:

1932 **Jack's the Boy**— Gainsborough (with Jack Hulbert)

1936 **Accused**— UA

     Jack of All Trades— Gau/Brit (with Johnny Boyle, Jack Hulbert)

1937 **Paradise for Two** (aka **The Gaiety Girls**)— UA (with Jack Donohue, Jack Hulbert)

     Take My Tip— Gau/Brit (with Jack Hulbert)

1938 **Hold My Hand**— ABPC (GB)

1940 **Sidewalks of London** (aka **St. Martin's Lane**)— Par

1947 **The Courtneys of Curzon St.**(aka **The Courtney Affair**)— Brit Lion (with Betty)

1954 **Laughing Anne**— Rep (with Betty)

1955 **Let's Make Up** (aka **Lilacs in the Spring**)— Gau/Brit (with Betty)

GEORGE BUNT

b. 1944

d. New York, New York, February 9, 1985

Dancer-choreographer who worked prolifically on stage projects around the country. From 1979 until his premature death of heart failure at the age of 41, he was the principal director-choreographer for the Melody Top Theater in Milwaukee.

Stage: Oh, Coward! (OB '72), *A Broadway Musical* (Bdwy '78, associate to Gower Champion), *Jolie* (OOT '78), *Lady Audley's Secret* (OB), *Reel American Hero* (Bdwy '81) ; multiple stock productions including *Camelot, L'il Abner, Minnie's Boys, Side by Side by Sondheim*

TV: "The Tonight Show," "Broadway My Street"

Film:

1974 **F. Scott Fitzgerald and "The Last of the Belles"**— Titus Prod/ABC (TV)

GREGG BURGE

b. Merrick, Long Island, 1960

This dynamic young tap dancing star first knew that he wanted to dance when he saw Sammy Davis, Jr. on "The Ed Sullivan Show." Beginning his dance studies at 7, he made his first TV commercial at the age of 10, eventually filming over 100 of them. While attending the High School of Performing Arts, he appeared on the popular children's television show, "The Electric Company" and after graduation, received a scholarship to Juilliard at 17. Featured stage appearances include *The Wiz, Sophisticated Ladies, Song and Dance* and *Oh Kay!* ('91 rev) on Broadway; Off Broadway in *Bojangles* and *Evolution of the Blues*; in the films **The Cotton Club** and **School Daze** and in the "Dance in America" TV special "Tap." He opened a dance school in Merrick, Long Island in 1985 and honed his choreographic abilities as assistant choreographer on *The Wiz, Song and Dance* and *Sophisticated Ladies*. He credits teacher Phil Black with inspiring him and his work.

Stage: One Mo' Time (OB), *Song and Dance* (Bdwy '85, tap choreo), *Conrack* (Goodspeed Opera House '92), *Hoops* (OOT '93, also appeared), *Abyssina* (North Shore Music Theatre, Mass. '95)

TV: Barcelona Summer Olympics Closing Ceremony ('92, also appeared)

Music Video: "Bad"— Michael Jackson (with Jeffrey Daniels, Michael Jackson, also appeared)

Film:

1985 **A Chorus Line**— Embassy (assistant to Jeffrey Hornaday, with Troy Garza, Brad Jeffries, Helene Phillips and Vickie Regan, also appeared)

HOVEY BURGESS

Mime performance artist and creator.

Film:

1980 **Popeye**— Disney/Par (with Sharon Kinney, Robert Messina, Lou Wills, Jr.)

RUBY BURNS

1994 **Even Cowgirls Get the Blues**— New Line Cinema (with Jann Dryer)

JEFF CALHOUN

b. Pittsburgh, Pennsylvania

One of the musical theatre's most promising director-choreographers in the 1990s, Calhoun started

Gregg Burge fronts **A Chorus Line** (L to R) Tony Fields, Nicole Fosse, Audrey Landers, Michael Blevins and Cameron English (Columbia, 1985).

his performance career at the age of 16 with the Kenley Players of Ohio, where he met his idol, mentor, and eventual co-collaborator, Tommy Tune. He appeared on Broadway in *Sophisticated Ladies*, *Seven Brides for Seven Brothers* and *My One and Only* (serving as associate choreographer and understudy to Tune), also dancing in the stage and film versions of **The Best Little Whorehouse in Texas**. Performances on television (**Copacabana**, '85, etc.) were among his last as he began focusing his energies and talent toward choreography and direction. After a six year period of directing on the West Coast, Tune invited him to collaborate on *The Will Rogers Follies* in 1991 and they have been co-creating stage works ever since. In a 1986 interview Calhoun expressed his views on choreography: "I'm not big on dance recital steps, I have trouble with that. When Fred Astaire gives you choreography the plot doesn't stop when he comes down and blows you away with his tap dancing. When his number starts, he greets you at the door, takes your coat, sits you down, pours you a drink, then the number is over. When he dances it makes sense, there's a reason for it."

Stage: How Do You Keep the Music Playing?, My One and Only (Bdwy '83, with Tommy Tune), *Bouncers* (LA '86), *Broadway at the Bowl* (Hollywood Bowl), *The Motion Picture Ball, Will Rogers' Follies* (Bdwy '91, assoc choreo with Tune, Tony

award), *Broadway Boys* (Takarazuka Theater, Japan, with Tune), *Grand Hotel* (Bdwy '91, assoc choreo with Tune), *Tommy Tune Tonight* ('92, also dir), *Grease* ('94 Bdwy rev, with Jerry Mitchell, Tony nom), *The Best Little Whorehouse Goes Public* (Bdwy '94, co-dir and choreo with Tune), *Buskers* (OOT '95, co-dir and choreo with Tune)

Film:
1986 **Weekend Warriors**— The Movie Store (also appeared)
1990 **Downtown**— Fox
Happy Together— Apollo

LYDIE CALLIER
1987 **One Woman or Two**—Orion

JAMES CAMERON
1985 **Return to Waterloo**— New Line Cinema

DAVID CAMPBELL
1957 **The Living Idol**— MGM (with José Silva)

TISHA CAMPBELL
b. Oklahoma City, Oklahoma, October 13, 1969
Tisha began her professional career as a 12-year-

old actress in the off-Broadway musical *Really Rosie* in 1981. She attended the Arts High School in Newark, New Jersey, and continued on the New York stage in *Mama, I Want to Sing*. She appeared in the films **Little Shop of Horrors**, **School Daze**, **Rooftops**, **Another 48 Hours**, **House Party** (her only choreography credit to date) and **House Party II**— usually finding an opportunity to dance. When interviewed as one of the stars of TV's "Martin," celebrating its 100th episode, she said, "I've been doing this for 20 years but people think I'm the new kid on the block."

Film:
1990 **House Party**— New Line Cinema (with A.J. Johnson, Kid 'n' Play)

EDUARDO CANSINO

b. Madrid, Spain, March 2, 1895
d. Pompano Beach, Florida, December 23, 1968
Classical Spanish dancer, choreographer and teacher who was one of Hollywood's first important dance instructors and the father of Margarita Carmen Dolores Cansino—who became "Rita Hayworth." Eduardo was trained by his father, Antonio, an acclaimed classic Spanish dancer and teacher, and arrived in America in 1913 to appear in vaudeville with his sister, Elisa, as the Dancing Cansinos. They were featured on Broadway in *Follow Me* (1916), where he met his future wife, Volga Hayworth. He moved to Los Angeles in 1927 to choreograph prologues and live stage shows at movie theatres. Contracted to be one of 20th Century–Fox's dance directors in 1935, he introduced young Margarita into his act and their appearances at a popular nightspot in Agua Caliente started her film career. He taught at Ernest Belcher's school before opening his own successful studio, where he taught for decades—introducing Spanish dance to generations of American dancers. It is unfortunate that a complete list of credits from Cansino's input to dance on film does not exist.

Nightclub/Concert: Acts for the Dancing Cansinos, the Royal Cansinos and Grace Poggi
Film:
1926 **La Fiesta**—Vitaphone (S) (also appeared)
1930 **Call of the Flesh**—MGM
        Golden Dawn—WB (with Larry Ceballos)
        Isle of Escape—WB
        Rogue of the Rio Grande—Sono Art
        Song of the Flame—WB (with Jack Haskell)
        Under a Texas Moon—WB
1935 **Dante's Inferno**—Fox (with Sammy Lee, also appeared with Rita)
1936 **Dancing Pirate**—UA (with Russell Lewis, also appeared as a member of the Royal Cansinos)
1940 **I'm Nobody's Sweetheart Now**—Univ

(with Louis Dapron , also appeared with the Dancing Cansinos)
1948 **The Loves of Carmen**—Col (with Robert Sidney)

ANTHONY CAPPS

1957 **Shake, Rattle and Rock**—AIP (with Val Raset)

GEORGE CARDEN

b. New South Wales, Australia, 1913
d. Sydney, Australia, May, 1981
Beginning his dance career with the successful J.C. Williamson musicals in Australia, Carden went to London in 1938 as principal male dancer at the famed Windmill Theater (depicted in the film **Tonight and Every Night**). During World War II he appeared in the revues *Sweet and Low* ('43) with Hermione Gingold and *Sweetest and Lowest* ('44) which he also choreographed. He remained in London to stage the shows at the London Palladium for thirteen years, also directing nine Royal Command Performances and becoming the resident choreographer for ITV television musical shows for eleven years. He returned to Australia in the 1960s to direct musicals, as well as make stage appearances. Until 1980, he choreographed the successful shows at the Bull 'n' Bush dinner theatre-restaurant in Sydney.

Stage: *Sweet and Lowest* (London, '44, also appeared), *Bet Your Life* (London '51)
TV: Numerous shows including "The Jimmy Jewel and Ben Warriss Show"
Film:
1958 **The Sheriff of Fractured Jaw**—Fox

CATHERINE CARDIFF

1985 **Came a Hot Friday**—Orion

KEVIN CARLISLE

Diminutive dancer with the trademark glistening white hair seen weekly as lead of the "Kevin Carlisle 3" (with Kathy Gale and Lorene Yarnell) on the musical TV series, "What's It All About, World?" in 1969, began his dance training at 17 in Birmingham, Michigan, with Marion Jones. He appeared in Bat'ya's act at the Dunes Hotel in Las Vegas ('62) and after dancing on Broadway, he began choreographing. From the mid-60s to 80s, his creativity was seen weekly on major television shows. Going into producing in 1970, he created, produced, directed and choreographed major musical shows and groups, including the "Solid Gold Dancers."

Stage: *Hallelujah, Baby!* (Bdwy '67)
TV: "The Garry Moore Show" ('64), "The Dean

Martin Show" ('65), "What's It All About World?" ('69, also appeared), "Doris (That's Day) Mary Ann Kappelhoff," "Dick Van Dyke Meets Bill Cosby" specials and the Don Knotts Series ('70), "Solid Gold" ('80), "Dream Girl U.S.A." ('86)

Film:
1995 **The Pebble and the Penguin**— WB

FREDDIE CARPENTER

b. Melbourne, Australia, February 15, 1908
d. London, England, January 19, 1989

Choreographer and director who began as a dancer in Australia at the age of 16. He moved to the United States to appear on Broadway in *John Murray Anderson's Almanac* ('29), London in *Bow Bells* ('32) and back to New York for Rodgers and Hart's *I'd Rather Be Right* ('37). He appeared in the British films **Ladies Day** ('43) and **Easy Money** ('48) and directed the 1948 film **Showtime**. He eventually returned to Australia to stage musicals for the J.C. Williamson Theater Group until his death.

Stage: *Tulip Time, Life Begins at Oxford Circus, The Town Talks, Mother Goose, And On We Go* and *Martiza* (England and Australia, cities and dates unknown); *How Do You Do, Princess* (London '36), *Bobby, Get Your Gun* (London '38), *The Dancing Years* (London '39), *Present Arms* (London '40), *Lady Behave!* (London '41), *The Love Racket* (London '43), *Big Boy* (London '45), *Ace of Clubs* and *Dear Miss Phoebe* (London '50), *Irene, Rodgers and Hammerstein's Cinderella, Hans Christian Andersen*, etc.

TV: "Tribute to Winston Churchill," "Noel Coward Revue," "Tarbuck's Luck"

Film:
1939 **She Couldn't Say No**— ABPC (GB)
1946 **Carnival**— GFD (GB) (with The Carpenter Corps de Ballet)
1950 **The Winslow Boy**— LFP/EL (GB)
1953 **My Heart Goes Crazy** (aka **London Town**)— UA

JOHN CARRAFA

b. 1955

"Movement can tell us things we don't know that can't be expressed in any other way. I'm interested in how movement identifies a person... And that's what Jerome Robbins is so great at: The way the characters move shows who they are," expresses Carrafa's approach to dance. While studying premed in college with the plan to become a doctor, Carrafa was also studying theatre and stagecraft, mime, clowning, juggling and tap and modern dance. Because of his exceptional dance talents he received a scholarship from the Massachusetts Council on the Arts in 1978 to study with Twyla Tharp in Boston. After one week of classes, he was

asked to join Tharp's company in which he remained from 1978 to 1987, appearing in the film **Hair** and on Broadway in *Singin' in the Rain* with the company. He assisted Tharp on three films and her stage version of *Singin' in the Rain* (translating Gene Kelly's and Stanley Donen's original film choreography for the stage) before launching his solo career. Interviewed in the *Los Angeles Times* (January 22, 1989) while creating the dance sequences for **Sing**, he said: "Film is like a language. Once I had figured out what the rules were, I started to be able to speak it. Eventually you start thinking in that language." Studying **West Side Story**, **Cabaret** and **All That Jazz** (plus experimenting with his own video camera and dancers) allowed him to explore the movement possibilities on camera before applying it to his film work. "I'm interested in choreography that doesn't look like choreography. It never made sense to me to just go and choreograph separate dances."

Stage: *Him, The Snowball, Club Soda, Bella, Belle of Byelorossia* and *Lucy's Lapses* (NY), *The Secret Garden* (Virginia Stage Co. '89) *Weird Romance* (WPA Theatre, NY '92), *Captains Courageous* (Goodspeed Opera House '94), *Love! Valor! Compassion!* (Bdwy '95)

TV: "thirtysomething"

Ballet/Dance Pieces: "Bach Cello Suite" (BalletMet, Columbus, Ohio)

Film:
1982 **Ragtime**— Par (assistant to Twyla Tharp)
1983 **Zelig**— WB (assistant to Twyla Tharp)
1984 **Amadeus**— Orion (assistant to Twyla Tharp)
1989 **Rooftops**— New Visions (with Jelon Vieira, assisted by Katherine LaNasa)
       Sing— TriStar (with Otis Sallid)
1992 **Brain Donors**— Par
1993 **The Night We Never Met**— Miramax
1994 **It Could Happen to You**— TriStar
1996 **City Hall**— Col

PEGGY CARROLL (SWANSON)

b. Oklahoma City, April 16, 1915
d. Los Angeles, California, March 3, 1981

Actress, dancer and choreographer who was "discovered" by film director Ernst Lubitsch in *The 9 O'Clock Revue* at the Music Box Theatre in Hollywood (choreographed by Hermes Pan) when she was 15 years old. Because she was still attending high school, she turned down his offer for a screen test but continued dancing in films. She was eventually contracted by RKO, became a Goldwyn Girl and assisted Pan on six Astaire-Rogers musicals at RKO. She then worked with Val Raset (with her actress-sister, Mary, eventually married Raset) at Columbia and as assistant choreographer at MGM. To keep her two careers separate she used the name "Jean Stevens" to appear as a featured actress from 1943–46 in such films as **Missing Juror** and **Return of the Durango Kid**. After taking a break from film work for several years, she returned in 1962 to assist Robert Tucker on **Gypsy**.

Film:
1942 **You Were Never Lovelier**— Col (with Fred Astaire, Val Raset)
1955 **Strange Lady in Town**— WB (with Antonio Triana)
1957 **The Helen Morgan Story**— WB (assistant to LeRoy Prinz)
　　Tammy and the Bachelor— Univ (with Kenny Williams, uncredited)
1962 **Gypsy**— WB (assistant to Robert Tucker, restaging Jerome Robbins' original work)

KAY CARSON
1965 **Winter a Go-Go**— Col

ALAN CARTER
b. London, England, December 24, 1920
Carter first studied dance and theatre at the Conti School and with Serafina Astafieva and Nicholas Legat and received his art education at Chelsea Polytechnic in London. He made his dance debut with the Vic Wells/Sadler's Wells Ballet in 1938 and after serving in the British Armed Forces during World War II, he returned to Sadler's Wells Ballet in 1946. He created his first ballet (*The Catch*) for the company and served as ballet master and danced in the films **The Red Shoes**, **The Tales of Hoffman** and **Invitation to the Dance.** He then formed, directed, choreographed and danced in the St. James' Ballet Company (1948–50), was ballet master and choreographer for the Empire Theatre, London (1951–53), ballet director at the Bavarian State Opera, Munich (1954–59) and choreographed for the Amsterdam Ballet (1959–60). From 1961–63, he served as guest professor of classical dance for the Royal Ballet. Other ballet direction and choreography assignments include the Opera House, Wuppertal, Germany (1964–68), Grand Theatre Bordeaux, France (1968–70), National Finnish Ballet (1971) and he founded, directed, designed and choreographed for the National Ballet of Iceland in Reyjavik (1973–75). He also guest-choreographed for companies in Israel, Norway, Turkey and Iran. Married to dancer Julia Claire, he served as Artistic co-director of the Elmhurst Ballet School from 1975–77 and has had multiple one man show painting exhibitions. The Carters continue to teach in the U.K. and he wrote, "In spite of my distant birth date, I continue to teach ballet and paint somewhat abstract ballet and contemporary dance subjects. With considerable pleasure, I also indulge in mu-

sical composition, using the miraculous new Technics piano. I have used the 'orchestrated' scores for local ballet productions."
Stage: *Annie Get Your Gun* and *My Fair Lady* (UK)
Ballet/Dance Pieces (Partial listing): "The Catch" ('46), "The Works," "The Prince of the Pagodas," "Ondine," "The Miraculous Mandarin," "Toccata," "Night Tryst," "Jonah," "Elements" ('75)
Film:
1951 **The Tales of Hoffman**— The Archers/ LFP/Loper (assistant to Frederick Ashton, with Joan Harris)
1953 **Invitation to the Dance**— MGM (assistant to Gene Kelly, with Jeanne Coyne, Carol Haney, also appeared)
1955 **The Man Who Loved Redheads**— UA
1956 **Ballerina** (aka **Rosen fur Bettina**)—(Ger)

JACK CARTER
b. Shrivenham, England, August 8, 1923
British dancer and choreographer who studied at Sadler's Wells Ballet School and with Olga Preobrajenska, making his dancing debut with Ballet Guild in 1946. Joining Continental Ballet, he also created his first choreography for the company. He choreographed for the Ballet der Lage Landen in Amsterdam (1954–57) and continued dancing with Ballets Russes, Ballet Rambert and the London Festival Ballet, where he became their choreographer from 1965–70. In 1961, he had choreographed an art film (**The Life and Loves of Fanny Elssler**) and his later international classic work as a choreographer took him to Japan, Sweden, Buenos Aires, Geneva and for multiple British companies.
Ballet/Dance Pieces (Partial listing): "Fantasies" ('46), "The Witch Boy," "Agrionia," "Beatrix," "Cage of God," "Swan Lake," "Pythones Ascendant," "Three Dances to Japanese Music," "Coppelia," "Don Juan de Manara," "Shukumei," "Lulu" ('76)
Film:
1964 **The Masque of the Red Death**— AIP

JANE CASSELL
1987 **The Hidden**— New Line
1990 **Pump Up the Volume**— New Line

JOE CASSINI
East Coast rock 'n' roll dancer who began performing in clubs which brought him to the West Coast. Dancing on TV, in films and in nightclubs, he soon became assistant to David Winters on TV (Ann-Margret special, '68, "The Spring Thing," '69, etc.) and nightclub projects (*Youthquake*, Riviera Hotel, LV '68). His expertise in rock movement soon led to directing and choreographing on his own.

TV: "The Barbara MacNair Show" ('69), "Kenny Rogers and the First Edition" ('71 series), specials for the Fifth Dimension and Bobby Sherman ('71); commercial for the Yellow Pages

Nightclub/Concert: acts for Brascia and Tybee ('70), Steve Allen ('70, also dir), Tybee Afra and Garrett Lewis ('71)

Film:
1995 **The Brady Bunch Movie**— Par (with Margaret T. Hickey Perez, "'Brady Bunch Variety Hour' choreographed by" credit)

GENE CASTLE

b. Utica, New York, September 13, 1946

"A major influence on my life both as a performer and choreographer is, without a doubt, Fred Astaire. For his style, his perfection, and for his humor," said this accomplished tap specialist who began dancing at the age of 5. "I was also influenced by Jerome Robbins ... for his ability to adapt his style to what's required for character. There's a wonderful logic to his choreography. He also had a tremendous sense of humor in much of his work." Gene attended the Children's Professional School and made his debut at 11 as an actor on TV's "New York Confidential" in 1957. Next appearing on Broadway in *Gypsy* ('59), he literally grew up on the New York stage from 1960 to 1968 in *Flower Drum Song, Best Foot Forward, High Spirits, Hot September, Henry, Sweet Henry, George M!* and *Oh, Kay!*, while studying dance at the School of American Ballet, jazz with Luigi and acting at the Herbert Berghoff Studio. Relocating to the West Coast, he appeared on stage in *Woman of the Year, Gone with the Wind, George M!* and *The Dybbuk*, in films **The Goodbye Girl** and **New York, New York** ('77) and on TV ("Look Up and Live," "Hullabaloo," the Bobby Darin and Ed Sullivan shows, etc.) Creating his first choreography for a TV pilot for "The Doc Severinson Show" in 1980, he wrote, "I want to continue directing and choreographing. The idea of just choreographing doesn't really appeal to me because I like to look at shows from the perspective of the whole. And try and figure out how best to make the elements come together."

Stage: *Cinderella* (Long Beach CLO), *Dennis, the Musical* (OOT tour), *Oh Coward!* (LA), *The Dybbuk* (Mark Taper Forum, LA); *On the Town* (San Jose CLO '93, also dir, Bay Area Theater Critics Circle Awards for choreo & dir)

TV: "The Doc Severinson Show" ('80 pilot, also appeared), "Bonnie and the Franklins" Special (also appeared)

Music Video: "Rappin' & Rhymin'," "Let's Tap" (instructional video starring Bonnie Franklin, also co-prod)

Miscellaneous: Industrials for Dr. Pepper

('89–present); for Princess Cruises: *Tin Pan Alley* ('90), *As Time Goes By* and *The Shooting Star* ('94, also co-wrote); American Cinema Awards and Friends of Childhelp Tributes

Film:
1982 **Kiss Me Goodbye**— Fox (also appeared)

NICK CASTLE (NICHOLAS JOHN CASACCIO)

b. Brooklyn, New York, March 21, 1910
d. Los Angeles, California, August 28, 1968

One of Hollywood's most important and prolific tap dancers, choreographers, producers and teachers, Nick Castle's immense talents and energies live on through the film direction work of his son, Nick Castle, Jr. As a child in New York young Nicholas Casaccio watched vaudeville routines and taught himself to dance. He began working in vaudeville in a dance team with Frank Starr on the Orpheum and Loew Circuits and also toured Europe. His Hollywood career began as Dixie Dunbar's tap teacher in the early '30s. Twentieth Century–Fox choreographer Jack Haskell hired him as an assistant and he began by teaching Shirley Temple, also coaching Norwegian skating star Sonja Henie in her film dance sequences. When Haskell left Fox, Castle was hired to replace him as dance director. After twenty films at Fox, he went to RKO, eventually working as a free-lancer for Republic, Columbia, and MGM. One of the most unique of Castle's creations was *The Wheelchair Revue* with a cast of World War II paraplegics — which preceded today's dance/movement exploration for the physically challenged by five decades. In *Dance Magazine*, February, 1947, he verbalized some of his approaches to musical numbers: "A number reaches its highest value when the camera is used to emphasize important movements and moods. Some gestures of tremendous significance are thus available to the choreographer... As to a large group dancing ... I prefer an intimate group of say four to five. I feel that the film audience is also inclined to lose interest in the film when a huge spectacle dance routine has been running for more than a minute... The star must motivate the number." From 1953 to 1962 his work was primarily at Paramount, where, because of his highly respected ability to create charming musical sequences for non-dancing stars and his extensive knowledge of the camera, he created most of the musical sequences for the Dean Martin and Jerry Lewis film series, continuing to supervise all of Lewis' dance numbers after the comedy team split up. He choreographed extensively for television and nightclubs in the 1950s and '60s and served as dance director for Universal, at the same time operating a successful dance studio. In 1989, his son, Nick, Jr. wrote and directed the film **Tap** in

Tap-master Nick Castle defines the style of a step for Donald O'Connor and Mitzi Gaynor in **Anything Goes** (Paramount, 1956) while an assistant goes over the steps.

tribute to his father, who died of a heart attack on his way to work on the Jerry Lewis TV Show at NBC. Castle offered his philosophy in a 1964 interview: "Many choreographers are not honest about themselves. Their choreography should not be an incident in their lives, but the very best that can offer... Always give your best." Castle gave us his best and is fondly remembered by dancers who worked for him: "You always had fun with Nick Castle!" He received the Gypsy Lifetime Achievement Award posthumously from the Professional Dancer's Society in 1992.

Stage: *Jump for Joy* (OOT '41, also co-dir), *Heaven on Earth* (Bdwy '48), *That's Life* (LA '54), *Joy Ride* (LA '56)

TV: The 28th Annual Academy Awards Show ('56), "The Eddie Fisher Show" ('57–59), "Oh, Susanna" ('57), "The Dinah Shore Chevy Show" ('62–63, with the Nick Castle Dancers), "The Judy Garland Show" ('63), "The Andy Williams Show" ('63–66), Caterina Valente series in Holland and Austria ('65), "The Jerry Lewis Show" ('67–68, with the Nick Castle Dancers), "Laugh-In,"

"Danny Thomas' Wonderful World of Burlesque," Specials for Tennessee Ernie Ford, Andy Griffith, Radio City Music Hall, etc.

Nightclub/Concert: Opening show at the Tropicana Hotel, Las Vegas ('57); staged over 300 nightclub acts including Frankie Avalon, Jack Carson & Cass Dailey, the Crosby Brothers, Billy Eckstine, Fabian, Eddie Fisher, Zsa Zsa Gabor, Al Hirt, Van Johnson, Lisa Kirk, Peggy Lee, Dean Martin & Jerry Lewis, Ann Miller, Debra Paget, Eleanor Powell, Buddy Rich, Dinah Shore, the Skylarks, Sarah Vaughan and Mae West

Miscellaneous: 1965 Golden Globe Awards Ceremony

Film:

1936 **One in a Million**— Fox (with Jack Haskell)

1937 **Life Begins in College**— Fox (with Geneva Sawyer)

    Love and Hisses— Fox (with Geneva Sawyer)

1938 **Arizona Wildcat**— Fox (with Geneva Sawyer)

    Hold That Co-ed— Fox (with George Murphy, Geneva Sawyer, also composer)

Josette— Fox (with Sawyer)
Just Around the Corner— Fox (with Bill Robinson, Sawyer)
Little Miss Broadway— Fox (with George Murphy, Geneva Sawyer, assisted by Audrene Brier)
My Lucky Star— Fox (with Harry Losee, Geneva Sawyer)
Rascals— Fox
Rebecca of Sunnybrook Farm— Fox (with Bill Robinson, Geneva Sawyer)
Sally, Irene and Mary— Fox (with Sawyer)
Straight, Place and Show— Fox (with Sawyer)
Up the River— Fox (with Bill Robinson, Sawyer)
While New York Sleeps— Fox (with Sawyer)
1939 The Boyfriend— Fox (with Sawyer)
Everything Happens at Night— Fox ("Skating numbers staged by" credit)
The Little Princess— Fox (with Ernest Belcher)
Swanee River— Fox (with Sawyer)
1940 Argentine Nights— Fox
Down Argentine Way— Fox (with Fayard Nicholas, Sawyer)
Young People— Fox (with Sawyer)
Youth Will Be Served— Fox
1941 Buck Privates— Univ
Hellzapoppin— Univ (with Richard Barstow, Eddie Prinz)
Hold That Ghost— Univ
In the Navy— Univ (with the Condos Brothers)
Keep 'Em Flying— Univ
Rookies on Parade— Rep (with Louis Dapron)
San Antonio Rose— Univ (with Louis Dapron)
Six Lessons from Madame La Zonga— Univ
1942 Joan of Ozark— Rep
Johnny Doughboy— Rep
The Mayor of 44th Street— RKO (with George Murphy)
Miss Annie Rooney— UA
Moonlight Masquerade— Rep
Orchestra Wives— Fox (with Fayard Nicholas, "Nicholas Brothers Dance Staged by" credit)
Ride 'Em Cowboy— Univ
1943 Around the World— RKO
Hit Parade of 1943— Rep
Nobody's Darling— Rep
Redhead from Manhattan— Col
She Had What It Takes— Col
Stormy Weather— Fox (with Katherine Dunham, Fanchon, Fayard Nicholas, Bill Robinson, Clarence Robinson)

This Is the Army— WB (with LeRoy Prinz, Robert Sidney)
Two Señoritas from Chicago— Col
What's Buzzin' Cousin?— Col (with Ann Miller, Val Raset)
1944 Lady in the Dark— Par (with Billy Daniel, Don Loper, "Circus" sequence)
Show Business— RKO (with George Murphy)
Something for the Boys— Fox
1945 Mexicana— Rep
Nob Hill— Fox
1946 Earl Carroll Sketchbook— Rep
Suspense— Mon
Thrill of Brazil— Col (with Jack Cole, Eugene Loring, Ann Miller, Frank Veloz)
1948 Lulu Belle— Col
Luxury Liner— MGM
Manhattan Angel— Col
The Saxon Charm— Univ
1949 Shamrock Hill— Eagle Lion
You're My Everything— Fox (with the Berry Brothers)
1950 Nancy Goes to Rio— MGM
Summer Stock— MGM (with Gene Kelly, Charles Walters)
1951 Rich, Young and Pretty— MGM
Royal Wedding— MGM (with Fred Astaire, assisted by Marilyn Christine, Dave Robel)
The Strip— MGM
1952 Everything I Have Is Yours— MGM (with Gower Champion)
I Dream of Jeannie— Rep
Jumping Jacks— Par
Skirts Ahoy— MGM
Stars and Stripes Forever— Fox (with Stephen Papich, Al White, Jr., "Springtime in New York" number)
1953 Here Come the Girls— Par (with the Four Step Bros)
Sweethearts on Parade— Rep
1954 Living It Up— Par
Red Garters —Par
Three Ring Circus— Par
1955 The Seven Little Foys— Par
You're Never Too Young— Par
1956 Anything Goes— Par (with Ernest Flatt, Roland Petit, assisted by Maggie Banks, Dick Humphreys)
The Birds and the Bees— Par
Bundle of Joy— RKO (assisted by Audrene Brier and Dick Humphreys)
Pardners— Par
That Certain Feeling— Par
1957 The Delicate Delinquent— Par
1958 Rock-a-Bye Baby— Par (assisted by Audrene Brier)
Sing, Boy, Sing— Fox

1960 **The Bellboy**— Par
       Cinderfella— Par (assisted by Helen Silvers)
1961 **The Errand Boy**— Par (assisted by Maurice Kelly)
       Pocketful of Miracles— Par (assisted by Gretchen Houser)
1962 **State Fair**— Fox (assisted by Maggie Banks)
1963 **Come Blow Your Horn**— Par (with Jack Baker, Maggie Banks)
1974 **That's Entertainment!**— MGM (with others)
1976 **That's Entertainment, Part II**— MGM (with others)
1986 **That's Dancing!**— MGM (with others)
1994 **That's Entertainment III**— MGM (with others)

SECONDINO CAVALLO

1961 **The Wonders of Aladdin**— MGM (Fr/Ital)

LARRY (HILARION OBISPO) CEBALLOS

b. Iqueque, Chile, October 21, 1887
d. Riverside, California, September 12, 1978

From his professional debut in 1889 to his retirement in 1951, Larry Ceballos' career spanned many decades and forms of entertainment. The colorful and prolific dance and film director was born in South America, when his Scotch-Mexican parents were performing there in an Italian circus. Larry's father was an acrobat/aerialist who worked from a hot air balloon and his mother performed "Iron Jaw" from a high wire. Larry made his debut with the family act in London at the age of 2 and while touring with Ringling Bros. and Barnum and Bailey Circus, he began dance studies with an Italian ballet master who staged dance sequences for the circus. After traveling with the circus for fifteen years, he appeared with his sister on Broadway in *Humpty Dumpty* (1904) at 17, and began formal dance training. When his Father died, young Larry and his sister formed an acrobatic vaudeville act, later creating an adagio dance act called the Fantastic Phantoms for which Larry began choreographing. Appearances in film shorts and more stage work continued as part of a dance team with Mona Desmond (Ceballos and Desmond) in vaudeville. Signed to dance in the 1915 London stage show *Shell Out*, when the dance director became ill, he took over and remained in England for four years before his work took him back to Broadway in 1920. After attaining success there as a dance director, he was brought to Hollywood by Warner Bros. in 1928 to create the musical sequences for film musicals — and Ceballos holds the distinction of being the first dance director ever given an on-screen credit for **Lights of New York** ('28). With a dance vocabulary primarily of buck, rhythm tap and soft shoe, Ceballos planned all of his musical numbers directly for the camera and staged each "cut" for specific camera angles ("A dance sequence is usually shot three or four times — long and medium shots and close-ups. If all of this film is handed to the cutter, it so confuses him that he chooses what he thinks is most effective and it is he who makes the final composition... I create my dance as a whole, watch it for eye focus and fatigue, and then cut it before I film it. In this way I use much less film, there is less wasted effort and the result is always a smoother, more pleasing dance sequence"— *The American Dancer*, June, 1938). He continued film and stage work, creating multiple prologues for Grauman's Chinese Theater and returned to England for several film jobs from 1937–38. Along with his dance direction work, from 1940–44 he directed a series of twenty five musical shorts for Universal: **Beat Me Daddy, Eight to the Bar, Congomania, Follies Parisienne, Hawaiian Rhythm, Torrid Tempos, Bagdad Daddy, Doin' the Town, In the Groove, Jumpin' Jive**, etc. In 1944 he was contracted by Republic to stage all of Roy Rogers and Dale Evans' musical numbers for their Western film series. Divorced from his wife Dorothy in 1935, he retired in 1951 and is survived by a daughter, Joy Griffiths.

Stage: *Greenwich Village Follies of 1920, '21, '23, '24, '25* (Bdwy), *Jack and Jill* (Bdwy '23), *Moonlight* (Bdwy '24), *Big Boy* (Bdwy '25, with Sammy Lee), *Americana 1925 & 1926* (Bdwy), *The Merry World* (Bdwy '26), *The Girl from Cooks* (London '27), *Fifty Million Frenchmen* (Bdwy '29), *Life of the Party* (OOT '42)

Nightclub/Concert: Earl Carroll's Nightclub (Hollywood)

Film:
1927 **Notorious Lady**— WB
1928 **The Larry Ceballos Revue**— Vitaphone (S) (a series of shorts including "Crystal Cave Cafe," "Undersea Revue," "Roof Garden Revue")
       Lights of New York— WB (first onscreen credit for a dance director)
       The Singing Fool— WB
1929 **The Gold Diggers of Broadway**— WB
       Honky Tonk— WB
       Is Everybody Happy?— WB
       On with the Show— WB (with Willie Covan)
       The Painted Angel— WB
       Paris— First Ntl
       Sally— First Ntl (with Theodore Kosloff, Albertina Rasch)
       The Show of Shows— WB (with Jack Haskell)

A studio portrait of Larry Ceballos, circa 1925. (Photo courtesy of Joy Griffiths.)

Smiling Irish Eyes— First Ntl (with Carl McBride, Walter Wills)
Stolen Kisses— WB
1930 **Dancing Sweeties**— WB
Golden Dawn— WB (with Eduardo Cansino)
Hold Everything!— WB
No, No Nanette— First Ntl (with Michio Ito)
Top Speed— WB
1931 **Bright Lights**— WB (with Busby Berkeley)
1933 **Diplomaniacs**— RKO
Footlight Parade— WB (completed the film for Busby Berkeley)
The Girl Without a Room— Par
Sitting Pretty— Par
So, This Is Africa— RKO
1934 **The Cat's Paw**— Fox
Murder at the Vanities— Par (with LeRoy Prinz)
She Made Her Bed— Par
Transatlantic Merry-Go-Round— UA (with Sammy Lee)
1935 **Redheads on Parade**— Fox
1936 **Follow Your Heart**— Rep
The Music Goes 'Round— Col (with Ananias Berry)
1937 **Make a Wish**— RKO
Rhythm Racketeer— BIFD (GB)

1938 **He Loved an Actress** (aka **Mad About Money** and **Stardust**)— Morgan/British Lion
Outside of Paradise— Rep
1940 **Melody Ranch**— Rep (with Ann Miller)
One Night in the Tropics— Univ
Sing, Dance, Plenty Hot— Rep
Spring Parade— Univ
1941 **Moonlight in Hawaii**— Univ
Pot o' Gold— UA
Sing Another Chorus— Univ (with Antonio)
1942 **Sleepytime Gal**— Rep
Yokel Boy— Rep
1943 **Follies Girl**— PRC
Tahiti Honey— Rep
1944 **The Cowboy and the Senorita**— Rep
The Lights of Old Santa Fe— Rep
San Fernando Valley— Rep
The Song of Nevada— Rep
Trocodero— Rep
The Yellow Rose of Texas— Rep
1945 **Along the Navajo Trail**— Rep
Bells of Rosarita— Rep
Dakota— Rep
Don't Fence Me In— Rep
Flame of the Barbary Coast— Rep
Man from Oklahoma— Rep
A Song for Miss Julie— Rep (with Anton Dolin)
Sunset in El Dorado— Rep
Utah— Rep
1946 **Meet the Navy**— BN/Anglo-American
Queen of Burlesque— PRC
1947 **Copacabana**— UA
Linda Be Good— PRC
1948 **The Babe Ruth Story**— Mon/AA
1950 **I'll Get By**— Fox (assisted by Roland Dupree and Margaret Kerry)
1951 **Valentino**— Col

CHRIS (CHRISTOPHER) CHADMAN

b. The Bronx, New York, 1948
d. New York, New York, April 30, 1995

This eventual dancer-choreographer auditioned for the High School of Performing Arts at the age of 11, was accepted and majored in ballet. After his first Broadway show *Darling of the Day* ('72), he met Bob Fosse during an Ed Sullivan show and Fosse eventually used him on Broadway in *Pippin* ('73), *Chicago* ('75), *Dancin'* ('79, in which he also assisted Fosse) and *Big Deal* ('86). During the creation of *A Chorus Line*, he participated in the original tape sessions with Michael Bennett — inspiring the "Gregory Gardiner" role by his recollections. Finally appearing in the show on Broadway, he never did play "Gregory," however, playing "Bobby" instead. Other Broadway shows: *Jimmy*, *Applause*, *Rockabye Hamlet* and *The Rothchilds*. Nightclub appearances include Chita Rivera's act and a solo engagement at the Barbaran Club in New York and he appeared in the film **The Flamingo Kid.** He made his full scale Broadway choreographic debut with *Merlin* ('83) and was associate choreographer to Fosse on *Big Deal* ('86). He began teaching at the Broadway Dance Center in 1990. Constantly inspired and encouraged by Fosse, he "auditioned" for the choreographic chores on the 1992 revival of *Guys and Dolls* by staging and choreographing several musical numbers from the show with dancer-friends. He got the job and won the 1992 Astaire Award for his Tony-nominated work on *Guys and Dolls*. In a October, 1992 *Dance Magazine* article about his new success, he said: "For me, if there's no motivation, there's no dance."

Stage: *Dancin'* (Bdwy '79, asst to Bob Fosse), *Merlin* (Bdwy '83, with Billy Wilson), *Big Deal* (Bdwy '86, associate choreographer with Bob Fosse), *Peter Allen and the Rockettes* (Radio City Music Hall, also dir), *Guys and Dolls* (Bdwy '92 rev, recipient of the '92 Astaire Award and Tony nom), *Fiorello!* (NY City Center '94 Concert rev), *A Funny Thing Happened on the Way to the Forum* (Bdwy '94 rev)

Nightclub/Concert: *Dancing in the Dark* ('79), *Chita* ('86, with Ron Field, Alan Johnson, Lisa Mordente)

Film:
1984 **The Flamingo Kid**— Fox (also appeared)
The Muppets Take Manhattan— TriStar
1991 **Scenes from a Mall**— Touchstone

GOWER CHAMPION

b. Geneva, Illinois, June 22, 1919
d. New York, August 25, 1980

Multi-talented dancer, singer, actor, choreographer and director who was discovered at the age of 13 by Ernest Belcher in a ballroom show at Bancroft Jr. High School in Hollywood. Moving from Illinois to Los Angeles at the age of 2, Gower had been studying ballroom dance from the age of 11 with Elissa Ryan and competing in ballroom competitions with a partner, Jeanne Tyler. To extend his dance training, he attended Belcher's dance school, where he studied with a junior high school classmate — and Belcher's daughter — Marge. At 15, he and Tyler placed first in a *Los Angeles Examiner* Spring 1935 ballroom exhibition contest staged by Veloz and Yolanda at the Coconut Grove in Los Angeles and were contracted for an engagement at the Grove, which was extended for thirteen weeks. After appearing as a member of the Hollywood Symphonic Ballet for Belcher in 1936, he and Tyler toured for four years as Gower and Jeanne and

appeared in the Vitaphone short **The Projection Room**, released in 1939. On Broadway, they danced in *Streets of Paris* ('39) and *The Lady Comes Across* and *Count Me In* in 1942. During World War II he enlisted in the Coast Guard and toured in the show *Tars and Spars*. After getting out of the service in 1946 and finding that Tyler had married and retired, Gower sought a new partner — with Ernest Belcher suggesting his daughter. In 1946, Marge and Gower created a popular adagio nightclub dance act (presenting what they called "Story ballets"), combining their extensive variety of dance techniques with the more traditional ballroom dances. They married in 1947. When Marge injured her ankle, Gower partnered Cyd Charisse in the film **Words and Music** ('48) and spent the time choreographing *Lend an Ear* (winning a Tony award) and *Small Wonder* in 1948. Upon her recovery, the team soared to national fame on TV in 1949 on "The Admiral Revue," the original Sid Caesar-Imogene Coca show. They continued to appear on all of the major television shows of the time (Ed Sullivan, Perry Como, Steve Allen, Dinah Shore, etc.), eventually having a show of their own. Making their film debuts as "Guest Stars" in **Mr. Music** ('50) for Paramount, they signed a contract with MGM to co-star in musical films with Gower choreographing all of their film routines. After a successful (and unprecedented for husband-and-wife stars) film career with Marge, he returned to the live theater to become one of Broadway's leading director-choreographers. Champion also directed the non-musical films **My Six Loves** ('63) and **Bank Shot** ('74). Winner of the *Dance Magazine* Award in 1949 in the "Musical Comedy" category for *Lend an Ear* and again in 1963, plus four Tony Awards for choreography and three for direction. On the opening night of his last show, *42nd Street* ('80), producer David Merrick made a curtain call speech, announcing to the shocked audience and cast that Mr. Champion had died, creating one of show business' most sensational legends. In 1993 he was posthumously awarded the Dance Library of Israel's Documents of Dance Award.

Stage: *Small Wonder* (Bdwy '48), *Lend an Ear* (LA and Bdwy '48, Tony Award), *Make a Wish* (Bdwy '51), *Three for Tonight* (Bdwy '55, also dir and co-star with Marge), *Bye Bye Birdie* (Bdwy '60, also dir, Tony Awards for choreo and dir), *Carnival* (Bdwy '61, also dir, Tony nom for dir), *Hello Dolly!* (Bdwy '64, also dir, Tony Awards for choreo and dir), *High Spirits* (Bdwy '64, also dir, replaced), *I Do I Do* (Bdwy '66, also dir, Tony nom for dir), *The Happy Time* (Bdwy '68, also dir, Tony Awards for choreo and dir), *Pretty Belle* (Bdwy '71, also dir), *Sugar* (Bdwy '72, also dir, 2 Tony noms), *Irene* (Bdwy '73 rev, dir only), *Mack and Mabel* (Bdwy '74, also dir, 2 Tony noms), *Rockabye Hamlet* (Bdwy

Gower Champion stretches while discussing a musical arrangement for a dance number with dance arranger Richard Priborg for **Three for the Show** (Columbia, 1953).

'76, also dir), *Annie Get Your Gun* (LACLO '77 rev, also dir), *A Broadway Musical* (Bdwy '78, also dir), *42nd Street* (Bdwy '80, also dir, Tony Award and Drama Desk awards for choreo)

TV: "The Admiral Revue" ('49, also appeared), Omnibus Spectacular "Fifty Five Minutes from Broadway," "Accent on Love," "A New Look at Love" ('59, also appeared), "The Dinah Shore Show," "The Bell Telephone Hour," Mary Martin Special, 42nd Annual Academy Awards Show ('69, also dir), Julie Andrews Special ('69, also prod, dir)

Nightclub/Concert: Acts for Gower and Jeanne (1935–42), Marge and Gower Champion (1946–50), Jane Powell ('58)

Film (All listings except two designate films in which Champion also appeared):

1939 **The Projection Room**— Vitaphone (S) (appears as Gower and Jeanne, uncredited)

1950 **Mr. Music**— Par (screen debut with Marge)

1951 **Show Boat**— MGM (with Robert Alton, appeared with Marge, uncredited)

Two Tickets to Broadway— RKO (with Busby Berkeley, Ann Miller, uncredited and assisted by Bobby Scheerer, did not appear)

1952 **Everything I Have Is Yours**— MGM (with Nick Castle, appeared with Marge)

Lovely to Look At— MGM (with Hermes Pan, appeared with Marge, uncredited)

1953 **Give a Girl a Break**— MGM (with Stanley Donen, Bob Fosse, Bill Foster, appeared with Marge)

1955 **Jupiter's Darling**— MGM (with Hermes Pan, appeared with Marge, uncredited)

Three for the Show— Col (with Jack Cole, appeared with Marge)

1957 **The Girl Most Likely**— RKO (choreo only, assisted by Jack Regas, did not appear)

MARGE CHAMPION (MARJORIE CELESTE BELCHER)

b. Los Angeles, California, September 2, 1919

Daughter of pioneering film choreographer and dance educator Ernest Belcher, this unique dancer, actress, teacher and choreographer began classes with her father at the age of 5 and grew up in Hollywood, working as the live-action model for Walt

Marge Champion lifts a leg in this 1957 publicity still taken in Cleveland, flanked by Jack Whiting on the left and her father, Ernest Belcher, on the right.

Disney as the title character in **Snow White and the Seven Dwarfs** ('37), the "Blue Fairy" in **Pinocchio** ('40), as well as the choreography for the hippos in ***The Dance of the Hours*** in **Fantasia** ('40). Briefly appearing with partner Louis Hightower in clubs and onstage in *Tonight at 8:30* on the West Coast, she began her onscreen film career with Hightower (as Louis and Celeste) in **Sunday Night at the Trocodero** (a '37 MGM short), continuing with a role in **The Story of Vernon and Irene Castle** ('39) and appeared in the western **Honor of the West** ('39) as "Marjorie Bell." She danced onstage in her father's Hollywood Bowl ballets and the LACLO productions of *Blossom Time* and *The*

Student Prince, had roles in *The Little Dog Laughed* (OOT '40) and *Portrait of a Lady* (OOT '41), and made Broadway appearances in *Dark of the Moon*, *Beggar's Holiday* and *What's Up?* She had first met Gower Champion in junior high school and later was reintroduced to him at her father's school. In 1946 they began to work together and created a landmark dance act which took them to unprecedented TV, Broadway (*Three for Tonight*, '55) and film stardom. With the decline of the movie musical, Gower began choreographing and directing exclusively for the stage and Marge assisted him on the various companies of *Bye Bye Birdie* and *Carnival* and was later associate choreographer to Tommy Tune on *Stepping Out* ('87). Separated from Gower in 1971, she continued as an actress in such films as **The Swimmer** ('67) and **The Party** ('68) and her later performance credits include **N.R.A.** (San Francisco Ballet '76) and *A 5-6-7-8-Dance* at Radio City Music Hall ('83). Calling her choreographic approach "Dance Design" ("It's like choreography, only with actors who are not dancers") she created works for stage, TV and film. Having taught dance at her father's studio from the age of 15, in later years, she joined the faculty of the Los Angeles Mafundi Institute. Honored with the Legend of Dance Award in 1991, she serves on the Board at Jacob's Pillow, the Williamstown Theatre Festival and was made a member of the Tony Award committee by the League of American Theaters in 1992. On July 12–13, 1995, the Film Society of Lincoln Center paid tribute to the Champion's contributions to dance on film.

Stage: And Where She Stops Nobody Knows (LA '76), *Stepping Out* (Bdwy '87, associate choreo with Tommy Tune), *Lute Song* (Berkshire Theatre Festival, also dir), *She Loves Me* (Berkshire Theatre Festival), *Ballroom* (Long Beach CLO '92)

TV: "The Awakening Land" mini-series ('81, also dialogue supervisor), "Ike" mini-series ('79, with Miriam Nelson)

Film:
1940 **Fantasia**—RKO (with George Balanchine)
1974 **Queen of the Stardust Ballroom**—Tomorrow Ent (TV) (Emmy winner, assisted by Frank Veloz)
1975 **The Day of the Locust**—Par (with Miriam Nelson)
1981 **When the Circus Came to Town**—CBS (TV)
        Whose Life Is It Anyway?—MGM

CHARLES (SPENCER) CHAPLIN
b. East Lane, Walworth, London, April 16, 1889
d. Corsier-sur-Vevey, Switzerland, December 25, 1977

Chaplin's comic genius and film innovations are so internationally acclaimed that his dance creativity is virtually ignored. Born of a theatrical mother and father, Chaplin made his first stage appearance at the age of 5. He toured for years in English music-hall, combining dance, pantomime and music for his performances, observing the vast array of talent around him and incorporating clog dance into his work. Making his American stage debut at the Colonial Theatre in New York on October 3, 1910, he began his legendary film career with the Keystone Company in 1914. He made scores of shorts until 1921, when he made his first "feature," **The Kid**. His film work always contained choreographed routines and sequences, invented by Chaplin himself, but uncredited. Martha Graham once said about the comic genius: "In a deep sense Chaplin is a dancer because he has always danced his roles. He also has a complete awareness of movement" and Nijinsky, Pavlova and W.C. Fields dubbed him "the greatest ballet dancer that ever lived." The true creator of dance as satire on film, he was finally given an honorary Oscar by the AMPAS in 1972.

Autobiography: "*My Autobiography*" (1954)
Film (All credits are for films which have traditional dance sequences in which Chaplin also appeared):
1914 **Tango Tangles**—Keystone (S)
        Tillie's Punctured Romance—Essanay
1915 **Burlesque on Carmen**—Essanay
1916 **The Count**—Essanay
1919 **Sunnyside**—First Ntl
1921 **The Idle Class**—First Ntl
1922 **The Pilgrim**—First Ntl
1925 **The Gold Rush**—UA
1936 **Modern Times**—UA
1940 **The Great Dictator**—UA
1955 **Limelight**—UA (with Andre Eglevsky, Melissa Hayden, Carmelita Maracci, received screen credit for choreo)

WILLIAM CHAPPELL
b. Wolverhampton Staffs, England, September 27, 1908
d. London, England, January 1, 1994

Named "one of the founding dancers of British ballet" in his obituary in *Dance Magazine*, this Renaissance man also choreographed, directed, designed costumes and scenery for film and stage productions, as well as being the author of *Studies in Ballet* ('48) and *Margot Fonteyn: Impressions of a Ballerina* ('51). After studying design at the Chelsea Arts School he was determined to become a dancer and began studying ballet with Marie Rambert at 17 and later with Léonide Massine and Bronislava Nijinska. He started his remarkable career as a

Charles Chaplin uses his dance talents for laughs in **The Great Dictator** (UA, 1940).

dancer with Ballet Rambert and later danced with the Ida Rubenstein, Ballet Club, Camargo Society and Vic-Wells ballet companies, while also making stage musical appearances in *Helen!* and *A Kiss in Spring* ('32). In addition to designing the decor and costumes for many ballets, he also designed the costumes for **The Winslow Boy** ('50) and appeared in the films **Flesh and Blood** ('51) and **The Trial** ('63). He directed plays and revues on the London stage (*Where's Charley?*, *Passion Flower Hotel*, etc.) until 1974.

    Stage (All London credits): *Evangeline* ('46, with Therese Langfield), *A La Carte* ('48), *The Lyric Revue* ('51, also dir), *The Globe Revue* ('52, also dir), *High Spirits* and *At the Lyric* ('53, also dir), *Going to Town* ('54, also dir), *Espresso Bongo* and *Living for Pleasure* ('58, also dir), *On the Avenue* ('61, also dir), *So Much to Remember* ('63, also dir)

    Film:
1952 **Moulin Rouge**— UA (also appeared)
1957 **The Prince and the Showgirl**— WB

NICO CHARISSE
    b. Athens, Greece, 1906
    d. Las Vegas, Nevada, April 14, 1970
    Dancer, choreographer, author and teacher who

began his career as one of eleven children who toured Europe and Africa as Mme. Charisse and her Children. Mother Calliope Charisse was a friend of Isadora Duncan and insisted that her entire family dance "to divert them from World War I." After touring Europe — and Mme. Charisse being decorated by the French government "for idealizing the concept of the French mother"— an RKO talent scout saw the family in Algiers and brought them to America in 1923. They appeared as headliners for the opening of the New York Hippodrome and toured on the Orpheum circuit in vaudeville. Nico (child #3) had begun his ballet training in 1916 with the Paris Opera. In 1926, he was the fencing master at the University of Michigan and began teaching ballet at the Fanchon and Marco school in Hollywood. It was there that he met and married student Tula Ellice Finklea, who would take the stage name "Cyd Charisse." After dancing as a member of the San Francisco Opera Ballet Company, Nico returned to Hollywood to open his own school, financed by tobacco heiress Doris Duke, who took private lessons there. Two of his sisters, Kathryn Etienne and Nenette Charisse, were among the most influential dance teachers in America (Nenette married choreographer Robert Tucker and her son, Paris Theodore, married Lee Becker). From

1944–46 Nico coached in New York and returned to Hollywood as dance director at MGM in 1946. He was contracted as dance master at Walt Disney Studios in 1948. Author of *Nico Charisse on Ballet for Today* ('51), in a chapter entitled "Ballet in Hollywood," he wrote: "Choreography for motion pictures differs quite a bit from work for the stage. To be effective it must be broader and slower and depend on group movement, counterpoint and composition rather then on a great deal of technical and animated intricacies." In the 1960s, he relocated to Las Vegas to open a theatrical agency, teach ballet, and give seminars around the country until his death three years later. He is survived by two sons, Nicky and Mark.

　　Nightclub/Concert: Earl Carroll Revues (NY '38), *Vegas A Go-Go* ('66), etc.

　　Miscellaneous: Glamorama (Beauty and Fashion Expo, LA '54)

　　Film:

1939 **Balalaika**— MGM (with Ernst Matray, uncredited for the *Prince Igor* ballet)

1940 **Rhumba Serenade**— Soundies Corp (S) (also appeared with Cyd Charisse, uncredited)

1943 **The Sultan's Daughter**— Mon (with John Alton)

1944 **Hollywood Canteen**— WB (assistant to LeRoy Prinz)

TONY CHARMOLI
b. Mountain Iron, Minnesota

Choreographer, producer and director whose prolific TV and nightclub creations have been seen by millions. His television choreography helped to change the face of— and set the standard for — televised dance sequences. One of nine children, he began his dance training in Minnesota with Ida Canossa. He danced with the Gertrude Lippincott group in Minneapolis and spent a summer with Ted Shawn's historic all male ensemble at Jacob's Pillow. After serving in the Air Corps during World War II — as well as dancing and directing for a USO troupe in the Panama Canal Zone — he attended St. Thomas College in St. Paul as a Speech and English major, graduating Cum Laude. He then moved to New York to study with Martha Graham, Roland Guerard, Hanya Holm, José Limon, Robert Pageant and Helen Platova. Following his interests in dance creation, he joined the Choreographer's Workshop and then helped form a group called Theatre Dance Inc. His first TV choreography was for a New York ABC-TV series "Stop the Music" in 1949 and he quickly became one of television's most acclaimed choreographers during its Golden Age. Receiving multiple Emmy awards for his choreography and the *Dance Magazine* Award ('54), his career progressed to television direction ("The

Bugaloos," "Captain and Tennille," "Lidsville," "Star Search" 1992–93, etc.)

　　Stage: Il Terrone Corre Sol Filo (Italy '54), *Ankles Aweigh* (Bdwy '55), *Dumas and Son* (Bdwy '67), *Viola, Violin and Viola D'Amore* (Rome '67), *Woman of the Year* (Bdwy '81)

　　TV (Partial listing): "Stop the Music" ('49), "Your Hit Parade" ('50–55, 2 Emmy nom, one Emmy award), "The Dinah Shore Chevy Show," "The Danny Kaye Show," "The Bell Telephone Hour," Specials for Cyd Charisse, Bobby Darin, Danny Kaye, Jane Powell ('61), "Around the World with Nellie Bly" ('60, also prod), "Rainbow of Stars" ('62), 40th Annual Academy Awards show ('67), "The Julie Andrews Hour" ('72–73, also dir, Emmy nom), "Mitzi … A Tribute to the American Housewife" ('73, Emmy award),"Shirley MacLaine — Gypsy in My Soul" ('75, Emmy award), "Cher" ('75–76), "John Denver and the Muppets," "Mitzi Zings Into Spring" ('77, Emmy nom), "Julie Andrews and Rudolph Nureyev — Invitation to the Dance," "Lily Tomlin — Sold Out" ('80, Emmys for dir and choreo)

　　Nightclub/Concert: Juliet Prowse Show (Winter Garden, NY '62); *Folies Bergère* (Tropicana Hotel, LV '64 & '68); acts for Kaye Ballard, the Beachboys, Cyd Charisse, Mitzi Gaynor, Bobbie Gentry, Lisa Kirk, Carol Lawrence, Eleanor Powell, Juliet Prowse, Dinah Shore, Kay Starr, Helen Traubel, Leslie Uggams, etc.

　　Miscellaneous: SHARE *Boomtown* Show ('65)

　　Film:

1965 **The Loved One**— MGM

1971 **What's the Matter with Helen?**— UA (assisted by Tad Tadlock)

NIGEL CHARNOCK
1992 **Edward II**— Fine Line Features (with Floyd Newsom)

XAVIER CHATMAN
1976 **Revenge of the Cheerleaders**— Monarch

FELIX CHAVEZ
b. Polvadera, New Mexico, January 3, 1933

Chavez's expertise in ballroom dance — particularly the Argentine Tango, Salsa, Bolero and other forms of Latin dance —finally found its way onto film in 1990 with **Lambada, the Forbidden Dance.** He studied drama at the University of New Mexico and ballet with Ballet Borealis in Minneapolis, Minn., appearing with them in *Scheherazade*, and then began his extensive ballroom training with the Arthur Murray, Fred Astaire and other leading ballroom dance studios and teachers. After serving in the Armed Forces during the Korean conflict (where he was also South Pacific middleweight boxing champion) drama studies continued at the Lee Strasberg Theatre Institute in Los Angeles. His career began as a performer: featured in plays in California, in Las Vegas in *Fantasia International*, on Sitmar and Royal Viking Cruise Lines and nightclubs throughout the world, before he concentrated on exhibition dancing and teaching. Winner of the Feather Award for his exhibition dancing with various partners, his choreography and staging talents also include fencing sequences.

TV: "Lifestyles of the Rich and Famous," "Saturday Night Dance Fever," "The Home Show," "Days of Our Lives," "Cara A Cara," commercials for General Telephone, etc.

Music Video: "The Art of Dancing Dirty" — instructional video

Film:

19?? **How to Murder a Millionaire** — CBS (TV)

1990 **Lambada, the Forbidden Dance** — Cannon (with Miranda Garrison)

SEAN CHEESMAN

With a healthy background of experience in music videos and television, Cheesman's film choreographic credits began with one of the biggest film hits of 1992, **The Bodyguard.**

TV: 1991 MTV Music Video Awards (Prince's appearance), "The Ryte Divine" Specials, "Guys Next Door"; commercials for Publix Supermarkets, Lotto (Spain).

Music Video (Partial listing): "I'm Every Woman" — Whitney Houston; "Insatiable," "Cream," "Diamonds and Pearls," "Get Off" — Prince; "Get on Up," "Go Go Dancer" — Carmen; "If," "This Time" — Janet Jackson; "Running Back to You," "You've Got That Look" — Vanessa Williams; "Scream" — Michael and Janet Jackson (with Tina Landon, Travis Payne, Lavelle Smith, MTV nom '95)

Nightclub/Concert: Karyn White 1989 tour

Miscellaneous: Industrials for Sun Ice, General Motors Olympic Promotions

Film:

1992 **The Bodyguard** — WB (also appeared)

SI-LAN CHEN

b. China

As the daughter of the Chinese foreign minister, this eventual dancer-choreographer was educated in England. Due to her father's assignments, she began her dance training in Russia with Kasyan Goleizovsky and after gaining the honor of being the first foreign artist to dance at the Moscow Con-

servatory since Isadora Duncan, she enjoyed success as a modern dance leader in Russia. Emigrating to the United States, she made her New York concert debut on January 30, 1938 with the *American Dancer* review observing, "Although ballet-trained, Miss Chen bases her compositions on free realistic movement more in the 'modern' manner with precise skill in execution... Her satires are pantomimically lucid — with mime not an interlude but woven into the fiber of the dance." With Miriam Blecher, Jane Dudley, Sophie Maslow and Lily Mehlman she formed the New Dance Group in 1938 and represented the Chinese government with performances at the 1939 New York World's Fair. In addition to her film choreography, She appeared in the films **The Keys of the Kingdom** ('44), **South Sea Sinner** ('50) and **Peking Express** ('51). In the mid '50s, she continued to present her choreographic works at the New York Ballet Club Choreographer's night.

Ballet/Dance Pieces (Partial listing): "Landlord on a Horse," "Two Chinese Women," "Shanghai Sketches," "Peach Blossom Lady," "National Dances of the Soviet East," "Deluxe Debutante," "Española," "Chinese Student — Dedication," etc.

Film:

1946 **Anna and the King of Siam** — Fox (also appeared)

1947 **Slave Girl** — Univ

ANNA CHESELSKA

1955 **Soldier of Fortune** — Fox (assistant to Stephen Papich)

1974 **The Girl from Petrovka** — Univ

YVAN CHIFRE

1975 **Lancelot du Lac** (aka **Lancelot of the Lake**)   (Fr/Ital)

JUN CHONG

Martial arts specialist.

Film:

1988 **Silent Assassins** — Action Bros (also appeared)

PATRICK CHU

b. Hong Kong

Chinese-born American dancer and choreographer.

Film:

1988 **Illusory Thoughts** — Patrick Chu Prod (also dir, writer, prod, star)

GEORGE CHUNG

Fight choreographer.
1986 **Low Blow**— Crown Intl

MARISA CIAMPAGLIA

1963 **The Vampire and the Ballerina** (aka **Seddok** and **Atom Age Vampire**)- Lopert

IMOGEN CLAIRE

British actress, dancer and choreographer who appeared in **Savage Messiah** and **Henry VII and His Six Wives** ('72), **Liztomania** and **Tommy** ('75), **Flash Gordon** ('80) and **Shock Treatment** ('81).
Stage: *Katie Mulholland* (Eng '83), *The Lion, the Witch and the Wardrobe* (Eng '84)
Film:
1988 **The Lair of the White Worm**— Vestron (also appeared)
1989 **The Rainbow**— Vestron

MALCOLM CLARE

1960 **Sands of the Desert**— Warner/Pathé
Tommy the Toreador— Warner/Pathé

CLIVE CLARK

1995 **Blue Juice**— Film Four International

LES CLARK

d. London, England, March, 1959
American dancer-choreographer who danced in such films as **Easter Parade** and worked closely with Dan Dailey as coach and dance-in for the star. In 1958, he appeared at the Sahara Hotel in Las Vegas and died the following year while working on a TV series in London with Dan Dailey.
Film:
1947 **Mother Wore Tights**— Fox (assistant to Seymour Felix with Angie Blue))
1948 **Give My Regards to Broadway**— Fox (assistant to Seymour Felix)
When My Baby Smiles at Me— Fox (assistant to Seymour Felix with Angie Blue)
You Were Meant for Me— Fox (with Kenny Williams)
1949 **You're My Everything**— Fox (assistant to Nick Castle)
1950 **I'll Get By**— Fox (assistant to Larry Ceballos)
My Blue Heaven— Fox (assistant to Billy Daniel, Seymour Felix)
1951 **Call Me Mister**— Fox (assistant to Busby Berkeley)
1953 **The Girl Next Door**— Fox (assistant to Richard Barstow, Michael Kidd)

1954 **White Christmas**— Par (assistant to Robert Alton)
1958 **I Married a Woman**— RKO (with Peggy Gordon)

RUSSELL CLARK

b. Philadelphia, Pennsylvania
Contemporary dance innovator, teacher, actor and producer whose father, Steve Clark, is a member of The Clark Brothers tap dancing team — who are still dancing. Living with his father in Europe and America, Russell studied dance in London, Paris and Boston with Consuelo Atlas, Yvonne Gobé, Molly Molloy and Albert Pesso. European stage performances were followed by acting and dancing appearances on film in **Xanadu** ('80), **Body Rock** ('84), **Vamp** ('86) and **Fright Night, Part II** ('89). As one of the leading dance figures in film and television in the '90s, Clark experiments with the latest technical advances ("morphing") and uses New Rock Jazz to create startling dance images. Nominated for an Emmy in 1985, he received Billboard and MTV Awards for his music video choreographic creation in 1986. With Tony Selznick he created Russell Clark Productions to encourage promising young dancers and they annually present a "Winner's Dance Industry Showcase."
Stage: *Water Engine*
TV (Partial listing): "Cop Rock" ('90), "Murder She Wrote," "American Music Awards," "The Tonight Show," "Arsenio Hall Show," "Falcon Crest," "Midnite Special," "Into the Night," "Red Shoe Diaries," "Super Model of the World" ('92), "Townsend Television" ('93, NAACP Image Award nom), "Melrose Place"; commercials for Pepsi, Sprite, Miller, Chrysler, McDonalds, Plymouth, Life Savers, Disneyland State Fair, Suntory Whiskey, Taco Bell, etc.
Music Video (Over 100— partial listing): "Badder"— Michael Jackson (with Michael Jackson); "This Song"— George Harrison; "Day in Day Out"— David Bowie; "I'm Not Perfect"— Grace Jones; "Sexual Healing"— Marvin Gaye; "Operator"— Little Richard; "Bad Boys"— Miami Sound Machine; "Rough Boys"— ZZ Top; "Give It Up and You Won't See Me Cry" and "Hold On"— Wilson Phillips; "3 O'Clock Jump"— Herb Alpert; "Do It to Me"— Lionel Richie; "Sex as a Weapon"— Pat Benatar; "Hearts on Fire"— Steve Winwood.
Night Club/Concert: Jade, Morris Day, Jeffrey Osbourne, Berlin, Irene Cara (African tour); Wilson Phillips, Stacy Earl, *Wade 200* with Brooke Shields
Miscellaneous: Ford Supermodels 1991
Film:
1976 **Cinderella**— Group 1
1980 **Xanadu**— Univ (associate to Kenny Ortega, with Gene Kelly, Jerry Trent, also appeared)

1982 **Annie**— Col (with Joe Layton, coach for Albert Finney)

    Blade Runner— WB

1984 **Body Rock**— New World (associate to Joanne Divito, Susan Scanlan — also appeared)

    Calendar Girl Murders— ABC (TV)

    Starman— Par (Jeff Bridges' movement coach)

1986 **Vamp**— New World (also appeared)

1988 **I'm Gonna Git You Sucka**— UA

    Moonwalker— WB (with Michael Jackson, Vincent Paterson)

    Two Moon Junction— Lorimar

1989 **Earth Girls Are Easy**— Vestron (with Sarah Elgart, ISO, Wayne "Crescendo" Ward, "Cause I'm a Blonde" number credit)

    Fright Night — Part 2— New Century — Vista

    Teen Witch— Trans World (with Bob Banas)

1990 **Rockula**— Cannon (with Toni Basil)

1991 **Cadence**— New Line

    Clifford— Dinosaur (associate to Vincent Paterson)

1992 **Desire and Hell at Sunset Motel**— Two Moon Releasing

    Doppleganger— Two Moon Releasing

    The Edge of Innocence— Triumph Releasing

    The Water Engine— Turner Pictures (TV)

1994 **House Party III**— New Line Cinema

1995 **The Crossing Guard**— Miramax

    Devil in a Blue Dress— TriStar

    Major Payne— Univ

HOPE CLARKE

b. Washington, D.C., March 23, 1941

In the 1993 TV special "Story of a People — Expressions in Black", this versatile African-American actress, dancer and choreographer said: "I never trained to be a choreographer and I never was interested in being a choreographer. This seemed to just happen. I was a performer and I've always been a performer and someone said: 'Why don't you try it? You've done so many shows' and so, I said: 'Okay' and I found out I have a very good eye. I think from my dance training my eye has been quite finely honed. I know where to put people on stage and how to make them move and that's how it happened…it wasn't something that I wanted to do … I never trained for it… It's nice to be the power!" She gained her wide dance vocabulary from studies at the Jones-Haywood School and with Alma Davis, Luigi and Matt Mattox and acting lessons from David Le Grant. Making her professional debut in 1960 in *West Side Story*, she continually appeared on and off-Broadway from 1961 to 1985

in *Kwamina*, Katherine Dunham's *Bambouche, Hallelujah Baby!, But Never Jam Today, Purlie, Don't Bother Me, I Can't Cope, Nigger Nightmare, Black Visions* and *Grind*, simultaneously appearing on television and in the films **Change of Mind, Book of Numbers, Going Home, In the Heat of the Night, A Piece of the Action** and **Beat Street**. As a soloist she danced with the Talley Beatty, Louis Johnson and George Faison dance companies, as well as Alvin Ailey's American Dance Theatre. Progressing from her successful performance career to choreography with *Dead Wood Dick: Legend of the West* at the LA Inner City Cultural Center in the early 1980s, she has since added direction (operas and musicals) credits to her diversified career. Winner of a Tony award for her innovative work in *Jelly's Last Jam* ('92) and critical praise for her 1995 staging and direction of *Porgy and Bess*, she credits Talley Beatty as being a major influence in her life and work.

Stage: *Deadwood Dick: Legend of the West* (LA), *Black Nativity* (Ford Theatre, D.C.), *Frida* (Houston Grand Opera/Brooklyn Academy of Music), *Spunk* (OOT), *Lost in the Stars* (NY), *O Freedom, To Broadway with Love* (Bdwy), *A— My Name Is Alice* (OB '84), *In the House of the Blues* (OB '85), *The Caucasian Chalk Circle* (Public Theater), *The Colored Museum* (Crossroads Theater Co., New Brunswick, NJ, '85), *Jelly's Last Jam* (Bdwy '92, with Gregory Hines and Ted L. Levy, Tony award), *A— My Name Is Still Alice* (OB '92), *Sweet and Hot— The Songs of Harold Arlen* (OOT '93), *Porgy and Bess* (Houston Grand Opera '95, dir), *The Tempest* (NY Shakespeare Festival '95)

TV: "The Colored Museum" and "Square One" (PBS); commercials for Carl's Jr., Earth, Wind and Fire

Music Video: "Rhythm of the Night"— Debarge; also videos for Earth, Wind and Fire

Nightclub/Concert: *Here's to the Ladies* (Alaska Black Caucus); acts for Earth, Wind and Fire, Robert Guillame, Deniece Williams,

Ballet/Dance Pieces: "Legacy" ('93)

Film:

1981 **Body and Soul**— Cannon (with Valentino)

FRANCES CLAUDET

b. Ottawa, Canada

Renowned ice choreographer and director whose live creations were seen for multiple seasons in *Ice Follies* productions. A Canadian figure skating champion, Olympic competitor and instructor, she began with the *Ice Follies* as a featured skater. Called "A patient but demanding overseer at countless rehearsals necessary to mould each routine into sheer perfection" in the *Follies* souvenir program, her early work was captured on film in 1939 by MGM.

Miscellaneous: *Ice Follies* ('38–65)
Film:
1939 **Ice Follies of 1939**—MGM (with Val Raset)

JOHN CLIFFORD

b. Hollywood, California, June 12, 1947

Born into a theatrical family, John Clifford made his professional debut at the age of 5 as a human prop for his parents' acrobatic act. He began dance lessons at 11 with Kathryn Etienne and was selected that year to appear as "The Prince" in New York City Ballet's *The Nutcracker* at Los Angeles' Greek Theater. After gaining further dance training at the American School of Dance in Hollywood from Irina Kosmovska and Eugene Loring, Clifford danced with the Ballet of Guatemala and Western Ballet. Earlier commercial performances on TV ("Death Valley Days," "The Danny Kaye Show" and a Carol Channing special) exposed him to various forms of dance and he began choreographing at the age of 16 with a Los Angeles summer stock production of *West Side Story*. He joined NYC Ballet in 1967, being promoted to soloist in 1973. He began to focus on choreography and created multiple works for NYC Ballet, Andre Eglevsky Ballet, San Francisco Ballet, Western Ballet, Royal Winnepeg Ballet and German Opera Ballet in Berlin. In 1974, he founded the Los Angeles Ballet, a landmark West Coast company. When the company experienced financial difficulties and disbanded in 1985, Clifford continued to contribute dance pieces to companies around the world.

Ballet/Dance Pieces (Partial listing): "Stravinsky Symphony" ('68), "Fantasies," "Prelude, Fugue and Riffs," "The Class," "Sarabande and Dance," "Night in the Tropics," "Symphony in E Flat," "Bartok No. 3," Concerto Fantasy," "Gershwin Concerto," "Souvenir de Florence" and "Escenas de Ballet" (Teatro Colon, '85)
Film:
1981 **Modern Problems**—Fox
1989 **Skin Deep**—Fox

LISA CLYDE

1994 **The Swan Princess**—Col/TriStar

JACK COLE (JOHN EWING RICHTER)

b. New Brunswick, New Jersey, April 27, 1914
d. Los Angeles, California, February 17, 1974
Legendary jazz-influenced dancer, actor, chore-

ographer and teacher who used many Asian and African dance forms and rhythms in his unique style, making drastic changes and immense contributions to stage and film dance during the 1940s and '50s. Taking his name from his stepfather, William Cole, he ran away from home at 16 to study and appear with the Denishawn troupe and subsequently danced with Ted Shawn's all-male group and the Doris Humphrey and Charles Weidman companies. He began his commercial career with partner Alice Dudley, debuting at The Embassy Club, New York, 1934, and they appeared in *Caviar* and *Thumbs Up* on Broadway in 1934, *Venus in Silk* (OOT) and *May Wine* (Bdwy) in 1935. Cole's other stage appearances include *The School for Husbands* (Bdwy '33, with the Weidman Troupe), *Princess Turandot* (Westport County Playhouse '37), *Nice Goin'* (OOT '39, with his dancers), *The Big Show* (Casa Mañana '39), *Keep 'Em Laughing* (Bdwy '42, also asst choreographer) and *Ziegfeld Follies* (Bdwy '43) and he made his solo Broadway choreographic debut with *Something for the Boys* ('43). Signed to open the Rainbow Room at the top of the RCA Building in Manhattan with Dudley, they created a sensation but eventually parted. He formed his first dance group in 1936 to appear at the Rainbow Room and throughout his career would continue to gather superb dancers who could interpret his one-of-a-kind style to appear in theaters and nightclubs throughout the country (Radio City Music Hall, the Roxy, Casa Mañana, Ciro's, Slapsie Maxie's, Chez Paree, Fairmont Hotel, Dunes Hotel, etc.), often with Cole himself dancing. Broadway choreographic successes brought him to films in 1941 and although his first film choreography (and onscreen appearance) in **Moon Over Miami** was deleted because of censorship concerns, his future work would be the highlight of the films themselves. Under contract as dance director, he created an unprecedented dance ensemble at Columbia from 1944 to 1948 and brought sensuality to all of the female stars he created numbers for: Mitzi Gaynor, Betty Grable, Rita Hayworth, Ann Miller, Marilyn Monroe and Jane Russell (plus protégé-assistant Gwen Verdon), continuing to cause havoc with the film censors of the day. His film work also includes several onscreen appearances, always done as a last minute replacement for an injured dancer. He returned to Broadway in 1950 to appear in *Alive and Kicking* and continued to alternately create innovative stage and film successes until his death. Called "an upstart" and a "rebel" because of his outspoken criticism of dance and other choreographers, he was also considered "The Father of Jazz Dance," credited with influencing all of the theater choreographers who succeeded him. Cole's work was based on feelings from the inside of the dancer, rather than superimposed movement from the outside and

Jack Cole, looking appropriately mysterious and exotic, in a deleted section from "Solitary Seminole" from **Moon Over Miami** (20th Century–Fox, 1941).

he was constantly travelling and studying ethnic dance forms to incorporate into his work. In his last years he taught at UCLA and the Morro-Landis Studios. He received the *Dance Magazine* Award in 1949 in the "Musical Comedy" category for his work in *Magdalena* and again in 1955, the first time the award was given for film choreography. In Tokyo in 1982, the American Dance Machine presented *Jack*, a musical based on his life and work,

starring Wayne Cilento. More biographical theatrical projects about his life are continually announced, but as of this writing, are unproduced. Inducted posthumously into the 1992 Theater Hall of Fame, in 1993 the Spectrum Dance Theater of Seattle, Wash., added "A Tribute to Jack Cole" to their repertoire. On February 4, 1994, the Film Society of Lincoln Center presented a tribute. He was honored in 1995 by LA Dance with a Lifetime

Achievement Award, accepted on his behalf of Gwen Verdon.

Biography: *Unsung Genius* by Glenn Loney (1984)

Stage: *Nice Goin'* (OOT '39, with Al White, Jr.), *Ziegfeld Follies* (also appeared) and *Something for the Boys* (Bdwy '43), *Allah Be Praised* (Bdwy '44), *Bonanza Bound* (OOT '47), *Alive and Kicking* (Bdwy '50, also starred with the Jack Cole Dancers), *Jollyana* (LACLO '52, with Jack Donohue), *Carnival in Flanders* (Bdwy '53, with Helen Tamiris), *Kismet* (Bdwy '53), *Candide* (Bdwy) and *Ziegfeld Follies* (OOT '56), *Jamaica* (Bdwy '57), *Donnybrook!* (Bdwy '61, also dir), *Kean* (Bdwy '61, also dir), *Magdalena* (LA and Bdwy '62), *A Funny Thing Happened on the Way to the Forum* (Bdwy '62), *Zenda* (OOT '63), *Foxy* (Bdwy) and *Royal Flush* (OOT '64), *Man of La Mancha* (Bdwy '65, Tony nom), *Chu-Chem* (OOT '66, also appeared), *Bomarzo* (NY City Opera '67), *Mata Hari* (OOT '67), *Lolita, My Love* (OOT '71, replaced by Danny Daniels, Dan Siretta)

TV (Partial listing): The Bob Hope Show, "Your Show of Shows," "The Hollywood Palace," "The Ed Sullivan Show," "Perry Como's Kraft Music Hall" ('59, also appeared), Phil Silvers' Pontiac Special ('59)

Nightclub/Concert: Multiple appearances for Ballet Intime and the Jack Cole Dancers; shows for the Casino du Liban (Beirut, Lebanon), the Riviera (Havana) Dunes Hotel, (LV '60); acts for Frankie Vaughn, Betty Grable, Mitzi Gaynor, Jayne Mansfield

Ballet/Dance Pieces (Partial/Alphabetical listing): "Anna and the King of Siam," "Bali: Play Dance" & "Love Dance," "Begin the Beguine," "Bolero," "Blue Prelude," "Cuban Love Dance," "East Indian Hunting Dance," "Georgia Revival Meeting," "Harlequin's Odyssey, "Irish Wake," "Japanese Lanterns," "Latin Impressions," "Les Fleurs du Mal," "Minnie the Moocher," "Nanigo," "Oriental Impressions," "Pawnee Indian War Dance," "Persian Market," "Pink Champagne," "Polynesian Faun," "Reefer Madness," "Reefer Joint at 4 A.M," "Requiem for Jimmy Dean" ('73), "Sing, Sing, Sing," "Spring in Brazil," "War Dance of the Wooden Indians," "Wedding of a Solid Sender" ('40), "West Indian Impressions"

Film:

1941 **Moon Over Miami**— Fox (with Hermes Pan, the Condos Bros, appeared but deleted from the release print)

1944 **Cover Girl**— Col (with Stanley Donen, Seymour Felix, Gene Kelly, Val Raset)

Jammin' the Blues— WB (S) (with Archie Savage)

Kismet— MGM (later retitled **Oriental Dream**)

1945 **Eadie Was a Lady**— Col (with Ann Miller, also appeared partnering Miller in "I'm Gonna See My Baby")

Tonight and Every Night— Col (with Val Raset, also appeared partnering Rita Hayworth in "What Does an English Girl Think of a Yank?")

1946 **Gilda**— Col

The Jolson Story— Col (with Audrene Brier, Miriam Nelson, "Dances staged by" credit)

Tars and Spars— Col (with Ann Miller)

Thrill of Brazil— Col (with Nick Castle, Eugene Loring, Ann Miller, Frank Veloz)

1947 **Down to Earth**— Col (assisted by Harriet Ann Gray)

1951 **David and Bathsheba**— Fox (assisted by Gwen Verdon)

Meet Me After the Show— Fox (with Steve Condos, assisted by Gwen Verdon, also appeared partnering Betty Grable in "Bettin' on a Man")

On the Riviera— Fox (assisted by Gwen Verdon, also appeared in the ensemble)

1952 **Lydia Bailey**— Fox (also appeared dancing with Carmen DeLavallade)

The Merry Widow— MGM (assisted by Gwen Verdon)

1953 **The Farmer Takes a Wife**— Fox (assisted by Gwen Verdon)

Gentlemen Prefer Blondes— Fox (assisted by Gwen Verdon)

The "I Don't Care" Girl— Fox (with Seymour Felix)

1954 **The River of No Return**— Fox

There's No Business Like Show Business— Fox (with Robert Alton)

1955 **Gentlemen Marry Brunettes**— UA (assisted by Gwen Verdon)

Kismet— MGM

Three for the Show— Col (with Gower Champion)

1957 —**Designing Woman**— MGM (assisted by Barrie Chase, also appeared as "The Choreographer")

Les Girls— MGM (with Gene Kelly, assisted by Alex Romero)

1959 **Some Like It Hot**— UA (with Wally Green, musical staging of Marilyn Monroe's numbers, uncredited)

1960 **Let's Make Love**— Fox (assisted by Maggie Banks)

1965 **Marilyn**— Fox (numbers from Marilyn Monroe's Fox films)

1966 **A Funny Thing Happened on the Way to the Forum**— UA (original stage work adapted by George and Ethel Martin)

1994 **That's Entertainment! III**— MGM (with others)

LEO COLEMAN

b. Louisiana

African-American dancer, actor, costume designer, illustrator and choreographer who studied with Katherine Dunham and first attracted attention as the "Mute" in the 1950 stage and 1952 film versions of Gian Carlo Menotti's opera, *The Medium*. Moving to Europe for greater opportunities, he appeared in **La Dolce Vita** ('60) and choreographed several Italian films.

Film:
1954 **Woman of the River**— Col (Fr/Ital)
1960 **It Started in Naples**— Par
1961 **Fury of the Vikings** (aka **Erik the Conqueror**)— AIP

ROSS COLEMAN
1986 **Rebel**— Vestron
1991 **Sweet Talker**— New Line

BARRY COLLINS
1980 **The Fiendish Plot of Dr. Fu Manchu**— Orion

DEAN COLLINS
Forties social dance specialist who also performed a Jitterbug speciality in **Always a Bridesmaid** ('43)
1946 **Junior Prom**— Mon (also appeared)

GENE COLUMBUS
b. Pittsburgh, Pennsylvania, August 24, 1940
About his single film choreographic credit, Columbus candidly wrote, "As for **Stranded**, I believe Miriam Nelson was called to do the movie and I was working for her during a TV special at ABC ... she couldn't deal with it and asked me if I would handle it as I always aspired to be a choreographer. I jumped at the chance and had a really good time." Raised in Denver, Colorado, he got his first dance training at the Ballet Theater School and started his performance career in the Denver Post Light Opera Company productions of *Oklahoma!* and *Annie Get Your Gun*. After co-founding the Ballet Center Company of Denver, his search for more extensive training sent him to California, where he studied at the American School of Dance and with Roland Dupree, Michel Panaieff and Claude Thompson. Making his professional debut on TV in "The Steve Allen Show" (dancing the Twist with Chubby Checker) he appeared onstage in Los Angeles and San Bernardino Civic Light Opera productions; in films (**Billie**, **Clambake**, **Dr. Dolittle**, **Funny Girl**, **How to Commit Marriage**, **Speedway** and **Valley of the Dolls**), and on television (the "Lucy" and Jerry Lewis shows; "The Hollywood Palace," "Polka Parade," "Shindig," etc). He

was also one of the few selected by George Balanchine for the short-lived Ballet Los Angeles. While assisting Rod Alexander on a 1968 Hawaiian production of *Hello, Dolly!*, he met his future wife, Becky Walker. Although his original dream was to direct for television, he continued performing, choreographing and gaining behind-the-scenes experiences. After serving as the assistant stage manager for a Bobbie Gentry tour, he acted as ballet master and stage manager for the touring arena show *Disney on Parade* from 1969–77. He remained with the Disney organization, currently producing live entertainment special projects and events at Walt Disney World. The father of two sons, Robert and John, his wife, Becky, operates the successful Columbus Center Dance Academy in Orlando, Florida.

Stage: *The Boy Friend* (Colorado College), Colorado Centennial Pageant

TV: Commercials for Burger Chef ('70), Ford Falcon

Ballet/Dance Pieces: Multiple works for Ballet Center, Denver; Visalia and San Bernardino Symphony Orchestras

Film:
1966 **Stranded** (aka **Valley of Mystery**)— Univ (also appeared)

DAVID AND FERNANDA CONDI
1957 **Love Slaves of the Amazon**— Univ

THE CONDOS BROTHERS
Frank: b. Greece, 1906
Nick: b. South Philadelphia, Pennsylvania, 1915. d. Los Angeles, California, July 9, 1988
Steve: b. Pittsburgh, Pennsylvania, October 12, 1918. d. Lyon, France, September 16, 1990

Awe-inspiring tap team whose father happened to own a restaurant opposite a theatre in Philadelphia, where eldest brother Frank watched some of the greatest tap acts in America perform and became fascinated. After teaching himself to dance in his bedroom, he joined the Dan Fitch Minstrels in 1922. With Mateo Olvera, he formed the act King and King and in 1927, they were featured on Broadway in *Artists and Models*. After splitting up that act in 1929, Frank created the Condos Brothers with middle brother Nick and they danced in *Earl Carroll's Vanities* ('32), toured Europe (where they made one British film) and appeared together for eight years. In 1933, Frank left the act to perform as a single, with 14-year-old Steve joining Nick. Frank finally retired as a performer in 1937, to become a teacher and assistant choreographer to Danny Dare and Chester Hale. The new team of Nick and Steve enjoyed the greatest film success and exposure ("We did all of our own choreography and were given freedom to improvise"). In 1943, Nick married comedienne Martha Raye and stopped performing to act as her business advisor. Steve then teamed with Jerry Brandow for TV, nightclub and films until the mid-fifties. Steve continued to perform on Broadway: *Say Darling*, '58, and *Sugar*, '72 (in which director-choreographer Gower Champion allowed him to improvise his tap solo each performance) and in the film **Tap** ('89). He died off-stage after a sensational solo performance in *Stars and Tap* at the Festival of Dance in Lyon, France, in 1990. They often choreographed their dance routines to jazz arrangements and are acknowledged to be the masters of "Wings"—flipping their feet to the sides and beating out five rapid tap sounds with each foot—which served as the climax of their act. While appearing on Broadway in *Sugar*, Steve claimed that Frank was "the man behind the success...He worked out our routines and developed a way of practicing and sets of exercises using all parts of the muscles in our bodies." One of the few white tap dancing groups to be accepted—and praised—by the great African-American artists. Author Sally Sommer wrote in Steve's obituary in *The Village Voice*: "Condos was a purist, a jazz/tap improviser who cared about the elegance and accents of his rhythms. A true percussionist, he never was interested in traveling through space. In fact, he stayed in one place, weaving a tapestry of sound."

Stage: *Artists and Models* (Frank and Matty King, Bdwy '27), *Earl Carroll's Vanities* (Frank and Matty King, Bdwy '32), *Sugar* (Steve only, Bdwy '72, with Gower Champion)

Film (Credits are for their routines):
1932 **Midshipmaid Gob**— Gau/Brit
1936 **Dancing Feet**— Rep (Nick only, with Joseph Santley)
1937 **Wake Up and Live**— Fox (with Jack Haskell)
1938 **Happy Landing**— Fox (with Harry Losee)
1939 **Broadway Buckaroo**— Vitaphone (S)
1941 **In the Navy**— Univ (with Nick Castle)
  Moon Over Miami— Fox (with Jack Cole, Hermes Pan)
1944 **Hey Rookie!**— Col (with Stanley Donen, Ann Miller, Val Raset)
  Pin Up Girl— Fox (with Fanchon, Hermes Pan)
  Song of the Open Road— UA (with George Dobbs)
1946 **The Time, the Place and the Girl**— WB (with LeRoy Prinz)
1951 **Call Me Mister**— Fox (with Busby Berkeley, John Wray, Steve only)

Meet Me After the Show— Fox (with Jack Cole — Steve with Jerry Brandow)
1953 **She's Back on Broadway**— WB (with Gene Nelson, LeRoy Prinz — Steve with Jerry Brandow)

KIM CONNELL

1985 **Perfect**— Col (with Natalie Brown, Jerry Jackson, "aerobics routines by")

BOBBY (ROBERT) CONNOLLY

b. New York, New York, 1895
d. Encino, California, February 29, 1944

Dance and film director who began his professional career as a child with the Cohan and Harris Minstrels and continued as a dancer and stage manager on Broadway in *Hitchy Koo* ('20). A graduate of the Massachusetts Institute of Technology, Connolly switched his interests from engineering to dance as an associate of Ned Wayburn, from whom he learned the art of dance direction. He assisted Wayburn on Broadway musicals and taught at his renowned New York school of dance, although Connolly never had a formal dance class himself. He solo staged and directed many important Broadway musicals before resigning from *The Ziegfeld Follies* in 1933, because of "a series of impossible conditions" and was replaced by John Murray Anderson. Declaring bankruptcy, he relocated to Hollywood to work as dance director. Signing a contract with Warner Bros. in 1934, he was assigned first to color shorts and was considered to be the studio's "Ace in the Hole" during their well-publicized litigation with Busby Berkeley. An article in the April 19, 1935 edition of the *Los Angeles Times* even trumpeted, "Dance Director Arriving Soon. Bobby Connolly, the dance director who has been signed by Warner Bros., will arrive here within the week. That looks like rivalry for Busby Berkeley, who has been the champion stager of numbers." When Berkeley finally left the lot, Connolly stayed at Warners until 1938, moving then to MGM until his death in 1944. Although Connolly's work was typical of stage dancing of the early period, he will be remembered by musical film fans for the "We're Off to See the Wizard" step performed by Judy Garland, Bert Lahr, Ray Bolger and Jack Haley in **The Wizard of Oz** ('39). He also directed the non-musical films **Expensive Husbands** and **The Devil's Saddle Legion** ('37) and **The Patient in Room 18** ('38) and was preparing to create the musical numbers on loan to Republic for **Atlantic City** when he died.

Stage: *Good Morning Dearie* (Bdwy '21), *The*

The Condos Brothers — in hideous black wigs — dance in front of the less-than-authentic-Native-American-chorus in "Solitary Seminole" from **Moon Over Miami** (20th Century–Fox, 1941).

Desert Song, Honeymoon Lane and *Kitty's Kisses* (Bdwy '26), *Funny Face* (with Fred Astaire), *Good News!, Judy* and *Rufus Le Maire's Affairs* (Bdwy '27), *The New Moon* and *Treasure Girl* (Bdwy '28), *Follow Thru, Spring Is Here, Show Girl, Bamboola* (also dir) and *Sons o' Guns* (also dir) (Bdwy '29), *Flying High* and *Princess Charming* (also dir) (Bdwy '30), *America's Sweetheart, East Wind* and *Free for All* (Bdwy '31), *Take a Chance, Ballyhoo of 1932* and *Hot-Cha!* (Bdwy '32) and *Humpty Dumpty* (OOT '32, replacing George Hale), *Melody* (Bdwy '33), *Ziegfeld Follies of 1931* and *1934* (Bdwy)

Film:

1933 **Moonlight and Pretzels**— WB
Take a Chance— WB

1934 **Flirtation Walk**— WB (with Ruby Keeler)
What, No Men?— WB (S)

1935 **Broadway Hostess**— WB (Academy Award nom: "Playboy from Paree" number)
G-Men— WB
Go Into Your Dance— WB (Academy Award nom: "Latin from Manhattan" number, with Busby Berkeley, Ruby Keeler, also appeared)
Shipmates Forever— WB (with Ruby Keeler)

Stars Over Broadway— WB (with Busby Berkeley)
Sweet Adeline— WB
Sweet Music— WB (with Johnny Boyle)

1936 **Cain and Mabel**— WB (Academy Award nom: "I'll Sing You a 1000 Love Songs" number)
Changing of the Guard— Vitaphone (S)
Colleen— WB (with Ruby Keeler)
Sing Me a Love Song— WB
The Singing Kid— WB (replacing Busby Berkeley)
Sons o' Guns— WB (also screenplay)

1937 **A Day at the Races**— MGM (with Dave Gould)
The King and the Chorus Girl— WB
Melody for Two— WB (with Robert Vreeland)
Ready, Willing and Able— WB (Academy Award nom: "Too Marvelous for Words" number, with Ruby Keeler)

1938 **Fools for Scandal**— WB (also dir)
Out Where the Stars Begin— Vitaphone (S)
Swing Your Lady— WB

1939 **At the Circus**— MGM

Dancer Teddy Blue (left) describes how she skated from Duluth, Minnesota, to Hollywood in 34 days, arriving just in time to be selected by Bobby Connolly (far right) for **The King and the Chorus Girl** (Warner Bros., 1937) to Sheila Ray and Helen Blizzard (photo courtesy of the Academy of Motion Picture Arts and Sciences).

Honolulu—MGM (with Sammy Lee, Eleanor Powell)

The Wizard of Oz—MGM (with Busby Berkeley, Ray Bolger, assisted by Arthur Appel and Donna Massin)

1940 **Broadway Melody of 1940**—MGM (with Fred Astaire, Eleanor Powell)

Two Girls on Broadway—MGM (with Eddie Larkin, George Murphy)

1942 **For Me and My Gal**—MGM (with Busby Berkeley, Gene Kelly, George Murphy)

Rio Rita—Loews (with Vincente Minnelli, David Robel)

Ship Ahoy—MGM (with Eleanor Powell)

1943 **I Dood It**—MGM (with Eleanor Powell)

Three Cheers for the Girls—Vitaphone (S) (with Busby Berkeley)

1974 **That's Entertainment!**—MGM (with others)

1976 **That's Entertainment, Part II**—MGM (with others)

1984 **That's Dancing!**—MGM (with others)

1994 **That's Entertainment! III**—MGM (with others)

GAIL CONRAD

1996 **Isle of Lesbos**—Duce Films Intl

JOHNNY CONRAD

1952 **Jack and the Beanstalk**—WB (with Johnny Conrad and His Dancers)

LOU CONTE

After dancing on Broadway and in road tours, Conte moved to Chicago to open a studio. Founder and artistic director of the Hubbard Street Dance Chicago since 1977 "creating a brand of Broadway-based, theatrical hoofing that makes viewers want to jump out of their seats and cheer" (*Dance Magazine*, August, 1988), Conte's company performs works by Bob Fosse, Margo Sappington, Twyla Tharp and his own original jazz-based dance creations.

Ballet/Dance Pieces (Partial listing): "New Country," "The '40s," "At the Rosebud"

Film:

1992 **A League of Their Own**—Col

DIANA CONWAY

1995 **Man of the House**—Disney

JO COOK

1970 **Moon Zero Two**—WB

LESLIE COOK

1994 **Forrest Gump**—Par (with Lisa Estrada)

RALPH COOPER

b. New York, circa 1910
d. New York, August 4, 1992

Ralph Cooper was once described by a dancer who had worked for him as, "He served as an idol when black children had precious few ... and he was one who would eternally encourage and offer you his hand." Despite his many talents, Cooper is best remembered as the producer and emcee at the fabled Apollo Theatre in Harlem, NY, for nearly fifty years. Beginning as a dancer in nightclubs in the 1920s, he also appeared at the Lafayette Theatre in Harlem in a dance act with Eddie Rector. Later, he led two bands, The San Domingans and the Kongo Knights. His handsome looks and suave personality moved him into film acting, with featured roles in the 1936 Fox films **Lloyds of London** and **White Hunter**. Realizing the potential of films for the large, untapped African-American audience, he co-founded Million Dollar Productions, a landmark company in the history of black cinema. He wrote, co-directed and cast himself in the lead in their first production (**Dark Manhattan**, '37) which led *Variety* to say: "Ralph Cooper, its star, is the stand-out." He continued writing screenplays, directing and starring in **Bargain with Bullets** ('37), **The Duke Is Tops** ('38), **Am I Guilty?** and **Gang War** ('40) for Million Dollar and Supreme. He then began his longtime career at the Apollo Theatre, eventually co-authoring the book *Amateur Night at the Apollo* in 1990. His son, Ralph Cooper II, carries on his elegant tradition.

Film:

1930 **Harlem Cabaret**—?

1936 **Poor Little Rich Girl**—Fox (with Jack Haskell, assisted by Geneva Sawyer)

LUCIA COPPOLA

1993 **Mina Tannenbaum**—IMA Films

DON CORREIA

b. San Jose, California, August 28, 1951

Correia began his dance training at the age of 5—after a teacher noticed him dancing in the corner when he visited classes with his sister—similar to the character of "Mike" he would eventually portray onstage in *A Chorus Line*. He attended San Jose State College before starting his show business career with the Ann Garvin Dance Company, a San Francisco-based group. After a stint with the Folies Bergere in Las Vegas he moved to Los Angeles for TV and nightclub work, adding to his skills as an actor-singer-dancer. He appeared on Broadway in *A Chorus Line, Perfectly Frank, Little Me, Sophisticated Ladies, A 5-6-7-8 Dance!* (Radio City Music Hall), *My One and Only* and attained Broadway stardom in the Gene Kelly role in *Singin' in the Rain*. Other performance credits include the nightclub acts of Ann-Margret, Goldie Hawn and Shirley MacLaine, on TV in "Baryshnikov on Broadway" and the Cheryl Ladd Special and he made his film debut in **Annie** ('82). Married to dancer-actress Sandy Duncan, they appeared together in *My One and Only* and a 1993 tour of *Cole*. He has since retired from performing and puts his talents into real estate and raising a family.

Film:
1988 **My Stepmother Is an Alien**— Col

MARILYN CORWIN
1989 **Fat Man and Little Boy**— Par (with Kurt Kaynor)

MELISSA COTTLE
1992 **The Man Without a World**— Milestone

EDWARD COURT
1937 **Pick a Star**— Hal Roach/MGM

ROBIN COUSINS
b. Bristol, England, August 17, 1957

Olympic Gold Medalist who has combined his multiple talents to become one of the best choreographers of ice dancing for the 1990s. Starting with dance lessons in Bristol, England, his hero was Gene Kelly and he "wanted to do musical comedy, but skating was very individual. I didn't have to do what everybody else was doing." He took his dance skills with him and began training on ice, appearing in his first competition at the age of 9. He went on to represent Great Britain for eight years and won all major international competitions in South Africa, England, Japan and Holland; was four-time British National Champion; three-time World Free Skating Gold Medalist and crowned his achievements with the 1980 Olympic Gold medal for his talents. He made his professional debut in NBC's "The Big Show" and continued to star in live and televised ice spectaculars. He created his own repertory Ice Theater Company and produces *Star Spangled Ice* annually at the Blue Jay Ice Castle near Lake Arrowhead, Calif., where he is artistic director for the training center there, which includes ballet and jazz dance classes. In 1991, he joined the NBC sports commentator team and received the MBE (Member of the British Empire) honor from Queen Elizabeth II, The People's Choice Award and was named "Professional Figure Skater of the Year" by *American Skating World* for his contributions to the sport of figure skating as a director, choreographer and commentator. Citing Gene Kelly, *Holiday on Ice* choreographer Stephanie Andros and Eliot Feld as major influences in his life and career, he noted: "In the days of Sonja Henie and the height of the

musical era, skating was high profile. It's taken some time, but it's nice to see it back in the forefront in TV and film." In 1995, he starred onstage in *The Rocky Horror Show* in London.

Stage: *Electric Ice* (Victoria Palace, London '82, also appeared and dir), *Ice Majesty* (Bristol Hippodrome '84, also dir), *Cinderella on Ice* (St. Louis Muny '90, also appeared)

TV: "Symphony of Sports" (1989–90), "Sudafed's Skating and Gymnastics Spectacular" (ABC '90, NBC '91, '92, also co-produced), "Beverly Hills 90210" ('92)

Miscellaneous: Performance pieces for Doug Mattis, Brian Orser, Tony Paul and Terry Pagana, Rosalyn Sumners, Debi Thomas, Charlene Wong, Paul Wylie; *The Wizard of Oz on Ice* ('95)

Film:
1985 **Fire and Ice**— Willy Bogner Prod.
1992 **The Cutting Edge**— MGM (also Technical advisor)

WILLIE COVAN
b. Atlanta, Georgia, March 4, 1898
d. Los Angeles, California, May 7, 1989

Legendary tap dancer and choreographer who was teacher and coach for some of Hollywood's greatest dancing stars. When Willie was 5 years old he began learning to dance from "Friendless" George in Chicago and at the age of 6 began a career as a pick tap dancer in minstrel shows. In 1910 he won an amateur tap contest and worked with Leonard Ruffin as Covan and Ruffin (Sammy Davis, Jr. once observed: "I've seen two great dancing acts, one was Bill Robinson and the other was Covan and Ruffin.") In 1915, Covan won the highly coveted Friday night contest which was part of the touring show *Old Kentucky* and "The judges gave Covan the prize and the audience came backstage after the show and carried him out on its shoulders. From then on, everybody in Negro show business knew about Covan." (*Jazz Dance*). In 1917 he formed the Four Covans with brother Dewey, Carita Harbert and his wife, Flo "Babe" Covan. The act combined acrobatic stunts, jazz and soft-shoe styles and toured the vaudeville and nightclub stages of the world, also appearing on Broadway in *Shuffle Along* ('22) and *Dixie to Broadway* ('24). After years of stage success, they made their film debut in **On with the Show** in 1929. Remaining in Hollywood, on the recommendation of Eleanor Powell to mogul Louis B. Mayer, he was contracted as MGM's staff tap dance instructor from the mid–1930s to '40s. Covan is credited with creating many classic tap dance steps (including the Rhythm Waltz Clog and Double Around the World with No Hands), but never received credit for his film choreographic contributions— which are many, but will sadly remain

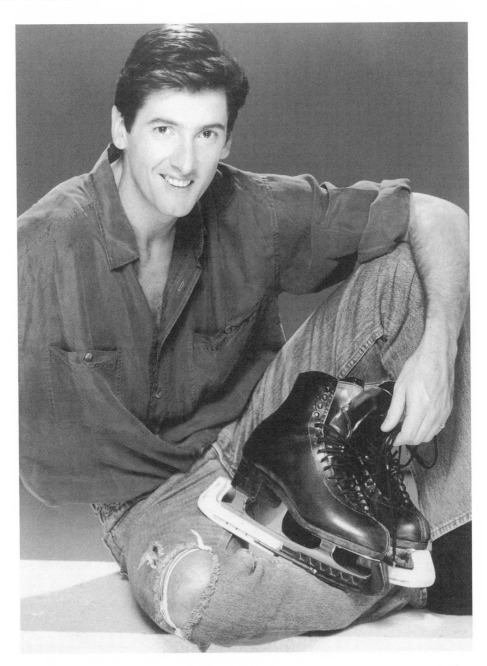

One of the newest ice-dancing choreographer to films, Olympic gold medalist Robin Cousins (photo by Richard Armas, courtesy of Robin Cousins).

unverified. Teaching until 1975, in 1981, he was finally honored with the PDS Gypsy Lifetime Achievement Award.

Film (Partial listing):

1929 **Fox Movietone Follies of 1929**— Fox (with Fanchon, appeared as part of The Four Covans, uncredited)

On with the Show— WB (with Larry Ceballos, appeared as part of The Four Covans, uncredited)

1938 **The Duke Is Tops**— Million Dollar (with Lew Crawford, also appeared, uncredited)

1953 **Small Town Girl**— MGM (with Busby Berkeley, Alex Romero, co-created Ann Miller's tap dance, uncredited)

AIMEE COVO

Stage: *Streetheart* (OB '84, asst to Rick Atwell)
Film:
1985 **Fast Forward**— Col (with Rick Atwell, Felix, Pamela Poitier, Gary Porter, Robin Summerfield, Charlie Washington.)

JEANNE COYNE

b. Pittsburgh, Pennsylvania, 1923
d. Los Angeles, California, May 10, 1973
One of the loveliest "unsung heroines" of screen dance, Jeanne Coyne was a talented dancer who had an important film choreographic career as assistant to Gene Kelly. As a girl in Pittsburgh, she had been a pupil of Kelly's. Arriving in New York in 1939, she worked with Robert Alton and Jack Cole on Broadway and relocated to Hollywood in 1942. With her expertise in ballet and jazz dance styles, she was hired to assist Kelly (with Carol Haney) and became a valuable member of MGM producer Arthur Freed's innovative movie musical unit. She married Stanley Donen in 1948, but the marriage lasted only one year. After Kelly divorced his first wife, Betsy Blair, Jeanne married him in 1960. The couple had two children (son, Timothy in 1962 and daughter Bridget, in 1963) before her premature death in 1973. Multiple film appearances include **On the Town** ('49 — featured in the *A Day in New York* Ballet), **Summer Stock** ('50) and **Kiss Me Kate** ('54 — dancing with Bobby Van in "From This Moment On").

TV: "Dancing Is a Man's Game" ('59, assistant to Kelly)

Film (All credits as assistant to Gene Kelly except*):
1952 **Singin' in the Rain**— MGM
1956 **Invitation to the Dance**— MGM (with Alan Carter, Carol Haney)
1957 **Les Girls**— MGM (with Jack Cole)
       Silk Stockings— MGM (assistant to Fred Astaire, Hermes Pan)

LEW CRAWFORD

1938 **The Duke Is Tops**— Million Dollar (with Willie Covan)

DON CRICHTON

b. Thompsonville (now "Enfield"), Connecticut, September 3, 1934
During his prolific career as a performer on the musical variety television shows of the 1960s and '70s, tall and handsome dancer-singer-actor Crichton partnered some of Hollywood's and Broadway's most glamorous stars (Julie Andrews, Rita Hayworth, Carol Lawrence, Chita Rivera, Lana Turner

and Gwen Verdon). Beginning his studies with tap lessons at the age of 4 and ballet at 6, his parents called a halt to dance studies to concentrate on a musical education. Convincing them that dance was his true love, he returned to classes with Helen Flanagan and Marjorie Fielding (Robert Alton's wife), opening his own studio while still in high school. At 17, he moved to New York to continue studying with various teachers and made his Broadway debut in the chorus of *Hazel Flagg* ('54). Robert Alton encouraged Crichton's talent and cast him in the film **The Girl Rush** and a New Frontier Hotel show in Las Vegas ('55). Other stage appearances include the *Ziegfeld Follies* (OOT '56) and a summer stock tour of Tallulah Bankhead's revue *Welcome Darlings* in 1956, multiple stock roles (*Meet Me in St. Louis, On the Town, Kiss Me Kate, The Boy Friend*) and being featured in the films **Thoroughly Modern Millie** and **Star!** He began his prolific TV performance career in 1956 on the Pat Boone, Patrice Munsel, Martha Raye and Larry Storch shows and subsequently became lead dancer on "The Garry Moore Show" ('60–64), "The Entertainers" (while simultaneously dancing on Broadway in *Fade Out— Fade In*, '64), "The Red Skelton Show" and the long-running "Carol Burnett Show" ('67–78). He made his choreographic debut with a Perry Como TV Special and his longtime association with Carol Burnett includes choreography for most of her recent TV, stage and film projects.

Stage: *From the Top* (Long Beach CLO '93)

TV (Partial listing): "The Love Boat" (choreographed for the Love Boat Mermaids, '85), "Bob Hope — The First 90 Years" ('92, Emmy nom), "Carol and Company," "The Golden Globe Awards," "The People's Choice Awards," "Linda in Wonderland," "The Tim Conway Show" (Emmy nom), "Alice," "Mama's Family," "Silver Spoons," "Amen," Three's Company," "Men, Movies and Carol" ('94); specials for Carol Burnett, George Burns, Perry Como, David Copperfield, Rodney Dangerfield, Bob Hope, the Osmonds and John Schneider

Nightclub/Concert: Tropicana Hotel, Atlantic City, Harry Blackstone tour

Miscellaneous: Ford Industrial (LV)

Film:
1981 **Chu Chu and the Philly Flash**— Fox
       Goldie and the Boxer Go to Hollywood— NBC/Col (TV)

JACK CROSBY

Beginning his career as assistant to LeRoy Prinz, this dance director worked steadily for ten years in films, but left very little behind in the way of details about his life and career — other than multiple mentions of his *not* being related to Bing Crosby.

Jeanne Coyne (center), listens as Gene Kelly discusses the cartoon sequence "Sinbad the Sailor" with William Hanna, for **Invitation to the Dance** (MGM, 1956).

Film:

1937 **Double or Nothing**— Par (assistant to LeRoy Prinz)

      Waikiki Wedding— Par (assistant to Prinz)

1938 **Dr. Rhythm**— Par

1939 **Hawaiian Nights**— Univ

1940 **South of Pago Pago**— UA

1941 **Playmates**— RKO

1944 **Dark Waters**— UA

      Knickerbocker Holiday— UA

      Lake Placid Serenade— Rep (with Felix Sadowski)

National Barn Dance— Par
1945 **People Are Funny**— Par
1946 **Whistle Stop**— UA
1947 **Unconquered**— Par
The Unsuspected— WB

VICTOR CUELLAR

Stage: Nostalgia Tropical (NY '93)
Film:
1985 **Patakin**— Cinema Guild

GEORGE CUNNINGHAM

b. New York, 1904
d. Los Angeles, California, April 30, 1962
Dance director, dancer and actor who began his varied career as assistant to Sammy Lee and producer of *Earl Carroll's Vanities* and *So This Is Paris* in New York. He relocated to Hollywood in 1925 to stage the dancing for many stage productions on the West Coast, among them the Los Angeles Civic Light Opera and prologues for the Paramount and United Artists theaters in Los Angeles. For four years he was dance director at MGM and coached stars Madeleine Carroll, Joan Crawford and Jeanette MacDonald. He also worked for Selznick, Paramount and Warner Bros. as a dance coach. Survived by a son and daughter.

Stage: Hollywood productions of *No, No Nanette, Lady Be Good, Nelly Kelly, The Music Box Revue* ('27) and *Castles in the Air, Hello Paris* (Bdwy '30), productions for the (Los Angeles Civic Light Opera): *New Moon* ('38 and '44), *The Desert Song, The Cat and the Fiddle, The Red Mill, Rose Marie* ('45 and '50), *The Three Musketeers* ('47)

Miscellaneous: The Ice Follies, Hansel and Gretel Ice Spectacular (Madison Square Gardens, NY)

Film:
1929 —**Broadway Melody**— MGM (also appeared)
The Hollywood Revue of 1929— MGM (with Ernest Belcher, Sammy Lee, Natasha Natova, Albertina Rasch, "assistant" credit, also appeared)
Our Modern Maidens— MGM (also appeared)
Thunder— MGM (also appeared)
1933 **Going Hollywood**— MGM (with Albertina Rasch)
1994 **That's Entertainment! III**— MGM (with others)

ROBERT CURTIS

1969 **The Witch**— Arco Film (Ital)

GROVER DALE (GROVER ROBERT AITKEN)

b. Harrisburg, Pennsylvania, July 22, 1935
Tony Award winning dancer, actor, choreographer and director who began dance lessons at the age of 9 in McKeesport, Pa. By the age of 13 he was assisting his teacher, Lillian Jasper, with classes and at 15 he opened his own studio. In 1953 he auditioned for the Pittsburgh CLO, beginning his career in musical theater. Moving to New York and working for June Taylor on the Jackie Gleason TV Show, his first professional stage appearance was a touring company of *Gentlemen Prefer Blondes*. After working in Summer stock at Camp Tamiment (with Carol Burnett and Joe Layton), he made his Broadway debut in *L'il Abner* ('56), also appearing at the Flamingo Hotel in Las Vegas and on TV's "The Colgate Comedy Hour" that same year. He then appeared in (and assisted Jerome Robbins on) *West Side Story* ('57) and Robbins' *Ballets: USA*. He also danced in Valerie Bettis' company at the Phoenix Theater. Off-Broadway in *Fallout* and *Too Much Johnson*, other Broadway shows include featured roles in *Greenwillow, Sail Away* (London '61 and Bdwy '62) and *Half a Sixpence*. Dale made his solo Broadway choreographic debut in 1971 with *Billy* and his unique performance abilities were featured in the films **The Unsinkable Molly Brown, Half a Sixpence, The Landlord** and **The Young Girls of Rochefort**. Married to actress Anita Morris and the father of son, James ("Our best production"), Dale founded the CRC (Choreographers Resourcenter) in 1992 and was named executive director of the National Academy of Dance. Anita's premature death in 1994 led Dale to create the Anita Morris Scholarship Fund to help new choreographers and as an important member of the team who created the film choreographer's union (MCC/SSDC) in 1993. Dale's energy, expertise and enthusiasm continues to vitalize the West Coast choreographic and dance community.

Stage: Fallout (OB '59, also appeared), *Billy* (Bdwy '71), *Rachel Lily Rosenblum and Don't You Ever Forget It* (OOT '73, with Tony Stevens, "choreographic supervision" credit), *Molly* (Bdwy '73), *Seesaw* (Bdwy '73, Tony Award winner, with Bob Avian, Michael Bennett, Tommy Tune), *The Magic Show* (Bdwy '74, also dir, Tony nom for dir), *King of Schnorrers* (OB '79, also dir), Ann Reinking's *One More Song/One More Dance* (Carnegie Hall, '84, also dir), *Mail* (Bdwy '90, also dir), *Jerome Robbins Broadway* (Bdwy '89, co-dir with Robbins, Tony Award for dir)

TV: "Today I'm 23" and "Look Up and Live" ('67)

Film:
1965 **Dance: Echoes of Jazz**— NET (TV) (with Donald McKayle)

1973 **The Way We Were**— Col
1981 **So Fine**— WB
1985 **Copacabana**— Dick Clark Cinema (TV) (Emmy nom)
1986 **Quicksilver**— Col
1988 **Aria**— Miramax (with Terry Gilbert, *Rigoletto* sequence)

ALICE DALGARNO

1969 **Sinful Davey**— UA

JACQUES (JOSEPH) D'AMBOISE (AHEARN)

b. Dedham, Massachusetts, July 28, 1934

Dancer, actor, choreographer and teacher who is one of America's most beloved male classical dancers. Raised on Staten Island, he began dance training while accompanying his sister, Ninette, to her ballet classes. After seven years of training at the School of American Ballet with George Balanchine, Anatola Oboukhoff, Vecheslar Swoboda and Pierre Vladimiroff, he joined New York City Ballet at 15. With his strong, raw, masculine appeal, he became a premier danseur with the company in 1953. As Balanchine's protégé, he had more works choreographed specifically for him than any other male dancer. One of the first ballet superstars to diversify their careers, he appeared on Broadway in *Shinbone Alley* ('57) and was featured in the films **Seven Brides for Seven Brothers** ('54), **Carousel** and **The Best Things in Life Are Free** ('56) and **A Midsummer Night's Dream** ('66). During the 1950's and 1960's, he guest-starred on most of the popular television shows ("The Bell Telephone Hour," "The Ed Sullivan Show," etc.) bringing his artistry to a wide American audience and leading the way to the acceptance of male ballet stars such as Mikhail Baryshnikov and Rudolph Nureyev. He danced and choreographed for the NYC Ballet from 1949–84. As founder and artistic director of the National Dance Institute (NDI), an unique organization which introduces the magic of dance to new generations of children each year since 1976, his work with the children of New York brought him new acclaim. The documentary **He Makes Me Feel Like Dancin'** ('84)— about his work with the NDI— won an Academy Award, six Emmy Awards, plus many others. Mr. d'Amboise is also the recipient of the Capezio Dance Award in 1990, the Award for Distinguished Service to the Arts by the American Academy of Arts and Letters in 1993 and co-author of *Teaching the Magic of Dance* with Hope Cooke ('83). Two of his four children, Charlotte and Christopher, are currently making their marks in the world of dance and theatre and in 1995, D'Amboise received the Kennedy Center Honors.

Stage: *Rosalinda* (LACLO, '68), *Peter and the Wolf* (NYC Center '68, also dir), 15 annual National Dance Institute Shows, *Rondelay* (OB '69), productions of *Roberta*, *Lady in the Dark*, *Peter Pan*, *A Thurber Carnival* and *The Shooting of Dan McGrew*

TV: Academy Awards Show, "Peanut Ballet" (PBS '90), "Phil Donahue: The 25th Anniversary" ('92)

Ballet/Dance Pieces (Partial Listing): "Pan America" ('60), "The Chase," "Quator," "Irish Fantasy," "Scherzo Opus 42," "Prologue," "Valse— Scherzo Concert Fantasy," "Celebration," "Tchaikovsky Suite No. 2" ('69), "Sarabande and Danse II," "Prologue and Saltarelli"

Film:
1983 **He Makes Me Feel Like Dancin'**— Edgar J. Shrink (winner of the Oscar for "Best Feature Length Documentary," also appeared)
       Stuck on You— Troma
1986 **Off Beat**— Touchstone (also appeared)

RITA D'AMICO (HYDE)

b. Philadelphia, Pennsylvania, December 25, 1936

After studying a variety of dance styles with Roland Dupree, this dancer and choreographer made her professional debut for Donn Arden at the Moulin Rouge in Hollywood as a young dancer. She appeared on stage (*West Side Story*, West Coast), in film (**Don't Knock the Twist**, **West Side Story**, **The Wonderful World of the Brothers Grimm**) and television ("The Nat King Cole Show," "Shindig," **The T.A.M.I. Show**, etc.), working with choreographers Nick Castle, Lee Scott and David Winters. Acting roles on television ("Dr. Kildare," "Mannix," "Mission Impossible," etc.), more dance studies with Jerry Grimes and eventual choreographic assignments filled her diversified career.

TV: "Bristol Court," "It's What's Happening," American Music Awards (asst)

Film:
1965 **Beach Ball**— Par (with Cholly Atkins)

BILLY DANIEL

b. Fort Worth, Texas, July 4, 1912
d. Beverly Hills, California, May 15, 1962

Dancer-choreographer who worked primarily for Paramount where he collaborated on twenty films as dance director from 1943–48. He was first "discovered" in 1939, starring in the St. Regis Roof Revue in New York which was directed by Mitchell Leisen. On Broadway he was featured with his partner, Pumpkin Parker, in *Let's Face It* ('41) and when Leisen relocated to Hollywood to direct films at Paramount, he invited Daniel to join him. Arriving in California, he made his West Coast debut at

Grover Dale (second from left) — of the longest flying legs in the world — kicks up his heels in **Half a Sixpence** (Paramount, 1967) with co-star Tommy Steele (to his right).

the Coconut Grove and danced in Paramount films from 1937–44 (**Zaza**, **Thrill of a Lifetime**, **Say It in French**, **Midnight**, **Bring on the Girls**) before being contracted to choreograph. Leaving Paramount after five years of varied dance creation assignments (from background period social dance to full-blown production numbers) he subsequently worked for Universal, 20th Century–Fox and MGM. In 1955 he was invited to Germany to choreograph films for Caterina Valente and other German musical stars during their '50s series of Pop musicals. Returning to America, he worked primarily in nightclubs until his death. In *Dance Magazine*, February, 1947, he stated: "From the standpoint of artistic development, I think dancing has hit its peak in Hollywood. There have been a few isolated attempts toward artistic development on the screen, but … radical changes sometimes prove disastrous in the movies and for this reason dance develops slowly." His name is often misspelled as Daniel*s*, so his credits get confused in print with the career of African-American singer Billy Daniels.

TV: "All Star Revue," hosted by Jack Carson ('50–52), "The June Havoc Show," "The Colgate Comedy Hour" ('54, also appeared), Multiple German Musical Variety shows

Nightclub/Concert: St. Regis Roof Revue (NY '39); Acts for Betty Grable (also appeared), Diane Hartman and Richard Allan, Sonia Henie, Marilyn Maxwell; production numbers at the Last Frontier (LV '54) and Ciro's (Hollywood)

Film:

1937 **Hold 'Em Navy** — Par

1944 **Brazil** — Rep (with Frank Veloz)
  Frenchman's Creek — Par (also appeared)
  Lady in the Dark — Par (with Nick Castle, Don Loper)
  The Three Caballeros — RKO (with Carmelita Maracci, Aloysio Oliveira)

1945 **Bring on the Girls** — Par (with Danny Dare)
  Duffy's Tavern — Par (with Dare)
  Kitty — Par
  Masquerade in Mexico — Par (also appeared, partnering Dorothy Lamour)
  The Stork Club — Par

1946 **Meet Me on Broadway** — Col
  Monsieur Beaucaire — Par (with Josephine Earl)

1947 **Golden Earrings** — Par
  Imperfect Lady — Par (with Earl)
  Ladies' Man — Par (with Dare)

Jacques d'Amboise and Melissa Hayden in a publicity photo for NYC Ballet's ***Stars and Stripes***, circa 1958.

The Perils of Pauline— Par
Road to Rio— Par (with Bernard Pearce)
The Trouble with Women— Par
Variety Girl— Par (with Dare, Pearce)
Welcome Stranger— Par

1948 **Dream Girl**— Par
The Emperor Waltz— Par
Enchantment— RKO
Footlight Rhythm— Par (S) (also dir)

Dorothy Dayton and Billy Daniel demonstrate dance steps during a promotional tour for **Zaza** (Paramount, 1938).

One Touch of Venus— Univ
The Paleface— Par
Rogue's Regiment— Univ
Sambamania— Par (S) (also dir)
1949 **Love Happy**— Rep
Red, Hot and Blue— Par
1950 **Love That Brute**— Fox
My Blue Heaven— Fox (with Seymour Felix, also appeared)
Wabash Avenue— Fox (assisted by Frances Grant, also appeared, partnering Betty Grable)
1952 **What Price Glory?**— Fox
With a Song in My Heart— Fox

1953 **Dangerous When Wet**— MGM (with Charles Walters)
Powder River— Fox
Scared Stiff— Par
1954 **The French Line**— RKO (assisted by Grant, also appeared as a French fashion designer)
1956 **Bonjour, Kathrin**—(Ger)
Girl with a Bad Memory—(Ger)
Kiss Me Again—(Ger)
Music Parade—(Ger)
You Are Music—(Ger)
1960 **The Tigress of Bengal** (aka **Journey to the Lost City**— AIP (with Robby Gay)

T. DANIEL

Mime/Movement artist and teacher.
Film:
1988 **Poltergeist III**— MGM

GRACIELA DANIELE

b. Buenos Aires, Argentina, December 8, 1939

"I like dance that tells a story," said director-choreographer Daniele, whose bold dance performance pieces expanded musical theater during the 1990s. "I allow my dancers to be like actors — to worry intellectually, emotionally about the parts they are playing … in the type of work that I do, the creative process is exactly like that of a play. The steps come last. Dance is another language of expression. Dancers can act and actors can dance and everybody can do it all." Her life in the theater began at the age of 7 when, because of a foot problem, a doctor prescribed ballet and she was accepted by the Teatro Colon in Buenos Aires and performed with the company for eight years ("I was a baby ballerina"). Moving to Paris, she danced with major companies internationally and after seeing *West Side Story* in 1963 ("As soon as I saw the show, I said, 'That's what I have to do!'") settled in New York in the early 1960s. There, she studied with Merce Cunningham, Martha Graham and Matt Mattox and performed on Broadway in *What Makes Sammy Run?* ('64), *Here's Where I Belong* and *Promises, Promises* ('68) and *Chicago* ('75). She began her choreographic career assisting Michael Bennett on *Coco* ('69) and *Follies* ('71). Her first solo choreography was "The Milliken Show," a major industrial show in 1976, which led to her multiple Broadway stage assignments. *Dance Magazine* (May, 1994) said of her work, "Daniele is not afraid to make audiences shiver" and she continues to explore new dance forms and innovative staging with her explosive works. About her own style, she said in *Theater Week* (July '95): "I find I am very grounded in ethnic stuff. I love to feel the floor. I'm very sensual … but when I look at my work, I don't see any style whatsoever." In 1995 she was director-in-residence at Lincoln Center Theater.

Stage: A History of the American Film (Bdwy '78), *The Most Happy Fella* (Bdwy '79 rev), *Girls, Girls, Girls* (OB '80), *Die Fledermaus* (Opera Company of Boston), *Naughty Marietta* (NYC Opera), *The Pirates of Penzance* (Bdwy '81, Tony nom & Drama Desk noms, LA Critics award), *Alice in Concert* (Bdwy '83), *Zorba* (Bdwy '83 rev), *The Rink* (Bdwy '84, Tony nom), *The Mystery of Edwin Drood* (Bdwy '85, Tony nom), *Smile* (OB '86, also dir), *Tango Apasionado* (Bdwy '88, also dir), *Dangerous Games* (Bdwy '90, also dir, Tony nom), *March of the Falsettos/Falsettoland* (Hartford '90, dir), *Once on This Island* (Bdwy '91, also dir, 2 Tony noms), *The Snow Ball* (OOT '91), *Captains Courageous* (OOT '92, also dir, Tony nom), *The Goodbye Girl* (Bdwy '93, Tony nom), *Herringbone* (Hartford, '93, also dir), *Hello Again* (Lincoln Center '94, also dir, 2 Drama Desk noms), *Chronicle of a Death Foretold* (Bdwy '95, also concept/dir, Tony nom), *A New Brain* (work-in-progress, NY '95), *Dancing on Her Knees* (NY '96, also dir)

Ballet/Dance Pieces: "Presley Pieces" (for ABT), "Cado Noche Tango," "El Nuevo Mundo" (Ballet Hispanico '92), "Stages"

Film:
1981 **Beatlemania**— American Cinema
1983 **The Pirates of Penzance**— Univ
1985 **Mirrors**— Leonard Hill Films/NBC (TV)
1986 **Haunted Honeymoon**— Orion
1991 **Naked Tango**— New Line Cinema (with Carlos Rivorola)
1994 **Bullets Over Broadway**— Miramax (assisted by Willie Rosario, *LA Dance* Awards nom)
1995 **Mighty Aphrodite**— Miramax (LA Dance Award)
1996 **Everyone Says I Love You**— Miramax

CINDY DANIELS

1991 **The Last Boyscout**— WB ("Cheerleader choreography by")

DANNY DANIELS (DANIEL GIAGNI)

b. Albany, New York, October 25, 1924

"I started at five and a half, and by the time I was ten years old I had just about everything in my feet that I was ever going to have," said Daniels in an April, 1980 *Dance Magazine* interview. One of the leading choreographers in contemporary stage and film work, he began tap lessons as a child in Albany and continued studying various forms of dance over the years with Elizabeth Anderson-Ivantzova, Vincenzo Celli, Edith Jane Falconer, Jack Potteiger, Thomas Sternfield and Anatole Vilzak. He began his performance career at age 6 and when his jazz band musician father moved the family to Los Angeles, Danny had a featured dance role in **The Star Maker** ('39). When the family relocated to New York, he debuted on Broadway in the choruses of *Best Foot Forward* ('41) and *Count Me In* ('42) and progressed to featured roles in *Billion Dollar Baby* ('45), *Street Scene* ('47), *Make Mine Manhattan* and *Kiss Me Kate* ('48) and with the Agnes DeMille Dance Theatre in 1953. Anna Sokolow, the choreographer of *Street Scene*, was responsible for Daniels becoming a choreographer himself— his first works were for summer stock at Camp Tamiment from 1954–55. His Broadway and television choreography led to his film career. In *Dance*

Magazine, December, 1965, he described the type of dance he most enjoys choreographing as "balletic jazz... Jazz plus the classic vocabulary adds up to a uniquely American style. Sure, it's a composite, but jazz has always been a composite, borrowing from many types of dance and turning them into something new and exciting. That's the kind of dance I'm comfortable in." Daniels often whimsically recreates the musical theatre of the past (**The Night They Raided Minskys**, **Indiana Jones and the Temple of Doom**) for contemporary audiences. His work is always filled with the sheer joy of dance and he has made such actors and actresses as Steve Martin (**Pennies from Heaven**) and Andrea Martin, Sheila McCarthy and Julie Walters (**Stepping Out**) dance as though they had been inspired by the spirit of Astaire and Rogers. Also a television director ("Gene Kelly's 50-Girls-50" and three HBO specials), he opened a dance school in Santa Monica in 1974 with wife, Bea (Bernice Grant, whom he married in 1947), and formed Danny Daniels Dance America Company. He danced on Gene Kelly's 1978 TV special "An American in Pasadena" with Kelly and Alex Romero. Winner of two Emmy Awards and one Tony Award for choreographic work, as well as being nominated twice as a performer. One of the founders of SSDC—where he served as president for three years and as a member of the Board of Directors for ten years—Daniels also taped a historic series of demonstration-interviews with Louis DaPron, Fred Kelly (Gene's brother), Hal Leroy, Fayard Nicholas and other tap greats for the dance archives of the New York Public Library at Lincoln Center and the Los Angeles Public Library. One of his sons, D.J. (Daniel Joseph) Giagni, served as Daniels' dance associate on multiple projects before starting his solo career.

Stage: *High Time* (Bdwy '53), *Shoestring '57* (Bdwy), *The Girls Against the Boys* (Bdwy '59), *Meet Me in St. Louis* (St. Louis Muny, '60), *All American* (Bdwy '62), *Best Foot Forward* (OB '63 rev, also dir), *Annie Get Your Gun* (NY City Center '63 rev, Tony nom), *High Spirits* (London and Bdwy '64, Tony nom), *Hot September* (OOT '65), *Walking Happy* (Bdwy '66, Tony nom), *Ciao Rudy* (Rome and Bdwy), *Love Match* (OOT '68, also dir), *1491* (Bdwy '69), *Lolita, My Love* (OOT '71, replacing Jack Cole, replaced by Dan Siretta), *Wonderful Town* (LACLO), *I Remember Mama* (Bdwy '79), *On a Clear Day You Can See Forever* (LACLO '80, also dir), *Tap Dance Kid* (Bdwy '83, with D.J. Giagni, Tony and Astaire Awards), *Follies in Concert* (NY '85, also TV)

TV: (Partial listing): "The Fabulous Fifties" ('60, Emmy Award), Bing Crosby special ('60), Danny Kaye Special ('61), "The Firestone Hour," "The Revlon Revue," the Martha Raye, Ray Bolger, Dick Van Dyke, Judy Garland, Patrice Munsel, Perry

Como, Eydie Gormé & Steve Lawrence and Milton Berle series; John Denver Special ('76, with D.J. Giagni, Emmy Award), "Will B. Able's Baggy Pants and Co. Burlesque" (HBO '78, also Prod)

Ballet/Dance Pieces: Morton Gould's "Tap Dance Concerto" ('52), "Hoofer Suite" ('56) and "Family Album" ('58)

Nightclub/Concert: *Gene Kelly's Wonderful World of Girls* ('70), Acts for Mitzi Gaynor, Arthur Godfrey, Leslie Uggams, George Gobel

Film:
1968 **The Night They Raided Minsky's**— UA ("Dances, Musical Numbers and sketches staged by" credit)
1969 **Stiletto**— AE
1972 **Richard**— Aurora City Group
1973 **Tom Sawyer**— UA
1981 **Pennies from Heaven**— MGM (assisted by Daniel Joseph Giagni and Randy Doney)
1982 **Piaf—The Early Years**— Fox
1983 **Zelig**— Orion/WB (with Twyla Tharp)
1984 **Indiana Jones and the Temple of Doom**— Par (assisted by Carolyn Hamilton)
1991 **Stepping Out**— Par (assisted by William Orlowski)

LOUIS DAPRON
b. Hammond, Indiana, February 3, 1913
d. Agoura, California, July 21, 1987

Tap dancer, choreographer and teacher whose dazzling tap skills created some of the 1940s' most energetic dance sequences. DaPron's mother and father were hoofers, so Louis started performing in vaudeville at the age of four. The family moved to Denver and opened a dance school, where teenage Louis taught and appeared in musicals at West High School. In 1930, 17-year-old Louis imitated Bojangles at a Chicago Convention of Dance teachers and in 1935, the family moved to Los Angeles, opening their school there. While appearing as the featured dancer at the Trocodero Nightclub in Hollywood, 22-year-old Louis was signed by Paramount to partner Eleanore Whitney in musical films. He made his film debut (also choreographing for himself) in **Three Cheers for Love** in 1937. After eight film appearances, he tried his luck in New York, but returned to Hollywood to assist LeRoy Prinz on **Dancing on a Dime** ('40). His first solo effort choreographing for other dancers (**Sweetheart of the Campus**, Ruby Keeler's last dance film) in 1941 led to a contract at Universal where he became the dancemaster for its Jivin' Jacks and Jills film musical series with dancing stars Donald O'Connor and Peggy Ryan. Working with O'Connor in multiple films and television shows, DaPron always supplied the sounds for Donald's taps—either live off-camera or pre or post recorded. DaPron holds the

A 1936 publicity still of Louis DaPron while he was under contract as a performer to Paramount (photo courtesy of the Academy of Motion Picture Arts and Sciences).

distinction of being the choreographer who appeared in the most films, performing his own work. He had his own school in Canoga Park and also taught at the California Dance Theatre in Agoura Hills. Receiving the PDS' first Gypsy Lifetime Achievement Award on February 8, 1987, just five months before his death, his hundreds of students carry on his unique tap heritage.

Stage: *Little Boy Blue* (Hollywood '50, directed by George Murphy)

TV: "Soap Box Playhouse" (KTLA), "Texaco Star Theatre: Here Comes Donald" ('54, Emmy nom), "The Perry Como Show" ('55–60, with the Louis Da Pron Dancers), "The Donald O'Connor Texaco Show" ('54–55), "The Julius LaRosa Show" ('57, with the Louis Da Pron Dancers), "Perry

Presents" ('59, with the Louis DaPron Dancers), "The Hollywood Palace," "The Smothers Brothers Comedy Hour" ('67–68, with the Louis DaPron Dancers), "Mayberry RFD," "Ben Vereen — Comin' at Ya" ('75), "Lucy Moves to NBC" ('80)

Nightclub/Concert: Acts for Mitzi Gaynor, Donald O'Connor, Ginger Rogers

Film:

1936 **The Big Broadcast of 1937**— Par (with LeRoy Prinz, also appeared)

College Holiday— Par (with Prinz, also appeared)

The Princess Comes Across— Par (also appeared)

Star Reporter Series—Par (S) (also appeared)

Three Cheers for Love— Par (with Danny Dare, also appeared)

1937 **All American Sweetheart**— Univ (also appeared)

Hideaway Girl— Par (also appeared)

1939 **Seeing Red**— WB (S) (also appeared)

1940 **La Conga Nights**— Univ

Dancing on a Dime—Par (assistant to Prinz)

I'm Nobody's Sweetheart Now— Univ (with Eduardo Cansino)

1941 **Blondie Goes Latin**— Col

Go West Young Lady— Col (with Ann Miller)

Melody Lane— Univ (also appeared)

Rookies on Parade— Rep (with Nick Castle)

San Antonio Rose— Univ (with Castle, also appeared)

Shadows in Swing— Univ (S) (also appeared)

Sweetheart of the Campus— Col (with Ruby Keeler)

Swing It Soldier— Univ (also appeared)

1942 **Almost Married**— Univ

Get Hep to Love— Univ

It Comes Up Love—Univ

Jivin' Jam Session— Univ (S) (also appeared)

Juke Box Jenny— Univ

When Johnny Comes Marching Home— Univ (with the Four Step Bros.)

1943 **Always a Bridesmaid**— Univ

Dixie— Par (with Seymour Felix, also appeared)

Follow the Band— Univ

He's My Guy— Univ (with Carlos Romero, also appeared)

How's About It— Univ (also appeared)

Mister Big— Univ

Moonlight in Vermont— Univ

She's for Me— Univ (also appeared)

Sweet Jam— Univ (S) (also appeared)

This Is the Life— Univ (with Fanchon)

Top Man— Univ

1944 **Babes on Swing Street**— Univ (also appeared)

Bowery to Broadway— Univ (with John Boyle, Carlos Romero)

Chip Off the Old Block— Univ

Follow the Boys— Univ (with Carmen Amaya, George Hale, Joe Schoenfeld)

The Ghost Catchers— Univ

Hey Rookie!— Col (with the Condos Bros., Stanley Donen, Ann Miller, Val Raset, also appeared)

Hi Good Lookin'— Univ (with Tip, Tap and Toe)

The Merry Monahans— Univ (with Carlos Romero)

Moon Over Las Vegas— Univ

Night Club Girl— Univ

Pardon My Rhythm— Univ

The Singing Sheriff— Univ (also appeared)

Slightly Terrific— Univ

Twilight on the Prairie— Univ

1945 **Blonde Ransom**— Univ (with Felix Sadowski

Her Lucky Night— Univ

Here Come the Co-Eds— Univ

Honeymoon Ahead— Univ

I'll Tell the World— Univ

On Stage Everybody— Univ

Patrick the Great— Univ

Penthouse Rhythm— Univ (also appeared)

See My Lawyer— Univ (with Carmen Amaya)

That Night with You— Univ (with Lester Horton)

That's the Spirit— Univ (with Carlos Romero)

1946 **Black Angel**— Univ (also appeared)

Cuban Pete— Univ

Girl on the Spot— Univ

Slightly Scandalous— Univ (also appeared)

1948 **Are You with It?**— Univ (also appeared)

Buddy Rich and His Orchestra— Univ (S) (also appeared)

The Countess of Monte Cristo— Univ

Feudin', Fussin' and A-Fightin'—Univ (also appeared)

1949 **There's a Girl in My Heart**— AA

Yes Sir, That's My Baby— Univ

1950 **Curtain Call at Cactus Creek**— Univ

One Too Many— Hallmark (also appeared)

1953 **Walking My Baby Back Home**— Univ

1956 **The Kettles in the Ozarks**— Univ (also appeared)

DANNY DARE

b. New York, March 20, 1905

d. Tarzana, California, November 20, 1996

Dancer, choreographer, director and producer who started dancing at the age of 6 when his mother enrolled him in Edward Neuberger's Social Dance classes, with fellow classmate, Seymour Felix. Although the family hardly had the extra money, his mother had ambitions for her talented son. Dance teacher Neuberger observed the child's talent and began private lessons. On his own, Dare began watching and imitating the dancers of the era, among them Fred Stone, much the way that today's street dancers learned their art. At 14 he was proficient enough to play Manhattan's Keith Theatre in a Gus Edwards Revue and at 17, he started dancing on Broadway in *The Passing Show* and *Five O'Clock Girl* ('27). He toured in Monte Carlo, London and Paris and had his own line of girls in Vaudeville. At 22, he directed the dances for *The Little Show* on Broadway in 1929 and then, went to Hollywood to begin his film musical career, becoming the dance director for Paramount in 1942. His assistants included Billy Daniel, Louis DaPron, Josephine Earl and Miriam Nelson. In 1944 he organized the Dance Director's Guild, but when he was contracted as a producer by Paramount, he could not hold office with the Guild and it soon disintegrated. He produced the films **Our Hearts Were Growing Up** ('46), **Variety Girl**, **Ladies Man**, **My Favorite Brunette** and **Road To Rio** ('47) and **Isn't It Romantic?** ('48). After his film career, he directed many stage and TV shows (Bob Hope and Frank Sinatra specials, "Damon Runyan," "Ford Theatre of the Air," "How To Marry a Millionaire" and "Here Comes the Showboat" series) and co-produced musicals with Sammy Lewis in California in the 1960s.

Stage: *Hot Chocolate*, *The Little Show* and *Sweet Adeline* (Bdwy '29), *Sweet and Low* (Bdwy '30), *You Said It* (Bdwy '31), *Tattle Tales* (Bdwy '33), *Hollywood Revels of 1933, '34, '36* (Bdwy, also dir), *Meet the People* (Bdwy '40, also dir), *They Can't Get You Down* (Hollywood '41)

Nightclub/Concert: Hollywood Restaurant (NY '35)

Film:

1930 **Fox Movietone Follies of 1930**— Fox (with Maurice Kusell, Max Scheck)

Let's Go Places— Fox

Not Damaged— Fox

Such Men Are Dangerous— Fox

1932 **Over the Counter**— MGM (S)

What an Idea!— Vitaphone (S) (with The Danny Dare Girls)

Wild People— MGM (S)

1935 **Speedy Justice**— Univ (S)

1936 **Three Cheers for Love**— Par (with Louis DaPron)

1937 **52nd Street**— UA (with George Tapps)

1938 **Start Cheering**— Col (with Hal Leroy)

1940 **Hit Parade of 1941**— Rep (with Ann Miller)

1942 **Holiday Inn**— Par (with Fred Astaire, assisted by Bernard "Babe" Pierce)

Maisie Gets Her Man— MGM

Panama Hattie— MGM (with the Berry Brothers, Sammy Lee)

Star Spangled Rhythm— Par (with George Balanchine, Jack Donohue, Katherine Dunham)

1943 **It Ain't Hay**— Univ (with the Four Step Brothers)

Lady of Burlesque— UA

Riding High— Par

1944 **And the Angels Sing**— Par

Here Comes the Waves— Par (with the Four Step Bros.)

Rainbow Island— Par

Up in Arms— Samuel Goldwyn

1945 **Bring on the Girls**— Par (with Billy Daniel)

Duffy's Tavern— Par (with Billy Daniel, also asst prod)

Incendiary Blonde— Par

Road to Utopia— Par

1948 **Isn't It Romantic?**— Par (with Josephine Earl, also prod)

NICOLE DARESCO

1982 **Bolero** (aka **Les Uns et les Autres**)— Double 13 (with Maurice Béjart, Ric Odums, Micha Van Joecke, Larry Vickers, also appeared)

EVA DARLOW

1985 **Hitler's SS: Portrait in Evil**— NBC (TV)

DENISE DARNELL

1992 **Mom and Dad Save the World**— Cinema Plus/HBO

MICHAEL DARRIN

Choreographer-director who began his performance career in Las Vegas cabaret extravaganzas (*Folies Bergère*, *Pzazz '70*, etc.) to become one of the leading club dance creators around the world.

TV: "Homefront," "Stand by Your Man," 1990 Academy Awards (with Paula Abdul, Emmy nom), 1990 American Music Awards (with Paula Abdul, Emmy winner), Gino Bramieri Show (Rome), "Le Sorcery" (HBO)

Music Video: "Cold Hearted Snake"—Paula Abdul

Nightclub/Concert (Partial listing): *Celebration* (Sun City, South Africa), *Pazaaz, Rage, Le Vamps, Zoom, Excitement* (Lake Tahoe), *Vive les Femmes* (Tokyo), *Ala-Ka-Zam, Sassy Class, Disco Fever* (LV), *Bottoms Up* (Atlantic City, Reno, Lake Tahoe, LV), Pink Lady's act

Miscellaneous: Industrials for Head Sportswear, America's Salute to the Astronauts

Film:
1994 **Dream Lover**— Propaganda Films

DANNI DASSA

Israeli dance choreographer and teacher who was a member of the staff of Benjamin Zemach's dance department at the University of Judaism in Los Angeles in the 1960s. Founder of the Sinjan (Coffee Pot) Dance Group and the Israeli Folk Company, he also had Casa Dassa, his own dance school.

Film:
1960 **The Story of Ruth**— Fox

IRVING DAVIES

b. South Wales, England

Running away from home at the age of 14 to dance, Davies made his professional debut in *Things Are Looking Up* and first appeared on the London stage in *Strike a New Note* in 1943. He continued in West End productions of *Strike It Again, Sigh No More, The Shepherd Show* and *Annie Get Your Gun*— where he would meet and begin his collaboration with Paddy Stone. After creating his first choreography for *Gay's the Word* in 1950, Davies, Stone and Beryl Kaye created Three's Company (a dance trio) in 1951 and toured Canada and the U.S., being featured on Broadway in the revue *Joyce Grenfell Requests the Pleasure ...* in 1955. Gene Kelly saw the trio and hired them for his film **Invitation to the Dance** ('56) in which Davies appeared as "The Crooner" in the *Ring Around the Rosie* ballet. Other film roles include **I'll Be Your Sweetheart, The Good Companions, As Long as They're Happy** and **Value for Money**. He began his film career co-creating with Stone and received his solo credit on his last (to date) film in 1977. He continues to be active in stage productions.

Stage: Gay's the Word (London '50, with Eunice Crowther), *Joyce Grenfell Requests the Pleasure* (London & Bdwy '55, with Paddy Stone, Alfred Rodrigues, Wendy Toye, also appeared), *Mister Venus* (London '58, with Paddy Stone), *Jorrocks* (Eng '66), *Come Spy with Me* (London '68), *The Amazons* (Nottingham, Eng '71), *So Who Needs Marriage?* (Eng '75), *The Biograph Girl* (Eng '80), *Jerome Kern Goes to Hollywood* (London & Bdwy '85), *Lust* (London '93)

TV: "The Liberace Show" ('69), "The John Davidson Show" ('69), "The Englebert Humperdinck Show" ('70, with the Irving Davies Dancers), George Gershwin Special (Danish TV '78)

Film:
1957 **The Good Companions**— ABF/AB Pathé (with Paddy Stone, also appeared)
1957 **As Long as They're Happy**— Rank (with Stone, also appeared)
Value for Money— Rank (with Stone, also appeared)
1977 **The Last Remake of Beau Geste**— Univ

JOAN DAVIS

British choreographer (not be confused with the successful American comedienne of the same name) who appeared in the film **Little Friend** ('34).

Film:
1939 **Lucky to Me**— Astor (GB)
1940 **Everything Is Rhythm**— Astor (GB)

MARK DAVIS

1994 **The Neverending Story III**— WB (with Brad Rapier)

DONA DAVIS-CLARKE

1988 **Elvira-Mistress of the Dark**— New World

D'DEE

1982 **Five Days One Summer**— WB
1984 **Le Bal**— Almi Classics (with Jacques Bense)

DOUGLAS DEAN

1942 **The Lady Is Willing**— Col

FARNESIO DEBERNAL

1993 **Like Water for Chocolate** (aka **Como Agua Por Chocolate**)— Miramax

PEDRO DECORDOBA

1959 **Thunder in the Sun**— Par

NICOLE DEHAYES

1993 **Germinal**— Guild (Fr/Bel/Ital)

HOWARD DEIGHTON

British dance director.

Film:
1935 **She Shall Have Music**— Imperial/Twickenham
1936 **Eliza Comes to Stay**— Imperial/Twickenham

ANNOUCHKA DeJONG

1995 **Babe**— Univ ("Hogget's Dance" choregraphy credit, *LA Dance* Award nom)

GEMZE DeLAPPE

b. Woodhaven, Virginia, February 28, 1922
Classical dancer, choreographer and educator who received acclaim for her longtime collaboration with Agnes DeMille. Her early music and dance training was at the Peabody Conservatory in Baltimore. At 6 she went to New York, auditioning at Carnegie Hall and winning scholarships to the Michel Fokine Ballet School and the Isadora Duncan School, at that time headed by Irma Duncan. She would eventually perform in concert with both groups. She attended Hunter College and the Ballet Arts School and studied with Yeichi Nimura, becoming his protégé. DeLappe made her musical stage debut in the national company of *Oklahoma!*, where she first met Agnes DeMille, and began a long association dancing in most of DeMille's shows. Broadway appearances include *Carousel* and *Brigadoon* ('47), *The King and I* ('51), *Paint Your Wagon* (also '51, for which she received the Donaldson Award), *Phoenix '55*, *Juno* ('59) and *Gorey Stories* ('78). She toured Asia for the State Department as a member of Rod Alexander's Dance Jubilee (1959–60) and also danced with DeMille's Dance Theater and American Ballet Theatre. Miss DeLappe appeared in the film **The King and I** (as "King Simon of Legree" in the **Small House of Uncle Thomas** ballet) and on TV in 1958 in DeMille's **Gold Rush**. She began her choreography and direction career assisting on the London production of *Oklahoma!* For many years she taught in the dance department at Smith College as well as being guest teacher at the National Academy of Arts in Champaign, Illinois, and Ballet Arts at Carnegie Hall.
Stage: *Something About Anne* (OOT), *The Birds* (Ann Arbor, Mich.), *Ladies Day* (Desilu Workshop, LA), *Oklahoma!* (Bdwy '79 rev, recreating DeMille's original choreo — as well as productions in London, Australia, NY City Center, Paris, Antwerp and Japan), revivals of *Carousel* (Volksoper, Vienna and Houston and Omaha Opera companies), *Finian's Rainbow*, *South Pacific*, *The Unsinkable Molly Brown*, *The King and I* (Volskoper, Munich, St. Louis Muny, Fisher Theatre, Detroit, '94)
Ballet/Dance Pieces: "Strangers" (National Academy of Dance, Champagne, Illinois), "Nocturne" (Smith College)

Film:
1969 **Justine**— Fox (assisted by Bill Ross)

MIGUEL DELGADO

b. Ciudad Juarez, Mexico
Born in Mexico to a dancing mother and musician father, this dancer, choreographer, producer and arts consultant was raised in Boyle Heights, Los Angeles. He learned his first dance at the age of 8 from his parents and at 17 began formal training in the U.S. and Mexico with Mexican dance from Carlos Casados, Javier de Léon, Amalia Hernandez, Encarnacion Martinez, Graciela Tapia and Florencio Yeseas; ballet with Tulio de la Rosas, Stefan Wenta and Sallie Whelan and modern with Alvin Ailey, Valentina Castro and Rosa Reina. He danced with Mexico's Ballet Folklorico and Ballet de las Americas and appeared on Mexico City TV in "Noches Tapatias." Making his professional acting debut in Los Angeles and on Broadway in *Zoot Suit* ('79 — also repeating his role in the film version), Delgado is the artistic director, choreographer and founder of Los Angeles' Teatro Mexicano y Danza. In addition to his dancecreations and movement consultant work, film roles include **Born in East L.A.** ('87), **Flatliners** ('90), and **Soldierboy**. Teaching Mexican folkloric dance throughout California and acting as consultant for Plaza de la Raza, he is on the staff at the UCLA.
Stage: *Hecuba* (Powerhouse Theatre), *Charlie Bacon and His Family* (South Coast Rep), *The Miser* (Odyssey Theater, LA), *La Llorana* (Mark Taper Forum), *La Virgen del Tepeyac* (El Teatro Campesina '91), *Salsa Opera* (Padua Hills, Cal), *Bandido* (LA '94), *Hollywood Olvidado!* (also creator)
TV: "Corridos" (PBS), commercials for Crest, Lawry's, Halston, Maruchan Foods, Scope, etc.
Film:
1981 **Body and Soul**—Cannon (movement coach with Hope Clarke, Valentino)
      Zoot Suit— Univ (movement coach with Patricia Birch, also appeared)
1987 **Born in East L.A.**— Univ (also appeared)
      In the Mood— Lorimar
      La Bamba— Col
1995 **Double Agent**— Disney
      My Family— New Line Cinema (also appeared)

CARMEN (PAULA) DELAVALLADE

b. Los Angeles, California, March 6, 1929
One of the leading American modern dancers in the 1950s and '60s, she was described by *Dance Magazine* in October, 1966 with "Few artists convey

The Lester Horton Dancers in a number from "Choreo '51," front row (L to R): Audree Covington, Carmen DeLavallade, Eva Valencia; back row: Don Martin, James Truitte and Pepe DeChazza.

the sensuous pleasure of movement as Carmen De Lavallade does." She began her dance training as a young girl with ballet lessons from Melissa Blake. Sensing her great potential, she was sponsored by Lena Horne to study modern dance with Lester Horton at his Dance Theatre in Hollywood. To diversify her dance technique, she also received ballet training from Carmelita Maracci. She made her professional debut with the Horton Dance Theatre in 1950 at the age of 17 and danced with him until his death in 1953. After attending Los Angeles City College, she went to New York and appeared onstage in *House of Flowers* ('54), *Ballet Ballads* ('61), *Hot Spot* ('63) and on TV in "Look Up and Live" ('61) and "5 Ballets of the 5 Seasons" ('67). She was featured with the Metropolitan Opera, Alvin Ailey, John Butler, Donald McKayle and Ballet Theatre Companies. Her own company performed at Jacob's Pillow in 1961. Appeared in the films **Abbott and Costello Meet Dr. Jekyll and Mr. Hyde, The Egyptian, Demetrius and the Gladiators, The Mole People, Lydia Bailey** (dancing with Jack Cole) and **Odds Against Tomorrow**. Married to multi-talented Geoffrey Holder on June 26, 1955 (while they appeared together in *House of Flowers*), she was featured in his dance company and in 1958 they appeared as a dance team at Radio City Music Hall and on a brief nightclub tour. Receiving the *Dance Magazine* award in 1966, she taught move-

ment for actors at the Yale Repertory Theater, periodically danced in New York and continues to appear onstage (*Island Memories*, '91).

Stage: *The Frogs* (Bdwy '74), *A Perfect Ganesh* (Manhattan Theatre Club '93), for the Met: *Porgy and Bess* ('90), **Lucia di Lammermoor** and **Die Meistersinger** ('92), *Rusalka* ('93)

Film:
1988 **The Serpent and the Rainbow**—Univ (with Juan Rodriguez)

TITO DeLUC
Italian dancer and choreographer.
Film:
1960 **Esther and the King**—Fox
     Maciste the Mighty—Panteon
1962 **Son of Samson**—(Fr/Ital/Yugo)
1976 **Madame Kitty**—Trans. Amer. Films (also appeared)
1980 **Caligula**—Penthouse Prod (with Pino Pennese)

MIKE DeLUTRY
Martial arts choreographer.
1959 **Arena of Fear**—Sascha/Lux

TONY DeMARCO

b. Buffalo, New York, 1898

d. West Palm Beach, Florida, November 14, 1965

As the male half of The DeMarcos with ten various partners — including eight wives (Mabel Scott, Renee DeMarco, Peggy Hooper, Maxine Arnold, Albertina Vitak, Patricia Bowman, Arlene Langem and Sally Craven), Tony DeMarco created one of America's most noted ballroom dance teams. He started his career with his sister in amateur contests and then teamed with first wife, Mabel Scott, to begin professional appearances in the early 1920s. He appeared on Broadway in 1930 in *Girl Crazy* and *Hot Cha!* ('32), *Boys and Girls Together* ('40, where he met future wife #8 and partner, Sally) and *Showtime* ('42). He achieved his greatest success with his second wife Renee, receiving top billing at the World's best nightspots — including an unprecedented four year run at the Persian Room at NY's Plaza Hotel. After making his film debut in 1935, he created a dance routine and partnered Joan Crawford in **The Shining Hour** in 1938, and always choreographed the ballroom dance routines which combined many styles for all live and film appearances. He appeared in three films and on TV (the Ed Sullivan Show, etc.) with last wife Sally, until the popularity of ballroom dance teams declined. He retired in 1957 to open a restaurant in Palm Beach, Florida, and manage his various real estate holdings. His *Variety* obituary stated "DeMarco ... was largely responsible for the image of ballroom dancers as symbols of class and elegance."

Film (Uncredited choreography for his own appearances):

    1935 **In Caliente** — WB (with Busby Berkeley)

    1938 **The Shining Hour** — MGM

    1943 **Crazy House** — Univ (with George Hale)

          The Gang's All Here — Fox (with Busby Berkeley)

    1944 **Greenwich Village** — Fox (with Seymour Felix, the Four Step Brothers)

AGNES (GEORGE) DeMILLE

b. New York, September 18, 1905

d. New York, October 7, 1993

A consummate storyteller who used words and dance with powerful effect. Her ballets and choreography for concert and the musical theater revolutionized dance worldwide with extension of plot and character and her stylized, bold steps. Daughter of William DeMille and niece of Cecil B., she moved from Harlem to Hollywood when she was 9 and grew up in the early film industry, appearing in the 1930 Publix short **The Ballet Class**. She began dance studies with Theodore Kosloff and continued with Margaret Craske and Marie Rambert. After receiving a degree in English at UCLA, she returned to New York and began her professional dance career as a soloist in concert in 1927, touring America and Europe. In 1928, she danced on Broadway in *The Grand Street Follies* and created her first choreography for a revival of the legendary musical *The Black Crook* in 1929 in Hoboken, New Jersey. While touring Europe in 1932 with her concert program, she met and studied with Anthony Tudor and they formed their own company. After her return to America, Uncle Cecil let her try out her dance talents by having her choreograph some of the dances in **Cleopatra** ('34) — although he fired her from dancing in the film. She made her ballet choreographic debut with ***Black Ritual*** for Ballet Theatre. Specializing in creating ballets based on American themes, her work revolutionized the musical theater form with *Oklahoma!* ('43) when her dances revealed the psychological depths of the characters and expanded the story. After *Oklahoma!* nearly every musical contained a "Dream Ballet" in an attempt to achieve what DeMille did — without the benefit of her genius. She was one of the first to use the term: "Choreographer" as her credit and became a director-choreographer on the Broadway stage with *Allegro* in 1947. Due to her phenomenal success with *Oklahoma!*, she was often announced as "signed" for films (**Where Do We Go from Here?**, **London Town**, etc.) but because of marriage and her successful stage and concert creations, her work did not reach the screen again until 1955. She started the Agnes DeMille Dance Theater in 1953 and choreographed many ballets for ABT and the Royal Winnipeg Ballet. In 1973, she organized and choreographed for the Heritage Dance Theatre. Along with her ongoing struggle for the recognition of choreographers and the importance of their contributions, she was elected the first president of SSDC, formed in 1965. Received the *Dance Magazine* Award in 1956, the Capezio Award in 1966, the Kennedy Center Honors in 1980, the White House National Medal of Arts in 1986 and a special Tony award in 1993. After suffering a major stroke in 1975, DeMille continued to lecture and write, being the author of thirteen books which chronicle the development of dance and theater in America during her time, her last book being *The Life and Work of Martha Graham* ('91). In a 1987 PBS documentary on her life, DeMille stated: "I would like one word on my tombstone — dancer."

Autobiographies: *Dance to the Piper* (1952), *And Promenade Home* (1958), *Speak to Me, Dance with Me* (1973), *Where the Wings Grow* (1977)

Stage: *The Black Crook* ('29 rev, Hoboken, NJ), *Flying Colors* (Bdwy '32, with Tamara Geva, Albertina Rasch), *Nymph Errant* (London '33), *Why*

Tony and Sally DeMarco sail across the floor in **Crazy House** (Universal, 1943).

Not Tonight (London '34), *Hooray for What?* (Bdwy '37, replaced by Robert Alton), *Swingin' the Dream* (Bdwy '39), *Oklahoma!* and *One Touch of Venus* (Bdwy '43), *Bloomer Girl* (Bdwy '44), *Carousel* (Bdwy '45) *Allegro* (Bdwy '47, also dir), *Brigadoon* (Bdwy '47, Tony Award), *Gentlemen Prefer Blondes* (Bdwy '49), *Paint Your Wagon* (Bdwy '51), *The Girl in Pink Tights* (Bdwy '54), *Goldilocks* (Bdwy '58, Tony nom), *Juno* (Bdwy '59), *Kwamina* (Bdwy '61, Tony Award), *110 in the Shade* (Bdwy '63), *Come Summer* (Bdwy '69, also dir)

Ballet/Dance Pieces (Partial listing): "Black Ritual" ('40), "Rodeo," "Three Virgins and a Devil," "Tally-Ho!," "Fall River Legend," "Strip Tease," "The Harvest According," "Rib of Eve," "The Rehearsal," "The Four Marys," "The Informer" ('87)

TV (Partial listing): Omnibus: "The Art of Ballet" and "The Art of Choreography" ('56), "Bloomer Girl" ('56), "Lizzie Borden" ('57), "Gold Rush" ('58)

Film:

1930 **Pathé Audio Review #30**—Pathé (S) ("The Black Crook" sequence)

1934 **Cleopatra**—Par (with LeRoy Prinz, billed as "Assistant Dance Director and Ballet Artist")

1936 **Romeo and Juliet**—MGM (assisted by Mary Meyer)

1955 **Oklahoma!**—Magna (with Gene Nelson, assisted by James Mitchell)

1956 **Carousel**—Fox (with Rod Alexander, "**Louise's Ballet**, derived from the original by" credit)

PAT (PATRICIA) DENISE

b. Vancouver, Canada

Strikingly beautiful blonde dancer, teacher and choreographer who studied with June Roper in Vancouver and made her professional debut as a "baby ballerina" for the Ballets Russes in 1940, billed as "Alexandra Denisova." Moving to Hollywood and focusing on commercial dance, she danced on TV and in films including **Easy to Wed** ('46),

Agnes DeMille arrives home from a concert tour of Europe and is met by the press, December 26, 1934.

Singin' in the Rain ('52), **Knock on Wood** ('53), **Three for the Show** ('55, dancing opposite Marge Champion in the **Swan Lake** ballet) and **Marjorie Morningstar** ('58). After assisting Hermes Pan on films and the landmark Fred Astaire TV specials, Jack Baker, and Hugh Lambert ('61 Bing Crosby

TV special), and, Jack Cole on *Zenda* ('63), she received her solo credits. "Dance-in" for Barrie Chase (**The George Raft Story**) and Cyd Charisse (**Party Girl**), she also taught at the George Zoritch school in California for many years.

TV: "Bonanza"

Film:
1953 **The Band Wagon**—MGM (assistant to Fred Astaire, Michael Kidd)
        Knock on Wood—Par (assistant to Kidd, also appeared)
1956 **Meet Me in Las Vegas**—MGM (assistant to Hermes Pan)
1957 **Beau James**—Par (assistant to Jack Baker)
        Funny Face—Par (assistant to Astaire, Pan, with David Robel)
        Les Girls—MGM (assistant to Jack Cole and Gene Kelly, with Alex Romero)
        Silk Stockings—MGM (assistant to Astaire, Eugene Loring, Pan with Angie Blue, David Robel)
1958 **Marjorie Morningstar**—WB (assistant to Jack Baker, also appeared)
1959 **The Big Circus**—AA (with Barbette)
1965 **The Flight of the Phoenix**—Fox

PAUL DeROLF

b. Terre Haute, Indiana, December 6, 1942

Dancer, actor, choreographer, director, teacher and film editor who started dancing as a child, studying with Deloris Blacker and Michel Panaieff. At the age of 7 he appeared on a popular local Los Angeles TV series, "Sandy Dreams" ('49) and began acting in films: **The Seven Little Foys** ('55), **The Ten Commandments** ('56), **I'll Take Sweden** and **The Buster Keaton Story** ('63) and on *TV:* "Bachelor Father," the Ed Sullivan and Donald O'Connor shows and as a regular on "Petticoat Junction"— on which he began his choreographic career. Stage appearances include a West Coast production of *West Side Story, Many Happy Returns* at the Desert Inn in Las Vegas and *Show Me America!* at Disneyland. He also danced in many musical films and television shows during the 1960s and '70s. His career moved into choreography, directing and teaching at a successful dance studio and rehearsal hall he owned and operated in the San Fernando valley. New success as a film editor arrived in the '90s and he relocated to Australia in 1993 for challenges in the growing entertainment industry there.

Stage: *Pinocchio* (Valley Children's Theater, Cal '65)

TV: "Petticoat Junction" (also appeared in a featured role), "The Beverly Hillbillies," "The Danny Thomas Show," "Private Benjamin," "LaVerne and Shirley," "Trapper John, M.D.," "T.J. Hooker," Shields and Yarnell Series, "Bosom Buddies," "Christmas at Walt Disney World"; specials for Johnny Mathis and Lou Rawls; commercials for Celenese Fortrel, Frito Lay, McDonalds, Meiji Chocolate, Schlitz Malt Liquor, Suntory Beer

Music Video: "40 Hour Week"—Alabama

Nightclub/Concert: Acts for the Mike Curb Congregation, Sandy Duncan, Trini Lopez, Debbie Reynolds and Shields and Yarnell

Miscellaneous: *Fantasy on Parade* (Disneyland); industrials for Pacesetters, 7–11

Film:
1978 **Rainbow**—Ten-Four Prod/NBC (TV)
1979 **1941**—Univ/Col (with Judy Van Wormer)
1981 **Evita Peron**—NBC (TV)
        For Ladies Only—NBC (TV)
1985 **My Wicked Wicked Ways**—CBS (TV)
1986 **The Karate Kid Part II**—Col (with Jose DeVega, Pat E. Johnson, Nobuko Miyamoto, Randall Sabusawa)

MARGUERITE POMERHN DERRICKS

Dancer, choreographer and teacher who is currently a member of the faculty at the Joe Tremaine Dance Center. Because of extensive publicity for her work in **Showgirls** ('95), her expertise in erotic dance will probably keep her well-in-demand in the future.

TV: "Circus of the Stars" ('93), "Melrose Place"; commercials for Pepsi, 7-Up

Music Video (Partial listing): Over 75 including "I Don't Go for That"—Quincy Jones; "Sex Cymbal"—Sheila E.; "I Got It Goin' On"—Tone Loc; "With Every Beat of My Heart"—Taylor Dane; "This Time It's for Real"—Donna Summer; "Show You Right"—Barry White

Miscellaneous: Industrials for ASICS, etc.

Film:
1991 **All I Want for Christmas**—Par
1992 **Wild Orchid II: Two Shades of Blue**—Triumph
1994 **Junior**—Univ
1995 **Showgirls**—MGM/UA (*LA Dance* Awards Nom)
1996 **Striptease**—Castle Rock (assisted by Michelle Elkin, Nancy O'Meara, Andrea Moen)

NINETTE DeVALOIS (EDRIS STANUS)

b. Baltiboys, Ireland, June 6, 1898

Internationally influential dancer, teacher, author, choreographer and director who (with Dame Marie Rambert) is regarded as one of the pioneers of British Ballet. As a child she began dance studies and toured in a theatrical troupe, The Wonder Children. Moving to London, she studied with Enrico Cecchetti and made her stage debut as a principal dancer in a pantomime at the Lyceum Theatre in 1914. She danced in revues, at the Royal Opera and joined Ballets Russes in 1923. In 1926, she opened a ballet school in London, The Academy of Choreographic Art. In 1928, she created her first ballet **Les Petits Riens** at the Old Vic and continued to create new ballets annually at the theatre. In 1931, she closed her first school and opened a new one at the newly rebuilt Sadler's Wells Theatre. Her company performed at the Old Vic and Sadler's Wells and was dubbed Vic-Wells Ballet — eventually to become the Sadler's Wells Ballet and finally, the prestigious Royal Ballet in 1957. During the early years of the Sadler's Wells Ballet, she appeared with the company. In 1947, she was awarded the Commander of the Order of the British Empire for her important role in the development of British Ballet and in 1951, Queen Elizabeth honored her as a "Dame of the British Empire." She authored *Invitation to the Ballet* ('37) and *Come Dance with Me* ('57). In 1963 she retired as director of the Royal Ballet, but continued as a life governor. In 1993, she was awarded an honorary doctorate of letters by Cambridge University, a special award by the Society of West End Theatres in London, the Vita per La Danza *Danza e Danza Magazine* award in Italy, the Order of Merit from Queen Elizabeth and a gala 93rd birthday tribute in the Royal Festival Hall in London.

Autobiography: *Come Dance with Me* (1957)

Biography: *Ninette de Valois — Idealist Without Illusions* by Katherine Sorley Walker (1987)

Ballet/Dance Pieces (Partial listing): "Les Petits Riens" ('28), "Le Creation du Monde," "The Haunted Ballroom," "The Rake's Progress," "The Gods Go A'Begging," "Orpheus and Eurydice," "Checkmate," "Job," "The Prospect Before Us," "Promenade," "Don Quixote" ('50)

Film:
1936 **As You Like It** — Fox

JOSE DeVEGA

b. San Diego, California, January 4, 1934
d. Westwood, California, April 8, 1990
Filipino-Columbian dancer, actor and choreographer whose life was cut tragically short by AIDS. Raised in San Diego, he moved to New York after high school to begin his stage performance career. His biggest opportunity arrived in 1957 when he was cast in the role of "Chino" on Broadway in *West Side Story*, reprising his role in the film. That dynamic performance led to roles in the films **Blue Hawaii**, **The Spiral Road** and **A Covenant with Death** ('66). He returned to the stage off–Broadway in *Your Own Thing* in 1968. Relocating to Europe in the early 1970s, he acted in the film **Ash Wednesday** and spent four years with the Modern Dance Company of Rome. When he returned to California for film and TV work, he joined Great Leap — an Asian-American arts organization — in 1981, choreographing, directing and performing in many of their productions which were in the fore-

front (along with the East-West Players) in the increasing awareness of the proper use of Asian-Americans in theatrical projects.

Film:
1986 **The Karate Kid Part II** — Col (with Paul DeRolf, Nobuko Miyamoto, Randall Sabusawa)

MONICA DEVEREUX

Dancer-choreographer married to screenwriter-director Chris Columbus.

Film:
1987 **Adventures in Babysitting** — Touchstone
1988 **Heartbreak Hotel** — Touchstone/Buena Vista
1991 **Backdraft** — Univ
      Only the Lonely — Fox (with Elizabeth Boitsov, "dance supervisor" credit)
1992 **Far and Away** — Univ

PAMELA DEVIS

British dancer-choreographer who appeared on film in **Value for Money** ('57) and had her own line of dancers in clubs and pantomimes.

Stage: "Jack and the Beanstalk" (London Palladium, '68)

Film:
1961 **Too Hot to Handle** — Wigmore/Topaz
1963 **The Dream Maker** (aka **It's All Happening**) — Univ (with Douglas Squires)
1995 **Haunted** — Lumiere Pictures (GB)

MELISSA DEXTER

1991 **Soapdish** — Par (with Tracy Singer)

MATTHEW (PHILIP) DIAMOND

b. New York, November 26, 1951
This successful television director first followed his brother, Dennis, through tap school and into the High School of Performing Arts. Studying every summer at Utah State ("I got into concert dance — the real thorough grounding, professional attitude, discipline, technique, and varied schools of training"), after graduation he made his professional debut in 1968 with the Norman Walker Dance Co. at Jacob's Pillow. Also appeared with Matteo and the Indo-American Dance Company, the NYC Opera, Louis Falco, Paul Sanasardo and José Limon companies. After receiving a B.A. in Literature from CCNY and appearing off–Broadway in *Love Me, Love My Children*, he began creating dance works. He formed his company (DIAMOND) which performed his choreographic pieces from 1979–83. From film choreography work he progressed to television director, directing segments of "Designing

Women," "Family Ties," "My Sister Sam," "The Golden Girls," "Guiding Light" (Emmy Award 1985–86), "Shining Times Station" (Emmy Award 1988–89), "Dance in America—Paul Taylor's *Speaking in Tongues*, Mark Morris' *Hard Nut* and "NBC's Out All Night" ('92, also prod) and "Not My Girl" on "Great Performances" 20th Anniversary Special ('92).

Ballet/Dance Pieces (Partial listing): "Dead Heat," "Thriller," "Hot Peppers," "3 of Diamonds," "Handful of Diamonds," "3 By Matthew Diamond" (all for DIAMOND); "Silent Film" (Utah Repertory Dance Theater '79), "Lunch" (Batsheva Dance Co. '79), "Implosion" (Bat-Dor '82), "A Night at the Ballet" (Washington Ballet '85)

Film:
1984 **Splitz**—Film Ventures
1985 **Maxie**—Orion

LUCINDA DICKEY

Actress, dancer and choreographer who began her film career in the ensemble of **Grease 2** but was quickly elevated to star status in **Breakin'**, **Breakin' 2: Electric Bugaloo** and **Ninja III—The Domination.**

Film:
1988 **Bloody Pom Poms** (aka **Cheerleader Camp**)—Atlantic (also appeared)

RANDY DIGRAZIO

Dancer-choreographer who appeared on Broadway in *Heathen!* ('71) and *Gigi* ('73).

Film:
1982 **Phi Beta Rockers**—?
1984 **Hardbodies**—Col

WILLY DIRTL

b. Vienna, Austria, 1931

Dancer-choreographer who studied ballet at the Vienna Staatsoper and danced as premiere danseur with the company from 1951. He appeared as guest soloist with the Belgrade Royal Opera Ballet ('64).

Film:
1964 **Die Fledermaus**—Casino/United
1968 **$100 a Night**—(Ger)

ANN (ANNE) DITCHBURN

b. Sudbury, Ontario, Canada, October 4, 1949

While starring in and choreographing the 1978 film **Slow Dancing in the Big City**, classical dancer Ditchburn was quoted in the UA press release for the film, "I would love to act again, but I would never give up choreography. And I think they can all feed each other and work together. I found that my progress as an actress was incredibly helped by the way I think as a choreographer. I make move-

ments through motivation and emotion." She began dance classes at 8 and entered the National Ballet of Canada School in 1967, made her debut with the company in 1968 and was promoted to soloist in 1976. While taking a one year leave-of-absence from the company in 1972, she went to London to study at Dance Centre and the Royal Ballet School. She began choreographing at the age of 16 during her last year of school (a three-minute "Listen 1") and continued to combine performance and choreography throughout her career. **Slow Dancing** director John Avildson was intrigued by a photo in the *New York Times* of her choreographing **Mad Shadows** and interviewed and signed her for her film debut. Created her own dance company, Ballet Revue, in 1983 and also appeared in the Canadian thriller **Curtains** that same year.

TV: Ice piece for Toller Cranston

Ballet/Dance Pieces (Partial listing): For the National Ballet of Canada: "Nelligan," "Kisses," "Nuts and Raisins," "Mad Shadows"; "Elouise" (Ballet Horizons, Vancouver)

Film:
1978 **Slow Dancing in the Big City**—UA (with Robert North, also appeared)
1982 **Six Weeks**—Univ (also appeared as "Assistant choreographer")

JOANNE DIVITO

b. Chicago, Illinois, March 10, 1941

Dancer, choreographer and director whose work in **Thank God It's Friday** captured the dance madness of the Disco era on film. After beginning her dance studies in Chicago with Edna McRae, she moved to Manhattan where she learned various dance forms at the Ballet Theatre, Ballets Russes, Joffrey and June Taylor schools, with Jaime Rogers and she studied choreography with Michael Bennett, Valerie Bettis and Anthony Tudor. She made her professional stage debut in NY State Theater productions of *Kismet* and *Annie Get Your Gun* ('65) and on Broadway in 1968 in *The Education of H.Y.M.A.N. K.A.P.L.A.N.* and *Finian's Rainbow* (NYC Center rev). Other performance credits include *Disney on Parade*, "The Raquel Welch Show" in Las Vegas and ballet engagements with the Illinois Ballet ('60–62), the Brooklyn Ballet ('62–63) and the Fibish Israeli Dance Company ('62–64). Made her choreographic debut with *Jockeys* at the Promenade Theatre, Off-Broadway in 1973 and her work continues to enhance all entertainment mediums.

Stage: *Jockeys* (OB '73), *Romance Language* (LA '85)

TV: "And Life Goes On," "Coach," "When We Were Young," "Head of the Class," "Dance Fever" ('79), "Santa Barbara," "Dream," "Goodtime

Choreographer-star Ann Ditchburn soars over Jaime Mercado in the climactic ballet sequence in **Slow Dancing in the Big City** (UA, 1978).

Girls"; commercials for Ace Hardware, Bridgestone Bikes, Dodge, General Foods, Mattel, McDonalds, Pillsbury, Polaroid, Pontiac, Schlitz, Seiko, etc.

Music Video: "I Feel for You"—Chaka Khan; "Go with the Impulse"—Cutting Crew; "I Want You"—Chico De Barge; "Like a Surgeon"—Weird Al Yanovic; "Swear"—Sheena Easton; "Human Touch"—Rick Springfield; "You Are"—Lionel Ritchie; "San Say"—Hiroshima; "Supernatural Love"—Donna Summer

Miscellaneous: *Kid Vid, Blast to the Past, Vid Squad* (Disneyland); Lotte World Theme Park, Seoul, Korea; fashion video for Norma Kamali; industrials for Mazda, Great Western, Valvoline

Film:

1977 **Harold Robbins' "79 Park Avenue"**— Univ (TV)

1978 **Almost Summer**—Univ/Motown

Thank God It's Friday—Col (assisted by Nancy Hammond)

1979 **Amateur Night at the Dixie Bar and Grill**—Univ (TV)

1980 **The Jayne Mansfield Story**—CBS (TV)

1983 **Eddie and the Cruisers**—Embassy

1984 **Body Rock**—New World (with Russell Clark, Susan Scanlan)

1985 **Little Treasure**—TriStar (with Chea Collette)

Once Bitten—Goldwyn

1986 **Bad Guys**—Interpictures

1989 **Wired**—Taurus Ent

1990 **Nite Angel**—Paragon Arts

HARLAND DIXON

b. Toronto, Canada, 1886

d. Jackson Heights, Long Island, N.Y., June 27, 1969

Celebrated character dancer who appeared as a featured performer on Broadway in some of the biggest successes of early American Musical Theater: *Broadway to Paris* ('12), *The Canary* ('18), *Dancing Around* ('14), *Hitchy Koo* ('17), *Tip Top* ('19), *Good Morning Dearie* ('21), *Ziegfeld Follies of 1923, Kid Boots* ('23), *Oh, Kay!* ('26), *Manhattan Mary* ('27), *Rainbow* ('28), *Top Speed* ('29) and

Anything Goes ('34). Dixon was first exposed to dance in gym class at the age of 12 and he continued to teach himself the steps and routines of the dancers he saw, developing an unique character style and repertoire: Big shoe dancing and a style of legomania known as Snap-Knee Eccentric. After winning an amateur contest in 1903, he and a partner, Jimmy Malone, began performing at stag "smokers" for money earned in a passed hat. Running away from home Dixon joined the cast of The George Primrose Minstrels in 1906 (modelling his dance style after Primrose) and then Lew Dockstaeder's Minstrels in 1907. After work in burlesque, he and new partner Jimmy Doyle created Dixon and Doyle and headlined from 1919–21 in vaudeville. His Broadway career flourished until the early thirties: "...suddenly the funny man was out. Everyone wanted ballet and dream sequences and schmalzy love stories with wholesome American backgrounds — operetta stuff" (Bert Lahr, *Jazz Dance*) and Dixon moved to dance direction at the Winter Garden Theatre from 1933–34. His brief film work from 1935–38 included appearances in Vitaphone shorts and dance direction and coaching for Grand National. He returned to New York to stage routines for nightclubs and hotels and appeared on the Broadway stage in *A Tree Grows in Brooklyn* ('51) and *Old Bucks and New Wings* ('62) before his death in 1969.

Film:
1935 **Dubarry Did It Right** — Vitaphone (S) (also appeared)
1937 **Flowers from the Sky** — Vitaphone (S) (also appeared)
       Something to Sing About — WB (with Angie Blue, John Boyle, also appeared)

PEGGY DIXON
1981 **Dragonslayer** — Par

GEORGE DOBBS
Dance and choreographer who appeared in the films **Footlight Serenade** and **The Lady Has Plans** ('42), **The Gang's All Here** ('43) and **Cover Girl** ('44).
Film:
1944 **Song of the Open Road** — UA (with the Condos Brothers)

KATHRYN DOBY (GLATTES)
b. Hungary, January 30, 1938
To escape the Hungarian revolution, this actress, dancer and choreographer emigrated to the United States as a teenager where she would personify "The

American Dream" and become an important collaborator to Bob Fosse and one of the quintessential exponents of his work. She arrived in New York and began her professional American career in 1963 dancing on television on the Ed Sullivan and Jackie Gleason Shows and the "Kraft Music Hall" and in the film **The Cardinal**. She first worked with Fosse in the national tour of *Little Me* ('64) and continued onstage in the Fosse-created shows *Pleasures and Palaces* ('65), *Sweet Charity* ('66), *Pippin* ('72) and *Chicago* ('75), as well as *Coco* and *Georgy* ('70). She appeared in the films **The Night They Raided Minskys** ('68), **Hello, Dolly!** and **Sweet Charity** ('69), **Cabaret** ('72) and **All That Jazz** ('79). She assisted Fosse on film, stage (*Pippin, Chicago* and *Dancin'*) and recreated his original work in various stage productions before she began her own choreographic career.
Stage: *Pippin* (Ntl. Tour '74, Theater an der Wien, Vienna '76)
TV: "Pippin" ('81); commercials for Vidal Sassoon Jeans, others
Miscellaneous: Multiple industrials, 1980–85
Film:
1969 **Sweet Charity** — Univ (assistant to Bob Fosse, also appeared)
1972 **Cabaret** — UA (assistant to Fosse, with John Sharpe, also appeared)
1979 **All That Jazz** — Fox (assistant to Fosse, with Gene Foote, also appeared as "assistant choreographer")
1981 **All the Marbles** (aka **The California Dolls**) — MGM
1983 **Star '80** — Ladd/WB (assistant to Fosse)
1985 **Fear City** — Zupnick-Curtis Enterprises Inc
       The Slugger's Wife — Col

ROYE DODGE
Well-known ballroom dance instructor with his wife, Jane.
Film:
1958 **This Angry Age** — Col (Fr/Ital)

ANTON DOLIN (SYDNEY FRANCIS PATRICK CHIPPENDALL HEALEY-KAY)
b. Sinfold, Sussex, England, July 27, 1904
d. Paris, France, November 25, 1983
England's first internationally acclaimed male ballet star, choreographer and author began his studies with Bronislava Nijinska. He made his stage debut as a child actor in *Peter Pan* and danced with the Diaghilev Ballets Russes from 1921 to 1929.

After Diaghilev's death, Dolin went to America in 1930 in *The International Revue*. Principal dancer with Sadler's Wells Ballet from 1931–33 and Ballets Russes ('39,'46–48), he was also the co-founder, director and leading danseur with the Markova-Dolin Company ('35–38, '45, '47–48). He danced with and choreographed for Ballet Theatre from its inception in 1940 until 1946. After appearing in a West Coast production of *Song Without Words* in 1949, he organized and danced with the London Festival Ballet until 1961. He wrote three autobiographies and *Pas De Deux: The Art of Partnering* ('49), *Alicia Markova, Her Life and Art* ('53) and *The Sleeping Ballerina — The Story of Olga Spessivtzeva* ('66). In addition to the films he also choreographed, his remarkable artistry as a performer can be glimpsed in the films **Dark Red Roses** ('30), **Forbidden Territory** ('38), **The Girl from Petrovka** ('74) and **Nijinsky** ('80). Recipient of the Order of the Sun, Lima, Peru in 1960, the Queen Elizabeth II Coronation Award of the Royal Academy of Dancing in 1957 and the *Dance Magazine* award in 1981. Artistic advisor of Les Grandes Ballets Canadiens until his death in 1983.

Autobiographies: Divertissement (1931), *Ballet Go Round* (1938), *Autobiography* (1960)

Stage: Earl Carroll's Vanities (Bdwy '27, with David Bennett), *That's a Good Girl* (London '28), *Walk with Music* (Bdwy '40), *Seven Lively Arts* (Bdwy '44, with Jack Donohue, also appeared), *The Mitford Girls* (London)

Ballet/Dance Pieces: "Rhapsody in Blue" and "Revolutionary Etude" ('27), "Quintet," "Capriccioso," "Bolero" (with Antonio Gades)

Film (All credits except one are for films Mr. Dolin also danced in):

1934 **Chu Chin Chow** — Gaumont (also appeared)

1935 **Invitation to the Waltz** — Gau/Brit (with Wendy Toye, also appeared)

1945 **A Song for Miss Julie** — Rep (with Larry Ceballos, also appeared with Alicia Markova)

1951 **Toast to Love** (aka **Yolanda**) — (Mex) (also appeared)

1953 **Ali Baba Nights** — Lippert

Never Let Me Go — MGM (also appeared)

EDWARD DOLLY

Stage (All London credits): *Mamzelle Kiki* ('24), *Turned Up* ('26), *Mr. Cinders* ('28), *Out of the Bottle* ('32)

Film:

1930 **Are You There?** — Fox

STANLEY (ISAAC) DONEN

b. Columbia, South Carolina, April 13, 1924

Imaginative dancer-choreographer who achieved even greater success and recognition as a film director, creating memorable musicals and lighthearted adventure films. After seeing **Flying Down To Rio** ("thirty or forty times") he started his dance studies as a child. At 16 he made his Broadway debut in the chorus of *Pal Joey* ('40) starring Gene Kelly, where their friendship began. He won further stage roles in *Best Foot Forward* ('41, in which he assisted Kelly) and *Beat the Band* ('42) and when *Best Foot Forward* was to be filmed, he was invited to Hollywood. While Kelly was making **Cover Girl** at Columbia, he asked Donen to join him as his assistant and Donen remained at Columbia as a dance director. Signing a seven-year contract with MGM, he continued working with Kelly on choreography, musical number staging, filming and direction and after his success co-directing **On the Town** ('49) with Kelly, producer Arthur Freed asked him to solo direct **Royal Wedding** ('51). Donen's film direction credits continued with the successful musicals **Singin' in the Rain** (with Kelly), **Give a Girl a Break**, **Seven Brides for Seven Brothers**, **Deep in My Heart**, **It's Always Fair Weather** (with Kelly), **Funny Face** and **The Pajama Game** — with his knowledge of dance and movement adding immeasurably in collaboration with choreographers Fred Astaire, Nick Castle, Gower Champion, Bob Fosse, Michael Kidd and Eugene Loring. Subsequent films include the comedies **Indiscreet**, **Kiss Them for Me**, **Once More with Feeling**, **Surprise Package**, **The Grass Is Greener**, **Charade**, **Arabesque**, **Two for the Road**, **Bedazzled** and **Blame It on Rio**. He spoke about his feelings concerning film in the documentary **MGM: When the Lion Roars**, "I always laugh about Jean-Luc Goddard's comment that film is truth 24 times a second because in my opinion, film is a lie 24 times a second. Everything is prearranged, pre-digested, rehearsed, thought out, worked out, written down and eventually photographed." Donen's colorful, rhythmic "lies" have gloriously entertained the world. He made his debut as a Broadway director with the stage version of *The Red Shoes* ('93).

Biography: Stanley Donen by Joseph Andrew Casper (1983), *Dancing on the Ceiling* by Stephen M. Silverman (1996)

Stage: Best Foot Forward (Bdwy '41, assisted Gene Kelly), *Call Me Mister* (Bdwy '46, staged some numbers), *Singin' in the Rain* (Bdwy '85, with Gene Kelly, film choreography recreated for the stage production by John Carrafa)

Music Video: "Dancing on the Ceiling" — Lionel Richie (dir only)

Film:

1943 **Best Foot Forward** — MGM (with J. M. Andrew, Jack Donohue and Charles Walters, also appeared)

Swing Out the Blues— Col
1944 **Beautiful But Broke**— Col
Cover Girl— Col (asst to Kelly, with Jack
Cole, Seymour Felix, Val Raset)
Hey, Rookie— Col (with the Condos
Bros., Ann Miller, Val Raset)
Jam Session— Col (with Miller)
Kansas City Kitty— Col
Stars on Parade— Col
1945 **Anchors Aweigh**— MGM (with Jack
Donohue, Kelly)
The Gay Señorita— Col. (with Antonio
Triana)
1946 **Holiday in Mexico**— MGM
No Leave, No Love— MGM
1947 **Killer McCoy**— MGM
Living in a Big Way— MGM (with Kelly)
This Time for Keeps— MGM ("dances
and water ballet by" credit)
1948 **The Big City**— MGM
A Date with Judy— MGM
The Kissing Bandit— MGM (with
Robert Alton)
1949 **On the Town**— MGM (with Kelly,
assisted by Alex Romero, also co-dir)
Take Me Out to the Ball Game— MGM
(with Busby Berkeley, Kelly, assisted by Alex
Romero, also co-scripted)
1951 **Double Dynamite**— RKO
1952 **Singin' in the Rain**— MGM (with Kelly,
also co-dir)
1953 **Give a Girl a Break**— MGM (with Gower
Champion, Bob Fosse, Bill Foster, also dir)
Sombrero— MGM (with Hermes Pan,
Jose Greco, staged Greco's dance)
1955 **It's Always Fair Weather**— MGM (with
Kelly, also co-dir)
1957 **Funny Face**— Par (with Fred Astaire,
Eugene Loring, "Songs staged by" credit, also dir)
1974 **That's Entertainment!**— MGM (with
others)
1976 **That's Entertainment, Part II**— MGM
(with others)
1978 **Movie, Movie**— WB (with Michael Kidd,
"Torchin' for Bill" number, also dir and prod)
1986 **That's Dancing!**— MGM (with others)
1994 **That's Entertainment III**— MGM (with
others)

JACK (JOHN) DONOHUE

b. New York, November 3, 1908
d. Marina Del Rey, California, March 27, 1984
An actor, dancer, dance director and film and
television director whose career spanned three
decades was described by Betty Garrett (who
worked with him in **Neptune's Daughter**) as, "A
delicious man with a wonderful sense of humor."

Above and beyond his talents for staging musical
numbers, he was most successful creating energetic,
acrobatic musical comedy sequences for Betty Hutton (**Star Spangled Rhythm**, '42), Red Skelton
(**Neptune's Daughter**, '49) and even Greer Garson
and Ricardo Montalban (a raucous Circus sequence
in **Julia Misbehaves**, '48). Of Irish descent, Donohue had no show business aspirations and after
graduating from St. Anne's Military Academy, he
got a job as a riveter. While on the job, he fell two
stories and broke both knees on a painter's scaffold.
Doctors suggested dance exercises for rehabilitation
and, after recovery, he saw an advertisement for an
audition for chorus boys and was hired for *Ziegfeld
Follies of 1927*. Without any formal dance instruction (but constant practice of dance routines in his
hotel room) dancing roles in the shows *Good News*
and *Shoot the Works* followed. While giving Broadway star Fred Stone's daughters, Paula and Dorothy,
dance lessons, Stone gave him a week's tryout as
"assistant dance director" to Merriel Abbott on
Smiling Faces in 1933. He assisted Bobby Connolly
on *Free for All* and *East Wind* ('31) *Take a Chance*
('32) and *Melody* ('33) and Albertina Rasch on *Face
The Music*, *Walk a Little Faster* and *Flying Colors*
('32). After being signed by Oscar Hammerstein to
do *Music in the Air* on Broadway, he was taken to
London by Hammerstein to do the ensembles for
Ball At the Savoy. He stayed in England for a year
doing dance direction and starring onstage, appearing opposite Lili Damita and Beatrice Lillie. He was
signed to take over Fred Astaire's stage role in the
London production of *The Gay Divorce* when Fox
brought him back to America and films as dance
director from 1934–36, primarily on Shirley Temple films. In 1937 he returned to England to choreograph films and also staged and starred in musicals and plays throughout Europe, as well as the
film **Smiling Along** ('38). He was staging musicals
in Sweden and Norway when World War II broke
out and he managed to return to America in 1940,
appearing on Broadway (*Higher and Higher*,
Panama Hattie, etc.) and returning as a dance director at various studios until signing with MGM in
December, 1942. He took a suspension from MGM
dance director chores to direct **Close-Up** at Eagle-
Lion in 1948 and eventually became a respected film
director with **The Yellow Cab Man**, **Watch the
Birdie**, **Lucky Me**, **Babes in Toyland**, **Top
Banana**, **Marriage on the Rocks**, **Assault on a
Queen** and many TV shows ("The Dinah Shore
Chevy Show," 81 Frank Sinatra Shows, 47 Red Skel-
ton Shows). His career is often confused with
Broadway song-and-dance star — also former iron
worker — Jack Donahue, who died in 1930. Sur-
vived by a son and daughter.

Stage: *Fast and Furious* (Bdwy '31), *A Little Racketeer* (with Albertina Rasch) and *Music in the Air*

(Bdwy '32), *Shady Lady* (Bdwy '33, also appeared), *Ball at the Savoy*, *Mr. Whittington* (with Buddy Bradley and Jack Buchanan) and *Jill Darling* (London '33), *Here's How!* (London '34, also appeared), *Going Greek* (London '37), *Wild Oats* and *Running Riot* (London '38), *White Plaster* (Sweden '38, also appeared), *Sitting Pretty* (London '39, also appeared), *Think of Something Else* (Norway '39), *Seven Lively Arts* (Bdwy '44, dir and asst choreo to Anton Dolin), *Are You with It?* (Bdwy '45), *Top Banana* (Bdwy '51, dir only), *Of Thee I Sing* (Bdwy '52 rev), *Jollyana* (LACLO '52, with Jack Cole, also dir), *A Night in Venice* (Jones Beach, '53–54), *Mr. Wonderful* (Bdwy '56, also dir), *Rumple* (Bdwy '57, dir only)

TV: "Colgate Comedy Hour" Summer series ('54, also dir, prod), Lux Christmas Show ('56), "The Stan Freburg Show" ('62, also dir)

Film:
1934 **Marie Galante**— Fox
      Music in the Air— Fox
1935 **Curly Top**— Fox
      Dressed to Thrill— Fox
      George White's Scandals of 1935— Fox (with Chester Hale)
      Life Begins at 40— Fox
      The Little Colonel— Fox (with Bill Robinson)
      The Littlest Rebel— Fox (with Robinson)
      The Lottery Lover— Fox
      Music Is Magic— Fox
      Thanks a Million— Fox
      Under Pressure— Fox
      Under the Pampas Moon— Fox (with Frank Veloz)
1936 **Captain January**— Fox
      Rhythm in the Air— Gau/Brit (also appeared)
1937 **Mayfair Melody**— Teddington
      Paradise for Two (aka **The Gaiety Girls**— UA (with Philip Buchel, Jack Hulbert)
1938 **Everything Happens to Me**— WB First National
      Keep Smiling— Fox
      The Singing Cop— WB First National
1941 **Louisiana Purchase**— Par (with George Balanchine)
      You're in the Army Now— Gau/Brit
1942 **The Fleet's In**— Par
      The Powers Girl— UA (with George Murphy)
      Priorities on Parade— Col (with Ann Miller)
      Star Spangled Rhythm— Par (with George Balanchine, Danny Dare, Katherine Dunham, uncredited)
      True to the Army— Col (with Miller)
1943 **Best Foot Forward**— MGM (with J.M. Andrew, Stanley Donen, Charles Walters)

Girl Crazy— MGM (with Busby Berkeley, Walters, staging of "Treat Me Rough" number)
      Salute for Three— Par
1944 **Bathing Beauty**— MGM (with Robert Alton, John Murray Anderson)
      Broadway Rhythm— MGM (with Alton, Don Loper, George Murphy, Walters)
      The Canterville Ghost— MGM
      Lost in a Harem— MGM
      Meet the People— MGM (with Sammy Lee and Walters)
      Music for Millions— MGM
1945 **Anchors Aweigh**— MGM (with Donen, Gene Kelly)
      Dangerous Partners— MGM
1946 **Easy To Wed**— MGM
      Love Laughs at Andy Hardy— MGM
      The Show-Off— MGM
      Two Sisters from Boston— MGM
1947 **It Happened in Brooklyn**— MGM
      Romance of Rosy Ridge— MGM
      Song of the Thin Man— MGM
1948 **Julia Misbehaves**— MGM
      On an Island with You— MGM
1949 **The Bribe**— MGM
      Madame Bovary— MGM
      Neptune's Daughter— MGM
      That Midnight Kiss— MGM
1950 **The Duchess of Idaho**— MGM (with Eleanor Powell)
1953 **Calamity Jane**— WB (assisted by Ernest Flatt)
1954 **Lucky Me**— WB (with LeRoy Prinz, assisted by Jack Boyle, also dir)
      A Star Is Born— WB (with Richard Barstow— when the film was so long in production, Barstow had to leave for other work and Donohue created several sequences)
1974 **That's Entertainment!**— MGM (with others)
1976 **That's Entertainment, Part II**— MGM (with others)
1992 **The Mambo Kings**— WB (with Kim Blank, Paul Pellicoro, Michael Peters— number from **Neptune's Daughter**)
1994 **That's Entertainment! III**— MGM (with others)

GAVIN DORIAN
1994 **Thumbelina**—WB (with Bruno "Taco" Falcon, "Live action reference choreography" credit)

DONALD DOUGLASS
1987 **Hollywood Shuffle**— Goldwyn

Jack Donohue "famed director of dances for Broadway and London hits signed as a dance director and actor by Fox" says this publicity still when Donohue began his first assignment on **Music in the Air** (1934) (photo courtesy of the Academy of Motion Picture Arts and Sciences).

MARA DOUSSE

1939 **Ball at the Castle** (aka **Ballo al Castello**)—(Ital)

ARTHUR DREIFUSS

b. Frankfurt, Germany, March 25, 1911
d. Studio City, California, December 31, 1993
As a child, Dreifuss was a prodigy pianist and conductor in Germany. He attended the University

of Frankfurt to pursue a writing and musical career. In 1928, he emigrated to New York, attending Columbia University Conservatory of Music and New York University, supporting himself as a pianist and arranger for Ziegfeld star, Jack Donahue. He began performing in Broadway shows, eventually producing. After moving to Hollywood and supporting himself by giving tap classes at the Fanchon and Marco school, he choreographed his first movie and then became a prolific motion picture producer, writer and director from 1939 to 1968 directing over 40 films for Allied Artists, American International, Columbia, Eagle-Lion, Grand National, Monogram, RKO and Universal (**Eadie Was a Lady, Juke Box Rhythm, Junior Prom, Riot on Sunset Strip, There's a Girl in My Heart**, etc.). In the 1950s and '60s he also produced, wrote and directed for television, taking just enough time off to teach classes in film technique at the University of Denver. The 1967 Columbia press release for a film about "hippies" that he wrote and directed lauds his multi-talents: "In a film like **The Love-Ins**, where music and dancing are almost as important as the dramatic talents of the stars ... a background of experience like Dreifuss' proved invaluable." In 1981 (at the age of 70) the multi-hyphenate Dreifuss announced he was starting a new career as a talent agent!

Film:
1936 **Hats Off** — Grand Ntl (with Victor Petroff)
1947 **Little Miss Broadway** — Col (with Victor McLeod, Betty Wright)

JANN DRYER
1994 **Even Cowgirls Get the Blues** — New Line Cinema (with Ruby Burns)

KATHERINE DUNHAM
b. Glen Ellyn, Illinois, June 22, 1912

A deservedly revered pioneer in ethnic and jazz dance, Katherine Dunham was once described as "a highly gifted creator of a modern technique which is firmly based in authentic origins." Her natural love of dance was encouraged in public schools in Joliet and when she began ethnology studies at the University of Chicago, she began ballet with Ludmilla Sperenza and taught dance to support her education. Constantly seeking to find a legitimate place for African-American dancers in classical dance, in 1931, she formed the first black dance company, Ballet Négre. In 1933, she made her dancing debut with the Chicago Opera and also appeared at the Chicago World's Fair in *La Guiabless*. She extensively researched dance in the Caribbean on fellowships during the mid 1930s and relocated to New York in 1940. Her concert "Tropics and Le Jazz Hot: From Haiti to Harlem" at the New York YMHA that year was a sensation. In 1943 she founded the Katherine Dunham Dancers, who appeared in nightclubs, on television and in concert for nearly three decades. Making her Broadway debut in *Pins and Needles* ('39) she appeared on Broadway in *Cabin in the Sky* ('40), and with her dancers in *Carib Song, Blue Holiday* and *Concert Varieties* ('45), *Bal Negre* ('46) and *Bambouche* ('62). Her appearances in commercial films gave much-needed exposure to black artists and her choreography made ethnic dance more acceptable to wide audiences. In 1945, she founded the Katherine Dunham School of Cultural Arts in New York City and the Performing Arts Training Center in East St. Louis in 1955, and has influenced generations of artists, as the "Dunham Technique" is still taught internationally. In *America Dances*, Agnes DeMille described some of Dunham's unique talents, "She had a very simple body technique. What she gave was her personality, and that was nothing short of magic, for she had a most unusual combination of qualities: seductiveness — very real and very sweet — and humor ... and always she seemed natural: indeed her large scenes seemed spontaneous — both totally deceptive impressions. Her large scenes were works of art and organized with great skill." Author of *Journey to Accompong, The Dance of Haiti; Island Possessed* and *Kasamance*. Winner of the *Dance Magazine* award in 1968, the Kennedy Center Honors in 1983, a 1993–94 Artslink Collaboration Projects grant and holder of a master's degree in anthropology from the University of Chicago. Widow of scenic and costume designer John Pratt and mother of daughter Marie-Christine, since the '60s, she has owned a large plantation in Haiti and continues to help its citizens through humanitarian efforts.

Autobiography: A Touch of Innocence (1959)
Biography: Katherine Dunham — A Biography by Ruth Beckford (1979)
Stage: Tropical Revue (Bdwy '43, also appeared), Blue Holiday, Carib Song and Concert Varieties (Bdwy '45, also appeared), Bal Negre (Bdwy '46) and Windy City (OOT '46, also asst dir), Bambouche (Bdwy '62, also appeared), Aïda (Metropolitan Opera '64), Peg (Bdwy '67)
Ballet/Dance Pieces (Partial listing): "L'ag'Ya" ('37), "Rara Tonga," "Tropics and Le Jazz Hot — From Haiti to Harlem," "Barrelhouse," "Batacuda," "Rites of Passage," "Plantation Dances," "Afrique," "Tropics," "Nanigo," "Bahaina," "Shango," "Florida Swamp Shimmy," "Flaming Youth," "Veracruzana," etc.
Films:
1941 **Carnival of Rhythm** — WB (S) (also appeared)
1942 **Cuban Episode** — Soundies Corp (S) (also appeared)
        Flamingo — Soundies Corp (S) (also appeared)

Pardon My Sarong— Univ (with Tip, Tap and Toe, "dances originated and staged by" credit)
The Spirit of Boogie Woogie— Soundies Corp (S) (also appeared)
Star Spangled Rhythm— Par (with George Balanchine, Danny Dare, Jack Donohue, also appeared)
1943 **Stormy Weather**— Fox (with Nick Castle, Fanchon, Fayard Nicholas, Bill Robinson, Clarence Robinson, also appeared)
1948 **Casbah**— Univ (with Bernard Pearce, also appeared)
1950 **Botta E Riposta**— Ponti-De Laurentis
1955 **Mambo**—(Ital) (also appeared)
1955 **Musica en la Noche**— Alianza Cinematographer
1959 **Green Mansions**— MGM
1966 **The Bible—in the Beginning**— Fox

ROLAND DUPREE

b. September 20, 1925
Highly successful Southern California dancer, choreographer and teacher who spent many years of his professional career performing before progressing into dance education and choreography. He danced as one of the Jivin' Jacks and Jills in **Always a Bridesmaid** ('43) and appeared in over twenty films from 1938 to 1957: **The Star Maker, You Can't Take It with You, Hey, Rookie!, Moonlight in Havana, Miss Annie Rooney, Maisie Goes to Reno, It Comes Up Love, Panama Sal**, etc. During the early '50s, he had a dance group (the Roland Dupree Trio) who worked in nightclubs and musical shorts. In 1978, he formed Dance Power to perform in clubs and the Los Angeles Jazz Company in 1979 for concert appearances. Opening the Roland Dupree Dance Academy in 1950, he was one of Hollywood's most successful and influential teachers and coaches (Juliet Prowse, Sylvie Varten, etc.), owning and operating the dance and rehearsal studio into the Eighties.
Stage: *Max, Point of View* and *Pal Joey* (LA '61), *Pal Joey* and *Silk Stockings* (Circle Arts Theater, San Diego, Cal, '61)
TV: "The Bob Hope Show" and 35th Academy Awards Show ('61), "The Jackie Gleason Show," "The Spike Jones Show," Peggy Fleming Special ('68), "Swing-in Fling" ('70), "Shields and Yarnell" ('77–78), commercials for Firestone, Pepsi Cola
Nightclub/Concert (Partial listing): *Let's Go Calypso* and *Come to the Mardi Gras* (Club Seville, LA, '57), *French Poodle* (NY '63), *Turn on '68* (Flamingo Hotel, LV); acts for Michael Callan, Helen Grayco, Barbara Luna, Gavin McCloud, Sheree North, Janis Paige and Lesley Ann Warren
Film:
1950 **I'll Get By**— Fox (asst to Larry Ceballos)

1957 **Panama Sal**— Rep (also appeared)
1960 **G.I. Blues**— Par (assistant to Charles O'Curran)
Hell to Eternity— AA
1961 **Gidget Goes Hawaiian**— Col

JUAN DUVAL
1930 **One Mad Kiss**— Fox

JOSEPHINE EARL
b. Boston, Massachusetts, circa 1910
d. Los Angeles, California, January 7, 1972
Eventually becoming one of the few female studio-contracted dance directors, Josephine began as a ballerina taking dance lessons from Mme. Lilla Viles Wyman in Boston at the age of 7. At 14 she graduated from Ivan Tarasoff's dance school in New York and made her professional debut as premiere danseuse with Anatole Bourman at the Strand Theater in New York. A stint in *The Greenwich Village Follies of 1934* followed and next, a tour with her own dance company (owned by Jack Pomeroy, an agent she would soon wed) and she opened her first dance school in New York. She was brought to the West Coast by Republic Pictures and was under contract there from 1939–41. She then moved to Paramount in 1942 as assistant to Danny Dare. Dare further encouraged her choreographic career when he hired her to create the dance sequences for **Isn't It Romantic?**, a film he produced for Paramount in 1947. In the April, 1953 issue of *Dance Magazine* she is credited with doing the first 3-D choreography for a commercial film in 1953 ("When she received her assignment she planned the three 18th century ballroom dances in the script for 'flat' film, Half-way through the picture it was decided that **Sangaree** should be shot in 3-D as well. As a result the twelve couples executing the dances are doing their performances in two different ways, one for the conventional type film, the other for 3-D.") She remained at Paramount until 1958, creating most of the dance and movement sequences for their comedies and dramas as well as operating the Josephine Earl Academy of Dance Art at 7616 Sunset Blvd. in Hollywood, which opened March, 1955. When her husband, Jack Pomeroy, died in 1965, she continued his talent agency until her death in 1972.
Nightclub/Concert: Shows for multiple nightclub venues (Babette Club, Atlantic City; Flamingo Hotel, LV, etc.); acts for the Andrews Sisters, Harry James, Johnny Silver and His Dolls
Film:
1940 **Barnyard Follies**— Rep
1943 **Gals, Incorporated**— Rep
Hoosier Holiday— Rep
Swing Your Partner— Rep

Dancer, choreographer and noted anthropologist Katherine Dunham, works out the rhythms with a drummer for her creations in **Green Mansions** (MGM, 1958).

1944 **You Can't Ration Love**— Par
1945 **Bombalera**— Par (S)
    Boogie Woogie— Par (S)
    Isle of Tabu— Par
    Star Bright— Par

1946 **Monsieur Beaucaire**— Par (with Billy Daniel)
1947 **Imperfect Lady**— Par (with Daniel)
1948 **Isn't It Romantic?**— Par (with Danny Dare)

1949 **A Connecticut Yankee in King Arthur's Court**— Par
　　　The Heiress— Par
　　　Sorrowful Jones— Par
1950 **Copper Canyon**— Par
　　　The Furies— Par
　　　My Friend Irma Goes West— Par
1952 **Hurricane Smith**— Par
　　　Son of Paleface— Par
1953 **Sangaree**— Par
　　　Shane— Par
1954 **Casanova's Big Night**— Par
1955 **The Far Horizons**— Par
1957 **Calypso Heat Wave**— Col
　　　Gunfight at the O.K. Corral— Par
　　　The Joker Is Wild— Par
　　　Teacher's Pet— Par (assisted by Hamil Petroff and Larri Thomas)
1958 **The Buccaneer**— Par
　　　Desire Under the Elms— Par
　　　Houseboat— Par (assisted by Larri Thomas)
1959 **Hound Dog Man**— Fox (assisted by Tommy Ladd and Winona Smith)
1960 **Flaming Star**— Fox
　　　North to Alaska— Fox
1961 **One Eyed Jacks**— Par (assisted by Tommy Ladd)
　　　The Right Approach— Fox (assisted by Erik Cooper)
1962 **Sergeants Three**— UA

CARLA EARLE

b. New York, August 29

Performer, choreographer, director and dance educator who attended the High School of Performing Arts in New York and received her dance training from Alvin Ailey, Bernice Johnson and at the Joffrey Ballet school. She made her professional stage debut in the touring company of *The Wiz* in 1978 (also dancing in the film and the '84 Bdwy revival). Other stage appearances include the 1979 international tour of *Bubbling Brown Sugar,* the 1980 tour of *Chicago* and dancing on Broadway in *42nd Street* and *Black Broadway.* After relocating to the West Coast, she worked in films (**Beaches, Coming to America, The Cotton Club** and **Tap**), television (Academy Awards Shows and Debbie Allen Specials) and made her choreographic debut with a promo commercial for the Los Angeles Lakers in 1988. Her teaching has allowed her to pass her knowledge and experiences on to the next generation. Encompassing a combination of styles (jazz, tap, Hip Hop and modern), her master workshops have taken her to Vancouver and Moosejaw, Canada, and Paris and Cannes, France. Naturally progressing into direction, she looks forward to more commercial and video directing chores and praises God for the blessings of her talents.

TV: "In Living Color" (also dir of dance sequences), "Soul Train," "The Mickey Mouse Club," "Nia Peeples Party Machine," "Burke's Law" ('93 pilot); commercials for Darkwing Duck, Hasbro, *Los Angeles Times,* Mattel and McDonalds

Music Video: "Hold On"— En Vogue; "Serious"— La Rue; "Talk to Myself"— Christopher Williams; "Countdown"— L.A. Posse; "Love's About to Change My Heart"— Donna Summer, "Darkwing Duck"

Nightclub/Concert:(also dir) En Vogue, Christopher Williams ('89), Marva Hicks, La Rue, Pretty in Pink and Donna Summer Tours

Film:
1991 **Iron Eagles II**— Ron Samuels/1st Film Int.

LORI EASTSIDE

b. Chicago, Illinois

A champion gymnast who channeled her energies into dance because of an injury, Eastside has created a unique career combining her exploration of physical wellness and her love of contemporary music with choreography and musical staging. After graduating from college, she moved to Great Britain and taught at the London Dance Centre. While in England, she found the opportunity to fulfill another ambition and joined her first rock group, The Lilettes. Returning to New York in 1980 she performed as lead vocalist for Kid Creole and the Coconuts for three years and then, left her live rock performance career behind when she choreographed her first film, **Get Crazy**— in which she also co-starred. After being Mick Jagger's personal trainer and choreographer from 1986–87, she continues to interweave contemporary music and dance in music videos, rock concerts and films.

Music Video: "Rock This Town"— The Stray Cats; "Tonight"— Kool and The Gang; "Beast of Burden"— Bette Midler; "This Is My Night"— Mick Jagger and Chaka Khan; "Harlem Shuffle"— The Rolling Stones (1986 *Billboard Magazine* Outstanding Achievement Award winner)

Nightclub/Concert: Mick Jagger tour ('89)
Film:
1983 **Get Crazy**— Embassy (also appeared)
1984 **Alphabet City**— Atlantic
1985 **Krush Groove**— WB
1987 **Back to the Beach**— Par
　　　China Girl— Vestron
1989 **Loverboy**— TriStar
1990 **Cry Baby**— Univ
1991 **Mannequin 2: On the Move**— Gladden Ent. Corp (assisted by Coco)
1993 **Tom and Jerry (The Movie)**— Miramax

PEARL EATON (ENDERLY)

b. 1898

d. Los Angeles, California, September 10, 1958

Sister of Mary, Doris and Charles Eaton — all major Broadway stars of the 1920s — this dancer, actress and choreographer appeared on Broadway as the dancing star of *Tick-Tack-Toe* ('20), *Earl Carroll's Vanities of 1925* and *She's My Baby* ('28). Married to Oscar Levant's brother, Harry, she had a line of dancers at Radio City Music Hall and taught tap (with Oscar Levant often playing piano for her classes). She left New York in 1928 when she was invited to relocate to Hollywood. Divorced from Levant in 1930, she was a dance director at RKO from 1929–31 and continued her performance career with appearances in the films **Tanned Legs** ('29) **Goin' to Town** ('35) and **Klondike Annie** ('36).

Stage: *Showboat* ('33 LA rev)

Film:

1929 **Rio Rita** — RKO
       Street Girl — RKO
1930 **The Cuckoos** — RKO
       Dixiana — RKO (with Bill Robinson)
       Hit the Deck — MGM
       Leathernecking — RKO
       Love Comes Along — RKO
1933 **Dance, Girl, Dance** — Invincible

MICHELE EHLERS

Arriving in China in 1982 to study Chinese and teach English, Ehlers' life and career took a new direction when she met Jamie H. J. Guan, a member of the Peking Opera. She began study of various Chinese performing arts and after marrying in China, Guan and Ehlers relocated to the United States. Approached by several schools to introduce Peking Opera techniques, they created a program of performance and lecture ("The Magic of the Monkey King") combining dance, drama, music and acrobatics which has been presented in multiple schools, universities and museums. When Guan was cast in the Broadway drama *M. Butterfly*, she and Guan were signed as Peking Opera consultants for the show, subsequently translating their work to film.

Stage: *M. Butterfly* (Bdwy '87), *The Woman Warrior* (LA '95)

Film:

1993 **M. Butterfly** — WB (with Jamie H.J. Guan, "Beijing Opera Choreography" credit)

SARAH ELGART

b. Chicago, Illinois, July 3, 1955

Dubbed "The Punk Gamine of Los Angeles Modern Dance" by the *Los Angeles Times*, Elgart has a career which moves from experimental dance and theater to commercial work with ease and regularity. As a child, she spent some of her growing years in Los Angeles, eventually moving to New York at the age of 20 to join Michael Sullivan's dance company, Mobius. She danced briefly with Donald Byrd's company before moving to Europe and study with disciples of Pina Bausch and Kurt Jooss at the Volk Wang Hoch Schule in Essen Werden, Germany. In 1979 she returned to Los Angeles and formed her own dance company, Pro Motion — which eventually became Sarah Elgart and Company. A workshop with Michael Kidd and Stanley Donen exposed her to dance on film and its possibilities and in 1983, she began working commercially for the Disney Channel. Along with films and television, she created a "Gestural Theater Group" (MADRES — Mothers and Daughters Reaching Empowered States) which continues to tour. Her television work has now moved into producing and directing. She served as Music Segment Producer for the Disney Channel's "New Mickey Mouse Club" and directed a film for the American Film Institute. In the August 15, 1986 issue of the *Hollywood Reporter*, her approach was described: "Elgart, who believes staging is an art in itself, said choreography involves more than dance and that she presumes there is a need for her services when actors are too inexperienced to improvise their own movements and gestures, directors are too busy or inexperienced to work with actors or sequences that are complicated enough to require a choreographer to help define characters. 'I'm interested in the evolution from ordinary walking and gestures to dance... My own dance works organically from the inside out, whereas my choreography in film works from the outside in... Each has its own challenges.'" A new baby, born in April, 1993, is one of the newest challenges within her busy and varied schedule.

TV: "The New Mickey Mouse Club," "L.A. Law," "Alien Nation," "thirtysomething"; commercials for Bugle Boy Jeans

Music Video (Partial listing): "Halo" — Depeche Mode; "Innocent Lover" — The Whispers; "It's No Crime" — Babyface; "Liverpool" — The Bangles; "Wilbury Twist" — Traveling Wilburys; over 35 for such artists as Patti LaBelle, Kenny Rogers, Ashford and Simpson, Alabama, Toto, the Pointer Sisters

Ballet/Dance Pieces: "Recess," plus multiple works for Sarah Elgart and Co.

Film:

1983 **Sudden Impact** — WB
1984 **Beverly Hills Cop** — Par
1986 **Fire with Fire** — Par
       Howard the Duck — Univ
       Modern Girls — Atlantic

1987 **The All Nighter**— Univ
1988 **It Takes Two**— UA
       Pass the Ammo— New Century/Vista
1989 **Earth Girls Are Easy**— Vestron (with Russell Clark, ISO, Wayne "Crescendo" Ward— "Brand New Girl" number)
1990 **Bad Influence**— Triumph (also appeared)
1993 **And the Band Played On**— HBO (TV) (with Myles Thoroughgood)

OSHRA EL KAYAM

A student of Martha Graham and a graduate of Juilliard, El Kayam danced with Batsheva and founded the Inter-Kibutzim Modern Dance Co., choreographing for them as well as Inbal, another Israeli dance group. In 1964, he began his own company.
Film:
1976 **Moses** (aka **Moses, the Lawgiver**)- ITC-RAI/AE (TV)

COCO ELLACOTT

Polynesian dancer and choreographer.
Film:
1979 **Hurricane**— Par
1981 **Beyond the Reef**— Univ

PETER ELLIOT

b. Yorkshire, England, 1956
A new category of specialized movement credit arrived on film in the '80s with such artists as Elliot, who pioneered in designing and teaching animal movement — dubbed "Primate Choreography." At he age of 6, he began exploring his athletic abilities through diving, boxing and as part of an acrobatics team which toured England. He enrolled in Drama School, specializing in movement and made his professional debut in English Music Hall Revues. After two years of intensive study of "Primate Behavior" he applied his knowledge to his first film, **Greystoke: The Legend of Tarzan**, portraying the male ape who raised Tarzan in a dazzling and sympathetic performance. Other film appearances include **Return to Oz**, **Quest for Fire** and **King Kong Lives**. His exploration of movement has now broadened to include "Alien Movement."
Film:
1984 **Greystoke: The Legend of Tarzan**— WB
1986 **Clan of the Cave Bear**— WB ("Clan Body Movement by" credit)
1995 **Congo**— Par (with Adam Shankman)

WARD ELLIS

b. Los Angeles, California, 1926
d. Los Angeles, California, May 4, 1985
Ellis began his career as a child, performing on radio, stage (*Gentlemen Prefer Blondes* and *Pal Joey* at the Greek Theater, Los Angeles), films (**The Strip**, **The Second Greatest Sex**, **Meet Me in Las Vegas**), television, and in nightclubs. His choreographic work began as an assistant in films to Robert Alton, Miriam Nelson and Jerome Robbins and on the Broadway stage with Robert Alton (*Hazel Flagg*, '53) and Gower Champion (*Three for Tonight*, '54). His solo work as a choreographer was primarily for television and nightclubs, being a pioneer in the creation of the young, high-energy song-and-dance groups like The Young Americans, The Doodletown Pipers and The Ward Ellis Dancers on television, nightclubs and in concert in the '60s.
   Stage: *Hardly a Kind Word About Anybody* (LA '62)
   TV: "The Paul Winchell-Jerry Mahoney Show" ('53–54), "The Hollywood Palace," "Romp," "The Bob Newhart Show" ('61–62) "The Ed Sullivan Show," "The Ford Show Starring Tennessee Ernie Ford," "The Dean Martin Show," "Stage '66," "The Roger Miller Show" ('66), "Our Place" ('67)
   Nightclub/Concert: Acts for Edie Adams, George Burns, Vicki Carr, Perry Como, The Doodletown Pipers (which he co-created), Pinky Lee, Johnny Mathis and the Young Americans (concert tour '64), Donald O'Connor, Andy Williams and Nancy Wilson
   Film:
1953 **Call Me Madam**— Fox (assistant to Robert Alton)
1954 **There's No Business Like Show Business**— Fox (assistant to Alton, with Ernest Flatt)
1955 **Bring Your Smile Along**— Col (assistant to Miriam Nelson)
1956 — **The King and I**— Fox (assistant to Jerome Robbins)
1957 **The Pied Piper of Hamelin**— Grand Ntl (TV)
       War Drums— UA
1964 **Three Nuts in Search of a Bolt**— Independent
1966 **The Big T.N.T. Show**— AIP

ANGNA ENTERS

b. New York, 1907
d. Tenefly, New Jersey, February 25, 1989
Called "The Vestal Virgin of the Theatre and applied arts" by *American Dancer* (November, 1934), as one of America's first acknowledged performance artists, Angna Enters' career was as colorful as her name. A dancer-mime, choreogra-

pher, painter, sculptor and author, she began dance studies in Milwaukee and in 1922, enrolled in the Art Students' League in New York. After studying dance and performing with Michio Ito, she gave her first solo performance in 1924. Creating the Theatre of Angna Enters in 1928 she presented pantomimes and theater pieces internationally, often in museums. She received a Guggenheim Scholarship to study in Greece in 1934 and a second one for study in Egypt the following year. She was placed under a unique contract with MGM to write scripts and direct, during which time she staged the "Comedia "D'el Arte" sequences in **Scaramouche.** Author of the screenplay **Tenth Avenue Angel** (1948), three autobiographies, a novel, *Among the Daughters,* a book about her work, *On Mime* and the plays *Love Possessed Juana: A Play of the Inquisition in Spain* and *The Unknown Lover,* produced by the Houston Little Theater. After retiring from performing in 1960, she became a master teacher at several American Colleges and Universities and held successful exhibitions of her paintings until she was confined to nursing homes in 1976.

Autobiographies: *First Person Plural, Silly Girl* and *Artist's Life*

Stage: Nearly 300 character vignettes for the Theater of Angna Enters including: "Ecclésiastique" ('24), "Moyen Age" ('26), etc

Film:
1952 **Scaramouche**— MGM (uncredited)

NATHALIE ERLBAUM
1990 **Henry and June**— Univ

DANIEL ESTERAS
Dancer and choreographer who currently produces and hosts the "Move to Groove Ball," a monthly showcase for choreographers and performance artists at Glam Slam, a funk club in Los Angeles. Not interested in "dance for dance's sake," Esteras constantly strives to create and present work that breaks new ground. Due to the amount of innovative work that has been displayed at the event since its beginning in 1992, Esteras has begun to develop as a television series.

Stage: *Peter and the Wolf* (Del Mar Theater Ensemble, Cal.)

TV: Daytime Emmy Awards ('86 and '90), "Santa Barbara"

Music Video: "I Wanna Dance with Somebody"— Whitney Houston; "New Dress"— Cheryl Lynn; "Sweat"— White Bread; "Uniform of Youth"— Mr. Mister; "Insatiable Woman"— Isley, Jasper, Isley; "Tender Love"— Force M.D.'s; "It's Shoko Time"— Bensdorf Shoko

Nightclub/Concert: *Wild Woman* (with Nancy Tricotin), Liisa Lipkin, Jeffrey Roy, Jackie Prete, Shelton Ray and Primal Heat, *Erodance Artheater*

Miscellaneous: Industrial/fashion shows for California Mart, Axxess Magazine, Jonathon Martin, White Stag, Surf Fetish, Style Auto

Film:
1992 **Exquisite Corpses**— Lorimar (TV)

LISA ESTRADA
Choreographer who specializes in cheerleading routines.

Film:
1992 **Buffy the Vampire Slayer**— Fox
1994 **Forrest Gump**— Par (with Leslie Cook)

KIRSTEEN ETHERINGTON
1983 **Videodrome**— Univ

BONNIE EVANS
b. Los Angeles, California, 1940

Dancer and choreographer who made her dancing debut at 13 in the LACLO productions of *Carousel* and *Song of Norway.* The 1955 production of *Kismet* took her to Broadway as one of the "Princesses of Ababu" and for the next four decades she would recreate Jack Cole's choreography for productions around the United States. Broadway shows also include an important role in *L'il Abner* ('56), which she recreated on film. Other film appearances include **Hello, Dolly!, The Music Man** and **The Wonderful World of the Brothers Grimm** and she danced as a "regular" on the Red Skelton ('51–64), Danny Kaye ('63–67) and Carol Burnett ('67–79) TV shows.

Stage: *Kismet* (Multiple productions, recreating Jack Cole's original work)

Film:
1959 **L'il Abner**— Par (assistant to Dee Dee Wood)
1987 **Walk Like a Man**— MGM/UA

JERRY EVANS
This highly successful dancemaker's career represents a strong case for how the fates and timing have helped write the story of dance on film. While a science major in college, Evans was already exploring his physical abilities in gymnastics, martial arts and fencing. When Steve Merritt returned to his home town to choreograph a San Jose Music Theatre production of *Hello, Dolly!,* Evans (along with childhood friend Jeffrey Hornaday) auditioned. "Merritt was forced to take anyone who showed up at the open calls... 'Football players, track people, baseball jocks — not a dancer among them.'" (*After*

Dark, Jan. '76). Nutured and taught by Merritt, Evans (at the late age of 21) and five of the other young men were encouraged to relocate to Hollywood, to continue studying with Merritt. Evans' natural dance talents and creativity led to his also assisting Merritt on TV shows ("The Midnight Special," Awards shows, etc.) In 1975, Merritt created an all-male song-and-dance quartet, Friends, with four of the San Jose hopefuls: Evans, Hornaday, Larry Coles and Tim Michaels. The group caught the eye of manager/producer Allan Carr (who was also Merritt's manager) and they were signed to appear with Petula Clark in nightclubs and on TV. After dancing on TV's "Baryshnikov in Hollywood" ('81), Evans began his solo choreographic career with commercials. From forty episodes of "Solid Gold" and two years of "The Tracey Ullman Show," Evans' dance contributions spread to film, music video and live tours and shows. Winner of the "Best Film Choreography" award from *LA Dance* in 1995 for his work on **The Mask**, he gratefully credits Steve Merritt as his mentor.

TV (partial listing): "The Midnight Special" (co-choreographer with Steve Merritt), "The Tracey Ullman Show" ('89, with associate Peggy Holmes), "Solid Gold," "Starting Over" (Reba McEntyre special); commercials for Budweiser, Chrysler Plymouth, Levis, Mc Donald's, Pepsi Cola, Ever Ready and Sprite

Music Video: "Promise of a New Day," "Vibeology"—Paula Abdul; also videos for Barbra Streisand, Smoking' Armadillos, the Stray Cats and Herb Alpert

Nightclub/Concert: Sylvie Vartan (Paris '91), Paula Abdul "Under My Spell" World Tour ('91, with Peggy Holmes), Chayanne World Tour ('93), Reba McEntyre tours ('93 and '94)

Film:
1984 **Getting Physical**— CBS Ent (TV)
     Heartbreakers— Orion
1985 **Weird Science**— Univ
1986 **Jumpin' Jack Flash**— Fox
1987 **Weeds**— De Laurentiis
1988 **Baja Oklahoma**— HBO (TV)
     The In Crowd— Orion (with Peggy Holmes, Lynn Taylor-Corbett and Linda Weisberg)
     Ladykillers— Rep (TV) (assisted by Holmes)
1989 **Dance to Win**— MGM (with Paula Abdul, assisted by Holmes)
     The Naked Gun— Par
1994 **The Mask**— New Line Cinema (assisted by Marlene Lang, *LA Dance* Award)
1996 **Edie and Penn**— 23rd St. Prod

DANIEL EZRALOW
b. Los Angeles, California
Modern ballet dancer who was described by Toni

Basil when she brought him into David Bowie's 1984 "Glass Spider" tour as: "Daniel was just incredible. David loved him because they both believed the show would work best if the choreography grew out of the music's strong images. And it was inspiring just to watch Danny dance. He's amazingly gifted, and gorgeous." He did not begin dance studies until he was 18, while a pre-med student at the University of California at Berkeley. Leaving college behind, he moved to New York and studied at the Alvin Ailey and Joffrey schools. Making his debut with the 5 by 2 Plus dance company, he subsequently danced with Lar Lubovitch, Paul Taylor and Pilobolus, where he was inspired to choreograph by Moses Pendelton—one of the Pilobolus founders ("Through that Pilobolus process, which acknowledges the collaboration of the dancers and the choreographers, we were taught a piece (***Bonsai***)... I was very involved in it; it was the immediate spark I needed to tell me: It's all right. You *can* choreograph. Anyone who wants to can try. That was my inspiration, Moses and that piece.") Performing and creating in many theatrical forms, he has choreographed for the London Contemporary Dance Theatre, the Paris Opera Ballet and Israel's Batsheva Dance Co., and danced and choreographed as a founding member of Momix and ISO. In 1995, he created and toured with "Daniel Ezralow's Heart Dances" and in 1996 was honored with the *LA Dance* Alterative Dance Award.

Stage: **Moby Dick** (Italy), **Florinda** (LA '95)
Music Video: Videos for Sting and U2
Ballet/Dance Pieces (Partial listing): For Pilobolus: "Parson Nibs and the Rude Beggars," "Minotaur"; For the Paris Opera Ballet: "Two Brothers" ('82) and "Soon" ('87)
Miscellaneous: Issey Miyake fashion show ('95)
Film:
1985 **Camorra**— Cannon
1989 **Earth Girls Are Easy**— Vestron (with Russell Clark, Sarah Elgart, ISO: Jamie Hampton, Ashley Roland, Morleigh Steinberg; Wayne "Crescendo" Ward)
1995 **Casa Riccordi**—(Ital)

GEORGE FAISON
b. Washington D.C., December 21, 1945
Dancer, choreographer, director, author and lyricist who was an important member of the creative team who brought *The Wiz* ('75) to the stage and screen. A native of Washington D.C., he attended Howard University studying dentistry but his interest in the theater soon led him in other directions. He studied dance with Alvin Ailey, Thelma Hill, Louis Johnson, Claude Thompson, James Truitte, Dudley Williams and with Capitol Ballet and studied and performed musical theater with the Amer-

ican Light Opera Company. Faison made his stage debut in *Thumby* (Long Wharf Theatre, '66) and joined the Alvin Ailey American Dance Theatre in 1967 as principal dancer for three years. He then appeared on Broadway in *Purlie* ('70) and founded his own dance company, The George Faison Universal Dance Experience, in 1971. After choreographing numerous ballets and stage works, he joined the ranks of director-choreographer with the off-Broadway production of *Apollo, Just Like Magic* (which he also wrote) in 1981. He produced the 30th Anniversary of the Alvin Ailey Dance Co. in 1989 and, with his Tony Award for *The Wiz*, holds the distinction of being the first black choreographer to win this award.

Stage: *Don't Bother Me, I Can't Cope* (Bdwy '72), *The Wiz* (Bdwy '75, with Geoffrey Holder, Tony Award, also lyricist), *1600 Pennsylvania Ave.* (Bdwy '76, also co-dir), *Apollo Just Like Magic* (OB '81, also writer-dir), *Sing Mahalia Sing* (OB, also writer-dir), *Tilt* (OB, also writer-dir), *The Mooney Shapiro Songbook* (Bdwy '81), *Porgy and Bess* (Radio City Music Hall '83, Tony nom), *Body and Soul* (OB '88), *Betsey Brown* (Princeton '91), *Golden Gate* (Theatre Toursky, Marseilles, France, '92, also writer), *American Jam Session* (Aix En Provence Jazz Festival '91, also writer), *Sweet 'n' Hot* (Bdwy '92), *Timon of Athens* (Bdwy '93), *C'mon and Hear—Irving Berlin's America* (OOT '94, also dir)

TV: CBS Jazz Special with Dionne Warwick, "Cosby Salutes Ailey" ('89, also conceived and prod), Earth, Wind and Fire HBO Special; commercials for Faava Shoes, AT & T; promotions for Avon and HBO

Music Videos: "Oasis"—Roberta Flack; "Movin'"—Betty Carter

Ballet/Dance Pieces (Partial listing): Works for the Alvin Ailey American Dance Theatre, Alvin Ailey Repertory Ensemble, Dayton Contemporary Dance Company, Eleo Pomare Dance Company, Capital Ballet of Washington D.C., Nanette Bearden Contemporary Dance Company, The George Faison Universal Dance Experience: "Slaves," "Reflections of a Lady," "Cafe America," "Gazelle" ('71), "Suite Otis" ('73)

Nightclub/Concert: Tours for Nick Ashford and Valerie Simpson, Earth, Wind and Fire, Roberta Flack, Eartha Kitt, Gladys Knight and the Pips, Stephanie Mills, Melba Moore and Stevie Wonder

Miscellaneous: Industrials for Lincoln/Mercury (starring Bill Cosby), Ford Motor Company, Associated Black Charities, American Express Celebrates Black History Month

Film:
1978 **The Secret Life of Plants**— Par
1984 **The Cotton Club**— Orion (with Claudia Asbury, Gregory Hines, Henry LeTang, Michael Meacham, Arthur Mitchell, Michael Smuin)

1991 **The Josephine Baker Story**— HBO (TV) (Emmy nom)

LOUIS FALCO
b. New York, August 2, 1942
d. New York, March 26, 1993

Calling his work "contemporary dance — not ballet or modern," Falco created theatrical pieces which portrayed ordinary people using movement to express their emotions, rather than the structured postures of classical dance. The son of immigrant Italian parents, he was first encouraged to study dance by a guidance counselor at the Henry Street Settlement House which his parents suggested he attend after school to "keep him off the streets." Awarded a modern dance scholarship at the Henry St. Playhouse School, he studied with Alwin Nikolais and Murray Louis and abandoned his dreams of becoming a photographer for the world of theatre and dance. While attending the High School of Performing Arts, he was noticed by Charles Weidman and at 17 made his professional dance debut with Weidman's company. After graduation, he was a member of the José Limon Dance Company, touring the U.S.A., South and Central America and the Far East for ten years (1960–70) while simultaneously appearing with the Weidman, Donald McKayle and Alvin Ailey companies; enriching his experience with musical theatre (*West Side Story* in stock) and opera (**Carmina Burana**) appearances and diversifying his dance skills at the Martha Graham, American Ballet Center and Ballet Theatre schools. In 1967 he formed his own group (Louis Falco Company of Featured Dancers) and began creating highly theatrical, experimental works — using rock groups and laserbeams for the first time in serious dance presentations. In 1977, while writing a movie script and planning a TV special, *Dance Magazine* wrote, "This involvement with film reveals the direction which Falco would like his work to take; to create a different kind of choreography specifically for film and eventually develop a film repertory company, along the lines of Ingmar Bergman's cohesive technical and performing group." He disbanded his group in 1983 to concentrate on movement and writing for films and television. His choreography for **Fame** created memorable images in dance of his former high school before AIDS robbed us of another innovator.

Stage: *Dude* (Bdwy '72), **Thais** (San Francisco Opera)

Music Video: Videos for Prince, the Cars, Ricky Scaggs

Ballet/Dance Pieces (Partial listing): "Argot" ('67), "Huescape," "Timewright," "Caviar," "Ibid," "Sleepers," "Soap Opera," "Pulp," "Two Penny Portrait" and "Kate's Rag" (for his own company);

Louis Falco (R) and assistant Bill Gonelle during the filming of "Hot Lunch Jam" on the streets of New York in **Fame** (MGM, 1980).

"Caravan" and "Escargot" (for Alvin Ailey American Dance Theater); "Black and Blue" (for the Paris Opera Ballet '82)

Film:
1980 **Fame** — MGM (assisted by Bill Gonelle)
1987 **Angel Heart** — TriStar
     Leonard: Part 6 — Col

BRUNO "TACO" FALCON

TV: "American Music Awards" ('93 with Michael Jackson)
Music Video: "The Floor" — Johnny Gill; "Feel For You" — Chaka Kahn
Nightclub/Concert: Michael Jackson's "Dangerous" World Tour ('93)
Film:
1991 **Bill and Ted's Bogus Journey** — Orion
1994 **Thumbelina** — WB (with Gavin Dorian, "Live action reference choreography" credit)

GIL FALSON

Australian choreographer.

Film:
1989 **Flirting** — Goldwyn

FANCHON (WOLF)

b. Los Angeles, California, circa 1895

Legendary dance director, film and stage producer, writer, lyricist, costume designer and prolific producer of prologues in movie theaters (live productions in conjunction with films, also called "Ideas") at the Fox Theatre Corporation chain (350 theaters) on the West Coast. She began performing at the age of 10 in amateur shows around Los Angeles and at 14 joined her brother, Michael Marco, as a popular dance team in nightclubs and theaters, eventually headlining on the Orpheum Circuit and the Ziegfeld Roof. Their act consisted of Marco playing the violin while Fanchon danced in and out of his arms. They started producing nightclub floor shows with *Pavo Real* in San Francisco in 1915 and in 1920, she and Marco produced *Sunkist*, their first musical revue for theaters, for which she also wrote the music and lyrics and designed the costumes. Together they created the Fanchon and Marco dynasty: contracted by the Fox West Coast theater chain from 1923 to 1932 to supply all of the live entertainment — eventually owning a theater circuit of their own, The Fanchonettes and Sunkist Beauties dance lines who appeared in World's Fairs, nightclubs and movie houses. Merging with the Ethel Meglin Studios in 1936, they also operated one of the most successful dance schools in Hollywood. An advertisement in *Variety*, January 3, 1933, boasted: "At present, she oversees all production at the mammoth Fanchon and Marco studios on Hollywood... Creates original ideas for shows... Supervises dance routines... Originates novel settings... Sets new designs for costumes and supervises their execution... Turns out more than fifty complete productions every year... And still finds time to be a wife, a mother, and a student of the times." Other Broadway work: *Satires of 1920* (wrote the music and lyrics), *Sunkist Revue* ('21, produced, wrote the songs and book and also appeared), *Stairway Idea* (wrote the songs, produced and directed). She produced the films **Turn Off the Moon** and **Thrill of a Lifetime**, becoming one of Hollywood's first female producers. Fanchon and Marco are reportedly the inspiration for James Cagney's role in **Footlight Parade**. At the height of their success their 50,000 square foot studio at 5600 Sunset Blvd in Hollywood contained five rehearsal stages, a wardrobe department, music library, booking agency and "Gag" library, with shows in 36 cities that used over 2,000 employees. After supplying dancing lines and original choreography and staging for films, from 1943 to 1945, she was contracted by Fox to "supervise" musical sequences. She then was contracted as a dance director at Republic. The Fanchon and Marco regime lasted until the mid-'50s, when the major movie theater chains stopped producing live presentations. Fanchon married William Simon in 1923 and one of their daughters is actress Faye Marlowe, who starred in **Rendezvous with Annie** ('46)—one of her mother's films. Fanchon's career is confused with the career of Fanchon Royer, another female film producer and she personifies some of the frustration involved in trying to document film dance creators. After a career filled with success, financial gain and respect from the industry, her death has been (to date) impossible to confirm.

Stage: Hundreds of "Ideas" (prologues) for the Fox Theater Chain, Concert at Barbizon-Plaza ('45)

Ballet/Dance Pieces: For the Hollywood Bowl: "Strauss Waltz: The Beautiful Blue Danube" ('33), "Prometheus" and "Hollywood" ('35, with Aida Broadbent, Marcel Silver), "Ballet in Blue"

Miscellaneous: Ice Follies ('34, also dir, billed as "Miss Fanchon")

Film:
1925 **The Eagle**— UA

1926 **Dance Madness**—? (S)
Kiki— First National
The Midnight Sun— Univ
1928 **Three Weekends**— Par
1929 **Alibi**— UA
Fox Movietone Follies of 1929— Fox (with Willie Covan, Edward Royce, also appeared)
Hearts in Dixie— Movietone (with Marco)
Innocents of Paris— Par (with Marco, LeRoy Prinz)
1935 **Beauty's Daughter**—? (S)
The Little Immigrant—? (S)
Paddy o' Day— Fox
Starlit Days at the Lido— MGM (S) (featuring the Fanchonettes)
This Is the Life— Fox (with Louis Dapron)
1936 **Song and Dance Man**— Fox
Sunkist Stars at Palm Springs— MGM (S) (featuring the Fanchonettes)
1937 **Cinema Circus**— MGM (S) (The Fanchonettes appear)
Thrill of a Lifetime— Par (with Prinz, Carlos Romero, also prod)
Turn Off the Moon— Par (with Prinz, The Fanchonettes appear)
1939 **Night at the Music Hall**— Col (S) (also appeared)
Night at the Trocodero— Col (S) (also appeared)
1943 **Stormy Weather**— Fox (with Nick Castle, Katherine Dunham, Fayard Nicholas, Bill Robinson, Clarence Robinson, "supervised musical numbers" credit)
Sweet Rosie O'Grady— Fox (with Hermes Pan, "supervised musical numbers" credit)
Wintertime— Fox (with James Gonzalez, Carlos Romero, Kenny Williams, "supervised musical numbers" credit)
1944 **Pin Up Girl**— Fox (with the Condos Brothers, Gae Foster, Pan, "supervised musical numbers" credit)
1945 **Where Do We Go from Here?**— Fox
1946 **Murder in the Music Hall**— Rep
Plainsman and the Lady— Rep
Rendezvous with Annie— Rep
Song of Arizona— Rep
1947 **Calendar Girl**— Rep
Campus Honeymoon— Rep (alsp prod)
Hit Parade of 1947— Rep
Northwest Outpost— Rep

GINGER FARLEY
1988 **Red Heat**— TriStar (with Mark Gonne)

WESLEY FATA
1994 **The Hudsucker Proxy**— Polygram/WB

MARGO FAUGHT
1989 **Diving In**— Maurer/Shaw

CONSUELO FAUST
1988 **Heat and Sunlight**— Snow Ball— New Front Alliance
1990 **The Spirit of 76**— Col

LUCY FAWCETT
1991 **Rebecca's Daughters**— Mayfair Ent./Palace Pictures (with Philippa White)

ELEANOR FAZAN
b. Kenya, Africa, May 29, 1930

Dancer, actress, choreographer and director who began her career on the British stage (*Her Excellency,* '49) and appeared in the films **Will Any Gentleman?** ('55), **Value for Money** ('57), **Inadmissable Evidence** ('68), **Savage Messiah** ('72) and **O Lucky Man!** ('73). She has multiple British television appearance credits, as well as directing and choreographing for films and stage.

Stage: *Grab Me a Gondola* (London '56, also co-dir), *Zuleika* (London '57, with Peter Powell and Alfred Rodrigues, also dir), *Chrysanthemum* (London '58 rev, also dir), *The Lily White Boys* (London '60), *The Pilgrim's Progress* (Eng. '64), *Mr. Polly* (London '77), *Noel and Gertie* (London, '91–92)

TV: "Carissima" (BBC '59, also co-dir)

Film:
1959 **Follow a Star**— Rank
1968 **Inspector Clouseau**— Mirisch/UA
1969 **Oh! What a Lovely War**— Par
1972 **Lady Caroline Lamb**— UA ("Dance movement" credit)
     The Ruling Class— AE
1979 **Yanks**— Univ
1980 **Heaven's Gate**— UA (with Tad Tadlock)
1982 **The Scarlet Pimpernel**— CBS (TV)
1983 **Lassiter**— WB (also appeared)
1985 **King David**— Par
1986 **Babes in Toyland**— NBC/Orion (TV)
1988 **Willow**— MGM
1990 **Mountains of the Moon**— Carolco/TriStar
1992 **The Lover**— Renn/Burrill/Films AZ
1993 **The Innocent**— Lakeheart/Sievernich Films

NICK FELIX
1983 **Tender Mercies**— U/AFD

SEYMOUR FELIX (FELIX SIMON)
b. New York, October 23, 1892
d. Los Angeles, California, March 16, 1961

Dubbed "The King of Dance" by Florenz Ziegfeld, Felix was a dancer, choreographer and film director who began his lengthy career as a vaudeville dancer at the age of 15 as one half of Felix and Care. At the insistence of his mother at the age of 5, his introduction to dance had been lessons at Edward Neuberger's Social Dance school with fellow classmate, Danny Dare. After performing for eight years with Care, a failed solo try convinced him to move to the other side of the footlights. Receiving notice for a burlesque show he staged the dances for (and requesting his name *not* to be listed on the program) he was hired to stage *Chuckles* in New York and London in 1922 and began his successful career staging musicals on Broadway in the early Twenties. Felix is credited with being one of the first to move dance away from the precision "line" to a more dramatically motivated integration (Felix was quoted in 1926, "No longer are routines a matter of speed and noise... Scrambled legs have become a bore. The important thing today is the so-called 'book' number.") He used dancers to create stage pictures, atmosphere and mood and was rewarded for his visionary work with the highest salary on Broadway. Felix was brought to Hollywood in 1928, although Busby Berkeley got the opportunity to bring *Whoopee*, one of Felix's greatest stage successes, to the screen. After dance direction on two films, he attempted the make the transition to film director with **Girls Demand Excitement** ('31) and **Stepping Sisters** ('32). Instead, he was contracted by MGM as a dance director in 1933, eventually becoming one of the three film dance directors to receive an Academy Award for his lavish work in **The Great Ziegfeld** ('36). Declaring bankruptcy in 1938, he was signed as dance director by 20th Century–Fox in 1944 and his film work continued into the 1950s at most of the major studios. Although acknowledged as an innovator on the Broadway stage, as dance and choreography changed drastically in the 1940s, his dance background and style were dated and Felix was relegated to creating period stage numbers for film musicals. Hired for his expertise with "Girly" numbers by the Flamingo Hotel in Las Vegas in 1953, he opened a dance studio in Westwood in 1954 and briefly worked in television before his death. Survived by a daughter.

Stage: *Chuckles* (U.S. and England '22), *Sun*

Showers (Bdwy '23), *Artists and Models, Big Boy, Hassard Short's Ritz Revue, Innocent Eyes* and *Top Hole* (Bdwy '24), *Sky High* and *June Days* (Bdwy '25), *Gay Paree, Hello Lola, Naughty Riquette* and *Peggy-Ann* (Bdwy '26), *Hit the Deck* (Bdwy '27), *Rosalie* and *Whoopee* (Bdwy '28), *Ziegfeld Midnight Frolics* (Bdwy '29, also dir), *Simple Simon* (Bdwy '30), *Strike Me Pink* (Bdwy '33)

Ballet/Dance Pieces: "The Hunting Ballet" (for Adeline Geneé)

TV: The George Gobel Show ('56)

Nightclub/Concert: Production numbers at the Flamingo Hotel (LV '53)

Film:

1929 **Sunnyside Up**— Fox
1930 **Just Imagine**— Fox
1932 **Stepping Sisters**— Fox (also dir)
1933 **The Prizefighter and the Lady**— MGM
1934 **The Cat and the Fiddle**— MGM (with Albertina Rasch)
　　　Hollywood Party— MGM (with Dave Gould, George Hale, Rasch)
　　　Kid Millions— UA (with George Murphy, Fayard Nicholas)
1935 **The Girl Friend**— Col
1936 **After the Thin Man**— MGM
　　　The Great Ziegfeld— MGM (with Ray Bolger, Academy Award winner: "Best Dance Direction": "A Pretty Girl is Like a Melody" number)
1937 **On the Avenue**— Fox
　　　Vogues of 1938— UA (with George Tapps)
1938 **Alexander's Ragtime Band**— Fox
　　　Everybody Sing— MGM (with Dave Gould)
1939 **Broadway Serenade**— MGM (with Busby Berkeley)
　　　Rose of Washington Square— Fox
1940 **Lillian Russell**— Fox
　　　Tin Pan Alley— Fox (with Fayard Nicholas)
1941 **Navy Blues**— WB
1942 **Yankee Doodle Dandy**— WB (replaced by LeRoy Prinz, with John Boyle)
1943 **Let's Face It**— Par
　　　Dixie— Par (with Louis Dapron)
1944 **Atlantic City**— Rep (with John "Bubbles" Sublett)
　　　Cover Girl— Col (with Jack Cole, Stanley Donen, Gene Kelly and Val Raset)
　　　Greenwich Village— Fox (with Tony DeMarco, the Four Step Brothers)
1945 **The Dolly Sisters**— Fox (assisted by Angie Blue)
1946 **Do You Love Me?**— Fox
　　　Three Little Girls in Blue— Fox (with Bernard Pearce)

A Fox publicity photo of Seymour Felix, circa 1935. (Photo courtesy of the Academy of Motion Picture Arts and Sciences).

1947 **Mother Wore Tights**— Fox (with Kenny Williams, assisted by Blue, Les Clark))
1948 **Give My Regards to Broadway**— Fox (with Williams, assisted by Clark)
　　　When My Baby Smiles at Me— Fox (assisted by Blue, Clark)
1949 **Dancing in the Dark**— Fox (assisted by Blue)
　　　Oh, You Beautiful Doll!— Fox
1950 **My Blue Heaven**— Fox (with Billy Daniel, assisted by Blue)
1951 **Golden Girl**— Fox
1952 **Down Among the Sheltering Palms**— Fox
1953 **The "I Don't Care" Girl**— Fox (with Jack Cole)
1974 **That's Entertainment!**— MGM (with others)
1994 **That's Entertainment! III**— MGM (with others)

FERN FELLER

1989 **The Chair**— Angelika

ANTHONY FERRO

Dancer-choreographer who was a member of Twyla Tharp's dance company from 1977–80, appearing with the group in **Hair** ('79).

Film:
1981 **Sharkey's Machine**— Orion/WB

RON (RONALD) FIELD
b. Queens, New York, 1934
d. New York, February 6, 1989
Dancer, choreographer and director whose interest in dance began in his Aunt Stella's dance studio in New York. He made his broadway debut at the age of 8 as a member of a children's chorus in *Lady in the Dark*. Attended the High School of Performing Arts and danced in *Seventeen* in 1951 (at 17!), *Gentlemen Prefer Blondes*, *Carnival in Flanders* ('53, billed as "Ronnie Fields"), *Kismet* and *The Boy Friend* ('55) and in cabarets as a Jack Cole Dancer. After choreographing in summer stock and at NY's Latin Quarter, he presented a concert of his own work "An Afternoon of Theatre and Dance" at the Brooklyn YMCA, which led to his first professional choreographic assignment for the critically acclaimed off–Broadway 1962 revival of *Anything Goes*. His subsequent work on Broadway brought him more recognition and three Tony awards. He appeared as "The Choreographer" in the 1985 TV movie **Mirrors** and was one of the dancemakers given a tribute on the 1984 Emmy Award TV show. After an international triumph staging the 1984 Olympic Opening Ceremonies in Los Angeles with a cast of 3,300 dancers, his career floundered, due to disappointments (his elaborate "Happy Endings" musical number had been edited from **New York, New York**), alleged substance use and erratic behavior. During the mounting of the 25th anniversary revival of *Cabaret* in 1987, he confided to star Alyson Reed that the work had restored his faith in his talent and he was on his way to creating new delights (*Sound Stage 10*) when he died of a brain lesion at the age of 55.
Stage: *Anything Goes* (OB '62 rev), *Nowhere to Go But Up* (Bdwy '62), *Cafe Crown* (Bdwy '64), *Cabaret* (Bdwy '66 & '87 rev, Tony award), *Showboat* ('66 rev), *Zorba* (Bdwy '68, Tony nom), *Applause* (Bdwy '70, also dir, 2 Tony awards), "On the Town" ('71 rev, also dir), *King of Hearts* (Bdwy '78, also dir), *Peter Pan* (Bdwy '80 rev, with Rob Iscove, "Production Supervised by" credit), *5-6-7-8 Dance!* (Radio City Music Hall '83, also dir), *Ashmedai* (NYC Opera), *Rags* (Bdwy '86, Tony nom), *Kiss Me Kate* (Royal Shakespeare Co., London '87)
TV: "Once Upon a Mattress" ('72), The 41st and 47th Annual Academy Awards Shows ('68 and '74), "Manhattan Transfer" ('75, also dir), "America Salutes Richard Rodgers and the Sound of His Music" ('76, Emmy winner), "Ben Vereen — His Roots" ('77, Emmy winner), Cheryl Ladd Special" ('79), "Baryshnikov on Broadway" ('80, Emmy

nom), "Goldie and Liza Together," Bette Midler — "Ol' Red Hair Is Back," " The Emmy, Grammy and Tony Awards Shows," "The Hollywood Palace," "The Ed Sullivan Show"
Nightclub/Concert: Acts for Ann-Margret (*AM-PM* '71), George Chakiris, Carol Lawrence, Shari Lewis, Tony Martin & Cyd Charisse ('74), Liza Minnelli and Chita Rivera; production shows for the Latin Quarter (NY), Carillon Hotel (Miami), Casino De Paris (Paris) and Casino Du Liban (Beirut)
Miscellaneous: Industrial for Lincoln-Mercury, 1984 Olympics Opening Ceremonies
Film:
1973 **Marco**— Tomorrow Ent/Cinerama
1976 **The Entertainer**— RSO (TV)
1977 **New York, New York**— UA

TONY (ANTHONY) FIELDS (CAMPOS)
b. Stafford, Kansas, 1959
d. Dunsmuir, California, February 27, 1995
Born in Kansas but raised in California, performer-choreographer Fields made his stage debut in the 9th grade in a community theater production of *Bye Bye Birdie*. He studied acting at the Pacific Conservatory in Hollywood and began his dance studies at the age of 20 at the Roland Dupree Dance Academy with Joe Bennett and Michael Peters. He made his professional debut in Debbie Reynolds' nightclub act. A four year stint on TV's as one of the original "Solid Gold" dancers was interrupted in 1984 when he left to assist Michael Peters (who, he called "my mentor, the major influence on my dancing, the teacher who brought out what was inside me") and dance in the music videos "Thriller," "Beat It" and "Running with the Night." After appearances in the films **Captain E-O**, **Protocol** and **Night Shift** he was cast as "Al" in **A Chorus Line** ('85) and other film roles include **Body Heat** and **Backstreet Dreams**. He died at the age of 36 of cancer.
Film:
1987 **Summer School**— Par
1989 **Phantom of the Opera**— 21st Century Film Corp (with Gyorgy Gaal)

ROY FITZELL
b. San Diego, California, 1929
Introduced to dance first at the age of 5 by Harry Hemphill, throughout the years this dancer, choreographer and teacher studied Spanish dance with José Cansino, tap with Johnny Boyle and ballet with Theodore Kosloff, Eugene Loring, Michel Panaieff and Simon Smemnoff. As "Roberto Fitzell," he

made his dancing debut at the age of 8 with Cansino's Spanish Dance company and was featured in Loring's Spanish ballet *Capitol of the World* which premiered on the TV show "Omnibus," December 6, 1953 and then was performed at ABT. Other ballet appearances include L.A.'s Ballet La Jeunesse and the San Francisco Ballet. He appeared as lead dancer in the LACLO productions of *Louisiana Purchase, Naughty Marietta, The Great Waltz, Plain and Fancy, Rosalinda, Fanny, Song of Norway* (also assisting Aida Broadbent) and *Carousel*. Other West Coast stage appearances include *The Boy Friend, Kiss Me Kate, Lend an Ear, Tongue in Cheek* and Debbie Reynolds' and Eleanor Powell's nightclub acts. He first appeared in films at the age of 14 in **Babes on Swing Street** and continued in **Dancing in the Dark** and **The Petty Girl**. After supplying the live action movement for "The March Hare" in Disney's **Alice in Wonderland**, he was featured in **L'il Abner, The Loves of Carmen, Never Steal Anything Small, Silk Stockings** and **Sweet Charity**. He began his choreographic work assisting Robert Sidney and his dance education career on the faculty of the American School of Dance, eventually serving as chairman of the Dance Department at the University of California at Irvine.

Stage: *The Red Mill* and *The Student Prince* (Greek Theatre, LA, '56, also appeared); For Harlequin Dinner Theater, Cal: *Anything Goes, The Pajama Game, West Side Story, Dames at Sea* (also dir), *The Unsinkable Molly Brown* (also dir), *South Pacific* (Casa Mañana, Texas), *Anything Goes* (Union Plaza Hotel, LV)

TV: "The Steve Allen Show" ('59), "The Judy Garland Show"

Nightclub/Concert: Eleanor Powell's act (also appeared)

Film:
1961 **The Fiercest Heart**— Fox
       The Second Time Around— Fox

BRAD FLANAGAN
1992 **Aladdin**— Walt Disney Pictures

ERNEST (OROVILLE) FLATT
b. Denver, Colorado, October 30, 1918
d. Taos, New Mexico, June 10, 1995

Dancer, choreographer and director who is primarily known for his innovative and prolific television work from the 1950s to the 1970s. In Englewood, Colorado, he won Charleston contests as a child and taught ballroom dance at 12. Moving to Hollywood, he seriously studied dance with Maria Bekefi, Ernest Belcher, Adolph Bolm, Walter Camyron, Eugene Loring and Michel Panaieff. After serving in World War II as a Coast Guard artillery gunner he toured in *Oklahoma!*, appeared in the LACLO dance ensembles of *Louisiana Purchase* ('47) and *Naughty Marietta* ('48) and helped Eugene Loring open the American School of Dance in Hollywood. He danced in many films, including **Tea for Two** ('50), **Singin' in the Rain** ('53), **West Point Story, Calamity Jane, An American in Paris** (featured dancer), **The 5,000 Fingers of Doctor T.** and **White Christmas** ('54, also assistant to Robert Alton) and began his choreographic career as an assistant to Alton, Jack Donohue, Gene Kelly, Eugene Loring and Charles Walters. After traveling to New York to assist Alton on *Me and Juliet* ('53), he made his solo choreographic debut with the LACLO 1955 revival of *Kiss Me Kate*. He returned to New York to choreograph for the Broadway stage and television, becoming one of the leading innovators in musical number concepts and choreography for the camera. His longterm association with Carol Burnett produced many years of sparkling, comedic musical numbers. His extensive knowledge of period movement and sense of humor reached its peak in the Broadway hit *Sugar Babies* ('79) and he was one of the choreographers paid tribute to in the 1984 Emmy Awards TV show.

Stage: For the LACLO: *Kiss Me Kate* ('55 rev), *Annie Get Your Gun* ('57 rev), *At the Grand* ('58) and *Showboat* ('60 rev); *Fade Out, Fade In* (Bdwy '64), *It's a Bird, It's a Plane, It's Superman* (Bdwy '66), *Lorelei* (Bdwy '74), *Sugar Babies* (Bdwy '79, also dir, Tony nom), *Honky Tonk Nights* (Bdwy '84), *Durante* (Canada '89–90).

TV (Partial listing): "Frosty Frolics" (KTLA, '53), "Annie Get Your Gun" ('57), "Kiss Me Kate," "Damn Yankees," "Your Hit Parade" ('55–58); The Ernie Flatt Dancers appeared on "The Garry Moore Show" ('58–63, Emmy Winner), "The Judy Garland Show" ('63–64), "The Entertainers" ('64–'65), "The Steve Lawrence Show" ('65) and "The Carol Burnett Show" ('68–77, Emmy winner '71, with 6 additional Emmy noms); "Julie and Carol at Carnegie Hall" (also assoc prod, Golden Rose Award winner), "Julie and Carol at the Met," "Bubbles and Burnett at the Met"; commercials include Tarrington Cigars and Bromo Seltzer

Nightclub/Concert: Acts for Ruth Buzzi, Dorothy Collins, Mitzi Gaynor, Giselle McKenzie and Juliet Prowse

Film:
1950 **The Toast of New Orleans**— MGM (assistant to Eugene Loring)
1953 **Calamity Jane**— WB (assistant to Jack Donohue)
1954 **The Country Girl**— Par (assistant to Robert Alton)

Popular "Solid Gold" dancers (clockwise from top): Paula Beyers, Helene Phillips, Tony Fields and Darcel Wynne (1978).

There's No Business Like Show Business— Fox (assistant to Alton, creating Donald O'Connor's numbers, with Ward Ellis)

White Christmas— Par (assistant to Alton)

1955 **The Girl Rush**— Par (assistant to Alton)

1956 **Anything Goes**— Par (with Nick Castle, Roland Petit, "Title Dance Direction" credit, also appeared)

KATE FLATT

1992 **Chaplin**— TriStar (with Johnny Hutch, Dan Kamin, Susanne McKenrick, "London crew — choreography" credit)

1995 **Restoration**— Buena Vista (with Quincy Sacks, "Court Dancers" credit)

CAROL FLETCHER

1994 **Tom and Viv**—Entertainment (GB)

RON FLETCHER

b. Dogtown (now "Edenville"), Missouri, May 29, 1921

Fletcher's career moved from serious dance to commercial theater and cabaret and on to health-related movement heralding the "physical fitness" boom of the 1980s in America. He began his dance training in St. Louis with George Murray ("he taught hoofing.") As a young man he went to New York to work for Saks Fifth Ave. and saw a Martha Graham concert which started his interest in serious dance. He received a scholarship from Graham, performed with her company and explored modern, jazz and ethnic dance with Jack Cole and other teachers. He made his commercial debut as featured dancer on Broadway in *Lute Song* in 1946, replacing choreographer Yeichi Nimura in the show because of the producer's fears of anti–Japanese audience reaction ("I was at the right place at the right time.") He partnered Nelle Fisher in multiple nightclub and Radio City Music Hall appearances and created Arden-Fletcher Productions with Donn Arden in 1949, supplying lines of dancers to clubs across America. A dance piece he choreographed at Camp Tamiment was seen by producer Arthur Lesser and incorporated into *Two on the Aisle*, leading to his first major choreographic effort, *Top Banana* on Broadway in 1951 (filmed in 1954). After being contracted by 20th Century–Fox for three years as dance coach and choreographer, his staging of an ice revue led to a long association with the *Ice Capades* as staging director and eventually, associate producer. His career then moved solely into creating shows for nightclubs around the country. Dropping out of the hectic demands of show business, he went back to school to study anatomy and movement and opened a studio in Beverly Hills in 1970, which explored fitness through dance, diet and a unique series of exercises created by Joseph Pilates ("The Pilates Technique") refocusing on physical fitness in America. In 1978, he wrote *Every Body Is Beautiful*, and continues to lecture and contribute to dance exercise and physical wellness into the '90s. "I get more gratification and pleasure out of teaching civilians and understanding how the body moves," sums up his evolution. Co-founder of the Choreographer's Workshop in New York and recipient of an honorary MS from Utah State University.

Stage: *Top Banana* (Bdwy '51)
TV: Multiple shows during the 1950s–'60s
Nightclub/Concert (Partial listing): The Lilliane Montevecchi Show: *Les Girls! Les Girls!, Kooks Tour* (Frontier Hotel, LV), *Gentlemen Prefer* (Sahara Hotel, LV), *Minsky's Follies* (Dunes Hotel, LV), *Fanny Hill* (Desert Inn, LV); Produced, directed and staged many revues and production numbers in Las Vegas from '49–60 (Desert Inn, Dunes, Riviera, Flamingo) as well as the Elmwood Casino; acts for Keefe Brasselle, Shirley Jones and Jack Cassidy
Miscellaneous: *Ice-Capades* ('54–66)
Film:
1954 **Top Banana**— UA
1961 **Snow White and the Three Stooges**— Fox

YANNI FLEURY
Choreographer for the Greek Folk Dances and Songs Society.
Film:
1957 **Boy on a Dolphin**— Fox
1985 **Scenario**— Greek Film Centre

JUDITH FLEX
1992 **The Waterdance**— Samuel Goldwyn

DENNY MARTIN FLINN
Dancer, choreographer, author and director who began his dance training on scholarship from the San Francisco Ballet School. While teaching dance at San Francisco State University, he explored his choreographic skills staging productions of *Carnival, How to Succeed…, The Boy Friend* and *The Apple Tree*. In 1970 he went to New York and appeared in *Show Me Where the Good Times Are* off-

Broadway and on Broadway in *Sugar* ('72), and from 1980 to 1982, appeared on Broadway and toured in the international company of *A Chorus Line* in the roles of "Greg" and "Zach." His experiences with the show propelled him to write the book *What They Did for Love— The Untold Story Behind the Making of A Chorus Line*. His writing work continues with a trilogy of mystery novels and co-story/screenplay of **Star Trek VI: The Undiscovered Country** ('91).

Stage: *Company* and *You're a Good Man Charlie Brown* (East Carolina University Summer Musical Theatre), *Rosalinda* and *Queen of the Dressmakers* (Allentown, Pa.), *Sugar* (reconstruction of Gower Champion's original work for '74 rev)
Film:
1988 **The Deceivers**— Cinecom

ISAAC FLORENTINO
1990 **Down the Drain**— Trans World

EUGEN D. FLOYD
1996 **Moving Target**— BG Prods

ANTAL FODOR
b. Barand, Hungary, January 1, 1941
Hungarian dancer-choreographer who studied at the Budapest State Ballet Institute and joined the Sopianae Ballet in 1959. Dancing with the company until 1968, he also began creating dance works. After joining the Budapest State Opera Ballet in 1968, he was appointed ballet master in 1971.
Ballet (Partial listing): "Ballo Concerto" ('66), "E Major Violin Concerto," "Metamorphosis," "Don Juan," "Bolero" ('77)
Film:
1991 **Meeting Venus**— The Bountiful Co/WB

BRIAN FOLEY
b. Canada
With dance and ice skating training and experience, Foley eventually became the choreographer for the Canadian World Team Skating Champions and his work covers all entertainment mediums.
Stage: *Toller Cranston's Ice Show* (Bdwy '77)
TV: "Family Christmas" (Billy Graham Christmas Special) and The Dorothy Hamill special.
Film:
1978 **Ice Castles**— Col (also appeared)
1985 **Heavenly Bodies**— MGM/UA (also appeared)
Joshua, Then and Now— Fox

NEISHA FOLKES

1996 **Rosewood**— Rosewood Prod

CLARENCE FORD

1995 **Billy Madison**— Univ

RONN FORELLA

b. New York, July 23, 1938
d. New York, January 18, 1989

Stationed in Florida with the Air Force, Forella began his study of dance at the late age of 21 with Edith Royal while majoring in Russian History at Rollins College, in Winter Park. He started his career as a dancer at the Atlanta Summer Theatre and then in touring productions of *The Unsinkable Molly Brown* ('62), *Annie Get Your Gun* and *Hot September* ('65). He enjoyed an active performance career on Broadway in *Promises, Promises* ('69), *Sweet Charity, Hallelujah Baby!, The Unsinkable Molly Brown* and *How Now Dow Jones*; TV ("The Hollywood Palace," the Perry Como, Ed Sullivan and Jonathon Winters shows and an Elvis Presley special); nightclubs and the film **Hello, Dolly!** ('69). With additional dance training from Don Farnworth and at the June Taylor and Joffrey schools, he opened his own school and then moved into choreography, first as an assistant, and then with a solo career creating for nightclubs, summer stock, the Broadway stage, television and film. In 1973, he founded Dance Con-Tin-U-Um and in 1975, 2d Century Dance Theatre (both jazz-ballet companies) and was guest choreographer for Southern Ballet Theatre. After his sudden death from a heart attack, a scholarship was established in his name by the 2d Century Dance Theater foundation.

Stage: *A Patriot for Me* (Bdwy '69, also asst dir), *Wild and Wonderful* (Bdwy '71), *Changes* (OB '79), multiple stock productions: *The Fantasticks, Promises, Promises*, etc.

TV: "The Great American Dream Machine" (PBS), the Mike Douglas, Merv Griffin, Dinah Shore, Pearl Bailey and Mary Tyler Moore shows

Nightclub/Concert: Acts for Wayne Cilento, Yvonne DeCarlo, Paul Jabarra, The Magid Triplets, Donna McKechnie, Liza Minnelli, Ann Reinking and Joan Rivers.

Film:
1974 **The Little Prince**— Par (with Bob Fosse)
1981 **Stripes**— Col (with Arthur Goldweit)
1986 **Playin' for Keeps**— Univ (with Lynette Barkley)

TRUDY FORREST

1994 **Little Women**— Col

BOB (ROBERT LOUIS) FOSSE

b. Chicago, Illinois, June 23, 1927
d. Washington

In *The Tony Award Book*, this superb artist is quoted about why he started to choreograph: "As a dancer, I was no choreographer's dream. I just couldn't pick up anyone else's style. I was very limited as a dancer. I had to adjust everyone's work to fit my own body." Graciela Daniele said about him, "He was the quintessential stylist, but I remember him saying, 'I don't know what style means. When I was a dancer, there were things I didn't do so well, so I hid them and that created a style.'" That distinctive style and his limitless imagination would make him a theatrical legend. His father, Sy, was a vaudeville performer and Fosse began studying tap, acrobatic and ballet dancing at the age of 9, making his professional debut at 13. He formed the dance team The Riff Brothers with Charles Grass in 1940 and at 17 was the opening act in a strip show, choreographing his first piece in 1942 ("That Old Black Magic") for a nightclub. He formed a dance team with first wife Mary Ann Niles (Fosse and Niles) and they appeared at such supper clubs as the Palmer House, Chicago, the Hotel Pierre and Plaza Hotel in New York and on all of the major musical television shows. Lead dancer on Broadway in the revue *Make Mine Manhattan*, he appeared with Niles in *Dance Me a Song* ('50) and the national company of *Call Me Mister*. He was also one of the lead dancers on television's "Your Hit Parade." After serving in the Navy he was brought to Hollywood and was featured in musical films (**The Affairs of Dobie Gillis, Give a Girl a Break** and **Kiss Me Kate** for MGM in 1953, and **My Sister Eileen** for Columbia in 1955). As the Golden Age of the musical film was over and proper roles for him were limited, he returned to the Broadway stage and began choreographing. He became one of the new breed of innovative director-choreographers in 1959 with *Redhead* and continued creating shows for — and collaborating with — his third wife, Gwen Verdon. Being brought back to Hollywood to recreate his stage successes on film, he also directed the dramatic films **Lenny** and **Star '80** and is the only director to win all three major awards in one year in 1973 for his work: Oscar for **Cabaret**, 2 Tony Awards for *Pippin* and an Emmy for the TV special "Liza with a 'Z'." His unique style is analyzed in *The Tony Award Book*: "...to treat the dancer's body as a collection of isolated parts. The convulsively hyperactive loins suddenly freeze, then release in neatly syncopated motion. Fosse's subtle use of rhythm and counterpoint brings the sexuality implicit in all dance to sharp, contemporary focus." Honored by the *Dance Magazine* award in

1962 and the *LA Dance* Heritage award in 1994, he is survived by a daughter, Nicole.

Biographies: *Razzle, Dazzle* by Kevin Boyd Grubb (1989) and *All His Jazz* by Martin Gottfried (1990)

Stage: *The Pajama Game* (Bdwy '54, Tony award), *Damn Yankees* (Bdwy '55, Tony Award), *Bells Are Ringing* (Bdwy '56, with Jerome Robbins), *New Girl in Town* and *Copper and Brass* (Bdwy '57, with Anna Sokolow), *Redhead* (Bdwy '59, Tony award), *Hail, the Conquering Hero* (Bdwy '61), *How to Succeed in Business Without Really Trying* (Bdwy '61, with Hugh Lambert, "musical staging" credit), *Little Me* (Bdwy '62, also co-dir, Tony Award for choreo), *Pal Joey* (NY City Center '63 rev, also appeared), *Pleasures and Palaces* (OOT '65, also dir), *Sweet Charity* (Bdwy '66 & '86 rev, also dir, Tony Award for choreo), *Pippin* (Bdwy '72, also dir, 2 Tony Awards), *Chicago* (Bdwy '75, also dir, Tony nom), *Dancin'* (Bdwy '78, also dir, Tony Award for choreo), *Big Deal* (Bdwy '86, also dir, Tony Award for choreo)

TV: (Partial listing): "The Ed Sullivan Show," "The Wonderful World of Entertainment" ('58); "Ford Startime" ('59), "The Seasons of Youth" ('61), "Liza with a 'Z'" ('73, also dir, Emmy award), "Pippin" ('81, original work recreated by Kathryn Doby)

Film:

1953 **The Affairs of Dobie Gillis** — MGM (with Alex Romero, also appeared)

Give a Girl a Break — MGM (with Gower Champion, Stanley Donen, Bill Foster)

Kiss Me Kate — MGM (with Hermes Pan, also appeared)

1955 **My Sister Eileen** — Col (assisted by Betty Scott, also appeared)

1957 **The Pajama Game** — WB (assisted by Patricia Ferrier)

1958 **Damn Yankees** — WB (assisted by Ferrier, also appeared performing "Who's Got the Pain?" with Gwen Verdon)

1967 **How to Succeed in Business Without Really Trying** — UA (with Dale Moreda recreating his original stage work)

1969 **Sweet Charity** — Univ (also dir, assisted by Kathryn Doby, Ed Gaspar, Paul Gleason, Sonja Haney, John Sharpe, Gwen Verdon)

1972 **Cabaret** — UA (also dir, Academy Award winner for Best Direction, assisted by Doby and Sharpe)

1974 **The Little Prince** — Par (with Ronn Forella, also appeared as "The Snake")

1979 **All That Jazz** — Fox (also script and dir, assisted by Doby and Gene Foote)

1983 **Star '80** — Ladd/WB (also dir, assisted by Doby)

1985 **That's Dancing!** — MGM (with others)

ALLAN K. FOSTER

b. 1879

d. November 2, 1937

Foster became the namesake of one of the most successful line dance groups on the Broadway stage of the 1920s (the Allan K. Foster Girls), because his wife had been a member of one of the original Tiller groups to first come to America. He wisely added acrobatics to the original precision marching-and-kicking to gain recognition and success and his acclaim led to collaboration on dozens of Broadway musicals. In addition to his dance direction work, he also directed *The Mimic World of 1921*, *The Rainbow* (London, '23) and *Spice of 1922* and produced *Hummin' Sam* on Broadway in 1933. It is assumed that his career was so successful in New York that he was not lured to remain in Hollywood.

Stage: (All Bdwy credits, except when noted otherwise): *The Debutante* and *Madame Moselle* ('14), *Alone at Last* and *Ned Wayburn's Town Topics* ('15), *Follow Me, The Girl from Brazil, Robinson Crusoe, Jr.* and *The Show of Wonders* ('16), *The Passing Shows of 1916*, *'17, '19, '22, '23, Doing Our Bit, Maytime* and *My Lady's Glove* ('17), *Girl o' Mine, Sometime, In and Out, The Melting of Molly* (OOT) ('18), *Hello Alexander, The Magic Melody, Monte Cristo, Jr.* and *Shubert Gaieties of 1919* ('19), *Frivolities of 1920* (with Edward Bower), *The Half Moon* and *Cinderella on Broadway* ('20), *Bombo, The Last Waltz, The Whirl of New York* and *Peggy* (OOT) ('21), *For Goodness Sake, The Lady in Ermine* (with Jack Mason), *Make It Snappy, The Rose of Stamboul, Sally, Irene and Mary, Springtime of Youth, Up in the Clouds* (with Vaughn Godfrey, Max Scheck), *Red Pepper* ('22), *Ted Lewis Frolic* ('23), *How's the King* (OOT, '25), *The Circus Princess* ('27), *A Night in Venice* ('29, with Busby Berkeley, Chester Hale), *Marching By* ('32), *Billy Rose's Jumbo* ('35)

Film:

1929 **The Cocoanuts** — Par (Allan K. Foster Girls appeared)

BILL FOSTER

b. Evansville, Indiana

When his family moved to Redwood City, California, young Foster began dance classes. Thinking dance was "sissy," he switched to acrobatics and began classes with Harry Cooper — joining Cooper's tumbling troupe with Ringling Bros. and Barnum and Bailey Circus at the age of 13 and touring for three years. After serving in 101st Airborne Division paratroopers, he was discharged in New York, where he met Michael Kidd. Encouraged to seriously study dance, he returned to California and took classes with Adolph Bolm, Louis DaPron and Eugene Loring. He began his performance career

Bob Fosse and Gwen Verdon perform "Who's Got the Pain?" in **Damn Yankees** (Warner Bros., 1958).

with club work in Las Vegas — where he also started choreographing — and appeared onstage in the L.A. production of *Little Boy Blue* in 1950. His work in the film musical began as a dancer in **The "I Don't Care" Girl**, **The Bloodhounds of Broadway**, and **Singin' in the Rain** ('52) and **Anything Goes** ('56).

He started his film choreographic career assisting Michael Kidd and was signed by 20th Century–Fox, and progressed to associate choreographer to Stanley Donen and Rod Alexander. His solo career began with two films for Pat Boone in 1957, who took Foster with him to New York to

Mitzi Gaynor (with George Reeder on her left and Bill Foster on her right) portrays a slinky hillbilly in Robert Sidney's staging from **Bloodhounds of Broadway** (20th Century–Fox, 1952).

stage his television series. After creating musical sequences for films and television (in 1959, he choreographed and directed 39 Canadian shows), he progressed to one of television's busiest and most prolific director-producers with over 75 shows, specials and series, including "Laugh-In," "Amen," "Chico and the Man," "Ironsides," "Tony Orlando and Dawn," "Applause" (with Lauren Bacall), "Omnibus," David Wolper's "Those Were the Days" and "Full House."

TV: "Pat Boone-Chevy Showroom" ('57–60), Danny Kaye special ('60), "Old Fashioned Thanksgiving" Special ('61), The Fred Waring Holiday Special (NBC '63), Meredith Willson special ('64), "The Ed Sullivan Show," "The Jimmy Dean Show," "Omnibus," "The Bell Telephone Hour," "The Big Record," "Kraft Music Hall" (one season), "Paris a la Mode" special

Nightclub/Concert: First Edition (Flamingo Hotel, LV '56)

Film:
1953 **The Band Wagon**—MGM (assistant to Michael Kidd)

The Girl Next Door—Fox (assistant to Kidd)

Give a Girl a Break—MGM (associate to Stanley Donen, with Gower Champion, Bob Fosse, uncredited)

Niagara—Fox (uncredited)

1956 **Carousel**—Fox (associate to Rod Alexander, also appeared)

The Best Things in Life Are Free—Fox (with Alexander, also appeared)

Teenage Rebel—Fox

1957 **April Love**—Fox

Bernadine—Fox

The Three Faces of Eve—Fox

1958 **Mardi Gras**—Fox

1961 **On the Double**—Par (assisted by Mary Jane Doerr)

GAE FOSTER
b. Los Angeles, California, circa 1900

Producer-choreographer of a famous line of girls who performed on stage, in films and at the world renowned Roxy Theatre in New York during the 1930s–40s, Foster also produced *Skating Vanities* — a unique roller-skating troupe. Coming from a poor family and wanting to dance from a very early age, she quit school at 14 to go to work. After four years she was able to afford lessons with Ernest Belcher and made her dancing debut in an Albertina Rasch ballet group. In 1918, she went to New York, studying with Ivan Tarasoff and dancing with Fokine. She returned to California, married and settled in San Francisco, where she joined the chorus of a Fanchon and Marco nightclub show in 1922. One year later, she became assistant to Marco and when Fanchon and Marco moved their headquarters to Los Angeles, Foster remained in San Francisco to produce their shows there. As Fanchon and Marco "units" came into great demand, she was transferred to Los Angeles where she produced a traveling unit on the average of one every two weeks for several years. After creating over 150 shows, she was sent to the Roxy Theatre in 1938 and began producing the stage shows and created The Gae Foster Girls. The mother of twins born in 1931, her sister, Nadine Gae, also went on to a successful dance career.

Stage: *Hellzapoppin'* (Bdwy '38), Roxy Theatre (NY, multiple shows from 1938)

Miscellaneous: *The New Aquacade Revue* (NY World's Fair, '40), *Skating Vanities* (also dir)

Film (Credits are for appearances of The Gae Foster Girls):
1937 **Script Girl** — Vitaphone (S)
1938 **The Candid Kid** — Vitaphone (S)
    Forget-Me-Knots — Vitaphone (S)
    The Knight Is Young — Vitaphone (S) (with Hal LeRoy)
    Prisoner of Swing — Vitaphone (S) (with Hal LeRoy)
    Up in Lights — Vitaphone (S)
1939 **A Fat Chance** — Vitaphone (S)
    One for the Book — Vitaphone (S)
    A Swing Opera — Vitaphone (S)
    Wardrobe Girls — Vitaphone (S)
1940 **All Girl Revue** — Vitaphone (S)
1944 **Pin Up Girl** — Fox (with Fanchon, Hermes Pan, Alice Sullivan, Skating Vanities appeared)

GEORGE FOSTER

Film:
1991 **Young Soul Rebels** — Prestige

THE FOUR STEP BROTHERS

1. Maceo Anderson: b. Charleston, South Carolina, September 3, 1910
2. Al Williams: b. Savannah, Georgia, 1911

d. Sherman Oaks, California, May 3, 1988
3. Sylvester Johnson
4. Freddie James (joined the act from 1939–43)
5. Prince Spencer: b. Jenkinsville, North Carolina, October 3, 1917
(joined 1941 — replacing Sylvester Johnson)
6. "Flash" McDonald: b. St. Louis, Mo., March 16, 1919
(joined 1943 — replacing Freddie James and appearing with the group in Europe)
7. Red Gordon
8. Sherman Robinson
9. Ernie (Sunshine Sammy) Morrison: b. New Orleans, Louisiana 1913
d. Lynwood, California, July 24, 1989
(An original member of the **Our Gang** film series, he joined the group in 1944 for two films)

Celebrated acrobatic "Flash" trio which contained some of the best Black American dancers throughout the years. The act was started in 1926 by three young African-American men who were not related: Al Williams, Maceo Anderson and Sylvester Johnson and throughout the years the personnel changed — but the sensational act did not ("At one time or another rhythm tap, Snake Hips, five-tap Wings, slides, Afro-Cuban movements, and the entire repertory of new acrobatics formed a part of the act" — *Jazz Dance*). The trio of youngsters had been inspired by such great tap dancers as Bill Robinson, Charles "Honi" Coles, Leonard Reed and the Condos Brother at the Lafayette Theater in Harlem. By the 1930s they became a quartet and appeared in films; toured internationally in nightclubs (The Cotton Club, Le Lido de Paris), were featured with Duke Ellington's Band from 1933–59 and starred in stage shows (Keith-Orpheum Circuit, Medrano Stadium, France, Radio City Music Hall and the Roxy Theatre), performing for Queen Elizabeth, Emperor Hirohito, the Prince of Laos, the King of Thailand and millions of fans. Their act was one-of-a-kind with a high energy level, shouts and clapping of their hands while they danced, culminating in a sensational "Challenge" from the four members, each with their own style and specialty. When the group broke up in 1959 the existing members went many directions. They celebrated 50 years in show business and co-produced and starred in a benefit at the London Palladium in 1982, also receiving a tribute at the Beverly Hilton Hotel on November 14, 1985. On July 14, 1988, they received a star on the Hollywood Walk of Fame. Prince Spencer appears in the film **Harlem Nights** as himself.

Film (Credits are for their own routines):
1930 **Check and Double Check** — RKO
1933 **Barber Shop Blues** — Vitaphone (S)
1942 **When Johnny Comes Marching Home Again** — Univ (with Louis DaPron)

Three of the Four Step Brothers can be seen with Bob Hope in this shot from **Here Come the Girls** (Paramount, 1953).

1943 **Hi Buddy**— Univ (with Dick Humphreys, Carlos Romero)

Rhythm of the Islands— Univ (with Lester Horton)

It Ain't Hay— Univ (with Danny Dare)

1944 **Carolina Blues**— Col (with Sammy Lee, Ann Miller)

Greenwich Village— Fox (with Tony DeMarco, Seymour Felix)

Shine On Harvest Moon— WB (with LeRoy Prinz)

1947 **That's My Gal**— Rep (with Hal Belfer)

1953 **Here Come the Girls**— Par (with Nick Castle)

1964 **The Patsy**— Par

JEAN-PIERRE FOURNIER

1990 **Heaven and Earth**— Triton (with Hiroshi Kuze)

DOROTHY FOX

b. St. Louis, Missouri

Dubbed a "modern satirical dancer" in a 1940 profile, Fox began her dance studies with Den-ishawn as a small child. After her graduation from finishing school, she was sent to Paris by her parents to study music, but chose dancing instead. She studied ballet with Svea Larsen, modern with Louis Hutton and Greek dancing with Raymond Duncan — one of Isadora's children. After making her professional debut with a ballet troupe in Paris, she danced in France, Italy and Prague. Returning to the U.S. she joined Hanya Holm's group and appeared on Broadway in *New Faces* ('35) where she teamed with Charles Walters. As Fox and Walters, they had a successful nightclub act, and appearing on Broadway in *Parade* and *Jubilee* (both '35). After the team separated in 1936, she continued club work with various partners. Forging a solo career with satirical pantomimes, she debuted at the Rainbow Room in New York, played London and returned to Broadway in *Sing Out the News* ('38) — as well as appearing in early television broadcasts. She began solo-staging shows with the 1940 Triangle show at Princeton and assisted Walters on *She Had to Say Yes* (OOT '41).

Ballet/Dance Pieces (partial listing): "The Chorus Girl's Day," "World Tour," "Serenade to a Wealthy Widow," etc.

Film:

1946 **Centennial Summer**— Fox

MICHAEL FRALEY

1991 **The Butcher's Wife**— Par ("skating choreography by" credit)

WILLY FRANZL

1962 **Forever My Love**— Par

DAMITA JO FREEMAN

b. Palestine, Texas

Expressive dancer, actress and choreographer whose potential was spotted by George Balanchine at the age of 8 and she was given a scholarship affiliated with the School of American Ballet to begin her training. She continued in Los Angeles with Irina Kosmovska at David Lichine's studio. After dancing with the Los Angeles Junior Ballet Company, she gained success dancing on Broadway in *Two Gentlemen of Verona* ('71), *Candide* ('74 rev) and *Platinum* ('78)— in which she was created "additional" choreography for Joe Layton. She started her TV choreographic career with Layton on Cher's "Fantasies" special and then, assisted Kenny Ortega on TV's "American Music Awards" and stage shows before getting her solo credits. She continues to mix acting appearances (**Private Benjamin**, **Bad Dreams**, **The Man with One Red Shoe**, **Rat Boy**, "L.A. Law," etc) with staging and choreography assignments.

    Stage: Siegfried and Roy Illusions (Japan '89, associate choreo with Joe Layton)

    TV (Partial listing): "The Tonight Show" (Natalie Cole's, Lisa Lisa & Cult Jam's and Cher's appearances), "Solid Gold" (Natalie Cole), "Dick Clark's '85 Summer Action Show," "Dionne and Friends," "American Bandstand" (The Supremes, the Fifth Dimension and the Spinners), "Cos," "Thea," etc.

    Music Video: "Neutron Dance" and "Baby, Come and Get It"— The Pointer Sisters; "Love Always"— El Debarge; Fashion Video — Coca Cola

    Nightclub/Concert: tours for Air Supply and The Commodores ('86), Cher, Natalie Cole, Whitney Houston ('88), James Ingram, The Pointer Sisters, Lionel Richie, Diana Ross and Sister Sledge; acts for James Brown, Dick Clark, Thelma Houston, Englebert Humperdinck, Anthony Newley and The Spinners

    Miscellaneous: 1984 Olympics Closing Ceremonies (also TV, asst to Joe Layton)

    Film:

1986 **My Chauffeur**— Crown Intl
1987 **Planes, Trains and Automobiles**— Par
    Valet Girls— Empire Pictures

NED FREEMAN

1939 **Winter Carnival**— UA

MASAYA FUJIMA

1956 **Teahouse of the August Moon**— MGM

LARRY FULLER

b. Sullivan, Missouri

Receiving his introduction to dance at the age of 4 from Miss Zoe, Larry Fuller continued during high school at the Marion Ford School of Dance in St. Louis. After making his professional debut with the St. Louis Muny Opera and staying for several seasons, he moved to New York to enrich his dance vocabulary ("What I really wanted to do was Broadway and movies. The MGM child, that was me! So I started seriously studying jazz to learn the kind of style that was being done on Broadway.") Interrupted by two years as one of the Jack Cole Dancers at the Dunes Hotel, Las Vegas, in 1960 ("one of the most valuable dance experiences in his life"), he continuously appeared on Broadway in the early '60s: *West Side Story, The Music Man, Redhead, Donnybrook!, Kean, Gravo Giovanni* and *No Strings*. While dancing in *Funny Girl* ('64), he asked choreographer Carol Haney if he could assist her and his career took a new direction. When Haney died, he helped to stage the national and London companies of the show and after assisting Peter Gennaro on the 1966 TV production of "Brigadoon," he made the decision to explore opportunities in Europe. There, his work was noticed by Harold Prince which led to his unique staging/directing chores that have kept him travelling between Europe and America throughout the years. When the change in the shooting schedule for **A Little Night Music** came into conflict with Patricia Birch's commitments, after the first day of filming, she left and Fuller completed the film. Interviewed in *Dance Magazine* (February, 1980), he expressed some of his views and goals, "…just to do funny song-and-dance numbers to entertain the folks — there are a lot of people who do that very well — is not enough. I want to do something that's got a little more meaning to it, that's all."

    Stage: Funny Girl (Dallas, Tex. '65), *Hello Sucker* (OOT '69, also dir), *The Pirate* (New Haven's Longwharf Theater), *Blood Red Roses* (Bdwy '70), *That's Entertainment* (OB '71), **Silverlake** (NYC Opera), *On the 20th Century* (Bdwy '78), *Evita* (Tony nom) and *Sweeney Todd* (Bdwy '79), *Merrily We Roll Along* (Bdwy '81), *A Doll's Life* and *Is There Life After High School?* (Bdwy '82), *Love* (OB '84, also dir), *Gotta Getaway* (Bdway '84, also dir), *Marilyn — The Musical* (London '84, also dir), *Time* (London '85), *Jekyll and Hyde* (Ntl tour '95);

Christopher Gable trades in his ballet slippers for tap shoes and becomes a movie star in **The Boyfriend** co-starring Twiggy and co-choreographed by Gable, Terry Gilbert, Gillian Gregory and Tommy Tune (MGM, 1971).

European productions: *On Your Toes, Candide, Funny Girl* (London), *West Side Story* and *Two Hearts in Quarter-Time* (Vienna Volksoper), *Girl Crazy, On the Town, Evita, Jesus Christ Superstar*

TV: "Brigadoon" CBS (with Peter Gennaro), The Tony and Emmy Awards Shows, "The Ed Sullivan Show," "Our Musical Heritage" series (WCBS-TV)

Nightclub/Concert: *Folies de Paris* (NY and Sahara Hotel, LV, '67); acts for Carol Channing and Lisa Kirk.

Ballet/Dance Pieces: "Jazz and the Dancing American" (Theater An Den Wien in Vienna), "Humours of Man" (London Festival Ballet)

Films:

1977 **A Little Night Music** — New World (with Patricia Birch)

　　The Boarding School (aka **The Passion Flower Hotel**) — (Ger)

GEORGE FULLWOOD

1978 **Deathsport** — New World

CHRISTOPHER GABLE

b. London, England, March 13, 1940

After acclaim as premier danseur with the Royal Ballet, this classical dancer switched careers to become an actor and choreographer. Yougn Gable studied at the Royal Ballet School and at 16 joined the Sadler's Wells Opera Ballet. The next year, he danced with the Covent Garden Opera Ballet. In 1957 he joined the Royal Ballet and danced leads in *La Bayadere*, *Swan Lake* and *Romeo and Juliet*. He retired from the world of classical dance in 1967 to concentrate on his acting career and appeared in 19 films from 1968–84 (among them, Ken Russell's films **Women in Love** and **The Music Lovers**, as well as TV specials for Russell). Other performances include **The Slipper and the Rose** ('76) and the successful London stage musical *Good Companions*. In 1982 he opened the Central School of Ballet in London and has been artistic director for Northern Ballet Theatre since 1987.

Ballet/Dance Pieces: (for Northern Ballet Theatre) "Don Quixote," "Giselle," "Romeo and Juliet," "Swan Lake"

Film:

1971 **The Boy Friend**— MGM (with Terry Gilbert, Gillian Gregory, Tommy Tune, also appeared)

ANTONIO GADES

b. Elda, Spain, 1936

Called by *Vogue Magazine* in 1964, "Spain's most brilliant young dancer (who) brings to flamenco what El Cordobes brings to the bullring: excitement, virility, audacity," this classical Spanish dancer and choreographer would go on to create dazzling all-dance films which found international acclaim. At the age of 14 he started dance training at Academie Palitos. He became a member of Ballet Espagnol de Pilar Lopez and danced with the company for ten years. He appeared with the Rome Opera (1961–62), the Festival of Two Worlds at Spoleto and La Scala (1962–63) and broadened his dance expertise by studying ballet with Anton Dolin in Paris. He made his film debut in 1963 in **Los Tarantos** with Carmen Amaya and in 1964, he created a sensation at the New York World's Fair in concert with his own company. Signed for a special appearance with Ann-Margret in his only American film, **The Pleasure Seekers**, he needed special permission from the Spanish government to leave the Spain Pavilion at the World's Fair for 10 days shooting in Hollywood. In the 1980s, he began collaborating with director Carlos Saura to create a series of all-dance films which moved classic Flamenco dance into exciting new directions.

Ballet/Dance Pieces: "Pavanne for a Dead Infanta," "Teatrino di Cristobal," "Bolero" (with Anton Dolin)

Film:

1963 **Los Tarantos**—(Span) (with Carmen Amaya, also appeared)

1964 **The Pleasure Seekers**— Fox (with Robert Sidney, also appeared)

1981 **Blood Wedding**— Libra (also appeared)

1983 **Carmen**— Orion (also appeared and wrote the screenplay)

1984 **Bizet's Carmen**— Triumph (Opera version)

1986 **El Amor Brujo**— Orion (also appeared and wrote the screenplay)

MALCOLM GALE

1986 **Killer Party**— UA/MGM

DON GALLAGHER

1944 **Jive Junction**— PRC (also appeared)

MARIA GAMBARELLI (AKA GAMBY)

b. Italy

Classical ballerina of Italian-American parents who studied as a child at the Metropolitan Opera Ballet School. She received the nickname "Gamby" while she was a member of the original Roxy Gang— one of the first entertainment groups to do nationwide radio broadcasts. She was premier danseuse at the Capitol Theatre, New York and with the Metropolitan Opera Ballet (1939–41). With Chester Hale, she founded the Gamby-Hale Ballet Girls, who appeared onstage and in films.

Film:

1929 **The Cocoanuts**— Par (with Allan K. Foster, Gamby-Hale Ballet Girls appeared)

1930 **Leave It to Lester**— Par

1935 **Here's to Romance**— Fox (also appeared)
Hooray for Love— RKO (also appeared)

CHRIS GANDOIS

1992 **Indochine**— Electric Pictures

1993 **Apres L'Amour**— Mayfair Ent

1994 **Une Femme Francaise**— Guild (FR/UK/Ger)

DIANE GARCIA

1987 **The Howling II**— Square Pictures

RICHARD GARCIA

1990 **Martians Go Home**— Taurus

PAT GARRETT

British artist whose first choreography was *Masterclass*, a dance work premiered in London. She appeared with many dance companies (including the EMMA Dance Company in 1980) and taught

Antonio Gades, the star choreographer of **Blood Wedding**, **Carmen** and **El Amor Brujo**.

at Leicester Polytechnic. Her stage contributions includes multiple movement creations for the Royal Shakespeare Company.

Stage: *The Three Penny Opera* and *The Pied Piper* (England, '91)

Film:
1985 **Santa Claus — The Movie** — TriStar
1986 **Little Ship of Horrors** — WB
1991 **King Ralph** — Univ
1992 **The Muppet Christmas Carol** — Disney

MIRANDA GARRISON (RANDY ROCHELLE GARRISON)

b. Long Beach, California, September 17, 1949

Garrison's versatile talents have allowed her to do a variety of things in front of and behind the camera in contemporary films. Although she studied briefly with Madame Kathryn Etienne as a child, most of her dance knowledge was gained as a street and club dancer. She attended the University of Las Vegas and Los Angeles City College Theatre Dept. and studied acting with Ron Sossi and the Odyssey Theatre Ensemble in Los Angeles. In 1972, she made her professional debut in *The Doo Dah Daze* for Toni Basil (Flamingo Hotel, LV) and continued nightclub work at the Latin Quarter, New York, and the Riviera Hotel, Las Vegas, for Kenny Ortega. Dramatic stage performances include Los Angeles productions of *Miller in Pieces, Peer Gynt, Another Part of the Forest* and *A Midsummer Night's Dream.* She began her choreographic career assisting Ortega on **Dirty Dancing** ('87), in which she also played a principal role. Among her twelve film performance credits are **Lambada: The Forbidden Dance, Mack the Knife, Salsa, Sunset** and **Xanadu.** One of the charter members of SSDC/MCC, she cites Toni Basil, Michael Martinez, Julie McDonald, Kenny Ortega and *Tango Argentino* as major influences in her life and career.

Stage: *All This and the Moonlight* (LA '92)

TV: "Dallas," "Equal Justice," "General Hospital," "Head of the Class," "Red Shoe Diaries" (asst to Russell Clarke), "Sibs," "Studio 5B" and "The Wonder Years"; commercials for 409 Cleaner, Miller Lite Beer, Publix, Rold Gold, Smart Foods, etc.

Music Video (Partial listing): "Twistin' the Night Away" — Rod Stewart; "La Isla Bonita" — Madonna; "Don't Walk Away" — Robert Tepper; "How to Salsa" (instructional video).

Film:
1987 **Dirty Dancing** — Vestron (assistant to Kenny Ortega, also appeared)
1988 **Roadhouse** — UA (assistant to Kenny Ortega)

Sunset — TriStar (with Miriam Nelson, also appeared)
Vibes — Col
1989 **Chances Are** — TriStar
Salsa — Cannon (associate to Kenny Ortega, also appeared)
Uncle Buck — Univ
1990 **Delirious** — MGM (assistant to Toni Basil)
Lambada: The Forbidden Dance — Cannon Intl (with Felix Chavez, also appeared)
Life Stinks — Brooksfilms (asst to Jeffrey Hornaday)
1991 **Ambition** — Miramax
The Marrying Man — Hollywood Pict (asst to Hornaday)
Mobsters — Univ (assistant to Basil)
My Friend Frank — Westgate
Naked Gun 2½: The Smell of Fear — Par (with Johnny Almaraz)
The Rocketeer — Touchstone (assisted by Almaraz)
1992 **A River Runs Through It** — Col (with Almaraz, Paul Pellicoro)
Sleepless in Seattle — TriStar
Straight Talk — Hollywood Pictures (with Paul Pellicoro)
1993 **Barbarians at the Gate** — HBO (TV)
Born Yesterday — Hollywood Pictures
Son-in-Law — Hollywood Pictures
1994 **Naked Gun 33⅓: The Final Insult** — Par (assisted by Michael Warwick)
When a Man Loves a Woman — Touchstone
Let It Be Me — Rysher Ent
Manhattan Merengue (aka **Rice, Beans and Ketchup**) — RBK Partners
1996 **Evita** — Cinergi (asst to Vincent Paterson)

TROY GARZA

b. Hollywood, California, August 20, 1954

From the ages of 6 to 16, Garza studied dance in California with Calle Bieber, Robert Regger and Carl Whitmer and made his professional debut in Gene Kelly's touring arena show, *Clownaround* in 1972. He enhanced his dance technique over the next five years with Joe Bennett, Stanley Holden and Claude Thompson, while performing in Las Vegas ("The Magic World of Mark Wilson," Charlie Rich's act), in the film **Lost Horizon** and multiple TV shows ("The Dean Martin Show" and "The Manhattan Transfer Show"). In 1976, he went to London with *A Chorus Line*, and studied there at the Royal Academy of Dramatic Arts. His long-running affiliation with *A Chorus Line* continued from 1977–90 on Broadway (also dance captain) and the national company (also supervisor). In 1979, he made his choreographic debut on Broadway with

Got Tu Go Disco and from 1990–94 appeared on and choreographed for TV's "Saturday Night Live." In clarifying his film choreographic credit, Garza candidly wrote: "Although I am credited as a 'Dance Assistant,' I was actually a technical consultant in that I taught Michael Bennett's tap combination to the film's cast." Citing Bob Avian, Bennett, Tim Cassidy, Gary Chryst, Christian Holder, Allegra Kent, T. Michael Reed, Timothy Scott and Carl Whitmer as major influences in his life and career, he continues to stage *A Chorus Line* internationally, as well as offering his creativity to other stage productions and teaching.

Stage: *Got Tu Go Disco* (Bdwy '79, with Jo Jo Smith), *Fourtune* (OB '79), *A Chorus Line* (South Africa '92, Holland '93 Long Beach CLO, '95, also dir), *Dreamgirls* (Long Beach CLO '93, associate di/choreo, *Drama-Logue* award), *No, No Nanette* and *Can Can* (Long Beach CLO '94, associate dir/choreo)

TV: "Saturday Night Live" (1990–94, multiple numbers for over 20 stars, including Kevin Bacon, Candice Bergen, Rob Lowe, Steve Martin, Patrick Swayze, Christopher Walken, etc., also appeared)

Nightclub/Concert: "Peter Allen at Westbury," Gary Chryst & Allegra Kent

Miscellaneous: Industrials for Jane Fonda/ Theoni Aldridge Activewear

Film:
1985 **A Chorus Line** — Embassy (with Gregg Burge, Jeffrey Hornaday, Brad Jeffries, Helene Phillips, Vickie Regan)

MYRNA GAWRYN
b. Montreal, Canada, September 5, 1953

"Seeing in terms of movement patterns, rhythms and shape makes my life and my work ... dance work, *all* work make sense," wrote this dancer, teacher and choreographer. Her diversified dance skills and technique were gained with extensive study in ballet from Margaret Hill, Stanley Holden and Stefan Wenta, modern from Rose Gold, Donald McKayle, Michelle Simmons and Lee Theodore and jazz from Russell Clark and Jaime Rogers. To encompass other aspects of theater and performance, she studied at the Laban School in New York and with the Company Theater in Los Angeles. Making her professional performance and choreographic debut with *Thighs* at the Company Theater in 1976, she continues experimenting in various mediums. From 1985–91, she produced, directed and choreographed Men Inside, a performing company composed of men in the CRC State Prison in Norco, California — an experience which "affected me greatly." Co-owner and director of Room to Move, a dance and performing arts studio in Venice, California, she named Rose Gold

and Lee Theodore as being very influential teachers in her life and work.

Stage (All LA productions): *Thighs* ('76), *Linke Vs. Redfield* and *I Am a Camera* ('84), *Hot House* ('85), *Creatures* ('87), *External Pressure* ('93)

TV: "Head of the Class," "On the Air," "Picket Fences"; commercials for Danskin, Honda, U.S. Bank, the Queen Mary, Shochu Sake (starring Gregory Hines)

Film (Credits are for films she also appeared in):
1985 **The Midnight Hour** — Circle Films/ABC (TV)
1991 **Teenage Mutant Ninja Turtles II — The Secret of the Ooze** — Fox
1993 **Armed and Innocent** — E.M.M. Prod/ CBS (TV)
   The Geek — Jersey Films

ROBBY GAY
1960 **Tigress of Bengal** (aka **Journey to the Lost City**) — AIP (with Billy Daniel)

HAZEL GEE
1061 **Follow That Man** — Epiney/UA

JEAN PIERRE GENET
1959 **Solomon and Sheba** — UA (with Jaroslav Berger)

PETER GENNARO
b. Metairie, Louisiana, 1924

Unique dancer-choreographer who was called "...may well be the greatest white jazz dancer in America" by *Dance Magazine* in 1974, Gennaro became one of television's major dancing stars in the 1950s and '60s. He began his career dancing in *American Jubilee* at the 1939 New York World's Fair. After getting out of the Service in 1946, he moved permanently to New York and took six months ballet study with Leila Haller and then continued his studies at the American Ballet Theatre Wing and with José Limon and Archie Savage. While dancing with the Chicago San Carlos Opera Ballet in 1948, he met future wife, Jean Kinsella. Gennaro appeared on Broadway in *Make Mine Manhattan* and *Kiss Me Kate* ('48), *Arms and the Girl* ('50), *Guys and Dolls* ('50–52), *By the Beautiful Sea* ('53), *The Pajama Game* ('54, where he received great acclaim introducing "Steam Heat" with Carole Haney and Buzz Miller) and *Bells Are Ringing* ('56). He began choreographing for the Broadway stage and embarked on his successful TV career as a performer-choreographer. His characteristic dance style was seen weekly on many TV shows. He

While rehearsing *Folies Bergère* at the Tropicana Hotel, Las Vegas in 1964, Peter Gennaro strikes a pose with a trio of saucy lovelies.

produced the shows at Radio City Music Hall from 1974–80. A Tony Award winner, Gennaro also received an honorary Doctorate of Fine Arts degree from Salve Regina College in Newport, Rhode Island and the *Dance Magazine* Award in 1964. Proud father of a son, Michael — who is a lawyer — and a daughter, Liza, who is following in her father's successful dancing footsteps.

Stage: *Seventh Heaven* (Bdwy '55), *West Side Story* (Bdwy '57, co-choreo with Jerome Robbins), *Fiorello!* (Bdwy '59, Tony nom), *The Unsinkable Molly Brown* (Bdwy '60), *Mr. President* (Bdwy '62), *Bajour* (Bdwy '64, Tony nom), *Jimmy* (Bdwy '69), *Irene* (Bdwy '73, Tony nom), *Annie* (Bdwy '77, Tony Award), *Bar Mitzvah Boy* (London '78), *The Neighborhood Playhouse at 50: A Celebration* (Bdwy '78), *Carmelina* (Bdwy '79), *One Night Stand* (Bdwy '80), *Little Me* (Bdwy '82 rev, Tony nom),

Singin' in the Rain (London '83), *Annie Warbucks* (OB '92)

TV (Partial listing): "The Polly Bergen Show" ('57–58, with the Peter Gennaro Dancers), "Your Hit Parade" ('58–59, with the Peter Gennaro Dancers), "The Bob Crosby Show" ('58, with the Peter Gennaro Dancers), "The Andy Williams Show" ('59, with the Peter Gennaro Dancers, also appeared), "Frankie Laine Time," "The Ed Sullivan Show," "The Perry Como Show" ('60–63, with the Peter Gennaro Dancers), "The Judy Garland Show" ('63–64, with the Peter Gennaro Dancers), 37th Annual Academy Awards Show ('64), "The Entertainers" ('65, with the Peter Gennaro Dancers), "The Hollywood Palace," Jeanmaire, Jim Nabors and "Rodgers and Hart Today" Specials ('66), "Brigadoon" (with Larry Fuller), "Kraft Music Hall" ('67–71), "Who's Afraid of Mother Goose?" Sepcial ('67)

Nightclub/Concert: *Folies Bergère* (Tropicana Hotel, LV '64–65)

Miscellaneous: Choreographed and produced the shows at Radio City Music Hall ('74–80)

Film:
1958 **Let's Rock**— Col
1964 **The Unsinkable Molly Brown**— MGM

EAMON GEOGHEGAN

1995 **Thin Ice**— ICA Projects (also appeared, "skating choreography by" credit)

PHIL GERARD

1986 —**A Fine Mess**— Col (Roller Skating Choreography)

GUSSA GERT

1958 **Attila**— Lux

TAMARA GEVA (TAMARA GEVERGEYEVA)

b. Petrograd (now St. Petersburg), Russia, 1906

Russian-born ballerina, actress, writer and choreographer who surprised the classical dance world when she scored a success on Broadway in *On Your Toes* in 1936. She studied at the Maryinsky Theatre and then left Russia at 16 with George Balanchine and Alexandra Danilova to perform in Germany and England, where they were seen by Diaghilev and invited to join his company. She was briefly married to Balanchine (she was 16, he was 18) and came to the United States with *Chavre Souris*. Signed by Florenz Ziegfeld to appear in *Whoopee*, she began her American career — alternating between

Ballet (ABT) and the stage in musicals (*On Your Toes, Three's a Crowd*) and comedies and dramas (*Idiot's Delight, The Trojan Women, Misalliance, Angel Street*) with dramatic film roles in **Night Club** ('29), **Girl Habit** ('31), **Their Big Moment** ('34), **Manhattan Merry-Go-Round** ('37), **Orchestra Wives** ('42) and **Night Plane from Chungking** and **Gay Intruders** ('48). She began choreographing for her own stage appearances ("I always created dances for myself which I could do easily … in *Three's a Crowd*, Albertina Rasch was the choreographer. Oh my! I said I was going to choreograph my own stuff. She raised hell… I was never all that interested in choreography, though. I did choreography for one film… I was Ben Hecht's assistant on that. I did the choreography and directed the last fifteen minutes. *Life* magazine called that the 'most frightening moment' of the year in films." (*Dance Magazine*, January, 1973). Geva wrote the TV documentary about Diaghilev for the BBC.

Autobiography: *Split Seconds* (1973)

Stage: *Flying Colors* (Bdwy '32, with Agnes DeMille and Albertina Rasch — with only Rasch receiving credit, also appeared)

Film:
1946 **Specter of the Rose**— Rep

D.J. (DANIEL JOSEPH) GIAGNI

b. New York, December 3, 1950

The son of Danny Daniels, D.J. began his study of dance with ballet at 17 ("very late") on a scholarship at ABT, at the San Francisco Ballet School and eventually tap with his father ("backwards"). A champion gymnast in high school, he also studied piano, composition and theory at the Manhattan School of Music. Making his professional debut in a 1970 Westbury Music Fair production of *Fiddler on the Roof*, he danced with the San Francisco Ballet, Joffrey Ballet (both '72) and Ballet Lyon ('73) before diversifying his performance experiences with the Lotte Goslar Pantomime Circus (1974–75), an LA Production of *Wonderful Town* ('76) and joined his father's Dance American Company in 1977. Multiple TV ("The John Denver Show," "Baggy Pants Burlesque," "Opening Nite," etc.) and film (**Lost Horizon, First Position**, etc.) appearances exposed him to the workings of the camera. With his tap expertise, he coached the New Mouseketeers and started his choreographic career assisting his father on TV and film projects (**Pennies from Heaven**—'81, in which he also appeared). Naming Andre Eglevsky, Igor Moiseyev, Rudolph Nureyev, Valentina Pereyaslavec, Anatole Vilzak, "Jerry Robbins and especially Danny Daniels who taught me to choreograph" as the major influences

Tamara Geva, described in the press release for this 1933 photo as a "Popular Musical Comedy Dancer," arrives in New York after a cruise.

in his life, he has since channeled his talents into making fine handcrafted furniture and choreographs projects which interest him.

Stage: *The Tap Dance Kid* (Bdwy '83, associate choreo with Danny Daniels, Tony and Astaire awards), *Harrigan 'n' Hart* (Goodspeed Opera House and Bdwy '84), *Personals* (OB '86), *Teddy and Alice* (Bdwy '87, "additional staging"), *Carni-*

val (Goodspeed Opera House), *Assassins* (Bdwy '92), *As You Like It* and *The Rocky Horror Show* (Actor's Theatre of Louisville), *The Apprenticeship of Duddy Kravitz* (Workshop and OOT), *Singin' in the Rain* (Birmingham Theatre), *Annie Get Your Gun* (Papermill Playhouse)

TV: John Denver Special ('76, asst to Danny Daniels), "Will B. Able's Baggy Pants and Co.

Burlesque" (HBO '78, asst to Danny Daniels), "All My Children," "Dream On," "How to Be a Man," "Mad About You," "Steve Martin's Best Ever Show"

Ballet/Dance Works: "Zeitgeist I & 2," "The Last of the Best" (DeAngelo Ballet European tour, also dir), "A Look at Partner Dancing," "Forward Motion" (San Diego Ballet)

Film:

1977 **Exorcist II: The Heretic**— WB (with the credit "Tap dance routine choreographed by Daniel Joseph Giagni" being nominated as one of "The Worst Credit Lines of All Time" in *The Golden Turkey Awards*, also appeared)

1981 **Pennies from Heaven**— MGM (assistant to Danny Daniels with Randy Doney)

1993 **Undercover Blues**— MGM

1995 **Pocahontas**— Walt Disney

DINO JOSEPH GIANNETTA

1979 **Summer Camp**— Borson/Seymour Borde

TERRY GILBERT

British artist who appeared in the film **Summer Holiday** ('63) and supplied atmospheric dance sequences for four of Ken Russell's films.

Stage: *House of Cards* (GB '63), *Treasure Island* (London '73, with Denys Palmer)

Film:

1969 **Women in Love**— UA

1971 **The Boy Friend**— MGM (with Christopher Gable, Gillian Gregory, Tommy Tune)

      The Devils— UA

      The Music Lovers— UA

1972 **Henry VIII and His Six Wives**— Anglo EMI

1984 **The Bounty**— Orion

1985 **Lost in London**— CBS (TV)

1988 **Aria**— Miramax (with Grover Dale)

DON GILLIES

1961 **The Mask**— WB

SALLY GILPIN

British dancer-choreographer who danced with the London Festival Ballet and diversified her career with appearances in the film **Half of Sixpence** ('67) and on television ("Pickwick" '69).

Stage: *Romance!* (GB '71), *Maggie* (London '77), *Foxy* (GB '77)

Film:

1971 **Macbeth**— Playboy/Col

1972 **The Public Eye**— Univ

1978 **Crossed Swords**— WB

TINA GIROUARD

1987 **The Big Easy**— Col

LESLI LINKA GLATTER

1985 **The Stuff**— New World

      To Live and Die in L.A.— New Century

PAUL GLEASON

b. Portland, Oregon

Dancer, choreographer and dance educator who arrived in Hollywood and received a scholarship to Eugene Loring's American School of Dance, eventually joining the faculty in 1956. As a close associate of Loring's, he assisted him on TV shows ("Cinderella" '64) and was a member of the Loring's Dance Players ('56) as well as co-founding the LA Dance Theater. He appeared in films, on TV and on stage, including the 1956 LACLO production of *Fanny* and the national touring company of *Camelot* ('63) and his direction — choreographic credits include an Army overseas entertainment unit while serving in the Armed Forces and multiple stock productions. His teaching assignments progressed from the Pasadena Playhouse to associate director of the American School of Dance and eventually dance director for the LACLO Musical Theatre Workshop ('72).

Stage: *The Hostage* (LA '64), *A Midsummer Night's Dream* and *Twelfth Night* (LA '66)

Nightclub/Concert: Act for George Chakiris

Film:

1987 **The Dead**— Vestron

MALCOLM GODDARD

British dancer and choreographer who appeared on the London stage in *Bob's Your Uncle* in 1948.

Stage (all London credits): *The Pied Piper* ('58), *Marigold* ('59), *The Maid of the Mountains* ('72), *Bordello* ('74)

TV: "Billy Cotton's Music Hall" (Brit TV, '64–65, with the Malcolm Goddard Dancers)

Nightclub/Concert: Act for Tommy Steele

Film:

1967 **Marat/Sade**— UA

1969 **Where's Jack?**— Par

RUTH GODFREY

Jack Cole dancer and assistant to LeRoy Prinz on many films.

Film:

1950 **West Point Story**— WB (with John Boyle, Gene Nelson, Eddie Prinz, LeRoy Prinz, Al White, Jr.)

1953 **Three Sailors and a Girl**— WB (with Nelson, assistant to Prinz)

1956 **The Ten Commandments**— Par (with Prinz)

PAUL GODKIN

b. Beaumont, Texas, December 28, 1914
d. Los Angeles, California, June 7, 1985
When he began his dance training at the age of 7 with Ann and Judith Sproule in Texas, Godkin also began to explore choreography ("Once a week each advanced student brought in a combination he had worked out by himself. In class, we taught each other our combinations, analyzed and criticized them. Those early experiments became a useful part of my background.") Moving to California, he studied with Ernest Belcher and Theodore Kosloff, making his stage debut at the Hollywood Bowl, dancing in **The Bartered Bride** with Agnes DeMille. In 1936, he toured with the Hollywood Symphonic Ballet and was "spotted" dancing the title role in Kosloff's **Petrouchka** in 1937 at the Bowl by George Balanchine and Zorina and invited to join Ballet Society and Ballet Caravan. After touring Europe and the U.S. in Ballets Russes de Monte Carlo, he diversified his career and made his Broadway musical comedy debut in *Great Lady* ('38). He also danced in *Stars in Your Eyes* and *Ballet Ballads* ('39—which included his first professional choreographic assignment, the ballet **Willie the Weeper**). After serving in the Navy in World War II, he returned to New York and *Beggar's Holiday* (Bdwy '46), *High Button Shoes* (Bdwy '47) and Jack Cole's *Bonanza Bound* (OOT '47). Moving to Hollywood, he danced in the film **Down to Earth**. He joined American Ballet Theatre as a soloist in 1949 and danced with the company (with future choreographers Jerome Robbins, Herbert Ross and Carmelita Maracci) for several years before concentrating on his choreographic career. Considered one of the pioneers of television choreography, his life-long friendship with Shirley MacLaine and her husband, Steve Parker, resulted in projects in multiple venues, including the ground-breaking *Holiday in Japan* revue in Las Vegas. In *Dance Magazine*, April, 1966, Godkin gave advice to future choreographers, "Be fearless in experimentation. Build up your own background of experience. Find your own vocabulary of movement. Try to keep away from the voids of derivativeness, but don't feel guilty if you use some of your predecessor's vocabulary. They did it, too."

Stage: *Ballet Ballads* (Bdwy '39, also appeared), *That's the Ticket* (OOT '48), *Plein Feu*—a Theatre Empire Revue for Maurice Chevalier and Colette Marchand (Paris '52, also appeared), *Go for Your Gun* (London), *Hair* (Munich, also dir)

TV: "Casey at the Bat" (CBS "Through the Crystal Ball" '49), "Shower of Stars" ('55), "A Drum Is a Woman" ('57, assisted by Donald McKayle), "The Ed Sullivan Show," "The Hallmark Hall of Fame," "The Dinah Shore Chevy Show" ('57), "Hello Kaye

Ballard, Welcome to Las Vegas" ('78), Danny Thomas Specials.

Nightclub/Concert: *Holiday in Japan, Europa '68* (also dir) and *Philippine Festival* (Frontier Hotel, LV), *Tonight the World* (Tally Ho Hotel, LV)

Film:
1955 **How to Be Very, Very Popular**—Fox (with Sonia Shaw, assisted by Dolores Naar)
1956 **Around the World in 80 Days**—UA (with José Greco)
1962 **My Geisha**—Par
1965 **John Goldfarb, Please Come Home**—Fox (assisted by Phyllis Sues)
1966 **Gambit**—Univ
     Our Man Flint—Fox
1970 **Pufnstuf**—Univ
1978 **Harvest Home** (aka **The Dark Secret of Harvest Home**)—Univ (TV)

JEANNETTE GODOY

b. San Bernardino, California, August 5, 1968
"It's amazing that I gained so much experience from my days as a drill team captain. All those years of choreographing huge squads of girls truly prepared me for my professional debut on the Bodeans' music video in March, 1990. From there it has been a constant working process where I continue to learn to be creative," wrote Latina Godoy in response to comments about her life and work. After beginning her dance training with Kevin Laughrun at Dancenter in San Bernardino, Glenda Hemsley, Kenneth Kreel and Marylynn Waterman at Riverside Ballet Theatre and Erie Ellis in L.A., the drill team training and experience she wrote about began while attending Central Middle School and John W. North High School in Riverside. She began choreographing for the drill team in the eighth grade and she continues to create in all mediums in the United States and Latin America.

TV: "Naruhodo the World" (Tokyo), "Ritmo Internacional" and "El Show de Marcano" (Telemundo), "Festival de Viña del Mar" and "Sabado Gigante" (Univision)

Music Video: "La Ola Latina"—Fernando Allende; "Love You Right"—Euphoria; "Baby Got Back"—Sir-Mix-a-Lot; "Let Me Be Your Only Man"—Xeno; "The Whistle Song"—Frankie Knuckles; "Rosechild"–Stress; "Old Glory"—Yomo & Maulkie; "Black, White and Blood Red"—Bodeans; "Pump It"—Icey Blue (asst); "I Thought You Were the One for Me"—Joey B. Ellis (asst); "Forever"—Bobby Womack; "Me Siento Bien"—Seguridad Social; "Cumbanchero"—Lisa M; "Te Amare"—Miguel Tomas

Nightclub/Concert: Shows for Gustavo Alarco, Fernando Allende, Coyote, Franco, Lisa M. ('92–93 tour), Miguel Tomas, etc.

Film:
1993 **CB4**— Univ

NAOMI GOLDBERG
1996 **The Hunchback of Notre Dame**— Disney

ARTHUR GOLDWEIT
1981 **Stripes**— Col (with Ronn Forella)

BEATRICE GOLLENETTE
1934 **Wine, Women and Song**— Chadwick

MARK GONNE
1988 **Red Heat**— TriStar (with Ginger Farley)

JAMES GONZALEZ
1942 **Iceland**— Fox (with Hermes Pan)
1943 **Wintertime**— Fox (with Fanchon, Carlos Romero, Kenny Williams)

TONY GONZALEZ
b. San Francisco, California
Tony's career started when he bet his brother that he could copy a dance step they were watching on Dick Clark's "American Bandstand." He won the bet and his gamble took him to Hollywood, where he danced in such films as **The Flintstones** ('94) and began his choreography career. Working extensively with NFL and NBA cheerleaders, his high-energy creativity is beginning to find its way into all mediums.
TV: "Summer Beach Tour" (ESPN '94), "Star Search '91 & '92"; "Third Rock from the Sun"; commercials for Nintendo, Visa, Bud Lite, Miller Lite, Pepsi
Miscellaneous: The LA Lakers, San Francisco 49ers, Sacramento Kings Girls, San Diego Chargers, Los Angeles Clippers and Golden State Warriors' girls
Film:
1993 **Wayne's World 2**— Par
1994 **Blue Chips**— Par

BILL GOODSON
Nightclub/Concert: Formidable (Moulin Rouge, Paris '88)
Film:
1979 **Roller Boogie**— Compass International (assistant to David Winters)
1984 **Breakin' 2 — Electric Bugaloo**— TriStar (with Shabba Doo)

1985 **Girls Just Want to Have Fun**— New World (with Steve LaChance, Otis Sallid)
The Jewel of the Nile— Fox

RAM GOPAL
b. Bangalore, India, November 20, 1916
Classic East Indian dancer, actor and choreographer who was one of the first masters of East Indian dance to be seen internationally (along with Uday Shankar). The son of a Sanskrit scholar and lawyer, he was sent to Indian dance masters as a child to learn the four classical schools of dance in Southern India and received his academic training in England. He opened his first school of classic Indian dance in Bangalore in 1935 and came to America in 1938, returning to India during World War II. After winning the All-India Festival in Delhi in 1947 he toured Europe with his dance company. On the faculty of many major international dance schools (Jacob's Pillow, etc.) he opened the Academy of Indian Dance and Music in London in 1962.
Autobiography: Rhythm in the Heavens (1957)
Ballet/Dance Pieces (Partial listing): "Dance of the Setting Sun," "Dances of India," "Legend of the Taj Mahal," etc.
Film (All credits are for his own film appearances):
1952 **Outpost in Malaya**— GFD
1954 **Elephant Walk**— Par
The Purple Plain— Rank/UA
1959 **Navy Heroes**— Group 3 Beaconsfield

PETER GORDENO
1992 **Carry On Columbus**— Island World Pic

LLOYD GORDON
1976 **The First Nudie Musical**— Par
1978 **Hot Tomorrows**— Crown Intl

PEGGY GORDON
1958 **I Married a Woman**— RKO (with Les Clark)

ANNA GORILOVICH
1955 **Mystery of the Black Jungle**— Rep

CHARLOTTE GOSSETT
1990 **Mr. and Mrs. Bridge**— Miramax (with Elizabeth Aldrich)

DAVE GOULD

b. Budapest, Hungary, March 11, 1899
d. Los Angeles, California, June 3, 1969

Prolific dance director who contributed greatly to the development of the film musical and holds the distinction of being the first of three Hollywood dance directors to receive an Oscar for their work. Although commonly spoken of as a "non-dancer" in later years by other dance directors, Gould started dance class at the age of 6, paying for the lessons by selling newspapers. He created an act with Ben Blue at the age of 14, and later toured in *Irene and Mary* with George M. Cohan. In a 1937 interview, his mother remarked, "It may be that Dave learned to walk like other babies, but it seems to me he always danced... I knew he would never do anything but dance." After attending Washington and Lee College he started his dance direction career on the Broadway stage. He soon was responsible for the musical numbers at the New York Paramount Theater for four years and the Capitol Theater in New York, as well as creating and producing a line of girls around the country appearing in nightclubs and movie theater prologues. Many of his musical numbers are classics and he is responsible for introducing assistant Hermes Pan to Fred Astaire on **Flying Down to Rio** in 1933. Hermes Pan later described Gould and his work methods: "He was a very quiet man. He was in charge of dance at RKO when I joined them. He wasn't a dancer, strangely enough. I don't think he could even do a time step. I guess you would call him more of a promoter type ... he promoted ideas. But he couldn't begin to do anything, to carry out anything in dancing. And that was fortunate for me, because, being in a dancing film for the first time with Astaire, I was the only one on his staff that danced. He was concerned with production and getting the big number together, and ideas and things, but my work was mainly with Astaire." Other assistants throughout the years included George King and Val "Mickey" Raset. He wrote the screenplay for **Gals, Incorporated** in 1942 and directed **Rhythm Parade** in 1943. In the mid–1940s, he also directed many soundies. His profile in the 1935–36 *Motion Picture Herald* reads: "5 feet, 10 inches tall; 170 pounds; black hair and brown eyes." Although Pan described him as "a very quiet man," his flamboyant life as a "Hollywood Dance Director" included three well-publicized marriages to showgirls. Survived by a son.

Stage: *Angela, Hello Yourself* and *Well, Well, Well* (Bdwy '28), *The Grand Street Follies* (Bdwy '29), *The Second Little Show* and *Fine and Dandy* (Bdwy '30), *The Gang's All Here* and *The Third Little Show* (Bdwy '31), *Hey Nonny! Nonny!* (Bdwy '32), *Sing Out the News* (Bdwy '38), *Fun for the Money* (OOT '41, also dir), *Hellzapoppin'* (Bdwy '49), *Shim Sham Revue* (OOT, also dir)

Nightclub/Concert: *Thrills of '43* (Florentine Gardens, Hollywood), *Hollywood Hilarities*, etc.

Miscellaneous: Victory Canteen Tour ('42)

Film:

1929 **Pathé Audio Review #17**— Pathé (S) (with The Dave Gould Girls)

1932 **Sea Legs**— Vitaphone (S) (with The Dave Gould Dancers)

Subway Symphony— Vitaphone (S) (with The Dave Gould Dancers)

1933 **Flying Down to Rio**— RKO (with Fred Astaire, assisted by Hermes Pan)

Melody Cruise— RKO

Yours Sincerely— Vitaphone (S) (with The Dave Gould Boys and Girls)

1934 **Cockeyed Cavaliers**— RKO (assisted by Pan)

Down to Their Last Yacht— RKO

Gay Divorcee— RKO (assisted by Pan)

Hips Hips Hooray— RKO (assisted by Pan)

Hollywood Party— MGM (with Seymour Felix, George Hale, Albertina Rasch)

Three on a Honeymoon— Fox

1935 **Broadway Melody of 1936**— MGM (with Carl Randall, Rasch — Academy Award winner Best Dance Direction: "I've Got a Feeling You're Fooling" number)

Folies Bergère— Fox (Academy Award winner: "Best Dance Direction": "Straw Hat" number)

The Perfect Gentleman— MGM

1936 **Born to Dance**— MGM (with Eleanor Powell, Academy Award nom: "Swingin' the Jinx" number)

Let's Dance— MGM (S)

1937 **Broadway Melody of 1938**— MGM (with Powell)

A Day at the Races— MGM (Academy Award nom: "All God's Chillun' Got Rhythm" number, with Bobby Connolly)

Rosalie— MGM (with Powell, Rasch)

1938 **Breaking the Ice**— RKO

Everybody Sing— MGM (with Seymour Felix)

1939 **Breaking the Ice**— RKO

1940 **The Boys from Syracuse**— Univ

It All Came True— WB

1941 **Lady for a Night**— Rep

1942 **Rhythm Parade**— Mon (also co-dir)

Sweater Girl— Par

1943 **Hands Across the Border**— Rep

Pistol Packin' Mama— Rep

Silver Skates— Mon

Youth on Parade— Rep

1944 **Casanova in Burlesque**— Rep

Dave Gould surveys exhausted dancers during rehearsals for **Broadway Melody of 1938** (MGM).

Lady, Let's Dance— Mon (with Michel Panaieff)
My Best Gal— Rep
Rosie the Riveteer— Rep
1946 **Digga Digga Doo**— RCM (S)
My Darling Clementine— Fox
1974 **That's Entertainment!**— MGM (with others)
1976 **That's Entertainment Part 2**— MGM (with others)
1994 **That's Entertainment! III**— MGM (with others)

PAT GOULD
1991 **One Good Cop**— Hollywood Pictures

RITA GRAHAM
1982 **National Lampoon's Class Reunion**— Fox

MARTY GRAIL
1944 **Since You Went Away**— UA (with Charles Walters)

CLAUDE GRANDJEAN
1956 **French Can Can**—(aka **Only the French Can**)— United Motion Picture Org

JOSÉ GRANERO
Spanish dancer-choreographer and dance educator currently teaching in Spain.
Ballet/Dance Pieces: "Bolero, Boleras" (Ballet Nacional Festivales de España)
Film:
1985 **The Court of the Pharaohs**—(Span)

STEVEN GRANGER
Tap dancer and teacher.
Film:
1943 **Calling All Kids**— MGM (S)

FRANCES GRANT
1957 **Jeanne Eagles**— Col

PAULINE GRANT
b. Birmingham, England, 1915
d. London, England, October 22, 1986

After studying dance at the Ginner-Mawer School and with Anthony Tudor and Vera Volkova, she formed her own ballet company in 1944. She began her choreography career creating works for the Sadler's Wells Opera, the Royal Opera House, Covent Garden and the Glyndebourne Opera, in which she also appeared as a soloist ('51–56). In 1949 she began choreographing for the Royal Shakespeare Company and diversified her career with musicals and ice shows. She was named ballet mistress for Sadler's Wells Opera in 1969 and then became a director and movement consultant for the English National Opera before her death.

Stage: *The Kid from Stratford* (London '48), *Belinda Fair* and *King's Rhapsody* (London '49), *The Olympians* ('50), *Zip Goes a Million* (London '51), *The Bohemian Girl* and *Love from Judy* (London '52), *Gavin and the Monster* (Britain '81)

Film:
1951 **Happy Go Lovely**— RKO (with Jack Billings)
1953 **Melba**— UA
1957 **Let's Be Happy**— AA (with Alfred Rodrigues)
1965 **The Amorous Adventures of Moll Flanders**— Par

JAMALE GRAVES

When asked to create music videos for C & C Music Factory, this dancer-choreographer suggested: "The best thing I can do is get a group of dancers for you, get to know you, work with you and pull you out." His success with the group led to multiple assignments in various mediums. "Being a choreographer, I understand that there is really not a thing called a new step. Everybody has a different interpretation. Its been done some place in some culture by someone before… But what makes it different is that person's heart and that person's feeling— how they take the movement and present it to you." ("Dance in America: Everybody Dance Now").

Stage: *A Woman Called Truth* (OB '90)
Music Video: "Gonna Make You Sweat"— C & C Music Factory ('91)
Film:
1994 **The War**— Univ

FELIX GRECO
1988 **The Blue Iguana**— Par

JOSÉ GRECO (COSTANZO JOSÉ GRECO)
b. Montorio-Nei-Frentani, Compobasso, Italy, December 23, 1919

Renowned classical Spanish dancer-director who, due to his great international exposure on television and in concerts, nightclubs and films in the 1950s, aided the universal recognition and acceptance of classic Spanish dance. Born of Spanish-Italian parents, he emigrated to Madrid at the age of 7 and then to New York at 10. Accompanying his sister, Norina, to Helene Veola's Spanish dance class in Manhattan, his natural ability allowed him to show his mother the entire class when he got home. He began classes with Veola and after dedicated study of Spanish dance (including with La Quica in Madrid), art and history, he made his debut as a soloist in 1935 with the Salmaggi Opera Co. He danced in **Carmen** at the NY Hippodrome Opera in 1937 and then, with partner Gloria Belmonte, appeared at NY's La Conga nightclub under the stage name of "Ramon Serrano." Invited to partner La Argentinita from 1941 until her death in 1945, he continued with her sister, Pilar Lopez, from 1946–48. In 1948, he choreographed his first dance work for the film **Manolete** and the following year, organized his own company. Prior to Greco's fame, classic Spanish dancing stars had primarily been females, but his appealing, dynamic and forceful performances made him one of the first internationally acclaimed male Flamenco stars. Although a naturalized American citizen, on April 8, 1962, he was decorated with the Cross of the Knight of Civil Merit from the Spanish Government along with the title of "Don." He retired from performing in 1975 to Marbella, where he operates a dance school while his Spanish Ballet Company continues to be active in the concert world, featuring his son and three daughters. His choreography uniquely combined classic Flamenco with ballet and exceptional heelwork and his personal appearances once had *The Scotsman* in Edinburgh praising, "…next time the authors of the encyclopedias revise their work, they might bracket after Spanish Dancing— See José Greco."

Autobiography: *The Gypsy in My Soul* (1977)
TV: The Perry Como, Bob Hope, Garry Moore, Dinah Shore and Ed Sullivan shows, "The Big Party," "The Voice of Firestone," "Walt Disney's Wonderful World of Color: Dances of Spain," Abbe Lane Special
Ballet/Dance Pieces (Partial listing): "Manolette" ('48), "Fiesta Goyesca," "Escenas Andaluzas," "El Cortijo," "Barcelona Suite," "Gintanerias en Triana," "Los Amantes de Sierra Morena," "In the Times of Goya" ('61)
Miscellaneous: *Ice Capades* ('57)
Film (All credits are for his solo dance sequences):
1950 **Manolete**—(Span)
1953 **Sombrero**— MGM (with Hermes Pan)
1956 **Around the World in 80 Days**— UA (with Paul Godkin)

José Greco defies gravity in a concert publicity photo (circa 1960).

1959 **Holiday for Lovers**— Fox
1965 **Ship of Fools**— Col
1972 **The Proud and the Damned**— Col

LISA GREEN
1986 **American Anthem**— Col

WALLY GREEN
Dancer, teacher and choreographer who appeared

in nightclubs (Dunes, LV '58) and was described in *Dance Magazine* (1965) as "well known exotic dance instructor who stages shows at the Pink Pussy Cat, The Body Ship and Club Largo has opened a studio in Oxnard, California." His first three film credits are in collaboration with director Billy Wilder.

   Nightclub/Concert: Act for Betty Garrett
   Film:
1959 **Some Like It Hot**— UA (with Jack Cole)
1963 **Irma la Douce**— Par

1964 **Kiss Me Stupid**— Par
1965 **The Hallelujah Trail**— Mirisch/UA

JOHNNY GREENLAND

British dancer-choreographer who danced in the film **The Young Girls of Rochefort** ('68).
Film:
1969 **Can Heironymous Merkin Ever Forget Mercy Humppe and Find True Happiness?**— Regional

GILLIAN GREGORY

Highly inventive British dancer, teacher, choreographer and director who started dancing at the age of 15. She performed in theater, cabaret, television and films before becoming an assistant choreographer to Gary Cockrell, who opened the first Dance Centre in London, where Gregory taught jazz, tap and classical ballet for six years. Her first choreographic assignment was **The Boy Friend** for director Ken Russell, where she added her tap expertise to the '30s satire. Celebrated tap students include Kenneth Branagh, David Essex, Christopher Gable, Bianca Jagger, Vanessa Redgrave, Terence Stamp, Emma Thompson and Twiggy. From choreographic creations for British stage, films and TV, she moved to also directing musicals (*Marry Me a Little, The Rocky Horror Picture Show, Joseph and His Amazing Technicolor Dreamcoat, Seven Brides for Seven Brothers, Mr. Wonderful—A Tribute to Sammy Davis, Jr.,* more) and continues to be a leading creative force in Great Britain. Her work encompasses a wide range of styles and periods, capturing the essence of the times, the culture and the dance movement with detail and humor.
Stage: *Kings and Crowns* (GB '78), *Bashville* (London '83), *Happy End* (London), *Chicago* (London), *Bugsy Malone* (London), *H.M.S. Pinafore* (London), *Nightingale* (London '83), *Me and My Girl* (London '85 and Bdwy '86, Tony Award), *Sophisticated Ladies* (London), *Tilly* (Buxton Festival), *The Merry Wives of Windsor* and *The Great White Hope* (Royal Shakespeare Company), *Seven Brides for Seven Brothers* (Haymarket Theatre, Leicester, GB '90, also dir), *Risky Kisses* (Queen's Theater, Hornchurch, GB '91), *Pal Joey* (Bristol Old Vic, '91 rev), *Annie Get Your Gun* ('92 rev and GB tour)
TV (All British credits): "The Songwriters," The Mike Reid Show, Irving Berlin and Jerome Kern specials, "Orpheus in the Underworld," "The Innes Book of Records," "Thompson," "Campion," "Virtual Murder"
Film:
1971 **The Boy Friend**— MGM (with Christopher Gable, Terry Gilbert, Tommy Tune)

1974 **Mahler**— UA
1975 **Tommy**— Col
1976 **Bugsy Malone**— Par
1977 **Valentino**— UA (assisted by Michael Vernon)
1979 **Quadrophenia**— Who Films
1980 **There Goes the Bride**— Vanguard
1981 **Reds**— Par
      Shock Treatment— Fox
1982 **Pink Floyd — The Wall**— MGM
1983 **Return of the Jedi**— Fox
1984 **Privates on Parade**— Orion
      Top Secret— Par
1987 **King Kong Lives** (aka **Queen Kong**)— DEG
1988 **Jane and the Lost City**— Blue Dolphin
1989 **Always**— Univ/UA (with Bob Banas)

JON GREGORY

A dancer-choreographer who created for films and nightclubs, Gregory was one of the last to be contracted by a major studio when was placed in charge of 20th Century–Fox's New Talent Workshop dance department in 1967. Among his dance assignments were to coach Michael Crawford and Marianne McAndrew for their numbers in **Hello, Dolly!** ('69).
TV: "The Frances Langford Show" (Pilot, '57)
Music Video: "If I Had a Hammer" and "Walk in the Sunshine" for Scopitone ('65)
Nightclub/Concert: Newcomers of 1928 (Desert Inn, LV '58), *Playgirls* ('60), *Get It On* (Tropicana Hotel, LV '67); Acts for Lita Baron, Peter Brecht, Mimi Dillard, Marilyn Maxwell, Constance Moore and Patrice Wymore
Film:
1955 **King's Rhapsody**— UA
1962 **Jack the Giant Killer**— UA
      Confessions of an Opium Eater (aka **Souls for Sale** and **Secrets of a Soul**)— AA
1963 **Shock Corridor**— AA
1968 **The Sweet Ride**— Fox

NANCY GREGORY

b. Ohio
Beginning her dance training at the Cincinnati Conservatory of Music, Nancy received her Masters degree in ballet. She performed in touring musicals and lectured and appeared as guest artist at universities before settling in Phoenix, Arizona, to teach musical theater and start a young audience program. Invited to teach aerobics to the Los Angeles Rams in 1982 ("The guys would call me 'Killer' because here I was, this skinny little blonde, out there killing them everyday with grueling workouts; they just couldn't keep up"), she began choreographing for

the Rams Cheerleaders. She was then invited to do the dances for Chippendales ("You want me to create dances for guys who take off their clothes in front of screaming women? C'mon, let's be serious. I'm from Ohio!"). From the diversity of children's theater to erotic male dance, she discussed her eclectic career in *Dance Magazine*, June, 1984: "The most important element in all my work is that I have a sense of humor. My idol is Jerome Robbins because no matter what he does, his work is always a lot of fun."

Stage: *The Wonderful Ice Cream Suit* (Pasadena Playhouse)

TV: "Starfest" (PBS)

Music Video: Videos for Kim Carnes, the Doobie Brothers, Cheryl Lynn and the Motels; "Muscle Motion" (Aerobic tape starring the LA Chippendales)

Nightclub/Concert: Los Angeles Rams *Cheerleader Entertainers* tour, *Chippendales* (NY, LA)

Miscellaneous: LA Rams Cheerleaders, *Alvin and the Chipmunks and the Magic Camera* ('84 touring arena show, also dir), *Thunder Cats* ('87 touring arena show, also dir)

Film:
1987 **Harry and the Hendersons**— Univ
1988 **The New Adventures of Pippi Longstocking**— Col
1994 **Little Rascals**— Univ

YURI (NIKOLAIEVICH) GRIGOROVICH

b. Leningrad, Russia, January 2, 1927
Described as "A brilliant classicist and an immensely gifted producer" in *The Concise Oxford Dictionary of the Ballet*, Grigorovich began his exploration of dance at the Leningrad Choreographic School. In 1946, at the age of 19, he graduated and joined the Kirov Ballet — also creating his first ballet, ***The Baby Stork***, that year. While dancing character roles for the company, he staged ***The Stone Flower*** to great success. After being the artistic director of the Ballet in the Leningrad State Theater, he was named chief choreographer and artistic director of the Bolshoi in 1964. Grigorovich ("under whose guidance the Bolshoi Ballet has shed its former athletic muscularity for a much slimmer and more elegant look") was responsible for most of the acclaimed contemporary ballets of the company. Married to Bolshoi prima ballerina Nathalya Bessmertnova, his thirty-year-long artistic rule of the Bolshoi was challenged by Vladimir Kokonin, the new general director of the theater, and on March 9, 1995, Grigorovitch resigned. After protests and confusion, former Bolshoi star dancer Vladimir Vasiliev was named artistic director on March 24.

Ballet/Dance Pieces: (Partial listing): For the Kirov: "The Baby Stork" ('46), "Stone Flower" ('57) and "Legend of Love"; for the Bolshoi: "Sleeping Beauty," "Spartacus," "Swan Lake," "Ivan the Terrible," "Angara," "Romeo and Juliet," "The Golden Age" ('82)

Film:
1966 **Bolshoi Ballet '67**— Par
1979 **Ivan the Terrible**— Corinth
    Spartacus— Corinth

UTAH GROUND

b. New York
Raised in New York, she made her professional dance debut with the Metropolitan Opera Ballet Co. In 1958, she relocated to Tyler, Texas, where she taught dance (with students including Sandy Duncan) and choreographed over sixty local musical productions.

Film:
1984 **Not for Publication**— Goldwyn

CECILIA GRUESSING

1980 **The American Success Company**— Col
    Loose Shoes— Atlantic

DORAIN GRUSMAN

b. Los Angeles, California
California-born Dorain began her career in dance studying with Burch Mann and eventually joined Mann's acclaimed American Folk Ballet company, touring from 1966 to '76. "This company and Burch Mann was the single most influential time and person in my life ... and as I approach my choreography. It was a brilliant experience. Wish you could have seen it! Someday, I hope my choreography reaches this experience." She also received dance training from San Christopher and Nicholas Tarnowsky and was selected by George Balanchine in 1964 to appear with the New York City Ballet at the Hollywood Bowl. Her performance career continued to include acting roles on television during the 1960s ("The Mary Tyler Moore Show," etc.) and dancing in films (**Pete's Dragon**, **Mame**) and she began her choreographic career assisting Tony Stevens on the Mary Tyler Moore and Cheryl Ladd TV specials and **The Best Little Whorehouse in Texas**. She made her solo choreographic debut on film with **Revenge of the Nerds** in 1984 and her career moves between music video, television and film work with great regularity, bringing her joy of movement to countless viewers, especially the thousands of people who perform her dance works daily to the popular "Sweatin' to the Oldies" Richard Simmons exercise videos.

TV (Partial listing): "Beach Boys Endless Summer," "Dancin' to the Hits," "Joanie Loves Chachi," "Kids, Inc.," "Mr. Belvedere," The Olson Twins "Mother's Day" Special, "Super Mario Brothers"

Music Video: "Martika's Kitchen," "Water," "I Feel the Earth Move"— Martika; "Sweatin' to the Oldies I–IV"— Richard Simmons

Films:

1982 **The Best Little Whorehouse in Texas**— Univ (asst to Tony Stevens, with Bruce Heath)

1984 **Footloose**— Par (with Charlene Painter, Lynn Taylor-Corbett, "Opening Credits" sequence)

Revenge of the Nerds— Fox

1985 **The Breakfast Club**— Univ

Fright Night— Col

1986 **The Whoopee Boys**— Par

1987 **Malibu Bikini Shop**— Intl Film Marketing

1989 **Troop Beverly Hills**— Col

1990 **Marked for Death**— Fox (with Steven Seagal)

Repossessed— Carolco

1992 **The Raven Dance**— Orphan Eyes Prod.

TATJANA GSOVSKY (ISSATCHENKO)

b. Moscow, Russia, March 18, 1901
d. Berlin, Germany, September 29, 1993

"The expressionists Kreutzberg and Mary Wigman have left traces in me. Salvador Dali and Jean Cocteau have inspired me. They all find echoes in my work. I do not imitate them, but I adopt them," remarked Gsovsky in a 1954 *Dance Magazine* article when asked about her influences. Although Russian-born, Gsovsky attained her great success in Germany as a ballet mistress, teacher, choreographer and author. The daughter of an actress, she began her dance studies in Petrograd at the age of 5 with Olga Preobrajenska and other classic masters. Emigrating to Germany in 1923, a severe accident ended her performing career and she began to choreograph and teach. Married to Victor Gsovsky (see following entry), they opened a school in Berlin in 1928 ("We had the common dream of wanting to help bring the Russian ballet and its wonderful methods to the young men and women devoted to the art of dancing"). In the early '30s, she created works for the Kuenstler Theatre in Berlin, the Dresden, Essen, Leipzig and Munich Opera companies and after serving as ballet mistress for the East Berlin State Opera, Teatro Colon and other international companies, she eventually founded Dance Theatre Berlin (aka Berliner Ballet) in 1955, retiring in 1965. Recognized as one of the most influential teachers for the post-war German generations of dancers and author of *Ballett in Deutschland*

('54), *The Concise Oxford Dictionary of the Ballet* calls her "one of the great personalities of German ballet history."

Ballet (Partial listing): "Don Juan" ('34), "Cartulla Carmina" ('43), "Prinzessin Turandot," "Don Quixote," "Die Chinesische Nachtigall," "Der Rote Mantel," "Menagerie," "The Idiot," "Apollon Musagete," "Hamlet," "The Seven Deadly Sins" ('60)

Film:

1954 **Der Zarewitsch**— (Ger)

1956 **Magic Fire**— Rep

VICTOR GSOVSKY

b. St. Petersburg, Russia, January 12, 1902
d. Hamburg, Germany, March 14, 1974

After studying with Eugenie Sokolova in St. Petersburg, Gsovsky began to teach at an early age. After marrying Tatjana Issatchenko, they arrived in Germany in 1924 and he served as ballet master for the Berlin State Opera, opening their school in 1928. He was chief choreographer for the UFA film company from 1930–33 — a period of great musical film activity under the creative direction of UFA head Erich Pommer — but, unfortunately, a precise list of Gsovsky's contributions is difficult to confirm, as the films contain no credit for "Choreography" or "Dance Direction." In 1937, Gsovsky left to tour with the Markova-Dolin company. As "one of the most internationally respected teachers of his generation" along with his years of private teaching in Paris (among his celebrated students are Heino Hallhuber, Colette Marchand, Serge Perrault and Violete Verdy), he also served as ballet master for Ballets de Champs Elysées, the Hamburg State Opera, the London Metropolitan Ballet, the Munich State Opera and the Paris Opera.

Ballet/Dance Pieces (Partial listing): "La Sylphide" ('45, Ballets de Champs Elysées), "Grand Pas Classique" ('49) "Hamlet," "Road to Light," "The Pearl," "Chemin de la Lumière" ('52, Munich State Opera)

Film (Partial listing):

1932 **Congress Dances** (aka **Der Kongress Tanzt**)— UFA

Ein Blonden Traum— UFA

1948 **A Lover's Return** (aka **Un Revenant**)— (Fr)

1954 **Par Odre Tu Tsar**—(Fr/Ger)

JAMIE H.J. GUAN

b. China, 1950

Guan began his studies with the Institute for Performing Arts in Beijing at the age of 10, eventually joining the company. When American Michelle Ehlers came to China in 1983, he introduced her to

Chinese performing arts and they eventually married. Relocating to the United States in 1984, they created "The Magic of the Monkey King" (a lecture-demonstration program about the Chinese musical acrobatic theater) and presented it to universities and museums across the country. When Guan was approached by the casting team of *M. Butterfly* to appear in the play, he and Ehlers were asked to create the Peking Opera sequences in the show, repeating their work in the film version.

Stage: *M. Butterfly* (Bdwy '88, also appeared), *F.O.B., Dragonwings, The Tempest, The Woman Warrior* (LA '95)

Film:
1993 **M. Butterfly**— WB (with Michele Ehlers, "Beijing Opera Choreography" credit)

JEAN GUELIS
b. Paris, France

After dancing with Paris Opera Ballet, Ballet International and Massine's Highlights, Guelis began choreographing and toured in his own works. He eventually became the choreographer at Le Crazy Horse in Paris and also created a successful line of dancers who appeared in French cabaret and on European TV. His two commercial film credits reflect his striptease expertise, rather than his ballet background.

Stage: *The Mad King* (Paris '60)
TV: "Mistral's Daughter" mini-series (CBS '84)
Ballet/Dance Pieces: "Sailor Dance" ('46)
Film:
1956 **Mademoiselle Strip Tease** (aka **Please Mr. Balzac**)— EGH/Hoch Prod
1965 **What's New Pussycat?**— UA

SHELAH (SHEILA) HACKETT
Dancer, actress and choreographer who was a member of the New Fanchonettes at the Los Angeles Paramount in the 1950s. She danced on Broadway in *Guys and Dolls,* where she met and married Michael Kidd. She assisted Kidd on *Destry Rides Again* ('50—in which she also appeared) and on *Wildcat* ('60). Film appearances include **Half Breed** ('52), **Oklahoma!** ('54), **The Opposite Sex** ('56) and **John Goldfarb, Please Come Home** ('64).

Film:
1958 **Merry Andrew**— MGM (assistant to Michael Kidd)
1966 **Not with My Wife, You Don't**— WB
1968 **Star!**— Fox (assistant to Kidd)
1969 **Hello, Dolly!**— Fox (assistant to Kidd)

GUY HAGGEGE
1994 **Elisa**— Gala (Fr)

CHESTER HALE
b. Jersey City, New Jersey, January 15, 1897
d. Redondo Beach, California, August, 1984

Classically trained ballet dancer, choreographer, teacher and Ice Show director. A graduate of military prep schools and the University of Chicago, while on vacation in New York, a night at the ballet changed the course of his life. He began training with Cecchetti and was selected by Nijinsky to be the first American to tour with Diaghilev's Ballets Russe at 19. He later joined Anna Pavlova's company and when Pavlova's tour ended in Buenos Aires, he worked as physical director at the YMCA there for ten months, toured Chile with an opera troupe and ended his balletic career with a Diaghilev tour. Finally settling in New York, he focused on the world of musical comedy and danced on Broadway in *As You Were, The Music Box Revue* and *The Ritz Revue*, becoming a protégé of director Hassard Short. After staging *The Music Box Revue* in London for Short, he did the dance direction for several Broadway shows and was hired by Major Bowes as ballet master and producer at the Capitol Theatre in New York (1924–34). Creating his own dance line for the Capitol (The Chester Hale Girls), they eventually appeared in Broadway shows, nightclub revues, films and prologues at movie theaters nationwide. He soon opened a successful school and studio on 56th street in New York. Signed by MGM as dance director in 1934, his profile in the 1937–38 editon of *Motion Picture Almanac* described him as "5 feet, 10 1/2 inches tall; weight: 165 pounds; dark brown hair and blue eyes." In 1943 he signed to stage *Ice-Capades* and began a long and successful association with the ice revue: "I knew nothing about skating but I decided to treat the ice like a new kind of dance floor... When I put it on ice, nothing fit! I decided then and there I would have to build the show right there on the ice... I realized ... the thrilling possibility of putting ballet on ice and what it would mean to add this terrific speed and space to the art of dancing."

Stage: *The Music Box Revue* (London, '23), *Hassard Short's Ritz Revue, Peg o' My Dreams* (also appeared) and *The Magnolia Lady* (Bdwy '24), *Harry Delmar's Revels* and *Lovely Lady* (Bdwy '27), *Houseboat on the Styx* and *A Night in Venice* (Bdwy '28), *Greenwich Village Follies of 1928 & '34* (Bdwy), *Murder at the Vanities* (Bdwy '33), *Annina* (OOT '34), *Frederika* and *Three Waltzes* (Bdwy '37), *Hollywood Hotel Revue* (New Zealand '38), *Frank Fay Vaudeville* (NY '39), *The Little Dog Laughed* (OOT '40), *Viva O'Brien* (Bdwy '42)

Nightclub/Concert: Dorchester, Park Lane (London '38–39), The Lido, (Venice, Italy '39), Casino Nacional (Havana '40—as part of their contract, the girls were required to "circulate at the Race Track"!)

Miscellaneous: *Sidewalks of New York* (NY World's Fair '39), RKO Palace Theatre (NY), *Ice-Capades* ('43–54), *Holiday on Ice* (1946–59)

Film:

1930 **Love at First Sight**— Chesterfield

1933 **The Big Casino**— Univ (S) (with The Chester Hale Girls)

1934 **George White's Scandals of 1934**— Fox
The Painted Veil— MGM
Student Tour— MGM

1935 **Anna Karenina**— MGM (with Ernest Belcher, Marguerite Wallman — credited for "The Mazurka")
David Copperfield— MGM
George White's Scandals of 1935— Fox (with Jack Donohue, Eleanor Powell)
Here Comes the Band— MGM
A Night at the Opera— MGM
The Night Is Young— MGM
Reckless— MGM (with Carl Randall)
A Tale of Two Cities— MGM

1936 **Rose Marie**— MGM ("Totem Pole dance staged by" credit)

1942 **Big Street**— RKO

GEORGE ("GEORGIE") HALE

b. 1901

d. New York, August 15, 1956

Tap dancer and choreographer whose dance staging on Broadway during the 1930s was seen in several groundbreaking Gershwin vehicles. He performed on Broadway in *The Rise of Rosie O'Reilly* ('23), *Greenwich Village Follies of 1924, Bye Bye Bonnie* and *Make It Snappy* ('27) before becoming a dance director. He subsequently produced *Hold Onto Your Hats* ('40), *The Lady Comes Across* ('42), *From Broadway to Paris* (also lyricist) and created industrials and packaged shows until his death in 1956.

Stage: *Heads Up* (Bdwy '29, also dir), *The New Yorkers, Strike Up the Band* and *Girl Crazy* (Bdwy '30), *Earl Carroll's Vanities of 1931* (Bdwy), *Of Thee I Sing* (Bdwy '31), *Humpty Dumpty* (OOT '32, replaced by Bobby Connolly), *Pardon My English* (Bdwy '33), *Red, Hot and Blue* (Bdwy '36, assisted by Al White, Jr.), *Paradise on Broadway* ('37), *International Revue* (European tour '37), *Shuffle Along* (Bdwy '52, also dir)

Nightclub/Concert: International Casino (NY '39), Versailles Club (NY '43), *All About Love* ('51, also dir)

Film:

1930 **Heads Up**— Par

1934 **Hollywood Party**— MGM (with Dave Gould, Albertina Rasch)
Many Happy Returns— Par (with Frank Veloz)

1935 **Princess O'Hara**— Univ

1943 **Crazy House**— Univ (with Tony De-Marco)

1944 **Follow the Boys**— Univ (with Carmen Amaya, Louis DaPron, Joe Schoenfeld, Frank Veloz)

SIANA LEE HALE

1979 **Rock 'n' Roll High School**— New World

MIKE HALEY

1985 **Fandango**— WB

JOEL HALL

b. Chicago, Illinois

Jazz idiom dancemaker who began his dance training with modern from Frances Alici and ballet at Ed Parish's school in Chicago ("He was just as quick at assimilating jazz, abstract, pop and ethnic idioms. 'From the first class I knew I wanted to be a choreographer. I needed the vocabulary.'") Moving to New York in 1969, he diversified his studies in jazz dance with Pepsi Bethel, Thelma Hill and Nat Horne. As lead dancer at Northeastern Illinois University, he also danced with the Chicago Moving Co. In 1974, he founded The Joel Hall Dancers of Chicago and opened his own studio, the New School of Performing Arts in 1976.

Stage: The Pearl Fishers (Chicago Opera)

Ballet/Dance Pieces (Partial listing): "Chicago," "Caliente," "Por Favor," "The Sorceress," "Nightwalker," "Uhuru," "Maison du Créateur de Rêves," etc.

Film:

1986 **Wildcats**— WB (with Paula Tracy Smuin)

HEINO HALLHUBER

b. Munich, Germany, 1927

German dancer-choreographer who studied with Erna Grebl, Victor Gsovsky and Pino Mlakar in Munich. He made his professional debut with the Munich State Opera in ***Don Juan*** ('49) and performed dozens of principal roles in classic, romantic and modern ballets for the company. He also gained additional recognition from multiple television appearances.

Film:

1977 **The Serpent's Egg**— Par

1985 **A Man Like Eva**— Promovision

ANN (ANNA) HALPRIN (SHUMANN)

b. Winnetka, Illinois, July 13, 1920

Performance art pioneer whose dancers and choreography are seen in one film, **Revolution**. After studying with Margaret H'Doubler and the Harvard School of Design, she danced with Doris Humphrey and Charles Weidman in *Sing Out Sweet Land* on Broadway. From 1948–55, she taught in San Francisco and made her professional choreographic debut in 1949 with the Pacific Dance Theatre company. In 1955 she began Dancers Workshop of San Francisco, which inventively combined the creativity of dancers, painters, architects and musicians. Her avant-garde works caused excitement — and controversy — within the dance world. In Russell Hartley's October, 1965 *Dance Magazine* review of her concert, her work was examined: "Miss Halprin's compositions, however far removed they may be from traditional notions of dance, can only be the creations of highly trained and imaginative dancers. Classicists may hesitate to call the productions dance — but only dancers can perform them... I had very much the feeling I had just lived through an event, or some sort of situation in which I had become personally involved, rather than having attended the theatre in any ordinary sense." Winner of the 1980 American Dance Guild's award "in recognition of her work as one of the nation's leading exponents of experimental dance."

Ballet/Dance Pieces (Partial listing): "Theme and Variations," "The Lonely Ones" ('49), "Five Legged Stools," "Stillpoint," "Visions," "The Flowerburger," "Birds of America, or Gardens Without Walls," "Parades and Changes," "The Bath," "Animal Ritual" ('71)

Film:

1968 **Revolution** — Lopert

JIMMY HAMILTON

1991 **House Party 2** — New Line Cinema (with Vernon Jackson, Kid 'n' Play)

CHRIS HAMMAN

1990 **Instant Karma** — MGM

JAMIE HAMPTON

Dancer-choreographer who began dancing at Dartmouth and joined Pilobolus in 1978. In 1983, he joined Momix — another collective dance/theatre group — and eventually was one fourth of ISO when they began in 1987. Discussing their collaborative process in a *Dance Magazine* interview (August, 1988), he said, "It's a challenge because,

on the one hand, you have to represent yourself, and you might be jealous of how much someone else can do. It's not necessarily harmonious at all times, but, on the other hand, you're all working for the same team. It's a very democratic way to work."

Film:

1989 **Earth Girls Are Easy** — Vestron (with Russell Clark, Sarah Elgart, ISO: Daniel Ezralow, Ashley Roland, Morleigh Steinberg; Wayne "Crescendo" Ward)

CAROL (CAROLYN) HANEY

b. New Bedford, Massachusetts, December 24, 1924

d. New York, May 10, 1964

Unique dancer, actress and choreographer who collaborated extensively with three of the greatest choreographers of the 20th century: Jack Cole, Bob Fosse and Gene Kelly. Starting her dance studies at the age of 5, she opened her own school in New Bedford (Miss Haney's School of the Dance) at the age of 15. In 1940 she went to Hollywood to study with Ernest Belcher, dance in nightclubs, work as a waitress and eventually join Jack Cole's dance group to appear in nightclubs across the country. After making her Broadway debut in 1945 in *Watch Out Angel* she also worked for Cole in *Bonanza Bound* ('47). While dancing in **Tea for Two**, star Gene Nelson noticed her ability with jazz and modern and after she helped him with his routines, he tried to convince Warner Bros. to place her under contract. Contracted instead to MGM from 1950–57, she assisted Cole and Gene Kelly, also appearing prominently in films (**On the Town, Kiss Me Kate, Invitation to the Dance** and **Summer Stock**). While assisting Kelly on **Brigadoon**, she heard about a new "George Abbott Show" and flew to New York to audition. When she got the show she took a leave of absence from the MGM contract, won a Tony award, and achieved Broadway immortality in *The Pajama Game* ('54) — reprising her pixiesque performance in the film. Her newfound stardom was responsible for featured appearances on all of the popular musical variety television shows of the period, which she often choreographed. After another stage appearance for Jack Cole in *Ziegfeld Follies of 1956*, she began choreographing for the Broadway stage. Married to actor Larry Blyden in 1955, they had two children and Haney was in the middle of a promising stage choreographic career when she caught pneumonia while staging the London production of *She Loves Me*. Returning to New York, she was in the midst of creating *Funny Girl* when she died unexpectedly.

Stage: *Flower Drum Song* (Bdwy '58, Tony nom), *Bravo Giovanni* (Bdwy '62, Tony nom), *She Loves Me* (Bdwy and London '63), *Jennie* (OOT '63, uncredited), *Funny Girl* (Bdwy '64, work completed by Larry Fuller, Tony nom)

TV (Partial listing): "The Broadway of Lerner and Lowe" ('62), "The Garry Moore Show" ('63–64), "The Perry Como Show," etc.

Miscellaneous: Industrials for Oldsmobile ('56–63)

Film (All credits as assistant to Gene Kelly):
1949 **On the Town**— MGM (also appeared)
1954 **Brigadoon**— MGM
1956 **Invitation to the Dance**— MGM (with Alan Carter, Jeanne Coyne, also appeared)

TOM HANSEN

b. Modesto, California, September 11, 1925

Originally inspired to dance by the '40s and '50s movie musicals, this Emmy-nominated television and stage choreographer only got one opportunity to place his creations on commercial film. He gained his dance education from Serge Ismalor, Anna Istomina and at the School of American Ballet and the Hanya Holm School in New York. Making his professional debut as a dancer at the Roxy Theatre in New York (1947), he appeared on Broadway in *Kiss Me Kate* (1948–50) and then began dancing on television ("Stop the Music," "Your Hit Parade," etc.) which led him to his choreographic career. While creating new numbers for the long-running *Jubilee!* at Bally's Hotel, Las Vegas, in 1995, he wrote, listing Tony Charmoli, Ernie Flatt and Bob Fosse as major influences in his life, and added: "I guess I was pretty good because I'm still at it at 70!"

Stage: *The Carol Channing Show* and *From A to Z* (Bdwy '60), for Sacramento Music Circus: *Bye Bye Birdie, Can Can, The Desert Song, Finian's Rainbow, The Music Man, My Fair Lady, Paint Your Wagon, 1776,* and *Tom Sawyer*

TV (Partial listing): "Your Hit Parade" ('58), "The Arthur Murray Party," "The Hollywood Palace," "The Dinah Shore Chevy Show," "The Ed Sullivan Show," "The Red Skeleton Show" (8 seasons, with the Tom Hansen Dancers, Emmy nom), "The Tim Conway Comedy Hour" ('70, with the Tom Hansen Dancers), "Your Hit Parade" ('74, with the Tom Hansen Dancers); specials for Steve Allen, Janet Blair, George Burns, Bing Crosby, Tennessee Ernie Ford ("Those Fabulous Fordies," '72 Emmy nom), Bob Hope, Ted Knight, Wayner Newton, Opryland, Roy Rogers & Dale Evans and Frank Sinatra; commercials for Newport cigarettes, Armstrong Flooring, Kings Island Dominion (starring Dick Van Dyke)

Nightclub/Concert: *Jubilee!* (MGM Grand/Bally's, LV), *Hello Hollywood Hello* (MGM Grand, Reno), *Lido de Paris, The Roaring Twenties* and *Keep America Smiling* (Harrah's, LV); acts for Steve Allen

& Jayne Meadows, Carol Channing, Dorothy Collins, Arlene Dahl, Elaine Dunn, Shirley Jones, Jim Nabors, Jane Powell and Juliet Prowse

Miscellaneous: Arena spectaculars: *Disney on Parade* (2 editions), *Peter Pan, Flintstones on Parade*; Marineland, John F. Kennedy Inaugural Gala, U.S. Air Force 40th Anniversary

Film:
1968 **Skidoo**— Par

JOHN W. HARKRIDER

b. Abilene, Texas, November 19, 1900

Actor, art-and-costume designer and staging director who enjoyed an eclectic theatrical career. He began his professional career playing juvenile leads in silent films with Theda Bara, Mary Pickford and Rudolph Valentino from 1917–18. After staging and design chores in New York (primarily for Florenz Ziegfeld), he designed the costumes for the films **Whoopee** ('30), **Roman Scandals** ('33), **Nana** ('36), **Swing Time** (also set design, '36), **Three Smart Girls** ('37, also art dir), **Top of the Town** and **My Man Godfrey**. He returned to acting in films in 1937: **Reported Missing, The Man Who Cried Wolf, One Hundred Men and a Girl** and **Merry-Go-Round of 1938**. He returned to New York, where he ran a successful male modeling agency for many years.

Stage: *The Ziegfeld Follies*
Film:
1930 **Glorifying the American Girl**— Par (with Ted Shawn, "Revue Finales Designed and Staged by" credit)

LIAM HARNEY
1994 **Blown Away**— MGM

JO ANN HARRIS
1986 **The Last Resort**— Concord

TODD HARRIS-GONZALEZ
1996 **Coyote**— Mallorca Ent

LINDA HART

Multi-talented Hart began her career at the age of 3, singing with her Grammy Award–winning Gospel music family, The Harts. Linda's diversified performing career has encompassed stage (*Anything Goes, Divine Madness: De Tour, Livin' Dolls, Pump Boys and Dinettes,* more), television ("The Johnny Cash Show," "Hill Street Blues," "Night Court," "The Garry Shandling Show," etc.), live tours with David Brenner, Bob Hope, Al Jarreau, Bette Midler and others, films (**Vamp**, **The Best of Times**, **Stella**, **A Perfect World**, etc.) and recordings (fourteen albums with her family, one solo album, the **Honkytonk Freeway** soundtrack, "After All These Years" single with her brother, Larry Hart, etc.). As the daughter of evangelists, she moved all over the United States, eventually settling in Detroit. Upon graduation from high school, she studied acting in Los Angeles, toured with The New Christy Minstrels and as one of Bette Midler's Harlettes before settling in New York and a serious stage career. In 1993 she was featured in the CBS tele-version of **Gypsy** as the trumpet-blowing "Miss Mazeppa" and her current performance career is visible in all mediums.

Film:
1986 **The Best of Times**— Univ (also musical dir and appeared)

ANDREA HARTFORD
1987 **Hell Squad**— Cannon

JACQUELINE HARVEY
1967 **Doctor Faustus**— Col (also appeared)

JACK HASKELL
Academy Award–nominated film choreographer who was one of 20th Century–Fox's dance directors from 1932–37. Described in *The Dance*, December, 1928 when he was one of Broadway's leading dance directors as, "He is first an artist, then a director of human beings. He has a cool, detached point of view which is frequently reflected in the charming humor of his numbers... Haskell habitually carries a walking stick with him when he is directing dances. His bald head lends him the appearance of an abbot ordering his flock about their devotions, in this case to the muse, Terpsichore." Independently wealthy, Haskell was also part-owner of a New York state chain of movie theatres.

Stage: *The Caberet Girl* (London '22), *Artists and Models, Song of the Flame* and *The Brown Derby* (Bdwy '25), *Some Day* (OOT '25), *The Girl Friend* (Bdwy '26), *The Five O'Clock Girl* (Bdwy '27), *Hold Everything!, Chee-Chee* and *The Optimists* (Bdwy '28), *Polly* (Bdwy '29), *The Purple Cow* (Bdwy), *The Vanderbilt Revue* (Bdwy '30), *Through the Years* (Bdwy '31)

Film:
1929 **The Show of Shows**— WB (with Larry Ceballos)
1930 **Bride of the Regiment**— First Ntl
Showgirl in Hollywood— First Ntl
Song of the Flame— First Ntl (with Eduardo Cansino)

Viennese Nights— WB
1993 **The Bowery**— Fox
Broadway Thru a Keyhole— UA/Fox
1934 **Myrt and Marge**— Univ
Search for Beauty— Par (with LeRoy Prinz)
1936 **Dimples**— Fox (with Bill Robinson)
One in a Million— Fox (with Nick Castle — Academy Award nomination: "Skating Ensemble" number)
Pigskin Parade— Fox
Poor Little Rich Girl— Fox (with Ralph Cooper, assisted by Geneva Sawyer)
Sing, Baby, Sing— Fox (assisted by Sawyer)
1937 **The Holy Terror**— Fox
This Is My Affair— Fox
Wake Up and Live— Fox (with the Condos Brothers)

MICHIYO HATA
1990 **Akira Kurosawa's Dreams**— WB

JENNIFER HATFIELD
1950 **A Ticket to Tomahawk**— Fox (with Kenny Williams)

KAREN HAZELWOOD
1985 **Night Patrol**— New World

BRUCE HEATH
b. Jamaica, New York, September 10, 1954
Acquiring his dance skills at the Gloria Jackson School of Dance, the High School of the Performing Arts and the California Institute of the Arts, Bruce danced with the Inner City Repertory Dance Co., the George Faison Universal Dance Company, the Chuck Davis and Fred Benjamin Dance companies. Theatre performances include Los Angeles productions of Leonard Bernstein's *Mass, $600 and a Mule* and *Evolution of the Blues* and he appeared on Broadway in *Dr. Jazz*, as well as assisting Michael Smuin on *Sophisticated Ladies* ('81). Film appearances include **Dr. Detroit**, **The Wiz**, **Funny Lady**, **Sparkle** and **Minstrel Man**. He also appeared in the nightclub acts of Ann-Margret, Lola Falana, Shirley MacLaine, Leslie Uggams and the Ike and Tina Turner Revue. Beginning his choreographic work as an assistant, he continues to create in all entertainment fields. As a dance educator, he opened the Rainbow Connection Dance School in Los Angeles.

Stage (All California theaters): *Five Guys Named Moe, Evolution of the Blues* (asst choreo), *The Book of the Crazy African*

TV: 1983 American Music Awards, Black Achievement Award, "Life Goes On," "Watch Me Move," "General Hospital"

Music Video: "Neutron Dance"— The Pointer Sisters, "Early in the Morning" and "Drop the Bomb"— Gap Band, "Too Much Mister"— Natalie Cole

Nightclub/Concert: Tours for Smokey Robinson, Teresa Tang, Candy Staton, Rita Moreno, Leslie Uggams, Chico De Barge, Beau Williams

Film:

1983 **Dr. Detroit**— Univ. (assistant to Carlton Johnson, also appeared)

1986 **Radioactive Dreams**— De Laurentis (with Michelle Simmons)

CATHARINE HEBERT

1991 **Dance with Death**— Concorde/New Horizons

HAROLD HECHT

b. New York, June 1, 1907
d. Beverly Hills, California, May 26, 1985

Hecht is one of the few dance directors to make the succesful transition to film producer. After beginning his career as a stage assistant to Richard Boleslavsky at the age of 16, he danced with the Metropolitan Opera Ballet and Martha Graham's Company. Gaining varied experience with the Neighborhood Playhouse, he went to Hollywood as a dance director for Busby Berkeley and eventually did several solo choreographic jobs in film and a ballet at the Hollywood Bowl. After serving in the military during World War II, Hecht became a literary agent and then, formed a successful partnership with James Hill and Burt Lancaster as Hecht-Hill-Lancaster Productions which produced **Marty** ('55 Best Film Oscar winner), **The Flame and the Arrow**, **Ten Tall Men**, **Apache**, **The Kentuckian**, **Bachelor Party**, **The Sweet Smell of Success**, **Separate Tables**, **The Birdman of Alcatraz**, **Taras Bulba** and **Cat Ballou**.

Ballet/Dance Pieces: "Skyscraper Ballet" (Hollywood Bowl '33)

Film:

1932 **Blondie of the Follies**— MGM
      Horse Feathers— Par
1933 **College Humor**— Par
      International House— Par
      She Done Him Wrong— Par
1934 **Bottoms Up**— Fox

ADRIAN HEDLEY

1985 **Lifeforce**— TriStar

SIR ROBERT HELPMANN

b. Mount Gambier, Australia, April 9, 1909
d. Sydney, Australia, September 28, 1986

Classical dancer, choreographer, director and actor who attended King Alfred's College in Australia and began his dance training with the Anna Pavlova Company while it was touring Australia. He danced in Adelaide, Australia, in musicals and then in 1933 left for England to train with the Vic-Wells School. He joined the Sadler's Wells company and became premier danseur in 1936. Helpmann made his stage acting debut in 1937 in *A Midsummer Night's Dream* and also acted in *Hamlet, Nude with Violin* and *He Who Gets Slapped*. Due to his superb acting/dancing talents, he became the Sadler's Wells Ballet's most acclaimed character dancer. He costarred in the dance films **The Red Shoes** and **Don Quixote** and his memorable non-dancing film acting credits include **One of Our Aircraft Is Missing**, **Henry V**, **Caravan** and **Chitty Chitty Bang Bang** (in which he will eternally frighten children as the demented child catcher). Helpmann was made a Commander of the Order of the British Empire in 1964 and knighted in 1968. In his later years he was director of the Australian Ballet.

Stage: Golden City (London '50), After the Ball (London, also dir), A Midsummer Night's Dream (Old Vic '54, also appeared), *Le Coq d'Or* (Royal Opera House '54, also dir), *Madame Butterfly* (Royal Opera House), Murder in the Cathedral (Old Vic, also dir)

Ballet/Dance Pieces (Partial listing): "Hamlet" ('42), "Comus," "Adam Zero," "Miracle in the Gorblas," "The Birds," "Yugen," "Electra," "The Display" ('64)

Film:

1936 **Rainbow Dance**— Gau/Brit (S) (also appeared)

1948 **The Red Shoes**— J. Arthur Rank (with Léonide Massine, also appeared)

SPENCER HENDERSON 3RD

b. Fort Worth, Texas, 1949
d. Fort Worth, Texas, November 14, 1993

Another of the promising young choreographers who had their lives and careers cut short by AIDS, Spencer Henderson studied dance in Washington, D.C., with the National Ballet and at the Joffrey and Harkness schools in New York. He began his career as a dancer in the Broadway shows *Promises, Promises* and *Zorba* ('68) and *Jesus Christ Superstar* ('71). After dancing with the Theater Dance Collection, he toured in Shirley MacLaine's, Liza Minnelli's and Chita Rivera's nightclub acts and

Sir Robert Helpmann surveys his several faces in **The Tales of Hoffman** (Lopert, 1965, choreographed by Sir Frederick Ashton) in which his brilliance as a dancing actor is captured.

appeared on television in the Emmy, Grammy, Golden Globe and People's Choice Awards shows. He began his choreographic career assisting Tony Stevens and Lynn Taylor-Corbett on films before his solo choreographic credit on **Steel Magnolias.**

Stage: *Up in One* (West Coast)

TV: "Forty" (a John Schneider special), "David Copperfield IV," "The Love Boat"

Film:

1982 **The Best Little Whorehouse in Texas**— Univ (assistant to Tony Stevens, with Dorain Grusman)

1984 **Footloose**— Par (assistant to Lynn Taylor-Corbett)

1989 **Steel Magnolias**— Rastar/TriStar (also appeared)

1990 **My Blue Heaven**— WB (assistant to Lynn Taylor-Corbett)

DONOVAN HENRY

TV: "Blossom," "Grammy Legends," commercial for Nintendo

Music Video: "I Wanna Girl"— Jeremy Jordan; "'Nuff Respect"— Big Daddy Kane; "Strictly Business"— LL Cool J

Nightclub/Concert: US3 '94 tour

Film:

1991 **New Jack City**— WB

1994 **Renaissance Man**— Cinergi

1996 **Don't Be a Menace**— Miramax

JOHN HENRY

1989 **Heart of Dixie**— Orion

WARREN HEYES

1990 **Chicago Joe and the Showgirl**— New Line

JOSEPH HACKETT HICKEY

1946 **Musical Masterpieces**— MGM (S)

GREGORY (OLIVER) HINES

b. New York City, February 14, 1946

Gregory Hines' talent and success have single-handedly brought tap dancing back to the big screen. He started dancing at the age of 2 1/2, and (inspired by the Nicholas Brothers) studied with Henry LeTang. For the fifteen years he appeared in nightclubs and theaters with brother Maurice as The Hines Kids and The Hines Brothers (1949–55). Their father (Maurice, Sr.) joined the act in 1963 and they became Hines, Hines and Dad. At 8, Gregory had made his Broadway debut in *The Girl in Pink Tights* ('54) and after "dropping out" in California from 1973–77, he returned to Broadway in *The Last Minstrel Show* and *Eubie!* ('78), *Comin' Uptown* ('79), *Black Broadway* ('80) and *Sophisticated Ladies* ('81) before his film career. Non-dancing film roles ("I feel like everything I do stems from my ability as a dancer, so these kinds of roles, while it's not like dancing, it is choreography") include **History of the World — Part I**, **Wolfen**, **Deal of the Century**, **Running Scared**, **Off Limits**, **White Lie**, **Total Destruction**, **T Bone 'n' Weasel** and **Renaissance Man**. He starred in "Tap in America"— an 1989 Emmy Award winning PBS special — and triumphantly returned to the Broadway stage in *Jelly's Last Jam* in 1992, winning the Astaire and Tony Awards for his performance. He made his film directorial debut with **White Man's Burden** in 1994.

Stage: *Blues in the Night* (OB '80), *Jelly's Last Jam* (Bdwy '92 with Hope Clark, Ted L. Levy, Tony nom, also appeared)

Film (Credits are for his own routines):

1984 **The Cotton Club** — Orion (with Claudia Asbury, George Faison, Henry LeTang, Michael Meachum, Arthur Mitchell, Michael Smuin)

1985 **White Nights** — Col (with Mikhail Baryshnikov, Roland Petit, Twyla Tharp)

1989 **Tap** — TriStar (with LeTang, "Improvography" credit)

NICKY HINKLEY

1993 **Deadly Advice** — Mayfair Ent

LYNNE HOCKNEY

b. England, October 10, 1956

British dancer, actress and choreographer who trained at the Royal Ballet School. After making her professional stage debut in *Falstaff* at Covent Garden in 1973 she appeared in the London stage productions of *Kiss Me Kate*, *Strauss*, *Queen of Spades* and *Pal Joey* as a dancer and actress before creating her first choreography for *Mask Plays* at the National Theatre in London. She also appeared in the film **Pink Floyd — The Wall** and on television in "The Innes Book of World Records," "Orfeo et Eurydice," "The Wonder Years" and Michael Nesmith's "TV Parts." In addition to her choreographic work, she teaches a workshop entitled "From Renaissance to Ragtime." She is an associate of the Royal Academy of Dancing and a founding member of the British Association of Choreographers.

Stage: *Mask Plays* (Ntl. Theatre, London), *Yakety Yak* (London), *Polly* (London), *The Wizard of Oz* (London), *Worzel Gummidge* (London '81, also appeared), *Romeo and Juliet* (British tour), *He's My Brother* (Leicester), *George Don't Do That!* (Beverly Hills '86, also appeared)

TV: "A Play" (BBC), "Sisters"

Film:

1983 **Another Pair of Aces** — CBS (TV)
       Princess Daisy — NBC (TV)
       Son of the Morning Star — ABC (TV)
1992 **Christmas in Connecticut** — TNT (TV)
1994 **It's Pat: The Movie** — Touchstone
       True Lies — Fox
1995 **Lawnmower Man 2** — New Line

STUART HODES

b. New York, 1924

After serving in the U.S. Army Air Corps during World War II, this modern dancer, choreographer and dance educator started studying dance with Martha Graham at the late age of 20. Obsessed with developing his technique, he added ballet classes with Lew Christensen and at the School of American Ballet. In 1947, he joined Graham's company (dancing with future wife, Linda) and became the leading male dancer, appearing with the company until 1958. Between engagements with Graham (and "to keep his family eating"), he made Broadway and touring appearances: *Paint Your Wagon* ('50), *The King and I* ('51), *By the Beautiful Sea* ('54), *Arabian Nights* (Jones Beach, '54), *Kismet* ('55), *Ziegfeld Follies* (OOT '56), *The Most Happy Fella* ('56), *Annie Get Your Gun* ('57 rev tour), Donn Arden's Latin Quarter Show ('58), *First Impressions* (also assisting Jonathon Lucas) and *Once Upon a Mattress* ('59), *Do Re Mi* and *Milk and Honey* ('61). His choreographic projects began with solo works performed in concert at the New York YM-YWHA ('50–53). He continued to earn further stage choreographic credits and experiences assisting Donald Saddler on Broadway and solo work for the Santa Fe Opera Company and the Harkness Ballet. Teaching on the faculties of the Martha Graham School, the High School of Performing Arts and the Juilliard School of Music Dance Department, he also headed the New York University Dance Dept.

Stage: First Impressions (Bdwy '50, asst to Jonathon Lucas, also appeared), summer stock productions of *Kiss Me Kate, Paint Your Wagon, Dark of the Moon* (Utah, '59–60); as assistant to Donald Saddler: *Milk and Honey* (Bdwy '61, also appeared), *We Take the Town* (OOT '62), *Sophie* (Bdwy '63), *To Broadway with Love* (NY World's Fair '64)

Ballet/Dance Pieces (Partial listing): "Lyric-Percussive," "Surrounding Unknown," "Drive," "Flak" (all '50); "I Am Nothing," "No Heaven in Earth," "Musette for Four," "Murmur of Wings," "Suite for Young Dancers," "Balaam," "La Lupa," "The Abyss" (for the Harkness Ballet, '65)

Film:
1979 **Voices**— UA

BOSCOE HOLDEN

British dancer and choreographer who was screen-tested for leading film roles while appearing at London's Churchill Club in 1953.

Film:
1965 **Dr. Terror's House of Horrors**— Par

GEOFFREY (LAMONT) HOLDER

b. Port-of-Spain, Trinidad, August 1, 1930

Called "Renaissance Man" by *Esquire* Magazine, Holder's impressive appearance and multi-talents allow him to move easily about within the Arts. He began performing with his brother, Boscoe's, dance company in Trinidad at the age of 7 (dancing a Lindy Hop with his sister) and studied native dances while attending Queens Royal College. When Boscoe left to tour Europe, Geoffrey became the director of the Trinidadian company and after Agnes DeMille saw them, she arranged an audition with impressario Sol Hurok — who brought Holder and the troupe to America in 1953. He appeared on Broadway in *Waiting for Godot* and *House of Flowers* ('54, in which he also assisted Herbert Ross) and was premier danseur for the Metropolitan Opera Ballet in 1955, also dancing with John Butler's Company. He eventually formed his own company, creating dance pieces based on ethnic sources for concert and TV appearances. As an actor, his film credits include **Annie, Doctor Dolittle, Live and Let Die, Swashbuckler** and *TV:* "Androcles and The Lion," "A Man Without a Country," "Aladdin," "The Bottle Imp," the 1989 Academy Awards Show and several nationally televised commercials. Married to dancer-choreographer Carmen DeLavallade since 1955, he is the winner of two Tony awards for his stage work and a Guggenheim Fellowship in 1957 for his painting.

Stage: I Got a Song (OOT '74), *The Wiz* ('75,

with George Faison, also dir and costume design, Tony awards for choreo and costumes), *Timbuktu* ('78, also dir and costume design), *Encore* (Radio City Music Hall '82)

Ballet/Dance Pieces (Partial listing): "Jeux des Dieux" (for Harkness Ballet), "Dougla" (for Dance Theatre of Harlem), "Three Songs for One"

Nightclub/Concert: Act for the Supremes.

Film:
1973 **Live and Let Die**— UA (also appeared)
1976 **Swashbuckler**— Univ (also appeared)

HANYA HOLM (JOHANNA ECKERT)

b. Worms-am-Rhein, Germany, March 3, 1893
d. New York, November 3, 1992

Modern dance pioneer and teacher whose exploration of dance diversified to include unique Broadway contributions which enlivened several smash hits of the 1950s. Unfortunately her one commercial film does not begin to hint at her greatness. In Germany, she attended the Hoch Conservatory and Dalcroze Institute and studied dance with Mary Wigman. Joining Wigman's group, she toured Europe for ten years as principal dancer, eventually becoming its chief instructor and co-director. She arrived in the United States in 1931 to found the N.Y. Mary Wigman School which become the Hanya Holm Studio in 1936. She organized her own company and toured the States in concerts, creating her first American ballet (*Trend*) in 1937. Her ballet *Metropolitan Daily* was the first modern dance to be televised in 1938 and her choreography for Broadway's *Kiss Me Kate* ('49) was the first to be Labonotated and accepted for copyright by the Library of Congress, which created an important procedure for future choreographers. She founded the Center of the Dance in the West in Colorado Springs in 1941 where she taught summer sessions for over 30 years and received an honorary degree of Doctor of Fine Arts from Colorado College. In 1958 she was honored by the Federation of Jewish Philanthropies for her contributions to modern dance and in 1961 became the head of the Musical Theatre Academy of N.Y. While working on the Broadway-bound *Here's Where I Belong* in 1968 (replaced by Tony Mordente), she talked about her sources of inspiration, "You must *feel* the timing and rhythm of every aspect of life. Timing enables you to say or do the right thing at the exact right moment… Rhythm, on the other hand, is the continuity of all these right movements… Everything has a form… Something beautiful happens in its outer and inner space." Winner of a New York Drama Critics Award in 1948, an Astaire award in 1987 and three *Dance Magazine* Awards: in 1939 for "Best group choreography," in the Musical Comedy category for *Kiss Me Kate* in 1949, and again in 1990. She continued to teach at the Juilliard School, the Nikolais-Louis Studio and Colorado College well into her '90s. The Hanya Holm Collection in the New York Public Library is an important chronicle of modern dance beginnings with Mary Wigman. In 1994, the White Oak Project performed her 1981 work *Jocose*.

Biography: Hanya Holm— *The Biography of an Artist* by Walter Sorrell (1969), *Hanya Holm: The Life and Legacy* (The Journal for Stage Directors and Choreographers, Volume 7, Spring/Summer 1993)

Stage: *The Golden Fleece* (Bdwy '41), *Ballet Ballads* (Bdwy '48), *Kiss Me Kate* (Bdwy '48 and London '49), *Blood Wedding* (Bdwy '49), *The Liar* and *Out of This World* (Bdwy '50), *My Darlin' Aida* (Bdwy '52), *The Golden Apple* (Bdwy '54), *Reuben, Reuben* (OOT '55), *The Ballad of Baby Doe* (Central City, Colo. '56, also dir), *My Fair Lady* (Bdwy '56 and London, Tony nom), *Where's Charley?* (London '57), *Camelot* and *Christine* (Bdwy '60), *Orfeo ed Euridice* (Vancouver '62, also dir), *Anya* (Bdwy '65)

TV: "Metropolitan Daily" ('38), "Pinocchio" ('57), "The Dance and the Drama" (Canadian TV '57), "Dinner with the President" ('63)

Ballet/Dance Pieces (Partial listing): "Bacchae" ('28), "Das Totenmal," "Trend," "Metropolitan Daily," "Tragic Exodus" ('39 — *Dance Magazine* Award for group choreography), "Parable," "The Gardens of Eden," "Prelude," "Ritual," "Ozark Suite," "Music for an Imaginary Ballet," "Theatrics," "Rota," "Four Nocturnes," "Jocose," "Capers" ('85)

Film:
1956 **The Vagabond King**— Par (assisted by Bella Lewitsky)

PEGGY HOLMES (MARGARET CERTO)

b. San Jose, California, December 3, 1962

After beginning her dance studies with tap, jazz, ballet and acrobatics at the age of 8 with Fran Atlas Lara at the Atlas School of Dance in San Jose, she started performing in annual dance recitals and in *West Side Story* for the San Jose CLO. At 19 she made her professional debut in TV specials for Televisa in Mexico City and moved to Los Angeles, where she studied with Hama and acted and danced on television ("Knot's Landing," American Music Awards, Academy Awards, Dick Clark specials, commercials, etc.), nightclubs (*Dream Street* at the Dunes Hotel, LV, Caesar's Palace in Atlantic City), stage (*Stars on 45, To Sir with Love*) and films

(**Gimme an "F," The In Crowd**, etc.) for eight years. She began her choreographic career as assistant to Jerry Evans and Steve Merrit, progressing to "Associate" with Evans and Kenny Ortega and simultaneously gaining her solo credits. Peggy was the first choreographer to sign a feature film Media Choreographer Council union contract for **I Love Trouble** in 1993. She credits Kenny Ortega for his support and guidance.

TV: "George Burns' 95th Birthday Special" (number for Ben Vereen), "Hull High" and "Dirty Dancing" (associate choreo with Kenny Ortega), "The Tracey Ullman Show" (associate choreo with Jerry Evans); commercial for Mercedes Benz

Nightclub/Concert: Michael Jackson's "Dangerous" tour ('92, associate dir with Kenny Ortega), Ben Vereen ('93–94 tour, also dir), and Paula Abdul's MTV tour (associate choreo with Jerry Evans)

Music Video: "How Can We Be Lovers?"— Michael Bolton, "Comfort of a Man"— Stephanie Mills; "I Fell in Love"— Carlene Carter

Ballet/Dance Pieces: "The Kin of Ata" (Choreographer's Resourcenter New Work Lab, LA '93, also dir)

Film:
1985 **Gimme an "F"**— Fox (assistant to Steve Merritt, also appeared)
1988 **The In Crowd**— Orion (assistant to Jerry Evans, also appeared)
       Ladykillers— ABC Circle Films (TV) (assistant to Evans)
1989 **Dance to Win**— MGM (assistant to Evans)
       The Fabulous Baker Boys— Fox
1992 **Encino Man**— Hollywood Pictures
       Newsies— Disney (with Kenny Ortega)
       Wayne's World— Paramount
1993 **Gypsy**— CBS (TV) (with Bonnie Walker recreating Jerome Robbins' original choreo and staging, "Movement consultant" credit)
       Hocus Pocus— Disney (with Ortega, *LA Dance* awards nom)
1994 **I Love Trouble**— Touchstone
1995 **Father of the Bride 2**— Touchstone
       Jury Duty— TriStar
1996 **A Very Brady Sequel**— Par (assisted by Cecilie Stuart)

VIOLET HOLMES

b. Queens, New York, 1928

Beginning dance classes at the age of 7, Violet was taken to Radio City Music Hall at the age of 14 by her mother and found her dream in the Rockettes ("It was just unbelievable, all that precision.") Beginning as a summer replacement in 1945 while still in school, this dancemaker and choreographer progressed from line captain to assistant-to-creator Russell Markert and finally to director-choreographer for the famous troupe when Market retired in 1971.

Stage: Multiple shows for Radio City Music Hall
Film:
1983 **Legs**— Radio City Music Hall Prod/ABC (TV)

HAROLD HOLNESS
1957 **Tarzan and the Lost Safari**— MGM

BONNIE ODA HOMSEY
b. Honolulu, Hawaii, September 15, 1951

Japanese-American dancer, actress and choreographer who studied ballet, modern, jazz and hula at her mother, Reiko Takakuwa Oda's, studio in Honolulu. After graduating from the University of Hawaii, she became a dance major at Juilliard, also taking acting with Sanford Meisner and Jose Quintero. She danced with the University of Hawaii Dance Theater ('68–73), the Ethel Winter company, the Metropolitan Opera Ballet ('71) and joined the Martha Graham company in 1973 to remain for six seasons. After forming her own group, Los Angeles Dance Theater in 1978, she returned to the Graham company for one year and acted in various Los Angeles stage productions, with television appearances including "Santa Barbara," "Knot's Landing," a recurring role in "Capitol," "The Trials of Rosie O'Neill" and "Dance in America." Film appearances include **Bobby's Story, Two Idiots in Hollywood, Nobody's Fool** and **Kalito**. In 1994, after raising three children, she revived the Los Angeles Dance Theater with Janet Eilber and they triumphantly presented works by such female dancemakers as Agnes DeMille, Isadora Duncan, Martha Graham and Helen Tamiris in the programs "The Indomitable Spirit of Women" and "Trailblazers: Dancers of Change."

Film:
1986 **Nobody's Fool**— Island Pic (also appeared)

STUART (GARY) HOPPS
b. London, England, December 2, 1942

English dancer-choreographer who studied at the Hettie Loman School, the London School of Contemporary Dance and with Merce Cunningham. He danced with the Hettie Loman and Meredith Monk companies from '62–69 and began choreographing for the Scottish Theatre Ballet. In 1970 he was founder-director of the Scottish Theatre Ballet's modern dance group, Movable Workshop, and progressed to choreography and direction for the musical stage and films in Great Britain.

Stage: *Worzel Gummidge* (Cambridge '81), *Carmen Jones* (London '91)

Film:
1974 **The Wicker Man**— WB
1982 **The Tempest**— World
1988 **White Mischief**— White Umbrella Films (assisted by Karen Halliday)
1993 **Much Ado About Nothing**— Goldwyn (assisted by Deni Sayer)
1994 **Mary Shelley's "Frankenstein"**— TriStar (assisted by Stacey Haynes)
1995 **Carrington**— Polygram
       Othello— Castle Rock
       Sense and Sensibility— Col/TriStar

JEFFREY HORNADAY
b. San Jose, California, 1956

At the height of his success, Hornaday described his approach to dancers in the September, 1985 issue of *Interview* magazine, "I use a method approach to choreography: if you treat dancers like actors you get a lot more from them. There's a whole school of contemporary choreographers who like to be powertrippers… I don't subscribe to this." At 9, he played bass in rock bands and at 13 began acting in San Jose community productions. At the age of 15 he saw the film **Cabaret** eighteen times and immediately signed up for dance classes in San Jose. After dropping out of high school, he moved to Southern California and continued classes at the Roland Dupree Dance Academy. At 19, he toured for two years with Petula Clark as a member of the performing dance group Friends. In 1977, he went to Mexico City to dance in a series of music videos, soon becoming assistant choreographer and eventually forming his own production team, learning about the camera, editing and other technical aspects of film. Returning to Hollywood, he danced on television on "Midnight Specials" and the Academy Awards Show and in the film **The Best Little Whorehouse in Texas** ('82). He decided to retire from performing and began studying directing with Lee Strasberg. After serving as an assistant on the 1983 "Miss Piggy" TV special, he began a relationship with Lesley Ann Warren (whom he also partnered in "Rolling Stone's 10th Anniversary" TV Special). It was Warren who recommended Hornaday to producer (and ex-husband) Jon Peters when Peters lamented not being able to find the right choreographer for his upcoming film— **Flashdance** … and the rest is film/dance history. The film's phenomenal success led Hornaday to become one of the '80s most sought-after film choreographers, but he shifted his career once again to directing with an ABC "Afterschool" special in 1984. He co-produced the 1988 film **The In Crowd** and directed **Shout** in 1991.

Music Video: "Say, Say, Say"— Michael Jackson & Paul McCartney; "Stand Back"— Stevie Nicks (also dir); videos for the Temptations, Alicia, Randy Jackson, Johnny Kemo, Nikki

Jeffrey Hornaday in rehearsal for **A Chorus Line** (Embassy, 1985), behind him (L to R) assistants Vickie Regan, Brad Jeffries and actress Yamil Borges.

Nightclub/Concert: Madonna's "Who's That Girl?" tour ('87, assisted by Helene Phillips) and her "Girlie Show" Tour ('93, also dir)

Film:

1983 **D.C. Cab**— Univ

Flashdance— Par

1984 **Romancing the Stone**— Fox

Streets of Fire— Univ

1985 **A Chorus Line**— Embassy (assisted by Gregg Burge, Troy Garza, Brad Jeffries, Helene Phillips, Vickie Regan)

1987 **Captain EO**— Disney (S) (assisted by Michelle Johnston, Phillips)

1989 **Tango and Cash**— WB

1990 **Dick Tracy**— Touchstone ("Musical Numbers Staged by" credit, assisted by Johnston)

Opportunity Knocks— Univ (assisted by Johnston)

1991 **Life Stinks**— Brooksfilms (assisted by Miranda Garrison)

The Marrying Man— Hollywood Pictures (assisted by Garrison)

1993 **Carlito's Way**— Univ

1995 **Birds of Prey**— BM5 Films

ROBIN HORNESS

1991 **The Fisher King**— TriStar

LESTER HORTON

b. Indianapolis, Indiana, January 23, 1906

d. Los Angeles, California, November 2, 1953

As a young boy, this eventual dance/theatre innovator visited many American Indian sites in his native Indiana, which started a deep interest within him to explore Indian culture, music and dance. He saw the Denishawn Troupe in 1922 and 1923, which encouraged him to start studying dance with Theo Hewes. He co-created *The Song of Hiawatha* in 1926–27 and came to California in 1928 with the show, staying to study with Michio Ito. His exposure to Ito's Japanese theatre techniques influenced Horton's approach to dance and theater and incorporating dialogue, revolutionary costume-and-prop design, he moved modern dance into "Total Theatre." In 1941, he opened his own dance school in Los Angeles and became a legendary dance/theater leader in California, teaching and nurturing many modern future dance greats, such as Alvin Ailey, Herman Boden, Janet Collins, Carmen and Yvonne DeLavallade, fashion designer Rudi Gernreich, Bella Lewitsky, James Mitchell,

Joyce Trisler and James Truitte. His dance troupe (California Ballet Co, started in 1934) created a sensation at the Hollywood Bowl in 1937 with his ballet *Le Sacre du Printemps*. To finance his serious work, he became a dance director at Universal Studios, doing the modern and ethnic dance pieces for films, while Louis DaPron created the tap and pop pieces for the studio. Horton presented his serious works at his Dance Theatre in Hollywood (beginning in 1946), but also had a very successful commercial dance company performing Afro-Cuban and Latin pieces in nightclubs. The day after his company opened at Ciro's nightclub in Hollywood, Horton died of a heart attack. Awarded the Indiana Society's designation as "The Outstanding American Artist From Indiana" in 1951, the Horton Technique is still taught in America, principally by Bella Lewitsky and James Truitte. In 1990 the Lester Horton Dance Awards were created by the Dance Resource Center of Greater Los Angeles to honor "all movement-based art" in the Los Angeles area. **Genius on the Wrong Coast**, a film documentary about Horton and his landmark work, was being prepared by former student and company member, Leila Goldoni, in 1993.

Biography: Lester Horton: Modern Dance Pioneer by Larry Warren (1977), a section of *Dancing in the Sun* by Naima Prevots (1987)

Stage: The Song of Hiawatha (Tour, '26–29), *Shootin' Star* (OOT '46), *Tongue in Cheek* (Los Angeles '49), *Girl Crazy* (LA '51 rev), *Annie Get Your Gun* (SF '51 rev,)

Nightclub/Concert: Happy Landing (LV '52), multiple numbers for the Lester Horton Dancers

Ballet/Dance Pieces (Partial listing): "Painted Desert Ballet"('34), "Conquest", "Siva-Siva," "Kootenai War Dance," "Voodoo Ceremonial," "Tawkish, the Star Maker," "Oriental Motifs," "Le Sacre du Printemps," "Salome," "Tierra Y Libertad!," "Something to Please Everybody," "Barrel House," "The Beloved," "Medea," "A Touch of Klee," "Liberian Suite," "Dedications in Our Time," "In the Ghetto," "The Park," "Salome"

Film:
1942 **Moonlight in Havana**— Univ (with Eddie Prinz)
1943 **Ali Baba and the Forty Thieves**— Univ (with Paul Oscard)
    Phantom of the Opera— Univ (staged Opera sequences)
    Rhythm of the Islands— Univ (with The Four Step Brothers, The Horton Dancers appeared)
    White Savage— Univ
1944 **The Climax**— Univ (staged Opera sequences)
    Cobra Woman— Univ (with Paul Oscard)
    Gypsy Wildcat— Univ
    Phantom Lady— Univ

An early 1940s publicity photo of Lester Horton.

1945 **Frisco Sal**— Univ
    Salome, Where She Danced— Univ
    Shady Lady— Univ
    Sudan— Univ
    That Night with You— Univ (with Louis DaPron)
1946 **Tangier**— Univ
    Tarzan and the Leopard Woman— RKO
1948 **Siren of Atlantis**— UA (assisted by Bella Lewitsky)
1949 **Bagdad**— Univ
1952 **Golden Hawk**— Univ
1953 **South Sea Woman**— WB (assisted by James Truitte)
    The 3-D Follies— RKO (also dir)

ANDRÉE HOWARD
b. London, England, October 3, 1910
d. London, England, March 18, 1967
British dancer, choreographer and designer who studied with Lubov Egorova, Olga Preobrajenska, Marie Rambert and Vera Trefilova. As a founder-member of Ballet Club, she began choreographing for the company, eventually creating works for Ballet Rambert, the London Ballet, Sadler's Wells and Edinburgh Festival Ballet, also designing the costumes and décor. In her later years she relocated to Turkey, producing the Turkish Ballet in Ankara and concentrating on her painting talents. She returned to London and committed suicide in her apartment with an overdose of drugs.

Stage: *Beau Brummell* (London '33, also appeared)

Ballet/Dance Pieces (Partial Listing): "Our Lady's Juggler" ('33), "The Mermaid," "Death and the Maiden," "Lady and the Fox," "La Fete étrange" "Carnival of the Animals," "The Fugitive," "The Sailor's Return," "Twelfth Night," "Assembly Ball," "Mardi Gras," "Selina," "A Mirror for Witches," "Veneziana," "Merrie England" ('60)

Film:
1946 **Woman to Woman**—(GB)
1952 **Secret People**—Ealing

HERMAN HOWELL

1972 **Georgia, Georgia**—Cinerama

BRUCE HOY

A natural athlete, Hoy was on the diving team at Columbia University when he began his dance studies with Eugene Loring. After making his stage debut in the 1947 Los Angeles Civic Light Opera production of *Louisiana Purchase*, he appeared on Broadway in *By the Beautiful Sea* ('54), *Arabian Nights* (Jones Beach '54) and *Silk Stockings* ('55), returning to California and the LACLO productions of *Fanny* ('57) and *Oklahoma!* ('59). He had a very successful career dancing in ballet (Ballet Theatre), TV ("Shindig," "The Edie Adams Show," etc.) and many films including: **Billie, Bye Bye Birdie, Funny Face, L'il Abner, Made in Paris, The One and Only Original Family Band, Pajama Party, Silk Stockings, When the Boys Meet the Girls**, etc. He began his choreographic career assisting Eugene Loring and Andre Tayir on films and TV projects. Married to dancer-actress Larri Thomas in 1964, he is now an artist.

Film:
1960 **Pepe**—Col (assistant to Eugene Loring)
1965 **Do Not Disturb**—Fox

TINA HUBBARD-GLOCKEL

1991 **The Neverending Story — The Next Chapter**—WB

JOHN "HI TECK" HUFFMAN IV

1991 **Cool as Ice**—Univ

JACK HULBERT

b. Ely, England, April 24, 1892
d. London, England, March 25, 1978
Popular British light comedy star who was called

"One of the magic figures of a golden period for British revue theatre" was a director, librettist, producer and choreographer with twenty-four film performance credits. Young Hulbert began his life-long passion for the stage as an audience member at a pantomime at the age of 5. Educated at Westminister and Cambridge, he made his first professional appearance on stage in *The Pearl Girl* in 1913 playing opposite his future wife, Cicely Courtneidge. They continued appearing together in twelve musicals on the London stage (*By the Way, Clowns in Clover, Under Your Hat, Full Swing*, etc.) and, from 1931–38, co-starred in films and were beloved by British audiences as "Cis and Jack." Jack was also a member of the police force during the day for seventeen years, eventually being in charge of the women's forces at Scotland Yard. When Jack (also the brother of Claude Hulbert—another popular British film and stage comedian) died in 1978, Dame Cicely never fully recovered and mourned until her death in 1980.

Autobiography: *The Little Woman is Always Right* (1975)

Stage: *Lady Mary* (London '28), *Under Your Hat* (London '38), *Full Swing* (London '42), *Something in the Air* (London '43), *Under the Counter* (London '45 and Bdwy '47, also dir), *Over the Moon* (London '53, also dir)

Film: (Choreography for his own dance routines):
1932 **Jack's the Boy**—Gainsborough (with Philip Buchel)
        Love on Wheels—Gau/Brit
1934 **Jack Ahoy!**—Gau/Brit
1936 **Jack of All Trades**—Gau/Brit (with Johnny Boyle, Buchel)
1937 **Paradise for Two** (aka **The Gaiety Girls**)—UA (with Buchel, Jack Donohue)
        Take My Tip—Gainsborough (with Buchel)

DICK (RICHARD WINSTON) HUMPHREYS

b. Lafayette, Indiana, September 17, 1929
d. Los Angeles, California, December 27, 1977
Actor, dancer and choreographer whose first professional appearance was at the age of 4. After winning competitions with his singing and dancing in stage and radio contests, he arrived in Hollywood when he was 9 and appeared onstage in Ken Murray's *Blackouts* and as a soloist with Veloz and Yolanda's concerts. While still attending Le Conte Junior High School, he was a member of Universal Studios' Jivin' Jacks and Jills and appeared in the films **Moonlight in Havana** ('42) and **Hi, Buddy** ('43). Graduating from Hollywood High

School in 1947, he was "discovered" by Eddie Cantor for a featured role in **If You Knew Susie** ('48). Further film credits include **Summer Stock** ('50) and **An American in Paris** ('51), **Meet Me in Las Vegas** ('56) and **Rock-a-Bye-Baby** ('57) and onstage in *That's Life* (LA '54). He worked as a assistant to Nick Castle and "dance-in" for the stars, which led to solo choreographic film credits. During the '60s, his talent was very much in demand in Las Vegas and he was signed as resident choreographer for the Riviera Hotel, assisted by Shirley Kirkes.

TV: "Juke Box Jury" ('56)

Nightclub/Concert: Production numbers at the Desert Inn (LV '60), Moulin Rouge (Hollywood '61), *Return of the Wildest* (Desert Inn LV '61), The Dick Humphreys Dancers at the Riviera Hotel (LV '63), *Ziegfeld Follies* (Thunderbird Hotel, LV '63, with Bob Banas), *Anything Goes* and *High Button Shoes* (Thunderbird Hotel, LV '64); acts for Jimmy Durante & Peter Lawford, Betty Grable (also appeared), Phil Harris, Louis Prima & Keely Smith

Film:
1956 **Anything Goes**— Par (assistant to Nick Castle with Maggie Banks)
         Bundle of Joy— RKO (assistant to Castle with Audrene Brier)
1961 **Twist All Night**— AIP
1964 **What a Way to Go!**— Fox (with Gene Kelly)

DONNIS HUNNICUTT
1978 **French Quarter**— Crown Int

GLENN HUNSICKER
1988 **A Tiger's Tale**— Atlantic

DAVID HURWITH
1988 **Sticky Fingers**— Spectra Films (also appeared)

CLAIRE HUTCHINS
1987 **The Sicilian**— Fox

LARRY HYMAN
Hyman began his training on a scholarship at the Maurice Béjart Multi-Disciplinary School in Brussels. Further exploration of dance and theater included study with Gemze DeLappe and Lee Theodore at the American Dance Machine School, Nenette Charisse, Danny Daniels, David Howard and Tatiana Riabouchinska. His stage work has won him multiple *Drama-Logue* awards.

Stage: **Blame It on the Movies** (Coast Playhouse, LA), **Salome** (Minnesota Opera), *Ghetto* (Mark Taper Forum, LA)

Film:
1989 **Bert Rigby, You're a Fool**— WB

CARL HYSON
American ballroom exhibition dancer who, with partner (and wife) Dorothy Dickson, began in vaudeville. They debuted on Broadway in *Ziegfeld Follies* of 1917 and 1918, continued in *Girl o' Mine* and *Rock-a-Bye Baby* ('18), *Morris Gest' Midnight Whirl* and *The Royal Vagabond* ('19) and *Lassie* ('20) and danced in the silent film **The Silver Lining** ('21) before being imported to London by producer Charles Cochran for *London, Paris and New York* in 1921. As Dickson became a leading British stage star, the couple divorced and Hyson went on to a diverse career of performing (Casino de Paris '32), producing (cabaret revues at the Grosvenor House, London, '33, etc.) and choreographing for stage and one film.

Stage: *Primrose* (London '24 with Laddie Cliff)

Film:
1935 **Honeymoon for Three**— Gaiety/ABF (with Leslie Roberts)

LUCY IGAZ
1985 **Mata Hari**— Cannon (with Senanda Kumar)

MADELEINE INGLEHEARN
1983 **The Wicked Lady**— MGM/UA

SUSIE (SUSAN) INOUYE
A graduate of USC, Japanese-American Inoue danced with the Asian American Dance Ensemble, appeared in the East-West Players productions of *And the Soul Shall Dance*, *Omen* and *Fortune Cookie*, the Mark Taper Forum production of *Zoot Suit*, Nobuko Miyamoto's *Women Hold Up the Sky* and on film in **Xanadu**.

Film:
1988 **Casual Sex?**— Univ
1990 **Rock-a-Doodle**— Sullivan/Bluth

ROB ISCOVE
b. Toronto, Canada, July 4, 1947

Dancer, choreographer and director who, as a scholarship student, studied at the Juilliard School of Music and danced with the Juilliard Dance Theatre. He appeared on Broadway in *Henry, Sweet Henry* ('67) before progessing into choreography. After a prolific television choreographic career, he focused his talents into direction. Among his television directing credits are "Mary" ('78), the special "Showstoppers: The Best of Broadway" ('82) and the drama "Breaking the Silence" ('92). He won an Emmy for Best Direction for "Romeo and Juliet On Ice" in 1983, which he also produced.

Stage: *Peter Pan* (Bdwy '80 rev, also dir, with Ron Field), *Copperfield* (Bdwy '81, also dir), *South Pacific* ('94 rev, Long Beach CLO, also dir)

TV (Partial Listing): "Jack — A Flash Fantasy" and "Clowns" (Canadian Broadcasting Company, also dir, prod and co-author), "Raquel Welch in Las Vegas" Special, "Mary"— The Mary Tyler Moore Variety Series, Ann-Margret Specials: "Ann-Margret Smith" ('76, Emmy nom), "Ann-Margret Olsson," "Ann-Margret — Rhinestone Cowgirl" ('77), "From Yankee Doodle to Ragtime" ('76), Steve Lawrence and Eydie Gorme Special ('78), "Glenn Campbell — The Musical West," Helen Reddy Special, Dorothy Hamill Special, "The Big Show" ('80), 50th Annual Academy Awards Show

Nightclub/Concert: Alice Cooper's concerts, nightclub acts for Ann-Margret, Raquel Welch and Sandy Duncan

Ballet/Dance Pieces: "Sessions" (Ntl Ballet of Canada, '76)

Film:
1973 **Jesus Christ Superstar**— Univ
1976 **The Duchess and the Dirtwater Fox**— Fox
    Silent Movie— Fox

MICHIO ITO

b. Japan, 1892
d. Tokyo, Japan, November 6, 1961
Groundbreaking dancer, choreographer and teacher who was one of the first to introduce Japanese theatre techniques and approach to dance to the western world. Beginning his exploration of theatre and dance in Japan with Noh and Kabuki studies, at 18, Ito went to Paris to study singing and explore world theater. Seeing Diaghilev's Ballets Russes in Paris and Isadora Duncan in Berlin reinforced his interest in dance and in 1912, he enrolled in the Dalcroze Institute in Hellerau. When World War I broke out, Ito left Germany in 1914 and moved to England. There, he met and shared ideas with many international artists, performing his unique blend of Oriental and Western dance in the homes of wealthy patrons and at the Coliseum Theatre in London. With his knowledge of Japanese theater forms, he collaborated with Ezra Pound and William Butler Yeats on *At the Hawk's Well*, an innovative dance/theater work. Moving to New York in 1916, he performed, choreographed, directed and taught at Carnegie Hall — among his students were Angna Enters, Martha Graham, Lester Horton, Luigi, Yeichi Nimura and other future experimenters. When he was offered a movie contract, he relocated to Los Angeles in 1929 to create a Japanese sequence in **No, No, Nanette**. He remained in California teaching, appearing in films (**Boo Loo** and **Spawn of the North**, '38) and creating dance dramas and ballets for the Hollywood

Bowl, Pasadena Rose Bowl, Redlands Bowl and Greek Theater until he was deported because of World War II to Japan. There, he choreographed a Japanese ballet company for the Special Services Division of the U.S. Army at the historic Ernie Pyle Theater in Tokyo (1945–54), produced a production of *The Mikado*, operated a television studio and arranged tours for Japanese dancers to the United States (*Holiday in Japan*, New Frontier Hotel, LV '59, etc.). He was planning the opening ceremonies for the 1964 Tokyo Olympics when he died.

Biography: *Michio Ito — The Dancer and His Dances* by Helen Caldwell (1977), a section of *Dancing in the Sun* by Naima Prevots (1987)

Stage: *At the Hawk's Well, What's in a Name?* (Bdwy '20), *Raymond Hitchcock's Pinwheel* (Bdwy '22), *The Greenwich Village Follies* (Bdwy '23, with Larry Ceballos), *Cherry Blossoms* (Bdwy '27, with Ralph Reader), *Players from Japan* (Bdwy '30)

Ballet/Dance Pieces (Partial listing): "Prince Igor" ('30), "Etenraku," "The Blue Danube" (Hollywood Bowl '37); works for Adolph Bolm's Ballets-Intime and the Neighborhood Playhouse (NY)

Film:
1930 **No, No Nanette**— First Ntl (with Larry Ceballos)
1932 **Madame Butterfly**— Par (assisted by Fujima Kansuma)
1938 **Spawn of the North**— Par (with LeRoy Prinz, also appeared)

RACHEL IZEN

1993 **U.F.O.**— Polygram

CARL JABLONSKI

b. Gary, Indiana, June 23, 1937
"I am blessed to have such great parents who enjoyed dancing so much," wrote this choreographer-director. "They led me into a career I love and work with wonderfully talented people." Singing and dancing from the age of 4, he studied with Frances Brumshagen (tap), Louise Glenn (ballet) and Ernest Geible (acrobatic) in Gary, Indiana from 1941–55. As his career took him to other locales, he continued training with Edward Caton, Harold Gordon and Frank Wagner. Making his professional debut at the age of 10 in The Atomic Six, an acrobatic troup, he later appeared at the St. Louis Muny ('54 and '55) and on Broadway in *Catch a Star* ('55) and *My Fair Lady* ('56). He joined Ballet Ho! de George Reich to tour Europe and choreographed his first work for the company. While in Paris, as principal danseur and assistant choreographer at the Olympia Music Hall, he made his film debut in **The Reluctant Debutante** ('59). Returning to the United States, he appeared on television (Garry Moore, Ed Sullivan, Jimmy Dean and Carol

Burnett shows) and began assisting one of his mentors, Ernest Flatt, on Mitzi Gaynor's club act, the Judy Garland TV series and *Fade Out, Fade In* ('64) and *It's a Bird, It's a Plane, It's Superman* ('66) on Broadway. Donn Arden then utilized Jablonski's talents in multiple international nightclub spectaculars. With the personal goal of "The fantasy, excitement and fun I've received is what I try to give back in my work and working with others," his work as a choreographer-director continues to be seen on stage, television, nightclubs and arenas.

Stage: *Gigi, Once Upon a Mattress* (Sacramento Music Circus); *Hello, Dolly!* (Atlantic City), *Song of Norway* (San Bernardino CLO), *Gypsy* (Long Beach CLO), *Dames at Sea* (La Mirada Theater, Cal), *Palm Springs Follies* ('94, also dir)

TV: Academy Awards Show, "NBC Follies" ('73 Emmy nom), "NBC Allstar Hour," "The Love Boat," "Fantasy Island," "Glitter," "The Way We Were," Marie Osmond and "Donny and Marie series, specials for Bob Hope, Suzanne Somers, etc.

Nightclub/Concert: Multiple shows for Donn Arden: Lido de Paris (Paris and Stardust Hotel, LV), *Pzazzz* (Desert Inn, LV), etc., *Minsky's Burlesque* (Hacienda Hotel, LV); acts for Sammy Davis, Jr., Florence Henderson, Ann Jillian, Suzanne Somers, John Schnieder tour with Alabama, Tony Martin & Cyd Charisse

Miscellaneous: Opryland Music Park, "Holiday on Ice," Ringling Bros. and Barnum and Bailey Circus (also dir), fashion shows for Bob Mackie, Gucci, Cole of California

Film:
1981 **Sizzle** (TV)—Aaron Spelling Prod

GEORGE JACK

Called "one of the film capital's leading lights of modern jazz" in a 1965 *Dance Magazine* profile, this dancer, choreographer and teacher gained valuable experience combining dance and the camera creating an award winning TV program in Caracas, Venezuela. A performing veteran of Las Vegas (the Sands and Riviera Hotels), the Long Beach CLO and Broadway (*Guys and Dolls, Goldilocks, Happy Town,* etc.), Jack's extensive training came from Merce Cunningham, Luigi, Jane and Roye Dodge and others. After being on the faculty of the American School of Dance, in 1967 he opened his own Dance and Theatre World studio in Santa Monica, California.

Stage: *Put on Your Hat* (Beverly Hills, '67)

TV: "El Show del Renny" ('64, Venezuela TV)

Ballet/Dance Pieces: Jazz dance work for Valentina Oumansky Dramatic Dance Ensemble ('66), work for Ballet Folklorico de Nueva Laredo ('67)

Film:
1967 **What Am I Bid?**—Liberty Intl

JERRY (REESE) JACKSON
b. Tulsa, Oklahoma, January 14, 1936

Dancer, choreographer, writer, director, composer, lyricist, costume designer and photographer who, because of a slight malformation in his feet, began dance studies for therapy with Wanda Newton in Bristow, Oklahoma. Pursuing a career as a concert pianist, he entered UCLA at 18 and was awarded a Bachelor of Arts degree in Art and a Masters degree in Advertising and Photography, with a minor in Music. His dance educators in California included David and Tanya Lichine, Carmelita Maracci, Carol Scotthorn and various teachers at the American School of Dance. He made his professional stage debut in a L.A. production of *Can Can* in 1954, and continued on stage in *Showboat* for the LACLO. He went into nightclub work as featured dancer at Bimbo's in San Francisco, the Moulin Rouge in Hollywood, Harrah's Tahoe and the New Frontier in Las Vegas, with television appearances on "The Danny Kaye Show," specials with Carol Channing and Cyd Charisse and partnering Barrie Chase on "The Carol Burnett Show." His choreographic career began in 1966 when Chase asked him to create a number for "Studio Uno," a TV show he was assisting Hermes Pan on in Italy. This led to staging the *Folies Bergère* in Paris and Las Vegas in 1967 with Pan. With his multi-talents, he soon became one of the world's most prolific and sought after nightclub/extravaganza creators, with shows he conceived, designed, directed and choreographed currently appearing at the Princess Casino in Freeport, Grand Bahamas, the Princess Hotel in Acapulco, Mexico, the Conrad International Hotel in Queensland, Australia, the Sandcastle Theatre in Guam and the Tropicana Hotel, Las Vegas.

Stage: *All Rooms Face the Ocean* (UCLA, '66), *Folies Bergere* (Paris '67–70), *Femme de Paris* (Melodyland, Cal. '68), *Man of La Mancha* and *Promises, Promises* (Sacramento Music Circus '72), *Casino de Paris* (Paris '75–78), *Cilla at the Palace* (Victoria Palace, London, also dir), *Seven Brides for Seven Brothers* (Bdwy '82), *Glitz* (Sandcastle Theatre, Guam, '91–present, also writer, dir, costume designer)

TV: Line Renaud Special (France '73), "Tony Orlando and Dawn" ('73–75), "Entertainment Awards" ('77), "Teatro Dieci" (Rome '77), "25th Anniversary of the Wonderful World of Disney" ('78); "The Hollywood Palace" (numbers for Barrie Chase), "Superstars of Magic" ('80), "Joan Rivers Comedy Hour," "Jimmy Durante Variety Awards" ('80), "Vegas Circus" ('81), "Let Me Off Uptown" ('84)

Nightclub/Concert (Partial listing): Barry Ashton Revues; *Flesh* (Caesar's Palace, LV '69), *Va Va Voom, Hot Flashes* and *Right On* (Sahara Hotel, LV '70), *Casino du Liban* (Beirut, Lebanon, '73–76, also dir), *Folies Bergère* (Tropicana Hotel, LV

'75–present, also conceived and dir), *Pinups* (Sahara Hotel LV '75–82), *Fire and Ice* (Hacienda Hotel LV, '80–84, also writer, dir, costume designer); acts for Gloria DeHaven, Sergio Franchi, Bobbie Gentry, Goldie Hawn, Abbe Lane, Lilliane Montevecchi, Tony Orlando and Dawn, Juliet Prowse and Line Renaud

Film:
1968 **Finian's Rainbow**— WB (assistant to Hermes Pan)
1974 **Godfather Part 2, The**— Par (with Steven Peck, created the Las Vegas sequences, uncredited)
1985 **Perfect**— Col (with Natalie Brown, Kim Connell)

MICHAEL (JOSEPH) JACKSON

b. Gary, Indiana, August 29, 1958
"Michael is dance. Michael breathes dance and every pore of his body is about dance and rhythm and music," said Vince Paterson about this superstar pop singer-dancer whose unique style of dancing warrants that he co-create all of his dance numbers with other choreographers. Growing up as a member of the Jackson Five, Michael was inspired by Fred Astaire but never received any formal dance training. While touring, young Michael began to pick up dance expertise observing such style-setting rock performers as James Brown. Signed by Motown, the five Jackson brothers found recording success and when sisters Janet and LaToya joined the act, they became The Jacksons, releasing a series of hit albums and starring in their own television series. Moving into a solo career, Michael's songwriting, singing and dancing talents led to unparalleled success, with his album "Thriller" being listed in the *Guinness Book of World Records* in 1984 as the most successful album in music industry history. Through his collaboration with choreographer Michael Peters on the music videos for "Beat It" and "Thriller," Jackson helped to change the form of the new medium. After his showstopping performance on "Motown at 25" in 1983 (in which he premiered The Moonwalk— a variation of a step he allegedly learned from "Soul Train" dancers), Fred Astaire, Hermes Pan and Gene Kelly all phoned to congratulate him. Although announcements of film projects are constantly made (**Peter Pan**, a film based on "Beat It," etc.) as of this writing, he has only made one feature film. In May 1994, he married Lisa Marie Presley but they divorced 20 months later.

TV: "Motown at 25" ('83, with Vincent Paterson), multiple appearances on the Grammy Awards Shows

Music Video (Partial listing): "Beat It," "Thriller" (with Michael Peters); "Smooth Criminal," "Black or White," "Speed Demon," "The Way You Make Me Feel" (with Vincent Paterson), "Billie Jean," "Bad" (with Gregg Burge, Jeffrey Daniels), etc.

Nightclub/Concert: Multiple tours ("Bad," "Dangerous," "Victory," etc.)

Film:
1978 **The Wiz**— Univ (with Carlton Johnson, Louis Johnson, Mabel Robinson)
1985 **That's Dancing!**— MGM (with others)
1987 **Captain E-O**— Disney (S) (with Jeffrey Hornaday)
1988 **Moonwalker**— WB (with Russell Clark, Vincent Paterson)

VERNON JACKSON

1991 **House Party 2**— New Line Cinema (with Jimmy Hamilton, Kid 'n' Play)

LEONID JACOBSON

1976 **The Blue Bird**— Fox (with Igor Belsky)

ANN JACOBY

Historical dance choreographer and teacher, based in Savignies, France.

Film:
1989 **Valmont**— Orion

JOANNE FREGALETTE JANSEN

1993 **The Ballad of Little Jo**— Fine Line Features ("Choreography/Movement Coach" credit)

KEVIN JEFF

1986 **She's Gotta Have It**— Island Pictures

HOWARD JEFFREY (SCHWARTZ)

b. Philadelphia, Pennsylvania, December 6, 1934
d. Los Angeles, California, November 2, 1988
Dancer, choreographer and film producer who arrived to films from the Broadway stage and Jerome Robbins' *Ballets:USA*. Howard came to California with his family as a child, first studying dance at Eugene Loring's American School of Dance. He acted on radio and began dancing professionally at the precocious age of 18 in the film **Hans Christian Andersen** ('52) and toured with Ballet Theatre, where he first met and worked with Nora Kaye, who would be influential in his future career. A South American tour with Ballets Alicia Alonso followed and he returned to films in **Anything Goes** ('56). He went to New York and appeared on Broadway in *Fiorello!* ('59, also assisting Peter Gennaro) and *West Side Story*. Returning to the West Coast to assist Robbins on the film version of **West Side Story** (primarily coaching Natalie Wood) he

The King of pop dance, Michael Jackson.

then assisted and toured in Robbins' **Ballets:USA** (1961–62). He began a long association with Herbert Ross (Nora Kaye's husband) first co-creating Elizabeth Taylor's drunken bump-and-grind in **Who's Afraid of Virginia Woolf?** ('66), continu- ing to assist him choreographically as Ross' career progressed to director. After gaining Barbra Streisand's confidence and friendship while assisting Ross on **Funny Girl**—in which he also appeared—he assisted Gene Kelly on **Hello, Dolly!**

(partnering Streisand in the title tune) and again assisted Ross and appeared in **Funny Lady**. Through Ross' mentorship, Jeffrey became a associate producer in 1977 on **The Seven Per Cent Solution** and **The Turning Point** and continued with producer credits on **Nijinsky, Looker, Divine Madness, Jinxed!, To Be or Not to Be** and **Protocol** and the television film **There Must Be a Pony!** ('86). A portion of Streisand's 1991 recording "Just for the Record" is dedicated to Howard, whose untimely death in 1988 was a great loss to the entertainment industry.

Stage: Georgy (Bdwy '70)

Nightclub/Concert: Acts for Anthony Newley, Debbie Reynolds, and Sylvie Varten (Olympia Theatre, Paris, '72)

Miscellaneous: Clownaround (Touring Arena Show directed by Gene Kelly, '72)

Film:

1961 **West Side Story**— UA (with Tommy Abbott, Maggie Banks, Tony Mordente, Jerome Robbins)

1966 **Inside Daisy Clover**— WB (assistant to Herbert Ross)

Who's Afraid of Virginia Woolf?— WB (assistant to Ross, uncredited)

1967 **Dr. Dolittle**— Fox (assistant to Ross)

1968 **Funny Girl**— Col (assistant to Ross, also appeared)

1969 **Hello, Dolly!**— Fox (assistant to Gene Kelly, also appeared)

1970 **On a Clear Day You Can See Forever**— Par

1971 **Willy Wonka and the Chocolate Factory**— Par

1975 **Funny Lady**— Col (assistant to Herbert Ross, also appeared)

BRAD JEFFRIES

b. San Jose, California, December 31, 1960

One of the 1990s' most successful and prolific choreographers, Jeffries studied dance with fellow students Jerry Evans and Steve Merritt and made his professional debut in the film **Grease 2** in 1982. After gaining stage experience on Broadway and on tour in *A Chorus Line* and *Dreamgirls*, he appeared on television in "Midnight Special," "American Music Awards" and the pilot for "Jump." His last performance was in Stevie Nicks' 1986 "Wild Heart" national tour, which he also choreographed. Assisting Jeffrey Hornady on **A Chorus Line**, he made his solo choreographic debut in 1985 with the film **Back to the Future** and Madonna's "Virgin" tour within weeks of one another. Nominated for both MTV's Best Choreography and American Music Video awards, he was named executive direc-

tor of dance for the Hong Kong Broadcasting Network in 1993.

TV: "Jack's Place," "Life Goes On," "Look of the Year," "Rachel Gun," "Rags to Riches," "Return Bruno," "The Tracey Ullman Show"

Music Video: "Open Your Heart," "Dress You Up," "Like a Virgin"— Madonna; "Heart"— Neneh Cherry; "Dare Me"— The Pointer Sisters; "Rooms on Fire," "I Can't Wait," "Talk to Me," "If Anyone Falls," "Stand Back"— Stevie Nicks; "Happy"— John Anderson; "Spanish Eddie"— Laura Brannigan; "Respect Yourself"— Bruce Ellis; "What Love Is"— Angeline Ball

Nightclub/Concert: Madonna's "Virgin" tour ('85), Stevie Nicks' "Wild Heart" tour ('86, also appeared), Laura Brannigan ('86 national tour), The Beach Boys summer ('89 tour)

Film:

1985 **Back to the Future**— Univ

A Chorus Line— Embassy (with Gregg Burge, Troy Garza, Jeffrey Hornaday, Helene Phillips)

1989 **Back to the Future**— **Part 2**— Univ

Bill and Ted's Excellent Adventure— Orion

1990 **Back to the Future**— **Part 3**— Univ

1991 **Don't Tell Mom the Babysitter's Dead**— WB

1992 **Death Becomes Her**— Univ (assisted by Cheryl Baxter)

1993 **The Beverly Hillbillies**— Fox

JHO JENKINS

1975 **Mahogany**— Par

TOM JOBE

b. Las Vegas, Nevada, 1953

d. London, England, December 8, 1992

American-born dancer and creator who studied at Southern Methodist University in Dallas before going to England to study at the London Contemporary Dance Theatre School. After joining the company in 1975, he became one of their leading male dancers and three years later he choreographed **9-5** for the group. His death at the age of 39 from complications from AIDS robbed the international creative community of yet another fine artist.

Film:

1981 **Time Bandits**— Avco Embassy ("Greek Dance choreographed by" credit)

A. J. JOHNSON

b. Fair Haven, New Jersey

Actress and dancer who has appeared in the films

Howard Jeffrey laughingly partners Barbra Streisand in **Funny Girl** (Herbert Ross, Columbia, 1968).

Dying Young, Pretty Hattie's Baby, House Party and **School Daze**.

Film:

1990 **House Party**— New Line Cinema (with Kid 'n' Play, also appeared)

ALAN JOHNSON

b. Ridley Park, Pennsylvania, February 18, 1937

This dancer, choreographer and director was first bitten by the theater bug when he saw *Make a Wish*

The only man who could tell Hitler what to do: Alan Johnson rehearses Mel Brooks in **To Be or Not to Be** (Fox, 1983, with Charlene Painter. Photo courtesy of Alan Johnson).

('51) playing Philadelphia on its way to Broadway. At the age of 18, he cut class to see **The "I Don't Care" Girl** and got his next inspiration: "It was a terrible film with three astonishing dance numbers choreographed by Jack Cole. My reaction was 'That's what dancing should be and that's how good I have to become.'" He went to New York, studied with Nenette Charisse, Peter Gennaro and Matt Mattox and made his professional dancing debut in the national tour of *Damn Yankees* in 1955. Broadway appearances include *New Girl in Town* and *West Side Story* ('57), *No Strings* ('62), *Anyone Can Whistle* and *Hallelujah Baby* ('64). His choreographic debut was at the Camden Music Fair in 1964 where he created the dances and musical numbers for their production of *Damn Yankees*. He then went to Vienna to stage *West Side Story* at the Volksoper, remaining in Austria and Germany for three years to create dance for TV and stage productions. After returning to the United States, he got the opportunity to work with one of his inspirations when he assisted Jack Cole on the 1963 West Coast production of *Zenda!*. He continued with stage work until he began his association with writer-director Mel Brooks and his hilarious staging of the "Springtime for Hitler" number in **The Producers** led to more film assignments. After multiple stage, TV and film choreographic credits, he directed the films **To Be or Not to Be** ('83) and **Solar Babies** ('86). One of the leading forces for the creation of SSDC/MDC (the film choreographer's union), he was one of the choreographers to be given a Tribute on the 1984 Emmy Awards TV show.

Stage: *Ballad for a Firing Squad* (OB '68), *Shirley Maclaine at the Palace* (Bdwy '76), *So Long 147th Street* (Bdwy '76), *The First* (Bdwy '81), *Shirley MacLaine on Broadway* ('84, also dir), *Ann Reinking — Music Moves Me* (OB '84, also dir), *Legs Diamond* (Bdwy '88, Tony nom), *Can Can* (natl tour '88), *The Chita Rivera Show* ('91), *Paper Moon* (OOT '93), *West Side Story* (World tour '95–96)

TV (Partial Listing): Anne Bancroft "Women in the Life of a Man" ('70), "George M" ('70 — Emmy nom), "Dames at Sea" ('71), "Jack Lemmon in 'S' Wonderful, S' Marvelous, S' Gershwin'" ('72, Emmy winner), "Cole Porter in Paris" ('73), Shirley MacLaine Specials: "If They Could See Me Now" ('74, Emmy nom), "Cos" ('76), The Grammy Awards, "Christmas at Disneyland" and "3 Girls 3" (all '77), "Where Do We Go from Here?" ('77, Emmy nom); "Every Little Movement" ('79, Emmy winner), and "Illusions" (Emmy nom); The 54th, 55th and 60th Academy Awards Shows ('81,'82,'87), "Texaco Star Theater" ('82), Emmy Awards ('84), Tony Awards ('87, '88), Irving Berlin's 100th Birthday, George Bush Inaugural Gala

Music Video: "Hitler" — Mel Brooks

Nightclub/Concert: acts for Peter Allen, Ann-Margret, Shirley MacLaine ('74–92), Bernadette Peters, Chita Rivera, Leslie Uggams and Pia Zadora

Ballet/Dance Pieces: "Royal Palace" (SF Opera '68), "Concerto in F" (Volksoper '69)

Miscellaneous: Industrials for Milliken, Lincoln Mercury, Pontiac, SHARE *Boomtown* Show ('94, with Charlene Painter and Randy Doney, also dir)

Film:

1967   **The Producers** — Embassy

1973   **The Naked Ape** — Univ

1974   **Blazing Saddles** — WB
       High Anxiety — Fox (uncredited)
       Young Frankenstein — Fox

1975   **The Adventures of Sherlock Holmes' Smarter Brother** — Fox

1977   **The World's Greatest Lover** — Fox

1981   **History of the World, Part 1** — Fox (assisted by Charlene Painter, also associate producer)
       Portrait of a Showgirl — CBS (TV)

1983   **To Be or Not to Be** — Fox (with Painter, also director, uncredited for choreography)

1995   **Dracula: Dead and Loving It** — Col

CARLTON JOHNSON

b. Washington D.C., 1924

d. Los Angeles, California, December 22, 1986

Well-loved jazz dance teacher, performer and choreographer who started dancing at the age of 3. Teaching himself how to tap, he formed a duo act called The Toppers, which appeared in D.C. nightclubs. At 13 he was asked by the D.C. Recreation Department to teach a tap class. His next dance group, The Del Rio Trio, appeared on D.C. television shows. He made his professional debut at 16 and studied ballet at the Jones-Haywood School and modern ballet with Louis Johnson, also dancing in Johnson's dance company. Moving to California for TV and film work, he taught modern jazz at Eugene Loring's American School of Dance and for twelve years at Cal State University, Long Beach. Stage appearances include Broadway with Katherine Dunham's troupe in *Bambouche* ('62), LACLO productions of *Show Boat* ('60 and '67) and *Kiss Me Kate* ('64 — also assistant choreographer) and *Carnival Island* (LA '60). Johnson assisted George Le Fave and appeared on "The Glen Campbell Show" ('69) and then danced for eight seasons on "The Carol Burnett Show" as one of the Ernest Flatt Dancers. His film choreography career began assisting Larry Maldonado in 1966 on **Movie Star, American Style** (aka **LSD, I Hate You!**) and he subsequently appeared in **The Blues Brothers**, **Finian's Rainbow**, **Sweet Charity** and **The Wiz**. He eventually formed the Carlton Johnson Jazz Ensemble and taught master classes at UC Irvine until his death.

Carlton Johnson in a publicity pose taken during his appearance in the 1967 Los Angeles Civic Light Opera production of *Show Boat*.

Stage: *Show Boat* (LACLO, with Lee Theodore), revues for Teatro Lirico (Mexico City, '66)

TV: Barbara McNair Special —"A Salute to Love," "Rene Simard Super Kid" (Canadian Special, '76)

Nightclub/Concert: *Watusi Wingding* (Stardust Hotel, LV), *Sunshine and Lollipops* (Desert Inn, LV), *Sahara Galore* (El Patio Club, Mexico City), *Lido de Paris*, *Skaterama A Go-Go* (Club La Fuente, Mexico City); acts for the Pointer Sisters, Sonny Charles and the Supremes

Ballet/Dance Pieces: "Compared to What?," "Jazz a la Carte," "Jazz at the Wilshire Ebell," "A Patch of Blue," "Strut," "Thank You," "The Way I Feel," "Walk"

Miscellaneous: Tomorrowland Revue (Disneyland '70)

Film:
1966 **Movie Star, American Style** (aka **LSD, I Hate You!**) — Famous Players (assistant to Larry Maldonado)

1978 **The Wiz** — Univ (assistant to Louis Johnson, with Mabel Robinson, also appeared)

1980 **The Blues Brothers** — Univ (also appeared)

1983 **Dr. Detroit** — Univ (assisted by Bruce Heath)

1987 **Ghost Fever** — Miramax

KENAN JOHNSON
1988   Windrider — MGM/UA

LOUIS JOHNSON
b. Statesville, North Carolina

Modern classical dancer, choreographer and teacher who moved to Washington D.C. to teach acrobatics at the YMCA and began his dance studies with Doris Jones and Claire Haywood. He was offered a scholarship to Balanchine's School of American Ballet, with fellow student, Chita Rivera. He made his debut with the NYC Ballet as guest artist in **Ballade** in 1952 and attracted attention on Broadway in *My Darlin' Aida* ('52), *House of Flowers* ('54), *Damn Yankees* ('55 — recreating his acrobatic dance role in the film version in '58), *Kwamina* ('61) and *Hallelujah, Baby* ('67). He created his first dance work (**Lament**) in 1953 and it was a sensation at the New York Ballet Club's annual Choreographer's Night. He subsequently choreographed works for his own company of dancers and the Dance Theater of Harlem. His Broadway dance contributions began with assisting Jack Cole on *Jamaica* ('57) and continued on-and-off Broadway with multiple projects. He was made artistic director for the D.C. Black Repertory Company and he taught in many prestigious schools across America. On the staff of the Negro Ensemble Co. in 1968, he has headed the dance program at the Louis Abrons Art Center in New York since 1987. In 1995, he was a recipient of the Lehman Award.

Stage: *The World's My Oyster* (OB '56), *Darwin's Theories* (OB '60), *Song of the Lusitanian Bogey* and *God Is a (Guess What?)* (OB '68), *Electra* (NY Shakespeare Fest '69), *Purlie* (Bdwy '70, Tony nom), *Lost in the Stars* (Bdwy '71), *A Ballet Behind the Bridge* (OB '71), *Treemonisha* (Bdwy '75), *Miss Truth* (OB '79), *A New York Summer* (Radio City Music Hall '79), **Aida** (Metropolitan Opera), *Daddy Goodness* (OOT '79), *Jazzbo Brown* (OB '80), *Booth Is Back in Town* (OOT '83), *Bessie Speaks* (Henry St. Settlement, NY '94)

Ballet/Dance Pieces (Partial listing): "Lament" ('53), "Wings," "No Way Out," "When Malindy Sings," "Forces of Rhythm," "Folk Impressions," "Ole," "Harlequin," "First Sin," "Trio," "Negro Spirituals," "Fontessa and Friends"
Film:
1970 **Cotton Comes to Harlem**— UA
1978 **The Wiz**— Univ (assisted by Carlton Johnson, Mabel Robinson)

MYRON JOHNSON
1993 **Bound and Gagged**— Cinescope

PAT E. JOHNSON
Beginning his career in 1974 as a film stuntman, Johnson progressed in this highly specialized art form to become one of Hollywood's leading Martial Arts choreographers and coaches.
Miscellaneous: *Mortal Kombat: The Live Tour* ('95)
Film:
1984 **The Karate Kid**— Col
1986 **The Karate Kid Part II** —Col
1989 **The Karate Kid III**— Col
1990 **Teenage Mutant Ninja Turtles**— New Line Cinema
1994 **The Next Karate Kid**— Col (assisted by Barbara Goldstone)
1995 **Mortal Kombat**— New Line (with Robin Show, "Fight Choreo" credit)

MICHELLE JOHNSTON
b. California, 1965
Michelle's ballerina mother, Wanda Johnston, first took her to ballet class when Michelle was four years old. Additional classes in acting, jazz and tap rounded out her education. At 16 she got her first job dancing in the film **One from the Heart** ('82) and that same year she went to Japan to dance in and choreograph for stage and TV shows. When she returned to California she appeared in the film **Staying Alive** ('83) and danced in and co-hosted the NBC-TV show "Rock Palace." Choreographer Jeffrey Hornaday cast her as "Bebe" in the film version of **A Chorus Line** and she began assisting him on Madonna's "Who's That Girl?" tour, music videos, and films. When Hornaday got the opportunity to direct **Shout**, he hired Johnston to make her solo choreographic film debut. In 1995, she played "Gay," a major role in **Showgirls** ("The only one," she notes, "who didn't take her top off.")
TV: "Tales from the Crypt," "Worlds of Wonder"; commercials for Chevron, Ford, Long John Silver, Lotto 5, McDonalds, Plymouth, Pringles, Reebok, Rice Krispies, etc.

Music Video: "Bounce Back"— Alisha; "Don't Say Goodbye"— Indecent Exposure; "Perpetrator"— Randy Jackson; "Birthday Suit"— Johnny Kemp; "All I Want"— The Temptations
Nightclub/Concert: Madonna's "Who's That Girl?"('87, assist to Hornaday) and '93 "Girlie Show" tours ('93, with Jeffrey Hornaday)
Film:
1987 **Captain E-O**— Disney (S)(assistant to Jeffrey Hornaday)
1990 **Dick Tracy**— Touchstone (assistant to Hornaday)
Opportunity Knocks— Univ (asst to Hornaday)
1991 **Shout**— Univ
1994 **Getting Even with Dad**— MGM
1995 **Grumpier Old Men**— WB (also appeared)
1996 **California Casanova**— Rumar

ROBERTA JONAY (JONES)
b. Philadelphia, Pennsylvania, October 15, 1922
d. Tarzana, California, April 19, 1976
Dancer, singer and choreographer who was raised in St. Petersburg, Florida, where she studied dance and performed in local stage productions. She received a scholarship to the Neighborhood Playhouse in New York and attended for two years studying acting. After making her professional debut dancing in nightclubs she was voted "Miss San Francisco" in 1937. She moved to Hollywood in 1943 to be featured in Earl Caroll's nightclub shows and was placed under contract to Paramount in December, 1943. She danced and acted extensively in Paramount films from 1944–48: **The Blue Dahlia, Duffy's Tavern, The Emperor Waltz, Golden Earrings, Here Come the Waves, Ladies' Man, Masquerade in Mexico, The Stork Club, Suddenly It's Spring** and **Variety Girl**, also assisting dance directors Danny Dare and Billy Daniel on many of the films. She went into stage work, performing the female lead in the 1947 touring production of *Allegro*.
Film:
1947 **Calcutta**— Par (with Asoka)

ROY JONES
1990 **The Raggedy Rawney**— L.W. Blair Films

AKU KADOGO
1989 **Young Einstein**— WB (also appeared as "African Lady")
1993 **Reckless Kelly**— WB (also appeared as "African Lady")

SIDNEY KALEFF
1986 **Rad**— TriStar

JAKOB KALUSKY

Israeli dancer and choreographer.
Stage: *From Israel with Love* (Bdwy '72)
Film:
1987 **Sleeping Beauty**— Cannon
    Snow White— Cannon
1988 **Appointment With Death**— Cannon

DAN (DANIEL RICHARD) KAMIN

b. New York, New York, September 17, 1946
   After being inspired by the film **Houdini** ('53), Kamin began expressing his creativity as a 12-year-old magician at other children's birthday parties and even competed on "Ted Mack's Original Amateur Hour" in 1962 — and lost! While attending Carnegie-Mellon University (1964–68), he was introduced to mime by professor Jewel Walker who had trained with Marcel Marceau's teacher, Etienne Decroux. From 1969–1971 he attended movement workshops (Esalen Institute, Dance Therapy Assoc. and Gestalt) and studied modern dance with Lucy Reynolds. His exploration of the movements arts led him to the appreciation of silent film masters Charles Chaplin ("He was like a god to me; like a religion") and Buster Keaton, and in 1970, he created *Silent Comedy ... Live!*, a tribute to their artistry. Continuing to create over 50 pure mime pieces for stage, symphony concert and television, he received multiple grants for his work and performed at the White House, London, Lincoln Center and across the United States. Also creating radio shows, short films and lecturing, he appeared as an actor in *Glengarry Glen Ross*, directed productions of *Waiting For Godot* and *The Lady from the Sea* and wrote and directed a musical revue, *That Gershwin Feeling*. Acknowledged as an authority on Chaplin, he authored *Charlie Chaplin's One-Man Show* in 1984 for Scarecrow Press and his writings on Chaplin and the art of mime have been published in such periodicals as *Movement Theatre Quarterly*, *Ballet News*, *Blackhawk Film Digest* and *Carnegie Technical*. He began his film work with appearances in **Creepshow 2** ('87) and **Diary of a Hit Man** ('91). When Kamin's book on Chaplin was given to Robert Downey, Jr. for research on his upcoming film role, Downey was instrumental in getting Kamin on the collaborative team of **Chaplin** as trainer, coach and comedy sequence creator.
   Note: All credits are for movement pieces Kamin created, wrote, choreographed, directed and appeared in:
   Stage: *Silent Comedy ... Live!* (Pittsburgh Playhouse '71), *The Talking Mime*, *The Pantomime Man*, *An Evening of Mime*, *Silent Comedy Theatre* ('81, with Michael Jon), *Masquerade* ('83), *The Corpo-*

zoid Man ('87), *Confessions of an Illusionist* ('88) *Welcome* (Choreographer's Continuum, Pittsburgh '94), *Slick Moves*
   TV: For PBS: "The Silent Art" ('71), "The Art of Mime" ('75), "Mister Rogers' Neighborhood," "The Pantomime Man" and "The Mime Idea" ('78)
   Nightclub/Concert: For Pittsburgh Symphony Orchestra: *Make Your Own Orchestra* and *Babar the Elephant* ('85), *The Mystery of the Lost Elephant* ('86), *Musical Structure and the Curious Stagehand* ('87), *The Magic of Mime* ('88), *Carnival of the Animals* (Phoenix Symphony '88), *Around the World in Eighty Minutes* and *From Russia with Love* ('89, with Michael Jon), *The Lost Elephant* (Baltimore Symphony '91)
   Ballet/Dance Pieces: Mime sequences for Pittsburgh Ballet Theatre productions of "Sleeping Beauty" ('79), "La Boutique Fantastique"
   Film:
1992 **Chaplin**— TriStar (with Kate Flatt, Johnny Hutch, Susanne McKenrick —"L.A. crew — Chaplin Choreography by" credit, also appeared)
1993 **Benny and Joon**— MGM/UA ("Physical comedy sequences choreographed by" credit, also appeared)
1996 **Mars Attacks**— WB

LISAN KAY (ELIZABETH HATHAWAY)

b. Conneaut, Ohio, May 4, 1910
   At the age of 14, this future dancer, choreographer and teacher joined the Chicago Civic Opera Company and studied with Ruth Austin, Yeichi Nimura, Serge Oukrainsky, Andreas Pavley and Vera Trefilova. She made her professional debut with the Chicago Civic Opera in their 1926 production of *Aïda* and subsequently toured the U.S. and Canada with the Pavley-Oukrainsky Ballet. Chosen by Nimura to be his partner in 1931, she toured with him until 1940. After performing the female lead dancer's role in *Lute Song* on Broadway (choreography by Nimura) in 1945, she remounted the show in London in '48. She married Nimura and worked briefly as a dance director at Republic Pictures before becoming an associate and teacher at the Ballet Arts School in New York.
   Stage: *Lute Song* (London '48, recreating Yeichi Nimura's original work)
   Film:
1944 **Storm Over Lisbon**— Rep (with Aida Broadbent)

KURT KAYNOR

1989 **Fat Man and Little Boy**— Par (with Marilyn Corwin)

A publicity still for Dan Kamin's 1995 "Slick Moves" tour (photo courtesy of Dan Kamin).

RUBY (ETHEL HILDA) KEELER

b. Dartmouth, Nova Scotia, Canada, August 25, 1909

d. Rancho Mirage, California, February 28, 1993

Famous 1930s dancer, actress and choreographer who popularized tap dancing on the screen in 1933 with **42nd Street** and then, revived it some 38 years later when she made a glorious "comeback" on Broadway in *No, No, Nanette* ('71). As the eldest of six children she emigrated to the United States when her family moved to New York. The teacher of her gymnasium class at St. Catherine of Sienna grammar school noticed her natural grace and ability during "rhythmic exercises" and suggested formal dance training. After lessons from Joe Price and Jack Blue's School of Rhythm and Tap in the Yorkville area of New York, she took ballet at the Metropolitan Opera school and attended Professional Children's School. She joined the chorus of *The Rise of Rosie O'Reilly* in 1923 at the age of 13 — lying that she was 16 to get the job. She refined her tap dance style and routines appearing in speakeasies and went on to other Broadway shows: *Bye Bye Bonnie, Lucky, The Sidewalks of New York* (all 1927), *Whoopee* (OOT, leaving the show before it reached Broadway in '28) and *Showgirl* (29). With her Broadway acclaim, she came to Hollywood to make films with her then-husband, Al Jolson. Her dance abilities, combined with her refreshing beauty and personality, made her one of filmdom's most beloved dancing stars — although her tap style was plodding, compared to Eleanor Powell, Ann Miller and other tap stylists of the era ("I did rhythm dance — which is usually better when done by a man"). After retiring from films in 1941 to raise her three children, she made "Comebacks" on "The Jerry Lewis Show" in 1963 and (after her husband, John Lowe, died in 1969) on Broadway in *No, No Nanette* in 1971, being reunited with Busby Berkeley. She collaborated in films with dance directors Berkeley ("I never knew how his dance numbers would turn out, but he's a genius") and Bobby Connolly, but was always responsible to create her own dance routines — a talent which was never credited.

Film:

1928 **Ruby Keeler** — Vitaphone (S)

1933 **Footlight Parade** — WB (with Busby Berkeley)

    42nd Street — WB (with Berkeley)

    Gold Diggers of 1933 — WB (with Berkeley)

1934 **Dames** — WB (with Berkeley)

    Flirtation Walk — WB (with Bobby Connolly)

1935 **Go Into Your Dance** — WB (with Berkeley and Connolly)

    Musical Memories — Par (S) (with Hal LeRoy)

    Shipmates Forever — WB (with Connolly)

1936 **Colleen** — WB (with Connolly)

1937 **Ready, Willing and Able** — WB (with Connolly)

MARY ANN KELLOGG

Dancer-choreographer who was a member of Twyla Tharp's company from 1979–87 and appeared on Broadway in *Singin' in the Rain* ('84). In 1995 her work created a sensation with the hilarious Judge Ito Dancers on "The Tonight Show."

TV: "As the World Turns," "The Tonight Show with Jay Leno" ('95)

Film:

1989 **Look Who's Talking** — TriStar

1990 **Look Who's Talking Too** — TriStar

1992 **Leap of Faith** — Par (with Sharon Kinney, Martin Morrisey)

1993 **Look Who's Talking Now** — TriStar

1994 **Guarding Tess** — TriStar

1995 **Clueless** — Par

1996 **The Rich Man's Wife** — Hollywood Pict

COLLEEN KELLY

1993 **Sommersby** — WB

GENE KELLY

b. Pittsburgh, Pennsylvania, August 23, 1912

d. Beverly Hills, California, February 2, 1996

Legendary dancing film star who changed the Movie Musical with his many innovations wrote in 1951: "If the camera is to make a contribution at all to dance, this must be the focal point of its contribution; the fluid background, giving each spectator an undistorted and altogether similar view of dancer and background. To accomplish this, the camera is made fluid, moving with the dancer, so that the lens becomes the eye of the spectator, *your* eye." As a member of a musical family, he began dance studies with teachers in the Pittsburgh area and by observing vaudeville acts. He eventually directed his family's successful dance school in Pittsburgh with brother, Fred, and sister, Jean, while choreographing local productions and appearing at nightclubs in an act with his brother. He attended the University of Pittsburgh and directed their annual "Cap and Gown" shows. He then studied ballet in Chicago with Berenice Holmes and in New York with Madame Ella Daganova. His first Broadway shows included *Leave It to Me!* ('38), *One for the Money* ('39) and *The Time of Your Life* ('40). During 1940 he choreographed summer stock

Dick Powell begs Ruby Keeler to **Go Into Your Dance** (Warner Bros., 1935).

productions of the musical *Two Weeks with Pay* and the square dances in *Green Grow the Lilacs*. He was "discovered" playing the lead role on Broadway in *Pal Joey* ('41) and brought to Hollywood. When he began his collaborative film work, he was greatly influenced by choreographer Robert Alton and director John Murray Anderson and he strove to create moods and character insight with his dances. He choreographed his own movement — plus that of the ensemble — in collaboration with collaborators Jeanne Coyne, Stanley Donen, Carol Haney, and Alex Romero. Kelly experimented with lighting, camera techniques and special effects to create his dance routines, truly integrating dance with film. He was one of the first to use split screens, double images, live action with animation and was almost singularly responsible for making the ballet form commercially acceptable to movie audiences with **On the Town**, **An American in Paris** and **Singin' in the Rain.** While serving with the Navy during World II, Kelly directed training films and subsequently directed the non-musical **The**

Tunnel of Love, **The Happy Road** and **Gigot** as well as one of the last major Hollywood musicals, **Hello, Dolly!** International acclaim includes a special Oscar, a Page One award in 1945 (for "inventive utilization of the motion picture camera in widening the scope of the dance on the screen"), an honorary Doctorate of Fine Arts from the Univ. of Pittsburgh, the *Dance Magazine* Award ('58), an American Film Institute Lifetime Achievement Award ('85), the Kennedy Center Honors ('82) and he was nominated a Chevalier of the Legion of Honor by the French Government in 1960 as well as being awarded France's Ordre des Arts et des Lettres in 1987. In 1993, Madonna asked him to supervise her "Girlie Show" tour — on-going confirmation of the man's talents and respect within the entertainment industry. In a 1994 TV interview, he revealed that "performing for me never worked. I preferred directing and choreographing." He died at the age of 84, but his genius continues to dance on film for the ages.

Biography: *Gene Kelly* by Clive Hirschhorn (1974), *The Films of Gene Kelly — Song and Dance Man* by Tony Thomas (1974)

Stage: *Two Weeks with Pay* (White Plains '40), *Green Grow the Lilacs* (Westport, Conn. '40 rev), *Best Foot Forward* (Bdwy '41), *Flower Drum Song* (Bdwy '58, dir only), *Singin' in the Rain* (Bdwy '85, with Stanley Donen, original film choreography used for stage production, adapted by John Carrafa and Twyla Tharp)

TV: "Dancing Is a Man's Game" ('59, Emmy nom), "Gene Kelly in New York, New York" ('65), "Gene Kelly and 50-Girls-50," "An American in Pasadena" ('78)

Nightclub/Concert: *Nights of Madness* (Diamond Horseshoe, NY '40), *Gene Kelly and 30-Girls-30*

Ballet/Dance Pieces: "Pas De Deux" (Paris Opera Ballet '60 — the first American-born choreographer to create a ballet for the Paris Opera), "Slaughter on Tenth Avenue" from **Words and Music** (original film choreography adapted by Jazz Dance America, NY '95)

Miscellaneous: *Clownaround* (Touring Arena show '72, with Howard Jeffrey, also dir)

Film (All credits, except one, are for films he also appeared in):

1942 **For Me and My Gal**— MGM (with Busby Berkeley, Bobby Connolly, George Murphy)

1943 **Dubarry Was a Lady**— MGM (with Charles Walters)

Thousands Cheer— MGM (with Don Loper)

1944 **Cover Girl**— Col (with Jack Cole, Stanley Donen, Seymour Felix, Val Raset)

1945 **Anchors Aweigh**— MGM (with Stanley Donen, Jack Donohue)

1946 **Ziegfeld Follies**— MGM (with Robert Alton, Fred Astaire, Eugene Loring, Walters, "The Babbit and the Bromide" number)

1947 **Living in a Big Way**— MGM (with Donen)

The Three Musketeers— MGM (action sequences)

1948 **The Pirate**— MGM (with Alton, Fayard Nicholas)

Words and Music— MGM (with Alton, assisted by Alex Romero)

1949 **On the Town**— MGM (with Donen, Ann Miller, assisted by Alex Romero, also co-dir)

Take Me Out to the Ballgame— MGM (with Busby Berkeley, Donen, assisted by Alex Romero)

1950 **Summer Stock**— MGM (with Nick Castle, Walters)

1951 **An American in Paris**— MGM (with Donen, assisted by Alex Romero, also dir) *"Special Award": Academy Award to Gene Kelly "in appreciation of his versatility as an actor, singer, director and dancer, and specifically for his brilliant achievements in the art of choreography on film."

1952 **Singin' in the Rain**— MGM (also co-dir with Donen, assisted by Jeanne Coyne)

1954 **Brigadoon**— MGM

Deep in My Heart— MGM (with Eugene Loring, Ann Miller)

1955 **It's Always Fair Weather**— MGM (with Donen, also co-dir)

1956 **Invitation to the Dance**— MGM (assisted by Alan Carter, Jeanne Coyne, Carol Haney, also prod and dir)

1957 **Les Girls**— MGM (with Jack Cole, assisted by Coyne, Alex Romero)

1960 **Let's Make Love**— Fox (with Cole)

1964 **What a Way to Go**— Fox (with Dick Humphreys)

1967 **Jack and the Beanstalk**— Hanna Barbera (TV)

The Young Girls of Rochefort— WB (with Norman Maen)

1974 **That's Entertainment!**— MGM (with others)

1976 **That's Entertainment Part II**— MGM (with others)

1980 **Xanadu**— Univ (with Kenny Ortega, Jerry Trent)

1982 **One from the Heart**— Zoetrope (with Kenny Ortega, "Musical number advisor" credit, did not appear)

1985 **That's Dancing!**— MGM (with others)

1993 **That's Entertainment! III**— MGM (with others)

PAULA KELLY
b. Jacksonville, Florida, 1944

Dynamic dancing actress who has gracefully moved from medium to medium with her multi-talents. Raised in Sugar Hill, Harlem, she studied on a scholarship at Juilliard as a Dance Major at 17. She began her career dancing with major companies: Alvin Ailey, Talley Beatty, Martha Graham, Pearl Lang, Donald McKayle and Arthur Mitchell. On Broadway, she appeared in *Something More, The Dozens, Metamorphoses, Story Theater, Bubbling Brown Sugar* and *Pippin* and co-starred in the national tour of *Sophisticated Ladies.* TV credits include "The Dean Martin Show," "The David Frost Show," "Medical Center," "The Young Lawyers," "Night Court," "The Richard Pryor Show," Harry Belafonte and Sammy Davis, Jr. Specials and "Gene Kelly in New York, New York." Critical acclaim onstage in *Sweet Charity* in London led to her being cast in the film. Other featured film role credits: **The Andromeda Strain, The Cool Breeze, Top of the Heap, Trouble Man,**

Soylent Green, **The Spook Who Sat by the Door** and **Uptown Saturday Night**. Between performance assignments she taught at the Mafundi Institute in Los Angeles. Married to film director Don Chaffey (**Chitty Chitty Bang Bang**, etc.), she moved to New Zealand in 1985 but, upon his death, returned to America and her stage and TV career.

Stage: *Alice* (OOT '78)

TV: "Clarence and the Ottoway" (PBS), "Peter Pan" (Hallmark Hall of Fame, associate choreographer to Michael Kidd, also appeared), 43rd Annual Academy Awards ('70)

Ballet/Dance Pieces: "Spirits of Naima" (LA Jazz Company, '81)

Film:

1970 **Alex in Wonderland**— MGM

1974 **Lost in the Stars**— American Film Theater (also appeared)

BERNADINE KENT

1979 **The Electric Horseman**— Col/Univ

LEO KHARIBIAN

b. Boston, Massachusetts

Expatriate dancer and choreographer who appeared in *West Side Story* in London 1959–61 and remained in Great Britain for stage and film work. Married to dancer Jennifer Till.

Stage: *Kiss Kiss* (London '62), *Pickwick* (London '63), *Queenie* (Eng '67), *Tom Brown's School Days* (London '72), *Decameron '73* (Eng)

Film:

1965 **Go Go Mania**— AIP

1968 **Don't Raise the Bridge, Lower the River**— Col

1975 **Monty Python and the Holy Grail**— Col

MICHAEL KIDD (MILTON GREENWALD)

b. New York, August 12, 1919

One of the driving forces in the evolution of dance on Broadway and in film, Michael Kidd majored in chemical engineering at NY City College while studying dance with Nenette Charisse, Muriel Stewart and Anatole Vilzak at the School of American Ballet. Making his performing debut in the musical *The Eternal Road* ('37) he appeared in *American Jubilee* at the NY World's Fair in 1938–39 (with another soon-to-be choreographer, Peter Gennaro). A soloist with Ballet Caravan in 1938 and with Eugene Loring's Company, he joined Ballet Theatre in 1942 and danced with the company until 1947, creating a sensation in **Billy the Kid** and **Fancy Free**. He also appeared on Broadway in *Con-*

cert Varieties in 1945, as part of "Jerome Robbins and Company." Kidd choreographed his only ballet, **On Stage**, in 1945 for Ballet Theatre which led him to be selected to choreograph *Finian's Rainbow* ('47) on Broadway. After several shows, he moved to the director-choreographer ranks with *L'il Abner* ('56). Although his first film choreography was an adaptation of a stage vehicle (*Where's Charley?*), his third film (**The Band Wagon**, '53) showed the brilliance he was capable of in collaborating on the original film musical form. His energetic, acrobatic choreography for **Seven Brides for Seven Brothers** further revolutionized film dance, utilizing the new CinemaScope filming process to its fullest. Kidd also appeared as an actor in the films **It's Always Fair Weather** ('55), **Smile** ('74) and **Skin Deep** ('89). In 1990 he was asked by Janet Jackson to co-choreograph her music video "Alright" with Anthony Thomas, which is a tribute to Kidd's work in **Guys and Dolls**. In the book *That's Dancing*, Kidd states: "I have found that the camera's ability to see more than the human eye allows an emphasis on close-ups at important moments and at the same time gives varying angles to the dance which stage audiences could not catch from their static position." Winner of five Tony awards, he directed the stage version of *The Goodbye Girl* in 1993 and in 1994 was honored by the Film Society of Lincoln Center as part of its "Capturing Choreography: Masters of Dance and Film" series.

Stage: *Finian's Rainbow* (Bdwy '47, Tony Award), *Hold It* and *Love Life* (Bdwy '48), *Arms and the Girl* (Bdwy '50), *Guys and Dolls* (Bdwy '50, Tony Award), *Can Can* (Bdwy '53, Tony Award), *L'il Abner* (Bdwy '56, also dir, co-prod, Tony Award for choreo), *Destry Rides Again* (Bdwy '59, also dir, Tony Award), *Wildcat* (Bdwy '60, also dir), *Subways Are for Sleeping* (Bdwy '61, also dir, with Marc Breaux, Tony nom), *Here's Love* (Bdwy '63), *Ben Franklin in Paris* (Bdwy '64), *Skyscraper* (Bdwy '65, Tony nom), *Breakfast at Tiffany's* (aka *Holly Golightly*, Bdwy '66), *The Rothchilds* (Bdwy '70, also dir, Tony nom), *Cyrano* (Bdwy '73, also dir), *Good News* (Bdwy '74 rev, also dir), *The Music Man* (NYC Center '80 rev, also dir)

TV: "Baryshnikov in Hollywood" ('81), 45th Academy Awards Show ('88)

Music Video: "Alright" ('90, with Anthony Thomas)— Janet Jackson

Ballet/Dance Pieces: "On Stage" ('45)

Miscellaneous: *Wonderworld* (NY World's Fair '64)

Film:

1952 **Where's Charley?**— WB (assisted by Beryl Kaye)

1953 **The Band Wagon**— MGM (with Fred Astaire, assisted by Bill Foster)

Michael Kidd and Janet Reed in **On Stage** for Ballet Theatre, Kidd's only ballet choreography, 1945.

The Girl Next Door— Fox (with Richard Barstow, assisted by Bill Foster)

1954 **Knock on Wood**— Par (assisted by Pat Denise)

Seven Brides for Seven Brothers— MGM (assisted by Alex Romero)

1955 **Guys and Dolls**— Samuel Goldwyn

1958 **Merry Andrew**— MGM (also dir)

1959 **L'il Abner**— Par (original work adapted for the screen by Dee Dee Wood)

1968 **Star!**— Fox (assisted by Shelah Hackett)

1969 **Hello, Dolly!**— Fox (assisted by Hackett)

1978 **Movie, Movie**— WB (with Stanley Donen, assisted by Jerry Trent)

1985 **That's Dancing!**— MGM (with others)

1994 **That's Entertainment! III**— MGM (with others)

KID (CHRISTOPHER REID) 'N' PLAY (CHRISTOPHER MARTIN)

Kid: b. New York, 1964
Play: b. New York, 1962

Comic duo who were among the first to successfully make the transition from rap recordings to films. Both grew up in the East Elmhurst section of Queens in New York and met in 1980. Kid fronted a band called Kid Cool Out, while Play (known as Playboy Mr. C.), was also performing. They joined forces and made their recording debuts. Success on the charts led them to films, which they starred in and also choreographed the musical numbers/party scenes for.

Film:
1990 **House Party**— New Line Cinema (with A.J. Johnson, Tisha Campbell)
1991 **House Party 2**— New Line Cinema (with Jimmy Hamilton, Vernon Jackson)

GEORGE KING

1939 **Dancing Co-ed**— MGM
 Idiot's Delight— MGM
1941 **Zis Boom Bah**— Mon

MATTY KING (MATEO OLVERA)

b. 1906
d. Florida, August 19, 1978

Self-taught dancer who teamed with Frank Condos on Broadway in the 1920s in *Artists and Models* and *Broadway Nights*. He then taught his brothers to dance and formed King, King and King, a successful nightclub tap trio who dressed in convict costumes (complete with ball-and-chain), did totally synchronized tap dancing and were famous for their toe stands. He appeared in the films **Golddiggers of 1935** and **Blues Busters** ('50) as well as being a dance director and coach at Warner Bros. He was hired to teach Larry Parks how to move like Al Jolson in **The Jolson Story**. His son, Matty King, Jr., continued in his dancing father's footsteps.

Film:
1937 **Confession**— WB
1938 **Freshman Year**— Univ
1939 **Swing, Sister, Swing**— Univ
1941 **Affectionately Yours**— WB
1942 **Wild Bill Hickok Rides**— WB
1943 **Murder on the Waterfront**— WB

1946 **The Jolson Story**— Col (with Audrene Brier, Jack Cole, Miriam Nelson, Val Raset, uncredited)

SHARON KINNEY

Modern dancer-choreographer who made her performance debut with the Paul Taylor Dance Company. She subsequently appeared with the companies of Ruth Currier, Twyla Tharp and Dan Wagoner. She created her first choreography in 1974 and has been a dance advisor at the Pratt Institute. Her first film choreography credit, **Popeye**, also features her playing the role of "Harry Hotcashes' Moll Named Cherry."

Stage: In Trousers (OB '80)
Film:
1980 **Popeye**— Par (with Hovey Burgess, Lou Wills, Jr.— also appeared)
1992 **Leap of Faith**— Par (with Mary Ann Kellogg)

SHIRLEY KIRKES

b. San Antonio, Texas, January 28, 1941

Dancer, actress, teacher, choreographer and Karate expert who began her dance studies with Jean and Jerry Grey in Texas at the age of 7 because of a serious bicycle accident. She studied ballet with the NYC Ballet, tap with Ernest Carlos and Bud Nash and Karate with Pat Johnson and Chuck Norris. Her performance career began when she won a beauty-and-talent contest and during the prize of "A week in California!" she auditioned for Donn Arden. After multiple lead dancer roles in Las Vegas: *Pzazz*, (Desert Inn '68), the Flamingo, Riviera, Sahara and Sands hotels and Betty Grable's nightclub act; she appeared as one of the Ernest Flatt Dancers on "The Carol Burnett Show" for many seasons. Extensive acting/dancing film and TV credits include "Blansky's Beauties," **Third Girl from the Left** ('73), **Funny Lady** ('75), **Silent Movie** ('76) and **Pennies from Heaven** ('81). She taught dance at UCLA, UC Northridge, Dance Center West and the Roland Dupree Academy of Dance. She made her choreographic debut with an industrial for Milliken and Yvonne Mounsey gave her the chance to choreograph her first full-length ballet, *The Ballad of Ishtar*, for the Westside Ballet in 1988. She also founded her own dance company in 1988: "Moving into forming our ballet company into a new look for tomorrow. Bringing children back to the art of dance through contemporary stories that they can relate to, as well as appreciate the commitment dancers have for their art... I don't want to just do abstract dancing. Our company is not exclusively into technique. Technique is the base, but I need emotionally oriented dancers because our work is built around stories."

Stage: *Movie Star* (Westwood Playhouse, Cal)

TV: "Cover Up," "Family Ties," "The Tony Randall Show"; pilots of "Beans of Boston," "Here's Boomer" and "Reno and Yolanda," "The Passion and the Dance" ('95); commercials for Acapulco Cigars, Casablanca Records, Gallo Wine

Ballet/Dance Pieces: (For Shirley Kirkes Ballet Co.): "Artist and the Lady," "Calling You," "Cambrian Kites," "Diane and Actaeon," "Dream Time," "Galaxy," "Ice," "Ishtar," "Rehearsal Frenzy," "Sultry Night," "Where Angels Live and Die"

Miscellaneous: Industrials for DuPont/Cole Swimwear, Milliken, Redkin Cosmetics; fashion shows for Dupont/Simplicity, Gabriele; dance video "Where Angels Live and Die"

Film:

1986 **Nothing in Common**— TriStar
     Three Amigos— Orion
1987 **Overboard**— MGM
1991 **Father of the Bride**— Touchstone
     Frankie and Johnny— Par

PATRICIA KIRSHNER

1960 **Foxhole in Cairo**— Par
1961 **The Devil's Daffodil**— Brit Lion

KATHLEEN KNAP

Knap studied a variety of dance styles in Missouri before forming KATNAP and KOMPANY, her own dance/theater group, which appeared successfully at clubs and discos throughout the Los Angeles area. Teaching in Southern California over the years, she currently heads the "Jazz and Disco" department at Academy West Dance School in Santa Monica, California.

TV: "Midnight Special"

Ballet/Dance Pieces: "A Jazz Tribute to Chuck Mangione" ('76)

Film:

1985 **Bachelor Party**— Fox

WAYNE AND DORIS KNIGHT

1988 **Betrayed**— UA

MARK (ALAN) KNOWLES

b. Lincoln, Nebraska, January 29, 1954

Crediting Cheryl Cutler, his first dance teacher, and choreographer Alex Romero ("one of my dearest friends, as well as my 'mentor'") as being major influences in his life and work, Mark Knowles is a performer-choreographer with an extremely wide range of dance studies: jazz with Roland Dupree, Ben Lokey, Michael Peters, Jaime Rogers and Joe

Tremaine; ballet with Margaret Hills, Dora Krannig and Vasilli Sulich; tap with Danny Daniels, Louis DaPron, Paul DeRolf, Stan Mazin, Alex Romero, John "Bubbles" Sublett, Jim Taylor and Lou Wills, Jr. and modern with Pam Finney, Murray Louis and Twyla Tharp. Knowles also received a B.A. in Theatre/Dance from Wesleyan University in 1976. Performance credits began in 1972 at the age of 13 with summer stock stage appearances in *Can Can*, *New Moon* and *David's Violin*, and he made his professional debut in *Le Lido de Paris* at the Stardust Hotel in Las Vegas in 1978. He continued to gain varied experience with multiple TV ("Hart to Hart," "John Denver and the Muppets," "Lily Tomlin: Sold Out," etc.) nightclub (Mitzi Gaynor's and Bobbie Gentry's nightclub acts), stage (*La Cage aux Folles*, *Sugar Babies*, *42nd Street*, etc.) and film (**Pennies from Heaven**, **The Best Little Whorehouse in Texas**) performances before making his choreographic debut in 1982 with stage productions. First place winner of the 1984 Duke Ellington Tap Dance contest, Knowles' successful stage dance creations keep him in demand in professional and community civic productions.

Stage (partial listing): *Grease* ('84 rev tour), *La Cage Aux Folles* (Buenos Aires, Sacramento Music Circus, Southeast Dinner Theatre, Sarasota Florida and Grand Dinner Theater, Anaheim, Cal.— Robby Award nom '88), *A Funny Thing Happened on the Way to The Forum* and *Return to the Forbidden Planet* (Alaska Festival Theatre, Anchorage), *The Boy Friend* (Sacramento Music Circus), *Me and My Girl*, *My One and Only* and *No, No Nanette* (Whittier/La Mirada CLO), *Bittersweet* (Long Beach CLO), *Singin' in the Rain* (Golden Apple Theater, Sarasota, Fla.), *Big Bang!* (Singapore '95), *The Goodbye Girl* (LA '96)

TV: "Boone," "Far Out," "Please, Mr. Postman," "Small Wonder," "CBS Thanksgiving Day Special" ('93)

Miscellaneous: Disneyland: ("Very Merry Christmas Parade" '91, "The World According to Goofy Parade" '92), Knott's Berry Farm (*Hot Tap*), industrials for the May Company, Avon, Honda, 7-11, Taco Bell, etc.; benefits for AIDS, Beverly Hills Educational fund

Film:
1984 **The Ice Pirates**— MGM/UA

JOSEF KONICEK

1968 **The Lady on the Tracks**— Royal (Czech)

MAURICE KOSLOFF

Teacher, choreographer and producer whose Hollywood dance school was one of the most successful during the 1930s–40s. Associate producer of Imperial Productions in 1939, he produced several shorts (**The Romance of Dancing**; **Button, Button**) and also produced the features **The Hoodlum** ('51) and **Movie Stuntmen** ('53). Unrelated to Theodore Kosloff (see next entry).

Nightclub/Concert: Florentine Gardens (Hollywood), personal appearances for the Dead End Kids

Film:

1935 **Jan of the Jungle**— Univ

THEODORE KOSLOFF

b. Moscow, Russia, January 22, 1882

d. Los Angeles, California, November 21, 1956

Pioneering dancer, actor, choreographer and teacher. With a grandfather and father who both conducted the Imperial Russian Theatre Orchestra, he began his classic training at the age of 10 at the Moscow Imperial Ballet School. Graduating in 1898 he joined the company in 1901, dancing with Pavlova and Nijinsky. He went to St. Petersburg to study with Nicholas Legat and was invited to Paris in 1909 by Diaghilev to join Ballets Russes. After the Bolshevik revolution — in which he lost all of his personal belongings — he emigrated to the U.S. in 1911, where he presented an evening of Russian Dance at the Winter Garden Theater in New York. He taught in New York and played the Keith Vaudeville Circuit with his dance troupe until 1917. While touring California, one of his former students, Jeannie McPherson, introduced him to her boss, Cecil B. DeMille, who, impressed with Kosloff's strong presence, invited him to appear in and choreograph dances for **The Woman God Forgot**. In 1919 he opened a very successful dance school in Los Angeles and was named ballet master for the California Opera Company in 1925, opening a second school in San Francisco at the same time. He was elected ballet director of both the Los Angeles and San Francisco Opera Ballets and was the first Russian to appear at the Hollywood Bowl, later creating several ballets for the unique outdoor theater. As an actor, he appeared in many films for DeMille from 1917–1930: **Adam's Rib, The Affairs of Anatol, Feet of Clay, Fools Paradise, Forbidden Fruit, The Golden Bed, King of Kings, Madame Satan, Something to Think About, Triumph, The Volga Boatman** and **Why Change Your Wife?** Because credits during the early days of films are so illusive, it is difficult to establish all of the films he contributed to, but his contributions to American dance through his teaching are well represented by his former students — among them Agnes DeMille, Paul Godkin, Edna McRae, Serge Oukrainsky and James Starbuck.

Stage: The Passing Show of 1915 (Bdwy), *A World*

A sutdio portrait of Theodore Kosloff, circa 1930.

of Pleasure (Bdwy '15), *See America First* (Bdwy '16), *Innocent* (Bdwy '23), *A Midsummer Night's Dream* (Hollywood Bowl '34)

Ballet/Dance Pieces (Partial listing): "The Romance of the Infanta" ('25), "Memories," "Scheherazade," "Spectre de la Rose," "Shingandi"; for the Hollywood Bowl: "Chopin Memories" ('32, also danced), "Dionysia" (Dallas Symphony '33), "Carmen" and "Petrouchka" ('37)

Miscellaneous: Multiple prologues for the Carthay Circle and Grauman's Chinese Theaters in Los Angeles, *Classics on Ice* ('50s)

Film:

1917 **The Woman God Forgot**— Famous Players (also appeared)

1918 **The Squaw Man**— Famous Players

1919 **Carmen**— Famous Players

  Don't Change Your Husband— Famous Players (with Ted Shawn)

1920 **Why Change Your Wife?**— Famous Players (also appeared)

1921 **The Affairs of Anatol**— Famous Players (also appeared)

  Fool's Paradise— Famous Players (also appeared)

  Forbidden Fruit— Famous Players (also appeared)

1922 **Manslaughter**— Famous Players

1923 **The Ten Commandments**— Famous Players

1924 **Feet of Clay**— Famous Players (also appeared)

1925 **The Golden Bed** — Par (also appeared)
1926 **The Volga Boatman** — Producers Distributing Co.(also appeared)
1929 **Dynamite** — MGM
1930 **Madame Satan** — Par (with LeRoy Prinz, also appeared)
        Sunny — First Ntl
1932 **Sign of the Cross** — Par (with LeRoy Prinz)
1935 **The Raven** — Univ
1949 **Samson and Delilah** — Par

SHO KOSUGI
b. Japan
Action film star and Martial Arts choreographer.
Film (All credits are for films he also appeared in):
1983 **Revenge of the Ninja** — MGM/UA
1984 **Ninja III: The Domination** — Cannon
1985 **9 Deaths of the Ninja** — Crown Intl
        Pray for Death — Amer Dist Group
1987 **Rage of Honor** — Trans World
1988 **Aloha Summer** — Hanauma Bay/Spectrafilm
        Black Eagle — Taurus (with Jean-Claude Van Damme)

EDMOND KRESLEY
b. Allentown, Pennsylvania
Performer, dancemaker, educator and historian who was an important member of the American Dance Machine — a company which recreated, documented and performed choreographic classics from the Broadway stage. His extensive dance education from 1954 to '87 encompassed a wide variety of techniques and lists over thirty names, including ballet with Nenette Charisse, Leon Danielian, Alexandra Danilova, Lisan Kay and Florence Lessing; jazz in the Jack Cole Technique and with Peter Gennaro, Luigi and Matt Mattox; tap with Honi Coles, Danny Daniels, Henry LeTang, Johnny Mattison; Indian with La Meri and Matteo; primitive with Katherine Dunham, Sevilla Fort and Spanish with Aide Alvarez. He made his professional debut at the age of 15 in Melody Circle summer stock in Allentown, Pa., and soon went to New York. Broadway appearances include *West Side Story* ('56), *Bye Bye Birdie* ('60), *All American* ('62); TV: "The Ed Sullivan Show," "Your Hit Parade," "The Sid Caesar Show" and "Hullabaloo." He had begun his choreography career assisting Danny Daniels on *All American* and he collaborated with Gower Champion on *Hello, Dolly!* ('64). As supervising archivist and associate director to Lee Theodore of The American Dance Machine, he recreated many Broadway dance classics, also appearing with the company (1980–86). In England during the early '80s, he choreographed and appeared on "The Hot Shoe Show," the major TV dance program of the decade. His teaching credentials include jazz and ballet at the International School of Ballet at Carnegie Hall, the NY Academy of Ballet, the Bridge Festival in France, Southern Methodist University and theatre dance for the American Dance Machine at Harkness House. Moving into direction, his creative input continues for stage and other venues.

Stage: All the King's Men (OB '74), Dash (London), Hallelujah, Hollywood! (Tel Aviv), Jack (Tokyo '82, based on the life and work of Jack Cole), Not So New Faces of '84 (NY), Don't Bother Me, I Can't Cope (12 companies, also dir), Jubilee (OB), Joe's Opera (OB), Tribute to Agnes DeMille (NY), Bye Bye Birdie (Ntl tour starring Tommy Tune, '91–92)

TV: "The Hot Shoe Show" (also appeared), "Tops of the Pops," "Whistle Stop," "The Terry Wogan Show" (all England), "Pop Rock" (Munich), "One Life to Live"

Music Video: "Total Eclipse of the Heart" — Bonnie Tyler; "Bad for Good" — Jim Steinman

Ballet/Dance Pieces: "Gould Tap Concerto" (Helsinki '85)

Film:
1985 **Rappin'** — Cannon

SENANDA KUMAR
1985 **Mata Hari** — Cannon (with Lucy Igaz)

SUDARSHAN KUMAR
1969 **Kenner** — MGM

MAURICE KUSELL
b.Champaign, Illinois, 1903
d. Los Angeles, California, February 2, 1992
Actor, dancer and choreographer whose parents were vaudevillians and he travelled the country with them, finally settling in Los Angeles. He made his film acting debut in **Love Never Dies** in 1916 and danced in Los Angeles nightclubs and musical revues such as *Annette Kellerman's Smiles of 1924* and *Harry Carroll's Pickens*. He opened a well-known dance school (in which Judy Garland was a student) in Hollywood in the 1920s. He began his dance direction work in silent films and continued into the early 1930s. When he died in 1992, he was survived by his wife, Linda, and two daughters.

Stage: Sunny and A Connecticut Yankee in King Arthur's Court (West Coast, also starred), Calling All Stars (Bdwy '34), Swing Along and Going Places (London '36)

Film:

1929 **Broadway**— Univ
College Love— Univ
The Great Gabbo— James Cruze Prod
1930 **Be Yourself**— UA
Fox Movietone Follies of 1930— Fox
(with Danny Dare, Max Scheck)
Hello Sister— Sono-Art
Puttin' on the Ritz— Univ
1931 **Reaching For the Moon**— UA

JEFF KUTASH

b. Cleveland, Ohio, 1946

"As a kid I was either fighting or dancing," said this street dancer, choreographer, director and producer whose innovative contemporary dance shows found success in Las Vegas, Atlantic City and other cabaret meccas. Quoted in the April 1986 issue of *Dance Magazine*: "I never took a dance lesson... I learned how to dance from the streets, but I learned how to choreograph from watching old movies," he began his professional dance career performing and choreographing for two Cleveland-based television shows, "Big Five" and "Upbeat." His brash self-confidence got him the jobs when he complained to the producer about the inept dancing on the shows and was hired to dance and choreograph himself. Supporting himself with dance competitions while working toward a dental degree at Ohio State and a business degree at Cleveland State, he moved to the West Coast in 1969 and was hired by Dick Clark to choreograph a TV special, "The Rock 'n' Roll Years," in 1970. He began his own group (Dancin' Machine) in 1974, which eventually grew to multiple companies touring clubs throughout the world. He trained John Travolta and influenced Deney Terrio, Shabba Doo and The Lockers. Kutash claims that Michael Jackson adapted The Moonwalk from one of his steps (The Backslide) which Jackson learned on a "Midnight Special" that Kutash co-produced and starred in. After a brief participation in films, Kutash continues to create nightclub shows which combine his street dance energy and business acumen to great success. In 1994, his *Splash* at the Riviera Hotel in Las Vegas was named "Best Show of the Year" for the tenth consecutive time.

Stage: Suite America ('75, also dir)

TV: "Big Five," "Up Beat," "The Rock 'n' Roll Years" ('70), The 20th Annual Grammy Awards, "Hot City Disco" ('78, also appeared), "Kicks" ('79, also host), "Midnight Special," Danny Thomas Christmas Special

Nightclub/Concert (Partial listing): *Jeff Kutash's Dancin' Machine* (multiple venues), *Dick Clark's Good Old Rock 'n' Roll* (Hilton, LV '74, also appeared), *Midnight Special* (Thunderbird Hotel, LV '76), *Splash* (Riviera Hotel, LV '84–95) *Splash*

II (Riviera LV '95); acts for Muhammed Ali, Cher and Bette Midler

Film:

1977 **Saturday Night Fever**— Par (with Jo Jo Smith, Deney Terrio, Lester Wilson — John Travolta's dance coach)

1986 **Knights of the City**— New World (with Dallace Winkler, also appeared)

1987 **Steel Justice**— Atlantic

THORSTEN KUTH

1993 **Decadence**— Mayfair (with Rodolopho Leoni)

HIROSHI KUZE

1990 **Heaven and Earth**— Triton (with Jean-Pierre Fournier)

SUSAN LABATT

1987 **Evil Dead 2: Dead by Dawn**— Rosebud Releasing (with Andrea Brown, Tam G. Warner)

STEVE LACHANCE

Performer, dance educator and creator who began his dance studies and career at a very early age in California with his sister, Manette. He made his Broadway debut in *Dancin'* ('79) and also appeared in the '80 Broadway revival of *Can Can*. Featured in the film **Body Beat** ('91), he also co-starred in two production numbers with Jasmine Guy on the 1993 Academy Awards Show. He currently teaches and choreographs in Europe.

Film:

1985 **Girls Just Want to Have Fun**— New World (with Bill Goodson, Otis Sallid, also appeared)

DERF LA CHAPELLE

1988 **Frantic**— WB

HUGH LAMBERT

b. Metuchen, New Jersey, 1930
d. Sherman Oaks, California, August 18, 1985

Lambert attended Christopher Columbus High School in the Bronx and after serving in the Air Force, attended radio announcer's school before starting modern dance classes at the late age of 20. He studied playwriting at the American Theatre Wing while dancing in Broadway shows: *Hazel Flagg, Wonderful Town* and *Can Can* ('53), *The Vamp* ('55), *Ziegfeld Follies* (OOT '56) and *Flower Drum Song* ('58 in which he danced for Carol

Haney). He began his choreographic work assisting Haney on a 1959 *Good News* Oldsmobile industrial (also appearing) and his career continued collaborating with Bob Fosse on *How to Succeed in Business Without Really Trying* in 1961. After successful solo TV work, he received an offer to do **Finders Keepers** in 1966. At first not certain about going to England, Herbert Ross strongly suggested that he do it: "You'll learn a lot about film choreography without putting your head on the block in Hollywood. The only way to learn about motion pictures is to do them" — as Ross had learned from his early British film musicals. While in England, Lambert also did stage and television work. Returning to America in 1968, he did one more film and continued with an active career in television, eventually moving into direction. With two children from a first marriage, his second marriage to Frank Sinatra's daughter, Nancy (December 12, 1970), produced two daughters and much of his career then concentrated on Nancy and her father's stage and TV work. In 1981, he directed President Reagan's inaugural gala and died from cancer in 1985.

Stage: *How to Succeed in Business Without Really Trying* (Bdwy '61, with Bob Fosse), *Don't Shoot, We're English* (London '65), *Flower Drum Song* (Stock)

TV (Partial listing): Gene Kelly's "Dancing Is a Man's Game" ('59), "The Ed Sullivan Show," "The Perry Como Show," "The New London Palladium Show" ('65), "The Adventures of Robin Hood" ('67), "The Hollywood Palace," "Laugh-In," "Movin' with Nancy Onstage" ('71, also prod), "'Ol Blue Eyes Is Back" ('71, also dir), "Dinah and Her New Best Friends" ('76); specials for Bing Crosby, Dean Martin, Dinah Shore and Dick Van Dyke

Nightclub/Concert: Acts for Abbe Lane, Nancy Sinatra and Connie Stevens; London Palladium revues ('65)

Miscellaneous: 1960 Presidential Inaugural Ball, multiple industrials

Film:
1967 **Finders Keepers** — UA
1968 **The One and Only Original Family Band** — Disney (assisted by Jim Hutchinson and Roberta Keith)

GINO LANDI

Leading Italian dancer-choreographer who works internationally in nightclub spectaculars, as well as film. He also currently directs and choreographs Italian stage and television, as one of Europe's most in-demand dance creators.

Nightclub/Concert: *Temptations* (Casino de Paris), *La Dolce Mini-Girls* (Riviera Hotel, LV '67), *Bottom's Up '70* (LV)

Film:

1965 **The Tenth Victim** — Embassy
1968 **Anyone Can Play** — Par
     La Traviata — Royal
1970 **Waterloo** — Mosfilm/Par
1971 **The Statue** — Cinerama
1972 **Roma** (aka **Fellini's Roma**) — Ultra Films
1976 **Fellini's Casanova** — Univ
1982 **The Meadow** — New Yorker
     Tempest — Col
1987 **Good   Morning,   Babylon** — Vestron
(assisted by Mirella Aguiaro)

BILL AND JACQUI (NEÉ JAQUELINE LEVY) LANDRUM

Bill b. Bakersfield, California, January 10, 1942
Jaqui b. Los Angeles, California, December 10, 1943

Successful husband-and-wife team of dancers, teachers and choreographers. Bill received extensive and varied dance training from Rosella Hightower, Gene Marinaccio, Paule Maure, Donald McKayle, Michel Panaieff, Jaime Rogers, Claude Thompson and Glen White and made his professional debut at Bimbo's nightclub in San Francisco in 1960. He appeared on Broadway in *All American* in 1962, danced in the films **Bedknobs and Broomsticks** and **The Unexpected Mrs. Polifax** and did international nightclub work at the Casino du Liban in Beirut ('63–64) and Mouche in Paris ('65). He appeared in the Las Vegas revues *Today USA* ('68) and *Let's Make Love* ('69) and became a member of the Donald McKayle Inner City Dance Company ('69–71), where he met future wife, Jacqui Levy. They both appeared in the 1972 Los Angeles production of *Tommy*. Jacqui had been introduced to Afro-jazz dance by Elle Johnson at the age of 12 while she was training to be a competitive ice skater. She became a member of the Jeni LeGon Afro-Dance company at 13 and received her varied dance background from the Lester Horton and Martha Graham Schools, Roland Dupree, Janet Eilber, Stanley Holden, Gene Marinaccio, Jaime Rogers and Claude Thompson. Choreographing since her grammar school show days, she made her professional debut with the Larry Maldonado Dancers ('64–68) and then joined McKayle's Inner City Dance company with Bill. Together, they began experimenting with dance and choreography and, after opening their own studio in 1976, the Landrum Dance Theatre debuted in 1977. Their creativity in dance experimentation eventually extended into films, television and music video.

Stage: (Bill): *West Side Story* (Cal '61, also appeared); (as a team): *Waves* (Cannes '72), *Christopher*

(OOT '76), *The Orestia* (OOT '77), *A Doll's House* (LA '83), *A Chorus Line* (USC, also dir)

TV: "Moonlighting" ('87, Emmy nom), "China Beach," The Wonder Years," "The Dolly Parton Show," "Fantasy Island," "Wally and the Beaver," Ed McMahon special, "The Making of Me" (Disney Special), "In Rap with Dance" (Cable, Emmy winner), Englebert Humperdinck special; commercials for Discover Card ('95 *LA Dance* Award), Pepsi Light, Sanyo

Music Video: "Rise"— Herb Alpert; "Voodoo Child"— Jimi Hendrix; "Work It"— Tina Marie; "Eternal Child"— Chick Corea; "I Know You by Heart"— Smokey Robinson

Ballet/Dance Pieces (For the Landrum Dance Theater — 1977–81): "All Is One But Not All Is Well," "Coming Out," "Inflatable Tear," "Suite Riviera," "When the Spirits Take You," "Where the Birds Go"

Film:

1986 **Blood Ties**— ABC (TV)
1987 **Clean and Sober**— WB
1989 **Great Balls of Fire**— Orion
1991 **Barton Fink**— Fox
    The Doors— Col (with Paula Abdul, also appeared, "dance coordinators" credit)
1992 **Basic Instinct**— TriStar
    Wrong Man— Viacom
1994 **Love Affair**— WB
    Empire— WB

MARCEA D. LANE

Performer-choreographer who danced in Michael Jackson's "Thriller" video and is on the faculty of the Joe Tremaine Dance Convention.

Film:

1987 **Crystal Heart**— NW (also appeared)

CHARLES LANG

1932 **A Bedtime Story**— Par

JACKY LANSLEY

1992 **Orlando**— Electric Pictures

DIANE LANTHROP

1990 **Metropolitan**— New Line Cinema

ALBERT LANTIERI

1975 **At Long Last Love**— Fox (with Rita Abrams, also appeared)

EDDIE LARKIN

1940 **Blondie Meets the Boss**— Col
    Little Nelly Kelly— MGM (with George Murphy)
    Two Girls on Broadway— MGM (with Bobby Connolly, George Murphy)

BARRY LATHER

b. Albany, New York, August 16, 1966

Commenting on his music video work, this dancer-teacher-choreographer-director recently said, "If its on video, everybody gets to see it and if its hip, everybody starts doing it. I try to get what's happening right on the street level or clubs … if you can give them to an artist, everybody gets to see them." Growing up in Atlanta in a family of dancers, Lather's exposure to and love of dance was enhanced through participating in dance conventions and watching "Soul Train." He moved to California as a young man and studied with Doug Caldwell and Joe Tremaine, soon joining Tremaine's Dance Conventions as their youngest instructor. In 1985, he began his professional performance career in the Disney 3-D film **Captain E-O** and was featured on TV in "Fame" and "Dancin' to the Hits." He also danced in Janet Jackson's music videos ("Nasty") and her TV appearances on the 1987 Grammy and American Music Awards shows (which he also choreographed). Jackson first hired him to choreograph her appearance on the 1986 Fuji TV Year End special in Japan and continued to encourage his transition from performer to choreographer. The recipient of MTV and two *Billboard* Awards for his music video creations, he married Cari French in 1993 and continues to create contemporary danceworks for stage, theme parks, TV, film, music video and on ice. Lather credits Bob Fosse, Janet and Michael Jackson, Michael Peters, Joe Tremaine, breakdancing and poppin' as major influences in his life and career. His students and dancers find his infectious energy and obvious love of dance hard to resist.

Stage: Stars on Ice (Tour '93–95)

TV: The Smothers Brothers Comedy Special, The American Music and Grammy Awards Shows ('87), "Top of the Pops" ('87), "The Arsenio Hall Show" ('91), MTV Music Video Awards ('91), "Roundhouse" (Nickelodeon '92–94), "Nancy Kerrigan's Disney Dreams on Ice" ('95); commercials for Carefree Bubble Gum, Dr. Pepper (starring Michael Jackson), Nike, Teddy Grahams, Pepsi, McDonalds, etc.

Music Video (Partial listing): "The Pleasure Principle"— Janet Jackson (MTV and *Billboard* awards); "We'll Be Together"— Sting (*Billboard* award); "Batdance"— Prince; "Electric Youth"— Debbie Gibson; "Kiss"— Tom Jones; "That Girl Wants to

Dance with Me"— Gregory Hines; "Jam"— Michael Jackson (MTV Award nom)

Nightclub/Concert: George Michael "Faith" tour ('88), Jodey Watley USA tour ('88), Debbie Gibson "Electric Youth" tour ('89), Paula Abdul "Spellbound" Tour ('91), "Le Ice Show" (Luxor Hotel, LV '95)

Miscellaneous: Euro Disneyland ('92), *Paramount on Ice: Legends* and *House of Groove* (Paramount Parks '95–96), competition routines for Brian Boitano, Katarina Witt and Kristi Yamaguchi

Film:
1993 **Super Mario Brothers**— WB

ANDREA LAWENT
1996 **Misery Bros.**—?
    Mrs. Winterbourne— TriStar

CHRISTINE LAWSON
1965 **She**— MGM

JOE LAYTON (JOSEPH LICHTMAN)
b. Brooklyn, New York, May 31, 1931
d. Key West, Florida, May 5, 1994
Preferring to be called a "stager," this dancer, choreographer, producer and director achieved great success with his innovative work on the Broadway stage and television. A graduate of the New York High School of Music and Art in 1948, he studied dance with Nenette Charisse and Joseph Levinoff. He started dancing on Broadway at the age of 16 in *Oklahoma!* and continued in *Miss Liberty, High Button Shoes, Gentlemen Prefer Blondes* and *Wonderful Town* and was a member of Ballet Ho! De George Reich in Paris ('45–46). He had begun his choreographic career staging shows at Fort Carson, Colorado ('53–55) while serving in the Army in Special Services and while in Europe, he choreographed pieces for a ballet troupe that played nightclubs. Returning to the U.S., he was hired to choreograph the 1958 season of shows at Camp Tamiment. There, he met Mary Rodgers (composer-daughter of Richard Rodgers) and one of the shows he collaborated on was her *The Princess and the Pea*— which would become *Once Upon a Mattress*. After assisting Dania Krupska on Broadway, his first New York solo choreographic assignment was a 1958 Off-Broadway revival of *On the Town*. The success of that show — and his important show business connections — led to prestigious Broadway and television assignments. In a 1959 *Dance Magazine* article focusing on his new success, he expressed his thoughts about dance and choreography, "I like dancers who are also good actors. Dancers have to be terribly human to put across a point of view. An audience isn't usually interested in dance steps. You can't give them sheer movement. If I were a great movement genius, it might be different. I work by telling a story. With me, the source of all choreography is mime. Maybe it's a result of my all-around theatrical background." After choreographing several shows, he joined the ranks of important director-choreographers with *No Strings* in 1962. While in London in 1963, Judy Garland asked him to choreograph musical sequences for her in **I Could Go On Singing**, but during filming, she forgot everything he created and improvised. His work on stage and television earned him many awards and acclaim. He directed the film **Richard Pryor Live on the Sunset Strip** and served as executive producer on the film **Annie**. Before his death, he was creative director of the entertainment division for Radio City Music Hall Productions. On April 6, 1995, his memory was honored in a spectacular tribute at the Wiltern Theatre in Los Angeles by leaders of the entertainment community.

Stage: *On the Town* (OB rev '58), *Once Upon a Mattress* (Bdwy '59), *The Sound of Music* (Bdwy & London '59), *Greenwillow* (Bdwy '60, Tony nom), *Tenderloin* (Bdwy '60), *Sail Away* (Bdwy & London '61), *Cock of the Walk* (OOT 62), *No Strings* (Bdwy '62, also dir, Tony award for choreo), *The Girl Who Came to Supper* (Bdwy '63, also dir), *On the Town* (London '63 rev), *Drat the Cat!* (Bdwy '65, also dir), *Sherry* (Bdwy '67, also dir), *George M!* (Bdwy '68, also dir, Tony Award for choreo), *Dear World* (Bdwy '69, also dir), *Carol Channing with 10 Stouthearted Men* (Bdwy '70, also dir, prod), *Two by Two* (Bdwy '70, also dir), *Gone with the Wind* (Tokyo, London, West Coast '72, also dir), *Lorelei* (Bdwy '73, also dir), *Bette Midler—Clams on the Half Shell* (Bdwy '75, also dir), *Platinum* (Bdwy '78, also dir), *Barnum* (Bdwy '80, also dir, Tony nom), *Bring Back Birdie* (Bdwy '81, also dir), *Rock and Roll—The First 5,000 Years!* (Bdwy '82, also dir), *Siegfried and Roy Illusions* (Japan '89, with Damita Jo Freeman), *The Life* (OB '90), *Ziegfeld* (London), *That's Life* (OOT '93), *The Lost Colony* (Manteo, N.C., wrote and dir, '73–93), *The Great Radio City Music Hall Spectacular starring the Rockettes* (Ntl tour '94, also dir)

TV (Partial listing): Mary Martin Easter Sunday Spectacular ('59), "The Gershwin Years" ('61); staged & directed four Barbra Streisand Specials — nominated for three Emmys, winning one for "My Name Is Barbra" ('65); "Androcles and the Lion" ('67, also dir), "And Debbie Makes Six" ('68), "The Hanna-Barbera Happy Hour" ('78, also dir); specials for Carol Burnett, the Carpenters, Cher, Willie Nelson, Olivia Newton-John, Dolly Parton and Diana Ross

Nightclub/Concert: *Carol Channing and Her Men* ('70), *Beyond Belief* starring Siegfried and Roy (Mirage Hotel, LV '90), Ann-Margret's Show at

Radio City Music Hall ('91); acts and shows for Carol Burnett, the Carpenters, Diahann Carroll, Cher, Harry Connick, Jr., Mac Davis, Joel Grey, Julio Iglesias, Jack Jones, Melissa Manchester, Bette Midler, Olivia Newton-John, Jeffrey Osborne, Dolly Parton, Lionel Richie, Kenny Rogers, Diana Ross, Connie Stevens, Travis Tritt, Raquel Welch and Trisha Yearwood

Ballet/Dance Pieces: Created four ballets for the Royal Ballet (incl. "Overture," "De Profundis" and "The Grand Tour") and one for the Joffrey ("Double Exposure")

Miscellaneous: Fashion Industry Show (Moscow, '59), 1984 Olympics Closing ceremonies, President Clinton's inaugural concert at Lincoln Memorial ('93), *Commitment to Life* benefit (AIDS Project LA, also dir)

Film:
1963 **I Could Go on Singing** — UA (work not performed)
1967 **Thoroughly Modern Millie** — Univ
1982 **Annie** — Col (with Russell Clark, Arlene Phillips, "Executive Producer and Musical Sequences Created By" credit)
1991 **For the Boys** — Fox ("Musical numbers devised by" credit)

HELEN LE COUNTE
1984 **Big Meat Eater** — New Line

SAMMY LEE (SAMUEL LEVY)
b. New York, May 26, 1890
d. Woodland Hills, California, March 30, 1968
Academy Award-nominated dance director whose Broadway shows and films were among the most popular and influential during the 1920s, '30s and '40s. A self-taught dancer ("At the age of four, he first discovered how interesting moving feet could be") Sammy danced for money on street corners. He began his professional career as a member of Gus Edwards Children's Revues and then teamed with Ruby Norton as Norton and Lee for six years on the vaudeville circuit and on Broadway in *The Firefly* ('12). After playing London in *The Belle of Bond Street*, in vaudeville with a new act (Sammy Lee and His Lady Friends) and back on Broadway in *Yip, Yip Yahank* ('18), he helped develop *The Gingham Girl* into a full-blown musical and began his dance direction career ("This was the turning point in my life. I had the chance to show what I could do... Numbers and changes of costumes had supplanted imagination and personalities; twenty, thirty of forty girls ... lost in mass formations... But I wanted something very different from this; girls with distinct personalities who did things that could really interest an audience ... every conceivable kind of dance step, and then such acrobatic stunts as only

a circus athlete could do — splits, cartwheels, flip-flops... They were hits, and their hit was my hit... I was no longer a hoofer." *The Dance*, January, 1929). Involved in the creation of many legendary stage musicals (*Lady, Be Good, Tip-Toes, Oh, Kay!, Show Boat*) in collaboration with George Gershwin, Jerome Kern and Fred and Adele Astaire, he also directed *Sweet Little Devil* ('24) and *Tell Me More* ('25) and produced *Cross My Heart* ('28) on the New York stage, before his success took him to Hollywood. He was signed by MGM and named head of their dance department and school in January, 1936, eventually also being contracted by Fox and Paramount. After nearly two decades of creating for films, he retired and was a patient for several years at the Motion Picture County Hospital before his death in 1968.

Stage: *Little Miss Charity* (Bdwy '20), *The Gingham Girl* (Bdwy '22), *Earl Carroll Vanities of 1923,* '24 (Bdwy), *Mary Jane Mc Kane* and *The Music Box Revue* (Bdwy '23), *Sweet Little Devil, Be Yourself* and *Lady Be Good* (Bdwy '24), *Big Boy* (with Larry Ceballos), *The Cocoanuts, Tell Me More* (also co-dir), *Tip Toes* and *No, No Nanette!* (Bdwy '25), *Betsy, Oh, Kay!, Queen High!* and *The Ramblers* (Bdwy '26), *Rio Rita, Show Boat, Talk About Girls, Yes, Yes Yvette* and *The Ziegfeld Follies of 1927* (Bdwy '27), *Cross My Heart* (also prod) and *Here's Howe!* (Bdwy '28), *Lady Fingers* and *Ziegfeld Midnight Frolics* (Bdwy '29), *Singin' the Blues* and *Billy Rose's Crazy Quilt* (Bdwy '31),

Miscellaneous: multiple prologues for Fanchon and Marco and others

Film:
1929 **Colortone Revue Series** — MGM (S)
    Cotton and Silk — MGM (S)
    The Doll Shop — MGM (S) (also dir)
    The Hollywood Revue of 1929 — MGM (with Ernest Belcher, Natacha Natova, Albertina Rasch, assisted by George Cunningham)
    It's a Great Life — MGM
    Lord Bryon of Broadway — MGM (with Albertina Rasch)
    The Road Show — MGM (S)
1930 **Chasing Rainbows** — MGM
    Children of Pleasure — MGM
    Doughboys — MGM
    Free and Easy — MGM
    Good News — MGM
    A Lady of Scandal — MGM
    A Lady's Morals — MGM
    Love in the Rough — MGM
    Manhattan Serenade — MGM (S) (also dir)
    March of Time — MGM (unreleased, with Albertina Rasch)
    Men of the North — MGM
    Montana Moon — MGM

They Learned About Women— MGM
Those Three French Girls— MGM
The Woman Racket— MGM
1933 Adorable— Fox
Arizona to Broadway— Fox
Broadway to Hollywood— MGM (with
Albertina Rasch)
Cavalcade— Fox
Dancing Lady— MGM (with Eddie
Prinz, assisted by Slavko Vorkapich)
I Loved You Wednesday— Fox
It's Great to Be Alive— Fox
Jimmy and Sally— Fox
Life in the Raw— Fox
Meet the Baron— MGM
My Lips Betray— Fox
Nertsery Rhymes— MGM (S) (number
from March of Time)
1934 Baby, Take a Bow— Fox
The Big Idea— MGM (S)
Bright Eyes— Fox
Caravan— Fox
Handy Andy— Fox
I Am Suzanne— Fox
Jailbirds of Paradise— MGM (S) (num-
ber from March of Time)
Some Call It Luck— Fox
Stand Up and Cheer— Fox
365 Nights in Hollywood —Fox (Acad-
emy Award nom:"Lovely Lady" and "Too Good to
be True" numbers)
Transatlantic Merry-Go-Round— UA
(with Larry Ceballos)
1935 Dante's Inferno— Fox (with Eduardo
Cansino)
Hooray for Love— RKO (with Maria
Gambarelli, Bill Robinson)
To Beat the Band— RKO
1936 Can This Be Dixie?— Fox
King of Burlesque— Fox
Star for a Night— Fox
Under Your Spell— Fox
1937 Ali Baba Goes to Town— Fox (Academy
Award nom: "Swing is Here to Stay" number)
The Goldwyn Follies— Goldwyn (with
George Balanchine)
Heidi— Fox
The Life of the Party— RKO
New Faces of 1937— RKO
1939 The Gracie Allen Murder Case— Par
Honolulu— MGM (with Bobby Con-
nolly, Eleanor Powell)
Rhumba Rhythm— MGM (S) (also dir)
1940 The House Across the Bay— UA
Hullabaloo— MGM
1941 Washington Melodrama— MGM
1942 Born to Sing— MGM
Cairo— MGM

Jackass Mail— MGM
Panama Hattie— MGM (with the Berry
Bros, Danny Dare)
1943 Hit the Ice— Univ (with Harry Losee)
Something to Shout About— Col (with
David Lichine)
1944 Carolina Blues— Col (with The Four
Step Brothers, Ann Miller)
Maisie Goes to Reno— MGM
Meet the People— MGM (with Jack
Donohue, Charles Walters)
Sensations of 1945— UA (with David
Lichine, Charles O'Curran, Eleanor Powell)
Two Girls and a Sailor— MGM
1945 Earl Carroll Vanities— Rep
Out of This World— Par
1946 Abilene Town— UA
1947 The Unfinished Dance— MGM (with
David Lichine)
1994 That's Entertainment! III— MGM (with
others)

SUE LEFTON
1980 Tess— Col

DIANA LEHAN
1991 Book of Love— New Line Cinema

RUFUS LEMAIRE
1929 Broadway Scandals— Col

TUTTE LEMKOW
b. Oslo, Norway, August 28, 1918
d. London, England, November 10, 1991
Born of Russian parents in Norway, this versatile
dance and mime creator began his entertainment
career with his brother in a dance act (The Lemkow
Brothers). He trained with the Bolshoi Theater,
studied dance in Oslo and became a member of the
National Theater of Oslo. Because of his Jewish
faith, he fled to Sweden in 1941 and continued dancing there, beginning his choreographic career as ballet master for Birgit Cullberg and her dance group.
He worked with director Ingmar Bergman and
actress Mai Zetterling (eventually marrying her) and
formed the new Norwegian Ballet Company after
World War II. In 1950 he moved to London, joining Ballet Rambert and remained in the United
Kingdom for over forty years working as an actor,
dancer and choreographer. He danced in the 1952
British/Canadian short Between Two Worlds and
appeared in over sixty films, among them Ben Hur,
The Pink Panther, Lawrence of Arabia, The Guns
of Navarone, Moulin Rouge, Woody Allen's Love
and Death, Raiders of the Lost Ark and Fiddler
on the Roof (portraying the "Fiddler"). He was

featured in the TV series "Red Sonja" and performed Franz Kafka's monologue *Report to an Academy* all over the world, receiving glowing reviews for his talent. His writing credits include the screenplay for **The Wild Duck** and "Thor the Viking" (with Anthony Shaffer) for British TV. He also managed to find the time and energy to own a successful pub in Chelsea.

Autobiography: *On Your Toes* ('89)
Stage: *Ernest* (Eng '59), *Who's Pinkus? Where's Chelm?* (London '67)
Ballet/Dance Pieces: "Spanish Suite" ('51)
Film:
1953 **The Captain's Paradise** — London/British Lion (also appeared)
1955 **Quentin Durward** — MGM
1957 **Fire Down Below** — Col (also appeared)
1958 **Bonjour Tristesse** — Col
1966 **Stop the World, I Want to Get Off** — WB ("Mime Director" credit)
1967 **Casino Royale** — Col
1973 **Theatre of Blood** — UA (also appeared)

MARIA LEONE
1993 **Mi Vida Loca** (aka **My Crazy Life**) — HBO

RODOLOPHO LEONI
1993 **Decadence** — Mayfair (with Thorsten Kuth)

LEON LEONIDOFF
b. Bendery, Romania, January 2, 1895
d. Palm Beach, Florida, July 29, 1989
Flamboyant personality whose career spanned five decades. As a child, he produced backyard shows in his small Romanian hometown. Following his father's wishes he studied medicine at the University of Geneva, but continued to explore his love for theater in the school's drama club. George Piteoff, a renowned Russian director, discovered Leonidoff's talent and invited him to join his performing troupe as assistant producer and lead dancer. As one of the founding members of Isba Russe, a group of young Russian performers, he travelled to the U.S. and the group made their American debut in 1920. Named ballet director at the Capitol Theatre on Broadway, he toured Canada, briefly opened a dancing school in Toronto but returned to New York in 1927 as director of production at the Roxy Theatre. In 1932 he was asked to produce the shows at the newly constructed Radio City Music Hall, where he remained senior producer until 1974, helping to create the Music Hall's voluminous library of musical spectaculars. He directed five Broadway shows and *Arabian Nights* (Jones Beach '54) and *Wonderworld* (NY World's Fair '64), but is best remembered by his Music Hall credit "Produced by Leonidoff," where his imagination dazzled millions of theatregoers during his forty-two year reign.

Stage: *The Nine-Fifteen Revue* and *The Well of Romance* (Bdwy '30)
Film:
1929 **The Talk of Hollywood** — Sono Art-World Wide
1931 **Pagliaci** — ?
1937 **When You're in Love** — Col
1941 **Sunny** — RKO (with Ray Bolger)

HAL LEROY (JOHN LEROY SCHOTTE)
b. Cheviot, Ohio, December 10, 1913
d. Hackensack, New Jersey, May 2, 1985
Gangly, eccentric tap dancing star who studied with Ned Wayburn and began dancing as a child, making his Broadway debut at 16 in *The Ziegfeld Follies of 1931*. He was featured on Broadway in *The Gang's All Here* ('31), *Strike Me Pink* ('33), *Thumbs Up* ('34), *Too Many Girls* ('39) and *Count Me In* ('42). Because of his stage success, he was brought to Hollywood to star as the title character in the **Harold Teen** film series and also appeared in **Wonder Bar**, **Start Cheering** and the film version of his Broadway success **Too Many Girls**, along with several musical shorts. His expertise allowed him to be one of the few Caucasian dancers allowed into the legendary Hoofer's Club and he continued performing in supper clubs, television and summer stock until 1984. LeRoy is credited with creating a style of rhythm with a Charleston foot known as the Tanglefoot Tap.

Film (Credits are for his own routines):
1931 **The High School Hoofer** — Vitaphone (S)
1932 **Tip, Tap, Toe** — Vitaphone (S)
1933 **Mr. Broadway** — Bdwy-Hollywood Prod
      Use Your Imagination — Vitaphone (S)
      The Way of All Freshmen — Vitaphone (S)
1934 **Harold Teen** — WB
      Picture Palace — Vitaphone (S)
      Private Lessons — Vitaphone (S)
      Syncopated City — Vitaphone (S)
      Wonder Bar — WB (with Busby Berkeley)
1935 **Main Street Follies** — Vitaphone (S)
      Musical Memories — Par (S) (with Ruby Keeler)
      Oh, Evaline — Vitaphone (S)
1936 **Rhythmitis** — Vitaphone (S)
      Wash Your Step — Vitaphone (S)
1937 **Swing for Sale** — Vitaphone (S)
      Ups and Downs — Vitaphone (S)
1938 **The Knight Is Young** — Vitaphone (S)
      Prisoner of Swing — Vitaphone (S)
      Start Cheering — Col (with Danny Dare)
1939 **Public Jitterbug #1** — Vitaphone (S)

1940 **Too Many Girls**— RKO (with Ann Miller, LeRoy Prinz)

FRED LESLIE

Stage: *The Beauty Prize* (London '32)
Film:
1935 **So, You Won't Talk?**— WB/First Ntl

KEITH LESTER

b. Guildford, England, April 9, 1904
British dancer-choreographer whose career moved gracefully from fouettés to fan dances. After studying with Anton Dolin, Michel Fokine, Nicholas Legat and other masters, he made his stage debut in London in 1923. He danced with the Markova-Dolin Ballet company in 1935 and began choreographing. In 1940 he formed the Art Theatre Ballet with Harold Turner but moved into commercial dance in 1945 and choreographed for the famed Windmill Theatre in London (immortalized in **Tonight and Every Night**) where he staged more than 150 shows. Returning to classical dance in 1965, he was named principal teacher at the London Royal Academy of Dancing.
Ballet/Dance Pieces (Partial listing): "David" ('35), "Pas de Quartre," "Pas de Déeses," etc.
Film:
1937 **Glamorous Night**— BIP-ABPC

HENRY LETANG

b. New York, 1915
LeTang's unique talents have kept him high in the ranks of America's greatest tap creators and dance educators. He started dancing at the age of 7 and received formal tap training from neighborhood schools and Buddy Bradley (as opposed to the mostly self-taught tap dancers of the 1920s and 30s), eventually opening his own school at 17. After his first onstage dancing job with the Claude Hopkins Orchestra at the Alhambra Theater and Harlem Opera House in New York, he appeared in nightclubs and theaters continuously during the 1930s and '40s, always creating his own show-stopping dance routines. After collaborating with other choreographers and creating tap sequences for several Broadway shows — without credit — he finally received well-deserved acclaim in 1988 with a Tony Award for *Black and Blue*, which premiered in Paris. He has had successful dance schools on the East and West Coasts since 1937 and among his students are Debbie Allen, Hinton Battle, Savion Glover, Gregory and Maurice Hines and Chita Rivera. While choreographing the film **Tap**, Maurice Hines commented on his legacy: "I think maybe Henry is the only tap choreographer who could have worked on

this movie. It's his image with the hoofers that lent this project credibility for them. They respect him and his ability to spot a person's strengths and choreograph for those strengths." LeTang described getting his choreography "off the top of my head. I never have a master plan, you have to be free to express yourself creatively." He currently teaches in Las Vegas.
Stage: *Crazy with the Heat* (Bdwy '41, with Catherine Littlefield, Carl Randall, uncredited), *My Dear Public* (Bdwy '43, uncredited, also appeared), *Dream with Music* (Bdwy '44, assisted George Balanchine, uncredited), *Shuffle Along* (Bdwy '52), *Broadway Dandies* (OB '74), *Eubie!* (Bdwy '78, with Billy Wilson, Tony nom), *Suddenly the Music Starts* (OB '79, also dir), *Sophisticated Ladies* (Bdwy '81, with Donald McKayle, Michael Smuin, Tony nom), *Stardust* (Bdwy '87 and '91 rev); *Black and Blue* (Paris and Bdwy '88, with Cholly Atkins, Frankie Manning and Fayard Nicholas, Tony award)
TV: "The Garry Moore Show" (7 seasons)
Nightclub/Concert: Acts for Jack Albertson, Debbie Allen, Hinton Battle, Lola Falana, Joe Frazier, Peter Gennaro, Joey Heatherton, Gregory & Maurice Hines, Lena Horne, Bette Midler, Sugar Ray Robinson, Leslie Uggams, Ben Vereen and Flip Wilson
Film:
1984 **Cotton Club**— Orion (with Claudia Asbury, George Faison, Gregory Hines, Michael Meacham, Arthur Mitchell, Michael Smuin)
1989 **Tap**— TriStar (with Gregory Hines)

CAREY LEVERETTE

b. 1925
d. North Hollywood, California, April 6, 1988
Dancer and assistant choreographer at MGM who appeared in the LACLO production of *Jollyanna* ('52), in Debra Paget's nightclub act and in films: **The Opposite Sex** ('56), **The Gazebo** ('59) and as a "Dance-in" for Pat Boone in **All Hands on Deck** ('61). Owning and operating Dance Arts Studio in Granada Hills, California, with his wife, Sally Sorvo, he changed careers in 1966 when he opened Donte's — a jazz club in North Hollywood. When the club began experiencing financial troubles more than twenty years later, Leverette was found mysteriously dead in the club's office the day *after* Escrow was to close on the sale to a new owner.
TV: "Designs for '60" (LA), "The Girl from UNCLE" ('66)
Nightclub/Concert: Desert Spa Hotel (LV '58)
Film:
1957 **The Oklahoman**— AA
1966 **What Did You Do in the War, Daddy?**— UA

RUSSELL LEWIS

b. 1908

d. Malibu, California, December 9, 1992

Dance director who eventually produced plays and musicals with partner Howard Young for over fifty years. After an early theatrical apprenticeship in Europe, Lewis arrived in Hollywood in the early '30s, where he served as dance director at RKO. In 1940, he and Young formed their partnership, producing stage productions for Broadway and touring units. In 1951 they established the Sacramento Music Circus, a tent theater which continues to be one of the most successful summer stock venues in the country. Despite few film choreography credits, he has the distinction of being one of the few dance directors to be nominated for an Academy Award in 1936 for **Dancing Pirate** (often erroneously reported as **Becky Sharp**, his other feature film credit.)

Film:

1934 **La Cucaracha** — RKO (S)

1935 **Becky Sharp** — RKO

1936 **Dancing Pirate** — RKO (with Eduardo Cansino, Academy Award nom: "The Finale" number)

SYLVIA LEWIS

b. York, Pennsylvania, April 22, 1931

Multi-faceted artist whose beauty and talents kept her in demand onscreen as a performer as well as offscreen as a choreographer. Classically trained at the Peabody Conservatory of Music, she moved to California as a child and studied with Louis DaPron, Edith Jane Falconer, Luigi, Madame Nijinska and Michel Panaieff in Hollywood. She began her career appearing in nightclubs and on stage and started in films as a dancer: **Living in a Big Way** ('47), **Hans Christian Andersen** and **Just for You** ('52) and **Red Garters** ('54). Cast as a featured soloist in 1953 low budget Sam Katzman epics for Columbia, she began choreographing her own numbers and progressed to featured roles in **Cha-Cha-Cha Boom** ('55), **The Conqueror** and **The Lieutenant Wore Skirts** ('56) and **The Ladies Man** ('57). Contracted by Universal as assistant dance director to Hal Belfer and Kenny Williams, she co-starred in Los Angeles and on Broadway in *Vintage '60* and *Billy Barnes L.A.* ('62) and was featured prominently on television on "Where's Raymond?" — The Ray Bolger Show (as Bolger's partner and co-choreographer), "The Bob Cummings Show" and multiple "Max Liebman Spectaculars." One of the founders of the Professional Dancers Society (PDS) in 1978, she continues to choreograph and in 1995, returned to performing in *Palm Springs Follies*.

Stage: *A Part of the Blues* (LA '57), *Little Mary Sunshine* (Hollywood '61, also appeared), *Billy Barnes L.A* (Bdwy and Hollywood '62, also

appeared), *Hollywood — Inside-Out* (Oregon), *Ain't Misbehavin'* (San Diego), *La Vie Parisienne* (West Coast), *South Pacific* (West Coast '93), *Palm Springs Follies* ('94–95, with Carl Jablonski, also appeared)

TV: "Where's Raymond" ('53, with Ray Bolger),"The Bob Cummings Show" ('61), "The Dick Van Dyke Show," "The Joey Bishop Show" ('62), "Peter Gunn," "Who's the Boss?"

Miscellaneous: Huis Ten Bosch Theme Park (Nagasaki, Japan '92)

Film:

1953 **The Siren of Bagdad** — Col (also appeared)

1954 **Destry** — Univ (assistant to Kenny Williams)

 Drums of Tahiti — Col (also appeared)

1955 **The Lieutenant Wore Skirts** — Fox (also appeared)

1956 **Hot Blood** — Col (with Matt Mattox, also appeared as "Dance In" for Jane Russell)

1957 **Spring Reunion** — Par

1961 **The Ladies Man** — Par (with Bobby Van, uncredited, also appeared)

1963 **For Love or Money** — Univ (also appeared)

1975 **Hearts of the West** — MGM

BELLA LEWITZKY

(sometimes spelled: "Lewitsky")

b. Llano del Rio, California, January 13, 1916

"I invented a kind of dance of my own when I was very young. I practiced it on our lawn at home in San Bernardino. I drew into it anyone who would be a willing member of my dance world," said this Southern California modern dance pioneer in an April 1967 *Dance Magazine* interview. She continued with, "I never danced to music, but to tendrils of thought or emotion which were more meaningful to me at the time. I played no phonograph records to 'inspire' me. I danced and made dance dramas to inside sounds. The qualities of movement I discovered probably weren't recognizable to anyone but me." The daughter of a Ukrainian emmigrant father, she saw her first modern dance at a Lester Horton class while in high school. At 19, she danced in Agnes DeMille's "Harvest Reel" at the Hollywood Bowl and then joined Horton's Dance group and Dance Theatre, becoming his leading female soloist (and often, inspiration) appearing as a speciality dancer with the troupe in *White Savage* ('43) and assisting him on his film work until 1950. Marrying fellow-dancer Newell Reynolds and relocating to Chicago, she formed her first company, Dance Associates, in 1951. She began raising a daughter, Nora, did periodic film work, taught at multiple schools and universities and finally formed her groundbreaking concert group, Lewitzky Dance Company, in 1965. In 1995, she announced that she would disband her company and concentrate on dance education. With the death of James Truitte,

Sylvia Lewis (far left), Luigi and the Gene Louis Dancers go "Latin" in a 1952 Nat "King" Cole short for Universal (photo courtesy of Sylvia Lewis).

Lewitzky is the surviving exponent of the Horton technique.

Film:

1948 **Siren of Atlantis**— UA (assistant to Lester Horton)

1950 **Tripoli**— Par

1951 **Prehistoric Women**— Eagle Lion

1956 **The Vagabond King**— Par (assistant to Hanya Holm)

DAVID LICHINE (LIECHTENSTEIN)

b. Rostov-on-the-Don, Russia, December 25, 1910
d. Los Angeles, California, June 26, 1972

As a child, Lichine fled with his family to Istanbul during the Russian revolution, eventually settling in Paris. There, he began to study dance at the age of 16 with Lubov Egorova and Bronislava Nijinska. He debuted with Ida Rubinstein's company in Paris in 1928, toured briefly in Pavlova's company and then danced with de Basil's Ballets Russes De Monte Carlo from 1932–41. He began creating dances for Ballets Russes and his repertoire of ballet choreography would eventually enrich

American Ballet Theatre, Borovansky Ballet, the Marquis de Cuevas' Grand Ballet de Monte Carlo, Les Ballets Des Champs Elysee (where he took Leslie Caron from the chorus for his ballet *La Rencontre* to make her an overnight star), the Royal Danish Ballet, La Scala, Teatro Colon and his own groups: London Festival Ballet, Ballet de la Ville des Anges (Ballet of the City of Los Angeles —'53) and Los Angeles Ballet Theatre. Arriving in America in 1942, after one Broadway show he began his film work. Lichine was usually responsible for the classic ballet sequences in his film credits — yet he also created such diverse works as the musical numbers for Mae West's **The Heat's On** and even appeared as Eleanor Powell's partner in a jitterbug number in **Sensations of 1945.** When choreographing an adagio in **Something to Shout About** ('43) he selected a young student, "Lily Norwood," to make her film debut as his partner — she would eventually become "Cyd Charisse." He directed a very successful school in Los Angeles from 1952 with his wife, Tatiana Riabouchinska, and they co-founded Ballet Society of Los Angeles in 1968.

Stage: *Beat the Band* (Bdwy '42), *The Waltz King* (OOT '43), *Rhapsody* (Bdwy '44, also dir), *Polonaise* (Bdwy '45)

David Lichine rests on the set of **The Heat's On** (Columbia, 1943).

TV: "This Is Your Music" Series ('55, also appeared), "Ozzie and Harriet" ('64, also appeared)

Ballet/Dance Pieces (31 works — Partial listing): "Nocturne" ('33), "The First Balloon," "La Creation," "Graduation Ball," "Les Imaginaires," "Le Pavillon," "Francesca Da Rimini," "The Gods Go A'Begging," "Prodigal Son," "Graduation Ball," "La Recontre," "The Nutcracker," "Runaway Mop" ('65)

Film:

1935 **Spring Night**— Par (S) (also appeared)

1943 **The Heat's On**— Col (also appeared)
The North Star— RKO
Something to Shout About— Col (with Sammy Lee, also appeared)
Song of Russia— MGM

1944 **Sensations of 1945**— UA (with Charles O'Curran, Eleanor Powell, also appeared)

1946 **Make Mine Music**— Disney ("Two Silhouettes" sequence, also appeared with Tatiana Riabouchinska)

1947 **The Unfinished Dance**— MGM (with Sammy Lee)
1953 **Tonight We Sing**— Fox
1958 **Fraulein**— Fox (also appeared)

SERGE LIFAR

b. Kiev, Russia, April 2, 1905
d. Lausanne, Switzerland, December 15, 1986
Classic ballet dancer-choreographer and director who is called "The chief architect of modern French ballet" by *The Concise Oxford Dictionary of the Ballet*. He began his studies with Bronislava Nijinska in Kiev and after joining Diaghilev's Ballets Russes in 1923, he continued his studies with Cecchetti, Nicholas Legat and Pierre Vladimiroff. As premier danseur with Ballets Russes from 1925, he danced many legendary roles (among them Balanchine's *The Prodigal Son* in 1929) and created his first choreography that same year. Ballet director and premier danseur for the Paris Opera (1929–45), he choreographed his only commercial film in France in 1938. Accused of being a collaborator during World War II, he left Paris in 1944 and formed Nouveau Ballet de Monte Carlo (1944–46), returning to the Paris Opera 1947–58. He founded the Paris Choreography Institute in 1947 and University of the Dance in 1957. From 1959, he worked as a freelance choreographer and ballet director internationally: the Netherlands Ballet, London Festival Ballet, Nice Opera, Teatro Colon, etc. He also authored over 25 books between 1935–67.
   Ballet/Dance Pieces (Partial listing): "Renard" ('29), "Creatures of Prometheus," "Bacchus and Aridne," "Salade," "L'apres-midi d'un Faune," "Alexandre le Grand," "Bolero," "Joan de Zarissa," "Les Mirages," "Le Chevalier et la Damoiselle," "A Night on Bald Mountain, "Snow White," "Firebird," etc.
   Film:
   1938 **Ballerina** (aka **La Mort du Cynge**)—(Fr)

TED LIN

b. Lynwood, California, March 14, 1958
Citing Bob Fosse's **All That Jazz**, Gene Kelly's **An American in Paris**, Busby Berkeley and Hermes Pan as major influences in his life and career, Lin was one of the leaders in filmed erotic dance as the new honesty arrived onscreen in the 1980s. He co-majored in dance and television at UCLA until 1982 and studied dance with Alvin Ailey, Joe Malone and at Steps and the Martha Graham School. After performing in various mediums — including a featured role in **Born in East L.A.**('87)—he then moved behind the camera. Choreographing from 1983–91, his talent as a cameraman and videotape operator progressed his career to writing, produc-

ing and directing in television and film. The future holds many directions for the multi-talented man, who says "Dance is divine — if it could last forever!"
   Stage: *The Lion, the Witch and the Wardrobe* ('90)
   TV: "Newhart," "Simon and Simon," "Our Planet Tonight" and "Surprise!, Surprise!" (Specials); commercials for Trejack Sportswear and "GP-1" Gasoline (Japan)
   Music Video: "Tonight's the Night" and "Singing Drive"— Yoko Oginome; "Winner Takes All"— Sammy Hagar; "Under the Influence"— Vanity
   Nightclub/Concert: *U.S. Male Revue* ('87), *Sexthetics* (Gallery event, '90)
   Miscellaneous: Industrial film for Mattel ("Dance Magic Barbie")
   Film:
   1987 **Stripped to Kill**— Concorde
   1988 **Purple People Eater**— Concorde (with Ben Lokey)
   1989 **Captain America**—21st Century Film Corp
         Dance of the Damned— Concorde
         Masque of the Red Death— Concorde
         Stripped to Kill II: Live Girls— Concorde
   1990 **Body Chemistry**— Concorde
   1991 **Our House**—New Line Cinema
   1992 **Poison Ivy**— New Line

TOMMY LINDEN
1962 **We Joined the Navy**— WB/Pathé

EARL LINDSAY

b. 1894
d. May 12, 1945
Lindsay's busy stage career in the 1920s led to his film assignments all within two years. His life and career from 1930–1945 is undocumented.
   Stage: *Silks and Satin* (Bdwy '20), *The Elusive Lady* (Bdwy '22), *Keep Cool* (Bdwy '24), *Gay Paree* (Bdwy '25), *The Great Temptations* (Bdwy '26), *Artists and Models, Bye, Bye, Bonnie* and *The Sidewalks of New York* (Bdwy '27), *Ups a Daisy* (Bdwy '28), *Ballyhoo* and *Luana* (Bdwy '30), *Page Miss Venus* (Bdwy, also dir)
   Film:
   1929 **The Dance of Life**— Par
         Sweetie— Par
         Why Bring That Up?— Par
   1930 **The Golden Calf**— Fox
         Happy Days— Fox

HILLAR LITOJA
1995 **When Night Is Falling**— Metro Tartan (Can) ("The Iron Dance" choreography credit)

BEN LOKEY

b. Birmingham, Alabama, December 15, 1944

This multitalented artist began his dance training with Neil Ness in Amarillo, Texas, and continued to enrich his skills and dance versatility over the years with Gene Castle, William Christensen, Louis DaPron, Paul DeRolf, Luigi, Matt Mattox, Michael Peters, and Stanley Williams. He studied acting with Herbert Berghof in New York and Jeff Corey, Martin Landau and the Actor's Studio in Los Angeles. Making his performance debut in summer stock productions of *Gypsy*, *The Music Man* and *Show Boat*, he danced as a principal with Ballet West and a soloist with the Pennsylvania Ballet. After receiving a BFA degree in dance and choreography and a MFA degree in stage direction, he returned to a performance career. He appeared on Broadway in *A Chorus Line* ('78), toured in Ann-Margret's nightclub act, was featured in the film **Breakin'** ('84) as one of the leads and made multiple film (**Sgt. Pepper's Lonely Hearts Club Band**, **Staying Alive, Captain E-O**), TV (15 specials) and music video ("Thriller," "Physical," etc.) appearances. His successful teaching career has taken him from private schools in California, Utah, Texas and Alabama to master classes at Universities in Sweden, California, Utah and Idaho with celebrity students including Olivia Newton-John, Juliet Prowse, Brooke Shields, John Travolta and Ben Vereen. He has recently applied his talents to casting and talent management.

Stage: *Run Through* (LA, *LA Weekly* Award winner), *Charly—A Love Song* (tour, also co-author, dir), West Coast and summer stock productions of *The King and I*, *Dark of the Moon* (also dir), *Where's Charley?*, *Man of La Mancha*, *Three Penny Opera* (also dir), *Guys and Dolls* and *Annie Get Your Gun*; for the Salt Lake Opera Company: *Die Fledermaus*, *L'Histoire du Soldat*, and *Amahl and the Night Visitors*; *The Best Little Whorehouse in Texas* (LV '94)

TV: "The Widget Shop" (Pilot), "Miss Teen U.S.A. Pageant" (asst choreo), "35th Annual Golden Globe Awards" (asst choreo)

Music Video: "Salsa" and "Lambada" (instructional videos—also appeared)

Nightclub/Concert: *Sizzle* (LV), *Red Hot Night*

Ballet/Dance Pieces: Los Angeles Jazz Co. ('79–80, also co-dir), "Jazz Unlimited Dance Co." (La Jolla, Cal.), "Hollywood Dancin'"

Film:

1988 **A Field So White**—Embryo Prod
      Purple People Eater—Concorde (with Ted Lin)

MARGARET LOOMIS

Dancer, actress and choreographer who began her studies with Denishawn, eventually appearing with the troupe. She went on to a successful acting career in silent films. Marrying Wayne D. Crook, she formed the Denishawn Club, holding monthly meetings with Denishawn dancers in the 1930s.

Film:

1917 **Rebecca of Sunnybrook Farm**—ART
1921 **Everywoman**—Famous Players-Lasky (also appeared)
      The Sheik—Famous Players-Lasky

DON LOPER (LINCOLN GEORGE HARD-LOPER)

b. Toledo, Ohio, August 29, 1906
d. Santa Monica, California, November 21, 1972

Multi-talented, elegant (and reportedly, arrogant) Don Loper began studying dance at the age of 4 and by the age of 12, he joined the Chicago Civic Ballet. At 14 he toured South America with Andres Pavley and Serge Oukrainsky. After organizing and directing a dance band, he began a ballroom dance act with a series of partners (with Beth Hayes at Radio City Music Hall in 1936, etc.) and appeared in European clubs and British films. Eventually pairing with Maxine Barrat, their success took them from Europe to Radio City Music Hall and the best of American supper clubs. They danced on Broadway in *One for the Money* and *Very Warm for May* ('39) and Loper was then signed to direct, produce and design the shows at the Copacabana in New York. Coming to Hollywood in 1942, he was first a dancer and assistant choreographer at Paramount before signing a unique contract with MGM to dance, choreograph, design sets and costumes, act, direct and produce. After six unrewarding years at MGM, he switched careers to become a renowned fashion designer—almost as famous for his champagne-in-hand fashion shows as his clothes, jewelry and cosmetics for the rich and famous. He continued in film as a costume designer: **Ruthless** ('48), **Rancho Notorious** ('52), **The Moon Is Blue** ('53), **The Big Combo** and **Not as a Stranger** ('55), **Paris Follies of 1956**, **Spring Reunion** ('57) and **Looking for Love** ('64). At the height of his career as a successful fashion and interior designer—and after three well-publicized marriages and several drunk driving incidents—the once graceful Loper fell from a ladder in his Bel Air home, punctured a lung and, after three months of hospitalization, died at the age of 66.

Nightclub/Concert: Copacabana (NY '38–42), *Be My Guest* (Mocambo, Hollywood '56, also prod)

Film:

1943 **Thousands Cheer**—MGM (dance specialty with Maxine Barrat)
1944 **Broadway Rhythm**—MGM (with Robert Alton, Jack Donohue, Charles Walters)

Ben Lokey supports Lucinda Dickey in **Breakin'** (Cannon, 1984).

Four Jills in a Jeep— Fox
Lady in the Dark— RKO (with Nick Castle, Billy Daniel, also partnered Ginger Rogers)
1944 **Belle of the Yukon**— RKO (also costume and set design)
1945 **It's a Pleasure**— RKO (also danced with Sonja Henie and associate producer)

ALBERTO LORCA

Classical Spanish dancer and choreographer currently teaching in Spain.

Ballet/Dance Pieces: "La Boda de Luis Alonso"
Film:
1959 **The Naked Maja**— UA
1972 **Bewitched Love** (aka **El Amor Brujo**)— (Span)

FRED LORD

British choreographer.
Film:
1930 **Loose Ends** — BIP

EUGENE LORING (LEROY KERPESTEIN)

b. West Allis, Wisconsin, August 12, 1911
d. Kingston, New York, August 30, 1982
Highly influential ballet dancer, choreographer and teacher who was one of the major innovators of ballet and Spanish dance sequences in films. A star athlete in Wisconsin, he had dreams of an acting career. After graduating from high school in 1929, he worked in a department store and became involved in an amateur little theater group ("Because I was so short, I was always cast as a boy or some weird character. I knew that it was good for actors to study dance, and so I took some lessons in order to improve my acting.") After making his professional debut with the Wisconsin Players, his love of dance guided him to New York to study at the School of American Ballet with George Balanchine. He joined Michel Fokine's company and made his dancing debut in 1934 in *Prince Igor* and *Scheherazade*, gaining acclaim in *Carnaval*. Joining Balanchine's company in 1936 (then known as American Ballet) he became an acclaimed soloist and helped to organize Ballet Caravan. His American folk ballet, *Billy the Kid* (created in 1938 for Ballet Caravan), was one of American ballet's landmarks. When Ballet Theatre was formed in 1940, Loring was part of it as both dancer and choreographer. Making a splash as an actor on Broadway in *The Beautiful People* in 1941, he alternated choreographing on stage with film work (having a unique contract with MGM to dance, act, direct, write, assistant produce and dance direct), also appearing as an actor in MGM's **National Velvet** and **Torch Song**. To strengthen his film work, he studied editing at NYU and researched and studied Mexican and Spanish dance in Mexico, eventually creating many Latin works for stage and screen. The creator and director of the famed American School of Dance in Hollywood ('47–74), where several generations of dancers, choreographers and actors studied, he also formed The Eugene Loring Dance Players which, after a previous start in New York in 1941, was revived in the Sixties and over the years would include future choreographers Jimmy Bates, Bonnie Evans, Paul Gleason, Howard Jeffrey, Michael Kidd and Roger Minami. In 1965 he founded the dance department at UC Irvine. Loring successfully collaborated with some of filmdom's best dancers and choreographers to create many memorable film dance sequences. As a winner of the *Dance Magazine* Award in 1967, he was honored for "Bridging the worlds of art and entertainment, he has made significant choreographic contributions to the development of an American style in ballet, films and musical comedy. As California educator, he has produced scores of versatile performers who bring quality to contemporary theatre dance."

Stage: *Carmen Jones* (Bdwy '43), *Park Avenue* (OOT '46), Greek Theatre, LA 1949 season: *Showboat*, *Annie Get Your Gun*, *Girl Crazy*, *New Moon* and *Carmen Jones*; *Buttrio Square* (Bdwy '52, also dir), *Three Wishes for Jamie* (Bdwy '52, with Ted Cappy, Herbert Ross), *The Great Waltz* (Bdwy '53 and LACLO '65), *Silk Stockings* (Bdwy '55), *Fanny* (LACLO '57), *The Devil and Daniel Webster* (Bdwy '59), *Kiss Me Kate* (Melodyland, Cal. '64), multiple annual stage productions at Loras College, Dubuque, Iowa ('55–68)

TV (Partial listing): Omnibus — "Capital of the World" ('53), "Crescendo" ('57), Donald O'Connor Special ('60), "The Shirley Temple Show," Rodgers and Hammerstein's "Cinderella" ('64), special for Cyd Charisse

Nightclub/Concert: Coconut Grove (LA '49)

Ballet/Dance pieces (23 works — Partial listing): "Harlequin for President" ('36), "Yankee Clipper," "Billy the Kid," "Prairie," "The Great American Goof," "Capital of the World," "The Man from Midian," "The Duke of Sacramento," "The Sisters," "The Funeral," "City Portrait," "Paradox," "Time Unto Time" ('80)

Miscellaneous: *Sand in Your Shoes* (Mormon Centennial pageant, '59), *Ice Capades* ('58, '65)

Film:
1944 **National Velvet** — MGM (also appeared)
1945 **Yolanda and the Thief** — MGM (with Fred Astaire)
1946 **Thrill of Brazil** — Col (with Nick Castle, Jack Cole, Ann Miller, Frank Veloz)
  Ziegfeld Follies — MGM (with Robert Alton, Fred Astaire, Gene Kelly, Charles Walters, the *La Traviata* sequence)
1947 **Fiesta** — MGM
  Something in the Wind — Univ (also appeared)
1948 **Mexican Hayride** — Univ
1949 **The Inspector General** — WB
1950 **The Petty Girl** — Col
  The Toast of New Orleans — MGM
1951 **Mark of the Renegade** — Univ
1952 **The Brigand** — Col
1953 **The 5000 Fingers of Doctor T** — Col
  The Golden Blade — Univ
  Torch Song — MGM (with Charles Walters, also appeared)
  The Veils of Bagdad — Univ
1954 **Deep in My Heart** — MGM (with Gene Kelly, *One Alone* Ballet for Cyd Charisse and James Mitchell)

"Former nightclub dancer" Don Loper "pauses next to one of his two pools at his elegant Beverly Hills home" in this publicity shot for one of his fashion shows in 1958.

1956 **Meet Me in Las Vegas**—MGM (with Hermes Pan, "Ballets Created by" credit)

1957 **Funny Face**—Par (with Fred Astaire, Stanley Donen, assisted by Pat Denise, Dave Robel)

Silk Stockings—MGM (with Fred Astaire, Hermes Pan, "All dances in which Fred Astaire appears choreographed by Hermes Pan; all others dances choreographed by" credit, assisted by Angela Blue, Pat Denise, Dave Robel)

1960 **Pepe**—Col (with Alex Romero, Ballet for Shirley Jones, Matt Mattox and Michael Callan, assisted by Bruce Hoy)

1994 **That's Entertainment! III**—MGM (with others)

TILLY LOSCH (OTTILIE ETHEL LEOPOLDINE LOSCH; LATER COUNTESS OF CARNARVON)

b. Vienna, Austria, November 15, 1907

d. New York, December 24, 1975

Exotic Viennese-born ballerina, stage star and painter who began her training at the age of 6 at the Vienna Opera Ballet School, later joining the company. In 1924 she had her first solo with the company in *Schlagobers*—with composer Richard Strauss himself conducting. While dancing and choreographing *A Midsummer Night's Dream* in 1927 at the Salzburg Festspeil for Max Reinhardt, she was spotted by English producer Charles B. Cochran and invited to London for Noel Coward's *This Year of Grace*. She resumed her stage work with Reinhardt and was featured in his productions, which brought her to America. She starred on Broadway in *Wake Up and Dream* ('29), *The Band Wagon* ('31—with Fred and Adele Astaire) and George Balanchine's *The Seven Deadly Sins*. She was then prima ballerina for Les Ballets company ('33) which her first husband, Edward James, financed for several seasons. After a highly scandalous divorce trial in 1934, she married the Earl of Carnarvon (whose father headed the fateful expedition to discover the tomb of King Tut) in 1939. They

Tilly Losch, portraying the fiery "Half-breed" mother of Jennifer Jones in a publicity still from her role in **Duel in the Sun** (Samuel Goldwyn, 1946).

were divorced in 1947. She made her final appearance on Broadway in *Topaze* in 1948 and retired to become an acclaimed portrait painter until her death.

Stage: *A Midsummer Night's Dream* (Salzburg '27, also appeared), *This Year of Grace* (London and Bdwy '28, also appeared), *Bitter Sweet* (London '29), *Wake Up and Dream* (Bdwy '29, also appeared), *The Gang's All Here* (Bdwy '31)

Film (All credits but one are for creating her own dance sequences):

1937 **Backstage** (aka **Limelight**)—GB (with Ralph Reader, also appeared)

The Garden of Allah—Samuel Goldwyn (also appeared)

The Good Earth—MGM (also appeared)

1946 **Duel in the Sun**—Samuel Goldwyn (with Lloyd Shaw, also appeared)

1947 **Song of Scheherazade**—Univ

HARRY (WALTER) LOSEE

b. 1901

d. December 16, 1952

Reviewing Losee's vaudeville act on June 6, 1932, the *Motion Picture Herald* wrote: "Harry Losee offers a character dance, portraying a red-skinned ethnic. He is graceful, supple and a keen student of the dance." This "keen student" would go on to become an Academy Award-nominated choreographer and stager of primarily ice skating film sequences. He began his dance career studying and performing with Ruth St. Denis and Ted Shawn and alternated a successful vaudeville and Broadway musical career (*A Tale of Araby* at the Roxy Theatre in 1930; the Harry Losee Trio at Radio City Music Hall in 1935; etc.) with film appearances in Hollywood. He danced in **Blood and Sand** ('22), **Man Hatters** and **The Thief of Bagdad** ('25) before moving into dance direction first on stage and then in film. He collaborated with Hermes Pan and Fred Astaire on **Shall We Dance** at RKO (creating the ballet sequences for Harriet Hoctor and corps) and was then signed by 20th Century–Fox to stage the ice skating spectaculars for Sonja Henie. Although ice was a totally new medium for him, his success with **Thin Ice** kept him at Fox for four years while he also staged Henie's live tours — often at night after filming. The relationship was successful — and sometimes, explosive. "Harry Losee's temperament was perfectly suited to working with Sonja... The dance was the thing whether on ice or on stage... I used to watch them really work out a number together. Sonja might say, 'I think it would work better over here' and Harry would say, 'I agree,' And the other way around... Harry, a teacher of ballet, had never seen a pair of skates before he saw Sonja ... but he got things from Sonja that nobody else did... Harry accepts no compromise. Sonja shakes her head when he says, 'Get out there and do it!' 'It cannot be done on ice,' she screams... It doesn't matter. I think sometimes they will kill each other, but when the practice is finished, they are both satisfied — laughing and hugging one another."(from *Queen of Ice, Queen of Shadows*, a biography about Henie). He also created ice dance sequences at Republic for their reigning ice queen, Vera Hruba-Ralston.

Stage: Keep Moving (Bdwy '34, asst to Robert Alton), *At Home Abroad* (Bdwy '35, with Gene Snyder), *The Show Is On* (Bdwy '36, asst to Alton), *Very Warm for May* (Bdwy '39, with Albertina Rasch)

Ballet/Dance Pieces: "A Tale of Araby" (Roxy Theatre '30), "The Passion of St. Sebastian" ('33)

Miscellaneous: multiple RKO vaudeville units ('30s), *Ice-a-Poppin'*, Sonja Henie Tour ('39), Coconut Grove Ice Revue (LA '40)

Film:
1925 **The Thief of Baghdad**— UA (also appeared)
1937 **Shall We Dance?**— RKO (with Hermes Pan, Fred Astaire)
    Thin Ice— Fox (Academy Award nom: "Prince Igor Suite" number)

You Can't Have Everything— Fox
1938 **Happy Landing**— Fox (with the Condos Brothers)
    My Lucky Star— Fox (with Nick Castle, Geneva Sawyer)
1939 **Second Fiddle**— Fox
1941 **Ice-Capades**— Rep
1942 **Ice-Capades Revue**— Rep
1943 **Hit the Ice**— Univ (with Sammy Lee)

EDWARD (M.) LOVE, JR.
b. June 29, 1948
d. New York, December 27, 1991
A graduate of Ohio University, Love began his career in 1973 with Alvin Ailey's American Dance Theater. Broadway appearances included *Raisin* ('73) *The Wiz*, *A Chorus Line* ('78), *Fortune and Men's Eyes* and *Dancin'*, as well as the Los Angeles company of *The Wiz*. He had acting roles in the films **Hair**, **To Kill a Cop** and **A Piece of the Action** and his direction and choreographic skills took him to Finland, France, Italy and Spain before his premature death.

Stage: Upstairs at O'Neal's (Bdwy Cabaret '82), *Williams and Walker* (also appeared), *Leader of the Pack* (OB '83), *American Jukebox* (Ntl tour, also dir), *A — My Name Is Alice* (OB and OOT, also dir), *Little Shop of Horrors* (Florida)

TV: "Natalie Cole's Big Break," "What's Alan Watching," "Shout" (Series pilot)

Music Video: "So Emotional"— Whitney Houston; "What's Love Got to Do with It?"— Tina Turner; "Jump Start"— Natalie Cole; videos for Billy Idol, Duran Duran, Steve Winwood and Chaka Kahn, Kurtis Blow, Lou Reed and Bette Midler

Film:
1984 **Exterminator 2**— Cannon
1988 **Hairspray**— New Line Cinema

DIA LUCA
1956 **Don Juan**— Akkrod/Times Film (Austral)

ANDY LUCAS
1992 **Becoming Colette**— Castle Hill

JONATHON LUCAS
b. Sherman, Texas, August 14, 1922
d. Los Angeles, California, February 5, 1991
Robust dancer, actor, choreographer and director who graduated as a psychology major at SMU but soon changed his career goals to dance, studying at the School of American Ballet in New York. After serving in the Navy during World War II, he danced at the Copacabana in New York and debuted

on Broadway in *A Lady Says Yes* ('45). He subsequently appeared in *Finian's Rainbow, Billion Dollar Baby, Small Wonder, Touch and Go, Around the World* and *The Golden Apple* (in which he won the 1954 *Theatre World* and Donaldson Awards for his performance). In his only dance appearance on film, he partnered Vera-Ellen in **Happy Go Lovely** ('51), and continued to perform on stage (*Carnival!* '61), television ("Sunday Comedy Hour" '54) and act as production assistant, choreographer and director for various mediums for the next forty years — from "The Mickey Mouse Club" to directing porno films under various pseudonyms. While producing a cabaret show at the Sandcastle Hotel in Guam in January, 1991, he fell and suffered internal injuries. He was rushed back to America, where he died.

Stage: First Impressions (Bdwy '59), *Vintage '60* (LA and Bdwy), *Seven Come Eleven* (Bdwy '63), "The Game Is Up" (Bdwy '64, also dir); multiple productions for Sacramento Music Circus, Fiesta Dinner Theater, Grand Dinner Theatre, Sebastian's Dinner Theatre and the Harlequin Dinner Theatre

TV: "The Martha Raye Show" ('55), The Esther Williams Cypress Gardens Special ('56), Rodgers and Hammerstein's "Cinderella" ('57), "The Eddie Fisher Show" ('58), "The Ernie Kovacs Show," "The Steve Allen Show" ('62), "The Dean Martin Show" ('65–74), "The Golddiggers" ('71, also dir), "The Milton Berle Show," "The Mickey Mouse Club," "The Barbara Mandrell Show," "Penthouse Pet of the Year" Specials

Nightclub/Concert: Sands Hotel (LV '56), *Upstairs at the Downstairs* (NY, also dir), *Gene Kelly's Wonderful World of Girls* (International Hotel, LV, with Tommy Tune), *Playgirls of 1961* with Marilyn Maxwell, Sheree North and Patrice Wymore; acts for George Chakiris, the Crew Cuts, Marlene Dietrich, the Fifth Dimension, Bobbie Gentry, Shirley Jones & Jack Cassidy, Gladys Knight & the Pips, the Lettermen, Julie London, Janis Paige, Eleanor Powell, Juliet Prowse, Jane Russell, Esther Williams ('57 European Tour) and Gretchen Wyler

Film:
1961   **The Two Little Bears** — Fox
1965   **Marriage on the Rocks** — WB
1969   **The Trouble with Girls** — MGM

OLGA LUNICK

Dancer-choreographer who first attracted notice with her appearances in *Marianne* (OOT '43) and *Glad to See You* (OOT '44), in early television dance shows on CBS in 1945 and Broadway roles in *Inside U.S.A* and *Ballet Ballads* in 1948. Her film roles include **The Golden Blade** ('53). She assisted Billy Daniel on the Eddie Cantor "Colgate Comedy Hour" and taught ballet and modern dance at Seymour Felix's Westwood dance studio ('54).

Stage: Moulin Rouge (LA '53, also appeared)
TV: "My Friend Irma," "Omnibus" ('53)
Film:
1952   **The Four Poster** — Col
         Rooty Toot Toot — UPA
1954   **Princess of the Nile** — Fox
1955   **Son of Sinbad** — RKO

DON LURIO

American expatriate who lives and works in Italy. After appearing in **The Bobo** ('67), he worked in European film, television and stage to become one of Europe's leading dancemakers.

Ballet/Dance Pieces: "The Broken Pate" (Ballet Theater Francais '58)
Film:
1968   **Candy** — Cinerama

GILLIAN LYNNE (PYRKE)

b. Bromley, Kent, England, 1928

Leading contemporary English dancer, choreographer and director who once discussed her childhood in the *L.A. Times* (June 20, 1985), "As a little girl I was a pain in the neck, apparently. I was always moving. My mother thought I had some disease like Saint Vitus Dance, so she took me to the doctor. He was very wise. He put some music on … and watched me leap about. He told my mother, 'Take her to dancing class — *now*!' I was five." She studied with Molly Lake, Madeleine Sharp and at the Royal Academy of Dancing and the Cone-Ripman School. After dancing with the Arts Theatre Ballet and Ballet Guild, at 16 she joined the Sadler's Wells Ballet, being rapidly promoted to soloist and then, prima ballerina ('45–51). While on tour to the United States with the Royal Ballet, she saw *Kiss Me Kate* and was so impressed that she decided to change her direction to musical theater. In 1951, Robert Helpmann encouraged her to audition for the London Palladium — she got the job and danced there for two years. After acting roles in the films **The Master of Ballantrae** ('53) and **The Last Man to Hang** ('56), she received further recognition in London stage musicals, among them being the Gwen Verdon role in *Can Can* ('62). In 1963, *Collages*, "a modern dance revue" she choreographed (and England's first jazz dance company) attracted notice and she was signed by Broadway producer David Merrick to do *The Roar of the Greasepaint—The Smell of the Crowd*. She has continued creating for films and London and Broadway stage successes, becoming one of England's leading exponent of musical stage dance. Her creativity with *Cats* (Olivier Award 1982) and *Phantom of the Opera* has brought her international recognition and acclaim. Married to New Zealand-born actor Peter Land since 1980, she described her work methods: "There's not much to help you out when you're actually working out dance steps. I try to think myself into the skin of the characters and how they would move and just hope my body will move that way. I can't do it in my head—I have to get out there and move."

Stage: *Collages* (Edinburgh Festival, '63), *The Roar of the Greasepaint— The Smell of the Crowd* (London and Bdwy '64), *Pickwick* (Bdwy '65), *The Match Girls* (Eng '65, also dir), *How Now Dow Jones?* (Bdwy '67), *Tomfoolery, Songbook, Bluebeard, Jeeves Take Charge, Phil the Fluter* (London '69), *Once Upon a Time* (London '72, also dir), *The Card* (London '73), *Songbook* (London '79), *Cats* (London and Bdwy '82, also assoc dir, Tony nom), *The Rehearsal* (London, '83), *Phantom of the Opera* (London and Bdwy '86), *Aspects of Love* (London '89, Bdwy '90), *Valentine's Day* (London '92); for the Royal Shakespeare Company: *A Midsummer Night's Dream, A Comedy of Errors, The Boyfriend, As You Like It, The Way of the World, Once in a Lifetime*; for the Royal Opera House, Covent Garden: **Midsummer Marriage, The Trojans, Parsifal** and **The Flying Dutchman**

TV (Partial listing): "The Muppet Show," "Easy Money" (dir), "Morte D'Arthur" (BBC), "Alice in Wonderland" ('85), "A Simple Man" ('88), "The Fool on the Hill" (Australia)

Ballet/Dance Pieces: "The Owl and the Pussycat" (Western Theatre Ballet '62), "Cafe Noir" (Houston Ballet '85)

Film:
1965 **It's a Wonderful Life** (aka **Swinger's Paradise**)—WB
Seaside Swingers—Embassy
Three Hats for Lisa—Seven Hills/WB Pathe
1967 **Half a Sixpence**—Par
1971 **200 Motels**—UA
1972 **Man of La Mancha**—UA
1975 **Mr. Quilp**—Avco Embassy
1983 **Yentl**—MGM/UA
1985 **National Lampoon's European Vacation**—Fox
1986 **Mr. Love**—WB

NIGEL LYTHGOE

b. England

After studying tap, jazz, modern, ballet and Greek ballet, Lythgoe began his career as a dancer. He completed his dance training in Liverpool, while also studying at a technical college. In 1969 he joined The Young Generation and in 1971 began choreographing for the group. His work has been primarily on European television, with an unusual English musical **The Apple** being his only com-

mercial film credit. His press release for the film noted: "Nigel and his terrific sense of humor and willingness to help out in *all* aspects of the filming ... made him a well-loved personality by everyone connected with the film."

Stage: Royal Command Performances, *Pull Both Ends* (London '72)

TV: "The Kessler Twins," "The Roberto Blanco Show," "Hello Peter," "Michael Schantze" (German TV), the Shirley Bassey series (British and Bahrain TV), Egyptian National Dance Company (Dubai TV)

Film:
1980 **The Apple**—Cannon

PONS MAAR

1985 **Return to Oz**—Buena Vista ("Mime Movement by" credit)

RANA MACK

1992 **South Central**—WB (also appeared as "Girl in Club")

ROY MACK

1930 **Lilies of the Field**—WB
Loose Ankles—WB

IRA MCAILEY

1991 **Pizza Man**—Meglomania Prod

CARL MCBRIDE

Assistant dance director at First National during the early '30s.

Film:
1929 **Smiling Irish Eyes**—First Ntl (with Larry Ceballos)
1930 **College Lovers**—First Ntl

BRENDAN MCDANIEL

1995 **Stonewall**—BBC (UK)

BRUCE MCDONALD

1995 **Mr. Holland's Opus**—Hollywood Pict

NEIL MCKAY

1988 **Gor**—Cannon

DONALD (COHEN) MCKAYLE

b. New York, July 6, 1930

This Tony-nominated dance innovator's work was analyzed in a review of one of his company's concerts in the June 1962 issue of *Dance Magazine* as: "Donald McKayle's view of existence is a comparatively simple one. In its simplicity lies part of its strength. He is convinced of the basic rightness of the man-woman relationship...and he harbors an honest compassion for the downtrodden. This compassion leads him to find their essential beauty." McKayle became interested in dance during his last year of high school and began studying on a scholarship at the New Dance Group with William Bales, Jane Dudley, Jean Erdman, Sophie Maslow and with Hadassah. He attended NY City College and continued studying dance at the Martha Graham School and with Nenette Charisse, Pearl Primus and Karel Shook. He made his debut with the New Dance Group in 1948, subsequently appearing with Dudley-Maslow-Bales, Jean Erdman, NYC Dance Theatre, NYC Opera Ballet, Anna Sokolow and Martha Graham companies. In 1951 he began creating original dance pieces for young choreographers' programs at Henry Street Playhouse and diversified his career dancing on Broadway in *Bless You All* ('51), *House of Flowers* ('55), *West Side Story* and *Copper and Brass* ('57, in which he assisted Anna Sokolow). He also assisted Bob Fosse on *Redhead* ('59) and appeared in the films **Edge of the City**, **Jazz on a Summer's Day** and **On the Sound**. His prolific teaching career has included classes at Bennington, Sarah Lawrence, the Neighborhood Playhouse, the Martha Graham School and Juilliard and currently is the artistic director and associate dean at the California Institute of the Arts, having been a member of their faculty since 1970. In 1995, he was honored with the California Dance Educator (CDEA) Award.

Stage: *Kicks and Co.* (OOT '61), *The Tempest* ('62), *As You Like It* and *Trumpets of the Lord* ('63), *Golden Boy* (Bdwy '64, Tony nom), *A Time for Singing* ('64), *Her First Roman* (OOT '67), *Black New World* ('67), *The Four Musketeers* (London '67), *I'm Solomon* (Bdwy '68), *The Emperor Jones* ('69), *Leonard Bernstein's Mass* (LA '72), *Raisin* (Bdwy '73, also dir, Tony noms for choreo and dir), *Doctor Jazz* (Bdwy '75, also dir, Tony nom for choreo), *The Last Minstrel Show* (OOT '78, also dir), *Evolution of the Blues* (LA '79), *Sophisticated Ladies* (Bdwy '81, with Henry LeTang and Michael Smuin, Tony nom), *Stardust* (OOT '90), *Shimmy* (in progress '94, also dir and creator)

TV: Bill Cosby Special ('68), "The Hollywood Palace" ('69), 43rd and 49th Academy Awards Show ('70 &'77), "The New Bill Cosby Show" ('72-73), "Free to Be You and Me" ('74), "Komedy Tonite" ('78), the Emmy Awards ('79)

Nightclub/Concert: Acts for Ann-Margret, Harry Belafonte, Helen Gallagher, Rita Moreno, Diana Ross and Mary Tyler Moore

Ballet/Dance Pieces (Partial Listing—Created ballets for his own company and the Alvin Ailey American Dance Theater): "Games" ('51), "Her Name Was Harrie," "Nocturne," "Rainbow 'Round My Shoulder," "Crosstown," "District Storyville," "Blood of the Lamb," "Blood Memories," "House of Tears" (Cleveland Ballet '92), "Ring-A-Levio" ('93), "Mysteries" and Raptures" (San Jose Ballet, '93)

Film:
1965 **Dance: Echoes of Jazz**—NET (TV) (with Grover Dale, also appeared)
1970 **The Great White Hope**—Fox
1971 **Bedknobs and Broomsticks**—Disney (assisted by Caroline Dyer)
1973 **Charley and the Angel**—Disney
1977 **Minstrel Man**—Roger Gimbel Prod/First Artists (TV) (Emmy nom)
1978 **Cindy**—Par/ABC (TV)
1980 **The Jazz Singer**—Samuel Goldwyn (with Shlomo Bachar)
1989 **Private Debts**—Chanticleer Films

SUSANNE MCKENRICK
1992 **Chaplin**—TriStar (with Kate Flatt, Johnny Hutch, Dan Kamin, "L.A. crew choreography" credit)

SUSAN MCKENZIE
Dancer-choreographer and dance educator who lives in Vancouver, Canada. She is a founder-member of Dancemakers and a co-founder of the Toronto Independent Dance Enterprise. With extensive stage credits, she is currently dance instructor to actors and dancers at the John Sullivan Hayes Program for Theatre Teaching.

Stage: Partial listing (All Canadian credits): *Sleeping Dogs Lie, Callumlillies, Horror High, The Dreamland, Glen, Coming Through Slaughter, Mirrorgame, Neverland, The Comedy of Errors*, (Stratford Festival '94-95)

Film:
1993 **Zero Patience**—Telefilm Canada
1995 **The Making of Monsters**—Telefilm Canada

BILL MACKEY
1979 **Freedom Road**—(TV) Zev Braun/NBC

SIR KENNETH MACMIL-LAN
b. Dunfermline, Scotland, December 11, 1930

d. London, England, October 29, 1992

Influential Scottish dancer and choreographer who often stated he had been inspired by Fred Astaire. At 16, he began his classical training at Sadler's Wells Ballet school from 1946 and was asked to join the company in 1948. While dancing, he made his choreographic debut in 1953 with **Son-ambulism** and subsequently choreographed for American Ballet Theater, Berlin Ballet, the Royal Ballet, the Royal Danish Ballet, Stuttgart Ballet and Theatre Ballet. Influenced by film and Britain's new theatrical realism, he created ballets which contained strong emotional content and dealt with contemporary problems. He was hailed for his creative, emotional pas de deux creations and his work on film was primarily in the vernacular of classical dance. Director of the Berlin Ballet from 1966–69 and the Royal Ballet from 1970–76, he was also artistic associate for American Ballet Theatre, 1984–89. Knighted in 1983, he died of a heart attack backstage at the Royal Opera House in London, in 1992, where they were performing his ballet **Mayerling**. At the time, he was also in the midst of choreographing a highly successful *Carousel* revival for London, which would eventually arrive to acclaim on Broadway in 1994, winning him a posthumous Tony Award.

Stage: *Ice Dancing* (Bdwy '78, with Norman Maen, Donald Saddler, Twyla Tharp), *Carousel* ('92 rev London & Bdwy '94, Tony award)

TV: Commercials on British TV (early '50s)

Ballet/Dance Pieces (66 works — Partial Listing): "Somnambulism" ('53), "Winter's Eve," "House of Birds," "Dances Concertantes," "Noctambules," "Journey," "The Burrow," "Agon, "Solitaire," "The Invitation," "The Rite of Spring," "Images of Love," "La Creation du Monde," "Romeo and Juliet" (first full-length ballet '65), "Concerto," "Las Hermanas," "Requiem," "Prince of the Pagodas," "Manon," "Winter Dreams," "The Judas Tree" ('92)

Film:
1960 **Expresso Bongo**— Continental
1966 **Romeo and Juliet**— Embassy
1977 **The Turning Point**— Fox (with Alvin Ailey, Sir Frederick Ashton, George Balanchine, Jean Coralli, John Cranko, Michel Fokine, Lev Ivanov, Harald Lander, Alexander Minz, Dennis Nahat, Jules Perrot, Marius Petipa)
1980 **Nijinsky**— Par
1988 **Little Nikita**— Col

MINNIE MADDEN
1988 **Dance or Die**— City Lights

WADE MADSEN
1996 **Crocodile Tears**— Crocodile Tears Prod

NORMAN MAEN
b. Ireland

Receiving his dance training in Ireland and Great Britain, Maen emigrated to America and danced in *Donnybrook!* and *Kean* on Broadway ('61), also assisting choreographer, Jack Cole. During the 1960s, his choreographic talents kept him moving back and forth between the United Kingdom, Canada and the United States, achieving great success on television, including an Emmy award for his work on "This is Tom Jones!" He eventually settled in London, where his dancemaking continues on stage and television.

Stage: *Vanity Fair* (London '62), *Man of La Mancha* (London '66), *Liz* (Eng '68), *Mr. and Mrs.* (London '68, with Ross Taylor), *Ice Dancing* (Bdwy '78, with Kenneth MacMillan, Donald Saddler, Twyla Tharp), *Some Like It Hot* (London, '92)

TV: Six years in Canadian variety shows, "This Is Tom Jones!" ('69–71, Emmy winner), "The Val Doonican Show" ('77), "Bonkers" ('78)

Nightclub/Concert: *Hallelujah Hollywood!* (MGM Grand, LV)

Film:
1967 **The Young Girls of Rochefort**— WB (with Gene Kelly, assisted by Pamela Hart, Maureen Bright)

SURIA MAGITA
1946 **Great Expectations**— Univ

ALEXANDRE MAGNO
b. Brazil

Describing his choreographic abilities as "ranging from Latin American styles to funk, sensual, partnering and strong theatrical works" this dancer-choreographer began acquiring solo choreographic credits in the early '90s.

Stage: *Hair, A Time to Dance; With Passion* (LA '94, also dir)

TV: "In Living Color," 62nd Academy Awards ('89), MTV Music Awards ('93), "Secrets of Hollywood" (Pilot & series), "Madonna Down Under" (HBO)

Music Video: Videos for Donna deLory, Induced Fantasy, Liberdade, Talk with God

Nightclub/Concert: Madonna's "Girlie Show" tour ('93), Chippendales tour ('94)

Film:
1992 **Liquid Dreams**— Northern Arts Ent.
1994 **Somebody to Love**— Lumiere Pictures
1995 **Lord of Illusions**— MGM/UA

TOMMY (THOMAS) MAHONEY
b. Texas

d. St. Paul, Minnesota, May 28, 1995

Holding the distinction of being one of the last studio contracted dance directors, Tommy Mahoney worked for Walt Disney Studios during their prolific television and theme park years. First contracted as a dance director by David O. Selznick and Howard Hughes, Mahoney was signed by Disney in the early Fifties. As the staff choreographer for "The Mickey Mouse Club" (1955–59) he created hours of musical numbers for Sharon Baird, Bobby Burgess, Annette Funicello and the rest of the popular Mouseketeers for their filmed and live stage appearances. When Disneyland opened, Walt Disney personally asked Tommy to stage the live shows there, including the *Golden Horseshoe Revue*, one of the longest-running shows as listed in the Guiness Book of World Records. He also supplied various entertainment for Knotts Berry Farm. Remembered and loved for his high energy and droll sense of humor, Mahoney is sadly missed.

Stage: R.S.V.P. (LA '60), Radio City Music Hall ('62), *The Runaway Toys* (SF '71), *Anything Goes* ('90 rev tour starring Mitzi Gaynor)

TV: "The Mickey Mouse Club" ('55–59), "The Golden Horseshoe," "The Bing Crosby Show" ('64), "Family Affair"

Nightclub/Concert: Up Your Frontier (LV '70, also wrote, dir)

Miscellaneous: Multiple shows and parades at Disneyland and Knotts Berry Farm, *Disney Night at the Hollywood Bowl*, *Ice-Capades*, *Crystal Palace Gaieties* (Astro World), Half-time show for New Orleans Saints ('67–68), Pro-Bowl Game Half-time show ('71), Opening Ceremonies (Lake Placid Olympics, '80), etc.

Film:
1958 **The Light in the Forest**— Disney
1959 **Darby O'Gill and the Little People**— Disney
1961 **The Absent Minded Professor**— Disney
       Babes in Toyland— Disney (with Ray Bolger, Jack Donohue, assisted by Joyce Horn and Bob Turk)
       The Parent Trap— Disney
1963 **Savage Sam**— Disney
       Summer Magic— Disney
1964 **Bikini Beach**— AIP
1980 **Airplane!**— Par

LEONE MAIL
1960 **The Would-Be Gentleman**—(Fr)

LARRY (LORENZO) MALDONADO
b. Indiana
d. Los Angeles, California, circa 1979

When he completed his service in the Navy, Maldonado relocated to the West Coast in 1949 and began his theatrical career in productions at the La Jolla Playhouse and San Diego's Circle Theater, studying dance with Marguerite Ellicott. Moving north to Hollywood, his dance studies there with Lester Horton and Carmelita Maracci redirected his energies away from teaching toward theater. As a dancer and art director for the Cabaret Concert Theater, he later joined the Horton Dance Theatre in 1954. After appearing on stage, TV and in films, he began nightclub work for Donn Arden and Dorothy Dorben as lead dancer and choreographer. In 1959, he founded The Larry Maldonado Dancers and while appearing in a New Jersey summer stock production of *West Side Story* in 1960, a fateful meeting with Barry Ashton led to a highly successful long-term career choreographing scores of shows for Ashton. His career continued in nightclubs and cabarets, with the Larry Maldonado Dancers successfully touring again from 1963 to '65, sponsored by Juliet Prowse. In 1966, he moved to Paris for two years, choreographing and appearing in the *Lido de Paris*.

Stage: Hans Christian Andersen (Players Ring Theater, LA '53), *A Night in Paradise* (Seattle World's Fair, '62)

Nightclub/Concert (Partial listing): *All About Dames* (Latin Quarter, NY), *Le Lido de Paris* (multiple productions in Paris and Stardust Hotel, LV), *Flapper Follies* (Art's Roaring '20s, San Diego '62), Larry Maldonado Dancers (Flamingo Hotel, LV '64), *Peep Hole Bunnies* (Showboat Hotel, LV '65), London Palladium ('67), *Today USA* (Tropicana Hotel, LV '68), *Pzazz* (Desert Inn, LV '68), *Hallelujah Hollywood* (MGM Grand, LV), *Philippine Playmates* (Tropicana Hotel, LV '70), Americana Hotel Revues (Miami and Puerto Rico '70), *Folies Bergère* (Tropicana Hotel, LV '71–73), *London Playgirl Revue* (Sands Hotel, LV '71), *Les Girls de Paris*, *The Wonderful World of Burlesque* (Silver Slipper, LV), *Hello Hollywood!* (MGM Grand Hotel, Reno, '78)

Ballet/Dance Pieces: "An American in Paris (Hollywood Bowl, '60), "The Wedding" and "The Marriage Vows" ('62)

Miscellaneous: Holiday on Ice ('68–70)
Film:
1966 **Movie Star, American Style** (aka **LSD, I Hate You!**)— Famous Players (assisted by Carlton Johnson)

HARRISON MANG
Martial arts choreographer.
1986 **No Retreat No Surrender**— New World

ANITA MANN

b. Detroit, Michigan, 1947

This vivacious one woman production team of the '90s began her dance training quite by accident at the age of 2 — her brother was pigeon-toed and a doctor suggested he take dance lessons. "I went along as his little sister, and knew from the first moment I walked into that dance studio in Detroit that I loved it and had found my home." When the family moved to St. Louis, she continued studies at the Ford School of Dance and started her career at 8 in *The King and I* at the St. Louis Municipal Opera. The family then moved to Los Angeles and her prolific performance career included films (**Love and Kisses**, **Bye Bye Birdie**, **Spinout**, etc.); TV ("Shindig," "Hullabaloo," Carol Burnett, Jerry Lewis, Lucille Ball and Danny Thomas shows, etc.), more stage (as "Anybodys" in *West Side Story*) and nightclubs (*Youthquake*, Sheila MacRae's act, etc.) in the '60s. She began her choreographic career at 18 assisting Jack Baker, Jack Regas, Alex Romero and David Winters and she attributes her interest and knowledge of the camera to working with Lucille Ball ("I was always interested in the camera, tracking, all the technical stuff... Lucy taught me everything I know about cameras. She was so fabulous and always wanted whatever it was done right.") As a solo choreographer, she found great acclaim with her work on "Solid Gold"—including Emmy nominations and a "Salute" on the 1984 Emmy Awards show. She progressed to the ranks of producer-director with continuing high-energy live productions, also raising two sons. In a *Drama-Logue* interview (May 19–25, 1994), she said: "Work breeds work, and I can honestly say I can't wait to get to work each day. I love what I do and thank God I get the chance to do it."

Stage: *Applause* (Long Beach CLO)

TV (Partial listing): "Solid Gold" (four seasons), "Top of the Month" ('72), "The Cher Show" ('75–76), "The New Zoo Revue," "The Keane Brothers Show" ('77); "The Muppets Go Hollywood" ('78, Emmy nom), 47th Academy Awards Show, "Entertainment Tonight" Tenth Anniversary Show (also prod, dir), "Perry Mason — The Silenced Singer," "Full House," "Miss Teen America Pageant," "The Smothers Brothers Show," "Super Night at the Super Bowl," "People's Choice Awards," "1981 Grammy Hall of Fame," "Golden Globe Awards" ('81), "The Jacksons," "The Muppets Go Hollywood" (Emmy nom), commercials for McDonald's, Manning House Coffee, Campbell's Soup, Winston Cigarettes, American Dairy Association

Music Video: "My Potential Boyfriend"— Dolly Parton; directed videos for Jane Fonda and Ozzy Osborne

Nightclub/Concert (Partial listing): *Doug Hen-*

ning Live on Stage (LV Hilton), *A.M. A Blast from the Past* (also dir, prod, '86–88, Hollywood, LV, Atlantic City), Engelbert Humperdinck World Tour (also dir, prod, '86–90), *Swing, Swing, Swing* (also dir, prod, Atlantic City '92, LV '93), *Hot Stuff* (Sands Hotel, LV '93–94), *A Blast from the Past* (Harvey's, Lake Tahoe '94); acts for Horace Heidt, Jr., the Pointer Sisters, Nancy Sinatra, Frankie Valli and the Four Seasons

Miscellaneous: *Sesame Street Live* ('80–81, touring Arena show, also dir), *Showtime America* and *The World's Greatest Illusions* (Busch Gardens), industrial for Chrysler (also dir, '88), *Soultown* (Disneyland '89, also dir), Royal Caribbean and Costa Cruise lines ('91–93, also prod, dir), NBC Affiliate Convention ('76–94), *The Mighty Morphin Power Rangers* (touring arena show, 94–95, also dir)

Film:

1965 **Love and Kisses**— Univ (also appeared)

1975 **The Legend of Valentino**— Spelling/Goldberg Prod. (TV)

1981 **The Great Muppet Caper**— Univ

1990 **The Lemmon Sisters**— Miramax

BURCH MANN (HOLTZMAN)

b. Wise County, Texas, August 16, 1908

d. Cedar City, Utah, June 25, 1996

Born and raised on her father's farm forty miles west of Dallas, she began dance studies when the family moved to Oklahoma. After graduation from high school she moved to New York, where she studied with Adolph Bolm, Michael Fokine and Mikhail Mordkin, beginning her professional career touring with Mordkin's company. While dancing in Lucia Chase's company (which eventually became the New York City Ballet) she made her solo choreographic debut at the Latin Quarter in New York. After choreographing for nightclubs and performing in and choreographing short films (Soundies) at the Edison studios in Brooklyn in the 1940s, she began the Burch Mann Dancers. In 1960 she opened a dance studio in Pasadena, California, and her company evolved into the American Folk Ballet in 1962 in which she used her classical background and training and adapted it to express American folk and social dance in a new form. "Folk history is the record of a people. It reveals a way of life, spiritual longings that are permanent, unchanging, universal... I wanted the dance company to capture the time of America's innocence when the people were like the land: open and generous, swift-springing and full of motion, industrious and honest: when a man's word was his bond." Since the group's inception it has dazzled audiences

Anita Mann (seated in front) danced with this collection of the "Hottest" dancers of the late '60s performing Toni Basil's staging in **The Cool Ones** (Warner Bros., 1967). From left to right: Terry (soon to be "Teri") Garr, Tom Cahill, Melanie Alexander, Debbie Watson, Gil Peterson, Jimmy Hibbard and Steve Ciro.

around the country and in historic appearances in Israel and Leningrad, Russia. Walt Disney saw the dance company and hired Ms. Mann to create dance on film at his studios. In 1982 she moved the company's headquarters to Cedar City, Utah, where she also served as a Distinguished Artist in Residence at Southern Utah State College. Among the many awards she received for her unique dance work were the George Washington Freedom Foundation Medal and the Dance in Action Award.

Stage: Cinderella (Cal. '67)

TV: "The Mickey Mouse Club" ('55), The Ed Sullivan Show, 43rd Annual Academy Awards Show ('70), American Spirit Special ('75)

Nightclub/Concert: Production numbers for the Latin Quarter, Havana-Madrid and Martinique (NY), the Mayfair (Boston)

Ballet/Dance Pieces (Partial listing for her own company): "Ox Driver's Song," "Unfenced Land," Indian Suite," "Dumbarton's Drums," "Sons and Daughters of Scotia," "Play Party at Stud Odom's Place," "Shady Grove," "Cotton Pickers," "River Baptizing," "Grand Ball at the Wingate Plantation," "Blues in My Heart," "Hot House Rag"; works for the Festival of the American West, Logan, Utah

Film:
1944 **Stepping Fast**— Soundies Corp. (S) (with The Burch Mann Dancers)
       Too Many Sailors— Soundies Corp. (S) (with The Burch Mann Dancers)
1976 **The Treasure of Matecumbe**— Disney

DANA MANNO
1976 **Leadbelly**— Par (also appeared)

CARMELITA MARACCI
b. Montevideo, Uruguay, 1911
d. Hollywood, California, July 26, 1987
Described as "one of the great dance figures of our time," this fabled Spanish dancer, teacher and American dance innovator was born of Italian-German parentage into a family of opera singers. The family moved to California when Carmelita was a child and she began studying modern with Anita Peters Wright at the age of 13, continuing with ballet with Luigi Albertieri and Enrico Zanfretta and Spanish dance with Hyppolito Mora. She quickly switched her energies to Spanish dance, interpreting it in her own unique style and integrating it

with classic dance in her choreography. While touring with her own company she made her New York dance debut at the YMHA Theatre in 1937. Becoming disillusioned by performing, she began teaching in Hollywood. During her nearly fifty-five years of teaching ballet, she became the mentor and inspiration for several generations of dancers and choreographers (among them Erik Bruhn, Leslie Caron, Agnes DeMille, Cynthia Gregory, Julie Newmar, Jerome Robbins and Donald Saddler). At the time of her death *Dance Magazine* wrote: "Once in a perverse while, a gifted artist manages to pass through this world almost unseen and unknown … Maracci, with her depth of imagination and theatrical daring, materialized in public view only briefly (Nov., 1987)." Her vision ("A dancer is not a robot. A dancer must have something to say, and say it…") lives on through her students.

Biography: A section of *Portrait Gallery* by Agnes DeMille (1990)

Ballet/Dance Pieces (Partial listing): "Piéce en Forme de Habañera" ('32), "Cantes Hondos," "Spain Cries Out," "Pavanna," "Viva Tu Madre," "The Nightingale and the Maiden," "Etude," "Cantine," "Fandanguillo," "Gavotta Vivace," "Life in the Raw España," "Narrative of the Bull Ring," "Rondo," "Circo de España" ('51, for Ballet Theatre)

Film:
1944 **Three Caballeros**—Disney (with Billy Daniel, Aloysio Oliveria)
1952 **Limelight**—UA (with Charles Chaplin, Andre Eglevsky, Melissa Hayden—ensembles by Maracci)

CAROLINE MARCADE

1995 **Up Down Fragile (Haut Bas Fragile)**—Pan Europenne

CLAUDE MARCHANT (MERCHANT-BROWN)

b. Charleston, South Carolina

Raised in Mt. Vernon, New York, and with only a few Irish Jig lessons and stage experience in a high school minstrel show, Marchant went to Manhattan to work in a feather factory at the age of 18. Classes in Harlem with Archie Savage led him to study with Katherine Dunham. Joining her legendary company in 1940 (where she gave him the stage name of "Marchant"), he appeared in *Cabin in the Sky* on Broadway, on film in **Carnival of Rhythm** ('41) and **Stormy Weather** ('43) and toured in nightclub, concert and theater performances. He would continue and enrich his dance vocabulary over the years studying with George Balanchine, Nenette Charisse, Lester Horton, José

Limon and Charles Weidman. Leaving Dunham and forming his own company in 1945, he also danced on Broadway in a revival of *Show Boat* ('46), on tour in *Caribbean Carnival*, at the Apollo Theatre and Carnegie Hall, for the Opening Ceremonies of the United Nations ('49) and multiple venues. In 1955 he relocated to Europe to act, sing and dance on stage, in nightclubs, TV, film (**Cleopatra, The Bible, Boccaccio '70, Juliet of the Spirits, Reflections in a Golden Eye**, etc.) and choreograph for Italian stage and films. He began teaching and created another dance company, with heiress Doris Duke studying and performing with the group. In 1967, Marchant was invited to help create a Ballet Academy at the University of Goteburg and in 1968 he headed the Ballet Academy Kursuerksamheten, both in Goteborg, Sweden, where he also formed the Marchant Dance Theater. Returning periodically to the U.S., he was given the Thelma Hill Performing Arts Center Men in Dance Award in 1981 and conducted workshops and seminars in Houston, Texas ('88, '90). For educating and inspiring scores of future dance artists, he has twice been recognized for his achievements in dance and dance education by the city of Goteburg, where he currently lives and teaches at The Dancehouse.

Stage: *Io e la Margherita* (Rome, Milan, '58–'60, also appeared); *Dark of the Moon* (Teatro del Servi, Italy, '61); *The Mysteries* (Rome, '62); *The Odyssey* and *Barouffa a Chioggia* (Villefrance, '68)

Ballet/Dance Pieces (Partial listing): "El Shango" ('46), "El Campesino," "Slave Suite," "Drum Dances," "Cuban Rhythms," "Brazilian Airs"; (Over 50 works for the Marchant Dance Theater incl.) "A Century of Popular Dance," "Don't Stop the Carnival," "God Rock," "I Got Rhythm," "Right On," "Salute to Duke," "Yerma," You Belong to the Night,""Bolero," Jazz Suite:"Le Jazz Hot!" ('90)

Nightclub/Concert: "Carnival" (UNICEF gala, '79); multiple revues for the Scandanavian Enskilda Bank ('87–95)

Miscellaneous: *Ice-Capades* ('48)

Film:
1959 **Sign of the Gladiator** (aka **Nel Segno di Roma**)—AIP (also appeared)
1967 **The Witches** (aka **La Streghe**)—Lopert

JEANNE MARIE

1986 **Stark—Mirror Image**—CBS Ent Prod (TV)

RUSSELL (ELDRIDGE) MARKERT

b. Westfield, New Jersey, August 8, 1899

d. Waterbury, Connecticut, December 1, 1990

Dancer-choreographer who is renowned as the creator of The Rockettes, the American equivalent of the famed English line dance group, The Tiller Girls. After serving in the Army during World War I, Markert began his dance training with Thelma Entwhistle in Brooklyn and started his career on Broadway when Sammy Lee selected him for the chorus of *Earl Carroll's Vanities of 1923*. While dancing in the next *Vanities*, he assisted David Bennett and moonlighted by entering Charleston contests. Sammy Lee, now Markert's agent, got him a job staging the numbers at Connie's Inn, a popular Harlem nightspot and introduced him to the Skouras brothers, Spyros and Charlie, who needed a dance director to create stage presentations at their Grand Central Theater in St. Louis. He went to St. Louis and started a line of girls (The Missouri Rockets — eventually becoming The Rockets) which played Publix Theaters and the Balaban and Katz circuit. Markert was asked to be the director of a precision dance line called The Roxyettes at New York's Roxy Theater in 1925 and the line went into several Broadway shows in 1928. In 1929, John Murray Anderson invited Markert to Hollywood, where, after his great success with **King of Jazz**, he was offered a contract to be dance director at both Samuel Goldwyn and Fox studios. Instead, he decided to return to New York to serve as dance director for the about-to-open Radio City Music Hall ("I've always wondered what my career would have been like had I accepted… But I turned down the offer. I missed my dancing troupe and wanted to see how my girls were doing.") When the spectacular Movie/Entertainment Palace opened in December, 1932, The Rockettes were born. For the next forty years Markert (assisted by Gene Snyder and Violet Holmes) created dance routines for his famous line of girls and alternated with Leon Leonidoff producing the shows at the Music Hall. He also produced *Roller Skating Vanities of 1948*, *Holiday on Ice* and *Ice-Capades*. He retired in 1972 with long-time assistant Violet Holmes continuing his work and legacy with the world-reknowned Rockettes.

Stage: *Greenwich Village Follies, Americana, Animal Crackers, Hello Daddy, Just a Minute* and *Rain or Shine* (Bdwy '28), *George White's Scandals of 1928 & 1936* (Bdwy), *Keep It Clean* (Bdwy '29), *Here Comes the Bride* (Bdwy '31), *George White's Music Hall Varieties* (Bdwy '32), Radio City Music Hall ('32–71), *Say When* (Bdwy '34)

Nightclub/Concert: Act for Dixie Dunbar

Miscellaneous: *Ice-Capades* ('41), *Roller Skating Vanities of 1946* (with Gae Foster), *Holiday on Ice* ('52)

Film:

1930 **King of Jazz** — Univ (with John Murray Anderson)

1934 **George White's Scandals of 1934** — Fox (with Chester Hale)

      Moulin Rouge — UA

GERRY MAROTSKI

1982 **I Love You** — Atlantic

DIANE MARTEL

1989 **Bloodhounds of Broadway** — Col

1993 **Life with Mikey** — Touchstone

GEORGE AND ETHEL MARTIN

George: b. Canton, Ohio, September 17, 1924

Ethel: b. New York, New York

Another of those rare husband-and-wife teams whose talent and working relationship allowed them solo creative contributions as well as collaborations in many performance mediums. George began his dance studies with William Reynolds in Canton, Ohio, and when he moved to New York he studied with Margaret Craske, David Lichine, Madame Swoboda and a creative genius who would greatly influence his life and career — Jack Cole. He spent the summer of 1942 at Jacob's Pillow on a scholarship and made his Broadway debut in *Lady in the Dark* that same year. He moved to the West Coast to appear in *The Waltz King* ('43), where he met Ethel at Republic Studios in 1944 on the set of **The Yellow Rose of Texas.** Ethel had made her professional debut as a child with her family in their vaudeville act. She began her dance lessons with tap from Sammy Burns and eventually Jazz and East Indian with Cole and classical Spanish with Carmelita Maracci. After making her Broadway debut in 1942 in *Let Freedom Ring* she and George became an integral part of Cole's legendary dance group, appearing in many films at Columbia and touring in their sensational nightclub act. After working in Cole's *Magdalena* on the West Coast and its brief Broadway run, George joined Kay Thompson's club act ('49–50) while Ethel appeared at the Lido de Paris. After Cole featured both of them on film (with Gwen Verdon) in **On the Riviera,** Ethel returned to the Broadway stage in *Something for the Boys* in 1951. In 1952, they both danced in a revival of *Pal Joey*, where George assisted Robert Alton. As Jack Cole had deserted Hollywood and the dying film musical, the Martins relocated permanently to New York. George worked continually on Broadway in *Carnival in Flanders* ('53), *Kismet* ('54, with Ethel), *The Ziegfeld Follies* ('56, assisting Cole), *Happy Hunting* ('57), *Rumple* ('58), *Kean* and *Donnybrook* ('61, assisting Cole), *A Funny Thing Happened on the Way to the Forum* ('62, with Ethel, assisting Cole) and *Zorba* ('68). Ethel's other

Broadway appearances include *New Girl in Town* ('57), *The Desert Song* ('58 rev) and *Foxy* ('64, assisting Cole). In 1968, Ethel created Four M Productions, Inc. and as president she produces video, multimedia, film, special events and live musical presentations for major corporations. With his extensive expertise of dance and musical theater, George became Production Stage Manager for many Broadway successes (*Follies, A Little Night Music, Evita, 42nd Street,* etc.), directing many of them internationally.

Stage: (George): *Pal Joey* (London '53), *Kismet* (London '55), *A Funny Thing Happened on the Way to the Forum* (recreation of Jack cole's original work, LV '64), *A Little Night Music* (London '73). (Ethel only): *The Selling of the President* (Bdwy '72, assisted by Rick Atwell), *Chapeau* (Bdwy '77), *Starting Here, Starting Now* (OB '77), *Lallapalousa* (NY Shakespeare Festival), *You're the Top* (NY, also dir), *Annie* (Australia, also dir), *Take One Step* (NY), *Company in Concert* (Long Beach CLO and NY '93)

TV: (Ethel only): "Electric Circus," "We the Women," the Ed Sullivan and Perry Como shows, "50th Anniversary of the Grand Ole Opry," "Look Up and Live," Daytime Emmy Awards Show.

Nightclub/Concert: *House of Love* (Dunes, LV '61, Ethel only)

Ballet/Dance Pieces: Recreated Cole's work for American Dance Machine (Ethel)

Miscellaneous: Industrials for Milliken ('63–66, both); George only: G.E. ('66–67), RCA ('66), Ford ('68).

Film:
1966 **A Funny Thing Happened on the Way to the Forum**— UA (adapting Jack Cole's original choreography)

LEE ANN MARTIN
1988 **Last Rites**— MGM (with Michelle Assaf)

BEATRICE MASSIN
1995 **Jefferson in Paris**— Touchstone (with Elizabeth Aldrich, "Dardanus" credit)

LÉONIDE MASSINE (LEONID FEDOROVITCH MIASSINE)
b. Moscow, Russia, August 8, 1895
d. Cologne, Germany, March 16, 1979
This classical ballet dancer and choreographer who was a dominant figure in international ballet in the 1930s and '40s once said: "To build movement in film, you can only show fragments of movement ... it is hard to obtain the feeling of depth ...

but for the individual dancer it is perhaps a greater showcase for his abilities." Born of a theatrical family, he studied acting and dancing at the Imperial School in Moscow with Enrico Cecchetti, Domashoff and Nicholas Legat. In 1913 he was discovered by Diaghilev (who "chanced to notice the way a fifteen-year-old boy walked across a stage") and was asked to join his company, making the decision for him between dance and acting. Diaghilev planned to train Massine as Nijinsky's replacement and he made his debut in 1914 in Fokine's ***Legende de Joseph*** at the Paris Opera, and was one of the sensations of Diaghilev's Ballets Russe. After Diaghilev's death, Massine debuted in America at the Roxy Theater. He danced with the Ballets Russes De Monte Carlo ('33–41, also ballet master and artistic director), Ballet National Theater ('41–44) and organized Massine's Highlights ('45–46). He had first choreographed at the age of 18 for the Russian Ballet and went on to create masterpieces for Ballet Theatre, Ballets Russes de Monte-Carlo and Sadler's Wells. While working on his first original film assignment, **Carnival in Costa Rica**, he spoke about his goals in the August, 1946 issue of *Dance Magazine*: "...to bring dancing to such a realistic point where all those concerned ... will forget the word 'ballet' ... to introduce dynamical dancing—in other words, to put more life in it. Everything so far has been artificial, static, staged... The time is approaching when ballet will break into motion pictures full strength. When that happens, we shall really go to town!"— prophesizing the impact **The Red Shoes** would have two years later. He had recorded all of his major dance works on 16mm film, so was no stranger to the camera. Massine is considered one of the legendary Russian dancers and choreographers and his works continue to be performed by Ballet companies around the world. Author of *Massine on Choreography* (1976), some of his finest works are captured on commercial film for all to see.

Autobiography: *My Life in Ballet* (1968)

Related Works: *Massine on Choreography* (1976)

Stage: *Still Dancing* (London '25), Roxy Theater (NY '28, also appeared), *Helen Goes to Troy* (Bdwy '44), *Vincent Youman's Ballet Revue* (OOT '44), *Vie La Parisienne* (NYC Center, '45), *Bullet in the Ballet* (London '46, also appeared)

TV: "Laudes Evangeli" ('62)

Ballet/Dance Pieces (72 works — Partial listing): "Soleil de Nuit" ('15), "Parade," "The Three Cornered Hat," "Le Sacre Du Printemps," "Le Belle Helene," "Symphonie Fantastique," "Gaite Parisienne," "Le Beau Danube," "Capriccio Espagnol," "Bacchanale," "Vienna 1814," "Saratoga," "Theme and Variations," "Clock Symphony," "La Valse," "Les Matelots," "Mercure," "Harold in Italy," "The New Yorker," "Rouge et Noir," "Choreartium,"

Léonide Massine soars through the air in **The Tales of Hoffman** (Lopert, 1965, choreographed by Sir Frederick Ashton).

"The Fall of the House of Usher," "The Good Humored Ladies" ('62)

Film:

1941 **The Gay Parisian**— WB (S) (Filmed version of *Gaieté Parisienne*)

        Spanish Fiesta— WB (S) (Filmed version of his *Capriccio Espagnol*)

1947 **Carnival in Costa Rica**— Fox (also appeared, assisted by Robert Bell)

1948 **The Red Shoes**— Rank (with Robert Helpmann, also appeared)

1951 **Neopolitan Carousel** (aka **Hurdy Gurdy**)— Gau/Brit (also appeared)

1959 **Honeymoon (Luna De Miel)**— (GB/Span) (with Antonio)

DAVID MASSINGHAM

1992 **Just Like a Woman**— Rank

TORRANCE MATHIS

Martial arts choreographer.

1985 **The Last Dragon**—TriStar (with Ernie Reyes, Sr. and Ron Van Clief)

ERNST MATRAY

b. Budapest, Hungary, 1891
d. Los Angeles, California, November 12, 1978

Multi-talented actor, director, screenwriter, producer and dance director. With a theatre-owner father and opera-singer mother, Ernst began acting in his teens and legendary German director Max Reinhardt persuaded his parents to allow him to study at the Deutsche Theatre in Berlin. From Reinhardt, he learned to choreograph crowd scenes and after many stage appearances in Reinhardt productions, he made his film debut in Reinhardt's **Venetian Night** in 1912. Forming his own film company in Berlin in 1913, Matray wrote, directed and starred in German films for over two decades, introducing Reinhardt colleague Ernst Lubitsch to films. He began his next career as a dance director and toured Great Britain and the United States with his own theater ensemble and dance group. Because of the success of his line of girls in American vaudeville (The Matray Ballet) he was signed by MGM in 1936 as a dance director and to appear as an actor in films. Despite his illustrious European dramatic stage and film career, he was to achieve success in American films as a dance director. At MGM he usually collaborated with his second wife, German actress-writer Maria Solveg, and their film choreography was mostly Eastern European-flavored folk dances and ballet sequences, along with coaching such non-dancing stars as Vivian Leigh for her role as a ballerina in **Waterloo Bridge** ('40) and Joan Crawford for her Swedish folk dance in **A Woman's Face** ('41). Matray continued screenwriting, one of his last scripts being the 1962 film **The Cabinet of Dr. Caligari**. He and Maria divorced in 1979 and she moved to Munich. He remarried and remained in touch with the film industry through the Hollywood Foreign Press until his death at the age of 87.

Stage: Multiple revues for Charles Cochran (London), *A la Carte* (OOT '46), *Pardon Our French* (Bdwy '50, with Maria Matray), *Parisian Life* (Vienna)

Film:
1938 **Sweethearts**— MGM (with Ray Bolger, Albertina Rasch)
1939 **Balalaika**— MGM (with Nico Charisse)
1940 **Bittersweet**— MGM
     Dance, Girl, Dance— RKO
     Florian— MGM (with Maria)
     Pride and Prejudice— MGM (also appeared)
     Waterloo Bridge— MGM (with Maria)
1941 **The Chocolate Soldier**— MGM
     Dr. Jekyll and Mr. Hyde— MGM
     A Woman's Face— MGM
1942 **I Married an Angel**— MGM (with Maria)
     Random Harvest— MGM
     The Seven Sweethearts— MGM
     White Cargo— MGM (with Maria)
1943 **Higher and Higher**— RKO
     The Human Comedy— MGM
     Presenting Lily Mars— MGM (with Charles Walters)
     Swing Fever— MGM (with Maria, Merriel Abbott)
1944 **Adventure in Musik** (Ger)
     Step Lively— RKO (with George Murphy)
1945 **Delightfully Dangerous**— UA
     George White's Scandals— RKO
1955 **Musik, Musik und Nur Musik** (Ger)

BRIGITTE MATTEUZI
1994 **Trois Couleurs: Rouge (Three Colors: Red)** (Fr/Swiss/Pol)

DARRYL MATTHEWS
1993 **Wrestling Ernest Hemingway**— WB

JESSIE MATTHEWS
b. London, England, March 11, 1907
d. London, England, August 20, 1981

Born into a poverty-stricken Soho family of 16 children, Jessie Matthews used her singing, dancing and comedy talents to leave her impoverished beginnings far behind and become England's "Dancing Divinity" and their top film star of the 1930s. A natural dancer ("I was a born dancer. It was something that was quite obvious—like breathing. As a child I did want to be an actress, but dancing was something I inherently loved, something I just did") she made her stage debut in *Bluebell in Fairyland* at the Alhambra Theatre in London at the age of 10. While appearing in Pantomimes, she formally studied dance with Elise Clare and at 15, appeared in *Music Box Revue* in 1923, for impressario Charles Cochran. She performed mime in silent films (**Straws in the Wind** and **The Beloved Vagabond**) and was cast in *Andre Charlot's Revue* which played London, New York and toured the U.S. and Canada. When the star, Gertrude Lawrence, became ill, Matthews replaced her and was soon elevated to a featured member of the cast. Other successful stage shows include *This Year of Grace* and *Awake and Dream* (her Broadway debut) with her first husband, Henry Lytton. Her greatest stage success in 1930, *Evergreen* (where she first worked with her future choreographic collaborator, Buddy Bradley), led to a longterm film contract with Gaumont British films. With her enchanting blend of ballet and rhythm tap, she choreographed her own routines on stage and film ("Rhythm dancing is a man's dance because it's so heavy with rhythm ... when a woman does it, it is usually ugly. I got away with it by adding Arabesques, spins and jumps to make it look expensive"—*Dance Magazine*, Sept., 1966). Her film musicals were so successful, several were imported to play Radio City Music Hall in New York. When Fred Astaire decided to do a film without Ginger Rogers, Matthews was the international film industry's obvious choice for **A Damsel in Distress** (1937). Instead, RKO cast a young contract actress, Joan Fontaine — and the rest is movie history (infamy?). Her next husband, Sonnie Hale, took over directing her films in 1937 and her success began to dwindle. After a non-musical film **Climbing High** (1938) and a comeback attempt in a low-budget thriller (**Candles at Nine**, 1944), she retired from the screen to raise an adopted daughter, Catherine, and work in repertory theater. In 1958, she played a small role in **Tom Thumb** and in 1963, was a member of the cast of a BBC radio soap opera, "The

Dale Family," which hired for 20 years. In 1966, the New York Gallery of Modern Art presented a retrospective of her musical films, but the public never fully recognized her choreographic contributions to dance on film. When asked about her inspirations, she named Tilly Losch, Margot Fonteyn, Alicia Markova and Fred Astaire: "While I admire Gene Kelly's technique and tremendous stride when he glides, Fred is fluent, graceful, gorgeous. He's only got to walk and he's dancing." What a pity the two never got to share their greatness on the permanence of film.

Autobiography: *Over My Shoulder* (1974)

Film: (Credits are for her solo routines, while Bradley choreographed the other dances)

1933 **Good Companions**— Gau/Brit (with Buddy Bradley)

1934 **Evergreen**— Gau/Brit (with Bradley)

1935 **First a Girl**— Gau/Brit (with Bradley, Ralph Reeder)

1936 **It's Love Again**— Gau/Brit (with Bradley)

1937 **Gangway**— Gau/Brit (with Bradley)

    Head Over Heels in Love— Gau/Brit (with Bradley)

1938 **Sailing Along**— Gau/Brit (with Bradley)

JAMES (JOHN/JOHNNY) MATTISON

b. Bayonne, New Jersey

Described in *Who's Who in Dance, 1940* as, "Tap, musical comedy, ballroom, eccentric and ballet dancer and teacher," Mattison had over twelve year's performing experience in vaudeville, movie shorts, prologues and nightclubs by that time. He began to produce vaudeville acts and units and numbers for Broadway shows ("through which he has become noted as a creator of original ideas and routines"). He danced in films (**Yankee Doodle Dandy**, etc.) and served as assistant at Warner Bros., RKO and MGM before being named dance director at Universal. After four films, he was succeeded by Louis DaPron. His teaching career eventually became his main focus and students over the years included Dan Dailey, Dixie Dunbar, Ray & Grace McDonald and John "Bubbles" Sublett (of Buck and Bubbles). His film credits are all within one year, so it assumed he concentrated on coaching and teaching. His daughter, Ethelyn, followed in her father's tap steps.

Stage: *Sea Legs* (Bdwy '37)

Film:

1942 **Broadway**— Univ

    Give Out Sisters— Univ

    Private Buckaroo— Univ

    What's Cookin'?— Univ

MATT (HAROLD HENRY) MATTOX

b. Tulsa, Oklahoma, August 18, 1921

"I've never classified myself as a jazz teacher, I prefer to talk about 'free-style dancing,' which means I have a choice of movement for any piece of music," said Mattox in a 1993 interview. To prepare for his career as one of America's leading stage and film dancers in the 1950s, Mattox started dance lessons at 11 ("5–6 years of tap and then I started ballet — and loved it!") studying with Ernest Belcher, Nico Charisse, Jack Cole, Louis Da Pron and Eugene Loring. After attending San Bernardino College and serving as a pilot in the Army during World War II, he made his Broadway debut in 1946 in *Are You with It?* Auditioning for Robert Alton in 1944, he was contracted by MGM to dance in their films. Being asked to join The Jack Cole Dancers at the age of 28, he appeared on Broadway in *Magdalena* ('48) and many films for Cole (**Gentlemen Prefer Blondes, The "I Don't Care" Girl**, etc.). Other appearances on Broadway include *Carnival in Flanders* ('53), *The Vamp* ('55), *Ziegfeld Follies* (OOT '56) and *Once Upon a Mattress* ('59) with LACLO roles in *Louisiana Purchase* ('47), *Three Wishes for Jamie* ('51), *The Song of Norway* ('52) and *Brigadoon* ('54).

In 1951 he created the dances for an Australian production of *Song of Norway* and received his first Broadway solo credit with *Say Darling* ('58). With his masculine, dark, good looks and strong dancing style, he was featured in films (**The Band Wagon, Dreamboat, The Girl Rush, Pepe, Seven Brides for Seven Brothers**, etc.) before retiring from performing in the '60s, creating a dance company and opening a studio in New York. He was one of the most sought-after dance teachers in Los Angeles and New York for many years and then, moved to London in 1970, to teach at the London Dance Centre and appear with his group JazzArt. The father of two daughters, his homebase has been France since 1975.

Stage: *Song of Norway* (Australia '51), *Out of Our Minds* (LA '53), *Say Darling* (Bdwy '58, also appeared), *The Pink Jungle* (OOT '59), **Aïda** (Metropolitan Opera, '59), *A Short Happy Life* (OOT '61), *Jennie* (Bdwy '63), *What Makes Sammy Run?* (Bdwy '64)

TV: Railroad Hour Series pilot ('53), "Crescendo" ('57, asst to Eugene Loring), "The Good Years" ('62), Bell Telephone Hour ('64)

Nightclub/Concert: Production numbers for the New Frontier Hotel (LV '56), *Revue La Parisienne* (Dunes Hotel, LV '60), act for Buddy Bryan and Joan Larkin ('53)

Ballet/Dance Pieces: "The Wild Party" ('61), "Birds" (Oslo, '75), multiple works for JazzArt

Film:
1953 **The Glory Brigade**— Fox
1956 **Hot Blood**— Col (with Sylvia Lewis, also appeared as "dance-in" for male star Cornell Wilde)

MAGGY MAXWELL
1969 **The Prime of Miss Jean Bodie**— Fox

MAYURA
Classic East Indian dance specialist.
Film:
1947 **Black Narcissus**— Archer Prod

STAN MAZIN
After graduating from high school in Philadelphia, Mazin attended the University of Miami. He began jazz, tap and ballet classes with Jack Stanly and decided to make dance his career, going on to study with Sevilla Fort, Aubrey Hitchins, Matt Mattox, Jack Potteiger and Sallie Whelan over the years. He went to New York and first danced in a jazz group headed by Claude Thompson and Jaime Rogers. Making his professional Broadway debut in 1964 in *High Spirits*, other stage appearances include *Bajour*, *The Boy Friend*, *Holly Golightly*, *How to Succeed in Business...*, *Walking Happy*, *West Side Story* and *Where's Charley?*. Mazin danced in Mitzi Gaynor's nightclub act and in films: **The Best Little Whorehouse in Texas**, **The Blues Brothers**, **History of the World — Part 1**, **Mame**, **Newsies** and **Pennies from Heaven**. TV appearances include multiple Oscar and Emmy Awards shows, "Laverne and Shirley" and ten seasons on "The Carol Burnett Show" as a member of the popular Ernest Flatt Dancers. He made his professional choreographic debut in 1979 with the stage work *Festival*.
  Stage: Jesus Christ Superstar (Harbor College, Cal '75), *Festival* (OB '79), *Walls* (LA, Robby Award — and Burt Reynolds Theater, Fla '82), *Guys and Dolls* (San Diego, *Drama-Logue* Award), *Chicago* (West Coast, '84, Robby and *Drama-Logue* Awards), *Anything Goes* (Long Beach CLO '87), *Bells Are Ringing* (West Coast '89, also dir), *Dames at Sea* (Long Beach CLO, also dir)
  TV: "Michael Nesmith's Television Parts," "Sister Kate," "Mama's Family," "Mr. Belvedere," "Babes"
  Nightclub/Concert: "Provoce," "Gershwin Show," "My Fairfax Lady," "Footlighters Ball" (Beverly Hilton, LA '81–92)
  Film:
1985 **Lust in the Dust**— New World

ALLEN MEACHAM
1965 **Man in the Dark**— Univ

MICHAEL MEACHAM
1984 **The Cotton Club**— Orion (with Claudia Asbury, Gregory Hines, Henry LeTang, Arthur Mitchell, Michael Smuin)

ANA MEDEM
1993 **La Ardilla Roja (The Red Squirrel)**— Sogetel

ALBERTO MENDEZ
1989 **The Spectre of War**—(Nicaragua)

ANA MERIDA
1989 **Old Gringo**— Col

STEVE MERRITT
b. San Jose, California, 1945
d. Los Angeles, California, January 24, 1993
  One of the leaders of erotic dance on stage and film, Merritt also was responsible for encouraging the careers of many, young budding choreographers (Jerry Evans, Peggy Holmes, Jeffrey Hornaday, etc.). He began his professional career as a dancer in Las Vegas and a member of Ann-Margret's nightclub act (also his first choreographic assignment in the early '70s) and continued with club work, combining jazz with street dance to create high-energy pieces. He then spent six years with "Televisa" in Mexico City, creating music videos and TV shows. In 1975 he formed a group of male dancers (Larry Cole, Jerry Evans, Jeffrey Hornaday and Tim Michaels) titled Friends, who appeared with Petula Clark in clubs and on television. While rehearsing, he said in *Dance Magazine*, "I choreograph from the solar plexus" with the writer commenting "...and that's where his dancers hit the spectator too." His work in **Gimme an "F"** contains one of the few sensual male dance routines in the history of American film and he staged the controversial Snow White/Rob Lowe 1988 Academy Award Ceremony Opening Number. He also contributed to the legacy of *Chippendales*, the landmark live dance show which celebrated male sensuality before his untimely death from AIDS.
  Stage (All as director-choreographer): *Beach Blanket Babylon* (Club Fugazi, SF '79–93), *Jukebox* (London '82), *Dream Street* (OOT '84), *Stars on 45* (LA), *The Chippendales* (London '91), *Night Dreams* (SF '92)
  TV: "The Midnight Special," Bill Cosby Special, "The Tonight Show with Johnny Carson," "The Mike Douglas Show," a Bing Crosby Christmas Special ('75), 61st Academy Awards Show ('88)

Mitzi Gaynor is flanked by two future choreographers: Marc Wilder (L) and Matt Mattox (R), as they sizzle in Jack Cole's highly enjoyable — and highly historically incorrect — "Comedia De'l Arte" version of "The Johnson Rag" in **The "I Don't Care" Girl** (20th Century–Fox, 1953).

Music Video: "Tall, Dark and Handsome" — The Chippendales ('87)

Nightclub/Concert: Vive Paris Vive (Aladdin Hotel, LV '74), *Dream Street* (Dunes Hotel, LV '81), Chippendales Revues (*Welcome to My Fantasy*, etc., 1986–93), *Night Dreams* (Dunes Hotel, LV '91); acts for Petula Clark, Sammy Davis, Jr., Friends, Tom Jones, Liza Minnelli and Pia Zadora

Miscellaneous: Industrials for IBM, Campbell Soup, Cadillac

Film:

1979 **Portrait of a Stripper** — Moonlight Prod/Filmways/CBS (TV) (with Sarah Tayir, "Dance sequence" credit)

1985 **Gimme an "F"** — Fox (assisted by Peggy Holmes)

GILBERT MEUNIERE

1985 **Amazons** — ABC Circle Films

SHEILA MEYERS

Dancer-wife of Jack Baker who also assisted him.

Film:

1962 **The Road to Hong Kong** — UA (with Jack Baker)

The Scarface Mob — Desilu (with Baker)

WILLIAM MILIÉ

b. Pittsburgh, Pennsylvania, November 27, 1929

American dancer, teacher and choreographer who found a welcome niche for his creative talents in Europe. Milié began his show business career as an ice skater at the age of 4. At 18 he began studying ballet and moved to New York, where he attended the Katherine Dunham and Metropolitan Opera Ballet Schools, studying with Margaret Craske, Myra Kinch, José Limon, Ted Shawn and Anthony Tudor. Summer stock and Broadway shows led to an appearance at Jacob's Pillow. After touring Germany in 1958 with American Festival Ballet, he remained in Munich, where he was greatly in demand choreographing for stage, TV, industrials and films. He began his Broadway Jazz Ballet group in 1961 and founded Munich's Depot Dance Studio in 1972, pioneering in teaching young German talent modern jazz, tap, gymnastics and singing, to create the new generation of German musical performers. Winner of the first prize in the 1960 Munich Choreography competition and the Bronze Rose award in Montreux in 1961.

Stage: Kiss Me Kate (Vienna, Munich '73), *Jedermann* (Salzburg Festival '73)

TV: "Continental Showcase," "Carmina Burana" ('75)

Ballet/Dance Pieces: "The Man with the Hat"

Miscellaneous: Fashion shows for Christian Dior, Frankfurt Fur Show, *Triumph '70* (Triumph International Brassiere Company)

Film:

1974 **A Free Woman**— New Yorker
1980 **The Formula**— MGM/UA
1981 **The Tales of the Vienna Woods**— Cinema 5

ANN MILLER (JOHNNIE LUCILLE COLLIER)

b. Chireno, Texas, April 12, 1923

Dynamic dancing actress and singer whose personal rat-a-tat, mile-a-minute tap style warranted that she choreograph all of her solo routines herself. When she was 3, her mother enrolled her in dancing school to cure rickets, but ballet was not her forté. Seeing Bill "Bojangles" Robinson in a personal appearance in Houston when she was 8 made her set her sights on tap, with Robinson giving her a first tap lesson. She soon was performing in clubs and local theaters. Moving to Los Angeles, she enrolled in the Fanchon and Marco Dance School, appearing as an "Extra" in films and in the revue *All Aboard*. Other appearances in vaudeville theaters led to nightclub bookings including the Bal Tabarin in San Francisco — a three week engagement which was held over for 16 weeks — where she was spotted by Benny Rubin, an RKO talent scout, and budding actress Lucille Ball. Her first film appearances at RKO led her to Broadway to star in *George White's Scandals of 1939*, creating a sensation with the dance number "The Mexiconga." She then went into *Too Many Girls* and when that successful show was filmed, she returned to Hollywood. She began a seven year contract with Columbia starring in a succession of Wartime musicals, where her solo routines were always the highpoint. In 1947 she was contracted by MGM when she replaced injured Cyd Charisse in **Easter Parade** and her exceptional talents were finally used to full advantage. As the Movie Musical went into decline

she returned to the stage to star in *Mame, Anything Goes,* and created another Broadway sensation in *Sugar Babies* in 1979, also touring with the show for many years. Non-musical film appearances include **The Devil on Horseback, Stage Door, You Can't Take It with You, Room Service, Having a Wonderful Time, Watch the Birdie, The Opposite Sex** and **The Great American Pastime**. She created some of the Movie Musical's most memorable tap dance moments — in collaboration with other choreographers and dance directors Busby Berkeley, Nick Castle, Jack Cole, Willie Covan, Louis DaPron, Stanley Donen and Hermes Pan. Miss Miller recently was awarded the Golden Boot award by the Western Film Association and the Professional Dancers Society 1993 Gypsy Lifetime Achievement award with Mickey Rooney.

Autobiography: Miller's High Life (1972)

Biography: Ann Miller — Tops in Taps by Jim Connor (1981)

Stage: George White's Scandals of 1939 (Bdwy), *Mame* (Bdwy and ntl tour '66, with Onna White), *Sugar Babies* (Bdwy and ntl tour '79, with Ernest Flatt)

TV: "The Hollywood Palace" (with Nick Castle, Louis DaPron), "Dames at Sea" ('71, with Alan Johnson), Campbell's "Great American Soup" commercial

Film (Credits are for the creation of her solo routines):

1936 **The Devil on Horseback**— Grand Ntl
1937 **Life of the Party**— RKO (with Sammy Lee)
      New Faces of 1937— RKO (with Lee)
1938 **Radio City Revels**— RKO (with Hermes Pan, Joseph Santley)
      Tarnished Angel— RKO
1940 **The Hit Parade of 1941**— Rep (with Danny Dare)
      Melody Ranch— Rep (with Larry Ceballos)
      Too Many Girls— RKO (with Hal LeRoy, LeRoy Prinz)
1941 **Go West Young Lady**— Col (with Louis DaPron)
      Time Out for Rhythm— Col (with LeRoy Prinz)
1942 **Priorities on Parade**— Par (with Jack Donohue)
      True to the Army— Par (with Donohue)
1943 **Reveille with Beverly**— Col
      What's Buzzin' Cousin?— Col (with Nick Castle, Val Raset)
1944 **Carolina Blues**— Col (with Lee, the Four Step Bros.)
      Hey Rookie!— Col (with the Condos Bros., DaPron, Stanley Donen, Raset)

Ann Miller (at top), faces the male chorus, with Jack Cole at top right — once again filling in for an injured dancer — in this number from **Eadie Was a Lady** (Columbia, 1945).

Jam Session— Col (with Donen)
1945 **Eadie Was a Lady**— Col (with Jack Cole)
Eve Knew Her Apples— Col
1946 **The Thrill of Brazil**— Col (with Nick Castle, Cole, Eugene Loring, Frank Veloz)
1948 **Easter Parade**— MGM (with Robert Alton, Fred Astaire, Castle)
The Kissing Bandit— MGM (with Alton, Donen)
1949 **On the Town**— MGM (with Donen, Gene Kelly)
1951 **Texas Carnival**— MGM (with Pan)
Two Tickets to Broadway— RKO (with Busby Berkeley, Gower Champion)
1952 **Lovely to Look At**— MGM (with Champion, Pan)
1953 **Kiss Me Kate**— MGM (with Bob Fosse, Pan)
Small Town Girl— MGM (with Busby Berkeley, Wille Covan, Alex Romero)
1954 **Deep in My Heart**— MGM (with Kelly, Loring)
1955 **Hit the Deck**— MGM (with Pan)

1974 **That's Entertainment!**— MGM (with others)
1976 **That's Entertainment Part 2**— MGM (with others)
1985 **That's Dancing!**— MGM (with others)
1994 **That's Entertainment! III**— MGM (with others)

RHONDA MILLER

TV: "Parker Lewis," "The Boys," "The Garry Shandling Show" (HBO)
Film:
1993 **The Naked Truth**—?
The Reluctant Vampire—?

AUREL MILLOSS (UREL DE MIHOLY; AKA AUREL VON MILLOSS)

b. Ujozora, Hungary, May 12, 1906

d. Rome, Italy, September 21, 1988

Premier danseur and choreographer for the Budapest, Cologne, La Scala, Rio de Janeiro, Rome, San Carlo, Sao Paulo and Vienna State Opera Houses who is credited with elevating the interest in dance in Italy. After having his "moment of truth" as a child seeing Nijinsky dance, Milloss studied at the Ecole Blasis in Belgrade and with Victor Gsovsky, Rudolph von Laban and Mary Wigman in Germany. His first important professional appearance was at the Berlin Opera in 1928, where his staging of the anti-tyranny-themed **Gaukelei** caused him to flee Hitler — and Germany. He moved from Paris to Hungary and started his Italian career at the San Carlo Opera in Naples in 1937. Along with his prolific dance creations for opera, he also created works for the Ballets de Champs-Elysées, Grand Ballet du Marquis De Cuevas and England's Festival Ballet. In 1960, he was named director of the Cologne Opera House but returned to Italy in 1966. After living in Rome since 1938 — although Hungarian born — he became a naturalized Italian citizen.

Ballet/Dance Pieces (Partial listing — over 300): "H.M.S. Royal Oak" ('32), "La Follia di Orlando," "Coup de Feu," "Marsia," "Anguish," Pulcinella," "Aeneas," "The Miraculous Mandarin," "Portrait de Don Quichotte," "Le Creature di Prometeo," "L'Allegra Piazzata," "The Firebird" ('82)

Film:
1951 **Quo Vadis** — MGM (with Madi Oblensky)

ROGER (AKINOBU) MINAMI

b. Honolulu, Hawaii, June 16, 1941

Japanese-American dancer, designer, photographer, producer, director and choreographer who attained success with cabaret productions in Las Vegas and Atlantic City (producing the longest running revues and winning the most entertainment awards for his thirteen Resorts International Casino Hotel productions there). Moving from Hawaii to California when he was 11, a production of *Flower Drum Song* triggered his interest in theater and dance and he began studying with Eugene Loring at the American School of Dance, eventually joining the Loring Dance Players. After attending Long Beach State College, his professional career began with West Coast productions of *The Music Man, Can Can, Wish You Were Here, The Pajama Game, Bells Are Ringing* and finally, *Flower Drum Song*. As one of the Hollywood's most sought-after dancers, he appeared on TV as a regular on Dick Clark's "Where the Action Is" ('65, also assistant choreographer) and in Ann-Margret's premiere nightclub

act ('67). In the early Seventies he moved to Las Vegas to be featured in shows (*Tower Sweets Revue, A Bare Touch of Vegas*, etc., winning the Best Male Performer awards for three consecutive years) and began his choreography career assisting Ron Lewis in Paris. After featured appearances in the film **Annie**, on Broadway in *The Act* ('77) and at Carnegie Hall in concert with Liza Minnelli and Obba Babatunde ('79), he concentrated his talents on highly acclaimed club shows, eventually relocating to Orlando, Florida.

Stage: *West Side Story* (Loras College, Iowa, with Eugene Loring, '67), Takarazuka Revue (Tokyo and Radio City Music Hall, NY)

TV: Frank Sinatra, Jr. special ('69)

Nightclub/Concert: (Partial listing): Casino de Paris ('68), multiple shows in Las Vegas, Atlantic City, Sun City, South Africa, Nassau (*Outrageous, Heatwave, Wild, Movin', Fascinatin' Rhythms, Pom Poms, Hot Cha Cha*, etc.)

Film:
1983 **Spring Break** — Col

REGINE MIRANDA
1987 **Opera Do Malandro** — Goldwyn

ARTHUR MITCHELL
b. New York, March 27, 1934

As America's first male African-American classical ballet soloist and creator of one of the world's most important dance companies, Arthur Mitchell has created opportunities in dance and served as an inspiration for hundreds of future black artists. With an introduction to dance of two years of tap lessons, he studied at the High School of Performing Arts in New York and was awarded a scholarship to the School of American Ballet. After dancing with the John Butler, Sophie Maslow, Donald McKayle and Anna Sokolow companies, he joined the New York City Ballet in 1955 and was promoted to soloist in 1959, amazing the dance world with his talent and charisma. Alternating commercial Broadway appearances (*House of Flowers, Noel Coward's Sweet Potato, Arabian Nights, Carmen Jones, Kiss Me Kate* and *Shinbone Alley*) and TV (The Jackie Gleason and Jinx Falkenberg shows, etc.) with his ballet work, Mitchell explored the full range of dance techniques — as well as beginning his choreographic career. When asked his feelings about "a ban on his dancing with a white partner on commercial TV... TV stations in the South refuse to carry it" when NYC Ballet's works were televised, Mitchell profoundly answered, "Bitterness is a waste of time. I'm a doer" (*Dance Magazine*, 1964). Under the U.S. Cultural Exchange Program, he developed the Brazilian Ballet for several

Ann Reinking is flanked by fellow choreographer-dancers Roger Minami and Geoffrey Holder in the "We Got Annie" number from **Annie** (Joe Layton, Arlene Phillips, Columbia, 1982).

years and the company debuted at Teatro Nova in 1967. Mitchell also choreographed his first film that year. After years of teaching black youngsters at the Katherine Dunham, Karel Shook and Jones-Haywood schools, in 1968, he founded the Dance Theater of Harlem with Shook, which was the world's first black classical company. Ballerina Virginia Johnson remembered Mitchell changing her life when she attended his Saturday dance class in Harlem; "He taught us to be black and in ballet, you had to be a fighter." The man who "wanted to do in classical ballet what Jackie Robinson was doing in baseball" is the recipient of the *Dance Magazine* award in 1975, the prestigious Kennedy Center Honors in 1993, the Handel Medallion of the City of New York award in 1994 and was declared a living landmark by the New York Landmarks Conservancy in 1995. His exquisite technique and presence as a performer is captured on film in **A Midsummer Night's Dream** ('66).

Stage: Shinbone Alley (Bdwy '57, asst to Rod Alexander), *Salome, Festival of Two Worlds* (Spoleto '61)

Ballet/Dance Pieces (Partial listing): For the Dance Theater of Harlem: "Ode to Otis" ('69),

"Fete Noir," "Le Corsaire," "Rhythmetron," "John Henry" ('88)

Film:

1967 **The Day the Fish Came Out**—International Classics (also appeared)

1977 **A Piece of the Action**—WB

1984 **The Cotton Club**—Orion (with Gregory Hines, Henry Le Tang, Michael Meacham, Michael Smuin)

JERRY MITCHELL

b. Detroit, Michigan, January 15, 1960

"Choreography was just something I always did," admitted this dancer-choreographer who was born in the Lincoln Park section of Detroit, but raised in Paw Paw, Michigan. Involved in school theater from the age of 8, he was always interested in dance but did not pursue it because: "I didn't want to be called 'Sissy.'" He created his first choreography for a "smash" production of *Aesop's Fallibles* for the Paw Paw Village Players, which he also directed, at the age of 12. When he broke his collar bone in a bicycle fall coming home from football practice at the age of 15, he talked his parents into letting him take tap lessons at the Meese Dance Studios in Paw Paw for physical activity. Within two weeks, he was asked to teach younger students. While a senior in high school, his parents and school officials allowed him to tour the country with The Young Americans' production of *West Side Story*, giving him school credit for his new experiences. He attended Webster College, studying ballet with Gary Hubler and after two years, went to New York to seriously study dance. At his very first NY audition, he was cast by Agnes DeMille in the 1980 revival of *Brigadoon* and continued on Broadway in *Barnum*, *Woman of the Year*, *On Your Toes*, *A Chorus Line* and *The Will Rogers Follies*. TV performances include "Moonlighting," the Academy, Grammy and Tony Awards Shows, "Night of 100 Stars," "One Life to Live" and the Kennedy Center Honors and he appeared on film in **The Best Little Whorehouse in Texas**. He began his choreography career assisting Michael Bennett on the workshop production of *Scandals* and accompanied Bennett to London to begin work on *Chess*, but when Bennett became ill, they left the show. He next assisted Jerome Robbins on *Jerome Robbins Broadway* ("I found out that Michael Bennett also left high school for a production of *West Side* and Robbins was his inspiration — It was like coming full circle") and Bob Avian on *Putting It Together* at the Manhattan Theatre Club and *Follies* in London. When Tommy Tune declined to do **Scent of a Woman**, Mitchell was called and got his first solo film credit. He credits three teachers in his life with "infusing and encouraging me with the idea of what I wanted to do," starting with his first teacher Cindy Meese ("When I left Paw Paw, I thanked her for teaching me to dance and she said; 'I didn't teach you to dance. You always had it in you. I just let it out'") and New York "inspirations" Nenette Charisse and Lee Theodore.

Stage: *Joseph and the Amazing Technicolor Dream Coat* (Minneapolis, Kudo Award from Minn/St. Paul press for best choreo), *Jeffrey* and *Lips Together, Teeth Apart* (OB), *Broadway Bares I–IV* (NY), *You Could Be Home Now* (NY), *Jekyll and Hyde* (Houston), *Hearts Desire* (Cleveland), *Grease* ('94 NY rev, assoc choreo with Jeff Calhoun)

Music Video: "I Wanna Dance with Somebody" — Whitney Houston

Miscellaneous: Gay Games IV (Opening Ceremony, NY '94)

Film:
1992 **Scent of a Woman** — Univ (with Paul Pellicoro)
1995 **Jeffrey** — Orion

NOBUKO (JOANNE) MIYAMOTO (AKA JOANNE MIYA & JOANNE MIYAMOTO)

b. Los Angeles, California

As one of the few female Asians with choreographic film credits, the multi-talented Miyamoto credits her parents with great support for her theatrical aspirations — a rarity among Japanese-American families. After starting ballet classes at the age of 7, she soon took vocal lessons. Appearing as "Joanne Miyamoto" in the film version of **West Side Story** ('61), she moved from stage roles in *Kismet* ('62 — as "Jo Anne Miya"), *Chu Chem* (OOT '66), *The King and I* and *West Side Story* to singing lead vocals with Warriors of the Rainbow, a mid–70s rock/jazz fusion band. Writing songs and stage performance pieces to explore her heritage and identity, as artistic director for Great Leap, Inc. and composer and lyricist of *Talking Story — Chapter 2*, she continues to use her talents to theatrically present the Asian-American experience.

Stage: *Chinatown*, *Chop Suey* (East-West Players, LA, also dir), *Women Hold Up Half the Sky* ('78)

Film:
1986 **The Karate Kid Part II** — Col (with Paul DeRolf, Jose DeVega, Randall Sabusawa)

ROBYN MOASE

Australian actress, dancer and choreographer.

Film:
1988 **Belinda** — Fontana Prod (also appeared)
        The Year My Voice Broke — Ave Pictures
1991 **Daydream Believer** — View Films

JOHN MONTE

1964 **Muscle Beach Party** — AIP

GOYO MONTERO

1991 **Beltenbros (Prince of Shadows)** — Metro Pictures (Span)

CINDY MONTOYA-PICKER

Long time associate to Paula Abdul on multiple television, music video, stage and film projects, she received her first solo choreographic credit for her film work in writer-director Mel Brooks' spoof **Robin Hood: Men in Tights**.

TV: Associate choreographer to Paula Abdul on the 1990 Academy Awards and The Tracey Ullman Shows; commercials for Mattel, M.C. Hammer doll, McDonalds, Taco Bell, etc.

Music Video: "Blowing Kisses" — Paula Abdul; "Time, Love and Tenderness," "Steel Bars," "Love

Is a Wonderful Thing"— Michael Bolton; "Pump It"— Icey Blue; "Do Me Right"— Guy; "Thought You Were the One for Me"— Joey B. Ellis; "This House"— Tracie Spenser; "I'm the One"— Steve Harvey; "Will You Marry Me?"

Nightclub/Concert: Associate to Paula Abdul on *Paula Abdul*, George Michael and Luther Vandross tours; Michael Bolton 1991 tour, Julio Iglesias tour ('94, with Dean Harvey)

Film:
1988 **Coming to America**— Par (assistant to Paula Abdul)
1989 **The Karate Kid Part III**— Col (asst to Abdul)
      She's Out of Control— Weintraub Ent Group (assistant to Abdul)
1990 **The Adventures of Ford Fairlane**— Fox (assistant to Aurorah Allain)
1993 **Robin Hood: Men in Tights**— Col/TriStar
1996 **Spy Hard**— Hollywood Pict

CLAUDIA MOORE
1995 **Exotica**— Miramax

VALERIE MOORE
1995 **Sugartime**— HBO (TV) (Also appeared as "The Choreographer")

BRAD AND JENNIFER MORANZ
1994 **Radioland Murders**— Univ

TEODORO MORCA
b. Spain

Dancer, choreographer and master teacher, who, with his wife, Isabel, created the Morca, Flamenco in Concert performing group. He chose classic Spanish dance after accidentally seeing a Flamenco concert when he was in his early 20's. After touring with José Greco, Lola Montez and others in Europe and the U.S., "He doesn't call himself a Spanish dancer anymore... Much of Morca's repertoire consists of 'Contemporary Theatre Compositions,' works set to Baroque music. While he retains the 'tension, essence, and coordination' of Spanish dance as the base of his choreography, Morca explains that he uses an 'individual approach' in creating dances." (*Dance Magazine*, April, 1978). He also teaches and lectures internationally, as well as choreographing for modern, ballet and ethnic companies. In 1976 he and Isabel opened their dance school in Bellingham, Washington, where they currently teach. He produced a six-part video series of Flamenco technique and is featured in a 1978 PBS special, "The Joy of Bach."

Film:
1974 **Zandy's Bride**— WB

LISA MORDENTE
Blessed with the talented genes of mother Chita Rivera and father Tony Mordente (see the following profile), Lisa Mordente has worked hard in various mediums to find her own place in the sun. Her credits as a performer include featured roles in *Platinum* ('78) and *Marlowe* ('81, Tony nom) on Broadway and on television in "Welcome Back Kotter" and "Viva Valdez," before she began her choreographic career. Married to singer-songwriter Donnie Kehr.

Stage: *The Who's Tommy* (Bdwy '93, asst to Wayne Cilento)
Nightclub/Concert: *Chita* ('86, also co-dir with Wayne Cilento), Liza Minnelli's "Stepping Out" tour ('93)
Film:
1978 **The End**— UA
1992 **Sister Act**— Touchstone (with Lester Wilson, "additional choreography by" credit)

TONY (ANTHONY) MORDENTE
b. Brooklyn, New York, 1935

When "His mother decided that he needed an additional outlet for his abundant energy," Anthony Mordente began his dance education at 13 with tap at Nellie Cooke's school in Brooklyn. He progressed to ballet study with Don Farnworth and attended the New York High School of Performing Arts. He made his professional dance debut at Jacob's Pillow in 1954 and that same year won a scholarship from the Ballet Theatre School. Because of "the driving energy, the alert way of cutting through the air, the sense of dancing-bravado" (*Dance Magazine*, September, '56), he was a soloist with Ballet Theatre and with the Radio City Music Hall Corps de Ballet. After a summer of stock at Camp Tamiment, he appeared on Broadway in *L'il Abner* and *West Side Story* (repeating his roles in the film versions) and danced on most of the popular television shows of the 1950s and '60s (Ed Sullivan, Sid Caesar, etc.) He began his choreographic career assisting Gower Champion on *Bye Bye Birdie* and remounted *West Side Story* for Jerome Robbins to great acclaim in Tokyo in 1965. He also assisted Michael Kidd on *Wonder World* at the 1964 NY World's Fair and *Ben Franklin in Paris* on Broadway. Former husband of Chita Rivera and father of Lisa Mordente, in the mid–70s, he transferred his talents to TV direction, with dozens of credits ("M.A.S.H.," "Keep on Truckin'," "The Harlem Globetrotters' Popcorn Machine," "Rhoda," "Nobody's Perfect," "The Rita Moreno Show," "The Tony Randall Show," etc.).

Stage: *West Side Story* (multiple productions), *Bye Bye Birdie* (London and LV), *How Do You Do I Love You?* (OOT '67), *Here's Where I Belong* (Bdwy '68)

TV: "The Jimmy Dean Show" ('66), "The Jim Nabors Hour" ('69–70), "The Melba Moore-Clifton Davis Show" ('72), "The Sonny and Cher Show" ('71–74), "The Mac Davis Show" ('74–75)

Film:
1961 **West Side Story**—UA (with Tommy Abbott, Maggie Banks, Howard Jeffrey, Jerome Robbins)

DALE MOREDA
Appeared on Broadway in multiple shows, among them *The Pajama Game* ('54) *How to Succeed...* ('61) and *Hallelujah, Baby* ('67).

Film:
1967 **How to Succeed in Business Without Really Trying**—Mirish/UA (adapted Bob Fosse's original stage choreography)

RUBEN MORENO
1995 **Boys on the Side**—WB (with Oscar Villela, "Folkloric Dance Co-ordinator" credit)

BRENTLEY MORGAN
1992 **Spring Break Sorority Babes**—Hit Ent

MARIAN MORGAN
A former Los Angeles school and dance teacher who realized the opportunities in film and created the Marion Morgan Dancers (among them Ramon Novarro) to appear onscreen and in prologues throughout the United States. Her film sequences were often bacchanales and Morgan "held the honors for interpretive work which occupied a distinct though minor place among the deluge of dance sequences in films" (*Dancing in Commercial Motion Pictures*).

Stage: *The Wishing Well* (Bdwy '29)
Film:
1926 **Don Juan**—WB
1927 **The Night of Love**—UA
1928 **The Private Life of Helen of Troy**—First Ntl
1930 **Paramount on Parade**—Par (with David Bennett)

MARTIN MORRISEY
1992 **Leap of Faith**—Par (with Sharon Kinney, "Hi Step Dance instructor" credit)

LOU MOSCONI
d. Hollywood, California, August 1, 1969

Tap-master who worked in vaudeville and on Broadway in *A World of Pleasure* ('15), *Hitchy-Koo* and *The Ziegfeld Follies* before moving to Hollywood where he taught tap for decades.

Film:
1931 **Laughing Sinners**—MGM

ANDREA MUELLER
1984 **Hot Moves**—Cardinal

GEORGE (LLOYD) MURPHY
b. New Haven, Connecticut, July 4, 1902
d. Palm Beach, Florida, May 3, 1992

The only performer-choreographer (to date) to become a U.S. Senator, Murphy—as the son of an renowned Olympic track trainer—was a gifted sportsman as a boy. He also possessed natural abilities as a dancer, which he used to form a dance team with Juliette Henkel and their success took them to London to be featured in a 1927 production of *Good News*. They were married and continued their stage success on Broadway (*Hold Everything, Shoot the Works, Of Thee I Sing* and *Roberta*). In 1933, he signed a contract with Samuel Goldwyn and moved to Hollywood to become one of its leading song-and-dance men. He was soon under contract to MGM and made forty-four musical, dramatic and comedy films during two decades for most of Hollywood's major film studios. His interest in politics led him to holding the office of vice-president and eventually, president of the Screen Actor's Guild. In 1952 he retired from the screen and put his energy into politics, representing the motion picture industry and being elected a California Senator in 1965. Murphy's easy-going Irish charm was only surpassed by his self-taught dance expertise. Winner of an honorary Academy Award in 1950 for "services in correctly interpreting the film industry to the country at large," Murphy usually choreographed or collaborated on his own dance routines in films.

Autobiography: *Say ... Didn't You Use to Be George Murphy?* (1970)

Film (Credits are for the choreography for his own routines):
1930 **Pathé Audio Review #13**—Pathé (S)
1934 **Kid Millions**—UA (with Seymour Felix, Fayard Nicholas)
1935 **After the Dance**—Col (with Albertina Rasch)
1936 **Violets in Spring**—MGM (S)
1937 **Broadway Melody of 1938**—MGM (with Dave Gould, Eleanor Powell)
 Top of the Town—Univ (with Gene Snyder)
 You're a Sweetheart—Univ (with Carl Randall)

Marion Morgan in a 1920s publicity pose.

1938 **Hold That Co-Ed**— Univ (with Castle, Sawyer)

    Little Miss Broadway— Fox (with Nick Castle, Geneva Sawyer)

1940 **Broadway Melody of 1940**— MGM (with Fred Astaire, Bobby Connolly, Eleanor Powell)

    Little Nellie Kelly— MGM (with Eddie Larkin)

    Two Girls on Broadway— MGM (with Connolly, Larkin)

1941 **A Girl, a Guy and a Gob**— RKO

    Rise and Shine— Fox (with Hermes Pan)

    Tom, Dick and Harry— RKO

1942 **For Me and My Gal**— MGM (with Busby Berkeley, Connolly, Gene Kelly)

    The Mayor of 44th Street— RKO (with Castle)

    The Powers Girl— UA (with Jack Donohue)

1943 **This Is the Army**— WB (with Castle, LeRoy Prinz, Bob Sidney)

1944 **Broadway Rhythm**— MGM (with Robert Alton, Jack Donohue, Don Loper, Charles Walters)

    Show Business— RKO (with Castle)

    Step Lively— RKO (with Ernst Matray)

Buddy Ebsen, Eleanor Powell and George Murphy relax on the set of MGM's **Broadway Melody of 1938**.

RICHARD MURPHY

1990 **Where the Heart Is**— Touchstone

BUD MURRAY

Dancer-choreographed who created the dance in most of the **Our Gang** shorts and all of the child actors' public appearances.
Film:
1938 **Our Gang Follies**—(S) Hal Roach

JOYCE MURRAY

Dancer-choreographer who was "said to be the first girl to do a tap dance for the talkies in **Broadway Melody**" (*Dance Magazine*, November 1942).
Film:
1942 **Once Upon a Honeymoon**— RKO

MIA NADASI

1976 **The Devil Within Her**— AIP

DANIEL NAGRIN

b. New York, May 22, 1917
Modern dancer and choreographer who graduated from James Madison High School and New York City College and studied dance with Nenette Charisse, Martha Graham, Hanya Holm, Anna Sokolow and Helen Tamiris (whom he later married). He made his musical stage debut in *Marianne* (OOT '43) and appeared in the dance companies of Sokolow, Tamiris and Charles Weidman. He soon began creating his own solo works and teaching. Broadway appearances (in which he also assisted Tamiris) include *Up in Central Park* ('45), *Annie Get Your Gun* and *Park Avenue* ('46), *Inside U.S.A.* ('48), *Bless You All* and *Touch and Go* ('50), *By the Beautiful Sea* ('54), and *Plain and Fancy* ('55). He was featured performing Tamiris' choreography in a Mexican modern ballet in the 1952 film **Just for You** with Florence Lessing and Miriam Pandor. In "In Quest of a Dance," an article he wrote for the September, 1951 issue of *Dance Magazine,* he expressed his methods of creating dances: "A dance … is a thread of movements poured out of a body.

Therefore, because it is so personal, the crucial question is not *how* you create a dance, but *why* you create a dance. Technique flows from philosophy. Content determines form... I believe one necessary element of ... success lays in the artist's *conscious* knowledge of *why* he dances." Nagrin's one film credit hardly gave him the chance to capture those thoughts on film. From 1957 he toured as one of America's leading solo dancers, lectured and taught. In 1994 he was one of the recipients of the 1993–94 Artslink Collaboration Projects grants and is currently on the staff of the Arizona State University dance department.

Stage: *Volpone* (OB '57), *The Emperor Jones* (Boston Arts Festival '64)

Ballet/Dance Pieces (Partial listing): "Strange Hero" ('48), "Man of Action," "Indeterminate Figure," "Three Ways," "Spanish Dances," "Jazz Three Times," "Blue Man," "Bounce Boy," "The Peloponnesian War," "Dance in the Sun," "Untitled" ('74)

Film:
1953   **His Majesty O'Keefe**— WB

NATACHA NATOVA

b. Russia, circa 1900

Fleeing Russia as a child with her parents during the Revolution, Natova eventually settling in Nice, France. Moving to Paris in her teens, she studied at the Paris Opera and was soon invited to join the company. Interested in the new "modern" ballet, she created an unique adagio act and was brought to America in *The Greenwich Village Follies of 1926*. She continued on stage, in vaudeville and was featured in the *Folies Bergère*. Also a painter and poet, Natova began creating ballets for theater (rather than concert) and when interviewed in *The Dance*, September, 1928, about her latest creation, she said," This machine age in which we live fascinates me, and I want to interpret it. You will observe that my stage set calls for a mechanical contrivance. It is supposed to manufacture men... I am to represent electricity." It is undocumented where her career went in the 1930s.

Film:
1929   **The Hollywood Revue of 1929**— MGM (with Ernest Belcher, Sammy Lee, Albertina Rasch)

ANTHONY Z. NELLE

b. Warsaw, Poland

Trained at the Imperial Ballet School in Warsaw, Nelle eventually danced with the prestigious company. During World War I he emigrated to Russia to produce opera ballet for the Kiev Civic Opera. He 1917 he produced musical comedies in Moscow and left Russia in 1920, to tour internationally with Pavlova's Ballet company as a character dancer. After arriving in America in 1922, he appeared in New York in *The Greenwich Village Follies* and remained in the country to act as production chief for the Roxy Theater and the Fox and Orpheum circuits. He then moved to Hollywood and worked briefly as a dance director for RKO. Returning to Europe in 1932, he served as dance director at UFA Studios in Germany (1932–39), at the Scala Theatre in Berlin and produced revues at the Coliseum, the Palladium and the Prince of Wales Theatres in London until World War II began. He returned once again to America to be dance director at the St. Louis Municipal Opera and to produce nightclub and vaudeville shows across the country. Married to dancer Margaret Donaldson, he was also a camouflage designer for the U.S. military.

Stage: Multiple prologues for the RKO, Keith and Orpheum theater circuits: *Les Sylphides, Scheherezade, Giselle, Polovetsian Dances, Grand Canyon Suite*, etc.; St. Louis Muny Opera (11 seasons)

Nightclub/Concert: Stevens Hotel, Chicago ('45, also prod)

Film:
1930   **Half Shot at Sunrise**— RKO (with Mary Read)

1932   **One Night in May**— UFA (German)
       A Woman Commands— RKO

GENE NELSON (EUGENE LEANDER BERG)

b. Seattle, Washington, March 24, 1920
d. Woodland Hills, California, September 16, 1996

Beyond his talents as a song-and-dance man and his likeable, accessible onscreen persona, it was Nelson's athletic and inventive choreographic talents which allowed him to become the Movie Musical's last leading male dance star. When accepting his *Dance Magazine* award in 1956, he wrote "I'm convinced that except in explicit fantasy, people like to see musical numbers spring from natural, ordinary situations... They enjoy seeing recognizable situations transposed for satiric, humorous or dramatic effects, I have earnestly tried, whenever possible, to follow this idea. I have wanted each dance to have a reason." Born in Seattle, his family moved to Los Angeles when he was 3. Trained in gymnastics since the age of 8, at 12, he saw **Flying Down to Rio** and Fred Astaire inspired him to dance. "My father was really a frustrated performer... He also loved to dance ... so when I became interested in dancing myself, I had a very supportive father." He studied dancing with Roy Randolph and Steve Granger ("Steve knew all of Bill Robinson's routines and he gave me private lessons") and he teamed with a friend, Ted Hanson, to perform as a duo at local benefits. After studying at the Fanchon and Marco School, he made his professional stage debut as a member of the Fanchon and Marco Juvenile Revue at the Paramount Theater in Los Angeles in 1935. Dance studies continued with tap from Nick Castle and ballet from Bert Privale. After graduating from high school at 18, he discovered ice skating: "I loved it — I was enamored with it — the sense of movement, the leaps and spins. I had a ball." He was selected to tour with Sonja Henie and appeared in two of her films (**Second Fiddle** and **Everything Happens at Night** in 1939) and at the Center Theater at Rockefeller Plaza in New York in *It Happens on Ice*. As a soldier during World War II he appeared on Broadway and in a worldwide tour in *This Is the Army*. His wife, the former Miriam Franklin, was under contract to Paramount, so after leaving the service in 1945, Gene joined her in California and was placed under contract to 20th Century–Fox. He made his film debut in **I Wonder Who's Kissing Her Now?** and also appeared in Fox's **Apartment for Peggy** ('48). Because of his youthful looks, the studio was not certain of what to do with him and they let his contract expire. When *Lend An Ear*, a revue that he was featured in on the West Coast went to Broadway in 1948, he was next contracted by Warner Bros. to star in their musical films, where he finally achieved Hollywood stardom. He choreographed his own dance material, creating many dazzling athletic tap solos — with the collaboration of his dancer-choreographer wife Miriam. Voted "Most Promising Newcomer" by the Hollywood Foreign Correspondents in 1950, he received screen credit for his choreography for the first time with **So This Is Paris** (1953). After his greatest success in **Oklahoma!** (in which he co-choreographed his number "Kansas City" with Agnes DeMille) he realized that the movie musical and the studio system itself were on the wane so he changed his focus to become a prolific film and television director in the 1960s and '70s: **Your Cheatin' Heart**, **Hootenanny Hoot**, **Kissin' Cousins**, **Harum Scarum**, "The Mod Squad," "Hawaii 5-0," "The F.B.I.," etc. He performed a glorious "Comeback" on Broadway in Stephen Sondheim's *Follies* in 1971, receiving a Tony nomination, and also appeared on Broadway in *Music! Music!* ('74). In the book *That's Dancing*, he praised the opportunities of dance on film: "It's a marvelous medium for dancing. The sky's the limit. You can do wonderfully imaginative things with film — it's like being a magician... In my heyday I could only do about four pirouettes without starting to fall, but with film I could do a dozen by cutting and editing. The magic of film is that you can create anything you want." Received the *Dance Magazine* award in 1955 and the Dance in Action award in 1981 and along with Astaire, credited Eleanor Powell, the Nicholas Brothers and Sonja Henie as major influences in his life. Survived by a daughter, Victoria, and two sons, Christopher and Douglas.

Stage: *Pal Joey* (Cal. '56, also starred), *Foolin' Ourselves* — A Billy Barnes Revue (Pre-Bdwy '57, also dir and star), *Startime* (Pantages Theater, Hollywood, also dir), *Darling I'm Yours* (SF), *Twain* (SF, also dir)

TV: "Shower of Stars" ("Showstoppers" and "Lend an Ear" '54), "The Eddie Fisher Show" ('58–59), The Chevy Summer Replacement and Gale Storm Shows, "America Pauses in September" ('59), Manny Sax Special, "The Best of Broadway," Coca Cola Special ('60)

Film: (All credits are for films he also appeared in):

1950 **The Daughter of Rosie O'Grady**— WB (with Miriam Nelson, LeRoy Prinz)

> **Tea for Two**— WB (with Miriam, Prinz)
> **The West Point Story**— WB (with John Boyle, Ruth Godfrey, Eddie Prinz, LeRoy Prinz, Al White, Jr.)

1951 **Lullaby of Broadway**— WB (with Miriam, Eddie Prinz, LeRoy Prinz, Al White, Jr.)

> **Painting the Clouds with Sunshine**— WB (with Miriam, LeRoy Prinz)
> **Starlift**— WB (with LeRoy Prinz)

1952 **She's Working Her Way Through College**— WB (with Miriam, LeRoy Prinz)

1953 **She's Back on Broadway**— WB (with Steve Condos, Miriam, LeRoy Prinz)

> **Three Sailors and a Girl**— WB (with LeRoy Prinz)

1954 **So This Is Paris**— Univ (with Lee Scott, first screen credit)

1955 **Oklahoma!**— Fox (with Agnes DeMille)

MIRIAM NELSON (NÉE FRANKLIN, LATER MEYERS)

b. Chicago, Illinois, September 21

Miriam began dance studies in her native Chicago and when her family moved to New York, she studied tap with Ernest Carlos at the age of 14. In a borrowed pair of toe shoes, she auditioned for Billy Rose's Casa Mañana, but instead made her professional debut with an act playing Troy and Schnectady. She eventually played the Casa Mañana and next, the Mayfair Club in Boston. After making her Broadway debut in 1938 in *Sing Out the News*, she went on to appear in *Yokel Boy* and *Very Warm for May* ('39), *Higher and Higher* and *Panama Hattie* ('40) and *Let's Face It* ('41), working with choreographers Robert Alton, Billy Daniel and Charles Walters and often selected to be line-captain. When her husband, Gene Nelson, joined the Signal Corps, Miriam went to Hollywood, where

Gene and Miriam Nelson with their son, Chris, in a Christmas, 1951, publicity photo taken in their Burbank home.

she signed a acting-dancing contract with Paramount and was featured in **Double Indemnity** and **Here Come the Waves** ('44), **Duffy's Tavern** and **Incendiary Blonde** ('45) and **Naughty Nanette** (a '46 short) and in **Cover Girl** ('44) and **The Jolson Story** ('46) for Columbia. First assisting Paramount dance director Danny Dare, she began choreographing and when Gene was signed by Warner Bros. to star in a series of musical films, she co-created many of his solo routines and coached Doris Day and his other female costars. Divorced from Nelson, she continued as one of Hollywood's busiest TV and film choreographers (along with her tap expertise, she specialized in staging party sequences), as well as being one of the pioneers of spectacular Arena show staging with *Disney on Parade* in 1969. As one of the founders of SHARE, she has staged and produced their annual fund-raising *Boomtown* shows for decades. Widowed after her second husband, producer Jack Meyers' death, she returned to the stage in longtime-friend Marge Champion's *Ballroom* at the Long Beach CLO in 1992.

Stage: *Wildcat* (OOT '62), *Festival Polynesia* (Hollywood Bowl, '66), *Anything Goes* (St. Louis Muny '72 rev), *Oklahoma!* (Bdwy '79 rev, "Kansas City" number), *Hoagy, Bix and Monk* (LA)

TV (Partial listing): "The Red Skelton Show" ('54), "Make Believe Ballroom," "Shower of Stars" ('54), Playhouse 90: "The Dingaling Girl" ('59), "The Bob Hope Show," "The Don Knotts Show," "Oh, Susanna" ('60), "Wagontrain," "The Farmer's Daughter," "The Hollywood Palace," "My Three Sons," The Lucy Show," "Away We Go" ('67, with The Miriam Nelson Dancers), 42nd Annual Academy Awards Show ('69), "Ike" ('79 mini series with Marge Champion); commercials include Chevron, K-Mart, Kentucky Fried Chicken, Kinney Shoes, McDonald's and Wendy's

Nightclub/Concert: Acts for Gene Barry, William Bendix, Janet Blair, Carol Channing, Gary Crosby, Barbara Eden, Gogi Grant, Steve Lawrence & Eydie Gorme, Howard Keel, Gordon & Sheila MacRae, Ann Miller, Anthony Newley, Donald O'Connor and Jane Russell; *La Parisienne* (Dunes Hotel, LV '60), *The Playmates*, the Flamingoettes (Flamingo Hotel, LV)

Miscellaneous: *Wives for Kennedy*—Fundraising

revue, ('60), *Onstage U.S.A.* and *Golden Horseshoe Revue* (Disneyland '69), *Disney on Parade* (touring arena show '69), SHARE Annual *Boomtown* parties ('53–95), Radio City Music Hall ('71), Opening of Madison Square Gardens, *Honor America* ('76), *Ice* (Radio City Music Hall), *Sesame Street Live* touring arena show, Thalians Ball ('94)

Film:

1945 **Duffy's Tavern**— Par (assistant to Billy Daniel, Danny Dare, also appeared in a featured number with Johnny Coy)

Incendiary Blonde— Par (assistant to Billy Daniel)

1946 **The Jolson Story**— Col (with Jack Cole, also appeared, ghosting for Evelyn Keyes in "Liza")

1950 **The Daughter of Rosie O'Grady**— WB (with Gene Nelson, LeRoy Prinz, also appeared)

Tea for Two— WB (with Nelson, Prinz)

1951 **Lullaby of Broadway**— WB (with Nelson, Eddie Prinz, Leroy Prinz, Al White, Jr.)

Painting the Clouds with Sunshine— WB (with Nelson, Prinz)

1952 **She's Working Her Way Through College**— WB (with Nelson, Prinz)

1953 **She's Back on Broadway**— WB (with Steve Condos, Nelson, Prinz)

1955 **Bring Your Smile Along**— Col (assisted by Ward Ellis)

Picnic— Col

1956 **He Laughed Last**— Col (assisted by Bob Street)

1957 **Public Pigeon Number One**— Univ

1960 **The Apartment**— UA

High Time— Fox

Visit to a Small Planet— Par

1961 **Breakfast at Tiffany's**— Par

Love in a Goldfish Bowl— Par

1962 **The Interns**— Col

1963 **A New Kind of Love**— Par

Soldier in the Rain— Par

1964 **Good Neighbor Sam**— Col

Honeymoon Hotel— MGM (assisted by Michelle Barton)

I'd Rather Be Rich— Univ (with Hal Belfer)

The New Interns— Col

Young Lovers— MGM

1965 **Cat Ballou**— Col

I'll Take Sweden— UA

In Harm's Way— Par

1966 **Hawaii**— UA

Murderer's Row— Col (assisted by Bob Street)

Walk, Don't Run— Col

1967 **Easy Come, Easy Go**— Par (with David Winters)

1969 **Bob and Carol and Ted and Alice**— Col

Cactus Flower— Col (assisted by Toni Kaye)

The Great Bank Robbery— WB (assisted by Larry Billman)

1973 **The Third Girl from the Left**— Playboy Films (TV)

1974 **Remember When**— Danny Thomas Prod./NBC (TV)

1975 **The Day of the Locust**— Par (with Marge Champion)

1978 **Ziegfeld, the Man and His Women**— Frankovich/Col (TV) (assisted by Tad Tadlock, Emmy nom)

1979 **Buck Rogers in the 25th Century**— Univ

10— Orion ("Dream Ballet" deleted)

1981 **Only When I Laugh**— UA

1982 **Yes, Giorgio**— MGM

1985 **Alice in Wonderland**— CBS/Irwin Allen (TV)

1988 **Sunset**— TriStar (with Miranda Garrison)

EVA NEMETH

1989 **Music Box**— Carolco/Tri-Star

LENORA NEMETZ

b. Pittsburgh, Pennsylvania

Dancer, singer and choreographer who began her professional career at the Pittsburgh Playhouse and Pittsburgh Civic Light Opera. She eventually was featured on Broadway in *Chicago*, *Working*, *Sweet Charity* and on TV in "Flora, the Red Menace." She co-starred on Broadway and on tour in *Up in One* with Peter Allen and appeared in *A Musical Christmas Carol* for the Pittsburgh CLO in 1994.

Stage: *America Kicks Up Its Heels* (OB '83), *Spotlight* (OOT '78)

Film:

1988 **Dominick and Eugene**— Orion

FLOYD NEWSON

1992 **Edward II**— Fine Line Features (with Nigel Charnok)

MBONGENI NGEMA (PRONOUNCED "BON-GEN-É EN-GÉ-MA")

b. Verulam, South Africa, 1955

Writer, composer, lyricist, actor, singer, choreographer and director who represents South Africa in film choreography listings. After growing up in the townships around Durban, he began his performance career as a guitar player for local theater pieces, in which he eventually began acting. Relocating to Soweto in 1979 to act, he wrote *Woza Albert!* in 1981 and established his own theater company, Committed Artists, becoming a leading figure in South African protest theater. As lead vocalist for the African Mbanganga group: The Soul Brothers and Music Unlimited Orchestra, he can be heard on best selling records. His stage creations eventually toured internationally and he won multiple awards for *Asinamali!* (including a Tony nomination for direction on Broadway). He next conceived the stage musical *Sarafina!*, as well as writing many of the songs and creating the choreography. When the musical was filmed he wrote the screenplay, played the role of "Sebela" and adapted his choreography for the camera.

Stage: *Township Fever* (OB '90, also dir, book), *Sarafina!* (Bdwy '91)

Film:

1993 **Sarafina!**— WB (with Michael Peters)

FAYARD NICHOLAS

b. Mobile, Alabama, October 20, 1914

Awe-inspiring dancer, actor, teacher and choreographer who — as the smaller-but-older half of The Nicholas Brothers — created dance numbers in films which always stopped the show. The Nicholas Brothers seemed to defy gravity with their athletic genius never seen before — or since. Their mother played the piano and father played the drums at the Standard Theater, Philadelphia, where young Fayard learned how to dance by sitting on the bandstand ("next to my Dad's drums") and nightly watching such great performers as Buck and Bubbles and The Berry Brothers perform. When Fayard was 10, he taught younger brother Harold to dance and their professional careers began as youngsters on a Philadelphia radio program, "The Horn and Hardart Kiddie Show." In 1932, they opened at the Cotton Club when Fayard was 14 and Harold was 8, making their first film appearance in **Pie, Pie Blackbird**, a Vitaphone short, that same year. After appearing in *The Ziegfeld Follies* and Broadway and *Lew Leslie's Blackbirds* in London, they were soon asked to be in feature films and continued for six decades in film, nightclubs, stage (America, Europe, Africa, South America) and TV. "As I always say, the Nicholas Brothers have done everything in Show Business but Opera!" and they *have*, including circus (Cirque Madrana in Paris) and ballet (Fayard recently portrayed the Grandfather in a San Diego production of **The Nutcracker**). The Brothers also appeared on Broadway in *Babes in Arms* ('37) and *St. Louis Woman* ('46, Harold only). Fayard choreographed everything for the Brothers' appearances prior to their work at 20th Century–Fox in the Forties, where he collaborated with Nick Castle. Castle ("who had wonderful ideas") encouraged them to create some of filmed dance's most incredible sights: dancing up walls, flying

splits over each other's heads, etc. After teaching at the Los Angeles Inner City Cultural Center, Fayard underwent several hip replacement operations but continues to make personal appearances while living happily at the Motion Picture Home with wife, Barbara. He made one purely dramatic film appearance in **The Liberation of L.B. Jones** in 1970. Long overdue recognition began when the Nicholas Brothers received the Kennedy Center Honors in 1991, the PDS Gypsy Award on Feb. 27, 1994 and the 1995 *Dance Magazine* award for being the National Treasures that they are. Fayard was quoted in the book *That's Dancing*: "We never called our dancing 'hoofing.' That's when you concentrate on your feet and don't care about your body and hands. We use it all."

Stage: *Cotton Club Parade* (Bdwy '32), *Ziegfeld Follies of 1936* (Bdwy), *Lew Leslie's Blackouts* (London '36), *Babes in Arms* (Bdwy '37, with George Balanchine), *Ziegfeld Follies of 1965* (Thunderbird Hotel, LV), *Black and Blue* (Bdwy '88, with Cholly Atkins, Henry LeTang, Tony award)

TV: Multiple appearances on most major musical variety shows, 53rd Annual Academy Awards Show ('80)

Film: (All credits are for the Brothers' film routines):

1932 **Pie, Pie Blackbird**— WB (S)

1934 **Kid Millions**— UA (with Seymour Felix)

1935 **All Colored Vaudeville**— Vitaphone (S)
  The Big Broadcast of 1936— Par (with LeRoy Prinz, Bill Robinson)
  Coronado— Par (with Prinz)

1936 **Black Network**— Vitaphone (S)
  Don't Gamble with Love— Col

1937 **Calling All Stars**— British Lion (S) (with John "Bubbles" Sublett)

1940 **Down Argentine Way**— Fox (with Nick Castle, Geneva Sawyer)
  My Son Is Guilty— Col
  Tin Pan Alley— Fox (with Seymour Felix)

1941 **The Great American Broadcast**— Fox
  Sun Valley Serenade— Fox (with Hermes Pan)

1942 **Orchestra Wives**— Fox (with Castle)

1943 **Choo Choo Swing**— Univ (S)
  Stormy Weather— Fox (with Castle, Katherine Dunham, Bill Robinson, Clarence Robinson)

1944 **Take It or Leave It**— Fox

1946 **Dixieland Jamboree**— Vitaphone (S)

1948 **The Pirate**— MGM (with Robert Alton, Gene Kelly)

1985 **That's Dancing!**— MGM (with others)

Fayard and Harold Nicholas in a publicity still taken for their nightclub appearances, circa 1940.

JIMMY NICKERSON

Fight choreographer.
Film:
1986 **Streets of Gold** — Fox
1989 **Fist Fighter** — Taurus

LISA NIEMI (HAAPANIEMI)
b. Houston, Texas, 1957

Blonde and beautiful actress-dancer Niemi met her husband-to-be, Patrick Swayze, while attending his mother Patsy's successful dance school in Houston at the age of 16. As a member of both the Harkness and Joffrey II Ballets, she also appeared in *Hellzapoppin'* ('76) with Jerry Lewis on tour before relocating to the West Coast in 1979 for Patrick's film career. They co-starred in the films **Grandview U.S.A.** and **Steel Dawn** and the 1985 stage production of *Without a Word* (a theatrical dance history of the Joffrey Ballet). Lisa made her Broadway debut in *The Will Roger's Follies* in 1993, reactivating her career.

Stage: *Without a Word* (LA '85, with Nicholas Gunn, Patrick Swayze, also appeared)

Film:

1985 **Grandview U.S.A.**—CBS (with Patrick Swayze)

BRONISLAVA (FOMINIT-SHNA) NIJINSKA (NIJINSKY)

b. Minsk, Russia, January 8, 1891

d. Pacific Palisades, California, February 21, 1972

The sister of the legendary Nijinsky, Madame Nijinska (as she is still referred to by all who studied with her) is regarded as "one of the formative choreographers of the twentieth century." After first studying dance with Enrico Cecchetti, she entered the Maryinsky Theatre Ballet School in St. Petersburg with her brother, Vaslav, in 1900 and studied there for eight years. Although she had made her stage debut at the age of 3 dancing with her parents in a Christmas program, her professional debut was at the Maryinsky Theatre. Joining Ballets Russes in 1911 with her brother (where Diaghilev changed her last name to avoid confusion), she soon rose in stature within the company. Leaving the company because of marriage and motherhood, she opened a school in Kiev and choreographed for the Kiev Opera. When she heard of her brother's illness, she managed to escape to Paris from Russia during the height of the Revolution. Returning to the Diaghilev company as a choreographer, she first staged portions of **Sleeping Beauty** in 1921 and eventually became Diaghilev's principal choreographer, creating eight ballets. She next formed her own company, Theatre De Danse, in Paris and continued to create works for major international companies, among them Ballet Theatre, Ballets Russes de Monte Carlo, Opera Russe a Paris, the Paris Opera, Vienna State Opera, Ida Rubinstein's company and Teatro Colon. After forming the Polish Ballet for the 1937 Paris Exposition, she settled permanently in California in 1939 and opened her school there, continuing to stage ballets for companies around the world, as well as inspiring generations of leading dancers with her training. Her one film credit is a result of her collaboration with Max Reinhardt. Inducted into the Whitney Hall of Fame of the National Museum of Dance in Saratoga Springs, NY, in 1994.

Autobiography: *Early Memories* (1981)

Ballet/Dance Pieces (70 works—Partial listing): "La Tabatiére" ('14), "Les Biches," "The Snow Maiden," "Chopin Concerto," "Les Noches," "Ren-

contres," "Aubade," "Les Comediens Jaloux," "Etude," "Harvest Time," "Rondo Capriccios" ('52)

Film:

1935 **A Midsummer Night's Dream**—WB

MIKE NOMAD

1984 **Splash**—Touchstone ("Swimming choreography by" credit)

CLEO NORDI

b. Kronstadt, Russia, 1899

Classical ballet dancer-choreographer who began her dance studies in Russia with Nicholas Legat and continued in Finland with George Gué and in Paris with Olga Preobrajenska and Vera Trefilova. She joined the Paris Opera Ballet in 1924 and then Anna Pavlova's company in 1926. She married Walford Hyden, Pavlova's conductor, and after Pavlova's death Nordi appeared in musicals in London, also choreographing. She opened her own school of ballet in London in the '40s, later guest teaching at the Royal Ballet and London Contemporary Dance Theatre schools into the Eighties.

Stage: *Magyar Melody* (London '39), *Sweet Yesterday* (London '45, with Frank Staff)

Film:

1946 **Caravan**—Eagle-Lion

ROBERT NORTH

b. Charleston, South Carolina, June 1, 1945

American-born dancer and choreographer who went to London and studied dance at the Royal Ballet School and joined the London Contemporary Dance Theatre during its inception in 1967. He became one of the company's leading dancers and choreographers. He briefly left the company to study and perform with Martha Graham, but returned as principal dancer in 1970 and continued creating for the company. His works have been performed by many dance companies around the world (Scottish Ballet, Dance Theatre of Harlem, Dance Umbrella and wife Janet Smith's Dance Group). He was appointed artistic director for Ballet Rambert and served from 1981–86.

Stage: *Pilgrim* (Eng '75)

Ballet/Dance Pieces: For London Contemporary Dance Theatre: "Conversation Piece" ('70), "One Was the Other" (with Noemi Lapzeson), "Brian," "Dressed to Kill," "Troy Game," "Scriabin Preludes," "Dreams with Silences," "Annunciation," "Songs, Lamentations and Praises," "Death and the Maiden"; For Ballet Rambert: "Running Figures," "Reflections," "Lonely Town, Lonely Street," "Pribaoutki," "Colour Moves" ('83)

Film:

Bronislava Nijinska (R) directs a very young Sid (sic) Charisse and William Hightower in the "Adagio" section of Nijinska's ballet ***Etude***, for a July 30, 1940 Hollywood Bowl performance.

1978 **Slow Dancing in the Big City**— UA (with Ann Ditchburn)

RUDOLPH (HAME-TOVITCH) NUREYEV

b. Mongolia (onboard a train between Lake Baikal and Irkutsk), March 17, 1938

d. Paris, France, January 6, 1993

Nureyev first made international headlines when he defected from his native Russia while appearing with the Kirov Ballet in Paris on June 17, 1961. Up until his death thirty-three years later, the headlines of the newspapers and periodicals of the world were filled with tales of his incredible performances and flamboyant lifestyle. Dancing first in folk dance classes, he began his formal training early, studying with the Ufa Opera Ballet. He entered the Leningrad Ballet School at the age of 17 and was accepted into the famed Kirov Ballet as a soloist in

Rudolph Nureyev (with Paolo Bortoluzzi) attempted to make the transition from international ballet sensation to film star with **Valentino**.

1958. After his defection, he immediately appeared with the Marquis de Cuevas Grand Ballet De Monte Carlo. Introduced to America on "The Ed Sullivan Show" in 1962, he was a guest artist with the Royal Ballet, where he partnered Dame Margot Fonteyn and created a sensation wherever they appeared with his superb technique and exotic personality. The media adored him and his high visibility in the "Jet Set" of the 1970s finally led to film stardom in **Valentino** and **Exposed**. He often restaged classic ballets, rather than choreographing, creating his first original work in 1966 (**Tancredi e Cantilena**) for the Vienna Opera Ballet. He became artistic director of the Paris Opera Ballet and served from 1983–89, during which time he created more than eleven ballets for the company. A 1988 Paris Opera Ballet program describes his choreographic goals for **Swan Lake** as "...further stripped down the plot to add dramatic force and remove some of the feebler parts while probing more deeply into the psychology of the characters." He remained as the com-

pany's principal choreographer until his failing health in 1992.

Winner of a *Dance Magazine* Award in 1973, he was decorated as a Commander of Arts and Letters by France's Minister of Culture and Education on October 8, 1992. His choreographic philosophy was once expressed to Martha Graham: "Steps don't mean anything until they come through the soul." Nureyev was pure soul, some of which can be seen in the 1973 documentary **I Am a Dancer.**

Autobiography: *Nureyev* (1962)

Biography: *Nureyev* by John Percival (1975), *Nureyev* by Clive Barnes (1982)

TV: "Spectre de la Rose" (German TV, '61)

Ballet/Dance Pieces (He restaged many ballets based on others' choreography, but his original choreographic works are): "Tancredi e Cantilena" ('66), "The Nutcracker," "Romeo and Juliet," "Manfred," "The Tempest," "Bach Suite," "Washington Square, " and "Cinderella" ('85)

Film:
1973   **Don Quixote**— Walter Read (after Marius Petipa, also dir and appeared)

MADI OBOLENSKY

Dancer-choreographer who was the trainer of the Bluebell Girls.

Film:
1951   **Quo Vadis**— MGM (with Aurel Milloss)
1954   **Romeo and Juliet**— UA
1956   **Helen of Troy**— WB

JOHN "CHA CHA" O'CON-NELL

1992   **Strictly Ballroom**— Miramax
1994   **Muriel's Wedding**— Miramax
1996   **William Shakespeare's Romeo and Juliet**— Fox

CHARLES O'CURRAN

b. Atlantic City, New Jersey, 1914
d. Granada Hills, California, June 26, 1984
In an article about his work as a dance director while filming **Somebody Loves Me** in 1952, O'Curran was described, "He doesn't just create the choreography. He doesn't simply dream up the concept of a routine. He doesn't only instruct the dancers. He does all these things and more. He takes a given set of lyrics, dramatizes it in movement and music, builds the entire routine and pays as much attention to the recording and interpretation of the lyrics as the actual terpsichorean movement of the performers." Nicknamed "Charlie," Irish-blonde O'Curran began his career performing in and staging vaudeville shows as a teenager, while also forming a band in Philadelphia. After competing as a marathon ballroom dancer, at 19 he danced at the *Folies Bergère* in Paris then returned to New York to direct musicals. In 1943 he moved to Hollywood, staged the highly successful all–Black revue *Sugar Hill* and produced film shorts. During his over-twenty-year career in films, he choreographed for most of the major studios, eventually being contracted to Paramount from 1952–60 as dance director. Married to Betty Hutton, he served as director, choreographer and producer of her live stage appearances — as well as receiving extensive press coverage as a highly visible "Star Spouse." Although many press releases throughout his career talked about film projects he planned to direct (especially with Hutton), he never made the transition. In fact, when Hutton demanded that he direct her next film and Paramount refused, she left the studio. They were divorced in 1955 and he married singer Patti Page, for whom he subsequently directed, staged and produced.

Stage: *Sugar Hill* (LA '44)
TV: "Satins and Spurs" ('54)
Nightclub/Concert: Acts for the Andrews Sisters, the Crosby Boys, Betty Hutton, Patti Page and Mae West

Film:
1943   **Swingtime Johnny**— Univ
1944   **Girl Rush**— RKO
        Moonlight and Cactus— Univ
        Music in Manhattan— RKO
        Sensations of 1945— UA (with Sammy Lee, David Lichine, Eleanor Powell, "Acrobatic Dances by" credit)
        Seven Days Ashore— RKO
1945   **Pan Americana**— RKO (with Antonio)
        Sing Your Way Home— RKO
1946   **Bamboo Blonde**— RKO
1947   **Honeymoon**— RKO (also appeared, partnering Shirley Temple)
1948   **Berlin Express**— RKO
        If You Knew Susie— RKO
        Miracle of the Bells— RKO
        Race Street— RKO
1949   **Roseanna McCoy**— RKO
1951   **Here Comes the Groom**— Par
1952   **Aaron Slick from Punkin Crick**— Par
        Glory Alley— MGM
        Road to Bali— Par
        Somebody Loves Me— Par
1955   **Artists and Models**— Par
1956   **Hollywood or Bust**— Par
1957   **Loving You**— Par
        The Sad Sack— Par
1958   **King Creole**— Par
1960   **Bells Are Ringing**— MGM (assisted by Bea Allen, Doris Avila)
        G.I. Blues— Par (assisted by Roland Dupree)
1961   **Blue Hawaii**— Par
1962   **Girls! Girls! Girls!**— Par (assisted by Maggie Banks)
1963   **Fun in Acapulco**— Par

KIMI OKATA

1993   **So, I Married an Ax Murderer**— TriStar (with Michael Smuin)

JODY OLIVER

1985   **Delivery Boys**— New World (with Nelson Vasquez, also appeared)

ALOYSIO OLIVERIA

1944   **Three Caballeros**— RKO (with Billy Daniel, Carmelita Maracci)

CHRISTINE OREN

1987 **Beauty and the Beast**— Cannon

KENNY ORTEGA

b. Palo Alto, California, April 18, 1950

Dancer, singer, choreographer, director and producer who protested in *Drama-Logue*, May 5, 1988: "I never *wanted* to be a dancer. I never *wanted* to be a choreographer. I loved acting and was fascinated by motion pictures and theater but I danced because it was just part of what we *did* ... I eventually got excited about choreography and the putting together of productions so one thing led to another." Ortega eventually created perhaps the most influential dance images on film in the 1980s (**Dirty Dancing** and **Salsa**). Growing up in Northern California in a supportive, loving, Hispanic family, he started dance lessons at 6 and made his acting debut at 13 in *Oliver* at the Circle Star Theatre in San Carlos. In 1968 he graduated from Canada College, where he had majored in theater and dance. After being one of the principals in the San Francisco and touring companies of *Hair* ('69 — later

Miranda Garrison and Kenny Ortega in a publicity still for **Dirty Dancing** (Vestron, 1987). (Photo courtesy of Miranda Garrison.)

crediting director Tom O'Horgan and choreographer Julie Arenal as inspirations) he began his choreographic-direction career staging The Tubes, a cutting edge multi-media, mixed-theatre Rock group. At a performance of The Tubes, Cher saw the act and hired Ortega to choreograph for her television show. He continued staging acts for rock luminaries and made his film choreographic debut assisting Toni Basil on **The Rose**. While co-choreographing **Xanadu** (with Jerry Trent and associate Russell Clark), the film's star, Gene Kelly, offered encouragement and expertise:"Basically you design the choreography with the camera in mind. So once the director takes it into the editing room, he's not

putting together *his* vision of *your* work." Ortega's optimistic energy and success with dance on film led to directing assignments on television ('88 debut with "Dirty Dancing" series) and film, with Disney's **Newsies** ('92) and **Hocus Pocus** ('93). Winner of numerous awards, including an American Dance Honors Award for **Dirty Dancing** and *LA Dance* Awards nominations.

Stage: *Toni Basil's Follies Bizarre* (also dir), *Marilyn: An American Fable* (Bdwy '83, also dir)

TV: "The Cher Show," "The Academy Awards Show," "Dirty Dancing" and "Hull High" ('90, with Peggy Holmes); Michael Jackson's "Dangerous" Special (also dir), Olivia Newton-John Special

Nightclub/Concert: Riviera Hotel, LV ('85), Caesar's Palace, Atlantic City; tours for Fleetwood Mac, Michael Jackson's "Dangerous" tour ('92, also dir, with Peggy Holmes), Billy Joel, Elton John, Kiss, Madonna, Bette Midler, Miami Sound Machine, Diana Ross, Rod Stewart and the Tubes (5 worldwide tours)

Music Video (Partial listing): "Material Girl"— Madonna (NARAS Award); "Physical"— Olivia Newton-John; "Young Turks," "Love Touch"— Rod Stewart; "I'm So Excited"— Pointer Sisters; "Allentown"— Billy Joel; "Gypsy"— Fleetwood Mac; "We All Sleep Alone," "Turn Back Time," "I Found Someone"— Cher; "Comin' Out of the Dark"— Gloria Estefan; "We're All in This Fight Together" ('92), "Techno Cumbia"— Serena; winner of an MTV Award for a Chayanne video

Miscellaneous: Member of the design team for the "Opening" and "Closing" ceremonies of the '96 Atlanta Olympics.

Film:
1979 **The Rose**— Fox (assistant to Toni Basil)
1980 **Xanadu**— Univ (with Russell Clark, Gene Kelly, Jerry Trent)
1982 **One from the Heart**— Col (with Gene Kelly, assisted by Cheryl Baxter)
1985 **St. Elmo's Fire**— Col
1986 **Ferris Bueller's Day Off**— Orion (with Wilbert Bradley)
    Pretty in Pink— Par
1987 **Dirty Dancing**— Vestron (assisted by Miranda Garrison, American Dance Honors award)
1988 **And God Created Woman**— Vestron
    The Great Outdoors— Univ
    Roadhouse— UA (assisted by Garrison)
    Salsa— Cannon (with Garrison, also appeared and co-prod.)
1989 **Shag**— Hemdale/TriStar
1992 **Newsies**— Walt Disney Pictures (with Peggy Holmes, also dir)
1993 **Hocus Pocus**— Walt Disney Pictures (with Holmes, also dir, *LA Dance* Awards nom)
1995 **To Wong Fu, Thanks for Everything, Julie Newmar**— Univ/Amblin (*LA Dance* Awards nom)

APRIL ORTIZ
1989 **Limit Up**— Sterling/MCEG

PAUL OSCARD
Dancer-choreographer who emigrated from Europe to head the creative staff at the Paramount Theatre, New York in 1933.

Film:
1935 **Goin' to Town**— RKO
1942 **Road to Morocco**— Par

1943 **Ali Baba and the Forty Thieves**— Univ (with Lester Horton)
    Happy-Go-Lucky— Par
1944 **Cobra Woman**— Univ (with Lester Horton)
1947 **Song of My Heart**— AA

COREY OUIMETTE
1991 **Sunset Strip**—?

ALEXANDER OUMANSKY
b. Russia, 1895
d. Honolulu, Hawaii, July 10, 1983
Dancer and choreographer who danced with Diaghilev's Ballets Russes de Monte Carlo and toured as an interpreter and secretary for Nijinsky. Emigrating to America in 1911, he went to England in 1929, to choreograph for the musical stage and films. While in London, he choreographed, directed and produced a series of six revuettes called "Sugar and Spice" for Gainsborough in the early 1930s. In a '30s edition of *The Dancing Times*, he expressed his views on creating ballet for film, "Creative ensembles are now superseding the stereotyped troupe dancing, which, besides being unimaginative in comparison, is pitifully restricted in its ability to convey a meaning to the audience... Cameras are placed at several different angles, all of them filming the ballet as it proceeds. When the dance is over, the film is developed, there are four or five different angles from which I can choose... Imagine the possibilities! The films are so mobile that the watcher can see everything." He created ballets throughout the world, opening the Hollywood Bowl with one of his ballets. He later founded the Magic Ring Theatre in Portland, Oregon and Honolulu, Hawaii. Survived by wife, Peggy, and daughter, dancer-choreographer Valentina, more details of Oumansky's contributions to dance on film will hopefully be unearthed.

Stage: *The Music Box Revue* (Bdwy '23, with Sammy Lee), *Rio Rita* (Prince Edward Theatre, London '25)

Film:
1930 **The Flame of Love**— Brit Intl Pictures
    Harmony Heaven— Brit Intl Pictures
    Why Sailors Leave Home— Brit Intl Pictures
193? **Alfresco**— Gainsborough (S) (also dir)
    Black and White— Gainsborough (S) (also dir)
    Classic Jazz— Gainsborough (S) (also dir)
    Darkie Melodies— Gainsborough (S) (also dir)
    Gypsyland— Gainsborough (S) (also dir)
    Toyland— Gainsborough (S) (also dir)

MICHAEL OWENS

1987 **The Bedroom Window**— DEG

CHARLENE PAINTER (NÉE MEHL)

b. St. Louis, Missouri

Dancer, actress and choreographer who was a great fan of the movie musical—especially Betty Grable. She began her dance studies as a child at the Lala Bauman School of Dance in St. Louis. After moving to New York in her teens, she made her Broadway debut in *The Music Man* ('60) and also appeared in Jerome Robbins' *Ballets: USA* ('61), *All American* ('62), *Tovarich* ('63), *Fade Out, Fade In* ('64), *On a Clear Day You Can See Forever* ('65), as well as the TV series "The Entertainers." After assisting choreographers Michael Bennett, Kevin Carlisle, Danny Daniels, Ron Field, Ernest Flatt, Peter Gennaro, Carl Jablonski, Alan Johnson, Michael Kidd, Tony Mordente, Marc Wilder and husband, Walter Painter, on dozens of films, television, nightclub and stage projects, she began her solo choreographic career. Also the mother of a son and a daughter, she received the Lehman Award in 1995.

Stage: *Doug Henning and His World of Magic* (Bdwy '84)

TV: Doug Henning Specials, "Santa Barbara," "Keep on Truckin'" ('75)

Nightclub/Concert: Acts for Nell Carter, Linda Carter, Debbie Reynolds

Miscellaneous: 8th Annual Professional Dancer's Society Awards Luncheon Show ('94, with Randy Doney), SHARE *Boomtown* Show ('94, with Alan Johnson & Randy Doney)

Film:

1981 **History of the World, Part 1**— Fox (assistant to Alan Johnson)

1983 **To Be or Not to Be**— Fox (with Johnson)

1984 **Footloose**— Par (with Dorain Grusman, Lynn-Taylor Corbett)

1985 **Protocol**— WB

ALFONSE L. PALERMO

1981 **True Confessions**— WB

DENYS PALMER

British dancer-choreographer.

Stage: *The Three Casketts* (London '56), *Antarctica* (London '57), *Mr. Burke, M.P.* (London '60), *Lock Up Your Daughters* (London '62), *Our Man Crichton* (London '64), *Something Nasty in the Woodshed* (Stratford, Eng. '65), *The Pursuit of Love* (Bristol, Eng. '67), *Treasure Island* (London '73, with Terry Gilbert)

Film:

1962 **Alive and Kicking**— 7 Arts (also appeared)

    Life Is a Circus— Brit Lion

1967 **Prehistoric Women**— Hammer/Seven Arts/ Fox

DAVID PALTENGHI

b. Christchurch, England, 1919

d. Windsor, England, 1961

Son of an English mother and a Swiss-Italian father, Paltenghi first studied ballet with Marie Rambert and Anthony Tudor. He joined Tudor's London Ballet in 1939 and remained with the company when it amalgamated with Ballet Rambert in 1940. As principal male dancer with the Sadler's Wells Ballet from 1941–47, he became interested in the possibilities for dance on film and in television and left the company to appear in the films **Sleeping Car to Trieste**, **Queen of Spades**, **Invitation to the Dance** ('51), and **The Black Swan** (a '52 3-D version of *Swan Lake* in which Paltenghi plays "The Prince") etc., as well as choreographing. Appearing as the commentator on a television series ("Ballet For Beginners"), he also created stage productions and occasionally danced as guest artist with Sadler's Wells and Rambert, creating major works for the latter. He retired as a dancer and became a stage director: *The Love Match* ('55), *Keep It Clean* ('56) and *Orders Are Orders* ('59) and television commercial and film choreographer until his death in 1961.

Stage: *Cage Me a Peacock* (London '48, also appeared)

Ballet/Dance Pieces: (Partial listing) For Ballet Rambert: "Eve of St. Agnes," "Prismatic Variations," "Scherzi Della Sorte," "Fate's Revenge"; for Canterbury Festival: "Canterbury Prologue"

Film:

1948 **Hamlet**— Rank (creating the Mime-play)

    Queen of Spades— ABF Pathe/Mon (also appeared)

1950 **Stage Fright**— WB

1951 **Hotel Sahara**— UA

1952 **The Black Swan**— Col (S) (also appeared)

1953 **The Sword and the Rose**— RKO (also appeared)

1954 **The Black Knight**— Univ (also appeared)

    Dance Little Lady— Gau/Brit

    You Know What Sailors Are— UA

1955 **Land of Fury**— Univ

1956 **Alexander the Great**— UA

    Port Afrique— Col

HERMES PAN (PANA-GIOTOPULOS)

b. Memphis, Tennessee, December 10, 1905

d. Beverly Hills, California, September 19, 1990

One of Hollywood's most acclaimed choreographers and dance directors whose innovations helped to create the "Golden Age" of the movie musical. With his sparkling eyes, impeccable behavior, remarkable dance vocabulary and expertise with the camera, Hermes Pan also appeared on screen frequently, partnering Betty Grable, Rita Hayworth and Lana Turner. The son of the Greek consul to the Southern states, Hermes first learned to dance from the blacks in Nashville, Tennessee, imitating their steps. At 14, he went to New York to begin his career dancing in amateur theatricals at Consolidated Edison and speakeasies in New York. He eventually danced on Broadway in *My Maryland* ('27), *Animal Crackers* ('28) and *Top Speed* ('29, also assisting LeRoy Prinz), where he first met Ginger Rogers. Relocating to Hollywood in 1930 with a dance act with his sister, Vasso Meade, he joined a touring production of *Cushman's Garden of Glorious Girls* ('30) for which he also staged the musical numbers and designed the costumes. Returning to Hollywood in 1933 to assist LeRoy Prinz on *Lucky Day*, he then assisted David Bennett on *The 9 O'Clock Revue*. When the show closed briefly because of troubles, it reopened with Pan redoing all of the numbers. Receiving favorable notices, an RKO talent scout signed him to choreograph a musical short for the studio. Instead, he began as an assistant to dance director Dave Gould, who assigned him to work with Fred Astaire on **Flying Down to Rio**. Astaire liked him and his input so much that they formed a lifelong association: revolutionizing dance-on-film with their choreography, dance scenarios, camera techniques and concepts for dance numbers. While Astaire concentrated on his choreography with Rogers and his other partners, Pan created the dance routines for the ensembles. During the 5–6 week rehearsal period Hermes would "Dance-in" for Rogers as they created the numbers and then, teach the choreography to her, also dubbing in her taps. Beyond his memorable association with Astaire and Rogers, when his RKO contract ended in 1939, he went on to choreograph ten films for Betty Grable, as well as some of Hollywood's greatest musical successes over a forty-year period. "When I hear music, I can almost see the motions of the music. It paints a picture for me. A lot of dancers see and feel that... But it's difficult to discuss abstract things like music and dance. Dancing is an emotional thing, an outburst of feeling that comes spontaneously." Along with his prolific film output, he also co-choreographed Astaire's Emmy Award–winning TV specials as well

as those for several other dance stars (Cyd Charisse, etc.). One of the three Academy Award–winning dance directors (**A Damsel in Distress**, '37), he was also honored by the National Film Society Achievement in Cinema Award in 1980, the Joffrey Ballet in 1986, the Gypsy Lifetime Achievement Award by the PDS on February 7, 1988 and by the National Theatre of Dance of Chateauvallon Toulon, France, in 1988. His contributions are those of one of the few film choreographers to be recognized by the serious dance world.

Stage: *Lucky Day* (Mayan Theatre, LA '32, assistant to LeRoy Prinz), *The 9 O'Clock Revue* (Hollywood, '32, with David Bennett), *As the Girls Go* (Bdwy '48)

TV (Partial listing): With Fred Astaire: "An Evening with Fred Astaire" ('59, Emmy award), "Another Evening with Fred Astaire," "Astaire Time," George Burns and Frances Langford Specials ('60), "Ford Startime" ('60), "Carol Channing and 101 Men," "Bell Telephone Hour — Sounds of America" ('61), "Hit Parade," "Remember How Great," "Think Pretty" ('64); "Studio Uno" (Rome, '65, assisted by Jerry Jackson), "The Hollywood Palace," etc.

Nightclub/Concert: Johnny Mathis Tour ('60), *La Parisiene* (Dunes Hotel, LV '60), *Folies Bergere* (Tropicana Hotel, LV '67–68)

Film:

1933 **Flying Down to Rio** — RKO (assistant to Astaire, Dave Gould)

1934 **Cockeyed Cavaliers** — RKO (assistant to Gould)

    Gay Divorcee — RKO (with Astaire, Gould)

    Hips, Hips Hooray — RKO (assistant to Gould)

    Strictly Dynamite — RKO

1935 **I Dream Too Much** — RKO

    In Person — RKO

    Old Man Rhythm — RKO

    Roberta — RKO (with Astaire)

    Top Hat — RKO (with Astaire, Academy Award nom: "The Piccolino" and "Top Hat" numbers)

1936 **Follow the Fleet** — RKO (with Astaire)

    Mary of Scotland — RKO

    Swing Time — RKO (with Astaire, Academy Award nom: "Bojangles of Harlem" number)

    A Woman Rebels — RKO

1937 **A Damsel in Distress** — RKO (with Astaire, assisted by Angie Blue, Academy Award winner: Best Dance Direction: "Fun House" number)

    Quality Street — RKO

    Shall We Dance — RKO (with Astaire, Harry Losee)

    Stage Door — RKO

1938 **Carefree**— RKO (with Astaire)
Radio City Revels— RKO (with Ann Miller, Joseph Santley)
1939 **Bachelor Mother**— RKO
The Story of Vernon and Irene Castle— RKO (with Astaire)
1940 **Second Chorus**— Par (with Astaire, appeared but sequence deleted)
1941 **Blood and Sand**— Fox (with Geneva Sawyer, "Fiesta Scenes Staged by" credit)
Moon Over Miami— Fox (with Condos Bros., assisted by Angie Blue, also partnered Betty Grable in "The Kindergarten Conga," his first onscreen appearance)
Rise and Shine— Fox (with George Murphy)
Sun Valley Serenade— Fox (with Fayard Nicholas)
That Night in Rio— Fox (assisted by Blue)
Weekend in Havana— Fox
1942 **Footlight Serenade**— Fox (assisted by Blue, also appeared partnering Betty Grable in "I Heard the Birdies Sing")
Iceland— Fox (with James Gonzalez)
My Gal Sal— Fox (with Val Raset, also appeared partnering Rita Hayworth to "On the Gay White Way")
Roxie Hart— Fox
Song of the Islands— Fox (assisted by Blue)
Springtime in the Rockies— Fox (assisted by Blue)
1943 **Coney Island**— Fox (assisted by Blue, also appeared partnering Grable to "There's Danger in a Dance")
Sweet Rosie O'Grady— Fox (with Fanchon, assisted by Blue, also appeared partnering Grable in "The Wishing Waltz")
1944 **Irish Eyes Are Smiling**— Fox
Pin Up Girl— Fox (with the Condos Bros., Fanchon, Gae Foster, Alice Sullivan, assisted by Blue, also appeared partnering Grable to "Once Too Often")
1945 **Diamond Horseshoe** (aka **Billy Rose's Diamond Horseshoe**)— Fox (assisted by Blue)
State Fair— Fox
1946 **Blue Skies**— Par (with Astaire, assisted by David Robel)
1947 **I Wonder Who's Kissing Her Now?**— Fox
The Shocking Miss Pilgrim— Fox (assisted by Blue)
1948 **That Lady in Ermine**— Fox (assisted by Blue)
1949 **The Barkleys of Broadway**— MGM (with Robert Alton, Astaire, "'Shoes with Wings On' directed by" credit)

1950 **Let's Dance**— Par (with Astaire)
A Life of Her Own— MGM (also appeared as "Specialty Dancer," partnering Lana Turner)
Three Little Words— MGM (with Astaire)
1951 **Excuse My Dust**— MGM
Texas Carnival— MGM (with Ann Miller)
1952 **Lovely to Look At**— MGM (with Gower Champion, Ann Miller)
1953 **Kiss Me Kate**— MGM (with Bob Fosse, Miller, assisted by Alex Romero — also appeared)
Sombrero— MGM (with José Greco)
1954 **The Student Prince**— MGM
1955 **Hit the Deck**— MGM (with Miller, assisted by Blue and Walton Walker)
Jupiter's Darling— MGM (with Busby Berkeley, Gower Champion)
1956 **Meet Me in Las Vegas**— MGM (with Eugene Loring, assisted by Pat Denise, Walton Walker)
1957 **Pal Joey**— Col (also appeared)
Silk Stockings— MGM (with Astaire, Loring, "All dances in which Fred Astaire appears choreographed by" credit, assisted by Blue, Pat Denise, Dave Robel)
1959 **The Blue Angel**— Fox
Never Steal Anything Small— Univ (assisted by Barrie Chase and Frank Radcliff)
Porgy and Bess— Samuel Goldwyn
1960 **Can Can**— Fox (assisted by Buddy Bryan and Gino Malerba)
1961 **Flower Drum Song**— Univ (assisted by Jimmy Huntley, Malerba and Becky Varno)
The Pleasure of His Company— Par (with Astaire)
1963 **Cleopatra**— Fox (assisted by Wilbert Bradley)
1964 **My Fair Lady**— WB (assisted by Varno and Radcliff)
1965 **The Great Race**— WB
1968 **Finian's Rainbow**— WB (with Astaire, Claude Thompson, assisted by Jerry Jackson)
1970 **Darling Lili**— Par (assisted by Bea Busch)
1973 **Lost Horizon**— Univ (assisted by Busch and Radcliff)
1974 **That's Entertainment!**— MGM (with others)
1976 **That's Entertainment Part 2**— MGM (with others)
1985 **That's Dancing!**— MGM (with others)
1993 **That's Entertainment! III**— MGM (with others)

MICHEL PANAIEFF

b. Novgorod, Russia, January 21, 1913
d. Los Angeles, California, February 8, 1982

Betty Grable dances "The Wishing Waltz" with choreographer Hermes Pan in **Sweet Rosie O'Grady** (20th Century–Fox, 1943).

Russian-born classical Ballet dancer, choreographer, actor and dance educator who escaped from Russia as a child during the Revolution with his English mother and Russian father. Settling in Sarajevo, he decided to become a dancer after seeing a performance of *Coppelia* at the age of 14. He began studying dance four years later at the Margarita Froman school and continued learning over the years at the State Theater in Zurich, with Lubov Egorova, Nicholas Legat and Olga Preobrajenska in Paris and at the School of American Ballet in New York. He made his dance debut with the Belgrade Royal

Opera Ballet and danced leading roles (among them the role of "Franz" in *Coppelia* over 150 times) with Ballets de Paris, Ballets Russes and the Rene Blum Ballet. Settling in California for choreographic and acting assignments, he created his first film choreography for **Lady, Let's Dance** starring ice-skating star Belita. After partnering her at the Hollywood Bowl in 1943, he served as a gunnery sergeant during World War II. Returning to the U.S. in 1946, he opened his Hollywood dance school and made many Southern California guest appearances (Redlands Bowl '47–49, etc.). His multiple film roles,

Michel Panaieff, one of Hollywood's leading ballet dancers, teachers and choreographers, partners an unknown stiff in **Rhapsody in Blue** (Warner Bros., 1945).

often portraying a Russian dancer or ballet master (a role he played in reality for Roland Petit's ballet group during their filming of **Hans Christian Andersen** in 1952), usually included creating his own choreography. In addition to the films listed in his choreographic credits, other film roles include **In Our Time, Fraulein** and **Silk Stockings.** In 1949 he formed the Santa Monica Civic Dancers and in 1956, Ballet Musicale. Adopting a son, David, he continued teaching, creating other groups, (Los Angeles Civic Ballet, Dance Theatre of Orange County) and made straight acting appearances in the films **The Prize** and **Seven Days in May** (both 1963). Never really given much of an opportunity to create more than brief ballet sequences for films, his major contribution to dance on film might be the influence of his popular school on La Brea Blvd. in Hollywood. As a training center, rehearsal hall, audition location and popular gathering place for professionals for almost forty years, the Panaieff Ballet Center — and the talented, exuberant little man who created and energized it — was an introduction to dance for several generations of future influential dance figures.

TV: "Dr. Kildare," "My Living Doll," "Mr. Terrific," "Concerto de General Motors" (Mexican TV, '53 — 44 weeks — also appeared)

Ballet/Dance Pieces (Partial listing): "Under the Circus Top," "Vesna," "The Seasons," "Forever Israel," "Fantaisie," "The Dress," "Songs Without Words," "La Danse et la Musique," "Dawn Till Dark," "Devil's Belt," "Pas de Quatre," etc.

Film (Credits are for the choreography for his own appearances):

1943 **Mission to Moscow**— WB (with LeRoy Prinz)

1944 **Lady, Let's Dance**— Mon (with Dave Gould)

1945 **Rhapsody in Blue**— WB (with Prinz)

1946 **Night and Day**— WB (with Prinz)

1956 **Gaby**— MGM

1966 **Torn Curtain**— Univ

TOM PANKO

Dancer-choreographer who appeared on Broadway in *L'il Abner* ('56), beginning his long-time association with Onna White, who was also in the cast.

Stage: Not While I'm Eating (OB '61), *Guys and Dolls* (LACLO '61 rev), *Golden Rainbow* (Bdwy '68), *Beau* (OOT '69), *One for the Money, Etc.* (OB '71)

TV: "The Roaring '20s" ('61)

Film:
1962 **The Music Man** — WB (associate to Onna White)
1963 **Black Gold** — WB
1968 **Oliver!** — Col (associate to White)
1969 **They Shoot Horses, Don't They?** — Palomar/ABC/ Cinerama (with Noble "Kid" Chissell, assisted by Alice Clift)

STEPHEN PAPICH

b. St. David, Illinois, May 22, 1925.

While growing up in Illinois, Papich began dance lessons at the age of 8, but his family returned to their native Jugoslavia and remained in Europe for eight years where young Stephen appeared with the Belgrade, Salzburg and Zagreb Opera companies. Returning to the United States at 13, he finished high school in Canton, Ill., and went to New York, where he studied under a scholarship with Katherine Dunham. After leaving the Armed Forces in 1945, he joined Dunham's dance troupe and began specializing in ethnic dance. In 1951 he was placed under contract to 20th Century–Fox where he created dances for their series of CinemaScope Biblical epics, also dancing in **South Pacific** ('58). After his contract with Fox ended, he produced his own group of dancers, Katherine Dunham's 1962 *Bambouche* tour, stage shows for the Hollywood Bowl and directed Josephine Baker in her last revues. Papich is the author of *Remembering Josephine* (1976).

Stage: For the Hollywood Bowl: *David* ('56), *Gay 90's Revue, Viennese* and *Fiesta Nights* ('59), *The California Story*

Nightclub/Concert: The Stephen Papich Company ('60); acts and shows for Josephine Baker, Dorothy Dandridge and Patricia Morrison

Film:
1952 **Stars and Stripes Forever** — Fox (with Nick Castle, Al White, Jr., also appeared, uncredited)
1953 **King of the Khyber Rifles** — Fox (with Asoka, assisted by Wiletta Smith, uncredited)
      The President's Lady — Fox
      The Robe — Fox
      Titanic — Fox
1954 **Demetrius and the Gladiators** — Fox
      Désirée — Fox
      The Egyptian — Fox
      The Silver Chalice — WB
1955 **The Rains of Ranchipur** — Fox
      Soldier of Fortune — Fox (assisted by Anna Cheselska)
      Untamed — Fox
      The Virgin Queen — Fox

NOEL PARENTI

b. Bakersfield, California

Parenti started his dance training at the age of 5 and by the time he was 16 he was appearing in Las Vegas productions (the Harry Belafonte and Mickey Rooney nightclub acts). With further study over the years from Natalia Clare, Ann Halprin, David Lichine and Wilson Morelli in California and the School of American Ballet, Met Opera Ballet School and American Ballet Theatre School in New York, Parenti danced with Clare's Ballet Co. and Ballet La Jeunesse, performed onstage in *Where's Charley?, Finian's Rainbow, West Side Story, On the Town, Redhead* and *Gypsy* and appeared in **The Music Man.** While serving in the Army, he created his first one-man show, *An Evening with Me*, which combined ballet, modern, musical comedy and mime. Upon discharge he returned to California in 1964 and appeared on TV in the Red Skelton and Danny Kaye shows. He created a one-man mime and dance show, touring from '65–67 and in 1968, settled in San Francisco with his wife, Rosalind.

Stage: Let's Laugh (LA '65)
TV: Morton Gould's "Concerto for Tap Dancers and Orchestra" (PBS '78, also appeared)
Nightclub/Concert: The Adventures of Noel Parenti ('65–67)
Film:
1961 **The Sergeant Was a Lady** — Univ

DAVID PARSONS

1991 **Fools Fire** — American Playhouse (TV) ("Masquerade choreography by" credit)

JULIA PASCALE

1991 **At Play in the Fields of the Lord** — Univ ("Indian dance movement and choreography" credit)

VINCENT PATERSON

b. Upland, Pennsylvania, May 4, 1950

Patterson is among the leading forces of taking dance in new and exciting directions in the 1990s. Receiving a Bachelor of Arts degree in direction and acting from Pennsylvania's Dickinson College in 1972, he moved to Tuscon, Arizona, to began dance training with Stephanie Stigers. He performed at the Tuscon Dance Gallery and the City Dance Theatre from 1975–76, choreographing his first work there in 1976. He relocated to L.A. to pursue a performance career, continuing his dance studies with Bill and Jacqui Landrum, Michael Peters, Sallie Whelen and Lester Wilson. He danced with the Landrum Dance Theater (1977–78) and then toured with Shirley MacLaine's nightclub and concert show. Other stage appearances include tours with Barbara Mandrell and the Osmonds. He appeared in the film **Footloose**, in music video ("Beat It," "Thriller," "Dancing on the Ceiling," "Totally Hot," etc.) on many TV specials, and, as Barbara Mandrell's partner, on her weekly TV series until his talents as a director and choreographer came into great demand. In PBS's "Dance in America: Everybody Dance Now," he discussed his agreement with Michael Jackson about filming dance for their music video "Smooth Criminal": "With dance, we both sort of felt that the master in shooting dance was Vincente Minnelli and we liked the technique of seeing the body. Of course, it's important to cut in for close-up... But we both really feel that it's important to see dance in full figure as much as possible." In 1994 he directed and choreographed the highly-acclaimed and Emmy-nominated "In Search of Dr. Seuss" for TV winning an Ace Award for Best Direction.

Stage: *Kiss of the Spider Woman* (Canada and London, '92, Bdwy, '93, Tony nom), *Commitment to Life IV and VI* (Wiltern Theatre, LA, dir)

TV: "Motown at 25" (Michael Jackson's number), "The Grammy Awards" ('88, Michael Jackson's number), Madonna's "Vogue" number on MTV Awards ('90) and her appearance on the 64th annual Academy Awards show ('91), "Mother Goose Rock 'n' Rhyme," "MGM: When the Lion Roars" ('92), "Body and Soul" (pilot, "Musical segment producer" credit), "In Search of Dr. Seuss" (TNT '94, also dir, Emmy nom); commercials for Antarctica Beer ('95 *LA Dance* Award nom), AT & T, Budweiser, Coors, Diet Pepsi (starring Ray Charles), Dupont, Holiday Health Spa, Kenwood, Levis, Lifesavers, McDonalds, Nike, Oldsmobile, Pepsi, Sony, Suntory Brandy, Taco Bell and Vidal Sassoon

Music Video (Partial listing): "Smooth Criminal," "Black or White," "Speed Demon," "The Way You Make Me Feel"—Michael Jackson; "Like a Virgin," "Holiday," "Express Yourself"—Madonna; "Trapped in the Body of a White Girl" and "Girl Fight Tonight"—Julie Brown; "Hot for Teacher"—Van Halen; "California Girls"—David Lee Roth; "I've Got My Mind Set on You"—George Harrison; "Stranglehold"—Paul McCartney; "Eternity"—Sheena Easton

Nightclub/Concert: Michael Jackson's "Bad" tour ('88, also dir), Madonna's "Blonde Ambition" Tour ('90, also co-dir), Chayanne, Sheena Easton and Donny Osmond tours

Film:
1987 **Mannequin**—Fox
1988 **Moonwalker**—WB (with Russell Clark, Michael Jackson)
1989 **The Mighty Quinn**—MGM/UA
1990 **Havana**—Univ

1991 **Clifford**—Dinosaur (with Russell Clark)
      Hook—Univ (with Kim Blank, Smith Wordes)
      Madonna—Truth or Dare (aka **In Bed with Madonna**)—Boy Toy Inc/Miramax
      MGM: When the Lion Roars—Turner Pict (TV)
1992 **Ruby**—Propaganda
1995 **Angus**—Turner Pictures
1996 **The Birdcage**—UA (assisted by Smith Wordes)
      Evita—Cinergi (assisted by Miranda Garrison)

BERNARD "BABE" PEARCE

Originally signed to do the dances for **The Sky's the Limit** ('43), Pearce was replaced by the film's star, Fred Astaire.

Nightclub/Concert: *The Magic Carpet Revue* (Dunes Hotel, LV Opening Show, June, 1955, with Val Raset)

Film:
1942 **Holiday Inn**—Par (assistant to Fred Astaire, Danny Dare)
1946 **The Kid from Brooklyn**—RKO
      Three Little Girls in Blue—Fox (with Seymour Felix, created the ballets)
1947 **Road to Rio**—Par (with Billy Daniel)
      Variety Girl—Par (with Billy Daniel, Danny Dare)
1948 **Casbah**—Univ (with Katherine Dunham)

STEVEN PECK (STEFANO IGNAZIO APOSTOLE PECORARO)

b. Brooklyn, New York, December 2, 1928

A self-taught dancer who performed at neighborhood bars as a child and went to the movies as often as possible to learn from George Raft, Gene Kelly and other film idols. He began competing in partner challenges at New York clubs, enhancing his natural talent and eye for movement with formal studies of ethnic dance with Katherine Dunham and adagio with "Pecky" and Renoff and Renova. Performing his own choreography, he made his professional debut at the Bella Taverna in NY in 1947 and created a sensational adagio act which took him to Hollywood nightclubs (Ciro's, Coconut Grove, Crescendo and the Mocambo) ... and to the attention of influential columnist Walter Winchell. In 1952, he created *Tantrums in Tempo* for the Crescendo nightclub in Hollywood—his professional choreographic debut. Strengthening his natural ability and style, he studied ballet with Gene Marinacchio and flamenco with José Cansino and began teaching Afro-Cuban Jazz and adagio at various schools. He opened his own studio in 1953, with Winchell dubbing him "Teacher of the Stars" because of his many celebrity students. Opening his own nightclub Club Seville in 1956, he continued coaching and partnering female stars on television, as well as winning a contract with MGM and one of the leading roles in **Some Came Running.** Acting classes with Jay Adler, the Anthony Quinn Acting Group and Lester Luther helped his multi-faceted career continue with acting appearances in dozens of films (**Bells Are Ringing, Two Weeks in Another Town, Lady in Cement, The Idolmaker, Rhinestone** etc.) and over 50 featured roles on television; writing, directing, choreographing and starring with The Steven Peck Jazz Dance Company and The Steven Peck Repertory Company and teaching and choreography assignments. Peck opened a second highly successful school and restaurant in Fullerton, California in 1971 and continues to pass on his unique talents, energy and philosophy to generations of young performers.

Stage (Partial listing for his theatre groups in California — also director, author and often appeared): *Concert in the Park, Jazz Soup, Isms, Cuban Overture, Above the Garbage, A Man Called George, Cafe Latino Funk, Blood, Peace and Charlie Cocaine, Dance Factory, Godfather — Tribute to Nino Rota* ('81)

TV: "The Steve Allen Show" ('56), "December Bride"

Nightclub/Concert: Adagio act with thirteen various partners, including Molly Molligan, Susan Jarrol and Lita Leon; *Tantrums in Tempo* (Hollywood, '52), act for Tommy Sands, *The Walter Winchell Revue* (Tropicana Hotel, LV '58)

Film:
1958 **The Gunrunners** — UA (also appeared)
1963 **Who's Been Sleeping in My Bed?** — Par
1966 **The Oscar** — Embassy
1974 **The Godfather, Part 2** — Par (with Jerry Jackson, choreographed his own "Tango" routine appearance with Tybee Afra)

PAUL PELLICORO
b. Levittown, New York
Describing himself as "a Hustle club kid of the '70s," Pellicoro has parlayed his talent and energy into becoming one of the '90s leading dance coaches. His extensive dance training included being a dance major at Adelphi University, over fifteen years with the top competitive Ballroom and Latin teachers, as well as jazz with Phil Black, Frank Hatchett and Luigi. Going into teaching himself in 1979 he researched the roots and authentic styling of Latin Dance and Argentine Tango in Brazil and throughout the Caribbean. In 1985 he travelled to

Argentina to study with Juan Carlos Lopez, the choreographer of *Tango Argentino*, and opened his popular Dancesport in Manhattan. Billed as "The Man who taught Al Pacino to Tango" after his two-month training of the star for **Scent of a Woman,** his other celebrity students include Gabrielle Anwar, Robert Duvall, Meryl Streep and actress-choreographer Miranda Garrison. He and partner Eleny Fotinos currently participate in international ballroom dance competitions.

Stage: Animalen (Swedish Opera)
Music Video: "City Streets" — Carol King (also appeared), Lambada and Swing instructional videos (also appeared)
Film:
1991 **Straight Talk** — Hollywood Pictures (with Miranda Garrison, uncredited)
1992 **The Mambo Kings** — WB (with Kim Blank, Jack Donohue, Michael Peters, uncredited consultant)
     A River Runs Through It — Col (with Johnny Almaraz, Miranda Garrison, uncredited)
     Scent of a Woman — Univ (with Jerry Mitchell)

PEDRO PABLE PENA
1994 **The Specialist** — WB (with the Miami Hispanic Ballet)

MOSES PENDLETON (ROBB PENDLETON)
b. Lyndonville, Vermont, March 28, 1948
One of the founder-members of the innovative dance/theater group Pilobolus in 1971, Pendleton graduated from Dartmouth College with a degree in English Literature, where he had started dance studies in his Senior year. The imaginative group choreographed collectively, creating mind-boggling visions of bodies in motion which dazzled the modern dance world ("If we amuse ourselves, chances are we'll amuse other people.") After a tour of Israel which deeply impressed him, Pendleton took the first name "Moses." In 1980 Pendleton created Momix (named after a milk supplement he fed to calves as a farm boy), another collaborative group which included Daniel Ezralow. In 1983 a documentary (**Moses Pendleton Presents Moses Pendleton**) was filmed presenting his work and philosophy. "'I never really saw myself as just a choreographer'... Pendleton comes up with the terms 'visualist' and 'fantasist'" (*Dance Magazine*, December 1994).

Stage: Carmen, The Magic Flute
TV: Italian television
Ballet/Dance Pieces (Partial listing): For Pilobolus:

"Shizen," "Lost in Fauna" (with Alison Chase); "Walklyndon," "Ciona," "Monkshood's Farewell," "Molly's Not Dead," "Ocellus, "Verticella;" for Momix: "Passion" ('94)
   Miscellaneous: 3-D IMAX film **Imagine**
   Film:
1991 **FX 2—The Deadly Art of Illusion**— Orion

GIUSEPPE PENNESE
1988 **Rent-a-Cop**— Kings Road Ent

PINO PENNESE
1980 **Caligula**— Penthouse (with Tito DeLuc)
1987 **The Barbarians**— Cannon
1989 **Adventures of Baron Munchausen**— Col (with Giorgio Rossi)

MARGARET T. HICKEY PEREZ
1995 **The Brady Bunch Movie**— Par (with Joe Cassini)

ROSIE PEREZ
   b. Brooklyn, New York
If Paula Abdul is the Super Pop Star of the '90s to come from the ranks of choreographers, colorful Latina Rosie Perez is certainly the first Actress of the Moment. Raised in New York and developing her own unique dance style in clubs ("I grew up in the clubs, and everybody who was in the clubs then is now in some aspect of the entertainment business"), she was discovered by a talent scout in a club and became a dancer on TV's "Soul Train." Moving to Los Angeles to study biochemistry, she was doing choreography for rock acts when film director Spike Lee saw her dancing in a club called Funky Reggae. He cast her in **Do the Right Thing**— in which she also choreographed her dance sequence. She was next signed by Robert Townsend to choreograph for the Fly Girls in his TV series "In Living Color." The ever-candid Perez revealed that when she walked onto the soundstage to begin rehearsals for the show, she announced to the professionally trained dancers: "Look, I'm not a real choreographer ... you know, I don't work like 5-6-7-8. If I feel a move, you gotta copy it. That's basically it." Nevertheless, she helped cause a sensation with the newest (and most popular) television dance troupe since the Solid Gold Dancers. Cast in **White Men Can't Jump**, she was immediately loved by audiences and cheered by critics ("A loveable Hispanic Clown, sort of a Desi Arnaz with cleavage"—

Vibe Magazine). She enjoyed great success as a film actress (**Untamed Heart, Fearless, It Could Happen to You, Somebody to Love**) and in September, 1994, a press release stated that she would "take a much needed break" from film stardom and go back to choreography.
   TV: "In Living Color" (Emmy nom)
   Music Video: "North on South Street"— Herb Alpert
   Nightclub/Concert: Acts for Bobby Brown, Heavy D, more
   Film:
1989 **Do the Right Thing**— Univ (with Otis Sallid, also appeared)

RENATO PERNIC
1983 **Twilight Time**— MGM/UA

BILLY PETCH
   b. Canada
Dancer-choreographer who achieved great success with international nightclub and cabaret shows.
   Nightclub/Concert: Talk of the Town (London), *Folies Bergére* (Paris & LV '61–62), *London Swings* (Sahara Tahoe, '66), *Casino de Paris* (Dunes Hotel, LV '68)
   Film:
1963 **What a Crazy World**— WB/Pathé

MICHAEL PETERS
   b. Williamsburg, Brooklyn, New York, 1948
   d. Los Angeles, California, August 27, 1994
"Dance was my saving grace. It was mine. I was a man without a country. When I danced everything else went away." (*Drama-Logue*, September 2–9, 1993) said dancer, director and choreographer Peters, whose work in music video in the 1980s revolutionized dance on film and gave him the nickname: "The Balanchine of MTV." Attending the High School of Performing Arts, his creativity bloomed at the Bernice Johnson Cultural Arts Center in Queens, where he began studying dance with Johnson. In 1966 his first professional job was a TV show in Rome, after which he assisted Lester Wilson on a German production of *Jesus Christ Superstar* and joined Lola Falana's nightclub act. He met Donna Summer in Germany and when they returned to America, she gave him his first solo choreographic assignment creating her "Love to Love You Baby" American concert tour. In 1968 he appeared in a stock production of *West Side Story*, choreographed by Michael Bennett, then was briefly a member of Alvin Ailey's and Talley Beatty's companies and danced on Broadway in *Purlie*, *Raisin* and *The Wiz*. Moving to California, he began

choreographing nightclub acts and dance pieces for various companies. After his first Broadway show (*Comin' Uptown*), he gained success — and a Tony award — co-choreographing *Dreamgirls* with Michael Bennett in 1981. His revolutionary music video collaborations with Michael Jackson ("Thriller," "Beat It") earned him the NAACP's 1983 Image Award and an American Music Award for Best Video Choreography. About his collaboration with Michael Jackson on the landmark music videos: "He had no training. I couldn't talk to him in dance terms. I had to talk to him like a musician." On the television show "Story of a People — Expressions in Black," Peters explained his approach to choreography: "I think I was born to dance… I get as much joy — if not more — in seeing others translate what I've envisioned. It doesn't matter whose body I put my work on because I design for whoever it is and for whatever their capabilities are. That's my job as a choreographer… My big thing in dance is story telling. I think that dance just for dance's sake to me is boring. Once you've seen somebody's technique, you've seen it, you know? But if somebody can portray an emotion — tell a story, that's interesting to me." One of the choreographers to be given a tribute on the 1984 Emmy Awards TV show, he was also one of the winners of the first *LA Dance* Awards for his work on **What's Love Got to Do with It?** (sharing the award with Otis Sallid for **Swing Kids**). His career moved into television direction (New Kids on the Block special, episodes of "Fresh Prince of Bel Air," "A Different World," "Knot's Landing") and music videos. While battling AIDS, Peters created some of his finest work and fought for recognition for choreographers, serving as an inspiration to the dance community with his artistry and bravery. *Time* Magazine's obituary acknowledged, "Peters' raucous choreography for music videos … helped gain recognition and legitimacy for the new art form."

Stage: *Rock the Ground* (LA Shakespeare Festival, '78), *Comin' Uptown* (Bdwy '79), *Dreamgirls* (Bdwy '81, with Michael Bennett, Tony award), *Leader of the Pack* (Bdwy '85, also dir), *To Sir with Love* (LA), *Electric Ice* (NY '85)

TV: "Centennial" ('78), 1983 Emmy Awards Show, 1984 Academy Awards Show, "Fame," "Liberty Weekend Closing Ceremonies" (Emmy Award), "Jackson Family Honors" ('94), "Comic Relief VI" ('94); commercials for Burger King, Dr. Pepper, McDonalds, Pepsi (starring the Jacksons), Sasson Jeans and Shasta soft drinks

Music Video: "Beat It," "Thriller"— Michael Jackson (MTV Award — with Jackson); "Running with the Night," "Hello"— Lionel Richie; "Love Is a Battlefield"— Pat Benatar; "Pieces of Ice"— Diana Ross; "Uptown Girl"— Billy Joel

Nightclub/Concert: Acts for Lucie Arnaz, Deb-

bie Reynolds, Connie Stevens, Donna Summer and Ben Vereen; Diana Ross' 1984 Central Park concert (also appeared)

Ballet/Dance Pieces: "Linear," "Altar Ego," "Who Are the Good Guys?" (Bernice Johnson Dance Co. '78), "Needlepoint Incantation" (Loretta Abbott & Al Perryman '78), "Love Fantasy" (LA Jazz Company, '81), "Quartet" (Ntl Ballet of Canada, '83), "The Awakening" (Spoleto Festival '84)

Film:

1977 **Scott Joplin**— Univ

1985 **That's Dancing!**— MGM (with others)

1991 **The Five Heartbeats**— Fox (assisted by Edgar Godineaux, Wayne "Crescendo" Ward))

1992 **The Mambo Kings**— WB (with Kim Blank, Jack Donohue)

1993 **The Jacksons: An American Dream**— ABC (TV) (Emmy Award)

Sarafina!— Miramax (with Mbongeni Ngema, *LA Dance* Award nom, assisted by Eartha Robinson)

Sister Act II— Disney (assisted by Eartha Robinson)

What's Love Got to Do with It?— Disney (assisted by Eartha Robinson, 1993 NAACP Image award nom and 1994 *LA Dance* Award winner)

ROLAND PETIT

b: Villemomble, France, January 13, 1924

Classical Ballet dancer, choreographer and director who has been described as "The Man who put sex in the ballet," Petit was born in a suburb of Paris, son of a French father and an Italian mother. He began his classical studies at the Paris Opera School at 11 and joined the Corps at age of 15 in 1939. At 17 he began choreographing and eventually giving solo recitals in 1944 (first ballet *Paul et Virginia*) and, always the rebel, left the Opera Ballet at 21 to choreograph for Les Vendredis de la Danse and co-form Les Ballets des Champs Elysees, premiering October 12, 1945, in which he was ballet master, choreographer and premier danseur. He eventually created his own group, Roland Petit's Ballets de Paris in 1948, which would change the face of classical dance with his inventive dance works combining music hall, classic ballet and generous helpings of sensuality. Among his dancers were future film leading ladies Leslie Caron, Jeanmaire and Colette Marchand. On December 29, 1954, he married Jeanmaire and created some of his most successful ballets, film work and stage shows for her. After tremendous notice in America for his revolutionary pieces, he was contracted by eccentric studio head Howard Hughes to film Petit's sensational *Carmen* in January 1951. The company

Jeanmaire gives the "Kiss of Life" to the near-dead Prince (Roland Petit) in the ***Little Mermaid Ballet*** from **Hans Christian Andersen** (Samuel Goldwyn, 1952).

remained on salary until August of that year, but the film was never made — although ***Carmen*** would be captured on film in **Black Tights**, ten years later. When George Balanchine, originally signed to choreograph **Hans Christian Andersen** for star Moira Shearer, dropped out — and Shearer became pregnant — Petit and Jeanmaire got their opportunity to create film dance history and Petit's international film credits began. Petit owned and produced shows for the *Casino de Paris* for five years during the 1970s. Since 1972 he has directed Ballet National de Marseille and to commemorate his 70th birthday, he created three new ballets for the Paris Opera in 1994.

Stage: *Zizi* (Bdwy '65), *Can Can* (Bdwy '81 rev, Tony nom)

TV: Max Liebman Spectaculars ('55), "Chemin de la Creation" ('65), "Show Roland Petit" ('71), "Top a Zizi" ('74), "Une Heure avec Roland Petit & Rudy Bryans" ('75), "Perfume Suit" ('76)

Nightclub/Concert: *La Revue Parisienne* ('64), multiple productions for the *Casino de Paris*

Ballet/Dance Pieces (Partial listing): "Sant de Tremplin" ('42), "Les Forains," "Le Rendez-vous," "Carmen," "Le Jeune Homme et La Mort," "Les Demoiselles de la Nuit," "The Diamond Cruncher," "The Devil in 24 Hours," "Ballabile," "Le Loup," "Lady in the Ice," "La Dame dans la Lune," "Cyrano de Bergerac," "Paradise Lost," "Passacaille," "Rhythm de Valses" and "Caméra Obscura: L'Amour Est Aveugle" ('94)

Film:

1952 **Hans Christian Andersen**— Samuel Goldwyn (also appeared as "The Prince" in ***The Little Mermaid Ballet***)

1955 **Daddy Long Legs**— Fox (with Fred Astaire, David Robel)

The Glass Slipper— MGM (with Charles Walters —"Ballets by" credit)

1956 **Anything Goes**— Par (with Nick Castle, Ernest Flatt)

1958 **Folies Bergère**—(Fr)

1962 **Black Tights**— Magna (also appeared)

1985 **White Nights**— Col (with Mikhail Baryshnikov, Gregory Hines, Twyla Tharp)

HAMIL PETROFF

Film director and producer who began his career as a dancer at the Hollywood Bowl in Theodore Kosloff's ***Petrouchka*** ('37) and appeared in the films **Sofia** ('48), **Samson and Delilah** ('49), **Phfft!** ('54) and **The Girl Rush** ('55). He assisted Jack Donohue on TV projects and Josephine Earl in films before earning his solo choreography credits.

He subsequently produced and directed **California** ('63) and **Runaway Girl** ('66).

TV: The Mickey Rooney Special ('60)

Miscellaneous: Ice-Capades, industrials for Jerry Fairbanks Prod., "Miss Universe" Pageant ('59)

Film:

1957 **Teacher's Pet**— Par (assistant to Josephine Earl)

1959 **The Beat Generation**— MGM

1962 **Mutiny on the Bounty**— MGM

DORIS PETRONI

1988 **Tango Bar**— Castle Hill (with Nelson Avila, Santiago Ayala, Lilliana Belfiore, Carlos Rivarola, Nelida Rodriguez, Norma Viola)

PEGGY PETTIT

1972 **Black Girl**— Cinerama (also appeared)

ARLENE PHILLIPS

b. Manchester, England

British dancer-choreographer-director who was one of the major forces in the musical theater boom in London in the 1980s. She began ballet classes at the age of 2½ in Manchester, England, and continued studies through college, also giving ballet lessons to children. Moving to London, she took her first jazz dance class and "never went back... I just stayed on with the same clothes and bags of things I'd arrived with." She started choreographing TV commercials in the early '70s, while simultaneously appearing onstage in Lindsay Kemp's *Flowers* (which she also choreographed) and *Oh! Calcutta!* in London. She came to prominence with her song-and-dance troupe Hot Gossip on "The Kenny Everett Video Show" on British television and subsequently created her own TV show ("The Very Hot Gossip Show"). Invited to the United States to create a new dance group for the syndicated series "Dancin' to the Hits," she has contributed internationally ever since. In her press release for **Annie**, Phillips explained that "her dance ideas come from almost anything she sees: 'a picture in a magazine, an old dress in a tatty show window,' and often by 'a great record that I hear. I even dream numbers... When I wake in the morning, costumes, sets, hair ... everything will be there'... She demanded of her dancers perfection and ... what she calls 'attack,' an inner strength that creates excitement for the audience. Her routines are not easy ... and they don't look it either." Her work in two of the last big musicals produced in Hollywood (**Can't Stop the Music** and **Annie**) assure her a place in film musical history.

Stage: *Flowers* (London and NY), *A Clockwork Orange* (Royal Shakespeare Co.), *Masquerade* (Young Vic), *Rock Nativity* (Eng '76), *Fire Angel* (London '77), *Masquerade* (Young Vic '82), *Starlight Express* (London '84 & Bdwy '86, Tony nom), *Time* (London), *Matador* (London '91), *Grease* ('93 London rev), *Starlight Express* ('94 LV rev, also dir)

TV (Partial listing): "The Very Hot Gossip Show," "Dancin' to the Hits," "The Hot Shoe Show," "The Benny Hill Show," "The David Essex Show," "Kenny Everett Video Show," "Ken Russell's ABC of Music," German Eurovision Song Contest, "The Royal Variety Show," specials for Donna Summer and Tina Turner; over 100 commercials for American Express, Burger King, Coca Cola, Dr. Pepper, Doritos, Levi Jeans, Miller Beer, 7-Up, TWA, etc.

Music Video: Videos for the Bee Gees, Culture Club, Duran Duran, Aretha Franklin, Whitney Houston, Elton John, Kiss, Freddie Mercury and Queen, George Michael, Olivia Newton-John, Cliff Richard and Tina Turner

Nightclub/Concert: *The Music of Andrew Lloyd Webber* (Intl. tour, also dir)

Film:

1979 **Escape to Athena**— Assoc Film Dist.

1980 **Can't Stop the Music**— EMI (assisted by Dan Levans, Heather Seymour)

1981 **The Fan**— Par

1982 **Annie**— Col

1983 **The Hunger**— MGM/UA

Monty Python's the Meaning of Life— Univ

1986 **Highlander**— Fox

Legend— Univ

1988 **It Couldn't Happen Here**— Liberty-Picture Music Intl.

Salome's Last Dance— Vestron (assisted by Wanda Rokicki)

1990 **White Hunter, Black Heart**— WB

HELENE PHILLIPS

b. Los Angeles, California

"For me, dancing is like breathing — it is the most natural and necessary element in my life!" said this dancer-choreographer who has successfully combined her gifts for dance composition with technical expertise to become an internationally well respected and sought-after dancemaker. Born and raised in Los Angeles, she began training on a scholarship at the Roland Dupree Dance Academy with Dupree, Jerry Grimes, Rick Miland, Delores Terry and Claude Thompson. While a Dance major at UCLA she made her professional debut at the age of 20 in popular West Coast clubs with KATNAP and KOMPANY ("We performed almost every night at a different disco or nightclub") and continued in fashion shows, industrials, films (**Dr. Detroit**, **Going Berserk**), stage (*Belz*— an original musical at Hollywood's Call Board Theater) and TV ("The Girl, Goldwatch and Dynamite," "Battle of Best" and the Academy Awards Show.) As one of the highly popular "Solid Gold" Dancers from 1979–81, she also assisted choreographer Kevin Carlisle. Her choreographic contributions continued in films assisting Dennon and Sayhber Rawles and Jeffrey Hornaday (also on Madonna's 1987 "Who's That Girl" tour). She gratefully credits Hornaday "For teaching me so much about the business," Rick Miland "For showing me a way to move, which I now teach to my students" and Shaun Earl "For continually reminding me all that I have to offer — as a person and as a choreographer." As for her approach to dance creation, she wrote, "When I'm choreographing I simply listen to the music and it tells me exactly what to do. I can make my song move the way it sounds!"

TV: "Temporarily Yours" (pilot), "Nightingales" (pilot & series), "Airwolf" (pilot), "Santa Barbara"; commercials for the Donnelly Directory, GE Cordless phone, Milde Sorte Cigarettes

Music Video: "Walk the Dinosaur"— Was Not Was; "Love the Way You Love Me"— Karyn White, "Weatherman Says"— Jack Wagner; "Fish for Life"— Karate Kid II; other videos for the Greg Kihn Band, Shaun Earl and Sweat

Nightclub/Concert: Broadway Dance Company (Japan)

Miscellaneous: industrials for Asics, L.A. Gear, Levi, Sports Chalet, Winterfest; shows for Q.E. II Cunard, Princess and Royal Viking Cruise ship lines (also dir)

Film:

1983 **Staying Alive**— Par (assistant to Dennon and Sayhber Rawles, also appeared)

1985 **Captain E-O**— Disney (S) (assistant to Jeffrey Hornaday, with Michelle Johnston)

A Chorus Line— Embassy (assistant to Jeffrey Hornaday with Gregg Burge, Troy Garza, Brad Jeffries, Vickie Regan, also appeared)

MURRAY PHILLIPS

1996 **Made in L.A.**— ZeaProd

BOY PILAPIE

Filipino dancer and choreographer.

Film:

1989 **Macho Dancer**— Strand Releasing

HARRY PILCER

b. United States, 1886
d. Cannes, France, January 15, 1961

Dashing performer and lyricist whose legendary romantic escapades inspired the standard "I'm Just Wild About Harry." A classmate of Fred and Adele Astaire's at Claude Alvienne's dance school in New York in 1904, he made his debut onstage in *The Heartbreakers* (OOT '11) and danced on Broadway in *Hello, Paris* that same year. He met and fell in love with the vivacious French star, Gaby Delys, writing the lyrics to "The Gaby Glide" for her show *Vera Violetta* ('11). He and Delys danced together on Broadway in the shows *The Honeymoon Express* ('13), *The Belle of Bond Street* ('14) and *Stop, Look and Listen* ('15), as well as the 1915 film **Her Triumph**. The dashing couple then went to Europe, where they were the toast of Paris. When their romance ended, Harry returned to New York to appear on Broadway in *Pins and Needles* ('22). He then was called back to the Folies Bergère and partnered Mistinguette — onstage and off. When the Germans occupied Paris in 1942, Pilcer lost all of his belongings and escaped to America, hoping to sell the story of Gaby Delys to films. He appeared in the film **Thank Your Lucky Stars** in 1942. When 20th Century–Fox film chief Darryl F. Zanuck heard that Pilcer was in Hollywood — and destitute — he hired him to play a 1920s cabaret star, as well as stage the nightclub sequence for **The Razor's Edge**, his last recorded theatrical work. Toward the end of his life, he worked at the Palm Beach Casino in Cannes. The epitome of the stylish, graceful and handsome gigolo, Harry Pilcer is remembered with awe.

Stage: The Genius (Bdwy '06)

Film:

1915 **Her Triumph**— Forrester-Parant (also appeared, uncredited)

1937 **Cinderella**—(Fr)

1946 **The Razor's Edge**— Fox (also appeared)

LITZ PISK

b. Vienna, Austria

"I'm not really a dancer at all," Pisk said when hired to act as dance consultant and choreographer for the film about the life of Isadora Duncan."I was more interested in the visual arts; however, for me, design and movement are very closely bound together." Studying costume design in Vienna with Max Reinhardt's famed stage designer, Oskar Strnad, she became involved with several dance groups inspired by Duncan, called the New School for the Art of Movement. At 16 she began classes with Elizabeth Duncan, Isadora's sister, and in 1933, she went to London to teach at the Royal Academy of Dramatic Arts. She later joined the Old Vic School as resident teacher of movement for actors where Vanessa Redgrave was a pupil. When Redgrave was signed for the film, Pisk began with six months training for the actress before filming.

Stage: As You Like It (London)
Film:
1968 **The Loves of Isadora** (aka **Isadora**) —
Univ (with Frederick Ashton)

ALEX PLASSCHAERT

b. Huntington Beach, California, March 23, 1932
This versatile dancer, actor, stuntman, choreog-rapher and director studied ballet with Ernest Belcher and Robert Rosselat and tap with Willie Covan, Louis DaPron and Al Ross. He attended East LA College and Pepperdine University, where he first gained his gymnastic training. Making his professional debut in the long-running Los Ange-les melodrama, *The Drunkard,* in 1953, his on-going performance career encompassed nightclubs (*Minsky's Follies, Le Lido de Paris, The Mickey Finn Show,* Dinah Shore's act, etc.), stage (*Vintage '60, Esther Williams' Spectacular* in London, etc.), films (**Babes in Toyland, Bye Bye Birdie, Can Can, Hello, Dolly!, Kissin' Cousins, Let's Make Love, Mary Poppins, The Unsinkable Molly Brown, The Wonderful World of the Brothers Grimm,** etc.) and television ("The Hollywood Palace," the Milton Berle, George Gobel, Bob Hope, Dean Martin, Dinah Shore and Andy Williams shows; Julie Andrews and Fred Astaire Specials, etc). After assisting Nick Castle in 1967 on "Laugh-In" and "The Jerry Lewis Show," he created his first solo choreography for "The Hollywood Palace" and combining his dance and acrobatic/stunt knowl-edge has continued for three decades to direct, stage and choreograph for various mediums. He cites Willie Covan, Gene Kelly, Donald O'Connor, Robert Rosselat, Disney second-unit director Art Viterelli and his Mom and Dad as being major influences in his life and career, writing: "A special treat to have worked with all these special and won-derful people. I have truly been blessed by God, before I ever knew him."
Stage: The Sammy Davis, Jr. Show (London '61), West Coast productions of *Annie Get Your Gun, Camelot, Can Can, Carousel, Hello, Dolly!, The Music Man, My Fair Lady, No, No Nanette, South Pacific* and *The Unsinkable Molly Brown*
TV: "The Hollywood Palace" (numbers for Buddy Ebsen, Raquel Welch), The Academy Awards Show (number for Debbie Reynolds), the Jerry Lewis, Oral Roberts, the Osmond and King Family series; Jack Benny and Lou Rawls Spe-cials
Nightclub/Concert: acts for Vikki Carr, Cyd Charisse & Tony Martin, Sammy Davis, Jr., The Osmond Bros., Mamie Van Doren; Line of "Watusi" Dancers at The Mint (LV '65)
Miscellaneous: Fantasy on Parade (Disneyland), *Disney on Parade* touring arena show, Magic Moun-tain, *The Dueling Pirates* (MGM Movieland, MGM Grand Hotel, LV '93, also dir)
Film:
1967 **The Adventures of Bullwhip Griffin** —
Disney (assisted by Ellen Plasschaert)
1978 **Superman — The Movie** — WB (uncredited)

ARTHUR PLASSCHAERT

1995 **The Man in My Life (aka L'Homme de Ma Vie)** — Gala (Fr/Can)

MAYA (MICHAILOVNA) PLISETSKAYA

b. Moscow, Russia, November 20, 1925
Daughter of a silent screen actress, this quintes-sential classical Russian ballerina, who won the *Dance Magazine* Award in 1965, began her studies at the Moscow Bolshoi Ballet School in 1934, where her uncle, aunt and brothers were members of the company. Dancing children's roles with the Bolshoi from the age of 11 she graduated in 1943, joining the company as a soloist, becoming prima ballerina in 1945. Dancing all of the major female roles for the company, she also made films as an actress (**Anna Karenina,** '68, etc.) but forfeited interna-tional film exposure when she dropped out of the title role in the first major Russian-American film collaboration **The Blue Bird** in 1976. Her first choreography for the Bolshoi was also *Anna Karen-ina* ('72), which is one of her commercial film cred-its. Ballet director for the Rome Opera from 1983–86 and Spain's Ballet del Teatro Lirico Nacional, she is married to composer Rodion Shchedrin. A 1964 documentary, **Plisetskaya Dances,** contains fascinating glimpses into her artistry and unique personality. In 1994, she was granted Spanish citizenship.
Biography: Maya Plisetskaya (1956)
Ballet/Dance Pieces: "Anna Karenina" ('72), "The Seagull" ('80)
Film:
1979 **Anna Karenina** — Corinth (also appeared)
1980 **The Seagull** — Corinth (also appeared)

ALBERTO PORTILLO

1990 **Ay! Carmela** — Palace Pic

JOSÉ POSSI

1985 **The Emerald Forest** — Fox

ELEANOR POWELL

b. Springfield, Massachusetts, November 21, 1913
d. Los Angeles, California, February 11, 1982
Acclaimed as Filmdom's premiere tap danseuse because of her unique dancing technique and

Marilyn Monroe is lovingly ogled by (L to R): James Elsegood, Bob Banas, Frank Radcliff, Jack Tygett, Herman Boden, Nick Navarro and Alex Plasschaert in **Let's Make Love** (Jack Cole, 20th Century–Fox, 1960).

strength, "Ellie" Powell actually began her dance training with ballet at 11 ("at a dollar a lesson, to make her more sociable"). She made her debut the following year in a Gus Edwards Children's Revue in Atlantic City, performing acrobatic ballet numbers. She appeared on Broadway in *The Optimists* ('28) and began tap classes in New York with John Boyle and Jack Donahue, who attached sand bags to her feet ("I could barely move, which is why I learned to dance so close to the floor"). She con-

tinued on Broadway (*Follow Thru*, *Fine and Dandy*, *Hot Cha!*, *George White's Musical Varieties*) and at the same time danced with big bands in New York, appeared at the Roxy Theater and Radio City Music Hall, and was the first tap dancer to appear at Carnegie Hall ('30). Seen by an MGM talent scout at New York's Casino de Paree, she was taken from Broadway to films. She always choreographed her own unique tap routines, usually creating while dancing to phonograph records. Like Fred Astaire and Gene Kelly, she constantly experimented with various props for her dances (capes, dogs, drum sticks, etc.) and for her unique lariat dance to "So Long, Sarah Jane" in **I Dood It**, she spent sixteen weeks working with rope expert Sam Garrett. Her unusual seven-year contract with MGM stipulated twelve weeks per year for rehearsals and choreography, often working with coach Willie Covan. In 1943 she wed actor Glenn Ford, had a son, Peter, in 1945, and retired from films, returning five years later for a "Guest Spot" in **The Duchess of Idaho.** In 1953 she hosted "Faith of Our Children," a religious television series. In a final dancing comeback in 1961, she appeared to great acclaim in nightclubs across America. Named by the Dance Masters of America "The World's Greatest Feminine Tap Dancer" in 1929, she is also the winner of a National Film Society Award, appropriately called The Ellie Award, in 1981. She died the following year.

Biography: Eleanor Powell—A Bio-Bibliography by Margie Schultz (1994)

Stage: The Optimists (Bdwy '28, with Jack Haskell), *Follow Thru* (Bdwy '29, with Bobby Connolly), *Fine and Dandy* (Bdwy '30, with Merriel Abbott, Dave Gould), *Hot Cha!* (with Bobby Connolly) and *George White's Music Hall Vanities* (Bdwy '32, with Russell Markert), *George White's Scandals* and *Crazy Quilt* (Ntl. tours, '33), *At Home Abroad* (Bdwy '35, with Robert Alton, Harry Losee and Gene Snyder)

TV: "Perry Como's Kraft Music Hall ('62), "The Bell Telephone Hour" ('63), "The Hollywood Palace" ('64)

Nightclub/Concert: Ambassador Hotel, Atlantic City ('25–26), Martins, Atlantic City ('27), Ben Bernie's, NY ('27–28), Carnegie Hall ('30), Radio City Music Hall and Roxy Theatre (NY '33), Casino de Paree (NY '34), multiple nightclub tours ('47–49, '53, '61–64)

Film (Credits are for Miss Powell's solo routines):
1935 **Broadway Melody of 1936**—MGM (with Dave Gould, Carl Randall, Albertina Rasch)
　George White's Scandals of 1935—(with Jack Donohue, Chester Hale, Russell Markert)
1936 **Born to Dance**—MGM (with Dave Gould)
1937 **Broadway Melody of 1938**—MGM (with Gould, George Murphy, coached by Johnny Boyle)
　Rosalie—MGM (with Ray Bolger, Dave Gould, Rasch)
1939 **Honolulu**—MGM (with Bobby Connolly, Sammy Lee)
1940 **Broadway Melody of 1940**—MGM (with Fred Astaire, Connolly, George Murphy)
1941 **Lady Be Good**—MGM (with the Berry Bros., Busby Berkeley)
1942 **Ship Ahoy**—MGM (with Connolly)

1943 **I Dood It**—MGM (with Connolly)
　Thousands Cheer—MGM (with Gene Kelly, Don Loper)
1944 **Sensations of 1945**—UA (with Sammy Lee, David Lichine, Charles O'Curran)
1950 **The Duchess of Idaho**—MGM (with Jack Donohue)
1974 **That's Entertainment!**—MGM (with others)
1976 **That's Entertainment, Part II**—MGM (with others)
1985 **That's Dancing!**—MGM (with others)
1993 **That's Entertainment! III**—MGM (with others)

MICHAEL MCKENZIE PRATT

1985 **Rocky IV**—MGM/UA

DICK PRICE

1963 **The Threepenny Opera**—Embassy

RICK PRIETO

Fight choreographer.
Film:
1988 **Hero and the Terror**—Cannon
1990 **Delta Force 2**—MGM

EDDIE (EDWARD A.) PRINZ

b. St. Joseph, Missouri, August, 1901
d. Los Angeles, California, July 28, 1967

Named after his father who operated a dance school in St. Joseph, Missouri, for over four decades, and as LeRoy Prinz's (see next entry) younger brother, with more dance expertise—but less ambition—Eddie assisted on scores of films, often not receiving credit. He did, however, create many musical numbers on his own. His credits are difficult to verify, for the name "Prinz" is assumed to be "LeRoy." Active in films for many decades, toward the end of his career Eddie served as production manager on television series, working on "Daktari" at the time of his death at the age of 66.

Stage: The Nine O'Clock Revue (Hollywood '31, also dir), *Earl Carroll's Vanities of 1940* (Bdwy)

Nightclub/Concert: Earl Carroll's Nightclub (Hollywood)

Miscellaneous: California Women's Cancer League show ('53)

Film:
1929 **Syncopated Trial**—Pathé (S) (with the Eddie Prinz Dancers)

Eleanor Powell and Fred Astaire rehearse their sensational duet in MGM's **Broadway Melody of 1940**.

1933 **Alice in Wonderland**— Par
Born Tough— Mon
Dancing Lady— MGM (with Sammy Lee)

Sweetheart of Sigma Chi— Mon
Too Much Harmony— Par (with LeRoy Prinz)
1934 **Babes in Toyland**— Hal Roach
1939 **Gone with the Wind**— MGM
That's Right, You're Wrong— RKO
1941 **Hellzapoppin'**— Univ (with Richard Barstow, Nick Castle)

1942 **Behind the Eight Ball**— Univ
Moonlight in Havana— Univ (with Lester Horton)
Passing the Buck— Univ
Shut My Big Mouth— Univ
1949 **Top o' the Morning**— Par
1950 **Tea for Two**— WB (with LeRoy, Al White, Jr., "Dances Staged By" credit)
West Point Story— WB (with Johnny Boyle, Ruth Godfrey, Gene Nelson, LeRoy Prinz, Al White)
1951 **The Lullaby of Broadway**— WB (with

Gene Nelson, Miriam Nelson, LeRoy Prinz, Al White)

    1953 **By the Light of the Silvery Moon**— WB (assistant to LeRoy, with Paul Haakon)

        The Jazz Singer— WB (assistant to LeRoy Prinz with Haakon and Donald Saddler)

        She's Back on Broadway— WB (assistant to LeRoy with Haakon, Saddler)

    1957 **Top Secret Affair**— WB

LEROY (JEROME) PRINZ

b. St. Joseph, Missouri, July 14, 1895

d. Wadsworth, California, September 15, 1983

This colorful Hollywood legend with over one hundred film credits began at Paramount as the dance director for Cecil B. DeMille in 1929 and subsequently supervised dozens of numbers at Warner Bros. for the next three decades. LeRoy's and Eddie's (see previous entry) father operated the "Prinz School of Social Dancing for Young Ladies and Gentlemen" in St. Joseph. At 15, LeRoy ran away from home to New York, where he learned some basic dance steps from "Buck" ("who, to the accompaniment of his harmonica, taught him tap dancing and Buck-and-Wing"). He joined the French Foreign Legion and in World War I, distinguished himself in action ("He was known as the crash ace. He was in fourteen crashes. Today he has a six-inch silver plate in his head"— *The American Dancer*, November, 1936) with the Canadian Royal Flying Air Corps 94th Aerial Squadron; Returning to the United States, he enrolled in Northwestern University, becoming interested in dramatics and he staged several successful musical productions in New York. His wanderlust took him to Florida and then, Mexico City, where he opened a dance school and taught The Charleston. His adventures continued and (according to Prinz), he moved to Havana ("But through a fight with a politician, wound up in the penitentiary on the Isle of Pines. In nine months he was released"), Europe, Chicago and eventually back to New York, where he supervised the musical numbers on 27 Broadway shows. After receiving a wire from friend Elsie Janis to come to Hollywood, he was hired as dance director for DeMille. While working on **Madame Satan**, DeMille told him that he didn't want a dance— he wanted "pageantry!" In his long association with DeMille, Prinz also acted as second unit director: moving extras, staging battles and creating the "pageantry!" DeMille wanted. He also privately coached stars such as Claudette Colbert and Marlene Dietrich, earning up to $250 an hour. He worked at Paramount for twelve years (1920–41) and when Seymour Felix was fired from **Yankee Doodle Dandy**, Prinz went to work for Warner Bros., where he directed all of their musical sequences

from 1941 to 1957. In *Dance Magazine* (Feb. '47), he was quoted: "We have already reached the zenith in big, spectacular numbers. Now Hollywood is beginning to rely on personality and individuality, ballet sequences that tell a story, and routines that blend into the picture… It is important that every dance director know camera technique as thoroughly as choreography, because screen dance must be planned especially for the camera." On his staff, Prinz had some of Hollywood's finest dance specialists (brother Eddie, John Boyle, Hal Belfer, Ruth Godfrey, Paul Haakon, Miriam Nelson, Al White, Jr., etc.) to create scores of musical numbers and dances: "My idea was a conception of ideas and presentation and shooting them … so it wasn't a question of worrying about steps… I've never learned a time step!… I conceived and staged and directed." He also brought in experts on every type of ethnic dance for his numbers— Hula to Rhumba— even bringing in Jig Dancers from Ireland for **My Wild Irish Rose** in 1947. Assistants and dancers who worked for him remember the entertaining stories he told about his adventurous exploits during rehearsals. In 1949 he won an Academy Award for Best Short Film for **A Boy and His Dog** and in 1956, opened the first of a proposed chain of fifteen Talent Centers in Sacramento, California. While accepting a plaque in 1981 from PDS for his prolific career, he laughed as he confessed, "I never could do a timestep … and I still can't." As a colorful entrepreneur and self-promoter, Prinz is unmatched in Hollywood history.

Autobiography: *Director's Guild of America Oral History* interviewed by Irene Kahn Atkins (1978)

Stage (Partial listing): *Headin' South* (Bdwy '28), *Earl Carroll's Sketch Book*, *Gay Paree*, *Great Day!* (assisted by Hermes Pan), *The Silver Swan* and *Top Speed* (Bdwy '29, assisted by Hermes Pan), *Earl Carroll's Vanities of 1930* (Bdwy), *Lucky Day* (Mayan Theatre, LA '32, assisted by Hermes Pan), *Tattle Tales* (Bdwy '33), *Folies Bergere* (Paris), *Bataclan Revue* (Spain)

TV: "The Korla Pandit Show" (KTLA, '54), Rock Hudson and Mae West's number on the 30th Academy Awards show ('57)

Nightclub/Concert: The Cotton Club, St. Regis Roof (NY '39, also prod), El Rancho Vegas (LV '54–55)

Miscellaneous: *Aqua Parade of 1949* (dir), *The Motor Pageant of Progress* (Hollywood '53), *West-O-Rama* (Ten State Fair Show '57)

Film:

1929 **Innocents of Paris**— Par (with Fanchon and Marco)

1930 **Madame Satan**— MGM (with Theodore Kosloff)

1931 **The Squaw Man**— Par

1932 **The Sign of the Cross**— Par (with Kosloff)

1933 **Hollywood Premier**—MGM (S)
   Too Much Harmony—Par (with Eddie
Prinz)
1934 **Bolero**—Par
   Cleopatra—Par (with Agnes De Mille)
   College Rhythm—Par
   Come on Marines—Par
   Mrs. Wiggs of the Cabbage Patch—Par.
   Murder at the Vanities—Par (with Larry
Ceballos)
   Search for Beauty—Par (with Jack
Haskell)
   She Loves Me Not—Par
   You Belong to Me—Par
1935 **All the King's Horses**—Par (Academy
Award nom: "Viennese Waltz" number)
   The Big Broadcast of 1936—Par (with
Fayard Nicholas, Bill Robinson, Academy Award
nom: "It's the Animal in Me" number)
   Coronado—Par (with Fayard Nicholas)
   The Crusades—Par
   The Lives of a Bengal Lancer—Par
   Rumba—Par (with Frank Veloz)
   Stolen Harmony—Par
1936 **Anything Goes** (later retitled **Tops Is the
Limit**)—Par
   The Big Broadcast of 1937—Par (with
Louis DaPron)
   College Holiday—Par (with DaPron)
   Collegiate—Par
   Millions in the Air—Par
   Show Boat—Univ (also appearing as
"Dance Director")
1937 **Artists and Models**—Par
   The Big Broadcast of 1938—Par
   Champagne Waltz—Par (with Frank
Veloz)
   Double or Nothing—Par (assisted by Jack
Crosby)
   High, Wide and Handsome—Par
   Mountain Music—Par
   This Way Please—Par
   Thrill of a Lifetime—Par (with Fanchon,
Carlos Romero)
   Turn Off the Moon—Par (with Fanchon)
   Waikiki Wedding—Par (Academy Award
nom: "Luau" number, assisted by Jack Crosby)
1938 **Artists and Models Abroad**—Par
   Bluebeard's Eighth Wife—Par
   The Buccaneer—Par
   College Swing—Par
   Every Day's a Holiday—Par
   Give Me a Sailor—Par
   Say It in French—Par
   Spawn of the North—Par (with Michio Ito)
   Stolen Heaven—Par
   Tropic Holiday—Par (assisted by José
Fernandez)

1939 **The Big Broadcast of 1939**—Par
   Cafe Society—Par
   The Great Victor Herbert—Par
   Man About Town—Par (with Merriel
Abbott)
   Midnight—Par
   Never Say Die—Par
   Paris Honeymoon—Par
   St. Louis Blues—Par
   The Star Maker—Par
   Union Pacific—Par
   Zaza—Par
1940 **Buck Benny Rides Again**—Par (with
Abbott)
   Dancing on a Dime—Par (assisted by
DaPron)
   Moon Over Burma—Par
   A Night at Earl Carroll's—Par
   Road to Singapore—Par
   Too Many Girls—RKO (with Hal LeRoy,
Ann Miller)
   Too Many Husbands—Par
1941 **All American Co-ed**—UA (also dir,
prod.)
   Aloma of the South Seas—Par
   Fiesta—WB (S) (also dir, prod)
   Las Vegas Nights—Par
   Road to Zanzibar—Par
   Time Out for Rhythm—Col (with Mil-
ler)
   You're the One—Par
1942 **The Hard Way**—WB
   Yankee Doodle Dandy—WB (with John
Boyle, Seymour Felix)
1943 **The Desert Song**—WB
   Mission to Moscow—WB (with Michel
Panaieff)
   Thank Your Lucky Stars—WB
   This Is the Army—WB (with Nick Cas-
tle, Bob Sidney)
1944 **Janie**—WB
   Hollywood Canteen—WB (with An-
tonio, Frank Veloz, assisted by Nico Cha-
risse)
   The Rhythm of the Rumba—WB (S)
(with Antonio Triana)
   Shine on Harvest Moon—WB (with
Four Step Bros.)
1945 **All Star Musical Revue**—WB (S) (Num-
bers deleted from **Hollywood Canteen**, with Busby
Berkeley)
   Rhapsody in Blue—WB (with Panaeiff)
   San Antonio—WB
1946 **Deception**—WB
   Night and Day—WB (with Panaieff)
   The Time, the Place and the Girl—WB
(with the Condos Bros.)
1947 **Cheyenne**—WB

LeRoy Prinz directs an unknown couple (circa 1940).

Escape Me Never—WB
My Wild Irish Rose—WB (with the Berry Bros., assisted by Hal Belfer)
Pursued—WB
1948 **April Showers**—WB

One Sunday Afternoon—WB (assisted by Belfer)
Two Guys from Texas—WB
1949 **Always Leave Them Laughing**—WB
It's a Great Feeling—WB

Look for the Silver Lining— WB (with Ray Bolger)

My Dream Is Yours— WB

1950 **The Daughter of Rosie O'Grady**— WB (with Gene and Miriam Nelson)

Tea for Two— WB (with Gene and Miriam Nelson, Eddie Prinz, Al White, Jr.)

The West Point Story— WB (with John Boyle, Ruth Godfrey, Gene Nelson, Eddie Prinz, Al White, Jr.)

1951 **I'll See You in My Dreams**— WB

Lullaby of Broadway— WB (with Gene and Miriam Nelson, Eddie Prinz, Al White)

On Moonlight Bay— WB (with Donald Saddler)

Painting the Clouds with Sunshine— WB (with Gene and Miriam Nelson, Al White, Jr. and assistants Ruth Godfrey and Paul Haakon)

Starlift— WB (with Gene Nelson)

1952 **About Face**— WB

April in Paris— WB (with Ray Bolger, Donald Saddler)

She's Working Her Way Through College— WB (with Gene and Miriam Nelson)

Stop, You're Killing Me— WB

The Story of Will Rogers— WB (assisted by Ruth Godfrey, Paul Haakon, Al White)

1953 **By the Light of the Silvery Moon**— WB (with Donald Saddler, assisted by Haakon, Eddie Prinz)

The Desert Song— WB

The Eddie Cantor Story— WB

House of Wax— WB

The Jazz Singer— WB (assisted by Haakon, Eddie Prinz and Saddler)

She's Back on Broadway— WB (with Steve Condos, Gene and Miriam Nelson, assisted by Haakon, Eddie Prinz, Saddler)

So This Is Love— WB

Three Sailors and a Girl— WB (with Gene Nelson, assisted by Ruth Godfrey)

1954 **Lucky Me**— WB (with Jack Donohue)

1956 **The Ten Commandments**— Par (with Godfrey)

1957 **The Helen Morgan Story**— WB (assisted by Peggy Carroll)

Sayonara— WB (also 2nd unit dir, winner of a special Golden Globe award)

1958 **South Pacific**— Fox (with Archie Savage, assisted by Joan Bayley and Ray Weamer, also 2nd unit dir)

1959 **The Big Fisherman**— Univ

JOSEF PROUZA

1995 **Big Beat**— Space Films Ltd

JEFF PRUITT

1995 **Mighty Morphin Power Rangers: The Movie**— Fox ("Oooze Fight Choreography" credit)

WANG QING

1995 **Shanghai Triad**— Electric Pict (China)

CARL RANDALL

b. Columbus, Ohio, 1898

d. Sydney, Australia, September 16, 1965

At the height of his success as a Broadway performer, Randall stated his theory for success in *The Dance*, April, 1928, "For every good step a ballet dancer has created, he has discarded dozens of ideas. Every ballet that has ever been arranged has grown out of dozens of discarded scenarios. A perfect ... dance is not something just arrived at by accident; it's the result of years of hard work. Sometimes in the flash of an inspired moment a wonderful idea comes, but any honest man will admit that the inspired moment is really a reflection of hundreds of other moments given to nursing pet ideas." Randall's parents owned a dance academy in Columbus, Ohio, and he began classes there as a child after his mother discovered him practicing ballet in the basement. Dancing first in vaudeville at 14 in an act called The Randall Children (with various female partners) his career soared on Broadway in such shows as *Oh Lady! Lady!!* and *The Princess Show* ('18), *The Ziegfeld Follies of 1915, 1916 and 1920, Ziegfeld Midnight Frolics of 1920 and 1921, Sunny Days* ('28), *The Third Little Show* ('31), *A Little Racketeer* ('32) and *Pardon My English* ('33), while simultaneously choreographing others. Whenever the Russian ballet was in New York, he would study with Fokine and Nijinsky. Associated for years with the Ziegfeld and Shubert organizations, he also created in Europe, staging shows for Maurice Chevalier and Mistinguett in London and France. In 1935 he was invited to Hollywood to partner Jean Harlow in **Reckless**, which he co-choreographed, and only remained there for two years, returning to greater success in stage work. In the late 1950s he went to Australia to produce a revival of *Annie Get Your Gun* and remained there until his death.

Stage: *Flora Bella* (Bdwy '16), *Fiddlers Three* (Bdwy '18), *Her Family Tree* (Bdwy '20), *Sonny Boy* (Bdwy '21, also appeared), *Greenwich Village Follies of 1922* (Bdwy), *The Music Box Revue* (Bdwy '24, also appeared), *Countess Maritza* (Bdwy '26, also appeared), *The Gay Divorce* (Bdwy '32, with Fred Astaire), *A Little Racketeer* (Bdwy '32, with Albertina Rasch), *Pardon My English* (Bdwy '33, with George Hale, also appeared), *Monte Carlo Follies* (Monte Carlo '33), *The Pure in Heart* (Bdwy '34), *Trans-Atlantic* (London), *The Illustrator's Show*

(Bdwy '36), *Knickerbocker Holiday* (Bdwy '38), *Stars in Your Eyes* (Bdwy '39), *Louisiana Purchase* (Bdwy '40, with George Balanchine), *Crazy with the Heat* (Bdwy '41, also appeared), *High Kickers* and *Sunny River* (Bdwy 41), *My Dear Public* (OOT '43, replaced by Henry LeTang), *The Passing Show of 1945* (OOT)

Film:
1935 **Broadway Melody of 1936**— MGM (with Dave Gould, Eleanor Powell, Albertina Rasch)
      Reckless— MGM (with Chester Hale, also appeared)
1937 **Merry-Go-Round of 1938**— Univ
      The Show Goes On— ABF (also appeared)
      You're a Sweetheart— Univ (with George Murphy)

ROY RANDOLPH
1937 **Nobody's Baby**— MGM

BRAD RAPIER
1994 **The Neverending Story III**— WB (with Mark Davis)

ALBERTINA RASCH
b. Vienna, Austria, 1896
d. Woodland Hills, California, October 2, 1967

The first Broadway dance director acknowledged to use classical ballet in her precision line work (called "Tiller-on-Toe"), Rasch—along with George Balanchine—believed deeply in the strength, talent and superiority of the American dancer. She had arrived in America at the age of 16 with nine years of training at the Imperial Opera Company in Vienna and was signed as prima ballerina at the Hippodrome Theatre in New York. She continued to dance in opera ballets in New York and Chicago, toured South America with Sarah Bernhardt and performed with Ballet Classique (her own dance group) in vaudeville across the United States, finally becoming prima ballerina at NY's Metropolitan Opera. She appeared on Broadway in *A Trip to Japan* ('09), *The International Cup* and *The Ballet of Niagara* ('10) and *The Firefly* ('12). In 1923, she opened her first school in New York and in 1924 created The Albertina Rasch Girls, a line of girls who would soon monopolize the Broadway stage, American and European tours and film musicals. Her first Broadway choreographic assignment was *George White's Scandals* in 1926 and she was the first to choreograph Gershwin's ***An American in Paris*** Ballet in *Showgirl* ('29) as well as his "Rhapsody in Blue" at the Hippodrome. She staged and choreographed some of the American musical theater's most successful shows before she was brought

to Hollywood in 1930 to create dances for some of the most important musical films of the 1930s and '40s. One of her Broadway credits (*Flying Colors*, '32) was the first American show to have separate black and white corps of dancers, although they were never integrated in the show. Her dancers also performed often at the Hollywood Bowl and in multiple prologues for Grauman's Chinese Theater. Married to film composer Dimitri Tiomkin for forty-one years until her death in 1967, because of her strict discipline, tapping cane and European "distance" from her dancers, she is still spoken of respectfully as "Madame Rasch."

Stage: *George White's Scandals* (Bdwy '26), *Lucky* (with David Bennett, also appeared), *My Princess, Rio Rita* and *Ziegfeld Follies of 1927* (Bdwy '27), *The Three Musketeers* (Bdwy '28, with Richard Boleslavsky), *Show Girl* and *Sons o' Guns* (Bdwy '29), *The Pajama Lady, Princess Charming* and *Three's a Crowd* (Bdwy '30), *The Band Wagon* (with Fred Astaire), *The Cat and the Fiddle, Everybody's Welcome, Laugh Parade* and *The Wonder Bar* (Bdwy '31), *A Little Racketeer* (with Carl Randall), *Face the Music, Flying Colors* (with Agnes DeMille and Tamara Geva) and *Walk a Little Faster* (Bdwy '32), *The Great Waltz* and *Pure in Heart* (Bdwy '34), *Jubilee* (Bdwy '35), *Very Warm for May* (with Harry Losee, Bdwy '39), *Boys and Girls Together* (Bdwy '40), *Lady in the Dark* (Bdwy '41), *Star and Garter* (Bdwy '42), *Marinka* (Bdwy '45)

Nightclub/Concert: Iridiem Room (St. Moritz Hotel, NY '36), *A Wilterhalter Revue* (Viennese Roof of the St. Regis Hotel, NY '37)

Ballet/Dance Pieces: For the Hollywood Bowl: Dimitri Tiomkin's "Choreographic Suite" ('30), "Tiomkin's Spanish Suite," "Cake-Walk," "Chant," "Ambition" ('33), "Carnaval" ('35), Suite from **The Great Waltz** ('38), "Le Tombeau de Couperin," "Dance of the Russian Sailors" from "The Red Poppy," "Mazurka," "Roumanian Rhapsody" ('39)

Miscellaneous: English Village (NY World's Fair '39)

Film:
1929 **Devil-May-Care**— MGM
      The Hollywood Revue of 1929— MGM (with Ernest Belcher, George Cunningham, Sammy Lee, Natacha Natova; the Albertina Rasch Girls appeared)
      Lord Byron of Broadway— MGM (with Sammy Lee)
      Sally— WB (with Larry Ceballos, Theodore Kosloff; the Albertina Rasch Girls appeared)
      Slave of Love— MGM
1930 **Crazy House**— MGM (S) (Albertina Rasch Ballet)
      Hell's Angels— UA
      The March of Time— MGM (with Sammy Lee, unreleased)

Our Blushing Brides— MGM

The Rogue Song— MGM (Albertina Rasch Ballet)

1931 **Angel Cake**— Vitaphone (S) (Albertina Rasch Girls)

The Devil's Cabaret— MGM (S) (number from **The March of Time**, the Albertina Rasch Girls)

Footlights— Vitaphone (S) (Albertina Rasch Girls)

The Musical Mystery— Vitaphone (S) (Albertina Rasch Girls)

1932 **Hello Good Times**— Vitaphone (S) (with Johnny Boyle; Albertina Rasch Girls)

1933 **Broadway to Hollywood**— MGM (with Sammy Lee; Albertina Rasch Girls)

Going Hollywood— MGM (with George Cunningham; Albertina Rasch Girls)

Hello Pop— MGM (S)

Plane Nuts— MGM (S)

Stage Mother— MGM

1934 **The Cat and the Fiddle**— MGM (with Seymour Felix)

Hollywood Party— MGM (with Felix, Dave Gould, George Hale)

Madame Du Barry— WB

The Merry Widow— MGM

Roast Beef and Movies— MGM (S)

1935 **After the Dance**— Col (with George Murphy)

Broadway Melody of 1936— MGM (with Dave Gould, Carl Randall; Albertina Rasch Girls)

1936 **The King Steps Out**— Col

1937 **The Firefly**— MGM (also appeared in "Guest Bit")

Rosalie— MGM (with Ray Bolger, Gould, Eleanor Powell)

1938 **The Girl of the Golden West**— MGM

The Great Waltz— MGM

Marie Antoinette— MGM

Sweethearts— MGM (with Bolger, Ernst Matray)

1940 **Broadway Melody of 1940**— MGM (with Fred Astaire, Bobby Connolly, George Murphy, Eleanor Powell)

1974 **That's Entertainment!**— MGM (with others)

1976 **That's Entertainment, Part II**— MGM (with others)

VAL "MICKEY" RASET

b. Russia, 1910

d. Hollywood, California, July 26, 1977

Classical dancer and choreographer who graduated from the Imperial Russian Ballet School. He toured with Diaghilev's company before coming to California, where he started choreographing and working as an assistant director. Married to actress Mary Carroll (whose sister, Peggy, often assisted Raset), he was one of MGM's dance directors (1935–40) before moving into television direction and production. His last documented job was as assistant director on the "Kojak" TV series ('75).

Stage: *The Girl from Nantucket* (Bdwy '45)

TV: "A Tale of Two Cities" (ABC, '53), Choreographed, directed and executive produced KTLA's "Polka Parade" ('50s–60s), "The George Gobel Show" ('59)

Nightclub/Concert: *The Magic Carpet Revue* (Opening show at the Dunes Hotel, LV June '55, with Bernard "Babe" Pearce)

Film:

1936 **The Gorgeous Hussy**— MGM

Moonlight Murder— MGM

Petticoat Fever— MGM

San Francisco— MGM

Trouble for Two— MGM

1937 **The Bride Wore Red**— MGM

Camille— MGM

The Good Old Soak— MGM

Maytime— MGM

1938 **Shopworn Angel**— MGM

Swiss Miss— Fox

1939 **East Side of Heaven**— Univ

Ice Follies of 1939— MGM (with Frances Claudet)

1940 **New Moon**— MGM

1942 **My Gal Sal**— Fox (with Hermes Pan)

Sing Your Worries Away— RKO

You Were Never Lovelier— Col (with Fred Astaire, Pan, assisted by Peggy Carroll)

1943 **Hello, Frisco Hello**— Fox

What's Buzzin' Cousin?— Col (with Nick Castle, Ann Miller)

1944 **Cover Girl**— Col (with Seymour Felix, Stanley Donen, Gene Kelly, assisted by Carroll)

Hey Rookie!— Col (with Condos Bros., Louis DaPron, Stanley Donen, Ann Miller, assisted by Carroll)

1945 **Tonight and Every Night**— Col (with Jack Cole)

1948 **Black Bart**— Univ

1951 **Hit Parade of 1951**— Rep

1952 **Abbott and Costello Meet Captain Kidd**— WB

The Return of Gilbert and Sullivan— Lippert

1956 **Shake, Rattle and Rock**— Sunset-American Intl (with Anthony Capps)

1960 **Heller in Pink Tights**— Par

Albertina Rasch advertises for Lucky Strike Cigarettes, 1929.

MAGGIE RASH

Beginning her career as a dancer and choreographer, she met future-husband, film director Steve Rash. After acting as associate director on his films **The Buddy Holly Story** and **Under the Rainbow** ('81) her career shifted into direction.

Film:
1978 **The Buddy Holly Story** — Entertainment Releasing (also assoc dir)

DENNON AND SAYHBER (NEÉ SARES) RAWLES

Dynamic jazz dancers, choreographers and teachers who work as a team in concert, films and television. Sayhber was lead dancer and assistant to Steven Peck when Dennon joined Peck's Jazz Company (1972–76), where they met and married in 1974. They created their own club show Energy Force (1977–78) and dance performance company, Jazz Dancers, Inc. (1979–present). Dennon's many performance credits include the films **New York, New York** ('77), **History of the World — Part 1** ('81) and **The Best Little Whorehouse in Texas** ('82); nightclub and TV appearances with Ann-Margret, Tony Martin and Cyd Charisse, Barbara Mandrell and "Baryshnikov on Broadway." Dennon assisted Michael Kidd on "Baryshnikov in Hollywood" ('81) and the Janet Jackson music video "Alright" ('90). They currently teach at UCLA, Moorpark College, Orange Coast College, the Idyllwild School of Music and the Arts and give master classes all over the country. They are the proud parents of daughter Jessica, born in 1981, and son Matthew, born in 1984.

Stage: Sayhber: *Gypsy* (Pierce College, Cal. '78)
TV: "$100,000 Name That Tune" (39 segments, '78–79, also appeared), "Bare Touch of Magic" (Canada '81), "Alfred Hitchcock Presents" ('86); commercials for Brahma Beer, Diet Slice, Shell Oil and Showtime
Nightclub/Concert: Jazzed Up (Japan '92); Ann-Margret and Toni Basil shows
Ballet/Dance Pieces (Partial listing — for Jazz Dancers, Inc.): "Tribute to Brubeck" ('79), "Jazz Meets Latin," "Kodachrome Suite," "The Rock in Jazz," "Turkish Bath," "Love on the Airwaves," "Tango Apasionad," "Busted for Boppin'," "Sentimental Journey," "Sooner or Later," "It's Alright with Us," "It's a Man's World" ('92), etc.

Film:
1983 **Staying Alive** — Par (assisted by Helene Phillips)
1984 **Voyage of the Rock Aliens** — Interplanetary
1987 **Club Life** — Troma (Dennon only)
1988 **Body Beat** — Vidmark

Jailbird Rock — Continental
1991 **Bugsy** — TriStar

ROBERT RAY

1985 **The Goolangatta Gold** — Rep (Australian)

RALPH READER

b. London, England, 1904
d. London, England, May 13, 1982

British stage, film and television actor, dance director, author, TV and radio star who appeared on Broadway in *The Passing Show* and *Big Boy* ('25) and became a dance director when Seymour Felix suggested him to the Shubert brothers. He returned to England in the 1930s, appearing in films and many London musicals and revues (which he also produced and directed) from 1934–68. In 1934 he also created the annual British Boy Scout fundraising revues known as *The Gang Shows*. He directed similar shows in Pittsburgh and Chicago, where he was made an Honorary Citizen of the state of Illinois. After the final edition in 1974, he retired. He was also the star of a British radio and TV series.

Autobiography: It's Been Terrific (1954)
Stage: Bad Habits of 1926, Yours Truly, The Greenwich Village Follies (all Bdwy '26), *The Three Sisters* (London '34).

Film:
1933 **I Adore You** — WB-First Ntl
1934 **Over the Garden Wall** — BIP
1935 **First a Girl** — Gau/Brit (with Buddy Bradley, Jessie Matthews)
       Hello Sweetheart — WB-First Ntl
       Squibs — Twickenham
1937 **Backstage** (aka **Limelight**) — Gau/Brit (with Tilly Losch, also appeared)
1938 **London Melody** (aka **Girl in the Streets**) — GFD
       Splinters in the Air — GFD (also appeared)

GENE REED

American-born dancer and choreographer who appeared at the Sahara Hotel in Las Vegas in 1958 and choreographed other American nightclub shows before he relocated to Europe in 1960. Based in Munich, he was one of the expatriate choreographic innovators in film and television there, becoming a celebrity with his own TV musical variety series and troupe of dancers. He returned to the United States, where he currently is creating the dances for *The Palm Spring Follies*.

Stage: The Palm Spring Follies (Cal '95)
TV: "The Gene Reed Show" (German TV, also the star)

Nightclub/Concert: *Le Crazy Horse Revue* (Paris and Hollywood '61)
Film:
1963 **Captain Sinbad**— MGM

VICKIE REGAN

Ballet/Dance Pieces: "Astaire" (Canadian Ballet, "Special Dance Advisor" credit)
Film:
1985 **A Chorus Line**— Embassy (with Gregg Burge, Troy Garza, Jeffrey Hornaday, Brad Jeffries, Helen Phillips, also appeared)

JACK REGAS

b. West Palm Beach, Florida, August 30, 1925

Dancer, choreographer and director who studied dance with Marge Hallick in San Diego and made his professional debut at the Roxy Theatre in New York in 1942. He started his film career as a teenager, eventually appearing in dozens of films (**The Band Wagon**, **The French Line**, **Gentlemen Prefer Blondes**, **Good News**, **Royal Wedding**, **Stars and Stripes Forever**, **The Strip**, **Tea for Two**, **Wabash Avenue**, **The West Point Story**, **Yolanda and the Thief**, **Ziegfeld Follies**, etc.) as one of the busiest contract dancers in Hollywood during the Forties and Fifties. Other live stage appearances include Judy Garland's and Betty Hutton's nightclub acts as well as the Los Angeles Civic Light Opera production of *Louisiana Purchase* in 1947. His transition to choreography began when he assisted Nick Castle and Gower Champion in films and Miriam Nelson on television ("Disneyland Opening" '55) and he made his solo choreographic debut with TV's "Shower of Stars" in 1957. Temporarily leaving Hollywood in 1964 for nine months, he served as director-choreographer for the Polynesian Cultural Center in Hawaii in 1964, returning annually to create their spectacular shows. After his prolific TV choreographic career he became a highly successful director, helming such series as "The Brady Bunch Comedy Hour" ('77), "Dance Fever" (1979–86), "Barbara Mandrell and Sisters," "The Mac Davis Show," "Star Search" and over 100 series and specials from 1972 until his retirement in 1989.

Stage: Best Foot Forward (Civic Playhouse, LA '56), *That Certain Girl* (Thunderbird Hotel, LV)

TV (Partial listing): Disney's "Tales of Andy Burnette" ('57), "The Summer Chevy Show" ('59), "Thriller," "The Arabian Nights," "G.E. Theater" and "Ford Startime" ('60), "The Bell Telephone Hour," "Laugh-In," "Kismet," Danny Thomas' "Wonderful World of Burlesque;" entire seasons of the John Byner, Glen Campbell, Nat "King" Cole, Phyllis Diller, Jimmy Durante & The Lennon Sis-

ters, John Gary, Spike Jones, Jerry Lewis, Giselle McKenzie, Bob Newhart, Louis Prima & Keely Smith, Jerry Reed, Roy Rogers & Dale Evans, Andy Williams and Flip Wilson Shows plus specials for Jack Benny, Pat Boone, Charo, Perry Como, Clifton Davis, Bob Hope, Burl Ives, Lennon Sisters and Bobby Vinton

Nightclub/Concert: Acts for The Beverly Hillbillies, Nat "King" Cole, Betty Hutton, Spike Jones, Abbe Lane, Shari Lewis, Giselle McKenzie, The Mitchell Boys Choir, The Osmond Brothers, Jane Powell (*Just Twenty— Plus Me* '64 concert tour) and Jane Russell

Miscellaneous: Polynesian Cultural Center show in Hawaii ('64–70), revues in New Zealand and Japan, *SHARE Boomtown* shows

Film:
1952 **Skirts Ahoy**— MGM (assistant to Nick Castle)
1957 **The Girl Most Likely**— RKO (assistant to Gower Champion)
      Peyton Place— Fox
1958 **In Love and War**— Fox
1963 **My Six Loves**— Par
1966 **Paradise, Hawaiian Style**— Par
1968 **Live a Little, Love a Little**— MGM (with Jack Baker, "Dream sequence by" credit)

GEORGE (FRANK) REICH

b. Long Island, New York, December 15, 1926

In describing George Reich, Graciela Daniele — who had been a member of his group — said in *Dance Magazine* (March, 1984), "George's dances for Ballet Ho! were really exciting, full of heat and energy, but never raw or undignified. And George was always so magnetic — blonde and handsome and extraordinarily talented. I don't think he realized how many dancers in the company considered him some sort of god." This American-born dancer, choreographer, director and producer would find his greatest success as an expatriate in Europe. Studying dance over the years with George Balanchine, Valerie Bettis, Anton Dolin, Rosella Hightower, José Limon, Alicia Markova, Roland Petit and Charles Weidman, he made his professional stage debut in *Sing Out Sweet Land* on Broadway ('46) and toured with the Markova-Dolin Ballet Company in 1947. He continued to appear on Broadway in *The Chocolate Soldier* ('47), *Inside U.S.A.* ('48) and *Touch and Go* ('49) and danced with Valerie Bettis' company in 1949. He first went to France to appear at the Lido de Paris for Donn Arden in 1949, subsequently performing at the Moulin Rouge, ABC and Olympia Theatres in Paris and created his first choreography at the Olympia Theatre in 1949. His acclaim continued and he found himself dancing in Roland Petit's Ballets de

Jack Regas creates a dance for Sally Forrest on a dramatic television special in the fifties (photo courtesy of Jack Regas).

Paris ('53), in French cabarets and theaters and television shows throughout Europe. In 1954, he formed his own company, Ballet Ho! de George Reich, combining ballet, modern jazz and acrobatic techniques and the revolutionary group was featured in French Music Halls, theatres and on television until 1970. Film appearances include **Daddy Long Legs**, **The Glass Slipper** and **La Garconne** ('55), **Black Tights** and **Taras Bulba** ('62) and his first film choreographic work (**Futures Vedettes**) helped to create the explosive "Sex Kitten" image for its star, former ballerina Brigitte Bardot. With partner Leonard Miller, Reich then formed Miller/Reich Productions and went on to become one of the foremost international cabaret show Producer-director-choreographers. He credits assistants Thom Allen, Joan Palethorpe and Vassili Sulich with being major influences in his life and career, along with Donn Arden, George Balanchine, Valerie Bettis, Anton Dolin, Alicia Markova and Roland Petit.

Stage: Paris Mes Amour (Olympia, Paris, '59), *Folies Bergere* (Bdwy '64)

TV: Shows for Montreal Radio Candada ('65–70) and dozens of musical variety shows in France, Italy and Germany

Nightclub/Concert (Partial listing): multiple shows from '50–present at The Lido, Moulin Rouge

Portraying the lovesick "Christian" in the *Cyrano de Bergerac* ballet from Roland Petit's all dance **Black Tights** (Magna, 1962), George Reich attempts to write a letter to his love, Roxanne.

and Olympia (Paris), Las Vegas, New York (Latin Quarter, Cafe Versailles), Lake Tahoe, Reno, Atlantic City, Los Angeles, *Fantastique* (Carillon Hotel, Palm Beach '75). etc.; acts for Josephine Baker, Brigitte Bardot, Marlene Dietrich, Sascha Distel, Lilliane Montevecchi and Edith Piaf

Film:

1955 **Futures Vedettes** (aka **Sweet Sixteen** & **Future Stars**)— Régie du Film/Del Duca (also appeared)

   Mam'zelle Pigalle (aka **Cette Sacrée Gamine**— Films de France

1958 **Gigi**— MGM ("Maxime's" and "Bois de Bologne" sequences, uncredited)
 Nez de Cuir— (Fr) (also appeared)
1963 **Julie the Redhead**— Les Films Matignon

HANNAH REINER
1968 **Where Angels Go ... Trouble Follows**— Col

TERRY REISER
1985 **Grace Quigley**— Cannon

CARLA RENALLI
Italian dancer and choreographer.
1961 **David and Goliath**— AA (Ital)

MICHEL RENAULD
1961 **Please, Not Now!**— Fox

MARTA RENZI
1983 **Lianna**— UA Classics

ERNIE REYES
Martial arts choreographer.
1985 **The Last Dragon**— TriStar (with Torrance Mathis, Ron Van Clief, Lester Wilson)

PACO REYES
Spanish dancer and choreographer.
1957 **The Pride and the Passion**— UA

PAT RICHARDS
1991 **George's Island**— Canada/New Line

DIETER RIESLE
1991 **American Note Blue**— (Ger)

LAURI RILEY
1988 **The Wizard of Speed and Time**— Hollywood

KEN RINKER
After assisting Twyla Tharp on the film version of **Hair** ('79) Rinker went on to solo film credits as well as having his own dance company in New York.
Stage: *Alice* (NY Shakespeare Festival), *Swing* (OOT '80)

Film:
1979 **Hair**— UA (assistant to Twyla Tharp)
1984 **Places in the Heart**— TriStar
1986 **Murphy's Romance**— Col

CHRISTOPHER (RONNIE) RIORDAN
b. Redwood City, California, November 25, 1937
Dancer, actor, choreographer, teacher, director and producer whose multi-faceted career has led him to his current position as artistic director for the Lyric Theater Company in Ashland, Oregon. Beginning his dance studies in Northern California, he made his professional stage debut at the Geary Theater in San Francisco at the age of 3. He moved to Los Angeles in 1956 and enhanced his techniques with ballet, tap and jazz at Roland Dupree's studio. There, he also began his extensive work in over 50 films as a dancer (**Clambake, The Go Go Set, Looking for Love, Made in Paris, My Fair Lady, Thoroughly Modern Millie, Viva Las Vegas**, etc.) and actor (**Camelot, The Gay Deceivers, Hot Rods to Hell, I'll Take Sweden, Somebody Up There Likes Me**, etc.). With many TV and stage credits, he partnered Barrie Chase on "The Hollywood Palace" and in her nightclub act. As an actor, he won LA acting awards for his stage performances in *Fly Blackbird, Light Up the Sky* and *Rope*. He began his choreographic career assisting Jack Baker at AIP during the Go Go Sixties and progressed to a solo career. In 1992, he directed, wrote and produced the PBS TV Special inducting his idol and mentor Fred Astaire into the Ballroom Dancer's Hall of Fame. When asked to summarize his career, he wrote: "I've been blessed in meeting the right people, making the right choices, keeping the best friends and having the love and respect of my son."
Stage: *Once Upon a Mattress* (Ashland, Oregon '94)
TV: Commercials for Kleenex and Hair Spray
Nightclub/Concert: *Champagne Cocktails* (Hollywood '60), George Chakiris' act (with Barrie Chase)
Film:
1966 **Dr. Goldfoot and the Bikini Machine**— AIP (assistant to Jack Baker)
 Fireball 500— AIP
 The Ghost in the Invisible Bikini— AIP (assistant to Jack Baker)
1967 **Thunder Alley**— AIP

CARLOS RIVAROLA
1988 **Tango Bar**— Castle Hill (with Nelson Avila, Santiago Ayala, Lilliana Belfiore, Doris Petroni, Nelida Rodriguez, Norma Viola)

1991 **Naked Tango** — New Line Cinema (with Graciela Danielle)

ERIC G. ROBARTS
1980 **Breaking Glass** — Par

JEROME ROBBINS (RABI-NOWITZ)
b. New York, October 11, 1918

Groundbreaking artist whose choreography and direction helped to change the face of American ballet, musical theater and dance on film. Like the character "Mike" in *A Chorus Line* (who sings "I Can Do That") it was Robbins' sister, Sonya, who was going to be the ballet dancer and changed his dreams for a career in chemistry when she taught him to dance. He started dance lessons with her from Gluck Sandor and Felicia Sorel of Dance Center in New York. He attended New York State Univ. but dropped out to continue his dance studies with Ella Daganova, Eugene Loring, the New Dance League, Yeichi Nimura, Anthony Tudor and Helene Veola — immersing himself in the techniques of ballet, modern, Spanish and Oriental dance. He began his professional appearances with the Sandor-Sorel Dance Center ('36) and danced in the Broadway choruses of *Great Lady* and *Stars in Your Eyes* ('38), *Straw Hat Revue* ('39) and *Keep Off the Grass* and *Concert Varieties* ('45). He joined the Corps de Ballet of American Ballet Theater in 1940 and was already dancing principal character roles by 1941. After being hired by producer Max Liebman to dance and choreograph at Camp Tamiment (1937–41) his first ballet choreography (*Fancy Free*, '44) was a sensation — and became the basis of *On the Town*, his first Broadway choreographic work. With *Peter Pan* ('54), he became a innovative director-choreographer. He had joined the New York City Ballet in 1948 and served as its associate artistic director from 1949–63, also forming his own company, *Jerome Robbins Ballets: USA* (1958–61). His work has won him five Tony Awards and two Academy Awards. He is also the recipient of the *Dance Magazine* Award in the "Ballet" category for *Age of Anxiety* — as well as a performance award for *The Prodigal Son* in 1950 and again in 1956 "for extending the expressive range for the Broadway musical theatre through his organic dance concepts in *West Side Story*," the rank of Chevalier de L'Ordre des Artes et Lettres from the French Government in 1964 and the 1981 Kennedy Center Honors.

Stage: *On the Town* (Bdwy '44), *Billion Dollar Baby* (Bdwy '45), *High Button Shoes* (Bdwy '47, Tony Award), *Peter Pan* (Bdwy '47, also co-dir), *Look Ma, I'm Dancin'* (Bdwy '48, also concept, co-dir), *That's the Ticket* (Bdwy '48, dir only), *Miss Liberty* (Bdwy '49), *Call Me Madam* (Bdwy '50), *The King and I* (Bdwy '51), *Two's Company* (Bdwy '52, dir only), *Wish You Were Here* (Bdwy '52), *The Pajama Game* (Bdwy '54, co-dir only), *Peter Pan* (Bdwy '54, also dir), *The Tender Land* (NYC Opera '54), *Silk Stockings* (Bdwy '55, replacing Eugene Loring), *Bells Are Ringing* (Bdwy '56, with Bob Fosse, also dir, Tony nom), *West Side Story* (Bdwy '57, also concept, dir, Tony Award), *Gypsy* (Bdwy '59, also dir), *Fiddler on the Roof* (Bdwy '64, also dir, 2 Tony Awards), *Jerome Robbins' Broadway* (Bdwy '89, also dir, with Grover Dale, Tony Award)

TV: "The Ford 50th Anniversary Show with Ethel Merman and Mary Martin" ('53), "Peter Pan" ('55, Emmy nom)

Ballet/Dance Pieces (Over 60 works — partial listing): for New York City Ballet: "Fancy Free" ('44), "Jones Beach" (in collaboration with George Balanchine), "The Cage," "Afternoon of a Faun," "Los Noces," "The Goldberg Variation," "Dances at a Gathering," "The Concert," "Glass Pieces," "In the Night," "Watermill," Interplay," "Age of Anxiety," "Pied Piper," "Fanfare," "The Concert," "Into the Night," "Allegro con Grazia," *West Side Story* Suite ('95)

Film:

1956 **The King and I** — Fox

1961 **West Side Story** — Mirisch (also co-dir, Academy Award Winner Best Direction with Robert Wise)

* "Special Award": Academy Award to Jerome Robbins "for his brilliant achievements in the art of choreography on film." Assistants credited: Tommy Abbott, Maggie Banks, Howard Jeffrey, Tony Mordente)

1962 **Gypsy** — WB (Robert Tucker adapting his original work)

1971 **Fiddler on the Roof** — Mirisch/UA (adapted by Tommy Abbott, Sammy Bayes)

1985 **That's Dancing!** — MGM

1993 **Gypsy** — CBS (TV) (re-created by Bonnie Walker)

DAVID "DAVE" ROBEL
Billed as "The Human Top," this dancer-choreographer appeared in vaudeville and on Broadway in *Rose Marie* ('36). His talents eventually led him to Hollywood, where he assisted Hermes Pan and was an associate of Fred Astaire's.

Stage: *High Button Shoes* (LA '56)

Miscellaneous: Thalian's show ('60)

Film:

1942 **Rio Rita** — Loews (with Bobby Connolly, Vincente Minnelli)

1946 **Blue Skies** — Par (assistant to Fred Astaire, Hermes Pan)

Director-choreographer Jerome Robbins is on his way to an Oscar as he instructs gang members in **West Side Story** (United Artists, 1961). Left to right: Gus Trikonis, George Chakiris, Nick Covacevitch, Andre Tayir.

1951 **Royal Wedding**—MGM (assistant to Nick Castle with Marilyn Christine)

1955 **Daddy Long Legs**—Fox (with Roland Petit, Fred Astaire, assisted by Ellen Ray)

The Girl in the Red Velvet Swing—Fox

1957 **Funny Face**—Par (assistant to Astaire, Eugene Loring, with Pat Denise)

Silk Stockings—MGM (assistant to Astaire, Eugene Loring and Hermes Pan, with Angela Blue, Denise)

1965 **A Very Special Favor**—Univ

LESLIE ROBERTS

British choreographer.
Film:
1935 **Honeymoon for Three**—ABFD (with Carl Hyson)

ANDREA ROBINOVITCH

1989 **Prom Night 3: The Last Kiss**—?

BILL ("BOJANGLES") ROBINSON

b. Richmond, Virginia, May 25, 1878
d. Richmond, Virginia, November 25, 1949

One of the greatest tap dancers to ever grace the screens and stages of the world, "Bojangles" teamed with Shirley Temple to create some of the Movie Musical's most beloved and lasting images. Originally named "Luther"—a name he hated—at the age of 8, he beat his older brother, Bill, in a fight and said he was taking his name. He began tap dancing as a boy for pennies on Richmond street corners and was "discovered" while working in a beer garden between vaudeville engagements. At the age of 12 he toured with a Minstrel show called *The South Before the War*. He arrived in New York in

Bill "Bojangles" Robinson performing his famed "Stair" dance.

1898 and got a job at Minors Theater in the Bowery and danced in restaurants on Coney Island and played vaudeville with a partner, George Cooper. Achieved acclaim on Broadway in *Blackbirds of 1928* and continued on stage in *Brown Buddies* ('30), *Blackbirds of 1933, The Hot Mikado* ('39), *All in Fun* ('40), *Hot from Harlem* (OOT '41) and *Memphis Bound* ('45). Famed for his neat, clean footwork and style of dancing up on his toes with few heel taps, he always choreographed his own dance routines, his most famous one being his "Stair Dance," which he performed with Shirley Temple in **The**

Little Colonel in 1935. The film **Stormy Weather** ('43) is loosely based upon his life story and April 29, 1946 was proclaimed "Bill Robinson Day" in New York to celebrate his sixtieth year in show business. At his funeral over one million people lined the streets of New York in silent tribute as his body moved to Evergreen Cemetary in Brooklyn.

Biography: *Mr. Bojangles* by Jim Haskins and N.R. Mitgang (1988)

Film (Credits are for his own routines):
1930 **Dixiana**— RKO (with Pearl Eaton)
1932 **Harlem Is Heaven**— Lincoln
1934 **King for a Day**— Vitaphone (S)
1935 **The Big Broadcast of 1936**— Par (with Fayard Nicholas, LeRoy Prinz)
     Hooray for Love— RKO (with Maria Gambarelli, Sammy Lee)
     In Old Kentucky— Fox
     The Little Colonel— Fox (with Jack Donohue)
     The Littlest Rebel— Fox (with Donohue)
1936 **Dimples**— Fox (with Jack Haskell)
1937 **One Mile from Heaven**— Fox
1938 **Just Around the Corner**— Fox (with Nick Castle, Geneva Sawyer)
     Rebecca of Sunnybrook Farm— Fox (with Castle, Sawyer)
     Road Demon— Fox
     Up the River— WB (with Castle, Sawyer)
1939 **It's Swing Ho — Come to the Fair**— Par (News)
1941 **By an Old Southern River**— Soundies Corp (S)
1942 **Let's Scuffle**— Soundies Corp (S)
1943 **Stormy Weather**— Fox (with Castle, Katherine Dunham, Fayard Nicholas, Clarence Robinson)

CLARENCE ROBINSON

Resident director and producer at the legendary Cotton Club who was one of the most successful African-American dance directors of the 1920s and '30s. The dancer Bill Bailey once said about Robinson: "He couldn't dance to pass a fly," but that didn't stop Robinson from packaging sensational displays by hiring great dancers to perform their own routines in Harlem nightclubs and at the Apollo Theatre, often having dancer Ristina Banks create the choreography. Dancer Cleo Haynes remembered, "He was the nicest man in the world to work for. He was our great one — our Ziegfeld. I don't know why the pages of black show business history choose to ignore him, because he was the top black producer. He did the Cotton Club and the Apollo... He launched the careers of many of our present-day performers." Although he is no relation to Bill "Bojangles" Robinson, his support and

encouragement of other artists made a tremendous impact on the history of Black dance in America.

Stage: *Keep Shufflin'* (Bdwy '28)
Nightclub/Concert: The Cotton Club (1931–'40), Mimo Professional Club, Moulin Rouge (LV '55)
Film:
1943 **Stormy Weather**— Fox (with Nick Castle, Katherine Dunham, Fayard Nicholas, Bill Robinson)

EARTHA ROBINSON

African-American dancer who appeared in films **School Daze** ('88) and began her choreography career as assistant to Debbie Allen, Michael Peters, Rosie Perez ("In Living Color") and Otis Sallid.

TV: "A Different World," "Fame," "Sisters," "News to Us" (HBO special)
Music Video: "Walk the Dog"— Karyn White; videos for Soula, Klymaxx, Sunset Marquis, Gap Band, Xscape and Sugar Babes
Concert/Nightclub: Tours for Karyn White ('92), Color Me Badd ('92), Luther Vandross and Atlantic Starr
Film:
1993 **Sarafina!**— Miramax (assistant to Michael Peters)
     Sister Act II— Disney (assistant to Peters)
     Sugar Hill— Beacon Films
     What's Love Got to Do with It?— Touchstone (assistant to Peters)
1995 **I Rhythm**—?
     Vampire in Brooklyn— Par
1996 **Bogus**— WB
     Eddie— Hollywood Pict

KELLY ROBINSON

1985 **The Hearst and Davies Affair**— ABC/Circle Films (TV)
1987 **The Big Town**— Col

ALFRED RODRIGUES

b. Cape Town, Africa, August 18, 1921
British dancer-choreographer who studied in Africa with C. Robinson and appeared in several Cape Town Univ. Ballet Club productions before creating his first choreography in 1938. He went to London in 1946, continuing his dance studies and appearing in the musical *Song of Norway*. He joined Sadler's Wells Ballet in 1947, becoming a soloist in 1949 and ballet master in 1953. He choreographed for many ballet and opera companies and eventually became primarily a successful choreographer of stage musicals in Europe. Married to former dancer Julia Farron.

Stage: *Jubilee Girl* (London '56, with Bert Stimmel and Peter Darrell), *Chrysanthemum* (London '58 rev), *Zuleika* (London '59 with Eleanor Fazan, Peter Powell, also dir), *The Quiz Kid* (London '59, also dir), *Is There Intelligent Life on Earth?* (GB '64), *Charlie Girl* (London '65), *Ann Veronica* (GB '69)

Ballet/Dance Pieces: For Sadler's Wells: "Ile des Sirenes" ('50), "Blood Wedding" ('53), "Cafe De Sports," "Saudades" ('55); for the Royal Ballet: "The Miraculous Mandarin" and "Jabez and the Devil;" "Romeo and Juliet," "Cinderella" and "Nutcracker" (La Scala); "Vivaldi Concerto" (Royal Danish Ballet); "Daphnis and Chloe," "La Sacre Du Printemps" and Orpheus" (for Warsaw Grand Opera)

Film:
1956 **Oh, Rosalinda!** (aka **Die Fledermaus**) — Gau/Brit
1957 **An Alligator Named Daisy** — Rank
      Let's Be Happy — ABE/Pathe(with Pauline Grant)
1959 **Tread Softly Stranger** — Gau/Brit

NELIDA RODRIGUEZ

Dancer who appeared in *Tango Argentino*, London '91.
Film:
1988 **Tango Bar** — Castle Hill (with Nelson Avila, Santiago Ayala, Lilliana Belfiore, Doris Petroni, Carlos Rivarola, Norma Viola — also appears)

ROGER THE SWEDE

1994 **Staggered** — Big Deal Pictures

ERIC ROGERS

1953 **Genevieve** — Univ

JAIME (JUAN) ROGERS

b. New York
Dancer, choreographer and teacher who was born in New York and raised in Puerto Rico and began his dance studies at 4. A graduate of the High School of Performing Arts and the Juilliard School of music, he danced with the Martha Graham and José Limon companies before debuting on Broadway in *Flower Drum Song* in 1958. He gained notice on Broadway in *West Side Story* ('61) and *Golden Boy* ('64, also assisting Donald McKayle) with his masculine dance style and intriguing multi-ethnic looks. Other stage appearances include *Kicks and Co.*(OOT '61) and *We Take the Town* (OOT '62) and he had his own touring dance troupe. He relocated to California for the film version of **West Side Story** (in the role of "Loco," '61) and remained there

to teach and choreograph. When he followed Debbie Allen as choreographer on the TV series "Fame" in 1985, an article in the *Los Angeles Times* described his style as "an exuberant, modern dance-based combination of geometrically balanced lines, driving rhythms and explosive leaps and turns. Rogers simply describes his style as 'clear.'"

Stage: The Education of $H*Y*M*A*N$ $K*A*P*L*A*N$ (Bdwy '68), *Golden Boy* (London), *Two Cities* (London '69)

TV: Elvis Presley Special (with Claude Thompson '68), "The Andy Williams Show" ('69–71), John Wayne Special ('70), Osmond Brothers Special ('71), "The Ken Berry Wow Show" ('72), "The Helen Reddy Show" ('73), "The Hudson Brothers Show" ('74), "Sonny Comedy Revue" ('74), "Mary's Incredible Dream" (Mary Tyler Moore special '75, Emmy nom), "The Sonny and Cher Show," Grammy and Emmy Awards shows, "Fame" ('85); commercials for Dr. Pepper

Nightclub/Concert: Acts for ABBA, Abbe Lane, etc.

Film:
1979 **Americathon** — UA
1980 **Wholly Moses!** — Col
1984 **Breakin'** — Cannon (with Shabba Doo)
1988 **Caddyshack 2** — WB

PERI ROGOVIN

1995 **How to Make an American Quilt** — Univ

ASHLEY ROLAND

Dancer and choreographer who has been a member of the collaborative Momix, ISO and ISOBOBS dance/theater groups. She began her dance career after ballet study with various teachers and at the North Carolina School of the Arts.
1989 **Earth Girls Are Easy** — Vestron (with Russell Clark, Sarah Elgart, ISO: Daniel Ezralow, Jamie Hampton, Morleigh Steinberg; Wayne "Crescendo" Ward)

ALEX ROMERO (ALEXANDER BERNARD QUIROGA)

b. San Antonio, Texas, August 20, 1913
One of the major dance on film contributors to the Hollywood musicals' final "Golden Age," Romero was born into a theatrical family. His father owned and operated an Opera House in Monterey, Mexico, and Alex started dancing in vaudeville and nightclubs at the age of 15 with his family's act ("Carlos and my brothers John and Oscar taught me the routines.") While touring the world he

Lee Scott, Gene Kelly and Alex Romero — three supreme dancers and choreographers — onscreen together in *A Day in New York* Ballet from **On the Town** (MGM, 1949).

learned acrobatics, tap, jazz, ballet ("Whatever I could pick up, in exchange for the little I knew") from the other acts on the bill. He also began choreographing, arriving early at the theater and "making things up." When the act disbanded because of World War II, he began dancing in films and was selected to be a member of Jack Cole's prestigious contract dance team at Columbia Studios, also touring with the Cole Dancers ("My real training came from the years I had with Jack Cole — he did it all, except tap. He did it all, better and more creative than most.") His career took a new direction when he was contracted by MGM in 1947 as a dancer — eventually being featured in **On the Town** ('49) in which he danced the *A Day in New York Ballet* with Gene Kelly, Lee Scott, Carol Haney, Jeanne Coyne and Vera-Ellen — and assisting Robert Alton, Cole, Kelly, Michael Kidd and Hermes Pan. He believes his first solo choreography was the "Thou Swell" number for June Allyson and the Blackburn Twins in **Words and Music** ('48 — "Robert Alton was too busy to do it"). He continued to assist between solo choreographic chores which contributed to films as they made their transition from the classic musical to rock 'n' roll. Making his one-and-only television appearance in the

TV comedy series "Please Don't Eat the Daisies" ('65), Romero's stage appearances include one of his brother's, Carlos' (see following entry) Fanchon and Marco revues at the Loews State Theater in Los Angeles and then, during the '70s, he appeared in *An American in Pasadena* with Gene Kelly and Danny Daniels (also TV) and *The Gene Kelly Show* in Atlantic City with Kelly and Roy Palmer. Naming Fred Astaire, Nick Castle, Jack Cole ("who really taught me to dance") and Gene Kelly as the major inspirations in his life, he added: "If I had my life to live over again, I would want it to be a re-run of this one! With one exception — I'd start dancing at age 3 — with teachers!"

Stage: *Happy Hunting* (Bdwy '56), *Pleasure Dome* (OB)

TV: "Fantasy Island," "Hart to Hart," "The Perry Como Show," "The Eddie Fisher Show" (one season), Debbie Reynolds specials, "Arthur Godfrey in Hollywood," the 32nd Academy Awards Show ('59), NAACP and "Who Tied the Can to Modern Man?" specials; "The Thornbirds" ('83), commercials for General Electric (featuring Debbie Reynolds) and Vons Markets

Nightclub/Concert: *Goodbye Broadway, Hello Gimp* (Ciro's, LA '56), production numbers at the

Riviera Hotel (LV); acts for Van Johnson, Howard Keel & Kathryn Grayson, Ann Miller, Jane Powell and Bobby Short

Miscellaneous: General Electric industrial

Film:

1948 **Words and Music**— MGM (assistant to Robert Alton, Gene Kelly)

1949 **The Barkleys of Broadway**— MGM (assistant to Alton, Fred Astaire)

    On the Town— MGM (assistant to Stanley Donen, Kelly, also appeared)

    The Red Danube— MGM

    Take Me Out to the Ballgame— MGM (assistant to Donen, Kelly)

1950 **Annie Get Your Gun**— MGM (assistant to Alton)

    The Outriders— MGM

    Pagan Love Song— MGM (assistant to Alton)

1951 **Across the Wide Missouri**— MGM

    An American in Paris— MGM (assistant to Kelly — also appeared)

    The Belle of New York— MGM (assistant to Alton and Astaire, with Marilyn Christine)

1953 **The Affairs of Dobie Gillis**— MGM (with Bob Fosse)

    The Band Wagon— MGM (assistant to Astaire, Michael Kidd, with Pat Denise)

    Kiss Me Kate— MGM (assistant to Hermes Pan)

    Small Town Girl— MGM (with Busby Berkeley, Willie Covan, Ann Miller)

1954 **Seven Brides for Seven Brothers**— MGM (assistant to Kidd)

1955 **I'll Cry Tomorrow**— MGM (assisted by Alex Ruiz)

    Love Me or Leave Me— MGM

    The Prodigal— MGM

1956 **The Fastest Gun Alive**— MGM

1957 **Jailhouse Rock**— MGM (assisted by Ruiz)

    Les Girls— MGM (assistant to Jack Cole, Kelly)

    Raintree Country— MGM

    Until They Sail— MGM (assisted by Patti Barker)

1958 **Tom Thumb**— MGM

1959 **The Gazebo**— MGM

    A Private's Affair— Fox (assisted by Ruiz)

    Say One for Me— Fox (assisted by Ruiz)

1960 **Pepe**— Col (with Eugene Loring, assisted by Ruiz)

1961 **The George Raft Story**— UA (assisted by Mary Menzies, Ruiz)

1962 **Four Horsemen of the Apocalypse**— MGM

    Whatever Happened to Baby Jane?— WB

The Wonderful World of the Brothers Grimm— MGM (assisted by Ruiz)

1963 **The Stripper**— Fox

1967 **Clambake**— MGM

    Double Trouble— MGM

1968 **For Singles Only**— Col

    Speedway— MGM

1971 **The Grissom Gang**— Cinerama

1975 **Hustle**— Par

1979 **The Frisco Kid**— WB

    Love at First Bite— AIP

1980 **Marilyn: The Untold Story**— Lawrence Schiller Prod/ABC (TV)

1981 **Zorro, the Gay Blade**— Fox

1985 **That's Dancing!**— MGM (with others)

1994 **That's Entertainment! III**— MGM (with others)

CARLOS (CHARLES) ROMERO

b. Monterrey, Mexico

Older brother of Alex Romero (see previous listing), he headed the family dance troupe with brothers John and Oscar on the Fanchon and Marco circuit, which Alex later joined. Carlos settled in California to assist Fanchon on production numbers in the 1930s for her successful chain of movie theater prologue productions and continued with his film career. He danced in films (**The Merry Widow**, '27) and his son, also named Carlos Romero, had a successful career as an actor in films.

Stage: Fanchon and Marco revues and prologues (Egyptian Theater, Loews State Theater, Los Angeles, etc.)

Ballet/Dance Pieces: "Fiesta de Boda" (Hollywood Bowl '35)

Miscellaneous: Ice Follies

Film:

1937 **Hollywood Party in Technicolor**— MGM (S)

    Thrill of a Lifetime— Par (with Fanchon, LeRoy Prinz)

1943 **He's My Guy**— Univ (with Louis DaPron)

    Hi Buddy— Univ (with Dick Humphreys, the Four Step Bros)

    Hi Ya Chum— Univ (with Eddie Prinz)

    Hi Ya Sailor— Univ

    Larceny with Music— Univ

    Never a Dull Moment— Univ

    Sing a Jingle— Univ

    Wintertime— Fox (with Fanchon, James Gonzales, Kenny Williams)

1944 **Bowery to Broadway**— Univ (with John Boyle, Dapron)

    Hat Check Honey— Univ

The Merry Monahans— Univ (with DaPron)
  Murder in the Blue Room— Univ
  Take It Big— Par
1945 **Men in Her Diary**— Univ
  Song of the Sarong— Univ
  That's the Spirit— Univ (with DaPron)

LIDYA ROMERO

1992 **Cabeza De Vaca**— Concorde

PACO ROMERO

1991 **Don Juan My Love**— Intl Film Exchange (Span)

GREG ROSATI

1991 **Blue Sky**— Orion ('95 *LA Dance* Award nom)

HERBERT ROSS

b. Brooklyn, New York, May 13, 1927

Former dancer-choreographer whose unique combination of talents make him the only person from the world of Ballet to become a highly successful film producer and director. He studied ballet with Madame Anderson-Ivantsova, Caird Leslie and Helene Platova and modern dance with Doris Humphrey. Other diverse training included acting with Herbert Berghof and painting with Hubert Landau. He began his career as an actor with a touring Shakespearean Company and then danced on Broadway in *Follow the Girls* and *Laughing Room Only* ('44), *Vincent Youman's Ballet Revue* (OOT '44), *Something for the Boys* ('45), *Beggar's Holiday* ('46), *Shootin' Star* (OOT '46), *Bloomer Girl* ('47), *Look Ma, I'm Dancin'* and *Inside U.S.A.* ('48) and *That's the Ticket* (OOT '49). On the strength of the phenomenal success of his very first ballet, *Caprichos* (sponsored by the New York Choreographer's Workshop, '49), he joined American Ballet Theatre as resident choreographer. With John Ward, he created the Ross-Ward Ballets in 1950, began choreographing on Broadway in 1951 and eventually formed his own company, Ballet of Two Worlds, to tour Europe in 1960. Although he had already choreographed his first film (**Carmen Jones**) in 1954 in the U.S., he was given a rare opportunity in 1960 to choreograph films in England for British pop music superstar Cliff Richard. After successfully directing *Wonderful Town* and *Finian's Rainbow* at NY City Center, he returned to Broadway, joining the ranks of director-choreographer. He also directed the non-musicals *Chapter 2* and *You Ought*

to Be in Pictures on Broadway and his career progressed to that of film director and producer of many (twenty four-to-date) highly successful films including **Dancers, Dr. Dolittle, Footloose, Funny Lady, Goodbye Mr. Chips, Nijinsky, The Owl and the Pussycat, Pennies from Heaven, Play It Again, Sam, The Secret of My Success, Steel Magnolias** and **Undercover Blues**. His 1977 film **The Turning Point** was the most commercially successful ballet film since **The Red Shoes**, causing Agnes DeMille to write in *America Dances*: "It remained, however, for Herbert Ross in **The Turning Point** to give us dancing, pure dancing, with all its vitality and strength and beauty and persuasiveness." Ross married former ABT legend Nora Kaye in 1959 and she closely collaborated on his stage and film work until her death. He then married Lee Radziwill in 1988. In 1993, he directed his first opera, *La Bohème*, for the Los Angeles Music Center Opera company. His honors include multiple Oscar and Tony nominations and the *Dance Magazine* Award in the "Ballet" category for *Caprichos* (called "sheer theatre magic" by the magazine) in 1950 and again in 1980 with a first-time-ever "Award of Distinction" with Nora Kaye ("...given in recognition of their work as collaborators in cinema; To Miss Kaye, as producer, and to Mr. Ross, as director, by which they have extended dance into cinema with profound, far-reaching influence on the public and on the American dance theater.") In 1994, he was one of the choreographers honored by the Film Society of Lincoln Center.

Stage: **A Tree Grows in Brooklyn** (Bdwy '51), *Three Wishes for Jamie* (Bdwy '52), *House of Flowers* (Bdwy '54, also dir, uncredited), *The Amazing Adele* (OOT '56), *Body Beautiful* (Bdwy '58), *Take Me Along* (Bdwy '59, with Onna White), *The Gay Life* (Bdwy '61, also dir, uncredited), *I Can Get It for You Wholesale* (Bdwy '62), *Tovarich* (Bdwy '63), *Anyone Can Whistle* (Bdwy '64, Tony nom), *Golden Boy* (Bdwy '64, with Donald McKayle), *Do I Hear a Waltz?* (Bdwy '65), *On a Clear Day You Can See Forever* (Bdwy '65), *The Apple Tree* (Bdwy '66, with Lee Theodore, "additional musical staging by" credit); Italy: *Reynaldo and Campo* ('62), *Rochelle in Aria, Delia in Scala*

TV: "The Milton Berle Show" ('54), "A Toast to Jerome Kern" and "Meet Me in St. Louis" ('59), "Four for Tonight" ('60, also co-dir), "Wonderful Town," "The Bell Telephone Hour," "The Fred Astaire Show" ('68, with Fred Astaire), "The Martha Raye Show," "The Fantasticks" (dir), "Follies in Concert" (dir)

Ballet/Dance Pieces (Partial listing): "Caprichos" ('49), "The Thief Who Loved a Ghost," "Pierrot and the Moon," "The Maids," "Paean," "Ovid Metamorphosis," "Tristan," "Angel Head," "Dialogues" and "The Dybbuk" ('60)

Director Herbert Ros shares a serious moment with choreographer/star Mikhail Baryshnikov on the set of **Dancers** (Cannon, 1987).

Nightclub/Concert: Acts for Eddie Albert & Margo, Constance Bennett, Diahann Carroll, Jerry Lewis, Patrice Munsel, Martha Raye

Film:

1954 **Carmen Jones** — Fox

1962 **The Young Ones** (aka **Wonderful to Be Young**) — WB/GB

1963 **Summer Holiday** — AIP

1966 **Inside Daisy Clover** — WB (assisted by Howard Jeffrey)

Who's Afraid of Virginia Woolf? — WB (uncredited, assisted by Howard Jeffrey)

1967 **Dr. Dolittle** — Fox (assisted by Howard Jeffrey, Nora Kaye, also dir)

1968 **Funny Girl** — Col (assisted by Howard Jeffrey and Nora Kaye)

1969 **Goodbye Mr. Chips** — MGM (also dir)

1975 **Funny Lady** — Col (assisted by Howard Jeffrey, also dir)

GIORGIO ROSSI

1989 **Adventures of Baron Munchausen** — Col (with Pino Penesse)

BIANCA ROSSINI

1988 **Moon Over Parador** — Univ

JANET (LESLIE) ROSTON

b. Los Angeles, California

When asked to comment about choreography, this dancemaker-educator wrote, "I think to be successful as a choreographer you have to be ready to work in any movement style. You never know when you'll have to draw on some ethnic or period style you learned way back when. The more you can absorb early on, the more ready you'll be." Rosten "absorbed" years of modern, ballet and jazz with dance studies in Los Angeles, New York and Paris — as well as a B.A. and M.A. in dance at UCLA — to build a firm foundation for her professional career.

She is currently director for the Dance program at Beverly Hills High School and choreographer in multiple theatrical venues.

Stage: West-Coast productions of *Nite-Club Confidential* ('86, also asst dir), *Partners, Hair, The Rocky Horror Show, It's a Bird, It's a Plane, It's Superman, Scarlet Letter: An Alternative Musical* and J.P. Nightingale Children's Theater tours.

TV: "The Charmings," "Elvis: Good Rockin' Tonight," "Murderous Passion" (NBC mini-series '95), multiple episodes of "Santa Barbara," "A League of Their Own" and "George"; commercials for Formula 409, Knott's Berry Farm, Lucky Supermarkets

Music Video: "Hot for Teacher" — Van Halen; "Gotta Get Love" — Timmy Thomas; "Oriental Dolls" — Frieda Parton; "James Brown Medley" — Soul Kings; "Ain't No Liberal" — The Foremen; videos for Rod Stewart, Geoffrey Osborne

Nightclub/Concert: Tours for Jack Mack and the Heart Attack, Trans X

Miscellaneous: Industrials for AVCO Finance, Stouffers Hotels, Sunkist, Polaroid

Film:

1985 **Remote Control** — Vista Films
      Teen Wolf — Atlantic Releasing Co
      3:15 — Dakota Ent

CAPRICE ROTH

1985 **Cocoon** — Fox (with Gwen Verdon, "Alien Choreography" credit)

ANN ROYAL

1954 **Jesse James' Women** — UA (with Jess Saunders)

EDWARD ("TEDDY") ROYCE

b. Bath, England, December 14, 1870
d. London, England, June 15, 1964

British director, producer and dance director who made his greatest impact as an important stage director-choreographer in collaboration with some of the American musical theater's most renowned composers (Rudolph Friml, Victor Herbert, Jerome Kern and Rodgers & Hart). Originally intending to be a scenic artist, Royce studied dance and after a brief performance career, he began staging dances and musical sequences for London musicals in 1903. One of the first director-choreographers on the modern musical stage, Royce may be best remembered for his creation of the "Runaround Dance" (or "The Oompah Trot" as it was dubbed in England) for Fred and Adele Astaire during rehearsals of *The Love Letter* in 1921. Astaire wrote in his autobiography *Steps in Time*: "Royce was a brilliant showman… He had a wonderful sense of timing and comedy values in addition to his other type dancing work. He was a slightly built man, five feet seven, with gray hair, sixty years of age (sic), and an accomplished dancer himself." From 1913–35 he directed and staged over thirty Broadway stage shows — among them the major successes *Sally, Irene, Kid Boots, Leave It to Jane, Ziegfeld Follies of 1920* and a raft of "Oh" shows: *Oh, Boy!, Oh, Lady! Lady!!, Oh, Look!,* and *Oh, My Dear!*

Stage: *Merrie England* (London '02), *The Earl and the Girl, A Princess of Kensington* and *Little Hans Andersen* (London '03), *The Catch of the Season* (London '04), *The Talk of the Town* (London '05), *The Beauty of Bath* (London '06), *The Gay Gordons* and *My Darling* (London '07), *Havana* (London '08), *Our Miss Gibbs* and *The Dollar Princess* (London '09, also dir), *The Girl in the Train* (London '10, also dir), *A Waltz Dream* (also dir), *Peggy, The Count of Luxembourg* (also dir) (London '11), *Gypsy Love* (London '12, also dir), *The Doll Girl* (Bdwy '13), *The Marriage Market* (London and Bdwy '13, also dir); *The Laughing Husband* (Bdwy '14), *Bric-a-Brac* (London '15, also dir), *Betty, Tina* and *The Miller's Daughter* (London '15, also dir), *The Happy Day* (London '16, also dir), *Betty* and *The Century Girl* (Bdwy '16), *Have a Heart, Oh, Boy!, Leave It to Jane, Kitty Darlin'* and *Going Up* (Bdwy '17, also dir), *Oh, Lady! Lady!!, The Rockabye Baby, The Canary* (Bdwy '18, also dir), *Come Along, She's a Good Fellow, Irene* and *Apple Blossoms* (Bdwy '19, also dir), *Lassie, Ziegfeld Follies, Kissing Time* and *Sally* (Bdwy '20, also dir), *Ziegfeld Follies, Good Morning Dearie* and *The Love Letter* (Bdwy '21, also dir), *Orange Blossoms* (Bdwy '22, also prod, dir), *The Bunch and Judy* (Bdwy '22, with Fred Astaire), *Cinders* and *Kid Boots* (Bdwy '23, also dir), *Annie Dear* (Bdwy '24, also dir), *Louie the 14th* (Bdwy '25, also dir), *The Merry Malones* (Bdwy '27, also dir), *Katja, the Dancer* (Australia '27, also prod), *She's My Baby* and *Billie* (Bdwy '28, also dir), *Open Your Eyes* (London '29), *Daphne* and *El Dorado* (London '30), *The Rose of Flanders* (LA '32), *A Waltz Dream* (London, '34, also dir), *Fritzi* (London '35, also dir, co-prod)

Film:

1929 **Fox Movietone Follies** — Fox (with Willie Covan and Fanchon, assisted by Gwen Davis)
      Married in Hollywood — Fox
      Words and Music — Fox (with Frank Merlin)

1934 **Along Came Sally** — Gainsborough/Gaumont

JACQUES RUET

1964 **Yesterday, Today and Tomorrow**— Embassy

ALTON RUFF

b. Texas, September 1

Dancing and singing actor-choreographer who majored in drama and dance at the University of Texas and then, moved to New York. There, he studied dance with Gerald Arpino, Peter Gennaro, Martha Graham, Aubrey Hitchins and Anthony Tudor and acting with Uta Hagen. After making his professional debut in the 1952 road company of *Oklahoma!*, he danced on Broadway in *The Pajama Game, New Girl in Town, Redhead* and *The Happiest Girl in the World*. Cast as one of Mitzi Gaynor's "Four Fellows" in her highly successful nightclub act, he moved to California, where he assisted Danny Daniels on the LACLO '75 revival of *Wonderful Town* and the film **Pennies from Heaven**, in which he also appeared. Other film dancing roles: **Funny Lady**, **Silent Movie** and **Mame**. His multiple television appearances include the Dean Martin, Garry Moore, Red Skelton, Carol Burnett and Jackie Gleason shows, "The Bell Telephone Hour," "The NBC Follies" and "Wonderful Town." Along with his prolific career as a performer, he began choreographing in 1982 with a stage production of Billy Barnes' *Movie Star* in California. Asked to name major influences in his life and career, Ruff credits Kevin Carlisle, Danny Daniels, Bob Fosse, Mitzi Gaynor, Carl Jablonski and Gwen Verdon,

Stage: *Movie Star* (Calif '82)

TV: "The Rich Little Show" ('76)

Nightclub/Concert: Act for Shirley Jones & Jack Cassidy

Miscellaneous: Industrials for Kawasaki, Levi Strauss; fashion shows for Bob Mackie

Film:

1981 **Pennies from Heaven**—MGM (assistant to Danny Daniels)

1983 **The Sting II**—Univ (with Ron Stein)

ALEX RUIZ

b. Tombstone, Arizona, October 27

"I became a choreographer out of self-defense," said Ruiz when asked about his start in dancemaking, "I just did not like what I was doing." Born in Arizona, his family moved to San Francisco when he was a baby and he began tap lessons as a child in Oakland, California. Making his professional debut at the age of 11 with jazz greats Count Basie and Lionel Hampton at the Hawaiian Gardens nightclub in San Jose, he soon realized that we would have to expand his dance technique and knowledge beyond tap. He moved to Hollywood to

study ballet with Edith Jane at the Falcon Studios and began making appearances in films. Disillusioned with the quality of dance in Hollywood films, he returned to San Francisco and joined the SF Ballet, also studying with Harold and Lew Christensen. When his ballet salary did not suffice for his newly-married status, he returned to Hollywood and continued dancing in films: **Jailhouse Rock** ('57), **Merry Andrew** ('58), **Babes in Toyland** and **West Side Story** ('64), etc., being a "Dance-In" for **Robin and the 7 Hoods** (also '64) and assisting Alex Romero before beginning his solo career. He also assisted Lee Scott on TV's "The George Gobel Show." Married to dancer-educator Sallie Whelan since 1956, they opened the LA Dance Center in 1974. Talking about his work in films and television, he stated that he got out of it because of the producers and directors: "They just minimalized what choreographers are doing." To do the quality of work he preferred, he created his own Dance Theatre USA in 1978 and the company continues to perform, most recently in Mexico.

Stage: *Kiss Me Kate* (Long Beach CLO '58), *The Pajama Game* and *Kismet* (Long Beach CLO '59), **Amahl and the Night Visitors**, *The Merry Widow* (Long Beach CLO '61), *Bye Bye Birdie, My Fair Lady* (Melodyland '64), *Carousel* (Melodyland '66)

TV: "Polka Parade" (with Sallie Whalen, '63–65)

Nightclub/Concert: Production shows at the Frontier and Flamingo Hotels (LV); acts for Dean Barlow & the Timekeepers, the Lee Sisters

Ballet/Dance Pieces (Partial listing): "How the West Was Lost," "Streetcar Named Desire," "Rain," "The Western," "The Petrified Forest," etc.

Miscellaneous: "Bal Sans Souci" Benefit (LA '65)

Film:

1957 **Jailhouse Rock**—MGM (assistant to Alex Romero)

1959 **A Private's Affair**—Fox (assistant to Romero)

Say One for Me—Fox (assistant to Romero)

1960 **I'll Cry Tomorrow**—MGM (assistant to Romero)

Pepe—Col (assistant to Romero)

1961 **The George Raft Story**—UA (assistant to Romero, with Mary Menzies)

1962 **The Wonderful World of the Brothers Grimm**—MGM (assistant to Romero)

1963 **Moonwalk**—MGM

A Ticklish Affair—MGM

1964 **Hush, Hush Sweet Charlotte**—Fox

1968 **The Scalphunters**—UA

CONNIE RYAN

1988 **The Courier**—Vestron

1990 **The Field**—Avenue

RANDALL SABUSAWA

In the credits of **Showgirls** (1995), Randy Sabusawa is listed as "New York casting associate."
1986 **The Karate Kid Part II**— Col (with Paul DeRolf, Jose DeVega, Nobuko Miyamoto)

QUINNY SACKS

1986 **Knights and Emeralds**— WB
1988 **Who Framed Roger Rabbit?**— Touchstone/BV (with David Toguri)
1990 **Tune in Tomorrow**— Cinecom
1995 **Restoration**— Miramax (with Kate Flatt, "Whittlesea Dancers" credit)

DONALD (EDWARD) SADDLER

b. Van Nuys, California, January 24, 1920
Dancer-choreographer who attended Los Angeles City College and received his dance training from Anton Dolin, Carmelita Maracci, Nijinska and Anthony Tudor in California, where he also began his professional dance appearances at the Hollywood Bowl. An alumnus of Ballet Theatre (1939–43), he made his Broadway debut in *Song of Norway* ('44) and while serving in the Armed Forces during World War II, he appeared in The Foxhole Ballet company. Returning to civilian life, he appeared in *High Button Shoes* ('47) and *Dance Me a Song* and *Bless You All* in 1950. His first choreography was the ballet **Blue Mountain Ballads** for the Markova-Dolin Company in 1949, before starting his prolific choreographic career in musical theater as assistant to Jerome Robbins on *Call Me Madam* in 1950. Saddler won the coveted Tony Award for his second Broadway show, *Wonderful Town*, and continued to make rich contributions to the musical stage. His all-too-brief film career began in 1952 assisting Helen Tamiris at Columbia and LeRoy Prinz at Warner Bros., before he returned to greater rewards in television, dance and theater work. Associate director for the Harkness Ballet Company (1964–70) and winner of the *Dance Magazine* Award in 1984.
Stage: For Dallas Fair Park Musical 1951 season: *Where's Charley?, Texas, L'il Darlin', The Song of Norway, I Married an Angel, Miss Liberty* and *The Merry Widow; Wish You Were Here* (Bdwy '52), *Wonderful Town* (Bdwy '53, Tony Award, also London), *John Murray Anderson's Almanac* (Bdwy '53), *Tobia La Candida Spia* (Italy '54, Silver Mask Award), *Shangri-La* (Bdwy '56), *When in Rome* (London '59), *Milk and Honey* (Bdwy '61), *We Take the Town* (OOT '62), *Morning Sun* (OB '63), *Sophie* (Bdwy '63), *To Broadway with Love* (NY World's Fair '64), *Knickerbocker Holiday* (LACLO '71), *No, No Nanette* (Bdwy '71, Tony Award), *Merman and Mar-*

tin on Broadway, *Much Ado About Nothing* (Bdwy '72, Tony nom), *Berlin to Broadway with Kurt Weill* (OB '72), *Tricks* (Bdwy '73), *Miss Moffat* (OOT '74), *A Midsummer Night's Dream* and *A Doll's House* (NY Shakespeare Festival '74), *Rodgers and Hart* (Bdwy '75), *The Robber Bridegroom* (Bdwy '76), *Hellzapoppin'* (OOT '76), *Oh Kay!* (OOT '78 rev, also dir), *Ice Dancing* (Bdwy '78, with Kenneth MacMillan, Norman Maen, Twyla Tharp), *The Grand Tour* (Bdwy '79), *Happy New Year* (Bdwy '80), *Say Hello to Harvey!* (Bdwy '81), *On Your Toes* (Bdwy rev '82, with George Balanchine, Tony nom), *I Hear Music — Frank Loesser and Friends* (OB '84), *The Golden Land* (OB '85), *My Fair Lady* (Bdwy '93 rev); Operas: **Aïda, La Perichole**
TV (Partial listing): "The Bell Telephone Hour" (3 seasons), "The Perry Como Show," Tony Awards Show, "Verna, U.S.O. Girl"
Nightclub/Concert: *La Nouvelle Eve* (El Rancho Vegas '61)
Ballet/Dance Pieces: "Blue Mountain Ballads" ('49), "This Property Is Condemned," "Winesburg, Ohio," "Dreams of Glory," "Koshare" ('66) and "Vaudeville" for Harkness Ballet; other ballets for the Joffrey Ballet, Markova-Dolin Ballet and Valerie Bettis Dance Company
Film:
1952 **April in Paris**— WB (with Ray Bolger, LeRoy Prinz)
  Just for You— Col (assistant to Helen Tamiris)
1953 **By the Light of the Silvery Moon**— WB (with LeRoy Prinz)
1955 **Young at Heart**— WB
  The Main Attraction— MGM (with Lionel Blair)
1975 **The Happy Hooker**— Cannon
1987 **Radio Days**— Orion

FELIX SADOWSKI

b. Poland
d. Chicago, Illinois, November 6, 1978
A member of the Polish Ballet, Sadowski, with his partner, Janina Frotovna, appeared in and choreographed their routines (usually combinations of ballet and Slavic folk dance) for several Hollywood films during the 1940s. Settling permanently in Chicago, he choreographed, produced and directed Polish films, theatre, TV ("Polka-Go-Round") and variety shows ("The Chainé Dancers") until he was beaten to death by an unknown assailant in 1978.
Stage: Halka ('53), **Mirele Efros** (Chicago '65)
TV: "Polka-Go-Round" ('62)
Film (Credits are for appearances with Frotovna):
1944 **Alaska**— Mon (with Jack Boyle)
  Lake Placid Serenade— Rep (with Jack Crosby)

1945 **Blonde Ransom**—Univ (with Louis DaPron)

RUTH ST. DENIS (DENNIS)
b. New Jersey, January 20, 1877
d. Hollywood, California, July 21, 1968
A cigarette poster of the Egyptian goddess Isis inspired little New Jersey farm girl Ruth Dennis in 1904 to become the exotic "Miss Ruth" of the veils, incense and American modern dance beginnings. She studied recitation, Delsarte mime and social dance with her mother, later studying ballet with Maria Bonfanti (of *The Black Crook*) and debuted in *Du Barry*, a David Belasco production in New York. It was Belasco who suggested she add the "St." and lose one "n" to her name. She also performed "skirt dancing" in early silent shorts. When Isis inspired her, she created her first dance recital of Oriental works in 1906, which toured "Smoking concerts" and vaudeville. Her success took her to Europe for three years, where she mystified the crowds. In 1915, with husband and partner Ted Shawn, she co-founded the Denishawn school in Los Angeles—acknowledged as the "First American platform of Modern Dance" (*The Concise Oxford Dictionary of Ballet*). The school trained many film personalities and she and Shawn choreographed for early silent films. Because they felt that film was not a serious enough art form (but paid the bills for their more esoteric efforts), it is difficult to document all of their contributions. The group and school also contributed several other film choreographers (Norma Gould, Margaret Loomis and Harry Losee). Many of St. Denis' dances were also filmed, as well as newsreels with footage of Denishawn. The Denishawn Dancers toured extensively throughout the world until 1932, gathering costumes, props and study of a wide variety of ethnic dances and ceremonies. When she separated from Shawn, St. Denis concentrated on religious dances for a period, but returned to Oriental dance, establishing the New York School of Natya with La Meri in 1940. She danced, lectured and taught until shortly before her death.
   Autobiography: *Ruth St. Denis: An Unfinished Life* (1939)
   Stage: *The Light of Asia* (Hollywood '18)
   Ballet/Dance Pieces (Partial listing): "Egypta" ('04), "Radha, the Dance of the Five Sense," "The Nautch," "The Insense," "The Cobras," "O-Mika," "White Jade," "The Dance of the Black and Gold Sari," "The Legend of the Peacock," "Chrysanthemum," "Theodora—Empress of Byzantium," "Masque of Mary" ('32), etc.
   Film:
1915 **The Lily and the Rose**
1916 **Intolerance**—Griffith (with Ted Shawn)

1917 **Cleopatra**—Fox (with Shawn)
1918 **Salome**—Fox

DOM SALINARO
b. Waterbury, Conn., December 10, 1932
This dance creator and educator made his professional performance debut in a production of *Oklahoma!* in Bridgeport, Conn. in 1954. After graduating from the University of Bridgeport with a BS in Journalism he moved to New York for study with Gerald Arpino, Vladimir Doukodovsky, Peter Gennaro and Matt Mattox and began appearing on Broadway in a raft of shows from 1955–66: *Bajour*, *The Boys from Syracuse*, *Breakfast at Tiffany's*, *Guys and Dolls*, *Milk and Honey*, *The Most Happy Fella*, *The Vamp*, *Walking Happy*, *What Makes Sammy Run?* and *Wonderful Town*, as well as a Summer stock season and a touring production of *West Side Story*. Relocating to the West Coast, he appeared in films (**Aria**, **History of the World—Part One**, **Sweet Charity** and **Topaz**) and on television (The Carol Burnett, Don Knotts, Jerry Lewis and Ed Sullivan shows, "The Hollywood Palace," Emmy Awards and multiple specials). He began his career as a dance educator of freestyle jazz in 1963 and over the years he has taught in New York, Los Angeles and in dance conventions across the country. Winner of the *L.A. Weekly*, *Drama-Logue* and Robby (3) Awards for his stage work, Salinaro credits, "I've had the great good fortune to have studied with some of the best dance teachers and to have worked with some of the world's finest and inspiring performers. My students and dancers have been my inspiration."
   Stage: *The Boys from Syracuse* (High School of the Performing Arts, NY), Twelve shows for Long Beach CLO ('70s and '80s) including *West Side Story* ('82, also dir, Robby Award for direction)
   TV: "Capitol," "Dinah's Place," "The Master," "The Waltons"; commercials for Eastman Kodak, One Day Auto Paint and Rheingold Beer
   Nightclub/Concert: Revues: *Have We Got a Song for You* (Chicago), *Ski Time* (Aspen Meadow, Colo.); acts for Joe Conley & Eric Scott, Ann Jillian
   Film:
1981 **Crazy Times**—WB (TV)
1982 **Mae West**—Hill-Mandelker Prod. (TV)
1983 **Girls of the White Orchid**—Hill-Mandelker Prod (TV)

KITSU SAKAKIBARA
1965 **Buddha**—Daici/UA (Jap)

OTIS SALLID
b. Harlem, New York
On the TV documentary, "Story of a People—

Otis Sallid directs Christina Ricci in the "Tag Team" video, filmed in conjunction with **Addams Family Values** (1991) (photo courtesy of Otis Sallid).

Expressions in Black," this multi-faceted dancer, choreographer, writer and director stated: "In my choreography in the films I make, I try to tell stories all the time. So, I come to it not by way of styles or being a great dancer, but by evoking an emotion that is atavistic somewhat and is in your dream memory. I came to choreography as a cook. I make good food you know? Choreography is making good soup. I believe enough in the black experience to share it." He began his extensive dance training at Harlem Youth Unlimited with teachers Alvin Ailey, Thelma Hill, Louis Johnson, Minnie Marshall and James Truitte. Awarded scholarships to both the High School of Performing Arts and Juilliard, he studied with Martha Graham, Benjamin Harkevy, José Limon and Anthony Tudor. Other theater training was received at the Negro Ensemble Co. and the Neighborhood Playhouse. When asked about his professional debut, he answered: "My mother's living room—I got paid." From the living room to Broadway, Sallid appeared in *Hallelujah Baby* ('67), *Purlie* ('70), *Two Gentlemen of Verona* ('71), *Don't Bother Me, I Can't Cope* ('72), *Me and Bessie* and *The Wiz* ('75), *Comin' Uptown* ('79)

and *The Dream on Monkey Mountain* with the Negro Ensemble Co. Dance company performances include Eleo Pomare, Kathy Posin and Dance Theatre of Harlem. He began his choreographic career in 1972 with works for his own dance company, New Art Ensemble, at the Edison Theater in New York. Sallid's company contained some of dance's newest forces: Debbie Allen, Hinton Battle, Ben Harney and Michael Peters. His choreographic talents soon led him to film and television work and then to direction: more than a dozen commercials for Coca Cola, Ford, McDonalds, Proctor and Gamble, Schlitz Malt Liquor and Sprite, an episode of "A Different World" and music videos for the group Arrested Development. When asked why he became a choreographer, he answered: "To help my people. To paint pictures of the future and to be a driving force in the race." Winner of a 1993 MTV Award and the Music Video Producers Association Award for best rap video, in 1994 Sallid was the co-winner (with Michael Peters) of the first *LA Dance* Awards for best film choreography for **Swing Kids**.

Stage: *Straws in the Wind* (OB '75), *Stand Up Tragedy* (Arena Stage, DC), *The Glorious Monster*

(Henry Street Settlement), *Le Film Noire* (NY Shakespeare Festival), *Happy with the Blues* (Manhattan Place Theatre), *A Night for Dancing* (LA '86, also dir), *Bee Hive* (OB '86), *Baby That's Rock and Roll — The Songs of Leiber and Stoller* (OOT '94, also conceived and dir)

TV: "Head of the Class," "Fame," 1984 Grammy Awards, Patti Labelle Special, "Henry Dances," "Showtime at the Apollo," "The Music of Your Life," "Pryor's Place," "Rock and Roll Mom," "Living Single"; commercials for Coca Cola, McDonalds, Procter and Gamble

Music Video: "Footloose"— Kenny Loggins; "I Feel for You"— Chaka Kahn; "Everyday People"— Arrested Development (also dir); "Just Want to Be Your Girl"— Anita Baker; "Addams Family Values" Tag Team video (also dir)

Nightclub/Concert: Patti Labelle, Herbie Hancock, James Ingram, Donna Summer, "Ready for the World" tour and *Debbie Allen at Radio City Music Hall*

Ballet/Dance Pieces: "Bachianas Brasileras," "Big Band," "Disco Lady," "Persechetti," "Every Mother's Child," "The Heat Is On," "Hour of Power," "Love Songs," etc.

Film:

1985 **Girls Just Want to Have Fun**— New World (with Bill Goodson, Steve LaChance)

1988 **School Daze**— Col

1989 **Do the Right Thing**— Univ (with Rosie Perez)

      Sing— TriStar (with John Carrafa)

1990 **Graffiti Bridge**— WB

1991 **A Rage in Harlem**— Miramax

1992 **Class Act**— WB

      Malcom X— WB (1993 NAACP Image Award nom)

1993 **Swing Kids**— Hollywood Pictures (*LA Dance* Award)

SCOTT SALMON

b. Wichita Falls, Texas, 1942
d. Los Angeles, California, July 17, 1993

Tony and Emmy Award-nominated choreographer-director who graduated from the University of Oklahoma in 1965 with a Bachelor of Arts degree in music education. He appeared on Broadway in *Mame* and *Pousse Cafe* ('66), in the 1967 Montreal Expo production of *Hellzapoppin'* and returned to Broadway in *Promises, Promises* and *George M!* ('68). Moving to the West Coast, he danced in *Minskys Follies* at the Dunes Hotel, Las Vegas, and joined Ann-Margret in her nightclub act. He started his choreographic career with the NY Shakespeare Festival and multiple stock productions for Dallas Summer Musicals, St. Louis Muny Opera and Kansas City Starlight Opera. After assisting Joe

Layton on *Two by Two* in 1970, he made his solo New York choreographic debut Off-Broadway with *More Than You Deserve* in 1974 and went on to acclaim and a Tony nomination for his work on *La Cage aux Folles* ('83). Moving easily between stage, film and television work with his artistry and energy, he began producing the SHARE (the renowned California Show Business charity group which benefits mentally retarded children) *Boomtown* shows, the "Princess Grace Benefit" and TV's "The Love Boat Reunion." In 1990 he began directing the Easter and Christmas Spectaculars for Radio City Music Hall and in 1991 directed the "Dedication of Mount Rushmore" with President and Mrs. Bush. His prolific career and joy-filled life were tragically cut short by an auto accident in 1993, at which time he was preparing to direct the 1994 edition of Ringling Bros. and Barnum and Bailey Circus.

Stage: *Two by Two* (Bdwy '70, assistant to Joe Layton), *More Than You Deserve* (OB '74), *Heaven Sent* (LA), *From Broadway* (West Coast, also dir), *La Cage aux Folles* (Bdwy '83, Tony nom), *Easter Extravaganza* (Radio City Music Hall ('90, also dir), *The Radio City Christmas Spectacular* ('92, also dir)

TV: Steve Martin (3) & David Copperfield Specials, The Grammy Awards, 57th Academy Awards Show (Emmy nom), The Barbara Mandrell Show ('81–82), "A Look Back" ('86), "The Comedy Hall of Fame" ('89), "Liberty Weekend," "NBC 60th Anniversary," "Television Academy Hall of Fame"

Nightclub/Concert: Acts for Ann-Margret, Chita Rivera

Miscellaneous: Anheiser Busch industrial ('82), Miss America Pageants ('84–92).

Film:

1979 **The Jerk**— Univ

1980 **The Last Married Couple in America**— Univ

      Stir Crazy— Col

1988 **Torch Song Trilogy**— New Line Cinema

DORIAN SANCHEZ

b. Fresno, California, February 28, 1959

Daughter of ballroom dancer-choreographer Frank Sanchez, Dorian began her dance studies with Pat Jackson at American Dance in San Luis Obispo, California. She continued studying at the Pacific Conservatory of the Performing Arts, with Bill Goodson at the New Breed Dance Theater and at Roland Dupree's Dance Academy in Los Angeles. She made her professional debut as a dancer in **S.O.B.** ('81) and continued in the films **Breakin' 2 — Electric Bugaloo**, **Dirty Dancing** and **Trains, Planes and Automobiles**. While appearing on television and stage she began assisting Kenny Ortega, making her solo choreographic debut with the music video "Love Overboard" for Gladys Knight and the Pips. In collaboration with Cher ("My teacher and mentor") she began creating tours and fitness videos. Stating: "I believe that I blend the best of street dancing with classical ballet — that makes a style that is very physical, energetic and sensual," her creativity now encompasses all mediums.

Stage: *Barry Manilow's Copacabana* (London '94)

TV: 35th Annual Grammy Awards ('93), "The Smothers Brothers Show," "The Tonight Show with Jay Leno," The Desi Awards, "Cher at the Mirage," Sally Jessy Raphaël, Arsenio Hall and Oprah Winfrey shows, "Dirty Dancing — The Concert Tour" (HBO), "Hot Latin Nights" ('95); commercials for Diet Coke, Target (starring Rita Moreno), etc.

Nightclub/Concert (Partial listing): Appolonia '90 tour, "Dirty Dancing — The Concert Tour" ('90, also co-dir), Cher "Love Hurts" tour ('92, also dir), Peter Gabriel "Secret World" tour ('93), Lorrie Morgan "Watch Me" tour ('93, also dir), Porno for Pyros world tour ('93, also co-dir); *Just Add Water* (Caesar's Tahoe), Barry Manilow (Caesar's Palace, Atlantic City), more

Music Video (Partial listing): "Love Overboard" — Gladys Knight and the Pips; "Pink Cadillac" and "Everlasting" — Natalie Cole; "Keep the Vibe Alive" — Herbie Hancock; "Love and Understanding" and "Shoop Shoop" — Cher; "Strange But True" — Times Two; "You Can't Buy My Love" — Kool Skool; "Let It Rain" — Sybil (also dir); Cher fitness videos, more

Miscellaneous: Industrials for Toyota, others

Film:

1991 **Elvis in Memphis** — (TV)
   The Hand and the Glove — (TV)

DIRK (DICK) SANDERS

b. Buitzenborg, Java, 1933

Dutch classic and modern dancer who studied with Kurt Jooss (1950–52) in Holland before moving to Paris. He appeared with Roland Petit's Ballets de Paris and in the films **Black Tights** and **A Very Private Affair** (both '62). He also toured the United States with Mary Martin's one-woman show, appeared on Broadway in *Cheri* and with Ballets de Paris, danced with Maurice Béjart's company and was featured on the major American musical variety television shows of the period. Married to actress Annie Fargé in 1960, he continued contributing to dance as a freelance director and choreographer, the major portion of his choreography being done for French television.

Stage: *Loin de Rueuil* (Paris '61), *The Boy Friend* (Paris '65)

TV: "C'est la Vie" ('66–67)

Ballet/Dance Pieces: "Recreation" (Maurice Béjart Ballet), "L'Echell" ('56, with Milko Sparemblek), "L'Emprise" and "Maratone Di Danza" ('57),

"Facettes," "Hop Hop" (for Ballet-Theatre Contemporain '70), etc.

Film:

1960 **Belles et Ballets** — Hermes (with Maurice Béjart, also appeared)

1961 **White Nights** — (Ital/Fr)

1962 **A Very Private Affair** — MGM (also appeared)

1969 **Castle Keep** — Col

JOSEPH SANTLEY (MANSFIELD)

b. Salt Lake City, Utah, January 10, 1889

d. West Los Angeles, California, August 8, 1971

Multi-talented creator who began his career appearing on Broadway at 9-years old in *Boy of the Streets*, followed by *From Rags to Riches*, *Billy the Kid* and *A Matinee Idol* in 1910. He had a prolific career as a Broadway performer, composer, lyricist, librettist, dance director and producer in seventeen productions including *All Over Town* ('15, also librettist and appeared), *She's a Good Fellow* ('19, appeared), *Rings of Smoke* ('20, composer), *Music Box Revues of 1921 and 1923* (appeared), *Daughter of Rosie O'Grady* ('25, composer), *Mayflowers* ('25, star and dir), *Lucky* and *Just Fancy* ('27, star, librettist, producer) and *Shamrock*, eleven of them costarring with his wife, Ivy Sawyer. He replaced Fred Astaire in *Gay Divorce* in London when Astaire left the stage for his film career. Santley also acted in early silent films. Co-director on **The Cocoanuts** ('29), he subsequently directed over 50 films from 1930–50, usually comedies and/or musicals for Republic Pictures: **There Goes the Groom** ('37), **Swing, Sister, Swing** ('38), **Melody and Moonlight** ('40), **Ice-Capades** ('41), **Joan of Ozark** ('42), **Sleepy Lagoon** ('43), **Rosie the Riveter** ('44), **Earl Carroll's Vanities** and **Make Believe Ballroom** ('45), etc.

Stage: *When Dreams Come True* ('13)

Film:

1936 **Dancing Feet** — Rep (with Nick Condos)

1938 **Radio City Revels** — RKO (with Ann Miller, Hermes Pan)

KARINE SAPPORTA

1991 **Prospero's Books** — Palace

JESS SAUNDERS

1954 **Jesse James' Women** — UA (with Ann Royal)

ARCHIE SAVAGE

Pioneering African-American jazz dancer, teacher and choreographer. As a member of the African Dance Troupe of the Federal Theatre Project, he appeared in the famed Orson Welles' production of

Archie Savage (R), in a publicity still for one of his dance company appearances, circa 1960.

the voodoo *Macbeth* in 1935. Other Broadway appearances include *Cabin in the Sky* ('40), *Carmen Jones* ('43), *Finian's Rainbow* ('47) and *South Pacific* ('49). After being a longtime member of Katherine Dunham's troupe, he formed his own dance company which appeared internationally. The Archie Savage Dancers appear in **The Glenn Miller Story** and **European Night** and Mr. Savage appears in **Tales of Manhattan** ('42), **His Majesty O'Keefe** ('53), **South Pacific** ('58), and Fellini's **La Dolce Vita** ('61).

Stage: *Life with the Lyons* (London '52, with Jack Hulbert)

Nightclub/Concert: Club Ebony (NY '48, also appeared)

Ballet/Dance Pieces: "Ballet Jazz" (Southern Calif. '56)

Film:

1944 **Jammin' the Blues**— Vitaphone (S) (with Jack Cole, also appeared)

1954 **Apache**— Hecht-Hill-Lancaster/UA

The Glenn Miller Story— Univ (with Kenny Williams, the Archie Savage Dancers appeared)

Vera Cruz— Hecht-Hill-Lancaster/UA

1958 **South Pacific**— Fox (with LeRoy Prinz, also appeared)

1960 **European Night**—(Ital) (Archie Savage and Dancers appeared)

1962 **Sodom and Gomorrah**— Fox

1967 **The Wild, Wild Planet**— MGM

KATINA SAWIDIS

1980 **The Long Riders**— UA

GENEVA SAWYER

b. Minneapolis, Minnesota, October 26, 1920

Educated at St. Margaret's School in Minneapolis and All Saints Episcopal School for Girls in Sioux Falls, South Dakota, young Geneva left school to create a vaudeville act with her sister, Francis. She moved to California and appeared in the legit *Hollywood Revue*, and while working on the film **Stand Up and Cheer**, was signed by Fox studios to a stock contract in 1934. She began her film choreographic career in 1936 as dance coach for Shirley Temple, teaching her the tap routines that Bill Robinson created. She first assisted Jack Haskell and then worked on multiple films with Nick Castle, becoming a full-fledged 20th Century–Fox dance director in 1941. Nothing has been located about her life and career after 1944.

Film:

1936 **Poor Little Rich Girl**— Fox (assistant to Jack Haskell)

Sing, Baby, Sing— Fox (assistant to Haskell)

1937 **Life Begins in College**— Fox (with Nick Castle)

Love and Hisses— Fox (with Castle)

1938 **Arizona Wildcat**— Fox (with Castle)

Hold That Co-ed— Fox (with Castle, George Murphy)

Josette— Fox (with Castle)

Just Around the Corner— Fox (with Castle, Bill Robinson)

Little Miss Broadway— Fox (with Castle, George Murphy)

My Lucky Star— Fox (with Castle, Harry Losee)

Rebecca of Sunnybrook Farm— Fox (with Castle, Bill Robinson)

Sally, Irene and Mary— Fox (with Castle)

Straight, Place and Show— Fox (with Castle)

Up the River— Fox (with Castle, Bill Robinson)

While New York Sleeps— Fox (with Castle)

1939 **The Boy Friend**— Fox (with Castle)

Swanee River— Fox (with Castle)

1940 **The Blue Bird**— Fox

Down Argentine Way— Fox (with Castle, Fayard Nicholas)

Johnny Apollo— Fox

Young People— Fox (with Castle)

1941 **Blood and Sand**— Fox (with Hermes Pan, "El Torero" dance)

Charlie Chan in Rio— Fox

Sun Valley Serenade— Fox (with Fayard Nicholas, Hermes Pan)

A Yank in the R.A.F.— Fox

1943 **Jitterbugs**— Fox

1944 **Home in Indiana**— Fox

In the Meantime Darling— Fox

Tampico— Fox

SHANDA (RUTH) SAWYER

b. Oakland, California, October 25, 1962

"I have always simultaneously been a performer, director, writer and producer. Never did the traditional dancer to choreographer progression," wrote Sawyer. The eclectic preparation for her career began with ten years of Cunningham technique in San Francisco and New York, tap with Camden Richman, Flamenco, middle Eastern, ballet, labonotation and Limon technique. She also did undergraduate work in dance, theater, video and pre-med at Lone Mountain. In 1973 she and her older sister Sharlyn created The Rom, a theatre/dance group which toured the Renaissance Pleasure Faires on the West Coast. From 1976–83, she appeared in San Francisco clubs and theaters with two subsequent groups that she also directed — Kos Kadas and The Rhythm Method — which satirized pop culture ("I love the surreal, humor and odd juxtaposition.") Film appearances include **The Green Line**, **Howard the Duck**, **'68, The Movie** and **Barbarians at the Gate**. "I'm probably more of a director than choreographer (I now split my career fairly between directing commercials, live and TV shows and choreography) because I work with dancers as if they are actors and form dances around scenarios, emotions, bizarre costumes, etc., more than 'steps.' When I work for directors, I can serve their vision because I can ask the right questions and really understand based on my own experience as a director." As the major influences in her life, she named "Marika Sakalavion (my teacher), Fellini movies as a teen in Berkeley, Fred Astaire, Michael Peters and especially Michael Kidd for his kind encouragement."

TV: "Roller Games," "The Show," "ABC Rocks," "Rock 'n' Reality" Special, "Legends of the Spanish Kitchen," "Sweet Nothing"; commercials for Acura, Cheerios, Doublemint, Kelloggs, Levi Strauss, Nintendo, and Pepsi (starring Hammer)

Music Video: "Here Comes the Hammer"— Hammer; "Surprise"—"A Chorus Line—The Movie"; "Condition of the Heart"—Khashif; "Eat the Rich" and "Screaming in the Night"—Krokus; "Boys Won't"—Greg Kihn; "And Dance"—Billy Preston; "Hard-Up"—Sylvester; "Love Stands Out"—C.C.

Film:
1980 **Haywire**— WB TV (TV)
1987 **'68 the Movie**— New World Pictures (also appeared)

SUSAN SCANLAN

Dancer, choreographer, director and producer who was one of music video's pioneers. While working on a video documentary of street dancers in Los Angeles, Scanlan was signed to choreograph **Body Rock**. With Joanne Divito, they combined the New York ("New York street dancing has more 'rocking' footwork. The feet move in a kind of boxing pattern") with Los Angeles ("California street dancing ... concentrates on movement from the waist up; it's very arms oriented") styles for the film's dance sequences.

Music Video: "All Night Long"—Lionel Ritchie
Film:
1984 **Body Rock**— New World (with Russell Clark, Joanne Divito)
1985 **Sweet Dreams**— TriStar

JOHN SCHAPAR
1961 **Bimbo the Great**— WB

CHRIS SCHECK
1991 **Ted and Venus**— Double Helix Films

MAX SCHECK

Another prolific Broadway dance director who was brought to Hollywood for the musical movie "boom" and after one film credit seemed to disappear into oblivion. Directed and choreographed the *Folies Bergere* in Paris and *Belmont Varieties* ('32) and *Two for Tonight* ('39) on Broadway.

Stage (all Bdwy credits unless noted otherwise):

The Rose Girl ('20); *Phoebe of Quality Street* ('21); *Chatter Box Revue, The Hotel Manager, Up in the Clouds* ('22); *Sunbonnet Sue* (OOT) ('23); *The Passing Show of 1924, The Student Prince* ('24); *A Night Out* (OOT), *Princess Flavia* ('25); *Katja, the Dancer* ('26); *Say When* ('28); *Through the Years* ('31)

Film:
1929 **Footlights and Fools**— WB

SCHEHERAZADE
1967 **The Long Duel**— Par

HOLLY SCHIFFER
1995 **Species**— MGM

TRUDI SCHOOP
b. Switzerland, 1903

Called "The Charlie Chaplin of the Dance" and "The Creator of the Comic Ballet" by dance reviewers, this Swiss modern dance pioneer first organized her Trudi Schoop Comic Ballet in 1931 and won second prize at the Paris Choreographer's Competition in 1932 for her work *Fridolin on the Road*. In the *American Dancer* review of her company's New York debut in 1936, her work was praised, "The cinematic quality of her ballets is apparent, first of all, in the strict ... economy of movement and gesture that underlies the dancing of her troupe. Loose movements have been eliminated entirely; every gesture expresses something, and every expression finds a gesture, a movement, a pose... Trudi Schoop has a tremendous advantage over most modern dancers ... her dancing and that of the troupe is based on ballet technique... She also knows the power of a close-up." She disbanded her company at the beginning of World War II, but then reformed in 1946 and toured for several years until she retired and concentrated on dance therapy work.

Stage: My L.A. (LA '51)
Ballet/Dance Pieces (Partial listing): "Fridolin" ('32), "Want Ads," "The Blonde Marie," "Hurray for Love," "Barbara"
Film:
1953 **The Village**— Wechsler (Ger)

HERBERT F. SCHUBERT
1979 **Just a Gigolo**— UA

BUDDY (EUGENE) SCHWAB
b. Detroit, Michigan, August 7, 1930
d. Detroit, Michigan, December 1, 1992

This dancemaker began his dance studies at the Top Hat Studio in Detroit. Relocating to New York, he studied with Adam Anderson and Nenette Charisse, making his professional Broadway debut at 18 in *As the Girls Go* in 1948. Other Broadway appearances include *Miss Liberty* ('49), *Guys and Dolls* ('50), *A Month of Sundays* (OOT '51) and *The Boy Friend* ('52). He began his choreographic career assisting Joe Layton on *Sail Away* and *No Strings* ('61), Jack Cole on *Zenda* ('63) and solo work on Off-Broadway shows, among them the New York revue *Pieces of Eight* at the Upstairs at the Downstairs. His humorous recreation of dances of the 1920s brought him acclaim for two revivals of *The Boy Friend* on stage and **Thoroughly Modern Millie** on film, with Joe Layton, a close associate and lifelong friend.

Stage: *The Boy Friend* (OB & LA '58 rev), *Fallout* (OB '59), *Pieces of Eight* (OB '59, also dir), *New Cole Porter Revue* (OB '65), *Hellzapoppin'* (Montreal Expo '67), *The Boy Friend* (Bdwy '69 rev), *Mack and Mabel* (Bdwy '74, asst to Gower Champion), *Winner Take All* (LA '76), *The Utter Glory of Morrisey Hall* (Bdwy '79), *Barnum* (10 productions worldwide including the London Palladium with Michael Crawford, also dir), *Camelot* (touring & Bdwy '80 rev, also dir)

TV: "The Hollywood Palace" ('68–70), "Movin'" ('70); specials for Burt Bacharach, Pearl Bailey, Diahann Carroll, Johnny Carson ("Johnny Carson's Sun City Special"), Sandy Duncan, Bob Hope and Barbra Streisand

Nightclub/Concert: Acts for Edie Adams, Bert Convy, Totie Fields, Tammy Grimes, Chita Rivera

Miscellaneous: *Ice-Capades* ('64)

Film:

1963 **The Cardinal**— Col
1967 **Camelot**— WB ("Musical staging associate" credit, assisted by Larri Thomas)
      Thoroughly Modern Millie— Univ (with Joe Layton, also appeared)

LARRY B. SCOTT

b. New York, New York, August 17, 1961

Actor who appears in films from the 1970's onward: **Thieves, A Hero Ain't Nothin' But a Sandwich, Iron Eagle, Revenge of the Nerds, Fear of a Black Hat**, etc.

Film:

1987 **Revenge of the Nerds II: Nerds in Paradise**— Fox (also appeared as "Lamar")

LEE SCOTT (LEE J. SNEDDON)

b. Ogden, Utah, March 4, 1925
d. Palm Springs, California, January 17, 1996

Jazz dancer, teacher and choreographer whose parents were railroad workers. Young Lee planned to be a machinist, although he had made his professional theatrical debut at 7 on the "Bob and Judy" radio show on station KLO in Ogden, Utah. While studying at the University of Utah, he sup-

ported himself as a blacksmith. His mother had enrolled him in dance classes as a child, and after serving in Special Services in World War II (where he played the drums and trombone in Desi Arnaz's band), he moved to Southern California, seriously studying ballet with Edith Jane Falconer, tap with Nick Castle and Louis DaPron, Modern and East Indian with Jack Cole and ballet with Edna McRae. He also studied percussion, trombone, piano and voice and was a graduate of the Don Martin Radio and Television School. After stage appearances at the Greek Theatre in 1948 (*The Student Prince, The Merry Widow*, etc.) he was cast as lead dancer in *My L.A.,* a 1951 Los Angeles stage show. Scott's film appearances include being featured with Gene Kelly and Alex Romero in the **A Day in New York Ballet** in **On the Town** ('49) and partnering Sally Forrest in dance sequences in the films **Excuse My Dust** (in which he also played a major role) and **The Strip** ('51). Scott had started choreographing in 1951, creating Kay Thompson's nightclub act, and he actively choreographed for films and television (hired first by War buddy Arnaz for "I Love Lucy") throughout the 1950s. He also had a troupe of dancers appearing in Southern California nightclubs. In 1950 he started modern jazz classes at the Falcon Studios in Hollywood, one of the first to offer instruction in jazz techniques for new generations of dancers and choreographers. Married to dancer Betty Scott, his teaching continued for decades, relocating to Las Vegas in 1992.

Stage: *Great to Be Alive* (Hollywood '53), *Happy Dollar* (LA '57), *Happy Town* (Bdwy '59, Tony nom)

TV (Partial listing): "I Love Lucy" ('50–55), "Bandstand Revue" ('51), The Johnny Carson Show ('52), "December Bride" ('53), The Eddie Fisher-George Gobel Show ('57), The George Gobel Show, a Bing Crosby Special and "The Chevy Show" ('58), The Steve Allen Show ('59–60), Ethel Merman Special ('60), The Rosemary Clooney Show ('61 series), etc.

Music Video: Scopitone musical shorts for Dinah Washington, Greenwood Country Singers, George and Teddy.

Nightclub/Concert: *Campelot* with Arthur Black, *I'm with You* (Nat "King" Cole Show, '60–61), acts for Patti Moore & Ben Lessy, Debra Paget, Kay Thompson, The Ritz Brothers, Lee Scott Dancers

Film:

1952 **Bela Lugosi Meets a Brooklyn Gorilla**— Real Art
      Harem Girl— Col
      Rainbow 'Round My Shoulder— Col
1953 **All Ashore**— Col
      Cruisin' Down the River— Col
      Let's Do It Again— Col (with Valerie Bettis)
      Miss Sadie Thompson— Col
      Salome— Col (with Asoka, Bettis, uncredited for "Dance of the Seven Veils")

Vera-Ellen uses Lee Scott as support in the "Miss Turnstiles" montage from **On the Town** (MGM, 1945).

1954 **Phfft!**—Col
　　　So This Is Paris—Univ (with Gene Nelson)
1955 **Ain't Misbehavin'**—Univ (with Kenny Williams)
　　　The Second Greatest Sex—Univ (assisted by Jack Harmon, Lucille Lamaar)
1956 **Dance with Me Henry**—UA
1957 **Monkey on My Back**—UA
1958 **Screaming Mimi**—Univ
1964 **Sex and the Single Girl**—WB
1966 **Las Vegas Hillbillys**—Wollner Bros
1978 **Hollywood Fever**—?

WALLY SCOTT
1960 **Peeping Tom**—Anglo Amalgamated Prod ("Rhythm Dance" credit)

STEVEN SEAGAL
b. Lansing, Michigan, April 10, 1951
　Action movie star and martial arts champion who brought his expertise to staging and choreographing the action scenes in his films. After mastering Aikido in Japan where he lived for several years, Seagal found an entré into films when he was the personal trainer for Hollywood super-agent Michael Ovitz. Ovitz managed to create a film package for Seagal to coproduce, cowrite and star in **Above the Law** ('88), without any previous acting or film experience. Formerly married to actress Kelly LeBrock,

his dark, brooding looks and physical agility made him one of the '90s top box-office stars.
　Film (All credits for films he also starred in):
1988 **Above the Law**—WB (also story)
1990 **Hard to Kill**—WB
　　　Marked for Death—Fox (with Dorain Grusman, also prod)
1991 **Out for Justice**—WB (also prod)
1992 **Under Siege**—WB (also prod)
1994 **On Deadly Ground**—WB (also dir)
1995 **Under Siege 2: Dark Territory**—WB

JOE SEKATSKI
1989 **Options**—Vestron

MARK SELLERS
1994 **8 Seconds**—New Line

ANNE SEMLER
1989 **Farewell to the King**—Vestron/Orion

VIRGINIA SEMON
1961 **Sanctuary**—Fox

SHABBA DOO (ADOLFO QUINONES)
b. Chicago, Illinois, 1955

"Shabba Doo" takes center stage in **Breakin'** (Cannon, 1984).

Called "The Bob Fosse of the street" and "The Baryshnikov of the pavement," this charismatic dancer, actor, choreographer and director has left his humble "street" beginnings far behind. Of Puerto Rican and African-American descent, he attended Robert A. Waller and Cooley High schools, adopting the street dance moniker "Shabba Doo" and perfecting his self-taught dance techniques on the streets and in the clubs of Chicago. He appeared on the popular TV program "Soul

Train" and danced on the streets of Chicago's "Old Town." Moving to Southern California in 1971 at the age of 16, he began his professional career as the youngest member of The Lockers, the legendary troupe of Pop and Lock dancers, joined and promoted by Toni Basil. Having only a background of being self-taught and dancing to his own inner rhythms and sounds, Basil taught him how to count music and to choreograph for other dancers. After sensational solo appearances in *Bette! Divine*

Madness on Broadway and on tour, he gathered dancers from "Soul Train" tapings and created his own dance troupe (The Shabba Doo Crew) that was featured in the TV show "The Big Show." With his dark good looks, heartbreaking smile and unique costuming (baggy pantaloons, French army jacket, headband and boxer boots) he went on to star in the dance films **Breakin'** and **Breakin' 2 — Electric Bugaloo** when commercial films finally decided to capitalize on the new dance phenomena. Not being content with the limitations of his career, he began directing music videos and in 1992, he made the transition to feature film director with **Rave-Dancing to a Different Beat**, based on his own story concept. Before the film was released, he expressed his hopes for its commercial success with today's audiences in *Dance Magazine*, July 1993: "The youth of today wants adventure. Theirs is an MTV viewpoint. They want information, information, information and *quick*! They love an element of danger in their lives, and their dancing is a cross between Twyla Tharp and Evel Knievel." At a Choreographers Resourcenter seminar in 1993, he admitted, "I always act on what I think... Your spirit makes the projects you work on special... Your spirit and love. Listening is the most important key to what you do."

Stage: *Stand-up Tragedy* (LA, *Drama-Logue* Award)

TV: "The Big Show," "Countdown at the Neon Armadillo"

Nightclub/Concert: Madonna's "Who's That Girl?" Tour ('87, also appeared)

Film:
1984 **Breakin'** — Cannon (with Jaime Rogers, uncredited for his own routines)
        Breakin' 2 — Cannon (with Bill Goodson, uncredited for his own routines)
1990 **Lambada** — WB (also appeared)
1995 **Rave — Dancing to a Different Beat** — Smart Egg Pictures (also dir)

DARI SHAI
1987 **Rumpelstiltskin** — Cannon

ADAM (MICHAEL) SHANKMAN
b. Santa Monica, California, November 27, 1964
This dancer-choreographer received his dance training from Myron Johnson of the Minnesota Children's Theater, the Juilliard School and Tina Bernal. Making his professional debut in a Michigan Opera Theater production of *West Side Story* in 1985, he continued onstage in **Die Fledermaus** (Detroit, '86), *Evita, Carnival* and *Oklahoma!* (Music Theater North, '87) and the 1988 revivals

On the Town (Arena Stage Theater), *Guys and Dolls* (Drury Lane, Chicago), *Leave It to Jane* and *The Boys from Syracuse* (Doolittle Theater, Hollywood). Dancing on TV on the 62nd Academy Awards show ('89) and on film in **Rockula** and **Midnight Cabaret**, he made his choreographic debut in 1990 with a music video for M.C. Shan. With a wealth of over 30 music videos, his experience with film work and dance/movement continues to grow. He names Jerome Robbins, Bob Fosse, William Forsythe, the work of Myron Johnson and Karen Azenberg ("These two choreographers nurtured me as a dancer and began me on this path") and Michael Bennett as major influences in his life and career.

Stage: *The Boys in the Band*, *West Side Story* (LA, *Drama-Logue* award), *Madness* and *The Emperor's Nightingale* (Minneapolis Black Box), *Guys and Dolls* (Chicago), *Vital Options* and Dancer's Alliance '91 benefits, *Eating Raoul* (Odyssey Theatre, LA '95)

TV: "Down the Shore," "Roundhouse," "Ellen," "The Arsenio Hall Show" (Kirov Ballet appearance), "Soul Train Awards" ('95), "Watten Das" (Germany); commercials for Diet Pepsi "Latin Market," the Energizer, ITT, Keystone Beer, McDonalds, Pepito Cookies, Rubbermaid, etc.

Music Video (Partial listing): "It Don't Mean a Thing" — M.C. Shann ('90), "Mystique" — Chic; "What About Now" — Robbie Robertson; "I'm Your Baby Tonight" — Whitney Houston; "Fair Weather Friend" and "Wrap My Body Tight" — Johnny Gill; "Feels Good" — Tony, Toni, Tone; "Keep Our Love Alive" — Stevie Wonder; "Jerk Out" — The Time; "Meet the Flintstones" — B 52's; "Last Teardrop" — Tanya Tucker; "Dancing Naked in the Rain" — The Blue Pearl; "We Can Get It On" — Rob & Fab; etc.

Nightclub/Concert: Tours for Milli Vanilli ('90), Ms. Adventure, Sophia Shinas ('93)

Film:
1992 **The Gun in Betty Lou's Handbag** — Touchstone
1993 **Addams Family Values** — Par (with Peter Anastos, Camp Chippewa sequence credit)
        Heart and Souls — Univ
        Weekend at Bernie's II — TriStar
1994 **Bad Girls** — Fox
        The Flintstones — Univ (*LA Dance* Awards nom)
        Milk Money — Par
1995 **Casper** — Univ
        Congo — Par (with Peter Elliott)
        Don Juan De Marco — New Line Cinema
        Miami Rhapsody — Hollywood Pictures
        Monster Bash — Greenhouse Films (with Lance McDonald)
        Tank Girl — MGM/UA
1996 **Mrs. Winterbourne** — Par
        Looney Tunes Tune Ups — WB
        The Relic — Par

LLOYD SHAW

1946 **Duel in the Sun**— Goldwyn (with Tilly Losch)

SONIA SHAW

With her husband, composer Bill Hitchcock, Sonia formed Shaw-Hitchcock Productions to create shows for nightclubs and industrials around the world.

TV: "Miss International Beauty Pageant" ('66)

Nightclub/Concert: Sahara Hotel, LV and Sahara-Tahoe (Dance Director, '57–68), *A La Carte, Skindo* (Rio de Janeiro), *Accent on Youth* (Bimbo's, SF, all '61); *Adam and Evil* ('67), Coconut Grove, LA ('69), *No Nudes Is Good News* ('71); acts for Marlene Dietrich, Yma Sumac

Miscellaneous: Industrials for Pure Oil, Signal Oil, Squirt Co., Union Oil, etc.

Film:

1955 **How to Be Very, Very Popular**— Fox (with Paul Godkin, "'Shake, Rattle and Roll' staged by" credit)

1962 **World by Night**— WB

MICHAEL SHAWN

b. Springfield, Illinois, July 3, 1944

d. New York, New York, April 28, 1990

This talented dancer-choreographer appeared on Broadway in *Golden Boy* ('64) and *Golden Rainbow* and *Promises, Promises* ('68) and was in the middle of a promising choreographic career when he was stricken with AIDS. He created show business history by filing a $2.75 million discrimination suit against the producers of *Legs Diamond* in 1988 when they let him go because of his being tested HIV-positive. He had created all of the choreography during the workshop period and was replaced for the Broadway debut by Alan Johnson. Ironically the star of *Legs Diamond*, Peter Allen, would also die from AIDS.

Stage: Onward, Victoria! (Bdwy '80), *Oh Brother!* (Bdwy '81), *Damn Yankees* (Paper Mill Playhouse '86 rev), *Peter Allen at Radio City Music Hall* ('88)

Nightclub/Concert: Act for Cycle Sluts ('76)

Film:

1971 **Willy Wonka and the Chocolate Factory**— Par (assistant to Howard Jeffrey)

1977 **The Goodbye Girl**— MGM/WB (also played the role of the choreographer)

TED (EDWIN MYERS) SHAWN

b. Kansas City, Missouri, October 21, 1891

d. Orlando, Florida, January 9, 1972

Named "The Father of American Dance," this pioneering modern dancer, choreographer and author changed dance in America with the Denishawn Dance Company (with his wife, Ruth St. Denis) and his revolutionary all male company. Raised in Denver, Colo., he entered the University of Denver to study the Ministry but became seriously ill and partially paralyzed due to poor medical treatment. To regain his strength, he began exercises, a strict health regimen and ballet studies with Hazel Wallack. After making his professional dance debut in Denver in 1911, he moved to Los Angeles, opened a dance school and made one of the earliest dance motion pictures, **Dance of the Ages** (with Norma Gould) in 1913. He met and married ethnic dance pioneer Ruth St. Denis in 1914 and they founded Denishawn, which would develop a generation of dance pioneers: Jack Cole, Martha Graham, Doris Humphrey, Charles Weidman, and others (D.W. Griffith ordered all his leading ladies to take dance classes with Denishawn). Continuing his unique dance career (basing much of his work on American thematic material) in concert, Shawn's many film contributions are difficult to verify. He appeared in and choreographed the Cecil B. DeMille film **Don't Change Your Husband** ('19) and the dance short **Arabian Duet** in 1922. After separating from St. Denis, he purchased a farmhouse in Jacob's Pillow, Massachusetts in 1930 and set out to prove that American men had the right to dance and formed his all male company in 1933. The Jacob Pillow's Dance Festival began in 1941, which has introduced most of the major international dance companies to America. The author of over a dozen books, Shawn received the Knighthood in the Order of Dannebrog in 1957 from King Frederick of Denmark and the *Dance Magazine* Award in 1969.

Autobiography: One Thousand and One Night Stands with Gray Poole (1960)

Stage: Falstaff (Bdwy '28, with Richard Boleslavsky)

Ballet/Dance Pieces (Partial Listing): "Minuet for Drums," "The Dreams of Jacob," "The Song of Songs," "Xochitl," "Cuadro Flamenco," "The Feather of the Dawn," "Job," "O Libertad," "Dance of the Ages," etc.

Film:

1913 **Dance of the Ages**— Edison (also appeared)

1916 **Intolerance**— Griffith (with Ruth St. Denis)

1917 **Cleopatra**— Fox (with Ruth St.Denis)

1919 **Don't Change Your Husband**— Artcraft (with Theodore Kosloff, also appeared)

1930 **Glorifying the American Girl**— Par (with John W. Harkrider, "Ballet Ensembles by" credit)

WILLIAM SHEPHARD

1974 **Phantom of the Paradise**— Fox (also appeared)

TED SHUFFLE

1958 **Hello London**— Regal Int (with George Baron, "ice choreography by" credit)

ROBERT (BOB) SIDNEY

Sidney's professional career began as an actor with the Theater Guild at the age of 15. He danced on Broadway in *Keep Off the Grass* ('40) and during World War II, he appeared in and choreographed the successful touring show *This Is the Army*, which is also his first film credit. As the movie musical was on the wane as he arrived to the medium, his talents were used to greater advantage by the television and nightclub mediums. For the 31st annual Academy Awards show in 1958, he staged Burt Lancaster and Kirk Douglas performing "It's Great Not to Be Nominated"— a number which stopped the show. His film credits show a wide range of dance styles and creativity and he was especially successful creating numbers for glamorous female dancing stars: Ann-Margret, Cyd Charisse, Mitzi Gaynor and Rita Hayworth. In the nineties, he has channeled his energy and renowned sense of humor to the Professional Dancers Society (PDS) as vice-president.

Stage: *This Is the Army* (Bdwy '42, with Nelson Barcliff, also appeared), *Nellie Bly*, *Three to Make Ready* and *Topletzky of Notre Dame* (Bdwy '46), *Along Fifth Avenue* (Bdwy '49), *Dance Me a Song* (Bdwy '50)

TV (Partial Listing): 31st and 39th annual Academy Awards ('58 & '66, also assoc prod), "Shower of Stars," "The Hollywood Palace," "The Pearl Bailey Show" ('71, with the Robert Sidney Dancers), "Bing Crosby Sounds of Christmas" and "The Perry Como Winter Show" ('71), Dean Martin Christmas Special ('76)

Nightclub/Concert: *Minsky's Follies* starring Tempest Storm (Dunes Hotel, LV '57); Acts for Jerry Antes, Cyd Charisse, Mitzi Gaynor, Betty Hutton and Debbie Reynolds

Miscellaneous: "Landslide"— Buick Industrial ('56)

Film:
1943 **This Is the Army**— WB (with Nick Castle, George Murphy, LeRoy Prinz, "Msgt Robert Sidney" credit)
1948 **The Loves of Carmen**— Col (with Eduardo Cansino, also appeared)
1952 **Bloodhounds of Broadway**— Fox
1954 **Susan Slept Here**— RKO
1956 **The Conqueror**— RKO
    The Opposite Sex— MGM (assisted by Ellen Ray)
    You Can't Run Away from It— Col
1957 **An Affair to Remember**— Fox
1958 **Party Girl**— MGM
1960 **Please Don't Eat the Daisies**— MGM (assisted by Frank Radcliff)
    Where the Boys Are— MGM
1962 **How the West Was Won**— MGM (assisted by Gloria DeWord)
1964 **Looking for Love**— MGM (assisted by Bob Street)
    The Pleasure Seekers— Fox (with Antonio Gades)
1965 **How to Murder Your Wife**— UA
1966 **The Silencers**— Col
    The Singing Nun—MGM
1967 **Valley of the Dolls**— Fox

JOSÉ SILVA

1957 **The Living Idol**— MGM (with David Campbell)

MARLENE SILVA

1982 **Xica**—(Brazilian)

DAN SIRETTA

b. Brooklyn, New York, July 19, 1942

Siretta received his solid dance and theater background from his studies of ballroom dance with Jimmy Trainor, ballet with Elizabeth Anderson-Ivantzova, Margaret Craske and Anthony Tudor and theater study at the High School of Performing Arts and Juilliard. A dancer in Broadway shows from 1959 (*Fiorello*, *Mr. President*, *The Girl Who Came to Supper*, *Drat! the Cat!*, *Walking Happy*, *Coco*, *Hello Dolly!* and *Sail Away*) and associate choreographer to Sammy Bayes in *Heathen!*, he was in the cast of *Lolita, My Love* ('71), on its way to Broadway when both Jack Cole and Danny Daniels quit, so Siretta began his professional choreographic career taking over the staging chores. He found a successful niche at the Goodspeed Opera House in East Haddam, Conn., reconceiving, staging and directing their celebrated revivals for fifteen years, serving as artistic director for three. Because of his specialization in period American dances, he lovingly recreated the movement for the neglected shows of George and Ira Gershwin, Jerome Kern and other famous American composers to great critical acclaim. His film career began with appearances in **Star!**, **Hello, Dolly!**, **Darling Lili** and **On a Clear Day, You Can See Forever**. His musical staging and choreography in the film **Those Lips, Those Eyes** humorously (and lovingly) captures the genre of

Rita Hayworth and Glenn Ford are flanked by choreographers in this scene from **The Loves of Carmen** (Columbia, 1948): Robert Sidney on the left, and at right, a young Roy Fitzell applauds.

Summer Stock musicals. Married to actress-dancer Nikki Sahagen, he cites "The Vaudevillian" (Jimmy Trainor) as a major influence in his life.

Stage: *Fiorello* (Remounting of orig. Bdwy show, Papermill Playhouse), *Lolita, My Love* (Bdwy '71); 30 revivals for the Goodspeed Opera House which often reached Broadway including: *Very Good Eddie* ('75), *Going Up* ('76), *Hit the Deck* ('76, also dir), *The Five O'Clock Girl, Whoopee!* ('79, Tony nom), *Tip-Toes* ('79), *Zapata* (Goodspeed '80), *Little Johnny Jones* ('81) and *Lady Be Good* ('87); *Sweet Adeline* ('77), *The Baker's Wife* (OOT '76, with Robert Tucker), *Take Me Along* (Bdwy '84 rev), *The Boy Friend* (London '84 rev), *Pal Joey* ('90 rev, also dir), *Oh Kay!* (Bdwy '90 rev, also dir, Tony nom), *The Most Happy Fella* (NYC Opera '91 rev), *I'll Be Seeing You* (Long Wharf Theatre), *The Shiek of Avenue B.* (NY '92, also dir)

TV: "Celebrating Gershwin" (PBS), commercials for McDonalds, Pepsi, etc.

Nightclub/Concert: *Stagedoor Canteen Revue* (NY '86), *The Rodgers and Hart Revue* ('91, also dir)

Ballet/Dance Pieces: "Indian Summer" (Alberta Ballet Co '92)

Miscellaneous: Industrials for Caribbiner

Film:
1980 **Those Lips, Those Eyes**—UA (also appeared)
1986 **Children of a Lesser God**—Par (with Nikki Sahagen)

MARY SKEAPING
b. Woodford, England, December 15, 1902
d. London, England, February 9, 1984

British classical dancer, dance educator, choreographer and dance historian who studied with Enrico Cecchetti, Margaret Craske and Lubov Egorova and toured with Anna Pavlova (1925–31) and the Nemtchinova-Dolin Company. Ballet mistress and teacher for Sadler's Wells (1948–51) and director of the Royal Swedish Ballet from 1953, Skeaping began specializing in recreating and mounting historical ballets at the Drottingholm Theatre in Sweden. She eventually was acknowledged as an international authority on the technique and style of court ballet of the 17th century. Awards include being made a Member of the Order of the British Empire in 1958 and awarded the Swedish Order of Vasa in 1961. She is also the author of "Ballet Under the Three Crowns" (a history of the Royal Swedish Ballet from 1637–1792) written for *Dance Perspectives* Magazine.

Ballet/Dance Pieces: "Cupid Out of His Humor" ('56), "The Return of Springtime" (reconstruction of an 1818 ballet), "Giselle" ('68)

Film:
1951 **The Little Ballerina**—Gaumont/Univ
1969 **Anne of the Thousand Days**—Univ

JO JO SMITH

Jazz dancer and teacher.

Stage: *Got Tu Go Disco* (Bdwy, '79, with Troy Garza)

TV: Bill Cosby special ('70)

Film:
1977 **Saturday Night Fever**—Par (with Jeff Kutash, Deney Terrio, Lester Wilson, "Dance consultant" credit)

WILETTA SMITH

1953 **King of the Khyber Rifles**—Fox (assistant to Stephen Papich)
    Man in the Attic—Fox
    Raiders of the Seven Seas—UA
    Second Chance—RKO

MICHAEL SMUIN

b. Missoula, Montana, October 13, 1938

"I always wanted to be a choreographer," said this multi-faceted dancemaker and director whose inspirations came at him from all directions. His dreams began in the local movie house in the forms of Fred Astaire and Gene Kelly and, at the age of 6, his mother took him to a performance of the Ballets Russe and it changed his life forever ("It was instantaneous. The curtain opened and this magic started happening, and I wanted to be a part of it. I wanted to make ballet, or do it, or somehow be in it.") After added inspiration by seeing Paul Draper dance, at the age of 7 he was taking tap lessons with Pauline Ellis and was performing around Montana as a member of The Wise Guys dance troupe. Miss Breen, Michael's Missoula ballet teacher, recognized his talent and sent him to Salt Lake City, where, at 13 he received a scholarship to study with William Christensen, brother of Lew Christensen, at the University of Utah. At 19 he was invited to join the San Francisco Ballet and after choreographing for the Bay Area Ballet and San Francisco Opera, he created *La Ronde* for the SF Ballet in 1961. He met his future wife, Paula Tracy, in the company, and with mutual dreams in their heads ("Paula and I wanted to spread our wings—maybe try Broadway, maybe form an act together, maybe join another ballet company—we

wanted it all!" *Dance Magazine*, January, 1988) they left for New York. Michael danced on Broadway in *Little Me* ('62) and he and Paula created a successful dance team (Michael and Paula), appearing in nightclubs and on television for three years. Invited to join American Ballet Theater in 1966, he choreographed for ABT and the Harkness and danced principal roles with ABT from 1969–73. Appointed director of the San Francisco Ballet in 1973, Smuin led the company to success with much-needed exposure through TV appearances on PBS' "Dance in America." In 1983, film director Francis Ford Coppola approached Smuin to choreograph the fight scenes in **Rumble Fish** and his film career—and ongoing collaboration with Coppola—began. He received the 1983 *Dance Magazine* Award and left the SF Ballet in 1985 to continue diversifying his career. Recipient of an Honorary Doctorate in Fine Arts from the University of Montana, he founded Smuin Ballets/SF in 1994.

Stage: *Carmen* and *Andrea Chenier* (SF Opera '59), *Candide* (LACLO '71), *Sophisticated Ladies* (Bdwy '81, with Donald McKayle, Henry LeTang, Tony nom, also dir), *Chaplin* (OOT '83, also dir), *Anything Goes* (Bdwy '87 rev—Tony, Drama Desk and Astaire Awards), *Shogun: The Musical* (Bdwy '90, also dir), *Fred Astaire in Rehearsal* (SF '92, also dir), *Damn Yankees* (OOT '93 rev), *Tannhäuser* (SF Opera '94), *Mack and Mabel* (London '95 rev)

TV: "Dance in America" presentations of SF Ballet productions: "A Song for Dead Warriors" and "Voice/Dance" (Emmy Awards), "Romeo and Juliet," "The Tempest Live with the San Francisco Ballet" (Emmy nom) and "Cinderella"

Music Video: "When You Wish Upon a Star"—Linda Ronstadt & Cynthia Gregory

Nightclub/Concert: Routines for Michael and Paula nightclub appearances ('63–66), Linda Ronstadt's "Canciones de mi Padre" tour (also dir)

Ballet/Dance Pieces (Partial Listing): for Bay Area Ballet: "Vivaldi Concerto" ('58); for American Ballet Theater: "The Catherine Wheel," "Gartenfest," "Pulcinella Variations"('68), "Cassation," "The Eternal Idol" and "Schubertiade"; Created 29 works for San Francisco Ballet including "La Ronde" ('61), "Trois Couleurs," "Highland Fair," "Sessions" and "Peter and the Wolf" ('91); "Medea" (Dance Theater of Harlem '93); "Hearts" (Hartford Ballet, '94); "Dances with Songs" (for Smuin Ballets/SF, '94)

Film:
1983 **Rumble Fish**—Univ
1984 **The Cotton Club**—Orion (with Claudia Asbury, Gregory Hines, Henry LeTang, Michael Meacham, Arthur Mitchell)
1986 **The Golden Child**—Par ("Movement Adviser" credit)

1989 **Fletch Lives**— Univ
1992 **Bram Stoker's Dracula**— Col (with Morleigh Steinburg, "Movement for the brides by" credit)
     Fletch Saved— Univ
1993 **The Joy Luck Club**— Hollywood Pictures
     So I Married an Ax Murderer— TriStar (with Kimi Okata)
1994 **Angie**—Hollywood Pictures
     Golden Gate— Goldwyn
     Wolf— Col
1995 **A Walk in the Clouds**— Fox

PAULA TRACY SMUIN

b. San Francisco, California, February 25
Dancer-choreographer who studied with Harold and Lew Christensen and attended the San Francisco Ballet School. She made her debut with the SF Ballet in 1956, where she met her future husband, Michael Smuin (see previous listing). They left the ballet company in 1962 and went to New York, where she danced on Broadway in *No Strings*. From 1963–66, she toured as half of the successful nightclub dance team Michael and Paula, before being invited to join American Ballet Theatre. She returned to the SF Ballet as a soloist in 1973.
Film:
1986 **Wildcats**— WB (with Joel Hall)
1988 **Tucker: The Man and His Dream**— Par
     Twins— Univ
1990 **Class Action**— Fox

GENE SNYDER

b. Richmond, Virginia, 1908
Snyder's French mother and American father appeared in vaudeville and gave him his first dance lessons. He began dancing as a child in Minneapolis on the Finkelstein and Rubin circuit, toured the Keith circuit with The Rosebuds, an all girl band, and returned to Minneapolis to enroll in the University of Minnesota. When the speakeasy he was performing in to pay his tuition was raided by the police, he was expelled. Back in vaudeville with Patsy Chapman, their act were booked into the Publix circuit, finally working its way to New York. When Patsy married, Snyder built his own vaudeville unit and worked his way across the country to California, where he met Russell Markert, who was doing **King of Jazz** (1930) and hired Snyder to dance in the film. Impressed with his tap expertise, Market advised Snyder to switch from performance to direction and soon offered him a job directing some of Markert's Roxyette lines. When Radio City Music Hall opened in 1932 (and the Rockettes were born), Snyder accompanied Markert to create dances for the successful troupe as co-director. Married to dancer Dixie Dunbar, Snyder assisted Markert and created precision tap routines for the Rockettes for many years.
Stage: *At Home Abroad* (Bdwy '35, with Robert Alton, Harry Losee), *Yokel Boy* (Bdwy '39), *It Happens on Ice* (NY '41, two editions, with Catherine Littlefield, also dir)
Film:
1937 **Top of the Town**— Univ (with George Murphy)

DINO CARAVALO SOLARI

1952 **O.K. Nero**—(Fr/Ital)
1966 **The Mongols**— Royal Film

ESTHER SOLER

1992 **Cronos**— October Films (Mexico)

PATRICE SORIERO

1989 **Miss Firecracker**— Corsair

TIMOTHY SPAIN

1988 **Shadow Dancing**— Shapiro-Glickenham Ent

MILKO SPAREMBLEK

b. Yugoslavia, 1928
Intensely dramatic ballet dancer and choreographer who began his studies at the Zagreb Opera Ballet school in his native Yugoslavia. Arriving in Paris in 1953 he studied with Serge Peretti and Olga Preobrajenska and danced with Les Ballets Janine Charrat (1954–56), Ballets de Paris (1956–58), the companies of Milorad Miskovitch and Maurice Béjart and began partnering Ludmilla Tcherina — dancing with her in one of his film credits, **The Lovers of Teruel**. His first choreographic work was *L'Echelle (The Ladder)* with Dirk Sanders for Miskovitch's company in 1956. When Béjart left the Brussels Opera Ballet in 1963, Sparemblek was named director. While choreographing *L'Absence*, a new work for the Harkness Ballet, he was described by *Dance Magazine* (November, 1969) as "someone who constantly tries to free himself from choreographic dogma." His advice to dancers and choreographers: "You must learn the 300 years of ballet's past, and then forget them all."
Stage: for the Metropolitan Opera: *Romeo and Juliet* ('67), *Orfeo* ('69)
TV: Multiple works for Belgian, French, German, Italian and Spanish TV
Ballet/Dance Pieces (Partial listing): "L'Echelle,"

"Quatuor," "Heros et Son Miroir," "Les Amants de Teruel," "Orfeo," "The Miraculous Mandarin," "7 Deadly Sins," "Climats," etc.

Film:
1962 **The Lovers of Teruel** — Monarch (also appeared)
1972 **Phedre** — ORTF (winner of the Prix Italia)

HEINZ SPORELI
b. Basel, Switzerland, July 8, 1941
Swiss dance artist who studied internationally with Walter Kleiber and at the School of American Ballet, American Ballet Center and London Dance Centre. After dancing with the Basel Ballet (1960–63), Cologne Ballet (1963–66), Royal Winnepeg Ballet (1966–67), Les Grandes Ballets Canadiens (1967–71) and Geneva Ballet (1971–73), he returned to Switzerland to act as ballet master for the Basel Ballet. He was named artistic director of the Dusseldorf Ballet in 1974, and, in 1995 he became director of the Zurich Ballet.
TV: "La Fille Mal Gardée" ('86, also appeared)
Ballet/Dance Pieces: Over 60 works including for the Basel Ballet: "Firebird" ('73), "Midsummer Night's Dream" ('76), "Ondine" ('78); "La Fille Mal Gardée" (Paris Opera '81), "Child Harold" (German Opera Ballet '81)
Film:
1990 **Silence Like Glass** — Moviestore Ent

DOUGLAS SQUIRES
1963 **The Dream Maker** (aka **It's All Happening**) — Brit Lion (with Pamela Devis)

JENNIFER STACE
Dancer-choreographer who appeared as one of the LA Knockers dance troupe in 1981.
Nightclub/Concert: Cher, Charo, Frank Zappa
Miscellaneous: Ice-Capades
Film:
1981 **Love Valentine** (TV) — Hickman Prod
     Separate Ways — Crown Intl
1985 **Just One of the Guys** — Col
1986 **Jo Jo Dancer, Your Life Is Calling** — Col

JAMES STARBUCK
b. Denver, Colorado, March 13, 1917
Dubbed "The Dean of Choreography" during the Golden Age of television musical variety shows by the press of the time, Starbuck began his life as an orphan abandoned at St. Vincent's church in Denver. He was adopted and raised in Colorado and after moving to California, he began his career as a child actor in stock productions. Noticed by choreographer Raoul Pausé, he was recruited to dance in a production of **Salome** at the Greek Theater in Berkeley and his dance career began. He attended the College of the Pacific and studied dance with Adolph Bolm, William Christensen, Martha Graham, Theodore Kosloff and made his professional dancing debut in 1934 with Ballet Moderne. He became a principal dancer with the San Francisco Opera Ballet at 18 (1935–38) and was a member of the Ballets Russe De Monte Carlo (1938–44). He appeared in Massine's 1941 Warner Bros. dance shorts **The Gay Parisian** and **Spanish Fiesta** and on Broadway in *Early to Bed* and *The Merry Widow* ('43), *Song of Norway* ('44), *Music in My Heart* ('47) and *Sleepy Hollow* ('48). Between Broadway engagements, he began his choreographic career staging musicals at Camp Tamiment, Pa. (1945–48), where he met entertainment director Max Liebman. When Leibman began producing for TV in 1949, he invited Starbuck to join him. Among the innovations that Starbuck introduced to early TV were the concepts of a group of dancers who appeared weekly in his specially created dance numbers and encouraging technicians to place wheels on the stationary cameras, rather than forcing the dancers to dance on a line or in a confining "box" of space ("It was really the problems of dance which forced the television camera to become more flexible.") Working with master comics Sid Caesar and Imogene Coca on "Your Show of Shows" his satires on classical ballet encouraged public interest in ballet and he began inviting such ballet stars as Alicia Markova and Maria Tallchief to begin making commercial TV appearances. Partnering celebrated female guest stars on "Arthur Murray's Dance Party," he became one of television's earliest dance celebrities. Unfortunately, only one theatrically released film contains his work ("Mostly, I had to locate and hire little people and stage battle scenes!")
Stage: *Mike Todd's Peep Show* (Bdwy '50), *Fanny* (OOT '54), *Strip for Action* (OOT '56), *Oh, Captain!* (Bdwy '58), *A Thurber Carnival* (Bdwy '60, also assoc dir), *Kismet* (Pepperdine College, Cal '75), *Much Ado About Nothing* (LA Shakespeare Co. '93)
TV (Partial listing): "Variety Showcase" ('48), "Admiral Broadway Revue" and "American Songs" ('49), "Inside U.S.A. with Chevrolet" ('50), "Your Show of Shows" ('50–54), "Arthur Murray's Dance Party," "Max Liebman Presents" ('55, Emmy Nom), "Shower of Stars" (with Ethel Merman, '58, Emmy nom), "Bell Telephone Hour," "The Big Record," "Frankie Laine Time" ('55), "Sing Along with Mitch" ('62–64); specials: "Marco Polo," "Heidi," "The Great Waltz," "Dearest Enemy," "The Maurice Chevalier Show"

Nightclub/Concert: Acts for Maurice Chevalier, Dorothy Dandridge, Lisa Kirk, Peter Lind Hayes & Mary Healey, Marguerite Piazza, "Sing Along with Mitch," Mia Slavenska & John Brascia

Ballet/Dance Pieces: For the Marquis De Cuevas Ballet: "The Bridge" ('56) and "Mal de Siecle" ('58); for Ballets Russe de Monte Carlo: "The Comedians" ('61); "The Nutcracker" (multiple productions including Buffalo, NY, Baltimore, Md., Ballet Theatre of L.A., etc.); "Pearl of Love," "Matinée/Soirée"

Miscellaneous: Industrial for Buick, Macy's Thanksgiving Day Parade, Orange Bowl Parade, Junior Miss America pageant

Film:
1956 **The Court Jester**— Par
1977 **The Night They Took Miss Beautiful**— Don Kirshner Prod (TV)

RON STEIN

Boxing choreographer.
Film:
1983 **The Sting II**— Univ (with Alton Ruff)

MORLEIGH STEINBERG

b. Los Angeles, California
Dancer-choreographer who began her dance career studying with Bella Lewitsky. She and her sister spent two years in Paris performing their dance/theatre pieces in outdoor concerts before she became a member of the collaborative dance groups Momix (1983–87) and ISO (1986–present, also cofounder). In 1992–93, she toured with the U2 "Zoo TV" tour "belly-dancing her way around the world," and in 1995, she appeared in Daniel Ezralow's "Heart Dances."

Music Video: Videos for Shawn Colvin, Lenny Kravitz, the Neville Brothers, U2, Rod Stewart, and Sting

Nightclub/Concert: U2 World tour ('92 and '93), Paula Abdul "Under My Spell" World tour ('93)

Ballet/Dance Pieces: Multiple works for ISO (with others)

Film:
1989 **Earth Girls Are Easy**— Vestron (with Russell Clark, Sarah Elgart, ISO: Daniel Ezralow, Jamie Hampton, Ashley Roland; Wayne "Crescendo" Ward)
1990 **Wild Orchid**— Vision
1992 **Bram Stoker's Dracula**— Col (with Michael Smuin)

GERALDINE STEPHENSON

British dancer-choreographer.

Stage (All Great Britain credits): *No Bed for Bacon* ('63), *The Rose and the Ring* (Stratford '64), *Mandrake* ('69), *Worzel Gummidge* (Birmingham '80), *Pride and Prejudice* (Royal Exchange Theater, Manchester '91)

TV: "Edward the King" ('79), "The Dancing Years" ('81)

Film:
1975 **Barry Lyndon**— WB
1977 **The Hunchback of Notre Dame**— BBC (TV)
1993 **Century**— Electric Pictures

TONY STEVENS (ANTHONY EDWARD PUSATERI)

b. Herculaneum, Missouri, May 2, 1948
"I never intended to be a choreographer," admitted Stevens when interviewed for this book. "I was going to be the next Gene Kelly!" To prepare himself for a performance career, he received extensive and varied dance studies from Lala Bauman, Nenette Charisse, Finis Jhung, Jaime Rogers, Michael Simms and Jo Jo Smith. Making his professional debut on a TV special in St. Louis at 16, he then appeared at the St. Louis Muny Opera at 18. He moved to New York where he became a much-in-demand performer, appearing in ten Broadway musicals, among them *Wonderful Town* ('67 rev), *The Boy Friend* ('69 rev), *On the Town* ('71 rev), *Hello, Dolly!* (Ntl. tour with Dorothy Lamour), *The Fig Leaves Are Falling, Georgy, Billy* and *Jimmy* ("In one year, I was in four legendary flops — but I got to watch some great people at work — George Abbott, Peter Gennaro.") His television appearances include the Ed Sullivan Show, Kraft Music Hall, "S' Wonderful, S' Marvelous, S' Gershwin," "Dames at Sea" and "Get Happy." His career changed directions when he was hired as associate choreographer on *Irene* (with Peter Gennaro), Gower Champion's 1977 productions of *Annie Get Your Gun* and *Rockabye Hamlet* and *Chicago* (with Bob Fosse). His solo choreographic career began with *Ringalerio* at the Studio Arena Theater in Buffalo, NY, and then, his first film, **The Great Gatsby** in 1974 (recommended to the producers by Peter Gennaro, who didn't want to do the film). His versatile career has been acknowledged by *LA Weekly* and *Drama Logue* Awards for Best Director for *Get Happy* at the Westwood Playhouse in Los Angeles, Top Ten Directors of 1985 in Japan for his production of *Chicago* and the Carbonell Award for Best Choreography for his work in *Guys and Dolls* at the Burt Reynolds Jupiter Theatre in Florida.

Stage: For the Burt Reynolds Jupiter Theatre: *The Best Little Whorehouse in Texas, Dreamgirls,*

Godspell, Guys and Dolls, The Music Man and *The Unsinkable Molly Brown*, (also dir of all listings); *Rachel Lily Rosenblum and Don't Ever You Forget It* (OOT '73, with Grover Dale), *Music! Music!* (NYC Center '74), *Rockabye Hamlet* (Bdwy '77, co-choreo with Gower Champion), *Sing Happy* (Bdwy '78, also dir), *Spotlight* (OOT '78), *Babes in Toyland* (Ntl. Tour '79), *Perfectly Frank* (Bdwy '80), *Get Happy* (Westwood Playhouse, LA '84, also dir), *Chicago* (Tokyo '85, also dir), *Wind in the Willows* (Bdwy '85), Takarazuka Revue (Japan), *The Unsinkable Molly Brown* (Tokyo, also dir), *Mike* (OOT '88), *Once Upon a Song* (OOT '90), *Mark Nadler: 7 O'Clock at the Top of the Gate* (OB '90, also dir), *Animal Crackers* ('92 rev, Goodspeed Opera House), *The Times* (Long Wharf Theater, '93), *Sayonara* (OOT '93–95), *Cabaret* (Theatre Apple, Tokyo '93, also dir), *The Body Shop* (OB '94), *Zombie Prom* (OB '95)

TV: "Broadway Plays Washington" (also dir), "Souvenirs"— Cheryl Ladd Special, "Mary"— Mary Tyler Moore Special ('78), "The Mary Tyler Moore Hour" ('79), "Dick Cavett Summer Show," "Magic of Music: Songwriters Hall of Fame," "Sing America, Sing," "How to Survive the '70s" (Special and variety series) "Lily Tomlin — Live and in Person," 1983 People's Choice Awards Show, "Disneyland's 30th Anniversary" ('85); commercials for Arrowwheat, Dearform, Dr. Pepper (3 years), Levi Stretch Jeans

Nightclub/Concert: *Pizazz '73* (NY, with Ron Fields), *Chita Rivera — Chita Plus Three* ('77, also appeared); acts for Bette Midler, Liza Minnelli and Bernadette Peters

Miscellaneous: Industrials for Avon, Ballys, GMC Trucks, IBM, Lincoln Mercury, Milliken, Pitney Bowes, Pontiac and Union Carbide (also dir)

Film:
1974 **The Great Gatsby**— Par (also appeared)
1982 **The Best Little Whorehouse in Texas**— Univ (assisted by Dorain Grusman, Spencer Henderson)
1984 **Johnny Dangerously**— Fox
       Where the Boys Are '84— TriStar
1988 **She's Having a Baby**— Par

ROD STEWART
1968 **My Secret Life**— Jack H. Harris Ent (also appeared)

KEPE STIRLING
1994 **Once Were Warriors**— Communicado ("Haka Choreography" by credit)

MIKE STONE
Martial Arts choreographer.
Film:
1981 **Enter the Ninja**— Cannon
1989 **American Ninja 3: Blood Hunt**— Cannon

PADDY (PATRICK) STONE
b. Winnepeg, Canada, September 16, 1924
d. Winnepeg, Canada, September 23, 1986
Canadian-born dancer, choreographer, director and teacher who trained at the Royal Winnepeg Ballet School and later at the School of American Ballet in New York. He was the first principal danseur for the Royal Winnepeg Ballet between 1938–46 but surprised the Canadian dance world when he suddenly decided to gain varied experience and went to Broadway to appear in *Annie Get Your Gun* in 1946. After the show took him to London, he also appeared in *Brigadoon* and briefly joined the Royal Ballet at Convent Garden but returned to the "commercial" world in 1951 when he co-created a song-and-dance trio (Three's Company) with Beryl Kaye and Irving Davies. They toured Canada and the U.S., and being seen by Gene Kelly, they were cast in his film **Invitation to the Dance** ('56). His first choreographic effort had been the ballet *Zigeuner* for the Royal Winnepeg Ballet in 1943 and after staging shows in London's West End, he gained success in all entertainment mediums. He also began teaching, to the delight (and sometimes horror) of budding British dancers, as his legendary temper often caused him to throw chairs at students. A dedicated poker player, his obituary read: "Paddy Stone will be remembered for having infused much of classical and musical theatre life with brilliant dance and choreographic talent, but his memory will be treasured by those who knew him as that of a man who inevitably carried an enormous spark of personality wherever he travelled."

Stage: *Joyce Grenfell Requests the Pleasure* (London & Bdwy '55, with Irving Davies, Alfred Rodrigues, Wendy Toye), *Mister Venus* (London '58, with Irving Davies), *Pieces of Eight* (London '59, also dir), *The Golden Touch* (London '60, also dir), *Autumn Show* (London Palladium), *One Over the Eight* (London '61, also dir), *Little Mary Sunshine* (London '62, also dir), *Maggie May* (London '64), *Twang!* (London '65, also dir), Takarazuka Revue (Japan, '65–68, also dir), *Cliff Richard at the Palladium* (London '68), *Good Old Bad Old Days* (London '73, also asst dir to Anthony Newley), *Mardi Gras* (London '76), *The Two Ronnies* (London '78)

TV: "Millie," "Piccadilly Palace," "ATV Music Hall" ('69), "The Des O'Connor Show" ('71)

Ballet/Dance Pieces: For the Royal Winnepeg Ballet: "Zigeuner" ('43), "Classico," "Variations on 'Strike Up the Band'" and "The Hand"; "Octetto" (Festival Ballet); "Bolero" ('81)

Film:

1957 **As Long as They're Happy** — Rank (with Irving Davies, also appeared)

The Good Companions ABF/Pathe (with Irving Davies, also appeared)

Value for Money — Rank (with Irving Davies, also appeared)

1958 **6.5 Special** — Anglo-Amalgamated (also appeared)

1968 **Great Catherine** — WB/7 Arts

1970 **Scrooge** — Cinema Center

1981 **S.O.B.** — Par (assisted by Jerry Trent, also appeared)

1982 **Victor/Victoria** — MGM

KENT STOWELL

1986 **Nutcracker** — Atlantic

SARA MILDRED STRAUSS

If Albertina Rasch could make a success of "Tiller-on-Toe," then Sara Mildred Strauss believed she could add modern dance to the popular line formula. Treasurer of the Concert Dancer's League (founded in 1930 with Agnes DeMille), Strauss left the concert field in 1933 for the more profitable stage and screen and opened her school on the roof of the Ziegfeld Theater in New York in 1934. In an interview with *American Dancer* (May, 1935), she expounded, "The modern dance, as the public demands it today, must be executed with feeling and faultless precision. Therefore I can't work with the type of dancer who thinks that a few tap steps and a split are sufficient equipment for group work. In order to get the best results, I give my girls a thorough training in the principles and techniques of the modern dance." The Strauss Dancers were the "Flavor of 1934–35," but not much was heard from them — or her — later.

Stage: *Ziegfeld Follies* and *America Sings* (Bdwy '34), *Calling All Stars* and *Ed Wynn Revue* (Bdwy '35)

Nightclub/Concert: A South American tour for the Strauss Dancers and appearances with the Boston Symphony ('34)

Film:

1935 **Sweet Surrender** — Univ (also appeared with the Strauss Dancers)

DESMOND F. STROBEL

1994 **Geronimo, an American Legend** — Col

CECILIE STUART

1996 **Meet Wally Sparks** — Meet Wally Prod

MALCOLM STUART

1966 **Way ... Way Out** — Fox

JOHN "BUBBLES" (WILLIAM) SUBLETT

b. Louisville, Kentucky, February 19, 1890(or 1902)

d. Baldwin Hills, California, May 18, 1986

Known as the "Father of Rhythm Tap," "Bubbles" Sublett opened the door to Jazz-Tap percussions with his intricate tap heel work and syncopated sounds. He created his first dance routine with his sister when he was 8 years old. At 10 he teamed with six-year-old Ford Lee "Buck" Washington to create Buck and Bubbles — one of Tap dancing's legendary teams who also performed comedy and songs. They began performing with an all-Black troupe and then in vaudeville in 1921 (Palace Theater, New York; Palladium, London) and theater (*In Bamville, Lew Leslie's Blackbirds of 1930* and *The Ziegfeld Follies of 1931*.) Being a self-taught dancer, "Bubbles" would see as many shows as he could, trying to learn the dancers' steps. "When he found a routine that he could not understand, he would go backstage and, under the guise of giving the dancers advice on their performance, he would get them to demonstrate the steps to him until he had memorized them." The act performed for over thirty years, inspiring such future dance greats as Fred Astaire, Nick Castle, Frank Condos, Paul Draper and Eleanor Powell. In 1935 Sublett originated the role of "Sportin' Life" in *Porgy and Bess* and when Buck and Bubbles dissolved, he continued to appear as a single in clubs, theaters (*Carmen Jones, Black Broadway,* etc.) and television, appearing at the age of 65 with Judy Garland at the Palace Theater in New York. One of his last appearances was a Newport Jazz Festival in New York at the age of 79. "Command Performances" include for the British Royal Family and he was awarded with testimonial scrolls from the City of New York and the City of Los Angeles, as well as an Award of Merit from the United States government for contributions to the Veterans of Vietnam. Before his death, he became an advisor for the John F. Kennedy Center in Washington.

Stage (also appeared in all entries): *George White Scandals of 1920* (Bdwy), *In Bamville* (Bdwy '23), *Lew Leslie's Blackbirds of 1930* (Bdwy), *Ziegfeld Follies* (Bdwy '31), *Porgy and Bess* (Bdwy '35), *Transatlantic Rhythm* (London '36), *Laff Time* (Bdwy '43)

Film (Credits are for choreography for Buck and Bubbles, unless noted otherwise):

1929 **Black Narcissus**— Pathé (S)
     Darktown Follies— Pathé (S)
     Foul Play— Pathé (S)
     Harlem Bound— Pathé (S)
     High Toned— Pathé (S)
     Honest Crooks— Pathé (S)
     In and Out— Pathé (S)
1934 **Nite in a Niteclub**— Univ (S)
1937 **Calling All Stars**— Brit Lion (with Fayard
Nicholas)
     Varsity Show— WB
1939 **Beauty Shoppe**—?
1943 **Cabin in the Sky**— MGM (Solo appearance, with Busby Berkeley)
1944 **Atlantic City**— Rep (with Seymour Felix)
1945 **Buck and Bubbles Laff Jamboree**—
Toddy Pictures
1948 **A Song Is Born**— RKO

SARA SUGIHARA

b. Boston, Massachusetts, November 21, 1953

Japanese-American dancer, composer, dance educator and choreographer who studied at the New York School of Arts and Sarah Lawrence College. After teaching for many dance companies in the U.S. and Europe, she now works as a free-lance artist.

Ballet/Dance Pieces (Partial listing): "Window" ('76), "Sleeping Birds," "The Gathering Water," etc.

Film:

1985 **Key Exchange**— Fox (also appeared)

PATRICK SWAYZE

b. Houston, Texas, August 18, 1952

The first choreographer to be tagged "The Sexiest Man Alive" by *People* magazine in 1991, this actor and singer was born into a performing family. Son of successful dance educator-choreographer Patsy Swayze (see next listing) and called "Buddy" by the family, he first appeared onstage at the age of 6, eventually dancing with the Houston Jazz Ballet, the Harkness and Eliot Feld Ballet companies. He appeared on Broadway in *Goodtime Charley* in 1975 (billed as "Pat Swayze"), toured with *Disney on Parade* ('74) and returned to Broadway in *Grease* ('78). He married Lisa Niemi, a dancer he had met at his mother's school, in 1974 and they relocated to the West Coast in 1979 when his acting career began to flourish. After multiple film and television roles, he achieved superstardom when he finally was able to combine his acting and dancing talents in the smash hit **Dirty Dancing** ('87). Other film roles include **Skatetown U.S.A.**, **The Outsiders**, **Uncommon Valor**, **Road House**, **Ghost**, **Point Break**, **Next of Kin**, **City of Joy**; **To Wong Fu, Thanks for Everything, Julie Newmar**, etc.

Stage: *Without a Word* (Beverly Hills Playhouse '85, with Nicholas Gunn, Lisa Niemi)
Film:
1985 **Grandview U.S.A.**— CBS (with Lisa Niemi, also appeared)

PATSY (YVONNE) SWAYZE

b. Houston, Texas, February 7, 1927

Choreographer-dance educator who credits "My multi-gifted parents whose talents, energy and drive were so influential and outstanding" for her diverse career. She began her dance training with Marcella Donovan Perry and studied various styles of dance with George Chaffee, Peter Gennaro, Corinne Henry, Robert Joffrey, Rudolph Khroder, Luigi, Matt Mattox, Robert Shelton and Jack Stanly. Winning the "Miss Houston" contest in 1944, she attended the University of Houston and made her professional debut in *Oklahoma!* at Theatre, Inc. For the same group, she created her first choreography for *The Golden Apple* and remained as resident choreographer-performer for fifteen years. She then opened and operated Houston's only theatrical training school, offering classes in musical comedy, ballet, jazz, tap and authentic country-western dance. Among her former students are Debbie Allen, Rick Odums, Randy Quaid, Kenny Rogers, Jacklyn Smith, Tommy Tune and her sons Don, Patrick and Sean and daughters Bambi and Vicki. Founder and artistic director of the Houston Jazz Ballet Company (1967–80), she moved to California where she currently operates a school in Simi Valley. Listed in *Who's Who of American Women* she served on the University of Houston faculty and received many awards and accolades from the state of Texas, including March 23, 1960 being proclaimed "Patsy Swayze Day" by the Mayor of Houston. In *LA Dance* (May/June, 1995) she advised aspiring choreographers, "Not everyone can choreograph. That's a gift, something you study. Be versatile. Learn everything you can... Get into live theater, community theater, musical theater, and local dance companies... Learn from the old pros. Go in and watch choreographers if they'll let you." At the 1994 *LA Dance* Awards banquet, Debbie Allen remembered: "When Patsy took me into her class, that's when I knew I could make it... And I love you for that, Patsy." The following year, *LA Dance* honored Patsy by giving her the Dance Educator Award of 1995.

Stage (Partial listing): For Theatre, Inc.: *Annie Get Your Gun, The Boy Friend, Finian's Rainbow, The Most Happy Fellow, West Side Story, Where's Charley?*; For Houston Playhouse Theatre Center: *Carnival, Gypsy, Half a Sixpence, Little Mary Sunshine, Seesaw*; For Houston Grand Opera: ***Aïda***, ***The Ballad of Baby Doe***, ***Carmen*** and ***Don Giovanni***

Patrick Swayze and Lisa Niemi in a publicity pose for **Steel Dawn** (Vestron, 1987).

TV: "Best of the West" PBS Children's shows; commercials for Bud Lite Beer, Mattel, McDonalds, IBM, Pepsi, etc.

Music Video: "Stand in the Fire"—Mickey Thomas; "She's Like the Wind"—Patrick Swayze and Lisa Niemi; "Swayze Dancing"—a "how-to" dance video with Patrick Swayze, Bambi Swayze, Lisa Niemi

Nightclub/Concert: Astro Dome Club, Ballerina Club, Congo Jungle Club, Glen Mc Carthy's Cork Club (all Houston); European concert tour for David Hasselhoff

Miscellaneous: Shows for Astro World Theme Park, Houston

Film:

1980 **Urban Cowboy**— Par
1982 **Liar's Moon**— Par
1988 **Big Top Pee Wee**— Par
1992 **Dead Again**— Par
    Thelma and Louise— Par (coach for Geena Davis)
1993 **Younger and Younger**— Vine International Pictures
1994 **Attack of the 50 Ft. Woman**— HBO
1995 **Problem Child 3: Junior in Love**— Telvan Prod (TV)

WANDA SZCZUKA
1986 **Pirates**— Cannon

TAD (THELMA) TADLOCK
b. Port Arthur, Texas

First studying dance with Florence Coleman in Port Arthur, Texas, when she was 4-years old, Tad went to New York at 18 and made her professional debut in *Make a Wish* ('51). While appearing on Broadway in such shows as *Top Banana*, *Pal Joey* and *Me and Juliet*, she voraciously took classes ("Ballet, tap, and modern and everything—Five classes a day!") at the School of American Ballet and with Jack Potteiger and Jack Stanly. Enjoying a career as an in-demand dancer during the "Golden Age of Television" in New York (Max Leibman Spectaculars, "Your Hit Parade," etc.) Tad also assisted Tony Charmoli and James Starbuck and began solo choreographing commercials in the 1960's. Her staging, choreography and direction career continues on TV and live venues, and she might be tagged "Miss Pageant" for her prolific work in that specialized venue. She names Florence Coleman, her first dancing teacher in Texas, and Tony Charmoli ("Worked for him as a dancer, now he directs 'The Pageants' and I choreograph—a good team!") as major influences in her life and career and adds: "High Light—I've choreographed for Tommy Tune!" ("Tap Dance in America," "All-

Star Salute to Ford's Theatre" and three "Miss U.S.A." pageants).

Stage: *Something More* (Bdwy '64, asst to Bob Herget), *The Student Prince* (Michigan '78), *Vincent* (LA), *Side by Side by Sondheim* (Michigan '92)

TV: "Your Hit Parade," "The Bell Telephone Hour," "Charlie's Angels," "Dance Fever," the Sid Caesar, Johnny Carson, Rich Little and Arthur Murray shows, Macy's Day Thanksgiving and Rose Bowl Parades, "Tap Dance in America" (PBS), "All Star Salute to Ford's Theatre," Super Bowl Half-Time Show, specials for Julie Andrews, Bing Crosby and Doc Severinson; multiple televised pageants (see "Miscellaneous")

Nightclub/Concert: The Young Americans *Gershwin* tour; acts and concerts for Bill Hayes & Ann Blythe, The King Family, Carol Lawrence; Latin Quarter, NY show

Miscellaneous: Industrials for Coca Cola, Dr. Pepper, Frito Lay, Honda, Kentucky Fried Chicken, Mattel, Miller Beer, Nestea, Oldsmobile, Toyota (also dir); SHARE *Boomtown* Shows (also dir & prod); Miss America, Miss Universe, Miss Teen USA, Miss USA, Miss Wool, College Queen and African-American Collegiate pageants (over 40, all televised—'81–present)

Film:

1971 **What's the Matter with Helen?**— UA (asst to Tony Charmoli)
1978 **Ziegfeld: The Man and His Women**— Col (TV) (asst to Miriam Nelson)
1980 **The Dream Merchants**— Col (TV)
    The Women's Room— WB (TV)
1981 **Body Heat**— WB (tap sequences for Ted Danson)
    Heaven's Gate— UA (with Eleanor Fazan—uncredited)
1983 **Rita Hayworth: The Love Goddess**— Susskind (TV) (also appeared as "The Choreographer")
1984 **Irreconcilable Differences**— WB
1990 **I Love You to Death**— TriStar

RUI TAKEMURA
1980 **Demon Pond**— Kino Intl (Japan)

LINDA TALCOTT
1995 **Blue in the Face**— Miramax

SUSANA TAMBUTTI
1986 **Tangos: The Exile of Gardel**—(Fr/ Argentina) (with Adolfo Andrade, Margarita Balli, Robert Thomas)

HELEN TAMIRIS (BECKER)

b. New York, April 24, 1905
d. New York, August 4, 1966
Beginning her dance training at 8 with Irene Lewisohn, this future American modern dance pioneer then studied with the Metropolitan Opera Ballet School and Michel Fokine. She toured South America with the Bracale Opera Company, danced with the Metropolitan Opera Ballet and appeared on Broadway in *The Music Box Revue* in 1927, also giving her first concert that year — which caught the attention of the dance world. Dividing her talents between serious dance and commercial work ("I think my whole career has been a history of breaking down the elitist fence around artists. I never fell for the insidious and false notion of art for art's sake. I am a worker, an artisan, a craftsman. I deplore cult thinking… When I functioned in the concert field, I always tried to reach the average person. I hated the idea of a small coterie of devotees.") her creations began enhancing all entertainment venues. In 1930 she organized the Dance Repertory Company (which combined the appearances of Martha Graham, Doris Humphrey, Charles Weidman and Agnes DeMille), toured Europe in concert and simultaneously taught at the School of American Ballet (1930–45). She also taught dance movement at the historic Group Theatre to such non-dancers as Elia Kazan, John Garfield and Franchot Tone. Impatient with Concert dance, her choreographic career on Broadway began with *Up in Central Park* in 1945. She became one of the leading creators of American stage dance for the next ten years, while continuing to create works for her company. With long-time partner and husband, Daniel Nagrin, she created the Tamiris-Nagrin Dance Co. in 1960. Recipient of the *Dance Magazine* Award in 1937 for a concert work and again in 1950 for her stage work on *Touch and Go*, in a June, 1955 *Dance Magazine* article she expressed her reasons for creating for the commercial theater with "I spent 18 years of beg, borrow, or steal… I got tired of listening to myself. How long can you be a missionary with nobody to listen?"

Stage: *Fiesta* (Bdwy '29), *Gold Eagle Guy* (Bdwy '34), *Marianne* (OOT '44), *Up in Central Park* (Bdwy '45), *Show Boat* (Bdwy '46 rev), *Annie Get Your Gun* (Bdwy '46), *Park Avenue* (Bdwy '46, replacing Eugene Loring), *Inside U.S.A.* (Bdwy '48), *Touch and Go* (Bdwy '49 — Tony Award), *Great to Be Alive!* (Bdwy '50), *Bless You All* (Bdwy '50), *Flahooley* (Bdwy '51), *Carnival in Flanders* (Bdwy '53, replacing Jack Cole), *By the Beautiful Sea* (Bdwy '54), *Fanny* and *Plain and Fancy* (Bdwy '55), *The Lady from Colorado* (Central City, Colo. '64)

Ballet/Dance Pieces (Partial listing — over 135 works): "Prizefight Studies," "Harmony in Athletics," "Rhapsody in Blue," "Triangle Dance," "Morning Ceremonial," "How Long Brethren?" ('37 *Dance Magazine* award), "Salut Au Monde," "Andelante," "Pioneer Memories," "Dance for Walt Whitman," "Memoir," "Women's Song," "Once Upon a Time" ('61), "Negro Spirituals," etc.

Film:
1948 **Up in Central Park**— Univ
1952 **Just for You**— Par (assisted by Donald Saddler)

MERYL TANKARD

1988 **Around the World in 80 Ways**— Alvie Film

GEORGE TAPPS (MORTIMER BECKER)

b. New York, 1920
When creating a dance for **Splendor in the Grass**, Tapps recalled in *Dance Magazine* (July '61), "Eliza Kazan asked him to be sure the dancer wouldn't feel the urge to do something artistic. 'Don't misunderstand…This will not make your reputation. What I want is something cheap and vulgar.' George admits it is that, a scene in a brassy speakeasy." One of the leading exponents of ballet-tap (along with Paul Draper), he studied at Ned Wayburn's school and made his professional debut at the age of 10 at the Maurice Diamond Club in New York, continuing in clubs and sharing the stages with Eddie Cantor, George M. Cohan, Ruby Keeler, George Raft and Sophie Tucker. He then appeared in the Broadway casts of *Americana* ('32), *I'd Rather Be Right* ('37) and replaced Gene Kelly in *Pal Joey* when Kelly left the show to go into films. After appearing in *Hello Beautiful* at the International Casino in New York in 1939 his unique tap pieces made him a popular nightclub attraction during the 1940s–50s when he headlined at the Plaza's Persian Room, New York's Versailles Club, Chicago's 5100 Club, Hollywood's Florentine Gardens and Cleveland's Hollander. His film appearances include **In This Corner, Katz' Pajamas** (two shorts), **52nd Street** and **Vogues of 1938**. He began his choreography career creating numbers for Merriel Abbott and her dancers. He eventually created his own dance company: George Tapps and Company. "Rediscovered" in 1977, Tapps performed a one-man concert (*What Ever Happened to Georgie Tapps?*) across the country.

Stage: *The Duchess Misbehaves* (Bdwy '46, replaced John Wray, also appeared), *Hilarities* (Bdwy '48), *A Midsummer Night's Dream* (Inner City Repertory, LA), *Lock Up Your Daughters* and *The Unknown Soldier and His Wife* (Pasadena Playhouse '68)

Nightclub/Concert: El Rancho, Moulin Rouge and Royal Nevada Hotels (LV '55–60), *Let It All Hang Out* (Sahara Hotel, LV '68)

Ballet/Dance Pieces (Partial listing): Tap renditions of "Ave Maria," "Blue Danube Waltz," "Bolero," "Danse Macabre," "Minute Waltz," "Ritual Fire Dance," etc.

Film:
1935 **In This Corner**— Vitaphone (S) (also appeared)
1936 **Katz' Pajamas**— Vitaphone (S) (also appeared)
1937 **52nd Street**— UA (with Danny Dare, also appeared)
        Vogues of 1938— UA (with Seymour Felix, also appeared)
1961 **Splendor in the Grass**— WB
1969 **Angel in My Pocket**— Univ (with Wilda Taylor)

VICKY TARAZI
1986 **Blue City**— Par

RON TASSONE
1993 **The Cemetary Club**— Touchstone

ANDRE TAYIR
b. Alabama, September 16, 1935
Dancer, choreographer, director and producer who began his dance studies in Atlanta, Ga. with Karen Conrad and Pittman Corey of the Southern Ballet Company. As a music major at the University of Georgia, he created his first choreography for a production of *Amahl and the Night Visitors* in 1954 and made his professional stage debut at Atlanta's Theatre Under the Stars in 1955. Migrating to New York he studied ballet with American Ballet Theatre and Arthur Mitchell and jazz with Matt Mattox and Buzz Miller. He toured with Columbia Concerts from 1960–64 and was brought to the West Coast by Jerome Robbins for the film version of **West Side Story** ('61), in which he played "Chile." While studying acting with Jeff Corey, Robert Ellenstein and Leonard Nimoy, he performed onstage (*West Side Story* and *A Taste of Honey*, Los Angeles, 1961–62) until his choreographic and directing career moved into high gear with prolific TV work during the active rock 'n' roll years. Proud father of a son and two daughters, he currently creates entertainment in Branson, Missouri.

Stage: The Jewel Box Revue (Ntl. tour '59), Catch My Soul (LA '67), Fabulous Palm Springs Follies (Palm Springs, Cal '91–94, also prod, dir)

TV (Partial listing): "Shindig" ('64–66), "Danny Thomas' Wonderful World of Burlesque" ('66–68),

"Where the Girls Are," "Laugh-In" ('68), "The Jonathon Winters Show" ('68), "The Andy Williams Show" ('70–71 with the Andre Tayir Dancers), "Andy Williams Presents Ray Stevens" ('70), "New Zoo Revue" ('72), "Wolfman Jack Show" ('75–76); specials for the Beatles ('64), Jack Benny, Bobby Darin, John Davidson, Andy Griffith, Noel Harrison, Don Knotts, Peggy Lee, Jim Nabors, Oral Roberts, The Supremes, Tiny Tim, Leslie Uggams, Dionne Warwick and Andy Williams (12 specials '72–80), etc.; commercials for American Oil, Granny Goose, Standard Oil

Music Video: "Kid Songs" (WB, 1985–93)

Nightclub/Concert: Acts and tours for JoAnne Castle, Andy Gibb, the Lennon Sisters, Gavin MacLeod, Jim Nabors, Tina Turner, Dionne Warwick, Tanya Welk and Andy Williams,

Film:
1966 **Last of the Secret Agents**— Par
1967 **Good Times**— Col (assisted by Maria Gahva)

WILDA TAYLOR (BIEBER)
b. Los Angeles, California, February 26, 1930
Stunning dancer, actress and choreographer who is a member of the dancing Bieber family with siblings Linda, Nita, Rod and Wanda. In Los Angeles she studied ballet with Egorova, Theodore Kosloff and Nijinskja, jazz with Jack Cole, tap with Louis DaPron and Spanish dance with José Cansino. At 18 she appeared at the Lido in Paris and, back in Hollywood, at the Greek Theater as featured ballerina in Lester Horton's works ('50) and with LACLO productions of *Song of Norway*, *Finian's Rainbow* and *Annie Get Your Gun*. She formed a dance company with David Lichine for a 1953 European tour, danced in Frankie Laine's nightclub act and her own Wilda Taylor Trio successfully toured nightclubs in 1963. Her film choreographic career began when she created her own number for **A House Is Not a Home** ('64). She assisted Earl Barton and had featured roles in **Frankie and Johnny**, **Harum Scarum** and **Roustabout** with Elvis Presley. Assisting Barton and Jack Baker, she worked on multiple sixties TV shows. After operating a boutique for several years in Toluca Lake, California, she returned to her acting career in 1990.

Stage: The Best of Burlesque (LA '60, with Jack Baker)

TV: "The Outsiders," The Steve Allen and Jack Paar shows

Film:
1964 **A House Is Not a Home**— Embassy (also appeared)
1965 **When the Boys Meet the Girls**— MGM (assistant to Earl Barton)

1966 **Frankie and Johnny**— MGM (assistant to Barton)

      Hold On!— MGM

      Out of Sight— Univ

1967 **The Fastest Guitar Alive**— MGM (also appeared)

1968 **P.J.**— Univ

1969 **Angel, Angel Down We Go** (aka **Cult of the Damned**)- AIP

      Angel in My Pocket— Univ (with George Tapps)

      The Love God?— Univ

WILHELMINA TAYLOR

1987 **The Believers**— Orion (also appeared)

LYNN TAYLOR-CORBETT

b. Denver, Colorado, December 2, 1946

When writing about her life and career, Taylor-Corbett recalled making her choreographic debut "in my basement, Littleton, Colorado at the age of 14." She studied dance with Harriet Andreson, at the Gwen Bowen School of Dance and with Constance Garfield Baker in Colorado, and in New York at the School of American Ballet, American Ballet Theatre, Harkness House and with Paul Sanasardo. Making her live stage debut in *This Was Burlesque* in 1965 (a rather unlikely beginning for her future career), she subsequently danced with the Alvin Ailey American Dance Theatre (1967–68), Anna Sokolow, Theatre Dance Collection and "millions of small dance companies." In 1970 she choreographed for the Interboro Ballet in New York. She made her Broadway debut in *Promises, Promises* in 1971 and also appeared in *Seesaw, Oklahoma!* and *A Chorus Line.* Her multiple talents allow her to move from stage to ballet to screen, with success in each venue. She credits her mother, Dorothy Johnson Taylor, as a major influence in her life, along with Emily Frankel, Rodney Griffin, Mary O'Keefe and Paul Sanasardo. Quoted in *Dance Magazine* (Nov. '92): "I cannot separate my intentions relating to dance from my overall purpose as a human being. There are issues I care deeply about, and these find their way into my dances. So perhaps I should be defined as a theatrical choreographer," she has contributed to NYC Ballet's "Diamond Project" in 1993 and 1994.

Stage: *Shakespeare's Cabaret* (Bdwy '80), *Boy's Breath* (NY, '84), *Merrily We Roll Along* (La Jolla, Cal.'85 rev), *Chess* (Bdwy '88), *Stop the World, I Want to Get Off* (Ntl tour), *Song of Singapore* (OB '91), *Theda Bara and the Frontier Rabbi* ('91, also dir), *Eating Raoul* (OB '92), *Jekyll and Hyde* ('92), *The Fields of Ambrosia* (George St. Playhouse, NJ '93), *Off Key* (OOT '93), *Hit the Lights* (Vineyard

Theater's Musical Lab '94), *Opal* (George Street Playhouse, NJ '95, also dir)

TV: "ABC Funfest" ('87, also co-author)

Music Video: video for Natalie Cole ('90)

Nightclub/Concert: Pat Metheny Japan Tour '89, *Sophie, Tottie and Bette* (Philadelphia, '92, also dir)

Ballet/Dance Pieces: "Great Galloping Gottschalk" and "Estuary" (ABT); "Mercury" (NYC Ballet); "Surfacing" and "Mystery of the Dancing Princess" (Miami City Ballet '95); works for Atlanta Ballet, Concordance (Paris), Gulbenkian Ballet (Lisbon), Hubbard St. Dance Company ("Case Closed" '87), Les Ballets Jazz, Pacific Northwest Ballet, Pennsylvania Ballet, Theatre Dance Collection

Miscellaneous: SSDC "Mr. Abbott Award" dinner ('93)

Film:

1984 **Footloose**— Par (with Myrna Gawryn, Charlene Painter, assisted by Spencer Henderson)

      Hey Babe!— Rafal

1988 **The In Crowd**— Orion (with Jerry Evans, Peggy Holmes, Linda Weisberg)

      My Blue Heaven— WB (assisted by Henderson)

1995 **O Holy Night**— Xmas Prod Inc

DENEY TERRIO

b. Florida, 1955

Disco era personality Terrio has the distinction of being the only Caucasian man to appear with the ground-breaking street dance troupe, The Lockers, on their first TV appearance. Member-choreographer Toni Basil recalled that the network had requested the group be integrated, so Basil selected Terrio to appear and appease the network ... although he never danced with the group again. A self-taught street and club dancer, he had arrived in Los Angeles from Florida and began entering dance contests, eventually winning the California State singles and couples championships. After a chance meeting with John Travolta's agent, he began coaching the star. The resulting publicity as Travolta's dance coach on **Saturday Night Fever** (even taking Travolta to contests at disco clubs "so he could get the feel of actual competition") led to Terrio making appearances in the films **Knights of the City**, **The Idolmaker** and **A Night in Heaven**— also creating the choreography for the latter two. After television appearances on "The Love Boat" and the Merv Griffin Show, he gained national fame as the Host of Griffin's TV series "Dance Fever" from 1979–85. When the Disco era ended, Terrio seem to boogie off into the distance. In 1993, Terrio once again surfaced and gained notoriety with one of the first same-sex sexual harassment suits

Bobby Thompson plays "percussionist" with Andre Tayir's head in **West Side Story** (United Artists, 1961) (photo courtesy of Bobby Thompson).

when he claimed that producer Merv Griffin "black-balled" him in the entertainment industry when he spurned his advances. The final outcome of the law-suit is unknown.

    Film:
    1977 **Saturday Night Fever**— Par (with Jeff Kutash, Jo Jo Smith, Lester Wilson, uncredited)
    1980 **The Idolmaker**— UA (also appeared)
    1983 **A Night in Heaven**— Fox (also appeared)

ALBERTO TESTA

b. Torino, Italy, December 23, 1922

    Italian dancer, critic and publicist who studied dance with the Léonide Massine and Margarita Wallman company schools. He worked as a chore-ographer for opera and films and taught "The His-tory of Dance" at the Rome National Academy of Dance. As the dance critic and correspondent for several magazines, he organized highly successful exhibits on Diaghilev's life and work in 1972 and 1977, as well as continually participating in dance festivals throughout Italy.

    Ballet/Dance Pieces: "The Songs of the Gulf of Naples" ('62)
    Film:
    1963 **The Leopard**— Fox
    1968 **Romeo and Juliet**— Par
    1977 **Jesus of Nazareth**— NBC/ITV (TV)
    1984 **La Traviata**— Univ

TWYLA THARP

b. Portland, Indiana, July 1, 1941

    Moving with her family to Rialto, California in 1949, the uniquely named Twyla was offered an eclectic education in the Arts: dance training at the Vera Lynn School of dance, piano, violin, drums, baton twirling and Flamenco. She began her seri-ous study of dance with Beatrice Collonette and over the years received varied training from John Butler, Merce Cunningham, Carmen DeLavallade, Martha Graham, Bella Lewitzky, Murray Louis, Luigi, Matt Mattox, Wilson Morelli, Alwin Niko-lais, Igor Schwezoff, Paul Taylor and Richard Thomas. After graduating from Barnard College she made her professional debut in Taylor's company in 1963, also creating her first choreography to *Tank Dive* that same year. With her extensive classical and modern background, she begin challenging dance itself and formed her own company, Twyla Tharp Dance — creating a sensation in the traditional dance world. From international success with her own company, she also choreographed original works for ABT and the Martha Graham Company. Her film work has been often in conjunction with director Milos Forman. Winner of the *Dance Magazine* Award in 1981, stage appearances with Mikhail Baryshnikov across the United States brought renewed acclaim in the early '90s. **I'll Do Anything,** her most recent film credit, is the subject of curiosity. At previews, audiences allegedly laughed at the musical sequences. They were edited completely and the film was released as a comedy. Hopefully the musical numbers — and Tharp's always innovative work — will be included on future video and laser disc releases of the film.

> **Autobiography:** *Push Comes to Shove* (1992)
>
> **Stage:** *Ice Dancing* (Bdwy '78, with Kenneth MacMillan, Norman Maen, Donald Saddler), *The Grand Tour* (Bdwy '78), *Singin' in the Rain* (Bdwy '85 with Stanley Donen and Gene Kelly, also dir)
>
> **TV:** "The Bix Pieces" ('73), "Twyla Tharp and 'Eight Jelly Rolls'" (England '74), "All About Eggs" ('74), "Sue's Leg, Remembering the Thirties" ('76), "Making Television Dance, a Videotape by Twyla Tharp" ('77), "Dance Is a Man's Sport Too" ('80), "Scrapbook Tape" ('82), "The Catherine Wheel" ('83, Emmy nom), "Baryshnikov by Tharp" ('84, Emmy winner)
>
> **Ballet/Dance Pieces** (Over 70 works — Partial listing): "Tank Dive" ('65), "Eight Jelly Rolls," "Deuce Coup," "As Time Goes By," "Sue's Leg," "Push Comes to Shove," "When We Were Very Young," "Sinatra Suite," "The Men's Piece," "Sextett," "Demeter and Persephone" (Martha Graham Company, '93)
>
> **Miscellaneous:** *After All* (ice work for John Curry, Madison Square Gardens, NY '76), *Three Fanfares* (Lake Placid Olympic Closing Ceremonies, '80)
>
> **Film:**
> 1979 **Hair**— UA (assisted by Ken Rinker)
> 1981 **Ragtime**— Par (assisted by John Carrafa)
> 1983 **Zelig**— Orion/WB (with Danny Daniels, assisted by Carrafa)
> 1984 **Amadeus**— Orion (choreography and staging of Opera sequences, assisted by Carrafa, Keith Young)
> 1985 **White Nights**— Col (with Mikhail Baryshnikov, Gregory Hines, Roland Petit)
> 1994 **I'll Do Anything**— Col (work deleted)

LEE THEODORE (NEÉ BECKER)

b. Newark, New Jersey, April 13, 1933
d. New York, September 3, 1987
Important American dance historian who first studied dance at the Mikhail Mordkin and Swoboda schools and attended the New York High School of Performing Arts. Upon graduation in 1950 she spent one summer at Camp Tamiment and then went into the Broadway cast of *Gentlemen Prefer Blondes.* She continued to appear on Broadway in *The King and I, John Murray Anderson's Almanac, Seventh Heaven* (in which she also assisted Peter Gennaro), *Damn Yankees, The Ziegfeld Follies, West Side Story* (gaining fame as the original "Anybodys") and *Tenderloin.* She also danced with the Slavenska-Franklin Ballet Company ('52) and created her first solo choreography for *Walk Tall*, a revue at the Playhouse-in-the-Round in Houston, Texas, in 1953. Being a painter herself, she married painter Yoram Kaniuk in 1955 and in 1962, she married another painter, Paris Theodore (the son of Nenette Charisse). In 1962 she formed Jazz Ballet Theatre with Michael Bennett, Eliot Feld, Dick Gain, Alan Johnson, Naomi Kimura, Jay Norman, Mabel Robinson and Jaime Rogers. She made her directorial debut with a 1968 revival of *West Side Story*, chosen by original creator Jerome Robbins for the task, and was also the director of Bill Baird's Puppet Theater. In 1975 she founded American Dance Machine, the historic company which recreated, documented, preserved and performed the work of famous Broadway choreographers ("I had the privilege of working as a dancer and assistant with what I call the masters, people like Jerome Robbins, Danny Daniels, Don Saddler, Jack Cole... I would be teaching at universities around the country and the kids wouldn't know who Jack Cole or Agnes DeMille were. Their work is part of our history and I began to feel it would be lost to this generation.") Her landmark company also included a dance school, featuring such instructors as Gemze DeLappe, Carmen DeLavallade, Agnes DeMille, Peter Gennaro and Gwen Verdon, with a branch in Tokyo. She was given the *Dance Magazine* award in 1982 for her Herculean efforts — and achievements.

> **Stage:** *Walk Tall* (Texas, '53), *Once Over Lightly* (Bdwy '55), *Graham Crackers* (OB '63), *The Perils of Scobie Prilt* (GB '63), *Baker Street* (Bdwy '65), *Flora, the Red Menace* (Bdwy '65), *The Apple Tree* (Bdwy '66, with Herbert Ross, Tony nom), *Showboat* (LACLO '67 rev), *Darling of the Day* (Bdwy '68), *Noel Coward's Sweet Potato* (Bdwy '68, also dir), *Livin' the Life* (OB '70, asst to John Butler), *Park* (Bdwy '70), *Hard Job Being God* (Bdwy '72), *Winnie the Pooh* (OB '72, dir only), *Davy Jones' Locker* (OB '73, dir only), *Pinocchio* (OB '73, dir

Disco king Deney Terrio on his television series, "Dance Fever" (1979–85).

only), *The Whistling Wizard and the Sultan of Tuffet* (OB '73, dir only), *The Prince of Grand Street* (OOT '78), *American Dance Machine* (Bdwy '78), *West Side Story* (Bdwy '80 rev, restaging of Jerome Robbin's original work with Tommy Abbott), *Jack* (Theatre Apple, Tokyo '82, dir only)

TV: The Steve Allen, Sid Caesar, Perry Como, Wayne & Schuster and Ed Sullivan Shows; "Little Red Riding Hood" Special, "Look Up and Live," "Kraft Music Hall" (with the Lee Becker Theodore Dancers '64), "Kiss Me Kate" ('68), "From the Ballroom to Broadway and Back" (Camera 3, PBS '80)

Ballet/Dance Pieces: "The Unicorn, the Gorgon and the Manticone" (Milan '62); "Dance Time-capsule" ('87)

Film:

1967 **The Honey Pot**— UA

1970 **The Song of Norway**— ABC (assisted by Avind Harum)

PETER THOEMKE

1982 **Purple Haze**— Triumph

ANTHONY THOMAS

It was music video that first offered the greatest opportunities — and challenges — to this rising dance artist ("A friend of mine had pointed out that do you realize that you and other choreographers help sell millions of albums?"—"Dance in America: Everybody Dance Now"). Creating the most exciting dance images he could imagine, Thomas excelled in the medium, combining classical and street dance ("I have my influence in technical dance but for the most part it comes from the street") in some of the most elaborate and technically original works for Janet Jackson and others. Winner of an MTV Best Choreography award for "Rhythm Nation," Thomas is one of the '90's most promising choreographic talents.

TV: 1990 NAACP Image Awards, 1992 American Music and Country Music Award shows, "MTV's Spring Break" ('94, with Tevin Campbell)

Music Video: "Rhythm Nation," "Miss You Much," "The Knowledge," "Black Cat," "Escapade," "Alright" (with Michael Kidd)— Janet Jackson; "Feels Good"—Tony, Toni, Tone; videos for Atlantic Starr and Wynonna Judd, more

Nightclub/Concert: Concert tours for Janet Jackson ("Rhythm Nation" '90), Wynonna Judd ('92), The Temptations, Luther Vandross ('93), etc.

Film:

1992 **Stay Tuned**— WB

  Toys— Fox

1995 **A Goofy Movie**— Disney

RANDALL THOMAS

1988 **The Night Before**— Kings Road Ent

ROBERT THOMAS

1986 **Tangos: The Exile of Gardel**—(Fr/Argentina) (with Adolfo Andrade, Margarita Balli, Susana Tambutti)

CLAUDE THOMPSON

b. Brooklyn, New York, 1937

Dancer, teacher and choreographer who started his performance career singing and dancing in small nightclubs at the age of 13. While attending the High School of Performing Arts, he made his Broadway debut at 15 in *My Darlin' Aida* ('52). Other Broadway appearances include *Jamaica*, *House of Flowers*, *Shinbone Alley*, *Mr. Wonderful* and *Bravo Giovanni* and he danced in Shirley Broughton's and Louis Johnson's dance companies in 1955. After working with Cantinflas, the Mexican film comedian, he partnered Nora Kaye for a Cannes Film Festival Gala and toured Europe. He appeared on television in "The Gershwin Years" ('61) and co-starred with Paula Kelly in the "Grand Opening" show for Caesar's Palace in Las Vegas: *Rome Swings*. He created The Claude Thompson Dancers, who toured with Sammy Davis, Jr. and made many television appearances. He got his first opportunity to choreograph for film when director Francis Ford Coppola was unhappy with Hermes Pan's work on **Finian's Rainbow**, asking Thompson to finish the film.

Stage: *Don't Bother Me I Can't Cope* (Bdwy '72, with George Faison), *Tommy* (LA '72, also dir), *Pal Joey* (LACLO '78)

TV: Specials for Harry Belafonte, Diahann Carroll, Mama Cass, Petula Clark, Sammy Davis, Jr., Robert Goulet, Lena Horne, Tom Jones, Eartha Kitt, Elvis Presley and Sylvie Varten; "America or Bust," "The NBC Follies," The Hollywood Palace, "Roots," "Harper Valley PTA" (Pilot '70)

Nightclub/Concert: *Flesh* (Bonanza Hotel, LV '69), *Paradise Found* (Hilton Hotel, Honolulu), The Claude Thompson Dancers (Sands Hotel, LV '72); acts for Harry Belafonte, Diahann Carroll, George Chakiris, Sammy Davis, Jr., Lena Horne, Quincy Jones, The Manhattan Transfer, Johnny Mathis, Juliet Prowse and Connie Stevens

Film:

1968 **Finian's Rainbow**— WB ("associate choreographer" with Fred Astaire, Hermes Pan)

1976 **King Kong**— Par

1985 **The Color Purple**— WB

1989 **Eddie and the Cruisers II: Eddie Lives!**— Alliance-Aurora/Scotti (assisted by Johnny Almaraz)

ROBERT (BOBBY) THOMPSON

b. Texas, 1934

d. Woodland Hills, California, June 13, 1984

Dancer and choreographer who had his blonde good looks darkened to play "Luis," one of the Sharks in **West Side Story** ('61). Other film appearances include **Can Can**, **Hello, Dolly!**, **The Music Man** and **Sweet Charity**. On TV in "Hello World," the Danny Kaye and Red Skelton shows, he briefly left Hollywood in 1964 to join a ballet company in Munich. Stage performance include the LACLO production of *Song of Norway* ('62), a West Coast tour of *West Side Story* ('64) and Ann-Margret's and Rhonda Fleming's club acts. In the field of choreography, he assisted Toni Basil, Aida Broadbent, Hugh Lambert, Walter and Charlene Painter and Buddy Schwab.

Stage: *West Side Story* (West Coast '64, asst to Michael Stuart)

Nightclub/Concert: *Doo Dah Daze* (Flamingo Hotel, LV '75, with Toni Basil), *Queens of the Silver Screen* (Holiday Inn, Bermuda)

Film:
1972 **Up the Sandbox** — First Artists (uncredited)
1982 **Jinxed!** — MGM/UA

NORMAN THOMSON
1962 **Almost Angels** — Buena Vista

MYLES THOROUGHGOOD
b. Philadelphia, Pennsylvania, March 3, 1960

Contemporary dance creator and educator stated, "Choreography offers me the infinite possibilities of expression through the universal language of movement" and cites Philadelphia College of Performing Arts jazz dance teacher Michelle Frampton Ed, entertainers Bette Midler and Gene Kelly, director-choreographer Sarah Elgart and manager Margie Chachkin as being major influences in his life and work. Growing up in Philadelphia he began his study of dance at the Philadelphia College of Performing Arts and drama with The Philadelphia Company. He made his professional debut as a dancer on the "Evening Magazine" TV show and created his first choreography for the Philadelphia's Cornucopia Dinner Theatre production of *Bluesin'*. He danced with the WAVES Jazz Dance Company from 1983–86, also choreographing works for the company. With his ongoing quest for technique and varied theater knowledge, he studied dance in New York with Phil Black and Shimon Braun and acting in Los Angeles with The Groundlings and The Actors Center. Stage performances include *Dancin' in the Streets* at the Tropicana Hotel in Atlantic City ('86), a national tour of *Satchmo* ('87), the Hong Kong Arts Festival and *Eleventh Hour* in 1988. His acting talents have been featured on TV in "Generations" and "This Week's Music" (as one of the series' "regulars"), "21 Jump Street," "What's Happening Now" and "Doogie Howser, M.D." In 1989 he began choreographing for the Disney Channel and has continued contributing to multiple entertainment venues with the Walt Disney company.

Along with his danceworks, he continues to give master classes across the country.

Stage: *Bluesin'* (Phil), *Open Doors* (Hollywood), *The Club That Never Closes* (LA, also dir and author)

TV: "The Mickey Mouse Club" ('89–95), 1990 Ace Awards, Inaugural Celebration ('93), "Festival of Lights" (CBC), "Regis and Kathie Lee," "The Party Machine," "Back to School," "Disney's Great American Celebration," Disney Christmas and Easter Parades, "Jungle Book" and "Back to School" specials (The Disney Channel)

Music Video: "What's Up Doc?" — Shaquille O'Neal & Fu-Schnickens; "That's Why" and "Peace, Love and Understanding" — The Party; The Disney Channel ('90–93); Professional Dance Teachers Association instructional dance video, Instructional Funk dance video

Nightclub/Concerts: *Dancin' in the Streets* (Tropicana Hotel, Atlantic City '86, also appeared), *Splash* (Riviera Hotel, LV '90 and Reno, '94); tours for the Mickey Mouse Club and The Party

Ballet/Dance Pieces: works for WAVES Jazz Dance Company (U.S. and European tours, '83–86) and M.A.D.R.E.S ("Abundance," "Every Woman's Evidence" and "Skin of the Rich"); "Pigment" (Glam Slam, LA, also appeared), "Social Circus" (LA '93)

Miscellaneous: Multiple stage shows and parades for Walt Disney World and EPCOT: *Galaxy Search*, *Ring in the New*, etc.

Film:
1993 **And the Band Played On** (TV) — HBO (asst to Sarah Elgart, also appeared)
At the Bluff — ?

LINDA THORSLUND
1990 **American Boyfriends** — Telefilm Canada

TIP, TAP AND TOE
Popular and innovative black acrobatic tap dance trio which was started in the late 1920s by original members Teddy Frazier, Sammy Green and Raymond Winfield. Freddie James and Prince Spencer (also members of The Four Step Brothers) joined the act for a brief period. After successes at the Palace and Paramount theaters in New York they were featured in *George White's Scandals of 1936*, before going into films. Among the innovations they introduced were exciting slides and lining up to tap the same sounds using different steps or the same steps making different sounds. Admired and copied by many other groups, "Honi" Coles once told the story that another group, (The Four Bobs) "sat in a Philadelphia theater all day until they copied the entire performance of 'Tip,Tap and Toe,' including

the mistakes." Evidently The Four Bobs could not copy the excitement — nor the fame — of the trio.

Film (All credits are for appearances of the trio):
1936 **By Request**— Vitaphone (S)
1937 **You Can't Have Everything**— Fox
1942 **Pardon My Sarong**— Univ (with Katherine Dunham)
1943 **All by Myself**— Univ
      Honeymoon Lodge— Univ (with Frank Veloz)
1944 **Hi Good Lookin'**— Univ (with Louis DaPron)

DAVID TITCHNELL
1987 **Slamdance**— Island Pic

RALPH TOBERT
1968 **Hammerhead**— Col

QUENTIN TODD
1936 **Amateur Gentleman**— Criterion (GB)

DAVID TOGURI
b. Vancouver, B.C. Canada, October 25

Canadian-born dancer and choreographer of Japanese ancestry who became a leading force in British theater, films and television. His dance educators included Errol Addison, Audrey de Voss, Andre Hardis, Luigi, Karel Shook and Boris Volkoff. He also attended the Ryerson Institute of Technology. He made his professional debut with the Volkoff Canadian Ballet in 1953 and stage appearances include Summer stock at the Melody Fair in Buffalo and Musicarnival in Cleveland (1953–55). After dancing in *Flower Drum Song* on Broadway he went to London with the show in 1960 and remained there to appear onstage in the Sammy Davis, Jr. Show ('61), *Six of One* ('63), *Chaganog* ('64) and *Charlie Girl* ('65). He also appeared in the films **Flower Drum Song**, **You Only Live Twice** and **Three Hats for Liza**. He then began his prolific stage, TV and film choreography-direction career in Australia, Canada, Great Britain and throughout Europe. His direction credits include *Camino Real* in Norway, *Robin Hood* in Canada and *Kiss Me Kate*, *Servant of Two Masters*, *Flea in Her Ear* and *Sweeney Todd* in England. His direction of the Australian production of *Guys and Dolls* won him the Best Musical Direction honor. Because of the ongoing success of the film **The Rocky Horror Picture Show**, his choreography and musical staging may be known and performed by more people around the world than any other film choreographer.

Stage: *Zorba* (London '71), *Tonight at 8:30* (London), *Cole* (London '74, also dir), *Censored Scenes from King Kong* (Eng. '77 & OB '80), *Shadow Play* (London), *Gulliver's Travels* (London); for the Royal Shakespeare Co.: *As You Like It, A Midsummer Night's Dream, Measure for Measure, The Tempest, Poppy* and *The Swan's Down Gloves; Robin Hood* (Young Vic '82, also dir), **Falstaff** and **Parsifal** (Convent Garden), *Hello, Dolly!* (London), *Wonderful Town* (London '86), *The Little Shop of Horrors* (Oslo), *Guys and Dolls* (London and Australia, also dir, SWET award), *Sugar* (West Yorkshire Playhouse, Eng '90), *Noel and Gertie* and *Swell Party* (London '91), *The Blue Angel* and *Spread a Little Happiness* (London '92)

TV: "Rock Follies" ('77), "The Good Companion," "Blue Money" (all British TV); commercials for Ariston, Burlington (featuring Petula Clark), Ford, Pepsi (featuring Tina Turner and David Bowie), Ryder Trucks

Music Videos: "Blue Jean"— David Bowie; "Break Every Rule"— Tina Turner; "Little Thing Called Love"— Freddie Mercury; also video for Barry Gibb.

Ballet/Dance Pieces: "Inochi" (Ballet Rambert '70)

Film:
1968 **The Devil's Bride** (aka **The Devil Rides Out**)— Fox
1975 **The Rocky Horror Picture Show**— Fox
1984 **Give My Regards to Broad Street**— Fox
1986 **Absolute Beginners**— Orion (assisted by Jonathon Thornton)
1988 **Who Framed Roger Rabbit?**— Touchstone/BV (with Quinny Sacks)
1989 **How to Get Ahead in Advertising**— WB
      Mack the Knife— 21st Century Film Corp
1990 **Memphis Belle**— WB
      Scandal— Miramax
1992 **Peter's Friends**— Goldwyn

MARIA FATIMA TOLEDO
Brazilian actress who was selected to work with the native Indians in **Medicine Man**. The press kit for the film describes her participation in the film with: "Not really 'choreography,' but supervising the Indian's participation in the film."

Film:
1992 **Medicine Man**— Hollywood Pictures ("Brazilian Indian choreographer" credit)

WENDY TOYE
b. London, England, May 1, 1917

One of the few female British film directors, Toye was born into a wealthy and cultured family and began dancing classes at a very early age, first appearing in public at the Royal Albert Hall at the age of 4. Frederic Franklin recalled in 1974, "The Toyes were close friends of all the great Russian artists in London. When Wendy was a little girl, she used to sit in Pavlova's dressingroom ... Diaghilev would have her beside him at the Covent Garden sessions. The Russians called her 'Toyshka,' and loved her because she was such a wonderfully gifted dancer." Blooming in this privileged environment, she won the English Charleston Competition and choreographed and produced *Mother Earth* at the Savoy Theater in London at 10. Two years later, she appeared at the Old Vic and in *Toad of Toad Hall,* joining Ninette deValois' Vic-Wells Ballet Company in 1930. Already "the darling of London before she turned 16," she was featured in nightclub shows (which she also choreographed), with Franklin as her partner, until they began touring with the Markova-Dolin Ballet in 1934. After appearing in the film **Invitation to the Waltz** ('36), she choreographed two films and the following year began staging all of the musical numbers for producer George Black's musicals and revues in London's West End, as well as making more onstage appearances. After her last onscreen appearance in **I'll Be Your Sweetheart** in 1945, she became one of Britain's first female director-choreographers of stage musicals. Her first film direction assignment was **The Stranger Left No Card**, a short which won an award at the Cannes Film Festival in 1951. She then devoted most of her creative energies to stage and film direction, directing six films from 1955–62 (**The Teckman Mystery**, **Three Cases of Murder**, **All for Mary**, **Raising a Riot**, **True as a Turtle** and **We Joined the Navy**) and continuing work on the London stage into the seventies.

Stage: (All London credits except *) *These Foolish Things* ('38), *Black and Blue, The Little Dog Laughed, Black Velvet* (also appeared) and *Who's Taking Liberty?* ('39), *Black Vanities* and *Gangway* ('40), *It's About Time* and *Best Bib and Tucker* ('42), *Hi-De-Hi, Strike a New Note, The Lisbon Story* and *Panama Hattie* ('43), *Jenny Jones* and *Strike It Again* ('44, also appeared), *Gay Rosalinda* and *Follow the Girls* ('45, also appeared), *Big Ben* and *The Shepherd Show* ('46, also dir), *Bless the Bride* ('47, also dir), *Tough at the Top* ('49, also dir), *And So to Bed* ('51, also dir), *Wild Thyme* ('55, also dir), *Joyce Grenfell Requests the Pleasure* (London and Bdwy* '55, with Irving Davies, Alfred Rodrigues and Paddy Stone), *Lady at the Wheel* ('58, also dir), *Virtue in Danger* ('63, also dir), *Robert and Elizabeth* ('64, also dir), *On the Level* ('66, also dir), *Show Boat* ('71 rev, also dir), *Stand and Deliver* ('72, also dir), *R Loves J* ('73, also dir), *Follow the Star* ('74, also dir)

Nightclub/Concert: Revues at the Grosvenor House (London '33)

Film:
1935 **Invitation to the Waltz**— BIP (with Anton Dolin)
1936 **Pagliaci**— UA

Southern Roses— GFD
1942 **The Young Mr. Pitt**—(GB)

LOFTI TRAVOLTA
1987 **Moonstruck**— MGM

JOE TREMAINE
b. Bastrop, Louisiana, December 20, 1938
Winner of the 1994 *LA Dance* Educators Award "for currently impacting future generations of dance artists," Tremaine's influence on filmed dance continues with his thousands of students over the years including dancers, choreographers and stars Paula Abdul, Ann-Margret, Jamie Lee Curtis, Jeff Goldblum and Goldie Hawn. Growing up in Oak Ridge, Louisiana, he began studying dance with Mary Lou Young and Pat Young Cook who immediately recognized the potential in their young student. He continued teaching himself while in high school ("When the other boys were playing cowboys and Indians, I always played being a teacher. It was an innate kind of thing") and later attended Northeastern Louisiana University, graduating with a double major in psychology and sociology. He studied with Valerie Smith while performing with the New Orleans Ballet Foundation and the New Orleans Opera and in New York he furthered his knowledge of ballet with Vincenzo Celli, jazz with Luigi, Matt Mattox and Jo Jo Smith and modern with Claude Thompson. After appearances in Cape Cod summer stock productions of *West Side Story* and *A Funny Thing Happened on the Way to the Forum*, while in the cast of Jones Beach's *Mardi Gras* ('65), choreographer June Taylor took him to "The Jackie Gleason Show" for the 1966–67 season. Other TV appearances included the Carol Burnett, Jerry Lewis, and Jonathon Winters shows and "Joey and Dad." He performed in Joey Heatherton's, Debbie Reynolds' and Raquel Welch's nightclub acts and attracted attention in 1969 in a group, Black, White and Fourteen (with Debbie Macomber and Burt Woods) in Las Vegas. Eugene Loring encouraged Joe to teach at his American School of Dance and in 1974 he began The Joe Tremaine Dance Center. Concentrating on dance education in 1981, he formed The Tremaine Dance Convention, which travels all over the United States, bringing the very best teachers in each field and having more than 50,000 students. In 1991 he opened his own studio in North Hollywood. His unique style ("fast, funky and very today") has developed into a "West Coast or L.A. style of dance." Among his awards are the 1988 Video Conference Award for Best Dance Instruction Video, the 1990 Gus Giordano Jazz Dance Award, the 1992 Dance Masters of America Jazz Dance Award, the Dance Educators of America Excellence in Dance

Award in 1993 and the proclamation of "Joe Tremaine Day" in Shreveport, La. by the entire state of Louisiana on June 17, 1993. He currently serves on the advisory board of Professional Dancers Society.

TV: Raquel Welch Special ('74), Barry Manilow Special ('76), "Doug Henning's World of Magic" ('78)

Nightclub/Concert: Black, White and Fourteen ('69, also appeared); acts for Lynne Latham, Diana Ross, Raquel Welch

   Miscellaneous: SHARE *Boomtown* Show ('81)

   Film:

   1969 **Flareup**— Fox

   1984 **The Ratings Game**— The Movie Channel (TV)

JERRY TRENT

   b. Danville, Illinois, January 25, 1941

Dancer-choreographer and director who has shifted into a rewarding career as an Emmy-nominated Foley Artist. He began his dance studies in Illinois with Florence Cizek, Warren Clark and Cathryn Cromwell and made his professional debut in 1957 in *Brigadoon* in Sullivan, Illinois, and appeared at the Del Prado Hotel in Chicago in 1962. He danced on Broadway in *Camelot* and in the NYC Center productions of *My Fair Lady* and **Carmina Burana**. Moving to the West Coast, he became one of the busiest film, nightclub and television dancers. Among his seventeen film credits are **Bedknobs and Broomsticks, Blazing Saddles, Funny Lady, Hello, Dolly!, Mame, Pete's Dragon** and **Sweet Charity**. He began working as assistant/associate choreographer with Michael Kidd on the LACLO productions of *Irma La Douce, The Sound of Music, Bells Are Ringing* and the national tour of *The Music Man* starring Dick Van Dyke. He assisted Hugh Lambert on a Nancy Sinatra TV special and the 1964 New York World's Fair and Bob Sidney and Buddy Schwab on nightclub acts. On film he assisted Marc Breaux, Michael Kidd, Paddy Stone and Onna White, before gaining his solo credits. In 1988 he became a Foley Artist, specializing in post-dubbing the dance sounds for such films as **Dancers**. He cites his family, wife Audrey, their son Christopher, and his love of dancing and performing as the major influences in his life. In 1994 he and Audrey were nominated for an Emmy for their Foley Artist contributions to "Star Trek— The Next Generation."

   Stage: *Winner Take All* (LA '76, with Buddy Schwab)

   Nightclub/Concert: Acts for Ann Dee and *Dondino* (also dir)

   Film:

   1977 **Pete's Dragon**— Disney (assistant to Onna White, with Fred Curt, Alice Clift, Pat Cummins, also appeared)

A publicity photo of Antonio Triana for an appearance in *Dance Fiesta 3* at the Philharmonic Auditorium in Los Angeles, circa 1957.

   1978 **Movie, Movie**— WB (assistant to Michael Kidd, also appeared)

       Sextette— Crown Intl (assistant to Marc Breaux, also appeared)

   1980 **Xanadu**— Univ (with Gene Kelly, Kenny Ortega)

   1981 **S.O.B.**— Par (assistant to Paddy Stone)

   1983 **Curse of the Pink Panther**— MGM

ANTONIO TRIANA

   b. Seville, Spain

Renowned dancer, choreographer and teacher who began study of the classic Spanish dance forms at the age of 8. Following a little girl to her classes with Manuel Otero, his puppy love soon turned to fascination with the dance and he became Otero's only male student. At 9 he made his debut dancing with the famed La Quica and continued in Flamenco clubs and theaters in Madrid. La Argentinita invited Triana to co-create and appear with her in a production of **El Amor Brujo** in Seville ("I believe this was truly the birth of 'Ballet Español' as we know it.") When the revolution began in Spain, Triana fled to Paris and toured North and South America with Argentinita, Pilar Lopez and eventually, Carmen Amaya. He created multiple works and soon formed The Trianas with family members (including daughter, Luisa) for concert, nightclub, TV and film work. Among his students are José Greco, Roberto Iglesias and Manolo Vargas. In a 1970 *Dance Magazine* interview, he expressed his views on the art of Flamenco, "…it must be spontaneous, and it must express an otherwise undefinable *gracia*— grace of living. Also, there has to be a quality of personal involvement in flamenco dance — and its motivation must be love. What the flamenco dancer is saying when he dances is: 'I can slap—but I can love." Married to former student Rita Vega since 1958, he founded Ballet Español in El Paso, Texas in 1985 and passed on his art to his two children.

Ballet/Dance Pieces: "El Amor Brujo," "La Vida Breve," "El Polo," "Zapataeado," "Bolero," "Alegrias"

Film:

1944 **Allergic to Love**— Univ (also appeared)
  The Bridge of San Luis Rey— UA (with John Boyle, also appeared)
  Lady and the Monster— Rep (also appeared)
  The Rhythm of the Rhumba— WB (S) (with LeRoy Prinz, also appeared)
1945 **The Gay Señorita**— Col (with Stanley Donen, also appeared)
1952 **The Fabulous Señorita**— Rep
  The Snows of Kilimanjaro— Fox
1955 **Strange Lady in Town**— WB (with Peggy Carroll, also appeared)
1958 **The Lady Takes a Flyer**— Univ (also appeared)
1959 **The Miracle**— WB

SOLANO TRINIDADE
1960 **Macumba Love**— UA

JAMES TRUITTE
  b. Chicago, Illinois, 1924
  d. Cincinnati, Ohio, August 21, 1995
Dancer-choreographer and exponent and teacher of the technique and works of Lester Horton. While a pre-med student at UCLA, Truitte began his dance studies with Janet Collins, Carmelita Maracci and Archie Savage, and first attended the Horton school in 1948. While performing in a West Coast revival of *Finian's Rainbow* in 1950, he became a member of the Horton Dance Theater, quickly being elevated to leading male dancer. When Horton died in 1953, Truitte began his life-long continuation of the Horton technique and restaging of his classic works. Truitte danced in the films **Mighty Joe Young** ('49), **The Golden Hawk** ('52), **Carmen Jones** ('54) and **South Pacific** ('58), as well as assisting Horton on his last film and gaining solo choreographic credits. In 1960 he became featured male soloist and associate artistic director with the Alvin Ailey American Dance Theatre and remained with the company until 1968. His extensive teaching credits included Ballet Akademien (Goteborg, Sweden), Barnard, Clark Center for the Performing Arts, Jacob's Pillow, UCLA and Vassar and since 1970, taught at the University of Cincinatti College Conservatory of Music, where he was

promoted to full professor in 1988. In 1992 he received an award for excellence for teaching, as well as an Ohio Dance Award for Sustained Achievement. He also had been artist-in-residence with the Dayton Contemporary Dance Company since 1976.

Ballet/Dance Pieces: "Liberian Suite," "Mirror, Mirror," "With Timbrel and Dance Praise His Name," "The Duke's Bard" and "Black Voices" as well as reconstruction/restaging of Horton Works: "The Beloved," "Dedication to Jose Clemente Orozco," "Guernica," "Face of Violence (Salome)," "Frevo"

Film:

1953 **South Sea Woman**— WB (assistant to Lester Horton, also appeared)
1956 **The Mole People**— Univ (with Kenny Williams, also appeared)
1957 **Calypso Joe**— AA (also appeared as one of the Lester Horton Dancers)
1960 **The Sins of Rachel Cade**— WB

ROBERT TUCKER
Dancer, actor and choreographer who appeared on Broadway in *One Touch of Venus* ('43), *The Waltz King* (OOT '44), *Look Ma, I'm Dancin'* and *Love Life* ('48) and *Miss Liberty* ('49). Tucker began his choreographic career assisting Jerome Robbins on *Peter Pan* ('54), Bob Fosse on *Bells Are Ringing* ('56) and *Sweet Charity* ('67) and Robbins again on *Gypsy* ('59). Married to dance educator Nenette Charisse and the father of two sons and two daughters, he also taught at Charisse's New York dance studio.

Stage: Bells Are Ringing (London '57), *Hail the Conquering Hero* (Bdwy '61, co-choreo with Bob Fosse), *Noel Coward's Sweet Potato* (Bdwy '68, with Lee Theodore), *Gypsy* ('74 rev, recreating Jerome Robbins' work), *Cowboy* (OOT '75, also dir), *A Musical Jubilee* (Bdwy '75), *Shenandoah* (Bdwy '75, Tony nom), *The Baker's Wife* (OOT '76, with Dan Siretta), *Angel* (Bdwy '78), *A Midsummer Night's Dream* and *The Merchant of Venice* (Stratford, Conn.)

Nightclub/Concert: Plaza 9 (Plaza Hotel, NY)

Film:

1962 **Gypsy**— WB (adapting Jerome Robbins' original work, assisted by Peggy Carroll)
1963 **Under the Yum Yum Tree**— Col
1964 **For Those Who Think Young**— UA
1966 **You're a Big Boy Now**— 7 Arts

WILLIAM TUELSETTO
1991 **London Kills Me**— Fine Line Features

TOMMY (THOMAS JAMES) TUNE
  b. Wichita Falls, Texas, February 28, 1939

Dubbed "A national treasure" by *Drama-Logue*, this actor, dancer, singer, choreographer-director is one of the leaders of musical theater in America. His father and mother met while ballroom dancing and young Tommy started dancing lessons when dance teachers came to Texas public schools looking for talent. His first teachers were Camille Hill and Emma Mae Horn. He studied acting and directing at the University of Texas and dance with Shirley Dodge. After touring in *Irma La Douce*, he created his first choreography for a Milwaukee Melody Top production of *Roberta* ('64) and made his Broadway debut in the chorus of *Baker Street* ('65). He first worked with Michael Bennett on *A Joyful Noise* ('66) and continued on Broadway in *How Now, Dow Jones* ('67). After his unique talents were featured in the film **Hello, Dolly!** ('69), Twiggy happened to see him on TV (as a featured regular on "Dean Martin Presents the Golddiggers") and told director Ken Russell about him for his filmization of **The Boy Friend**—in which Tune appeared and choreographed portions of the miles of dance. He returned to Broadway in *Seesaw* (choreographing his own tap routines) and won a Tony Award for his performance. Lovingly recreating the joy of nostalgic dance routines, he has managed to combine his successful director-choreographer career with stage performances (*My One and Only*, *Bye Bye Birdie* ('91 rev) and *Tommy Tune Tonight* ('92–93). He also directed the plays *The Club* ('76) and *Cloud 9* ('81). Winner of the *Dance Magazine* award in 1984, eight Drama Desk awards, two Obies and nine Tony awards for his stage work—the only person to date to have received awards in four different categories. 1994 awards include the Unihealth America Pinnacle award for community service and the Michelangelo Shoe award. He returned to the stage in 1995 starring in *Buskers*.

Stage: *Roberta* (Melody Top, Milwaukee '64), *Canterbury Tales* (OOT '69), *Seesaw* (Bdwy '73, with Michael Bennett and Bob Avian, also appeared), *Hellzapoppin'* (OOT '76, with Donald Saddler), *The Best Little Whorehouse in Texas* (Bdwy '79, Tony nom), *A Day in Hollywood—A Night in the Ukraine* (Bdwy '80, also dir, Tony award for choreo with Thommie Walsh), *Nine* (Bdwy '82, also dir, Tony award for dir, nom for choreo), *My One and Only* (also dir and appeared, Tony award for choreo), *Stepping Out* (Bdwy '87, assisted by Marge Champion, also dir), *Grand Hotel* (Bdwy '89, with Jeff Calhoun, also dir), *Will Rogers Follies* (Bdwy '91, with Calhoun, also dir, 2 Tony awards), *Bye Bye Birdie* ('91 rev tour, also appeared), *The Best Little Whorehouse Goes Public* (Bdwy '94, also co-dir with Calhoun)

TV: "Dean Martin Presents the Golddiggers" ('69–70, assistant to Jonathon Lucas, also appeared) *Nightclub/Concert:* *Gene Kelly's Wonderful World*

of Girls (Las Vegas Hilton, with Jonathon Lucas), *Atop the Village Gate* ('75, also dir and appeared), *Beach Blanket Babylon* (San Francisco '93)

Miscellaneous: Adolph Zukor's 100th Birthday Party at Paramount ('73)

Film:

1971 **The Boy Friend**—MGM (with Christopher Gable, Terry Gilbert, Gillian Lynne)

1991 **Postcards from the Edge**—("I'm Still Here" musical staging for Shirley MacLaine, uncredited)

JANE TURNER

1995 **Goldeneye**—UA

BETTY UTEY

Dancer and actress who appeared in the films **Pal Joey** and **Tarnished Angels** ('57) and **Merry Andrew** and **Party Girl** ('58). At the time of her one film choreographic credit, she was married to the film's director, Nicholas Ray.

Film:

1961 **King of Kings**—MGM ("Salome's Dance")

VALENTINO

b. Alabama

The single-named dancer and choreographer began performing in Alabama as a child before moving to New York. There he attended the High School of Performing Arts, also taking dance classes at the New York School of Ballet and American Ballet Theatre School. After dancing with the Harkness Ballet, he made his acting debut in *The Me Nobody Knows* and an Australian production of *Hair*. His eclectic career includes recording in England, nightclub performances, appearing in *The Wiz* and fashion shows.

Film:

1981 **Body and Soul**—Cannon (with Hope Clarke)

BOBBY VAN

b. New York, 1933

d. Los Angeles, California, July 31, 1980

As the son of Harry King, dance director of *The Ziegfeld Follies of 1937*, young Bobby was surrounded by dance and theater from an early age. He attended the Metropolitan Vocational School of Music and the New York College of Music, making his Broadway debut in *Alive and Kicking* in 1950. He then made his screen debut in **Because You're Mine** ('52), performing "Pagan Love Song." As one of the last song-and-dance players placed under contract to MGM, he appeared in **Skirts Ahoy** ('52), **Small Town Girl**, **Kiss Me Kate** and **The Affairs of Dobie Gillis** ('53). Subsequent film

James Truitte as the title character in ***According to St. Francis***, from *Choreo '54*, a concert by the Horton Dance Theatre in Los Angeles.

roles include **The Navy vs. the Night Monsters** ('66) and **Lost Horizon** ('73). He made a triumphant return to Broadway in *No, No, Nanette* with Ruby Keeler in 1971 and continued onstage in *Dr. Jazz* ('75). Married to dancer-actress Elaine Joyce, he hosted the TV shows "The Fun Factory" ('76) and "Make Me Laugh" ('79) before his premature death from a heart attack. Sylvia Lewis recalled that Van merely "supervised" the musical numbers in **The Ladies' Man**, his one choreographic credit.

Film:
1961 **The Ladies' Man**—Par (with Sylvia Lewis)

JEAN-CLAUDE VAN DAMME (VAN VARENBERG)

b. Brussels, Belgium, October 18, 1960

The "Muscles from Brussels" action film star started studying karate, bodybuilding and ballet at the age of 9 to build up his slight, spindly frame. Winning the Mr. Belgium bodybuilding title at 18 and the European Professional Karate Association middleweight champion the following year, he opened a successful gym in Brussels but his childhood dreams of the movies urged him to go to the United States. He arrived in Hollywood in 1981 determined to become a film star and, after help from action star Chuck Norris and producer Menahem Golan, he began his rise to the top of the highly competitive action star heap. Called "The Astaire of kickboxing flicks" by *Entertainment Weekly*, the small (5'8") but mighty actor has the curious distinction of being the choreographer with the most photographed bare butt in contemporary film—sharing that honor with actor-director Mel Gibson.

Film (All credits are for films he also appeared in):
1988 **Black Eagle**—Taurus (with Sho Kosugi)
 Bloodsport—Cannon
1989 **Cyborg**—Cannon
 Kickboxer—Cannon
1990 **Death Warrant**—MGM
1991 **Double Impact**—Col (also story, prod)
 Lionheart—Univ (with Anthony Van Laast, also screenplay)
1992 **Universal Soldier**—TriStar
1993 **Hard Target**—Univ
 Nowhere to Run—Col
1994 **Street Fighter**—Univ
 Timecop—Univ

PIETER VAN DER SLOOT

Ballet/Dance Pieces: "La Bateau Lore" (West Germany's Tahnz-Theater '85)

Film:
1960 **Legions of the Nile**—Fox
1963 **Hercules Conquers Atlantis** (aka **Hercules and the Captive Women** and **Hercules and the Conquest of Atlantis**)—Golden Era (Fr/Ital)

ANTHONY VAN LAAST

British dancer, director and choreographer who trained at the London Contemporary Dance Theatre School, soon joining the company and beginning his choreographic work. He diversified his career with stage and television credits and the notoriety for his prolific West End Theater work led to film credits and international success. Van Laast is currently artistic director for the Souls in Motion dance company.

Stage: *Song and Dance* ('82, London and Australia), *Blondel* (London '83), *Peter Pan* (London), *Annie Get Your Gun* (London), *The Hired Man* (London '84), *A Little Night Music* (London), *Budgie* (London), *Candide* (London), *Into the Woods* (London '90), *Radio Times* (London '92), *Chess* (revised '92 version for UK tour), *Joseph and the Amazing Technicolor Dreamcoat* ('92 rev, London, Canada, Bdwy), *Hair* ('93 rev, London, Olivier award nom), **Requiem Variations** (Omaha Opera '94); For the Royal Shakespeare Company: *The Maid's Tragedy*, *Peer Gynt*, *The Merry Wives of Windsor*, *Romeo and Juliet*, *A Midsummer Night's Dream*, *The Beggar's Opera*; For the English National Opera: *The Mikado*, *A Midsummer's Marriage*

TV: "The Hot Shoe Show" ('85), "Bluebell," "The Queen Mother's 90th Birthday Gala," "Maria's Child" ('92)

Nightclub/Concert: *EFX* (MGM Grand Hotel, LV '95, also co-dir); acts and shows for Kate Bush, Kid Creole & The Coconuts, Cleo Laine, Elaine Paige, Siegfried & Roy, Wayne Sleep & Dash

Ballet/Dance Pieces: For London Contemporary Dance Theatre: "Outside-In" ('72, with Micha Bergese), "Just Before" ('78)

Film:
1981 **Excalibur**—Orion/WB
 Outland—WB
1982 **The Nutcracker**—Rank
1983 **The Final Option**—MGM/UA
 Never Say Never Again—UA (also appeared)
1987 **Hope and Glory**—Col
1991 **Lionheart**—WB (with Jean-Claude Van Damme)
1994 **Princess Caraboo**—TriStar

JUDY VAN WORMER

Dancer-choreographer who appeared in films

(**Bye Bye Birdie**), television (The Smothers Brothers and Pearl Bailey Shows) and nightclubs (*Youthquake*) during the '60s and '70s.

Film:
1979 **1941**— Univ/Col (with Paul DeRolf)

MARTIN VARGAS (FERNANDO MARTIN CAURIN)

b. Villamarchante, Spain, March 5, 1925
Making his debut as a singer and dancer when he was 14-years old in Valencia, this classic Spanish dancer-choreographer toured Italy and eventually partnered La Argentina on tours throughout South and Central America and successful appearances in New York. Remaining for six years in the United States, he performed classical Spanish dance concerts and was invited to Hollywood to dance and choreograph for films. Returning to Spain, he appeared at Barcelona's Gran Teatro del Liceo and partnered Pilar Lopez. After appearing as premier danseur and serving as ballet master for del Teatro de la Zarzuela for ten years, he joined Ballet Nacional Español, where he was Maestro and choreographer for the troupe. Relocating to Valencia, he currently teaches at Centro de Danza Carmen Lopez and heads Martin Vargas' Ballet de Valencia.
Stage: "La Leyenda del Beso," "Serrano," "50 Años de Recuerdo," "Katiuska," etc.
Film:
1958 **Maracaibo**— Par (also appeared)

NELSON VASQUEZ

1985 **Delivery Boys**— New World (with Jody Oliver, also appeared)

SABRINA VASQUEZ

1993 **Tombstone**— Hollywood Pictures

DAVID VAUGHAN

1955 **Killer's Kiss**— UA

FRANK VELOZ

b. Washington D.C., February 5, 1902
d. Los Angeles, California, February 27, 1981
Renowned ballroom dancer and choreographer who was the male half of Veloz and Yolanda (with the former Yolanda Cassaza), an immensely popular dance team during the 1930s and '40s. The team began in 1927, being named "New York State Dance Champions" after winning forty dance contests. Creating a unique dance act with Veloz choreo-graphing all of their routines, they eventually starred in theaters (*The Love Call, Pleasure Bound*), nightclubs (New York, Chicago, Havana, Miami, Los Angeles), were the first ballroom team to appear in concert at Carnegie Hall ('38) and were also featured in several films. They eventually opened their own club (The Iris in Florida) and a successful chain of dance schools. One of their films, **Cavalcade of the Dance** is a fascinating montage of American social dance. Veloz' film choreography for films he did not appear in are for Latin dances (Beguine, Tango, etc.) for such stars as Ricardo Montalban, George Raft, Lana Turner and Vera Zorina. The couple divorced in 1962, after thirty-four years of marriage. With a son and daughter surviving them, Yolanda died March 24, 1995 at the age of 84.
Film (All choreographic credits except three are for films the dance team appeared in):
1934 **Many Happy Returns**— Par (with George Hale)
1935 **Rumba**— Par (with LeRoy Prinz)
     Under the Pampas Moon— Fox (with Jack Donohue)
1937 **Champagne Waltz**— Par (with Prinz)
1941 **They Met in Argentina**— RKO (choreo only)
1942 **The Pride of the Yankees**— RKO
1943 **Cavalcade of the Dance**— WB (S)
     Honeymoon Lodge— Univ (with Tip, Tap and Toe)
1944 **Brazil**— Rep (with Billy Daniel)
     Follow the Boys— Univ (with Carmen Amaya, Louis DaPron, George Hale, choreo only)
     Hollywood Canteen— WB (with Antonio, Prinz)
1945 **All Star Musical Revue**— WB (S) (numbers deleted from **Hollywood Canteen**)
1946 **Thrill of Brazil**— Col (with Nick Castle, Jack Cole, Eugene Loring, Ann Miller)
1953 **Latin Lovers**— MGM (choreo only)
1974 **Queen of the Stardust Ballroom**— CBS/Tomorrow Ent (TV) (assistant to Marge Champion)

TONY VENTURA

1986 **Ginger and Fred**— MGM/UA (assisted by Isabella Paolucci)

GWEN (GWYNNETH) VERDON

b. Culver City, California, January 13, 1925
Flame-haired American Musical Theater legend who began her dance studies with her mother Gertrude, a Denishawn dancer, while very young

because of being "knock-kneed." She continued her education with Ernest Belcher, Aida Broadbent, Eduardo Cansino and Nenette Charisse in Hollywood. Chosen "Miss California" at the age of 14, she danced with Broadbent's ballet corps in Los Angeles Civic Light Opera and Hollywood Bowl productions in her early teens and appeared briefly in a comedy ballroom team. After a brief marriage, motherhood and a three year interlude from dance, she returned to enhance her dance vocabulary studying with La Meri, Carmelita Maracci and, replacing Carol Haney, she joined Jack Cole's company in nightclubs and onstage: *Bonanza Bound* (OOT '47) and *Alive and Kicking* (Bdwy '50). She had begun her choreographic career as assistant to Cole on *Magdalena* (Bdwy '48) and films — often dancing onscreen, coaching the female stars (Marilyn Monroe once said, "If Gwen can't teach you a routine, you're rhythm bankrupt with incompatible feet") and dubbing taps for Dan Dailey's dance sequences. Between assistant assignments with Cole, she did her solo film choreographic work from 1950–53 ("...she insists that she is not the least bit creative that way. 'I did a sort of spiritual for the film **The Mississippi Gambler**. It was for four boys and me, but one can always protect oneself from criticism by saying it was for camera angles. I get a brilliant dance idea about once in five years.'" *Dance Magazine*, August, 1956). She also assisted Donn Arden on a Lido show in Paris in 1950. After leaving Hollywood and film to create a sensation on Broadway in *Can Can* ('53), she starred in *Damn Yankees, Redhead, New Girl in Town, Sweet Charity* and *Chicago*, all created by husband Bob Fosse for her, becoming the definitive dancing/singing star of American musicals. On March 24, 1963, the Fosse's welcomed a daughter, Nicole, who would go on to a performance career. After her divorce from Fosse, she continued to assist him on the film version of **Sweet Charity**, staging the second company of *Chicago*, serving as dance mistress on *Dancin'* ('78) and appearing in films and TV shows (**Cocoon, Cocoon 2, The Cotton Club, Legs, Nadine**, etc.). Recipient of the Donaldson, Grammy, *Dance Magazine* ('61) and four Tony awards for her stage performances: *Can Can* ('54), *Damn Yankees* ('56 — luckily preserved on film), *New Girl in Town* ('58) and *Redhead* ('59), Verdon also has the distinction of being the quintessential exponent of two of America's most brilliant choreographer's (Cole and Fosse) work.

Stage: As assistant to Jack Cole: *Magdalena* (Bdwy '48) *Alive and Kicking* (Bdwy '50); *Dancin'* (asst to Bob Fosse)

Film:
1951 **David and Bathsheba**— Fox (assistant to Jack Cole — also appeared)

Meet Me After the Show— Fox (assistant to Cole, also appeared)

On the Riviera— Fox (assistant to Jack Cole, also appeared)

1952 **Dreamboat**— Fox (uncredited — also appeared)

The Merry Widow— MGM (assistant to Cole, also appeared)

1953 **The Farmer Takes a Wife**— Fox (assistant to Cole, also appeared)

Gentlemen Prefer Blondes— Fox (assistant to Cole)

The Mississippi Gambler— Univ (also appeared)

1969 **Sweet Charity**— Univ (assistant to Bob Fosse, Shirley MacLaine's coach)

1985 **Cocoon**— Fox (with Caprice Roth, also appeared)

LARRY VICKERS
Dancer-choreographer who appeared on Broadway in *Purlie* ('69). Moving to Europe, he choreographed for French cabaret revues, with his work being filmed in **Bolero**. Returning to the U.S., he assisted Lester Wilson on *Grind* ('84) and appeared in Shirley MacLaine's nightclub act.

Nightclub/Concert: *Femmes, Femmes, Femmes* (Moulin Rogue, Paris '83)

Film:
1980 **Loving Couples**— Fox
1982 **Bolero** (aka **Les Uns et les Autres**)— Double 13 (with Maurice Béjart, Nicole Daresco, Rick Odums, Micha Van Joecke)

RENEE VICTOR
1991 **Kiss Me a Killer**— Califilm
1995 **Neon Bible**— Artificial Eye/Mayfair (GB)

JELON VIEIRA
Afro-Brazilian, jazz and modern dancer and teacher currently in New York. Capoeira (Brazilian combat dance) specialist.

Film
1989 **Rooftops**— New Visions (with John Carrafa, "Capoeira choreography by" credit, assisted by Byron Easley)

OSCAR VILLELA
1995 **Boys on the Side**— WB (with Ruben Moreno, "Ballet Folkloric Azteca" credit)

NORMA VIOLA
1988 **Tango Bar**— Castle Hill (with Nelson Avila, Santiago Ayala, Lilliana Belfiore, Doris Petroni, Carlos Rivarola, Nelida Rodriguez)

Publicity pose of Martin Vargas, circa 1965.

ADRIANO VITALE

1961 **The Pharaoh's Woman**— Univ

DARIA VOBORNIKOVA

1994 **Faust**— Heart of Europe Prague K Prod

ROBERT (RICHARD) VREE-LAND

b. 1909

d. Los Angeles, California, October 12, 1969

After a performance career and several film choreographic credits, Vreeland became a unit production manager and assistant director on many films.

Frank Veloz and Yolanda in a 1948 publicity still.

He served as chairman of the Director's Guild of America council.

Film:

1937 **Melody for Two**—WB (with Bobby Connolly)

1940 **City for Conquest**—WB

1941 **Footsteps in the Dark**—WB

TAUNIE VRENON

1987 **Necropolis**—Empire

PHILIPPA WAITE

1991 **Rebecca's Daughters**—Mayfair Ent/Palace Pictures (with Lucy Fawcett)

KIM WALKER

1995 **Billy's Holiday**—Miramax

MARGUERITE (AKA MARGARET & MARGHERITA) WALLMAN

b. Vienna, Austria, July 22, 1904

d. Monte Carlo, May 2, 1992

Ballet mistress and opera director who began her career as a dancer with the Diaghilev Ballets Russes and ballet mistress of the Vienna State Opera Ballet until 1926. She turned to modern dance, studying with Mary Wigman, eventually founding and directing Wigman's Berlin school. From 1929–32

Gwen Verdon, surrounded by Bob Fosse memorabilia, hosts "Bob Fosse: Steam Heat," a PBS presentation on "Dance in America," 1990.

she taught in New York, formed her own company (Dancegroup 1930), became dance director at the Salzburg Festival and then worked in Hollywood briefly for MGM. Because of World War II she fled Europe and was ballet mistress at Teatro Colon in Buenos Aires. Named choreographer for the Teatro alla Scala, Milan in 1952, she became a renowned international stager of opera, including the Metropolitan Opera in New York (1964–66). She retired to Monte Carlo in the 1970s to write her memoirs. The various spellings of her first name are a result of her international work.

Ballet/Dance Pieces: "Legend of Joseph" (Teatro alla Scala)

Film:

1935 **Anna Karenina**—MGM (with Ernest Belcher, Chester Hale — the Moscow Opera Ballet scene)

1948 **Where Words Fail** (aka **Donde Mueren Las Palabras**)—Argentina

1950 **The Little Woman of the Moulin Rouge**—(Ital)

1954 **Aida**—Oscar/EF

1958 **Beautiful But Dangerous**—Fox

ARTHUR WALSH

Actor, dancer and choreographer who appeared in twenty-two films from **Blonde Fever** in 1944 to **Battle Cry** in 1959.

Film:

1945 **Twice Blessed**—MGM

CHARLES WALTERS

b. Pasadena, California, November 17, 1911

d. Malibu, California, August 13, 1982

"I'll never understand why more choreographers haven't made it as directors; after all, dialogue is movement and rhythm" said this dancer-choreographer who successfully made the transition to director — creating some of Hollywood's most memorable musical films. When he finished high school he decided to become a dancer and worked in local night clubs. While in the cast of a Pasadena production of *Lo and Behold* he was told by producer Leonard Sillman that "if he ever came to New York," Sillman would hire him. After touring with partner Dorothy Fox (Fox & Walters) in a Fanchon and Marco vaudeville unit, he arrived in New York where Sillman cast him in *New Faces of 1934*. Other Broadway appearances include *Fools Rush In* ('34),

Jubilee and *Hit Parade* ('35), *The Show Is On* ('36), *Between the Devil* ('37) and *I Married an Angel* ('38). Seen at the Versailles Club in New York by Robert Alton, he was encouraged by Alton, finally gaining notice co-starring with Betty Grable in Alton's *DuBarry Was a Lady* ('39). When Seymour Felix's work was unacceptable to Gene Kelly in the film version of **Dubarry**—and Alton was unavailable—Kelly hired Walters to stage one number in the film. "I think I'm the only dance director who ever read a script to find out what the characters were all about," Walters stated, as he successfully staged the number and then was hired to redo all of Felix's work. Walters stated that the first number he staged and directed the camera for was "The Brazilian Boogie" in **Broadway Rhythm** ('44). Promoted by producer Arthur Freed, he eventually evolved into an acclaimed director of MGM musical films (**Easter Parade, Lili, Billy Rose's Jumbo, Good News, The Unsinkable Molly Brown, The Barkleys of Broadway, Summer Stock, The Glass Slipper** and **High Society**) and continued to stage the musical sequences in his films ("I have always done the 'stars' numbers—the so-called 'intimate book' numbers.") It is acknowledged that Walters had the rare ability to choreograph for the camera as well as for the dancers.

Stage: Sing Out the News (Bdwy '38), *She Had to Say Yes* (OOT '40, also appeared), *Banjo Eyes* (Bdwy '41, dir only), *Let's Face It* (Bdwy '41, also dir), *St. Louis Woman* (Bdwy '46)

Film:

1942 **Seven Days Leave**—RKO

1943 **Best Foot Forward**—MGM (with J. M. Andrew, Stanley Donen and Jack Donohue)

Dubarry Was a Lady—MGM (with Gene Kelly)

Girl Crazy—MGM (with Busby Berkeley, Donohue, also appeared)

Presenting Lily Mars—MGM (with Ernst Matray, also appeared, partnering Judy Garland)

1944 **Broadway Rhythm**—MGM (with Robert Alton, Donohue, Don Loper, George Murphy)

Meet Me in St. Louis—MGM

Meet the People—MGM (with Donohue, Sammy Lee)

Since You Went Away—UA (with Marty Grail)

Three Men in White—MGM

1945 **Abbott and Costello in Hollywood**—MGM (also appeared)

Her Highness and the Bellboy—MGM

Thrill of a Romance—MGM

Weekend at the Waldorf—MGM

1946 **The Harvey Girls**—MGM (with Alton, Ray Bolger)

Ziegfeld Follies—MGM (with Alton, Fred Astaire, Gene Kelly, staged "Madame Crematon," the Judy Garland sequence)

1947 **Good News**—MGM (with Alton, also dir)

1948 **Summer Holiday**—MGM

1950 **Summer Stock**—MGM (with Nick Castle, Gene Kelly, staged "Get Happy" after Castle went on to other work, also dir)

1953 **Dangerous When Wet**—MGM (with Billy Daniel, also dir)

Lili—MGM (assisted by Dorothy Jarnac, also dir and appeared)

Torch Song—MGM (with Eugene Loring, also dir and appeared, partnering Joan Crawford)

1956 **High Society**—MGM (also dir)

1964 **The Unsinkable Molly Brown**—MGM (with Peter Gennaro, also dir)

1974 **That's Entertainment!**—MGM (with others)

1976 **That's Entertainment Part II**—MGM (with others)

1985 **That's Dancing!**—MGM (with others)

1994 **That's Entertainment! III**—MGM (with others)

RANDY WANDER

1993 **Boiling Point**—String of Pearls Prod Inc

WAYNE "CRESCENDO" WARD

Dancer-choreographer whose film appearances include **Naked Gun 33 1/3—The Final Insult** ('93).

TV: "In Living Color" (pilot), Diana Ross special

Nightclub/Concert: Sammy Davis Jr. (Harrah's Tahoe, also dir), The Pointer Sisters ('87–90 tours)

Film:

1989 **Earth Girls Are Easy**—Vestron (with Russell Clark, Sarah Elgart, ISO—"Co-choreographer" credit for "Deca Dance," also appeared)

1991 **The Five Heartbeats**—Fox (assistant to Michael Peters)

TAM G. (GREENOUGH) WARNER

b. Los Angeles, California, October 12, 1950

When she would return in tears from failed auditions as a young dancer, her father "...who was an astrologist, always said; 'You know, I'm telling you. Your career is going to be on the other side of the table.'" She first studied dance with San Mann, at

Director/choreographer Charles Walters partners Joan Crawford onscreen in **Torch Song** (MGM, 1953).

Burch Mann's School in Alhambra until the age of 16. She then studied ballet with Evelyn LeMone and made her professional debut on a TV special that Jaime Rogers choreographed (in the classic tale of "Taking-a-friend-to-an-audition:" "I got it, My friend didn't.") She danced on TV (a Jim Nabors special, etc.) and live stage work (Mark Wilson's and David Copperfield's magic shows, industrials, etc.) and got her first chance to assist choreographer

Tad Tadlock on a Mark Wilson show because ("Mark suggested me because I knew the magic stuff.") Her staging-direction work has been in constant demand for live venues and to date she has two film credits: **Evil Dead 2** ("I did the 'Headless Corpse Dance,' which became an animated sequence") and **Mr. Saturday Night** ("Lester Wilson couldn't do two scenes, so he suggested me"). She cites Tad Tadlock ("She taught me alot about basic staging") and Disney's Barnette Ricci as major influences in her career. "It's interesting that two women realized my potential and gave me a chance to learn and grow with them."

Stage: West Coast productions of *Damn Yankees*, *Finian's Rainbow*, *L'il Abner* and *Once Upon a Mattress*

TV: "Children of China," "Magic of China," "Hocus Pocus" and "Mumbo Jumbo" (HBO), Superbowl XXI

Nightclub/Concert: Shows for Princess Cruises, *American Oldies*

Miscellaneous: Disneyland: *Fantasy on Parade*, *Main Street Electrical Parade*, *Circus Fantasy*, etc. and Lotte World (Seoul, Korea), **Pocahontas** Premiere (NY '95); industrials for Best Western, Daihatsu, Disney Home Video, Mattel, Pepsi, 7-Up, etc.

Film:
1987 **Evil Dead 2: Dead by Dawn** — Rosebud Releasing Corp.(with Andrea Brown, Susan Labatt)
1992 **Mr. Saturday Night** — Col (with Lester Wilson, uncredited)

SHEILA WARTSKI
South African dancer-choreographer.
1965 **Dingaka** — Embassy
     Kimberley Jim — Embassy

TEXI WATERMAN
Choreographer for the Dallas Cowboys Cheerleaders.
Film:
1979 **Dallas Cowboys Cheerleaders** — ABC/Aubrey-Hammer Prod (TV) (also appeared as herself)
1980 **Dallas Cowboys Cheerleaders II** — ABC/Aubrey-Hammer Prod

BOBBY WATSON
1970 **Brotherly Love** — MGM

CATHY CARTHERS WAYNE
1990 **Two Evil Eyes** — (Ital)

DENNIS WAYNE (WENDELKEN)
b. St. Petersburg, Florida, July 19, 1945
Charismatic dancer-choreographer who was called in 1983: "That 'bad lad of ballet' with the beach-boy good looks and romantic reputation to match" has had a truly dramatic life and career. At the age of 3 he debuted in his family's acrobatic vaudeville act (Taffy, Terry and Trio) and won the 1963 Best Dancer award while attending New York's High School of Performing Arts. He made his dance debut in 1962 with the Norman Walker Company and danced with the Harkness Ballet ('63) and Joffrey ('70). In 1972, he and dancer Bonnie Mathis were savagely attacked by an intruder and after recovery, he formed American Ballet Company in 1973. Joining American Ballet Theatre as a soloist, he also appeared in the films **Summer Wishes, Winter Dreams** ('73) and **In the Beginning** ('74). He resigned from ABT in 1975 to form his own company, Dancers, with funding help and support from Joanne Woodward. On March 25, 1980, while appearing in Paris with the company, he was in a serious automobile accident, injuring his back and hip. Miraculously, he opened a dance school the next year and by 1983 was dancing again, forming Dennis Wayne Dancers. At the time of their New York debut, he stated "...I believe if you have a gift from God to dance, it's sacrilegious not to... Dance has often alienated people, because it's 'cultural.' I believe dance is about communication. And I want to break a barrier. I want people to laugh. There is not enough laughter."

Ballet/Dance Pieces:(Partial listing) "Andante," "Just Another Dance"

Film:
1973 **Summer Wishes, Winter Dreams** — Col (also appeared)
1983 **Echoes** — Continental (also appeared)

BOBBY WELLS
1988 **A Night in the Life of Jimmy Reardon** — Fox

STEFAN WENTA
Although his film credits do not reflect the seriousness of his dance career, Wenta was premier danseur and choreographer for Warsaw's Great Opera and Ballet Theatre, co-founder of Le Ballet European with Léonide Massine and artistic director of the Los Angeles Western Ballet. He taught at George Zoritch's school in Hollywood and formed the Wenta Ballet in 1970.

Ballet/Dance Pieces: "Roumanian Rhapsody #1" ('68), "7 Trumps for the Tarot Cards," "Alice in Wonderland," "Behind the Beauty Mask"

Film:
1967 **In Like Flint** — Fox
1976 **Logan's Run** — MGM

ELIZABETH WEST
1958 **Inbetween Age** — AA

AL WHITE, JR.

b. 1878

d. January 7, 1957

Tap specialist who assisted Georgie Hale on the 1936 Broadway production of *Red, Hot and Blue* before going on to a solo stage career. His film work was primarily as assistant to LeRoy Prinz and dance coach at Warner Bros. during the early 1950s.

Stage: *Salute to Spring* (St. Louis Muny '37, with Theodore Adolphus), *Gentleman Unafraid* (St. Louis Muny '38), *Nice Goin'* (OOT '39), *Star and Garter* (Bdwy '42), *A Connecticut Yankee* (Bdwy '43 rev, with William Holbrook), *Memphis Bound* (Bdwy '45), *Texas Li'l Darlin'* (Bdwy '49)

Nightclub/Concert: *Hello Beautiful* (International Casino NY '39)

Film:

1950 **Tea for Two**— WB (with Eddie & LeRoy Prinz, Gene & Miriam Nelson, "Dances Staged By" credit

   West Point Story— WB (with Johnny Boyle, Gene Nelson, Eddie Prinz, LeRoy Prinz)

1951 **The Lullaby of Broadway**— WB (with Nelson, Eddie and LeRoy Prinz)

1952 **Sound Off**— Col

   Stars and Stripes Forever— Fox (with Nick Castle, Stephen Papich)

MARC WHITE

b. Barbados, West Indies

Born in the West Indies, he emigrated to Australia at the age of 5, where he began classical ballet classes. Adding jazz and contemporary dancer to his repertoire, at 19 he was accepted by the New Zealand School of Dance. For six years, he toured with Limbs Dance Company internationally and formed his own jazz dance company, Full of Piranhas in Wellington. Appearing in the hit stage show, *Ladies Night*, he relocated to Sydney, Australia, to begin teaching and choreographing. Given the challenge of creating musical numbers for three non-dancing actors wearing high heels for the first time, Marc White planted himself firmly on the Dance on Film map with his work on **The Adventures of Priscilla, Queen of the Desert**, his first commercial film credit.

Stage: *Cats, Mardi Gras*

Miscellaneous: The Diva Awards

Film:

1994 **The Adventures of Priscilla, Queen of the Desert**— Polygram Filmed Ent (*LA Dance* award nom)

ONNA WHITE

b. Powell River, British Columbia, Canada, March 24, 1922

Broadway choreographer who transferred her tal-ents to film — creating some of the finest musical numbers at the end of the Golden Age of the Movie Musical and receiving a special Academy Award in 1968 for **Oliver!** Moving from Canada to the United States in 1939, she began studying with Harold, Lew and William Christensen and started her career as a dancer with the San Francisco Ballet, dancing all of the classical leads ("What used to kill me was that I was always the Swan Queen or something, when I wanted to do the sexy parts.") She made her Broadway debut in *Finian's Rainbow* in 1947 ("You know, after all those **Swan Lakes**, I'd never been so happy in my life! I adored it — just to be able to let myself go!") and also danced in *Hold It!* ('48), *Regina* ('49) *Arms and the Girl* ('50) and *Silk Stockings* ('55). She began her choreographic career assisting Michael Kidd while also dancing in *Guys and Dolls* ('50) and then recreating his original work in New York City Center and Las Vegas productions of *Guys and Dolls* and *Finian's Rainbow*. "Sometimes I couldn't remember what Mike had done, so I had to make up things myself, and I suppose this was my first choreography. Also, during the same time, I broke my foot, and I've never danced since, thank God. The next year, City Center asked me to stage *Carmen Jones* on my own. Joshua Logan saw it and flipped, and before I knew it, I was off to London to stage the dances for *Fanny*. After that came *Music Man*" (*Dance Magazine*, March, 1967). Her innovative stage choreography led her to films. Nominated eight times for Tony awards, she received the *Drama-Logue* Award for *A Little Night Music* and the Gypsy Lifetime Achievement Award from the Professional Dancer's Society in 1991.

Stage: *Guys and Dolls* and *Finian's Rainbow* (recreating Michael Kidd's work, LV and NYC Center '55), *Carmen Jones* (NYC Center) and *Fanny* (London '56), *The Music Man* (Bdwy '57, Tony nom), *Whoop-Up* (Bdwy '58, Tony nom), *Take Me Along* (Bdwy '59, Tony nom), *Irma La Douce* (Bdwy '60, Tony nom), *Let It Ride* (Bdwy '61), *Hot Spot* (Bdwy '63), *I Had a Ball* (Bdwy '64), *Fanny* (London & NYC Center '65 rev), *Half a Sixpence* (Bdwy '65, Tony nom), *Mame* (Bdwy '66, Tony nom), *Ilya Darling* (Bdwy '67, Tony nom), *A Mother's Kisses* (OOT '68), *1776* (Bdwy '69), *Gantry* (Bdwy '70, also dir), *70 Girls, 70* (Bdwy '71), *Gigi* (Bdwy '73), *Billy* (London '74), *Goodtime Charley* (Bdwy '75), *I Love My Wife* (Bdwy '77, Tony nom), *Working* (Bdwy '78), *Home Again, Home Again* (OOT '79), *Charlie Girl* (London '86), *A Little Night Music* (LA '90 rev), *Sweet, Smart Rodgers and Hart* (LA '93)

TV: "Hansel and Gretel"

Nightclub/Concert: acts for Vivian Blaine, Ginger Rogers, Gretchen Wyler

Miscellaneous: *Disney on Parade* and *The Wizard of Oz* (Touring Arena Shows)

Mary Costa watches Onna White as she demonstrates a step during rehearsals for **The Great Waltz** (MGM, 1972).

Film:
1962 **The Music Man**— WB (assisted by Tom Panko)
1963 **Bye Bye Birdie**— Col
1968 **Oliver!**— Col (with Panko, Honorary Academy Award for"Outstanding Achievement in Choreography")
1972 **The Great Waltz**— MGM
  1776— WB
1974 **Mame**— WB (assisted by Martin Allen)
1977 **Pete's Dragon**— Disney (with associate Martin Allen, assisted by Alice Clift, Pat Cummins, Fred Curt, Jerry Trent)

MARC WILDER

b. Italy, 1933
d. Los Angeles, California, April 18, 1983
Described by the *Hollywood Reporter* as "one of the best dance partners for female dancers in the history of the film musical" this handsome dancer-choreographer was featured with Mitzi Gaynor and Matt Mattox in **The "I Don't Care" Girl** ('53), and partnered Cyd Charisse in the *Sleeping Beauty* bal-

let in **Meet Me in Las Vegas** ('56) and Shirley MacLaine in the *Adam and Eve* ballet in **Can Can** ('60). Coming to America from Italy at the age of seven, he began his dance training studying tap in Hollywood with Ethel Meglin (of The Meglin Kiddies fame) at the age of 10. He then studied ballet with Eugene Loring at the American School of Dance at 18. Stage appearances include on Broadway in *Kismet* ('53) and *Vintage '60*, in the LACLO productions of *The Chocolate Soldier* and *Rose Marie* ('50) and *Zenda* ('63) and the La Jolla Playhouse 1956 revival of *Pal Joey*. Making his film debut in **With a Song in My Heart** ('51) he danced in over twenty-five films (**Gentlemen Prefer Blondes, The Best Things in Life Are Free, The Opposite Sex, State Fair, Houseboat, The Tender Trap, Second Chance, Frankie and Johnny, When the Boys Meet the Girls**, etc.) with his last film appearance in **Mame** ('72). He also appeared on all of the major musical variety television shows during the 1950s–60s (Glen Campbell, George Gobel, Bob Hope, Dinah Shore and Andy Williams) and the Fred Astaire specials. Wilder's choreographic credits include assisting Gene Kelly on a 1959 TV

Kenny Williams guides Barbara Stanwyck through her musical moves for **All I Desire** (Universal, 1953) (photo courtesy of Dick De Neut).

special and Jack Cole on the '62 revival of *Kismet*. Despite all of his contributions to dance on film, this gentle, upbeat and well-loved man is instead remembered as one of the first entertainment industry AIDS casualties.

    Stage: *Seventeen* (Hollywood '56), *Bye Bye Birdie* (Santa Rosa, Calif '63)
    Film:
1969 **The April Fools**—National General

ANITA WILLIAMS
1992 **Pure Country**—WB ("Line dance choreography by" credit)

KENNY WILLIAMS
    Dancer, choreographer and assistant director who started his career appearing in films: **Fifth Avenue Girl** ('39), **Irish Eyes Are Smiling** ('44), **Diamond Horseshoe** ('45), **When My Baby Smiles at Me** ('48) and **Slattery's Hurricane** ('49). Beginning as a dance director at Twentieth Century–Fox during the 1940s, he collaborated on multiple projects with Dan Dailey. When Dailey's Fox contract ended and he began making films for Universal, Williams went with him and from 1951–65, he was head of Universal's dance department, giving classes to all of their contract players as well as creating the choreography for many of their films.

TV: "Burlesque," multiple commercials during the 1960s.

Film:

1943 **Wintertime**— Fox (with Fanchon, James Gonzalez, Carlos Romero)

1944 **The Lodger**— Fox

1945 **Doll Face**— Fox

1946 **If I'm Lucky**— Fox

1947 **Mother Wore Tights**— Fox (with Seymour Felix, also appeared)

1948 **Fort Apache**— RKO

When My Baby Smiles at Me— Fox (with Felix)

You Were Meant for Me— Fox (with Les Clark, also appeared)

1950 **A Ticket to Tomahawk**— Fox (with Jennifer Hatfield)

When Willie Comes Marching Home— Fox (also appeared)

1952 **Meet Me at the Fair**— Univ (also lyricist)

1953 **Abbott and Costello Meet Dr. Jekyll and Mr. Hyde**— Univ

All I Desire— Univ

1954 **Destry**— Univ (assisted by Sylvia Lewis)

The Glenn Miller Story— Univ (with Archie Savage)

Magnificent Obsession— Univ

Naked Alibi— Univ

Sign of the Pagan— Univ (assisted by Isabel Mirrow)

1955 **Ain't Misbehavin'**— Univ (with Lee Scott)

Cult of the Cobra— Univ

Pete Kelly's Blues— WB

1956 **The Mole People**— Univ (with James Truitte)

Tammy and the Bachelor— Univ (with Peggy Carroll)

1957 **Kelly and Me**— Univ

Man of a Thousand Faces— Univ (assisted by Bill Chatham)

1958 **Appointment with a Shadow**— Univ

The Big Beat— Univ

Once Upon a Horse— Univ

1965 **The War Lord**— Univ

LOYD WILLIAMSON

1985 **Maria's Lovers**— Cannon

LOU WILLS, JR. (SHERMAN CHARLES BIENER)

b. Yonkers, New York, December 26, 1927

Acrobatic tap dancer, actor, choreographer, producer and director who started his career with a sensational Broadway debut at 14-years old in *Best Foot Forward* in 1941. Changing his professional

name to mirror mentor and teacher Lou Wills, he also studied dance with Sammy Burns, Madame Alexandra Fedorova, Tommy Hyde, John Mattison, Johnny Sager and Charlotte Steinberg. He continued on Broadway in *One Touch of Venus* and *Something for the Boys* ('43), *Laffing Room Only* ('44), *Are You with It?* ('45), *Make Mine Manhattan* ('48), *A Tree Grows in Brooklyn* ('51) and *Lovely Ladies, Kind Gentlemen* ('70). Starring in his own highly successful nightclub act, Wills toured the major nightclubs in America for decades as well as appearing in films, and on television ("Dancing Is a Man's Game," "Mr. Merlin," "Hank," "Married: With Children," "Roseanne," etc.). His choreography and dance coaching for Robin Williams on the "Mork and Mindy" TV series led to doing the same for Williams on the film *Popeye*. As an associate producer and producer on television projects, his work has won Emmy nominations and awards. His resumé mentions a "Ph.D. in Schtick and Hobnobbery" and he lists Sammy Burns, Gene and Fred Kelly and Lou Wills, Sr. as major influences in his life and career.

Stage: Top Banana, The Pajama Game and Funny Girl tours, Wish You Were Here (St. Louis)

TV: "We Opened in New Haven" (Showtime), "The Erotica Roast," "Mork and Mindy," "Four Stars for Showtime," "Dinah," "Wide World of Entertainment"; commercials for Bab-O, Beauty Rest Mattress, Milton Bradley Toys, Silva Krim, Speedy Muffler and Studebaker-Lark (also dir)

Nightclub/Concert: Anatomy of Burlesque, The Ken Murray Show (Riviera Hotel, LV '59, also appeared); acts for Milton Berle, Michael Callan, Jan Rado and Connie Stevens, as well as his own act.

Film:

1947 **My Wild Irish Rose**— WB (with the Berry Bros., LeRoy Prinz, created own acrobatic tap routine)

1980 **Popeye**— Par (with Hovey Burgess, Sharon Kinney)

1982 **Cannery Row**— MGM

BILLY (WILLIAM ADOLPHUS) WILSON

b. Philadelphia, Pennsylvania, April 21, 1935

d. New York, New York, August 14, 1994

When asked why he became a choreographer, Wilson answered: "Even as a child it seemed to extend naturally from my dancing, like a line extending and broadening." He had begun his stage career at the age of 7 in Philadelphia and made his professional stage debut at 17 at Club Harlem in Philadelphia. He gained his dance education at the Sidney King School of Dance and with Anthony

Tudor at the Philadelphia Ballet Guild, while also attending Pierce Business College and Temple University. When he moved to New York in his teens, he studied with Karel Shook and at the Katherine Dunham School. He made his New York debut in the 1956 City Center production of *Carmen Jones* and appeared on Broadway in *Bells Are Ringing* (1956–57) and *Jamaica* ('57) and went to London that year with *West Side Story*. In Europe, he became a soloist for the National Ballet of Holland (1958–64), and was loaned to a London revue *New Cranks*. In Holland he appeared on TV and was featured on stage in *Kiss Me Kate*. He remained in Europe for ten years, creating ballets and working in all mediums. After returning to America, he headed the dance departments at Brandeis University and the National Center for Afro-American Artists. He also directed several "Hasty Pudding" shows at Harvard. Listed in *Who's Who Among Black Americans*, he was associate professor at Carnegie-Mellon University, School of Drama and Fine Arts. He listed among his inspirations Tad Johnson and Mildred Holloway of Philadelphia public schools, Sonia Gaskell, Serge Lifar, Karel Shook, Anthony Tudor and his two children, Alexis and Parker.

Stage: Odyssey (Bdwy '74), *Bubbling Brown Sugar* (Bdwy '75, Tony nom), *Guys and Dolls* (Bdwy '76 rev, also dir), *Eubie* (Bdwy '78, with Henry LeTang), *Stop the World I Want to Get Off* (Bdwy '78 rev), *Merlin* (with Christopher Chadman) and *Dance a Little Closer* (Bdwy '83), *Josephine* (Europe '91, also dir), *The Cotton Club* (London '91, also dir), *Dancin' in the Streets* (Boston)

TV: "Zoom" ('69–73), "Blues and Gone" ('81), Alka Seltzer commercial with Sammy Davis, Jr.

Ballet/Dance Pieces: "Concerto in F" (Alvin Ailey Co.), "Joplinesque," "Phoenix Rising," "Black Light," "Lizt," "I Told Jesus," "Mirage," "Lullaby for a Jazz Baby" ('82), "Rosa" (Capitol Ballet, Washington D.C.), "Opus One," "Ginastera" (Dance Theater of Harlem), "The Winter in Lisbon" ('92, Alvin Ailey Co.)

Nightclub/Concert: Acts for Cab Calloway, Nell Carter, Billy Daniels, Sergio Franchi

Film:
1978 **Stop the World — I Want to Get Off** (aka **Sammy Stops the World**) — Spec Event Ent

LESTER WILSON
b. April 13, 1942
d. Los Angeles, February 14, 1993

Dancer, choreographer and teacher who was among the most creative and beloved of contemporary film choreographers. He graduated from Jamaica, N.Y. High School and was a psychology major at New York City College when he took his first dance class — which changed his life. After win-

ning a scholarship to Juilliard he studied with Lucas Hoving, Mary Hinkson and Donald McKayle and also at Martha Graham's school. While dancing at the African Room nightclub in New York he was noticed by Bob Fosse (a man he credited as a mentor and inspiration) who cast him in a Lincoln Center revival of *Pal Joey*. He appeared on Broadway in *Golden Boy* and *Anyone Can Whistle* ('64), danced in *Hellzapoppin'* at the 1967 Montreal Expo and was a member of the Alvin Ailey, Donald McKayle and Talley Beatty dance companies. After touring Europe with Sammy Davis, Jr. he remained there, dancing at the Olympia in Paris ('68), choreographing and staging shows in Munich, Berlin and Vienna, becoming a pop recording and TV star and being the first American to win the German equivalent of an Emmy Award for his television work. He returned to America in the early '70s, where he remained — appearing on Broadway in *Me and Bessie* ('75) and eventually settling on the West Coast to choreograph and direct in all entertainment mediums. Among the awards he received are multiple Emmy nominations for his TV work. Broadwayites were certain he would have been nominated for a Tony award for his work on *Grind* in 1985 — a year that the award category was eliminated by the Tony committee, angering the theatre/dance community. His last work was direction of a "Tribute to Peter Allen" a week before his sudden death from a heart attack. A scholarship for promising young dancers has been created in Wilson's name by the Choreographers Resourcenter.

Stage: Golden Boy (London), *Jesus Christ Superstar!* (Berlin), *Promises, Promises* (Vienna), *Harlem Rhythm* (Australia, also dir), *$600 and a Mule* (LA '73, also dir), *Me and Bessie* (Bdwy '75, also appeared), *Three Musketeers* (Bdwy '84 rev), *Grind* (Bdwy '85), *George and Ira Gershwin: A Musical Tribute* (LA '93)

TV: Specials for himself (Europe), George Burns, Lynda Carter, Sammy Davis, Jr., Olivia Newton-John and Marie Osmond; "Sabato Sera" (Italian TV '66), Motown's 25th (Emmy nom) & 30th Anniversary Shows, "Lola Falana: Lola!" ('75, Emmy nom), "Van Dyke and Company" ('76), "Comic Relief," "Diana Ross' Red Hot Rhythm and Blues," "The Redd Foxx Comedy Hour" ('77–78), "Uptown: A Musical Comedy History of the Apollo Theater" ('79), "Ebony, Ivory and Jade" ('79), "Lily Tomlin for President," "The Smothers Brothers Comedy Hour," "Saturday Night Live," "60 Years of Seduction" ('81, Emmy nom), Emmy Awards ('81,'90,'92), "Solid Gold" ('87–88), "America's Dance Honors" ('91, Emmy nom)

Music Videos: "It's Over Now" — Luther Vandross; "Dirty Looks" — Diana Ross; "Hold Me, Squeeze Me" — Ann-Margret

Nightclub/Concert: Acts for Ann-Margret (15

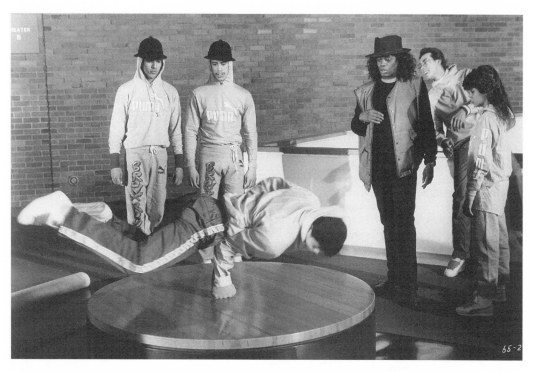

Lester Wilson (at right, wearing the hat) watches his young street dancers try out various Breakdance combinations for **Beat Street** (Orion, 1984).

years), Vicki Carr, Sammy Davis Jr., Lola Falana, Redd Foxx, Aretha Franklin, Johnny Holliday (Paris), Thelma Houston, Gladys Knight & The Pips, Marilyn McCoo, Julia Migenes (Paris), Liza Minnelli (Paris), Rita Moreno, Bonnie Pointer, Luther Vandross, Pia Zadora

Film:

1975 **Funny Lady**—Col (assistant to Herbert Ross)

1976 **Sparkle**—WB

1977 **Saturday Night Fever**—Par (with Jeff Kutash, Jo Jo Smith, Deney Terrio)

1984 **Beat Street**—Orion

1985 **The Last Dragon**—TriStar (with Torrance Mathis, Ernie Reyes, Ron Van Clief)

1986 **The Men's Club**—Atlantic

1988 **Scrooged**—Par

1991 **Hot Shots**—Fox (assisted by Rick Rozzini)

1992 **Mr. Saturday Night**—Col (with Tam G. Warner)

Sister Act—Touchstone (with Lisa Mordente)

1993 **Breakin' Through**—Disney

Fatal Instinct—MGM

Hot Shots—Part Deux—Fox

Made in America—WB (assisted by Rick Rozzini and Richard Montoya, "In loving memory of" credit, *LA Dance* award nom)

ROBIN WINBOW

1971 **Puppet on a Chain**—Cinerama

DALLACE WINKLER

Dancer who appeared in the made-for-TV film **Copacabana** ('85) and worked frequently as assistant to Jeff Kutash.

Film:

1986 **Knights of the City**—New World (with Jeff Kutash, also appeared)

DOMINI WINTER

1986 **Sky Bandits**—Galaxy Intl

DAVID WINTERS (WEIZER)

b. London, April 5, 1939

"Discovered at the age of 12 by a CBS talent scout while singing in a Hungarian restaurant," this dancer, actor, choreographer, teacher, director and producer was one of the most influential choreographers of the 1960s in films and television. Born in London, he moved with his family to Canada in 1947 and finally to New York in 1954, where he began dance lessons. He danced as a youngster on Broadway in *On Your Toes* ('54), *Shinbone Alley,*

One More River, West Side Story and *Gypsy* ('59) and Off-Broadway in *Sandhog, Sing to Me Through an Open Window* and *Half-Past Wednesday* ('61), simultaneously acting on most of the major television shows in New York at the time. He went to Hollywood to make the film version of **West Side Story** ('61, as "Arab"), became interested in films and television and started teaching jazz classes and choreographing for the rock-oriented film stars. He continued performing with acting roles in **Roogie's Bump** ('54), **Rock, Rock, Rock** ('56), **The Last Angry Man** ('59), **Captain Newman M.D.** ('63) and **The New Interns** ('64). With assistants Toni Basil and Anita Mann, Winters was one of the first choreographers to actually choreograph Rock dance steps. After a successful career as a choreographer, he progressed to direction (his first job being "The Monkees" TV show) and then producing. Directed the non-musical films: **Linda Lovelace for President** and **Racquet** (also prod '79), **The Last Horror Film** ('84, also writer, prod). In 1992 he was quoted in the *Hollywood Reporter*: "When I was a choreographer I was always upset because the directors never photographed my dances in the way I wanted them photographed. So I became the director and the choreographer. But then there was a little guy called a producer who used to tell me, 'We can't afford this; you can't do that,' So I became the producer, director, choreographer and sometimes writer... But I had never thought about distribution." Winters is now chairman of the board of Action International Pictures Distribution.

Stage: **Goosebumps** (SF '80, also dir)

TV (Partial listing): Liberace special ('62), "Ozzie and Harriet" and "Shindig" ('64), "The Breaking Point," "Hullabaloo" ('65), "The Monkees," "Swing Ding at TJ" ('66), "Movin' with Nancy" ('68—Emmy "Special Achievement Award"), "Monte Carlo—C'est La Rose" ('68 special with Princess Grace of Monaco), "Ann-Margret—From Hollywood with Love" ('69, Emmy nom), "Raquel" ('71, also dir, prod), The Leslie Uggams special, "The Big Show" ('80)

Nightclub/Concert: Youthquake (Riviera Hotel, LV '68); acts for Ann-Margret, Barbara Eden, Joey Heatherton and Raquel Welch

Film:

1964　**Kitten with a Whip**—Univ
　　　　Pajama Party—AIP
　　　　Send Me No Flowers—Univ
　　　　Viva Las Vegas—MGM (assisted by Maggie Banks)

1965　**Billie**—UA (assisted by Donna McKechnie)
　　　　Bus Riley's Back in Town—Univ (assisted by Basil)
　　　　Girl Happy—MGM
　　　　The T.A.M.I. Show—AI (assisted by Basil)

Tickle Me—AA
1966　**Made in Paris**—MGM (assisted by Banks)
　　　　The Swinger—MGM (assisted by Banks)
1967　**Easy Come, Easy Go**—MGM (with Miriam Nelson)
1976　**A Star Is Born**—WB
1979　**Roller Boogie**—UA (assisted by Bill Goodson)
1988　**Little Dragons**—AIP (also dir)

DEE DEE WOOD

b. Boston, Massachusetts, June 7, 1925

With her husband, Marc Breaux, this dancer, choreographer and director gave the movie musical some of its most memorable musical numbers. After training at the School of American Ballet, she became a member of Katherine Dunham's Experimental Dance Group. She began dancing on Broadway and first worked with Michael Kidd in *Guys and Dolls* in 1950, eventually becoming his assistant. Other Broadway appearances include *Can Can* ('53) and *Li'l Abner* ('56)—in which she assisted Kidd, appeared on the cover of *Life* Magazine and met her future husband, Breaux. After they were wed in September, 1955, she was featured on TV in "Caesar's Hour" and "The Colgate Comedy Hour." Wood received her first film choreographic credit for the "restaging" of Kidd's original stage work for **Li'l Abner**. Collaborating with Breaux, their work kept them in demand in television and films for the next decade. No longer married to nor working with Breaux, she continues to add her multiple talents to a wide variety of entertainment projects as director and choreographer.

Stage: **Do Re Mi** (Bdwy '60, with Breaux), Billy Barnes' *Movie Star* (West Coast '84)

TV: With Breaux: "The Bell Telephone Hour," "The Andy Williams Show," Pat Boone Special, "The Hollywood Palace," "Music from Shubert Alley" ('59), "Of Thee I Sing" ('72)

Wood only: (partial listing): "The Perry Como Show," "The Cher Show" ('75, Emmy nom), specials for Bette Midler, Diana Ross and the King Family, the Country Music Awards, "The Billy Crystal Comedy Hour" ('82, with the Dee Dee Wood Dancers), "Burlesque Is Alive and Living in Downtown Burbank," "Debbie Reynolds—The Sound of Children," "John Denver and Friend Frank Sinatra," "The Bert Convy Show," "Laugh In," "Pure Goldie," "Dream On," "Dorothy Hamill's Nutcracker on Ice," "Fifth Annual Comedy Awards," "Welcome Home America," "25 Years of Mouseketeers," "Liberty Weekend Closing Ceremonies" (Emmy Award)

Miscellaneous (partial listing): *Disney on Parade* (Touring Arena Show, with Breaux), SHARE *Boom-*

town parties, XXIII Olympiad Opening and Closing Ceremonies ('84), Super Bowl '90 and '94 Halftime Shows, The Pope's Visit to America, Fiesta Bowl 1991 Halftime Show, USA Olympic Festival Opening Ceremonies ('91)

Film:
1959 **Li'l Abner** — Par ("staged" Michael Kidd's original choreography, assisted by Bonnie Evans, Bobby Karl)
1962 **40 Pounds of Trouble** — Univ (with Breaux)
1964 **Mary Poppins** — Disney (with Breaux)
1965 **The Sound of Music** — Fox (with Breaux, assisted by Phil Laughlin and Larri Thomas)
1967 **The Happiest Millionaire** — Disney (with Breaux)
1968 **Chitty Chitty, Bang Bang** — UA (with Breaux)
1980 **In God We Trust** — Univ
1988 **Beaches** — Touchstone

SMITH WORDES

TV: Julie Brown special (Showtime), "In Search of Dr. Seuss" ('94, asst. to Vince Paterson), commercial for Levis
Music Video: "Black or White" — Michael Jackson
Nightclub/Concert: Sheena Easton ('90 –95 tours)
Film:
1990 **Deadly Dancer** — AIP
1991 **Hook** — Amblin/Univ (assistant to Vince Paterson, with Kim Blank)
1994 **Beverly Hills Cop III** — Par
1996 **The Birdcage** — UA (assistant to Vince Paterson)

JOHN WRAY

d. 1994
Dancer, choreographer and director. Married to Rae MacGregor, he created the choreography for The Toastettes on "Toast of the Town" (the Ed Sullivan Show) during the heyday of the musical variety television show. In 1961 he relinquished the choreography chores and made the transition to director.
Stage: New Faces of 1943 (Bdwy), *Call Me Mister* (Bdwy '46), *The Duchess Misbehaves* (Bdwy '46, replaced by George Tapps)
TV: "Toast of the Town — The Ed Sullivan Show" ('54–61, then dir until '71)
Film:
1945 **Wonder Man** — RKO
1951 **Call Me Mister** — Fox (with Busby Berkeley, Steve Condos)

CHRISTOPHER WREN

1985 **Tender Is the Night** — Showtime Ent

MONI YAKIM

Mime artist and educator.
Film:
1975 **Jacques Brel Is Alive and Well** — American Film Theatre ("movement by" credit)
1987 **Robocop** — Orion

TADASHI YAMASHITA

1985 **Sword of Heaven** — Trans World (also appeared)

SAUL YBARRA

1993 **The Coneheads** — Par

KEITH YOUNG

TV: "Soul Train Awards" ('95, Baby Face's appearance); commercial for Bonita Banana
Music Video: (Partial listing): "Where Is My Love" — Baby Face and El Debarge; "Hungah" — Karyn White
Concert/Nightclub: Earth, Wind and Fire Japan Tour ('94–95), Baby Face Tour ('95), Gladys Knight tour ('95), Robert Gallup Magic Show
Film:
1984 **Amadeus** — Orion (assistant to Twyla Tharp)
1996 **Grace of My Heart** — Grammercy
House Arrest — Rysher Ent

HECTOR ZARASPE

b. Tucaman, Argentina, 1931
This dancer-choreographer's major contributions to dance have been made through his teaching and he said, "One of my most cherished memories is of Nureyev introducing me as his teacher" (*Dance Magazine*, October, 1969). Zaraspe began his exploration of the world of dance as a small child learning folk dancing from his father, whose livelihood was farming but as a dancer was "reknowned in his neighborhood for his inventiveness and fine rhythmic sense." At the age of 10 his family moved to Buenos Aires and Hector began Spanish, modern and finally, ballet lessons four years later with Esmee Bulnes. Already making his professional debut in public festivals, he danced with Teatro Colon from 1949–52. With government assistance he started a school for children who could not afford lessons in

Buenos Aires in 1951. In 1954 he went to Spain and founded Liceo Coreografico y Musical de Madrid, taught ballet to major Spanish dance companies and staged festivals. In Spain he also choreographed for stage, television and the two internationally released films listed below, as well as several Spanish films. He taught briefly in London in 1963, and after touring with Antonio's Ballet De Madrid, moved to New York in 1964, where he became a member of the faculty of Joffrey's American Ballet Center. As personal coach of Spanish and classic techniques, Zaraspe has not only trained Rudolph Nureyev but also Margot Fonteyn and Maya Plisetskaya and has been guest teacher for the Royal Ballet and the National Ballet of Holland. From 1971–73 he was director of the Rio de Janeiro Teatro Municipal and Brazil's National Ballet. Currently a member of the Juilliard dance faculty.

Stage: Carmen (NYC Opera), for American Opera Center: **La Traviata, Orpheo, La Rondine, The Masked Ball**; *Tango Pasion* (Bdwy '93)

TV: Various programs for Madrid TV ('54–62): "La Vida Alegre," "El Rey Lear"

Miscellaneous: Religious festivals (Vigo, '54 and Madrid, '55–60), Madrid Industrial & Agricultural Fair ('62)

Film:

1959 **John Paul Jones**— WB

1960 **Spartacus**— Univ (staged the battle sequences filmed in Spain)

1963 **55 Days at Peking**— Samuel Bronston Prod

MICHELLE ZEITLIN
b. Princeton, New Jersey, December 23, 1962

Actress, dancer and choreographer who started her dance training at the age of 4 with the National Ballet of Canada school. At 17 she relocated to New York after receiving a scholarship with the Joffrey Ballet. Dance teachers included Rick Atwell, Meredith Baylis, Robert Denvers, Billis Godson, Stanley Holden and Michael Owens. Studying theater arts and acting at the Banff School of the Arts, Theatrecraft Playhouse and with Harold Kennedy, she made her professional debut in *Gypsy* at the Theatre Guild of Wisconsin. Other performance credits include dancing with the Joffrey Concert Group and Westside Ballet in Los Angeles, the workshop production of *Scandals* (in which she also assisted Michael Bennett) and productions of *Evita, My Fair Lady, Man of La Mancha*, etc. She created her first solo choreography for Tiberios restaurant in Los Angeles in 1980. She appeared as a regular on the TV series "Fame" and multiple television shows, as well as the films **Back to the Future—Part 2, La Bamba** and **Detective**. Her choreo-

graphic career led her to extensive work in Japan and forming More Zap Productions for her various projects.

TV: Robert Townsend HBO Special ('88, asst. to Russell Clark), "L.A. Dance Trax" (Pilot, '88), "Feisty Fairytales" (Pilot, '92)

Ballet/Dance Pieces: "Switched on Bach" (Banff Festival '80), "Escape" ('90), "Babar"

Music Video: "Misty," "Ebony and Ivory," "The Way We Were," "The Last Waltz" (All in Japan), "Private Dancer" (Erotic Dance series)

Miscellaneous: Spruce Goose/Queen Mary New Year's Eve Rock 'n' Roll Party, fashion shows for Nike, Rockport Shoes, "Miss Teen America" 1990 pageant; industrials for American Film Market, Executive Life Insurance, Fitness Expo '87, Mobil/Australia,

Film:

1989 **Hollywood Story**— United Ent

1991 **Danse Macabre/Terror in St. Petersburg**— 21st Century Film Corp (also appeared)

BENJAMIN ZEMACH
b. Russia, 1901

Because his brother, Nachum, was an actor, this Academy Award nominated dance director began his exploration of theater studying with Stanislavsky in Moscow in 1917. Nachum eventually created Habimah (a Hebrew Theatre in Moscow) with Benjamin and Benjamin's formal dance training began in 1918 with Dalcroze Eurythmics and members of the Russian Imperial Ballet. When Habimah came to America to perform in 1927, the Zemach Brothers accompanied it to New York. Selecting a racial subject as a focus for his creativity, Benjamin's dance/theater pieces involved Judaic history and ritual and used the spoken word, an innovation for that time. In 1935 a dancer remarked in *The American Dancer*, "The thing that makes Benjamin Zemach's dances so delightful to me is that they are built on a spiral, whether he is conscious of it or not. Each movement is a natural growth from the one that proceeded it. His dancing is thus fluent; not a series of steps." In 1932 he gave his first concert in Los Angeles as part of the L.A. Olympic Festival. At the Hollywood Bowl, he danced with Martha Graham, Doris Humphrey and Charles Weidman and presented his unique theater pieces. His Oscar-nominated "Hall of Kings" number in **She** is generally acknowledged to be one of the first times an art dance (with its use of masks and abstract movement) is an integral part of a filmed story. Finally discouraged by Hollywood's misuse of dance, he returned to New York in 1936 to direct and choreograph *Road of Promise* for Max Reinhardt. He remained there until 1947, opening a school and teaching many actors, among them Alan Arkin, Herschel Bernardi, Lee J. Cobb and Sam Jaffe. Returning to the West Coast he served as director of the theater arts department and head of the dance department of the University of Judaism in Los Angeles since 1947, retiring and emigrating to Israel in 1971. Mr. Zemach is the subject of a 1969 short film: **The Art of Benjamin Zemach**.

Biography: A section of *Dancing in the Sun* by Norma Prevots (1987)

Stage: *Road of Promise* (Bdwy '36), *Pins and Needles* (Bdwy '37)

Ballet/Dance Pieces (Partial listing): "The Beggar's Dance," "Roumanian Rhapsody," "Tocatta and Fugue," "Ruth," "Farewell to Queen Sabbath," "Fragments of Israel" (Hollywood Bowl '33), "The Victory Ball" (Hollywood Bowl '35), "The Eternal Road," "Yome Yome," "Hodoya," "Bialik," "The Camel"

Film:

1935 **The Last Days of Pompeii**— RKO

She— RKO (Academy Award nom: "Hall of Kings" number)

1963 **Night Tide**— AIP

LACHEN ZINOUNE

1988 **The Last Temptation of Christ**— Univ

1990 **The Sheltering Sky**— WB

APPENDIX TO PART II: FILMS AND THEIR CHOREOGRAPHERS

Aaron Slick from Punkin Creek—Charles O'Curran

Abbott and Costello in Hollywood—Charles Walters

Abbott and Costello Meet Captain Kidd—Val Raset

Abbott and Costello Meet Dr. Jekyll and Mr. Hyde—Kenny Williams

Abilene Town—Sammy Lee

About Face—LeRoy Prinz

Above the Law—Steven Seagal

The Absent Minded Professor—Tommy Mahoney

Absolute Beginners—David Paltenghi

Accused—Philip Buchel

Across the Wide Missouri—Alex Romero

Action Jackson—Paula Abdul

The Addams Family—Peter Anastos

Addams Family Values—Peter Anastos, Adam Shankman

Adorable—Sammy Lee

Adventure in Musik—Ernst Matray

Adventures in Babysitting—Monica Devereaux

Adventures of Baron Munchausen—Pino Pinesse, Giorgio Rossi

The Adventures of Bullwhip Griffin—Alex Plasschaert

The Adventures of Ford Fairlane—Aurorah Allain

The Adventures of Priscilla, Queen of the Desert—Marc White

Adventures of Sherlock Holmes' Smarter Brother—Alan Johnson

Affair in Trinidad—Valerie Bettis

An Affair to Remember—Robert Sidney

The Affairs of Anatol—Theodore Kosloff

The Affairs of Cellini—Adolph Bolm

The Affairs of Dobie Gillis—Bob Fosse, Alex Romero

Affectionately Yours—Matty King

After the Dance—George Murphy, Albertina Rasch

After the Thin Man—Seymour Felix

The Age of Innocence—Elizabeth Aldrich

Aida—Marguerite Wallman

Ain't Misbehavin'—Lee Scott, Kenny Williams

Airplane!—Tommy Mahoney

Akira Kurosawa's Dreams—Michiyo Hata

Aladdin—Brad Flanagan

Aladdin and His Lamp—Asoka

Alaska—Jack Boyle, Felix Sadowski

Alex in Wonderland—Paula Kelly

Alexander the Great—David Paltenghi

Alexander's Ragtime Band—Seymour Felix

Alfresco (S)—Alexander Oumansky

Ali Baba and the Forty Thieves—Lester Horton, Paul Oscard

Ali Baba Goes to Town—Sammy Lee

Ali Baba Nights—Anton Dolin

Alibi—Fanchon

Alice in Wonderland (1933)—Eddie Prinz

Alice in Wonderland (1985) (TV)—Miriam Nelson

Alive and Kicking—Denys Palmer

All American Co-Ed—LeRoy Prinz

All American Sweetheart—Louis DaPron

All Ashore—Lee Scott

All By Myself—Tip, Tap and Toe

All Colored Vaudeville (S)—Fayard Nicholas

All Girl Revue (S)—Gae Foster

All Hands on Deck—Hal Belfer

All I Desire—Kenny Williams

All I Want for Christmas—Marguerite Derricks

The All Nighter—Sarah Elgart

All Star Musical Revue (S)—Antonio, Busby Berkeley, LeRoy Prinz, Frank Veloz

All That Jazz—Bob Fosse

All the King's Horses—LeRoy Prinz

All the Marbles (aka *The California Dolls*)—Kathryn Doby

Allergic to Love—Antonio Triana

An Alligator Named Daisy—Alfred Rodrigues

Almost Angels—Norman Thomson

Almost Married—Louis DaPron

Aloha Summer—Sho Kosugi

Aloma of the South Seas—LeRoy Prinz

Along Came Sally—Edward Royce

Along the Navajo Trail—Larry Ceballos
Alphabet City—Lori Eastside
Always—Bob Banas, Gillian Gregory
Always a Bridesmaid—Louis DaPron
Always Leave Them Laughing—LeRoy Prinz
Amadeus—Twyla Tharp
Amateur Gentleman—Quentin Todd
Amateur Night at the Dixie Bar and Grill (TV)—
   JoAnne Devito
Amazons—Gilbert Meuniere
Amberwaves—Johnny Almaraz
Ambition—Miranda Garrison
American Anthem—Lisa Green
American Boyfriends—Linda Thorslund
American Graffiti—Toni Basil
An American in Paris—Stanley Donen, Gene
   Kelly
American Ninja 3: Blood Hunt—Mike Stone
American Note Blue—Dieter Riesle
The American Success Company—Cecilia Gruess-
   ing
Americathon—Jaime Rogers
El Amor Brujo (1972) (aka *Bewitched Love*)—
   Alberto Lorca
El Amor Brujo (1986)—Antonio Gades
The Amorous Adventures of Moll Flanders—Pauline
   Grant
Anchors Aweigh—Stanley Donen, Jack Donohue,
   Gene Kelly
And God Created Woman—Kenny Ortega
And the Angels Sing—Danny Dare
And the Band Played On (TV)—Sarah Elgart,
   Myles Thoroughgood
And the Moon Dances (*Bulan Tertusak Ilalang*)—
   Maria D. Hoetomo
Angel, Angel, Down We Go (aka *Cult of the
   Damned*)—Wilda Taylor
Angel Cake (S)—Albertina Rasch
Angel Heart—Louis Falco
Angel in My Pocket—George Tapps, Wilda Taylor
Angels and Insects—Kim Brandstrup
Angie—Michael Smuin
Angus—Vincent Paterson
Anna and the King of Siam—Si-Lan Chen
Anna Karenina (1935)—Ernest Belcher, Chester
   Hale, Marguerite Wallman
Anna Karenina (1979)—Maya Plisetskaya
Anne of the Thousand Days—Mary Skeaping
Annie—Joe Layton, Arlene Phillips
Annie Get Your Gun—Robert Alton
Another Pair of Aces (TV)—Lynne Hockney
Another Part of the Forest—Jeanette Bates
Antonio and Rosario (S)—Antonio
Anyone Can Play—Gino Landi
Anything Goes (1936) (aka *Tops Is the Limit*)—
   LeRoy Prinz
Anything Goes (1956)—Nick Castle, Ernest Flatt,
   Roland Petit

Apache—Archie Savage
The Apartment—Miriam Nelson
The Apple—Nigel Lythgoe
Appointment with a Shadow—Kenny Williams
Appointment with Death—Jakob Kalusky
Apres L'Amour—Chris Gandois
The April Fools—Marc Wilder
April in Paris—Ray Bolger, LeRoy Prinz, Donald
   Saddler
April Love—Bill Foster
April Showers—LeRoy Prinz
La Ardilla Roja (*The Red Squirrel*)—Ana Medem
Are You There?—Edward Dolly
Are You with It?—Louis DaPron
Arena of Fear—Mike DeLutry
Argentine Nights—Nick Castle, Geneva Sawyer
Aria—Grover Dale, Terry Gilber
Arizona to Broadway—Sammy Lee
Arizona Wildcat—Nick Castle, Geneva Sawyer
Armed and Innocent (TV)—Myrna Gawryn
Around the World—Nick Castle
Around the World in 80 Days—Paul Godkin, José
   Greco
Around the World in 80 Ways—Meryl Tankard
The Art of Love—Hal Belfer
Artists and Models (1937)—LeRoy Prinz
Artists and Models (1955)—Charles O'Curran
Artists and Models Abroad—LeRoy Prinz
As Long as They're Happy—Irving Davies, Paddy
   Stone
As You Like It—Ninette DeValois
At Long Last Love—Rita Abrams, Albert Lantieri
At Play in the Fields of the Lord—Julia Pascale
At the Bluff—Myles Thoroughgood
At the Circus—Bobby Connolly
Athena—Valerie Bettis
Atlantic City—Seymour Felix, John "Bubbles"
   Sublett
Atom Age Vampire (aka *Seddok* and *The Vampire
   and the Ballerina*)—Marisa Ciampaglia
Attack of the 50 Foot Woman (TV)—Patsy Swayze
Attila—Gussa Gert
Awakenings—Patricia Birch
Ay! Carmela—Albert Portillo
Babe—Annouchka DeJong
The Babe Ruth Story—Larry Ceballos
Babes in Arms—Busby Berkeley
Babes in Toyland (1934)—Eddie Prinz
Babes in Toyland (1961)—Ray Bolger, Jack Dono-
   hue, Tommy Mahoney
Babes in Toyland (1986) (TV)—Eleanor Fazan
Babes on Broadway—Busby Berkeley
Babes on Swing Street—Louis DaPron
Baby, Take a Bow—Sammy Lee
Bachelor Mother—Hermes Pan
Bachelor Party—Kathleen Knap
Back to the Beach—Lori Eastside
Back to the Future—Brad Jeffries

Back to the Future — Part 2 — Brad Jeffries
Back to the Future — Part 3 — Brad Jeffries
Backdraft — Monica Devereux
Backstage (aka *Limelight*) — Tilly Losch, Ralph Reader
Bad Girls — Adam Shankman
Bad Guys — Joanne Divito
Bad Influence — Sarah Elgart
Bagdad — Lester Horton
Baja Oklahoma (TV) — Jerry Evans
Le Bal — D'Dee, Jacques Bense
Balalaika — Nico Charisse, Ernst Matray
Ball at the Castle (*Ballo al Castello*) — Mara Dousse
The Ballad of Little Jo — JoAnn Fregalette Jansen
Ballerina (aka *La Mort du Cygne*) (1938) — Serge Lifar
Ballerina (aka *Rosen Fur Bettina*) (1956) — Alan Carter
La Bamba — Miguel Delgado
Bamboo Blonde — Charles O'Curran
The Band Wagon — Fred Astaire, Michael Kidd
The Barbarians — Pino Pinnese
Barbarians at the Gate (TV) — Miranda Garrison
Barber Shop Blues (S) — Four Step Bros.
The Barkleys of Broadway — Robert Alton, Fred Astaire, Hermes Pan
Barnyard Follies — Josephine Earl
Barry Lyndon — Geraldine Stephenson
Barton Fink — Bill and Jacqui Landrum
Basic Instinct — Bill and Jacqui Landrum
Bathing Beauty — Robert Alton, John Murray Anderson, Jack Donohue
Be Yourself — Maurice Kussell
Beach Ball — Cholly Atkins, Rita D'Amico
Beach Blanket Bingo — Jack Baker
Beaches — Dee Dee Wood
The Beat Generation — Hamil Petroff
Beat Street — Lester Wilson
Beatlemania — Graciela Daniele
Beau Brummel — Ernest Belcher
Beau James — Jack Baker
Beautiful But Broke — Stanley Donen
Beautiful But Dangerous — Marguerite Wallman
Beauty and the Beast — Christine Oren
The Beauty Shoppe (S) — John "Bubbles" Sublett
Beauty's Daughter (S) — Fanchon
Becky Sharp — Russell Lewis
Becoming Collette — Andy Lucas
Bedknobs and Broomsticks — Donald McKayle
Bedroom Window — Michael Owens
A Bedtime Story — Charles Lang
Beetlejuice — Chrissy Boccino
Behind the Eight Ball — Eddie Prinz
Bela Lugosi Meets a Brooklyn Gorilla — Lee Scott
The Believers — Wilhelmina Taylor
Belinda — Robyn Moase
Bella Donna — Ernest Belcher

The Bellboy — Nick Castle
The Belle of New York — Robert Alton, Fred Astaire
Belle of the Yukon — Don Loper
Belles et Ballets — Maurice Bejart, Dirk Sanders
Belles on Their Toes — Angie Blue
Bells Are Ringing — Charles O'Curran
The Bells of Rosarita — Larry Ceballos
Beltenbros (*Prince of Darkness*) — Goyo Montero
Bengal Brigade — Asoka
Benny and Joon — Dan Kamin
Berlin Blues — Giorgio Aresu
Berlin Express — Charles O'Curran
Bernadine — Bill Foster
Bert Rigby, You're a Fool — Larry Hyman
Best Foot Forward — J.M. Andrew, Stanley Donen, Jack Donohue, Charles Walters
The Best Little Whorehouse in Texas — Tony Stevens
Best of the Best 2 — George Alexander
The Best of Times — Linda Hart
The Best Things in Life Are Free — Rod Alexander, Bill Foster
Betrayed — Wayne and Doris Knight
Between Two Women — Jeanette Bates
The Beverly Hillbillies — Brad Jeffries
Beverly Hills Cop — Sarah Elgart
Beverly Hills Cop III — Smith Wordes
Bewitched Love (aka *El Amour Brujo*) — Alberto Lorca
Beyond the Reef — Coco Ellacott
The Bible — In the Beginning — Katherine Dunham
Big — Patricia Birch
The Big Beat (1958) — Kenny Williams
Big Beat (1995) — Josef Prouza
The Big Broadcast of 1936 — Fayard Nicholas, LeRoy Prinz
The Big Broadcast of 1937 — Louis DaPron, LeRoy Prinz
The Big Broadcast of 1938 — LeRoy Prinz
The Big Broadcast of 1939 — LeRoy Prinz
The Big Casino — Chester Hale
The Big Circus — Barbette, Patricia Denise
The Big City — Stanley Donen
The Big Easy — Tina Giroud
The Big Fisherman — LeRoy Prinz
The Big Idea — Sammy Lee
Big Meat Eater — Helen LeCounte
The Big Store — Arthur Apell
Big Street — Chester Hale
The Big T.N.T. Show — Ward Ellis
Big Top Pee Wee — Patsy Swayze
The Big Town — Kelly Robinson
Bikini Beach — Tommy Mahoney
Bikini Party and the Haunted House — Jack Baker
Bill and Ted's Bogus Journey — Bruno "Taco" Falcon
Bill and Ted's Excellent Adventure — Brad Jeffries

Billie—David Winters
Billy Bathgate—Patricia Birch
Billy Madison—Clarence Ford
Billy Rose's Diamond Horseshoe (aka *Diamond Horseshoe*)—Hermes Pan
Billy Rose's Jumbo—Barbette, Busby Berkeley
Billy's Holiday—Kim Walker
Bimbo the Great—John Schaper
The Bird of Paradise—Busby Berkeley
The Birdcage—Vincent Paterson
The Birds and the Bees—Nick Castle
Birds of Prey—Jeffrey Hornaday
Bittersweet—Ernst Matray
Bizet's Carmen—Antonio Gades
Black and White (S)—Alexander Oumansky
Black Angel—Louis DaPron
Black Bart—Val Raset
The Black Castle—Hal Belfer
Black Eagle—Sho Kosugi, Jean-Claude Van Damme
Black Girl—Peggy Pettit
Black Gold—Tom Panko
The Black Knight—David Paltenghi
Black Narcissus (1929) (S)—John "Bubbles" Sublett
Black Narcissus (1947)—Mayura
Black Network (S)—Fayard Nicholas
The Black Swan (S)—David Paltenghi
Black Tights—Roland Petit
Blade Runner—Russell Clark
Blazing Saddles—Alan Johnson
The Blind Bargain—Ernest Belcher
Blonde Ransom—Louis DaPron, Felix Sadowski
Blondie Goes Latin—Louis DaPron
Blondie Meets the Boss—Eddie Larkin
Blondie of the Follies—Harold Hecht
Blood and Sand—Hermes Pan, Geneva Sawyer
Blood Ties (TV)—Bill and Jacqui Landrum
Blood Wedding—Antonio Gades
Bloodhounds of Broadway (1952)—Bob Sidney
The Bloodhounds of Broadway (1989)—Diane Martel
Bloodsport—Jean-Claude Van Damme
Bloody Pom Poms (aka *Cheerleader Camp*)—Lucinda Dickey
Blown Away—Liam Harney
The Blue Angel—Hermes Pan
The Blue Bird (1940)—Geneva Sawyer
The Blue Bird (1976)—Igor Belsky, Leonid Jacobson
Blue Chips—Tony Gonzalez
Blue City—Vicky Tarrazi
The Blue Danube—Ernest Belcher
Blue Hawaii—Charles O'Curran
The Blue Iguana—Felix Greco
Blue in the Face—Linda Talcott
Blue Juice—Clive Clark
Blue Skies—Fred Astaire, Hermes Pan, David Robel

Blue Sky—Greg Rosatti
Bluebeard's Eighth Wife—LeRoy Prinz
The Blues Brothers—Carlton Johnson
The Boarding School (aka *The Passion Flower Hotel*)—Larry Fuller
Boardinghouse Blues—Berry Bros.
Bob and Carol and Ted and Alice—Miriam Nelson
Body and Soul—Hope Clarke, Valentino
Body Beat—Dennon and Sayhber Rawles
Body Chemistry—Ted Lin
Body Heat—Tad Tadlock
Body Moves—Linda Bernabei
Body Rock—Joanne Divito, Susan Scanlan
The Bodyguard—Sean Cheesman
Bogus—Eartha Robinson
La Boheme—Ernest Belcher
Boiling Point—Randy Wander
Boléro (1934)—LeRoy Prinz
Bolero (aka *Les Uns et les Autres*) (1981)—Maurice Béjart, Nicole Daresco, Ric Odums, Micha Van Joecke, Larry Vickers
Bolshoi Ballet '67—Yuri Grigorovich
Bombalera (S)—Josephine Earl
Bonjour Kathrin—Billy Daniel
Bonjour Tristesse—Tutte Lemkow
Boogie Woogie (S)—Josephine Earl
Book of Love—Diana Lehan
The Boost—Zina Bethune
Born in East L.A.—Miguel Delgado
Born Reckless—Jack Baker
Born to Dance—Dave Gould, Eleanor Powell
Born to Sing—Busby Berkeley, Sammy Lee
Born Tough—Eddie Prinz
Born Yesterday—Miranda Garrison
Botta e Riposta—Katherine Dunham
Bottoms Up—Harold Hecht
Bound and Gagged—Myron Johnson
The Bounty—Terry Gilbert
The Bowery—Jack Haskell
Bowery to Broadway—John Boyle, Louis DaPron, Carlos Romero
The Boy Friend (1939)—Nick Castle, Geneva Sawyer
The Boy Friend (1972)—Christopher Gable, Terry Gilbert, Gillian Gregory, Tommy Tune
Boy on a Dolphin—Yanni Fleury
The Boys from Syracuse—Dave Gould
Boys on the Side—Ruben Moreno, Oscar Villela
The Brady Bunch Movie—Joe Cassini, Margaret T. Hickey Perez
Brain Donors—John Carrafa
Bram Stoker's Dracula—Michael Smuin, Morleigh Steinberg
The Brass Bottle—Hal Belfer
Brazil—Billy Daniel, Frank Veloz
Breakfast at Tiffany's—Miriam Nelson
The Breakfast Club—Dorain Grusman

Breakin' 1— Jaime Rogers, Shabba Doo

Breakin' 2: Electric Bugaloo— Bill Goodson, Shabba Doo

Breakin' Through— Lester Wilson

Breaking Glass— Eric G. Robarts

Breaking the Ice— Dave Gould

Brewster's Millions— Buddy Bradley

The Bribe— Jack Donohue

Bride of the Regiment— Jack Haskell

The Bride Wore Red— Val Raset

The Bridge of San Luis Rey— John Boyle, Antonio Triana

Brigadoon— Gene Kelly

The Brigand— Eugene Loring

Bright Eyes— Sammy Lee

Bright Lights— Busby Berkeley, Larry Ceballos

Bring on the Girls— Billy Daniel, Danny Dare

Bring Your Smile Along— Miriam Nelson

Broadway (1929)— Maurice Kusell

Broadway (1942)— James Mattison

Broadway Buckaroo— Condos Bros.

Broadway Hostess— Bobby Connolly

Broadway Melody— George Cunningham

Broadway Melody of 1936— Dave Gould, Eleanor Powell, Carl Randall, Albertina Rasch

Broadway Melody of 1938— Dave Gould, George Murphy, Eleanor Powell

Broadway Melody of 1940— Fred Astaire, Bobby Connolly, George Murphy, Eleanor Powell, Albertina Rasch

Broadway Rhythm— Robert Alton, Jack Donohue, Don Loper, George Murphy, Charles Walters

Broadway Scandals— Rufus LeMaire

Broadway Serenade— Busby Berkeley, Seymour Felix

Broadway Thru a Keyhole— Jack Haskell

Broadway to Hollywood— Sammy Lee, Albertina Rasch

Broken Blossoms— Ernest Belcher

Brotherly Love— Bobby Watson

The Buccaneer (1938)— LeRoy Prinz

The Buccaneer (1958)— Josephine Earl

Buccaneer's Girl— Hal Belfer

Buck and Bubbles Laff Jamboree— John "Bubbles" Sublett

Buck Benny Rides Again— Merriel Abbott, LeRoy Prinz

Buck Privates— Nick Castle

Buck Rogers in the 25th Century— Miriam Nelson

Buddha— Kitsu Sakakibara

The Buddy Holly Story— Maggie Rash

Buddy Rich and His Orchestra (S)— Louis DaPron

Buffy the Vampire Slayer— Lisa Estrada

Bugsy— Dennon and Sayhber Rawles

Bugsy Malone— Gillian Gregory

Bull Durham— Paula Abdul

Bullets Over Broadway— Graciela Daniele

Bundle of Joy— Nick Castle

Burlesque on Carmen— Charles Chaplin

Bus Riley's Back in Town— David Winters

The Butcher's Wife— Michael Fraley

By an Old Southern River— Bill Robinson

By Request (S)— Tip, Tap and Toe

By the Light of the Silvery Moon— LeRoy Prinz, Donald Saddler

Bye Bye Birdie (1963)— Onna White

Bye Bye Birdie (1995) (TV)— Ann Reinking

Cabaret— Bob Fosse

Cabeza de Vaca— Lidya Romero

Cabin in the Sky— Busby Berkeley, John "Bubbles" Sublett

The Cable Guy— LTC Choreography

Cactus Flower— Miriam Nelson

The Caddy— Jack Baker

Caddyshack 2— Jaime Rogers

Cadence— Russell Clark

Cafe Society— LeRoy Prinz

Cain and Mabel— Bobby Connolly

Cairo— Sammy Lee

Calamity Jane— Jack Donohue

Calcutta— Asoka, Roberta Jonay

Calendar Girl— Fanchon

Calendar Girl Murders (TV)— Russell Clark

California Casanova— Michelle Johnston

The California Dolls (aka *All the Marbles*)— Kathryn Doby

Caligula— Tito DeLuc, Pino Pennesse

Call Me Madam— Robert Alton

Call Me Mister— Busby Berkeley, Steve Condos, John Wray

Call of the Flesh— Eduardo Cansino

Calling All Girls (S)— Busby Berkeley

Calling All Kids (S)— Steven Granger

Calling All Stars (S)— Fayard Nicholas, John "Bubbles" Sublett

Calypso Heat Wave— Josephine Earl

Calypso Joe— James Truitte

Came a Hot Friday— Catherine Cardiff

Camelot— Buddy Schwab

Camille— Val Raset

Camorra— Daniel Ezralow

Campus Honeymoon— Fanchon

Campus Sleuth— Jack Boyle

Can-Can— Hermes Pan

Can Heironymous Merkin Ever Forget Mercy Humppe and Find True Happiness— Johnny Greenland

Can This Be Dixie?— Sammy Lee

The Candid Kid (S)— Gae Foster

Candy— Don Lurio

Cannery Row— Lou Wills, Jr.

Can't Buy Me Love— Paula Abdul

Can't Stop the Music— Arlene Phillips

The Canterville Ghost— Jack Donohue

Captain America— Ted Lin

Captain Cosmos— Nigel Binns

Captain E-O (S)— Jeffrey Hornaday, Michael Jackson

Captain January— Jack Donohue

Captain Sinbad— Gene Reed

The Captain's Paradise— Tutte Lemkow

Caravan (1934)— Sammy Lee

Caravan (1946)— Cleo Nordi

The Cardinal— Buddy Schwab

Carefree— Fred Astaire, Hermes Pan

Caribbean Gold— Asoka

Carlito's Way— Jeffrey Hornaday

Carmen (1919)— Theodore Kosloff

Carmen (1983)— Antonio Gades

Carmen Jones— Herbert Ross

Carnival— Freddie Carpenter

Carnival in Costa Rica— Léonide Massine

Carnival of Rhythm (S)— Katherine Dunham

Carolina Blues— Sammy Lee, Ann Miller, Four Step Bros.

Carousel— Rod Alexander, Agnes DeMille

Carrington— Stuart Hopps

Carry on Columbus— Peter Gordeno

Casa Riccordi— Daniel Ezralow

Casanova in Burlesque— Dave Gould

Casanova's Big Night— Josephine Earl

Casbah— Katherine Dunham, Bernard Pearce

Casino Royale— Tutte Lemkow

Casper— Adam Shankman

Castle Keep— Dirk Sanders

Casual Sex?— Susie Inouye

Cat and the Fiddle— Seymour Felix, Albertina Rasch

Cat Ballou— Miriam Nelson

Cat Women of the Moon— Betty Arlen

Cats Don't Dance— Deborah Bray, Gene Kelly

The Cat's Paw— Larry Ceballos

Cavalcade— Sammy Lee

Cavalcade of the Dance (S)— Frank Veloz

Caverns of Vice (aka *Das Nachtlokal zum Silbermond*)— Ernesto Bittner

CB4— Jeannette Godoy

The Cemetery Club— Ron Tassone

Centennial Summer— Dorothy Fox

Century—Geraldine Stephenson

Cha-Cha-Cha-Boom— Earl Barton

Chain of Desire— Karole Armitage

The Chair— Fern Feller

Champagne Waltz— LeRoy Prinz, Frank Veloz

Chances Are— Miranda Garrison

Changing of the Guard (S)— Bobby Connolly

Chaplin— Kate Flatt, Johnny Hutch, Dan Kamin, Susanne McKenrick

Charley and the Angel— Donald McKayle

Charlie Chan in Rio— Geneva Sawyer

Chasing Rainbows— Sammy Lee

Check and Double Check (S)— Four Step Bros.

Cheerleader Camp (aka *Bloody Pom Poms*)— Lucinda Dickey

Cheyenne— LeRoy Prinz

Chicago Joe and the Showgirl— Warren Heyes

Children of a Lesser God— Nikki Sahagen, Dan Siretta

Children of Pleasure— Sammy Lee

The Children's Hour— Maggie Banks

China Girl— Lori Eastside

Chip Off the Old Block— Louis DaPron

Chitty Chitty, Bang Bang— Marc Breaux, Dee Dee Wood

The Chocolate Soldier— Ernst Matry

Choo Choo Swing (S)— Fayard Nicholas

A Chorus Line— Gregg Burge, Troy Garza, Jeffrey Hornaday, Brad Jeffries, Helene Phillips, Vickie Regan

Chorus of Disapproval— Sandra Blair

The Christian— Ernest Belcher

Christmas in Connecticut (TV)— Lynne Hockney

Chu Chin Chow— Anton Dolin

Chu Chu and the Philly Flash— Don Crichton

Cinderella (1937)— Harry Pilcer

Cinderella (1976)— Russell Clark

Cinderella Jones— Busby Berkeley

Cinderfella— Nick Castle

Cindy (TV)— Donald McKayle

Cinema Circus (S)— Fanchon

Cinerama Holiday— Donn Arden

City Beneath the Sea— Hal Belfer

City for Conquest— Robert Vreeland

City Hall—John Carrafa

City of Women— Leonetta Bentivoglio

Clambake— Alex Romero

The Clan of the Cave Bear— Peter Elliott

Class Act— Otis Sallid

Class Action— Paula Tracy Smuin

Classic Jazz (S)— Alexander Oumansky

Clean and Sober— Bill and Jacqui Landrum

Cleopatra (1917)— Ruth St. Denis, Ted Shawn

Cleopatra (1934)— Agnes De Mille, LeRoy Prinz

Cleopatra (1963)— Hermes Pan

Clifford— Russell Clark, Vincent Paterson

The Climax— Lester Horton

Club Life— Dennon Rawles

Clueless—Mary Ann Kellogg

Cobra Woman—Lester Horton, Paul Oscard

Cockeyed Cavaliers—Dave Gould

Cocoon— Caprice Roth, Gwen Verdon

Colleen— Bobby Connolly, Ruby Keeler

College Holiday— Louis Dapron, LeRoy Prinz

College Humor— Harold Hecht

College Love— Maurice Kussell

College Lovers— Carl McBride

College Rhythm— LeRoy Prinz

College Swing— LeRoy Prinz

Collegiate— LeRoy Prinz

The Color Purple— Claude Thompson

Colors— Patrick Alan

Colortone Revue (S)— Sammy Lee

Come Blow Your Horn— Jack Baker, Maggie Banks, Nick Castle

Come On Marines— LeRoy Prinz

Comin' 'Round the Mountain— Hal Belfer

Coming to America— Paula Abdul

The Commancheros— Hal Belfer

Como Agua por Chocolate (aka *Like Water for Chocolate*)— Farnesio DeBernal

The Coneheads— Sal Ybarra

Coney Island— Hermes Pan

Confession— Matty King

Confessions of an Opium Eater (aka *Souls for Sale* and *Secrets of a Soul*)— Jon Gregory

La Conga Nights— Louis DaPron

Congo— Peter Elliott, Adam Shankman

Congress Dances (aka *Der Kongress Tanzt*)— Victor Gsovsky

A Connecticut Yankee in King Arthur's Court— Josephine Earl

The Conqueror— Robert Sidney

Cool as Ice— John "Hi Teck" Huffman IV

The Cool Ones— Toni Basil

Copacabana (1947)— Larry Ceballos

Copacabana (1985) (TV)— Grover Dale

Copper Canyon— Josephine Earl

Coronado— Fayard Nicholas, LeRoy Prinz

The Corsican Brothers— Adolph Bolm

Cotton and Silk (S)— Sammy Lee

The Cotton Club— Claudia Asbury, George Faison, Gregory Hines, Henry LeTang, Michael Meachum, Arthur Mitchell, Michael Smuin

Cotton Comes to Harlem— Louis Johnson

The Count— Charles Chaplin

The Countess of Monte Cristo— Louis DaPron, Don Loper

The Country Girl— Robert Alton

The Courier— Connie Regan

The Court Jester— James Starbuck

The Court of the Pharaohs— Jose Granero

The Courtneys of Curzon Street (aka *The Courtney Affair*)— Philip and Betty Buchel

Cover Girl— Jack Cole, Stanley Donen, Seymour Felix, Gene Kelly, Val Raset

The Cowboy and the Señorita— Larry Ceballos

Cowboy in Manhattan— Aida Broadbent

The Cowboy Way— Patricia Birch

Coyote— Todd Harris-Gonzalez

Crazy House (1930) (S)— Albertina Rasch

Crazy House (1943)— Tony De Marco, George Hale

Crazy Times (TV)— Dom Salinaro

Crocodile Tears— Wade Madsen

Cronos— Esther Soler

Crossed Swords— Sally Gilpin

The Crossing Guard—Russell Clark

Cruisin' Down the River— Lee Scott

The Crusades— LeRoy Prinz

Cry Baby— Lori Eastside

Crystal Heart— Marcea D. Lane

Cuban Episode (S)— Katherine Dunham

Cuban Pete— Louis DaPron

La Cucaracha (S)— Russell Lewis

The Cuckoos— Pearl Eaton

Cult of the Cobra— Kenny Williams

Cult of the Damned (aka *Angel, Angel, Down We Go*)— Wilda Taylor

Curly Top— Jack Donohue

The Curse of the Pink Panther— Jerry Trent

Curtain Call at Cactus Creek— Louis DaPron

The Cutting Edge— Robin Cousins

Cyborg— Jean-Claude Van Damme

D.C. Cab— Jeffrey Hornaday

Daddy Long Legs— Fred Astaire, Roland Petit, David Robel

Dakota— Larry Ceballos

Dallas Cowboys Cheerleaders (TV)— Texi Waterman

Dallas Cowboys Cheerleaders II (TV)— Texi Waterman

Dames— Busby Berkeley, Ruby Keeler

Damn Yankees— Bob Fosse

A Damsel in Distress— Fred Astaire, Hermes Pan

Dance: Echoes of Jazz (TV)— Grover Dale, Donald McKayle

Dance Americana (S)— Rod Alexander

Dance, Girl, Dance (1933)— Pearl Eaton

Dance, Girl, Dance (1940)— Ernst and Maria Matray

Dance Little Lady— David Paltenghi

Dance Madness (S)— Fanchon

The Dance of Life (1929)— Earl Lindsay

Dance of Life (1951)— Valerie Bettis, José Limon

Dance of the Ages (S)— Ted Shawn

Dance of the Damned— Ted Lin

Dance or Die— Minnie Madden

Dance Pretty Lady— Sir Frederick Ashton

Dance to Win— Paula Abdul, Jerry Evans

Dance with Death— Catharine Hebert

Dance with Me Henry— Lee Scott

The Dancer of Paris— Ernest Belcher

The Dancers (1930)— Ernest Belcher

Dancers (1987)— Mikhail Baryshnikov

Dancing Co-Ed—George King

Dancing Dolls (S)— Johnny Boyle

Dancing Feet— Nick Condos, Joseph Santley

Dancing in the Dark— Seymour Felix

Dancing Lady— Sammy Lee, Eddie Prinz

Dancing on a Dime— LeRoy Prinz

Dancing Pirate— Eduardo Cansino, Russell Lewis

Dancing Sweeties— Larry Ceballos

Dangerous Partners— Jack Donohue

Dangerous When Wet— Billy Daniel, Charles Walters

Danse Macabre/Terror in St. Petersburg— Michelle Zeitlin

Dante's Inferno— Eduardo Cansino, Sammy Lee

Darby O'Gill and the Little People— Tommy Mahoney
The Dark Crystal— Jean Pierre Amiel
Dark Red Roses— George Balanchine
Dark Sands— John Boyle
The Dark Secret of Harvest Home (aka *Harvest Home*) (TV)— Paul Godkin
Dark Waters— Jack Crosby
Darkie Melodies (S)— Alexander Oumansky
Darktown Follies (S)— John "Bubbles" Sublett
Darling Lilli— Hermes Pan
Das Nachtlokal zum Silbermond (aka *Caverns of Vice*)— Ernesto Bittner
A Date with Judy— Stanley Donen
The Daughter of Rosie O'Grady— Gene Nelson, Miriam Nelson, LeRoy Prinz
David and Bathsheba— Jack Cole
David and Goliath— Carla Renalli
David Copperfield— Chester Hale
A Day at the Races— Bobby Connolly, Dave Gould
The Day of the Locust— Marge Champion, Miriam Nelson
The Day the Bubble Burst (TV)— Bobby Banas
The Day the Fish Came Out— Arthur Mitchell
Daydream Believer— Robyn Moarse
The Dead— Paul Gleason
Dead Again— Patsy Swayze
Deadly Advice— Nicky Hinkley
Deadly Dancer— Smith Wordes
Death Becomes Her— Brad Jeffries
Death Warrant— Jean-Claude Van Damme
Deathsport— George Fullwood
Decadence— Thorsten Kuth, Rodolopho Leoni
The Deceivers— Denny Martin Flinn
Deception— LeRoy Prinz
Deep in My Heart— Gene Kelly, Eugene Loring, Ann Miller
The Delicate Delinquent— Nick Castle
Delightfully Dangerous— Ernst Matray
Delirious— Toni Basil, Miranda Garrison
Delivery Boys— Jody Oliver, Nelson Vasquez
Delta Force 2—Rick Prieto
Demetrius and the Gladiators— Stephen Papich
Demon Pond— Rui Takemura
Dennis the Menace
Der Kongress Tanzt (aka *Congress Dances*)— Victor Gsovsky
Der Zarewitsch— Tatjana Gsovsky
Desert Legion— Asoka
The Desert Song (1943)— LeRoy Prinz
The Desert Song (1953)— LeRoy Prinz
Designing Woman— Jack Cole
Desire and Hell at Sunset Motel— Russell Clark
Desire Under the Elms— Josephine Earl
Désirée— Stephen Papich
Destry— Kenny Williams
The Devil Dancer— Ernest Belcher

Devil in a Blue Dress— Russell Clark
Devil-May-Care— Albertina Rasch
The Devil on Horseback— Ann Miller
The Devil Within Her— Mia Nadasi
The Devils— Terry Gilbert
The Devil's Bride (aka *The Devil Rides Out*)— David Toguri
The Devil's Cabaret (S)— Albertina Rasch
The Devil's Daffodil— Patricia Kirshner
Diamond Horseshoe (aka *Billy Rose's Diamond Horseshoe*)— Hermes Pan
The Diamond Queen— Asoka
Dick Tracy— Jeffrey Hornaday
Die Fledermaus (1964)— Willy Dirtl
Die Fledermaus (1955) (aka *Oh, Rosalinda!*)— Alfred Rodrigues
Diferente— Alfredo Alaria
Digga Digga Doo— Dave Gould
Dime with a Halo— Maggie Banks
Dimples— Jack Haskell, Bill Robinson
Dingaka— Sheila Wartski
Diplomaniacs— Larry Ceballos
Dirty Dancing— Miranda Garrison, Kenny Ortega
Divas (TV)— LTC Choreography
Divine Madness— Toni Basil
Diving In— Margo Faught
Dixiana— Pearl Eaton, Bill Robinson
Dixie— Louis DaPron, Seymour Felix
Dixieland Jamboree (S)— Fayard Nicholas
Do Not Disturb— Bruce Hoy
Do the Right Thing— Rosie Perez, Otis Sallid
Do You Love Me?— Seymour Felix
Dr. Detroit— Carlton Johnson
Doctor Dolittle— Herbert Ross
Doctor Faustus— Jacqueline Harvey
Doctor Goldfoot and the Bikini Machine— Jack Baker
Dr. Jekyll and Mr. Hyde— Ernst Matray
Dr. Rhythm— Jack Crosby
Doctor Terror's House of Horrors— Boscoe Holden
Doctor, You've Got to Be Kidding— Earl Barton
Doll Face— Kenny Williams
The Doll Shop (S)— Sammy Lee
The Dolly Sisters— Seymour Felix
Dominick and Eugene— Lenora Nemetz
Don Juan (1926)— Marion Morgan
Don Juan (1956)— Dia Luca
Don Juan De Marco— Adam Shankman
Don Juan My Love— Paco Romero
Don Quixote— Rudolph Nureyev
Don't Be a Menace— Donovan Henry
Don't Change Your Husband— Theodore Kosloff, Ted Shawn
Don't Fence Me In— Larry Ceballos
Don't Gamble with Love— Fayard Nicholas
Don't Knock the Rock— Earl Barton
Don't Knock the Twist— Hal Belfer

Don't Raise the Bridge, Lower the Water — Leo Kharibian

Don't Tell Mom the Babysitter's Dead — Brad Jeffries

The Doors — Paula Abdul, Bill and Jacqui Landrum

Doppleganger — Russell Clark

Double Agent — Miguel Delgado

Double Crossbones — Hal Belfer

Double Dynamite — Stanley Donen

Double Impact — Jean-Claude Van Damme

Double or Nothing (1936) (S) — Johnny Boyle

Double or Nothing (1937) — LeRoy Prinz

Double Trouble — Alex Romero

Doubling for Romeo — Ernest Belcher

Dough Boys — Sammy Lee

Down Among the Sheltering Palms — Seymour Felix

Down and Out in Beverly Hills — Bob Banas

Down Argentine Way — Nick Castle, Fayard Nicholas, Geneva Sawyer

Down the Drain — Isaac Florentino

Down to Earth — Jack Cole

Down to Their Last Yacht — Dave Gould

Downtown — Jeff Calhoun

Dracula: Dead and Loving It — Alan Johnson

Dragonslayer — Peggy Dixon

Dragonwyck — Arthur Appell

Dream Girl — Billy Daniel

Dream Lover — Michael Darrin

The Dream Maker (aka *It's All Happening*) — Pamela Devis, Douglas Squires

Dream Merchants (TV) — Tad Tadlock

Dreamboat — Gwen Verdon

Dreams (aka *Akira Kurosawa's Dreams*) — Michiyo Hata

Dressed to Thrill — Jack Donohue

Drums of Tahiti — Sylvia Lewis

Dubarry Did It Right (S) — Harland Dixon

Dubarry Was a Lady — Charles Walters, Gene Kelly

The Duchess and the Dirt Water Fox — Rob Iscove

The Duchess of Idaho — Jack Donohue, Eleanor Powell

Duel in the Sun — Tilly Losch, Lloyd Shaw

Duende y Misterio Del Flamenco — Antonio

Duffy's Tavern — Billy Daniel, Danny Dare

The Duke Is Tops — Willie Covan, Lew Crawford

Dutch Treat — Eddie Baytos

Dynamite — Theodore Kosloff

Eadie Was a Lady — Jack Cole, Ann Miller

The Eagle — Fanchon

Earl Carroll Sketchbook — Nick Castle

Earl Carroll Vanities — Sammy Lee

Earth Girls Are Easy — Russell Clark, Sarah Elgart, ISO: Daniel Ezralow, Jamie Hampton, Ashley Roland, Morleigh Steinberg, Wayne "Crescendo" Ward

East Side of Heaven — Val Raset

Easter Parade — Robert Alton, Fred Astaire, Ann Miller

Easy Come, Easy Go — Miriam Nelson, David Winters

Easy to Love — Busby Berkeley

Easy to Wed — Jack Donohue

Echoes — Dennis Wayne

Eddie — Eartha Robinson

Eddie and the Cruisers — Joanne Divito

Eddie and the Cruisers II: Eddie Lives! — Johnny Almaraz, Claude Thompson

The Eddie Cantor Story — LeRoy Prinz

The Edge of Innocence — Russell Clark

Edie and Penn — Jerry Evans

Edward II — Nigel Charnock, Floyd Newson

The Egyptian — Stephen Papich

Ein Blonden Traum — Victor Gsovsky

Eldfageln (aka *The Firebird*) — Maurice Béjart

Eleanor and Franklin (TV) — Bob Banas

The Electric Horseman — Bernadine Kent

Elephant Walk — Ram Gopal

Elisa — Guy Haggege

Eliza Comes to Stay — Howard Deighton

Elvira: Mistress of the Dark — Dona Davis-Clark

Elvis in Memphis (TV) — Dorain Sanchez

The Emerald Forest — José Possi

The Emperor Waltz — Billy Daniel

Empire — Bill and Jacqui Landrum

Enchantment — Billy Daniel

Encino Man — Peggy Holmes

The End — Lisa Mordente

Enemies of Women — Ernest Belcher

Enter the Ninja — Mike Stone

The Entertainer (TV) — Ron Field

Erik the Conqueror (aka *Fury of the Vikings*) — Leo Coleman

The Errand Boy — Nick Castle

Escape Me Never (1935) — Sir Frederick Ashton

Escape Me Never (1947) — LeRoy Prinz

Escape to Athena — Arlene Phillips

Esther and the King — Tito DeLuc

European Night — Archie Savage

The Europeans — Elizabeth Aldrich

Eve Knew Her Apples — Ann Miller

Even Cowgirls Get the Blues — Ruby Burns, Jann Dryer

Ever Since Venus — Jack Boyle

Evergreen — Buddy Bradley, Jessie Matthews

Every Day's a Holiday — LeRoy Prinz

Everybody Sing — Seymour Felix, Dave Gould

Everyone Says I Love You — Graciela Daniele

Everything Happens at Night — Nick Castle

Everything Happens to Me — Jack Donohue

Everything I Have Is Yours — Nick Castle, Gower Champion

Everything Is Rhythm — Joan Davis

Everything's on Ice — Dave Gould

Everywoman — Margaret Loomis

Evil Dead 2: Dead by Dawn—Andrea Brown, Susan Labatt, Tam G.Warner

Evita—Vince Paterson

Evita Peron (TV)—Paul DeRolfe

Excalibur—Anthony Van Laast

Excuse My Dust—Hermes Pan

Exorcist II: The Heretic—D.J. Giagni

Exotica—Claudia Moore

Expresso Bongo—Kenneth MacMillan

Exquisite Corpses (TV)—Daniel Esteras

Exterminator 2—Edward Love

F. Scott Fitzgerald and "The Last of the Belles" (TV)—George Bunt

The Fabulous Baker Boys—Peggy Holmes

The Fabulous Dorseys—Charles Baron

The Fabulous Señorita—Antonio Triana

Fair Wind to Java—Asoka

Fame—Louis Falco

The Fan—Arlene Phillips

Fandango—Mike Haley

Fantasia—George Balanchine, Marge Champion

The Fantasticks—Michael Smuin

Far and Away—Monica Devereux

The Far Cry—Ernest Belcher

The Far Horizons—Josephine Earl

Farewell to the King—Anne Semler

The Farmer Takes a Wife—Jack Cole

Fashions of 1934—Busby Berkeley

Fast Forward—Rick Atwell, Aimee Covo, Felix, Pamela Poitier, Gary Porter, Robin Summerfield, Charlie Washington

Fastest Guitar Alive—Wilda Taylor

Fastest Gun Alive—Alex Romero

A Fat Chance (S)—Gae Foster

Fat Man and Little Boy—Marilyn Corwin, Kurt Kaynor

Fatal Instinct—Lester Wilson

Father of the Bride—Shirley Kirkes

Father of the Bride 2—Peggy Holmes

Faust—Daria Vobornikova

Fear City—Kathryn Doby

Feet of Clay—Theodore Kosloff

Fellini's Casanova—Gino Landi

Fellini's Roma (aka *Roma*)—Gino Landi

Une Femme Française—Pat Garrett

Ferris Bueller's Day Off—Wilbert Bradley, Kenny Ortega

Feudin', Fussin' and A-Fightin'—Louis DaPron

Fiddler on the Roof—Tommy Abbott, Sammy Bayes, Jerome Robbins

Fiddlers Three—Buddy Bradley

The Field—Connie Ryan

A Field So White—Ben Lokey

The Fiendish Plot of Dr. Fu Manchu—Barry Collins

The Fiercest Heart—Roy Fitzell

Fiesta (1942) (S)—LeRoy Prinz

Fiesta (1946)—Eugene Loring

La Fiesta (S)—Eduardo Cansino

The Final Option—Anthony Van Laast

Finders Keepers—Hugh Lambert

A Fine Mess—Phil Gerard

Finian's Rainbow—Fred Astaire, Hermes Pan, Claude Thompson

Fire and Ice—Robin Cousins

Fire Down Below—Tutte Lemkow

Fire with Fire—Sarah Elgart

Fireball 500—Ronnie (Christopher) Riordan

The Firebird—Maurice Béjart

The Firefly—Albertina Rasch

Fires Within—Ron Arciaga

First a Girl—Buddy Bradley, Jessie Matthews, Ralph Reader

The First Nudie Musical—Lloyd Gordon

The Fish That Saved Pittsburgh—Debbie Allen

The Fisher King—Robin Horness

Fist Fighter—Jimmy Nickerson

Five Days One Summer—D'Dee

The Five Heartbeats—Michael Peters

The Five Pennies—Earl Barton

Five Weeks in a Balloon—Hal Belfer

Flame of Araby—Hal Belfer

The Flame of Calcutta—Asoka

The Flame of Love—Alexander Oumansky

The Flame of the Barbary Coast—Larry Ceballos

Flamenco—Antonio

Flaming Star—Josephine Earl

Flamingo (S)—Katherine Dunham

The Flamingo Kid—Christopher Chadman

Flareup—Joe Tremaine

Flashdance—Jeffrey Hornaday

The Fleet's In—Jack Donohue

Fletch Lives—Michael Smuin

Fletch Saved—Michael Smuin

Flight from Folly—Buddy Bradley

The Flight of the Phoenix—Pat Denise

The Flintstones—Adam Shankman

Flirtation Walk—Bobby Connolly, Ruby Keeler

Flirting—Gil Falson

The Floorwalker—Charles Chaplin

Florian—Ernst and Maria Matray

Flower Drum Song—Hermes Pan

Flowers from the Sky (S)—Harland Dixon

Fluffy—Hal Belfer

Flying Down to Rio—Fred Astaire, Dave Gould, Hermes Pan

Flying High—Busby Berkeley

Folies Bergère (1935)—Dave Gould

Folies Bergère (1958)—Roland Petit

Follies Girl—Larry Ceballos

Follow a Star—Eleanor Fazan

Follow That Man—Hazel Gee

Follow the Band—Louis DaPron

Follow the Boys—Carmen Amaya, Louis DaPron, George Hale, Frank Veloz

Follow the Fleet—Fred Astaire, Hermes Pan

Follow Thru— David Bennett
Follow Your Heart— Larry Ceballos
Fools' Fire— David Parsons
Fools for Scandal— Bobby Connolly
Fools Paradise— Theodore Kosloff
Footlight Parade— Busby Berkeley, Larry Ceballos, Ruby Keeler
Footlight Rhythm (S)— Billy Daniel
Footlight Serenade— Hermes Pan
Footlights (S)— Albertina Rasch
Footlights and Fools— Max Scheck
Footloose— Dorain Grusman, Charlene Painter, Lynn Taylor-Corbett
Footsteps in the Dark— Robert Vreeland
For Ladies Only (TV)— Paul DeRolf
For Love or Money— Sylvia Lewis
For Me and My Gal— Busby Berkeley, Bobby Connolly, Gene Kelly, George Murphy
For Singles Only— Alex Romero
For the Boys— Joe Layton
For Those Who Think Young— Robert Tucker
Forbidden Fruit— Theodore Kosloff
Forbidden Music— John Boyle
Forever My Love— Willy Franzl
Forget-Me-Knots (S)— Gae Foster
Forget Paris— Debbie Allen, Lisa Estrada
The Formula— William Milié
Forrest Gump— Leslie Cook, Lisa Estrada
Fort Algiers— Hal Belfer
Fort Apache— Kenny Williams
Foul Play (S)— John "Bubbles" Sublett
Four Friends— Julie Arenal
The Four Horsemen of the Apocalypse (1962)— Alex Romero
Four Jacks and a Jill— Ray Bolger, Aida Broadbent
Four Jills in a Jeep— Don Loper
The Four Poster— Olga Lunick
Four Rooms— Sissy Boyd
Fox Movietone Follies of 1929— Willie Covan, Fanchon, Edward Royce
Fox Movietone Follies of 1930— Danny Dare, Maurice Kussell, Max Scheck
Foxhole in Cairo— Patricia Kirshner
Frankie and Johnny (1966)— Earl Barton
Frankie and Johnny (1991)— Shirley Kirkes
Frantic— Derf La Chapelle
Fraulein— David Lichine
Freddie Steps Out— Jack Boyle
Free and Easy— Sammy Lee
A Free Woman— William Milié
Freedom Road (TV)— Bill Mackey
French Can Can (aka *Only the French Can*)— Claude Grandjean
The French Line— Billy Daniel
French Quarter— Donnis Hunnicutt
Frenchman's Creek— Billy Daniel
Fresh from Paris (aka *Paris Follies of 1956*)— Donn Arden

Freshman Year— Matty King
Fright Night— Dorain Grusman
Fright Night— *Part 2*— Russell Clark
The Frisco Kid— Alex Romero
Frisco Sal— Lester Horton
Fun in Acapulco— Charles O'Curran
Funny Bones— Christine Avery
Funny Face— Fred Astaire, Stanley Donen, Eugene Loring
Funny Girl— Herbert Ross
Funny Lady— Herbert Ross
A Funny Thing Happened on the Way to the Forum— Jack Cole, George and Ethel Martin
The Furies— Josephine Earl
The Furnace— Ernest Belcher
Fury of the Vikings (aka *Erik the Conqueror*)— Leo Coleman
Futures Vedettes (aka *Sweet Sixteen* and *Future Stars*)— George Reich
FX 2— *The Deadly Art of Illusion*— Moses Pendleton
G-Men— Bobby Connolly
G.I. Blues— Charles O'Curran
Gaby— Michael Panaieff
The Gaiety Girls (aka *Paradise for Two*)— Philip Buchel, Jack Donohue, Jack Hulbert
The Gal Who Took the West— Hal Belfer
Gals, Incorporated— Josephine Earl
Gambit— Paul Godkin
The Gang's All Here— Busby Berkeley
Gangway— Buddy Bradley, Jessie Matthews
The Garden of Allah— Tilly Losch
Garden of the Moon— Busby Berkeley
Gay Divorcee— Fred Astaire, Dave Gould, Hermes Pan
The Gay Parisien (S)— Léonide Massine
The Gay Señorita— Stanley Donen, Antonio Triana
The Gazebo— Alex Romero
The Geek— Myrna Gawryn
The Gem of the Ocean (S)— Richard Barstow
Gems of MGM (S)— Ernest Belcher
General Crack— Ernest Belcher
Genevieve— Eric Rogers
Gentlemen Marry Brunettes— Jack Cole
Gentlemen Prefer Blondes— Jack Cole
George Balanchine's The Nutcracker— George Balanchine
The George Raft Story— Alex Romero
George White's Scandals of 1934— Chester Hale, Russell Markert
George White's Scandals of 1935— Jack Donohue, Chester Hale, Eleanor Powell
George White's Scandals of 1945— Ernst Matray
George's Island— Pat Richards
Georgia, Georgia— Herman Howell
Germinal— Nicole Dehayes
Geronimo: An American Legend— Desmond F. Strobel

Get Crazy— Lori Eastside
Get Hep to Love— Louis DaPron
Get Yourself a College Girl— Hal Belfer
Getting Even with Dad— Michelle Johnston
Getting Physical (TV)— Jerry Evans
The Ghost Catchers— Louis DaPron
Ghost Fever— Carlton Johnson
The Ghost in the Invisible Bikini— Jack Baker
Gidget Goes Hawaiian— Roland Dupree
Gigi— George Reich, Charles Walters
Gigolo— Ernest Belcher
Gilda— Jack Cole
Gilda Live— Patricia Birch
Gimme an "F"— Steve Merritt
Ginger and Fred— Tony Ventura
A Girl, a Guy and a Gob— George Murphy
Girl Crazy— Busby Berkeley, Jack Donohue,
　Charles Walters
The Girl Friend— Seymour Felix
The Girl from Petrovka— Anna Cheselska
Girl Happy— David Winters
The Girl in the Red Velvet Swing— David Robel
Girl in the Streets (aka *London Melody*)— Ralph
　Reader
The Girl Most Likely— Gower Champion
The Girl Next Door— Richard Barstow, Michael
　Kidd
The Girl of the Golden West— Albertina Rasch
Girl on the Spot— Louis DaPron
Girl Rush (1944)— Charles O'Curran
The Girl Rush (1955)— Robert Alton
Girl with a Bad Memory— Billy Daniel
The Girl Without a Room— Larry Ceballos
Les Girls— Gene Kelly, Jack Cole
Girls! Girls! Girls!— Charles O'Curran
Girls in the Night— Hal Belfer
Girls Just Want to Have Fun— Bill Goodson, Steve
　LaChance, Otis Sallid
Girls of the White Orchid (TV)— Dom Salinaro
Give a Girl a Break— Gower Champion, Stanley
　Donen, Bob Fosse, Bill Foster
Give Me a Sailor— LeRoy Prinz
Give My Regards to Broad Street— David Toguri
Give My Regards to Broadway— Seymour Felix
Give Out Sisters— James Mattison
Glamourous Night— Keith Lester
The Glass Slipper— Roland Petit, Charles Wal-
　ters
The Glenn Miller Story— Archie Savage, Kenny
　Williams
A Global Affair— Hal Belfer
Glorifying the American Girl— Ted Shawn, John
　H. Harkrider
Glory Alley— Charles O'Curran
The Glory Brigade— Matt Mattox
Go Go Mania— Leo Kharibian
Go Into Your Dance— Busby Berkeley, Bobby
　Connolly, Ruby Keeler

Go West, Young Lady— Louis DaPron, Ann Miller
The Godfather, Part 2— Jerry Jackson, Steven
　Peck
The Godless Girl— Ernest Belcher
Godspell— Sammy Bayes
Goin' to Town— Paul Oscard
Going Hollywood— George Cunningham,
　Albertina Rasch
The Gold Rush— Charles Chaplin
The Golden Bed— Theodore Kosloff
The Golden Blade— Eugene Loring
The Golden Calf— Earl Lindsay
The Golden Child— Michael Smuin
Golden Dawn— Eduardo Cansino, Larry Ceballos
Golden Earrings— Billy Daniel
Golden Gate— Michael Smuin
Golden Girl— Seymour Felix
The Golden Hawk— Lester Horton
The Golden Horde— Hal Belfer
GoldenEye— Jane Turner
Goldie and the Boxer Go to Hollywood (TV)— Don
　Crichton
Goldiggers in Paris— Busby Berkeley
The Goldiggers of Broadway— Larry Ceballos
Goldiggers of 1933— Busby Berkeley, Ruby Keeler
Goldiggers of 1935— Busby Berkeley
Goldiggers of 1937— Busby Berkeley
The Goldwyn Follies— George Balanchine, Sammy
　Lee
Gone with the Wind— Eddie Prinz
Good Companions (1933)— Buddy Bradley, Jessie
　Matthews
The Good Companions (1956)— Irving Davies,
　Paddy Stone
The Good Earth— Tilly Losch
Good Morning, Babylon— Gino Landi
Good Neighbor Sam— Miriam Nelson
Good News (1930)— Sammy Lee
Good News (1947)— Robert Alton, Charles Wal-
　ters
The Good Old Soak— Val Raset
Good Times— Andre Tayir
The Goodbye Girl— Michael Shawn
Goodbye, Mr. Chips— Herbert Ross
A Goofy Movie— Anthony Thomas
The Goolangatta Gold— Robert Ray
Gor— Neil McKay
The Gorgeous Hussy— Val Raset
Grace of My Heart— Keith Young
Grace Quigley— Terry Reiser
The Gracie Allen Murder Case— Sammy Lee
Graffiti Bridge— Otis Sallid
The Grand Parade— Richard Boleslawski
Grandview U.S.A.— Lisa Niemi, Patrick Swayze
Grease— Patricia Birch
Grease 2— Patricia Birch
The Great American Broadcast— Fayard Nicholas
Great Balls of Fire— Bill and Jacqui Landrum

The Great Bank Robbery— Miriam Nelson
Great Catherine— Paddy Stone
The Great Dictator— Charles Chaplin
Great Expectations— Suria Magita
The Great Gabbo— Maurice Kusell
The Great Gatsby— Tony Stevens
The Great Muppet Caper— Anita Mann
The Great Outdoors— Kenny Ortega
The Great Race— Hermes Pan
The Great Victor Herbert— LeRoy Prinz
The Great Waltz (1938)— Albertina Rasch
The Great Waltz (1972)— Onna White
The Great White Hope— Donald McKayle
Great Ziegfeld— Ray Bolger, Seymour Felix
The Greatest Show on Earth— John Murray
  Anderson, Barbette
The Green Grass of Wyoming— Angie Blue
Green Mansions— Katherine Dunham
Greenwich Village— Tony De Marco, Seymour
  Felix, Four Step Brothers
Greystoke: The Legend of Tarzan— Peter Elliott
The Grissom Gang— Alex Romero
Ground Zero— Tony Bartuccio
Grumpier Old Men— Michelle Johnston
Guarding Tess— Mary Ann Kellogg
The Gun in Betty Lou's Handbag— Adam Shank-
  man
Gunfight at the O.K. Corral—Josephine Earl
The Gunrunners— Steven Peck
Guns, Girls and Gangsters— Jack Baker
Guys and Dolls— Michael Kidd
Gypsy (1962)— Jerome Robbins, Robert Tucker
Gypsy (1993) (TV)— Peggy Holmes, Jerome Rob-
  bins, Bonnie Walker
Gypsy Soul (*Alma Gitana*)— Lozano
Gypsy Wildcat— Lester Horton
Gypsyland (S)— Alexander Oumansky
Hair— Twyla Tharp
Hairspray— Edward Love
Half a Sixpence— Gillian Lynne
Half Shot at Sunrise— Anthony Nelle, Mary Read
The Hallelujah Trail— Wally Green
Hamlet— David Paltenghi
Hammerhead— Ralph Tobert
The Hand and the Glove (TV)— Dorian Sanchez
Hands Across the Border— Dave Gould
Handy Andy— Sammy Lee
Hans Christian Andersen— Roland Petit
The Happiest Millionaire— Marc Breaux, Dee Dee
  Wood
Happy Days— Earl Lindsay
Happy Go Lovely— Jack Billings, Pauline Grant
Happy-Go-Lucky— Paul Oscard
The Happy Hooker— Donald Saddler
Happy Landing— Condos Bros, Harry Losee
Happy Together— Jeff Calhoun
Hard Target— Jean-Claude Van Damme
Hard to Kill— Steven Seagal

The Hard Way— LeRoy Prinz
Hardbodies— Randy DiGrazio
Harem Girl— Lee Scott
Harlem Bound (S)— John "Bubbles" Sublett
Harlem Cabaret— Ralph Cooper
Harlem Is Heaven— Bill Robinson
Harlow— Jack Baker
Harmony Heaven— Alexander Oumansky
Harold Robbins' "79 Park Avenue" (TV)— JoAnne
  Divito
Harold Teen— Hal LeRoy
Harry and the Hendersons— Nancy Gregory
Harum Scarum— Earl Barton
Harvest Home (aka *The Dark Secret of Harvest
  Home*)— Paul Godkin
The Harvey Girls— Robert Alton, Ray Bolger,
  Charles Walters
Has Anybody Seen My Gal?— Hal Belfer
Hat Check Honey— Carlos Romero
Hats Off— Arthur Dreifuss, Victor Petroff
Haunted— Pamela Devis
Haunted Honeymoon— Graciela Daniele
Haut Bas Fragile (*Up Down Fragile*)— Caroline
  Marcade
Havana— Vincent Paterson
Hawaii— Miriam Nelson
Hawaii Calls— Augie Auld
Hawaiian Nights— Jack Crosby
Haywire (TV)— Shanda Sawyer
He Laughed Last— Miriam Nelson
He Loved an Actress (aka *Mad About Money* and
  Stardust)— Larry Ceballos
He Makes Me Feel Like Dancin'— Jacques d'Am-
  boise
Head— Toni Basil
Head Over Heels in Love— Buddy Bradley, Jessie
  Matthews
Heads Up— George Hale
The Hearst and Davies Affair—(TV) Kelly Robin-
  son
Heart and Souls— Adam Shankman
Heart Like a Wheel— Bob Banas
Heart of Dixie— John Henry
Heart of Maryland— Ernest Belcher
Heartbreak Hotel— Monica Devereux
Heartbreakers— Jerry Evans
Hearts in Dixie— Fanchon
Hearts of the West— Sylvia Lewis
Heat and Sunlight— Consuelo Faust
The Heat's On— David Lichine
Heaven and Earth— Jean-Pierre Fournier, Hiroshi
  Kuze
Heavenly Bodies— Brian Foley
Heaven's Gate— Eleanor Fazan, Tad Tadlock
Heidi— Sammy Lee
The Heiress— Josephine Earl
The Helen Morgan Story— LeRoy Prinz
Helen of Troy— Madi Oblensky

Hell Squad— Andrea Hartford
Hell to Eternity— Roland Dupree
Heller in Pink Tights— Val Raset
Hello, Dolly!— Shelah Hackett, Michael Kidd
Hello, Frisco, Hello— Val Raset
Hello Good Times (S)— Johnny Boyle, Albertina Rasch
Hello London— George Baron, Ted Shuffle
Hello Pop (S)— Albertina Rasch
Hello Sister— Maurice Kusell
Hello Sweetheart— Ralph Reader
Hell's Angels— Albertina Rasch
Hellzapoppin'—Richard Barstow, Nick Castle, Eddie Prinz
Henry and June— Nathalie Erlbaum
Henry VII and His Six Wives— Terry Gilbert
Her Highness and the Bellboy— Charles Walters
Her Lucky Night— Louis DaPron
Her Triumph— Harry Pilcer
Hercules Conquers Atlantis (aka *Hercules and the Captive Women* and *Hercules and the Conquest of Atlantis*)— Pieter Van Der Sloot
Hercules, Samson and Ulysses— Wilbert Bradley
Here Come the Co-Eds— Louis DaPron
Here Come the Girls— Nick Castle, Four Step Brothers
Here Come the Waves— Danny Dare
Here Comes the Band— Chester Hale
Here Comes the Groom— Charles O'Curran
Here's to Romance— Maria Gambarelli
Hero and the Terror— Rick Prieto
Heroes of the Street— Ernest Belcher
He's My Guy— Louis Dapron, Carlos Romero
Hey Babe!— Lynn Taylor Corbett
Hey, Rookie!— Condos Brothers, Louis DaPron, Stanley Donen, Ann Miller, Val Raset
Hi Buddy— Four Step Brothers, Dick Humphreys, Carlos Romero
Hi, Good Lookin'—Louis DaPron, Tip,Tap and Toe
Hi Ya Chum— Eddie Prinz, Carlos Romero
Hi Ya Sailor— Carlos Romero
The Hidden— Jane Cassell
Hideaway Girl— Louis DaPron
High Anxiety— Alan Johnson
High School Hero— Jack Boyle
The High School Hoofer (S)— Hal LeRoy
High Society— Charles Walters
High Spirits— Micha Bergese
High Tide— David Atkins
High Time— Miriam Nelson
High Toned (S)— John "Bubbles" Sublett
High, Wide and Handsome— LeRoy Prinz
Higher and Higher— Ernst Matray
Highlander— Arlene Phillips
Hips, Hips, Hooray— Dave Gould
His Majesty O'Keefe— Daniel Nagrin

History of the World, Part 1— Alan Johnson
The Hit Parade of 1941— Danny Dare, Ann Miller
The Hit Parade of 1943— Nick Castle
The Hit Parade of 1947— Fanchon
The Hit Parade of 1951— Val Raset
Hit the Deck (1930)— Pearl Eaton
Hit the Deck (1955)— Ann Miller, Hermes Pan
Hit the Ice— Sammy Lee, Harry Losee
Hitler's SS: Portrait in Evil (TV)— Eva Darlow
Hocus Pocus— Peggy Holmes, Kenny Ortega
Hold 'Em Navy— Billy Daniel
Hold Everything!— Larry Ceballos
Hold My Hand— Philip Buchel
Hold On!— Wilda Taylor
Hold That Co-Ed— Nick Castle, George Murphy, Geneva Sawyer
Hold That Ghost— Nick Castle
Holiday for Lovers— José Greco
Holiday in Mexico— Stanley Donen
Holiday Inn— Fred Astaire, Danny Dare
Hollywood Canteen— Antonio, LeRoy Prinz, Frank Veloz
Hollywood Fever— Lee Scott
Hollywood Hotel— Busby Berkeley
Hollywood or Bust— Charles O' Curran
Hollywood Party— Seymour Felix, Dave Gould, George Hale
Hollywood Party in Technicolor (S)— Carlos Romero
Hollywood Premier (S)— LeRoy Prinz
Hollywood Revue of 1929— Ernest Belcher, George Cunningham, Sammy Lee, Natacha Natova, Albertina Rasch
Hollywood Shuffle— Donald Douglass
Hollywood Story—Michelle Zeitlin
The Holy Terror— Jack Haskell
Home in Indiana— Geneva Sawyer
L'Homme de Ma Vie (*The Man in My Life*)— Arthur Plasschaert
Honest Crooks (S)— John "Bubbles" Sublett
Honey— David Bennett
The Honey Pot— Lee Theodore
Honeymoon (1947)— Charles O'Curran
Honeymoon (1959) (aka *Luna da Miel*)— Antonio, Léonide Massine
Honeymoon Ahead— Louis DaPron
Honeymoon for Three— Carl Hyson, Leslie Roberts
Honeymoon Hotel— Miriam Nelson
Honeymoon Lodge— Tip,Tap and Toe, Frank Veloz
Honky Tonk— Larry Ceballos
Honolulu— Bobby Connolly, Sammy Lee, Eleanor Powell
Hook— Kim Blank, Vincent Paterson, Smith Wordes
Hooray for Love— Maria Gambarelli, Sammy Lee, Bill Robinson
Hoosier Holiday— Josephine Earl

Hootenany Hoot— Hal Belfer
Hope and Glory— Anthony Van Laast
Horse Feathers— Harold Hecht
Hot Blood— Sylvia Lewis, Matt Mattox
Hot Moves— Andrea Mueller
Hot Rhythm— Jack Boyle
Hot Shots— Lester Wilson
Hot Shots: Part Deux— Lester Wilson
Hot Tomorrows— Lloyd Gordon
Hotel Sahara— David Paltenghi
Hound Dog Man— Josephine Earl
House Across the Bay— Sammy Lee
House Arrest— Keith Young
A House Is Not a Home— Wilda Taylor
House of Wax— LeRoy Prinz
House Party— A. J. Johnson, Tisha Campbell, Kid N' Play
House Party II— Jimmy Hamilton, Vernon Jackson, Kid N' Play
House Party III— Russell Clark
Houseboat— Josephine Earl
How the West Was Won— Robert Sidney
How to Be Very, Very Popular— Paul Godkin, Sonia Shaw
How to Commit Marriage— Jack Baker
How to Get Ahead in Advertising— David Toguri
How to Make an American Quilt— Peri Rogovin
How to Murder a Millionaire— Felix Chavez
How to Murder Your Wife— Robert Sidney
How to Stuff a Wild Bikini— Jack Baker
How to Succeed in Business Without Really Trying— Bob Fosse, Dale Moreda
Howard the Duck— Sarah Elgart
The Howling II— Diane Garcia
How's About It— Louis DaPron
Huckleberry Finn— Marc Breaux
The Hudsucker Proxy— Wesley Fata
Hullabaloo— Sammy Lee
The Human Comedy—Ernst Matray
The Hunchback of Notre Dame (1924)— Ernest Belcher
The Hunchback of Notre Dame (1977) (TV)— Geraldine Stephenson
The Hunchback of Notre Dame (1996)— Naomi Goldberg
The Hunger— Arlene Phillips
The Hurdy Gurdy (aka *Neopolitan Carousel*)— Léonide Massine
Hurricane— Coco Ellacott
Hurricane Smith— Josephine Earl
Hush, Hush Sweet Charlotte— Alex Ruiz
Hustle— Alex Romero
I Adore You— Ralph Reader
I Am Suzanne— Sammy Lee
I Could Go on Singing— Joe Layton
The I "Don't Care" Girl— Jack Cole, Seymour Felix
I Dood It— Bobby Connolly, Eleanor Powell

I Dream of Jeannie— Nick Castle
I Dream Too Much— Hermes Pan
I Live for Love— Busby Berkeley
I Love Melvin— Robert Alton
I Love Trouble— Peggy Holmes
I Love You— Gerry Marotski
I Love You to Death— Tad Tadlock
I Loved You Wednesday— Sammy Lee
I Married a Woman— Les Clark, Peggy Gordon
I Married an Angel— Ernst and Maria Matray
I Rhythm— Eartha Robinson
I Was an Adventuress— George Balanchine
I Wonder Who's Kissing Her Now— Hermes Pan
Ice-Capades— Henry Losee
Ice-Capades Revue—Henry Losee
Ice Castles— Brian Foley
Ice Follies of 1939— Frances Claudet, Val Raset
The Ice Pirates— Mark Knowles
Iceland— James Gonzalez, Hermes Pan
I'd Rather Be Rich— Hal Belfer, Miriam Nelson
Idiot's Delight— George King
The Idle Class— Charles Chaplin
The Idol Dancer— Ernest Belcher
The Idolmaker— Deney Terrio
If I'm Lucky— Kenny Williams
If You Knew Susie— Charles O' Curran
I'll Cry Tomorrow—Alex Romero
I'll Do Anything— Twyla Tharp
I'll Get By— Larry Ceballos
I'll See You in My Dreams— LeRoy Prinz
I'll Take Sweden— Miriam Nelson
I'll Tell the World— Louis DaPron
Illusory Thoughts— Patrick Chu
I'm Gonna Git You Sucka— Russell Clark
I'm Nobody's Sweetheart Now— Eduardo Cansino, Louis DaPron
Imitation of Life— Donn Arden
Imperfect Lady— Billy Daniel, Josephine Earl
In and Out (S)— John "Bubbles" Sublett
In Bed with Madonna (aka *Madonna — Truth or Dare*)— Vincent Paterson
In Caliente— Busby Berkeley, Tony DeMarco
The In Crowd— Jerry Evans, Lynne Taylor-Corbett, Linda Weisburg
In God We Trust— Dee Dee Wood
In Harm's Way— Miriam Nelson
In Like Flint— Stefan Wenta
In Love and War— Jack Regas
In Old Kentucky— Bill Robinson
In Person— Hermes Pan
In the Good Old Summertime— Robert Alton
In the Meantime Darling— Geneva Sawyer
In the Mood— Miguel Delgado
In the Navy— Nick Castle, Condos Brothers
In the Nick— Lionel Blair
In This Corner (S)— George Tapps
Inbetween Age— Elizabeth West
Incendiary Blonde— Danny Dare

Indiana Jones and the Temple of Doom— Danny Daniels

Indochine— Chris Gandois

The Innocent— Eleanor Fazan

Innocents of Paris— Fanchon and Marco, LeRoy Prinz

Inside Daisy Clover— Herbert Ross

Inspector Clouseau— Eleanor Fazan

The Inspector General— Eugene Loring

Instant Karma— Chris Hamman

International House— Harold Hecht

The Interns— Miriam Nelson

Interview with the Vampire— Micha Bergese

Intolerance— Ruth St. Denis, Ted Shawn

Invitation to the Dance— Jeanne Coyne, Carol Haney, Gene Kelly

Invitation to the Waltz— Anton Dolin, Wendy Toye

Irene (1926)— Ernest Belcher

Irene (1940)— Aida Broadbent

Irish Eyes Are Smiling— Hermes Pan

Irma La Douce— Wally Green

Iron Eagles II— Carla Earle

Irreconcilable Differences— Tad Tadlock

Is Everybody Happy?— Larry Ceballos

Isadora (aka *The Loves of Isadora*)— Frederick Ashton, Litz Pisk

Isle of Escape— Eduardo Cansino

Isle of Lesbos— Gail Conrad

Isle of Tabu— Josephine Earl

Isn't It Romantic?— Danny Dare, Josephine Earl

It Ain't Hay— Danny Dare, Four Step Brothers

It All Came True— Dave Gould

It Comes Up Love— Louis DaPron

It Could Happen to You— John Carrafa

It Couldn't Happen Here— Arlene Phillips

It Happened at the World's Fair— Jack Baker

It Happened in Brooklyn— Jack Donohue

It Only Happens with You (aka *Let It Be Me*)— Miranda Garrison

It Started in Naples— Leo Coleman

It Takes Two— Sarah Elgart

It's a Great Feeling— LeRoy Prinz

It's a Great Life— Sammy Lee

It's a Pleasure— Don Loper

It's a Wonderful Life (aka *Swinger's Paradise*)— Gillian Lynne

It's All Happening (aka *The Dream Maker*)— Pamela Devis, Douglas Squires

It's Always Fair Weather— Stanley Donen, Gene Kelly

It's Great to Be Alive— Sammy Lee

It's Love Again— Buddy Bradley, Jessie Matthews

It's Pat: The Movie— Lynne Hockney

It's Swing Ho— Come to the Fair (S)— Bill Robinson

Ivan the Terrible— Yuri Grigorovich

Jack Ahoy!— Jack Hulbert

Jack and the Beanstalk (1952)— Johnny Conrad

Jack and the Beanstalk (1967) (TV)— Gene Kelly

Jack of All Trades— Philip Buchel, Johnny Boyle, Jack Hulbert

Jack the Giant Killer— Jon Gregory

Jackass Mail— Sammy Lee

Jack's the Boy— Philip Buchel, Jack Hulbert

The Jacksons: An American Dream (TV)— Michael Peters

Jacqueline Susann's Valley of the Dolls (TV)— Earl Barton

Jacques Brel Is Alive and Well— Moni Yakim

Jailbird Rock— Dennon and Sayhber Rawles

Jailbirds of Paradise (S)— Sammy Lee

Jailhouse Rock— Alex Romero

Jam Session— Stanley Donen, Ann Miller

Jammin' the Blues (S)— Jack Cole, Archie Savage

Jan of the Jungle— Maurice Kosloff

Jane and the Lost City— Gillian Gregory

Janie— LeRoy Prinz

The January Man— David Allan

The Jayne Mansfield Story (TV)— JoAnne Divito

Jazz Boat—Lionel Blair

The Jazz Singer (1927)— Ernest Belcher

The Jazz Singer (1953)— LeRoy Prinz

The Jazz Singer (1980)— Shlomo Bachar, Donald McKayle

Jeanne Eagles— Frances Grant

Jefferson in Paris— Elizabeth Aldrich, Beatrice Massin

Jeffrey— Jerry Mitchell

Jenny Be Good— Ernest Belcher

The Jerk— Scott Salmon

Jesse James' Women— Ann Royal, Jess Saunders

Jesus Christ Superstar— Rob Iscove

Jesus of Nazareth (TV)— Alberto Testa

The Jewel of the Nile— Bill Goodson

Jimmy and Sally— Sammy Lee

Jinxed!— Robert Thompson

Jitterbugs— Geneva Sawyer

Jive Junction— Don Gallagher

Jivin' Jam Session (S)— Louis DaPron

Jo Jo Dancer, Your Life Is Calling— Jennifer Stace

Joan of Ozark— Nick Castle

John Goldfarb, Please Come Home— Paul Godkin

John Paul Jones— Hector Zaraspe

Johnny Apollo— Geneva Sawyer

Johnny Dangerously— Tony Stevens

Johnny Doughboy— Nick Castle

The Joker Is Wild— Josephine Earl

Jolson Sings Again— Audrene Brier

The Jolson Story— Audrene Brier, Jack Cole, Miriam Nelson

The Josephine Baker Story (TV)— George Faison

Josette— Nick Castle, Geneva Sawyer

Joshua Then and Now— Brian Foley

Journey to the Center of the Earth— Joan Bayley

Journey to the Lost City (aka *Tigress of Bengal*)— Billy Daniel, Robby Gay

The Joy Luck Club— Michael Smuin
Jubilee Trail— Jack Baker
Juke Box Jenny— Louis DaPron
Juke Box Rhythm— Hal Belfer
Julia Misbehaves— Jack Donohue
Julie the Redhead— George Reich
Jumpin' Jack Flash— Jerry Evans
Jumping Jacks— Nick Castle
Junior— Marguerite Derricks
Junior Prom— Dean Collins
Jupiter's Darling— Gower Champion, Hermes Pan
Jury Duty— Peggy Holmes
Just a Gigolo— Herbert F. Schubert
Just Around the Corner— Nick Castle, Bill Robinson, Geneva Sawyer
Just for You— Helen Tamiris
Just Imagine— Seymour Felix
Just Like a Woman— David Massingham
Just One of the Guys— Jennifer Stace
Justine— Gemze DeLappe
Kansas City Kitty— Stanley Donen
The Karate Kid— Pat E. Johnson
The Karate Kid Part II— Paul DeRolf, Jose DeVega, Pat E. Johnson, Nobuko Miyamoto, Randall Sabusawa
The Karate Kid Part III— Paula Abdul, Pat E. Johnson
Katz' Pajamas (S)— George Tapps
Kazablan— Shimon Braun
Keep 'Em Flying— Nick Castle
Keep Smiling— Jack Donohue
Keep Your Seats Please— John Boyle
Kelly and Me— Kenny Williams
Kenner— Sudarshan Kunar
The Kettles in the Ozarks— Louis DaPron
Key Exchange— Sara Sugihara
Kickboxer— Jean-Claude Van Damme
The Kid from Brooklyn— Bernard Pearce
The Kid from Spain— Busby Berkeley
Kid Millions— Seymour Felix, George Murphy, Fayard Nicholas
Kiki (1926)— Fanchon
Kiki (1931)— Busby Berkeley
Killer McCoy— Stanley Donen
Killer Party— Malcolm Gale
Killer's Kiss— David Vaughan
Kimberly Jim— Sheila Wartski
The King and I— Jerome Robbins
The King and the Chorus Girl— Bobby Connolly
King Creole— Charles O'Curran
King David— Eleanor Fazan
King for a Day— Bill Robinson
King Kong— Claude Thompson
King Kong Lives (aka *Queen Kong*)— Gillian Gregory
The King of Burlesque— Sammy Lee
The King of Jazz— John Murray Anderson, Russell Markert

The King of Kings— Betty Utey
The King of the Gypsies— Julie Arenal
King of the Khyber Rifles— Asoka, Stephen Papich
King Ralph— Pat Garrett
The King Steps Out— Albertina Rasch
The Kings of Caroline— Toni Basil
The King's Rhapsody— Jon Gregory
Kismet (1941) (aka *An Oriental Dream*)— Jack Cole
Kismet (1955)— Jack Cole
Kiss Me a Killer— Renee Victor
Kiss Me Again— Billy Daniel
Kiss Me Goodbye— Gene Castle
Kiss Me Kate— Bob Fosse, Ann Miller, Hermes Pan
Kiss Me Stupid— Wally Green
Kissin' Cousins— Hal Belfer
The Kissing Bandit— Robert Alton, Stanley Donen, Ann Miller
Kitten with a Whip— David Winters
Kitty— Billy Daniel
Knickerbocker Holiday— Jack Crosby
The Knight Is Young (S)— Gae Foster, Hal LeRoy
Knights and Emeralds— Quinny Sacks
Knights of the City— Jeff Kutash, Dallace Winkler
Knock on Wood— Michael Kidd
Krush Groove— Lori Eastside
Kuffs— Karole Armitage
Labyrinth— Charles Augins, Cherly McFadden
The Ladies' Man (1947)— Billy Daniel
The Ladies' Man (1961)— Sylvia Lewis, Bobby Van
Ladies of the Chorus— Jack Boyle
Lady and the Monster— Antonio Triana
Lady Be Good— Busby Berkeley, Berry Bros, Eleanor Powell
Lady Caroline Lamb— Eleanor Fazan
Lady for a Night— Dave Gould
Lady in the Dark— Nick Castle, Billy Daniel, Don Loper
The Lady Is Willing— Douglas Dean
Lady, Let's Dance— Dave Gould, Michel Panaieff
Lady of Burlesque— Danny Dare
A Lady of Scandal— Sammy Lee
The Lady on the Tracks— Josef Konicek
The Lady Takes a Flyer— Antonio Triana
Ladykillers (TV)— Jerry Evans
A Lady's Morals— Sammy Lee
The Lair of the White Worm— Imogen Claire
Lake Placid Serenade— Jack Crosby, Felix Sadowski
Lambada— Shabba Doo
Lambada: The Forbidden Dance— Felix Chavez, Miranda Garrison
Lancelot du Lac (aka *Lancelot of the Lake*)— Yvan Chiffre
Land of Fury— David Paltenghi
Larceny with Music— Carlos Romero

Larry Ceballos Revue (S)— Larry Ceballos
Las Vegas Hillbillys— Lee Scott
Las Vegas Nights— LeRoy Prinz
Lassiter— Eleanor Fazan
The Last Boyscout— Cindy Daniels
The Last Days of Pompeii— Benjamin Zemach
The Last Dragon (aka *Berry Gordy's the Last Dragon*)— Torrance Mathis, Ernie Reyes, Sr., Ron Van Clief
The Last Married Couple in America— Scott Salmon
The Last of the Secret Agents— Andre Tayir
The Last Remake of Beau Geste— Irving Davies
The Last Resort— Jo Ann Harris
Last Rites— Michelle Assaf, Lee Ann Martin
Last Tango in Paris— R.G. Barsi
The Last Temptation of Christ— Lachen Zinoune
Latin Lovers— Frank Veloz
Laughing Anne— Philip and Betty Buchel
Laughing Sinners— Lou Mosconi
A Lawless Street (aka *The Marshall of Medicine Bend* and *My Gun Commands*)— Jerry Antes
Lawnmower Man 2: Beyond Cyberspace— Lynne Hockney
Leadbelly— Dana Manno
A League of Their Own— Lou Conte
Leap of Faith— Mary Ann Kellogg, Sharon Kinney, Martin Morrisey
Leathernecking— Pearl Eaton
Leave It to Lester— Maria Gambarelli
Legend— Arlene Phillips
The Legend of Valentino (TV)— Anita Mann
Legions of the Nile— Pieter Van Der Sloot
Legs (TV)— Violet Holmes
The Lemon Sisters— Anita Mann
Lenny— Bob Fosse
Leonard: Part 6— Louis Falco
The Leopard— Alberto Testa
Let It Be Me— Miranda Garrison
Let's Be Happy— Pauline Grant, Alfred Rodrigues
Let's Dance (1936) (S)— Dave Gould
Let's Dance (1950)— Fred Astaire, Hermes Pan
Let's Do It Again— Valerie Bettis, Lee Scott
Let's Face It— Seymour Felix
Let's Go Native— David Bennett
Let's Go Places— Danny Dare
Let's Make Love— Jack Cole, Gene Kelly
Let's Make Up (aka *Lilacs in the Spring*)— Philip and Betty Buchel
Let's Rock— Peter Gennaro
Let's Scuffle (S)— Bill Robinson
Lianna— Marta Renzi
Liar's Moon— Patsy Swayze
The Lieutenant Wore Skirts— Sylvia Lewis
Life Begins at 40— Jack Donohue
Life Begins in College— Nick Castle, Geneva Sawyer
Life in the Raw— Sammy Lee

Life Is a Circus— Denys Palmer
A Life of Her Own— Hermes Pan
The Life of the Party— Sammy Lee, Ann Miller
Life Stinks— Miranda Garrison, Jeffrey Hornaday
Life with Mikey— Diane Martel
Lifeforce— Adrian Hedley
The Light in the Forest— Tommy Mahoney
Lights of New York— Larry Ceballos
The Lights of Old Santa Fe— Larry Ceballos
Like Water for Chocolate (aka *Como Agua Por Chocolate*)— Farnesio De Bernal
L'il Abner— Michael Kidd, Dee Dee Wood
Lilacs in the Spring (aka *Let's Make Up*)— Philip and Betty Buchel
Lili— Dorothy Jarnac, Charles Walters
Lilies of the Field— Roy Mack
Lillian Russell— Seymour Felix
The Lily and the Rose— Ruth St. Denis
Limelight (1937) (aka *Backstage*)— Tilly Losch, Ralph Reader
Limelight (1952)— Charles Chaplin, Andre Eglevsky, Melissa Hayden, Carmelita Maracci
Limit Up— April Ortiz
Linda Be Good— Larry Ceballos
Lion Heart— Anthony Van Laast, Jean-Claude Van Damme
Liquid Dreams— Alexandre Magno
The Little Ballerina— Mary Skeaping
The Little Colonel— Jack Donohue, Bill Robinson
Little Dragons— David Winters
Little Egypt— Hal Belfer
The Little Immigrant (S)— Fanchon
Little Miss Broadway (1938)— Nick Castle, George Murphy, Geneva Sawyer
Little Miss Broadway (1947)— Arthur Dreifuss, Victor McLeod, Betty Wright
Little Nelly Kelly— Eddie Larkin, George Murphy
A Little Night Music— Patricia Birch, Larry Fuller
Little Nikita— Kenneth MacMillan
The Little Prince— Ron Forella, Bob Fosse
The Little Princess— Ernest Belcher, Nick Castle
Little Rascals— Nancy Gregory
Little Shop of Horrors— Pat Garrett
Little Treasure— Chea Collette, Joanne Divito
The Little Woman of the Moulin Rouge— Margarita Wallman
Little Women— Trudi Forrest
The Littlest Rebel— Jack Donohue, Bill Robinson
Live a Little, Love a Little— Jack Baker, Jack Regas
Live and Let Die— Geoffrey Holder
The Lives of a Bengal Lancer— LeRoy Prinz
The Living Idol— David Campbell, José Selva
Living in a Big Way— Stanley Donen, Gene Kelly
Living It Up— Nick Castle
The Lodger— Kenny Williams
Logan's Run— Stefan Wenta
London Kills Me— William Tuckett

London Melody (aka *Girl in the Streets*) — Ralph Reader

London Town (aka *My Heart Goes Crazy*) — Freddie Carpenter

The Long Duel — Scheherazade

The Long Riders — Katina Sawidis

Look for the Silver Lining — Ray Bolger, LeRoy Prinz

Look Who's Talking — Mary Ann Kellog

Look Who's Talking Now — Mary Ann Kellog

Look Who's Talking Too — Mary Ann Kellog

Looking for Love — Robert Sidney

Looney Tunes Tune Ups — Adam Shankman

Loose Ankles — Roy Mack

Loose Ends — Fred Lord

Loose Shoes — Cecila Gruessing

Lord Byron of Broadway — Sammy Lee, Albertina Rasch

Lord of Illusions — Alex Magno

Los Tarantos — Carmen Amaya, Antonio Gades

Lost Angels — B.H. Barry

Lost Horizon — Hermes Pan

Lost in a Harem — Jack Donohue

Lost in Alaska — Hal Belfer

Lost in London (TV) — Terry Gilbert

Lost in the Stars — Paula Kelly

The Lottery Lover — Jack Donohue

Lousiana Purchase — George Balanchine, Jack Donohue

Love Affair — Bill and Jacqui Landrum

Love and Hisses — Nick Castle, Geneva Sawyer

Love and Kisses — Anita Mann

Love at First Bite — Alex Romero

Love at First Sight — Chester Hale

Love Comes Along — Pearl Eaton

The Love God? — Wilda Taylor

Love Happy — Billy Daniel

Love in a Goldfish Bowl — Miriam Nelson

Love in the Rough — Sammy Lee

The Love-Ins — Hal Belfer

Love Laughs at Andy Hardy — Jack Donohue

Love Me or Leave Me — Alex Romero

Love on Tap (S) — Merriel Abbott

Love on Wheels — Jack Hulbert

Love Slaves of the Amazon — David and Fernanda Condi

Love That Brute — Billy Daniel

Love Thy Neighbor — Merriel Abbott

Love Valentine (TV) — Jennifer Stace

The Loved One — Tony Charmoli

Lovely to Look At — Gower Champion, Ann Miller, Hermes Pan

The Lover — Eleanor Fazan

Loverboy — Lori Eastside

The Lovers of Tereul — Milko Sparemblek

A Lover's Return (aka *Un Revenant*) — Victor Gsovsky

The Loves of Carmen — Eduardo Cansino, Robert Sidney

Loves of Isadora (aka *Isadora*) — Frederick Ashton, Litz Pisk

Loving Couples — Larry Vickers

Loving You — Charles O'Curran

Low Blow — George Chung

LSD, I Hate You! (aka *Movie Star, American Style*) — Larry Maldonado

Lucky Me — Jack Donohue, LeRoy Prinz

Lucky to Me — Joan Davis

Lullaby of Broadway — Gene Nelson, Miriam Nelson, Eddie Prinz, LeRoy Prinz, Al White

Lulu Bell — Nick Castle

Luna de Miel (aka *Honeymoon*) — Antonio, Léonard Massine

Lust in the Dust — Stan Mazin

Luxury Liner — Nick Castle

Lydia Bailey — Jack Cole

M. Butterfly — Michele Ehlers, Jamie H.J. Guan

Mac and Me — Marla Blakely

Macbeth — Sally Gilpin

Macho Dancer — Boy Pilapie

Maciste the Mighty — Tito DeLuc

Mack the Knife — David Toguri

Macumba Love — Solano Trinidade

Mad About Money (aka *He Loved an Actress* and *Stardust*) — Larry Ceballos

The Mad Genius — Adolph Bolm

Madame Bovary — Jack Donohue

Madame Butterfly — Michio Ito

Madame du Barry — Albertina Rasch

Madame Kitty — Tito DeLuc

Madame Satan — Theodore Kosloff, LeRoy Prinz

Made in America — Lester Wilson

Made in L.A. — Murray Phillips

Made in Paris — David Winters

Mademoiselle Striptease (aka *Please Mr. Balzac*) — Jean Guelis

Madhouse — Chrissy Bocchino

Madonna — Truth or Dare (aka *In Bed with Madonna*) — Vincent Paterson

Mae West (TV) — Dom Salinaro

The Magic Christian — Lionel Blair

Magic Fire — Tatjana Gvosky

Magnificent Obsession — Kenny Williams

Mahler — Gillian Gregory

Mahogany — Jho Jenkins

The Main Attraction — Lionel Blair, Donald Saddler

Main Street Follies (S) — Hal LeRoy

Maisie Gets Her Man — Danny Dare

Maisie Goes to Reno — Sammy Lee

Major Payne — Russell Clark

Make a Wish — Larry Ceballos

Make Mine Laughs — Antonio, Ray Bolger

Make Mine Music — David Lichine

The Making of Monsters — Susan McKenzie

Making the Grade — Ernest Belcher

Malcom X — Otis Sallid

The Malibu Bikini Shop — Dorain Grusman

Mambo— Katherine Dunham

The Mambo Kings— Kim Blank, Jack Donohue, Michael Peters

Mame— Martin Allen, Onna White

Mam'zelle Pigalle (aka *Cette Sacrée Gamine*)— George Reich

Man About Town— Merriel Abbott, LeRoy Prinz

Man from Oklahoma— Lary Ceballos

The Man in My Life (aka *L'Homme de Ma Vie*)— Arthur Plasschaert

Man in the Attic— Wiletta Smith

Man in the Dark— Allen Meacham

The Man in the Santa Claus Suit (TV)— Diane Arnold

A Man Like Eva— Heino Hallhuber

Man of a Thousand Faces— Kenny Williams

Man of La Mancha— Gillian Lynne

Man of the House— Diana Conway

The Man Who Loved Redheads— Alan Carter

The Man Without a World— Melissa Cottle

Manhattan Angel— Nick Castle

Manhattan Merengue (aka *Rice, Beans and Ketchup*)— Miranda Garrison

Manhattan Serenade (S)— Sammy Lee

Mannequin— Vincent Paterson

Mannequin 2: On the Move— Lori Eastside

Manolete— José Greco

Manslaughter— Theodore Kosloff

Many Happy Returns— George Hale, Frank Veloz

Maracaibo— Martin Vargas

Marat/Sade— Malcolm Goddard

The March of Time— Sammy Lee, Albertina Rasch

Marco— Ron Field

Mardi Gras— Bill Foster

Maria Gallante— Jack Donohue

Maria's Lovers— Loyd Williamson

Marie Antoinette— Albertina Rasch

Marilyn— Jack Cole

Marilyn: The Untold Story (TV)— Alex Romero

Marjorie Morningstar— Jack Baker

Mark of the Renegade— Eugene Loring

Marked for Death— Dorain Grusman, Steven Seagal

Marriage on the Rocks— Jonathon Lucas

Married in Hollywood— Edward Royce

The Marrying Man— Miranda Garrison, Jeffrey Hornaday

Mars Attacks— Dan Kamin

The Marshall of Medicine Bend (aka *The Lawless Street* and *My Gun Commands*)— Jerry Antes

Martians Go Home— Richard Garcia

Mary Lou— Jack Boyle

Mary of Scotland— Hermes Pan

Mary Poppins— Marc Breaux, Dee Dee Wood

Mary Shelley's "Frankenstein"— Stuart Hopps

The Mask (1961)— Don Gilles

The Mask (1994)— Jerry Evans

The Masque of the Red Death (1964)— Jack Carter

Masque of the Red Death (1989)— Ted Lin

Masquerade in Mexico— Billy Daniel

Mata Hari— Lucy Igaz, Senanda Kumar

Maxie— Matthew Diamond

Mayfair Melody— Jack Donohue

The Mayor of 44th Street— Nick Castle, George Murphy

Maytime— Val Raset

Me and Him— Barbara Allen

The Meadow— Gino Landi

Medicine Man— Maria Fatima Toledo

Meet Danny Wilson— Hal Belfer

Meet Me After the Show— Jack Cole, Steve Condos

Meet Me at the Fair— Kenny Williams

Meet Me in Las Vegas— Eugene Loring, Hermes Pan

Meet Me in St. Louis— Charles Walters

Meet Me on Broadway— Billy Daniel

Meet the Baron— Sammy Lee

Meet the Navy— Larry Ceballos

Meet the People— Jack Donohue, Sammy Lee, Charles Walters

Meet Wally Sparks— Cecilie Stuart

Meeting Venus— Antal Fodor

Melba— Pauline Grant

Melody and Moonlight— Aida Broadbent

Melody Cruise— Dave Gould

Melody for Two— Bobby Connolly, Robert Vreeland

Melody Lane— Louis DaPron

Melody Parade— Jack Boyle

Melody Ranch— Larry Ceballos, Ann Miller

Memphis Belle— David Toguri

Men in Her Diary— Carlos Romero

The Men in Her Life— Adolph Bolm

Men of the North— Sammy Lee

The Men's Club— Lester Wilson

Merry Andrew— Michael Kidd

Merry-Go-Round of 1938— Carl Randall

The Merry Monahans— Louis Dapron, Carlos Romero

The Merry Widow (1934)— Albertina Rasch

The Merry Widow (1952)— Jack Cole

Metropolitan— Diane Lanthrop

Mexican Hayride— Eugene Loring

Mexicana— Nick Castle

MGM: When the Lion Roars (TV)— Vince Paterson

Mi Vida Loca (aka *My Crazy Life*)— Maria Leone

Miami Rhapsody— Adam Shankman

Michael— JoAnne Fregalette Jansen

Midnight— LeRoy Prinz

The Midnight Hour— Myrna Gawryn

The Midnight Sun— Fanchon

Midshipmaid Gob— The Condos Brothers

A Midsummer Night's Dream (1935)— Bronislava Nijinska

A Midsummer Night's Dream (1966)— George Balanchine

Mighty Aphrodite— Graciela Daniele

Mighty Morphin Power Rangers: The Movie— Jeff Pruitt

The Mighty Quinn— Vince Paterson

Milk Money— Adam Shankman

The Milkman— Hal Belfer

The Milky Way (S)— Merriel Abbott

Million Dollar Mermaid— Busby Berkeley, Audrene Brier

Millions in the Air— LeRoy Prinz

Mina Tannenbaum— Lucia Coppola

The Minotaur— Adriano Vitale

Minstrel Man (1944)— John Boyle

Minstrel Man (1977) (TV)— Donald McKayle

The Miracle— Antonio Triana

Miracle of the Bells— Charles O'Curran

Mirrors (TV)— Graciela Daniele

The Misery Bros.— Andrea Lawent

Miss Annie Rooney— Nick Castle

Miss Firecracker— Patrice Soriero

Miss Sadie Thompson— Lee Scott

Mission to Moscow— Michel Panaieff, LeRoy Prinz

The Mississippi Gambler— Gwen Verdon

Mr. and Mrs. Bridge— Elizabeth Aldrich, Charlotte Gossett

Mister Big— Louis DaPron

Mr. Broadway (S)— Hal LeRoy

Mr. Hobbs Takes a Vacation— Maggie Banks

Mr. Holland's Opus— Bruce McDonald

Mr. Love— Gillian Lynne

Mr. Music— Gower Champion

Mr. Quilp (aka *Quilp*)— Gillian Lynne

Mr. Saturday Night— Tam G. Warner, Lester Wilson

Mistress— Julie Arenal

Mobsters— Toni Basil, Miranda Garrison

Modern Girls— Sarah Elgart

Modern Problems— John Clifford

Modern Times— Charles Chaplin

The Mole People— James Truitte, Kenny Williams

Mom and Dad Save the World— Denise Darnell

The Mongols— Dino Solari

Monkey on My Back— Lee Scott

Monsieur Beaucaire— Billy Daniel, Josephine Earl

Monster Bash—Lance McDonald, Adam Shankman

Montana Moon— Sammy Lee

Monty Python and the Holy Grail— Leo Kharibian

Monty Python's the Meaning of Life— Arlene Phillips

The Moon of Manakoora (S)— Augie Auld

Moon Over Burma— LeRoy Prinz

Moon Over Las Vegas— Louis DaPron

Moon Over Miami— Jack Cole, Condos Bros., Hermes Pan

Moon Over Parador— Bianca Rossini

Moon Zero Two— Jo Cooke

Moonlight and Cactus— Charles O'Curran

Moonlight and Pretzels— Bobby Connolly

Moonlight in Havana— Lester Horton, Eddie Prinz

Moonlight in Hawaii— Larry Ceballos

Moonlight in Vermont— Louis DaPron

Moonlight Masquerade— Nick Castle

Moonlight Murder— Val Raset

Moonstruck— Lofti Travolta

Moonwalk— Alex Ruiz

Moonwalker— Russell Clark, Michael Jackson, Vincent Paterson

La Mort du Cygne (aka *Ballerina*)— Serge Lifar

Mortal Kombat— Pat E. Johnson, Robin Show

Moses (aka *Moses the Lawgiver*) (TV)— Oshra Elkayam

Mother o' Mine— Ernest Belcher

Mother Wore Tights— Seymour Felix, Kenny Williams

Moulin Rouge (1934)— Russell Markert

Moulin Rouge (1952)— William Chappell

Mountain Music— LeRoy Prinz

Mountains of the Moon— Eleanor Fazan

Movie, Movie— Stanley Donen, Michael Kidd

Movie Star, American Style (aka *LSD, I Hate You!*)— Larry Maldonado

Moving Target— Eugen O. Floyd

Mrs. Wiggs of the Cabbage Patch— LeRoy Prinz

Mrs. Winterbourne— Andrea Lawent, Adam Shankman

Much Ado About Nothing— Stuart Hopps

The Muppet Christmas Carol— Pat Garrett

Muppet Treasure Island— Pat Garrett

The Muppets Take Manhattan— Chris Chadman

Murder at the Vanities— Larry Ceballos, LeRoy Prinz

Murder at the Windmill (aka *Mystery at the Burlesque*)— Jack Billings

Murder in the Blue Room— Carlos Romero

Murder in the Music Hall— Fanchon

Murder on the Waterfront— Matty King

Murderer's Row— Miriam Nelson

Muriel's Wedding— John O'Connell

Murphy's Romance— Ken Rinker

Muscle Beach Party— John Monte

Music Box— Eva Nemeth

Music for Millions— Jack Donohue

The Music Goes 'Round— The Berry Bros., Larry Ceballos

Music in Manhattan— Charles O'Curran

Music in the Air— Jack Donohue

Music Is Magic— Jack Donohue

The Music Lovers— Terry Gilbert

The Music Man— Tom Panko, Onna White

Music Parade— Billy Daniel

Musica en La Noche— Katherine Dunham

Musical Masterpieces (S)— Joseph Hackett Hickey

Musical Memories (S)— Ruby Keeler, Hal LeRoy
The Musical Mystery (S)— Albertina Rasch
Musik, Musik und Nur Musik— Ernst Matray
Mutiny on the Bounty— Hamil Petroff
My Best Gal— Dave Gould
My Blue Heaven (1950)— Billy Daniel, Seymour Felix
My Blue Heaven (1990)— Lynne Taylor-Corbett
My Chauffeur— Damita Jo Freeman
My Crazy Life (aka *Mi Vida Loca*)— Maria Leone
My Darling Clementine— Dave Gould
My Dream Is Yours— LeRoy Prinz
My Fair Lady— Hermes Pan
My Family— Miguel Delgado
My Friend Frank— Miranda Garrison
My Friend Irma Goes West— Josephine Earl
My Gal Sal— Hermes Pan, Val Raset
My Geisha— Paul Godkin
My Gun Commands (aka *The Lawless Street* and *The Marshall of Medicine Bend*)— Jerry Antes
My Heart Goes Crazy (aka *London Town*)— Freddie Carpenter
My Lips Betray— Sammy Lee
My Lucky Star— Nick Castle, Harry Losee, Geneva Sawyer
My Secret Life— Rod Stewart
My Sister Eileen— Bob Fosse
My Six Loves— Jack Regas
My Son Is Guilty— Fayard Nicholas
My Stepmother Is an Alien— Don Correia
My Wicked, Wicked Ways (TV)— Paul DeRolf
My Wild Irish Rose— Berry Bros., LeRoy Prinz
Myra Breckenridge— Ralph Beaumont
Myrt and Marge— Jack Haskell
Mystery at the Burlesque (aka *Murder at the Windmill*)— Jack Billings
Mystery of the Black Jungle— Anna Gorilovich
Naked Alibi— Kenny Williams
The Naked Ape— Alan Johnson
The Naked Gun— Jerry Evans
Naked Gun 2 1/2: The Smell of Fear— Johnny Almaraz, Miranda Garrison
Naked Gun 33 1/3: The Final Insult— Miranda Garrison
The Naked Maja— Alberto Lorca
Naked Tango— Graciela Daniele, Carlos Rivorola
The Naked Truth— Rhonda Miller
Nancy Goes to Rio— Nick Castle
National Barn Dance— Jack Crosby
National Lampoon's Class Reunion— Rita Graham
National Lampoon's European Vacation— Gillian Lynne
National Velvet— Eugene Loring
The Naughty Nineties— John Boyle
Navy Blues— Seymour Felix
Navy Heroes— Ram Gopal
Nearly Eighteen— Jack Boyle
Necropolis— Taunie Vrenon

Nel Signo di Roma (aka *Sign of the Gladiator*)— Claude Marchant
Nell— Susan Bonawitz-Collard
The Neon Bible— Renee Victor
Neopolitan Carousel (aka *Hurdy Gurdy*)— Léonide Massine
Neptune's Daughter— Jack Donohue
Nertsery Rhymes (S)— Sammy Lee
Never a Dull Moment— Carlos Romero
Never Let Me Go— Anton Dolin
Never Say Die— LeRoy Prinz
Never Say Never Again— Anthony Van Laast
Never Steal Anything Small— Hermes Pan
The Neverending Story: The Next Chapter— Tina Hubbard-Glocker
Neverending Story III— Mark Davis, Brad Rapier
The New Adventures of Pippi Longstocking— Nancy Gregory
New Faces of 1937— Sammy Lee, Ann Miller
New Faces of 1952— Richard Barstow
The New Interns— Miriam Nelson
New Jack City— Donovan Henry
A New Kind of Love— Miriam Nelson
New Moon— Val Raset
New York, New York— Ron Field
Newsies— Peggy Holmes, Kenny Ortega
The Next Karate Kid— Pat E. Johnson
Nez du Cuir— George Reich
Niagara— Bill Foster
Nickelodeon— Rita Abrams
Night and Day— Michel Panaieff, LeRoy Prinz
A Night at Earl Carroll's— LeRoy Prinz
Night at the Music Hall (S)— Fanchon
A Night at the Opera— Chester Hale
Night at the Trocodero (S)— Fanchon
The Night Before— Randall Thomas
Night Club Girl— Louis DaPron
Night Club Revels (S)— Merriel Abbott
A Night in Heaven— Deney Terrio
A Night in the Life of Jimmy Reardon— Bobby Wells
The Night Is Young— Chester Hale
The Night of Love—Marion Morgan
Night Patrol— Karen Hazelwood
The Night They Raided Minsky's— Danny Daniels
The Night They Took Miss Beautiful (TV)— James Starbuck
Night Tide— Benjamin Zemach
The Night We Never Met— John Carrafa
Night World— Busby Berkeley
Nijinsky— Kenneth MacMillan, Léonide Massine
Ninja III: The Domination— Sho Kosugi
Nite Angel— Joanne Divito
Nite in a Niteclub (S)— John "Bubbles" Sublett
No Leave, No Love— Stanley Donen
No, No Nanette (1930)— Larry Ceballos, Michio Ito
No, No Nanette (1940)— Ray Bolger, Aida Broadbent

No Retreat, No Surrender— Harrison Mang
Noah's Ark— Eduardo Cansino
Nob Hill— Nick Castle
Nobody's Baby— Roy Randolph
Nobody's Darling— Nick Castle
Nobody's Fool— Bonnie Oda Homsey
Norma Jean and Marilyn (TV)— Mary Ann Kellogg
North— Patricia Birch
The North Star— David Lichine
North to Alaska— Josephine Earl
Northwest Outpost— Fanchon
Not Damaged— Danny Dare
Not for Publication— Utah Ground
Not with My Wife, You Don't— Shelah Hackett
Nothing in Common— Shirley Kirkes
Notorious Lady— Larry Ceballos
Nowhere to Run— Jean-Claude Van Damme
The Nutcracker (1982)— Anthony Van Laast
Nutcracker (1986)— Kent Stowell
The Nutcracker (1993) (aka *George Balanchine's Nutcracker*)— George Balanchine
O, Holy Night—Lynn Taylor-Corbett
Off Beat— Jacques d'Amboise
Oh, Evaline! (S)— Hal LeRoy
Oh, Rosalinda! (aka *Die Fledermaus*)— Alfred Rodrigues
Oh, What a Lovely War!— Eleanor Fazan
Oh, You Beautiful Doll!— Seymour Felix
O.K. Nero— Dino Solari
Oklahoma!— Agnes DeMille, Gene Nelson
The Oklahoman— Carey Leverette
Old Gringo— Ana Merida
Old Man Rhythm— Hermes Pan
Oliver!— Tom Panko, Onna White
On a Clear Day You Can See Forever— Howard Jeffrey
On an Island with You— Jack Donohue
On Deadly Ground— Steven Seagal
On Moonlight Bay— LeRoy Prinz, Donald Saddler
On Stage Everybody— Louis DaPron
On the Avenue— Seymour Felix
On the Double— Bill Foster
On the Riviera— Jack Cole
On the Sunny Side of the Street— Audrene Brier
On the Town— Stanley Donen, Gene Kelly, Ann Miller
On with the Show— Larry Ceballos, Willie Covan
On Your Toes— George Balanchine
Once Bitten— Joanne Divito
Once Upon a Honeymoon— Joyce Murray
Once Upon a Horse— Kenny Williams
Once Upon a Time in America— Julie Arenal
Once Were Warriors— Kepe Stirling
The One and Only Genuine and Original Family Band— Hugh Lambert
One-Eyed Jacks— Josephine Earl
One for the Book (S)— Gae Foster

One from the Heart— Gene Kelly, Kenny Ortega
One Good Cop— Pat Gould
One in a Million— Nick Castle, Jack Haskell
One Mad Kiss— Juan Duval
One Mile from Heaven— Bill Robinson
One Night in May— Anthony Nelle
One Night in the Tropics— Larry Ceballos
One Sunday Afternoon— LeRoy Prinz
One Too Many— Louis DaPron
One Touch of Venus— Billy Daniel
One Woman or Two— Lydie Callier
Only the French Can (aka *French Can Can*)— Claude Grandjean
Only the Lonely— Elizabeth Boitsov, Monica Devereaux
Only When I Laugh— Miriam Nelson
Opera do Malandro— Regine Miranda
Opportunity Knocks— Jeffrey Hornaday
The Opposite Sex— Bob Sidney
Options— Joe Sekatski
Orchestra Wives— Nick Castle, Fayard Nicholas
An Oriental Dream (aka *Kismet*)— Jack Cole
Orlando— Jacky Lansley
Orphans— Lynette Barkley
The Oscar— Steven Peck
Othello— Stuart Hopps
Our Blushing Brides— Albertina Rasch
Our Gang Follies (S)— Bud Murray
Our House— Ted Lin
Our Man Flint— Paul Godkin
Our Modern Maidens— George Cunningham
Out for Justice— Steven Seagal
Out of Sight— Wilda Taylor
Out of the Blue— Buddy Bradley
Out of This World— Sammy Lee
Out Where the Stars Begin— Bobby Connolly
Outland— Anthony Van Laast
Outpost in Malaya— Ram Gopal
The Outriders— Alex Romero
Outside of Paradise—Larry Ceballos
Over the Counter (S)— Danny Dare
Over the Garden Wall— Ralph Reader
Overboard— Shirley Kirkes
P.J.— Wilda Taylor
Paddy O'Day— Fanchon
Padlocked— Ernest Belcher
Pagan Love Song— Robert Alton
Pagliaci (1931)— Leon Leonidoff
Pagliaci (1936)— Wendy Toye
Paint Your Wagon— Jack Baker
The Painted Angel— Larry Ceballos
The Painted Veil— Chester Hale
Painting the Clouds with Sunshine— Gene Nelson, Miriam Nelson, LeRoy Prinz
The Pajama Game— Bob Fosse
Pajama Party— David Winters
Pal Joey— Hermes Pan
The Paleface— Billy Daniel

Palmy Days— Busby Berkeley
Panama Hattie— Berry Bros, Danny Dare, Sammy Lee
Panama Sal— Roland Dupree
Pan-Americana— Antonio, Charles O'Curran
Par Ordre du Tsar— Victor Gsovsky
Paradise for Two (aka *The Gaiety Girls*)— Philip Buchel, Jack Donohue, Jack Hulbert
Paradise, Hawaiian Style— Jack Regas
Paramount on Parade— David Bennett, Marion Morgan
Pardners— Nick Castle
Pardon My Rhythm— Louis DaPron
Pardon My Sarong— Katherine Dunham, Tip, Tap & Toe
The Parent Trap— Tommy Mahoney
Paris (1929)— Larry Ceballos
Paris Follies of 1956 (aka *Fresh from Paris*)— Donn Arden
Paris Honeymoon— LeRoy Prinz
The Party— Natalia Borisova
Party Girl— Bob Sidney
Pass the Ammo— Sarah Elgart
Passing the Buck— Eddie Prinz
Passion Flower Hotel (aka *The Boarding School*)— Larry Fuller
Patakin— Victor Cuellar
Pathé Audio Review #13 (S)— George Murphy
Pathé Audio Review #17 (S)— Dave Gould
Pathé Audio Review #30 (S)— Agnes DeMille
Patrick the Great— Louis DaPron
The Patsy— Four Step Brothers
The Pebble and the Penguin— Kevin Carlisle
Peeping Tom— Wally Scott
Peggy Sue Got Married— Toni Basil, Chrissy Bocchino
Pennies from Heaven— Danny Daniels
Penthouse Rhythm— Louis DaPron
People Are Funny— Jack Crosby
Pepe— Eugene Loring, Alex Romero
Perfect— Natalie Brown, Kim Connell, Jerry Jackson
The Perfect Gentleman— Dave Gould
The Perfect Model— Rosemary Barnes
The Perils of Pauline— Billy Daniel
Pete Kelly's Blues— Kenny Williams
Peter Rabbit and the Tales of Beatrix Potter— Frederick Ashton
Peter's Friends— David Toguri
Pete's Dragon— Martin Allen, Onna White
Petticoat Fever— Val Raset
The Petty Girl— Eugene Loring
Peyton Place— Jack Regas
Phantom Lady— Lester Horton
Phantom of the Opera (1925)— Ernest Belcher
Phantom of the Opera (1943)— Lester Horton
Phantom of the Opera (1989)— Tony Fields, Gyorgy Gaal
Phantom of the Paradise— William Shephard

The Pharaoh's Woman— Adriano Vitale
Phedre— Milko Sparemblek
Phfft!— Lee Scott
Phi Beta Rockers— Randy DiGrazio
Piaf—The Early Years— Danny Daniels
Pick a Star— Edward Court
Picnic— Miriam Nelson
Picture Palace (S)— Hal LeRoy
Pie, Pie Blackbird— Fayard Nicholas
A Piece of the Action— Arthur Mitchell
The Pied Piper of Hamelin (TV)— Ward Ellis
Pigskin Parade— Jack Haskell
The Pilgrim— Charles Chaplin
Pin Up Girl— Condos Brothers, Fanchon, Gae Foster, Hermes Pan, Alice Sullivan
Pink Floyd— The Wall— Gillian Gregory
The Pink Jungle— Hal Belfer
Pink Nights— Shaun Allen
The Pirate— Robert Alton, Gene Kelly, Fayard Nicholas
Pirate Movie— David Atkins
Pirates— Wanda Szczuka
The Pirates of Penzance— Graciela Daniele
Pirates of Tortuga— Hal Belfer
Pistol Packin' Mama— Dave Gould
Pizza Man— Ira McAiley
Places in the Heart— Ken Rinker
Plainsman and the Lady— Fanchon
Plane Nuts— Albertina Rasch
Planes, Trains and Automobiles— Damita Jo Freeman
Play It Cool— Lionel Blair
Playin' for Keeps— Lynette Barkely, Ronn Forella
Playmates— Jack Crosby
Please Don't Eat the Daisies— Robert Sidney
Please Mr. Balzac (aka *Mademoiselle Striptease*)— Jean Guelis
Please, Not Now!— Michel Renault
The Pleasure of His Company— Fred Astaire, Hermes Pan
The Pleasure Seekers— Antonio Gades, Robert Sidney
Pocahontas— D.J. Giagni
Pocketful of Miracles— Nick Castle
Poison Ivy— Ted Lin
Police Academy: Mission to Moscow— Boris Baranovsky
Polly (TV)— Debbie Allen
Poltergeist III— T. Daniel
Poor Little Rich Girl— Ralph Cooper, Jack Haskell
Popeye— Hovey Burgess, Sharon Kinney, Robert Messina, Lou Wills, Jr.
Porgy and Bess— Hermes Pan
Port Afrique— David Paltenghi
Portrait of a Showgirl (TV)— Alan Johnson
Portrait of a Stripper (TV)— Steve Merritt, Sarah Tayir

Postcards from the Edge— Tommy Tune
Pot o' Gold— Larry Ceballos
Powder River— Billy Daniel
The Powers Girl— Jack Donohue, George Murphy
Pray for Death— Sho Kosugi
Prehistoric Women (1951)— Bella Lewitzky
Prehistoric Women (1967)— Denys Palmer
Presenting Lily Mars— Ernst Matray, Charles Walters
The President's Lady— Stephen Papich
Pretty in Pink— Kenny Ortega
Pride and Prejudice— Ernst Matray
The Pride and the Passion— Paco Reyes
Pride of the Yankees— Frank Veloz
The Prime of Miss Jean Brodie— Maggy Maxwell
The Prince and the Showgirl— William Chappell
Princess Caraboo— Anthony Van Laast
The Princess Comes Across— Louis DaPron
Princess Daisy (TV)— Lynne Hockney
Princess of the Nile— Olga Lunick
Princess O'Hara— George Hale
Priorities on Parade— Jack Donohue, Ann Miller
Priority Blues (S)— Merriel Abbott
Prisoner of Swing (S)— Gae Foster, Hal LeRoy
Private Buckaroo— James Mattison
Private Debts— Donald McKayle
Private Lessons (S)— Hal LeRoy
The Private Life of Helen of Troy— Marion Morgan
The Private Life of Sherlock Holmes— David Blair
Private School— Paul Abdul
A Private's Affair— Alex Romero
Privates on Parade— Gillian Gregory
The Prizefighter and the Lady— Seymour Felix
Problem Child 3: Junior in Love (TV)— Patsy Swayze
The Prodigal— Alex Romero
The Producers— Alan Johnson
The Projection Room— Gower Champion
Prom Night III— Andrea Robinovitch
Promise Her Anything— Lionel Blair
Prospero's Books— Karine Saporta
Protocol— Charlene Painter
The Proud and the Damned— José Greco
The Public Eye— Sally Gilpin
Public Jitterbug #1 (S)— Hal LeRoy
Public Pigeon Number One— Miriam Nelson
Pufnstuff— Paul Godkin
Pump Up the Volume— Jane Cassell
Puppet on a Chain— Robin Winbow
Pure Country— Anita Williams
Purple Haze— Peter Thoemke
Purple People Eater— Ted Lin, Ben Lokey
The Purple Plain— Ram Gopal
Pursued— LeRoy Prinz
Puttin' on the Ritz— Maurice Kusell
Quadrophenia— Gillian Gregory
Quality Street— Hermes Pan

Quartet— Elizabeth Aldrich
Queen Kong (aka *King Kong Lives*)— Gillian Gregory
Queen of Burlesque— Larry Ceballos
Queen of Spades— David Paltenghi
Queen of the Nile— Wilbert Bradley
Queen of the Stardust Ballroom (TV)— Marge Champion
Quentin Durward— Tutte Lemkow
Quicksilver— Grover Dale
Quilp (aka *Mr. Quilp*)— Gillian Lynne
Quo Vadis— Auriel Milloss, Madi Obolensky
Race Street— Charles O'Curran
Rad— Sidney Kaleff
Radio City Revels— Ann Miller, Hermes Pan, Joseph Santley
*Radio Days—*Donald Saddler
The Radio Parade of 1935 (aka *Radio Follies*)— Buddy Bradley
Radioactive Dreams— Bruce Heath, Michelle Simmons
Radioland Murders— Brad and Jennifer Moranz
A Rage in Harlem— Otis Sallid
Rage of Honor— Sho Kosugi
The Raggedy Rawney— Roy Jones
Ragtime— Twyla Tharp
Raiders of the Seven Seas— Wiletta Smith
Rainbow (TV)— Paul DeRolf
The Rainbow— Imogen Claire
Rainbow Dance (S)— Robert Helpmann
Rainbow Island— Danny Dare
Rainbow 'Round My Shoulder— Lee Scott
The Rains of Ranchipur— Stephen Papich
Raintree County— Alex Romero
Random Harvest— Ernst Matray
*Rappin'—*Edmond Kresley
Rascals— Nick Castle
The Ratings Game (TV)— Joe Tremaine
Rave — Dancing to a Different Beat— Shabba Doo
The Raven— Theodore Kosloff
The Raven Dance— Dorain Grusman
The Razor's Edge— Harry Pilcer
Reaching for the Moon— Maurice Kusell
Ready, Willing and Able— Bobby Connolly, Ruby Keeler
Rebecca of Sunnybrook Farm (1917)— Margaret Loomis
Rebecca of Sunnybrook Farm (1938)— Nick Castle, Bill Robinson, Geneva Sawyer
Rebecca's Daughters— Lucy Fawcett, Philippa Waite
Rebel— Ross Coleman
Reckless— Chester Hale, Carl Randall
Reckless Kelly— Aku Kadogo
The Red Danube— Alex Romero
Red Garters— Nick Castle
Red Heat— Ginger Farley, Mark Gonne
Red, Hot and Blue— Billy Daniel

Red Riding Hood— Barbara Allen

The Red Shoes— Robert Helpmann, Léonide Massine

The Red Squirrel (aka *La Ardilla Roja*)— Ana Medem

Redhead from Manhattan— Nick Castle

Redheads on Parade— Larry Ceballos

Reds— Gillian Gregory

The Relic— Adam Shankman

The Reluctant Debutante

The Reluctant Vampire— Rhonda Miller

The Remains of the Day— Elizabeth Aldrich

Remains to Be Seen— Jeanette Bates

Remember When— Miriam Nelson

Remote Control— Janet Roston

Renaissance Man— Donovan Henry

Rendevous with Annie— Fanchon

Rent-a-Cop— Guiseppe Pennese

Repossessed— Dorain Grusman

Restoration— Kate Flatt, Quinny Sacks

The Return of Gilbert and Sullivan— Val Raset

Return of the Jedi— Gillian Gregory

Return to Oz— Pons Maar

Return to Waterloo— James Cameron

Reveille with Beverly— Ann Miller

Un Revenant (aka *A Lover's Return*)— Victor Gvosky

Revenge of the Cheerleaders— Xavier Chatman

Revenge of the Nerds— Dorain Grusman

Revenge of the Nerds 2: Nerds in Paradise— Larry B. Scott

Revenge of the Ninja— Sho Kosugi

Revolution— Ann Halprin

Rhapsody in Blue— Michel Panaieff, LeRoy Prinz

Rhumba Rhythm (S)— Sammy Lee

Rhumba Serenade (S)— Nico Charisse

Rhythm in the Air— Jack Donohue

Rhythm of the Islands— Lester Horton, Four Step Brothers

Rhythm of the Rumba (S)— LeRoy Prinz, Antonio Triana

Rhythm Parade— Dave Gould

Rhythm Racketeer— Larry Ceballos

Rhythmitis (S)— Hal LeRoy

Rice, Beans and Ketchup (aka *Manhattan Merengue*)— Miranda Garrison

Rich Girl— Robert Alvarez

The Rich Man's Wife— Mary Ann Kellogg

Rich, Young and Pretty— Nick Castle

Richard— Danny Daniels

Ride 'Em Cowboy— Nick Castle

The Ride to Hangman's Tree— Hal Belfer

Riding High— Danny Dare

The Right Approach— Josephine Earl

Rio Rita (1929)— Pearl Eaton

Rio Rita (1942)— Bobby Connolly, Vincente Minnelli, David Robel

Riot on Sunset Strip— Hal Belfer

Rise and Shine— George Murphy, Hermes Pan

Rita Hayworth: The Love Goddess (TV)— Tad Tadlock

The River of No Return— Jack Cole

A River Runs Through It— Johnny Almaraz, Miranda Garrison, Paul Pellicoro

Road Demon— Bill Robinson

The Road Show (S)— Sammy Lee

Road to Bali— Charles O'Curran

Road to Hong Kong— Jack Baker, Sheila Meyer

Road to Morocco— Paul Oscard

Road to Rio— Billy Daniel, Bernard Pearce

Road to Singapore— LeRoy Prinz

Road to Utopia— Danny Dare

Road to Zanzibar— LeRoy Prinz

Roadhouse— Miranda Garrison, Kenny Ortega

Roast Beef and Movies (S)— Albertina Rasch

Rob Roy— Gillian Barton

The Robe— Stephen Papich

Roberta— Fred Astaire, Hermes Pan

Robin and the 7 Hoods— Jack Baker

Robin Hood: Men in Tights— Cindy Montoya-Picker

Robocop— Moni Yakim

Rock-a-Bye Baby— Nick Castle

Rock-a-Doodle— Susie Inouye

Rock Around the Clock— Earl Barton

Rock 'n' Roll High School— Siana Lee Hale

Rock 'n' Roll Revue— Cholly Atkins

The Rocketeer— Miranda Garrison

Rockula— Toni Basil, Russell Clark

Rocky IV— Michael McKenzie Pratt

The Rocky Horror Picture Show— David Toguri

Rogue of the Rio Grande— Eduardo Cansino

The Rogue Song— Albertina Rasch

Rogue's Regiment— Billy Daniel

Roller Boogie— David Winters

Roma (aka *Fellini's Roma*)— Gino Landi

Roman Scandals— Busby Berkeley

Romance of Rosy Ridge— Jack Donohue

Romance on the High Seas— Busby Berkeley

Romancing the Stone— Jeffrey Hornaday

Romeo and Juliet (1936)— Agnes DeMille

Romeo and Juliet (1954)— Madi Oblensky

Romeo and Juliet (1966)— Kenneth MacMillan

Romeo and Juliet (1968)— Alberto Testa

Romeo and Juliet (1996) (aka *William Shakespeare's Romeo and Juliet*)— John "Cha Cha" O'Connell

Rooftops— John Carrafa, Jelon Vieira

Rookies on Parade— Nick Castle, Louis DaPron

Rooty Toot Toot— Olga Lunick

Rosalie— Ray Bolger, Dave Gould, Eleanor Powell, Albertina Rasch

The Rose— Toni Basil

Rose Marie (1936)— Chester Hale

Rose Marie (1954)— Jeanette Bates, Busby Berkeley

Rose of Washington Square— Seymour Felix

Roseanna McCoy— Charles O'Curran
Roseland— Patricia Birch
Rosen fur Bettina (aka *Ballerina*)— Alan Carter
Rosencrantz and Guildenstern Are Dead— Ivica
  Boban
Rosewood— Neisha Folkes
Rosie!— Hal Belfer
Rosie the Riveteer— Dave Gould
Roustabout— Earl Barton
Roxie Hart— Hermes Pan
The Royal Ballet— Frederick Ashton
Royal Wedding— Fred Astaire, Nick Castle
Ruby— Vincent Paterson
Ruby Keeler (S)— Ruby Keeler
The Ruling Class— Eleanor Fazan
Rumba— LeRoy Prinz, Frank Veloz
Rumble Fish— Michael Smuin
Rumplestilskin— Dari Shai
The Running Man— Paula Abdul
Rush— Alex Arizpe
The Sad Sack—Charles O'Curran
Safety in Numbers— David Bennett
Sailing Along— Buddy Bradley, Jessie Matthews
St. Elmo's Fire— Kenny Ortega
St. Louis Blues— LeRoy Prinz
St. Martin's Lane (aka *Sidewalks of London*)—
  Philip Buchel
Sally— Larry Ceballos, Theodore Kosloff,
  Albertina Rasch
Sally, Irene and Mary— Nick Castle, Geneva Sawyer
Salome (1918)— Ruth St. Denis
Salome (1953)— Asoka, Valerie Bettis, Lee Scott
Salome vs. Shenandoah— Ernest Belcher
Salome, Where She Danced— Lester Horton
Salome's Last Dance— Arlene Philips
Salsa— Miranda Garrison, Kenny Ortega
Salt and Pepper— Lionel Blair
Salute for Three— Jack Donohue
Sambamania (S)— Billy Daniel
Sammy Stops the World (aka *Stop the World, I
  Want to Get Off*)—Billy Wilson
Samson and Delilah— Theodore Kosloff
Samson and the Seven Miracles of the World—
  Wilbert Bradley
San Antonio— LeRoy Prinz
San Antonio Rose— Nick Castle, Louis DaPron
San Fernando Valley— Larry Ceballos
San Francisco— Val Raset
The San Francisco Story— Hal Belfer
Sanctuary— Virginia Semon
Sandokin the Great— Wilbert Bradley
Sands of the Desert— Malcolm Clare
Sangaree— Josephine Earl
Santa Claus: The Movie— Pat Garrett
Sarafina!— Mbongeni Ngema, Michael Peters
Sarge Goes to College— Jack Boyle
Saturday Night Fever— Jeff Kutash, Jo Jo Smith,
  Deney Terrio, Lester Wilson

Savage Sam— Tommy Mahoney
Savages— Patricia Birch
The Saxon Charm— Nick Castle
Say It in French— LeRoy Prinz
Say One for Me— Alex Romero
Sayonara— Leroy Prinz
The Scalphunters— Alex Ruiz
Scandal— David Toguri
Scaramouche— Angna Enters
Scared Stiff— Billy Daniel
The Scarface Mob— Jack Baker, Sheila Meyers
Scarlet Angel— Hal Belfer
The Scarlet Pimpernel (TV)— Eleanor Fazan
Scenario— Yanni Fleury
Scenes from a Mall— Christopher Chadman
Scent of a Woman— Jerry Mitchell, Paul Pellicoro
School Daze— Otis Sallid
Scott Joplin— Michael Peters
Screaming Mimi— Lee Scott
Script Girl (S)— Gae Foster
Scrooge— Paddy Stone
Scrooged— Lester Wilson
The Sea Beast— Ernest Belcher
Sea Legs (S)— Dave Gould
The Seagull— Maya Plisetskaya
Search for Beauty—Jack Haskell, LeRoy Prinz
Seaside Swingers— Gillian Lynne
Second Chance— Wiletta Smith
Second Chorus— Fred Astaire, Hermes Pan
Second Fiddle— Harry Losee
The Second Greatest Sex— Lee Scott
The Second Time Around— Roy Fitzell
The Secret Life of Plants— George Faison
Secret People— Andrée Howard
Secrets of a Soul (aka *Souls for Sale* and *Confessions
  of an Opium Eater*)— Jon Gregory
Seddok (aka *Vampire and the Ballerina* and *Atom
  Age Vampire*)— Marisa Ciampaglia
See My Lawyer— Carmen Amaya, Louis DaPron
Seeing Red (S)— Louis DaPron
Send Me No Flowers— David Winters
Sensation Hunters— Phyllis Avery
Sensations of 1945— Sammy Lee, David Lichine,
  Charles O'Curran, Eleanor Powell
Sense and Sensibility— Stuart Hopps
Separate Ways— Jennifer Stace
Serenade— Ernest Belcher
Sergeant Deadhead— Jack Baker
The Sergeant Was a Lady— Noel Parenti
Sergeants Three— Josephine Earl
Serpent and the Rainbow— Carmen DeLavallade,
  Juan Rodriguez
The Serpent's Egg— Heino Hallhuber
Seven Brides for Seven Brothers— Michael Kidd
Seven Days Ashore— Charles O'Curran
Seven Days' Leave— Charles Walters
The Seven Little Foys— Nick Castle
The Seven Sweethearts— Ernst Matray

Sex and the Single Girl— Lee Scott

Sex Kittens Go to College— Jack Baker

Sextette— Marc Breaux

Sgt. Pepper's Lonely Hearts Club Band— Patricia Birch

Shadow Dancing— Timothy Spain

Shadows in Swing (S)— Louis DaPron

Shady Lady— Lester Horton

Shag— Kenny Ortega

Shake, Rattle and Rock— Anthony Capps, Val Raset

Shall We Dance— Fred Astaire, Harry Losee, Hermes Pan

Shamrock Hill— Nick Castle

Shane— Josephine Earl

Shanghai Triad— Wang Qing

Sharkey's Machine— Anthony Ferro

She (1935)— Benjamin Zemach

She (1965)— Christine Lawson

She Couldn't Say No— Freddie Carpenter

She Done Him Wrong— Harold Hecht

She Had What It Takes— Nick Castle

She Loves Me Not— LeRoy Prinz

She Made Her Bed— Larry Ceballos

She Shall Have Music— Howard Deighton

The Sheik— Margaret Loomis

The Sheltering Sky— Lachen Zinoune

The Sheriff of Fractured Jaw— George Carden

She's a Sweetheart— Jack Boyle

She's Back on Broadway— Steve Condos, Gene Nelson, Miriam Nelson, LeRoy Prinz

She's for Me— Louis DaPron

She's Gotta Have It— Kevin Jeff

She's Having a Baby— Tony Stevens

She's Out of Control— Paula Abdul

She's Working Her Way Through College— Gene Nelson, Miriam Nelson, LeRoy Prinz

Shine On Harvest Moon— Four Step Bros., LeRoy Prinz

The Shining Hour— Tony DeMarco

Ship Ahoy— Bobby Connolly, Eleanor Powell

Ship of Fools— José Greco

Shipmates Forever— Bobby Connolly, Ruby Keeler

Shock Corridor— Jon Gregory

Shock Treatment— Gillian Gregory

The Shocking Miss Pilgrim— Hermes Pan

Shopworn Angel— Val Raset

Shout— Michelle Johnston

Show Boat (1936)— LeRoy Prinz

Show Boat (1950)— Robert Alton, Gower Champion

Show Business— Nick Castle, George Murphy

Show Folks— Ernest Belcher

The Show Goes On— Carl Randall

Show of Shows— Larry Ceballos, Jack Haskell

The Show Off— Jack Donohue

Showgirl in Hollywood— Jack Haskell

Showgirls— Marguerite Derricks

Shut My Big Mouth— Eddie Prinz

The Sicilian— Claire Hutchins

Sidewalks of London (aka *St. Martin's Lane*)— Philip Buchel

Sign of the Cross— Theodore Kosloff, LeRoy Prinz

Sign of the Gladiator (aka *Nel Signo di Roma*)— Claude Marchant

Sign of the Pagan— Kenny Williams

Silence Like Glass— Heinz Sporeli

The Silencers— Bob Sidney

Silent Assassins— Jun Chong

Silent Movie— Rob Iscove

Silk Stockings— Fred Astaire, Eugene Loring, Hermes Pan

Silken Shackles— Ernest Belcher

The Silver Chalice— Stephen Papich

Silver Skates— Dave Gould

Since You Went Away— Marty Grail, Charles Walters

Sincerely Yours— Jack Baker

Sinful Davey— Alice Dalgarno

Sing— John Carrafa, Otis Sallid

Sing a Jingle— Carlos Romero

Sing Another Chorus— Antonio, Larry Ceballos

Sing, Baby, Sing— Jack Haskell

Sing, Boy, Sing— Nick Castle

Sing, Dance, Plenty Hot— Larry Ceballos

Sing Me a Love Song— Bobby Connolly

Sing Your Way Home— Charles O'Curran

Sing Your Worries Away— Val Raset

Singin' in the Rain— Stanley Donen, Gene Kelly

The Singing Cop— Jack Donohue

The Singing Fool— Larry Ceballos

The Singing Kid— Bobby Connolly

The Singing Marine— Busby Berkeley

The Singing Nun— Robert Sidney

The Singing Sheriff— Louis DaPron

The Sins of Rachel Cade— James Truitte

The Siren of Atlantis— Lester Horton

The Siren of Bagdad— Sylvia Lewis

Sis Hopkins— Aida Broadbent

Sister Act— Lisa Mordente, Lester Wilson

Sister Act II: Back in the Habit— Michael Peters, Eartha Robinson

Sitting Pretty— Larry Ceballos

Six Lessons from Madame La Zonga— Nick Castle

Six Weeks— Ann Ditchburn

Sizzle (TV)— Carl Jablonski

Skatetown U.S.A.— Bobby Banas

Ski Patrol— Jeff J. Adkins

Skidoo— Tom Hansen

Skin Deep— John Clifford

Skirts Ahoy— Nick Castle

Sky Bandits— Domini Winter

Sky Symphony (S)— Merriel Abbott

The Skydivers— Bob Banas

The Sky's the Limit— Fred Astaire, Bernard Pearce

Slamdance— David Titchnell

Slave Girl— Si-Lan Chen
Slave of Love— Albertina Rasch
Sleeping Beauty— Jacob Kalusky
Sleeping with the Enemy— Patricia Birch
Sleepless in Seattle— Miranda Garrison
Sleepytime Gal— Larry Ceballos
Slightly French— Jack Boyle
Slightly Scandalous— Louis DaPron
Slightly Terrific— Louis DaPron
The Slipper and the Rose— The Story of Cinderella—Marc Breaux
Slow Dancing in the Big City— Ann Ditchburn, Robert North
The Slugger's Wife— Kathryn Doby
Small Town Girl— Busby Berkeley, Willie Covan, Ann Miller, Alex Romero
Small Town Idol— Ernest Belcher
The Small World of Sammy Lee— Lili Berden
Smile— Jim Bates
Smiling Faces (S)— Merriel Abbott
Smiling Irish Eyes— Larry Ceballos, Carl McBride, Walter Wills
A Smoky Mountain Christmas (TV)— Paula Abdul
The Snow Devils— Wilbert Bradley
Snow White— Jakob Kalusky
Snow White and the Three Stooges— Ron Fletcher
The Snows of Kilimajaro— Antonio Triana
So Fine— Grover Dale
So, I Married an Ax Murderer— Kimi Okata, Michael Smuin
So This Is Africa— Larry Ceballos
So This Is Love— LeRoy Prinz
So This Is Paris— Gene Nelson, Lee Scott
So, You Won't Talk?— Fred Leslie
Soapdish— Melissa Dexter, Tracy Singer
Sodom and Gomorrah— Archie Savage
Soldier in the Rain— Miriam Nelson
Soldier of Fortune— Stephen Papich
Solomon and Sheba— Jaroslav Berger, Jean Pierre Genet
Sombrero— Stanley Donen, José Greco, Hermes Pan
Some Call It Luck— Sammy Lee
Some Like It Hot— Jack Cole, Wally Green
Somebody Loves Me— Charles O'Curran
Somebody to Love— Alexandre Magno
Something for the Boys— Nick Castle
Something in the Wind— Eugene Loring
Something to Shout About— Sammy Lee, David Lichine
Something to Sing About— Angie Blue, John Boyle, Harland Dixon
Something to Talk About— Toni Basil
Somersby— Colleen Kelly
Son-in-Law— Miranda Garrison
The Son of Ali Baba— Hal Belfer
Son of Paleface— Josephine Earl
Son of Samson— Tito DeLuc

Son of Sinbad— Olga Lunick
Son of the Morning Star (TV)— Lynne Hockney
Song and Dance Man— Fanchon
A Song for Miss Julie— Larry Ceballos, Anton Dolin
A Song Is Born— John "Bubbles" Sublett
Song of Arizona— Fanchon
Song of My Heart— Paul Oscard
The Song of Nevada— Larry Ceballos
Song of Norway— Lee Theodore
Song of Russia— David Lichine
Song of Scheherezade— Tilly Losch
Song of the Flame— Eduardo Cansino, Jack Haskell
Song of the Islands— Hermes Pan
Song of the Open Road— Condos Bros, George Dobbs
Song of the Sarong— Carlos Romero
Song of the Thin Man— Jack Donohue
Sons o' Guns— Bobby Connolly
Sons of the Desert— David Bennett
Sorrowful Jones— Josephine Earl
Souls for Sale (1923)— Ernest Belcher
Souls for Sale (1962) (aka *Secrets of a Soul* and *Confessions of an Opium Eater*)— Jon Gregory
The Sound of Music— Marc Breaux, Dee Dee Wood
Sound Off— Al White
Soup for One— Julie Arenal
South Central— Rana Mack
South of Pago Pago— Jack Crosby
South Pacific— LeRoy Prinz, Archie Savage
South Sea Woman— Lester Horton, James Truitte
Southern Roses— Wendy Toye
The Spanish Dancer— Ernest Belcher
Spanish Fiesta (S)— Léonide Massine
Sparkle— Lester Wilson
Spartacus (1960)— Hector Zaraspe
Spartacus (1979)— Yuri Grigorivich
Spawn of the North— Michio Ito, LeRoy Prinz
The Specialist— Pedro Pable Pena
Species— Holly Schiffer
Specter of the Rose— Tamara Geva
The Spectre of War— Alberto Mendez
Speedway— Alex Romero
Speedy Justice (S)— Danny Dare
The Spider— Buddy Bradley
Spike of Bensonhurst— Michele Assaf
Spinout— Jack Baker
The Spirit of Boogie Woogie (S)— Katharine Dunham
The Spirit of 76— Consuelo Faust
Splash— Mike Nomad
Splendor in the Grass— George Tapps
Splinters in the Air— Ralph Reader
Split Second— Troy Baker
Splitz— Matthew Diamond
Sports à la Mode (S)— Merriel Abbott

Spotlight Scandals— Jack Boyle
Spring Break— Roger Minami
Spring Break Sorority Babes— Brentley Morgan
Spring Night (S)— David Lichine
Spring Parade— Larry Ceballos
Spring Reunion— Sylvia Lewis
Springtime (aka *Spring Song*)— Jack Billings
Springtime in the Rockies— Hermes Pan
Spy Hard— Cindy Motoya-Picker
The Squaw Man (1918)— Theodore Kosloff
The Squaw Man (1936)— LeRoy Prinz
Squibs— Ralph Reader
Squizzy Taylor— David Atkins
Stage Door— Hermes Pan
Stage Door Canteen— Ray Bolger
Stage Fright— David Paltenghi
Stage Mother— Albertina Rasch
Stage Struck— Busby Berkeley
Stagecoach— Maggie Banks
Staggered— Roger the Swede
Stand Up and Cheer— Sammy Lee
Star!— Michael Kidd
Star Bright— Josephine Earl
Star '80— Bob Fosse
Star for a Night— Sammy Lee
A Star Is Born (1954)— Richard Barstow, Jack Donohue
A Star Is Born (1976)— David Winters
The Star Maker— LeRoy Prinz
Star Reporter Series (S)— Louis Da Pron
Star Spangled Rhythm— George Balanchine, Danny Dare, Jack Donohue, Katherine Dunham
Star Struck— David Atkins
Starburst (aka *He Loved an Actress* and *Mad About Money*)— Larry Ceballos
Stark: Mirror Image (TV)—Jeanne Marie
Starlift!— Gene Nelson,LeRoy Prinz
Starlit Days at the Lido (S)— Fanchon
Starman— Russell Clark
Stars and Stripes Forever— Nick Castle, Stephen Papich, Al White Jr.
The Stars Are Singing— Jack Baker
Stars on Parade— Stanley Donen
Stars Over Broadway— Busby Berkeley, Bobby Connolly
Start Cheering— Danny Dare, Hal LeRoy
State Fair (1945)— Hermes Pan
State Fair (1961)— Nick Castle
The Statue— Gino Landi
Stay Tuned— Anthony Thomas
Staying Alive— Dennon and Sayhber Rawl
Steal Big, Steal Little— Julie Arenal
Steel Justice— Jeff Kutash
Steel Magnolias— Spencer Henderson 3rd
Stella— Patricia Birch
Step Lively— Ernst Matray, George Murphy
Stepping Fast (S)— Burch Mann

Stepping Out— Danny Daniels
Stepping Sisters— Seymour Felix
Sticky Fingers— David Hurwith
Stiletto— Danny Daniels
The Sting II— Alton Ruff, Ron Stein
Stir Crazy— Scott Salmon
Stolen Harmony— LeRoy Prinz
Stolen Heaven— LeRoy Prinz
Stolen Kisses— Larry Ceballos
Stonewall— Brendon McDaniel
Stop the World, I Want to Get Off (1966)— Tutte Lemkow
Stop the World, I Want to Get Off (1978) (aka *Sammy Stops the World*)— Billy Wilson
Stop, You're Killing Me— LeRoy Prinz
The Stork Club— Billy Daniel
Storm Over Lisbon— Aida Broadbent, Lisan Kay
Stormy Weather— Nick Castle, Katherine Dunham, Fanchon, Fayard Nicholas, Bill Robinson, Clarence Robinson
The Story of Ruth— Danni Dassa
The Story of Three Loves— Frederick Ashton
The Story of Vernon and Irene Castle— Fred Astaire, Hermes Pan
The Story of Will Rogers— LeRoy Prinz
Straight, Place and Show— Nick Castle, Geneva Sawyer
Straight Talk— Miranda Garrison
Stranded (aka *Valley of Mystery*)— Gene Columbus
Strange Lady in Town— Peggy Carroll, Antonio Triana
Strauss' Great Waltzes (aka *Waltzes from Vienna*)— Buddy Bradley
Street Fighter— Jean-Claude Van Damme
Street Girl— Pearl Eaton
Streets of Fire— Jeffrey Hornaday
Streets of Gold— Jimmy Nickerson
La Streghe (aka *The Witches*)— Claude Marchand
Strictly Ballroom— John "Cha Cha" O'Connell, Paul Mercurio, Antonio Vargas
Strictly Business— Emilio "Stretch" Austin
Strictly Dynamite— Hermes Pan
Strike Me Pink— Robert Alton
Strike Up the Band— Busby Berkeley
The Strip— Nick Castle
Stripes— Ronn Forella, Arthur Goldweit
Stripped to Kill— Ted Lin
Stripped to Kill II: Live Girls— Ted Lin
The Stripper— Alex Romero
Striptease— Marguerite Derricks
Stuck on You— Jacques d'Amboise
The Student Prince—Hermes Pan
Student Tour— Chester Hale
The Stuff— Leslie Linko Glatter
Subway Symphony (S)— Dave Gould
Such Men Are Dangerous— Danny Dare
Sudan— Lester Horton

Sudden Impact— Sarah Elgart
Sugar Hill— Eartha Robinson
Sugartime (TV)— Valerie Moore
The Sultan's Daughter— John Alton, Nico Charisse
Summer Camp— Dino Joseph Giannetta
Summer Holiday (1948)— Charles Walters
Summer Holiday (1963)— Herbert Ross
Summer Job— Bob Banas
Summer Magic— Tommy Mahoney
Summer School— Tony Fields
Summer Stock— Gene Kelly, Nick Castle, Charles Walters
Summer Wishes, Winter Dreams— Dennis Wayne
Sun Valley Serenade— Fayard Nicholas, Hermes Pan, Geneva Sawyer
Sunbonnet Sue— Jack Boyle
Sunday in New York— Maggie Banks
Sunkist Stars at Palm Springs (S)— Fanchon
Sunny (1930)— Theodore Kosloff
Sunny (1941)— Ray Bolger, Leon Leonidoff
Sunnyside— Charles Chaplin
Sunnyside Up— Seymour Felix
Sunset— Miriam Nelson, Miranda Garrison
Sunset in El Dorado— Larry Ceballos
Sunset Strip— Corey Ouimette
The Super— Lola Blank
Super Mario Brothers— Barry Lather
Superman — The Movie— Alex Plasschaert
Surviving Picasso— Elizabeth Aldrich
Susan Slept Here— Robert Sidney
Suspense— Nick Castle
The Swan— Angie Blue
The Swan Princess— Lisa Clyde
Swanee River— Nick Castle, Geneva Sawyer
Swashbuckler— Geoffrey Holder
Sweater Girl— Dave Gould
Sweet Adeline— Bobby Connolly
Sweet Charity— Bob Fosse
Sweet Dreams— Susan Scanlan
Sweet Genevieve— Audrene Brier
Sweet Jam (S)— Louis DaPron
Sweet Music— John Boyle, Bobby Connolly
The Sweet Ride— Jon Gregory
Sweet Rosie O'Grady— Fanchon, Hermes Pan
Sweet Sixteen (aka *Futures Vedettes*)— George Reich
Sweet Surrender— Sara Mildred Strauss
Sweet Talker— Ross Coleman
The Sweetheart of Sigma Chi— Eddie Prinz
Sweetheart of the Campus— Louis DaPron, Ruby Keeler
Sweetheart of the U.S.A.— Jack Boyle
Sweethearts— Ray Bolger, Ernst Mattray, Albertina Rasch
Sweethearts on Parade— Nick Castle
Sweetie— Earl Lindsay
Swing Fever— Merriel Abbott, Ernst and Maria Matray

Swing for Sale (S)— Hal LeRoy
Swing It Soldier— Louis DaPron
Swing Kids— Otis Sallid
A Swing Opera (S)— Gae Foster
Swing Out the Blues— Stanley Donen
Swing Parade of 1946— Jack Boyle
Swing Time— Fred Astaire, Hermes Pan
Swing Your Lady— Bobby Connolly
Swing Your Partner— Josephine Earl
Swing, Sister, Swing— Matty King
The Swinger— David Winters
Swinger's Paradise (aka *It's a Wonderful Life*)— Gillian Lynne
Swingtime Johnny— Charles O'Curran
Swiss Miss— Val Raset
The Sword and the Rose— David Paltenghi
Sword of Heaven— Tadashi Yamashita
Syncopated City (S)— Hal LeRoy
Syncopated Trial (S)— Eddie Prinz
Tahiti Honey— Larry Ceballos
Take a Chance— Bobby Connolly
Take Her She's Mine— Hal Belfer
Take It Big— Carlos Romero
Take It or Leave It— Fayard Nicholas
Take Me Out to the Ball Game— Busby Berkeley, Stanley Donen, Gene Kelly
Take Me to Town— Hal Belfer
Take My Tip— Philip Buchel, Jack Hulbert
A Tale of Two Cities— Chester Hale
The Tales of Hoffman— Frederick Ashton
The Tales of the Vienna Woods— William Milié
Talk of Hollywood— Leon Leonidoff
The Tall Guy— Charles Augins
The T.A.M.I. Show— David Winters
Tammy and the Bachelor— Peggy Carroll, Kenny Williams
Tampico— Geneva Sawyer
Tangier— Lester Horton
Tango and Cash— Jeffrey Hornaday
Tango Bar— Nelson Avila, Santiago Ayala, Lilliana Belfiore, Doris Petroni, Carlos Rivarola, Nelida Rodriguez, Norma Viola
Tango Tangles— Charles Chaplin
Tangos: The Exile of Gardel— Adolfo Andrade, Margarita Balli, Susana Tambutti, Robert Thomas
Tank Girl— Adam Shankman
Tap— Gregory Hines, Henry LeTang
Tapeheads— Cholly Atkins, Eddie Batos
Tarnished Angel— Ann Miller
Tars and Spars— Jack Cole
Tarzan and the Leopard Woman— Lester Horton
Tarzan and the Lost Safari— Harold Holness
Tea for Two— Gene Nelson, Miriam Nelson, Eddie Prinz, LeRoy Prinz
Teacher's Pet— Josephine Earl
Teahouse of the August Moon— Masaya Fujima
Ted and Venus— Chris Scheck

Teen Witch— Bob Banas, Russell Clark
Teen Wolf— Janet Roston
Teen Wolf Too— Randy Allaire
Teenage Mutant Ninja Turtles— Pat Johnson
Teenage Mutant Ninja Turtles II: The Secret of the Ooze— Myrna Gawryn
Teenage Rebel— Bill Foster
Tell It to a Star— Aida Broadbent
Tempest (1958)— Gino Landi
Tempest (1982)— Stuart Hopps
Temple of Venus— Ernest Belcher
The Ten Commandments (1922)— Theodore Kosloff
The Ten Commandments (1956)— Ruth Godfrey, LeRoy Prinz
Ten Thousand Bedrooms— Jack Baker
Tender Is the Night (1962)— Hal Belfer
Tender Is the Night (1985)— Christopher Wren
Tender Mercies— Nick Felix
The Tenth Victim— Gino Landi
Tess— Sue Lefton
Texas Carnival— Ann Miller, Hermes Pan
Thank God It's Friday— Joanne Divito
Thank Your Lucky Stars— LeRoy Prinz
Thanks a Million— Jack Donohue
That Certain Feeling— Nick Castle
That Lady in Ermine— Hermes Pan
That Midnight Kiss— Jack Donohue
That Night in Rio— Hermes Pan
That Night with You— Louis Dapron, Lester Horton
That Thing You Do!— Toni Basil
That's Dancing!— Robert Alton, Fred Astaire, Busby Berkeley, Ray Bolger, Johnny Boyle, Bobby Connolly, Stanley Donen, Bob Fosse, Dave Gould, Michael Jackson, Ruby Keeler, Gene Kelly, Ann Miller, Fayard Nicholas, Hermes Pan, Michael Peters, LeRoy Prinz
That's Entertainment!— Robert Alton, Fred Astaire, Busby Berkeley, Nick Castle, Bobby Connolly, Stanley Donen, Jack Donohue, Seymour Felix, Dave Gould, Gene Kelly, Michael Kidd, Ann Miller, Hermes Pan, Eleanor Powell, Albertina Rasch, Charles Walters
That's Entertainment Part II— Robert Alton, Fred Astaire, Busby Berkeley, Nick Castle, Jack Cole, Bobby Connolly, Stanley Donen, Jack Donohue, Bob Fosse, Dave Gould, Gene Kelly, Ann Miller, Hermes Pan, Eleanor Powell, Albertina Rasch, Alex Romero, Charles Walters
That's Entertainment! III— Robert Alton, John Murray Anderson, Fred Astaire, Busby Berkeley, Nick Castle, Jack Cole, Bobby Connolly, George Cunningham, Stanley Donen, Jack Donohue, Seymour Felix, Dave Gould, Gene Kelly, Michael Kidd, Sammy Lee, Eugene Loring, Ann Miller, Hermes Pan, Eleanor Powell, Alex Romero, Charles Walters

That's My Gal— Hal Belfer, Four Step Brothers
That's Right, You're Wrong— Eddie Prinz
That's the Spirit— Louis DaPron, Carlos Romero
Theatre of Blood— Tutte Lemkow
Thelma and Louise— Patsy Swayze
There Goes My Baby— Kim Blank
There Goes the Bride— Gillian Gregory
There's a Girl in My Heart— Louis DaPron
There's No Business Like Show Business— Robert Alton, Jack Cole
They Learned About Woman— Sammy Lee
They Met in Argentina— Frank Veloz
They Shoot Horses, Don't They?— Tom Panko
The Thief of Bagdad— Harry Losee
Thin Ice (1937)— Harry Losee
Thin Ice (1995)— Eamon Geoghegan
The Thin Man Goes Home— Jeanette Bates
The Third Girl from the Left (TV)— Miriam Nelson
This Angry Age— Raye Dodge
This Could Be the Night— Jack Baker
This Is My Affair— Jack Haskell
This Is My Life— Pat Birch
This Is the Army— Nick Castle, George Murphy, LeRoy Prinz, Bob Sidney
This Is the Life— Louis DaPron, Fanchon
This Time for Keeps— Stanley Donen
This Way Please— LeRoy Prinz
This'll Make You Whistle— Buddy Bradley
Thoroughly Modern Millie— Joe Layton
Those Lips, Those Eyes— Dan Siretta
Those Redheads from Seattle— Jack Baker
Those Three French Girls— Sammy Lee
Thousands Cheer— Gene Kelly, Don Loper, Eleanor Powell
Three Amigos— Shirley Kirkes
Three Caballeros— Billy Daniel, Carmelita Maracci, Aloysio Oliveria
Three Cheers for Love— Louis DaPron, Danny Dare
Three Cheers for the Girls (S)— Busby Berkeley, Bobby Connolly
The Three-Cornered Hat—Antonio
The Three Faces of Eve— Bill Foster
Three for the Show— Jack Cole, Gower Champion
Three Hats for Lisa— Gillian Lynne
Three Little Girls in Blue— Seymour Felix, Bernard Pearce
Three Little Words— Fred Astaire, Hermes Pan
Three Men in White— Charles Walters
The Three Musketeers— Gene Kelly
Three Nuts in Search of a Bolt— Ward Ellis
Three on a Honeymoon— Dave Gould
Three Ring Circus— Nick Castle
Three Sailors and a Girl— Gene Nelson, LeRoy Prinz
Three Weekends— Fanchon
Threepenny Opera— Dick Price

Thrill of a Lifetime— Fanchon, LeRoy Prinz, Carlos Romero

Thrill of a Romance— Charles Walters

Thrill of Brazil— Nick Castle, Jack Cole, Eugene Loring, Ann Miller, Frank Veloz

Thumbelina— Gavian Dorian, Bruno "Taco" Falcon

Thunder— George Cunningham

Thunder Alley— Ronnie (Christopher) Riordan

Thunder in the Sun— Pedro De Cordoba

A Ticket to Tomahawk— Jennifer Hatfield, Kenny Williams

Tickle Me—David Winters

A Ticklish Affair— Alex Ruiz

A Tiger's Tale— Glenn Hunsucker

The Tigress of Bengal (aka *Journey to the Lost City*)— Billy Daniel, Robby Gay

Till the Clouds Roll By— Robert Alton

Tillie's Punctured Romance— Charles Chaplin

Timberjacks— Jack Baker

Time Bandits— Tom Jobe

Time Out for Rhythm— Ann Miller, LeRoy Prinz

The Time, the Place and the Girl—Condos Bros., LeRoy Prinz

Timecop— Jean-Claude Van Damme

Tin Pan Alley— Seymour Felix, Fayard Nicholas

Tip, Tap, Toe (S)— Hal LeRoy

Titanic— Stephen Papich

To Be or Not to Be— Alan Johnson, Charlene Painter

To Beat the Band— Sammy Lee

To Live and Die in L.A.— Lesli Linka Glatter

To Wong Foo, Thanks for Everything, Julie Newmar— Kenny Ortega

The Toast of New Orleans— Eugene Loring

Toast to Love (aka *Yolanda*)— Anton Dolin

Tom and Jerry (The Movie)— Lori Eastside

Tom and Viv— Carol Fletcher

Tom, Dick and Harry— George Murphy

Tom Sawyer— Danny Daniels

Tom Thumb— Alex Romero

Tombstone— Sabrina Vasquez

Tomcat: Dangerous Desire— Barbara Bourget

Tommy— Gillian Gregory

Tommy the Toreador— Malcolm Clare

Tonight and Every Night— Jack Cole, Val Raset

Tonight We Sing— David Lichine

Too Hot to Handle— Pamela Devis

Too Many Girls— Hal LeRoy, Ann Miller, LeRoy Prinz

Too Many Husbands— LeRoy Prinz

Too Many Sailors (S)— Burch Mann

Too Much Harmony— Eddie Prinz, LeRoy Prinz

Top Banana— Jack Donohue, Ron Fletcher

Top Hat— Fred Astaire, Hermes Pan

Top Man— Louis DaPron

Top o' the Morning— Eddie Prinz

Top of the Town— George Murphy, Gene Snyder

Top Secret— Gillian Gregory

Top Secret Affair— Eddie Prinz

Top Speed— Larry Ceballos

Tops Is the Limit (aka *Anything Goes*)— LeRoy Prinz

Torch Song— Eugene Loring, Charles Walters

Torch Song Trilogy— Scott Salmon

Torn Curtain— Michel Panaieff

Toyland (S)— Alexander Oumansky

Toys— Anthony Thomas

Train Ride to Hollywood— Jack Baker

Transatlantic Merry Go Round— Larry Ceballos, Sammy Lee

La Traviata (1968)— Gino Landi

La Traviata (1984)— Alberto Testa

Tread Softly Stranger— Alfred Rodrigues

The Treasure of Matecumbe— Burch Mann

Tripoli— Bella Lewitzky

Triumph of the Spirit—Teddy Atlas

Trocodero— Larry Ceballos

Trois Coleurs: Rouge— Brigette Matteuzi

Troop Beverly Hills— Dorain Grusman

Tropic Holiday— LeRoy Prinz

Tropic Zone— Jack Baker

Trouble for Two— Val Raset

The Trouble with Girls— Jonathon Lucas

The Trouble with Women— Billy Daniel

True Confessions— Alfonse L. Palermo

True Lies— Lynne Hockney

True to the Army— Jack Donohue, Ann Miller

Tucker: The Man and His Dream— Paula Tracy Smuin

Tuff Turf— Bob Banas

Tune in Tomorrow— Quinny Sacks

Turn Off the Moon— Fanchon, LeRoy Prinz

The Turning Point— Alvin Ailey, Frederick Ashton, George Balanchine, Jean Coralli, John Cranko, Michel Fokine, Lev Ivanov, Harald Lander, Kenneth MacMillan, Alexander Minz, Dennis Nahat, Jules Perrot, Marius Petipa

Twelfth Night—Stuart Hopps

Twenty Million Sweethearts— Busby Berkeley

Twice Blessed— Arthur Walsh

Twilight on the Prairie— Louis DaPron

Twilight Time— Renato Pernic

Twinkletoes— Ernest Belcher

Twins— Paula Tracy Smuin

Twirl (TV)— Michelle Assaf

Twist All Night— Dick Humphreys

Twist Around the Clock— Earl Barton

Two Blondes and a Redhead— Audrene Brier

Two Evil Eyes— Cathy Carthers Wayne

Two Faced Woman— Robert Alton

Two for the Seesaw— Maggie Banks

Two Girls and a Sailor— Sammy Lee

Two Girls on Broadway— Bobby Connolly, Eddie Larkin, George Murphy

Two Guys from Texas— LeRoy Prinz

The Two Little Bears— Jonathon Lucas
Two Moon Junction— Russell Clark
Two Señoritas from Chicago— Nick Castle
Two Sisters from Boston— Jack Donohue
Two Tickets to Broadway— Busby Berkeley, Gower Champion, Ann Miller
Two Weeks with Love— Busby Berkeley
U.F.O.— Rachel Izen
Uncle Buck— Miranda Garrison
Unconquered— Jack Crosby
Under a Texas Moon— Eduardo Cansino
Under Pressure— Jack Donohue
Under Siege— Steven Seagal
Under Siege 2: Dark Territory— Steven Seagal
Under the Boardwalk— Bob Banas
Under the Pampas Moon— Jack Donohue, Frank Veloz
Under the Yum Yum Tree— Robert Tucker
Under Your Spell— Sammy Lee
Undercover Blues— D.J. Giagni
The Unfinished Dance— Sammy Lee, David Lichine
Union Pacific— LeRoy Prinz
Universal Soldier— Jean-Claude Van Damme
Les Uns et les Autres (aka *Bolero*)— Maurice Bejart, Nicole Daresco, Ric Odums, Micha Van Joecke, Larry Vickers
The Unsinkable Molly Brown— Peter Gennaro, Charles Walters
Unsuspected— Jack Crosby
Untamed— Stephen Papich
Until They Sail— Alex Romero
Up Down Fragile (aka *Haut Bas Fragile*)— Caroline Marcade
Up in Arms— Danny Dare
Up in Central Park— Helen Tamiris
Up in Lights (S)— Gae Foster
Up the River— Nick Castle, Bill Robinson, Geneva Sawyer
Up the Sandbox— Bobby Thompson
Ups and Downs (S)— Hal LeRoy
Urban Cowboy— Patsy Swayze
Use Your Imagination (S)— Hal LeRoy
Used People— Patricia Birch
Utah— Larry Ceballos
The Vagabond King— Hanya Holm
Valentino (1951)— Larry Ceballos
Valentino (1977)— Gillian Gregory
Valet Girls— Damita Joe Freeman
Valley of Mystery (aka *Stranded*)— Gene Columbus
Valley of the Dolls— Bob Sidney
Valmont— Ann Jacoby
Value for Money— Irving Davies, Paddy Stone
Vamp— Russell Clark
The Vampire and the Ballerina (aka *Seddok* and *Atom Age Vampire*)— Marisa Ciampaglia
Vampire in Brooklyn— Eartha Robinson
Van Nuys Blvd.— Sandy Hendricks Adler

Variety Girl— Billy Daniel, Bernard Pearce
Varsity Show— Busby Berkeley, John "Bubbles" Sublett
The Veils of Bagdad— Eugene Loring
Vera Cruz— Archie Savage
A Very Brady Sequel— Peggy Holmes
A Very Private Affair— Dirk Sanders
A Very Special Favor— David Robel
Vibes— Miranda Garrison
Victor/Victoria— Paddy Stone
Videodrome— Kirsteen Etherington
Viennese Nights— Jack Haskell
The Village— Trudi Schoop
Village of the Giants— Toni Basil
Violets in Spring (S)— George Murphy
The Virgin Queen— Stephen Papich
Visit to a Small Planet— Miriam Nelson
Viva Las Vegas— David Winters
Vogues of 1938— Seymour Felix, George Tapps
Voices— Stuart Hodes
The Volga Boatman— Theodore Kosloff
Voyage of the Rock Aliens— Dennon and Sayhber Rawles
Wabash Avenue— Billy Daniel
Waikiki Wedding— LeRoy Prinz
Wake Up and Live— Condos Bros, Jack Haskell
Walk, Don't Run— Miriam Nelson
A Walk in the Clouds— Michael Smuin
Walk Like a Man— Bonnie Evans
Walking My Baby Back Home— Louis DaPron
Walking on Air— Buddy Bradley
Waltzes from Vienna (aka *Strauss' Great Waltzes*)— Buddy Bradley
The War— Jamale Graves
War Drums— Ward Ellis
The War Lord— Kenny Williams
Wardrobe Girls (S)— Gae Foster
Wash Your Step (S)— Hal LeRoy
Washington Melodrama— Sammy Lee
The Water Engine (TV)— Russell Clark
The Waterdance— Judith Flex
Waterloo— Gino Landi
Waterloo Bridge— Ernst and Maria Matray
The Way of All Freshmen— Hal LeRoy
Way... Way Out— Malcolm Stuart
The Way We Were— Grover Dale
Wayne's World— Peggy Holmes
Wayne's World 2— Tony Gonzalez
We Can't Have Everything— Ernest Belcher
We Joined the Navy— Tommy Linde
Weeds— Jerry Evans
Weekend at Bernie's II— Adam Shankman
Weekend at the Waldorf— Charles Walters
Weekend in Havana— Hermes Pan
Weekend Warriors— Jeff Calhoun
Weird Science— Jerry Evans
Welcome Stranger— Billy Daniel
The West Point Story— John Boyle, Ruth Godfrey,

Gene Nelson, Eddie Prinz, LeRoy Prinz, Al White, Jr.

West Side Story— Tommy Abbott, Maggie Banks, Howard Jeffrey, Tony Mordente, Jerome Robbins

What a Crazy World!— Billy Petch

What a Drag! (*Pedale Douce*)— Cedric Brenner

What a Way to Go!— Dick Humphreys, Gene Kelly

What Am I Bid?— George Jack

What an Idea! (S)— Danny Dare

What Did You Do in the War, Daddy?— Carey Leverette

What Happened to Father— Ernest Belcher

What, No Men?— Bobby Connolly

What Price Glory?— Billy Daniel

Whatever Happened to Baby Jane?— Alex Romero

What's Buzzin' Cousin?— Nick Castle, Ann Miller, Val Raset

What's Cookin'?— James Mattison

What's Love Got to Do with It?— Michael Peters

What's New Pussycat?— Jean Guelis

What's So Bad About Feelin' Good?— Michael Bennett

What's the Matter with Helen?— Tony Charmoli, Tad Tadlock

When a Man Loves a Woman— Miranda Garrison

When Johnny Comes Marching Home— Louis DaPron, Four Step Brothers

When My Baby Smiles at Me— Seymour Felix, Kenny Williams

When Night Is Falling— Hillar Lotoja

When the Boys Meet the Girls— Earl Barton

When the Circus Came to Town (TV)— Marge Champion

When Willie Comes Marching Home— Kenny Williams

When You're in Love— Leon Leonidoff

Where Angels Go...Trouble Follows— Hannah Reiner

Where Did You Get That Girl?— John Boyle

Where Do We Go from Here?— Fanchon

Where the Boys Are (1960)— Robert Sidney

Where the Boys Are '84— Tony Stevens

Where the Heart Is— Richard Murphy

Where Words Fail (aka *Donde Mueren Las Palabras*)— Margharita Wallman

Where's Charley?— Ray Bolger, Michael Kidd

Where's Jack?— Malcom Goddard

While New York Sleeps— Nick Castle, Geneva Sawyer

Whistle Stop— Jack Crosby

White Cargo— Ernst and Maria Matray

White Christmas— Robert Alton

White Hunter, Black Heart— Arlene Phillips

White Mischief— Stuart Hopps

White Nights (1961)— Dirk Sanders

White Nights (1985)— Mikhail Baryshnikov, Gregory Hines, Roland Petit, Twyla Tharp

White Savage— Lester Horton

Who Framed Roger Rabbit?— Quinny Sacks, David Toguri

Wholly Moses!— Jaime Rogers

Whoopee— Busby Berkeley

The Whoopee Boys— Dorain Grusman

Who's Afraid of Virginia Woolf?— Howard Jeffrey, Herbert Ross

Who's Been Sleeping in My Bed?— Steven Peck

Whose Life Is It Anyway?— Marge Champion

Why Bring That Up?— Earl Lindsay

Why Change Your Wife?— Theodore Kosloff

Why Sailors Leave Home— Alexander Oumansky

The Wicked Lady— Madeleine Inglehearn

The Wicker Man— Stuart Hopps

Wild Bill Hickok Rides Again— Matty King

Wild Orchid— Morleigh Steinberg

Wild Orchid II: Two Shades of Blue— Marguerite Derricks

The Wild Party— Patricia Birch

Wild People (S)— Danny Dare

The Wild, Wild Planet— Archie Savage

Wildcats— Joel Hall, Paula Tracy Smuin

William Shakespeare's Romeo and Juliet (1996)— John "Cha Cha" O'Connell

Willow— Eleanor Fazan

Willy Wonka and the Chocolate Factory— Howard Jeffrey

The Wind in the Willows— Arlene Phillips

Windrider— Kenan Johnson

Wine, Women and Song— Beatrice Gollenette

The Winslow Boy— Freddie Carpenter

Winter à Go-Go— Kay Carson

Winter Carnival— Ned Freeman

Wintertime— Fanchon, James Gonzalez, Carlos Romero, Kenny Williams

Wired— Joanne Divito

The Witch— Robert Curtis

The Witches (aka *Le Streghe*)— Claude Marchant

With a Song in My Heart— Billy Daniel

Without You, I'm Nothing— Karole Armitage

The Wiz— Carlton Johnson, Louis Johnson, Mabel Robinson

The Wizard of Oz— Busby Berkeley, Ray Bolger, Bobby Connolly

The Wizard of Speed and Time— Lauri Riley

Wolf— Michael Smuin

A Woman Commands— Anthony Nelle

The Woman God Forgot— Theodore Kosloff

Woman of the River— Leo Coleman

The Woman Racket— Sammy Lee

A Woman Rebels— Hermes Pan

Woman to Woman— Andrée Howard

A Woman's Face— Ernst Matray

Women in Love— Terry Gilbert

The Women's Room (TV)— Tad Tadlock

Wonder Bar— Busby Berkeley, Hal LeRoy

Wonder Man— John Wray

Wonderful to Be Young (aka *The Young Ones*)— Herbert Ross

The Wonderful World of the Brothers Grimm— Alex Romero

The Wonders of Aladdin— Secondino Cavallo

Words and Music (1929)— Frank Merlin, Edward Royce

Words and Music (1948)— Robert Alton, Gene Kelly, Alex Romero

Working Girl— Patricia Birch

World by Night— Sonia Shaw

The World in His Arms— Hal Belfer

The World's Greatest Lover— Alan Johnson

The Would-Be-Gentleman— Leone Mail

Wrong Man— Bill and Jacqui Landrum

Wyoming Mail— Hal Belfer

Xanadu— Gene Kelly, Kenny Ortega, Jerry Trent

Xica— Marlene Silva

A Yank in the R.A.F.— Geneva Sawyer

Yankee Doodle Dandy— John Boyle, Seymour Felix, LeRoy Prinz

Yanks— Eleanor Fazan

The Year My Voice Broke— Robyn Moarse

The Yellow Rose of Texas— Larry Ceballos

Yentl— Gillian Lynne

Yes, Giorgio— Miriam Nelson

Yes Sir, That's My Baby— Louis DaPron

Yesterday, Today and Tomorrow— Jacques Ruet

Yokel Boy— Larry Ceballos

Yolanda (aka *Toast to Love*)— Anton Dolin

Yolanda and the Thief— Fred Astaire, Eugene Loring

You Are Music— Billy Daniel

You Belong to Me— LeRoy Prinz

You Can't Have Everything— Harry Losee

You Can't Ration Love— Josephine Earl

You Can't Run Away from It— Robert Sidney

You Can't Take It with You— Aida Broadbent

You Know What Sailors Are— David Paltenghi

You Were Meant for Me— Les Clark, Kenny Williams

You Were Never Lovelier— Fred Astaire, Peggy Carroll, Val Raset

You'll Never Get Rich— Robert Alton, Fred Astaire

Young at Heart— Donald Saddler

Young Einstein— Aku Kadogo

Young Frankenstein— Alan Johnson

The Young Girls of Rochefort (aka *Les Demoiselles de Rochefort*)— Gene Kelly, Norman Maen

The Young Lovers— Miriam Nelson

The Young Mr. Pitt— Wendy Toye

The Young Ones (aka *Wonderful to Be Young*)— Herbert Ross

Young People— Nick Castle, Geneva Sawyer

Young Soul Rebels— George Foster

Younger and Younger— Patsy Swayze

Your Cheatin' Heart— Hal Belfer

You're a Big Boy Now— Robert Tucker

You're a Sweetheart— George Murphy, Carl Randall

You're in the Army Now— Jack Donohue

You're My Everything— Berry Bros., Nick Castle

You're Never Too Young— Nick Castle

You're the One— LeRoy Prinz

Yours Sincerely (S)— Dave Gould

Youth on Parade— Dave Gould

Youth Will Be Served— Nick Castle

Zandy's Bride— Teodoro Morca

Zaza— LeRoy Prinz

Zelig— Danny Daniels, Twyla Tharp

Zero Patience— Susan McKenzie

Ziegfeld: The Man and His Women (TV)— Miriam Nelson, Tad Tadlock

Ziegfeld Follies— Robert Alton, Fred Astaire, Gene Kelly, Eugene Loring, Charles Walters

Ziegfeld Girl— Busby Berkeley

Zis Boom Bah— George King

Zoot Suit— Patricia Birch

Zorro the Gay Blade— Alex Romero

Part III. Index

Stage and *printed works* are in *italics*, **operas** and **ballets** in **bold italics**, "song titles," "television," "radio" and "music videos" are in "quotation marks." Films are printed in **bold**. Page numbers in **boldface** indicate photos. (S) = Short subject. The dance form of ballet is not listed, as the classic form is included throughout the entire book. Most other dance forms/styles, however, are listed.